shakespearean criticism

"Thou art a Monument without a tomb,
And art alive still while thy Book doth
   live
And we have wits to read and praise to
   give."

*Ben Jonson, from the preface
to the First Folio, 1623.*

Mr. WILLIAM
SHAKESPEARES

COMEDIES,
HISTORIES, &
TRAGEDIES.

Published according to the True Originall Copies.

Martin Droeshout sculpsit London.

LONDON
Printed by Isaac Iaggard, and Ed. Blount. 1623.

Frontispiece to the First Folio (1623). By permission of the Folger Shakespeare Library.

ISSN 0883-9123

Volume 12

shakespearean criticism

Excerpts from the Criticism of
William Shakespeare's Plays and Poetry,
from the First Published Appraisals
to Current Evaluations

Sandra L. Williamson
James E. Person, Jr
Editors

Stephen B. Barnard
Lawrence J. Trudeau
Associate Editors

 **Gale Research Inc.** • *DETROIT* • *NEW YORK* • *LONDON*

STAFF

Sandra L. Williamson, James E. Person, Jr., *Editors*

Stephen B. Barnard, Lawrence J. Trudeau, *Associate Editors*

Joseph C. Tardiff, Debra A. Wells, *Assistant Editors*

Jeanne A. Gough, *Production & Permissions Manager*
Linda M. Pugliese, *Production Supervisor*
David G. Oblender, Suzanne Powers, Maureen A. Puhl,
Linda M. Ross, Jennifer VanSicle, *Editorial Associates*
Donna Craft, James G. Wittenbach, *Editorial Assistants*

Victoria B. Cariappa, *Research Manager*
H. Nelson Fields, Judy L. Gale, Maureen R. Richards, *Editorial Associates*
Paula Cutcher, Alan Hedblad, Jill M. Ohorodnik, *Editorial Assistants*

Sandra C. Davis, *Permissions Supervisor (Text)*
Kimberly F. Smilay, Josephine M. Keene, *Permissions Associates*
Maria L. Franklin, Michelle M. Lonoconus, Camille P. Robinson,
Shalice Shah, Denise M. Singleton, Becky Stanko, *Permissions Assistants*

Patricia A. Seefelt, *Permissions Supervisor (Pictures)*
Margaret A. Chamberlain, *Permissions Associate*
Pamela A. Hayes, Lillian Quickley, *Permissions Assistants*

Mary Beth Trimper, *Production Manager*
Evi Seoud, *Assistant Production Manager*

Art Chartow, *Art Director*
C. J. Jonik, *Keyliner*

Laura Bryant, *Production Supervisor*
Louise Gagné, *Internal Production Associate*

Since this page cannot legibly accommodate all the copyright notices, the Acknowledgments constitute an extension of the copyright notice.

While every effort has been made to ensure the reliability of the information presented in this publication, Gale Research Inc. neither guarantees the accuracy of the data contained herein nor assumes any responsibility for errors, omissions, or discrepancies. Gale accepts no payment for listing; and inclusion in the publication of any organization, agency, institution, publication, service, or individual does not imply endorsement of the editors or publisher. Errors brought to the attention of the publisher and verified to the satisfaction of the publisher will be corrected in future editions.

The paper used in this publication meets the minimum requirements of American National Standard for Information Sciences—Permanence Paper for Printed Library Materials, ANSI Z39.48-1984. ∞™

Gale Research Inc.
835 Penobscot Bldg.
Detroit, MI 48226-4094

Library of Congress Catalog Card Number 86-645085
ISBN 0-8103-6136-1
ISSN 0883-9123

Printed in the United States of America

10 9 8 7 6 5 4 3

Contents

Preface

Shakespearean Criticism (SC) provides students, teachers, and other interested readers valuable insight into Shakespeare's plays and non-dramatic poems. Volumes 1 through 10 of the series offer a broad range of interpretations and effectively present a unique historical overview of the critical response to each Shakespearean work. A multiplicity of viewpoints derives from the nearly two hundred periodicals and books excerpted for each volume of *SC*. The excerpts document the critical reaction of scholars and commentators from the seventeenth century to the present day. Students and teachers at all levels of study can benefit from *SC*, whether they seek information for class discussions and written assignments, new perspectives on traditional issues, or the most noteworthy and innovative analyses of Shakespeare's artistry.

Scope of the Work

Beginning with volume 11 in the series, SC will trace the history of Shakespeare's plays on the stage and in important films through eyewitness reviews and retrospective evaluations of individual productions, comparisons of major interpretations, and discussions of staging issues. Each entry is designed to appeal to students of the theater, including undergraduates, graduates, specialists, actors, and directors, as well as to the general reader. The chronological overview provides a unique perspective on the evolution of principal interpretations. Volume 12, the second number in the series, delineates the production record of four Shakespearean comedies: *The Merchant of Venice, A Midsummer Night's Dream, The Taming of the Shrew,* and *The Two Gentlemen of Verona.*

Starting in 1990, *SC* will also compile an annual volume including approximately fifty of the most noteworthy essays published on Shakespeare during the previous year. The essays, reprinted in their entirety, will have been recommended to Gale by an international panel of distinguished scholars.

Organization of the Plays in Performance Series

Each entry consists of the following elements: an introduction, excerpts and complete texts of performance criticism, and an annotated bibliography of further reading.

The *introduction* outlines prevalent and enduring interpretations of the play, summarizes notable productions by prominent actors and directors, and characterizes the critical response to individual productions.

The *reviews and retrospective accounts* section includes immediate responses, by theater critics and others, to selected productions; recollections of notable performances; and reconstructions of legendary stagings. This section may also include excerpts from the diaries of actors and directors, accounts of rehearsals, and interviews that first appeared in newspapers or periodicals. For the benefit of the reader, commentary on a single production is grouped together, and individual productions are presented chronologically. Coverage of each production begins with the name of the principal artist or artists associated with it, the year of the production, and the theater where it was presented. In the case of film adaptations, the title, director, and date of the film are given. This is followed by a paragraph outlining the general significance of the performance, the principals involved, and the critical reception.

The *comparisons and overviews* section includes comparative evaluations of two or more performances and surveys of different actors' representations of a role in different historical periods. Among the productions covered here may be ones that are treated individually in the *reviews and retrospective accounts* section. Readers should consult the *cumulative index to artists* (see below) to determine if commentary on the work of a particular actor or director appears in more than one place in the entry.

The *staging issues* section includes practical and theoretical discussions of questions associated with theatrical representation, including characterization, choreography, costumes, and stage design. Infrequently, comparisons of important productions of a play or commentary on staging issues connected with it are not obtainable; when this is so, a play entry will comprise fewer than three sections.

All of the individual essays are preceded by *explanatory notes* as an additional aid to students using *SC*. The explanatory notes summarize the commentary and furnish previous publication information, such as original title and date, for reprinted and translated publications. The notes also provide background information on the critic.

A complete *bibliographical citation* designed to facilitate the location of the original essay or book follows each piece of criticism. If an essay first appeared without a signature but its author can be determined, this is noted in the citation.

Within the text of the criticism, some parenthetical information (such as publisher names, journal titles, footnotes, or page references) has been deleted to provide smoother reading of the text. Whenever necessary, act, scene, and line designations have been changed to conform to *The Riverside Shakespeare*, published by Houghton Mifflin Company.

Within each entry are *illustrations* of principal and supporting actors as they appeared in the play. These illustrations include paintings and sketches of eighteenth- and nineteenth-century performers, photographs of modern productions, and stills from film adaptations.

The annotated bibliography of *further reading* appearing at the end of each entry suggests additional reading on the performance history of the play. Explanatory notes summarize each essay listed here.

Additional Features

A *list of plays and poems* covered in the series follows the Preface. This listing indicates which works are treated in existing or forthcoming volumes.

A *chronological guide to selected productions* of each play precedes the entries. This guide indicates the principal actors and directors associated with individual productions, as well as the dates and locations of the productions.

Each volume also contains a list of *selected studies of Shakespearean production*. These are seminal works on the history of Shakespearean plays in performance which offer important background information.

So that readers may quickly locate commentary on specific actors, directors, producers, and designers, a *cumulative index to artists* has been added to *SC*. Each artist's name is followed by a list of the plays he or she has appeared in or presented and the volume and initial page number where substantial commentary on the artist can be found.

To help students locate essays by specific commentators, *SC* includes a *cumulative index to critics*. Under each critic's name are listed the plays and non-dramatic poems on which the critic has written and the volume and page where the commentary begins.

SC also provides a *cumulative index to topics*. This feature identifies the principal topics in the criticism and stage history of each work. The topics are arranged alphabetically, and the volume and initial page number are indicated for each excerpt that offers innovative or ample commentary on that topic.

As an additional aid to students, the *SC* performance series offers a *glossary* of terms relating to theaters, festivals, acting companies, and technical elements frequently mentioned by critics and used in the introductions to the play entries. The glossed terms are identified by small capital letters when they first appear in the introductions.

A Note to the Reader

Students who quote directly from any volume in the Literature Criticism Series in written assignments may use the following general forms to footnote reprinted criticism. The first example pertains to material drawn from periodicals, the second to material reprinted from books.

[1]Sears Jayne, "The Dreaming of *The Shrew*," *Shakespeare Quarterly,* XVII (Winter 1966), 41–56; excerpted and reprinted in *Shakespearean Criticism,* Vol. 9, ed. Mark W. Scott and Sandra L. Williamson (Detroit: Gale Research, 1989), pp. 381-85.

[2]Maynard Mack, *King Lear in Our Time* (Methuen & Co., 1966); excerpted and reprinted in *Shakespearean Criticism*, Vol. 11, ed. Sandra L. Williamson and James E. Person, Jr. (Detroit: Gale Research, 1990), pp. 132-36.

Suggestions Are Welcome

The editors encourage comments and suggestions from readers to expand the coverage and enhance the usefulness of the series. In response to various recommendations, several features have been added to *SC* since the series began, including the list of plays and poems covered in each volume, the glossary, the topic index, and the sample bibliographic citations noted above. Readers are cordially invited to write the editors or call our toll-free number: 1-800-347-GALE.

Acknowledgments

The editors wish to thank the copyright holders of the excerpted criticism included in this volume, the permissions managers of many book and magazine publishing companies for assisting us in securing reprint rights, and Anthony Bogucki for assistance with copyright research. We are also grateful to the staffs of the Detroit Public Library, the Library of Congress, the University of Detroit Library, Wayne State University Purdy/Kresge Library Complex, and the University of Michigan Libraries for making their resources available to us. Following is a list of the copyright holders who have granted us permission to reprint material in this volume of *SC*. Every effort has been made to trace copyright, but if omissions have been made, please let us know.

COPYRIGHTED EXCERPTS IN *SC*, VOLUME 12, WERE REPRINTED FROM THE FOLLOWING PERIODICALS:

American Jewish Archives, v. XXIII, April, 1971. ©1971 by the American Jewish Archives. Reprinted by permission of the publisher.—*Cahiers Elizabéthains,* n. 12, October, 1977; n. 14, October, 1978; n. 16, October, 1979; n. 30, October, 1986. All rights reserved. All reprinted by permission of the publisher.—*Canadian Art,* v. XIX, July-August, 1962.—*The Canadian Forum,* v. XLII, September, 1962.—*The Christian Science Monitor,* July 25, 1966; January 23, 1981. © 1966, 1981 The Christian Science Publishing Society. All rights reserved. Both reprinted by permission from *The Christian Science Monitor.*—*Drama,* London, n. 130, Autumn, 1978; n. 142, Winter, 1981. Both reprinted by permission of the British Theatre Association.—*Drama Survey,* v. 2, Fall, 1962 for a review of "The Taming of the Shrew" by Wes Balk. Copyright 1962 by The Bolingbroke Society, Inc. Reprinted by permission of the author.—*Educational Theatre Journal,* v. XIX, October, 1967; v. XXIII, October, 1971; v. 26, March, 1974; v. 27, December, 1975; v. 28, October, 1976. © 1967, 1971, 1974, 1975, 1976 University College Theatre Association of the American Theatre Association. All reprinted by permission of the publisher.—*Encounter,* v. XXXV, July, 1970. © 1970 by Encounter, Ltd. Reprinted by permission of the publisher.—*Essays and Studies,* n.s. v. 26, 1973. © The English Association 1973. All rights reserved. Reprinted by permission of the publisher.—*Film Quarterly,* v. XXI, Fall, 1967 for a review of "The Taming of the Shrew" by Stephen Farber. © 1967 by The Regents of the University of California. Reprinted by permission of the author.—*The Financial Times,* September 14, 1961; March 3, 1967; April 6, 1967; August 4, 1967; July 24, 1970; May 5, 1978; October 24, 1980. © The Financial Times Limited 1961, 1967, 1970, 1978, 1980. All reprinted by permission of the publisher.—*The Guardian,* July 24, 1970. © Guardian and Manchester Evening News Ltd., 1970. Reprinted by permission of Los Angeles Times—Washington Post News Service.—*Horizon,* Alabama, v. II, January, 1960 for "In Search of Shylock" by Walter Kerr. © 1960, renewed 1988 American Heritage Publishing Company, Inc. Reprinted by permission of the author.—*The Illustrated London News,* v. 250, April 15, 1967; v. 257, August 8, 1970; v. 257, September 12, 1970. © 1967, 1970 The Illustrated London News & Sketch Ltd. All reprinted by permission of the publisher.—*International Theatre Annual,* n. 5, 1961. © John Calder (Publishers) Ltd. 1961. Reprinted by permission of the publisher.—*Journal of Canadian Studies/Revue d'études canadiennes,* v. XI, February, 1976. Reprinted by permission of the publisher.—*The Listener,* v. LXXVII, March 9, 1967; v. 97, May 19, 1977; v. 99, May 11, 1978; v. 104, October 30, 1980; v. 106, September 10, 1981. © British Broadcasting Corp. 1967, 1977, 1978, 1980, 1981. Reprinted by permission of the publisher.—*Literature/Film Quarterly,* v. 8, 1980. © copyright 1980 Salisbury State College. Reprinted by permission of the publisher.—*London Magazine,* n.s. v. 7, December, 1967. © London Magazine 1967. Reprinted by permission of the publisher.—*Modern Language Notes,* v. XXXVI, June, 1921. Copyright 1921 by The Johns Hopkins University Press. All rights reserved. Reprinted by permission of the publisher.—*The Nation,* New York, v. 195, July 14, 1962; v. 211, July 6, 1970. Copyright 1962, 1970 *The Nation* magazine/ The Nation Company, Inc. Both reprinted by permission of the publisher./ v. 185, August 31, 1957; v. 187, July 5, 1958. Copyright 1957, renewed 1985; copyright 1958, renewed 1986 *The Nation* magazine/ The Nation Company, Inc. Both reprinted by permission of the publisher.—*New Statesman,* v. LXII, September 22, 1961; v. LXIII, April 27, 1962; v. 73, March 3, 1967; v. 80, September 4, 1970; v. 95, May 12, 1978; v. 97, May 4, 1979; v. 102, July 24, 1981. © 1961, 1962, 1967, 1970, 1978, 1979, 1981 The Statesman & Nation Publishing Co. Ltd. All reprinted by permission of the publisher.—*New York Herald Tribune,* June 21, 1962; June 22, 1962. © 1962 I.H.T. Corporation. Both reprinted by permission of the publisher.—*The New York Times,* November 27, 1927; October 1, 1935; October 20, 1935; February 6, 1940. Copyright 1927, 1935, 1940 by The New York Times Company. All reprinted by permission of the publisher./ June 22, 1960; June 22, 1962; July 30, 1970; August 28, 1970. Copyright © 1960, 1962, 1970 by The New York Times Company. All reprinted by permission of the publisher./ July 1, 1955; July 23, 1957; March 19, 1958; June 23, 1958; April 13, 1960. Copyright © 1955, renewed 1983; copyright © 1957, renewed 1985; copyright, © 1958, renewed 1986; copyright © 1960, renewed 1988 by The New York Times Company. All reprinted by permission of the publisher.—*Nineteenth Century Theatre Research,* v. 9, Summer, 1981 for "The Aesthetics of Beerbohm Tree's Shakespeare Festivals" by Ralph Berry. Reprinted by permission of the publisher and the author.—*The Observer,* April 22, 1962; August 30, 1970; May 15, 1977; July 19, 1981. All reprinted by permission of The Observer Limited, London.—*Plays and Players,* v. 9, November, 1961; v. 10, August, 1963; v. 14, June, 1967; v. 17, June,

1970; v. 17, September, 1970; v. 18, October, 1970; v. 24, July, 1977; n. 338, November, 1981; n. 347, August, 1982; n. 393, June, 1986. © 1961, 1963, 1967, 1970, 1977, 1981, 1982, 1986 Plusloop. All reprinted with permission of the publisher.—*Punch,* v. CCXLIV, June 26, 1963; v. 252, April 12, 1967; v. 259, August 5, 1970; v. 281, September 16, 1981; v. 290, June 25, 1986. © 1963, 1967, 1970, 1981, 1986 by Punch Publications Ltd. All rights reserved. May not be reprinted without permission.—*Saturday Review,* v. XLV, July 7, 1962; v. XLV, July 14, 1962; v. LIII, July 11, 1970. © 1962, 1970 *Saturday Review* magazine.—*The Saturday Review,* New York, v. XL, July 27, 1957. © 1957, renewed 1985 Saturday Review magazine.—*The Shakespeare Newsletter,* v. XVII, September, 1967. Reprinted by permission of the publisher.—*Shakespeare Quarterly,* v. XIII, Autumn, 1962; v. XXI, Autumn, 1970; v. 27, Winter, 1976; v. 30, Spring, 1979; v. 32, Summer, 1981; v. 32, Autumn, 1981; v. 33, Summer, 1982; v. 33, Autumn, 1982. © The Folger Shakespeare Library 1962, 1970, 1976, 1970, 1981, 1982. All reprinted by permission of the publisher.—*Shakespeare Survey: An Annual Survey of Shakespearian Study and Production,* v. 14, 1961; v. 16, 1963; v. 20, 1967; v. 24, 1971; v. 31, 1978; v. 32, 1979; v. 35, 1982; v. 36, 1983. © Cambridge University Press, 1961, 1963, 1967, 1971, 1978, 1979, 1982, 1983. All reprinted with the permission of Cambridge University Press.—*Sight and Sound,* v. 36, Spring, 1967. Copyright © 1967 by The British Film Institute. Reprinted by permission of the publisher.—*The Spectator,* v. 207, September 22, 1961; v. 218, March 10, 1967; v. 225, August 1, 1970; v. 225, September 5, 1970; v. 243, May 5, 1979; v. 256, June 21, 1986. © 1961, 1967, 1970, 1979, 1986 by The Spectator. All reprinted by permission of *The Spectator.*—*Studies in English Literature, 1500-1900,* v. XVIII, Spring, 1978 for "The Original Ending of 'The Taming of the Shrew': A Reconsideration" by Karl P. Wentersdorf. © 1978 William Marsh Rice University. Reprinted by permission of the publisher and the author.—*The Sunday Times,* London, May 15, 1977; July 19, 1981. © Times Newspapers Limited 1977, 1981. Both reproduced from *The Sunday Times,* London by permission.—*Theater,* v. 13, Summer-Fall, 1982 for "A Dance for Our Disbeliefs: The Current 'A Midsummer Night's Dream' of the RSC." by Gary Jay Williams. Copyright © by *Theater,* formerly *yale/theater* 1982. Reprinted by permission of the publisher and the author.—*Theatre Arts,* v. XLI, September, 1957 for "The Stratford Story: Connecticut Version" by Alice Griffin. Reprinted by permission of the author.—*Theatre History Studies,* v. III, 1983. Copyright © 1983 by the University of North Dakota. Reprinted by permission of the publisher.—*Theatre Journal,* v. 32, March, 1980; v. 33, October, 1981. © 1980, 1981, University and College Theatre Association of the American Theatre Association. Both reprinted by permission of the publisher.—*Theatre Notebook,* v. XXIII, Winter, 1968-69 for "Samuel Phelp's 'A Midsummer Night's Dream' " by Richard Foulkes; v. XXXI, 1977 for "Helen Faucit and Ellen Terry as Portia" by Richard Foulkes; v. XXXVI, 1982 for "An Unholy Alliance: William Poel, Martin Harvey and 'The Taming of the Shrew' " by Jan McDonald. All reprinted by permission of the respective authors.—*Theatre Research,* v. 3, 1963. © Oxford University Press 1963. Reprinted by permission of the publisher.—*Theatre Survey,* v. XVII, November, 1976; v. XVIII, November, 1977. Copyright © 1976, 1977 American Society for Theatre Research, Inc. Both reprinted by permission of the publisher.—*Time,* New York, v. 95, May 18, 1970. Copyright 1970 Time Inc. All rights reserved. Reprinted by permission from *Time.*—*Time and Tide,* v. 42, September 21, 1961.—*The Times,* London, August 29, 1970 for "Life and Joy" by Peter Brook and Ronald Hayman. © Times Newspapers Limited 1970. Reprinted by permission of the Peters Fraser and Dunlop Group Ltd and Peter Brook./ April, 18, 1962; April 24, 1962; June 14, 1963; February 28, 1967; April 1, 1967; April 6, 1967; August 4, 1967; April 29, 1970; July 24, 1970; August 28, 1970; May 5, 1978; October 24, 1980; August 26, 1981; September 4, 1981; June 17, 1982; June 12, 1986. © Times Newspapers Limited 1962, 1963, 1967, 1970, 1978, 1980, 1981, 1982, 1986. All reproduced from *The Times,* London, by permission.—*The Times Literary Supplement,* n. 3972, May 19, 1978; n. 3995, October 27, 1978; n. 4048, October 31, 1980; n. 4087, July 31, 1981; n. 4094, September 18, 1981. © Times Newspapers Ltd. (London) 1978, 1980, 1981. All reproduced from *The Times Literary Supplement* by permission.—*yale/theatre,* v. 4, Summer, 1973 for " 'The Concord of this Discord': Music in the Stage History of 'A Midsummer Night's Dream' " by Gary Jay Williams. Copyright © by *Theater,* formerly, *yale/theatre,* 1973. Reprinted by permission of the publisher and the author.

COPYRIGHTED EXCERPTS IN *SC*, VOLUME 12, WERE REPRINTED FROM THE FOLLOWING BOOKS:

Allen, Shirley S. From *Samuel Phelps and Sadler's Wells Theatre.* Wesleyan University Press, 1971. Copyright © 1971 by Wesleyan University. Reprinted by permission of the publisher.—Berry, Ralph. From *On Directing Shakespeare: Interviews with Contemporary Directors.* Croom Helm, 1977. © 1977 Ralph Berry. Reprinted by permission of the publisher.—Billington, Michael. From *The Modern Actor.* Hamish Hamilton, 1973. Copyright © 1973 by Michael Billington. Reprinted by permission of the publisher.—Brown, John Russell. From *Shakespeare's Plays in Performance.* Edward Arnold (Publishers) Ltd., 1966. © John Russell Brown 1966. Reprinted by permission of the publisher.—Cottrell, John. From *Laurence Olivier.* Prentice-Hall, Inc., 1975. Copyright © 1975 by John Cottrell. All rights reserved. Reprinted by permission of the author.—Cusack, Sinead. From "Portia in 'The Merchant of Venice'," in *Players of Shakespeare: Essays in Shakespearean Performance.* By twelve players with the Royal Shakespeare Company, edited by Philip Brockbank. Cambridge University Press, 1985. © Cambridge University Press 1985. Reprinted with the permission of the publisher.—Drew, John. From *My Years on the Stage.* E. P. Dutton & Company, 1922. Copyright 1921, 1922, by The Curtis Company. Copyright, 1922, by E. P. Dutton & Company. Renewed 1949 by Susanah K. Tarkington. All rights reserved. Reprinted by permission of the publisher, E. P. Dutton, a division of Penguin Books USA Inc.—Felheim, Marvin. From *The Theater of Augustin Daly: An Account of the Late Nineteenth Century American Stage.* Cambridge, Mass.: Harvard University Press, 1956. Copyright © 1956 by the President and Fellows of Harvard College. Renewed 1984 by Charlotte Darrow Felheim. Excerpted by permission of the publishers and the Literary Estate of Marvin Felheim.—Fitzsimons, Raymund. From *Edmund Kean: Fire from Heaven.* Hamish Hamilton, 1976. Copyright © 1976 by Raymund Fitzsimons. Reprinted by permission of the author.—Guthrie, Sir

Tyrone. From an introduction to "The Merchant of Venice," in *Shakespeare: Ten Great Plays*. By William Shakespeare, edited by Tyrone Guthrie. Golden Press, 1962. Copyright © 1962 by Western Publishing Company, Inc. Used by permission of the publisher.—Haring-Smith, Tori. From *From Farce to Metadrama: A Stage History of "The Taming of the Shrew," 1594-1983*. Greenwood Press, 1985. Copyright © 1985 by Tori Haring-Smith. All rights reserved. Reprinted by permission of Greenwood Publishing Group, Inc., Westport, CT.—Holderness, Graham. From *Shakespeare in Performance: The Taming of the Shrew*. Manchester University Press, 1989. © Graham Holderness 1989. Reprinted by permission of the publisher.—Jorgens, Jack J. From *Shakespeare on Film*. Indiana University Press, 1977. Copyright © 1977 by Indiana University Press. All rights reserved. Reprinted by permission of the author.—Kennedy, Dennis. From *Granville Barker and the Dream of Theatre*. Cambridge University Press, 1985. © Cambridge University Press 1985. Reprinted with the permission of the publisher and the author.—Kirstein, Lincoln. From "On Producing 'A Midsummer Night's Dream'," in *A Midsummer Night's Dream*. By William Shakespeare, edited by Charles Jasper Sisson. Dell Publishing Co., Inc., 1960. © copyright, 1960, by Western Printing and Lithographing Company. Renewed 1988 by Dell, a Division of Bantam, Doubleday, Dell Publishing Group, Inc. Reprinted by permission of the Literary Estate of C. J. Sisson.—Manvell, Roger. From *Shakespeare and the Film*. Praeger Publishers, 1971. © 1971 in London, England, by Roger Manvell. All rights reserved. Reprinted by permission of the publisher.—Mazer, Cary M. From *Shakespeare Refashioned: Elizabethan Plays on Edwardian Stages*. UMI Research Press, 1981. Copyright © 1981, 1980 Cary M. Mazer. All rights reserved. Reprinted by permission of the publisher.—McDonald, Jan. From " 'The Taming of the Shrew' at the Haymarket Theatre, 1844 and 1847," in *Essays on Nineteenth Century British Theatre*. Edited by Kenneth Richards and Peter Thomson. Methuen & Co. Ltd., 1971. © 1971 Methuen. Reprinted by permission of the publisher.—Miller, Jonathan. From *Subsequent Performances*. Faber & Faber, 1986. © 1986 by Jonathan Miller. All rights reserved. Reprinted by permission of Faber & Faber Ltd.—Miller, Tice L. From "The Taming of the Shrew," in *Shakespeare Around the Globe: A Guide to Notable Postwar Revivals*. Edited by Samuel L. Leiter. Greenwood Press, 1986. Copyright © 1986 by Samuel L. Leiter. All rights reserved. Reprinted by permission of Greenwood Publishing, Inc., Westport, CT.—Pepys, Samuel. From *The Diary of Samuel Pepys, 1662, Vol. II*. Edited by Robert Latham and William Matthews. University of California Press, 1970 by G. Bell & Sons, Ltd. Reprinted by permission of the publisher.—Proudfoot, Richard. From "Peter Brook and Shakespeare," in *Drama and Mimesis*. Cambridge University Press 1980. © Cambridge University Press, 1980. Reprinted with the permission of the publisher.—Robinson, Henry Crabb. From two diary entries in *The London Theatre, 1811-1866: Selections from the Diary of Henry Crabb Robinson*. Edited by Eluned Brown. The Society for Theatre Research, 1966. © Eluned Brown. Reprinted by permission of the publisher.—Rossi, Alfred, and Paul Rogers. From an interview in *Astonish Us in the Morning: Tyrone Guthrie Remembered*. By Alfred Rossi. Hutchinson & Co., Ltd., 1977. © Alfred Rossi 1977. Reprinted by permission of the publisher.—Shattuck, Charles H. From *Shakespeare on the American Stage: From Booth and Barrett to Sothern and Marlowe, Vol. 2*. Folger Shakespeare Library, 1987. © 1987 by Associated University Presses, Inc. Reprinted by permission of the publisher.—Simon, John. From *Uneasy Stages: A Chronicle of the New York Theater 1964-1973*. Random House, 1975. Copyright © 1975 by John Simon. Reprinted by permission of Random House, Inc.—Sprague, Arthur Colby. From *Shakespearean Players and Performances*. Cambridge, Mass.: Harvard University Press, 1953. Copyright 1953 by the President and Fellows of Harvard College. Renewed 1981 by Arthur Colby Sprague. Excerpted by permission of the publisher and the author.—Stewart, Patrick. From "Shylock in 'The Merchant of Venice'," in *Players of Shakespearean Performance*. By twelve players with the Royal Shakespeare Company, edited by Philip Brockbank. Cambridge University Press, 1985. © Cambridge University Press 1985. Reprinted with the permission of the publisher.—Styan, J. L. From *Max Reinhardt*. Cambridge University Press, 1982. © Cambridge University Press 1982. Reprinted with the permission of the publisher.—Styan, J. L. From *The Shakespeare Revolution: Criticism and Performance in the Twentieth Century*. Cambridge University Press, 1977. © Cambridge University Press 1977. Reprinted with the permission of the publisher and the author.—Tynan, Kenneth. From *Curtains: Selections from the Drama Criticism and Related Writings*. Atheneum Publishers, 1961. All rights reserved. Copyright © 1961 by Kenneth Tynan. Reprinted by permission of the Literary Estate of Kenneth Tynan.—Wells, Stanley. From an introduction to *A Midsummer Night's Dream*. By William Shakespeare, edited by Charles Kean. Cornmarket Press, 1970. Reprinted by permission of the author.—Williams, Simon. From "The 'Shakespeare-Stage' in Nineteenth-Century Germany" in *Shakespeare and the Victorian Stage*. Edited by Richard Foulkes. Cambridge University Press, 1986. © Cambridge University Press 1986. Reprinted with the permission of the publisher.

PHOTOGRAPHS AND ILLUSTRATIONS APPEARING IN *SC*, VOLUME 12, WERE RECEIVED FROM THE FOLLOWING SOURCES:

The Shakespeare Centre Library, Stratford-upon-Avon: **p. 48**; Photograph by Angus McBean. Harvard Theatre Collection: **pp. 50, 243, 351, 354, 355**; Photograph by McKague, Toronto: **p. 56**; Tom Holte Theatre Photographic Collection, Shakespeare Centre Library: **pp. 66, 247, 474**; Photograph by Anthony Crickmay: **p. 75**; Photograph by Joe Cocks: **pp. 98, 104, 491**; The Billy Rose Theatre Collection, The New York Public Library at Lincoln Center, Astor, Lenox and Tilden Foundations: **pp. 192, 343, 347**; UA Sixteen: **p. 215**; British Theatre Museum, London: **p. 235**; Photograph by David Farrell: **p. 255**; The Shakespeare Centre and the Governors of the Royal Shakespeare Theatre: **p. 261**; Photograph by Zoë Dominic: **p. 360**; Photograph by Gordon Goode. The Governors of the Royal Shakespeare Theatre: **p. 362**; Photograph by Douglas Jeffery. © RSC: **p. 383**; © RSC: **p. 386**; *The Financial Times*: **p. 391**; © BBC: **p. 402**; Photograph by Houston Rogers: **pp. 462, 464, 468**; Donald Cooper/Photostage: **p. 494**.

List of Plays and Poems Covered in *SC*

[The year or years in parentheses indicate the composition date of the work as determined by G. Blakemore Evans in *The Riverside Shakespeare*]

Volume 1

The Comedy of Errors (1592-94)
Hamlet (1600-01)
1 and *2 Henry IV* (1596-98)
Timon of Athens (1607-08)
Twelfth Night (1601-02)

Volume 2

Henry VIII (1612-13)
King Lear (1605)
Love's Labour's Lost (1594-95)
Measure for Measure (1604)
Pericles (1607-08)

Volume 3

1, 2, and *3 Henry VI* (1589-91)
Macbeth (1606)
A Midsummer Night's Dream (1595-96)
Troilus and Cressida (1601-02)

Volume 4

Cymbeline (1609-10)
The Merchant of Venice (1596-97)
Othello (1604)
Titus Andronicus (1593-94)

Volume 5

As You Like It (1599)
Henry V (1599)
The Merry Wives of Windsor (1597)
Romeo and Juliet (1595-96)

Volume 6

Antony and Cleopatra (1606-07)
Richard II (1595)
The Two Gentlemen of Verona (1594)

Volume 7

All's Well That Ends Well (1602-03)
Julius Caesar (1599)
The Winter's Tale (1610-11)

Volume 8

Much Ado about Nothing (1598-99)
Richard III (1592-93)
The Tempest (1611)

Volume 9

Coriolanus (1607-08)
King John (1594-96)
The Taming of the Shrew (1593-94)
The Two Noble Kinsmen (1613)

Volume 10

The Phoenix and Turtle (1601)
The Rape of Lucrece (1593-94)
Sonnets (1593-99)
Venus and Adonis (1592-93)

Volume 11 (Performance Series)

King Lear
Othello
Romeo and Juliet

Volume 12 (Performance Series)

The Merchant of Venice
A Midsummer Night's Dream
The Taming of the Shrew
The Two Gentlemen of Verona

Forthcoming

Volume 13: *Shakespearean Criticism Yearbook*

Chronological Guide to Selected Productions

(* indicates productions covered in the excerpts)

The Merchant of Venice

Date	Artist(s)	Theater / Company
1605	Richard Burbage King's Men	Whitehall
1701–35	George Granville Thomas Doggett Thomas Betterton	Lincoln's Inn Fields
* 1741	Charles Macklin	Drury Lane
1784	J. P. Kemble Sarah Siddons	Drury Lane
* 1814	Edmund Kean	Drury Lane
1823	W. C. Macready	Covent Garden
1875	The Bancrofts Ellen Terry	Prince of Wales
* 1879	Henry Irving Ellen Terry	Lyceum
* 1932	Theodore Komisarjevsky	Shakespeare Memorial Theatre
1938	John Gielgud Peggy Ashcroft	Queen's
* 1953	Michael Redgrave Peggy Ashcroft	Shakespeare Memorial Theatre
* 1955	Tyrone Guthrie Frederick Valk	Stratford Festival, Ontario
1956	Margaret Webster Emlyn Williams Margaret Johnston	Shakespeare Memorial Theatre
* 1957	Morris Carnovsky Katharine Hepburn	American Shakespeare Theatre
* 1960	Michael Langham Peter O'Toole	Shakespeare Memorial Theatre
* 1962	Joseph Papp George C. Scott	New York Shakespeare Festival

* 1970	Jonathan Miller Laurence Olivier	Old Vic / National
1971	Terry Hands Emrys James Judi Dench	Royal Shakespeare Company
* 1978	John Barton Patrick Stewart	The Other Place, Stratford-upon-Avon
1989	Peter Hall Dustin Hoffman	Royal Shakespeare Company

A Midsummer Night's Dream

Date	Artist(s)	Theater / Company
* 1662	Thomas Killigrew	The King's Servants
* 1692	Thomas Betterton	Dorset Garden
* 1755 and 1763	David Garrick	Drury Lane
* 1816	Frederick Reynolds	Covent Garden
* 1826 and 1841	Edmund Simpson	Park Theatre
1833	Alfred Bunn	Drury Lane
* 1840	Madame Vestris	Covent Garden
* 1843	Ludwig Tieck Felix Mendelssohn	Potsdam Court
* 1853	Samuel Phelps	Sadler's Wells
* 1854	William Burton	Burton's Theatre
* 1854	E. A. Marshall	Broadway Theatre
* 1856	Charles Kean	Princess's
1859	Laura Keene	Keene's Theatre
* 1873–96	Augustin Daly	Daly's Theatre, et al.
1889–1915	F. R. Benson	Shakespeare Memorial Theatre, et al.
* 1900 and 1911	Herbert Beerbohm Tree	Her Majesty's
* 1905–39	Max Reinhardt	Neues, Deutsches, et al.
* 1914	Harley Granville-Barker	Savoy
1931	Harcourt Williams Ralph Richardson	Old Vic

* 1937	Tyrone Guthrie Ralph Richardson Vivien Leigh	Old Vic
1945	Nevill Coghill John Gielgud Peggy Ashcroft	Haymarket
* 1951	Tyrone Guthrie Paul Rogers	Old Vic
* 1958	Jack Landau Morris Carnovsky	American Shakespeare Theatre
* 1959–68	Peter Hall	Royal Shakespeare Company
1960	Benjamin Britten	Aldeburgh Festival
1967	John Hancock	Theatre de Lys
* 1970	Peter Brook	Royal Shakespeare Company
1975	Robert Brustein	Yale Repertory
1976–77	Robin Phillips	Stratford Festival, Ontario
* 1977	John Barton Patrick Stewart	Royal Shakespeare Company
* 1981	Ron Daniels	Royal Shakespeare Company
1989	John Caird	Royal Shakespeare Company

The Taming of the Shrew

Date	Artist(s)	Theater / Company
1594(?)	Chamberlain's Men	Newington Butts
1754	David Garrick	Drury Lane
* 1844 and 1847	J. R. Planché Benjamin Webster Robert Strickland Louisa Nisbett	Haymarket
* 1856	Samuel Phelps	Sadler's Wells
* 1867	Henry Irving Ellen Terry	Queen's
* 1870	Miss Alleyne Boothroyd Fairclough	Globe Theatre
* 1887 and 1888	Augustin Daly Ada Rehan John Drew	Daly's Theatre, New York Gaiety, London

* 1913	John Martin Harvey William Poel	Prince of Wales
1929	Douglas Fairbanks Mary Pickford	(Film Adaptation)
* 1935 and 1940	Alfred Lunt Lynn Fontanne	The Guild, New York
1947	John Burrell Trevor Howard	New Theatre

* 1953–54	George Devine
	Marius Goring and
	  Keith Michell
	Yvonne Mitchell and
	  Barbara Jefford
		Shakespeare Memorial Theatre

1954	Tyrone Guthrie	Stratford Festival, Ontario

* 1960 and 1961	John Barton and
	  Maurice Daniels
	Peggy Ashcroft and
	  Vanessa Redgrave
	Peter O'Toole and
	  Derek Godfrey
		Shakespeare Memorial Theatre

* 1962	Michael Langham John Colicos	Stratford Festival, Ontario
* 1967	Franco Zeffirelli Richard Burton Elizabeth Taylor	(Film Adaptation)
* 1967	Trevor Nunn Michael Williams Janet Suzman	Royal Shakespeare Company
1973	Clifford Williams	Royal Shakespeare Company
* 1978–79	Michael Bogdanov Jonathan Pryce Company Paola Dionisotti	Royal Shakespeare
* 1980	Jonathan Miller John Cleese	(BBC Television)
1982–83	Barry Kyle	Royal Shakespeare Company
* 1986	Toby Robertson Timothy Dalton Vanessa Redgrave	Theatre Royal, Haymarket
1987	Jonathan Miller Fiona Shaw	Royal Shakespeare Company

The Two Gentlemen of Verona

Date	Artist(s)	Theatre / Company
* 1762	Benjamin Victor David Garrick	Drury Lane
1790 and 1808	J. P. Kemble	Drury Lane
* 1821	Frederick Reynolds	Covent Garden
1841	W. C. Macready	Drury Lane
1848	Charles Kean	Haymarket
* 1895	Augustin Daly Ada Rehan	Daly's Theatre, New York Daly's Theatre, London
* 1896 and 1910	William Poel	Merchant Taylors' Hall His Majesty's
* 1938	B. Iden Payne	Shakespeare Memorial Theatre
1952	Denis Carey John Neville	Bristol Old Vic
* 1957-58	Michael Langham Keith Michell Barbara Jefford	Old Vic Phoenix, New York
* 1957	Stuart Vaughan Jerry Stiller Ann Meara	New York Shakespeare Festival
* 1960	Peter Hall Derek Godfrey	Shakespeare Memorial Theatre
* 1970	Robin Phillips Ian Richardson Helen Mirren	Royal Shakespeare Company
* 1975	Robin Phillips David Toguri	Stratford Festival, Ontario
* 1981	David Ostwald	Oregon Shakespearean Festival
* 1981	John Barton	Royal Shakespeare Company
1983	Don Taylor	(BBC Television)

THE MERCHANT OF VENICE

The Merchant of Venice ranks with *Hamlet* as one of the most frequently performed plays in Shakespearean stage history, an astonishing fact given that a period of nearly 150 years lapsed after the initial production before the play was revived. Records document two performances by the KING'S MEN before James I and the court at Whitehall, February 10 and 12, 1605. No evidence survives, describing the nature of this first production, although some scholars speculate that Richard Burbage likely created the role of Shylock and played the character in a comic style. On 11 January 1701 George Granville, later Lord Lansdowne, presented his adaptation of Shakespeare's *Merchant,* entitled *The Jew of Venice,* at LINCOLN'S INN FIELDS. Granville deleted characters and whole scenes and added others, including a masque. He also rewrote a great deal of the verse and shifted the emphasis of the drama away from Shylock to Bassanio, played by the popular actor Thomas Betterton, in order to create the type of romantic comedy so popular at the time. Thomas Doggett, a leading comic actor of his generation, won plaudits for his low-comic portrayal of Shylock; Granville's production, after moving to Covent Garden in 1714, continued to draw large audiences until its close in 1735. (Further evidence of the prevailing approach to staging the play is provided by William Dunlap, in his *A History of the American Theater.* Dunlap reports that *The Merchant of Venice* was "the first play performed in America by a regular company of comedians," in Williamsburg, Virginia, 15 September 1752.)

Nicholas Rowe, the editor of the first critical edition of Shakespeare's plays (1709) and author of the first authoritative Shakespeare biography (1709), presaged the iminent revolution in interpretation and re-evaluation of Shylock when he remarked, in the latter work, that despite Doggett's commendable, comic performance, a tragic conception of the character would be more appropriate: "tho' we have seen that Play Receiv'd and Acted as a Comedy, and the Part of the Jew perform'd by an Excellent Comedian, yet I cannot but think it was design'd Tragically by the Author. There appears in it such a deadly Spirit of Revenge, such a savage Fierceness and Fellness, and such a bloody designation of Cruelty and Mischief, as cannot agree either with the Stile or Characters of Comedy." Charles Macklin shared Rowe's conception of Shylock, although perhaps for reasons more mercenary than academic, and sought to bring that interpretation to the stage.

Macklin was a prominent Irish actor, who found himself in 1741 lacking the artistic reputation and public approval he dearly desired. In restoring Shakespeare's *The Merchant of Venice,* and supplanting Granville's travesty, Macklin envisioned transforming the play into a star vehicle that would establish him at the top of his profession. Macklin encountered considerable opposition from the managers of the Drury Lane theater as well as the cast, who were convinced that anything other than a comic rendering of Shylock and the play would inevitably fail. Thus, Macklin, who also directed the production, concealed his true intent in rehearsals, but on opening night, he proceeded with his innovative interpretation. According to accounts of the performance, Macklin's malevolent, cunning, ferocious Shylock overwhelmed his skeptical audience and drew wide admiration. Francis Gentleman, who lauded Macklin's villainous appearance and facile manner of modulating his passions, declared that Macklin "through the whole displays . . . unequalled merit." Macklin's performance is said to have inspired the couplet, often attributed to Alexander Pope, "This is the Jew / That Shakespeare drew." Macklin's success is even more remarkable in light of the fact that the cast of his production, including James Quin as Antonio and, most notably, Kitty Clive as Portia, retained their comic impersonations as developed in Granville's adaptation. Shylock remained a key figure in Macklin's repertoire, last performed by the aged actor on 7 May 1789.

Beginning in the late eighteenth century, prominent actors such as John Henderson, John Philip Kemble, and George Frederick Cooke began to introduce elements of dignity and pathos into their conceptions of Shylock, tempering the image of sheer malevolence crafted by Macklin. This sentimentalizing tendency prepared the way for the two greatest Shylocks of the nineteenth century, Edmund Kean and Henry Irving. These two actors portrayed Shylock not as a comic figure, as in the first half of the eighteenth century, nor as a malicious villain, as in the second half, but as a wise, tragic figure, more sinned against than sinning.

Kean was developing a reputation for fine, impassioned, tragic acting in provincial productions when the managers of the Drury Lane theater, spurred by stagnant ticket sales, contracted the young actor to perform in London. When Kean arrived in London, however, the conservative managers reneged on their promise of allowing the actor the role of his choice, Shylock. Kean remained steadfast, and eventually the managers acquiesced, granting Kean a single rehearsal on the morning preceding his first performance, 26 January 1814. Kean, like Macklin, subdued his volatile, passionate acting style in rehearsal, so as not to alarm the suspicious Drury Lane company, but held nothing back in performance. Appearing for the first time in the play's stage history in a black wig, rather than a conventional, stereotypical red one, Kean attained the climax of his fiery, captivating performance in the scene with Solanio, Salerio, and Tubal, Act III, Scene i. Douglas Jerrold, who witnessed Kean's Shylock, reported approvingly that Kean struck his audience "like a chapter of Genesis." Kean, as the pioneer of the romantic style of acting, played Shylock, in the words of William Winter, "as a creature of murderous malice, and yet of distinctively Hebraic majesty." William Hazlitt, regarded as one of the principal founders of formal, dramatic criticism and a leading figure in the romantic movement, aided the ascendance of Kean by extolling the latter's virtues throughout his career on the stage. Although Hazlitt occasionally contested Kean's conception of a character, as in the case of his half-tragic, victimized Shylock, he averred that as a performer, Kean was unrivalled: "His style of acting is, if we may use the expression, more significant, more pregnant with meaning, more varied and alive in every part, than any we have almost ever witnessed. The character never stands still; there is no vacant pause in the action; the eye is never silent. For depth and force of conception, we have seen actors whom we should prefer to Mr. Kean in Shylock; for brilliant and masterly execution, none."

Henry Irving, the second preeminent Shylock of the period, was the most successful actor-manager of the late nineteenth century. According to his grandson, Laurence Irving, he once declared: "Looking back on my life's work and attempting—in all humility—to appraise it, I feel certain of one thing—mine is the only great Shylock." Indeed, Irving's production of *The Merchant of Venice,* featuring his long-time Lyceum partner Ellen Terry as Portia, ranks as one of his most celebrated and popular productions, appearing more than 250 times in its first run alone. His portrayal of Shylock is regarded as one of his very finest Shakespearean roles. Irving indulged in the Victorian taste for lavish sets, as developed by Charles Kean and the Bancrofts, and his *Merchant* was no exception. Yet the production owed its success to much more than visual splendor. Critics praised the restoration of the fifth act, which was often omitted in previous productions because the perceived star, Shylock, makes his final exit at the end of Act IV. Terry's winsome, radiant portrayal of Portia won near unanimous acclaim. Joseph Knight, the *Athenaeum* critic, exclaimed, "The beauty of Miss Terry's Portia is incontestable." The *Saturday Review* critic wrote of Terry, "Every changing phase of the part is rendered with the highest instinct and art, and every change seems natural and easy."

Irving's portrait of Shylock, inspired by a trip he made to the Levant, and following in the tradition established by Kean, depicted an aristocratic, proud figure, a grieved widower, and loving father. Although his rage and bitterness occasionally surfaced, he retained his dignity and composure throughout. The pinnacle of the performance was generally thought to be the Trial Scene, and Irving's especially poignant exit. The *Spectator* critic was moved to comment, "his Shylock is Mr. Irving's finest performance, and his final exit is its best point." To enhance his conception of a tragic Shylock, Irving added a scene in which Shylock returns to his house just after Lorenzo has swept Jessica away, Act II, Scene vi. Irving slowly crossed a canal bridge and knocked twice at his door, silently waiting for his absent daughter to answer as the curtain fell. Of Irving's Shylock, Clement Scott remarked, "in point of variety, incisiveness and subtlety of expression, it ranks higher than anything the actor has yet attempted." Over time, it has been said, Irving endowed his Shylock with more vindictiveness and overt malice. In any case, Irving's *Merchant* remained very popular and enjoyed considerable success during Irving's eight tours of America as well.

In the twentieth century, producers and actors continued to reinterpret the play, typically seeking some middle ground between the two extreme conceptions of Shylock, the malicious villain and the sentimentalized, tragic victim. William Poel, a highly influential English actor, producer, and founder of the Elizabethan Stage Society, advocated unadorned, swiftly-paced productions reminiscent of Elizabethan stage conventions and rejected Victorian abuses such as elephantine sets and sentimentalized characterizations. Poel conceived of Shylock as a villain, in the manner that Shakespeare conceived of the character, so Poel felt. Although some critics felt Poel went too far in reaction to Irving, Poel emerged as a harbinger of later twentieth-century productions that

sought to restore dramatic balance between the tragic, mercantile world of Shylock and Antonio in Venice and the comic, fairy-tale world of Portia and her suitors in Belmont. Thus, in contrast to early eighteenth- and nineteenth-century productions that presented *The Merchant of Venice* as a star vehicle, twentieth-century productions, with some exceptions, sought to reconcile the two story lines, the bond-plot and the casket-plot, and restore the romance-comedy aspect.

Another influential early-twentieth-century figure was Harley Granville-Barker, an English actor, playwright, director, and critic who emphasized simplicity in staging, set design, and costuming, believing that elaborate scenery obscures the poetry which is of central importance to Shakespeare's plays. In his *Prefaces to Shakespeare* (1930), Barker declared, "*The Merchant of Venice* is a fairy tale," and argued that as long as the director observes this dictum, the production will unfold naturally and coherently. Thus, Barker intimated that productions which deviate from this simple prescription and treat the story realistically, as tragedy rather than romance-comedy, are likely to unravel under the strain of inconsistency. Many producers and critics took Barker's words to heart.

In the early 1930s, the director of the Shakespeare Memorial Theatre at Stratford-upon-Avon, W. Bridges-Adams, invited Theodore Komisarjevsky, a Russian producer and director gaining notoriety in Europe, to serve as guest director. During his tenure at Stratford, Komisarjevsky produced six Shakespearean plays, including *The Merchant of Venice* in 1932. English critics reacted somewhat skeptically to Komisarjevsky's controversial productions, arguing that the producer had become enamored with the mechanical capabilities of the theater itself, and that his direction was overly theatrical, involving clumsy scene changes. Yet critics also recognized Komisarjevsky's innovative, artistic spirit, and they praised his effort to emphasize the elements of romance and comedy in *The Merchant of Venice*. This *Merchant,* according to critics, appeared as an extended revel, featuring an opening masque, elaborate, caricatured sets, "fantasticated" casket scenes, and, significantly, a virtually uncut text with the original scene order. Randle Ayrton portrayed a villainous, thoroughly unsentimental Shylock, generally well received by critics.

In the 1950s, within a span of only five years, three critically-acclaimed productions of *The Merchant of Venice* reached the stage. Most critics felt the strongest point of Denis Carey's 1953 Stratford-upon-Avon production was the performance of Peggy Ashcroft as Portia, the "jewel of the evening," according to Kenneth Tynan. Michael Redgrave's portrayal of Shylock was reminiscent of Macklin's: a compelling figure of rage and animosity, unflinching in his desire for vengeance. Critics protested that Redgrave ignored the character's guile, self-mockery, and humor; Tynan, again, maintained that Redgrave failed to "fuse the villainy of the part with its sardonic comedy."

In 1955, Tyrone Guthrie mounted a production of *The Merchant of Venice* at Stratford, Ontario, that earned plaudits for its direction, "a brilliant total interpretation," according to Henry Hewes. Guthrie infused the play with many comic touches in an effort to rekindle the comic mood of the drama and balance the two dominant plots. To achieve this balance, as many critics noted, Guthrie sought to elevate Antonio's role in the production, as a character who unites Belmont and Venice. Frederick Valk played a passionate, vengeful Shylock, who also conveyed a sense of dignity. The Canadian novelist Robertson Davies called Valk's performance "an astounding exhibition of mounting emotion." Alice Griffin deemed Francis Hyland's Portia "an ideal heroine for Shakespearean comedy."

In 1957, Katharine Hepburn drew considerable attention to the play when she appeared as Portia in Jack Landau's American Shakespeare Festival production at Stratford, Connecticut. Although Hepburn took star billing, Morris Carnovsky's Shylock won most of the critical praise. Like Guthrie, Landau conceived of the play as romantic comedy, and Carnovsky's portrayal of Shylock as comic villain aptly suited this framework. Alice Griffin pronounced Carnovsky's performance "a full-length, subtly executed, excellent portrait." Hepburn was not so fortunate. According to Claire McGlinchee, Hepburn's "voice is not the instrument for Shakespeare's poetic lines." Griffin was more charitable in her appraisal, although she conceded that Hepburn's Portia was "not so much Shakespeare's as her own familiar brand of heroine."

To the satisfaction of most critics, Michael Langham's 1960 production of *The Merchant of Venice* at Stratford-upon-Avon marked a reversion to the tragic representation of Shylock. Peter O'Toole impressed his audience with his powerful, magnetic performance as a witty, dignified Shylock. A. Alvarez commended O'Toole for transforming the character "from an ambiguous figure hovering somewhere between caricature and melodrama into a major tragic hero." Dorothy Tutin offered an enchanting Portia, somewhat overshadowed, most critics felt, by the tragic dimensions of O'Toole's captivating performance. A disciple of Guthrie, Langham demonstrated a technique which occasionally led to gratuitous devices and reminded some critics of Guthrie's stress on stage business and theatricality. But for the most part, reviewers welcomed the emphasis on romance-comedy. Langham employed a late-eighteenth-century set and costumes, to the occasional mystification of the critics.

Joseph Papp's version of *The Merchant of Venice* was one of the inaugural productions in the new Delacorte theater in Central Park, as part of the New York Shakespeare Festival in 1962. Once again, Shylock, as portrayed by George C. Scott, was presented neither as an Irving-esque tragic victim nor as an outright villain, but as a very real character embracing elements of both extremes. Nan Martin's Portia failed to excite critics, but many other cast members were commended, especially those in comical roles, such as the princes of Morocco and Arragon, and Launcelot Gobbo, played by James Earl Jones, Gerald McGonagill, and John Call, respectively. Most reviewers praised Papp's lively staging, "a realistic, crowd-pleasing melodrama spiced with slapstick"; however, some critics decried the appearance of the maskers clad in what appeared to be Ku Klux Klan hoods.

One of the most significant and controversial twentieth-century productions of *The Merchant of Venice* was mounted in 1970 by the British National Theatre. This production was especially noteworthy for two reasons: first, because of the appearance of Laurence Olivier, one of the most venerated actors of the twentieth century, as Shylock; and second, because director Jonathan Miller undertook to adapt Shakespeare's portrait of Venice to a late-nineteenth-century setting. Critics surmised that Miller sought to illuminate parallels between the mercantile world of *fin de siècle* Venice (and by parallel, England) and the image of Renaissance Italy that Shakespeare envisioned. Debate swirled over whether Miller's adaptation was successful, merely a distraction, or a distortion of the text. Although many reviewers acknowledged the originality and power of Miller's interpretation, some felt that the emphasis on Venice, and consequently on Olivier's Shylock, regardless of its own merits, diminished the romance and poetry of Belmont. Irving Wardle, who admired Miller's inventive adaptation, commented that it was "not exactly the play that Shakespeare wrote," and Don Moore termed Miller's production "a thoughtful, interesting, and colorful misinterpretation of *The Merchant of Venice*." Some critical rebukes were harsher and contended that Miller's adaptation threw the play out of balance, errantly purporting that the fundamental function of the play is to address the nature of capitalism, rather than mercy. As for Olivier's Shylock, no critic had the audacity to challenge the technical brilliance of the master's performance, referred to by Michael Billington as "the best of its generation," although considerable dissension arose concerning Olivier and Miller's interpretation of the role. For example, Clive Barnes granted the performance's technical brilliance, but affirmed that it was "ill-judged." Kenneth Muir, a distinguished British critic and Shakespearean editor, argued that Miller's conception of Shylock as the "cultured," persecuted hero of *The Merchant of Venice* is unsupported by and, in fact, antithetical to Shakespeare's text. Thus, in the theater, reviewers typically could not help being swept away by Olivier's classical-style, virtuoso performance, which culminated with a plaintive wail delivered offstage following Shylock's final exit. But most critics objected that this Shylock did not accord with Shakespeare's character. Julia Trevelyan Oman designed the handsome *belle époque* scenery.

In 1978, John Barton and the Royal Shakespeare Company staged a very well-received rendition of *The Merchant of Venice*. The hallmark of the production was Patrick Stewart's dynamically-performed and thoughtfully-conceived portrayal of Shylock. Stewart, attempting to rid the role of its "Jewishness," the caricature of Shylock, sought to de-emphasize the heroic or tragic aspects of the character and thus humanize him. J. W. Lambert deemed Stewart's "educated, almost donnish" Shylock "richly characterised," and Roger Warren called it "a virtuoso performance encompassing all the variety of the part, now quietly colloquial, now impassioned." Complementing Stewart's interpretation was Barton's restrained, well-balanced direction, lauded by most critics. Some reviewers also drew attention to Barton's skillful use of the intimacy created by the relatively small theater, the Other Place, focus on the play's pivotal scenes.

REVIEWS AND RETROSPECTIVE ACCOUNTS OF SELECTED PRODUCTIONS

PERFORMANCE:

Charles Macklin • Drury Lane • 1741

BACKGROUND:

Macklin was a prominent Irish actor who is credited with discarding George Granville's adaptation, *The Jew of*

Venice, and reviving Shakespeare's text, *The Merchant of Venice.* Having passed the age of fifty and concerned to establish his artistic reputation, Macklin convinced Charles Fleetwood, a manager of the Drury Lane theater, to play Shakespeare's original, rather than Granville's adaptation. When the cast and company learned that Macklin intended to play Shylock in the tragic spirit as a grim, sinister character rather than conventional comic figure, as played by Thomas Doggett, they turned hostile, prompting Macklin to conceal his true intentions for the role. On opening night, according to William Winter, Macklin appeared on stage costumed in "long, wide trousers, loose black gown, a three-cornered red hat, and a piqued beard. He probably wore red hair as had been customary." Macklin's revolutionary conception of a spiteful, non-comic Shylock won the approval of his audience, despite the fact that the remainder of the cast continued to perform their roles in the conventionally prescribed manner of low comedy. Macklin's performance is said to have inspired the couplet, often attributed to Alexander Pope, "This is the Jew / That Shakespeare drew." The cast included James Quin as Antonio, Kitty Clive as Portia, and Hannah Pritchard as Nerissa.

COMMENTARY:

Francis Gentleman   (essay date 1770)

[*Gentleman, an Irish actor and playwright, was the author of* The Dramatic Censor: or Critical Companion *(1770) and contributed the introductions to John Bell's 1774 edition of Shakespeare's plays. In the excerpt below, Gentleman declares that Macklin "through the whole displays . . . unequalled merit." Specifically, Gentleman commends the actor's appearance, his ferocity, and his facile manner of alternating passions.*]

Shylock, whose peculiarity of character and language we have hinted, is a most disgraceful picture of human nature; he is drawn, what we think man never was, all shade, not a gleam of light; subtle, selfish, fawning, irrascible and tyrannic; as he is like no dramatic personage but himself, the mode of representation should be particular; as to figure and features, any person and countenance, by dress and other assistance, may be made suitable; however, there is no doubt but Mr. MACKLIN looks the part as much better than any other person as he plays it; in the level scenes his voice is most happily suited to that sententious gloominess of expression the author intended; which, with a sullen solemnity of deportment, marks the character strongly; in his malevolence, there is a forcible and terrifying ferocity; in the third act scene, where alternate passions reign, he breaks the tones of utterance, and varies his countenance admirably; in the dumb action of the trial scene, he is amazingly descriptive; and through the whole displays such unequalled merit, as justly entitles him to that very comprehensive, though concise compliment, paid him many years ago, "This is the Jew, that SHAKESPEARE drew." (pp. 291-92)

Francis Gentleman, "The Merchant of Venice," in his The Dramatic Censor; or, Critical Companion, *Vol. 1, 1770. Reprint by AMS Press Inc., 1975, pp. 278-98.*

George Christoph Lichtenberg   (letter date 2 December 1775)

[*Lichtenberg describes Macklin's costume and appearance as Shylock, and the indelible impression he created upon uttering Shylock's first line. At one stroke, according to Lichtenberg, Macklin established the character's calm, determined, avaricious villainy.*]

I have seen the Shylock of Macklin, so well known for his high deserts, his lawsuit, and his physiognomy. You know that the announcement of Macklin as Shylock sounds as attractively on the play-bill as Garrick in Hamlet. It was the evening on which he appeared for the first time after his suit was decided. When he appeared he was received with great applause, thrice given, each time lasting a quarter of a minute. It is not to be denied that the sight of this Jew suffices to awaken at once, in the best-regulated mind, all the prejudices of childhood against this people. Shylock is none of your petty cheaters, who can talk for an hour over the excellence of a pinchbeck watch-chain. He is slow, calm in his impenetrable cunning, and when he has the law on his side he is unflinching, even to the extreme of malice. Picture to yourself a somewhat strong man, with a sallow, harsh face and a nose which is by no means lacking in any one of the three dimensions, a long double chin or dewlap; and in making his mouth, Nature's knife seems to have slipped and gone all the way to his ears, at least on one side, so it seemed to me. His cloak is black and long, his pantaloons also are long and broad, and his hat three-cornered and red, probably in accordance with the style of the Italian Jews. The first words which he utters are spoken slowly and deliberately: *'Three thousand ducats'* [I. iii. 1]. The *th* and the *s* twice occurring and the last *s* after the *t* have a lickerish sound from Macklin's lips, as if he were tasting the ducats and all that they can buy; this speech creates for the man, upon his first appearance, a prepossession which is sustained throughout. Three such words, thus spoken and at the very first, reveal a whole character. In the Scene in which he first misses his daughter he appears hatless, with hair all flying, some of it standing up straight, a hand's breadth high, just as if it had been lifted up by a breeze from the gallows. Both hands are doubled up, and his gestures are quick and convulsive. To see a man thus moved, who had been hitherto a calm, determined villain, is fearful. (pp. 374-75)

George Christoph Lichtenberg, in a letter on December 2, 1775, in A New Variorum Edition of Shakespeare: The Merchant of Venice, *edited by Horace Howard Furness, thirteenth edition, J. B. Lippincott Company, 1888, pp. 374-75.*

William Cooke   (essay date 1804)

[*Cooke recounts Macklin's interest and motive in restoring Shakespeare's text, the actor's deceptively subdued rehearsals, and his eventual triumph on opening night.*]

Chance presented *The Merchant of Venice* to [Macklin's] notice, which, however, strange now to conceive, had laid upon the shelf since the year 1701, to make room for an alteration from the same play by Lord Lansdowne, called *The Jew of Venice;* in which the celebrated Dogget performed the *Jew* almost in the style of broad farce. Macklin saw this part with other eyes; and, very much to the credit of his taste and understanding, as well as a proper estimation of his own powers, he found he could build a reputation by reviving the original

Charles Macklin as Shylock.

of Shakespeare, and playing the character of Shylock in a different manner. The attempt was arduous, and subject to many miscarriages, and in particular to public prejudice; but a consciousness of being right will generally give great confidence—Macklin felt this consciousness, and was determined on the trial.

As soon as resolved, he communicated his design to the Manager, who gave his consent to bringing it out merely as a revived piece, which might bring money to the treasury. The play was therefore announced to be in preparation; and Macklin, who always loved the character of a *Theatrical Drill Serjeant,* now entered into it with all his heart and mind, by casting the parts himself, ordering frequent rehearsals, &c. &c. but when he came to affix to himself the character of *Shylock,* and intimated his design to play it *seriously,* the laugh was universal.—His best friends shook their heads at the attempt; whilst his rivals chuckled in secret, and flattered him with ideas of success, the surer to work out his destruction.

His keen observation, and suspicious temper, clearly saw the train that was laying for him, which he not only seemingly overlooked, but so far assisted, that at every rehearsal, whilst he enjoined the rest of the performers to do their best, he himself played both under his voice and general powers, carefully reserving his fire till the night of representation. His fellow

performers were by this conduct completely trapped, insomuch that many of them threw off all reserve, and publicly said, "That this hot-headed, conceited Irishman, who had got some little reputation in a few parts, had now availed himself of the Manager's favour, to bring himself and the Theatre into disgrace." Fleetwood heard this, and seriously applied to Macklin to give up the part: but the latter was too conscious of his own excellence to lose such an opportunity: He frankly told the Manager, "that he was deceiving a set of men who envied him; but that he would pledge his life on the success of the play; and that, in the end, it would be highly serviceable to them both."

The long-expected night at last arrived, and the House was crowded, from top to bottom, with the first company in town. The two front rows of the pit, as usual, were full of critics, "Who, Sir, (said the veteran,) I eyed through the slit of the curtain, and was glad to see there, as I wished, in such a cause, to be tried by a *special jury.* When I made my appearance in the green-room, dressed for the part, with my red hat on my head, my piqued beard, loose black gown, &c. and with a confidence which I never before assumed, the performers all stared at one another, and evidently with a stare of disappointment. Well, Sir, hitherto all was right—till the last bell rung—then, I confess, my heart began to beat a little: however, I mustered up all the courage I could, and, recommending my cause to Providence, threw myself boldly on the stage, and was received by one of the loudest thunders of applause I ever before experienced.

"The opening scenes being rather tame and level, I could not expect much applause; but I found myself well listened to—I could hear distinctly, in the pit, the words, 'Very well—very well, indeed!—This man seems to know what he is about,' &c. &c. These encomiums warmed me, but did not overset me—I knew where I should have the pull, which was in the third act, and reserved myself accordingly. At this period I threw out all my fire; and, as the contrasted passions of joy for the Merchant's losses, and grief for the elopement of Jessica, open a fine field for an actor's powers, I had the good fortune to please beyond my warmest expectations—The whole house was in an uproar of applause—and I was obliged to pause between the speeches, to give it vent, so as to be heard. When I went behind the scenes after this act, the Manager met me, and complimented me very highly on my performance, and significantly added, "Macklin, you was right at last." My brethren in the greenroom joined in his eulogium, but with different views—He was thinking of the increase of his treasury—they only for saving appearances—wishing at the same time that I had broke my neck in the attempt. The *trial scene* wound up the fulness of my reputation: here I was well listened to; and here I made such a silent yet forcible impression on my audience, that I retired from this great attempt most perfectly satisfied.

"On my return to the green-room, after the play was over, it was crowded with nobility and critics, who all complimented me in the warmest and most unbounded manner; and the situation I felt myself in, I must confess, was one of the most flattering and intoxicating of my whole life. No money, no title, could purchase what I felt: And let no man tell me after this, what Fame will not inspire a man to do, and how far the attainment of it will not remunerate his greatest labours? By G–d, Sir, though I was not worth fifty pounds in the world at that time, yet, let me tell you, I was *Charles the Great* for that night." (pp. 90-4)

Of his *Shylock,* in "The Merchant of Venice," we have a number of living witnesses, as evidences of its being one of the finest pieces of modern acting; and there are passages in it, particularly in the third act, which exhibit the contrasting passions of grief for his daughter's elopement, and joy at Antonio's misfortunes, which demand an uncommon versatility of powers. This, and the whole of the trial scene, we may safely pronounce, have not been equalled, at least, since Macklin had possession of the part. Many have since attempted it, and with considerable success; such as the late Mr. Henderson, the present Mr. Murray, and Mr. Cooke; each of whom would be principals, but for Macklin's superior abilities, which have placed them in the second class. To Henderson's Shylock, the veteran himself paid this compliment, when asked, Whether he was entitled to that popular applause which he received? "Sir, there is no putting out the light of the sun—the young fellow has very considerable merit." At Murray's Shylock, he was so insensible, (such was the deranged state of Macklin's intellect at the time,) that he frequently asked, in the course of the representation, what play it was? He then seemed to recollect himself, and screw up his attention to the scene; but Nature was too imbecile for any sort of mental combination. All these succeeding Shylocks, though just and pleasing portraits of the character, wanted the original firmness and colouring of Macklin's pencil. There was, beside his judgment, which went to the study of every line of it, such an iron-visaged look, such a relentless savage cast of manners, that the audience seemed to shrink from the character; nor could they recover the true tone of their feelings, till the merchant was liberated from the fangs of such a merciless creditor. Cooke seems to be nearest the original of any we have ever seen. (pp. 404-06)

> *William Cooke, in his* Memoirs of Charles Macklin: Comedian, *1804. Reprint by Benjamin Blum, Inc., 1972, 444 p.*

John Doran (essay date 1865)

[*Doran contextualizes Macklin's restoration of Shylock and the text of* The Merchant of Venice. *The author also describes the opening-night audience's favorable reaction to Macklin's revolutionary interpretation of Shylock.*]

For some years, Macklin . . . failed to reap the distinction he coveted. The attainment was made, however, in 1741, when he induced Fleetwood to revive Shakespeare's *Merchant of Venice,* with Macklin for Shylock. There was a whisper that he was about to play the Jew, as a serious character. His comrades laughed, and the manager was nervous. The rehearsals told them nothing, for there, Macklin did little more than walk through the part, lest the manager should prohibit the playing of the piece, if the nature of the reform Macklin was about to introduce should make him fearful of consequences. In some such dress as that we now see worn by Shylock, Macklin, on the night of the 14th of February, 1741, walked down the stage, and looking through the eyelet-hole in the curtain, saw the two ever-formidable front rows of the pit occupied by the most highly-dreaded critics of the period. The house was densely crowded. He turned from his survey, calm and content, remarking, "Good! I shall be tried to night by a Special Jury!"

There was little applause on his entrance, yet the people were pleased at the aspect of a Jew whom Rembrandt might have painted. The opening scene was spoken in familiar, but earnest accents. Not a hand yet gave token of approbation, but there occasionally reached Macklin's ears, from the two solemn rows of judge and jury in the pit, the sounds of "Good!"—"Very good!"—"Very well, indeed!"—and he passed off, more gratified by this, than by the slight general applause intended for encouragement. As the play proceeded, so did his triumph grow. In the scene with Tubal, which Doggett in Lansdowne's version had made so comic, he shook the hearts, and not the sides of the audience. The sympathies of the house went all for Shylock; and at last, a storm of acclamation roared pleasantly over Macklin. So far all was well; but the trial scene had yet to come. It came; and there the triumph culminated. The actor was not loud, nor grotesque; but Shylock was natural, calmly confident, and so terribly malignant, that when he whetted his knife, to cut the forfeit from that bankrupt there, a shudder went round the house, and the profound silence following, told Macklin that he held his audience by the heart-strings, and that his hearers must have already acknowledged the truth of his interpretation of Shakespeare's Jew. When the act-drop fell, Old Drury shook again with the tumult of applause. The critics went off to the coffeehouses in a state of pleasurable excitement. As for the other actors, Quin (Antonio), must have felt the master-mind of that night. Mrs. Pritchard (Nerissa), excellent judge as she was, must have enjoyed the terrible grandeur of that trial-scene; and even Kitty Clive (Portia) could not have dared, on that night, to do what she ordinarily made Portia do, in the disguise of young Bellario; namely, mimic the peculiarities of some leading lawyer of the day. And Macklin?—Macklin remarked, as he stood among his fellows, "I am not worth fifty pounds in the world; nevertheless, on this night am I Charles the Great!"

Pope pronounced Macklin to be the Jew that Shakspeare drew; and he asked the actor, why he dressed Shylock in a red hat? Macklin replied, it was because he had read that the Jews in Venice were obliged, by law, to wear a hat of that colour;—which was true. (pp. 312-13)

> *John Doran, "Charles Macklin," in his* "Their Majesties' Servants": Annals of the English Stage, from Thomas Betterton to Edmund Kean, *revised edition, Wm. H. Allen & Co., 1865, pp. 310-18.*

Toby Lelyveld (essay date 1960)

[*Lelyveld describes the background and substance of Macklin's imaginative conception of Shylock. In addition, he discusses the nature of the production itself, which included, for example, many songs; Macklin's appearance and costume; and the critical reception.*]

When Charles Macklin announced his intention to depart from the comic tradition that had been established by way of the Granville version of *The Merchant of Venice,* the play had been off the boards for more than two years. He encountered nothing but derision and discouragement on the part of his colleagues at the Drury Lane. They believed that a serious treatment of Shylock would be only an arrogant and presumptuous display. But Macklin did not permit himself to be dissuaded. After deliberately underacting at rehearsals, in order to avoid the criticism of his associates, he presented a characterization of Shylock on February 14, 1741 that was to become the precursor of an interpretation for many of the great tragedians who were to undertake the role.

We have no direct information as to the acting version that

Macklin used. No Macklin prompt-book of the play is extant. It may be assumed with some certainty, however, that the Bell edition of 1774 follows his text in most essentials. From the Bell edition we conclude that Macklin cut lines in many scenes. In Act I of the Bell version, Portia's jibes at the English and the Scotch are deleted. Francis Gentleman's inclusion of footnotes, however, compensates for the omissions throughout the edition. Bell opens Act II with the Gobbo scene, ignoring Morocco and later, Arragon. Macklin retained both suitors. Tubal had been overlooked by Granville, but he served as such an effective foil for Shylock that he was now restored to the *dramatis personae*. The trial scene was kept almost intact; only five important lines are excised from it. Act V was entirely faithful to Shakespeare. (p. 21)

The Shylock that Macklin created was not likeable. On the contrary, the aspects of Shylock's personality that were stressed most by Macklin made the money-lender appear to be something of a monster. Macklin counted upon a shock-effect, and so fierce was this new Shylock that audiences were startled into taking him seriously for the first time. It was Macklin's underscoring of the Jew's malice and revengefulness that first established Shylock as a significant dramatic character. He was relentless, savage, ominous, venomous. So malignant was this Shylock that the spectators, unaccustomed to such a display of passion on the stage, could not distinguish between the actor and his role and believed that in private life, Macklin was some sort of devil. As a matter of fact, Macklin had killed a fellow-actor in a quarrel over a wig in 1735. He had been tried for murder, and although he had been acquitted, playgoers probably recalled his violent disposition and associated it with the character he now portrayed.

The question of what it was that attracted Macklin to the Shakespearean play can hardly be resolved. Perhaps he was responding, more or less consciously, to a public demand for Shakespeare's plays in greater purity of text and plot. It may be, too, that having achieved but slight distinction in minor plays, he was seeking a vehicle that would display his talents to better advantage, and found it in *The Merchant of Venice*, long overshadowed by the Granville version.

Possibly the best reason that Macklin had for undertaking to play Shylock was an awareness of his own personal suitability to the role. Portraits of him show dark, piercing eyes, an aquiline nose of considerable proportions, a short upper lip, a protruding lower lip and a massive jaw. He was above medium height, erect, athletic, robust without being corpulent. His face, even without make-up, suggests what Dickens later may have had in mind when he created Fagin.

The spirited Kitty Clive was cast as Portia, and doubtless this was a final concession to the farcical mood of the Granville era. She romped through the part in a flippant manner, mimicking Lord Mansfield, the famous lawyer, and introduced comical stage "business" in the trial scene in order to imitate his peculiarities which were then delighting London. Her burlesque of the young judge must have made Macklin's iron-visaged Shylock appear incongruous and ridiculous.

Shortly after Macklin's Shylock was introduced, Portia was given a song and it became the practice to list it in playbills: "Portia—With a Song." It was soon necessary for Lorenzo, Nerissa and Jessica, as well, to sing, and the number of musical selections continued to increase. In addition to the interpolated songs, novelties were introduced at the end of Acts III and IV which served to slacken the pace of the play. Evi-

dently the eighteenth-century playgoer was in no greater hurry than his ancestors had been in Samuel Pepys' day. There was no attempt to sustain the play's unity by a discriminating choice of appropriate selections. Such extraneous pieces as *The Belle of the Village,* at the close of Act III and a dance entitled *The Arcadian Festival,* following Act IV, literally served as divertissements. This concern with giving the public its money's worth in a variety program lasted until almost the close of the nineteenth century. Every sort of extravaganza, from acrobatic stunts to opera, shared the bill with *The Merchant of Venice.* Even with these distractions, the play continued to hold its own.

Although Macklin's genius brought about the innovation of a serious reading of Shylock's lines, a number of contemporary critics believed that he did not seem to have delved deeply enough into the character of the Jew and that he never succeeded in making the character come to life. His lasting popularity in the role, therefore, remains something of a puzzle. (pp. 22-4)

Much has been written concerning Macklin's effort to dress his characters appropriately. Macklin's Shylock wore a loose black gown, long wide trousers and a skull-cap. His beard was short, red, wispy and pointed. This costume may represent a first attempt at historically accurate dress for Shylock, or it may be a further adaptation of the costume of Pantalone. William Cooke, Macklin's biographer [*Memoirs of Charles Macklin, Comedian*], describes a dinner at which Pope, who was said to have seen Shylock on the third night of the first run, asked Macklin why he wore a *red* hat. The reply was that Macklin had read that Jews in Italy, particularly in Venice, wore hats of that color.

> "And pray, Mr. Macklin, do players in general take such pains?"
> "I do not know, Sir, that they do; but I had staked my reputation on the character, I was determined to spare no trouble in getting at the best information."
> "It was very laudable," said Pope.

This little scene may never have taken place, but Pope's admiration of Macklin's performance has crystallized into a tradition which has been handed on for endless quotation in the doggerel couplet invariably attributed to Pope:

> This is the Jew
> That Shakespeare drew.

During the long years that Macklin played the role of Shylock he must have found it necessary to modify his costume several times, and a number of changes are shown in later engravings, in which we find him in pantaloons and a Quaker collar that were much like the costumes worn by the Christians in the play. The pointed underchin beard, the skull-cap and the conspicuous hook nose remained as his "Jewish" markings. His acting style in this part was evidently considered an authentic reproduction of Jewish manners and it was thought that much research had gone into it [*Connoisseur,* 31 January 1754]:

> When a comedian, celebrated for his excellence in the part of Shylock, first undertook that character, he made daily visits to the centre of business, the 'Change and the adjacent Coffee-houses, that by a frequent intercourse and conversation with the "unforeskinned race" he might habituate himself to their air and deportment. . . .

William Cooke records what purports to be Macklin's description of his first performance of *The Merchant of Venice:*

> The opening Scenes, being rather tame and level, I could not expect much applause; but I found myself well listened to,—I could hear distinctly, in the pit, the words, 'very well—very well, indeed!—This man seems to know what he is about', &c. These encomiums warmed me, but did not overset me—I knew where I should have the pull, which was in the Third Act, and reserved myself accordingly. At this period, I threw out all my fire; and, as the contrasted passions of joy for the Merchant's losses, and grief for the elopement of Jessica, opens a fine field for an actor's powers, I had the good fortune to please beyond my warmest expectations. The whole house was in an uproar of applause—and I was obliged to pause between the speeches, to give it vent, so as to be heard. . . . The trial Scene wound up the fulness of my reputation: here I was well listened to; and here I made such a silent, yet forcible, impression on my audience, that I retired from this great attempt most perfectly satisfied. . . .

Something of the pathetic quality of Shylock's plight may have come through in Macklin's interpretation. [Thomas] Davies [in his *Memoirs of the Life of David Garrick*] says that it made some tender impressions on the spectators. Macklin's fierceness, contrasting as it did with the sentimentalization of Shylock by later actors, would make it appear that these impressions were aroused by the character and not by the characterization. An account that probably has Macklin in mind describes Shylock, without Davies' reservation, as an abhorrent person [Francis Gentleman, in his *Dramatic Censor*]:

> The wretched state to which Shylock . . . is reduced, is so agreeable a sacrifice of justice, that it conveys inexpressable satisfaction to every feeling mind. . . . [He is] . . . a most disgraceful picture of human nature; he is drawn, what we think man never was, all shade, not a gleam of light; subtle, selfish, fawning, irrascible and tyrranic. . . .

(pp. 25-7)

Frances Gentleman did not doubt that Macklin looked the part better than any other Shylock actor. He describes the range of emotion that Macklin demonstrated as the play progressed:

> . . . in the level scenes his voice is most happily suited to the sententious gloominess of expression the author intended; which, with a sullen solemnity of deportment, marks the character strongly; in his malevolence there is a forcible and terrifying ferocity; in the Third Act scene, where alternate passions reign, he breaks the tones of utterance and varies his countenance admirably; in the dumb action of the Trial Scene, he is amazingly descriptive.

Lichtenberg, the German critic, saw Macklin play the part late in life. His observations [in his *Vermischte Schriften*] on the subject are the best we have:

> Picture to yourself a somewhat portly man, with a yellowish coarse face, a nose by no means deficient in length, breadth or thickness, and a mouth, in the cutting of which Nature's knife seems to have slipped as far as the ear, on one side at least, as it appeared to me. . . . The first words he speaks on coming on the stage are slow and full of import. 'Three thousand ducats.' The two *th's* and the two

s's, especially the last after the *t,* Macklin mouths with such unction, that one would think he were at once testing the ducats and all that could be purchased with them. This at starting at once accredits him with the audience in a way which nothing afterwards can damage. Three such words, so spoken in the situation, mark the whole character. In the scene where, for the first time he misses his daughter, he appears without his hat, with his hair standing on end, in some places at least a finger's length above the crown, as if the wind from the gallows had blown it up. Both hands are firmly clenched and all his movements are abrupt and conclusive. To see such emotion in a grasping, fraudulent character, generally cool and self-possessed, is fearful . . .

The effect was not intended to recommend Shylock to our sympathy. The writer concludes: "It is not to be denied that the sight of this Jew suffices to awaken at once in the best regulated mind, all the prejudices of childhood against this people."

[James] Boaden [in his *Memoirs of the Life of John Philip Kemble*] was another who recalled the latter-day Shylock of Macklin:

> His acting was essentially manly,—there was nothing of trick about it. His delivery was more level than modern speaking, but certainly more weighty, direct, and emphatic. His features were rigid, his eye cold and colourless; yet the earnestness of his manner, and the sterling sense of his address, produced an effect in Shylock that has remained to the present hour unrivalled. Macklin, for instance, in the Trial Scene, 'stood like a TOWER,,' as Milton has it. He was 'not bound to *please*' anybody by his pleading; he claimed a right grounded upon LAW, and thought himself as firm as the Rialto. To this remark it may be said, 'You are here describing Shylock.' True; I am describing Macklin.

John Bernard [in his *Retrospections of the Stage*] is not nearly so respectful. He evidently regrets the passing of the musical style which the new school of acting had superseded. He remembers Macklin as "broad-breasted, shaggy-browed, hooked-nosed . . . as rough and husky as a cocoanut, with a barking or grunting delivery more peculiar than pleasing, which to musical ears made him something like a bore. . . ."

There are, however, few disparaging notes in the chorus of praise for Macklin's performance. [John] Doran [in his *"Their Majesties' Servants"*] recalls the reaction of the audience to the trial scene:

> The actor was not loud, nor grotesque; but Shylock was natural, calmly confident, and so terribly malignant, that when he whetted his knife . . . a shudder went round the house and the profound silence following told me that he held his audience by the heart-strings, and that his hearers must have already acknowledged the truth of his interpretation of Shakespeare's Jew. . . .

Before long, Macklin's Shylock became the standard by which to measure the interpretations of other actors in the role. The author of the *Dramatic Censor* found Sheridan's treatment of Act I as admirable as Macklin's, but inferior in the third and fourth acts. King was not as cruel of feature or voice as Macklin and therefore, not as good. Yates' conception was "insipid" and "disgraceful" because he did not conceive Shakespeare's (or was it Macklin's?) meaning. His manner must have differed considerably from that of the master; it was described as "a quaint snip-snap mode of expression."

We have some notion of the disturbing quality of Macklin's performance when we read how George II, on one occasion, was so moved by the actions of this Shylock, that he could not sleep the night he witnessed it. *The Morning Post and Daily Advertiser* [9 November 1781] reported of another performance, that when Shylock whetted his knife, " . . . Mr. Macklin was so highly characteristic in the part, that a young man who was in the pit fainted away."

(pp. 30-2)

[I]nterest in Macklin's Shylock continued unabated. Macklin played the role nearly fifty years. We read, how, at Covent Garden

> The house was uncommonly crowded and brilliant, and his reception very great. This wonderful old man, like Anteus, seems to acquire fresh vigour. . . .

Two years later, the press notes that at the same theatre:

> . . . a crowded audience was collected . . . by what may be truly termed a phenomenon, a man in the ninetieth year of his age, sustaining a character that requires the strongest exertions of faculties in their meridian blaze, and not merely sustaining them, but embodying them with such a force that would make the most inanimate spectator "live o'er the scene." A few trivial lapses of memory excepted, his performance of the character betrayed no symptoms of declension to the observation even of the oldest. On his entrance all hands and voices united in expressing the warm pleasure which the sight of him, who had entertained their fathers, and still retained the powers vigorous as the stoutest of their sons. . . .

Added to the arduous role was the inconclusion in the program of *Love à la Mode,* in which the veteran appeared as Sir Archy. But old age was beginning to leave its inevitable marks on him. The loss of his teeth made his nose and chin appear to be more prominent. James Quin, a rival actor, remarked on the "cordage", not lines, in Macklin's face. With any other role, this would have been disastrous, but it suited the harsh and stern-faced Shylock that Macklin depicted. He had grown deaf and was unable to hear the prompter. Now his memory failed him and at last the Nestor of the stage, as he was called, was compelled to withdraw from the theatre. (pp. 36-7)

There had been no dearth of Shakespearean actors in Macklin's time. His portrayal of a despicable Shylock never changed to suit the spirit of the times. But what he did, he did with such expertness that he was able to withstand the innovations that surrounded him. Even while he was in his dotage, he retained the title of having no equal in the role of Shylock. What he lacked in versatility—and his earlier failures with Macbeth and Richard testify to his limited range—he more than made up in the consistent and vigorous characterization of an avaricious and unrelenting Shylock. (p. 37)

> *Toby Lelyveld, in her* Shylock on the Stage, *The Press of Western Reserve University, 1960, 149 p.*

PRODUCTION:

Edmund Kean • Drury Lane • 1814

BACKGROUND:

Kean's portrayal of Shylock established his reputation as his generation's preeminent tragedian. Douglas Jerrold reported that Kean, as Shylock, impressed his audience, "like a chapter of Genesis." Kean's success in this, his London stage debut, at the age of twenty-seven, is even more remarkable in light of the considerable obstacles he encountered in bringing his performance to the public. The Drury Lane managers who had contracted to bring the young Kean to London to spark attendance repeatedly brushed aside his requests to play the leading role, Shylock. Kean remained steadfast, and eventually the managers acquiesced, granting Kean a single rehearsal, on the morning preceding his first performance, 26 January 1814. In the face of the company's antagonism, Kean rehearsed with restraint, subduing his passionate style and convincing his wary auditors that he was bound for failure. Upon the play's performance, however, Kean drew raves from the small but appreciative audience. Kean appeared in a black wig, instead of the traditional red one, and he chilled his audience with his fiery impersonation of a vindictive Shylock. Yet Kean also introduced an element of nobility to his performance, an interpretation that was adopted and amplified by many subsequent actors, most notably Henry Irving. According to William Winter, Kean "presented the Jew as a creature of murderous malice, and yet of distinctively Hebraic majesty." William Hazlitt, one of the principal founders of Romantic dramatic criticism, enhanced his own reputation as a critic by identifying Kean as among the most significant actors of his age. Although Hazlitt occasionally contested Kean's conception of a character, as in the case of Kean's near-tragic Shylock, the critic averred that as a performer, Kean was unmatched: "For depth and force of conception, we have seen actors whom we should prefer to Mr. Kean in Shylock; for brilliant and masterly execution, none."

COMMENTARY:

William Hazlitt   (review date 27 January 1814)

[*Hazlitt was an eminent English essayist and critic whose work, typically focusing on characterization, reflects the influence of Romanticism. One of the first great dramatic critics, his reviews were published in the* Examiner, *the* Morning Chronicle, *the* Champion, *the* London Magazine, *and the* Times. *Some of these were subsequently collected in his* The Round Table *(1817) and* A View of the English Stage *(1818). In the review below, originally published in the* Morning Chronicle, *Hazlitt concedes that Kean's fiery, passionate style was impressive and won the sustained applause of his audience. Ultimately, however, it contradicted the critic's conception of Shylock: "The fault of his acting was an overdisplay of the resources of the art, which gave too much relief to the hard, impenetrable, dark groundwork of the character of Shylock."*]

Mr. Kean (of whom report had spoken highly) last night made his appearance at Drury-Lane Theatre in the character of Shylock. For voice, eye, action, and expression, no actor has come out for many years at all equal to him. The applause, from the first scene to the last, was general, loud, and uninterrupted. Indeed, the very first scene in which he comes on with Bassanio and Antonio, shewed the master in his art, and at once decided the opinion of the audience. Perhaps it was the most perfect of any. Notwithstanding the complete success of Mr. Kean in the part of Shylock, we question whether he will not become a greater favourite in other parts. There was a lightness and vigour in his tread, a buoyancy and elasticity of spirit, a fire and animation, which would accord better with almost any other character than with the morose, sullen, inward, inveterate, inflexible malignity of Shylock. The character of Shylock is that of a man brooding over one idea, that of its wrongs, and bent on one unalterable purpose, that of revenge. In conveying a profound impression of this feeling, or in embodying the general conception of rigid and uncontroulable self-will, equally proof against every sentiment of humanity or prejudice of opinion, we have seen actors more successful than Mr. Kean; but in giving effect to the conflict of passions arising out of the contrasts of situation, in varied vehemence of declamation, in keenness of sarcasm, in the rapidity of his transitions from one tone and feeling to another, in propriety and novelty of action, presenting a succession of striking pictures, and giving perpetually fresh shocks of delight and surprise, it would be difficult to single out a competitor. The fault of his acting was (if we may hazard the objection), an over-display of the resources of the art, which gave too much relief to the hard, impenetrable, dark groundwork of the character of Shylock. It would be endless to point out individual beauties, where almost every passage was received with equal and deserved applause. We thought, in one or two instances, the pauses in the voice were too long, and too great a reliance placed on the expression of the countenance, which is a language intelligible only to a part of the house.

The rest of the play was, upon the whole, very respectably cast. It would be an equivocal compliment to say of Miss Smith, that her acting often reminds us of Mrs. Siddons. Rae played Bassanio; but the abrupt and harsh tones of his voice are not well adapted to the mellifluous cadences of Shakespear's verse. (pp. 179-80)

> *William Hazlitt, in an excerpt from* The Collected Works of William Hazlitt, *edited by A. R. Waller and Arnold Glover, J. M. Dent & Co., 1903, pp. 179-80.*

William Hazlitt   (review date 2 February 1814)

[*Hazlitt iterates that Kean's interpretation of the role of Shylock was questionable, but he affirms that the actor's performance was unrivalled: "For depth and force of conception, we have seen actors whom we should prefer to Mr. Kean in Shylock; for brilliant and masterly execution, none." Hazlitt's review was originally published in the* Morning Chronicle.]

Mr. Kean appeared again in Shylock, and by his admirable and expressive manner of giving the part, fully sustained the reputation he had acquired by his former representation of it, though he laboured under the disadvantage of a considerable hoarseness. He assumed a greater appearance of age and feebleness than on the first night, but the general merit of his playing was the same. His style of acting is, if we may use the expression, more significant, more pregnant with meaning, more varied and alive in every part, than any we have almost ever witnessed. The character never stands still; there is no vacant pause in the action; the eye is never silent. For depth and force of conception, we have seen actors whom we should

prefer to Mr. Kean in Shylock; for brilliant and masterly execution, none. It is not saying too much of him, though it is saying a great deal, that he has all that Mr. Kemble *wants* of perfection. He reminds us of the descriptions of the 'far-darting eye' of Garrick. We are anxious to see him in Norval and Richard, and anticipate more complete satisfaction from his performance of the latter part, than from the one in which he has already stamped his reputation with the public.

Miss Smith played Portia with much more animation than the last time we saw her, and in delivering the fine apostrophe on Mercy, in the trial-scene, was highly impressive.

> *William Hazlitt, in an excerpt from* The Collected Works of William Hazlitt, *edited by A. R. Waller and Arnold Glover, J. M. Dent & Co., 1903, p. 180.*

William Hazlitt   (essay date 1817)

[*Hazlitt commends Kean's revolutionary portrayal of Shylock, asserting that nothing in the text specifically contradicts Kean's interpretation; thus, according to Kean as well as Hazlitt, Shylock need not be portrayed as old nor as single-mindedly obsessed with revenge.*]

When we first went to see Mr. Kean in Shylock, we expected to see, what we had been used to see, a decrepid old man, bent with age and ugly with mental deformity, grinning with deadly malice, with the venom of his heart congealed in the expression of his countenance, sullen, morose, gloomy, inflexible, brooding over one idea, that of his hatred, and fixed on one unalterable purpose, that of his revenge. We were disap-

Edmund Kean as Shylock.

pointed, because we had taken our idea from other actors, not from the play. There is no proof there that Shylock is old, but a single line, "Bassanio and *old* Shylock, both stand forth" [IV. i. 175]—which does not imply that he is infirm with age—and the circumstance that he has a daughter marriageable, which does not imply that he is old at all. It would be too much to say that his body should be made crooked and deformed to answer to his mind, which is bowed down and warped with prejudices and passion. That he has but one idea, is not true; he has more ideas than any other person in the piece; and if he is intense and inveterate in the pursuit of his purpose, he shews the utmost elasticity, vigour, and presence of mind, in the means of attaining it. But so rooted was our habitual impression of the part from seeing it caricatured in the representation, that it was only from a careful perusal of the play itself that we saw our error. The stage is not in general the best place to study our author's characters in. It is too often filled with traditional common-place conceptions of the part, handed down from sire to son, and suited to the taste of *the great vulgar and the small.*— " 'Tis an unweeded garden: things rank and gross do merely gender in it!" [*Hamlet,* I.ii.135-37] If a man of genius comes once in an age to clear away the rubbish, to make it fruitful and wholesome, they cry, " 'Tis a bad school: it may be like nature, it may be like Shakespear, but it is not like us." Admirable critics! (pp. 170-71)

> *William Hazlitt, "The Merchant of Venice," in his* Characters of Shakespear's Plays & Lectures on the English Poets, *The Macmillan Company, 1903, pp. 165-71.*

The Theatrical Observer   (review date 15 February 1825)

[*The critic praises Kean's portrayal of Shylock, especially in the scene with Tubal (Act III. Scene i), and in the trial scene (Act IV. Scene i), although he contends that Kean played too passively as the scene closed. The actor could enhance the dramatic effect, according to the critic, by overtly demonstrating his anguish.*]

There was one of the most brilliant houses of the season here last night, on the occasion of Mr. Kean's performance of *Shylock,* which character he appeared in for the second time this season. We spoke of this representation at some length on the former occasion, and we cannot add to the terms of our approbation, which could hardly go the length the actor merited for some parts of his talented performance: but we may again remark as we have already several done, that his powers are greatly distinguished in the scene with *Tubal,* where he learns at once the misfortunes of *Antonio,* and the extravagance of his daughter. His transitions from joy at the one account, and bitter anguish at the other, were marked with masterly effect. Then, in the scene of the Trial he was as great as ever: shewing the deep-rooted hatred, and cruelty of persecution which the Jew is influenced by, in his conduct towards the unfortunate Merchant. We think, however, the effect of the close of this fine piece of acting might be further heightened by a more agitated proof of his feelings. We are aware of Mr. Kean's idea—he considers the Jew so completely overwhelmed by the reverse the law has brought upon him, that he ought to represent the mind in calm though bitter anguish. This style, true as it may be to nature, loses all effect on the stage, by the circumstance of the only power of expression to indicate this state of feeling, lying in the features, which in this character, being much concealed by the beard, &c. are

neutralized, and the whole expression left to the perfect stillness of the frame, the clenched hands, and downcast eyes. It is certain, that the termination of this scene fails to support and give full point to the previous excellent acting; and we strongly recommend to Mr. Kean to re-consider whether he could not, without violating nature, add to the effect, by shewing the Jew in his state of reverse, still a man of violent passions, although something chastened by the overthrow of his longed-for vengeance.

The other characters of this fine Play were very ably supported, as we have before mentioned. Mrs. West, Mrs. Orger, Miss Povey, Mr. Browne. Mr. Pope, Mr. Harley, Mr. Horn, Mr. Hughes, &c, giving to their several parts much effect. Might we, however, say to Mrs. West, in respect of her delivery of the beautiful apostrophe to Mercy, to *equalise* her tones as much as possible, and be abstemious of her *emphases.* Why do not performers take a pen in their hands, and mark the *few* words that in any passage require *force* of delivery. This would enable them, generally, to avoid that false emphasis, which destroys the true effect of a fine speech. Although we have made this remark in respect of Mrs. West's delivery of the encomium on Mercy, yet we cannot withhold from her the praise of general impressiveness which her manner produces, and which may with those who do not pretend to any critical notice, pass current for being very finely spoken. Mrs. West is a very clever lady, and one who in many respects merits the approbation of her audience, and the approval of critical judges; and on this account we the more freely offer our humble opinion with a view to her standing still higher in her profession. *False emphasis* is the ruin of many an otherwise good performer—it requires only a strict reference to the meaning of words, and to the purport of a sentence, to avoid this too common fault. The Ballet of *The Rossignol,* and the Pantomime, concluded the performances.

> *A review of "The Merchant of Venice," in* The Theatrical Observer, *No. 1002, February 15, 1825, pp. 1-2.*

William Hazlitt?   (essay date 1828)

[*The author reflects on the power of Kean's original, innovative interpretation of Shylock in 1814 and affirms that the vitality and inventiveness of his performance has not been diminished by the passage of fourteen years.*]

It was some time since we had seen Mr. KEAN's *Shylock.* Fourteen years ago we were desired to go and see a young actor from the country attempt the part at Drury-lane; and, as was expected, add another to the list of failures. When we got there, there were about fifty people in the pit, and there was that sense of previous damnation which a thin house inspires. When the new candidate came on, there was a lightness in his step, an airy buoyancy and self-possession different from the sullen, dogged, *gaol-delivery* look of the traditional *Shylocks* of the stage. A vague expectation was excited, and all went on well; but it was not till he came to the part, when leaning on his staff, he tells the tale of Jacob and his flock with the garrulous ease of old age and an animation of spirit, that seems borne back to the olden time, and to the privileged example in which he exults, that it was plain that a man of genius had lighted on the stage. To those who had the spirit and candour to hail the lucky omen, the recollection of that moment of startling, yet welcome surprise, will always be a proud and satisfactory one. We wished to see after a lapse of time and other changes, whether this first impression would still keep "true touch," and we find no difference. Besides the excellence of the impassioned parts of Mr. KEAN'S acting, there is a flexibility and indefiniteness of outline about it, like a figure with a landscape background—he is in Venice with his money-bags, his daughter and his injuries, but his thoughts take wing to the East, his voice swells and deepens at the mention of his sacred tribe and ancient law, and he dwells delighted on any digression to distant times and places, as a relief to his vindictive and rooted purposes. Of all Mr. KEAN'S performances, we think this the most faultless and least *mannered*, always excepting his *Othello*, which is equally perfect and twenty times more powerful.

William Hazlitt?, in a review of "The Merchant of Venice," in The Examiner, *No. 1050, March 16, 1828, pp. 179-80.*

W. L. Rede? (essay date 1834)

[*The author relates the inauspicious conditions and events that preceded Kean's triumphant debut as Shylock, and provides details of the 1814 performance. Particularly memorable in this exhilarating performance were Kean's black wig, a first in the play's stage history, and the climax of the action in Act III, Scene I, depicting Shylock with Salanio and Tubal.*]

A stranger in the porter's-room of a theatre royal, gentle reader, is generally looked upon as a "suspicious person," and soon becomes subject of general inquiry amongst the gossips of the theatre; but Kean was not unknown, though his *purpose* was; he was known to Mrs. Bartley, for he had played Glenalvon to her Lady Randolph, &c.; he was known to Rae, to Elliston, to T. Dibdin—to Hughes and Oxberry, intimately: the two latter actors knew his powers well, but Hughes, who had had the latest evidence of them, was himself but a novice in the theatre, having only appeared two months before Kean. Several ill-natured stories have been currently repeated respecting the insults Kean received, but his sensitiveness made him misconstrue much, and, humble as his manner was, it was truly a *proud* humility. It has been said that he had no dressing-room assigned him: this is untrue; he did not choose to dress in the place allotted him by Mr. Wroughton (then the stage-manager,) and in dudgeon went to the supernumeraries' room and dressed there; but though, only the day previous to his appearance, he had received a letter from his theatrical friends advising him against his rash attempt— though Mr. Knight had volunteered his opinion that "Mr. Kean had better pass his evenings in the front, trying to improve himself by witnessing the performance of good actors"—though Mr. Rae had passed him in the hall without recognising him—though the committee had said "*he could not do*"—though a certain set of underlings had christened him, in their jocularity, "Mr. Arnold's hard-bargain," Kean was not *actually* dispirited: stung in heart and mind he certainly was; but the night before his appearance he said, "Let me once set my foot before the float (i.e. the stagelights,) and I'll let them see what I am." In fact, he had one great attribute of genius—its irrepressibility: all real and all imagined slights (and he was always too apt to imagine the existence of neglect towards him) only confirmed his resolution; he did not come there merely to appear, he came there to succeed; he relied on his own powers and on the public judgment, and the little, submissive, meek, and frightened man that had rehearsed Shylock was wholly lost when he assumed the gaberdine and beard. Very little interest appeared to be excited in the the-

atre; at the call of "last music," i.e. the commencement of the overture, the first peeper through the curtain announced the fact of its being a "shy domus," which was replied to by "What did you expect? there'll be nothing till half-price;" intimating that the pantomime might attract, but the new tragedian would not. On went Rae as Bassanio, in an especial ill-humour, and the early scenes of the play were altogether enacted with a listless and careless spirit. At last, the prompter gave the word "No. 3" to the call-boy, and he went to the green-room to call Shylock to his duty; but Shylock was not in the green-room, and hadn't been there: the boy went up to the dressing-room that had been allotted to the "new gentleman"—he was not there. Somewhat alarmed at this irregularity, the call-boy was hurrying back to report the fact, when he saw Shylock standing ready at the place at which he was to make his entrance; as in duty bound, the young functionary said "You're called, Sir." "Thank you," was the reply; and those were the only words (save those of Shakspeare) that Kean uttered that night, until the end of the fourth act, Shylock's last scene. Stage-fright (which has been compared to sea-sickness) he certainly did not suffer from; he dreaded the green-room more than a thousand audiences; the pent-up hopes of years were now too near fulfilment for him to know the "taste of fear." Scene 3d, Act 1.—Shylock and Bassanio entered; his reception was cordial, not rapturous; he acknowledged it rather slightly, and began: the wings (i.e. stage entrances) were not over-crowded, though it is common for the actors to come to see a new one's first scene; however, "come one, come all,"—it mattered little then; "he *had* got his foot to the float." Kean began to bestir himself the instant Bassanio left the stage; he was warmly applauded at the lines

> If I can catch him once upon the hip,
> I will feed fat the ancient grudge I bear him.
>
> [I. iii. 46-7]

When he replied to Antonio's sneer,

> Is your gold and silver ewes and rams?
> I cannot tell—I make it breed as fast,—
>
> [I. iii. 95-6]

there was laughter and applause; the scene went well, and as the act fell, a comedian who had been looking on went into the green-room—a comedian who is himself, in his peculiar walk, an admirable actor—and addressing some one who had just entered, said, "I say! he's got a *black* wig and beard; did *you* ever see Shylock in a black wig?" This is not quoted as an instance of ill-nature, for it was not said in that spirit, but as a proof of what a slight impression had been made on the mind of the actor in question by the new tragedian. Shylock does not reappear until Scene 4 in the second act; and, of course, it was expected Kean would have gone into the green-room. Hollow as the professions might have been, had he done so he would there have been congratulated on his success; for badly as the actors of the theatre royal, Drury-lane, might be suspected of wishing towards the interloper, they would not have been wanting in such an outward mark of decency; but Kean prowled about behind the scenes, didn't require the attention of the call-boy, but was at his post when wanted. In his speech to Jessica (Mrs. Bland) he was much applauded, and the audience had become extremely attentive, which was particularly shown by their approbation at his exit in this scene, when their plaudits must be considered rather as a sign of their general satisfaction than as extorted by his delivery of

Safe bind, safe find,—
A proverb never stale in thrifty mind.

[II. v. 54-5]

Act 3 commenced, Bassanio, Antonio, and Gratiano, and, in fact, all the characters save Shylock, Tubal, Salarino, and Salanio, were quietly seated in the green-room, when the dread rumble of reiterated plaudits burst on their ears—"Again! again!! *What* could it be" not "*Who* could it be?" for of that there was now no doubt. The green-room was cleared in an instant, and every character was at the wing to look at "the little man in the *black* wig," who was raging like a lion in the great scene with Tubal: the applause was, considering the scanty number of the audience, prodigious; as Oxberry very drolly said, "How the devil so few of them kicked up such a row was marvellous!" At the end of this scene Kean ran up stairs to the room where he had dressed to avoid his congratulators, and in the deep recesses of his own proud heart buried his joys. It appeared to those who were unused to Kean's enunciation, that he had become hoarse from exertion, but in fact he was never in better voice. However, after him went Messrs. Raymond and Arnold, one bearing negus and the other oranges; and believe me, "my pensive public," the fact of those great functionaries having done this proves that the impression he had made was by no means a slight one. The trial scene (though highly applauded) was rather an anti-climax in effect: such, in fact, it always was, for his scene with Salanio and Tubal was so overwhelming, that nothing could exceed it. Shylock ends in the fourth act, and before the play was over, Kean had left the theatre.

> W. L. Rede?, *"Recollections of Kean," in* The New Monthly Magazine, *Vol. III, May, 1834, pp. 345-52.*

Edmund Kean as Shylock.

Bryan Waller Procter   (essay date 1835)

[*Procter recounts the events leading up to Kean's debut on the London stage as Shylock, the obstacles he encountered, and his eventual triumph in winning the plaudits of both audience and critics.*]

On Wednesday, the 26th of January, 1814, the Drury Lane play-bills intimated that "their Majesties' servants" would that evening perform Shakspeare's play of *The Merchant of Venice.* Among the principal actors announced, were,—as Portia, Miss Smith; Antonio, Mr. Powell; Bassanio, Mr. Rae; Lorenzo (with songs), Mr. Phillips; Lancelot, Mr. Oxberry; Gratiano, Mr. Wrench; and "*Shylock, Mr. Kean,* from the Theatre Royal, Exeter." This was the day "big with the fate" of Kean and the acting drama.

Never was any thing less propitious; the winter was in its height (the cold severe and the snow two feet deep upon the ground); the actor himself was friendless; and he had undergone three months of want, anxiety, and discouragement. No paragraphs (those insidious prologues to a first appearance) had trumpeted his approach; no brother-actor had taken him by the hand, or cheered him up to stand his forth-coming trial; and he had not had one single rehearsal! Until the morning of the very day on which he was to make his *debut,* he had never gone through a scene with the actors who were to be fellow-labourers with him in the play. What occurred to interrupt the common custom of theatres we are not competent to say.

At last, however, the play was put in rehearsal; this was not until the morning of the 26th, the very day on which he was to appear. In obedience to the call, Kean attended at the theatre, to walk through his part. Mr. Raymond, the stage-manager, and the several actors specified in the bill of the evening, were there. Every one was very civil, and as cold as the season. The actors at the side scenes (Kean heard of this afterward, though he could not then distinguish anything) were liberal of their prophecies:—"He will be sure to fail." However, our hero went through the speeches of Shylock, or rather he was in the *act* of repeating them (giving some of his peculiar effects to each), when Raymond, the manager, could withhold his advice no longer. "This will *never* do, Mr. Kean," said he, with a superior smile; "it is an innovation, sir; it is totally different from any thing that has ever been done on these boards."—"Sir," returned our hero (we can imagine something of his tone here, however repressed it might have been),—"Sir, I *wish* it to be so."—"It will not do, Mr. Kean, be assured of it," returned the manager carelessly. "Well, sir," replied the other, "perhaps I may be wrong; but, if so, *the public* will set me right." Finding remonstrance of no avail, Mr. Raymond left the refractory actor to perform the "Road to Ruin" his own way. (pp. 127-28)

After dinner, Kean prepared for the awful evening. His stock of "properties" was very scanty. He tied up his wig and collar, however, and an old pair of black silk stockings, in a pocket-handkerchief, thrust them into his greatcoat pocket (his coat with "the great capes"), and trudged through the snow to Drury Lane.

It was a cold and dismal evening; and when the curtain drew up, there were but few persons in the theatre. And even those few, it is presumed, were less disposed to be pleased than they would have been at a more genial season. For there is a predisposition to pleasure or otherwise on such occasions; and a portion of the praise or censure which is showered upon actors, owes its origin to the previous comfort or discomfort of the spectator. There were one or two sound critics in the house, however, and these determined—not the quantity of applause, but the quality of reputation, which should belong to the new performer. And it is always thus. We hear, indeed, of this and that thing or person being allowed by all "the world" to be best,—pre-eminent beyond rivalry or doubt. We hear of certain rare beauties, and exalted flavours, which are allowed excellent by "the world,"—passages of Milton—deep and subtle thoughts in Shakspeare—the odour of violets—the white muscle of the haunch—the callipash and the callipee, and so forth. Alas! "the world" has nothing to do with these high and weighty matters. All is determined by the critics,—by the half a dozen men of taste and genius who support the credit of their age. The coarse palate of the public, of the multitude, cannot apprehend such delicacies. It admits them, indeed; and they become, in time, truths,—commonplaces; not because they are generally felt, but because, by a fine providence, the many and the ignorant admit and follow, in instinctive obedience, the lessons of the few and the wise.

When Kean first entered upon the stage, that evening, the spectators saw that something decisive (good or bad) was about to happen. His quick, flashing, and intelligent eye, and his quiet resolute bearing, denoted a sure result,—Cæsar, or nothing. "I could scarcely draw my breath," said Dr. Drury to Kean on the following day, "when you first came upon the stage. But directly you took your position, and leaned upon your cane, I saw that all was right." Kean was received with the usual encouraging plaudits bestowed on a new actor; and he acknowledged them with a bow eminently graceful. This was so far in his favour. His audience now took notice of him, and saw a figure and countenance that Titian would have been pleased to paint. His thin, dark face, full of meaning, and taking, at every turn, a sinister or vigilant expression, was just adapted to the ascetic and revengeful Shylock—He spoke,—"Three thousand ducats? well!" [I.iii.1]—and you were satisfied that there would be no failure. As he proceeded, the feeling of the audience went altogether with him. His reply to Bassanio (who says, Be assured you may take his bond), "I *will* be assured I may," [I.iii.29]—obtained applause; and his fine retort on Antonio (which shames, or ought to cast shame on the Christian merchant,)

> Fair Sir, you spit on me on Wednesday last;
> You spurned me such a day; another time
> You called me—dog; and for these courtesies
> I'll lend you thus much moneys—
>
> [I.iii.126-29]

was received with acclamations. At one time, it was feared that his voice would fail, and the manager hurried after him with a glass of negus, as a restorative; but it was an idle apprehension. He went on, still gaining ground, until he arrived at the scene with Salarino, where those fierce and unanswerable interrogations on behalf of the Jew ("Hath not a Jew eyes" [III. i. 59], &c.) are forced from him: when, knitting himself up, he gave them forth with terrible energy, and drew down a thunder of applause. And in this way he went on, victorious, to the end; gathering glory after glory, shout after shout, till the curtain fell. Nothing like that acting—nothing like that applause, had, for many previous years, resounded within the walls of ancient or modern Drury. It was a new era. The actor and the theatre were both poor, and each, separately, was unable to rise. But together—like certain salts and other substances which are formidable only in conjunction—

they were competent to encounter any thing. That day was golden-lettered in theatrical annals. The audience went home wondering and delighted; the committee more than content; the actor himself triumphant. (pp. 129-31)

Bryan Waller Procter, in an excerpt from his The Life of Edmund Kean, *Harper & Brothers, 1835, pp. 127-35.*

Raymund FitzSimons　(essay date 1976)

[*FitzSimons describes Kean's debut as Shylock in the half-empty Drury Lane theater, the commotion the actor stirred among the acting company and the spectators, and the favorable reaction of the press. This last included William Hazlitt, writing his first dramatic criticism, and the conservative London* Times, *historically partisan to the classic declamatory school of acting exemplified by John Philip Kemble.*]

The day of Kean's début was cold and miserable. A heavy fall of snow two days previously was thawing slowly, covering the streets with deep slush, and a drizzling rain had set in, which was to continue all day. Only one rehearsal had been allotted him and this was called for twelve o'clock on the day of the performance. Until then he had never gone through a scene with any of the players who were to act with him that night. The stage manager was George Raymond, generally known as 'Bustling' Raymond, and neither he nor any of the players gave Kean a word of encouragement. The atmosphere was one of defeat, for they were certain he would fail, like all the other provincial tragedians who had come and gone in the past few weeks.

That night Kean set out for Drury Lane. He could not afford a carriage, and trudged through the slush, carrying a bundle containing his stage costume. At the theatre, he was offered a dressing-room to himself, for on that night at least he was the star, but he refused this because of the attitude of the committee towards him, and he changed below the stage with the supporting actors. They were startled when they saw him lay out a black wig and beard. The news spread quickly backstage that the strange little man from Exeter had rejected the traditional red wig worn by every Shylock since the days of Shakespeare himself. Even Charles Macklin, who, seventy-three years previously, had been the first to interpret the part as a tragic instead of a comic one, had retained the red wig. This was the first of the many surprising events that were to happen at Drury Lane that night.

There were few people in the theatre. The boxes were completely empty and the pit and gallery barely half full. The weather had inclined people to stay at home rather than sit on the cheerless benches at Drury Lane to witness the failure of yet another provincial tragedian. The actors expected no more to come until half-price, for obviously the only attraction of the evening was the afterpiece, with the comedian, Jack Bannister, playing in a farce entitled *The Apprentice*. The curtain rose and *The Merchant of Venice* began.

Alexander Rae, as Bassanio, listlessly expounded his love for Portia. The prompter told the call-boy to summon Kean, but the boy found him already waiting in the wings. When he made his entrance as Shylock, and stood listening gravely to Bassanio's request for money, a ripple of expectancy ran through the thin audience. They sensed that this was no ordinary actor. Dr. Drury told him later: 'I could scarcely draw my breath when you came upon the stage. But directly you took your position, and leaned upon your cane, I knew that all was right.'

Bassanio said, 'Be assured you may take his bond,' and Shylock's sardonic reply, 'I *will* be assured I may' [I. iii. 28-9] drew the first applause of the evening. Then his mood changed, as with the garrulity of age, he told the story of Jacob and his flock. By the time he had finished, everyone in the vast cold theatre had been warmed into responsive life. When he addressed Antonio, the contempt in his voice drew further applause.

> Hath a *dog* money? is it possible
> A *cur* can lend three thousand ducats . . .
>
>   [I. iii. 121-22]

The expressions playing rapidly over his thin, pallid face wore, in turn, sinister, vigilant, ascetic and revengeful. His arms and hands were in constant play; his whole body was eloquent. No one in the audience had seen anything like this.

By the end of the second act, the theatre had filled up a little. A new comic opera, *A Farmer's Wife,* advertised for first production that night at Covent Garden, had been withdrawn at the last minute, and some of those disappointed crossed over to see the new tragedian at Drury Lane. But even with these additions, the theatre was far from full. The newcomers were in time to see the remarkable playing of Kean in the first scene of the third act, between Shylock, Solanio and Salarino. Shylock said: 'He hath disgraced me and hindered me half-a-million; laughed at my losses, mocked at my gains, scorned my nation, thwarted my bargains, cooled my friends, heated mine enemies . . .' [III. i. 54-8] He hurried through the catalogue of wrongs Antonio had done him, accentuating each one in a high-pitched voice, but when he reached the climax—'and what's his reason? I am a Jew' [III. i. 58]—he came down by a sudden transition to a gentle suffering tone on the words, *'I am a Jew.'* The natural simplicity he gave to the words touched the heart of the audience. Then he continued, with passionate recrimination in his voice, 'If you prick us, do we not bleed? if you tickle us, do we not laugh? . . .' [III. i. 64-5] The audience were on their feet, greeting each savage interrogation with roars of approval.

The players seated in the green room were startled by the din. They rushed to the wings in time to see Shylock raging like a lion in the dialogue with Tubal. Dr. John Doran, the theatre historian, wrote: '[His] anguish at his daughter's flight, his wrath at the two Christians who make sport of his anguish; his hatred of all Christians, generally, and of Antonio in particular; and then his alternations of rage, grief, and ecstasy, as Tubal relates the losses incurred in the search of that naughty Jessica, her extravagances, and then the ill-luck that has fallen upon Antonio;—in all this, there was such originality, such terrible force, such assurance of a new and mighty master,—that the house burst forth into a very whirlwind of approbation.' William Oxberry, who played the role of Launcelot Gobbo, wrote: 'How the devil so few of them kicked up such a row was marvellous.'

In the trial scene in the fourth act, Kean consolidated his triumph. When urged by Portia to accept Bassanio's offer of three times the sum owed in place of a pound of Antonio's flesh, he replaced the traditional severity of Shylock's reply, 'An oath, an oath, I have an oath in heaven' [IV. i. 228], with the bantering tone of a man who knows that things are going his way. Again, his reply to Portia's entreaty to procure a surgeon for charity's sake, 'I cannot find it; 'tis not in the bond'

[IV. i. 262], was accompanied by a delightful chuckle instead of the sneer given by Macklin and other actors. Doran wrote: 'His calm appearance at first, his confident appeal to justice; his deafness, when appeal is made to him for mercy; his steady joyousness, when the young lawyer recognises the validity of the bond; his burst of exultation, when his right is confessed; his fiendish eagerness, when whetting the knife:— and then, the sudden collapse of disappointment and terror, with the words, 'Is *that*—the *LAW?'* [IV. i. 34]—in all was made manifest, that a noble successor to the noblest of the actors of old had arisen. Then, his trembling anxiety to recover what he had before refused; his sordid abjectness, as he finds himself foiled, at every turn; his subdued fury; and, at the last (and it was always the crowning glory of his acting in this play) the withering sneer, hardly concealing the crushed heart, with which he replied to the jibes of Gratiano, as he left the court,—all raised a new sensation in an audience, who acknowledged it in a perfect tumult of acclamation. As he passed to his dressing-room, Raymond saluted him with the confession, that he had made a hit; Pope, more generous, avowed that he had saved the house from ruin.'

With the trial scene, Kean's part was over and by the time the play finished, he had already left the theatre. He hurried home to tell Mary of his triumph and he burst in upon her, shouting exultantly, 'Mary, you shall ride in your carriage, and Charlie shall go to Eton.'

Only two newspapers, the *Morning Post* and the *Morning Chronicle,* had sent their dramatic critics to Kean's début. The *Morning Post* praised his expressive face, his intelligence and mastery of his art. The critic for the *Morning Chronicle* was William Hazlitt. He was thirty-five years old and he had worked for the newspaper since the spring of the previous year. He had started as Parliamentary correspondent, but in October the editor, James Perry, had appointed him dramatic critic. Perry had no idea that in Hazlitt he had a genius on his staff and he sighed at the length of the dramatic criticisms that landed daily on his desk. He had been asked by the Drury Lane committee to report kindly on Kean's début, and he had instructed Hazlitt accordingly. Hazlitt recalled: 'I had been told to give as favourable an account as I could: I gave a true one. I am not one of those who, when they see the sun breaking from behind a cloud, stop to ask others whether it is the moon. Mr. Kean's appearance was the first gleam of genius breaking athwart the gloom of the Stage.'

It was a remarkable stroke of destiny that Kean's début coincided so closely with that of Hazlitt as a critic, for in Hazlitt he was to have a chronicler worthy of his performances. But if this was fortunate for Kean, it was equally so for Hazlitt. For years he had brooded on the characters of Shakespeare until they had become part of his blood and spirit, but he was beginning to doubt that he would ever see them fully realised on the stage of a theatre. He was to find in Kean not only an understanding of Shakespeare that matched his own, but the power to give expression to it, visible and tangible, on the boards of Drury Lane. To this, Hazlitt was to respond ardently, and his accounts of Kean's performances are written with a passion unequalled in the history of dramatic criticism. With Kean's début as Shylock, Hazlitt embarked on a voyage of discovery that he would not have believed possible this side of the grave. 'Before the night was ended,' he wrote, 'I had hailed in such poor words as I could muster at the moment, the advent, I might almost say the portent, of Edmund Kean.'

While the Drury Lane committee were pleased with Kean's reception, two favourable reviews and the applause of a small audience did not completely allay their uncertainty as to how the great majority of playgoers would react to him. Kemble had made the classical style of acting fashionable and many people might not care for Kean's rapidity and energy. The committee had not enough confidence in him to alter their schedule and his next performance did not take place until 1 February, almost a week later. This was his real test. The audience was double that of his début and included many connoisseurs of the drama. With the exception of *The Times,* all the newspapers were represented. Hazlitt had come again to see whether Kean could sustain his previous performance, and he was not disappointed. He wrote in the *Morning Chronicle:* 'His style of acting is, if we may use the expression, more significant, more pregnant with meaning, more varied and alive in every part, than any we have almost ever witnessed. The character never stands still; there is no vacant pause in the action; the eye is never silent.'

Leigh Hunt's *Examiner* was equally enthusiastic. Thomas Barnes was covering the theatre in place of Hunt, who was in prison for a libel on the Prince Regent. Like Hunt, Barnes was totally opposed to the artificiality of Kemble and his school. He wrote of Kean: 'There was an animating soul distinguishable in all he said and did, which at once gave a high interest to his performance, and excited those emotions, which are always felt at the presence of genius—that is, at the union of great powers with a fine sensibility. It was this that gave fire to his eye, energy to his tones, and such a variety and expressiveness to all his gestures, that one might almost say "his body thought".'

On 3 February Kean gave his third performance as Shylock. The prestigious *Times,* which would never have condescended to report on a completely unknown actor, was now sufficiently interested to send their critic. He wrote: 'We have seldom seen a much better Shylock. If he be inferior to Kemble in those peculiarities which distinguish that great actor, and to Cooke, in the force which he, above most performers, must give to particular passages, he need have no fear of a successful competition with any other man on the stage who attempts the sordid and malignant Jew.' This was praise indeed, for *The Times* had always favoured the classical style of Kemble. In the eyes of the committee, this review, above all others, set the seal of approval on Kean. They began to hope that in him they had at last found the tragedian they were seeking. (pp. 52-7)

> *Raymund FitzSimons, "The Saviour of Drury Lane," in his* Edmund Kean: Fire from Heaven, *Hamish Hamilton, 1976, pp. 48-75.*

PRODUCTION:

Henry Irving-Ellen Terry • Lyceum • 1879

BACKGROUND:

Henry Irving's *The Merchant of Venice* was one of his most successful Shakespearean productions, presented more than 250 times in its first run, and his Shylock is often regarded as his finest Shakespearean performance.

Critics praised the elaborate, detailed sets; Irving's restoration of the fifth act; Ellen Terry's beguiling portrayal of Portia; and Irving's portrait of Shylock "as the venerable Hebrew patriarch, the lonely, grieved widower, and the affectionate, while austere, father." Irving's poignant, final exit at the conclusion of Act IV is often singled out as the performance's apex. The *Spectator* critic wrote, "his Shylock is Mr. Irving's finest performance, and his final exit is its best point." Two eminent critics, Clement Scott and Joseph Knight, likewise classified Irving's performance as first-rate, "higher than anything the actor has yet attempted," and celebrated the production as "a credit to our time," and "superior to anything of its class that has been seen on the English stage by the present generation." According to most critics, Ellen Terry's portrayal of Portia captured the quintessence of the character, "a true Shakespearean replica," in the words of Scott, although some critics demurred, including Theodore Martin—the husband of another distinguished nineteenth-century Portia, Helena Faucit—and Henry James, who objected that "Miss Terry has too much nature, and we should like a little more art." Irving's *Merchant,* which debuted in London on 1 November 1879, first played in America, where the play was Irving's most popular, on 6 November 1883 at the Star Theater in New York. Over time, it has been said, Irving's Shylock became more vindictive and less sympathetic; and it has been suggested that Irving originally adopted his sympathetic portrayal of the character, for which he is often remembered, because he felt he lacked the physical attributes necessary to render the character's full villainy.

COMMENTARY:

Dutton Cook   (review date November 1879)

[*Cook asserts that Irving's portrayal of "old Shylock" as subdued, infirm, victimized but ultimately dignified, ranks among the actor's finest performances. "I never saw a Shylock that obtained more commiseration from the audience," Cook reports, noting that Irving's conception undermined the status of the Christians in the drama. Cook expresses his regrets that Irving ignored the convention of running the Belmont and Venice scenes together and instead restored Shakespeare's original pattern of alternating scenes. Of Terry, the critic affirms that "a more admirable Portia there could scarcely be."*]

An actor who has appeared with applause as *Hamlet* and *Othello, Macbeth* and *Richard,* must feel almost constrained to essay the character of *Shylock.* In times past, of course, *Shylock* was handed over to the low comedians to do their worst with; and Shakspeare's words, more or less, were delivered by the old-fashioned Jew of the streets, three-hatted, carrying an old-clothesman's bag, and afflicted with the guttural accents of Houndsditch. This absurdity was expelled from the stage by Macklin in the first instance, whose example was followed, after intervals, by Cooke and Kean; so that *Shylock* now comes before us essentially a tragic character. It had seemed to me, from the time of Mr. Irving's first experiments with the Shakspearean repertory, that, in the part of *Shylock,* he would find peculiar opportunities for the employment of his art; his power as an actor greatly consisting in the portrayal of definite character and special individuality as opposed to the more abstract and ideal creations. His best successes, to my thinking, have arisen from his presentment of strong personalities in which the prosaic element has prevailed over the poetic. His *Richard* I have always accounted his most complete achievement, and I am now much disposed to rank his *Shylock* with his *Richard*. No doubt *Shylock,* as a stage figure, has long worn the impress of Edmund Kean's genius; but there is a sort of natural Statute of Limitations in regard to histrionic traditions and prescriptions; and the lapse of nearly half a century has a good deal blunted, so to say, Kean's points, and rendered nugatory the old conventions of performance. Mr. Irving's *Shylock,* I may say at once, is not the *Shylock* of the patent theatres; nor must the violence of tone, the fierceness of gesture, the explosions of passion, so long associated with the part, be looked for at the Lyceum. I have known *Shylocks* who have seemed from first to last in a frenzy of malignancy, whose every speech had a certain detonating quality, and with whom ranting and raving were as close and continuous habits of life; and I must own that very cordial applause was wont to wait upon those excesses of representation. It is not only that Mr. Irving has not sufficient physical force for such clamorous exhibitions, but his conception and treatment of the character are altogether more subdued. He plays in a minor key, as it were; sufferance appears genuinely the badge of his tribe; long oppression and the custom of submission have tamed and cowed him until intolerable wrong blows the grey ashes of his wrath red-hot again; he is veritably "old *Shylock,*" as he describes himself and as the *Doge* addresses him: the years weigh upon him, he is infirm of gait, his face manifests the furrows of care and the pallors of sickness; and if he has stinted *Launcelot Gobbo,* his servant, in the matter of food, he has not been more liberal to himself. Mr. Irving is always picturesque. His *Shylock* is carefully arrayed, if without the traditional red cap which Venetian law compelled the Jews to wear, and by no means fails in artistic qualities of expression, line, and colour. The performance is altogether consistent and harmonious, and displays anew that power of self-control which has come to Mr. Irving this season as a fresh possession. Every temptation to extravagance or eccentricity of action was resolutely resisted, and with the happiest results. I never saw a *Shylock* that obtained more commiseration from the audience; for usually, I think, *Shylock* is so robustly vindictive and energetically defiant, as to compel the spectators to withhold from him their sympathies. But Mr. Irving's *Shylock,* old, haggard, halting, sordid, represents the dignity and intellect of the play; beside him, the Christians, for all their graces of aspect and gallantry of apparel, seem but poor creatures. His hatred of them finds justification in his race and his religion, and in the fact that they, his mental inferiors, are his tyrants; and when he is plundered by them alike of his child and his gold, his detestation turns naturally not so much to blind fury as to a deadly purpose of revenge. There is something grandly pathetic in the fixed calm of the Jew as he stands in the judgment-hall, a figure of Fate inexorably persistent, demanding the penalty of his bond; he is no mere usurer punishing a bankrupt debtor; if he avenges private injuries, he also represents a nation seeking atonement for centuries of wrong. By what a technical quibble is he denied justice, and tricked out of both penalty and principal! What a pitiful cur is *Gratiano* to yelp at his heels! One's sympathies follow the baffled and persecuted Jew as he slowly withdraws from the court; it is impossible to feel much interest in the release from peril of that very dull personage *Antonio.*

This was Mr. Irving's best scene, as it is of course the climax of the play. In the earlier passages he seemed bent, I thought, upon varying his tones too frequently, dropping into a collo-

quial manner too suddenly; while his interview with *Tubal* suffered somewhat from an accidental failure of memory on the part of his playfellow. But the representation was upon the whole singularly complete; the success of Mr. Irving's new venture was, indeed, never questionable for a moment. I regret, however, that his acting edition of the play has not dispensed with much scene-shifting which now oppresses and delays the performance; in this respect the arrangements of Mr. Charles Kean in 1858 and of Mr. Bancroft in 1875 were more to be admired. For modifications of this kind to suit the conditions of modern performance are, I hold, quite permissible. Shakspeare changed his scenes so often because there were, in fact, no scenes to change; much stage-management was then effected by the imagination of the spectators, whose thoughts "pieced out" the imperfections of the performance. "The Merchant of Venice" is one of the least compact of Shakspeare's works; *Shylock,* the most prominent character, disappears at the end of the fourth act; and the two plots—the caskets and the "merry bond"—are very slightly connected: *Shylock* and *Portia* only meeting in the trial scene. Mr. Bancroft, I remember, contrived very happily to pack the Belmont scenes closely together; and Mr. Kean's second act required no change of scene—the "exterior of *Shylock's* house" sufficed throughout. Mr. Irving, retaining the *Prince of Morocco,* has dismissed the *Prince of Arragon* from the cast: both these suitors, however, appeared alike at the Princess's and at the Prince of Wales's Theatre. Happily the *Portia* of 1875—who rendered memorable a revival that was otherwise rather ill-starred, for all the taste and refinement of its scenic decorations—Miss Ellen Terry, lends her invaluable assistance to Mr. Irving at the Lyceum; and a more admirable *Portia* there could scarcely be. Nervous at first, and weighed down possibly by the difficulty of equalling herself and of renewing her former triumph, the lady played uncertainly, and at times with some insufficiency of force; but as the drama proceeded her courage increased and her genius asserted itself. Radiantly beautiful in her Venetian robes of gold-coloured brocaded satin, with the look of a picture by Giorgione, her emotional acting in the casket-scene with *Bassanio;* her spirited resolve, confided to *Nerissa,* to prove "the prettier fellow of the two" [III. iv. 64]; her exquisite management of the most melodious of voices in the trial before the *Doge;* the high comedy of the last act—these left nothing to be desired, and obtained, as they deserved, the most enthusiastic applause. *Antonio* and *Gratiano* were but weakly interpreted; Mr. Johnson proved an acceptable *Launcelot,* versed in the humours of the part; and there was decided merit in the stalwart mien and natural feeling of Mr. Barnes's *Bassanio.* Miss Alma Murray appeared as *Jessica,* and Miss Florence Terry as *Nerissa,* both actresses finding favour with the audience. The new scenes by Mr. Hawes Craven and others are excellently artistic, and the costumes and furniture very handsome and appropriate. (pp. 390-93)

Dutton Cook, "The Merchant of Venice," in his Nights at the Play: A View of the English Stage, *Chatto and Windus, 1883, pp. 390-93.*

Clement Scott　(review date 2 November 1879)

[*Scott was an English dramatic critic who wrote for the* Daily Telegraph *and was editor of the* Theatre *during the last quarter of the nineteenth century. His writings, including* From 'The Bells' to 'King Arthur' *(1896), a collection of reviews of opening night performances at the Lyceum theater, reflect his aversion to contemporary theater and the emergence of real-*

Henry Irving as Shylock.

ism, which he perceived as an affront to moral sensibility. In the review below, originally published on 2 November 1879, Scott affirms that Irving's production "is a credit to our time," and recognizes Irving's pathetic, dignified Shylock as one of the actor's highest achievements: "in point of variety, incisiveness and subtlety of expression, it ranks higher than anything the actor has yet attempted." The critic terms Terry's beguiling performance "a true Shakespearean replica."]

The latest contribution to the art series of Shakespearean revivals at the Lyceum, however much criticism it may evoke, will, unquestionably, bind closer the sympathies of the intelligent public with the name, the fame, the energy, and the industry of Henry Irving. Once more all who are interested in the higher aims and aspirations of the drama have been summoned to see something done for Shakespeare; and once more strong-hearted work is crowned with success. The *Merchant of Venice,* presented as a picture of rare splendour; the character of Shylock personated in a style that rivets the attention, absorbs the interest, and draws out the intellectual faculties of the audience; a Portia who will live beyond the present day as one of the most gracious and charming of Shakespearean memories; an atmosphere of general intelligence and wholesome co-operation; and a scene which fascinates the eye by its colour, its harmony, and its tastes, are points not to be neglected in these days of theatrical depression. On the contrary, they are valuable gifts that cannot be too highly esteemed.

It is a common trick of theatrical controversy to ignore the present and deplore the past, to ridicule the new school and applaud the old, to draw hasty conclusions on the decline of the Shakespearean drama, and to drag down ambitious enterprise with the power of contemptuous indifference; but we have no hesitation in saying that such as profess to want so much, and own to finding so little, are, indeed, hard to please, if in the revived *Merchant of Venice* they cannot gratify their intellectual faculties, and enliven their higher tastes. For, let it be remembered, that there is much more present in this performance than the mere success of an individual actor or actress, and far deeper significance than the presence of a new Shylock or an ideal Portia. It is not given to the whole world to think alike, and there may be minds as unstirred by the pathetic dignity of Mr. Irving's Shylock, as by the winsome vivacity of Miss Ellen Terry's Portia. They may see, unmoved, the intense comedy and facial force of the one, and pass over the disciplined gaiety of the other; they may sneer at individual bits, and neglect the consideration of the whole; they may linger on defects, and fail to acknowledge the true notes of human passion; but they are unjust in their strictures, and prejudiced in their opinions if they cannot gather from such a performance as this a renewed promise and a brighter hope. Every age cannot bring forth a genius, but the young playgoers of today may be proud of the opportunity that gives to their dramatic education and their theatrical tastes the study of such works as Mr. Irving puts before them. Let criticism say what it will, this *Merchant of Venice,* viewed in its completeness, is a credit to our time.

First, then, as to the Shylock of Mr. Irving. It is no new theory that the old Jew commands the sympathies of generous men, whatever Shakespeare may have intended. Let us grant the fixity of his purpose, the implacability of his nature, the terribleness of his revenge, and still the heart is stirred to see him the victim of a legal quibble, the butt of an impudent courtier, and condemned to the most merciless fate by the very judges who had preached to him about mercy. Shakespeare might or might not have intended subtly to uphold the grandeur of a down-trodden race, but certainly it has hitherto been most difficult to harmonise the man Shylock with the tricks of theatrical tradition. We all know how Edmund Kean succeeded, by blending the human Jew with the showy effects of his art, the night when he turned his antagonists into worshippers, and arriving at home, promised his wife a carriage, his boy a career, and broke down with that passionate regret, "If Howard had but lived to see it!" But even Kean's greatest admirer, praising as he did the majesty of the personation, complained that his natural gifts ill accorded with the requirements of his character. "We question," wrote Hazlitt, "if he will not become a greater favourite in other parts. There was a lightness and vigour in his tread, a buoyancy and elasticity of spirit, a fire and animation, which would accord better with almost any other character than the morose, sullen, inward, inveterate, inflexible malignity of Shylock."

Mr. Henry Irving has determined to give us a new Shylock, and to discard theatrical tradition. If he puzzles the student of the past, he will please the surveyor of the text. If he chills the trial scene with his studious neglect of time-honoured business, he finishes off with admirable art the brief career of a gloomy and disappointed life. What we lose in effect we gain in persuasion; for though the hungry rapacity of Shylock is toned, the mind is enlivened with that ever present picture of a proud, pale, and hopelessly crushed man, who is speechless in the hands of fate, and dazed as if in a dream when he bows at the decision that confiscates his fortune and seeks to change his religion. The unworthy vulgarity of a stage Shylock is never for an instant suggested by Mr. Irving. He might make many points by obeying tradition and discarding consistency; but he prefers to put before us a proud, resolute, and religious man, sincere in his ancient faith, tender in his recollections, as hard and inflexible as adamant when his revenge becomes a madness, cold and impassive in the demand for his rights, crushed with horror at the injustice that is his doom. But let us take the new Shylock briefly from the moment when he first comes upon the scene in his sober, yet picturesque, garments. With clearcut features and grey, wolf-like, hungry face, twisting his thin wisp of a beard as he leans over his stick and inwardly meditates on Bassanio's proposal for a loan. We are reminded of a scene in the life of Edmund Kean, told by Dr. Drury, the head master of Harrow. "Shylock leant over his crutched stick with both hands and looking askance at Bassanio said, 'Three thousand ducats?' paused, bethought himself and then added, 'Well?' 'He is safe,' said Dr. Drury." And so was Mr. Henry Irving when he looked across the footlights into distance after the tumult of applause had subsided and gave as it were the keynote to the character he had conceived.

For the purposes of criticism, Mr. Irving's Shylock may be divided into three distinct chapters—first in the scene with Antonio and Bassanio we have the irony of humour and the subtlety of sarcasm; second, in the Tubal scene the exhibition of frenzied passion; and, lastly, the majestic dignity of the trial. The first division of the picture will, in point of variety, incisiveness and subtlety of expression, rank higher than anything the actor has yet attempted. We have to go to a certain scene in *Louis XI* to find its parallel, but this is more composed and less restless. For what do we see both in soliloquy and dialogue? Not only the religious aspirations of the old Hebrew and the intense fervour of his antipathies, as expressed in such words as, "He hates our sacred nation" [I. iii. 48], but an admirable humour and cynicism in a retort like, "I will be assured I may, and that I may be assured I will bethink me!" [I. iii. 29-30] or as such a change as is contained in the sneer, "O, Father Abram! what these Christians are, whose own hard dealings teach them to suspect the thoughts of others!" [I. iii. 159-61] Nor is the scene unrelieved by sympathetic touches of art of the finest kind. Dignified, self-contained, cynical as Shylock is, there is just one effusive moment when, the bargain all arranged, he says, "This kind will I show. Go with me to the notary" [I. iii. 143-44], and touches the breast of Antonio. The shrinking horror of contact reminds the Jew of his mistake, and he bows with polished courtesy, tinged with the most subtle sarcasm. The action conveys a world of thought. But scarcely a moment of the dialogue was unrelieved by some variety of intonation or facial expression—at one moment the half-laughing sneer that a pound of man's flesh was not so profitable as that of mutton, or of goats, and at another the recital with the fervour of interest of some old passage in the history of Jacob.

Thus early in the play the sympathies of the audience were artfully enlisted, for the man whose good offices were sought by the man who had insulted him. The scene on the discovery of loss of daughter and ducats was not, on the whole, so successful. True, the actor was slightly put out by a blunder on the part of Tubal, but the expression of incontinent rage and prostration of nervous energy, was occasionally not in tune. The great speech was started in too high a key, and, though

it won the finest burst of applause of the whole evening, Mr. Irving was not at this moment seen at his best. True, no doubt, it was to nature, this distraught, half-maddened old man, rushing from one thing to another, and worn out with the fatigue of his own frenzy; but the strain was very great and a little painful. Yet mark what power and variety there must be in the actor, who, a few seconds after this hysterical declamation, could subside tranquilly into the calm and almost inspired delivery of the pathetic words: "No satisfaction, no revenge; nor no ill-luck stirring but what lights o' my shoulders; no sighs, but o' my breathing; no tears, but of my shedding!" [III. i. 94-6] This pathetic outburst restored the lost balance of the composition, and, from that instant, all went well again.

The fever was over, and the calm was regained, with only one short interval of very bitter and emphatic scorn in the restored scene, where Antonio prays for mercy at the Jew's hands, and is relegated in disgust to the gaoler. This is a good introduction, for it flavours the unrelenting inflexibility of the revenge, and leads up well and efficiently to the isolated dignity of the trial. A finer picture the Stage has seldom seen than that painted Venetian hall, backed with spectators, lined with mediæval soldiery in their quaint costumes, and coloured with faultless taste. All tradition is discarded. Shylock is not accompanied to the judgement-seat by a crowd of eager admirers, Tubal, and the rest, who support one of their own people. No; there he stands, pale, alone, and defiant, the very picture of calm and unruffled determination. He has appealed unto Cæsar, and unto Cæsar has he gone, and there is something splendid even in his vindictiveness. In the presence of so majestic a figure, the jests of Gratiano are ribald and offensive; all eyes are turned upon the relentless features of the cold-cut face. Never was facial expression so successfully used in the exhibition of character, and even Portia seemed to shudder under the icy gaze of this determined man. We read of Kean's "steady joyousness," his "burst of exultation, when his right is confessed," his "fiendish eagerness when whetting the knife"; but none of this was here. All was calm and terrible, making the audience almost shudder at the concentrated hate, that was so near a climax.

If Mr. Irving's Shylock was true at first, it could be played in no other way now. It is a bold, defiant protest against mere tradition, and those who have followed it, must observe to the end. With the turning of the tables comes a sudden collapse. The knife and scales the Jew had brought out from the concealment of his gaberdine, drop like lead from his hands. Astonishment and horror sit upon Shylock's countenance, and with a piteous and far-seeing gaze, he accepts the inevitable. At this moment, the gibes of Gratiano are painful to the interested and pitying audience, and one feels inclined to resent such determined cruelty, insult being added to injury. That such a man, so firm in his faith, so determined in his revenge, and so consistent in his characteristics, should ever accept the religion of his enemies as part, is a point that must be argued out with Shakespeare. Mr. Irving gets out of the difficulty in the best possible manner by the lost air of dreaminess that makes the lips answer while the mind is astray. Shylock's occupation is gone, the world and his oppressors have been too strong for him, sufferance is the badge of all his tribe, and, at least, he accepts his fate like a hero. "The withering sneer hardly concealing the crushed heart," with which the insulted Jew receives the last impertinence of Gratiano, provides Mr. Irving, as it did Kean, with a magnificent exit, that crowned a very conspicuous and undoubted triumph.

Ripened and matured by experience, finish, fancy, and taste, the Portia of Miss Ellen Terry becomes the most bewitching of Shakespearean creations. Good as it was years ago at the Prince of Wales's Theatre, it is better now. The love is more expressive and tender, the gaiety more wilful and abandoned, the style more pronounced. At anxious moments sudden fitful gusts of nervousness seemed to distract and dismay the actress, but no accidents of the kind took away from the unrivalled merit and wayward charm of so pure a conception. When Portia explains to Nerissa her plan and future pranks, it is the very thistle-down of light and breezy humour; not for an instant is womanliness abandoned or excess displayed; the little tricks of imitation and suggestion, the sketches of the conceited and self-sufficient man so soon to be represented are in the finest spirit of gaiety; and in all Miss Terry enchanted her audience. Those tender and trembling accents in her voice were of the greatest value in the speech for mercy at the trial, and those were ill-advised who left before the last act, which contains some gems of Shakespearean poetry, and a scene of comedy in which Portia literally surpassed herself. These seem high compliments; but even those whose inclinations are wedded to old traditions and past favourites, would recognise here a singular adaptability, a gracious ideality, and a Portia who seems to contain the echo of Shakespeare's heroine. Whether she lounges idly on the sofa as Nerissa describes her lovers, or nervously trembles when the Prince of Morocco chooses from the caskets, or with maidenly grace accepts the wooing of Bassanio, or revels in the contemplation of her frolic, or tremblingly administers justice, or hurries homewards to enjoy the vexation of her lover in the comedy of the ring, the Portia of this modern stage is a true Shakespearean replica, sufficient in itself to compel the attention of dramatic connoisseurs.

For the rest there is some careful and unambitious acting, that for the most part may receive the negative compliment of doing little harm when it failed in creating a very strong impression. The Nerissa was, no doubt, an unfortunate mistake in more ways than one, for she is an individual character, and not a feeble echo of Portia. There should be contrast, and not diminutive imitation. Under any circumstances the employment of sisters would be hazardous, but in this case a very distressing attack of nervousness blunted the activity of Miss Florence Terry, and jeopardised several important scenes. Mr. Tyars and Mr. Beaumont, as the Prince and the Duke, spoke their lines well, but perhaps the most useful example of manly bearing and spirited elocution was the Bassanio of Mr. Barnes, who made his way with the audience by good, sound, and honest work. Launcelot Gobbo and old Gobbo are awkward characters, but Mr. Johnson and Mr. C. Cooper got out of the difficulty very well; and in the part of Jessica it was pleasant to hear the silvery voice and intelligent utterance of Miss Alma Murray. In the distant future, when a dramatic school exists, it will be possible, perhaps, for the general elocution to be better than it is at present. Shakespeare's verse cannot be rattled off like modern comedy dialogue without destroying its beauty.

In architectural and romantic painting, Mr. Hawes Craven, Mr. W. Telbin, Mr. W. Hann, and Mr. W. Cuthbert have advanced even upon former Lyceum glories, and as regards decoration and appropriate detail, a play could not have been better mounted. So, when at the close of the evening, Mr. Irving was enthusiastically called before the curtain, it was natural that he should express intense pleasure at the demonstrative expressions of approval. Another bold effort has been re-

warded with success, and, for once, an exception will be found to the old theatrical rule that *The Merchant of Venice* is an unremunerative play. Scholars, students, and mere idle spectators have here before them, the generous result of much anxious labour and devotion to dramatic art. (pp. 163-70)

Clement Scott, " 'The Merchant of Venice'," in his From "The Bells" to "King Arthur", John MacQueen, 1896, pp. 163-70.

The Illustrated London News (review date 8 November 1879)

[*The critic commends many aspects of Irving's production, including the restoration of Act V and much of the stage business. As for Irving's performance, the critic deems it a new interpretation in some respects, noteworthy for the "sparks of humanity" struck by Irving's Shylock and the contrast and depth afforded to a character often flatly depicted as the villain. Ellen Terry's Portia revealed "a charming simplicity and naivete" that could be perfected with the addition of more force in the trial scene.*]

The *Merchant of Venice* . . . has been made the vehicle for considerable spectacular display. Mr. Irving must be complimented on his disposition of the scenes, and the general arrangement of effective stage business. To the regular acting copy additions have been made from the original Shaksperean text. The last act, so often and regrettably omitted in representation, is given. The first casket scene in the third act, introducing the Prince of Morocco, and portraying the natural sophistry which induces him to place his choice on the wrong casket, is also a welcome innovation. Of course, there is one drawback to these restorations—the length of the performance, which on the first night was protracted to a late hour. The audience, however, evinced no signs of impatience; and the final fall of the curtain, close upon midnight, was the signal for loud and repeated plaudits. A criticism of the play itself would, at this late date, and after the numerous able dissertations on the subject, be superfluous. "*The Merchant of Venice,* says one of Shakspeare's commentators, "since the restoration of Charles II., has been one of the most popular plays on the English stage, and the appearance of Shylock has been the ambition of its greatest actors." We are prepared, from our own personal experiences, to endorse this statement. From time immemorial the character has been essayed by our most eminent tragedians, and Mr. Henry Irving but adds another to the list of its numerous exponents. In some respects the last-named gentleman gives an entirely new rendering of the wily and, in our opinion, somewhat oppressed Israelite. Of the reviled Jew he gives, as far as possible, a humanised portraiture, exhibiting, as points of contrast to his craft, avarice, and greed of vengeance, sparks of humanity that lie dormant in him, especially evidenced in his feeling for his daughter, Jessica, and his inordinate love of his despised and persecuted race. The actor makes the most of this phase of the character, and thus relieves it from the tedium of perpetual execration which otherwise pervades it. Even after the Jew's desertion by his daughter, Mr. Irving introduces the paternal element as interposing between him and his maledictory utterances. His acting in this scene was exceedingly fine. Some exception might be taken in the earlier scenes to the violence of the transition from a feeling of abject servility to one of intense hatred, the same coming upon the audience occasionally with the force of a concussion. But, as a whole, the performance is an artistic study, and adds another to the list of Mr. Irving's histrionic triumphs. The rôle of Portia fell to the lot of Miss Ellen Terry. This lady's success in the character has already been chronicled. Her acting throughout, especially in the earlier portions of the play, is characterised by a charming simplicity and naïveté. A little more force infused into the celebrated trial-scene, where Portia turns the tables on the uncompromising Jew, and the assumption would be perfect. The Antonio of Mr. Forrester, the Bassanio of Mr. Barnes, and the Gratiano of Mr. F. Cooper were all deserving of high commendation. Mr. S. Johnson gave an effective rendering of Launcelot Gobbo. The characters of Nerissa and Jessica found able representatives in Miss Florence Terry and Miss Alma Murray. The minor parts were adequately filled. The costumes are magnificent, and the views of Venice, executed by Messrs. Telbin, Craven, Hann, and Cuthbert, are graphically depicted. We prognosticate a long run for this successful Shakespearean venture.

A review of "The Merchant of Venice," in The Illustrated London News, *Vol. LXXV, No. 2108, November 8, 1879, p. 442.*

Joseph Knight   (review date 8 November 1879)

[*Knight was an English dramatic critic who wrote for the* Athenaeum. *Some of his reviews are collected in his* Theatrical Notes *(1893). In the originally unsigned review reprinted below, Knight heralds Irving's production and performance as "superior to anything of its class that has been seen on the English stage by the present generation." Knight praises the playing of the comic scenes and Irving's dignified portrayal of Shylock, and he especially lauds Irving's final exit. Terry's performance as Portia, according to the reviewer, was remarkable for its beauty, delivery of verse, and interpretation.*]

The performance of *The Merchant of Venice* at the Lyceum is remarkable in many respects. Considered as interpretation it is superior to anything of its class that has been seen on the English stage by the present generation, while as a sample of the manner in which Shakspeare is hereafter to be mounted it is of highest interest. In thus speaking we do not confine our praise to what may be called the upholstery portion of the accessories. An immense stride has been made in the direction of a thoroughly satisfactory presentation of the early drama, and the foundation is established of a system of performances which will restore Shakspeare to fashion as an acting dramatist, and will render attractive to the student, whatever his culture, that observation of the acted drama of Shakspeare which is indispensable to a full estimate of his powers. A background which is at once striking, natural, and unobtrusive is supplied, and from this the action receives added intelligibility. Constant attention has been paid to the trial scene, and one actor of eminence after another has contributed something to the fidelity or the dramatic value of the representation. Mr. Irving has, however, found something new and striking to add to this scene, and the presence, in the crowd of spectators of the trial, of a knot of eager and interested Jews, among whom the sentence condemning Shylock to deny his religion falls like a thunderbolt, and the explosion of popular wrath against this body which the result of the trial produces, are instances of ingenious and intelligent explanation and comment in the shape of action.

There are those doubtless who will regard such additions as futile or worse. Their effect upon the vivacity of the interpretation and upon the interest of the public is, however, great, and there is nothing whatever in the play itself to render such

things impertinent. It has been the fashion of late to close the performances of *The Merchant of Venice* at the end of the trial scene, and to bring down the curtain upon the defeat and despair of the Jew. A natural result of this course has been to foster the delusion that the play is a tragedy. It is in truth a romantic drama; it might even be called a tragicomedy set in a fantastic framework which is indispensable to the plot. That a very serious interest is inspired in Shylock is true. It is, however, highly improbable that an audience of Shakspeare's time, when prejudice against Jews still existed, felt the tragedy of the story as it has since been felt. In the very dislike to the Hebrews which animated those whose fathers or grandfathers might have seen them burned at the stake was found the cause why the notion of tragedy never suggested itself to early audiences. That Shylock to the time of Macklin was presented as a comic character is known, and the description by Macklin of the difficulties he encountered in trying to substitute the Jew of Shakspeare for that of Granville, Lord Lansdowne, is one of the most familiar of theatrical anecdotes. When the last act is put on the stage, the extreme sadness of the central interest ceases to be felt. Lord Lansdowne in his last act presents Lorenzo and Jessica rejoicing over Shylock's enforced apostasy. Shakspeare, with infinitely higher taste, makes no mention of the Jew except when Nerissa instructs Lorenzo and Jessica that they are chosen his heirs. To an audience, indeed, of the time of Shakspeare the penalty undergone by Shylock can scarcely have presented itself as very serious. Taking, then, *The Merchant of Venice* to be what it is, a play founded on one of the stories of the *Pecorone* of Ser Giovanni Fiorentino, with the substitution of the story of the three caskets, which comes from the *Gesta Romanorum,* for that of a species of Circe who in the Italian story sends her lovers to sleep by means of a potion and by a not too modest expedient robs them of their treasures, it must be classed with the romantic comedies. As such it lends itself readily to the kind of additions now made, and the revels in the Venetian streets and the pictures of a gay and frolic life are altogether in keeping. It may be incidentally mentioned, as it is a fact on which little if any stress has been laid, that Shakspeare's indebtedness to the Italian novel does not end with the character of Shylock and the attempted exaction of the forfeit. The scene of the framework or underplot, which in the story is more closely welded into the main action than in the play, is Belmonte, and the court of the lady, who is a widow, is not unlike that of Portia. Her waiting-woman, moreover, is wedded by Giannetto, the hero, to his friend Ansaldo, who may answer to Gratiano. Of none of these things is there any trace in the story from the "Gesta Romanorum," which is supposed to have supplied the idea of the caskets.

Mr. Irving's presentation of Shylock is in his later and happier vein. It is too restless in the scene with Tubal, the violent shaking of the head and one or two similar things suggesting snappishness rather than passion. In some respects, however, it has singular merits. The final exit of the Jew is one of the most impressive things we can recall; the comedy passages are introduced with full effect, and much melancholy dignity is assigned Shylock. The entire performance is thoughtful and scholarly, and likely to raise Mr. Irving's reputation. Whether in one belonging to a persecuted race there should be so open valiancy of hate, or whether more servility is to be expected, is a matter on which keen controversy may be waged. The beauty of Miss Terry's Portia is incontestable. An instance of perfect exposition is presented, and the business introduced is always subtle, poetical, and significant. Got up in exact imitation of those stately Venetian dames who still

---

gaze down from the pictures of Paolo Veronese, Miss Terry looks in every respect the Lady of Belmont of the story or the play. Her delivery is just and pure, and her performance is a remarkable instance of interpretation. In other respects the representation is noteworthy for general excellency of bearing and for *ensemble* rather than for the merit of single performances. Mr. Johnson's *Launcelot Gobbo* deserves, however, praise for its moderation, and the *Jessica* of Miss Alma Murray, the *Bassanio* of Mr. Barnes, the gallants (*Salanio, Salarino, Gratiano,* and *Lorenzo*) of Messrs. Elwood, Pinero, Cooper, and Norman Forbes form portions of a representation that may be pronounced satisfactory. There were shortcomings in the delivery of the verse, and there were other respects in which improvement might be effected. So considerable an advance is, however, this representation upon anything previously seen, censure seems churlish. The reception of the performance was enthusiastic. (pp. 302-06)

Joseph Knight, in an excerpt from his Theatrical Notes, *Lawrence & Bullen, 1893, pp. 302-06.*

The Saturday Review (review date 8 November 1879)

[*The critic avers that Irving's Shylock appeared too dignified in the early scenes, but that the performance reached its impressive pinnacle in Act IV: "Nothing could be finer than Mr. Irving's acting at this point, which is the climax of a scene the power and imagination of which can scarcely be rivalled." The critic deems Terry's Portia faultless.*]

The production by Mr. Irving at the Lyceum of *The Merchant of Venice* was eagerly expected and had a double source of certain attraction. The beauties of Miss Ellen Terry's Portia were already known; those of Mr. Irving's Shylock had to be discovered. The character of Shylock has given food for much discussion. It is well known that modern interpretations of the part have differed entirely from those given by the actors who, before the days of Macklin, treated the part from the point of view of the most grotesque comedy; and a good many people have told us how Shakspeare intended it to be treated. Mr. Hawkins, in the current number of the *Theatre* magazine, has argued very ingeniously and interestingly, from the fact that *The Merchant of Venice* appeared during the excitement caused by the iniquities of the Jew physician, Rodrigo Lopez, that the play was intended by its author as "a plea for toleration towards the Jews." The theory is well worked out and hangs well enough together, since it is admitted that, supposing this to have been Shakspeare's intention, his position as a manager, bound to please his public, hampered him in its execution. But we have always been of opinion that theorizing as to Shakspeare's intentions and the meanings of his characters, however interesting it may be as an exercise of ingenuity, has little practical import. It will hardly seem probable that Shakspeare was in the habit of sitting down with a set purpose to teach certain moral lessons by means of certain characters, to be rendered in certain definite ways; and yet one might infer from the work of commentators that this was the case. No manager or play-writer could believe that any part would ever be given in precisely the same way by any two actors, except so far as it might be done by servile imitation; and, indeed, to make this possible would involve a degradation of character to caricature. Such a broad rule as that Shylock ought not to be played as a low-comedy part, or that Lear ought not to be from beginning to end a drivelling idiot, may of course be laid down; but one has surely no more right to expect an actor to execute a part

in the way imagined to be right by commentators than to demand that a painter should seize just this or that aspect of a great historical subject. The enthusiasm aroused by Mr. Irving's Shylock, even in those who find his rendering of the character differ from their view of it, goes, however, to prove that, as has been suggested, an elaborate analysis of Shakspeare's characters made from studying the text is valuable chiefly as a mental exercise.

Mr. Irving presents Shylock as a picturesque figure, with an air as of a man feeling the bitterness of oppression, and conscious of his own superiority in all but circumstance to the oppressor—a feeling which is finely indicated when, in talk with Antonio, he touches the Christian merchant, and, seeing the action resented, bows deprecatingly, with an affectation of deep humility. He dwells with concentrated bitterness on the expressions of hatred to Antonio in the speech beginning "How like a fawning publican he looks" [I. iii. 41]; and here, in the implacable determination of "If I can catch him once upon the hip, I will feed fat the ancient grudge I bear him" [I. iii. 46-7], we have the prologue, as it were, to the intense revengefulness of the last scene. It may be noted that since the first night Mr. Irving's performance has gained in leading up consistently to its climax—as consistently, that is, as is possible in the case of a human creature worked on by mixed emotions which sometimes baffle scrutiny. The point which on the first night seemed most striking to many people in the general scope of the actor's representation was that his Shylock was intended to be, before all things, dignified, and it was thought that his acting in the scene when he bewails the loss of his daughter and his ducats was at variance with the rest of the performance. It would perhaps be neither easy nor desirable to make Shylock altogether dignified at this point; but it is not the less true that Mr. Irving has improved the rendering of this scene, and, with it, the whole value of his representation.

To return, however, to Mr. Irving's first scene, we may note specially the bitterness of subdued scorn in the speech beginning "Signior Antonio, many a time and oft in the Rialto you have rated me" [I. iii. 106-07], and the diabolical mockery of good humour with which he proposes the "merry bond." In the next scene in which the Jew appears we have again his hatred and desire for revenge marked strongly in the resolution to go forth to supper "in hate, to feed upon the prodigal Christian" [II. v. 14-15], and to part with Launcelot "to one that I would have him help to waste his borrowed purse" [II. v. 50-1]; and at the end of the act Mr. Irving has introduced a singularly fine touch of invention. Lorenzo has fled with his stolen bride and her stolen money, and a crowd of masquers has crossed the stage and disappeared over the picturesque bridge with laughter and music. Then Shylock is seen, lantern in hand, advancing, bent in thought; and, as he comes close to his robbed and deserted house, the curtain falls. The effect, however, would, to our thinking, be doubled if the curtain had not fallen for a moment and been raised again just before this appearance of Shylock—if the masquers had disappeared in sight of the audience, and the sounds of revelry had died away in the distance. It may be conjectured that the dropping of the curtain signifies the interval of time which might naturally elapse between the elopement and Shylock's return; but this is, we think, needless. Mr. Irving, in the scene already referred to of the third act, is now less vehement than might have been expected; the Jew's passion seems to have exhausted him, but is not for that the less intense in itself. He is overweighted with trouble, and the delivery of the words "no ill luck stirring, but what lights o' my shoulders; no sighs, but o' my breathing; no tears, but o' my shedding" [III. i. 94-6], is charged with the pathos of the heaviest grief, and it may be the importance given by the actor's feeling and art to this passage which makes one think that less than its due value is given to the following passage about Leah's ring.

It is, however, in the fourth act, as is fitting, that the actor's complete triumph is attained, and in this there seems to us no room for anything but admiration. From the moment of his entrance to that of his finding his revenge torn from him he is the very incarnation of deadly, resistless hatred. While he listens to the Duke's speech in mitigation he has the horrible stillness and fascination of the rattlesnake. When he answers, his speech is that of a man possessed of his purpose, coldly tenacious of his rights. His object has been gained, and the passion which has been concentrated on it will not deign to waste itself in supporting a position that is unassailable. His scorn of Gratiano's railings seems bitter from habit, and not because he is one whit moved by them. There is something appalling in his aspect when he stands waiting for the long desired moment with the knife in one hand the scales in the other, and his pointing to the bond with the knife as he asks, "Is it so nominated in the bond?" [IV. i. 259] is admirably conceived and executed. When the moment of defeat arrives it strikes him like lightning, but its effect, like that of his expected triumph, is so powerful that it cannot find expression in any accustomed use of gesture or attitude. He is still in his despair as in his victory; but it is the stillness of one suffering instead of threatening death. Where he before inspired terror, he cannot now but command respect for the very awfulness of his downthrow. He leaves the court with a dignity that seems the true expression of his belief in his nation and himself. His mind is occupied with greater matters than the light jeers of Gratiano, and to these jeers he replies with three slow downward movements of the head, which are infinitely expressive of his acceptance of that which has befallen him and of his power to bear himself nobly under its weight. "Gratiano speaks an infinite deal of nothing " [I. i. 114], and what he says at this moment seems empty indeed when answered with this silent eloquence. Nothing could be finer than Mr. Irving's acting at this point, which is the climax of a scene the power and imagination of which can scarcely be rivalled.

The striking excellences of Miss Ellen Terry's Portia are, if anything, bettered by being transferred to a larger stage than that on which they were first presented to a London audience. Every changing phase of the part is rendered with the highest instinct and art, and every change seems natural and easy. The tenderness; the love so fine that it finds no check to open acknowledgment; the wit, the dignity; and in the last scene the desire to be merciful and to inspire mercy, giving way to a just and overwhelming wrath, and followed again by the natural playfulness of the lady who is not the less a great lady because she indulges it, are alike rendered with a skill that one must call perfect. As feats of acting the assumption to Nerissa of a bragging youth's manner, and the exit in the trial scene are specially remarkable; but it is needless to point out in detail the patent beauties of a performance with which we can find no fault.

The cast for the other characters might perhaps have been better devised. Mr. Forrester's Antonio is disappointingly monotonous and tedious, and Mr. Barnes, who has lately acted very well in a part of a different kind, fails to give grace or interest to Bassanio. Mr. Tyars speaks the words set down for the Prince of Morocco with intelligence and discretion; Mr. Beaumont represents the Duke of Venice with remarkable dignity; and Mr. F. Cooper makes of Gratiano a more pleasant person than he is sometimes made on the stage. With regard to the mounting of the play, Mr. Irving says, in a note prefixed to his published version, "I have endeavoured to avoid hampering the natural action of the piece with any unnecessary embellishment; but have tried not to omit any accessory which might heighten the effects," and he has, it seems to us, carried out his intention with remarkable taste and judgment. (pp. 571-72)

A review of "The Merchant of Venice," in The Saturday Review, *London, Vol. 48, No. 1254, November 8, 1879, pp. 571-72.*

The Spectator　　(review date 8 November 1879)

[*The critic praises Irving's "entirely novel and unexpected" portrayal of a near-tragic Shylock, "Mr. Irving's finest performance," and cites Irving's dramatic final exit as "its best point." Terry's Portia, the critic contends, is without rival, and the "casket scenes" rank among the most beautiful "beheld on any stage"; however, the critic protests that Terry did not sufficiently disguise herself in the trial scene.*]

That no artist has so much actual enjoyment of success as the actor, and that no fame is so evanescent as his, has been generally accepted as a truth. But only the first part of the saying is altogether true; the last part will, at least, bear modification. Were it entirely and unfailingly true, neither actors nor spectators would be beset by traditions, no fulfilled renown would interpose its laurels between the student-artist and the dramatist's creation; or stir the air about his audience with the distant echo of its trumpets. On the contrary, the traditions of the great actors of the past are always with us,—and although we cannot point to handiwork of theirs in stone or on canvas, they are the most interesting of memories, because the *aiguillon* of curiosity and question pricks all discussion of them. Did Garrick give this passage so? Did the Siddons make that point? And what was Edmund Kean's reading? They come to the play with us, when it is a great play, and the actors are great actors, or approaching greatness, and is not that the survival of fame? Of all plays, *The Merchant of Venice* is that one which the spectator would, we fancy, go to see with the "historical" association most strongly in his mind, and also that one in which the actors of the great parts would be most pressed and overshadowed by the tradition of their predecessors. That was, however, no "historical" Shylock which Mr. Irving set before the closely-packed audience assembled on last Saturday evening to see Shakespeare's finest comedy put upon the stage of the Lyceum as it has certainly never previously been put upon any stage, and acted as it has not often been acted. Probably, to every mind, except that of Shakespeare himself—in which all potential interpretations of his Shylock, as all potential interpretations of his Hamlet, must have had a place—the complex image which Mr. Irving presented to a crowd more or less impressed with notions of their own concerning the Jew whom Shakespeare drew, was entirely novel and unexpected; for here is a man whom none can despise, who can raise emotions both of pity and of fear, and make us Christians thrill with a retrospective sense of shame. Here is an usurer indeed, but no more like the customary modern rendering of that extortionate lender of whom Bassanio borrowed "monies," than the merchants *dei Medici* were like pawnbrokers down Whitechapel way; an usurer, indeed, and full of "thrift," which is rather the protest of his disdain and disgust for the sensuality and frivolity of the ribald crew out of whom he makes his "Christian ducats," than of his own sordidness; an usurer indeed, but above all, a Jew! One of the race accursed in the evil days in which he lives, but chosen of Jehovah in the olden time wherein lie his pride, and belief, and hope,—the best of that hope being revenge on the enemies of himself and all his tribe, now wearing the badge of sufferance, revenge, rendered by the stern tenets of a faith which teaches that "the Lord, his God, is a jealous God, taking vengeance," not only lawful, but holy. A Jew, in intellectual faculties, in spiritual discipline, far in advance of the time and the country in which he lives, shaken with strong passion sometimes, but for the most part fixed in a deep and weary disdain. He is an old man, but not very aged, so that the epithet "old" used to him is not to be mistaken for anything but the insolence it means; a widower,—his one pathetic mention of his "Leah" was as beautiful a touch as ever has been laid upon the many-stringed lyre of human feeling;—the father of a daughter who amply justifies his plain mistrust of her, an odious, immodest, dishonest creature, than whom Shakespeare drew no more unpleasant character, and to whom one always grudges the loveliest loveliness that ever were spoken, especially when it is borne in mind that the speaker, Lorenzo, was at best a receiver of stolen goods. Mr. Irving's Shylock is a being quite apart from his surroundings. When he hesitates and questions with himself why he should go forth to sup with those who would scorn him if they could, but can only ridicule him, while the very stealthy intensity of scorn of them is in him, we ask, too, why should he? He would hardly be more out of place in the "wilderness of monkeys" [III. i. 122], of which he makes his sad and quaint comparison, when Tubal tells him of that last coarse proof of the heartlessness of his daughter "wedded with a Christian,"—the bartering of his Leah's ring. What mean, pitiful beings they all are, poetical as is their language, and fine as are the situations of the play, in comparison with the forlorn, resolute, undone, baited, betrayed, implacable old man, who, having personified his hatred of the race of Christians in Antonio, whose odiousness to him, in the treble character of a Christian, a sentimentalist, and a reckless speculator, is less of a mere caprice than he explains it to be. He reasons calmly with the dullards in the Court concerning this costly whim of his, yet with a disdainful doubt of the justice that will be done him; standing almost motionless, his hands hanging by his sides—they are an old man's hands, feeble, except when passion turns them into gripping claws, and then that passion subsides into the quivering of age, which is like palsy—his grey, worn face, lined and hollow, mostly averted from the speakers who move him not; except when a gleam of murderous hate, sudden and deadly, like the flash from a pistol, goes over it, and burns for a moment in the tired, melancholy eyes! Such a gleam there came when Shylock answered Bassanio's palliative commonplace, with,—

Hates any man the thing he would not kill?

　　　　　　　　　　　　　　　　[IV. i. 67]

At the wretched gibes of Gratiano, and the amiable maundering of the Duke, the slow, cold smile, just parting the lips and touching their curves as light touches polished metal, passes over the lower part of the face, but does not touch the eyes or lift the brow. This is one of Mr. Irving's most remarkable facial effects, for he can pass it through all the phases of a smile, up to surpassing sweetness. Is it a fault of the actors

or of ours that this Shylock is a being so absolutely apart, that it is impossible to picture him as a part of the life of Venice, that we cannot think of him "on the Rialto" before Bassanio wanted "monies," and Antonio had "plunged," like any London city-man in the pre-"depression" times, that he absolutely begins to exist with the "Three thousand ducats,—well!" [I. iii. 1] These are the first words uttered by the picturesque personage to whom the splendid and elaborate scene, whose every detail we have previously been eagerly studying becomes merely the background. He is wonderfully weird, but his weirdness is quite unlike that of any other of the impersonations in which Mr. Irving has accustomed us to that characteristic; it is impressive, never fantastic,—sometimes solemn and terrible. There was a moment when, as he stood in the last scene, with folded arms and bent head, the very image of exhaustion, a victim, entirely convinced of the justice of his cause, he looked like a Spanish painter's *Ecce Homo*. The likeness passed in an instant, for the next utterance is:—

My deeds upon my head. I crave the law,
The penalty and forfeit of my bond.
　　　　　　　　　　　　　　　　[IV. i. 206-07]

In the opinion of the present writer, his Shylock is Mr. Irving's finest performance, and his final exit is its best point. The quiet shrug, the glance of ineffable, unfathomable contempt at the exultant body, Gratiano, who, having got hold of a good joke, worries it like a puppy with a bone, the expression of defeat in every limb and feature, the deep, gasping sigh, as he passes slowly out, and the crowd rush from the Court to hoot and howl at him outside, make up an effect which must be seen to be comprehended. Perhaps some students of Shakespeare, reading the Jew's story to themselves, and coming to the conclusion that there was more sentiment than legality in that queer, confused, quibbling Court, where judge and advocate were convertible terms, may have doubted whether the utterer of the most eloquent and famous satirical appeal in all dramatic literature, whose scornful detestation of his Christian foes rose mountains high over what they held to be his ruling passion, drowning avarice fathom-deep in hatred, would have gratified those enemies by useless railing, and an exhibition of impotent rage. But there is no "tradition" for this rendering, in which Mr. Irving puts in action for his Shylock one sense of Hamlet's words:—"The rest is silence!" [V. ii. 358] The impression made by this consummate stroke of art and touch of nature upon the vast audience was most remarkable; the thrill that passed over the house was a sensation to have witnessed and shared.

Although Mr. Irving sinks the usurer in the Jew in a quite novel manner, he does not do so too entirely, departing from Shakespeare's intention arbitrarily; he only reverses the general estimate of the intensity of Shylock's two master passions. Both are present, always, and his last effort to clutch the gold, when the revenge has escaped his grasp, his cunning, business-like, "Give me my principal, and let me go!" [IV. i. 336] is an admirable point. Throughout the entire performance the actor's best qualities are at their best, and his characteristic faults are hardly apparent. The picturesqueness of his appearance is largely assisted by the grave, flowing robe and shawl-girdle which he wears; his self-restraint fails not before his Christian foes; Shylock's passionate agony is in soliloquy, or when only Tubal, a Jew, like him, who understands him, and their common holy faith, and what dogs these Christians are, as well as "Father Abraham" himself understands it, is with him. In the scene with Tubal, the sentence, "The curse never fell upon our nation till now,—I never felt it till now!" [III. i. 85-6] is as finely delivered as Mr. Irving's "I know,—I was a Dauphin myself once," in his "Louis the Eleventh." There was a fine effect—and it, too, thrilled the house—in the third scene of the first act. In the striking of the terrible bargain between Antonio and the Jew, Shylock touches the Christian lightly on the breast; Antonio recoils, and Shylock, without breaking his discourse, bows low, in apologetic deprecation of his own daring and the merchant's indignation, while his face is alight for an instant with a gleam of hatred and derision truly devilish.

Of Miss Ellen Terry's Portia, it is almost superfluous to speak, except for one's own gratification, for it has been long and well known to be of an excellence without rival or compeer. Probably no more beautiful sight than the "casket scenes" have ever been beheld on any stage, with this consummate actress, in her golden-hued, gold-fringed, satin robes, with her beautiful face, her sweet, flexible voice, her graceful, exquisitely appropriate movements and gestures, her sweet, womanly perplexity, girlish fun, swiftly growing passion, and gracious wifely surrender, amidst surroundings which are almost ideally perfect. If only Portia's "black boy," the inevitable adjunct to the state of a Venetian or Florentine lady of that period, had a monkey with a silver chain sitting upon his arm, Paolo Veronese might be as well satisfied with the *mise-en-scène* as Shakespeare with the acting; and how plainly the presence of the exotic and expensive pet would point the moral of Jessica's ambition, and her ill-behaviour in the matter of the "turquoise" which Shylock "had from Leah when he was a batchelor" [III. i. 122]. Miss Terry constantly reminds one, by her vigorous, lithe movement, and the graceful carriage of her head, of one of the most charming of pictures, the elder Leslie's beautiful Juliet on the terrace, with the nurse, leaning on her stick, in the background. The sweetness, the spirit, the grace of Miss Terry's Portia make one feel all the more strongly the injustice that is done the Jew, and the approval of that injustice which Shakespeare takes for granted. Portia is so dutiful a daughter, that she risks all her future happiness rather than be "forsworn" to her dead father by traversing his quaint conceit, and most beautifully does Miss Terry put this point; but she eagerly welcomes Jessica after she has deserted and robbed her father, and what is her reason? That father is a Jew, therefore *hors la loi* of human nature and Christian charity, even as that gentle Doctor of Laws interprets it. "She hath deceived her father, and may you!" [*Othello*, I. iii. 293] says Desdemona's deserted parent; and Othello sees the truth of the hint, and remembers it. "And true she is, as she hath proved herself" [II. vi. 55], says Lorenzo, just before he goes off with the Jew's daughter under his cloak and the Jew's casket under his arm.

Miss Ellen Terry is so true an artist, that she ought to be able to rise above every consideration which would impair her rendering of a character in which she is so nearly perfect as that of Portia. That a pretty woman cannot be induced to disguise herself, is said to be an article of faith with managers, but it ought not to hold good, or bad, in the case of such an actress as she is. It probably would not do so, if Miss Terry could at all realise how very near she goes to making her own share in the trial scene ridiculous, and how seriously she weakens the effect of the exquisite acting which precedes it, especially of the lovely bit of gleeful humour in which she boasts to Nerissa how, "when they are both accoutred like young men, she'll prove the prettier fellow of the two" [III.

v. 63-4], by refusing to adopt the slightest precaution to prevent the recognition of her by her bridegroom, by the Duke, by all the people in the Court, who must have been perfectly familiar with the famous beauty of Belmont. To say nothing of the absurdity of a quantity of curling hair under the berretta of a lawyer in a piece costumed with such elaborate accuracy in other respects, the absence of all pretence at incognito enfeebles the effect of her graceful, but not very impressive delivery of the famous lines in this scene, and impinges upon the comedy of both the "situation" and the dialogue in the fifth act. Miss Terry's artistic sense is unconsciously affected by her wilful departure at this point from the earnestness and truth of her artistic delineation; she has suddenly become inconsistent, and the whole scene, in which her Portia might easily be made worthy of Mr. Irving's Shylock, suffers. Nerissa stares at her resplendent mistress too much—though perhaps not a man or woman of us had the heart to blame her for that—and is not quick enough to wait on her, or lift her fan, or sympathetically snatch the key when Bassanio makes his good shot at the great prize; but Miss Florence Terry is as yet "unschooled, unpractised," and "happy in this, she is not yet so old but she may learn."

All those liberties which Mr. Irving has taken with the text of the play are not only allowable, but welcome. It is to be wished that his good-taste had suggested just one more alteration,—only one, for we suppose the heavy fooling of Launcelot Gobbo must remain, like those detestable rhymes in *Hamlet*, on pain of accusation of treason against Shakespeare, who was, no doubt, proud of his bad puns. That one is the omission of Gratiano's horrid jest when Shylock is whetting his knife on the edge of his shoe,—"Not on thy sole, but on thy soul, harsh Jew, thou mak'st thy knife keen" [IV. i. 123-24]. Could not this flagrant vulgarity be discarded? It is as execrable as the "more remains behind" [III. iv. 179] with which Hamlet, adding a poor joke to murder, draws aside the arras to have a look at dead Polonius.

A review of "The Merchant of Venice," in The Spectator, *Vol. 52, No. 2680, November 8, 1879, pp. 1408-09.*

Theodore Martin (review date December 1879)

[*Martin, the husband of Helena Faucit, praises the scenery and staging of Irving's production, but is critical of the characterization. He sees Antonio, for example, reduced to insignificance, upsetting the balance of the play. Terry's Portia, a rival of Faucit's interpretation of the role, failed "in its most essential point," according to Martin, in the trial scene. Terry's portrayal lacked dignity, the critic declares, and she exhibited inadequate restraint in her fondness for Bassanio. Martin saves his kindest words for Irving's Shylock, "perhaps, as a whole, his best Shakespearian performance," both in interpretation and execution.*]

The recent production of *The Merchant of Venice* at the Lyceum is another of Mr. Irving's hopeful efforts towards the improvement of the general level of stage representation. To say that it is wholly satisfactory is impossible; for with the best intentions on Mr. Irving's part, the means for such a representation are not within his reach. (p. 648)

In scenery, appointments, and in stage arrangements every reasonable wish is fulfilled. The local colouring is well preserved, and a fine framework and background provided for the figures of the picture. Venice, with its noble architecture, its busy port, its ruffling gallants, its stately halls, is well suggested. Nor can a fairer Belmont, both within and without, be desired for the "lady richly left" [I. i. 161] who is its owner, and "of such wondrous virtues" [I. i. 163] that they outvie her wealth. The eye is pleasantly regaled, but not distracted by the scenic accessories. So far all is well. The same may be said of the costumes, which are well studied in contrasts of colour, true to the period, and handsome.

But have the characters of the play been equally well studied and made out? Passing for the moment over Shylock and Portia, what is to be said of the Antonio, Bassanio, Gratiano, Salanio, and Salarino, the Nerissa and the Jessica?

Antonio, the Merchant, who gives his name to the play, and who is a character of really first importance, is reduced by the actor to an insignificance which disturbs the balance of the drama. Let us consider for one moment what Antonio is, as Shakespeare drew him. The words which begin the play are spoken by him, and in them he strikes the first note of the not too sad minor key which ever and anon is heard in a faint undertone throughout it. He is kept prominently in view all through the play, and becomes an important feature at its close. In fact, his fortunes are the pivot on which the play turns, and therefore it is called the *Merchant of Venice*. It is his generous friendship which enables Bassanio to try his fortune at Belmont; it is the peril at which he does this act of affection which creates the main interest of the piece, and brings out the distinctive qualities of its two most important characters, Shylock and Portia. He, the great and honoured Christian merchant, is the contrast and foil to the oppressed and rancorous Jewish money-broker. It is the knowledge of what a friend he is that makes Portia face the task, from which her natural timidity would have shrunk—

> The kindest man,
> The best conditioned; an unwearied spirit
> In doing courtesies;
>
> [III. ii. 292-94]

and the very last things Portia says show us, that in helping his friend to win her, he will not, as he feared he might, lose that friend for himself. In the man there is a dignity which, coupled as it is with a large and kindly heart, wins him the mingled affection and respect of the young Venetian nobles by whom he is surrounded. See how Salanio speaks of him in the speech beginning.

> A kinder gentleman treads not the earth,
>
> [II. viii. 35]

where the parting from Bassanio, and the pang it cost him, are described;

> His eye being big with tears,
> Turning his face, he put his hand behind him,
> And, with affection wondrous sensible,
> He wrung Bassanio's hand, and so they parted.
>
> [II. viii. 46-9]

Observe Salarino's rejoinder—"I think he only loves the world for him" [II. viii. 50] and his call to his friends to join him in trying to beguile the heaviness of the now solitary Merchant. Again, Portia's words tell us how Shakespeare would have us think of Antonio, when she rates him as worthy to be the peer of her Bassanio—

> For in companions,
> That do converse and waste the time together,

> There needs must be some like complexion
> Of lineaments, of manners, and of spirit.
>
> [III. iv. 11-12, 14-15]

In all ways, therefore, Antonio is a personage of primary importance. So far from this, however, the Antonio of the Lyceum is from first to last presented in a manner so feeble, so commonplace, that he seems as little fitted to be the object of Shylock's "lodged hate," as of the love and respect which he commands from every other person of mark in the play.

In citing, as we have done, two brief passages of what is spoken by Salanio and Salarino, enough has been cited to show that they are not the skipping feather-brained fops who are presented to us at the Lyceum,—gentlemen, who run off their words at a gallop, as if they were acting in a farce, and who seem to think that rushing to and fro upon the stage is the legitimate mode of expressing the vivacity of high-bred Venetian gentlemen. What would have been thought of them in Venice, if they had borne themselves in this fashion on the open streets? There is not one of them that is not a man of breeding as well as of brains. Gay, brightwitted gentlemen they are, with youth and health and fine spirits. But they are gentlemen; and what each of them says is marked by distinct character, and shows him to be a man who both thinks and observes well and closely in a fashion of his own. The Salanio, the Salarino, and the Lorenzo of the Lyceum, on the contrary, are all of the same type, "as like one another as halfpence are" [*As You Like It,* III. ii. 354], a sort of weak Gratianos—anything, in a word, but persons to whom a man of Antonio's staid and thoughtful character would have said, "Your worth is very dear in my regard" [I. i. 62]. Only the Lorenzo (Mr. N. Forbes) aims at giving significance and emphasis to his part; but even he does not do so until we see him in the famous moonlight scene of the fifth act. Up to that point he is, like the rest, little better than a well-dressed fop.

Gratiano is an ungracious part at the best, and requires from the actor a high-bred and airy grace to carry off his frivolity without annoyance to the audience. Still, there must have been a charm about the fellow, else Bassanio, who hits off his character in a sentence, as "speaking an infinite deal of nothing more than any man in Venice" [I. i. 114-15], would never have taken him with him when he went to Belmont, or when he returned thence to Venice on his sad errand to Antonio. But he has the fault of many excellent fellows of not knowing when to hold his tongue; and when he carries this vice into the court of Venice, and baits the Jew with ill-timed banter, we are apt to lose patience, and to share Shylock's contempt for his wits. A skilful actor will therefore take care to keep Gratiano's "skipping spirit" well toned down. This seems to be felt by Mr. F. Cooper, the Gratiano of the Lyceum; and except that in his performance the tone and quality of a high-bred gentleman are not sufficiently suggested and maintained, it is upon the whole not unsatisfactory.

Why Jessica and Nerissa should have been regarded as of so little importance as to be intrusted to two young ladies, who would be weak in the smallest of comediettas, one is at a loss to conceive. In the case of Nerissa it is inexcusable, for Nerissa is the companion of Portia. She is not the lady's maid, but the lady-in-waiting, with whom the great Italian heiress makes free interchange of her thoughts; and much of the impression which Portia has to make in her first scene depends upon the way Nerissa's portion of the dialogue is maintained. It is not to the insipid undeveloped girl into which Nerissa is turned at the Lyceum, that Portia would hold discourse of her lovers in a strain so intellectual and so brilliant; neither would such a Nerissa venture to remind her friend of the Venetian, "a scholar and a soldier, who came hither in the company of the Marquis of Montferrat" [I. ii. 114], as being "of all the men that ever her foolish eyes looked upon, the best deserving a fair lady" [I. ii. 117-19]. On the way this is done depends much of the effect of Portia's rejoinder: "I remember him well; and I remember him worthy of thy praise" [I. ii. 120-21], which should be given, but is not given by Miss Ellen Terry, in a way to let it be seen that Bassanio was no braggart in telling Antonio, in a previous scene, that "sometimes from her eyes he did receive fair speechless messages" [I. i. 163-64]. As little would such a Nerissa be chosen by Portia to aid her in her enterprise at Venice. If this be a specimen of the way the demand is to be met for completeness and *ensemble* in the production of Shakespeare, much good advice has been thrown away in vain. To degrade Nerissa to the level of a *soubrette* is to lower Portia. She wisely judged men by their friends, and the audience insensibly judges of Portia by the same rule. It would have been impossible for the real Portia to have had a Nerissa who did not show some "like complexion" to herself "in manners and in spirit." But, indeed, it would be idle to dwell upon the want of judgment which could place a character of this importance in such hands.

Of the Portia we find it impossible to speak in the terms of unqualified rapture with which Miss Ellen Terry's performance has generally been greeted. We place our ideas of Portia high,—not higher, however, than Shakespeare meant them to be placed, by speaking of her as

Nothing undervalued
To Cato's daughter, Brutus' Portia,

[I. i. 165-66]

by the elaborate care with which he has depicted the impression she produced on all around her, and by the way he has developed her charms of heart and mind throughout the action of the piece. She is the ideal of the high-born woman, gloriously endowed in body and in mind, and with her intellect cultivated to the highest point to which female culture could be brought. Only such a woman could have carried out the task which her old friend Bellario's illness forced upon her, preventing him, as it did, from obeying the Doge's summons, and coming to Venice to determine the question at issue between Antonio and Shylock. It is with the knowledge, and upon the express recommendation of the great jurisconsult, that she takes his place. He knew that he could safely trust her to make a sound exposition of the points on which to rely for the discomfiture of the Jew. For observe, his own reputation was at stake, and any break-down on Portia's part would have compromised his character fatally with the Doge. But she had, as he well knew, the knowledge and the "undaunted mettle" to carry her through an enterprise to which she was prompted, not merely by love, but by humanity. She had the higher power, which enabled her to use the knowledge in her own way, and the noble forebearance of the Christian woman, to keep in the background her weapon for discomfiting the Jew, until she had found that every appeal either to his heart or to his avarice was of no avail.

It is in the trial scene that the character of Portia culminates. Her appearance there may surprise us; but the actress should previously have made us feel that she is equal to what she has undertaken. It is the splendid development of the splendid qualities of heart and mind, with which all we have previously heard and seen of her have made us familiar. Severe as the

ordeal is to which she is exposed, the noble gravity and self-command with which she bears herself throughout the scene, should seem but a natural phase of her strong and beautiful nature. Most subtly, too, the womanly element breathes throughout her treatment of the situation, even while her penetrating look and intellectual vigour held the Jew firmly in her grasp. She proves him, step by step, to see if he be indeed the wretch "void of any dram of mercy" [IV. i. 5-6] she has been told he is; and leads him on to an avowal of the malice which nothing short of Antonio's death will appease. From that point she has him at her mercy; and, since he would have nothing but his bond to the letter, she discomfits him by holding him to the letter of his bond. The tender woman's heart, that has up to a certain point had pity for the Jew, is from that moment sternly closed against him, and she becomes as grandly stern as the mouthpiece and organ of the court in declaring the law, as she had hitherto been beautiful and persuasive in her appeals to the better feelings for which she had given Shylock credit. Her arguments are no "pretty sophisms," as an admiring critic of Miss Terry's Portia in one of the leading journals called them. She has law and reason on her side. The Jew is self-convicted of compassing the death of a Venetian citizen; and it is by no legal quibble, but by the laws of Venice—"thyself shall see the act " [IV. i. 314] she tells the Jew—that she defeats his purpose.

If we are right in this conception of Portia, then Miss Terry's impersonation fails in its most essential point. Even those who have racked the language of panegyric in its praise have shrunk from claiming unqualified admiration for her in the trial scene. They might well do so, for at no one point in it does she indicate that she appreciates the situation, or how it should be treated. The words are spoken, but so spoken that one marvels why they should issue from the lips of one who looks so little in earnest, who takes so little note of Shylock, of Antonio, of the Doge, and of the court, every one of whom it is her business to impress by the manner in which she discharges the function of determining the matter at issue, which has been delegated to her by the Duke.

We have spoken first of this scene because it is the touchstone of the actress's powers, and because our love of Shakespeare forbids us to be blinded by the attractions of either actor or actress to any failure in a due conception of the characters he has drawn for us with so firm a hand. But the shortcomings of Miss Terry, in our apprehension, begin at an earlier stage. She turns the character "to favour and to prettiness;" but she does not even aim at the distinction and the dignity which essentially belong to it. She is not the great lady of Belmont, the self-possessed queenly creature, whose very presence turns men of ordinary mould into poets, and attracts, even while she holds them at bay in admiring reverence. She fails especially to suggest the Portia that, as Shakespeare most carefully makes us aware, would have sacrificed even her love for Bassanio, deep as we see it is, had he failed to win her by the process appointed by her father. How little this feature of the character is felt by the actress is made apparent in her treatment of the passage where she urges Bassanio to tarry, "to pause a day or two" [III. ii. 1], before he tries his fortune with the caskets. Throughout all this fine speech she holds him caressingly by the hand, nay, almost in an embrace, with all the unrestrained fondness which is conceivable only after he had actually won her. This, too, when all eyes are fixed upon her, and when her demeanour would have made her secret known to all the world ih the last way a lady would court under any circumstances, but especially when, had her lover chosen wrong, she must have been parted from him at once and for ever. There is altogether a great deal too much of what Rosalind calls "a coming-on disposition" [*As You Like It,* IV. i. 132] in Miss Terry's bearing towards her lover. It is a general fault with her, but in Portia it is painfully out of place.

A similar forgetfulness of what truth to the character and the situation demands, while the Prince of Morocco is making choice among the caskets, is visible in the far too marked demonstrativeness with which Miss Terry follows his movement from casket to casket. The room is full of people, servants, and others, any one of whom could tell in a second from Miss Terry's looks and movements when, in the words of the old game, he was hot, and when he was cold, and could have sold the information to the next wooer that arrived. It requires subtler touches than this lady seems to have at command, to indicate, without exaggerating, the emotion proper to a nature disciplined like Portia's to self-command.

There is, notwithstanding what we have said, much that is agreeable and attractive in Miss Terry's Portia, and no one will be surprised that uncritical people, who have not made their own separate study of the play, should be delighted with it. What we do wonder at, however, and most deeply regret, is the unmeasured terms of praise with which the critics of nearly all the journals have received it. Our wonder would be greater, if most of their criticisms did not at the same time show how little pains the writers had taken to make themselves masters of Shakespeare's text and of the intentions it reveals. One can only hope that Miss Terry's good sense will protect her from accepting too greedily the eulogies of undiscriminating admirers. They are certainly doing their best to spoil her.

To the same insidious influence Mr. Irving is exposed, to a degree that, for his sake, would make us welcome the appearance of some other actor who should carry off a little of the extravagant enthusiasm of which he has at present the monopoly. But Mr. Irving has the undoubted merit of not having been misled by it into dealing carelessly with his art. His Shylock is a decided advance, and perhaps, as a whole, his best Shakespearian performance. It is based upon a broad clear conception, and carried out in all its details with great finish and great picturesqueness. Mr. Irving makes no attempt to create special sympathy for Shylock, but shows him—as Shakespeare, we fancy, meant him to be shown—as a man in whom the persecution of his race, and the indignities inflicted on himself by those with whom he had to cope upon the mart, had begot a settled abhorrence of all Christian men, intensified and concentrated into "a lodged hate" of Antonio. Antonio has treated him with contumely, has thwarted him in trade, has "hindered him of half a million" [III. i. 55], has denounced his usuries, and, finally, baffled his revenge by "delivering from his forfeitures many that have at times made moan to" [III. iii. 22-3] the Christian merchant. "Cursed be my tribe if I forgive him" [I. iii. 51-2], are among Shylock's first words; and he means to the letter what he says when he vows, if once "he catches him upon the hip, he will feed fat the ancient grudge he bears him" [I. iii. 46-7]. Of course Shylock has affections of some kind. What man has not? But Shakespeare has been at no pains to call attention to this side of his character. His servant and his daughter have little to say in his praise, and it will never do to lay great stress on his tenderness over his turquoise ring, which he had "of Leah when he was a bachelor" [III. i. 122]. Pity for him Shake-

speare certainly did not set himself to excite, beyond that pity which one feels for any human creature hardened by cruel usage, by the persecution of his religion, by sordid avarice, and finally, maddened, by the elopement of his daughter with a Christian, into the cunning, stony-hearted, merciless wretch, whose own calculated device in "the merry bond" is fitly turned against him to his ruin.

This is the man Mr. Irving sets before us. If he had a voice that did not break into painful dissonances in transports of passion, and greater robustness of *physique* to give emphasis to his rage, there would be little left to desire. No man, be his conception ever so fine, can go farther than his physical resources will carry him; and it is ungracious to point to failures in particular passages, when, merely from a defect of this kind, the actor cannot make out thoroughly all he would. Notably this is obvious in the famous scene with Tubal, where the wild transitions of rage and disappointment and vindictive menace are better suggested than expressed. The fine scene just before with Salanio and Salarino fails somewhat of effect from the same cause. But one forgets the cracked and screaming tones, and the occasional want of articulateness, in the powerful action, the visible intensity of the feeling, the thoroughness with which the ruling idea is worked out.

In his first interview with Antonio, however, Mr. Irving commits what seems to us a grievous mistake. When Shylock changes from reproach to fawning in the speech beginning, "Why, look now, how you storm!" [I. iii. 137] he comes close up to Antonio, and touches him on the breast with an air of familiar entreaty. Antonio recoils from him with contemptuous scorn, and Shylock bows low, while he winces at the rebuke. This has been praised as a fine stroke of truth. But is it so? Antonio has just told Shylock that he is "as like to spit on him again, to spurn him too" [I. iii. 131]. Would Shylock with these words fresh in his ears, forget himself so far as to lay a finger on the haughty merchant, never haughtier than at that moment, when asking a loan from a man he despised? Again, is such an action conceivable in one who feels the pride of race so strongly as Shylock? For one of "the sacred nation" like himself to touch the Christian merchant would in his mind be viewed as nothing less than contamination and defilement. The momentary stage effect, which Mr. Irving gains by the introduction of this novelty, is surely dearly purchased at the sacrifice of all probability.

Mr. Irving's treatment of the trial scene is excellent. He never forgets, as most Shylocks have done, that he is in the great court of Venice, and he bears himself with a restrained intensity suitable to the situation. He lays no stress upon the incident of whetting the knife, but deals with it as merely something by the way. It is in the calm, immovable rigidity of aspect, in the concentrated force which he throws into his words, that he leaves, and rightly leaves, the audience to read the triumphant inflexibility of his purpose. This contrasts finely with the momentary flashing out of a passionate delight, where Portia's words to Antonio, "You must prepare your bosom for his knife" [IV. i. 245], seem to put within his grasp the object of his hate. It contrasts still more finely with the total collapse of mind and body, when at a glance the full significance of the words—"This bond doth give thee here no jot of blood" [IV. i. 306], bursts upon his keen intellect. In these words, and what follows, he seems to receive his death-blow. It matters little whether they strip him of his fortune, or tell him, as the condition of saving his life, that he shall presently become a Christian. His doom is written. His pulse will soon cease to beat. We feel the prop is in effect gone "that doth sustain his life." But he keeps a firm front to the last, and has a fine curl of withering scorn upon his lip for Gratiano, as he walks away to die in silence and alone. As he leaves the scene, we feel that we care not to know how this or that great actor of other days has treated it. This treatment is good, and it is a fitting climax to the Shylock of the previous acts. (pp. 649-56)

> *Theodore Martin, in an originally unsigned essay titled "Theatrical Reform: The 'Merchant of Venice' at the Lyceum," in* Blackwood's Edinburgh Magazine, *Vol. CXXVI, No. DCCLXX, December, 1879, pp. 641-56.*

Henry James (essay date 1881)

[*James was an American novelist, short story writer, critic, and essayist of the late nineteenth and early twentieth centuries. He is regarded as one of the greatest novelists of the English language and is also admired as a lucid and insightful critic. Although he composed several dramatic works, few were produced; however, some of his novels have since been successfully adapted for the stage. In addition, James was a frequent contributor to many prominent American journals, including the* North American Review, *the* Nation, *and the* Atlantic Monthly. *In the following excerpt, James praises the picturesqueness of Irving's production, but asserts that the performances themselves fell short. Although he reserves judgment on Irving's conception of a sentimentalized Shylock, James asserts that the actor was neither "excited nor exciting, and many*

Ellen Terry as Portia.

of the admirable speeches, on his lips, lack much of their incision." Likewise, James discerns flaws in Terry's superficially pleasing performance, which would improve with polish: "To our own English vision Miss Terry has too much nature, and we should like a little more art."]

Upward of two years ago the Lyceum passed into the hands of Mr. Henry Irving, who is without doubt at present the most distinguished actor in England. He had been acting at the Lyceum for some years before, while the house was under the management of the late Mr. Bateman, and then of his widow, who has within a few months, with a great deal of courage and zeal, attempted to awaken the long dormant echoes of Sadler's Wells—a theatre which had its season of prosperity (many years ago), but which finally, in its out-of-the-way position, was left stranded by ebbing tides. Mrs. Bateman, to whom much of the credit of originally introducing Mr. Irving to the public belongs, succeeded in some degree, we believe, in turning the tide back to the little theatre to which the late Mr. Phelps's "revivals" at one period attracted the town. Mr. Irving for the last two years, then, has had his own way at the Lyceum, and a very successful way it has been. Hamlet and Shylock have constituted the stock of his enterprise, though he has also acted several of the parts in which he built up his reputation—Richelieu; Eugene Aram and Charles I., in Mr. W. G. Wills's plays; Louis XI., in a translation of Casimir Delavigne's rather dull drama, and Matthias in *The Bells.* During the whole of last winter, however, *The Merchant of Venice* held the stage, and this performance disputes with that of *Hamlet* the chief place in his list of successes as an actor. Among his triumphs as a manager, the former play, we believe, quite heads the list; it has every appearance of being an immense financial success, and startling stories are told of the great sums of money it brings in to the happy lessee of the theatre. It is arranged upon the stage with a great deal of ingenuity and splendour, and has a strong element of popularity in the person of Miss Ellen Terry, who is the most conspicuous actress now before the London public, as the picturesque Shylock of her Portia is the most eminent actor. Mr. Irving has been a topic in London any time these five years, and Miss Terry is at least as much of one. There is a difference, indeed, for about Mr. Irving people are divided, and about Miss Terry they are pretty well agreed. The opinion flourishes on the one side that Mr. Irving is a great and admirable artist, and on the other the impression prevails that his defects outnumber his qualities. He has at least the power of inspiring violent enthusiasms, and this faculty is almost always accompanied by a liability to excite protests. Those that it has been Mr. Irving's destiny to call forth have been very downright, and many of them are sufficiently intelligible. He is what is called a picturesque actor; that is, he depends for his effects upon the art with which he presents a certain figure to the eye, rather than upon the manner in which he speaks his part. He is a thoroughly serious actor, and evidently bestows an immense deal of care and conscience upon his work; he meditates, elaborates, and, upon the line on which he moves, carries the part to a very high degree of finish. But it must be affirmed that this is a line with which the especial art of the actor, the art of utterance, of saying the thing, has almost nothing to do. Mr. Irving's peculiarities and eccentricities of speech are so strange, so numerous, so personal to himself, his vices of pronunciation, of modulation, of elocution so highly developed, the tricks he plays with the divine mother-tongue so audacious and fantastic, that the spectator who desires to be in sympathy with him finds himself confronted with a bristling hedge of difficulties.

He must scramble over the hedge, as best he can, in order to get at Mr. Irving at all; to get at him, that is, as an exponent of great poetic meanings. Behind this hedge, as we may say, the actor disports himself with a great deal of ingenuity, and passes through a succession of picturesque attitudes and costumes; but we look at him only through its thorny interstices. In so doing, we get glimpses of a large and various ability. He is always full of intention, and when the intention is a matter of by-play, it is brilliantly carried out. He is, of course, much better in the modern drama than in the Shakespearean; because, if it is a question of sacrificing the text, the less we are obliged to sacrifice the better. It is better to lose the verses of Mr. Wills than to fail to recognize those of the poet whom the French have sometimes spoken of as Mr. Williams. Mr. Irving's rendering of Shakespeare, however, is satisfactory in a varying degree. His Macbeth appeared to us wide of the mark, but his Hamlet is very much better. In *Macbeth,* as we remember his performance, he failed even to look the part satisfactorily—a rare mistake in an actor who has evidently a strong sense of what may be called the plastic side of the characters he represents. His Hamlet is a magnificent young prince: few actors can wear a cloak and a bunch of sable plumes with a greater grace than Mr. Irving; few of them can rest a well-shaped hand on the hilt of a sword in a manner more suggestive of the models of Vandyke. The great trouble with the Hamlet was that it was inordinately slow—and this, indeed, is the fault throughout of Mr. Irving, who places minutes between his words, and strange strides and balancings between his movements. Heat, rapidity, passion, magic—these qualities are the absent ones, and a good general description of him is to say that he is picturesque but diffuse. Of his Shylock during last winter, it was often said that it presents his faults in their mildest and his merits in their highest form. In this there is possibly a great deal of truth; his representation of the rapacious and rancorous Jew has many elements of interest. He looks the part to a charm, or rather we should say, to a repulsion, and he might be painted as he stands. His conception of it is a sentimental one, and he has endeavoured to give us a sympathetic, and, above all, a pathetic Shylock. How well he reconciles us to this aspect of the character we ourselves shall not undertake to say, for our attention was fixed primarily upon the superficial execution of the thing, and here, without going further, we found much to arrest and perplex it. The actor struck us as rigid and frigid, and above all as painfully behind the stroke of the clock. The deep-welling malignity, the grotesque horror, the red-hot excitement of the long-baffled, sore-hearted member of a despised trade, who has been all his life at a disadvantage, and who at last finds his hour and catches his opportunity—these elements had dropped out. Mr. Irving's Shylock is neither excited nor exciting, and many of the admirable speeches, on his lips, lack much of their incision; notably the outbreak of passion and prospective revenge after he finds that Antonio has become forfeit, and that his daughter has fled from him, carrying off her dowry. The great speech, with its grim refrain: "Let him look to his bond!" [III. i. 47] rising each time to an intenser pitch and culminating in a pregnant menace, this superb opportunity is missed; the actor, instead of being "hissing hot," as we have heard Edmund Kean described at the same moment, draws the scene out and blunts all its points. (pp. 138-41)

Miss Terry is at present his constant coadjutor, and Miss Terry is supposed to represent the maximum of feminine effort on the English stage. The feminine side, in all the London theatres, is regrettably weak, and Miss Terry is easily distin-

guished. It is difficult to speak of her fairly, for if a large part of the public are wrong about her, they are altogether wrong, and one hesitates to bring such sweeping charges. By many intelligent persons she is regarded as an actress of exquisite genius, and is supposed to impart an extraordinary interest to everything that she touches. This is not, in our opinion, the truth, and yet to gainsay the assertion too broadly is to fall into an extreme of injustice. The difficulty is that Miss Terry has charm—remarkable charm; and this beguiles people into thinking her an accomplished actress. There is a natural quality about her that is extremely pleasing—something wholesome and English and womanly which often touches easily where art, to touch, has to be finer than we often see it. The writer of these lines once heard her highly commended by one of the most distinguished members of the Comédie Française, who had not understood a word she spoke.

> "Ah, Miss Terry, for instance; I liked her extremely."
> "And why did you like her?"
> "Mon Dieu, I found her very natural."

This seemed to us an interesting impression, and a proof the more of the truism that we enjoy things in proportion to their rarity. To our own English vision Miss Terry has too much nature, and we should like a little more art. On the other side, when a French actress is eminent she is eminent by her finish, by what she has acquired, by the perfection of her art, and the critic I have just quoted, who had had this sort of merit before his eyes all his life, was refreshed by seeing what could be achieved in lieu of it by a sort of sympathetic spontaneity. Miss Terry has that excellent thing, a quality; she gives one the sense of something fine. Add to this that though she is not regularly beautiful, she has a face altogether in the taste of the period, a face that Burne-Jones might have drawn, and that she arranges herself (always in the taste of the period) wonderfully well for the stage. She makes an admirable picture, and it would be difficult to imagine a more striking embodiment of sumptuous sweetness than her Ophelia, her Portia, her Pauline, or her Olivia, in a version of Goldsmith's immortal novel prepared for the Court Theatre a couple of years ago by the indefatigable Mr. Wills. Her Ophelia, in particular, was lovely, and of a type altogether different from the young lady in white muslin, bristling with strange grasses, whom we are accustomed to see in the part. In Miss Terry's hands the bewildered daughter of Polonius became a somewhat angular maiden of the Gothic ages, with her hair cropped short, like a boy's, and a straight and clinging robe, wrought over with contemporary needlework. As for her acting, she has happy impulses; but this seems to us to be the limit of it. She has nothing of the style, nothing of what the French call the authority, of the genuine *comédienne.* Her perception lacks acuteness, and her execution is often rough; the expression of her face itself is frequently amateurish, and her voice has a curious husky monotony, which, though it often strikes a touching note in pathetic passages, yet on the whole interferes seriously with finish of elocution. This latter weakness is especially noticeable when Miss Terry plays Shakespeare. Her manner of dealing with the delightful speeches of Portia, with all their play of irony, of wit and temper, savours, to put it harshly, of the school-girlish. We have ventured to say that her comprehension of a character is sometimes weak, and we may illustrate it by a reference to her whole handling of this same rich opportunity. Miss Terry's mistress of Belmont giggles too much, plays too much with her fingers, is too free and familiar, too osculatory, in her relations with Bassanio. The mistress of Belmont was a great lady, as well as a tender and a clever woman; but this side of the part quite eludes the actress, whose deportment is not such as we should expect in the splendid spinster who has princes for wooers. When Bassanio has chosen the casket which contains the key of her heart, she approaches him, and begins to pat and stroke him. This seems to us an appallingly false note. "Good heavens, she's touching him!" a person sitting next to us exclaimed—a person whose judgement in such matters is always unerring. (pp. 142-44)

In speaking of the performances of Shakespeare at the Lyceum just now as "inadequate," we meant more particularly that no representation of Shakespeare can be regarded as at all adequate which is not excellent as a whole. Many of the poet's noblest and most exquisite speeches are given to secondary characters to utter, and we need hardly remind the reader how the actors who play secondary characters (putting, for the moment, those who play primary ones quite aside) are in the habit of speaking poetic lines. It is usually a misery to hear them, and there is something monstrous in seeing the most precious intellectual heritage of the human race so fearfully knocked about. Mr. Irving has evidently done his best in distributing the parts in *The Merchant of Venice,* and with what sorry results this best is attended! What an Antonio! what a Bassanio! what a Nerissa! what a Jessica! The scene between Lorenzo and Jessica on the terrace at Belmont, in which the young lovers, sitting hand in hand, breathe out, in rhythmic alternation, their homage to the southern night—this enchanting scene, as it is given at the Lyceum, should be listened to for curiosity's sake. But who, indeed, it may be asked, can rise to the level of such poetry? who can speak such things as they should be spoken? Not, assuredly, the untrained and undedicated performers of whom the great stock of actors and actresses presenting themselves to the English and American public is composed. Shakespeare cannot be acted by way of a change from Messrs. Byron and Burnand, Messrs. Robertson and Wills. He is a school and a specialty in himself, and he is not to be taken up off-hand by players who have been interpreting vulgarity the day before, and who are to return to vulgarity on the morrow. (pp. 145-46)

Henry James, in an originally unsigned essay titled "The London Theatres," in Scribner's Monthly *Vol. XXI, No. 3, January, 1881, pp. 354-69.*

Joseph Hatton   (essay date 1884)

[*Hatton recounts Irving's opening night in Boston and quotes Irving extensively about his conception of Shylock as "the type of a persecuted race; almost the only gentleman in the play and the most ill-used." In his remarks, Irving responds to conservative critics who contested his departure from tradition in presenting a dignified Shylock.*]

On the first night of the *Merchant of Venice* at Boston, Irving played Shylock, I think, with more than ordinary thoughtfulness in regard to his original treatment of the part. His New York method was, to me, a little more vigorous than his London rendering of the part. Considerations of the emphasis which actors have laid upon certain scenes that are considered as especially favorable to the declamatory methods possibly influenced him. His very marked success in Louis no doubt led some of his admirers in America to expect in his Shylock a very hard, grim, and cruel Jew. Many persons hinted as much to him before they saw his impersonation of this

much-discussed character. At Boston I thought he was, if possible, over-conscientious in traversing the lines he laid down for himself when he first decided to produce the "Merchant" at the Lyceum. Singularly sensitive about the feelings of his audiences, and accustomed to judge them as keenly as they judge him, he fancied the Boston audience, which had been very enthusiastic in their applause on the previous nights, were not stirred as they had been by his other work in response to his efforts as Shylock. The play, nevertheless, was received with the utmost cordiality, and the general representation of it was admirable. I found a Londoner in front, who was in raptures with it. "I think the carnival, Belmont, and court scenes," he said, "were never better done at the Lyceum."

At the close of the piece, and after a double call for Irving and Miss Terry, I went to his dressing room.

"Yes," he said, "the play has gone well, very well, indeed; but the audience were not altogether with me. I always feel, in regard to this play, that they do not quite understand what I am doing. They only responded at all to-night where Shylock's rage and mortification get the better of his dignity."

"They are accustomed to have the part of Shylock strongly declaimed; indeed, all the English Shylocks, as well as American representatives of the part, are very demonstrative in it. Phelps was, so was Charles Kean; and I think American audiences look for the declamatory passages in Shylock, to compare your rendering of them with the readings they have previously heard. You omit much of what is considered great business in Shylock, and American audiences are probably a little disappointed that your view of the part forbids anything like what may be called the strident characteristics of most other Shylocks. Charles Kean ranted considerably in Shylock, and Phelps was decidedly noisy,—both fine, no doubt, in their way. Nevertheless they made the Jew a cruel butcher of a Jew. They filled the stage with his sordid greed and malignant desire for vengeance on the Christian, from his first entrance to his final exit."

"I never saw Kean's Shylock, nor Phelps's, nor, indeed, any one's. But I am sure Shylock was not a low person; a miser and usurer, certainly, but a very injured man,—at least he thought so. I felt that my audience to-night had quite a different opinion, and I once wished the house had been composed entirely of Jews. I would like to play Shylock to a Jewish audience." (pp. 224-26)

"I look on Shylock," says Irving, in response to an invitation to talk about his work in that direction, "as the type of a persecuted race; almost the only gentleman in the play, and most ill-used. He is a merchant, who trades in the Rialto, and Bassanio and Antonio are not ashamed to borrow money of him, nor to carry off his daughter. The position of his child is, more or less, a key to his own. She is the friend of Portia. Shylock was well-to-do—a Bible-read man, as his readiness at quotation shows; and there is nothing in his language, at any time, that indicates the snuffling usurer which some persons regard him, and certainly nothing to justify the use the early actors made of the part for the low comedian. He was a religious Jew; learned, for he conducted his case with masterly skilfulness, and his speech is always lofty, and full of dignity. Is there a finer language in Shakespeare than Shylock's defence of his race? 'Hath not a Jew eyes; hath not a Jew hands, organs, dimensions, senses, affections, passions; fed with the same food; hurt with the same weapons; subject to the same diseases; healed by the same means; warmed and cooled by the same winter and summer, as a Christian is?' [III. i. 59-64] As to the manner of representing Shylock, take the first part of the story; note his moods. He is, to begin with, quiet, dignified, diplomatic; then satirical; and next, somewhat light and airy in his manner, with a touch of hypocrisy in it. Shakespeare does not indicate at what precise moment Shylock conceives the idea of the bond; but he himself tells us of his anxiety to have Antonio on the hip.

> I will feed fat the ancient grudge I bear him.
> He hates our sacred nation, and he rails,
> Even there where merchants most do congregate,
> On me, my bargains, and my well-won thrift,
> Which he calls interest.
>
> [I. iii. 47-51]

"His first word is more or less fawning; but it breaks out into reproach and satire when he recalls the insults that have been heaped upon him. 'Hath a dog money?' and so on; still he is diplomatic, for he wants to make reprisals upon Antonio: 'Cursed be my tribe if I forgive him!' [I. iii. 51-2] He is plausible, even jocular. He speaks of his bond of blood as a merry sport. Do you think if he were strident or spiteful in his manner here, loud of voice, bitter, they would consent to sign a bond having in it such fatal possibilities? One of the interesting things for an actor to do is to try to show when Shylock is inspired with the idea of this bargain, and to work out by impersonation the Jew's thought in his actions. My view is, that from the moment Antonio turns upon him, declaring he is 'like to spit upon him again' [I. iii. 130-31], and invites him scornfully to lend the money, not as to his friend, but rather to his enemy, who, if he break, he may with better force exact the penalty,—from that moment I imagine Shylock resolving to propose his pound of flesh, perhaps without any hope of getting it. Then he puts on that hypocritical show of pleasantry which so far deceives them as to elicit from Antonio the remark that 'the Hebrew will turn Christian; he grows kind' [I. iii. 178]. Well, the bond is to be sealed, and when next we meet the Jew he is still brooding over his wrongs, and there is in his words a constant, though vague, suggestion of a desire for revenge, nothing definite or planned, but a continual sense of undeserved humiliation and persecution:—

> I am bid forth to supper, Jessica.
> There are my keys. But why should I go?
> I am not bid for love. They flatter me;
> But yet I'll go in hate, to feed upon
> The prodigal Christian
>
> [II. v. 11-15]

"But one would have to write a book to go into these details, and tell an actor's story of Shylock."

"We are not writing a book of Shylock now, but only chatting about your purpose and intention generally in presenting to the public what is literally to them a new Shylock, and answering, perhaps, a few points of that conservative kind of criticism which preaches tradition and custom. Come to the next phase of Shylock's character, or, let us say, his next dramatic mood."

"Well, we get at it in the street scene: rage,—a confused passion; a passion of rage and disappointment, never so confused and mixed; a man beside himself with vexation and chagrin.

> My daughter! Oh my ducats! Oh, my daughter!
> Fled with a Christian! Oh, my Christian ducats!

> Justice! the law! my ducats and my daughter!
>
> [II. viii. 15-17]

"I saw a Jew once, in Tunis, tear his hair, his raiment, fling himself in the sand, and writhe in a rage, about a question of money,—beside himself with passion. I saw him again, self-possessed and fawning; and again, expressing real gratitude for a trifling money courtesy. He was never undignified until he tore at his hair and flung himself down, and then he was picturesque; he was old, but erect, even stately, and full of resource, and as he walked behind his team of mules he carried himself with the lofty air of a king. He was a Spanish Jew,—Shylock probably was of Frankfort; but Shakespeare's Jew was a type, not a mere individual: he was a type of the great, grand race,—not a mere Hounsditch usurer. He was a man famous on the Rialto; probably a foremost man in his synagogue; proud of his descent; conscious of his moral superiority to many of the Christians who scoffed at him, and fanatic enough, as a religionist, to believe that his vengeance had in it the element of a godlike justice. Now, you say that some of my critics evidently look for more fire in the delivery of the speeches to Solanio, and I have heard friends say, that John Kemble and the Keans brought down the house for the way they thundered out the threats against Antonio, and the defence of the Jewish race. It is in this scene that we realize, for the first time, that Shylock has resolved to enforce his bond. Three times, during a very short speech, he says, 'Let him look to his bond!' 'A beggar that was used to come so smug upon the mart; *let him look to his bond;* he was wont to call me usurer; *let him look to his bond;* he was wont to lend money for a Christian courtesy; *let him look to his bond* ' [III. i. 46-50]. Now, even an ordinary man, who had made up his mind to 'have the heart of him if he forfeit' [III. i. 127] would not shout and rave and storm. My friend at Tunis tore his hair at a trifling disappointment; if he had resolved to stab his rival he would have muttered his intention between his teeth, not have screeched it. How much less likely still would this bitterly persecuted Jew merchant of Venice have given his resolve a loud and noisy utterance! Would not his settled hate have been more likely to show itself in the clinched hand, the firmly planted foot, the flashing eye, and the deep undertones in which he would utter the closing threat: '*Let him look to his bond*'? I think so."

"And so do the most thoughtful among your audiences. Now and then, however, a critic shows himself so deeply concerned for what is called tradition that he feels it incumbent upon him to protest against a Shylock who is not, from first to last, a transparent and noisy ruffian."

"Tradition! One day we will talk of that. In Davenant's time,—and some dare to say he got his tradition from Shakespeare himself—they played Shylock as a comic character, in a red wig; and to make it, as they thought, consistent, they cut out the noblest lines the author had put into his mouth, and added some of their own. We have no tradition in the sense that those who would insist upon our observance of it means; what we have is bad,—Garrick played Othello in a red coat and epaulettes; and if we are to go back to Shakespeare's days, some of these sticklers for so-called tradition forget that the women were played by boys. Shakespeare did the best he could in his day, and he would do the best he could if he were living now. Tradition! It is enough to make one sick to hear the pretentious nonsense that is talked about the stage in the name of tradition. It seems to me that there are two ways of representing Shakespeare. You have seen

David's picture of Napoleon and that by Delaroche. The first is a heroic figure,—head thrown back, arm extended, cloak flying,—on a white horse of the most powerful, but unreal, character, which is rearing up almost upon its haunches, its forelegs pawing the air. That is Napoleon crossing the Alps. I think there is lightning in the clouds. It is a picture calculated to terrify; a something so unearthly in its suggestion of physical power as to cut it off from human comprehension. Now, this represents to me one way of playing Shakespeare. The other picture is still the same subject, 'Napoleon crossing the Alps'; but in this one we see a reflective, deep-browed man, enveloped in his cloak, and sitting upon a sturdy mule, which, with a sure and steady foot, is climbing the mountain, led by a peasant guide. This picture represents to me the other way of playing Shakespeare. The question is, which is right? I think the truer picture is *the right* cue to the poet who himself described the actor's art as to hold, as it were, the mirror up to nature."

"Which should bring us very naturally back to Shylock. Let us return to your brief dissertation at the point where he is meditating vengeance in case of forfeiture of the bond."

"Well, the latest mood of Shylock dates from this time,—it is one of implacable *revenge*. Nothing shakes him. He thanks God for Antonio's ill-luck. There is in this darkness of his mind a tender recollection of Leah. And then the calm command to Tubal, 'Bespeak me an officer' [III. i. 126] What is a little odd is his request that Tubal shall meet him at the synagogue. It might be that Shakespeare suggested here the idea of a certain sacredness of justice in Shylock's view of vengeance on Antonio. Or it might be to accentuate the religious character of the Jew's habits; for Shylock was assuredly a religious Jew, strict in his worship, and deeply read in his Bible,—no small thing, this latter knowledge, in those days. I think this idea of something divine in his act of vengeance is the key-note to the trial-scene, coupled, of course, with the intense provocation he has received.

> Thou calledst me dog before thou hadst a cause;
> But since I am a dog, beware my fangs!
> The duke shall grant me justice.
> . . . . Follow not,
> I'll have no speaking; I will have my bond.
>
> [III. iii. 6-13]

"These are the words of a man of fixed, implacable purpose, and his skilful defence of it shows him to be wise and capable. He is the most self-possessed man in the court. Even the duke, in the judge's seat, is moved by the situation. What does he say to Antonio?

> I am sorry for thee; thou art come to answer
> A stony adversary.
>
> [IV. i. 3-4]

"Everything indicates a stern, firm, persistent, implacable purpose, which in all our experience of men is, as a rule, accompanied by an apparently calm manner. A man's passion which unpacks itself in oaths and threats, which stamps and swears and shouts, may go out in tears, but not in vengeance. On the other hand, there are those who argue that Antonio's reference to his own patience and to Shylock's fury implies a noisy passion on the part of the Jew; but, without taking advantage of any question as to the meaning of 'fury' in this connection, it seems to me that Shylock's contempt for his enemies, his sneer at Gratiano:—

> Till thou canst rail the seal from off my bond,
> Thou but offend'st thy lungs to speak so loud
>
> [IV. i. 139-40]

and his actions throughout the court scene, quite outweigh any argument in favor of a very demonstrative and furious representation of the part. 'I stand here for law!' [IV. i. 142] Then note when he realizes the force of the technical flaws in his bond,—and there are lawyers who contend the law was severely and unconstitutionally strained in this decision of the court,—he is willing to take his bond paid thrice; he cannot get that, he asks for the principal; when that is refused he loses his temper, as it occurs to me, for the first time during the trial, and in a rage exclaims, 'Why, then, the devil give him good of it!' [IV. i. 345] There is a peculiar and special touch at the end of that scene which, I think, is intended to mark and accentuate the crushing nature of the blow which has fallen upon him. When Antonio stipulates that Shylock shall become a Christian, and record a deed of gift to Lorenzo, the Jew cannot speak. 'He shall do this,' says the duke, 'or else I do recant the pardon' [IV. i. 391-92]. Portia turns and questions him. He is hardly able to utter a word. 'I am content' [IV. i. 394], is all he says; and what follows is as plain an instruction as was ever written in regard to the conduct and manner of the Jew. 'Clerk, draw a deed of gift' [IV. i. 394], says Portia. Note Shylock's reply, his last words, the answer of the defeated litigant, who is utterly crushed and borne down:—

> I pray you give me leave to go from hence;
> I am not well; send the deed after me,
> And I will sign it.
>
> [IV. i. 395-97]

"Is it possible to imagine anything more helpless than this final condition of the Jew? 'I am not well; give me leave to go from hence!' How interesting it is to think this out! and how much we all learn from the actors when, to the best of their ability, they give the characters they assume as if they were really present, working out their studies, in their own way, and endowing them with the characterization of their own individuality! It is cruel to insist that one actor shall simply follow in the footsteps of another; and it is unfair to judge an actor's interpretation of a character from the stand-point of another actor; his intention should be considered, and he should be judged from the point of how he succeeds or fails in carrying it out." (pp. 227-36)

Joseph Hatton, "Boston and Shylock," in his Henry Irving's Impressions of America, *James R. Osgood and Company, 1884, pp. 214-36.*

Bernard Shaw (review date 22 September 1896)

[*Shaw, an Irish dramatist and critic, was the major English playwright of his generation. His hostility toward Shakespeare, evident in his criticism of the poet's work, was based in large measure on his belief that Shakespeare's reputation as a dramatist was inflated and that his plays interfered with the acceptance of Henrik Ibsen and the new social theater he so strongly advocated. Shaw served as theater critic for the* Saturday Review *from 1895 to 1898. In addition,* Ellen Terry and Bernard Shaw: A Correspondence *(1931) affords further insight into Shaw's views on drama. In the excerpt below, from an 1896 review of Irving's Lyceum production of* Cymbeline, *Shaw maintains that Irving invented his own characters with little concern for the text. Taking Irving's Shylock as an example, Shaw ar-*

gues that debating the merits of Irving's interpretation of Shylock is futile, because Irving "was simply not Shylock at all."

A prodigious deal of nonsense has been written about Sir Henry Irving's conception of this, that, and the other Shakespearean character. The truth is that he has never in his life conceived or interpreted the characters of any author except himself. He is really as incapable of acting another man's play as Wagner was of setting another man's libretto; and he should, like Wagner, have written his plays for himself. But as he did not find himself out until it was too late for him to learn that supplementary trade, he was compelled to use other men's plays as the framework for his own creations. His first great success in this sort of adaptation was with the *Merchant of Venice.* There was no question then of a bad Shylock or a good Shylock: he was simply not Shylock at all; and when his own creation came into conflict with Shakespeare's, as it did quite openly in the Trial scene, he simply played in flat contradiction of the lines, and positively acted Shakespeare off the stage. This was an original policy, and an intensely interesting one from the critical point of view; but it was obvious that its difficulty must increase with the vividness and force of the dramatist's creation. Shakespeare at his highest pitch cannot be set aside by any mortal actor, however gifted; and when Sir Henry Irving tried to interpolate a most singular and fantastic notion of an old man between the lines of a fearfully mutilated acting version of *King Lear,* he was smashed. On the other hand, in plays by persons of no importance, where the dramatist's part of the business is the merest trash, his creative activity is unhampered and uncontradicted; and the author's futility is the opportunity for the actor's masterpiece. (pp. 56-7)

> *Bernard Shaw, "Blaming the Bard," in his* Dramatic Opinions and Essays with an Apology, Vol. 2, *Brentano's, 1906, pp. 51-60.*

Ellen Terry   (essay date 1908)

[*Terry belonged to a distinguished, English acting family. She began her career at the age of nine as Mamillius in* The Winter's Tale *and rose to prominence with Henry Irving at the Lyceum Theatre. In the excerpt below, Terry relates her experience playing Portia at the Lyceum and describes the enduring effect of Theodore Martin's uncomplimentary* Blackwood's Edinburgh Magazine *review of her performance. Terry also remarks on Irving's Shylock, defending it against those critics who claimed it lacked pathos.*]

The Lyceum production of *The Merchant of Venice* was not so strictly archæological as the Bancrofts' had been, but it was very gravely beautiful and effective. If less attention was paid to details of costumes and scenery, the play itself was arranged and acted very attractively and always went with a swing. To the end of my partnership with Henry Irving it was a safe "draw" both in England and America. By this time I must have played Portia over a thousand times. During the first run of it the severe attack made on my acting of the part in *Blackwood's Magazine* is worth alluding to. The suggestion that I showed too much of a "coming-on" disposition in the Casket Scene affected me for years, and made me self-conscious and uncomfortable. At last I lived it down. (pp. 200-01)

The unkind *Blackwood* article also blamed me for showing too plainly that Portia loves Bassanio before he has actually won her. This seemed to me unjust, if only because Shakespeare makes Portia say *before* Bassanio chooses the right casket:

> One half of me is yours—the other half yours—
>
> *All yours!*
>
> > [III. ii. 16]

Surely this suggests that she was not concealing her fondness like a Victorian maiden, and that Bassanio had most surely won her love, though not yet the right to be her husband.

"There is a soul of goodness in things evil," and the criticism made me alter the setting of the scene, and so contrive it that Portia was behind and out of sight of the men who made hazard for her love.

Dr. Furnivall, a great Shakespearean scholar, was so kind as to write me the following letter about Portia:

> Being founder and director of the New Shakespeare Society, I venture to thank you most heartily for your most charming and admirable impersonation of our poet's Portia, which I witnessed to-night with a real delight. You have given me a new light on the character, and by your so pretty by-play in the Casket Scene have made bright in my memory for ever the spot which almost all critics have felt dull, and I hope to say this in a new edition of 'Shakespeare.'

(He did say it, in "The Leopold" edition.)

> Again those touches of the wife's love in the advocate when Bassanio says he'd give up his wife for Antonio, and when you kissed your hand to him behind his back in the Ring bit—how pretty and natural they were! Your whole conception and acting of the character are so true to Shakespeare's lines that one longs he could be here to see you. A lady gracious and graceful, handsome, witty, loving and wise, you are his Portia to the life.

That's the best of Shakespeare, *I* say. His characters can be interpreted in at least eight different ways, and of each way some one will say: "That is Shakespeare!" The German actress plays Portia as a low comedy part. She wears an eighteenth-century law wig, horn spectacles, a cravat (this last anachronism is not confined to Germans), and often a mustache! There is something to be said for it all, though I should not like to play the part that way myself.

Lady Pollock, who first brought me to Henry Irving's notice as a possible leading lady, thought my Portia better at the Lyceum than it had been at the Prince of Wales's.

> Thanks, my dear Valentine and enchanting Portia," she writes to me in response to a photograph that I had sent her, "but the photographers don't see you as you are, and have not the poetry in them to do you justice . . . You were especially admirable in the Casket Scene. You kept your by-play quieter, and it gained in effect from the addition of repose—and I rejoiced that you did not kneel to Bassanio at 'My Lord, my governor, my King' [III. ii. 165]. I used to feel that too much like worship from any girl to her affianced, and Portia's position being one of command, I should doubt the possibility of such an action . . .

I think I received more letters about my Portia than about all my other parts put together. Many of them came from university men. One old playgoer wrote to tell me that he liked me better than my former instructress, Mrs. Charles Kean. "She mouthed it as she did most things. . . . She was not real—a staid, sentimental 'Anglaise,' and more than a little stiffly pokerish."

Henry Irving's Shylock was generally conceded to be full of talent and reality, but some of his critics could not resist saying that this was *not* the Jew that Shakespeare drew! Now, who is in a position to say what *is* the Jew that Shakespeare drew? I think Henry Irving knew as well as most! Nay, I am sure that in his age he was the only person able to decide.

Some said his Shylock was intellectual, and appealed more to the intellect of his audiences than to their emotions. Surely this is talking for the sake of talking. I recall so many things that touched people to the heart! For absolute pathos, achieved by absolute simplicity of means, I never saw anything in the theater to compare with his Shylock's return home over the bridge to his deserted house after Jessica's flight. (pp. 201-04)

> Ellen Terry, *"Work at the Lyceum,"* in her The Story of My Life: Recollections and Reflections, *The McClure Company, 1908, pp. 174-207.*

W. Graham Robertson   (essay date 1931)

[*Robertson fondly recalls his childhood experience of watching Ellen Terry's performance as Portia at the Lyceum in 1879. The author remarks that Irving's heroic, sympathetic portrayal of Shylock, although "magnificent and unforgettable," nevertheless "upset the balance of the play and it ruined Portia's Trial Scene."*]

I had reached the ripe age of thirteen and had for years been an earnest student of fairy-tales, ballads and romances. In the course of my studies I was continually coming across dazzlingly beautiful ladies, princesses lovely as the day, radiant fairies, exquisite though distressed heroines. There was never any doubt as to the beauty of these ladies; it took you flat aback at first sight and you knew at once that you were in the presence of a Fairy or a Princess or at least of an ill-used step-daughter—which came to the same thing in the end. And there seemed to be any amount of these amazing creatures about; in fact nothing very interesting ever happened to any lady who was not beautiful as the day.

I looked round me in the solid, comfortable, mid-Victorian world. There were pretty girls and girls who were not pretty; there really seemed very little difference between them. They roused no particular interest, and as to taking one flat aback—well, it was not in their line. I concluded, after some research, that the race of Fairy Princesses was extinct, and I didn't much mind. I had never been able to fit one of these ladies very comfortably into my schemes for the future, and the removal of her figure from my Air Castle—where she had naturally occupied a very handsome suite of apartments—left me a nice lot of room.

But one day in 1879 I was taken by my mother to see *The Merchant of Venice* at the Lyceum Theatre. I was delighted to find Venice all that I had pictured it, and soon old friends began to take shape: Antonio, Bassanio—rather stouter than I had fancied—and above all, the terrible, fateful Shylock with his pale face and glittering eyes. Then came Belmont and Nerissa and—O, my goodness! Flat aback was I taken in quite the correct and conventional style.

There she was at last, from head to foot all gold—the Impossible She—the Fairy Lady, beautiful as the day! As I had imagined, there was no mistake about it. The Princess suite in my Air Castle was opened at once and thoroughly aired—it might be wanted at any minute. In fact, before I could turn round, there was the Lady installed.

'Portia, Miss Ellen Terry,' read the programme.

Well, she solved many difficulties.

If Miss Ellen Terry were possible anything might be possible, including dragons and roc's eggs. The Gates of Elf Land had been closing; Miss Ellen Terry flung them wide again: the Lady Beauty had revealed herself just as I was about to say, "I don't believe there's no such a person."

And what was she like? How is it possible to describe to a generation that knows her not the beauty of Ellen Terry? Her portraits will remain showing an appealing, arresting personality, a haunting glance, a grace of softly falling raiment, but no portrait can reflect a shadow of her beauty.

Pale eyes, rather small and narrow, a broad nose slightly tilted at the tip, a wide mouth, a firm, large chin, pale hair, not decidedly golden, yet not brown—by no means a dazzling inventory of charms, yet out of these was evolved Ellen Terry, the most beautiful woman of her time.

I knew that her radiance was not the mere glamour of the stage, for I was, at that age, a hardened theatre-goer. I was familiar with the machine-made beautiful fairies and Princesses of Pantomime and had accepted them placidly, as a child accepts bad illustrations to an interesting book. But here was no painted show from the land of Make Believe—here was the real thing.

Her charm held everyone, but I think pre-eminently those who loved pictures. She was *par excellence* the Painter's Actress and appealed to the eye before the ear; her gesture and pose were eloquence itself.

She was a child of the studio, having always been much with artists, and during her brief married life she must have sat almost continuously to her husband, G. F. Watts, who afterwards destroyed many of his studies made from her, but the few that escaped are among his very best works. The wraith-like Ophelia, the eager, wistful youth in 'Watchman, what of the night?' the running girl in blue with clasped hands, which he presented to her after time had swept away all bitterness between them, and best of all, the picture called 'Choosing' in which she stands against dark camellia leaves, a girl of sixteen in a dress of golden brown with beribboned sleeves—her wedding dress, designed by Holman Hunt—are records of a period which left a great mark upon her art.

She had learnt to create Beauty, not the stage beauty of white-wash and lip salve, but the painter's beauty of line, harmony and rhythm.

Meanwhile I was sitting absorbed in *The Merchant of Venice*. What stands out most clearly in that wonderful evening? In spite of the gracious charm of the Fairy Lady, what rises first and last in my mind is the face of Henry Irving.

The memory of the Lady's Portia (oddly enough, I never saw it again) is like a dream of beautiful pictures in a scheme of gold melting one into another; the golden gown, the golden hair, the golden words all form a golden vision of romance and loveliness; but of Irving's Shylock I seem to remember every movement, every tone.

Later on, when I came to compare it with his other parts (Irving could never be compared with anyone but himself), it was not among my favourites. His readings of characters were nearly always most sympathetic to me, but I feel that, for once, he was wrong about Shylock.

His dignified, heroic, intensely aristocratic Martyr was magnificent and unforgettable, but it upset the balance of the play and it ruined Portia's Trial Scene.

How small and mean sounded her quibbling tricky speeches when addressed to a being who united the soul of Savonarola and the bearing of Charles the First, with just a touch of Lord Beaconsfield that made for mystery.

After her best effect we momentarily expected the doge to rise exclaiming, "My dear sir, pray accept the apology of the Court for any annoyance that this young person has caused you. By all means take as much of Antonio as you think proper, and if we may throw in a prime cut off Bassanio and the whole of Gratiano we shall regard your acceptance of the same as a favour."

Still, right or wrong, his Shylock was a living thing, a haunting, memorable figure, and I left the theatre with the profoundest sympathy for the noble, ill used Jew and with the name Ellen Terry graven indelibly on my heart. (pp. 53-6)

> *W. Graham Robertson, "Of the Lady of Belmont and Albert Moore," in his* Time Was: The Reminiscences of W. Graham Robertson, *Hamish Hamilton Ltd., 1931, pp. 53-62.*

Arthur Colby Sprague (essay date 1953)

[*An American critic and scholar, Sprague is the author of* Shakespeare and the Audience: A Study in the Technique of Exposition *(1935),* Shakespeare and the Actors: The Stage Business in His Plays, 1660-1905 *(1944),* Shakespearian Players and Performers *(1953),* Shakespeare's Histories: Plays for the Stage *(1964), and* Shakespeare's Plays Today: Some Customs and Conventions of the Stage *(1970). In the excerpt below, Sprague employs numerous critical references in order to recreate a comprehensive picture of Henry Irving's Shylock, including the derivation of his conception, and the popular and critical response. Sprague suggests that Irving may have adopted his sympathetic portrait of Shylock out of physical necessity rather than for intellectual reasons.*]

On October 20, 1905, Henry Irving, like David Garrick before him, was laid to rest in the Abbey. It was in keeping with what he had accomplished for himself and his calling. The knighthood Queen Victoria had conferred a few years earlier, adding to the formal "Rise, Sir Henry," her own words, "It gives me very great pleasure, sir," carried much the same meaning. He was one among the Great Victorians and, like Garrick once more, a national figure.

A few weeks after his death appeared a pathetic little volume of poetical tributes [*Tributes to the Memory of the Late Sir Henry Irving,* 1905]. The writers were without exception obscure men—provincial journalists, country clergymen, and the like. They praise Irving for the most part as a good and worthy man, one who had purified the stage, sowing "white lily-flowers where other pois'nous weeds," one who would now, in a better world, be greeted by Tennyson as well as

Shakespeare. A generation later, on the eve of the Second World War, came another commemorative volume, the splendid and desirable book, *We Saw Him Act.* This time, the writers, now a distinguished company, unite in praising Irving as an artist. For the demurrers and detractors, the Archers and Bernard Shaws, they express only contempt. It is as if, in their lifetime, there had been but one theatre, the Lyceum, and one supremely gifted actor, the man whose memory they were honoring. The applause of other days echoes anew. Surely, we must believe, it was deserved!

Yet no other player of comparable rank, not even Edmund Kean, remained so long unrecognized; no other, when recognition came, was so widely or destructively criticized. Irving, we are assured over and over again, could neither walk nor talk. He was a painstaking and even inspired stage manager, but quite incapable of tragic acting on any level of true excellence. Some of those who remembered the old patent theatre days simply could not understand the enthusiasm of the inexperienced. Edward Fitzgerald [in his *Letters to Fanny Kemble*], having looked in at "the famous Lyceum Hamlet" early in the spring of 1879, "soon had looked, and heard, enough."

> It was incomparably the worst I had ever witnessed, from Covent Garden down to a Country Barn. . . . When he got to "Something too much of this," I called out from the Pit door where I stood, "A good deal too much," and not long after returned to my solitary inn.

By that time, however, Macready was a generation away; and where, save in the provinces, and America, were there any who respected the traditions for which he had stood? Their doom already determined in Macready's own day, they were discarded or forgotten. Phelps at Sadler's Wells had carried them bravely forward. So, in a measure, had Charles Kean. It was in the eighteen-sixties that actors of the old school began to find themselves no longer wanted. In London, Shakespeare spelled ruin—save, momentarily, with the foreigner Charles Fechter, who exulted in overthrowing tradition, which he called, not very happily, "that worm-eaten and unwholesome prison, where dramatic art languishes in fetters."

Irving as a very young man was coached by a member of Phelps's company. During his long years of apprenticeship in the provinces, he had sometimes the good fortune to appear with traditional actors like Barry Sullivan and the young Edwin Booth. But he was scarcely qualified to go far in their ways, even if he had desired to follow them, which is more than doubtful. Rather, he learned from many sources, and applied his knowledge shrewdly, Fechter and melodrama teaching him the effectiveness of pure miming; Charles Kean, a regard for historical accuracy. As a Shakespearian actor, he was very original, very "modern." Archer, indeed, exaggerated only legitimately when he asserted of English acting [in his *The Theatrical World of 1897*] that "the objects and methods of Macready were very much the same as those of Betterton; the objects and methods of Sir Henry Irving, even when he deals with the same material, are utterly dissimilar."

Those who held out for the older style of Shakespearian acting had only distant memories to cite, and standards which, in England at any rate, had long been unmet. Irving satisfied such influential conservatives as Clement Scott and William Winter. It was rather from the left, from men associated with the new movement in drama, that he continued to be assailed. With Garrick, as we have seen, began the preëminence of the actor in the English theatre. Lamb's paradoxical essay, "On the Tragedies of Shakspeare," is in the first instance a protest against the exaltation of the player at the expense of the poet. It was an actor's theatre still when, in the eighteen-seventies, Irving mounted a long-vacant throne. But, with the passing of time, another theatre, realistic in intent, very serious, very self-conscious, came into being—an author's theatre. Pinero, it was remarked, would already have arranged every detail of performance when one of his mature plays reached the actors, so that they had only to follow his instructions. Shaw, in his sagacious little pamphlet *The Art of Rehearsal,* tells the dramatist how to get his own way with the players.

Now Irving gave nothing by Shaw, or Henry Arthur Jones, and such contemporary dramas as he did give (Tennyson's *Becket* is a dignified exception) were wanting in vitality. Shakespeare yielded him parts in which he could star— though not enough of them—and he drew upon the store of elder tragedians and did *Richelieu* and *Louis XI.* No wonder there was grumbling! Jones, in his unfinished *Shadow of Henry Irving,* insists gloomily upon "the eternal distinction, an opposition sometimes amounting to a pull-devil-pull-baker rivalry between the Drama and the Theatre." He grants that "Irving's acting and management at the Lyceum remain the supreme achievement of the English Theatre in all its annals"; but "by very reason of his being such a great actor and with this incomparable position he was the greatest enemy of the English Drama."

In the autumn of 1879, however, Ibsen and the new realism were still unknown to English playgoers, and they were full of enthusiasm for the Lyceum and its new manager. At the close of the season before, he had promised them a number of curious revivals and did, indeed, open with Macready's old war horse *The Iron Chest.* But soon after—as early as October 8—he changed his plans and set to work on the first new Shakespearian play to be given at his own theatre, *The Merchant of Venice.* On Saturday, November 1, a little over three weeks later, it was ready for performance, ran for two hundred and fifty nights, and remained thereafter in Irving's "working *répertoire.*" In all, he is said to have played Shylock over a thousand times.

The preface to Irving's acting edition of *The Merchant of Venice* contains an admirably concise statement of his ideals as a producer:

> I have endeavoured to avoid hampering the natural action of the piece with any unnecessary embellishment; but have tried not to omit any accessory which might heighten the effects. I have availed myself of every resource at my command to present the play in a manner acceptable to our audiences.

In the course of an interview some years later, when the actor was in America, he answered criticism that the play's success was chiefly owing to its *mise en scène* by pointing out how little time (twenty-three days!) he had had for its preparation. The elaborate mounting of plays at the Lyceum began, he said, with the productions of 1880-81. Percy Fitzgerald explains [in his *Sir Henry Irving*] that "the whole effect," which was of great beauty, "was produced by the painting, not by built-up structures"; there was "none of that overloading of illustration without *a propos,* which was such a serious blemish in later productions." He questions, it is true, whether there had not been some overemphasis on externals even in *The Merchant of Venice.* "At the same time, it must be said that this system of reviving the tone of the era seems quite

un-Shakespearian. These revels and Venetian dances and gondolas, put in for 'local colour,' have little to do with high tragedy and dramatic interest." But there were few playgoers, in 1879, who would have shared his doubts.

Irving's acting text seems, at first glance, badly mutilated. Not only are some entire episodes omitted—the discomfiture of the Prince of Arragon; Jessica's talk with Launcelot Gobbo, discreditable to Shylock; Portia's, with Lorenzo and Nerissa, just before she sets forth from Belmont; and, more excusably, the scene in Belmont following her departure— but others are cut so drastically as to seem no longer themselves. Thus the scene of Bassanio's choosing among the caskets is reduced by more than a third, with over seventy lines omitted—and Portia was Ellen Terry! It is all the more striking that such mention of the text as occurs when Irving first produced the play, and when, four seasons later, he brought it to America, is usually complimentary. In particular, his "restoration" of the fifth act is frequently cited. Booth and a good many others had been accustomed to treat the play as a sort of tragedy and lowered their curtain upon the defeat of Shylock. Clement Scott noticed [in his *From "The Bells" to "King Arthur"*] that on the first night some of the spectators left at the close of the Trial Scene. They were "ill-advised" to do so. As the run proceeded, Irving, not without protest, dropped the fifth act altogether, and substituted an afterpiece by Wills.

J. H. Barnes, "handsome Jack" Barnes, as he was called, appeared as Bassanio in the production of 1879. In his autobiography [*Forty Years on the Stage*], Barnes takes exception to the idea of Shylock as a wronged man for whom we should feel only sympathy. He had, he says, talked over the character with Irving in 1901, and thought "he was almost disposed to agree with my view." Could it be that the Shylock Irving "played and made so famous" was not "absolutely the Shylock he would have played if he had possessed a greater amount of physical power?" During the early rehearsals, Barnes fancied that he was aiming at this other, more truly Shakespearian character, only to find it, at certain points, beyond his reach. William Winter [in his *Shakespeare on the Stage*] quotes Irving as having said in his presence that Shylock was "a bloody-minded monster—but you mustn't play him so, if you wish to succeed; you must get some sympathy with him"; and Robert Hichens [in *We Saw Him Act*, H. A. Saintsbury and Cecil Palmer, eds.] after a talk with the great actor, was left with much the same impression, that Irving's treatment of the part had been conditioned by his desire to score heavily in it. Both explanations—the shrewd surmise that audiences of his day would prefer a sympathetic Jew, and the realization that he himself could not, like Kean, bring them to their feet with outbursts of passion—are likely to have weighed with Irving. After all, he had the fortunes of the Lyceum to consider as well as his own prestige. And who could say with confidence that this carefully wrought interpretation of his was wide of the mark?

Those who wrote of that first Shylock of 1879 divide, with few exceptions, into three groups. Some—and they are the largest group—were enthusiastic about Irving's conception of the part; a few wholly disagreed with it; and still others maintained that the actor had presented not one Shylock but two, that the impersonation was inconsistent with itself. One Shylock, according to *The Times,* was "erect, composed, dignified," and "almost by his bearing compelling our sympathies where they are most keenly raised against him." The other was "a screaming incoherent old man, who seemed to have lost his wits together with his daughter and his ducats." *The Saturday Review* [15 November 1879] agreed that the scene in which the Jew bewails his losses was out of keeping with the rest. *Punch,* perhaps with greater subtlety, was satisfied that "Mr. IRVING'S conception of the character, its truth to SHAKESPEARE, and to nature," lay in its very inconsistency.

> If Mr. IRVING is firm one moment, tottering another, now hobbling, now striding: now bent and broken, anon upright and sturdy; if at one time he raves and scolds like a virago, and at another is calm, impassive, and unrelenting as destiny,—I say that this is SHAKESPEARE'S own *Shylock,* a character all lights and shades.

Yet Dutton Cook [in his *Nights at the Play*] found the performance "altogether consistent and harmonious"—this Shylock, "old, haggard, halting, sordid, represents the dignity and intellect of the play"; and another critic [*The Theatre,* 1 December 1879] felt that the part, as Irving represented it, had taken on "a sad and romantic interest, an almost tragic elevation and grace." Among the dissentors several have famous names. Ruskin, who had been quoted in *The Theatre* as having told Irving that his impersonation was "noble, tender, and true," protested that although admiring "Mr. Irving's own acting of Shylock . . . I entirely dissent (and indignantly as well as entirely) from his general reading and treatment of the play." Henry James referred to the conception as "a sentimental one," then turned his attention to matters of technique. Irving as the Jew, he wrote comprehensively [in *Scribner's Monthly,* January 1881], was "neither excited nor exciting." In later years, both Shaw [in his *Dramatic Opinions and Essays*] and Henry Arthur Jones joined the attack. "He was simply not Shylock at all" (writes the former) and in the Trial Scene "positively acted Shakespeare off the stage." And Jones [in his *The Shadow of Henry Irving*] calls the final exit,

> undoubtedly a great piece of acting. It was, however, quite ex-Shakespearean, if not anti-Shakespearean. It illustrates a frequent habit and method of Irving—that of getting his greatest effects not in, and by, the text and obvious meaning of his author, but in his own extraneous bits of business.

A densely crowded audience waited for their first sight of the new Shylock. They saw him enter with Bassanio, at the beginning of Scene 3, against "a view of the Palace of St. Mark, with a quay on which porters are landing bales of merchandise" [*The Theatre;* 1 December 1879]. A man of between fifty and sixty, old but not decrepit, he was dressed in a sober brown robe, with an oriental, shawl-like girdle and a black cap across which ran a yellow line. In his hand, as was traditional, he carried a stick. The face was gaunt and wolfish, with a wisp of iron-grey beard. Certainly, as even James admitted, he looked the part!

In Boston, on an evening some years later, Irving talked about Shylock, and had much to say about this first, long scene. He traced the Jew's changing moods. "He is, to begin with, quiet, dignified, diplomatic; then satirical; and next, somewhat light and airy in his manner, with a touch of hypocrisy in it." Although "his first word is more or less fawning," he presently,

> breaks out into reproach and satire when he recalls

the insults that have been heaped upon him. "Hath a dog money?" [I. iii. 121] and so on; still he is diplomatic, for he wants to make reprisals upon Antonio: "Cursed be my tribe if I forgive him!" [I. iii. 51-2] He is plausible, even jocular. He speaks of his bond of blood as a merry sport. Do you think if he were strident or spiteful in his manner here . . . they would consent to sign a bond having in it such fatal possibilities?

Clement Scott, who for all his limitations was a good critic of acting, calls attention to many details in Irving's performance of the scene. "Scarcely a moment of the dialogue was unrelieved by some variety of intonation or facial expression," such as "the half-laughing sneer that a pound of man's flesh was not so profitable as that of mutton, or of goats," or "the recital with the fervour of interest of some old passage in the history of Jacob." In the long aside beginning:

> How like a fawning publican he looks!
>
> [I. iii. 41]

the actor dwelt "with concentrated bitterness on the expressions of hatred to Antonio . . . and here, in the implacable determination of

> If I can catch him once upon the hip,
> I will feed fat the ancient grudge I bear him.
>
> [I. iii. 46-7]

we have the prologue, as it were, to the intense revengefulness of the last scene" [*The Saturday Review,* 8 November 1879]. Irving himself raises the interesting question of when the idea of the bargain first occurs to Shylock—of when, to speak more accurately, the coming of the hideous thought should be indicated by the actor. He had chosen the moment at which Antonio, turning upon the Jew, declares "he is 'like to spit upon him again' [I. iii. 131], and invites him scornfully to lend him the money, not as to his friend, but rather to his enemy. . . . From that moment I imagine Shylock resolving to propose his pound of flesh" [in Hattan, *Irving's Impressions of America*]. Putting on a show of servility, he came close to his victim and touched him lightly on the breast. Antonio recoiled in disgust and Shylock, sensitive to the rebuke, bowed low. He could afford to wait.

During the second act, Shylock has little to do. But just at the end, Irving invented for him and invented brilliantly. Jessica's elopement had been elaborately staged. The scene showed the Jew's house, "with a bridge over the canal which flows by it, and with a votive lamp to the Virgin on the wall. There a barcarolle is sung by some Venetians on a gondola, and a number of masqueraders rush merrily past" [*The Theatre,* 1 December 1879]. As the sound of their laughter and music died away, the curtain descended. (Can it have been that at this point some of the critics scurried for the lobbies? At any rate, what follows passes unmentioned in a good many contemporary accounts of the performance.) After a few moments, the curtain was raised once more, showing the same scene, but now silent and deserted. Shylock appeared, "lantern in hand, advancing, bent in thought," and as he drew close to the house—still unaware that it is now empty—the curtain fell. In later performances, he sometimes knocked at the door.

Edmund Kean had made Shylock's scene of mingled menace and lamentation, at the beginning of Act III, the climax of his performance. Irving could not. The expression of violent emotion in torrents of speech was denied him. On the first night, moreover, he was upset by a bad slip of memory on Tubal's part (*Punch* fancies what would have happened to the unfortunate actor had he been with Macready!). Irving had not yet learned how to make the most of his powers. He ranted "after a fashion and in a language wholly unintelligible" [*The Times,* 3 November 1879]. Yet Sir Theodore Martin assures us [in *Blackwood's Magazine,* December 1879] that as a spectator he was able to forget "the cracked and screaming tones, and the occasional want of articulateness, in the powerful action, the visible intensity of the feeling, the thoroughness with which the ruling idea is worked out." Scott too, though admitting there were faults, remained cordial.

> The expression of incontinent rage and prostration of nervous energy, was occasionally not in tune. The great speech was started in too high a key, and, though it won the finest burst of applause of the whole evening, Mr. Irving was not at this moment seen at his best . . . the strain was very great and a little painful.

A moment later, however, came "the calm and almost inspired delivery of the pathetic words: 'No satisfaction, no revenge . . . no tears but of my shedding . . .' and, from that instant, all went well again." [in Scott]. In America, a few years later, Irving was thought to have reached a "summit and climax" in his speaking of the same words [William Winter in *The New York Tribune*]. It is not, perhaps, without significance that in talking of the traditional playing of this scene he then dwelt upon the desirability of avoiding excess. Shylock would be unlikely to give his terrible resolve "a loud and noisy utterance" [Hattan].

Irving's best scene was still to come—that of the trial. The setting was a splendidly painted hall adorned with portraits of Venetian worthies. It was "lined with mediaeval soldiery in their quaint costumes" [Scott]; and spectators, including a little knot of eager Jews, watched the proceedings. Shylock, entering slowly, remained "standing almost motionless, his hands hanging by his sides . . . his grey, worn face, lined and hollow, mostly averted from the speakers who move him not; except when a gleam of murderous hate, sudden and deadly . . . burns for a moment in the tired, melancholy eyes"—as he asked, for instance,

Hates any man the thing he would not kill?

[IV. i. 67]

At the taunts of Gratiano, "and the amiable maundering of the Duke," a "slow, cold smile, just parting the lips . . . passes over the face, but does not touch the eyes or lift the brow" [*The Spectator,* 8 November 1879]. The stillness, or even listlessness, of this Shylock is remarked on again and again. While he listened to "the Duke's speech in mitigation," we are told, somewhat inexactly, he had "the horrible stillness and fascination of the rattlesnake" [*The Saturday Review,* 8 November 1879].

It was noticed that Irving, unlike many earlier Shylocks, laid no emphasis upon the grim action of whetting the knife. When Bassanio made his offer of twice the amount owed—

For thy three thousand ducats here is six—

[IV. i. 84]

Shylock's refusal was accompanied by his tapping the bag of jingling coins three times with the point of his knife; and it was again with the knife's point that he later showed the

young judge what was and what was not specified in the bond, leaning eagerly over the other's shoulder as he did so.

With the deadly "A sentence! Come, prepare!" [IV. i. 304] the scene leaps to climax—and the next moment, Shylock is defeated. In Irving's performance, he stood as if dazed, his utter collapse marked by the dropping of the scales and knife from his hands. The "last effort to clutch the gold . . . his cunning, business-like, 'Give me my principal, and let me go!' [IV. i. 336]" was "an admirable point" [*The Spectator,* 8 November 1879]. Then came what was to be one of Irving's most famous moments—equalled, it may be, only by the frenzied action at the close of the Play Scene in *Hamlet.* It is well described by *The Spectator:*

> Shylock is Mr. Irving's finest performance, and his final exit is its best point. The quiet shrug, the glance of ineffable, unfathomable contempt at the exultant booby, Gratiano, who, having got hold of a good joke, worries it like a puppy with a bone, the expression of defeat in every limb and feature, the deep, gasping sigh, as he passes slowly out, and the crowd rush from the Court to hoot and howl at him outside, make up an effect which must be seen to be comprehended.

And still speaking of this exit, the writer adds that the impression it produced "upon the vast audience was most remarkable; the thrill that passed over the house was a sensation to have witnessed and shared." Is it any wonder if some preferred, as we have seen, not to stay on, after that, for Shakespeare and his fifth act?

In Shylock, Irving's mannerisms were found less conspicuous, less obstructive to a full success, than they were in most of his other rôles. After all, a certain strangeness of speech and gait may be granted the Jew, and even become him.

A great deal has been written about these mannerisms, and they remain mysterious. The late Sophia Kirk, daughter of the John Foster Kirk who knew and wrote about Macready, once told me of going with her brother to see Irving for the first time. They had heard he had a wooden leg. But which leg? After comparing notes at the close of the performance, they were satisfied—*both were!* Yet Irving could upon occasion walk well, and gracefully, just as he was capable, at rehearsals, of pronouncing "God" otherwise than "Gud."

All sorts of explanations were offered. Were the mannerisms deliberately assumed, as some of Irving's admirers insisted to the last, or were they involuntary? And if involuntary, were they due to mere nervousness, as on such unfortunate first nights as that of *King Lear*? Ellen Terry suggested as a means of overcoming self-consciousness, that he avoid long waits at the side before his entrances, and in *The Merchant of Venice* he followed her advice successfully.

Apologists for Irving, when not actually extolling his mannerisms, made light of them. At first distracting, they might be readily forgotten as one became accustomed to them. . . . Such too was Irving's dignity, his absorption in his characters, his command of audiences, that ridicule of him found no expression in the theatre. "Never once at the Lyceum," writes Sir Max Beerbohm [*The Saturday Review,* 21 October 1905], "did I hear a titter. Irving's presence dominated even those who could not be enchanted by it." It was possible, notwithstanding, to feel the enchantment and still deplore Irving's lapses of speech as a grave defect in his art. The Bostonian critic Henry Austin Clapp states the conservative position admirably [in *The Atlantic Monthly,* March 1884]. The mere "mannerisms," as they were called, Clapp takes as evidence that the actor had not mastered his craft; and the demand that they be lightly dismissed from consideration was much

> as if an acquaintance were to recommend for confidential clerk a young man who was a little weak on the score of honesty and accuracy, but, aside from these trifling mannerisms, had every desirable qualification. . . . If there were such a crime as linguamatricide, Mr. Irving would have suffered its extreme penalty long ago; for night after night he has done foul murder upon his mother-tongue.

The voice itself, he goes on to describe as possessing "very little resonance, and almost no richness of tone; it is high-pitched, and has a narrow range; he seems absolutely incapable of *sustained* power and variety in speech." There were others who agreed. Henry James found the voice "without charm . . . a thick unmodulated voice"; and Bernard Shaw described it [in *Ellen Terry and Bernard Shaw: A Correspondence,* Christopher St. John, ed.], in comparison with Barry Sullivan's, as "a highly cultivated neigh."

Thus it was that the grandeur of the Shakespearian music, which earlier actors would summon up, however mechanically, through their declamatory method, was flatly denied Irving. But had not much the same thing been true of Macready before him? How came it about, then, that Irving could so startle and offend—or startle and delight—as he did, for instance, on his first visit to America? The explanation lies, I believe, as much in the sensational success of his methods as in their novelty. He was picturesque himself, and a master of pictorial effect. Clapp was inclined to say that Irving's face was "without exception the most fascinating" he had "seen upon the stage. Once beheld, it will not out of the memory." His hands were beautiful and he used them with extraordinary skill. Above all, he possessed in a degree only matched, perhaps, by Garrick among English actors, that quality of personal attraction which writers on the theatre despair to explain. You could not help watching Irving while he was on the stage. You saw him after the fall of the curtain—it might be for years to come—as the Jew, or Hamlet, or the half-crazed burgomaster, Mathias, in *The Bells.* And what is more remarkable this might hold good even when the actor's view of a character was not your own.

Alfred Darbyshire, the architect, has a tale to tell of Irving's obscure days as a minor actor at Manchester under Charles Calvert. Darbyshire "was watching a rehearsal at the Theatre Royal, when someone came up to Calvert and asked the question, 'Why on earth did you engage that raw fellow?' (pointing to Irving). Calvert replied by touching his forehead with his forefinger" [in Calvert's *The Art of the Victorian Stage*]. And Irving had brains. With little education, and no interests, seemingly, outside those of his profession, he thought, observed, and invented with a devotion to the theatre which was sometimes considered fantastic. No detail was beneath his notice. Robert Ganthony [in his *Random Recollections*], a very minor actor who did Stephano in *The Merchant of Venice,* gives an anecdote by way of illustration.

> If genius be the faculty of taking pains, Irving must be a genius, for if it were the last performance of a play, and he saw something that would improve it, he would adopt it. Months after we had been playing the "Merchant" he called me to him and said,

> "It would be better, Ganthony, if your spurs jingled a little more as you entered and crossed the stage." I accordingly had two metal discs put in each, the sound from which should have satisfied all the requirements of dramatic art.

For Irving was a producer as well as an actor, and it is not always easy to distinguish one side of his achievement from the other. Is the homecoming of Shylock across that Venetian bridge to be regarded as a feat of stage-management or an unusually elaborate piece of original "business"? It scarcely matters, really, since as we have seen this *Merchant of Venice* kept Shylock ever to the fore. Yet if in some sense a production at the Lyceum was no more than a frame for Irving himself, it was a frame splendidly wrought and gilded—a work of art. And though his methods of presenting Shakespeare may seem to us who only read of these performances, cumbersome and even a little prosaic, they appeared quite otherwise to audiences of his own day. Thus Irving's Romeo, I read in an anonymous little book on the actor, published in 1883 [*Henry Irving: A Short Account of His Public Life*], could not altogether pass unchallenged, nor could his Benedick,

> but for pure enjoyment of a play—or *going to the play* as we say—an evening spent in the society of those beautifully-dressed, admirably-graceful ladies and gentlemen, in that Lyceum-land where, as in the Isle of the Lotus-eaters, it is "always afternoon," is perfect. When we leave we have indeed "been to the play—not merely looked on at a performance, but *been* there—to the home of chivalry, romance, ease, and wealth, where nothing sordid can ever enter, though malice and all uncharitableness creep in to make it human.

(pp. 104-20)

Arthur Colby Sprague, "Irving as Shylock," in his Shakespearian Players and Performances, *Cambridge, Mass.: Harvard University Press, 1953, pp. 104-20.*

Herbert W. Kline   (essay date 1971)

[*Kline analyzes Irving's near-tragic, dignified portrayal of Shylock within the context of alternative interpretations throughout the play's stage history. Kline also describes the primarily favorable popular and critical response to Irving's subdued, untraditional Shylock in the course of eight American tours. The* Merchant of Venice *was Irving's most successful production in America, according to the author.*]

With the exception of Hamlet, none of Shakespeare's creations have been given a wider range of interpretation by professional actors than Shylock, the Jewish protagonist of *The Merchant of Venice.* Stage history records three distinct conceptions of the character: as a clown, as a malicious villain, and as a near-tragic man of dignity. Though there is little information about the original performance of Shylock (the play was first published in 1600), it is known that for more than a hundred years after his creation the character was presented wearing the red fright wig of a low comic. For most of these years, Shylock cavorted on English stages in productions like George Granville's *The Jew of Venice* (1701), a travesty of Shakespeare's play. Then, in 1741, Charles Macklin rescued Shylock from the comedians. His was a deadly serious, malicious portrayal, and it prompted the famous couplet, usually attributed to Alexander Pope, "*Here is the Jew*

/ *That Shakespeare drew.*" For a century after his performance, all the great Shylocks, in varying degrees of severity, were related to the tradition which Macklin initiated.

The American theatre, which always drew heavily upon England for theatrical inspiration and approval, had its share of venomous Shylocks. George Frederick Cooke, the first prestigious British actor to visit America, portrayed the character as a depraved usurer for early nineteenth-century audiences. In the trial scene he deviously whetted his knife on the floor in anticipation of collecting the pound of flesh. The great British actors Edmund Kean and William Charles Macready and America's first native-born star Edwin Forrest played similar Shylocks for American audiences as the century moved on. Even the gentle Edwin Booth, America's finest actor, continued the tradition of Macklin. *The New York Times* [4 February 1867] described his 1867 characterization of the Jew as "a fierce malignity," and noted that Booth could not resist "all the miserable old business of sharpening the knife." It is not surprising that the portrayals of Shylock in this country during the first three quarters of the nineteenth century emphasized the venomousness of the character. Tradition is a strong force in the theatre. In addition, a creeping anti-Semitism in America was characteristic of the years before and after the Civil War. In 1862, General U. S. Grant issued his notorious Order Number 11, which accused "Jews as a class" of wartime trading violations and expelled them from the territory subject to his control, but this was only the most odious of a series of restrictive acts by the Union Army aimed at Jewish merchants. In 1877, Joseph Seligman, whose banking firm had helped Lincoln finance the war, was as a Jew refused admission to the Grand Union Hotel in Saratoga Springs. These are two instances of the Jew-baiting which made news during the period. Little wonder that at this time a number of Judeophobic farces, similar to George Granville's early eighteenth-century travesty, caught the fancy of American theatregoers. The malicious Shylocks and their grotesque farcical counterparts offered only a distasteful picture of the Jew to American audiences. It was not until 1883 that theatregoers in this country were able to see a markedly different interpretation. In that year the London Lyceum Theatre, headed by the great actor-manager Henry Irving, toured America.

Irving was a strange figure in the theatrical world. His thin, ungainly body and heron's stride delighted the caricaturists. His voice was weak, his pronunciations were strange, and he was never able to master the music of Shakespeare's verse. Unfit to be a traditional actor, he gained acclaim as an innovative one. He foreswore the oratorical and frequently ranting style of the older tragedians and adopted the techniques of the "new school" of acting. This acting was dependent on the ability to produce on stage the actually observable details of human behavior—including the natural by-play which has become commonplace in contemporary realistic acting—in order to develop more natural, individualized characters. Such acting had been seen only in lightweight domestic comedies when Irving took it up. He was the first to use it in plays from the traditional repertory.

According to Bram Stoker, Irving's business manager, the role of Shylock had not appealed to Irving until he made a summer yachting trip to Morocco and the Levant in 1879. "When I saw the Jew in what seemed his own land and in his own dress," he said [in Stoker's *Personal Reminiscences of Henry Irving*], "Shylock became a different creature. I began

to understand him; and now I want to play the part. . . ." Irving's production of *The Merchant of Venice* opened in November, 1879, and was a tremendous Lyceum success. It played two hundred and fifty consecutive nights, the play's longest run till that time.

The Theatre for December, 1879, gives a vivid analysis of Irving's innovative performance:

> Irving evidently believes that Shakespeare intended to enlist our sympathies on the side of the Jew. . . . the bearing of this Shylock is distinguished by a comparatively quiet and tranquil dignity. . . . In point of dignity and culture he is far above the Christians with whom he comes in contact, and the fact that as a Jew he is deemed far below them in the social scale is gall and wormwood to his proud and sensitive nature.

According to Toby Lelyveld [in his *Shylock on the Stage*] Irving transformed Shylock "from antagonist to protagonist, shifted sympathy to him," and, for the first time, "Shylock took his place among the great figures of tragedy"—despite the fact that he was appearing in a comedy. It would be a mistake to infer that Irving's tragedy-oriented, sympathetic portrayal was an altruistic attempt to alter the picture of the stage Jew which decades of malignant and farcical Shylocks had fostered. There is evidence which suggests that Irving's characterization was prompted by the actor's recognition that he lacked the power required in a traditional interpretation. J. H. (Jack) Barnes, who played Bassanio in the production, almost apologetically declared [in *Forty Years on the Stage*]:

> . . . at the early rehearsals I saw him "make shots" at the big scheme, and, with his great mentality, recognize that it was out of his reach, and so, by degrees, he came to develop, with consummate art, a Shylock he could encompass.

Irving's Shylock appears to have been a compromise with his limitations.

Whatever the motives for Irving's conception, he treated American audiences to a production of *The Merchant of Venice* unlike any ever seen before in this country. For once Irving had decided to embody a dignified Jew, he used all the theatrical elements at his command. He began by making Shylock clearly distinct from the Venetian society which surrounded him. Shylock's garb was that of a Levantine Jew, an alien in Venice, and therefore more saturated with Judaism than those of his religion who had rubbed shoulders with Europeans. The costume "suggested that Shylock kept his household and himself apart from Western custom." On his head was a tightly fitting black cap with a yellow bar on the front, suggesting a discriminatory racial badge.

Irving used his imaginative skills in stage management to further the sympathetic atmosphere. A memorable moment occurred at the end of the scene in which Shylock's daughter had run away with her gentile lover. The stage, depicting the street before Shylock's house, was momentarily filled with a group of gaily dressed masqueraders. The whirl of the crowd passing through provided a moment of striking contrast with the silence which followed, in the midst of which Shylock appeared over a Venetian bridge. When he knocked on his door for admission and no one answered, his realization of the deception became apparent. The curtain lowered on the picture of the still, lonely figure. Later, in the trial scene, Irving added a sympathetic touch. To the crowd of spectators at the trial, he added "a knot of eager and interested Jews, among whom the sentence condemning Shylock to deny his religion falls like a thunderbolt" [Laurence Irving, in his *Henry Irving: The Actor and His World*]. The use of this group and the "explosion of popular wrath against this body, which the result of the trial produces," were examples of Irving's intelligent use of action as commentary.

But the prime generator of sympathetic audience response was, of course, Irving's dignified portrayal of Shylock. The following description of his acting [in *Laurence Irving*] of the last moments of the trial scene is sufficient illustration of his innovative performance.

> The whole history of the Jewish race was illustrated in his expression at the bare mention of his turning Christian. At the loathed word (and Antonio purposely gave a long pause) Shylock, who could no longer speak, lifted his head slowly and inclined it backwards over his left shoulder. His eyelids, which hung heavily over his dimmed eyes, were open to their full and his long pleading gaze at Antonio showed how bitterly he felt the indignity. Then, as he slowly turned his head, he raised his eyes fervently; his lips murmured incoherent words as his whole body resumed a dreamy, motionless attitude.
>
> When Shylock grasped the severity of his sentence, his eyelids became heavy as though he was hardly able to lift them and his eyes became lustreless and vacant. The words "I am not well . . ." [IV. i. 396] were the plea of a doomed man to be allowed to leave the court and to die in utter loneliness. But Gratiano's ill-timed jibe governed Shylock's exit. He turned. Slowly and steadily the Jew scanned his tormentor from head to foot, his eyes resting on the Italian's face with concentrated scorn. The proud rejection of insult and injustice lit up his face for a moment, enough for the audience to feel a strange relief in knowing that, in that glance, Shylock had triumphed. He inclined his head slightly three times and took three steps toward the door of the court. (Irving had a mystical belief in threefold action.) As he reached the door and put out his hand toward it, he was seized with a crumpling convulsion. It was but a momentary weakness indicated with great subtlty. Then, drawing himself up to his full height once more, Shylock bent his gaze defiantly upon the court and stalked out.

The passage indicates that Irving's characterization was thoroughly modern, both in technique and intention. As an acted performance, Irving aimed at revealing the inner feelings of Shylock by the use of carefully selected external signs. In addition, the staging of the scene makes it clear that Irving was attempting to prevent the audience from feeling any sense of elation at the victory of the Christians; the presentation of Shylock as a dignified, deep-feeling human being is quite clear. Theatre critics in America agreed with the reviewer who wrote that Irving's rendering of the role of Shylock was "a more subdued one than any to which American play-goers have been accustomed and it is in many respects a bold departure from the established traditions of the stage." Some condemned Irving's untraditional performance. "An idealized Shylock," wrote one of them [Boston *Globe*, 13 December 1883], " . . . is as incongruous as a glorified Richard III or a saintly Iago. . . ." However, the major portion of critical opinion agreed with the New York writer [in *The Spirit of the*

Stage, 10 November 1883] who claimed that Irving's playing enabled Shylock to become "a natural and probable character, instead of a raving scene-chewer and impossible monstrosity."

In city after city, the humanizing of Shylock was recognized and applauded for its enlightening effect on audiences' perception of the famous stage Jew. In Philadelphia, it was noted [in *The Evening Bulletin,* 24 December 1895] that Irving's portrayal "shows the Jew as something more than the mere incarnation of avarice," and the reviewer found it possible to sympathize with Shylock "in the midst of persecution." A Brooklyn writer declared that the presentation "carried the sympathies of the auditors with the Jew, and revealed his judges fairly in the light of persecutors." And a Chicago reviewer [in the *Chicago Tribune,* 10 January 1884] stated that "the actor interprets the intrinsic dignity which Shakespeare, with the justice and unconsciousness of genius, gave to Shylock." Irving's playing of the trial scene impressed a Boston critic, because it was played "without artifice or bombast, but with a dignified and quiet intensity which was very touching" [Boston *Sunday Globe,* 14 January 1894]. These are, indeed, enlightened statements from the critics who for decades had endorsed, and even demanded, a venomous Shylock.

A late nineteenth-century Chicago journalist [in the *Tribune,* 10 January 1884], in an exaggerated estimate of the period's liberal attitude toward Jews, wrote the best paean to Irving's performance:

> It is a nineteenth century Shylock. It is a creation only possible to our age, which has pronounced its verdict against medieval cruelty and medieval blindness. Two hundred years ago the world would have rejected the impersonation which Irving gave last night. Today the world accepts it. The future will vindicate it.

The future did vindicate Irving's performance, if vindication was ever necessary, for his characterization of the role was the progenitor of the best Shylocks seen on our contemporary stages.

The Merchant of Venice was the most popular play in the Lyceum's American repertory, for it was the only production which Irving included on each of the eight tours of this country which his company made from 1883 to 1904. Frequently used as a replacement for productions which failed to attract audiences, the play always made money. Irving's Shylock, then, was a milestone for Americans, for not only was it performed in Boston, New York, Philadelphia, and Chicago, but also in Scranton, Toledo, Memphis, Omaha, and a host of other cities and towns. It was the role with which most Americans identified Irving, and people would frequently travel for miles to see the production for a second or third time. Though it would be a mistake to argue that Irving was responsible for any major sociological change in attitude toward Jews, it seems defensible that his widespread playing of his unique characterization helped to engender an attitude of sympathy and understanding for the stage Jew, where before there had been only scorn. Perhaps most importantly, Irving showed American actors that a Shylock based on higher motives than simple maliciousness could be a viable stage creation. (pp. 63-72)

Herbert W. Kline, "The Jew That Shakespeare Drew?" in American Jewish Archives, *Vol. XXIII, No. 1, April, 1971, pp. 63-72.*

Richard Foulkes   (essay date 1976)

[*Foulkes relates the manner in which Irving staged the Trial scene (Act IV, Scene i), in contrast to two of the very most lavish nineteenth-century productions of* The Merchant of Venice: *those by Charles Kean in 1858 and the Bancrofts in 1875. Irving's staging, Foulkes contends, reflected his emphasis on acting rather than pageantry.*]

For the mid-nineteenth-century actor-manager the enduring attractions of *The Merchant of Venice* were supplemented by the opportunities which it gave for the current fashion of lavish scenery. The two major London productions which preceded Henry Irving's in 1879, those of Charles Kean in 1858 and the Bancrofts in 1875, were more notable for their scenic than histrionic display. The tone is set by Kean's characteristic program note: "In the production of *The Merchant of Venice* it has been my object to combine with the poet's art a faithful representation of the picturesque city: to render it again palpable to the traveller who has actually gazed upon the seat of its departed glory; and, at the same time, to exhibit it to the student, who has never visited it." For the Bancrofts a visit to Venice with their scenic designer George Gordon in the late summer of 1874 was an essential preliminary to their production the following year: "Our ultimate object was to get to Venice, where we had arranged to meet our scenic artist at the beginning of September, to see what nooks and spots we best could choose for our proposed bold attempt to place *The Merchant of Venice* upon our little stage" [*Mr. and Mrs. Bancroft On and Off Stage Written by Themselves*]. Five years later, in the summer of 1879, Henry Irving visited Venice during his trip aboard the Baroness Burdett-Coutt's steamer "The Walrus," and he "explored the city, collecting prints and pictures for Hawes Craven with nothing more definite in his mind than a revival of *Othello* or perhaps *Venice Preserved*" [Laurence Irving, in his *Henry Irving*]. However on 8 October, a few weeks after his return to London, Irving broached the idea of a production of *The Merchant of Venice* to Stoker and Loveday: "I am going to do *The Merchant of Venice*. . . . I never contemplated doing the piece which did not ever appeal very much to me until when we were down in Morocco and the Levant. . . . When I saw the Jew in what seemed to be his own land and his own dress, Shylock became a different creature. I began to understand him; and now I want to play the part as soon as I can. I think I shall do it on the first of November" [Bram Stoker, in his *Personal Reminiscences of Henry Irving*].

The difference in emphasis is remarkable. Irving's inspiration came not from seeing bricks, mortar, and water, but from seeing people; his motivation was an urgent personal desire to act Shylock, not to mount a painstakingly researched historical pageant. Accordingly the Lyceum production was swiftly and inexpensively mounted in accordance with Irving's declared principles: "In producing 'The Merchant of Venice' I have endeavoured to avoid hampering the action of the piece with any unnecessary embellishment; but have tried not to omit any accessory which might heighten the effects" [Henry Irving, in his edition of *The Merchant of Venice*]. Small wonder that Ellen Terry, who had previously played Portia in the Bancroft production, which she regarded [in her "Scenery in Shakespeare's Plays"] as "from many points of view the most beautiful production with which I have ever been associated," should remark [in her *The Story of My Life*], "The Lyceum production of 'The Merchant of Venice' was not so strictly archaeological as the Bancrofts' had been, but it was very gravely beautiful and effective. If less attention was paid to details of costume and scenery the play itself was arranged and acted very attractively and always went with a swing." This represents a clear contrast with the Bancroft production which for all its scenic splendor was not a popular success.

The trial scene (IV. 1) is bound to be central to a production of *The Merchant of Venice* and managers and designers deliberated about the most appropriate setting for it. Kean recorded the source for his staging of the scene: "This scene represented the Sala dei Pregadi, or Hall of the Senators. . . . The authority for the six senators in red (in this scene) is taken from the picture at Hampton Court Palace, where the Doge of Venice, in state, is receiving Sir Henry Wootton, ambassador from James the First. The picture is by Odoardo Fialletti, better known as an engraver than a painter, and who was living at Venice when Sir Henry Wootton was ambassador there." A comparison between Fialletti's picture and Kean's designs in the Victoria and Albert Museum shows that his debt extended beyond the six senators to the total concept of the trial scene in his production. The nature of Kean's priorities is evident from his biographer's comment on the scene [J. W. Cole, in his *The Life and Theatrical Times of Charles Kean FSA*]: "The architecture and ornament are punctiliously preserved. . . . He has . . . succeeded in embodying the most impressive court of justice that has ever been subjected to the criticism of a theatrical audience."

The architect E. W. Godwin was archaeological adviser to the Bancrofts, and W. Moelwyn Merchant records [in his *Shakespeare and the Artist*] that Godwin's "first choice of the room in the Ducal Palace would have been the *Sala del Maggior Consiglio,* 'but as this hall measures no less than 154 by 74 feet, it is next to impossible to represent it in anything like the dignity of its true size on any stage other than exceptionally large ones.' He therefore chooses the *Sala dello Scrutinio.* . . ." However when the Bancrofts and George Gordon visited the palace they "saw plainly that the Sala della Bussola was the only one within our means to realise, and this room we decided should be accurately reproduced for the trial of Antonio and Portia's pleading on his behalf." Thus Godwin's plans were superseded by Gordon's.

Undoubtedly one of Charles Kean's major contributions to theatre design was his concept of diagonal staging, and as Godfrey Turner remarked in 1887 [in his "First Nights of My Young Days"]: "That manager's method of stage perspective has not been improved upon. However complicated and built-out the scenery might be, its place was always diagonal, which greatly favoured the effect of a procession." Diagonal staging was used most effectively in many of Kean's lavish productions, notably *King Richard II,* for the lists at Coventry and the interpolated episode of Richard's entry into London with its great procession. However, Kean's staging of the trial scene following Fialetti's picture was squared firmly on the center of the stage. In his plans for the trial scene Godwin wrote: "Considering all the circumstances of the case I again propose a diagonal set for this scene"; his plan was to place the Doge and Magnificos on a raised platform stage right with Shylock, Portia, and Antonio grouped around a table beneath them and with "the general public . . . indicated by very small groups near the entrances EE, especially at that near N."

Percy Fitzgerald [in his *Henry Irving*] recorded the effect of Irving's setting for the trial scene: "But the Court scene, with its ceiling painted in the Verrio style, its portraits of Doges, the crimson walls with gilt carvings, and the admirable arrangements of the throne, etc., surely for taste, contrivance, and effect has never been matched. The work of the whole is virtually done by the painting, not by built-up structures." By relying on painting for his effect Irving was using a simpler and less expensive method than the architecturally based sets used by Kean and Bancroft and planned by Godwin. However, the plan for the trial scene preserved in Irving's promptbook shows a striking similarity to Godwin's. The staging is diagonal and incorporates the same three essentials: (1) the Doge's throne (stage left instead of stage right), (2) the table for Portia and Shylock, significantly more central in Irving's plan, and (3) the crowds present in both plans, but in Irving's placed at the rear of the stage where they would not distract attention from the principals. By 1879 Godwin and Ellen Terry (Irving's Portia) were no longer living together and there is no evidence that he was involved in the production, though he was to have a hand in *The Cup* in 1881. Nevertheless, the theatrical world of London in the 1870s was sufficiently small to allow the possibility that Irving was aware of Godwin's plans, particularly in view of Ellen Terry's close involvement with both men. It is through Ellen Terry that further evidence about Irving's staging of the trial scene can be traced. Among the numerous, but on the whole not very informative, promptbooks for *The Merchant of Venice* at Smallhythe, one contains the black and white reproduction of a picture which can be identified as Paris Bordone's *Fisherman handing the ring to the Doge Grandenigo,* the original of which is in the Academy, Venice. A comparison between the picture and Irving's setting plan reveals an extremely close resemblance. The Doge is situated on the right of the picture as he was from the audience's viewpoint on the Lyceum stage, and he and the Magnificos who flank him (four on each side in the picture and on stage) are raised on a platform reached by a short flight of steps. Unlike the archaeologically minded Kean and Bancroft, Irving gave no source for his designs and indeed it is unlikely, at this stage in his career at least, that he would have followed a model rigidly. Bram Stoker records that when Irving broached the idea of producing *The Merchant of Venice* he had already formulated his ideas for the production, and Stoker refers to Irving's proposal for the staging of the "Casket" scene. More than likely Bordone's painting was among the prints and drawings which Irving collected for Hawes Craven during his visit to Venice, even if the actor brought it home only in his mind's eye.

As Irving himself testified, the inspiration which he gained from his visit to Venice and the Levant was not focused on architecture and archaeology, but on acting Shylock; and, invariably, the scenery was an accompaniment to the acting, not an end in itself as it tended to be for Kean. Consequently, the design for the trial scene fulfilled the major function of centering the action on Shylock, who was positioned at or near the table which occupied the center of the stage. The Doge was situated in accordance with *his* importance in the play and in such a way as to ensure that Shylock (and indeed Portia) did not have his back to the audience when addressing the judges. Lyceum audiences did not pay to see Henry Irving's back. The crowning glory of Irving's Shylock is his exit: "In the opinion of the present writer [*The Spectator,* 8 November 1879], his Shylock is Mr. Irving's finest performance, and his final exit its best point. The quiet shrug, the glance of ineffable, unfathomable contempt at the exulting booby Gratiano, who, having got hold of a good joke, worries it like a puppy with a bone, the expression of defeat in every limb and feature, the deep, gasping sigh, as he passes slowly

out, and the crowd rush from the court to hoot and howl at him outside, make up an effort which must be seen to be comprehended." For such an exit, the climax of Irving's performance as Shylock, nothing less than the maximum width of the stage would suffice, and Irving made full use of every inch of it. From *The Bells* onwards Irving's instinct for entrances and exits was unfailing, and three years after *The Merchant of Venice* he was to insist on *going down* into a vault for the tomb scene in *Romeo and Juliet,* with the result that his designers provided him with two flights of steps down which to make his entrance. In the trial scene W. Cuthbert's design performed the primary function of setting "the Governor's" Shylock to advantage. As Edward Gordon Craig, son of Godwin and protégé of Irving, wrote [in his *Henry Irving*]: "He set out not to produce a play . . . but to act one. Irving was an actor, and an actor only: all he did and all he thought, rightly or wrongly, was inspired or done as an actor." (pp. 312-17)

Richard Foulkes, "The Staging of the Trial Scene in Irving's 'The Merchant of Venice'," in Educational Theatre Journal, *Vol. 28, No. 3, October, 1976, pp. 312-17.*

Edward M. Moore (essay date 1976)

[*Moore asserts that Irving took considerable liberties with Shakespeare's text of* The Merchant of Venice *in order to convert the play into a melodrama focusing on his own virtuouso performance as a sympathetic, heroic figure.*]

Henry Irving was by far the most celebrated actor during the last quarter of the nineteenth century. He had few rivals, and literally none in Britain. But I believe no other actor has caused such extensive and continual controversy regarding his genius. From the beginning of his triumph, shortly after he joined the company of Hezekiah Bateman at the Lyceum in 1871, until long after his death in 1905, his devotees claimed for him a place among the greats of the past: Alleyn, Burbage, Betterton, Garrick, Edmund Kean; indeed, the claim is still occasionally heard today. No less a man of the theater than Gordon Craig wrote [in his *Henry Irving*], twenty-five years after Irving's death, "I have never known of, or seen, or heard of, a greater actor than was Irving." Certainly Irving made the Lyceum the most celebrated theater in England, and not even his severest critics denied his status as the head of his profession. He was the first actor in history to be knighted, and he was given burial in Westminster Abbey. And yet, the best critics of the day were from the first almost unanimous in their condemnation of his acting, and, after he took over the management of the Lyceum in 1878, of his productions. With none of the other "greats" of the stage was there any such distinguished chorus of dissent. A glance at the list of parts Irving performed and plays he produced reveals that he did nothing—absolutely nothing—for contemporary drama. His greatest successes (aside from Hamlet, Shylock, and Benedick) were *The Bells, Charles I, Louis XI, Eugene Aram,* and later *Faust, Dante, King Arthur,* and finally Tennyson's *Becket.* Only the last gives either Irving or Victorian drama any credit, and even the Poet Laureate's noble effort is of questionable merit; along with the other plays it died with Irving. One should remember that England—indeed all Europe—was undergoing a genuine movement both in dramatic literature and in its production precisely during the height of Irving's career. With this movement he had nothing to do, and the fact is even more striking in view of his absolute pre-eminence as actor and manager.

When one looks at his Shakespearean productions, Irving's services to the stage are, if anything, even more discreditable. In his twenty-three years as chief actor and sole manager of the most prominent theater in England, he produced twelve of Shakespeare's plays. Samuel Phelps, a generation earlier, had produced thirty-one in eighteen years at Sadler's Wells—more, in fact, than could be seen anywhere in London during Irving's career. I will have something to say about almost all of Irving's Shakespearean productions, and will consider a few of them in detail. I think it will become apparent that students of Shakespeare have little reason to be grateful for what Irving *did* for Shakespeare, and may very well wish he had produced fewer than twelve of his plays. (pp. 195-96)

Irving produced *Macbeth* in 1875, *Othello* in 1876 (neither was successful), and, in the fall of 1879, *The Merchant of Venice,* by all accounts his most famous Shakespearean performance (if not production). In London, the provinces, and America, Irving played Shylock over one thousand times; and, according to his grandson [Laurence Irving, in his *Henry Irving: the Actor and his World*], when Irving's Lyceum was gone, he told a group of friends in 1902: "Looking back on my life's work and attempting—in all humility—to appraise it, I feel certain of one thing—mine is the only great Shylock."

But Irving's Shylock was hardly Shakespeare's. Irving made the whole play revolve around the character he played; indeed, in the spring of 1879 he even cut out the entire last act in order to play *Iolanthe* in the same billing, an action that brought a fiery denunciation from F. J. Furnivall, among others. Irving's impersonation of Shylock climaxed a nineteenth-century tradition (which had roots in the eighteenth) of playing Shylock for all the pathos, justified resentment, and nobility that could be imposed upon Shakespeare's Jew. A definite development in this direction can be traced from George Frederick Cooke's performance in 1803, through Kean's in 1814, Macready's in 1823, and Charles Kean's in 1858; but Irving climaxed it. According to William Winter, Irving purposely and consciously distorted the character and the play in order to gain his own effects; Winter says [in his *Shakespeare on the Stage*] that Irving told him, "Shylock is a bloody-minded monster,—but you musn't play him so, if you wish to succeed; you must get some sympathy with him." The statement is revealing in making clear Irving's approach to Shakespeare (as well as to any other playwright); he cared nothing about realizing a play as written, but only about making his effects; and as splendid as these no doubt were, most of us would rather have Shakespeare's.

In *The Merchant of Venice,* Irving's attitude led him to play so directly against the text that, after Shylock's outburst in III, i, "I would my daughter were dead at my foot," *etc.* (lines 88ff.), Irving paused, hid his face in his hands, and murmured an anguished "No, no, no, no, no!" and in the subsequent self-pitying lines on his losses, he opened his robe and smote himself continually, slowly, and heavily on his bare breast. An examination of his studybook reveals that he also cut most of Shylock's ravings about the loss of his ducats, though not, of course, of his daughter. He delivered the speech about Jacob (I, iii, 71ff.) "in a reverential fervor," betraying "his conviction that whatever Jacob did was right and just" [Laurence Irving]. And there was the celebrated effect imported from *Rigoletto*: after Jessica's elopement, which took place

with a group of Venetians in a gondola singing a barcarolle, several sets of masqueraders rushed by and the curtain fell; there was a moment of silence; the curtain then rose on Shylock silently walking in the moonlight across the bridge and deserted streets to his home. Originally, the curtain fell as he reached his door, later only after he had knocked several times. This bit of business caught on and was carried further and further by Irving's imitators. The sympathetic effect here is as contrary to the impression of Shakespeare's play as is the pictorial effect to his dramaturgy: this is not an occasion when the audience's attention should be focussed on Shylock's grief.

The trial scene was the climax of the play, but was presented as a victory for Shylock. Irving introduced a crowd of Jews as attendants to Shylock, primarily to emphasize the Jewish persecution theme, which he exploited. Dutton Cook says [in his *Nights of the Play*] of Irving's Shylock, "if he avenges private injuries, he also represents a nation seeking atonement for centuries of wrong"; consequently, his entourage received the sentence that Shylock must deny his religion "like a thunderbolt." Shylock acted with dignity and determination throughout. The final touch was added to the performance at his exit. Here is the description by Irving's grandson:

> At the end of Portia's verdict he dropped the scales and stood as though mesmerized; when at last he spoke his voice was heavy and thick, though there was still the trace of a sneer in it. . . . Shakespeare makes Shylock accept the situation very suddenly, but Irving managed to suggest that Shylock had accepted it with only half his mind—that of the usurer. The other half was still stunned. . . . His last words came with difficulty and were spoken with unutterable sadness.

When he heard that he must become a Christian,

> his lips murmured incoherent words as his whole body resumed a dreamy, motionless attitude. When Shylock grasped the severity of his sentence, his eyelids became heavy as though he was hardly able to lift them and his eyes became lustreless and vacant. The words "I am not well . . ." were the plea of a doomed man to be allowed to leave the court and to die in utter loneliness. But Gratiano's ill-timed jibe governed Shylock's exit. He turned. Slowly and steadily the Jew scanned his tormentor from head to foot, his eyes resting on the Italian's face with concentrated scorn. The proud rejection of insult and injustice lit up his face for a moment, enough for the audience to feel a strange relief in knowing that, in that glance, Shylock had triumphed. . . . As he reached the door and put out his hand towards it, he was seized with a crumpling convulsion. It was but a momentary weakness indicated with great subtlety. Then, drawing himself up to his full height once more, Shylock bent his gaze defiantly upon the court and stalked out.

Even Ellen Terry [in her *The Story of My Life*] disapproved of Irving's Shylock in this scene, and for very good reasons:

> I had considered, and still am of the same mind, that Portia in the trial scene ought to be very *quiet.* I saw extraordinary effect in this quietness. But as Henry's Shylock was quiet, I had to give it up. His heroic saint was splendid, but it wasn't good for Portia.

The cutting of the play was typically Irvingesque. There was actually less of Shakespeare's text than in either of the two most scenically lavish and textually spare productions before him, Charles Kean's in 1858 and the Bancrofts' in 1875. Passages—indeed, whole scenes—which tended to discredit Shylock were simply cut out, such as Jessica's conversation with Launcelot (II, iii) and the scene between Jessica, Lorenzo, and Launcelot after Portia leaves Belmont (III, v). The Prince of Arragon was not in the play at all, the first scene with Morocco was omitted (though part of his speech there was given in the second), and over seventy lines of Bassanio's speech in choosing the casket were cut—this whole scene (III, ii) being reduced by over one-third. These cuts also reduced the shifting from Venice to Belmont and back by four times, a necessity with elaborate scenery, though, as with *Hamlet,* this production was not as grandiose as later ones were to be.

I think the charge that Irving made Shakespeare's plays into melodramatic virtuoso pieces for himself—even before he became elaborately scenic—is substantiated by the examination of . . . *The Merchant of Venice.* He used the plays to excite and arouse emotion in an audience by displays of passion and pathos, but had no interest in attempting to resolve the emotions he was so accomplished in arousing; and it is precisely the resolution of emotion that Shakespeare's plays so marvellously effect. Even Clement Scott, Irving's most influential devotee, in an early review speaks of "an irresistible but still unhealthy excitement" that characterizes his acting. That Irving possessed a magnetic stage presence is undeniable, and that he perfected a technique appropriate to arousing certain emotions to the highest possible pitch is no less deniable. But this effect was largely one of mannerisms—his peculiar gait and voice were most frequently mentioned—and finely executed bits of "business." Coquelin [in his *The Art of Acting*] said of him: "Irving cannot avoid seeking after the picturesque even in his slightest movement," and William Archer [in his *Henry Irving, Actor and Manager: A Critical Study*] talks of his "feverish anxiety to fill up with 'business' every moment he is on stage." Gordon Craig's long and brilliant description [in his *Henry Irving*] of his Mathias demonstrates this judgment. Henry A. Clapp, in a well thought-out article [in his *Reminiscences of a Dramatic Critic*]—favorable to Irving, but conscious of his faults—sums up Irving's qualities:

> Mr. Irving's style has in no respect the sustained quality; it is, so to speak, altogether staccato; there are no sweeps or long strokes in it, but everything is accomplished by a series of light, disconnected touches or dabs, the total effect of which, when the subject is not too lofty, is agreeable and harmonious.

In addition to an ability to deliver blank verse, Shakespeare calls precisely for the "sustained quality," broad strokes, and overall conception and presentation, contrasts of character with character and scene with scene to make a total impression. All of this was foreign to Irving's methods; he tended to make any play revolve around himself, to fill any bare sketch of a character with his own "noble melancholy." (pp. 201-04)

> Edward M. Moore, "Henry Irving's Shakespearian Productions," *in* Theatre Survey, *Vol. XVII, No. 2, November, 1976, pp. 195-216.*

PRODUCTION:

Theodore Komisarjevsky • Stratford-upon-Avon • 1932

BACKGROUND:

Komisarjevsky was a Venetian-born Russian producer and director of plays and operas who journeyed to England following the Russian Revolution. In the early 1930s, he was invited to serve as guest director at Stratford, where he remained for several years. During his tenure, he produced six Shakespearean plays, which were at first somewhat skeptically received and controversial, but also innovative. Komisarjevsky sought to restore and emphasize the perspective of romantic comedy in *A Midsummer Night's Dream,* in part through sheer theatricality. To achieve this, he opened the production with a masque; designed extravagant sets and "fantasticated" the casket scenes; restored the text virtually to its original, uncut form; and observed the Shakespearean scene order. He also divested Shylock, played by Randle Ayrton, of some of the sympathetic traits attributed to the character by many nineteenth-century interpreters of the role and turned Venice into a carnival. Ayrton's unsentimentalized, villainous Shylock was generally well-received by the critics. Fabia Drake played Portia, Wilfrid Walter played Antonio, and Eric Lee performed Bassanio.

COMMENTARY:

The Times, London   (review date 26 July 1932)

[*The* Times *reviewer avers that Komisarjevsky's production, although striking, was "reckless and affected"; further, that the spectacle, including the "fantasticated" casket-plot, became monotonous. Ayrton's unsentimental portrayal of Shylock earned the critic's approbation, as did Drake's Portia, "played . . . with strength and charm."*]

It is possible that an Elizabethan finding himself in the Memorial Theatre tonight would have recognized in Mr. Randle Ayrton's Shylock the Jew he had been accustomed to see played at the Globe. If he retained his taste for a little Jew-baiting he might have laughed uproariously at the despairing rage of the crafty alien usurer hoist with his own petard. Moral sensibility does not lend itself to such laughter, but we may confess that the hardening process so skilfully applied by the actors to our hearts is good for the play. Since we are not asked to regard Shylock as a wholly tragic, half-heroic character, we can the more easily overlook the vital flaw in characterization which opposes to revengeful cruelty so little of Christian charity. A hatred so personal and so much like bestial savagery must be checked, we feel, if not by law, then by quibbles.

Mr. Ayrton is careful not to let the avoidance of modern sentimentalism take him too far in the other direction. His Shylock is a great deal more than the easy butt for Elizabethan Christians that may have been in Shakespeare's mind when he started on the play. He labours to impress on us Shylock's immense intellectual superiority and to convey Shakespeare's very Shakespearian divination that the Jew is also a human being, but he refrains deliberately from giving the character credit for an impersonal desire to be revenged on the oppressor of his race. Only once does this Shylock claim the tragic dignity which belongs to a more impersonal hatred, and that is when he pleads the cause of a common humanity to Salario and Salarino, wasting upon those exquisites his superb burst of passionate logic. For the rest of the play he is moved by a hatred that is beyond our sympathy. We know that he has at least three good reasons for loathing Antonio, but Mr. Ayrton persuades us that beneath these motives there is something vulpine and instinctive. Rightly, he lets himself be dismissed from the Court without the least straining after heroic gesture, making an exit that well befits the crushed and sordid usurer who, once persuaded that the law has played him false, would now be only too content to take his three thousand ducats and let the Christian go. In his chief outline, then, Mr. Ayrton's conception of the part wins its way with us; and before the end of the run the impression of subtlety and intellectual power for which he labours will doubtless be firmer.

Mr. Theodore Komisarjevsky is the first producer to be invited to the new theatre, and, perhaps because he has fallen too much in love at first sight with the machinery, the production, though striking, is reckless and affected. The masque with which he chooses to open the play is in itself a charming thing. Certainly it sets before us the histrionic Venice of the untravelled Elizabethan, a place where youth may flaunt itself under the sparkling lights of gaiety, frivolity, and idleness, and where even trade has about it the glamour of the East. But the spectacle does work which Salario and Salarino are later to do better in words, and there is something to be said, as Shakespeare thought, for beginning with strict realism the telling of stories as incredible as the stories of the pound of flesh and the caskets. Mr. Komisarjevsky has frankly fantasticated the story of the caskets, beginning each episode with a *tableau vivant* which has a dainty porcelain grace, and is well enough until the *tableau* leaves the level of the stage and comes to rest on a roof garden. The purpose of this device is to show us the shining, desirable Portia poised on high, while her unwelcome suitors blunderingly woo her on a lower level, and to let her descend later to Bassanio's level. The effect of this is hardly worth the disturbance of our vision while acting is taking place on the higher stage.

The costumes are of no period and can scarcely be said to attain to any definite unity. No curtains are lowered between the scenes, and the audience has the spectacle of massive scenes rising and falling and wheeling themselves together in sections, a spectacle which becomes somewhat monotonous, while the sudden appearances of Jessica and Gobbo on the top of high towers outside the proscenium are definitely irritating. Miss Fabia Drake played Portia with strength and charm, though she would be well advised to drop her comic make-up in the court scene. Mr. Eric Lee made a Bassanio we could not utterly despise, and there were many neat minor sketches.

A review of "The Merchant of Venice," in The Times, *London, July 26, 1932, p. 10.*

Ivor Brown   (review date 31 July 1932)

[*Brown was a British author, dramatic critic, and editor. As a critic, he regularly contributed to such periodicals as the* Guardian, *the* Saturday Review, *the* Observer, Sketch, *and* Punch. *His works include* Shakespeare in His Time *(1960),* Shakespeare and His World *(1964), and* Shakespeare and the Actors *(1970). In the review below, Brown concedes that* The Merchant of Venice *is not a great play, but he praises Komisarjevsky for the imagination and inspiration to make an extended*

revel of Shakespeare's drama. The critic commends the "fantastication" of the casket-scenes. Ayrton's "strong, clear, sardonic, and never sentimentalized" performance as Shylock, and Drake's "enchanting" Portia. "There are mistakes," Brown writes, "such as over-employment of the movable-stages. But there is invention, and it is the invention of a true theatrical artist."]

The world of the theatre is so often embittered with jealousies that one is the more pleasantly impressed by magnanimous co-operations. It is not every producer who welcomes a colleague to his particular stage, especially when that colleague is a man of genius. Mr. Bridges Adams has done finely to insist on broadening the Stratford basis, finely and wisely. For Stratford, with its notable new theatre, must become a national institution as well as continuing to guard its local tradition. Mr. Adams's policy of hospitality for all creative and original minds is generous and will, I am sure, be rewarded. To call in Mr. Komisarjevsky was a brave beginning: true, his *King Lear* at Oxford had proved him a great Shakespearean director, but to entrust *The Merchant* to his hand was certainly to invite a violent cleavage with tradition in the very town where authority is likely to be strongest and Bensonian memories abound. Those who want an endless repetition of the old way may be shocked. Mr. Bridges Adams knows that well enough. But he believes in the therapeutic value of discreet upheavals. Mr. Komisarjevsky has obliged him, and us, by making the upheaval witty and gracious. There are mistakes, such as over-employment of the movable stages. But there is invention, and it is the invention of a true theatrical artist. There are two contemporary fashions in Shakespearean production. One is to say "This play is not dead ritual. It is about actual human beings, whose problems are your own. To drive that into minds deadened by the class-room, we shall dress our Hamlet as you are dressed, the more easily to make you see your own image." The other is to say: "This play is no longer acceptable as a tale to be believed. We do not ask your rational attention. But it is a gorgeous fairy-story, and we shall fancy-dress it for your delight." One method suits one play, one another. Mr. Komisarjevsky has fancy-dressed *The Merchant of Venice.* His production has no period but that of eternal masquerade. It opens and closes with a little masque of pierrots whose false noses bid us sniff a moonshine aroma. Shylock is properly left in his true Elizabethan habit; he is a wicked old scamp to be detested of the audience, a scamp with drollery inherent, but meriting all the punishment that comes his way. Mr. Randle Ayrton's performance is strong, clear, sardonic, and never sentimentalised or expanded with irrelevant goings-on. Here the production stays properly on earth; for the rest, it skips and takes the air of fancy. It draws Portia from the china-shop and Morocco, a perfect golliwog, from the toy-shop. And why not? Who in these days will endure without a yawn a solemn rendering of the casket-nonsense? The producer has every right to fantasticate to the top of his bent.

So what might be a moribund ritual of Bardolatry becomes a revel, charioted on sliding glimpses of Venetian bridges and skied in a Belmont loggia that rises on a lift. "First floor, caskets. Second floor, roof garden." There are even casements further flung for Jessica, and Gobbo, a zany out of Harlequin's world, makes perilous flight from home by way of a rope. Let it be said at once that this is a "take it or leave it" production. If you take the play seriously, be warned. If it seems to you, as it does to me, one of the least attractive reaches of the canon, too brutal here, too silly there, then there is real delight in this translation of it to a totally unreal and timeless world of Merry Andrews and musical dolls dancing in the finery of any age, so it be fine. There are weaknesses, as I said. The sliding scenery slides slowly and too often, and there is not enough obeisance to the lyrical beauty of the words. But then Shakespeare made a tactical error in giving his most glorious lines to Lorenzo, a small part. The company, for the most part, break tradition with judgment. Miss Fabia Drake's Portia is enchanting, persuading us alike of the great lady's wit and warmth, yet always gracing the artificial picture which Mr. Komisarjevsky has so cunningly composed. There is a fine spirit, too, in Mr. Isham's Gratiano and Miss Coxhead's Nerissa, while the Gobbos mitigate the dullness of their parts with ample antics from the world of Pantaloon. This production may be said to merge titles. "The Merchant, or What You Will." For my part, it is as I like it, but then I never did much like *The Merchant*.

> *Ivor Brown, in a review of "The Merchant of Venice," in* The Observer, *July 31, 1932, p. 7.*

Ralph Berry   (essay date 1983)

[*Berry chronicles Theodore Komisarjevsky's years at Stratford, England, when he served as guest director for several Shakespearean productions, including* The Merchant of Venice. *According to Berry, Komisarjevsky's* Merchant *was noteworthy for its theatricality, extravagant sets, a "virtually uncut text" faithful to the Shakespearean scene order, an opening masque,*

and its overall interpretation of the work as a romantic comedy.]

'I am not in the least traditional,' said Theodore Komisarjevsky [in an interview with *The Daily Telegraph*, 26 July 1932] in his motto-statement to the press shortly before the opening of his first Stratford production. This was no other than the truth, and Komisarjevsky went on to illustrate it in six remarkable productions at the Shakespeare Memorial Theatre, from 1932 to 1939. They amused, astonished, and outraged. They gave the Theatre what international distinction it possessed during an otherwise lean period. They anticipated much of what has come to be regarded as normal, on today's stage. Even so, Komisarjevsky's seven seasons at Stratford have until recently been thought of as the work of a brilliant prankster, a professional *enfant terrible*. It is time to review as a whole Komisarjevsky's work at Stratford.

To begin with, the Stratford seasons contain almost all of Komisarjevsky's Shakespearian work on the English-speaking stage. His *King Lear* at Oxford in 1927 (with Randle Ayrton as Lear) was a pilot for the Stratford *Lear* of 1936. The notorious *Antony and Cleopatra* (New Theatre, 1936) was his only Shakespearian production of the 1930s in London. There is a late appendix, which I shall deal with in its place. Otherwise, there is nothing of substance; and Komisarjevsky was generally known as a director of modern plays, above all as a master of Chekhov. It is in that capacity that

Theodore Komisarjevsky and Lesley Blanch's setting for Komisarjevsky's 1932 production.

Gielgud praises him highly in his memoirs. When Komisarjevsky came to direct *The Merchant of Venice* at Stratford in 1932, he was a month short of his fiftieth birthday: his reputation was already made, almost entirely outside Shakespeare.

That *Merchant of Venice,* and the productions that followed, saw Komisarjevsky always in the same capacity: he was a guest director. He had no institutional standing, though his annual invitation was recurring after 1934. He was in the first instance invited by the Memorial Theatre's director, W. Bridges-Adams. After Bridges-Adams resigned, in 1934, his successor, Ben Iden Payne, continued to invite Komisarjevsky. However, Sally Beauman states [in her *The Royal Shakespeare Company: A History of Ten Decades*] that 'his continuing presence at Stratford was due to the fact that Archie [Sir Archibald Flower, Chairman of the Board of Governors], and not Iden Payne, championed him. Archie appreciated the fact that Komisarjevsky productions attracted publicity and sold tickets.' It is a fascinating alliance, the autocrat and the revolutionary. Later in the 1930s, Sir Archibald must have seen Komisarjevsky as a shield against the criticisms increasingly levelled at the SMT. There, at least, was a symbol of modernity and innovation. And in box-office terms, Komisarjevsky never failed.

If Komisarjevsky's status as guest director remained constant, so did his role. Throughout the decade he remained an *enfant terrible* and foe to the traditional. He gave enormous offence to the traditionalists, few pains being comparable to the violation of a fixed idea. The Stratford theatre records are studded with letters to the local press and reviews from the less wary of critics, which after some wrenchingly reluctant tribute to Komisarjevsky's artistry ask *'But is it Shakespeare?'* The rhetorical identification of Shakespeare, and a certain way of playing him, is a ploy of long standing. As against this order of pain, Komisarjevsky gave great pleasure. Four of his productions were comedies, all were spectacular. How influential they were is now emerging. No less than Peter Brook has acknowledged the ancestry, if not the paternity, of Komisarjevsky: *'Titus Andronicus* was a *show;* it descended in an unbroken line from the work of Komisarjevsky.'* There are other parallels between Komisarjevsky's work, and that of the post-war directors.

The new Shakespeare Memorial Theatre, built after the old theatre was destroyed by fire, opened in 1932; and the stage machinery that came with it ravished Komisarjevsky. His sets for *The Merchant of Venice* made delighted use of a chance for extravagant artificiality. Venice was a city of leaning towers and crooked houses, which split down the middle for the Belmont scenes. The pillar topped by the Lion of St Mark's departed stage right, while the Bridge of Sighs exited stage left. From the depths emerged the Belmont loggia, Portia and co. in tableau positions, rather in the style of the old cinema organ. Ivor Brown was reminded of a department store lift, 'First floor, caskets. Second floor, roof garden.' The sliding of Venice to and from the wings grew a little tedious to many spectators, who complained that illusion was wantonly destroyed. But Komisarjevsky wished to sustain the note of unabashed theatricality. And this was necessary, for he was bent on overthrowing the Irving / Benson / Tree model of the play, which still held sway at Stratford, that of *The Merchant of Venice* as a quasi-tragedy. As Komisarjevsky saw it, the play was a romantic comedy.

Hence the opening, a masque of grotesque black and white pierrots to the music of Bach's Toccata and Fugue in D

Minor. They were shooed away by Launcelot Gobbo as Harlequin, and the play proper began. The *commedia dell'arte* touches were extended to Old Gobbo, as Pantaloon, and the Prince of Morocco as a golliwog. Komisarjevsky made further use of masks in the court scene: 'I shall try to bring out the power of that scene by having all the senators of the Doge's court sitting round in a uniform dress, their faces covered by uniform masks. Not a human face will be visible but Portia's, and in the background there will be painted a shadowy ensemble of the court crowd—the sort of people who gloat over sensations in our present-day courts. The *commedia* had the last word, for 'at the end . . . it is Harlequin Gobbo who makes the final exit, yawning and stretching in relief that his labours are over'. None of your alienated Antonios left alone on stage here.

This was a carnival Venice, the revellers ('fast, bright young people like the crowd we have in London today') attired in Venetian Renaissance garb with monstrous ruffs, by no means the setting for a major social issue or a human problem *à clef.* The casket scenes were treated with heartless vivacity, Nerissa shamelessly leading on Bassanio with the emphasized rhymes of 'Tell me where is fancy *bred* . . .' [III. ii. 63]. It follows that Shylock could not dominate the production. 'I shall not have a sympathetic Shylock. The point of Shylock is revenge, and revenge can never be sympathetic.' The reviewers took, with some surprise, to the astringent and unsentimentalized Shylock of Randle Ayrton. He seemed to them a Shylock such as the Elizabethans might have perceived, an old rascal who got his deserts.

The reviewers made little, however, of a feature that looked to the future. Komisarjevsky played a virtually uncut text. A few lines in Shylock's court speech, the bagpipe-urine reference, went (presumably a minor Bowdlerization). There are trifling deletions at 2.2.121-6; 3.1.18; 3.2.72; and 5.1.32-3. Otherwise, Komisarjevsky followed the text meticulously. Moreover, he followed the Shakespearian scene order. Since the prompt-book is a palimpsest—it was used originally for the 1929 production at Stratford—one can see through the erasures that he reduced the number of indicated scenes from eighteen to fifteen. This was a fluid, speeded-up version; and Komisarjevsky allowed a single interval only. Of course, he played some tricks with inflections. One reviewer noted that Morocco, upon finding he had chosen the wrong casket, intoned 'O hell! What have we here?' in the manner of a motorist who had burst a tyre. But all the fantastications were created out of a text that was itself untouched. That should be remembered, as we contemplate Komisarjevsky's dream-Venice, with its sprightly and inventive stagecraft, inexhaustible high spirits, and continuous delight in its own artifice. The reviewers, with varying degrees of delight and regret, acknowledged the theatrical virtuosity that had transformed a stereotype. And Komisarjevsky had a mere ten days to rehearse it. (pp. 73-5)

Ralph Berry, "Komisarjevsky at Stratford-upon-Avon," in Shakespeare Survey: An Annual Survey of Shakespearian Study and Production, *Vol. 36, 1983, pp. 73-84.*

PRODUCTION:

Michael Redgrave and Peggy Ashcroft • Stratford-upon-Avon • 1953

BACKGROUND:

Critical appraisals of the various performances in Denis Carey's Stratford production were quite divided, although critics were almost unanimous in finding fault in the direction and disparaging the stale, conventional, fairy-tale interpretation; the flimsy, second-rate scenery; and the improbable characterization. Michael Redgrave played Shylock as a raging, spiteful character who was compelling when enraged but who failed to convey Shylock's guile. According to Kenneth Tynan, Redgrave was unable to "fuse the villainy of the part with its sardonic comedy." As for the production's Portia, Tynan affirms that the "jewel of the evening is Peggy Ashcroft's Portia," although at least one critic felt her portrayal lacked the character's "necessary hardness." Harry Andrews played Antonio, Tony Britton played Bassanio, and Hutchinson Scott designed the sets.

COMMENTARY:

Kenneth Tynan   (review date 1953)

[*Tynan was a prolific dramatic critic and author whose reviews appeared over three decades in the* Spectator, *the* Observer, *and the* New Yorker. *Laurence Olivier appointed Tynan the first literary manager of the British National Theatre in 1963, with which he remained affiliated until 1973. In the review below, Tynan avers that Redgrave's performance appeared forced and overplayed. The critic contends that this Shylock "simply could not fuse the villainy of the part with its sardonic comedy." The highlight of this awkwardly staged production, Tynan states, was Ashcroft's Portia.*]

Whenever I see *The Merchant of Venice,* I while away the blanker bits of verse by trying to pull the play together in my mind. Does Shylock stand for the Old Testament (an eye for an eye, etc.) and Portia for the New (mercy, etc.)? And if so, what does that make Antonio, the shipping magnate whose bond unites the two plots? Does he represent the spirit of Protestantism? These metaphysical hares chase each other round and round; and when I have done, the play remains the curate's egg it always was. Or, rather, the rabbi's egg, because so much depends on Shylock. Which brings us to the Problem of Michael Redgrave, now, as always, at the turning-point of his career.

The difficulty about judging this actor is that I have to abandon all my standards of great acting (which include relaxation and effortless command) and start all over again. There is, you see, a gulf fixed between good and great performances; but a bridge spans it, over which you may stroll if your visa is in order. Mr. Redgrave, ignoring this, always chooses the hard way. He dives into the torrent and tries to swim across, usually sinking within sight of the shore. Olivier pole-vaults over in a single animal leap; Gielgud, seizing a parasol, crosses by tight-rope; Redgrave alone must battle it out with the current. The ensuing spectacle is never dull, but it can be very painful to watch.

His conception of Shylock is highly intelligent—a major prophet with a German accent, a touch of asthma, and lightning playing round his head. But who cares for conceptions? It is the execution that counts. And here Mr. Redgrave's smash-and-grab methods tell against him. His performance is a prolonged wrestling match with Shylock, each speech being floored with a tremendous, vein-bursting thump; the process also involves his making a noise like a death-rattle whenever he inhales, and spitting visibly whenever he strikes a "p" or a "b."

Some things he did superbly. At the end of the court scene, even after Portia had warned him that to take the pound of flesh would expose him to the death penalty, you felt that this cheated tyrant would be maniac enough to hang the consequences and start carving. There were also hints that Mr. Redgrave did not deny Shylock a sense of humour: he discovered a sensational new pun in his delivery of the speech about "water-rats" and "pi-rates." But he simply could not fuse the villainy of the part with its sardonic comedy. And I begin to think that no English player ever will. It needs a Continental actor to switch from fun to ferocity in a split second: Englishmen take at least half a minute to change gear. And when they are playing in their high-tragedy manner, as Mr. Redgrave is, they find it practically impossible to change gear at all.

Now, Shylock is a proud and successful financier with a chip on his shoulder; he is not an abject slave bearing a yoke of lead. Mr. Redgrave cringes and crumples every time Antonio opens his mouth—you would think he had never seen a Christian before. He should, of course, outsmile the lot of them. Like the other Shakespearean rogues, Richard III, Iago, and Claudius, Shylock must wear a cloak of charm. Even Antonio describes him as "kind," and the bond must

Michael Redgrave as Shylock.

seem to be what Shylock calls it, "merry." Mr. Redgrave gives us nothing more merry than a twisted leer. Or perhaps I should say a twisted Lear. Because I shall be much surprised if his performance as the mad king, later in the season, is vocally or physically very different from last Tuesday's Jew. I hope one day to see this actor playing a part insincerely, with his mind on other matters. Then the defences might come down, and the great Shakespearean performance that surges within him might at last be let out.

The jewel of the evening is Peggy Ashcroft's Portia, a creature of exquisite breeding and uncommon sense. She speaks the poetry with the air of a woman who would never commit the social gaffe of reciting in public, with the result that the lines flow out newly minted, as unstrained as the quality of mercy itself. Her handling of the tiresome princelings who come to woo her is an object lesson in wit and good manners; later, in the court-room, we wept at her compassion; and the last act, invariably an anti-climax, bloomed golden at her touch.

Apart from the fiery furnace that is Mr. Redgrave and the cool zephyr that is Miss Ashcroft, the production is pretty tepid stuff. The scenery (flimsy pillars, as usual) looks fine in silhouette, and on one occasion, when the sky inadvertently turned green, assumed extraordinary beauty. But I tire of settings that seek to represent nowhere-in-general; how one longs to see everywhere-in-particular! The trial was well staged—but why must Shylock always be alone? Surely all the Jews in Venice would turn up for his triumph?

I cannot imagine what Donald Pleasence was trying to make of Launcelot Gobbo, who is not, I suggest, an organ-grinder's monkey. Yvonne Mitchell is wasted on Jessica. On the credit side, Tony Britton's Bassanio is an attractive scamp; and Robert Shaw, cast as Gratiano, delighted us and himself by giving a fiery and determined performance of Mercutio. (pp. 42-4)

Kenneth Tynan, in a review of "The Merchant of Venice," in his Curtains: Selections from the Drama Criticism and Related Writings, *Atheneum Publishers, 1961, pp. 42-4.*

Roy Walker   (review date 21 March 1953)

[*Walker extols Redgrave's portrayal of Shylock, a "venomous and menacing monster" that aptly contrasted with Portia. Redgrave's depiction of villainy, he states, was matched antithetically by Ashcroft's portrait of goodness as Portia.*]

There has been a glut of goods on the Rialto this year. Shylocks come in three standard shades, black, red or grey, with character to match. Paul Rogers was a Rathbony artist in villainy at the Vic. At the King's, Hammersmith, last week, Donald Wolfit prefaced his coming Wandering Jew with a sympathy-compelling Semitic victim of notorious wrong. Now Stratford starts its Coronation season with its thirty-seventh Shylock, Michael Redgrave's guttural and asthmatic hybrid of Caliban and Lear, a venomous and menacing monster. It is superbly done and surely this interpretation does most to bring out the antithesis between Portia and the Jew that unites Belmont and Venice on the judgment day.

Here too is a Portia of a goodness to match his misanthropy, Peggy Ashcroft exquisitely witty and tender by turns and beautiful in glowing blue and a yellow as golden as sunshine on daffodils—until she strides into court in German field-

grey. The important thing here is not male impersonation but the vision of justice transfigured by mercy, the true gold standard of love triumphing over love of gold and the old law of revenge. 'So may the outward shows be least themselves' [III. ii. 73] is not a cue for the costumier and Portia no lead soldier. Most of Hutchinson Scott's other designs were graceful and one specially remembers the raven loveliness of Yvonne Mitchell's Jessica lying in Lorenzo's arms in a dress of gleaming white, 'The moon sleeps with Endymion'.

Denis Carey's production is Bristol-fashion, with an unexpectedly moving love scene between Portia and Bassanio (Tony Britton), a handsomely gaunt Antonio (Harry Andrews) and a singer (Deny Graham) whose music was indeed the food of love. But the logic of the setting is absurd. A cluster of arcades opens like the claws of a crab to Shylock's house; but in this first act no scenic distinction at all is made between Venice and Belmont and afterwards it is only a sort of winter garden.

No matter. All eyes were on lovely Peggy anyway. She and Shylock have brought Glen Byam Shaw's first venture as Director triumphantly to port while, as Michael Redgrave aptly reminded us at the end, Anthony Quayle and the other Stratford company are wandering in the Antipodes where, to the scandal of Shakespearean scholarship, Desdemona has just married Cassio.

Roy Walker, in a review of "The Merchant of Venice," in Time & Tide, *Vol. 34, No. 12, March 21, 1953, p. 366.*

Peggy Ashcroft as Portia, 1953.

Ivor Brown   (review date 22 March 1953)

[*In the review below, Brown praises the cast and direction of Carey's straightforward, powerful, and unadorned production. Redgrave's defiant, vengeful Shylock loomed "large in stature, voice and gesture." Ashcroft's "subtle-sweet performance" was most effective in the Belmont scenes, according to the critic.*]

Amid the Shakespearean plethora of 1953 it would be natural for managements and their producers to seek distinction by display or fantastic novelty. Stratford-upon-Avon, however, opens its new season in a mannerly, middle-of-the-road, way without exhibitionism or stuntsmanship. *The Merchant of Venice* is an obvious temptation to the stuntsmen, but Denis Carey has directed it with just enough furniture and a scrupulous regard for clear speech of the text. No gabbling or throw-it-away methods here and no effort to score irrelevant points. Peggy Ashcroft is a lady-like Lady of Belmont, witty when wit is needed, but never bubbling over with a forced foam of gaiety; her country-seat suits her better than the law-court. (She is so natural and the Trial Scene so intensely theatrical.) During the inevitable tedium of the Casket Scenes it is full compensation, though a trifle hard on the suitors, to watch the emotions play on her features; this is subtle-sweet performance. Miss Ashcroft cannot keep sincerity out of it: she turns the preposterous Belmont fairy-tale into something actual and the house pulses with true feeling. In this her Bassanio, Tony Britton, assists her, for he is not at all the slick, brassy adventurer but so serious a lover and so sensitive a type that he might jump into Romeo's shoes.

Michael Redgrave's Shylock conforms to the general pattern of honest, unaffected performance. He shows us a villainous vessel of anti-Christian hatred, the carrion-crow who is given no false plumage of a dove. Large in stature, voice and gesture, this Shylock does not snivel or cringe, but spits defiance. There is ample pain in his "my turquoise" and the "wilderness of monkeys" [III. i. 122-23] speech. But it is the pathos of frustrated avarice and so cannot drive at our deeper sympathies. Yvonne Mitchell's Jessica is charming and I welcome Donald Pleasence and Noel Howlett to Stratford, wishing them better parts than those of the Gobbi. Under Leslie Bridgewater's direction and with Julian Slade's composition there is a modest supply of fairly traditional music, a delightful change after the ghastly modernist noises now so often inflicted on the Bard. Anthony Quayle, now leading an immensely successful Stratford tour in New Zealand despite some odd assertions to the contrary, would have liked the first fruits of the care-taker government.

Ivor Brown, "Men and Ghosts," in The Observer, *March 22, 1953, p. 11.*

Peter Fleming   (review date 27 March 1953)

[*Fleming protests that Carey's direction accentuated the inherent improbabilities in the text and within the characters. Redgrave aptly rendered Shylock's passion, vindictiveness and pride, but he was less successful in conveying the character's "guile and opportunism," which led to some incongruities and appeared as gratuitously theatrical, according to the critic. Fleming commends Ashcroft's Portia.*]

The stage, when the curtain rises, is seen to be dominated by an enormous gilt pergola: the sort of thing that, if you were a wealthy eccentric and had plenty of wire netting, would be very handy for keeping vultures in. Salerio is lying flat on his back on the ground—I know that he and Solanio are supposed to bored stiff by Antonio's introspective mood; I know that in very hot countries the humbler members of the community are often to be seen recumbent in the streets; but I maintain that expensively dressed young gentlemen did not, while sober, adopt this posture in sixteenth-century Venice. Nor, when they parted from each other, did they almost invariably do so at the double. Nor—But enough has been said to indicate my suspicion that Mr. Dennis Carey's stylish production is on the wrong lines. With the exception of Shylock, everyone in *The Merchant of Venice* behaves in a highly improbable manner. The producer's aim should surely be to lessen, not to increase, our difficulty in accepting them as human beings. Neither the brittle chic of the *décor*, nor the neo-Bensonian antics of the Venetians, nor a trial scene during which two-thirds of those present remain as impassive as waxworks assists in the achievement of this aim.

Mr. Michael Redgrave is, of all our eminent actors, the most difficult to spit upon. It is not easy to fawn on or cringe to men half a head shorter than yourself, and this Shylock, though it is a powerful and intelligent performance, does not quite come off. In pathos, in rage, in pride of race, he is excellent; but the guile and opportunism—the, as it were, feminine side of the Jew's character—are not given their full effect. The rich, dove-grey robe in which Mr. Redgrave plays the part does not suggest an alien intruder from the ghetto, and when in the trial scene he starts to sharpen his knife on the sole of his boot we are suddenly aware of incongruity; what should have seemed a natural, squalid act becomes, when done by this dignified, sensitive Shylock, merely theatrical.

Miss Peggy Ashcroft's Portia is a fine piece of work, though perhaps a little lacking in high spirits. Mr. Harry Andrews does his usual yeoman service as Antonio, and Mr. Tony Britton's Bassanio is personable and pleasant.

Peter Fleming, in a review of "The Merchant of Venice," in The Spectator, *Vol. 190, No. 6509, March 27, 1953, p. 373.*

T. C. Worsley   (review date 28 March 1953)

[*Worsley disparages the lack of fresh interpretation in the conventional, fairy-tale rendition of the Stratford play, although he concedes that Carey's production had its merits. Redgrave offered a "blood-curdling performance," although somewhat anachronistic in context. Ashcroft made "something wholly individual and unique" of Portia, but she lacked the necessary hardness for the part.*]

[The] first production of the season is yet another *Merchant of Venice*, the third major production of this previously unpopular play within three months. Does the play, as a result, win a place once more in our affections? Well, at least we are encouraged to hope that one day we may see a perfect production, one that will resolve the various difficulties that the play presents. Mr. Denis Carey's production does not do that; it is a pleasant and charming fairy-tale production in the current idiom. It does not bring any fresh interpretation to bear on the play; it plays, agreeably enough, familiar variations in the contemporary style. We always hope for more than this, of course, and tend to forget that we are lucky to get as much. Twenty years ago a production like this would be exceptional; now it is the general rule.

From the Bristol Old Vic Mr. Denis Carey has brought his designer and his composer, and both show up well. Mr.

Hutchinson Scott's set is a light and airy filigree construction suggesting, well, light and air—nothing very much more definite; but it is easy to manage, and leaves the detail as the Shakespearean purists believe correct for the imagination of the audience to fill in. The dresses are graceful and romantic: and the romantic is the note that is struck most clearly (the humour is rather feeble). Shylock's scenes apart, the best passage is that where Bassanio comes to Belmont to make his choice. A promising newcomer, Mr. Tony Britton, was the Bassanio. He has, in the bud, what Miss Peggy Ashcroft has in the full flower, namely quality, a power to distil and project a romantic flavour of personality that lifts the audience up above the everyday world. The two together—she quite still to one side, but in her very stillness suggesting an agitation of doubt and hope, he restlessly moving from casket to casket in an agony of doubt—raise this scene far above the common level. Miss Ashcroft is not otherwise, to my mind, an ideal Portia—she lacks any streak of hardness—but needless to say she makes something wholly individual and unique of the part.

Completely at odds with the contemporary taste of the rest of this production is Mr. Redgrave's broad violent Piranesi Jew. Nothing here of quiet English good taste: an almost old-fashioned actor-manager performance with all the stops out. One can imagine something like it having been given by a Beerbohm Tree. The difficulty of playing Shylock is today almost a sociological difficulty. Neither audience nor actor can separate their interpretations completely from the overtones rising from our age of persecution. If an actor could be found who could play Shylock in the way many think Shakespeare meant it to be played, as a figure of fun, even then no audience would be able to stand it. On the other hand ennobling Shylock—even so much for instance as Mr. Paul Roger's did at the Old Vic recently—throws out the play in another direction, for it throws into even higher relief the caddishness of the Christians. Mr. Redgrave's Jew is singularly uncompromising for these days. He is the other side of the Jewish problem as fanatically full of race hatred as his persecutors and the kind of Jew whose Jewishness invites persecution. And no nonsense about it. It is a blood-curdling performance.

Altogether, this is one of those productions which will, I should judge, be ten times better after five performances. On the first night no one had quite caught the pitch of the theatre and roughnesses in the lighting and elsewhere will smooth themselves out.

T. C. Worsley, *"From Belmont to Forres,"* in The New Statesman & Nation, *Vol. XLV, No. 1151, March 28, 1953, p. 367.*

PRODUCTION:

Tyrone Guthrie and Frederick Valk • Stratford, Ontario • 1955

BACKGROUND:

Guthrie's *Dream* production earned acclaim for its direction, "a brilliant total interpretation," according to Henry Hewes. Critics praised Guthrie's many comic touches in his effort to place Shylock in balance with the generic demands of the play as romance-comedy. Many critics discerned a special emphasis in Guthrie's production on Antonio, played by Robert Goodier, as a character who unites the two plots, Belmont and Venice. Frederick Valk played a passionate, vengeful Shylock who nevertheless conveyed a sense of dignity, despite his often overt villainy. Robertson Davies called Valk's performance "an astounding exhibition of mounting emotion," although one critic protested that Valk's verbal delivery was hampered by his middle-European accent. Francis Hyland was widely praised for her portrayal of Portia, "an ideal heroine for Shakespearean comedy," according to Alice Griffin. The highly acclaimed cast included William Shatner as Gratiano, Helen Burns as Nerissa, Donald Harron as Bassanio, and Lorne Greene as Morocco. Tanya Moiseiwitsch was the production's designer.

COMMENTARY:

Brooks Atkinson   (review date 1 July 1955)

[Atkinson finds Guthrie's production theatrically exciting, but notes that the poetry, the verse-speaking, was sacrificed in the process, especially by Valk. However, the production offered many pleasing touches and a strong cast, handsomely costumed by Tanya Moiseiwitsch.]

As a professional iconoclast, Tyrone Guthrie is just the man to rescue *The Merchant of Venice* from respectability. His production of the Shakespeare comedy, which opened in the festival tent last evening, is beautiful, humorous, tumultuous and melodramatic.

For everything that Shakespeare can do, Dr. Guthrie can do as if it had never been done before. The Shakespeare story is an old one that was never very sensible. But around Frederick Valk's exuberant, apoplectic Shylock, Dr. Guthrie has spun his masquerades, his romantic interludes with broad comedy flourishes and a trial scene that might have come straight out of Kydd or Webster. Give Dr. Guthrie a whiff of blood and he in turn can give the audience goose pimples with a grim rack on which Antonio, weak with horror, is roped and blindfolded and coldly plucked for the slaughter.

There is a price for this sort of theatrical originality. It comes at the expense of the poetry. Not very much of this *Merchant* is beautifully spoken. While they are getting on with the story, the actors throw most of the dialogue away. Frances Hyland, a slender, enchanting Portia with a reedy voice, does speak the invocation to mercy with loveliness, which is an act of mercy in itself. And Donald Harron, an ideal Bassanio, speaks with grace and clarity.

But Mr. Valk, who is a Middle European by birth, has not yet mastered English words or English rhythms, and he leaves most of Shylock's intellectual eminence unexpressed. It is up with the excitement, it is down with the poetry. This is the price Dr. Guthrie charges for a highly enjoyable show.

Most of us will be willing to pay it. For Dr. Guthrie always gives good measure in the goods he traffics in. He has made something cheerful out of Launcelot Gobbo, one of the worst parts Shakespeare ever wrote. By paying very little attention to the lines, Ted makes the part brash and chuckled-headed and very good company. In Eric House's acting, the perfunctory part of the Prince of Arragon, together with comic entourage, is a wonderful caricature of dullness and condescension.

As Gratiano, William Shatner has a boyish swagger that refreshes another commonplace part. And Helen Burns' Nerissa is the freshest egg in the basket. Instead of following her mistress with fawning devotion, Miss Burns regards her with quizzical astonishment as if she does not believe that Portia can be so witless and outrageous. Very good stuff.

Thanks to Tanya Moiseiwitsch, everyone looks extraordinarily handsome. The lighting is gay. The costumes are glorious in stunning whites with golden adornment, in azure blue and other sweet colors; and the designs are original, carefully tailored and flowing. Whenever Shakespeare falters for a split second, Dr. Guthrie sends his armies of pike-bearers up through the ramps carrying fluttering pennants on elegant poles. These gaily caparisoned bits are frivolously theatrical. Since he has no respect for the conventions, Dr. Guthrie makes bright every corner.

Ever since the Stratford festival announced *The Merchant of Venice* the familiar charge of anti-Semitism has been raised against it. Without taking time to go into the subject of English culture in Shakespeare's day, let's admit that the play is anti-Semitic. It might also be observed that Mr. Valk's acting robs Shylock of most of his distinction. Although Mr. Valk is a vigorous, interesting actor, he cannot convey much of Shylock's lonely thinking or the shades of Shylock's feeling.

But if we are to get touchy about religious matters, the Christians might file a counter-suit against Shakespeare for libel and slander—a more serious indictment, since he lived among Christians and presumably was one. In the *Merchant* his Christians are not only fools and prodigals: They are also heartless, arrogant, vindictive and cruel, and they violate most of the principles their Lord tried to teach them. Trust Dr. Guthrie to put the bitter facts on the line. When the trial goes against Shylock, the Christians taunt and jeer him with an animal ferocity that would be horrifying if *The Merchant of Venice* were a sensible play.

It isn't. But Dr. Guthrie had made a stimulating show out of it.

Brooks Atkinson, "New Shylock," in The New York Times, *July 1, 1955, p. 13.*

Henry Hewes   (review date 23 July 1955)

[*Hewes is an American dramatic critic who wrote for the* Saturday Review *from 1951 to 1977. In the review below, Hewes commends Guthrie not only for "finding a brilliant total interpretation for* The Merchant of Venice," *but also for restoring the comic spirit of the play. A key element of Guthrie's interpretation was the acknowledgement of "the physical love between Bassanio and Antonio" which helped put "Shylock back in proportion with the whole story.*]

It hardly needs affirming, but this year's festival is a badge of the strength of this three-year-old organization's production techniques. For this season Canada's Stratford has chosen to revive its *Oedipus Rex,* to feature native talent in the key roles of *Julius Caesar,* and to do *The Merchant of Venice* with an unheralded English actor in the part of Shylock. The result has been to shift the focus of interest away from individual performances or the exploration of less familiar plays

to the skill with which these better-known works have been mounted. (p. 21)

The drawbacks in performance of the first two shows happily fade in the benign glow of the third production, *The Merchant of Venice.* Here director Tyrone Guthrie has really made this play back into a comedy that is all of a piece. By acknowledging the physical love between Bassanio and Antonio (who is, after all, the title character) Mr. Guthrie lends the play a logical base. Antonio is established as a man ready to make any sacrifice for the good of the boy he loves. And the final scene, usually so anticlimactic, becomes meaningful when Antonio swears to Portia that Bassanio will never more "break faith advisedly" [V. i. 253]. Robert Goodier is physically right as Antonio, and Donald Harron catches the ambiguity of Bassanio's position beautifully.

The building up of Antonio and Bassanio accomplishes something else. It puts Shylock back in proportion with the whole story. As the usurer Frederick Valk injects a certain amount of stubborn humor and playfulness into Shylock's early scenes. Later he doesn't dwell too much on Shylock's personal tragedy, being content to work for the maximum effectiveness of the story in which he has, after all, earned his comeuppance by plotting the cruel murder of Antonio. The more he relishes this murder in advance the more satisfying is its last-second prevention.

As Portia Frances Hyland is a fetching little minx. When she comes to the famous "quality of mercy" [IV. i. 184] speech she is wise enough neither to declaim it or throw it away. Rather she lets it become a natural and sincere plea to Shylock. And when Shylock makes a gesture of obdurateness the speech turns from pleading into angry denunciation.

And it is in the staging of the many minor bits that Tyrone Guthrie demonstrates that on top of finding a brilliant total interpretation for *The Merchant of Venice* he can also come up with some highly inventive embroidery that preserves the comic spirit of a play too many directors seem to have forgotten is a comedy. Inevitably this embroidery places the emphasis on the devices used rather than on the acting. Such antics as Launcelot Gobbo's running up the steps on one side of the balcony to tell Jessica a secret while Shylock is descending the steps on the other side, just barely not noticing, or the deadpan zombie-like Prince of Aragon reading a piece of ticker-tape drawn from the mouth of a miniature statue are remembered long after one has forgotten the characters themselves.

Another device which helps the play enormously is the use of a choir to enhance the scenes at Belmont. This makes possible a lot of lovely dancing that gives the play a much-needed booster of gaiety. And when the fully realized Mozartian finale comes to a happy close Mr. Guthrie leaves Antonio onstage alone sadly dropping the letter which has brought him good news about his saved ships, as he meditates over the loss of his most precious argosy, Bassanio.

Tanya Moiseiwitsch does the production proud with rich but never ponderous Venetian costumes and a marvelous Piero della Francesca motif for the choir. As long as Miss Moiseiwitsch and her crew of artisans are around, Stratford, Ontario, will be worth making reservations to see, no matter what reservations are made about the interpretations and the castings. (pp. 21-2)

Henry Hewes, "The Bard in Canada," in The Saturday Review, *New York*, Vol. XXXVIII, No. 30, July 23, 1955, pp. 21-2.

Alice Griffin   (review date September 1955)

[Griffin praises both the director and cast of this "brilliant" production. Griffin avers that it "was a directorial and acting triumph that both [Goodier's] Antonio and [Valk's] Shylock were portrayed as intensely human beings," infusing the play with a rare unity. In addition, Griffin lauds Hyland as an ideal heroine for Shakespearean comedy.]

A brilliant *Merchant of Venice* and a revival of last season's *King Oedipus* were contributions to modern theatre of which the 1955 Stratford Shakespearean Festival in Canada might well be proud. For the third consecutive summer season, capacity audiences in the blue tent beside the Avon at Stratford, Ontario, saw productions staged by Tyrone Guthrie that were as emotionally exciting as they were thought-provoking.

As *The Merchant of Venice* and *King Oedipus* revealed, one reason for the great appeal of his productions of the classics is that the play's central theme is clearly revealed and maintained throughout, and the dramatic elements—character interpretation, spectacle and plot—are developed with variety, richness and imagination within the framework of that theme, and always in relationship to it. Thus in *The Merchant of Venice* he stressed the moral idea, contained in the "quality of mercy" speech, that justice should be tempered with mercy. Shylock stands for justice, Antonio for mercy. Although Antonio has less to say and do than Shylock, the former, who has the title role, was prominent throughout this production. It was his figure that unified the two strands of the plot, the romantic Portia-Bassanio episodes set at Belmont and the pound-of-flesh story set in Venice of corrupt wastrels as uncharitable as Shylock.

It was a directorial and acting triumph that both Antonio and Shylock were portrayed as intensely human beings, and it was through the audience's feelings for these principals that the larger theme was realized. As effectively played by Robert Goodier, Antonio was an older man, deeply attached to young Bassanio, hurt at the youth's suit for the hand of Portia but generously agreeing to finance it. At the trial, though fearful, he was almost eager to die for Bassanio. After he had been saved and, in return for the justice demanded for him, had asked mercy for Shylock, Antonio came to Belmont in the final scene, the odd figure in black among the three pairs of happy lovers. At the very end of the play, his lone figure occupied the stage as, brooding, he let slip away the letter containing the good news of the return of his argosies.

Frederick Valk's Shylock was a worthy addition to the gallery of memorable Shakespearean performances. When we first met him here, Shylock was portrayed as an efficient businessman considering the loan to Bassanio. When Antonio was mentioned as guaranteeing the bond, Shylock's emotions deepened—he hated the merchant in an almost routine way because he was Christian, but intensely despised him because Antonio loaned money gratis and was a threat to Shylock's own financial existence. This Shylock had dignity and self-assurance which perhaps stemmed from his intense attachment to three things: his business (moneylending, which Christians were not permitted to practice), his Jewish faith and his family—specifically, his daughter Jessica. To the man who threatened the security of any one of these—as did Anto-

nio to Shylock's business—he would be unrelenting in his revenge.

Valk brought much variety to his dynamic Shylock, who was so intelligent and capable that it was only a brief flashing of the eyes that warned us that the "pound of flesh" proposal was not just a jest. His "Hath not a Jew eyes?" [III. i. 59] passage was delivered as the logical working of a keen mind, not as a plea for pity, for he never stooped to the Venetians. After the loss of his daughter to the Venetian ne'er-do-wells, along with the money with which he carried on his business, a distraught Shylock came on the scene. Resembling a bearded Old Testament prophet, he roared for revenge and justice. Wounded by the loss of the things he held dear and which gave him his former dignity, he now directed his hate against the generous Antonio, who at this point is himself suffering in silence the hurt given him by Bassanio. To remind us of the importance of Shylock's family to the moneylender, who is not merely lamenting the loss of his ducats, Valk gave a quietly sad reading of the lines about his wife Leah.

The clash between Antonio and Shylock came to a vivid climax in the trial scene, which opened with a processional entry from all aisles of the auditorium—by clerks, red-robed justices and the retinue of the presiding Duke. The tension mounted through Shylock's defiance of the pleas of mercy, his sharpening of the knife and approach to the bare-breasted, panting Antonio. Defeated by the same unrelenting justice on which he had depended, Shylock fell across the rail of the dock where Antonio had been seated. In his last moments on the stage Shylock still held the audience's sympathy because he was a man who had some admirable traits, but not enough to overcome his personal hurt and find charity and mercy for those who had wronged him. Following Antonio's statement of excessive conditions for Shylock's reprieve, the Christians in the court drive Shylock out with jeers; and here director Guthrie pointed up the irony that they too have not learned that mercy should temper justice.

In contrast to the Rialto scenes, those at Portia's home at Belmont were ones of sheer enchantment. Her wooing by the Princes of Morocco and Arragon were storybook episodes with wonderfully comic contributions by Lorne Greene, as the huge, saber-swinging Moor attired in exotic white robe and turban, and Eric House as the bloodless little Arragon in black and white, accompanied by learned doctors who prompt his speech. Frances Hyland is an ideal heroine for Shakespearean comedy, blending warmth, wit and vitality with a grace of movement that makes her appealingly beautiful in the romantic episodes and charmingly engaging in the disguise scenes. This Portia could not conceal her love for Bassanio nor her anxiety that he choose the right casket. At the trial scene, her stalling for time and finally hitting on a solution added much more suspense than having Portia come in coldly efficient, already knowing how she will trap Shylock.

The romantic heroes of Shakespeare's comedies are often as dull as his heroines are delightful, yet Donald Harron expertly achieved the difficult job of making Bassanio likeable. Moving in both plots, he brought romantic fervor and comedy to the wooing scenes and a special sensitivity to his scenes with Antonio. Nerissa was delightfully interpreted by Helen Burns as an earthy, good-humored, slow-thinking foil for the quicksilver wit of her mistress, and Nerissa's suitor, the blunt Gratiano, was well played by William Shatner. The ring episode in the final scene of moonlight and merriment was beautifully fluid in its staging: The patterned dance movements of the actors matched the mannered lines. The open stage was used to good advantage here, as well as in the casket scenes and the masking episode of Jessica's elopement. In the latter a small group of actors moving purposefully, and a few properties provided the pageantry. Tanya Moiseiwitsch's costumes stressed the influence of Botticelli; the men were attired in rich Renaissance hues and the women in pastels, while the robes of Jessica and Shylock suggested an Eastern flavor. The properties made by Brian Jackson demonstrated the careful attention to each detail of the production; the gold, globe-like casket and the silver, temple-like one resembled gorgeous Renaissance *objets d'art,* while the lead one was a black oblong banded with leaden strips. (pp. 30-1, 91-2)

> Alice Griffin, "Shakespeare and Sophocles at Stratford," *in* Theatre Arts, *Vol. XXXIX, No. 9, September, 1955, pp. 30-1, 91-3.*

Robertson Davies   (review date 1955)

[*Davies is a well-regarded and popular Canadian novelist. In the review below, he provides a thorough, actor-by-actor appraisal of Guthrie's* The Merchant of Venice, *a production, the reviewer reports, that "never strayed from the adult's fairy-tale conception of the play." Davies commends Goodier's Antonio, a role that received special emphasis in Guthrie's interpreta-*

tion, Hyland's excellent performance as Portia, and Valk's Shylock, faithful to Shakespeare's delineation of the character as a villain: "His conception was powerful rather than subtle. . . . It was an astounding exhibition of mounting emotion."]

Shylock is an extremely attractive role and it has been played in many different ways. There is a persistent tradition that it was once played as a comedy part, and that it was thus that Shakespeare intended it. Nobody with much knowledge of Shakespeare could believe anything of the sort. But it is true that there was a comic Shylock in a play called *The Jew of Venice,* written by Lord Lansdowne, and performed first in 1701. This comment on it from *Biographia Dramatica, or A Companion to The Playhouse* (published in 1764), gives us a notion of its quality:

> This play is altered from Shakespeare's *Merchant of Venice,* and in some respects with judgement. The introduction of the feast, more particularly where the Jew is placed at a separate table, and drinks to his money as his only mistress, is a happy thought; yet, on the whole, his Lordship has greatly lessened both the beauty and effect of the original; which, notwithstanding this modernized piece, aided by magnificence and music, still stands its ground, and will ever continue one of the darling representations of the theatre. . . . In this play, as Rowe remarks, the character of Shylock (which

Frances Hyland as Portia and Donald Harron as Bassanio. Act III, scene ii.

was performed by Dogget) is made comic, and we are prompted to laughter instead of detestation.

Dogget was a famous low comedian, and he played Shylock in Lansdowne's play in a red wig; but I can find no record of Shakespeare's play having been performed with a comic Shylock—though I was solemnly taught when I was a schoolboy that this was so, and that we were very clever people to have discovered that Shakespeare might secretly have meant him to be serious.

That detestation which the eighteenth century writer mentions has sometimes been as remote from popular taste as the idea of a comic Shylock is to us. During the nineteenth century several eminent actors played Shylock as a man desperately wronged, and driven almost to madness. The greatest of these, Sir Henry Irving, created a Shylock so aristocratic of demeanour, and so distinguished of intellect, that the play became his personal tragedy. He did not, however, go so far as some earlier players, who finished the play at the end of the Trial Scene, concluding that when Shylock had made his final exit there was nothing of any consequence to follow. For at least a century this was Shylock's play. It is only in comparatively recent times that the balance of the plot has been rediscovered, and the fairy-tale nature of the whole piece brought forward, and for this, as for so many other illuminations of Shakespeare, we are indebted to the late Harley Granville-Barker. (pp. 51-2)

The state of the world in our time has given the character of Shylock an importance which is not inherent in it as an element in the play. But the Stratford production put stress on another element in the piece which has been much neglected. It is called *The Merchant of Venice,* and the Merchant is Antonio. Yet we have been accustomed to seeing the play performed in such a way that Antonio was a rather dull character of secondary interest. Dr. Guthrie has chosen to emphasize the very warm friendship which exists between Antonio and Bassanio, bringing it forward as a homosexual romance. But if this attitude toward the play gains favour, and the growing interest in, and sympathy for, the plight of homosexuals increases, our grandchildren may see the day when well-organized groups of homosexuals protest against the presentation of the play because it shows one of their number heartlessly betrayed by a young man for whom he has undergone the utmost danger.

The revelation of this theme in the play may give offence in some quarters, but it cannot easily be argued down. Even so careful and sober a scholar as the late Sir Edmund Chambers has drawn attention to it. Once again we must bear in mind that this play was written primarily for the Renaissance world and not for our own, and that in that world, with its attachment to Greek ideals of life, homosexuality was not held in horror. And nowadays people who have had opportunities to see something of life under varied circumstances know that homosexual love is by no means uncommon, and that it is no more necessarily gross or degrading than romantic love between men and women. The homosexual is quite as often a courageous, intelligent and admirable person as his heterosexual brother, and it is his personal character, rather than his sexual disposition, which makes his love noble or despicable. We are shown Antonio as a man much respected, and the terms in which his love for Bassanio are made known are restrained. His sadness at the beginning of the play, which puzzles his companions, becomes clear enough when we find that Bassanio wants his help to win Portia. And, in the scene

of the Trial, what are we to make of this, his last speech before Shylock exacts his penalty:

> I am arm'd and well prepared;
> Give me your hand, Bassanio, fare you well,
> Grieve not that I am fallen to this for you;
> For herein Fortune shows herself more kind
> Than is her custom: it is still her use
> To let the wretched man outlive his wealth,
> To view with hollow eye and wrinkled brow
> An age of poverty; from which lingering penance
> Of such misery doth she cut me off.
> Commend me to your honourable wife,
> Tell her the process of Antonio's end,
> Say how I lov'd you, speak me fair in death;
> And when the tale is told, bid her be judge
> Whether Bassanio had not once a love.
>
> [IV. i. 264-77]

In the Stratford production this element in the play was handled with discretion, but it was unmistakable, and it added greatly to the effect of the whole, for it carried into the lyrical Fifth Act some of the quality of the Trial Scene. To the theme of the Three Caskets and the Pound of Flesh was added a third, fully as powerful as either—a theme of Renunciation. This has always been an attractive element in drama; such popular favourites as *The Only Way* were built on nothing else. When the lovers had left the stage at the end of the play, we saw the lonely figure of Antonio, holding in his hand the letter which tells of the restoration of his fortunes; but he has lost his love, and as the letter drops from his fingers and the lights fade, we feel a bittersweet pang for him which gives the play, on the modern stage, a new and important dimension.

Much has been written about Shakespeare and homosexuality, and the Sonnets have been a battle-ground for sixty years where those who wish to claim him as a homosexual genius contend with those who take a larger view of his nature. There can be no doubt that Shakespeare understood homosexuality, as he understood murder, remorse and romantic love—as well as the ludicrous and repellent aspects of heterosexual love where it has grown rank. *The Merchant of Venice* adds nothing to the arguments on either side, but when the affection of Antonio for Bassanio is given its full weight in the play many things in it are illuminated which had formerly been dark.

The Stratford production never strayed from the adult's fairy-tale conception of the play; it was like a story from Bandello or Boccaccio richly brought to life. Where the play is serious it was finely serious, but it never substituted mere solemnity for seriousness. Some detailed attention has already been given to the treatment of the Renunciation theme in the play; it was tellingly but delicately stated, and Antonio's affection for Bassanio was in that tradition of the love of an older man for a younger—a love which is at once passionate, and yet paternal and protective—which is familiar in the Greek and the Renaissance world. The theme of the Three Caskets was all in a vein of romantic fantasy. The caskets themselves were objects of beauty, and it was a good moment when the Prince of Arragon took the fool's head from the silver casket, and read its message on a long tongue which pulled out of its mouth like a tape. The theme of the Pound of Flesh was treated as full-blooded melodrama. The first encounter of Antonio and Shylock was marked by a reapportionment of lines which was effective and, unless I am very much deceived, correct. In all printed texts Shylock's speech at this point begins:

How like a fawning publican he looks!
I hate him for he is a Christian!

[I. iii. 41-2]

But in this production the first of these lines was given to Antonio, in whose mouth it makes more sense than if it is spoken by Shylock. Why would the proud merchant seem 'fawning', even to his enemy? The tension of this relationship mounted irresistibly to the point in the Trial Scene where Antonio is brought up from the depths of the prison, tied to a hurdle and ready for the knife. There was a splendour of danger about the Trial, right until the moment of Portia's triumph, for in this production she did not arrive full of guileful certainty, and armed with a quibble by her cousin Bellario; she found her solution on the stage, before our eyes, and struck down her opponent almost on the spur of the moment. This is not the kind of thing which commends itself to the realists, and it does not bear close examination in retrospect, but it is a splendidly thrilling stage effect. The play, it must be repeated, is meant to be enjoyed as it progresses, and this was the highest of many pinnacles of excitement.

The production, as always when Dr. Guthrie is in charge, was marked by brilliance and delicacy of imagination. We are used to seeing the suitors for Portia sharply differentiated, but not so sharply as here, where the scimitar-flourishing Moor is contrasted with a Prince of Arragon who seemed to be the most obscure and most haemophilic of all the Hapsburgs. The caskets were carried by girls dressed in costumes of golden, silver and leaden hues—Miss Lead being so sadly unequal to her heavy task that she often had to be helped by Portia's servant, Balthasar. During the scene of Jessica's elopement we were given just enough of the atmosphere of a Venetian carnival to suggest the atmosphere of a rich and gay city, but we were never allowed to weary of it. The costumes and the properties were in Miss Tanya Moiseiwitsch's best manner—fanciful, striking but never marred by opulence for its own sake. All the elements of the production were united to suggest, but never to insist upon, the splendour of Venice. The eye was fully satisfied, but never wearied or distracted.

The hearing, also, was happily ministered to, for as part of Portia's household there was an excellent choir which sang unaccompanied music by John Cook, to supplement the action where it was needed. The music was most effective at two high points in the play. The first of these was when Bassanio made his choice among the caskets; the choir welcomed him, as it had done in the case of the other suitors, but it sang 'Tell Me Where is Fancy Bred' [III. ii. 63] while he took a pause for quiet deliberation. As he stood in the centre of the stage, considering his choice, attendants with crowned and ribboned standards wove in and out among the actors, creating a pattern which was beautiful in itself, and helpful to the action of the play. Dr. Guthrie's productions move at great speed, and sometimes a rest is needed. Bassanio's long pause provided such a moment of rest, and the music was given full opportunity to create an atmosphere of romance.

Similarly in the Fifth Act, during the love scene between Lorenzo and Jessica, we were given enough music to support the lines, but before Portia's entrance we were allowed to hear it for some little time without other sound. It was a splendid device to give us a moment of respite after the excitement of the Trial Scene, to suggest the romantic beauty of the night, and to prepare the stage for one of the most charming of Shakespearean finales. We carried away from this production a

sense of having heard music which, without obtruding on the play, had lent its own quality to it, and which had laid its own gentle restraint on the sometimes breathless pace of the action.

The production contained a variety of good performances. The Gobbos are among the stumbling-blocks for modern audiences. We have lost the Renaissance relish for this particular type of jocosity; we have our own strange appetites, as an evening with radio or television will show, but the run-of-the-mill, flat-footed foolery of Shakespeare's day is not the run-of-the-mill, flat-footed foolery of our own, and as a general thing we endure Launcelot Gobbo and his father, knowing that they cannot last long. Ted Follows and William Hutt made Canadian rustics of the Gobbos, which gave them some freshness, though no more wit than before. Old Gobbo's hat was a splendid creation, and he provided us with one moment of true pathos when he discovered that his son was not dead. But the scene between father and son is an uncomfortable one for an audience today; we do not think blindness funny, and we cannot greatly like a son who pretends to be dead in order to make his father weep. Dr. Guthrie is not a man to soften such a scene as this, and he is right not to do so; let us by all means see what a Renaissance English audience considered funny, so long as we are not obliged to think it funny ourselves. Through the remainder of the play Ted Follows did what Launcelot has to do capably, but he has not the true comedian's gift of making bricks without straw.

Some mention has already been made of the two suitors who do not win Portia. Lorne Greene was a figure of tawny majesty as the Prince of Morocco and his first entrance was a fine sight, but he was not able to continue at this high pitch, and grew a little dull before he had made his choice. It would have been interesting to see him blacker; no doubt a Moroccan is coffee-coloured, but it is probable that Shakespeare thought of the Prince as a Negro, and a coal-black face under the huge white turban which Miss Moiseiwitsch had decreed would have made a fine effect. But the monotony of voice which betrayed Mr. Greene in *Julius Caesar* was apparent in this smaller part, also.

As Eric House played him, the Prince of Arragon was one of the fine creations of the production. Pale, clad in black and shadowed by three Tutors who wore those shovel hats traditionally associated with the Spanish clergy, he was chilling, repellent and yet also pitiable. When he moved, he was a bored procession of one; when he spoke, it was from a body in which the white corpuscles had long taken the upper hand; he touched nothing which was not given to him by one of his clerical keepers; even the three caskets were snatched from their virgin attendants by these Arragonian vultures. Yet there was a true nobility about him. When he found the fool's head in the silver casket it was his Tutors who showed dismay and chagrin, not he. He read its bitter message to the end, and even improvised a few limping lines in the same metre, to show that he, like Bottom, could gleek upon occasion. Prisoner of his great inheritance though he might be, there was a spark of gallantry in this dreadful little prince, and though he was a figure of fun we admired him. To convey so much of a character in a single scene is a considerable achievement.

The court of Venice must impress more by its dignity than by its intellect; it exists simply to tremble before Shylock, and the grander it is, the more effective the scene. Miss Moiseiwitsch had robed the Magnificoes in several different reds, which suggested that they had all bought their ceremonial robes at different times, like Peers at a Coronation. There were enough of them to make an impressive show, and a background for Robert Christie, who played the Duke. He had chosen to characterize this not very clearly drawn ruler as an eccentric, humming-and-hawing old aristocrat; it was well done, but would not the scene be stronger if the Duke were not quite so realistic, so matter-of-fact? The Duke is the visible sign of the might of Venice, and Shylock sets him at naught; would not a Duke more awesome in his dignity be more useful to the production? There are characters in Shakespeare who are not much more than walking and talking scenery, and the Duke is one of them. To give him too much individual character may be to lessen his effectiveness in the play.

There is some confusion in the texts of this play about the friends of Bassanio and Antonio, known to actors as The Salads. Sometimes they appear simply as Salanio and Salarino, as they did in this production, but occasionally the first of the two is called Solanio, and now and then an intruder named Salerio finds his way into the text. The late Stephen Leacock claimed to have known a man who discovered a Saloonio in this play. It is not of much consequence, for they are ungrateful parts, designed chiefly to 'feed' cues to more important characters. And, as Salarino, that is what Edward Holmes did, though not always accurately. But as Salanio, Lloyd Bochner provided a surprise in Act Two, in the scene in which he describes Shylock's rage and despair when he finds that his daughter has fled. There was a bitterness of mockery in this which was startling, and extremely valuable to the play, for it gave us a strong sense of the enmity that Shylock had incurred, and of the storm that was brewing. The venom of the Christians' hatred of the infidel was strongly accented in this production, and here we were given one of its most shocking manifestations. Once again we were reminded that Stratford's repertory system enables producers to cast powerful actors in comparatively minor roles.

The conception of the role of Antonio, the Merchant of the title, which brought a new quality to this production, has already been discussed. The part was played by Robert Goodier with dignity and restraint. His sadness was not a matter of sighs and gloomy looks, contrasting with the lightheartedness of his companions; it was an inner quality, which he seemed at pains to conceal. He played Antonio, indeed, very much in the manner of Sidney Carton, which was precisely the right note to hit. In many productions Antonio seems to be a nuisance in the Fifth Act; he is a stranger and he is in low spirits, even though he has escaped death and has recovered his fortunes; unless we see him as a deserted lover his melancholy in the last act of the play is hard to excuse. But it was in that light that we saw him at Stratford, and his melancholy gave an agreeably sombre contrast to the high spirits of the three pairs of lovers. And as he was the last figure that we saw on the stage, the play closed, not with Gratiano's racy joke about guarding Nerissa's ring, but with the melancholy man whom we had seen when the play began, and thus Antonio's misfortune bracketed the whole of the action. Many playgoers, who had seen *The Merchant of Venice* many times, must have felt, as I did, that they had seen Antonio for the first time.

The love story of Lorenzo and Jessica is to that of Bassanio and Portia as the moon is to the sun. Their situation is strongly romantic, and they have one of the great lyric scenes of the play. But to persuade the audience to accept them it is not enough to put two handsome young people into the roles, and hope that all will be well. To create an atmosphere of romance is one of the most difficult tasks that can be required of an actor or an actress; it demands a technique so difficult and so fine that very few people acquire it until they are considerably past the age of the characters they are called on to play. A director has his choice: he can give such parts to players who have youth and beauty of precisely the type that is wanted, and hope that the audience will forgive some lightweight acting; or he can find players who are fully capable of extracting the last ounce of romantic beauty from the lines, but whose appearance is no longer dewy. Dr. Guthrie chose the former course, and cast Neil Vipond and Charlotte Schrager as Lorenzo and Jessica.

Their appearance was in every way suitable, and Miss Schrager has just the type of beauty for the semi-Oriental dress which Miss Moiseiwitsch gave her. But neither was fully audible, and neither was skilled in speaking poetry. To do this it is not enough to look poetic and feel poetic; it is necessary to be able to understand the poetry thoroughly and to have a technique by which that understanding can be conveyed to a large audience. Mr. Vipond and Miss Schrager cannot justly be blamed because they lack such a technique; it takes years to acquire it. Therefore, though they made a gallant attack upon their roles, they cannot be said to have succeeded in them. It was not that they failed the play; it was simply that they did not understand the degree of intensity with which the other actors were performing. And for this reason they came to us faintly, and rather charmingly, like music heard intermittently across a lake on a summer evening. But much could be forgiven them because of their appearance.

With Gratiano and Nerissa we felt no such lack of vigour. William Shatner is one of the most promising of the younger actors at Stratford; he has zest and attack, and an exuberance which is very winning. He has also that rare quality of masculinity which is so valuable on the stage. There are excellent actors who, without being in any way effeminate, lack masculine appeal; and there are actors who are so in the grip of what Max Beerbohm called 'manlydom' that they are nuisances on the stage, for their manlydom expresses itself in all the most obvious ways—in noise, in overbearing mannerism, and in rumbustiousness; but the really masculine actor is the one who has masculine grace and gentleness and charm combined with virility, and Mr. Shatner is one of these lucky ones. He played Gratiano as a bore, with a ready and rattling laugh—but a young bore, to whom all may be forgiven for his gaiety; what such a man would be at forty we are not obliged to enquire. It was an excellent performance, which deepened suddenly and repellently in the Trial Scene. As this progressed Gratiano became more and more enraged until, as Shylock was about to leave the court, he spat full in his face. It was a shocking moment, but it was a moment of truth. For which of us has not had the experience of seeing a friend betray himself in some ugly passion, showing as in a lightning-flash a dark abyss in his nature at which we had not guessed? Here we saw that, like so many jolly good fellows, Gratiano could be a dangerous and brutal man.

Nerissa was played by Helen Burns in a style that admirably complemented that of Portia and Gratiano at once. Where her mistress was dashing and adventurous, she was reluctant and apprehensive; the exploits which Portia proposed with all the careless enthusiasm of a leader, she considered with the realistic eye of a follower who would undoubtedly be called upon to do much of the work. Where Gratiano was bold and winning, she was reserved and guarded. Her whole performance was a beautifully controlled and witty commentary on the extravagances of those around her. Miss Burns is especially gifted in the matter of her face, which mirrors her thoughts with fine subtlety; it is not that she pulls faces, or indulges in the 'double-takes' and eye-rollings of comedians of the baser sort; it is rather that she follows the action with an alert blankness of expression which imperceptibly changes to incredulity, or misgiving, or disappointment, or secret glee without any discernible movement of the features. Such a moment was her entrance in the Trial Scene, dressed as the lawyer's clerk; a less confident clerk was never seen, but her terror was given to us without tricks. This was a comic performance on a high level, and it added much to the quality of the whole.

Bassanio, far more than Lorenzo, demands high romance from the actor. The character does not bear logical examination; there is no point in probing Bassanio for psychological subtleties. What is required of the actor is to fill out the sketch which Shakespeare has given to the dimensions of the hero in a fairy-tale. Bassanio has some fine poetry to speak, and some telling situations in which to display himself. It is up to him to make the most of his opportunities. He needs a heroic presence, a fine voice, and the ability to suggest romance on the highest level.

Donald Harron is not an obvious choice for such a role as this, for he is primarily a comedian. There is about his personality a crisp and sparkling quality which is a very different thing from the warm effulgence of the romantic hero. He can submerge it in such a part as that of Octavius in *Julius Caesar;* the chilly calculation of that ambitious youth is well within his scope. He can give us a hero who is not entirely heroic—who has a dash of character—as he did when he played Bertram in *All's Well That Ends Well.* But Bassanio has no character other than that of Prince Charming; the actor must, so to speak, bring his character with him. That is what Mr. Harron did, and he gave us a Bassanio who was handsome, witty, and at the same time oddly boyish and gauche. These latter attributes were assumed; Mr. Harron need not be boyish or gauche unless he chooses. Apparently he assumed these qualities in order to make Bassanio likeable, because he could not play the part in the high heroic strain in which it is written.

It must be said at once that there are not many actors who could do so. That quality of high romance is out of fashion nowadays except in ballet, where we see it exemplified in the great *danseur noble*—Youskevitch, for example. We are assured by critics of an earlier era that several actors of the late Victorian and Edwardian period possessed it; those of us who have seen some of those actors after their youth had gone have recognized what they must have been at their best; the passing of time had sometimes marred romance with pomposity, but a glowing tenderness and splendour was still fitfully apparent. But this is not in Mr. Harron's line.

If he did not show us the full romantic quality of Bassanio he gave us much for which we were grateful. His ardour in describing Portia to his friend was moving, and his deep concern when he was to make his choice among the caskets was finely suggested. But when he turned to claim the waiting Portia he gave a giggle which was not that of a triumphant suitor in the noble mould. In all of Bassanio that was capable

of being played as comedy he delighted us, but the moments of high romance eluded him.

Perhaps this would not have been a subject for comment if Portia had not been at her best in these very moments. Frances Hyland is an actress who appears to do everything by art and nothing by nature. This is not said in dispraise, but in an attempt to explain her style of acting; she is a splendid technician; she never struggles or seems possessed by an idea which she cannot communicate. She had determined on a Portia who was a very great lady, and she conveyed that idea with complete success. We wanted her to be won by a Bassanio who was a very great gentleman.

The brilliance of Miss Hyland's technique may be illustrated by an instance from the Trial Scene. She approached the Mercy Speech so gently that we were never troubled by that sense that a Gem from Shakespeare was coming, which even very good actresses cannot always avoid. She was well into the speech before we recognized it as something we had all memorized at school. And, at one point, she seemed to hesitate, to be unsure of what she should say next. A great many people were deceived into thinking that she had forgotten one of the best-known speeches in Shakespeare. But it was a telling effect, carefully conceived and successfully carried out.

Portia's conduct in the Trial Scene has been taken by many actresses as the foundation for her whole character. A woman who can argue down an opponent who has silenced the whole might of Venice must, they feel, be a woman of weighty intellect. And so they have played Portia somewhat heavily, as though all her wit and exuberance in the other scenes of the play were the relaxations of a female Blackstone. But it was not Dr. Guthrie's idea that Portia should come to court with her sleeves full of aces; she pretended to be assured, but she was feeling her way until she found the solution to the case in a law-book, just in the nick of time. This was in keeping with the conception of the play as a fairy-tale. It also disposed of the difficulty which the other interpretation brings with it, which makes Portia seem to be playing cat-and-mouse with Shylock, admitting the justice of his case only to hurl him from a higher precipice at the end. This Portia appeared in court obviously hoping that Shylock could be bought off, and when he refused the money she was in a desperate predicament. When an appeal to mercy, and an offer of money, had failed, she fell back upon her mother-wit and it served her well. This was consistent with the Portia whom we had seen mocking her unwanted suitors, and who had surrendered herself to Bassanio in a speech of great tenderness and nobility.

Many descriptions are to be found of performances of Portia by great actresses of the past which leave us full of admiration for them. But until recent times they did not give us Shakespeare's Portia in full, for they shrank from certain passages which, in the words of one eminent Victorian critic, 'virtue and taste must always wish to be excised from this otherwise supreme conception of pure womanhood'. Nowadays we are not so convinced that pure womanhood may not relish a joke about sex; purity, we feel, is at least as much a matter of how a thing is said, as of what is said. The lines in which Portia and Nerissa reproach their husbands for the loss of their rings do not seem to us to be outside the range of ladies of high spirits, who know how to turn a phrase. Miss Hyland was able to give us this side of Portia with all the lightness it demands. *The Merchant of Venice* is, among many other attributes, a comedy of sex, and it is good to see all the wit of the Fifth Act restored and played for its full effect.

Let us not leave this performance without commenting on the grace of Miss Hyland's stage deportment. She moves like a dancer, and wears her costumes perfectly. We are fortunate indeed that we need not look outside Canada for an actress who can give such splendid life to one of Shakespeare's loveliest heroines.

Shylock, much more than Portia, has been the subject of extreme and often misplaced ingenuity. The actor-managers of the nineteenth and early twentieth century, determined to make *The Merchant of Venice* into a play in which they could star, with a leading lady, laid heavy emphasis on Shylock's misfortunes as a father; they squeezed remarkable pathos out of his single reference to Leah, who gave him the turquoise (and who is never, it must be pointed out, identified as his wife); his references to his Jewish faith were solemnly underlined. Sir Henry Irving built up the part by a device which is so striking that it won the approval of discerning critics in his day; after the elopement of Jessica with Lorenzo, when the masquers had dispersed and the stage was empty, Shylock, with his staff and lantern, was seen to return to his home, crossing a bridge which spanned a canal; he knocked at his door, and as the curtain fell he was waiting for his daughter to open it. This is a fine imaginative stroke, and I for one would like to have seen it. Sir Herbert Beerbohm Tree, with his restless anxiety to go Irving one better, did the same thing but continued the action until Shylock had let himself in with his own latchkey, only to rush back upon the stage in an ecstasy of grief and rage. That was too much. Other actors cut out Salanio's description of Shylock's public rage, and introduced a scene in which the Jew stormed across the stage, pelted by jeering children. Of several Victorian actors it was said that they made this role typify the suffering of the whole Jewish race. To such excesses does the star system lead when it is applied to ensemble plays. For *The Merchant of Venice* is an ensemble play, and Shylock is one of four leading parts.

In many ways his part is the best and most memorable, but that is not the same thing as a part to which all others are subordinate. If the play is turned into a background for a personal creation it ceases to be the play that Shakespeare wrote.

Frederick Valk played Shylock as the character appears in the text. He did not attempt to make the Jew a type of all Jews; he was content to make him one man, and that the villain of the play. His conception was powerful rather than subtle. He did not attempt to surprise us with ingenious sidelights on Shylock; his aim was to astonish and appal us with a full-blooded depiction of a man driven to an extreme course of action by ill usage, and in this he succeeded fully. His performance mounted like a great wave from the first scene in which he appears until the end of the Trial Scene, where his passion reached its height, and broke upon the beach. It was an astounding exhibition of mounting emotion, possible only to an actor of great physical and vocal resource. This was acting of a kind which we have not seen before at Stratford—acting which is uncommon in the English-speaking world, though a style favoured in Europe—and it roused the first-night audience to give Mr. Valk a standing ovation, which he had clearly not expected.

There were those who said that this tribute was because Mr. Valk, himself a Jew, had appeared as a Jew of villainous temperament. I for one do not believe this to be true; comparatively few people are obsessed by this question of who is, and who is not, of the Jewish faith, and theatre audiences do not reserve their warmest approbation for shows of good sportsmanship. It was a tribute to a stirring piece of acting, as was the similar ovation given to Alec Guinness on the first night of *Richard III*.

One somewhat unexpected characteristic of this Shylock was his geniality in his first scene. He did not fawn; he faced Bassanio and Antonio firmly, and with a hint of ironic insolence. He suggested the bond with the forfeit of a pound of flesh not as a calculated scheme to murder his enemy, but as a spur-of-the-moment joke, obviously thinking it the most ridiculous thing in the world. His treatment of Launcelot Gobbo was impatient, but not harsh, and in his passages with Jessica he was fatherly, but not sentimentally so. This Shylock, in his early scenes, was a man as much at ease in his world as the restrictions laid upon his race would permit.

This early sense of well-being provided an excellent contrast with Shylock as he appeared when robbed of his daughter and his money. If we see a Shylock who is too subtle and nervous, his rancorous pursuit of revenge does not greatly surprise us; this man, who seemed so sure of himself, presented a shocking figure when he became obsessed with the desire to kill his enemy. Yet there was no raving, no sobbing—only a frightening force of purpose, when he confronted his Christian tormentors. The great speech which begins 'To bait fish withal' [III. i. 53], which has always been a high moment in any performance of this part, was given by Mr. Valk with quiet fury. It was in the scene which follows, with Tubal, that he gave way to violent emotion.

Sir Henry Irving referred to certain parts in the plays in his repertoire as 'table-legs', because upon their firm support rested an important section of his own performance. Tubal is a table-leg. Bruno Gerussi was suitably firm and helpful, but he was dressed in the only really bad costume in the production; no actor can rise above a rig-out that makes him look like a bearded lady who has allowed herself to run to fat. Beyond this handicap, a good performance was discernible. Tubal was phlegmatic, and gave Shylock his news, good and bad, with the same air of resignation. Shylock's exultation when he heard of Antonio's misfortune was close to madness, but in the next scene, when he met his enemy with the gaoler, he was utterly self-possessed, and icy in his refusal of mercy.

Shylock appeared in the Trial Scene plainly assured of his victory. He barely concealed his contempt for the proceedings, and his reply when the Duke suggested mercy to him was given in the tone of a sharp rebuke. It is unusual to see a Shylock as bold as this, but the concept fits well with the fairy-tale nature of the play; Shylock is the powerful evil magician before whom even the constituted powers of law are abashed. He was patronizing and almost jaunty in his attitude toward the young judge who came to settle the case, and frankly contemptuous of Gratiano. His certainty of success was so great that even when Portia uttered the judgement which reduced his hopes to ruin he did not at first comprehend it. He looked at her incredulously, and laughed the laugh that we had first heard when he proposed the bond to Antonio. Then, as the reality of his situation broke upon him he lost, but only for a moment, his self-possession, and quickly recovered it to meet his altered situation.

It is easy for Shylock to garner sympathy at the end of the

Trial Scene by suggesting that he is suddenly stricken by mortal illness; Richard Mansfield used to thrust his knife under his gaberdine in such a way that Shylock seemed to have stabbed himself; he made his exit as though bleeding to death. There is no warrant for such extreme antics. Shylock is a villain, and he meets a villain's fate. But if he is true to his villainy we admire him as we admire any show of constancy, however wrong-headed. Mr. Valk did not play for our sympathy at the end by tricks; he showed us, instead, a man whose world has fallen into ruins. He hardly seemed to notice the Christians who exulted in so un-Christian a fashion all around him. It was his inner agony which possessed him; physical insult was an old story to him, but spiritual defeat was a new experience. And so we saw him leave the court, surrounded by a cruel mob, but by his own reckoning completely alone.

Though some of the words of criticism in the foregoing may seem to suggest a pernickety dissatisfaction, they are intended only to record particular aspects of what was, considered as a whole, a noble and heart-warming production of a great comedy. It is the fashion in some critical circles at present to decry anything which may be labelled as 'escape'. Yet *The Merchant of Venice* is escape. It contains nothing of that realism which gives photographic detail of the accidents of daily life: it is, on the contrary, a fine example of that other realism which provides us with a poetic distillation of our deepest wishes and our richest emotional experience. Shakespeare was at home with both these varieties of realism, and knew the value of both, but he gave unquestioned precedence to the latter. (pp. 53-79)

Robertson Davies, "The Merchant of Venice," in Thrice the Brinded Cat Hath Mew'd: A Record of the Stratford Shakespearian Festival in Canada 1955 by Robertson Davies and others, Clarke, Irwin & Company Limited, 1955, pp. 45-80.

PRODUCTION:

Morris Carnovsky and Katharine Hepburn • American Shakespeare Theatre • 1957

BACKGROUND:

Although Katharine Hepburn took star billing in Jack Landau's production at Stratford, Connecticut, critics agreed that Morris Carnovsky's Shylock was the real showpiece. Within Landau's conception of the play as romantic comedy, Carnovsky's conception of Shylock as comic villain operated aptly to balance the drama, according to the critics. "This Shylock of Morris Carnovsky," affirmed Alice Griffin, "is a full-length, subtly executed, excellent portrait." Hepburn's Portia was not as successful and appeared strained to some witnesses. Claire McGlinchee asserted that Hepburn's "voice is not the instrument for Shakespeare's poetic lines," whereas Griffin commended Hepburn's performance but conceded that "her Portia is not so much Shakespeare's as her own familiar brand of heroine." Donald Harron played Bassanio, Lois Nettleton played Nerissa, Earle Hyman appeared as the Prince of Morocco, and Richard Warring appeared as An-

tonio. Rouben Ter-Arutunian designed the sets, and Motley the costumes.

COMMENTARY:

Henry Hewes   (review date 27 July 1957)

[*Although the production fell short of what it should be, in the critic's estimation, it still had its merits, notably Carnovsky's "true" portrayal of Shylock. Carnovsky, according to Hewes, successfully evoked the character's humour as well as his rage, thus preserving the balance of the play. In her performance as Portia, Hepburn appeared to be "overdoing the obvious."*]

While the American Shakespeare Festival Theatre's production of *The Merchant of Venice* falls short of what it should be, it is the occasion for the best major performance in the three-year-history of the Festival. Moreover, it is a performance with roots in our theatre, one which should inspire finer performances in many future American productions.

The role of Shylock has always been a difficult one: how to play this old usurer without transforming the play from a comedy to a tragedy? But in this performance Morris Carnovsky manages to portray a true Shylock, and one who does not destroy the balance of the play. Carnovsky captures the prototype of all men who allow their businesses to obsess them to the point where they narrow their perspectives, spoil their manners, and miss out on the good things in life. This is not to say that he underplays the racial characteristics. His arguments are filled with a lively Jewish humor. Indeed, his plot against Antonio's life does not grip him in earnest until a Christian has badly hurt him by eloping with both his daughter and his jewels. Most audacious and appropriate is the first-act curtain director Jack Landau has devised, with Shylock silently discovering the open door to his house.

In Act II Mr. Carnovsky gives us Shylock's towering rage, and lust for revenge on all Christians, without raising or lowering the old Jew's stature. When in the midst of his grief he hears that Antonio's ships have been lost, he breaks out into a magnificently ludicrous dance of glee. Even in the courtroom he gets a fine laugh, when he berates the men for offering to sacrifice their wives with "These be Christian husbands" [IV. i. 295]. This humor only makes the characterization more complete, and when Shylock finally leaves, sick at heart, he is an unforgettable picture of a human made small by his own smallnesses.

To the part of his daughter, Jessica, Dina Doronne brings a remarkable warmth and reality, particularly when she professes embarrassment at appearing before her fiancé in men's tights. Earle Hyman's Morocco has a nice bit of hilarious horseplay with "four virgins of his clime" [II. i. 10]. Rouben Ter-Arutunian's scenery and Motley's costumes add elegance, and Virgil Thomson's music lightness, to the sad comedy. But the rest is only occasionally effective, with scenes often slowing down.

After a declamatory and posturing beginning there comes a brilliant entrance for the play's star. A platform supporting two closed doors moves forward on a bare stage and has no more than rolled to a stop when Katharine Hepburn bursts through the portal. And though we are immediately too conscious of the familiar voice and delivery, we are given reason to hope. For her first scene is her best. As she describes her suitors she is content really to see them in her mind's eye, without the tension that results when she tries to "act." She is also amusing when, as Bassanio ponders which casket to choose, she repeats all the singer's words that rhyme with "lead." And in moments of embarrassment her trick of suddenly descending from her normal high pitch to a low tone produces a laugh or two. But for the most part Miss Hepburn is overdoing the obvious, or illustrating the familiar. For the "quality of mercy" speech [IV. i. 184] she has the sound notion of delivering it not as an oration but as a plea. But this device chops up the speech without offering the compensation of emotional involvement by Miss Hepburn with Shylock and the court around her, and the play is badly let down.

But, fortunately, an audience drawn here to see a glittering star attempt Portia can go home having seen a real theatre artist achieve Shylock.

Henry Hewes, "Shylock Achieved," in The Saturday Review, New York, Vol. XL, No. 30, July 27, 1957, p. 22.

Claire McGlinchee (review date Autumn 1957)

[*McGlinchee declares that Carnovsky's Shylock "embodied all the qualities that are looked for in this character." The critic also praises Harron's and Warring's performances. Hyman's ranting Morocco was a disappointment, as was Hepburn, according to McGlinchee: "Her voice is not the instrument for Shakespeare's poetic lines."*]

The second play of the season, *The Merchant of Venice*, stands out in many ways, not only as superior to the group's previous achievements but as the best *Merchant of Venice* seen for a number of years. It was Shylock's play. Most people, it is true, go to this play to see Shylock. Here they were richly rewarded, for Morris Carnovsky's Jew embodied all the qualities that are looked for in this character. He was a greedy, vengeful, injured, conniving, even cruel man, with dignity, loyalty to his tribe, and a touch of kindness in his farewell to Jessica and his word of praise for Lancelot Gobbo. He spoke his lines impressively.

Donald Harron gave a life and vitality to Bassanio that is too often missing. He balanced well his passionate affection for Portia and his sincere devotion to his more than generous friend Antonio. Richard Waring's Antonio sustained an admirable dignity, from his first premonitory sadness to the final happiness in the knowledge that his ships have "safely come to road".

Katherine Hepburn was not a fully satisfying Portia. Her voice is not the instrument for Shakespeare's poetic lines. She evinced little feeling for the rhythms and delivered the "quality of mercy" speech [IV. i. 184] in so halting a manner as to convey the impression that she had forgot her lines. The scene with the Prince of Morocco was a travesty. Earle Hyman had nothing of the dignified graciousness and proud, poised speech of Shakespeare's prince. He ranted, menacing with wild gestures of his scimitar the lady he hoped to win. She cowered and shook from head to foot, revealing all too obviously her dislike and fear of him. Indeed, she had shown so much unnecessary emotion over Morocco and the excellently absurd Prince of Arragon (Stanley Bell) that the eager fluster with which she watched Bassanio make his choice of casket lost some of its effect. Yet, here, for the first time, Miss Hepburn gave her audience a measure of the charm of Portia. Beautifully gowned in this scene, she was plainly—alas too

plainly, for she overacted—the young woman eager to have the man of her choice select the leaden casket which contained her portrait.

Too many of Miss Hepburn's entrances were made on the run, as if the famous stage direction from *Winter's Tale* had been reversed to "Enter Portia, pursued by a bear". Even a child walks occasionally, and Portia was, after all, a young woman of distinction. Miss Hepburn's courtroom scene had its good moments, but no group of people on the serious business that had brought the Duke, Shylock, Antonio, Bassanio and the others to the court would have been fooled by the clowning entrance of Portia and Nerissa as Balthasar and his clerk.

Why was the romantic poetry of the final scene spoiled by transposing to the end and parceling out to the three pairs of lovers the beautiful antiphonal duet of "In such a night" quatrains [V. i.] by which Jessica and Lorenzo should weave for us the magic spell that is Belmont?

One minor bit that deserves praise was the perfect singing by Russell Oberlin (the matchless counter-tenor) at the second curtain, of "For I the ballad will repeat" [*All's Well That Ends Well*, I. iii. 60] to an unpublished setting by Virgil Thompson. Deservedly it got one of the warmest rounds of applause in the entire performance.

The variety in similarity that Mr. Reuben Ter-Arutunian devises for stage effects against those by now famous slat blinds is truly fascinating. In this play, a suggestion of Venetian windows outlined in gold; a wiry but graceful Rialto Bridge which must have been stronger than it looked to withstand the too frequent traffic and obvious posing that was its fate; a curtain of prettily flowered ribbons that indicated Portia's house—these were good. Less effective were the architectural gingerbread of the caskets and the way in which they were juggled about; two of them were even carried off the stage before Bassanio had made his final choice. There was an excess of processions of entourages of the various suitors hurrying over the bridge, and an unnecessary number of revelers flitting rather aimlessly about Shylock's house. A few such figures are enough to suggest the contrast between the carnival spirit and the loneliness that awaits Shylock on his return home after Jessica's elopement.

The supporting roles were well cast. Richard Easton's Lancelot Gobbo was noteworthy, the scene with old Gobbo being particularly well done. John Colicos' Gratiano, Richard Lupino's Lorenzo, Dina Doronne's Jessica, and Lois Nettleton's Nerissa deserve commendation. (pp. 508-09)

Claire McGlinchee, "Stratford, Connecticut, Shakespeare Festival 1957," in Shakespeare Quarterly, Vol. VIII, No. 4, Autumn, 1957, pp. 507-10.

Euphemia Van Rensselaer Wyatt (review date September 1957)

[*Wyatt affords special attention to the staging of Landau's production, including the unconventional use of the scales in the trial scene (Act IV, Scene i), the set designs, and Motley's costumes.*]

Was it revenge or vengeance? The key to Shylock's character lies in the motive. Macklin, Macready and Edwin Booth made their Shylock a man festering with the infection of personal hate but it was vengeance in the sense of stern justice which prompted the rather Mosaic character created by Edmund Kean and the elder Booth which moved one spectator to liken Kean to a "chapter out of Genesis." David Warfield's Shylock was a pitiful old widower; George Arliss played him as a suave Oriental; Luther Adler as a middle-aged trader. Richard Mansfield angled for pathos; Moskovitch for comedy.

Morris Carnovsky in the American Stratford production is a fine figure who might be one of the Minor Prophets but who lacks—as all the modern Shylocks I have seen have lacked—the tensity of a great personality like Sir Henry Irving whom I saw when I was eight years old but remember far more distinctly than Arliss. Sir Henry based his characterization on the study of a Levantine Jew, scholarly and dignified but who, once he has let hatred corrode his soul, becomes malignant.

The keynote of the present production is anti-Semitism. Carnovsky's Shylock is governed by a rather impersonal spirit of Hebraic justice against the racial discrimination he has endured. His vengeance adheres to the letter of the law and he sharpens his knife as he might a lawyer's pencil. His most important speech is, of course, "Hath not a Jew, eyes?" [III. i. 59] etc., which he addresses squarely to the public.

To further this interpretation, however, a serious break has been made in the traditional staging, a break which also is in contradiction to the text. When Portia asks, "Are there balances here to weigh the flesh?" the question now becomes purely rhetorical as the most prominent property on the stage is an oversize pair of scales. Their presence not only takes some of the bite out of Portia's defense but obliterates a sinister detail of Shylock's business scrupulosity when he replies, "I have them ready" [IV. i. 256]. It was then he formerly drew them out of his belt. Clever staging in the trial scene places the populace supposedly in the pit thus reducing the need for supernumeraries and giving Shylock the opportunity for a dramatic exit as he descends into the jeering crowd.

With Booth, Irving and Belasco the sets were joyously Venetian, with Jessica sometimes eloping in a gondola. There is no hint of Venice at Stratford which has the usual slattish background except that in the middle of the stage there stands a gracefully fragile arched bridge whose height predicates agility in the company. The bridge also forces the action downstage where, drenched in golden light, the baleful slats can be forgotten. Some enchanting ribbon streamers indicate Portia's villa in Belmont and there the bridge serves as grand staircase. At the trial, draped with tapestry, it is the Judge's seat with Portia at a podium on a lower level. The play opens with Gratiano and Lorenzo meeting on the bridge and greeting Antonio below. After Shylock has passed over it, a gilded arabesque doorway slides under the bridge and there emerges Portia in shimmering yellow.

And what a lovely Portia! Young, high-spirited, tender, Miss Katharine Hepburn's highborn Venetian lady is also very much in love; her eagerness giving personal interest to the pageantry of the caskets. These are borne in by pages who, sitting cross-legged on the edge of the stage, hold them aloft like lanterns. Earle Hyman as Morocco is tremendously impressive with his white robes and turban and white-robed black suite whom an agitated Portia leads up her stairway. Tall Arragon's exaggerations are good comedy as played by Stanley Bell, and Bassanio shows how he managed to spend so many of Antonio's ducats when he appears in richest cerise

heralded by six varlets in pink with flower-bedecked staves. Portia welcomes him in white with roses trailing across the bouffant skirts which she must hold up with both hands. She is full of lithe grace as she runs about the stage or sinks in a billowing curtsy to the floor.

Ellen Terry wore crimson at the Trial but Miss Hepburn is in a dull-colored gown with severe black head-piece; her deep voice abetting her authority as she dominates the scene. Her "Quality of Mercy" speech [IV. i. 184] is saved from rhetoric by being addressed privately to Shylock but also loses importance. The baiting of Bassanio and Gratiano with the rings is high comedy chiming prettily with the poetry of the last act.

Thanks to the direction of Jack Landau, Motley's costumes, Jean Rosenthal's lighting, Virgil Thomson's music, to the Bassanio of Donald Harron, the Antonio of Richard Waring, the Gratiano of John Colicos, the Shylock of Carnovsky and the radiance of Miss Hepburn this is the finest and most delightful production so far presented *at the American Shakespeare Festival Theater* (Stratford-on-the-Housatonic). (pp. 467-69)

Euphemia Van Rensselaer Wyatt, in a review of "The Merchant of Venice," in The Catholic World, *Vol. 185, No. 1110, September, 1957, pp. 467-69.*

Alice Griffin　(review date September 1957)

[*Griffin asserts that in the context of romantic comedy, Carnovsky's villainous Shylock was aptly conceived and performed: "This Shylock of Morris Carnovsky is a full-length, subtly executed, excellent portrait." Hepburn offered a "sprightly, graceful and thoroughly winning" performance, although "her Portia is not so much Shakespeare's as her own familiar brand of heroine."*]

As directed by Jack Landau, *The Merchant of Venice* is a sunlit comedy, briefly clouded over by the threat of Shylock, but resolving itself in moonlight and mirth. When the curtain rises, a graceful Venetian bridge is seen, stretching from one end of the stage to the other, with Antonio, Salerio and Solanio strolling across it. It is here that Antonio pauses while Shylock comments below, "How like a fawning publican he looks!" [I. iii. 41] From the streets of Venice we are transported to the fairy-tale atmosphere of Belmont, where exotic processions of the Princes of Morocco and Arragon cross the bridge (now a stairway) to choose from the three caskets, as Jean Rosenthal's lighting and Virgil Thomson's music evoke the magic mood.

Throughout, this mood is one of music and hope, of young love and devotion between friends, of mercy tempering justice, an atmosphere in which evil exists but is bound to be thwarted. Within this framework of comedy, it is proper that Shylock be played as a villain, rather than as a sentimental, self-pitying hero. This Shylock of Morris Carnovsky is a full-length, subtly executed, excellent portrait. With a slight Yiddish inflection and a wealth (but never an excess) of gestures, the Shylock of this production is a man of authority and business when we first meet him in his gabardine tunic of gray and yellow. His evil and hatred grow out of the personal affronts to which he is subjected and under which he smarts. His "Hath not a Jew eyes?" [III. i. 59] is delivered in a vengeful tone, not a pitying one, and at the final insult from the Venetians who steal his daughter and his ducats, he becomes a beast turned desperate. When Tubal interrupts with the news of Antonio's losses, Shylock seizes on the collection of the pound of flesh as revenge for his own recent injuries and all his former ones. Maddened by grief, he spreads his fingers wide, raises his hands above his head, and dances in jubilation around Tubal. His self-love and his blindness to human values deserve his final treatment and ejection from the court and from the play.

Dominating the scenes at Belmont is a sprightly, graceful and thoroughly winning Katharine Hepburn, handsome in a series of stunning gowns by Motley. Her Portia is not so much Shakespeare's as her own familiar brand of heroine, from *Alice Adams* to *Summertime:* tremulous, shy, touching in her awkwardness and comic in her eagerness in the presence of the man she loves. She brings to the role a good sense of comedy. Miss Hepburn handles the prose and comic lines well, but her flat, nasal tones fail to do justice to the lyric passages, such as the "quality of mercy" speech [IV. i. 184]. She is fortunate in having as her vis-à-vis the Bassanio of Donald Harron, whose steadfast ardor is a good foil for her taut heroine. Of their memorable scenes together, their adroit and comic debate over the ring stands out especially. The young Venetians are well depicted, including Richard Lupino's lyrical Lorenzo, Kendall Clark's stalwart Solanio, and the Gratiano of John Colicos, who, with fine voice, movement and presence, makes of the role a minor-league Mercutio, full of gusto and humor. Richard Easton's oafish Lancelot Gobbo and Stanley Bell's foppish Arragon are valuable comic assets.

For this production, designer Ter-Arutunian adds to the Venetian blinds not only the bridge mentioned above, but a number of devices which localize his basic, unlocalized setting. Traced in metal, Shylock's house or Portia's chamber comes sliding down the raked stage; strips of ribbon fall from above for Belmont, while the blinds at the rear of the stage lift, and through an archway gleams a blue and silver backdrop. Although this machinery all moves rapidly and smoothly, it is sometimes distracting.

After the villain has been thwarted in the courtroom and thrust from the play, the short final scene restores the mood of magic, and the work closes on this note, as the three couples stroll about the stage reciting between them the beautiful lyric lines (transposed from the beginning of the act), "In such a night as this . . . " [V. i. 1]. (p. 70)

> *Alice Griffin, "The Stratford Story: Connecticut Version," in* Theatre Arts, *Vol. XLI, No. 9, September, 1957, pp. 68-70.*

PERFORMANCE:

Peter O'Toole and Michael Langham • Stratford-upon-Avon • 1960

BACKGROUND:

Critics lauded O'Toole's powerful, magnetic performance of the sympathetic interpretation of Shylock. A. Alvarez commended O'Toole for transforming the character "from an ambiguous figure hovering somewhere between caricature and melodrama into a major tragic hero." Dorothy Tutin's Portia, although perhaps not as captivating as O'Toole's Shylock, was likewise skillfully conceived and performed. Michael Langham's direction, reminis-

cent of Tyrone Guthrie's 1955 effort, according to John Russell Brown, emphasized the romantic-comedy elements of the play and satisfied most reviewers, although at least one critic labeled Langham's stage business "gratuitous horseplay." Patrick Allen played Antonio, and Desmond Heeley devised the late-eighteenth-century designs.

COMMENTARY:

W. A. Darlington　(review date 13 April 1960)

> [*Darlington commends Langham's "excellent romantic account of the play" and the two "first-rate" principal performances of O'Toole and Tutin.*]

The new season at the Shakespeare Memorial Theatre here got into its full stride tonight with a distinguished performance of *The Merchant of Venice,* which, in spite of its preposterous plot, should have the most sure grip on the public favor of any of the Shakespeare comedies.

The director was Michael Langham from the theatre at Stratford, Ont., who practiced no eccentricities (unless putting the cast into eighteenth-century costume counts as eccentric) and gave an excellent romantic account of the play.

He had a first-rate Shylock in Peter O'Toole and a first-rate Portia in Dorothy Tutin. If these two parts are well played, little can go wrong with this comedy.

Mr. O'Toole is a Shylock of the kind that Sir Henry Irving invented—not so much a stage villain as a man cruelly ill-used who sees his chance of revenge and takes it cruelly.

Instead of the snarling, cringing, malignant Jew we sometimes see, Mr. O'Toole gives us a tall figure, a handsome face and a dignified, almost noble, carriage.

Miss Tutin's Portia is enchanting in the love scenes, authoritative at the trial and charmingly gay when the comic opportunities come along.

The whole company gives solid support and already shows signs of welding into a team.

> *W. A. Darlington, "Stratford Group Gives 'Merchant'," in* The New York Times, *April 13, 1960, p. 46.*

Alan Brien　(review date 22 April 1960)

> [*Director Langham "loaded on the business," especially in the casket scenes, which proved theatrically effective, according to Brien; however, the distracting visual business obscured the verse as well as "the central theme of the play which is the ambiguity of appearances." O'Toole's powerful performance impressed the reviewer, but Tutin appeared "a little underweight for Portia."*]

Of all modern Shakespeare directors, Tyrone Guthrie is most apt to take the wildest liberties with the author, Michael Langham, the director of the new Stratford *Merchant,* is a pupil who yet keeps the master's high spirits reined in. To set the play in the late eighteenth century neither helps nor hinders the fairy-tale fluidity of the improbable plot though through it he builds up a night-world of brutal, swaggering gallants, eloping heiresses, masked rioters and melancholy romantics where music, laughter and bird song underscore the restless action. In the casket scenes, he has loaded on the business—the Prince of Arragon is played by Ian Richardson as a Goya ninny with a white camel-face. He is accompanied by a ravaged duenna and fusty tutor, and during his runaway speech the maid holding the silver casket faints with strain and boredom. All this is theatrically effective: it distracts the ear from the verse by filling the eye. But it also obscures the central theme of the play which is the ambiguity of appearances—what Bassanio calls 'the seeming truth which cunning times put on to entrap the wisest' [III. ii. 100-01].

Shakespeare is a poet as well as a story-teller just because he is able to transmute a familiar string of incidents into a significant and powerful chain of images. The casket which conceals the jewelled prize behind a lead facade, the beautiful girl who secretes her message of mercy beneath a lawyer's gown, the Jew's bond which turns his revenge back on his own breast—all three devices echo and re-echo in action and in words the same message. Even Shylock's careful choice of the story of Jacob, who thrived by changing the colour of his lambs, and Launcelot Gobbo's cruel gulling of his blind father are part of the pattern. It is hard to be sure how far Shakespeare himself was conscious of the ironies his images bred in this atmosphere of bluff and double-bluff, hoax and counter-hoax. Does Bassanio mean to hint that Portia may be wrong and Shylock wronged when he says:

> In law, what plea so tainted and corrupt,
> But being seasoned with a gracious voice,
> Obscures the show of evil? In religion,
> What damned error, but some sober brow
> Will bless it, and approve it with a text?

[III. ii. 75-9]

Is it merely accidental that all the famous lovers invoked by Lorenzo and Jessica during their 'In such a night as this' [V. i. 1] speech should be unhappy and deserted victims of unruly passion? These are legitimate intuitions and suppositions that production should illuminate and underline. Like almost all other Shakespearian directors, Mr. Langham is too busy ingeniously, and often entertainingly, encrusting the surface of the play to spare much time uncovering the roots.

Oddly enough, this petit point throws in vivid relief the figure of that pitiful stage monster, Shylock, the Caliban of the stock exchange. Mr. Langham's judges and spectators in the trial scene all groan and moan and throw up their hands in over-drilled unison like the chorus in a Kentucky minstrel show. This is silly but its very silliness helps to magnify Peter O'Toole's performance which has a strength and integrity and size rare at today's Stratford. Apart from an occasional tendency to overdo the Yiddisher mummer (as a friend said to me afterwards—'Shylock is obviously a Sephardic Jew, why should he speak with an Ashkenazi accent?') Peter O'Toole hits the role smack below the heart. His Jew, like Falstaff and like Iago, has no choice but to be the thing he is. He looks so right, neither cringing nor noble, but the pedigree alien among a pack of home-grown mongrels, the nouveau Richelieu caught in a rugger scrum. Around him the Christians scrounge and gamble for money and love, why should he too not suffer genuinely at the loss of his ducats and his daughter? Peter O'Toole's Shylock is not a grotesque—his desire for revenge, for acceptance, for profits, for love springs from normal and convincing human ambitions. The familiar lines come alive in his mouth and his readings of them have an authority and impact which only a true heroic actor can

enforce. The rest of the cast are good enough on a knee-high scale—especially Dinsdale Landen as Launcelot, Jack MacGowran as Old Gobbo and Patrick Wymark as Gratiano—though Dorothy Tutin is a little underweight for Portia, Patrick Allen too thick-necked for Antonio, and Ian Holm hardly red-blooded enough for Lorenzo. (pp. 572-73)

Alan Brien, "The Show of Evil," in The Spectator, *Vol. 204, No. 6878, April 22, 1960, pp. 572-73, 575.*

A. Alvarez (review date 23 April 1960)

[*Alvarez asserts that O'Toole's authority, magnetism, and intelligence combined to transform Shylock "from an ambiguous figure hovering somewhere between caricature and melodrama into a major tragic hero." O'Toole's compelling performance compensated for the "gratuitous horseplay" of some of Langham's staging, the critic remarks. Although Tutin's performance could not match O'Toole's for power, according to Alvarez, it was at least superficially pleasing.*]

Two weeks ago I boded darkly for Stratford's new regime when Peter Hall sacrificed *The Two Gentlemen of Verona* to those two deities, Mimsy, God of Atmosphere, and Watchit, God of Stage Mechanics. Mercifully, the skies have brightened with the Memorial Theatre's second production. *The Merchant of Venice* is a more rewarding play than *Two Gentlemen,* and Michael Langham's production is proportionately fertile and intelligent.

Stratford's stage and resources being what they are, it would take a positively saintly asceticism not to overproduce. Moreover, Desmond Heeley's eighteenth-century designs are so

Dorothy Tutin as Portia.

beautiful and Maurice Daniels's lighting so subtle that they begin to compete with the play. The temptation is to look more than to listen, as though the speeches were there simply to orchestrate the scenery. Langham counteracts this by bringing the minor characters resolutely up to date. Patrick Wymark's Gratiano is not merely a bluff, cheerful fellow, he is also the club bore who runs on like a river while all around him throw up their hands. The Prince of Arragon (Ian Richardson), washed-out and black-suited, with mother and tutor to match, turns his choice of caskets into a ceremonial parody of bloodless nobility. Jessica escapes into a strange, nightmare carnival and the Gobbos (Jack MacGowran and Dinsdale Landen) add a little sympathetic, modern knockabout to their humour. If the producer really believes his audiences need a palliative to the poetry, this is the way to do it. But it's a pity that Langham then spoilt his subtleties by gratuitous horseplay: a servant staggering under the weight of a casket, singers getting the giggles, grimace capping grimace. There is a point at which a production becomes so sophisticated that it sinks back again into mere naivety. But in all fairness, Langham reaches it only at moments.

All the faults and hesitations, however, all the skylarking and parade, were annulled by Peter O'Toole's Shylock. I don't know what it is that suddenly produces, in all the polished adequacy of English acting, a great performance. Whatever the quality may be, O'Toole has it. One ingredient, certainly, is authority: the ability to grip an audience by its throat even while speaking slowly and hardly above a whisper. Another is sheer physical presence: like Olivier, O'Toole has an animal magnetism no matter what he is doing or who else is present; for example, while the trial rages around him, he sits deliberately sharpening his knife on his shoe; he is intent but quiet, not a movement is demonstrative, yet one can't take one's eyes off him, for all that the Venetians scurry about noisily, Portia is laying down the law and Antonio (Patrick Allen, who was impressive on his own terms) is stripped and manacled for execution. Then there is his intelligence: each word and gesture is thought out and disciplined without for a moment appearing over-rehearsed; everything seems less to be premediated than to emerge from a central conception of the character. These all add up to—what? An inwardness, a certain inner tension: without histrionics, O'Toole imposes on the audience a pressure of emotion and dignity which transforms Shylock from an ambiguous figure hovering somewhere between caricature and melodrama into a major tragic hero.

As Portia, Dorothy Tutin wisely did not try to compete with him. She has none of that kind of authority. Her talent is all of the surface: a matter of delicacy and prettiness, with a touch of pertness and a sensitive voice that was at times so finely tuned as to sound almost piping. She was bright and easy in the comic scenes, lightly romantic where romance was needed; in the trial scene, what she lacked in strength she made up in cleverness.

A. Alvarez, "A Great Shylock," in New Statesman, Vol. LIX, No. 1519, April 23, 1960, p. 586.

Peter Roberts   (review date May 1960)

[*Roberts lauds Langham's mirthful, inventive directing, and his effort to integrate and balance the two plots. O'Toole's imaginative, subtle, and tragic Shylock was compelling, the critic maintains, but also revealed how the play resists unifica-*

tion when interpreted in this manner. Tutin appeared charming as Portia but lacked the requisite sense of command and gravity for the trial scene.]

More tricked up Shakespeare, I groaned, as the lighting cleared to reveal Venetian Magnificoes dressed like characters from a Sheridan comedy. First *Hamlet* in plus-fours, much later *All's Well That Ends Well* in Edwardian costume, then *Henry V* in battle-dress—and now a Georgian *Merchant of Venice* with Belmont looking like a animated Gainsborough! But I did not groan on for long in this vein. For Michael Langham's production deftly and simply knits up the double plot of the caskets and the bond and gives to both plenty of invention that was neither self-conscious nor too clever by half.

Perhaps he was a little over-zealous in breaking up Gratiano's *Let me play the fool* [I. i. 79] with interruptions of his own devising, but the usually dull Gobboes and the drearier casket-hunters were all genuinely funny. The Prince of Arragan, provided with a mimed mother and tutor and a delivery reminiscent of royal speechifying at its worst was, in particular, a joy.

But no director, no matter how inventive, can give *The Merchant of Venice* the unity it ceased to have the day Shylock began to be played as a tragic and not a comic character. And Peter O'Toole's Jew was decidedly tragic. In the first place he was a comparatively young man, tall and upright, with a beard and hair only just touched with grey. His imaginative and subtle interpretation made one realise how infinitely Shakespeare improved on Marlowe's *Jew of Malta*. He also showed up the Gratiano—Lorenzo crew for the shallow, irresponsible, thieving louts that they are. Mr. O'Toole delivered the well-worn lines with remarkable freshness often choosing *mezza voce* where so many of his predecessors have pulled the stops right out. Where, for instance, many have opted for a sobbing Shylock at the close of the court scene, he is happy with a very little ironical laugh and an unemotional, but whispered, "I am content" [IV. i. 394]. Because this was so complex and so real a character, I have never before felt so conscious of the lack of unity in the play, nor so uneasy at the moonlight revels at Belmont which follow the trial.

Most of my Portia's have been *grandes dames* at Belmont and moralising blue-stockings at court in Venice. Dorothy Tutin is everywhere quite different. At home she is full of bubbling girlishness, with something of the "coming on" disposition Ellen Terry is supposed to have favoured in this part. At court, she looks so slight a figure, one sympathises with this Duke's astonished question, "Come *you* from old Bellario?" [IV. i. 169] Whilst I like to think of Portia as a greater and more serious character than Miss Tutin gives her credit for, I was nevertheless delighted with her charming performance.

For the rest, Denholm Elliott makes a dashing Bassanio, Patrick Wymark a fat and jolly Gratiano, and Patrick Allen a grave and honest Antonio.

Peter Roberts, in a review of "The Merchant of Venice," in Plays and Players, Vol. 7, No. 8, May 1960, p. 15.

John Russell Brown   (review date 1961)

[*Brown is a British scholar, director, editor of several Shakespearean plays, and associate director of the British National Theatre. His works include* Shakespeare and his Comedies

(1957), Shakespeare's Plays in Performance *(1966),* Shakespeare's Dramatic Style *(1970),* Free Shakespeare *(1974),* Shakespeare in Performance: An Introduction through Six Major Plays *(1976), and* Shakespeare and His Theatre *(1982). In the review below, Brown affirms that "the outstanding aspect of the production was Peter O'Toole's Shylock." The success of O'Toole's interpretation was assisted by Langham's directing, which, among other things, elevated Shylock by demeaning the Christian characters. In addition, Brown discerns the influence of Tyrone Guthrie, Langham's predecessor at Stratford, Ontario, upon the production's staging.]*

By one stroke Michael Langham in directing *The Merchant of Venice* at Stratford-upon-Avon showed that he was concerned to give meaning and form to the production: in the trial-scene, after Shylock has said that he is 'content' and Gratiano that he would have had him hanged, a crowd circles round the Jew jeering at him, and he stumbles to the ground; Portia moves across, the crowd falls back silent, and Shylock rises face to face with the boy-like lawyer who has spoken of mercy and of fines. There were no words for them to speak, but the point of the moment was to show that all had been done, that the two were irreconcilable. Possibly such an emphasis would have been better made earlier, where Shakespeare directed the two to confront each other, but, together with other details, it ensured that the trial was as exciting as it usually is and more clearly the necessary centre of both the Venetian and Belmont strands of the plot.

The merriment of the fifth act at Belmont often seems detached and irrelevant after the drama of the fourth, and here again Langham's resource was to emphasize a theme, that of friendship. This was long prepared for: for example, Antonio's 'Fie, fie' in the first scene, when Salerio accuses him of being in love, was forcefully spoken and followed by an emphasizing moment of embarrassed silence, and the description of the parting of Antonio and Bassanio was listened to in such a way that the answering 'I think he only loves the world for him' [II. viii. 50] sounded no less than a measured truth. By such means Langham was able to present Antonio's silent figure in Act V as the merchant of Venice who had just given all his wealth in love to Portia; at the end he was left alone on the stage, seated and idly playing with the piece of paper which had given him the irrelevant news that all his argosies were 'richly come to harbour' [V. i. 277]. This silent, isolated drama had something of the force of the silent, isolated drama as the other merchant of Venice departed from the court of law without the 'means by which *he* lived' [IV. i. 377]. While the confrontation of Shylock and Portia gave meaning to a moment, the treatment of Antonio throughout the play allowed the end to draw strength from the whole.

Nevertheless, the outstanding aspect of the production was Peter O'Toole's Shylock. The reprieve from a persistent quest of vitality, which enabled individual points to be emphasized, also allowed one performance to tower above the others. This was less through the longer speeches than in short phrases, snatches or bites at single words: 'I *hate* him . . . If I can *catch* him . . . [I. iii. 42-6] Even on *me* . . . I have an oath in *heaven* . . . [IV. i. 228], Is *that* the law?' [IV. i. 314] Sometimes this effect was delayed or reversed, as when he waited for the third 'let him *look* to his *bond*' [III. i. 50] before fully realizing and uttering his hatred, slowly and quietly. Occasionally the sudden snarl seemed irrational or perverse, as in '. . . who *then* conceiving' [I. iii. 87] His was not a pathetic Jew: 'no tears but of my shedding' [III. i. 96] was not said for sympathy, but with ritualistic beating on his breast. He ex-

pressed pain here and at the memory of Leah by showing his effort to bear it himself, with clenched control. After this the trial disappointed at first, for Shylock had not the intellectuality to carry off the long, quietly taunting speeches; these were broken with movement and self-regarding feeling, as when 'If every ducat . . .' was said with quiet voice and almost closed eyes. But as Portia drew the trial towards an issue, the shorter phrases—a shouted 'I stand for judgement . . .' [IV. i. 103] stilled an angry court—and the intense sharpening of the knife had full power. After the collapse of his 'rights' Shylock regained some of his strength with his dignity; he laughed at the sparing of his life and prided himself still on his sense of right—'send the deed after me, And I *will* sign it' [IV. i. 396-97].

All along O'Toole was aided by his director. The tripping music of a masque off-stage gave strength by contrast to his farewell to Jessica. His costume was more dignified than usual, so that when he returned after his daughter's flight with his gown torn and muddied the audience was at once aware of a great reversal. Neither director nor actor stressed the 'inhumanity' of Shylock: his rapaciousness was not evident, for he was dressed too well for a miser; he walked too upright to suggest cunning or unbridled hatred; in the savagery of the court scene he was controlled. Moreover, this 'magnificent Shylock', as one review called him, was opposed by a gushing, nervous, trivial band of Christians.

Presumably this was another of the director's ideas for the play, for it was consistently maintained. Antonio, who was given considerable prominence, was a sombre figure, with little joy in his generosity. The others were light. Lorenzo was brisk and Jessica unaccommodating. The crowd in the trial-scene was callow, mechanical in its reactions, and cheaply exultant. The first two casket scenes were played for the comedy that could be extracted from, or given to, the wooers, while Portia's predicament and desires were almost lost to sight. The caskets did not stand still and mysterious, but were carried around by three pretty girls. Lest the audience took the Bassanio casket scene too intently, Portia was dressed in swirling pink, moved about and often spoke loudly across the stage to Bassanio. While Bassanio was 'commenting on the caskets' and the song was sung, a collapsible arbour was carried across the stage to encircle Portia. During the soliloquy, 'How all the other passions fleet to air' [III. ii. 108], attention was drawn away from the speaker to a crowd of servants moving around stage to encircle Bassanio. There was little opportunity for warm intimacy, modesty, deep intelligence. In Act V there was such emphasis on gaiety, with chasing round in circles and patronizing Antonio, that Portia's underlying confidence and pleasure in Bassanio, and her good sense, could scarcely show through. Fortunately Miss Tutin played the role, and through the ebullience managed to suggest a star-eyed eagerness, and in the trial scene, without the dignity of the usual robes, spoke the mercy speech with clarity and a solemnity that seemed to come from beyond Portia's own powers or consciousness.

In all this Langham directed consistently and with an intellectual grasp of the basic conflicts of the play. While the Shylock was not cunning, rapacious or inhuman in pursuit of revenge and the Portia did not appear wise in love, by pointing the form of the play, its crises, contrasts, repetitions, developments, the director ensured that the audience was involved in the play as a whole; under this condition, false emphasis and wayward characterization cannot destroy its holding power.

For the last five years Michael Langham has directed plays at Stratford, Ontario, and this has probably influenced some details of his work. His choice of a low, dark setting, changing little except in lighting and furniture as the action moves from Venice to Belmont, might be explained by his familiarity with Ontario's open, basically unchanging stage. At the Memorial Theatre, the single set gave fluency, as did Hall's for *Troilus,* but lacked emotive, visual appropriateness—a considerable loss on a picture-frame stage. The eighteenth-century costumes are more difficult to explain; they may have been chosen to give elegance to the gaiety of this Belmont, or possibly the example of Tyrone Guthrie, his predecessor as Director of the Canadian Festival, encouraged Langham to experiment in this way. Indeed Guthrie, who directed *The Merchant of Venice* in Ontario's Stratford in 1955, often seemed to be behind this production: he had directed the caskets to be carried by three maids who moved about 'freely'; his Aragon was accompanied by 'three black-clad tutors' (Langham's had one and a mother); for cutting the pound of flesh, his Antonio was tied to a 'sort of frame' which seemed 'symbolical of crucifixion' (Langham used a simpler pillory); his crowd indulged itself in 'jeering and jostling and even spitting' at the trial; his Antonio was left 'lonely and dispirited' at the close of the play [as reported in *The Ottawa Citizen,* 30 June 1955]. In both productions a 'choir' sang on stage for Portia's pleasure and the lovers 'wreathed' around during the ring-jests of Act V [as reported in *The Toronto Globe,* 1 July 1955] If these details represent direct indebtedness, it is still quite clear that in total effect, especially in their Shylocks and the oppositions of the trial scene, the two productions were wholly disparate. Besides giving strong and embracing form to his production, Langham had learned and assimilated the experience of another director and of the opportunity of working on another kind of stage. (pp. 135-37)

> John Russell Brown, *"Three Directors: A Review of Recent Productions,"* in Shakespeare Survey: An Annual Survey of Shakespearian Study and Production, *Vol. 14, 1961, pp. 129-37.*

PERFORMANCE:

George C. Scott and Joseph Papp • New York Shakespeare Festival • 1962

BACKGROUND:

Papp's production earned high marks from critics for its acting and its staging. Critics lauded George C. Scott's portrayal of Shylock, balanced between tragic victim and villain. Nan Martin received mixed notices, but many other cast members were commended, especially such comical parts as the princes of Morocco and Arragon, and Launcelot Gobbo, played by James Earl Jones, Gerald McGonagill, and John Call, respectively. Reviewers expressed appreciation for Papp's lively staging, "a realistic, crowd-pleasing melodrama spiced with slapstick," perhaps not innovative, but certainly entertaining. However, more than one critic objected to the appearance of the maskers clad in what appeared to be Ku Klux Klan hoods.

COMMENTARY:

Judith Crist　(review date 22 June 1962)

> [*Crist deems Scott's Shylock a "completely satisfying performance"; a bitter, vindictive character, but also an aggrieved father whose daughter has left him. Martin's Portia started slowly but grew in authority, whereas James Earl Jones disappointed as Morocco, according to Crist. Papp's direction was merely adequate, Crist writes, and the stage often appeared bare, animated only by the presence of Scott's Shylock.*]

It's Shylock's play—or, more specifically, George C. Scott's, in the New York Shakespeare Festival's opening production in Central Park.

Mr. Scott's performance is, perhaps, the sole excuse for the revival of *The Merchant of Venice* because it is one of the least satisfying of the comedies for a modern-day audience, an irritating clash of social comment involving personal tragedy with redundantly trivial romances that move us not at all in their buffooneries. There is a wearying alternation of scenes that jerk us from the intensities of Shylock's involvements to the idiocies of insouciant courtships. In this work at least the comedy distracts from rather than intensifies the drama and the drama underlines the trivia of the comedy.

It is Mr. Scott who brings life to the strangely bare and sparsely populated stage, who creates a man amid the vapid pastel-colored Venetians dawdling along the levels set between two decorative towers, who makes the drama more than a play of words. His Shylock, a far cry from the cringing handwringer or cerebral conniver of previous productions, is an interesting man—one wracked with bitterness but given to self-satire, a man who suggests a bargain in terms of almost ironic jest but demands his pound of flesh in the screaming, searing tones of one weighted by generations of injustice. He is a man who talks of the loss of his ducats, but permits the talk to be underlined with the half-shamed tones of a grieving father; he lets a gesture of tenderness obtrude, a hint of understanding edge his bitterness. There is a magnificently heartbreaking moment as he tries to rip apart the scarf his daughter has lost in flight—then he relaxes, clutches it with fleeting warmth—and discards it wryly. His is a completely satisfying performance.

Others pale beside it—and not entirely to the discredit of the actors. But once Shylock has won your heart, a number of others lose character.

Albert Quinton's Antonio seems to grow in pomposity, although Mr. Quinton's diction is, as always, a joy and one of the festival's major assets. Another festival veteran, John Call, makes of Launcelot Gobbo a fey clown; Mr. Call works fiercely at the role—and it is particularly rewarding as he and Frank Groseclose achieve a perfect duet of malapropisms in their father-and-son scene. Nan Martin's Portia is a bit too sweet-mouthed in the earlier scenes; the fiery sophistication this actress has lent other Shakespearean heroines is missing. But when she softens with love she lends her lines enchantment—and her courtroom speeches have authority.

There is little subtlety in the script, of course—and some of the performers add none. James Earl Jones is disappointing as the Prince of Morocco, playing the role in almost minstrel-show style and, worse, garbling the rhythm of his lines. Gerald E. McGonagill lends a little more finesse to the utterly aristocratic Prince of Arragon and Ben Hayes as Gratiano and Bette Henritse as Nerissa add a much-needed and pleasant gaiety to the proceedings.

The others are adequate—and adequate is all that can be said for the direction provided by Joseph Papp and Gladys Vaughan. For once the stage—and this is a handsome new one in the permanent theater designed by Eldon Elder and sparsely but attractively dressed by Ming Cho Lee—is somehow bare; the Rialto is deserted, with only a couple of players pausing to converse from time to time. Only in a masque scene—a finely dramatic moment when white-robed revelers descend upon the bewildered Shylock—is any use made of the far reaches of the stage. And only in the court scene, with crimson-costumed guards, an impressive tapestry and weighty furniture, is any sense of a rich and colorful Venetian period evoked.

The costumes and the performers seem part of a watercolor; only Mr. Scott provides the needed slash of scarlet.

> *Judith Crist, in a review of "The Merchant of Venice," in* The New York Herald Tribune, *June 22, 1962, p. 9.*

Arthur Gelb   (review date 22 June 1962)

[*Gelb praises all aspects of this "stylish, opulent and beautifully acted production," including Scott's "perfectly balanced Shylock" and Martin's "dignified and flawlessly articulate" Portia.*]

After having been rained out two nights in a row in Central Park, the New York Shakespeare Festival finally opened its season last evening with a stylish, opulent and beautifully acted production of *The Merchant of Venice.*

Producer-director Joseph Papp in past years fought former Parks commissioner Robert Moses to a standstill over the issue of free Shakespeare in the park. Now he has withstood the protests of the New York Board of Rabbis, and wrought a thing of objective gaiety, humor and pathos from one of Shakespeare's most felicitous plays.

To deal, first, with the unavoidable issue of the recently renewed charges of anti-Semitism against the play, two salient facts must be pointed out.

While Shakespeare undeniably shared the anti-semitism of his day, the argument as presented is so exaggerated and remote from contemporary aspects of the religious problem, that it is absurd to believe today's theatregoers could be swayed by it. The subtle manifestations of anti-Semitism that exist in our present society do not hinge upon Shakespeare's uninhibited image of the Jew as usurer.

Secondly, the festival has found in George C. Scott a perfectly balanced Shylock—neither apologetic, nor stridently aggressive. Mr. Scott plays Shylock superbly, as a multi-dimensional human being, turned almost psychotically villainous through accumulated persecution, both real and imagined.

His rages are monumental, his grievances ferociously imaginative. Mr. Scott shows evidence of being one of our most persuasive and versatile actors.

Though Shylock is not an attractive man, in Mr. Scott's hands he is certainly picturesque. He is also a pathetic victim, whose motivations cannot fail to elicit sympathy.

Under Mr. Papp's assured direction, the character manages to make the Christians—and, indeed, the human race in general—appear something less than unsmirchedly noble.

If this interpretation strays from what some scholars regard as Shakespeare's intent, Shakespeare himself must take the blame. He was too honest an artist to turn the mirror away from human nature, for the sake of propaganda.

It must also be pointed out that while the dynamic and irrepressible Mr. Papp has judiciously avoided the pitfall of turning the play into an overly-sympathetic argument for Shylock, he has somewhat slyly introduced a visual image that smacks of un-Shakespearean propaganda; the participants in the masque scene who taunt Shylock wear hooded white robes that deliberately evoke the the garb of the Ku Klux Klan.

In addition to Mr. Scott's fiery and tormented Shylock, the production boasts a Portia who is both lovely to look at and self-confident. As Nan Martin plays her, Portia is graceful, coquettish, dignified and flawlessly articulate. Her rendering of the trial scene is memorable.

Albert Quinton is an eloquent and restrained Antonio; Lee Richardson is a quixotic Bassanio; Bette Henritze is a pert and witty Nerissa; Ben Hayes is an impetuous Gratiano, and James Earl Jones makes a lively and amusing scene of the casket-picking episode, in the role of a vain and cocky Prince of Morocco.

In fact, all the members of the large company live up to Mr. Papp's confidence in them; John Call as a bumbling, double-talking Launcelot Gobbo; Jane McArthur as a sweet and fluttery Jessica; Richard Jordan as an avid Lorenzo—and others too numerous to single out for praise.

As for the new Festival theatre itself, it is all that a Shakespeare theatre should be. Its sweeping platform stage has been decked out by Ming Cho Lee in delicate lattice-work, a bridge and airy flights of steps to represent Venice.

Mr. Lee has also provided two lovely panels of free-standing tapestry that unroll impressively to furnish a rich background for Portia's house and a stately one for the courtroom scene. Theoni V. Aldredge's costumes have dash and splendour without ostentation. And David Amram has written his usual appropriate background score to underline the vivid pageantry of the action.

Mr. Papp recently said that the amount of work that had gone into the festival to date could have built a duplicate of New York City. It was meant as a joke, of course, but it is true to say that very few men have labored as ardently and tirelessly to such worthy effect as Mr. Papp. He finally has his People's Theatre, and surely Shakespeare himself would have been proud of it.

> *Arthur Gelb, in a review of "The Merchant of Venice," in* The New York Times, *June 22, 1962, p. 14.*

Robert Hatch   (review date 14 July 1962)

[*Hatch lauds the entire cast as well as the thoughtful staging of Papp's production. In addition, Hatch replies to those critics who deem the play anti-Semitic. Papp's production "makes it perfectly clear," he declares, "that* The Merchant of Venice *is an anti-Semitic play only to those who are already anti-Semites."*]

The 1962 season opened with *The Merchant of Venice,* to be followed (July 16) by *The Tempest* and (August 13) by *King Lear.* As always happens when *The Merchant of Venice* is produced, there have been protests from official Jewish quarters, made the more uneasy this time because one of the performances was shown on television. I cannot argue with Jews who deplore the play—they have suffered much in the name of Shylock—but the fact is, and Mr. Papp's production makes it perfectly clear, that *The Merchant of Venice* is an anti-Semitic play only to those who are already anti-Semites.

As performed here by George C. Scott, Shylock is a proud, powerful man, deeply committed to his traditions and driven to the point of insanity by the hostility and (worse) contempt of the proper Venetians. He demands the forfeit of Antonio's pound of flesh, and certainly it is a piece of wicked vengeance to act so. But the Christians, making much of their superior charity, demand of Shylock the forfeit of his God (he must turn Christian), and they lack the excuse for their cruelty of years of persecution.

The Merchant of Venice is one of Shakespeare's dark comedies, and its lyricism, its buffoonery, bawdry and high spirits, do not hide the ugliness of its main narrative. It is possible to neutralize the gall by making of Shylock a monster or a clown, but when he is played with straightforward clarity, when as here the whole motivation of the play is lucid, one feels that somehow the Antonio-Portia-Bassanio crowd has gotten away with it again. The fact that Portia lives in the suburbs does nothing to allay this social itch. The play is really about the momentum of the organization, with some of the most darling lovers in all Shakespeare thrown in to make it a treat for a summer's night.

Nan Martin plays Portia with fine spirit and wit, and she is very lovely; her voice sounded a little harsh at times, perhaps she was not trusting the microphones at the start of the run. Lee Richardson is a properly dashing (and feckless) Bassanio, Bette Henritze a most winning Nerissa. James Earl Jones is spectacularly funny as the Prince of Morocco without falling into the trap of caricaturing his own race (he keeps it personal). John Call stops the show as Launcelot Gobbo, but I have seen Mr. Call in several such roles, and I begin to suspect that he has invented an all-purpose Shakespearean clown. Gobbo, after all, is not Fluellen and Fluellen is not Dogberry; but in Central Park they are all becoming John Call.

Ming Cho Lee has designed a set of cantilevered grace and strength that is bodied out with light and on occasion with two beautiful screens that fill the central opening; Theoni Aldredge designed vivid and flattering costumes on a budget that must have far exceeded the pin money formerly spent on festival dress.

Mr. Papp, finally, staged *The Merchant of Venice* with the directness, the clarity of speech and movement and (with one or two lapses) the confidence in Shakespeare's stage sense that is the hallmark of the Central Park seasons. (pp. 17-18)

> Robert Hatch, in a review of "The Merchant of Venice," in The Nation, New York, Vol. 195, No. 1, July 14, 1962, pp. 17-18.

Henry Hewes   (review date 14 July 1962)

[*Although Papp's production avoided wrestling with the ambiguities and complexities of Shakespeare's text, according to*

Hewes, the result was "a realistic, crowd-pleasing melodrama spiced with slapstick." Scott's Shylock, balanced between tragic victim and stage villain, stood above the rest, although the hilarious casket scenes, featuring James Earl Jones and Gerald McGonagill, and the Launcelot Gobbo scenes featuring the popular John Call, threatened to steal the show.]

The inaugural New York Shakespeare Festival presentation in the new 2,300-seat Delacorte Theatre in Central Park was auspicious in many ways.

The Festival's new outdoor amphitheatre has been designed by Eldon Elder and the Park Department to meet the needs of a company whose style and approach has evolved through trial and error over a valiant seven-year period of performing on a low budget under makeshift conditions for audiences unfamiliar with professional theatre. It is not too different from the temporary theatre that the Festival used on the same site (Belvedere Lake) two seasons ago. The main improvements appear to have been the construction of a more steeply pitched auditorium that partially surrounds an open stage, the erection of permanent lighting towers and comfortable control booths for operators who used to work under conditions comparable to those faced by polar expeditions, and a loud-speaker system which is less objectionable than most, partly because of its intelligent planning, and partly because its operator can hear and control it. The stage itself contains tracks to permit the sliding off and on of the rear facade; a trap door at the back, through which scenery can be raised on poles to duplicate the effect in indoor theatres of lowering a backdrop; and a number of circular sockets in the stage floor into which poles can be firmly screwed. And, of course, the stage itself is sown with the familiar tank-trap posts that contain the concealed microphones.

Against Ming Cho Lee's stylish and graceful setting of ancient Venetian blinds in natural wood, the presentation of *The Merchant of Venice* flows smoothly. Like most of the New York Shakespeare Festival attractions, it seems to make little attempt to provide insights into Shakespeare's ambiguities, and it refuses to trade on the glories of his verse. It performs the play as a realistic, crowd-pleasing melodrama spiced with slapstick.

The Festival's own George C. Scott, whose opening-night performance of Shylock drew some minority dissent as being too mannered, displayed on the second night a nicely controlled mixture of passion and economical directness. He played the role neither as the miserable victim of a discriminatory society, nor as a stock villain.

While, as perhaps is the case in real life, we do not quite see the point where the man made his catastrophically wrong decision, we do see a number of places where Shylock permitted his not entirely unjustified hatred of Antonio to affect his better judgment. However, he makes it fairly clear that under the conditions that prevailed in his society, Shylock had a right to try to improve the conditions of his money-lending profession by eliminating a man like Antonio who lent money without interest, thereby lowering the rate. But the exciting thing about Mr. Scott's performance is its rapidly thought-through deliveries, always fresh and jumping, and his willingness to serve up the grotesque and despicable parts of Shylock when it serves the purpose of the scene.

The cast around him is less fortuitous. Albert Quinton's slow-speaking Antonio may be an attempt to show us why Shylock dislikes him, but it becomes tiresome over the course of the play. Lee Richardson and Ben Hayes as Bassanio and Gratiano bring out only a portion of the fun and irony that lie in these roles. And Nan Martin's Portia, which is most effective when she is treating the audience as her ally and confidant, doesn't always avoid the danger of smugness.

On the other hand, director Joseph Papp has amusingly staged the two scenes in which we see the undesirable suitors choose the caskets, with James Earl Jones and Gerald E. McGonagill most entertaining as the self-centered princes. And he has paid so much attention to the usually shortened Lancelot Gobbo scenes that John Call becomes the virtual star of this production. At his first entrance he even receives as much of a hand as does Mr. Scott, and it is clear that this chubby little clown has from his past performances as Puck and Dogberry found a home in the hearts of Central Park audiences. He is in the music-hall tradition and by technique and byplay gets laughs no one probably ever got before from the usually tedious equivocations of this obnoxious servant. And perhaps because he does it all so gently and unmaliciously, we tend not to resent him as much as his actions warrant. Indeed, the park audience loves him and the entire production so uncritically that a reviewer can only feel churlish at not fully sharing their enthusiasm.

> *Henry Hewes, " 'You Have a Friend at Shylock's',"
> in* The Saturday Review, *Vol. XLV, No. 27, July 14, 1962, p. 15.*

Alice Griffin   (review date Autumn 1962)

[*Griffin identifies Scott's "original and compelling performance" as Shylock as the ultimate source of success of Papp's production. By contrast, Martin failed to realize Shakespeare's Portia, Griffin argues, resembling instead "a soap-opera heroine." The critic commends the design and staging aspects of the production, but demurs that cloaking the maskers in what appeared to be Ku Klux Klan hoods was a false step.*]

The great success of *The Merchant of Venice* as the opening production (June 19-July 7) was due mainly to the brilliant portrayal of Shylock by George C. Scott. This writer had the good fortune to see (and report in these pages) Mr. Scott's Richard III in the early years of the Festival, and the same originality was present in his Shylock, plus a greater depth which has come with the actor's maturity in his art. It was a dynamic interpretation, rich in depth, exciting in its invention. Mr. Scott's Shylock was any human being who finds himself the oddball—defensive, alert to possible injury, cornered and desperate when baited, gleeful in revenge when the tables are turned. He was an emotional man trying to control his emotions until the final outbreak, when he leaped, snarling and savage, at his enemy's throat when Shylock is told he must convert to Christianity. Mr. Scott's reading of the lines was excellent, preserving what poetry is given to Shylock, in such lines as "I had it of Leah when I was a bachelor" [III. i. 121], and when Shylock is with his enemies, giving the man who hated music a rapid, rasping speech. He smiled often, not an evil or a servile smile, but one that covered desperation. In its parts and as a whole, this was an original and compelling performance.

The direction by Mr. Papp and Gladys Vaughan maintained excellent pace, and included many touches designed to clarify the action and the characters. Both the costumes by Theoni V. Aldredge and music by David Amram contributed greatly to the production. Ming Cho Lee's effective setting utilized

a central structure suggesting the inner and upper stages (as in Jessica's elopement). For the Belmont scenes a tapestry was raised between two slender poles at the center back; the seal of Venice in red was the background in a similar fashion for the court action. The one false note in the production was clothing the maskers in Ku Klux Klan costumes.

Nan Martin's portrayal of Portia conveyed to the audience little if anything of Shakespeare's characterization; her movements and voice were closer to those of a soap-opera heroine. None of the myriad details in her depiction added up to an understandable interpretation, either classic or modern. Bette Henritze was effective as Nerissa, and John Call and Frank Groseclose provided amusing moments as Lancelot Gobbo and Old Gobbo respectively. (p. 554)

> *Alice Griffin, "The New York Season 1961-1962,"
> in* Shakespeare Quarterly, *Vol. XIII, No. 4, Autumn, 1962, pp. 553-57.*

PERFORMANCE:

Laurence Olivier and Jonathan Miller • National Theatre • 1970

BACKGROUND:

The British National Theatre's production of *The Merchant of Venice* was especially noteworthy for two reasons: first, it featured Laurence Olivier, whom many consider the preeminent actor of his generation, as Shylock; and second, the production's director, Jonathan Miller, undertook to adapt Shakespeare's portrait of Venice to a late-nineteenth-century setting. The advantage derived from Miller's setting, critics surmised, was the illumination of parallels between the heartless, mercantile world of *fin de siècle* Venice, and by parallel, England, and the context Shakespeare envisioned, Renaissance Italy. Most critics acknowledged the originality and power of Miller's interpretation, but some felt that the emphasis on Venice—and consequently on Olivier's Shylock—despite its own merits, nevertheless diminished the romance and poetry of Belmont. Through his adaptation and focus on Shylock, Miller, some critics contended, threw the play out of balance and errantly purported that the fundamental function of the drama is to address the nature of capitalism, rather than mercy. Reviewers typically judged Olivier's Shylock technically flawless, but perhaps ultimately misdirected or "ill-judged." One poignant moment in Olivier's performance came with the conclusion of Act IV, just after Shylock has left the stage following his forced conversion; from offstage, Olivier delivered a plaintive wail. The cast included Joan Plowright as Portia, Derek Jacobi as Gratiano, Anthony Nicholls as Antonio, and Jeremy Brett as Bassanio. Julia Trevelyan Oman designed the handsome *belle époque* scenery.

COMMENTARY:

Irving Wardle   (review date 29 April 1970)

[*Wardle asserts that Miller and Oman's late-nineteenth-century setting successfully emphasized "the obvious financial element of the play" and mocked late-Victorian sentimentality. Although Wardle grants that Miller's inventive adaptation*

[*was interesting, the critic concedes that it was "not exactly the play that Shakespeare wrote." Olivier's radically new interpretation of Shylock showed "the kind of monster into which Christian societies transform their aliens," Wardle contends; the critic ranks Olivier's as the finest acting of his generation. In addition to the solemn spectacle of Venice, Miller's production also contained "some excellent fun," involving the Gobbos and Portia's princely suitors.*]

Modern dress Shakespeare has been tried and found useless as our own society is too close to serve as a lens to bring the past into focus. But periods other than our own, midway between ourselves and Shakespeare and possessing strongly defined characteristics, are one of the strongest interpretive mediums at the director's disposal as Jonathan Miller reconfirms in this late nineteenth century production of what might better be called *The Merchants of Venice*.

It is, notoriously, a divided piece; part insipid fairy tale, part a pioneering masterpiece in Christian-Semitic relationships. Tenuously holding the two parts together is the theme of money; and in Dr. Miller's version this thread has thickened into a steel cable.

From our first view of Julia Trevelyan Oman's set, a bare businesslike square with a couple of curtained upstage houses that open like jewel caskets, this is clearly not a romantic Venice but a Tuscan centre of private bankers and merchant venturers. And our first view of Anthony Nicholls's Antonio is of a sombre top-hatted figure, arriving preoccupied as if from a company meeting, hardly attending to the surrounding chatter until he is left alone with Bassanio over a cafe table, to whom he then addresses a curt, "Well?" Jeremy Brett's Bassanio, squirming and ill-at-ease in leading up to his plea for yet another loan, grows lyrical when he gets to the point. "In Belmont is a lady *richly* left" [I. i. 161], at which an off-stage violin strikes up.

The setting, in other words, works in two ways. It emphasizes the obvious financial element of the play, and it also unmasks the romantic element as so much flimsy sentimental decoration. The whole apparatus of treacly late-Victorian sensibility is wheeled into position to reduce the love-affairs to so much beribboned marzipan. Pastiche Mendelssohn. Portia's boudoir bursting with tastelessly ornate furnishings and status-affirming dresses, all bespeak a greedy philistine society whose real life goes on in counting houses and legal chambers like the sober leather-seated room where Shylock comes to judgment.

This, of course, is not exactly the play that Shakespeare wrote. One should be more charmed by Portia than one is by Joan Plowright's auburn frizzed homebuilder, not to mention Mr. Brett's caddish adventurer (who takes a distinctly arrogant line with his social inferiors). If the production is perverse, it shows this most in the nocturne for Jessica and Lorenzo; this Shakespearian hymn to the power of music is played indoors by a couple of householders—a stolid pipe-smoking Lorenzo who spreads a handkerchief before exposing his natty suit to the floor, and a Jessica (Jane Lapotaire) who drops off to sleep during his speech. It fits the production, but it creaks.

However, to come to the main business of the evening, it forms a necessary framework for Laurence Olivier's Shylock which marks a total departure from stage tradition. Olivier jettisons altogether the rabbinically bearded tribal figure (on his lips the very word "tribe" approaches a sneer). He is not

a Jew of the Renaissance ghetto, but one who has come into his own in a mercantile age and can almost pass for a Christian merchant: in his morning suit, gold spectacles, and top hat he is indistinguishable from Antonio.

Within, however, he has been incurably maimed by the process of assimilation. His delivery is a ghastly compound of speech tricks picked up from the Christian rich: posh vowels and the slipshod terminations of the hunting counties. "I am debatin' of my present state" [I. iii. 53], he spits out, fingering a silver-topped cane, and then spoils the gesture by dissolving into paroxysms of silent, slack-jawed laughter. Olivier's face has exchanged its familiar contours for a fleshy, apoplectic countenance whose very lips have somehow grown thick and flabby. The voice is thin and nasal, except when it hits those ringing top notes, and altogether the performance disdains the easy process of making Shylock "sympathetic"; instead it shows the kind of monster into which Christian societies transform their aliens.

Two moments stand out: his jubilant dance on first hearing of Antonio's shipwreck, and finally his response to the court sentence, slowly bludgeoned to his knees with every fresh stroke, and then collecting himself for a dignified exit, which he follows, off stage, with a long, withdrawing and hardly human wail. We have not seen greater acting since *The Dance of Death*.

It would be unfair to leave the impression that the production is entirely schematic. It also contains some excellent fun. Jim Dale's Launcelot is easily the best I have seen, and almost redeems that wretched part with the addition of legitimately inventive clowning.

The first casket scene is also splendidly burlesqued. Dr. Miller, happily, has resisted the temptation to take the Prince of Morocco too seriously, and Tom Baker plays him as a wild refugee from the minstrels who draws a shriek of panic from the two girls. Charles Kay's Arragon is even better: tottering into the contest as if from a ducal old folks' home he has entirely lost control of his motor faculties, and, left to himself, would keep walking or putting sugar into his coffee for ever. The performance is beautifully shaped, and here, for once, seems to have brought his knowledge of pathology to the service of the theatre.

Irving Wardle, "Merchants All," in The Times, *London, April 29, 1970, p. 9.*

Time   (review date 18 May 1970)

[*The critic contends that although Miller "takes a one-sided view of the play," emphasizing the heartless, mercantile Venetian world at the expense of the romance and poetry of Belmont, "it is a strong side." The effect of Miller's interpretation was to place Shylock firmly at the drama's center, according to the critic, and Olivier's "unorthodox" performance of the role, although not at all sentimentalized, was captivating.*]

Under the shadow of a Venetian palazzo, the figure strides onstage in the regalia of an affluent Victorian gentleman—top hat, frock coat, gloves and cane. Is this some cultured character out of the pages of Henry James? One of the gentry from *The Forsyte Saga*? Hardly. It is Shakespeare's "wolvish, bloody" Shylock, in a provocative new production of *The Merchant of Venice* by London's National Theatre.

The director is the multidexterous Jonathan Miller, who for

the past year has been making a name in England as a Shakespearean interpreter. For his Old Vic debut, he has removed *Merchant* from its traditional Renaissance setting and placed it in that most mercantile of periods, the late 19th century. In his staging, the characters as well as the furniture are ornate, substantial, richly upholstered. The verse is flattened into realistic conversational accents. The play's extravagances are trimmed to the tone and dimensions of a leather-cushioned board room.

The point is as clear as it is contemporary. Money and goods are what the Venetian world turns on. But in Miller's conception, the obsession is shared not only by Shylock and his fellow usurers but also among those who look down on Shylock—Christian merchants, lovers, well-born ladies. All levels of society are driven by the engine of commerce, in marriage contracts no less than in other transactions.

A director who sees the countinghouse at the center of the play cannot take seriously Portia's enchanted realm of Belmont, with its fairy-tale plot and flowery sentiments. Miller treats it as either hypocritical or irrelevant. He turns the casket scenes into occasions for extravaganzas of comic stage business. In the famous lyric dialogue between Lorenzo and Jessica ("In such a night as this . . . " [V. i. 1], he makes Lorenzo a pipe-puffing bore and has Jessica fall asleep. Thus he undercuts the romantic element of the play, the key to what Shaw called the work's "humanity and poetry." In a world ruled by money, Miller suggests, poetry and magic have no currency.

In short, Miller takes a one-sided view of the play, but it is a strong side. For one thing, it makes the play more than ever Shylock's play. And as Shylock, Miller has Laurence Olivier—at 62, performing the role for the first time in his career. In keeping with the period setting, Olivier does away with the hooked nose, greasy locks and biblical rantings that have served stage Shylocks down through the centuries. His is a Jew who has come out of the ghetto and into his own, proving that you can teach an old dog nouveau tricks.

Yet if this Shylock is more or less domesticated, he is not quite tamed. His fashionable top hat comes off to reveal a yarmulke on his head. His upper-class speech breaks down into a breathy canine laugh or into red-faced rages of snarling and spitting. Once, after his humiliation in court, his dignity falls away completely and he lapses off-stage into a piercing primeval wail of lamentation. Disappointingly to some, this is as near as Olivier comes in this characterization to performing at full classical pitch. Nor does he modulate to softer emotions. He tears angrily through the "Hath not a Jew eyes" speech [III. i. 59], from which most Shylocks wring the last drop of pathos.

Like the production as a whole, Olivier makes no easy appeal to the audience's sympathies, but holds to an avid, harshly funny portrayal of the cruelty of human justice and the bitter ironies of human mercy. At the end of Shakespeare's text, Jessica and the merchant, the two characters whose triumphs have been bought at the cost of Shylock's downfall, pause alone and silently onstage before the final curtain. The moment apparently is intended by Director Miller to evoke Shylock, and it works. Such is the flinty power of Olivier's unorthodox performance that his unseen presence dominates the stage at that moment as few actors ever do when they are actually on it.

"A 19th Century Shylock," in Time, *Vol. 95, No. 20, May 18, 1970, p. 72.*

Peter Ansorge   (review date June 1970)

[*Ansorge laments that Miller's provocative conception of the play was somewhat lamely executed. In addition, the critic demurs, the closed society suggested by Miller's late nineteenth-century setting clashed with the free-flowing rhythms of Elizabethan drama. As a result, the Belmont scenes were poorly integrated, and many of the roles, although intriguingly begun, eventually unraveled—or, as in Olivier's case, devolved into a classical or conventional rendering that belied the originality of their conception.*]

A standing response on the part of a German Jew in 1920s Berlin to the question 'How many Jews in a Germany of thirty-five million?' was the clipped reply, 'Thirty-five million—because every anti-Semite knows an *exception* Jew.' After reading the jubilant commentaries on the Miller-Olivier *Merchant of Venice* one is tempted to re-phrase this chilling example of Kosher humour as, 'Every dramatic critic knows an *exception* Shylock'.

For nothing seems more likely to indicate the confusion which still exists over the strange role of the Jewish people in the history of Christian civilisation than the various explanations which have been offered about the meaning of Olivier's Shylock (no more numerous, however, than the suggestions offered publicly by Miller himself). A Disraeli opportunist? A Rothschilds banker? A Svevo businessman—a degenerate outcast driven to declaring a tribal war on society? A devil in a frock coat? An angel broken by his enemies' crucifix? As ever, we are wont to pay our money and reshape Shakespeare's Jew after the images of our own consciences.

Let me say that I bow to no Lévi-Strauss fan in my admiration of Jonathan Miller, the theoretician. Spend an evening in the company of Miller and you will be taken on a magical mystery tour of Western Civilisation: a thrilling, cross-cutting intellectual adventure covering some of the most important discoveries of our time. But it is precisely because I felt so little of that imagination to be in actual evidence on the stage of the Old Vic that it would be misleading to praise Miller for a production which in theory he has conceived compellingly but, at best, put very uncertainly into practice. It might be claimed that such a criticism doesn't take into account the inconsistency of the text of *The Merchant of Venice*—the contradictions and bitter taste left embarrassingly on the palate of the play itself.

Yet cast your minds back to the 1964 RSC production of Marlowe's *Jew of Malta*. Precisely by facing the barbarism beneath the blank verse, by unleashing a furious conflict between Jew and Christians in Ralph Koltai's austere, simple and pace-crazy setting—an underlying contemporary meaning was established. The pace slowed down only once, to allow Marlowe's Jew to come to the front of the stage and announce, 'This is the life we Jews are used to lead. For Christians do the like . . . ' Without ever pointing out the fact in reflective theory, the production showed us the startling manner in which Christian society has been so often disposed to treat a section of its most gifted people—the Jews.

Miller's production concentrated on a very different context. The Piazza of Venice's San Marco had been reconstructed, with precision and research from the designer Julia Trevelyan Oman, complete with towering steeples, sinister shadows, fin de siecle bric-a-brac. For Miller had chosen to present his Shylock inside a fabricated society, wandering through sophisticated salons, and sipping aperitifs in Florian's of San Marco Square. Antonio and Bassanio, with top hats and canes, emerged from the lush background to discuss their financial affairs in calm and quiet. Yet it is a fact that such a setting is appropriate in accommodating the life-style and leisurely reflections of a nineteenth-century novelist. It doesn't easily absorb the violent, quick-changing rhythms of the Elizabethan drama—which were designed to portray human experience in an *open* context, as opposed to the *closed,* private world of the nineteenth-century novel. That world and incidentally its anti-Semitism, was most perfectly chronicled by Marcel Proust (one authority whom Miller seems to have missed out on)—the caste systems, ritual hatreds and boredom which finally exploded in the Dreyfus Affair.

Had the production kept to a strict presentation of the hidden taboos and careful prejudices lurking beneath the fabrication and sophistication of this Venice we might well have been given the production that many of the reviewers thought they had, in fact seen. But the producer didn't keep to any specific code of character or period as, for instance, Zeffirelli had done so outrageously in his Sicilian take-over of *Much Ado About Nothing.* Once the action moved inside Belmont and amongst the caskets, everything was thrown to the gods, including the elaborate scenery. The Prince of Morocco hopped in and out as a diplomatic Al Jolson minstrel just back from the colonies; the Prince of Arragon crawled towards his silver casket as senility personified (wrecking the sense that we were watching a Jamesian choice of spouse and income on the part of Portia). 'Where is fancy bred' [III. ii. 63], was chanted by two Victorian aunties as a rousing, drawing-room ditty.

I suspect that Miller had despaired of relating the Belmont scenes to the grim Venetian conflicts. Instead of cutting or reworking the text, these scenes were played for any and every laugh that could be milked from them. It took away all sense of unity from the production and we were left admiring the colourful sets and applauding the jolly performances of the National Theatre Company—not least Jim Dale's Carry-On-Shakespeare treatment of the wretched Launcelot Gobbo.

The failure to integrate the smaller roles made it difficult to define the important ones. In the concluding moments Jane Lapotaire's Jessica (solitary in the final spotlight) was given a context and place in the scheme of the production. Derek Jacobi's anti-Semitic Gratiano probably came closest to how the producer had originally conceived the Venetians. Joan Plowright's Portia was an original creation: a new rich, snobby spinster who, apart from a determination to buy a husband (preferably with a lower income than herself) was utterly indifferent to the events taking place around her. Though Miller has related this Portia both to the Lady of Shalott and to Isabel Archer in James' *Portrait of a Lady,* he hasn't related her to *The Merchant of Venice.* Her appearance at the trial scene made no sense at all and her conventional delivery of 'The Quality of Mercy' [IV. i. 184] in saintlike whispers undercut much of the originality that had fired Plowright's performance in the earlier scenes.

It used to be claimed (by Jews) that only a real Jew could play Shylock convincingly. This isn't true of course but there is a measure of truth in the fact that a modern audience wishes to see something of Shylock's inner, unspoken suffering—the secret image he has of himself. After 1900 it was a tradition

in German Theatre to play a scene, not written by Shakespeare, after Shylock returns to his house and faces the flight of his daughter. The actor would race through the house, lighting up the rooms one by one, crying 'Jessica! Jessica!' and finally letting out a piercing scream of regret and suffering. Olivier saves the scream till his final moment of leaving the stage but, from the point of view of motivation, he adds very little to the inner life of Shylock. We first see him as a relaxed businessman who occasionally grimaces when uttering a mis-timed vowel, a quiet cackle, a swallowed insult. The original bond is suggested as a joke, a bait for Antonio to catch his sober tongue upon. Yet once Olivier crumbles the business man is forgotten—his animal nature usurps his reason and we watch another version of Othello falling back into dark, tribal blood rites. The Venetian setting dwindles into a cardboard background for an 'heroic' performance.

It is almost as though Olivier had listened to the wandering, conflicting ideas of his director more for the purposes of his delivery than for an interpretation. Olivier's Shylock isn't a Jew, but an actor with a Jewish director up his sleeve. For this reason the rehearsals for *The Merchant of Venice* may well have been more engaging to watch than the actual performance which, to my mind, reveals just a few pale flickers of meaning borrowed from an original luminous conception. (pp. 39-43)

Peter Ansorge, in a review of "The Merchant of Venice," in Plays and Players, *Vol. 17, No. 9, June, 1970, pp. 39-43.*

Laurence Olivier as Shylock and Joan Plowright as Portia.

John Weightman   (review date July 1970)

[*Weightman analyzes the legitimacy and effect of Miller's adaptation of* The Merchant of Venice *to a late nineteenth-century setting. Although Miller's treatment illuminated some interesting ironies and the Christians' hypocrisy, the ultimate effect was to strip the Belmont scenes of their lyricism and render the fairy-tale plot an irrelevant absurdity. A depoeticised Portia is no match for a realistic Shylock. Thus, according to Weightman, the process of elevating Shylock's status necessitated the dismantling of the Belmont scenes and the sacrifice of much of the magic of the verse.*]

The wonderful thing about Shakespeare is that he is practically unbreakable. Stretch him this way and that, turn him upside down, inflate some characters and deflate others, do all the men as women and all the women as men, make him pop or baroque or existentialist, and he survives just as well as when it was the fashion to make him the perfect English gentleman, the patriot, the Christian. "Others abide our question, thou art free"—free to be turned into anything that the spirit of the times or the genius of the producer happens to be concerned with. The explanation, I suppose, is that Shakespeare operates at a quite unusual level of intellectual interchangeability; he has no opinions, prejudices, or contours, only marvellously expressed perceptions arranged in loose masses which are open to infinite manipulation. Thus Jonathan Miller is able to take *The Merchant of Venice* out of the 16th century, that is out of the violence and colourfulness of the Renaissance, and reset it in the late 19th century or *belle époque* period, the great philistine epoch following the Industrial Revolution, and it still functions up to a point. True, it shudders and jumps, and there are considerable phenomena of rejection, yet for the duration of the evening the experiment is an acceptable and fascinating one.

But why, it may be asked, was such an experiment necessary? The reason is, no doubt, that Shakespeare's one and only treatment of the Jewish question is now rather difficult to handle in a straight manner. It would be embarrassing to do Shylock traditionally, as a bearded figure in exotic garb snarling out his hatred of the Christians. Our present concern with the racial question creates no difficulty with Othello; he can be presented as a race-conscious blackamoor, because there is no irredeemable evil in his character, and in any case the main burden of guilt is borne by the enigmatic, and quite European, Iago. But Shylock, in Shakespeare's text, is clearly a diabolic pole of the action, in contrast to the strong, white radiance of Portia. He still has a great deal of the medieval monster about him, and as he whets his knife on the sole of his shoe in ghoulish preparation for revenge, he is meant to thrill the audience with memories of all the dark sacrifices the Jews were supposed to indulge in. He is a blood-thirsty bigot, living in a state of war with the Gentiles, and only tolerated by them because he fulfils a necessary and despised role, like an Untouchable. It is true that he has a beautiful daughter who elopes with a Gentile and is received into polite society, but it is frequently the case that mythic monsters have beautiful daughters, since the fear inspired by the monster can stimulate sexual interest in the beauty that has come from the beast.

In short, Shakespeare quite frankly accepts anti-Semitism in those places where he exploits the traditional concept of the Jew. Of course, he offsets this concession to popular feeling by the big speeches in which Shylock asserts his common humanity, but the play, on a literal reading, is weighted against the Jew, as was no doubt inevitable in the religious and socio-logical conditions of the time. The virtuous Antonio spits on Shylock as a matter of course, the clown Gobbo is keen to leave him, his daughter abandons him without a qualm, the Duke speaks to him with dignified contempt, and Portia not only gets the better of him in the trial scene, like a virgin quelling a dragon, but also reduces him to poverty and abjuration. Then Gentile society, after expelling the Jewish monster from within its midst, enjoys a happy postlude of poetry and music, full of classical references—"In such a night as this. . . ." [V. i. 1] The play can be read as a sort of cleansing ceremony and if, even so, Shylock rather than Portia remains the dominant figure, this is because the Devil always tends to steal the show when he gets half a chance, and Shakespeare is too good a writer not to give him a whole chance.

Dr. Miller undertakes to turn this anti-Semitic play, if not into a frankly pro-Semitic one, which would be too sentimental a thing to do, at least into an "unpleasant" one, in which all the characters are tarred more or less with the same brush. The first effect of transferring the action to the late 19th century is that the gap between Jew and Gentile is immediately narrowed. Instead of being an exotic figure from the ghetto, Shylock looks like a gentleman on the Stock Exchange, in fact exactly like the orthodox English Jews I see every Jewish holiday going past my window in their Sabbath best on their way to the synagogue. Sir Laurence Olivier does a perfect imitation of the first- or second-generation immigrant with a business in the City and a house in Ranulf Road. This makes nonsense of a number of lines in the play about the radical difference between Antonio, who is "The Merchant of Venice" of the title and Shylock, the usurer. Shakespeare's monster labours under the weight of the Church's reprobation, because he lives on usury. No doubt, by the time of the Renaissance, many hidden forms of usury were practised by Christian merchants, but the official condemnation still survived. At any rate, Shakespeare takes it as being fully valid. Antonio lends money without interest, and the business of the pound of flesh (which Shakespeare picked up from traditional sources, as he picked up the story of the three caskets) is more credible if we see it as a mythic reaction to the horror of usury. Antonio can accept the stipulated form of compensation as a grim Jewish / Christian jest, precisely because he is not used to thinking in terms of interest and can therefore conceive of the pound of flesh as a kind of metaphor. But by the end of the 19th century, usury was a universally accepted principle, the Jews were perfectly integrated in this respect, or rather Christian society had been integrated to them, Disraeli had been Prime Minister, Edward VII had close Jewish friends, the Rothschilds were at the height of their power, and so on. It is impossible to imagine a rich, 19th-century Jew whetting his knife on the sole of his boot to carve his due out of a Christian, and in fact Dr. Miller has to transfer the gesture from Shylock to an assistant. Dr. Miller may argue that the knife and the pound of flesh remain valid as symbols of the hostility still latent between Jew and Gentile. This is quite true, but a serious credibility gap arises from the fact that the Gentiles have to speak as if usury were foreign to them, when their dress proclaims that they are living in the heyday of capitalism. This is the major difficulty that Dr. Miller has not managed to solve. Since both Shylock and Antonio are in 19th-century dress, they cannot speak to each other as if they belonged to different worlds, yet Shakespeare's rhetoric and symbolism are based on the assumption that they do. Therefore the two actors, Sir Laurence Olivier and Anthony Nicholls, have to give muted performances which, however interesting, impose a strain on the actual language of the text.

While thus scaling Shylock down from the status of medieval monster to the more comprehensible role of sardonic, literal-minded, modern English Jew, Dr. Miller subtly discredits the Gentiles by undermining their poetry and introducing a strong element of "Beyond the Fringe" farce into the action. Frequently, when a character launches into a purple passage, background music strikes up in such a way as to make the lyricism just a shade too sweet to be tolerable. What, in Shakespeare's text, is presumably meant as direct enjoyment of lyrical emotion is pushed, by the 19th-century music, in the direction of Victorian phoneyness. A doubt is cast on Bassanio's feeling for Portia by the musical underlining of *"In Belmont is a lady richly left"* [I. i. 161]. *"Tell me where is fancy bred"* [III. ii. 63] becomes a hilarious ballad sung by two simpering ladies. Even the transcendent lyricism of Act V, Scene I [ll. 9-10]—

> In such a night
> Stood Dido with a willow in her hand . . .

is brilliantly ruined by Lorenzo being made to pace up and down with a pipe in his mouth, like an enthusiastic but slightly crass *Eng. Lit.* don quoting Shakespeare rather than acting him. In a sense, this is beautifully effective, because it emphasises the fact that Shakespeare is not at all scrupulous about where he brings in his poetry. It doesn't necessarily reinforce truth of character or situation, but may be stuffed in in handfuls simply to elevate the mood. Dr. Miller doesn't want the Gentile characters to benefit indiscriminately from such an advantage, and so he systematically sabotages their higher flights. He goes so far as to extinguish Portia's great solo: *"The quality of mercy is not strained. . . ."* [IV. i. 184] I imagine that most famous actresses of the past must have stood in the attitude of the Statue of Liberty to declaim this tirade; Miss Plowright leans across the table and, in a flat voice, develops the argument exactly in the manner used by Mrs. Barbara Castle when, as Minister for Transport, she defended the merits of the breathalyser on television.

The general effect of this process is to tarnish Shylock's adversaries. Bassanio is a rather jaded playboy who borrows three thousand ducats in order to court a wealthy heiress and so restore his fortunes. Portia is a mature, bustling lady who knows exactly which pretty young man she wants and immediately takes control of his life, although she makes a formal statement of submission. Lorenzo, Gratiano, etc., are all part of a rather heartless, upper-class set who look upon the disagreement with the Jew as an episode which interrupts the even tenor of their privileged lives. The only profoundly serious, metaphysical character is Shylock; when he has been defeated, browbeaten, deprived of his possessions and forced into apostasy, he staggers off into the wings and sets up a howl of pain comparable to the bellowing of Oedipus in the moment of tragic revelation. This howl is echoed right at the end of the play when, contrary to any indication laid down by Shakespeare, Jessica is left on the stage to muse alone while a Jewish chant rises in the silence. As Dr. Miller has arranged things, this chant sounds genuine, whereas the neo-Platonic ecstasy which had preceded it by a few minutes—

> Look how the floor of heaven
> Is thick inlaid with patines of bright gold. . . .
>
> [V. i. 59]

was made to seem like Pre-Raphaelite decoration. It is really a considerable achievement to stand Shakespeare on his head

in this way on the stage of the National Theatre, with the co-operation of such a body of remarkable actors.

Dr. Miller's vigorous shifting of the emphasis reminds us again of some curious incidental features of the play. Perhaps they are just accidents, resulting from the fact that Shakespeare threw the borrowed elements together with more concern for immediate theatrical excitement than for fundamental coherence. But with him one can never be sure; they may be mysterious quirks of genius.

The story of the caskets is the main puzzle. Is it just a lot of nonsense that cannot be significantly related to the main action? Dr. Miller treats it as such and gets some of his funniest effects by guying the two unsuccessful suitors. The Prince of Morocco is turned into a naive, loud-mouthed barbarian (a touch of anti-wog racialism here?), while the Prince of Aragon becomes a doddering, sententious ancient who brings the house down with a lot of business about putting endless lumps of sugar into his coffee-cup. There is no need to listen to what they actually say; they create their impact merely through their comic stage presence. And since they are completely ridiculous, they devalue the whole operation. It is a foregone conclusion that Bassanio will choose rightly because, impoverished though he is, he is the only man in the running. In any case, Portia has already chosen him, and it is difficult to believe that such a strong-minded lady is really subject to an irrational condition laid down in her father's will. Moreover, the test itself is childish; how can such an international series of suitors have consistently chosen the wrong caskets? Portia dismisses the earlier ones as fools when she describes them to Nerissa, but why should she be courted only by nitwits if, as Bassanio says,

> . . . the four winds blow in from every coast
> Renowned suitors. . .?
>
> [I. i. 168-69]

But perhaps it is significant that, in Shakespeare's text, the two visible suitors, the Princes of Morocco and Aragon, are *not* figures of fun; they are bombastic heroes who might have come out of a tale of chivalry, and they have a touch of unreality about them, when they are compared to Bassanio.

Suppose we say that the casket business is not nonsense, to be "Beyond-The-Fringed" to the last degree to make it tolerable for a modern audience, but myth, or perhaps more accurately a mixture of myth and realism characteristic of the transition from the medieval to the Renaissance world? Bassanio, after a hectic youth, is attracted to the lady who is going to save him both materially and emotionally, and she is the first woman who is more important to him than Antonio. She is a princess in the tower of Belmont, only to be reached by the knight who successfully passes a ritual test imposed by her father. It can happen that even a strong-minded woman has been so conditioned by her father that she is only free to choose according to the concept of maleness she has derived from him. Portia's viciousness about the earlier suitors may be an expression of her sexual impatience while she is waiting for the man she knows to be the right one. Also, all women are caskets, to be unlocked rightly or wrongly according to the behaviour of the man. One would expect an affinity between Portia and the gold casket, because her locks—

> Hang on her temples like a golden fleece. . . .
>
> [I. i. 170]

yet she does not respond to the gold and silver of high romance. The man who gets her is neither Morocco nor Aragon, who opt for gold and silver, but Bassanio (much in need of gold and silver) who opts for the workaday realism of lead. Why? Perhaps because there is a fundamental, mysterious prosiness about the sexual relationship, which is stronger than the illusions of romance. And this prosiness may not be simply economic, although economics come into it; it is a sort of resolved hostility, such as is represented by the amiable bickering about the ring, which intrudes so surprisingly on the trial scene.

It may well be that my suggestions are nonsense too, but I feel that Shakespeare was getting at something deeper than mere nonsense in all this. It is important for the balance of the play that Portia, like Shylock, should move between myth and realism. If she is depoeticised from the start and turned into a straightforwardly competent, not-suffering-fools-gladly sort of person, such as Miss Plowright is bound to present in this production, she no longer comes down from the heights of allegorical sublimity to the middle ground of humanity for the meeting with Shylock, who has come up from the lower depths. She needs to be both allegorical Lady and woman, if she is to make sense of the various levels of action through which she passes. Dr. Miller shows that Shakespeare's poetry is not always to be taken at its face value, and this is a major strength; but I wonder if the pattern of ironies and sublimities is not a good deal more complex than his interpretation allows. (pp. 54-6)

John Weightman, "Dr. Miller's Transplant," in Encounter, *Vol. XXXV, No. 1, July, 1970, pp. 54-6.*

Harold Clurman (review date 6 July 1970)

[*Aside from the late nineteenth-century setting of Miller's* The Merchant of Venice, *Clurman remarks, "the production marks no startling departure from previous interpretations of recent years." Although Clurman concedes that Olivier's performance was "superb," the critic asserts that like the production as a whole, it lacked "a sense of grandeur," and unity.*]

The sensation of the late London season is the National Theatre's production of *The Merchant of Venice.* The main attraction is Laurence Olivier's Shylock, though there are other novelties in the occasion.

The play has been staged by Jonathan Miller, who was one of the stars of *Beyond the Fringe* and who has recently been marking time by refurbishing Lewis Carroll and Shakespeare with contemporary conceits. The revue touch is especially effective in the casket scene in which the Prince of Morocco is played as a modern African potentate, and the Prince of Arragon is burlesqued as a senile and purblind idiot. But there is less humor in the rest.

Miller mitigates the anti-Semitic aspect of the play. Thus when Bassanio witnesses Shylock's extreme humiliation, he is markedly affected and does all he can to stop his friend Gratiano from viciously guying the suffering Jew. Even Antonio, played as a respectable Victorian British businessman, is shaken when he hears Shylock's terrible sobbing immediately after he has left the court in defeat. The play begins and ends with what sounds very much like a traditional Hebrew chant of lamentation.

I have always thought of *The Merchant of Venice* as an ironic comedy about "capitalist" hypocrisy. Antonio and his companions—their whole society in fact—live on unearned income. Most of them are wastrels parading as gentlemanly gay blades. They hate the Jew for being a moneylender which was virtually the only profession open to one of his religion in the 16th century. But they require his money when they have been profligate in the use of their funds. After they escape the consequences of their improvidence and bankrupted the Jew they turn once more to their thoughtless fun and games. This explains the last act, superfluous even fatuous, unless the play is so understood.

Something of this comes through in Miller's production, but hardly enough. Still I suspect that the interpretation I have suggested is based on the assumption that every one of Shakespeare's plays is a coherent whole. I am not at all convinced that this is so. Shakespeare was a giant among poet-dramatists, but he was also a popular play-maker, and when he wrote *The Merchant* he was dealing with a tricky theme. He planned to write a play with lots of laughs and pretty diversions, a melodramatic comedy which would also contain the menace of a fantastic creature, a *Jew,* who in the England of his day was an unknown phenomenon, since the Jews had been banished many years before.

But because Shakespeare was a genius he could not create an entirely false character, and Shylock became a highly complex one: an ogre to the groundlings, a man of fierce and understandable passion for the more aware. He has been denatured by the cruelty of his situation as an "alien" in a corrupt society. On several occasions in these columns I have referred to him as "the poisoned conscience of Venice." He is no "hero" and just as certainly not the laughable villain the Elizabethans must have taken him to be.

What I saw at the National Theatre is a clever show with hints and overtones of contemporary significance and a *reasonable* portrait of the pivotal character. Except for the late 19th-century English mode in which the play is set, the production marks no startling departure from previous interpretations of recent years.

As performance, Olivier's Shylock is superb. His beardless make-up possesses a striking resemblance to some Anglo-Jewish tradesmen of Austrian or German origin often seen today in London. His delivery and readings are wonderful in their clarity and eloquence. With great conviction he conveys the justified resentment of the persecuted. The famous "Hath not a Jew eyes" [III. i. 59], is not special pleading but the exasperation of a man fed up to the teeth with injustice. Storming about the stage his protest rises tempestuously from within him but is not addressed to anyone in particular.

Shylock here is reduced to middle-class proportions. The slight Germanic accent conspires to enhance this impression. (There is in the whole idea of making Shakespeare a man of our day, whether in a "Marxist" or "existentialist" vein, something basically middle class.) What is lacking in Olivier's Shylock—and the production generally, more a thing of good and less good bits and patches than a satisfactory whole—is a sense of *grandeur.* Without it Shakespeare's stature is diminished.

I was an interested observer, even at moments an admiring one, at this *Merchant.* But it did not move me nor did it cause me to see the play in a new light. Intelligence and skill had gone into its making, but I felt less involved than I did in the ephemeral pieces I saw on some of the other evenings.

Just as there hardly exists a truly tragic drama in the contemporary theatre, there are virtually no genuine tragedians. The last one I can remember seeing was Chaliapin, and between 1916 and 1922 John Barrymore struck me as having that potential. Laurence Olivier is not essentially a tragedian. He is a romantic actor, a brilliant delineator of (often comic) characters. He has extraordinary power, scope and charm, and he is certainly the most dazzlingly accomplished player today on the English-speaking stage.

> *Harold Clurman, in a review of "The Merchant of Venice," in* The Nation, *New York, Vol. 211, No. 1, July 6, 1970, p. 30.*

Henry Hewes   (review date 11 July 1970)

[Hewes contends that Miller primarily aimed to poke fun at the absurdity of Victorian life, a conception supported by Olivier's intentionally muted, but original and fine portrayal of Shylock. In the critic's estimation, "the majority of the production moves quickly and humorously along."]

With Daniel-like judgment, the Queen has just decreed that henceforth Sir Laurence Olivier be known as Lord Olivier. The honor is clearly deserved, for Olivier not only has proved himself one of the greatest actors in theatrical history, but has worked tirelessly to lead the National Theatre to its present high estate. Indeed, the National Theatre's gain has inevitably cost the theatergoing public a few major Olivier performances that might have had the time to create had he not assumed the responsibility of administration.

Therefore, to see Olivier as Shylock in *The Merchant of Venice,* his first attempt at a major role since his tremendous performance in *The Dance of Death* two years ago, is a keenly anticipated opportunity. And although it is a less overpowering display of the actor's emotional capacities than a number of his past triumphs, it is a highly original conception, in which the actor places all of his famed skill and concentration at the service of the production.

Director Jonathan Miller has set the play in what appears to be polished Victorian England. It is a poisonously unfair society run by gentlemen who manipulate inherited wealth so that the money and gracious living it permits can be kept on the special preserve of the well-born. In such a society, Shylock is a nonmember attempting during business hours to dress and speak like the frock-coated, top-hatted gentlemen merchants with whom he does business. But underneath the top hat, he wears a yarmulke, which symbolizes his other allegiance. At night he returns to his daughter, Jessica, and is content to live as a Jewish banker, whose shrewdly earned wealth gives him status among the elders of his own religion. On the other hand, her father's obsession with money rather repels Jessica, who overcompensates by deciding to elope with Lorenzo, here portrayed as a snobbish middle-aged gentile.

The first confrontation between Shylock and Antonio is strictly a demonstration of how the clever usurer merrily outdoes the staid and joyless merchant, to whom business has become a meaningless, though necessary, ritual. Olivier is gleefully crafty as he puns about pi-*rats,* and begins the famous "Many a time and oft in the Rialto" [I. iii. 106-07] speech with his face hidden behind a newspaper. After cataloguing the past snubs of the man who now seeks his financial assistance, he scolds Antonio as he might a naughty but already

forgiven child with "What *should* I say to you?" [I. iii. 120]. When he frivolously suggests the penalty of a pound of flesh "to be cut off and taken in what part of your body pleases me" [I. iii. 150-51], he has a momentarily improper thought, and the audience joins him in quick laughter. In fact, there is a touch of music-hall humor as Olivier feigns disinterest in closing the deal but then snaps it up eagerly when Antonio accepts.

However, after Jessica elopes with his jewelry, Olivier's Shylock becomes insanely vengeful. "Has not a Jew eyes?" [III. i. 59] is not a plea for ecumenical compassion, but an angry assertion of his body's uncontrollable compulsion to total revenge for all other past humiliations he has prudently suffered from hostile and cold-hearted "Christians." Similarly, his joy at hearing of Antonio's losses is expressed in a brief, spastic attempt at dancing.

In the trial scene, we see that Shylock is clearly mad in his undauntable expectation that he will get justice and thereby, with propriety, achieve his irrational and cruel revenge. The audience laughs when Portia punctures Shylock's overconfidence. But soon thereafter we inevitably sympathize with the woeful plaintiff turned defendant. When Shylock is asked if he is content with his severe sentence, he snaps to catatonic attention like an obedient soldier and loudly replies with military punctiliosity, "I am content" [IV. i. 394]. A moment later, after he has been led off stage, we hear an anguished crescendo of a wail, as if Shylock's wretched soul had died within him.

It is a splendid performance, and its significance is reinforced when, at the end of the play, Jessica is clearly ashamed of having betrayed her father and of having thereby impelled him into the irrational acts that led to his living death. As she stands holding the will that Shylock has been forced to make leaving his estate to Lorenzo, we hear a Jewish chant. It is the prayer for the dead.

However, *The Merchant of Venice* is a comedy, and Olivier has deliberately kept his tragic moments as brief as possible. Thus, the majority of the production moves quickly and humorously along. A great deal of the fun comes from the absurdity of Victorian life. Director Miller makes fun of it at the same time as he seems to be making a point about the lack of deep emotion and the insensitivity toward others that went with much of white Anglo-Saxon Protestant living in those days.

He also invents outrageously here and there. In the casket-choosing scene, one of the suitors is portrayed as a senile octogenarian. And Miller gets a marvelous comic effect by having the old man absent-mindedly put lump after lump after lump of sugar into his demitasse. But then, just as he is about to drop yet another lump into the cup, he suddenly looks at his hostess and puts it back in the sugar bowl instead.

Joan Plowright gives us a strong-willed Portia who sees through all the decorums and elaborate speeches. Indeed, one feels she would not be above tampering with the caskets in order to assure her marriage to the suitor of her choosing. Yet, she has never been more sophisticatedly comic, getting her humor more with rapid twinkles of insight than with elaboration or circumlocution. Jane Lapotaire as Jessica and Anthony Nicholls as Antonio are the most memorable of the rest of the cast, perhaps because in this production they are represented as the two most deeply saddened characters in the play, and because they are also the two who stand together at the final curtain with the recognition that wealth may buy marriage partners and friends but not the kind of love they wish to have reciprocated.

Julia Trevelyan Oman's scenery and costumes nicely suggest the compromise between the Victorian and Venetian, and the whole production moves more swiftly and smoothly than any other I have seen of this play. It is a fine example of the efficiency the National Theatre has attained and of how a dedicated man of the theater can put his extraordinary talent at the service of his company to give a performance of beautifully controlled explosiveness and variety.

> *Henry Hewes, " 'The Merchant' Ltd.," in* Saturday Review, *Vol. LIII, No. 28, July 11, 1970, p. 20.*

Clive Barnes   (review date 30 July 1970)

[*Barnes chastises Miller for gratuitously adapting his* Merchant *to a more modern setting, a grafting that yielded no new meaning, according to the critic. Barnes concedes that some of Miller's excesses were pardonable because the play itself is "fundamentally unstageable." Olivier's performance was technically superb, but "ill-judged." The reviewer reserves special commendation for Brett's Bassanio and Oman's sets.*]

I can see a thin and tenuous reason for staging Shakespeare in modern dress. The director is indicating with an archly lifted eyebrow how absolutely madly contemporary it all is. Mind you, if he needs to put Hamlet in jeans to prove his relevance, you are, I think, entitled to wonder how much he knows about relevance.

Jonathan Miller, director of *The Merchant,* has not placed the play in either the Shakespearean time capsule—after all, what period did Shakespeare want?—or modern dress. Rather he has taken a fin de siecle Venice, full of sighs and popinjays, which offers a great opportunity, beautifully taken, to his designer, Julia Trevelyan Oman, but remains a weak Tyrone Guthrie-like jape against the play.

By transplanting the play in this arbitrary, yet trendy fashion, Mr. Miller gains nothing but an air of peculiarity that innocent souls may confuse with originality. It is a confidence trick, of course, but then Mr. Miller has never lacked for confidence.

One of the difficulties of *The Merchant* nowadays is to explain away its anti-Semitism, which Mr. Miller tends to ignore. He gives us a very friendly Shylock, gently aiming at discreet tragedy. He underplays the Belmont scenes. He makes Lorenzo an ass and has Jessica apparently in love with Launcelot Gobbo. In short, Mr. Miller is making an honest attempt to stage a fundamentally unstageable play, and his excesses should be viewed with tolerance if not approval.

Laurence Olivier's Shylock is admittedly an elegant piece of stagecraft. Mr. Miller, a great humorist, once described himself as "a Jew, but, you know, not Jewish." It would be an admirable description of this Shylock. Olivier is marvelous—a boardroom Shylock, stuffed with interest rates, impersonal to the point of credibility. A robot business man with Hebraically ethnic overtones. It is a great performance. Great, but ill-judged.

Of the rest, the company is as splendid as the circumstances will allow. Joan Plowright is less than ideal as Portia—the quality of mercy and almost everything else is all too strained—but Anthony Nicholls makes a sensibly bluff Antonio. Jeremy Brett, in the production's best performance, is a grimly aggressive Bassanio, and Jim Dale is sweet enough, yet not too sweet, as the younger Gobbo.

Miss Oman gives us the Venice we have all dreamed of, reading authors as various as John Ruskin and Thomas Mann. Miss Oman is a great designer of nuance. You could trust her with a mist.

> *Clive Barnes, "London Companies Shine on Subsidies," in* The New York Times, *July 30, 1970, p. 39.*

Don Moore   (review date October 1971)

[*Moore finds Miller's production "a thoughtful, interesting, and colorful misinterpretation of* The Merchant of Venice." *In Moore's view, Miller goes astray in focusing on the theme of capitalism, Shylock, and the Venetian plot, rather than the theme of charity as developed by Portia, Bassanio, and Antonio.*]

I am beginning to wonder if we ever will have a major production of *The Merchant of Venice* which will capture the nuances and complexities of that play, that is, a non-polarized production in which Shylock does not come off as a victimized figure of great sympathy, humiliated by people of lesser worth than he. Certainly, we are aware that there are some terribly human elements in Shylock, and have some cause to wonder about the ethics of the others. For an extreme view of Shylock-as-victim, we can turn to Harold Goddard's *The Meaning of Shakespeare.* But most modern critics preface their discussion of Shylock as does Herbert Bronstein in a recent essay (*Shakespeare Quarterly,* XX): "No critical card tricks, no juggling of lines, can obscure the fact that Shylock is a greedy usurer who dreams of money bags and is implacable in his demands for Antonio's pound of flesh. . . . He is also comic in his parsimony and meanness." Walter Kerr has written of Shylock's comic ancestry in the figure of Pantalone (*Thirty Plays Hath November*); and J. R. Brown in his Arden edition states that "no matter how harshly the Christians treat him [Shylock] remains the Jew who intends to kill his enemy, a harsh, cynical, and ruthless villain."

But none of this avails, to my knowledge, in recent theatre. Orson Welles continues to pop up on unlikely television variety shows doing a long composite monologue drawn from Shylock's speeches, leaving millions of viewers convinced that Shakespeare wrote a play exclusively concerning religious intolerance. And in 1970, Britain's National Theatre mounted a critically acclaimed, sellout, hold-over production which has already influenced some college productions in the United States. I found Jonathan Miller's production a thoughtful, interesting, and colorful misinterpretation of *The Merchant of Venice.*

The scene was late nineteenth century Venice (read "England"); Julia Oman's set was a colonnaded golden piazzetta which opened out on one side to reveal Shylock's house, and on the other, Portia's, the latter crammed with the apparatus of Victorian upper-class domesticity. And the play itself became crammed with Victorian upper-class hypocrisy. Bassanio and his friends were transformed into spendthrift playboys; Antonio was a fiftyish, top-hatted wealthy businessman definitely in love with the young Bassanio (there were at least four protracted meaningful looks and three arm-claspings); Joan Plowright's Portia was a rather bossy head of an assured and wealthy household; and Lorenzo became a second-rate philosopher who punctuated his music-and-the-heavens speech in Act V with stabs of his pipe, after carefully spreading a handkerchief for Jessica to sit upon. (She dozed.)

And there was Laurence Olivier, the world's most interesting actor, as Shylock. Here was a middle-class Shylock in shiny top hat (with skull cap underneath), sleek morning coat (no "Jewish gaberdine" here), and slight Germanic accent replete with a dropped final "g" and faltering "ow" sounds, in all resembling the Anglo-Jewish tradesman of European origin often seen in London today. This was a man aping his betters, doing his subtle best to keep up with them. At length and with great conviction Olivier conveyed the resentment of the persecuted: the antagonized Jew broke through the Victorian veneer, even as his Othello stripped away his crucifix and fell into a pagan crouch. Yet only in his single finger repeatedly stabbing at the bond did we have traces of the maniacal Shylock readers so often see. Otherwise, our sympathy went out to him well before the trial scene, in such moments as at the end of Act III, Scene i, when Olivier, in spite of the raucous assonance which ends the scene with Tubal, knelt with a prayer shawl over his head and shoulders. That they were to meet at the synagogue further to plan a murder was not to be considered.

The trial scene took place in a small private room. Portia's speech on mercy was dealt with as if in a line rehearsal, although Shylock listened intently. When events had reached their climax, Shylock was literally wilting with arms half-spread against the wall on stage right, suggesting an inverse crucifixion. Bassanio was visibly affected, and did his best via looks and movements to stop Gratiano from his happy verbal persecution. Antonio too was shaken when, after Shylock had stumbled off, he heard the terrible sobbing from stage right. And no one can out-sob Laurence Olivier.

The fifth act, as you may imagine, was anticlimactic. Jessica throughout emphatically resisted Lorenzo, and was obviously adrift in memory and uncertainty amid the smugness of this Belmont. The gentlemen had escaped the consequences of their improvidence; it was time again to party. The entire Shakespearean emphasis on harmony and order was turned awry: music, moonlight, and love gave way to a quietly distraught Jessica, an ineffective Lorenzo, and a final curtain which left Antonio and Jessica alone on stage looking at each other as we heard, as at the beginning of the play, a disembodied voice intoning the Kaddish, a Jewish song of mourning. The spirit of Shylock was mighty yet.

And thus ended *The Merchant of Venice,* a production which conclusively proved that Shakespeare wrote it as a bitterly ironic tragi-comedy about capitalist hypocrisy, with Shylock, as one reviewer felt, representing an emergent yeoman culture which as yet cannot penetrate the feudal remnants of the old order, an order which itself is not fully integrated in the New Capitalism.

But is *The Merchant of Venice* about capitalism or charity? I would like someday to see a production which would give us an eloquent Bassanio ready to give and hazard all he has, in contrast to Shylock's fanatical desire to get as much as he deserves; an Antonio who shares his wealth without expecting return, who takes risks and is ready to sacrifice his life for his friend; a Portia who is not always a glib logician but also a woman of thought and feeling. And I would like once to hear a Jessica give proper emphasis to her lines in II, iii [18-

19], "But though I am a daughter of his blood / I am not to his manners." For it is manners, not religion, that is for me the focal point of the play. Perhaps Shylock is a Jew and a villain in order effectively to symbolize tendencies Shakespeare deplored in any race: there are moments indeed when the Christians seem a bit suspect. Gratiano, for one, is hardly an example of Christian charity; and Portia's great speech is aimed at us all. But the play is, I think, more about the "manners" of charity and less about the crises of capitalism than at the National. The final emphasis in *The Merchant of Venice* is on love and harmony, on giving and receiving. The role of Shylock is powerful; but there are things to be done in the other roles also.

Future directors might do well to read the last act first. (pp. 349-51)

Don Moore, in a review of "The Merchant of Venice," in Educational Theatre Journal, *Vol. XXIII, No. 3, October, 1971, pp. 349-51.*

Kenneth Muir   (essay date 1973)

[*A British critic, educator, and translator, Muir has published numerous volumes of Shakespearean criticism, including* Shakespeare and the Tragic Pattern (*1959*), Shakespeare as Collaborator (*1960*), A New Companion to Shakespeare Studies (*1971*), Shakespeare's Tragic Sequence (*1972*), The Sources of Shakespeare's Plays (*1977*), *and* Shakespeare's Comic Sequence (*1979*). *In addition, he has edited several of Shakespeare's plays, written book-length critical studies of* King Lear *and* Antony and Cleopatra, *and served as the editor of* Shakespeare Survey *from 1965 to 1980. In the excerpt below, Muir argues that Miller's interpretation of Shylock as the "cultured," persecuted hero of* The Merchant of Venice *has no foundation in the play and is, in fact, antithetical to Shakespeare's text.*]

In the recent National Theatre production of *The Merchant of Venice,* the modern dress of Shylock immediately reminded the audience of the Nazi persecution of the Jews. This was clearly the director's intention, and Shylock emerged as the baffled hero of the play. It need hardly be said that this interpretation runs counter to the text. Shylock's real role is that of villain, as we can see from his first aside:

How like a fawning publican he looks!
I hate him for he is a Christian;
But more for that in low simplicity
He lends out money gratis, and brings down
The rate of usance here with us in Venice.
He hates our sacred nation; and he rails . . .
On me, my bargains, and my well-won thrift,
Which he calls interest.

[I. iii. 41-51]

This hatred may spring partly from Antonio's contemptuous rudeness, but it is fanned by religious and especially economic motives. There is nothing in Shakespeare's character to suggest the generous, cultured Jew portrayed by Laurence Olivier: he is a miser, and he hates music—two indications of what the poet thought of him. Of course, there are moments in the play when we are allowed to pity him; but even the scene where he hears of the sale of the ring given him by his dead wife shows that he is more perturbed by the loss of his ducats than of his daughter. If the sympathies of the audience are enlisted for Shylock—because of our modern feelings of guilt—the fourth act will be tragic and the last act will be imbued with bitterness. One can imagine an admirable play in which a noble and cultured Jew is hounded to death by a pack of Philistines, in which Bassanio pursues Portia's fortune rather than her person, in which Jessica is a treacherous thief with Lorenzo her accomplice, and in which the Duke's court is as obviously corrupt as the one where Volpone is tried—but Shakespeare's script cannot be used to mean anything like this. I have more sympathy with the point of view expressed in a recent pamphlet, wrong-headed as it is, that *The Merchant of Venice* should not be staged so long as people remember Belsen and Dachau. One might reply that so long as people remember the concentration camps, the play is unlikely to do any harm. (pp. 25-6)

Kenneth Muir, "The Pursuit of Relevance," in Essays and Studies, *n.s. Vol. 26, 1973, pp. 20-34.*

Michael Billington   (essay date 1973)

[Billington presents a scene-by-scene analysis of Olivier's Shylock, "the best of its generation." He asserts that the performance's success is attributable to the acuity of its conception, the charisma of the actor, and the compelling spectacle of a "full-scale piece of heroic acting being given in an orderly, mercantile late-nineteenth-century setting," playing off "the tension between period and style."]

'One talks vaguely of genius,' wrote Matthew Arnold, 'but I had never till now comprehended how much of Rachel's superiority was purely in intellectual power, how eminently this power counts in the actor's art as in all art, how just is the instinct which led the Greeks to mark with a high and severe stamp the Muses.' Arnold was right. For, although several things conspire to make Olivier's Shylock the best of its generation, the greatest of these are its 'high intellectual power' and sheer interpretative originality.

The key point about Olivier's Shylock (a frock-coated prosperous Jew with a skull-cap under his top-hat reminiscent of George Arliss as Disraeli) is that he knows his revenge upon Antonio is inextricably tied up with Venice's credibility as an international trading area (a point highlighted by Julia Trevelyan Oman's realistic nineteenth-century setting with its hint of St. Mark's Square). Antonio himself realises that if the course of law be denied it 'will much impeach the justice of the state Since that the trade and profit of the city consisteth of all nations' [III. iii. 29-31]. And therefore in the Trial Scene Shylock's 'If you deny me . . . THERE IS NO FORCE IN THE DECREES OF VENICE' [IV. i. 102] is driven in like a series of hammer-blows. Allied to this implacable conviction that he has the city by the short hairs is Olivier's conception of Shylock as an outsider who is tolerated by Venetian society just so long as he continues to play the role that is expected of him. I was reminded of something James Baldwin wrote in *Notes of a Native Son.* 'It is part of the price the Negro pays for his position in society that he is almost always acting. A Negro learns to gauge precisely what reaction the alien person facing him desires and he produces it with disarming artlessness.' So it is with Olivier's Jew.

A second reason for the performance's power is Olivier's familiar ability to seize on a line or a moment and impale it forever on our memories. Thus Shylock's last words to the court—'I am content' [IV. i. 394]—are delivered with rigid, poker-stiff back, eyeballs bulging and hands clapped firmly to the sides like a carefully-welded toy soldier: clearly the man is undergoing some kind of fit and so we are prepared for the earth-shaking, off-stage death-cry that follows his exit.

And a third reason for the performance's magnetism is that it offers us the terrifying and exhilarating spectacle of a full-scale piece of heroic acting being given in an orderly, mercantile late-nineteenth-century setting. It is like seeing a tiger unleashed in a drawing-room. It would be a great performance in Renaissance costume; it becomes even greater because of the tension between period and style. But to show how the performance works in detail let me analyse it scene by scene.

ACT I. Scene 3

First impression is of a wealthy urban financier who has adopted the alien's mask of politeness and false *bonhomie*. He is constantly laughing (after 'Antonio is a good man' [l. 12] he emits a dangerous chuckle) and making weak Gentile puns (like the one about the 'pi-rats') which drop into the conversation like boulders into a garden-pool. He is the smiler with the knife under the cloak. And early on he plants the verbal mannerisms: the dropping of the final 'g' on verbs ('I was debatin' of my present store' [l. 53]), the pinched strangulated vowel sounds that evoke the ghetto origins ('For sufferance is the badge of all *ower* tribe' [l. 110]). And, as always with Olivier, one is struck by the mimetic vigour. 'Your worship was the last man in our mouths' [l. 60] is accompanied by a rolling masticatory jaw movement. Likewise when he describes how Jacob, while Laban's ewes were breeding, 'peeled me certain wands' [l. 84], he inserts his stick with a corkscrew movement through his outstretched left hand brilliantly summoning up both the peeling-process and animalistic copulation. The element of icy racial fury under the bland exterior only emerges in the speech to Antonio about the insults he has repeatedly borne—and he highlights this fury simply through a sharp emphasis on the word 'You'. '*You* come to me and *you* say "Shylock, we would have moneys"—*you* say so; *you* that did void *your* rheum upon my beard, [ll. 115-17]. Yet in proposing the bond he resorts to the mask of joviality that he has adopted for purely commercial transactions. In talking of a 'merry sport' he jauntily puts his stick over his shoulder like a young Chevalier. And he does a marvellous false exit when it looks as if the bond will not be unanimously accepted, spinning round on his heel the very split second Antonio cries out, 'Yes, Shylock'. Thus the scene comes full circle and returns to the note of benevolent amiability on which it began. In the course of ten minutes Olivier has given us the complete architecture of the scene; filled in the outline with some staggering detail; and laid the whole basis of the characterisation for the rest of the play.

ACT 2. Scene 5

The scene where he bids farewell to Jessica. Decked out in white tie, tails and with a watch-chain across a spreading corporation, he resembles more than ever a role-playing alien. Immediately he introduces a note of menace by asking of Gobbo 'Who bids thee call?' and then dropping his voice to a whisper on 'I did not bid thee call' [l. 7]. And he introduces a typically eccentric touch by placing the keys for Jessica on the thumb of his right hand where most actors would simply hand them to her. He also introduces a whole new concept of Gobbo on 'the patch is kind enough but a *huge* feeder' [l. 46], suddenly producing an image of a boy with a gargantuan Dickensian appetite (scarcely borne out, one must admit, by Jim Dale's attenuated, bird-like frame). It is a short scene but Olivier reinforces the earlier impression of a stern patriarch prepared to dissemble in front of the Christians just so long as it suits his purpose: in the previous scene, do not forget,

Shylock has told us that he will not eat with the Christians, yet here he is going off to supper with them.

ACT 3. Scene 1

This is the key scene where you really know what a Shylock is made of. . . . O'Toole did it brilliantly in Michael Langham's 1960 Stratford production, rending his gown of watered silk and allowing the desire for revenge to increase in direct proportion to his disgust with his daughter's behaviour. Olivier's treatment has less of a straightforward linear curve; but he leaves particular moments branded on the memory. He begins the scene on the balcony of his house eavesdropping on Salanio's news of Antonio's misfortunes and feverishly searching for his daughter. He comes down to street level visibly distracted and confused. He rests for support on a side rail with his back to us and is obviously more obsessed by news of his daughter's flight than anything else. Antonio's name is mentioned and he then turns slowly round on 'Let him look to his bond' [ll. 49-50] so that we see the dawning realisation of the consequences of the merchant's loss. He prowls restlessly round the stage like a caged wolf itemising Antonio's insults and stiffens suddenly on 'I am a Jew' [l. 58] as if summoning up all his racial pride. In this context, 'Hath not a Jew eyes?' [l. 59] becomes not a sentimental plea for pity but a clarion-call to revenge—the word Olivier insistently emphasises. And for that key word he devises an extraordinary gesture that consists of slapping the right hand into the palm of the left and shooting the thumb of the left hand outwards: it suggests a butcher slapping a piece of meat on to a weighing machine and has exactly the right blend of coarseness and brutality.

With Tubal's arrival he retires to his house and emerges with Jessica's dress draped over his shoulder, stroking it gently as if to console himself for the loss of two thousand ducats. On 'I would my daughter were dead at my feet' [ll. 87-8] he hurls it to the ground as if the folds of cloth did indeed contain Jessica and tramples on it as if to exorcise her spirit for ever. His frame bursting with a flood of contradictory emotions, he breaks into some ancient Sephardic dance on the news of Antonio's ill-fortune; and as suddenly snaps out of that by picking up Jessica's dress and twirling it rapidly round his arm like a bandage on the news of the ring that was exchanged for a monkey. Telling Tubal that he would not have given it for a wilderness of monkeys, he elongates all the vowel sounds on the word 'wilderness' as if to suggest an eternity of pain and anguish. At this point one suspects he has studied carefully what Irving did with the role. 'He contrived to suggest,' according to his biographer, 'in his delivery of the word "wilderness" of monkeys a vast emptiness signifying Jessica's life of frivolous and trifling amusement and his contempt for it—an example of his ability to make an effective point out of an apparently insignificant word.' Olivier's final touch is masterly. For 'Go Tubal and meet me at our synagogue' [l. 129] he takes up his Jewish prayer shawl, holds it up to his face and lightly kisses its hem; and then drapes it round his head before setting off to his devotions. The veneer of bourgeois amiability has now been torn aside to expose the naked racial hostility underneath.

ACT 3. Scene 3

Sixteen lines only for Shylock in this short scene with Antonio and the Gaoler. Yet Olivier still manages to reveal a new facet of the character: an implacable, iron resolve. He signifies this by a harsh, reiterated emphasis on the word 'bond'.

And he fortifies it on 'I'll have no speakin' ' [l. 17], ramming the point home by forming the shape of a mouth with a rounded thumb and forefinger. He exits with sublime confidence using one of his favourite tricks: that of leaving part of himself trailing behind as he departs. In *Rebecca* there is an extraordinary shot of him going out of a door momentarily leaving his hand caressing a support; in *Coriolanus* he let a hand linger on a pillar after his body had already gone past; and here he places his stick on his shoulder as if it were a rifle and exits slowly upstage so that for a second or two all we can see is the tip of the stick after he has gone out.

ACT 4. Scene 1

A stony adversary: Olivier here exemplifies the Duke's words. And the reason, as I suggested earlier, is that Shylock knows that it is the integrity and honour of Venice that is on trial. Thus he enters jauntily, swinging a black briefcase, as if off for a day at the races. Confident of the outcome, he is anxious to get on with the business, drumming his fingers on the table and scarcely bothering to turn round to answer Bassanio's queries. Like Irving, Olivier also unerringly hits the key word in any speech. The slaves purchased by the Christians are abjectly used because 'you *bought* them' [l. 93]. And in the same speech the pound of flesh he demands of [Antonio] is also 'dearly *bought*'. He chuckles knowingly on Antonio's 'I am a tainted wether of the flock' [l. 114] which instantly tells us that the Merchant's homosexuality was a common secret. And his reaction to the 'quality of mercy' speech [l. 184] is a derisive 'Huh'. This is a man who can at last afford to show his true religious and racial animosity.

Olivier brings his exultation to the boil on hearing Portia's initial declaration in his favour, even doing a spring-heeled leap. But this is the turning-point in the scene: from here on Shylock's fortunes trace a downward curve which Olivier plots with startling intensity. He has Antonio halfway out of the door to execute sentence before Portia halts him with 'Tarry a little' [l. 305]. Learning that his lands will be confiscated if he sheds Christian blood, he enquires anxiously 'Is that the law?' [l. 314] peering at a dusty legal tome. He realises that he cannot even retrieve his initial capital, hurries towards the door and is stopped just as he has reached the side-rail. Portia puts the boot in by telling him of the legal penalties against an *alien*. The last word is like a dagger in his heart. He obviously knows exactly what is to come: jaw sagging, he turns round to utter a cry that just will not come like that of Weigel in *Mother Courage*. His quivering hand reaches out for the rail to steady himself; he can stand everything except Antonio's vicious demand that he become a Christian, at which he flops over the rail, his head hurtling towards the floor until he is rescued by two Jewish friends. They prop him up while he says 'I am content' [l.394], and his rigid frame is carried from the court. A few seconds elapse before a cry is heard—sharp and intense at first and then barbarically extended—that reminds one of a wolf impaled on a spike and dying a slow death, or of some savage mastiff gradually having the life squeezed out of it as it is forcibly put down. Shylock has returned to his forefathers. (pp. 82-9)

Michael Billington, "The Great Ones," in his The Modern Actor, *Hamish Hamilton, 1973, pp. 68-94.*

Patrick Sullivan (essay date 1974)

[*Sullivan provides a comprehensive, scene-by-scene analysis of*

Miller's production, addressing critical issues raised by the play and the production as they unfold. According to Sullivan, Miller's highly original interpretation paradoxically sought to restore the "essential moral energy of The Merchant of Venice.*"]*

What follows is a critical account of the Jonathan Miller-Laurence Olivier *Merchant of Venice,* first performed in 1970 by The National Theatre and since revived (the production will be taped for the 1973-74 American television season). This production became a focus of critical controversy from its premiére. I have tried to recall my response to the play in such a way that the critical issues are met not so much logically or thematically but organically, as they are presented and developed by the performance itself. I have checked my account with other scholars and teachers who saw the play, and I am reasonably sure that my interpretation is a representative one. Yet there are many places where I have seen the play differently from other commentators.

The curtain rises on a grand emptiness. Soft, sad yellow light illuminates a three-storied, ornate Romanesque house front. Silence seems natural to this place; conversation and music are efforts at dispelling a void, at overcoming a man-made cityscape, grand, remote, constricting and weighty. Antonio enters like a man returning from a funeral. With a profile like the old professor's in Bergman's *Wild Strawberries,* Anthony Nicholls' Antonio, dressed in Edwardian tuxedo and top hat, wearily comes to center stage, leans heavily on his walking stick, looks sad, aloof, resigned: the play has begun.

Director Jonathan Miller's decision to make Antonio an old man heightens the contrast between his languor and the young Gratiano's ebullient cynicism. Derek Jacobi's Gratiano is a character of considerable prominence in this production. In these opening moments the audience's attention goes in two directions: we listen to Gratiano spin out his fancy and we note the distance in more than age between him and Antonio. Antonio cannot be reached, and can draw on social energies only when Bassanio enters and Antonio is at last moved to sit down with his friend at a side-walk table. Listlessness gives way to paternal concern and affection.

Bassanio (Jeremy Brett) shows genuine affection for Antonio. The younger man is ill at ease in his recurring request for funds. He appears charming and corruptible, not decadent or prodigal in the manner of his biblical prototype. He is returning to a father of sorts; but here the son seeks to *go from* not *return to,* and the father is to provide the fortunate wind and sails. In Brett's performance there is a marked fearfulness lurking behind most of his speech and gestures. He is therefore seen as vulnerable in ways which Antonio, if he cannot duplicate, can sympathize with and understand. The scene establishes the characteristic responses of both men. Antonio shows a chilled, isolated painfulness in his life he can forget only in the presence of Bassanio. Bassanio conveys the sense that only with Antonio can he feel himself integral, responsible, a man without 'performance' or pretense. Bassanio's speech softens his inner dubieties, but through his stage movement and particularly his eyes he portrays a subtle confusion about the meaning his life holds up to him now. That Bassanio is not all that young or innocent deepens our sympathies for him. Bassanio is Antonio's young surrogate in quest of the Golden Fleece. Gratiano's departure allows Antonio and Bassanio's half-articulated intimacy to reach out to the audience. The contact is, however, sad: both of them silently give signs of recognizing that they have communicated only so much of their true state of mind, that their bond is deep but remains distant in expression and in effect on their lives. After all, love is what Bassanio knows and shows; money is what he needs and uses.

Portia's Belmont is humorously, ludicrously bright yellow. Joan Plowright's characterization, from the moment she delights in the self-mocking delivery of her first line "By my troth, Nerissa, my little body is aweary of this great world" [I. ii. 1-2], carries the audience to a place very different from the brooding and fretful Venetian world of Antonio and Bassanio. Here in Belmont Portia plays with feelings and persons, one of them being herself, with comic impunity and power. We learn the terms of her possible marriage, and the international list of contenders. The world of Portia leaps into more emotional and complex relief when Bassanio's name is recalled. Miss Plowright finds herself smiling in eager pleasure but also afraid of such emotions, given the conditions of her marriage. She appears momentarily more vulnerable and complicated than we shall perhaps ever witness again. Most of her life calls for her to 'pull things off,' 'make things work,' maintain power over herself and her feelings, yet there is also a woman's yearning—she isn't young—for a man she carries in her heart more than she has ever allowed herself to carry in her words or hopes.

Joan Plowright erases once and for all the Granville-Barker image of Portia as more elevated, more 'musical,' than the witty and stable socialite she plays here. The romance in Portia is in her wit, her ability to perform with delight and irony; but she does not invest herself with larger archetypal meanings. From the beginning we like Plowright's Portia more than we admire her. She is not erotically fetching nor romantically beautiful. The force of her femininity is social, it is articulate, and it grows from and into a mannered and even artificial society. We enjoy Belmont now, but we are not asked to identify with its values or imaginatively embrace its heroine. If Portia is a happily mocking woman, she is also snobbish and sophisticated in a self-knowing but not totally pleasant way. Scene two is zestful and honest fun, but the biases and barbs are evident along with the humor and gaiety.

We travel back to Venice. Olivier as Shylock enters with Bassanio. Shylock walks with a shuffle, he is portly, somber and affluent in appearance (Olivier holds his mouth in such a manner as to alter his facial expressions and facilitate the accent of a Jew). This Shylock reveals no suppressed malevolence. Our first response to him, in fact, is more like one we would give to a character who humored or amused us. Gradually we realize that Shylock enjoys his situation with Bassanio because it is rare and delicious to him. The fact that Bassanio is asking for money from Shylock is the only means of contact between them and the only means Shylock has to feel himself 'familiar' with the Christian.

Then Antonio enters, and Shylock appears eager to continue the rare occasion: he takes on the manner of genteel humor which is an unsuccessful if pleasant enough mask for his defensiveness. Shylock's bulk is solid and secure-looking, but his manner is very much that of an abused pariah half-willing to show that he misses the fellowship of men like Antonio who move in the Venice beyond the ghetto. This is not to suggest that Shylock has started out as a sentimentalized version of the Shakespearian villain. Rather, Miller presents us here with an initial vision of Shylock as a nominally self-confident and secure Jew who nevertheless fears a situation where Antonio and his world could spit on his likes again.

Shylock in this scene does not really want to offer Antonio his friendship and trust, but he does not want to hurt him either. This Shylock does not seem initially given to malevolent deception. When the bond is made, it appears to be a means of extracting them all from a situation turned sour and foreboding with Antonio's harsh and cruel response to Shylock's expansive accusations of the "Jewish Gabardine" speech. Shylock puts aside the badge of sufferance and seizes the occasion to voice the indignities he has known for all too long. When Antonio again turns on him spitefully and with as supercilious a confidence as he had "Wednesday last" on the Rialto, Shylock turns quickly back to a *modus operandi* less charged with hostility and verbal violence. If there is only the pretense of kindness between these two men at the end of the scene, and an extraordinary if subtle tension between them throughout the scene (they circle about the stage keeping their distance from one another), there is not the grim sense that Shylock is covertly manipulating Antonio into a position where the roles of predator and victim can be reversed. Shylock preserves throughout the scene a control over himself which does not seem in the service of some sinister purpose. He remains canny, even secretive, but secretive principally for purposes of self-protection and self-preservation.

From what has been said so far about Shylock, it becomes clear how crucial was Miller's choice to excise Shylock's soliloquy: "How like a fawning publican he looks / I hate him for he is a Christian . . ." [I. iii. 41-2]. In not allowing access to Shylock's consciousness in this manner, Miller has changed the scene to one in which no simple, clear, and crude explication of human evil is available. The critical issue here is why Miller made such a cut and whether such a cut is defensible. Miller has taken from Shylock the single most obvious indication of his villainy, that is, Shylock's intention to act on his hatred by means of the bond: "If I can catch him once upon the hip / I will feed fat the ancient grudge I bear him" [I. iii. 46-7]. The rest of the soliloquy is dramatized shortly after when his and Antonio's hostility comes to the fore. But the way that hostility is shown in Miller's handling is not principally in terms of Shylock's "ancient grudge" but in terms of the ancient antagonism between a representative of the dominant majority and a representative of the wealthy but disinherited minority.

Miller's thinking may have been that a modern sensibility and social vision would balk at a soliloquy which made Shylock the evil scapegoat. However, it is often argued that the scene *with* the soliloquy makes for a more complex dramatic situation. In this case Shylock is malevolent, but his evil is made coherent and even attractive by the way Antonio and his supposedly Christian society have "fed fat" Shylock's grudge. The audience must then work with a villain whose evil is apprehended not so much with an easy-minded understanding of evil as abhorrent and even physically unnatural (à la *Richard the Third*) but as conditioned, if not created, by the society which abuses him so consistently. With the soliloquy, therefore, *The Merchant of Venice* is not necessarily a less complex or tough-minded drama.

There are other possible reasons for Miller's choice. He may have felt along with several other students of the play that Shakespeare's real dramatic interests in the play are not well served by the soliloquy, that it is a mistake, a vehicle of explication which, though satisfying to an Elizabethan audience, is unacceptable to a modern one. Shakespeare may here assign hatred to Shylock, but such an assignment neither explains him well nor explicates the play's action.

While the latter point of view may have some bearing on Miller's reading of this scene and the rest of the play, it seems more likely that he stands close to W. H. Auden when he writes [in his *The Dyer's Hand,* 1962]:

> Recent history has made it utterly impossible for the most unsophisticated and ignorant audience to ignore the historical reality of the Jews and think of them as fairy-story bogeys with huge noses and red wigs. An Elizabethan audience undoubtedly still could—very few of them had seen a Jew—and, if Shakespeare had so wished, he could have made Shylock grotesquely wicked like the *Jew of Malta.* The star actors who, from the eighteenth century onwards have chosen to play the role, have not done so out of a sense of moral duty in order to combat anti-Semitism, but because their theatrical instinct told them that the part, played seriously, not comically, offered them great possibilities.

The "theatrical instinct" in Miller's interpretation here and elsewhere seems both original and significant. Shylock's "great possibilities" are marred by a soliloquy which allows actor and audience to respond to him "comically" or melodramatically as the villain. The scene in Miller-Olivier's hands achieves a concentration of effect the soliloquy would seriously undermine. Moreover, the excision of the soliloquy allows the audience to discover and feel Shylock's grudge rather than hear about it and then have it illustrated. The absence of the soliloquy delivers the scene to a place where audience and actor are pulled much closer together. Olivier's performance allows the menacing aspects of Shylock's character to build up over a series of scenes rather than register themselves obtrusively in his first scene.

Olivier gives us a Shylock who readily converts goodness into economic solvency and kindness into money-lending. Shylock's energy is too cagey and deliberate not to suggest the destructive potentialities of his nature. But we also feel that his nature is not fully known, first of all by himself. He is vulnerable in ways we have seen Bassanio and even Antonio to be, but Shylock seems not to know such ways of being. On the contrary, he seems dangerously self-persuaded that his mercantile mind is sufficient, that he has control over his world. Under the nervous but also knowing laughter Shylock ventilates in his first scene, he hides from society and also from himself. This is part of Shylock's richness "played seriously" by Laurence Olivier.

The next sequence (Act Two in the text) is characterized by comings and goings. Launcelot and Jessica go from Shylock, Shylock himself goes from his home to dine at the house of the heathen Christians, Lorenzo and Jessica will follow Bassanio and Gratiano from Venice, the Princes of Morocco and Arragon come and go from the comic court of Belmont, and the going of Antonio's fortunes is suggested before too long. When we do come back to Shylock in Venice, then, we are ready for important changes in both him and the situation. Miller suffuses this sequence of his first act with a rich blend of farcical comedy and disquieting poignancy. Launcelot's argument with himself possesses a light, child-like playfulness and innocence; he has no real animosity for Shylock and he is obviously fond of Jessica as a sort of soul-mate. The game he plays with his father is hardly engineered for laughs alone—they are both persons rather lost in a big world. More significant for the play as a whole, Jessica is an anxious and hardly seductive young girl in love. She is never at ease with herself; she is troubled with confusions which she cannot articulate but which will dominate her actions to the end. Shylock shows his disturbed nature as he argues with himself about leaving his home on such a night after he has had foreboding dreams of "money bags" and when the siren masques of Venice threaten to create a world beyond the control of his mercantile mind. Lorenzo and Jessica are the Romeo and Juliet of *The Merchant of Venice,* but in the company of Gratiano they are both seen to be blind and partly ludicrous. Lorenzo is heavy-footed and dull-witted. His protestations of love are cloddishly conventional; his behavior coupled with Jessica's fretful naivete and awkwardness provide just the right context for Gratiano's pivotal speech:

> Who riseth from a feast
> With that keen appetite that he sits down?
> Where is the horse that doth untread again
> His tedious measures with the unbated fire
> That he did pace them first? All things that are
> Are with more spirit chased than enjoyed.
> How like a younger or a prodigal
> The scarfed bark puts from her native bay,
> Hugg'd and embraced by the strumpet wind!
> How like the Prodigal doth she return,
> With over-weathered ribs and ragged sails,
> Lean, rent, and beggar'd by the strumpet wind!
>
> [II. vi. 8-19]

This speech captures a dominant mood of the play: a sense of defeatedness in life, a sense that man's "keen appetites" become dulled not by conscience but by satiety and dissatisfaction with the whimsies of accident, fortune, misfortune here beyond man's knowledge or responsibility. One feels that Venetian life is not so much decadent as it is defeated. While Gratiano's cynicism is enriched by his awareness of both the embracing and the beggaring of the "strumpet wind," the unusual repetition of that last phrase accentuates a motif with significance for the play as a whole, as we shall see. Gratiano's sense of life explicates and judges Jessica and Lorenzo's situation. Miller paces down the action so that a speech like Gratiano's can resonate with an authority a more fast-paced and feverish dramatic action would disallow.

We feel a painfulness in human life even at Belmont when free-swinging farce gives way to silencing ridicule as Arragon reads his judgment from the casket. Morocco is blusteringly funny, a minstrel-show Prince whose heavy-voiced, Othello-like manners offer a parody of Olivier's Moor. Portia's courteousness toward and fearful mockery of him gives the scene a blend of farcical action and revelation of character. With Arragon the comedy accelerates even more: his is a doddering, eighty-year-old, near-blind, wheezing, small figure of a man whose presence brings the whole business of the suitors to a hilarious comic catastrophe. But when he reads the judgment of the casket, we listen intently and sympathetically to this same figure as he is told he should have been wise ere he was old. While in the text itself Morocco is in fact a more sympathetically portrayed type than is Arragon, under Miller's direction Morocco stays more completely within the confines of farce whereas Arragon's final moments and exit off stage possess a quiet desparation growing out of his dim awareness of senile folly. The play stands at the limits of laughter as Arragon slowly departs. These moments provide an emotional preparation for Shylock's exit, broken and alone, from the courtroom of Venice. Comic justice and ridi-

cule are impermanent and beyond a certain point dangerous tools in coming to terms with human experience.

We return to a Venice of mean confusion. Solanio and Salerio cruelly bait Shylock over the loss of his daughter: "My own flesh and blood to rebel / Out upon it, old carrion! Rebels is it these years? / I say my daughter is my flesh and blood" [III. i. 34-8]. And Shylock comes out of his complex feelings about Jessica to return their fire: "Hath not a Jew eyes? . . . Why revenge. The villainy you teach me I will execute, and it shall go hard but I will better the instruction" [III. i. 59-73]. Olivier shapes the speech so that it moves inexorably to its final statement, one uttered with a concentrated, quiet power more foreboding and grim than anything we have heard before. There is real malice seething beneath the words; there are no questions in Shylock's mind, no attempt to "convert" his audience or justify himself. Shylock is feeling deprived and threatened, but he is also feeling confident in a power he before lacked over the hateful Christian world.

The exchange with Tubal tells us more. Miller moves the two of them into a darkened room of Shylock's house. We see and hear Shylock in his own surroundings. The place is one of a ghettoed Jew, well-to-do but also isolated and defensive. We have the sense that whatever community Shylock does have will be revealed here if anywhere.

Yet here again Shylock does not allow us a warm or compassionate sympathy for him. While we do feel the familial bonds broken by Jessica, and the humiliation of Shylock's losses, we find him speaking in a tone of exaggerated heartbreak:

> Why, there, there, there, there! A diamond gone cost me two thousand ducats in Frankfort! The curse never fell upon our nation till now; I never felt it till now. . . . Why, thou loss upon loss! the thief gone with so much, and so much to find the thief; and no satisfaction, no revenge! nor no ill luck stirring but what lights o' my shoulders; no sighs but o' my breathing; no tears but o' my shedding.
>
> [III. i. 83-96]

Olivier's Shylock holds Jessica's cape outstretched as if it were a limp body and lets it drop to the floor. His agony is both intense and suffocating: his confused feelings cannot issue out to other persons. His counting the cost of his loss deprives us of warmly identifying with him as a man deeply wronged, deeply bereaved of companionship and love. His sense of loss robs him of experiencing another man's pain: Tubal's "Yes, other men have ill luck too. Antonio as I heard in Genoa . . ." [III. i. 97-8] recalls for Shylock his opportunity for revenge, forgotten in self-pitying preoccupation with himself.

Our sympathies for Shylock here do not so much diminish as they recede, and we are watching him from a more distant and critical perspective. He is revealing a need to compensate hastily for his own suffering. Within the bondage of the mercantile mind is what can be termed a malignant whimsy almost childish in the way we feel it: "I am glad of it. I'll plague him. I'll torture him. I am glad of it" [III. i. 116-17]. Shylock's earlier "The curse never fell upon our nation till now; I never felt it till now" [III. i. 85-6], was a sentiment incapable of providing real insight; he rushes toward the more familiar converse of his advertised "sufferance"—vindictiveness. Olivier's Shylock is now too old to learn, too alone to feel an enlarging human concern. He is insulated strikingly from Tubal, most importantly from himself. The scene shows us a man deprived of a daughter now as of a wife earlier, but a man who will not be broken by human pain, who will not even really face it.

His world is a sort of combined fortress and safe: the safe has been broken into and the losses registered, but the fortress now has a prisoner for the first time, the debtor Antonio. Another prisoner here is Shylock himself. Shylock has no community, and he seems to sense this basic human need at the scene's end when he quietly tells Tubal to meet him at the synagogue. At this scene's conclusion Olivier turns away in a mood of stalwart isolation. He attempts to move away from his most malicious feelings which his religion may have a part in controlling or at least channeling (he dons a prayer shawl as he turns his back on the audience).

Shylock's threatening presence is displaced for awhile by a return to Belmont and Bassanio's penultimate encounter with the caskets. Miller has Portia clearly eager to accept Bassanio: her social presence provides a veneer over her inner joy and humorously eager anticipation. Bassanio is self-possessed, gracious, enjoying his happy status as the favored suitor at Belmont. He and Portia exchange sentiments in a manner pleasing to the conventions of the social order yet transcending them in their warmth and willingness to acknowledge themselves before one another. Portia's speech "You see me, Lord Bassanio, where I stand / Such as I am" [III. ii. 149-50], possesses a new beauty and delight as she gives herself over to full-felt joy. And Bassanio's reply "Madam, you have bereft me of all words" [III. ii. 175], resonates here with a special fitness. Sincerity and conventionality are happily wed. Plowright's Portia ingratiates herself because her obvious age makes for feelings about the match a younger Portia would not carry with her.

The funniest and also most startling aspect of the scene (III. ii) is the way Miller handles the song "Tell me, where is fancy bred . . ." [III. ii. 63]. Three good-sized, matronly looking ladies come in suddenly from off stage. The rest of the case freezes (Bassanio's bemused resignation emphasizes the hilarity of the moment), and the song is delivered with boisterous comic speed. The ladies do not give the slightest sign of understanding what they are singing; they have locked-on smiles which tell us that they are performing to please and that they are plumply complacent. The song is hardly delivered at all; it is discharged. Yet its effect is to swing the various phases of the scene into greater harmony with one another.

This absurd interlude facilitates the turn from social glitter and gamesmanship to Bassanio's serious, introspective commentary on the significance of "ornament." The farce of the song disappears immediately as Bassanio begins, "So may the outward shows be least themselves; / The world is still deceived with ornament" [III. ii. 73-4] This pleasing prodigal directs our attention to the ultimate seriousness of the man about to choose the right casket. Belmont is silent and attentive as Bassanio speaks. In the song's wake comes a speech of restorative seriousness and power. The attractiveness of Belmont takes on a richness now we have not felt before. Bassanio's perspective effortlessly discards the treacherous trappings of "ornament" and show. He expresses a capacity for intimacy and trust we saw before with Antonio in the first scene. We witness here two persons who are happily complete individually and together. We know the play must go on, that it will be only moments before Antonio's letter blasts forever from the play the festive feelings of this love match. But for one moment the world has appeared solidly good on its own

terms. In this performance we feel players and audience have earned the right to affirm romance and promise. For, unlike Lorenzo and Jessica, and unlike Shylock, Bassanio and Portia possess a power, a control first of all over themselves.

We return to Venice menaced by Shylock's insistence on the terms of the bond: "I'll have no speaking; I will have my bond" [III.iii. 17]. Shylock's malignant singleness of purpose pulls us quickly into a world totally opposed to the happy fulfillment of the previous scene. Antonio's bleak resignation reveals an adopted fatalism rather than an overcome righteousness. When Shylock scorns the "Christian intercessors," he does it out of the need to control himself by sustaining willful power over others. This is the same Shylock who before scorned himself for dining with Christians and who ordered Jessica to shut up his house from the masquers' music. But now Shylock has legal sanctions to go on the offensive. His voice and movement suggest a man holding himself sadistically, rigidly to a disreputable course of action. Shylock has learned not to express deep-seated emotions publicly as he did previously with Solanio and Salerio. Shylock has locked away his heart from the intercessors—and from himself also. We are ready for the climactic revelations of the trial scene.

The curtain goes up on a silent court chamber. A large table divides the stage in halves. The duke enters quitely; there is a work-a-day ritualized, routine matter-of-factness to him which makes us watch him closely. These first few minutes strike a note held the entire scene. There is a real sense of wonder at this scene: no courtiers, guards milling about; no grand entrances; no color at all. Miller places the public nature of the words and acts in a setting which suggests the closeness and quiet of privacy. Voices will seldom be raised here, movement will be held to a minimum. This is perhaps the most subdued and informal beginning to the trial scene in the history of the play's performance. The ordinary conduct of legal business is at hand; the stuffy smug air of the Duke is in keeping with his surroundings.

The various entrances are quiet and somber. Antonio is limply resigned, Bassanio confused and displaced, Gratiano surly and vindictive. Shylock appears proper, confident; only the stark tenseness of his face betrays his ferocious determination. Shylock moves to the left side of the table; Antonio and Bassanio are up stage on the right. The scene's spatial balance remains consistent throughout the trial scene: Antonio will almost be led off on the right side, then after the reversal Shylock will be led off to a chamber out of sight on the left.

The Duke's speech to Shylock at once presumes and subverts the generosity of spirit it invokes. The Duke asks for "human gentleness and love" [IV. i. 25]. But he speaks condescendingly to Shylock at every turn, and his "We all expect a gentle answer, Jew" [IV. i. 34], contains a barely hidden taunt and challenge. Shylock's reply is forthright, clear-minded: he acknowledges "a lodged hate and a certain loathing" [IV. i. 60] as the roots of his behavior. He shows a growth in self-confidence by returning Bassanio's ridicule with rhetorical questions and jibes: "Hates any man the thing he would not kill?" [IV. i. 67].

Shylock stubbornly invites the courtroom's condemnation of his conduct: "I'll not answer that . . . are you answered yet? . . . Now for your answer . . . Are you answered?" [IV. i. 42-62]. Shylock is ready for the abuse, he even welcomes it because he feels now the power to silence or check both the Duke and Bassanio. Shylock's examples mockingly bestialize the human world ("What, would thou have a serpent sting thee twice?" [IV. i. 69]). His world has become so barren that he can turn private hatred into legal murder. For Shylock, cruelty is the currency of the world, and he will use it. If the bond will cost Antonio his life, it will also apparently cost Shylock his humanity. He removes himself to a place of apparent invincibility; at the same time he brings to the surface the full burden of the hostility he has carried about so long. The world has become sadistically simple for Shylock: with the law as his defense, he will give license to his hatreds. Without mannerisms of vengeful delight but with a sense of self-satisfied control and imminent victory, Shylock abrasively demands his pound of flesh: " 'Tis mine, and I will have it / If you deny me, fie upon your law!" [IV. i. 100-01].

When Portia enters disguised as Balthasar, the presence of a woman subtly alters the mood of the court. There is momentary comedy as Portia quickly sweeps by Bassanio to avoid recognition. She moves rapidly to establish herself directly opposite Shylock at the front of the table, and delivers the "mercy speech" leaning toward him. This speech has an unearthly remoteness and rapidity to it. It is clearly a prologue to a later action, an action of cruel justice bearing no more respect for the mercy involved here than did Antonio's previous remarks about Shylock: "You may as well do anything most hard / As seek to soften that—than which what's harder?—His Jewish heart" [IV. i. 78-80]. Shylock's lack of repentance is duplicated by Antonio's. This kind of mutual destructiveness makes the values of Portia's speech unable to redeem Shylock or to redeem the world of Antonio either. We look to other means of resolving this conflict of inveterate hostilities.

For a few minutes Shylock believes that Portia furthers his own cause. His applause—"O wise and upright judge!" [IV. i. 250]—carries with it a sense of relief: Shylock has waited until now to see how Balthasar's presence will effect the court and he feels more secure once he hears what he thinks is an advocate for strict justice. Yet it is important that in Olivier's handling of the role here he never luxuriates in a sense of victory, he always appears ready to strike but also suspicious, which prepares us for his change shortly after.

The scene moves to the moment of reversal as Shylock presses Portia to "pursue sentence." We see Bassanio's grief, distanced from it though we are by Portia's and then [Nerissa's] flippant asides regarding their husbands' protestations. Shylock picks up on their remarks and recalls the provocative marriage of his Jewish daughter to a Christian. The connections are again solidly made between his avoidance of self-laceration and the outrage he has bound himself to commit:

> Would any of the stock of Barrabas
> Had been her husband rather than a Christian!
> We trifle time. I pray thee, pursue sentence.
>
> [IV. i. 296-98]

Shylock leads Antonio toward the exit on the right of the stage. The moment of reversal comes; the suspended blade falls—and it falls on Shylock. He comes back around to the left side of the table as Portia delivers the first part of her "mere justice":

> Tarry a little; there is something else.
> This bond doth give thee here no jot of blood;
> The words expressly are "a pound of flesh."
> Take then thy bond, take thou thy pound of flesh;
> But in the cutting it if thou dost shed

> One drop of Christian blood, thy lands and goods
> Are, by the laws of Venice, confiscate
> Unto the state of Venice.
> GRATIANO: O upright judge! Mark, Jew. O
>   learned judge!
> SHYLOCK: Is that the law?
> PORTIA: Thyself shalt see the act;
>   For, as thou urgest justice, be assur'd
>   Thou shalt have justice more than thou desir'st.
>
> [IV. i. 305-16]

These lines are given extraordinary power because the world has shifted its axes with breathless speed, and everyone falteringly begins to cope with the change. Gratiano's first outburst is more a testing of the air than a volley: he waits, after his first "learned judge," to see if indeed what he thinks has happened is really the case. Shylock, even more, is caught in a moment of stunned incredulity. But his reaction is quickly to accept the interpretations of the court and beat a retreat from the now non-existent support of law. Then Portia goes on the grim offensive: her "justice more than thou desir'st" [IV. i. 316] will soon give way to "Why doth the Jew pause?" [IV. i. 335] and the even more cruel, "Tarry Jew / The law hath yet another hold on you" [IV. i. 346-47]. Portia has become an instrument of the state. Suddenly and thoroughly the law of Venice fits in easily with Gratiano's Jew-baiting malice: "A second Daniel! a Daniel, Jew! / Now, infidel, I have you on the hip" [IV. i. 333-34] (Bassanio moves to Gratiano to restrain him in his fit). When Shylock is blocked from recovering even his principal, he says as he moves to leave, "Why, then the devil give him good on it! / I'll stay no longer" [IV. i. 345-46]. But Portia blocks his departure with the harshest blow of all, a blow struck against the *alien* Shylock: he has sought the life of a citizen and must therefore lose his property and sue the Duke for his life. Portia concludes: "Down, therefore, and beg mercy of the Duke" [IV. i. 363].

Shylock has moved to a railing on the left side of the stage where he takes his last blow. His body sways under it; and as Antonio renders his mercy on Shylock, he slumps forward over the bar in abject defeat. The audience anxiously wonders if he has fainted, or worse. His last words before slumping forward were "You take my life / When you do take the means whereby I live" [IV. i. 376-77]. We know the cost involved in taking house and money from Shylock. Then too, Antonio's sincere attempt to mitigate his despair only intensifies it: Shylock must become a Christian under coercion, so even more of his "life" becomes Lorenzo's and Jessica's.

It is primarily the repeatedness of the blows which insures our sympathetic feelings for Shylock and our sense of the court's menace. The law and its prosecutors rob him of any semblance of worth, integrity, decency. He is killed by weapons he could never take up and do battle with himself. As W. H. Auden has noted and as Miller-Olivier made an important aspect of the trial scene, Shakespeare makes the death blow a blow struck against an alien:

> . . . in the trial scene Shakespeare introduces an element which is not found in *Pecorone* or other versions of the pound-of-flesh story. After Portia has trapped Shylock, through his own insistence upon the letter of the law of Contract, she produces another law by which any alien who conspires against the life of a Venetian citizen forfeits his goods and places his life at the Doge's mercy. Even in the rush of a stage performance, the audience cannot help

reflecting that a man as interested in legal subtleties as Shylock would, surely, have been aware of the existence of this law and that, if by any chance he has overlooked it, the Doge surely would very soon have drawn attention to it. Shakespeare, it seems to me, was willing to introduce what is an absurd implausibility for the sake of an effect which he could not secure without it: at the last moment, when, through his conduct, Shylock has destroyed any sympathy we may have felt for him earlier, we are reminded that, irrespective of his personal character, his status is one of inferiority. A Jew is not regarded, even in law, as a brother.

As Shylock's head bends over the rail, the audience notes the skull cap on his head, the signature of his alien way of life, a cap which called so little attention to itself when he sat at the table opposite Portia. And to her question, "Art thou contented, Jew? What dost thou say?" Shylock is raised up, then held to say "I am content" [IV. i. 393-94] at such a desperately strident pitch that we feel his shattered sense of life as a centuries old social fact.

To the jeering and coarse mockery of Gratiano, making sinister humor of Shylock's baptism, Shylock is led off stage. The silence of his departure gives way to the sound of his unforgettable wailing off stage. For what seems a long tortured time we witness Shylock's invisible breakdown, one which restores him to his humanity at last and brings visible regret and guilt to those on stage.

The painfulness of this moment is in large part due to that same defeatedness which is at the heart of the play's vision. Once again Venice has won, but betrayed its own brutal biases in the process. The court's silent recognition of Shylock's tear-ridden pain is still private, generating no public scrutiny of the social weaponry it has so thoroughly utilized in destroying Shylock. These few moments of introspection end in Antonio's striking the table when Shylock's loud sobs continue undiminished. Antonio's gesture indicates self-criticism and second thoughts; but he and the rest are trapped in gestures, not actions. Shylock, however, has been trapped not by gestures but by the action of the court. The silence suggests grounds for a common humanity and suffering; the silence also suggests the distance between such fragmentary feelings and the harshness of conventional behavior and social practice. All the Duke can say as they all move away from such a state of mind is (to Portia), "Sir, I entreat you home with me to dinner" [IV. i. 401]. Their faint-hearted breast-beating is over, no more crying is heard from offstage. The comedy around the giving of the rings begins, but the atmosphere is too heavy for any easy-minded laughter. The dramatic question in the air is: how to go back to Belmont now that to some extent the world has ended, with a bang and then a whimper.

Whether Act V can be played successfully has been a staple of Shakespeare criticism for some time. Miller brings to the final act a vision consistent with his treatment of the play as a whole. He and Olivier clearly intended the Edwardian dress and milieu to release the audience from the confining tradition of pretending to view the play as Elizabethans did. Any director or actor of distinction may want to *understand* how the Elizabethans viewed Jews but their theatrical imaginations would hardly stop there. Miller and Olivier designed a vision of the classic which would speak to a modern, post-Dachau audience and thereby comment on the moral sensibilities and the uneasiness we must face and carry with us.

Slowly, quietly, we are transported back to Belmont. It is outdoors at night, in the grounds beside the house, the light a rare and moody glow of white and green. We feel as though we are awakening into a sort of dream vision or falling asleep into one. Lorenzo starts, "The moon shines bright. In such a night as this . . ." [V. i. 1] and the scene turns into a labored exchange of love courtesies between two persons who seem unable to make contact with one another. Lorenzo falls easily into his role of the complacent, well-secured gentleman lover; he puffs his pipe with the manners of a middle-aged businessman. And he seems to take Jessica for granted; his gaze is over and above her own. She looks to him for recognition of her insecurities and does not find him receptive. They are awkward lovers, he not intimidated enough and she intimidated too much. She appears lonely and alone. A world characterized earlier by Gratiano reappears: "All things that are / Are with more spirit chased than enjoy'd" [II. vi. 12-13].

The lyricism of their verse is one thing; their actual behavior with each other is another matter. Lorenzo's discourse on "the touches of sweet harmony" [V. i. 57] becomes a way for him to fill in the awkward gaps. Jessica says, "I am never merry when I hear sweet music" [V. i. 69], and she says it with an expression asking for Lorenzo's attention. But from him she receives a discourse that avoids speaking *to* her and talks *about* something else:

> The reason is, your spirits are attentive.
> For do but note a wild and wanton herd
>
> . . . .
>
> The man that hath no music in himself . . .
>
> [V. i. 70-83]

This speech becomes an ironic commentary on how little Lorenzo hears Jessica's own sad music and how indeed the music brings in a note of sadness which his idle and pompous chatter denies. They both seem isolated and lonely, but Lorenzo tries to find in the comforts of Belmont sufficient compensation. For Jessica, her alien status becomes more marked each time she cannot 'connect' with Lorenzo. She can scarcely play the pleased loved one's role Lorenzo assumes for her. She is hurt by Lorenzo's self-absorption, complacency, remoteness. Defeatedness in a new form hangs in the air, this time in Belmont: "Who riseth from a feast / With that keen appetite that he sits down?" [II. vi. 8-9].

This reflective and critical mood—action being held back to allow the previous scene to take its place in the play's ongoing movement—Portia brings to a higher level when she speaks of the candle's beams from her house ("So shines a good deed in a naughty world" [V. i. 91]) and of how sweet the music sounds coming as it does at night ("How many things by season season'd are" [V. i. 107]). Portia's relaxed seriousness upon returning home prepares us for the comedy of the rings to be worked out as well as the conclusion to come after a period of light and lively play.

Yet this opening of the final scene suggests how we have never really returned with emotional fulness to Belmont. The courtroom and its memories have cast a shroud over our return to Belmont. Belmont can dispel the ghosts of Venice for awhile, but in the end Shylock is recalled and Belmont is marked with emotions which grow out of ones we have experienced in Venice. Portia says she has "some good comforts" [V. i. 289] for Lorenzo, and Nerissa adds:

> There do I give to you and Jessica,

From the rich Jew, a special deed of gift,
After his death, of all he dies possess'd of.

[V. i. 291-93]

Again the weight of Shylock's tears come down on us, especially so because Antonio's joy at the recovery of his fortunes turns sour so quickly as he contrasts his fortune to Jessica's.

The older two pairs of lovers and Lorenzo go inside, leaving the stage empty except for Jessica and Antonio. He stands reading his letter about his argosies "richly come to harbour suddenly" [V. i. 277]. As he reflects, he seems to play over the experience of the entire play; in particular, the strumpet wind's perverse way seems to have a large share of his thoughts. When he sees Jessica seated in awed fear and trembling at the fate of her father and the anxiety of her own station, Antonio moves from a reflective state of mind to a defeated gesture of faint-hearted disgust at how things have turned out: he slowly crumples up the letter and walks off stage—helpless, alone, weakened, yet also sadly invulnerable, "fortunate."

Jessica is left alone on stage. Her eyes remain riveted on the document which tells her what we have already witnessed and with what she must try to come to terms. The more she studies, the more she seems to see her father—helpless, alone, weakened, and unfortunate. She sees also her own actions, her attempts at escape and her feelings of being brought up short now by those same actions and the fate of her people. Jessica is left on stage; nobody—even if they tried—could come to her and help her. Portia's "good comforts" have turned out to be terrible mirrors of misfortune and moral irresponsibility, of a sadness no one there but Jessica can really comprehend. Antonio's own isolation allows him some access to her state of mind, but he finally must leave the stage, in a sense out of respect for her own pain. And then at last, her own music comes: a Kaddish chant for single male voice opens the final moments of the play to the collective plight and lamentation of the Jewish experience. It is a note that can be held only so long, but it is a note that sounds within itself the crying of Shylock and the inner struggles of Jessica, never so completely his daughter as now. Nothing sentimental or sententious here; these final moments capture a feeling for life sad and sobering.

The importance of Olivier's Shylock and Miller's *Merchant of Venice* rests in the fact that this highly original interpretation takes the Shakespearian back to the play and the audience back to themselves and their deepest intuitions about life. Miller's direction is that of a moral visionary. With a production like this one, performance becomes itself a critical act, one capable of regenerating a vision which avoids 'benign' anti-semitism on the one hand and stodgy moralism (or amoralism) on the other. While this production has not been nor will be free from dislike or censure, I am also certain that students of Shakespeare and the theatre must take it seriously as an effort at discovering and dramatizing the essential moral energy of *The Merchant of Venice*. For Shakespeare as for literature more generally, tradition and the individual talent need to stay married for the continuous realization of great art. (pp. 31-44)

Patrick J. Sullivan, "Strumpet Wind—The National Theatre's 'Merchant of Venice'," in Educational Theatre Journal, *Vol. 26, No. 1, March, 1974, pp. 31-44.*

John Cottrell   (essay date 1975)

[*Cottrell relates the circumstances by which Olivier came to play Shylock, his preparation for the role, and some critical responses to his performance.*]

In 1970 Olivier was cajoled and caressed into taking on a major new stage role—his first in three years. Jonathan Miller was to direct *The Merchant of Venice* with a late nineteenth-century setting. Two actors were unsuccessfully approached to play Shylock. Finally, under pressure from Tynan among others, Sir Laurence agreed to take it on, and he came back characteristically with a portrait worked out with infinite care and attention to detail. He wore a shiny top hat over his skullcap and a Disraeli-style curl on his forehead; the not quite immaculate cut of his striped trousers and the affected dropping of his final g's gave subtle evidence of the pseudo upper-class gentility of this frock-coated Jew; and the slightly protruding upper teeth that showed when he smiled was another touch neatly designed to give the man an unsavory visual image. Nor had Olivier lost any of his penchant for physical invention, though one most striking piece of business—an infernal dance of triumph based on Hitler's *schadenfreude* skip at the signing of the armistice in the Forest of Compiegne—was, in fact, suggested by the director. "One rather needed to throw in this kind of contribution in exchange for concessions on the other side," says Jonathan Miller. "Some measure of give-and-take was essential; after all, at the beginning there was a real danger of Olivier shaping a too grotesque caricature, a full-blown hooked nose and all the rest. You can only go so far in seeking to restrain an actor of such stature and individual technique. He is so experienced at building up a strong characterization of his own design, and he is naturally wary of suggestions that seem to be incompatible with his own strong ideas."

Predictably, critical opinion of that characterization is sharply divided. Michael Billington, who gives an admirably didactic scene-by-scene analysis of the performance in his book *The Modern Actor,* calls this Shylock "the best of its generation," especially because of its "high intellectual power" and "sheer interpretative originality." Richard Findlater thought it suffered to some extent from the implausibilities of the 1890s setting, "yet in spite of that obstacle Olivier demonstrated once again that separates good acting from great acting, even when a great actor is below his summit." Herbert Kretzmer (*Daily Express*) was among critics who rated it less highly: "Not even the genius of Sir Laurence Olivier can bring life sour of substance to Shylock. . . . It is a performance of awesome technique, as one would expect, but it is lacking in both pity and truth." And Harold Hobson (*Sunday Times*), whose profound admiration of Olivier goes back as far as *The Rats of Norway* (1933), was unusually blunt: "Dancing with glee at Antonio's misfortunes, coming to court to cut off a pound of flesh with a briefcase more prominent than a knife, and after sentence apparently falling down stairs offstage, Sir Laurence will not be remembered for his Shylock. Or if he is, he will be singularly unlucky."

Yet here again Olivier was running absolutely true to form. He had presented another fascinating demonstration of the actor's art, one which the diligent theatergoer could see again and again and each time discover something afresh; at the same time, he gave an interpretation that for some unyielding purists was too often at variance with the lines Shakespeare wrote. Typically, it divided opinion without failing for an instant to command attention; and even those who disapproved

90

of the overall effect hastened to acknowledge its stunning moments. It was, needless to say, another overwhelming success in box-office terms, indeed a double Olivier triumph since Joan Plowright also came across effectively with a Portia of striking authority. (pp. 359-61)

John Cottrell, "The Second Term," in his Laurence Olivier, Prentice-Hall, Inc., 1975, pp. 357-68.

Helen Krich Chinoy   (interview date 1976)

[*In the interview below, director Miller describes his production process, the identification of a central idea or image distilled from the text brought to realization on the stage. The director likens the process to story-telling, the narration of a dream or vision. Miller concedes that "great actors" may challenge the director's vision, and in the case of* Merchant, *Olivier and Miller did "a lot of horse-trading"; however, the director takes credit for suggesting much of Olivier's acclaimed stage business, including Shylock's off-stage wail at the conclusion of Act IV, Scene I.*]

"There is no mystery about it," replies Jonathan Miller when you ask him how he goes about transforming plays, especially those of Shakespeare burdened with centuries of critical and theatrical commentary, into immediate revelations. "You can do it or you can't do it. It's like bike riding. You learn directing by directing; you learn each time you do a play." As he folds and unfolds his long limbs in rhythms that recall the frenetic gangling mimic of *Beyond the Fringe,* he disavows the know-how of the trade, the tricks, devices, and special techniques one is supposed to master. You can learn what you need, as Miller did, on the job. "The mystery is in the head."

It is his unique emphasis on "plays as embodiments of ideas about life" that has made Miller an important interpreter of Shakespeare in the last few years. Neurosurgeon, medical historian, comedian, television personality, film maker, associate director of the National Theatre, and now associate director of the Greenwich Theatre, Miller came to directing by chance. During the run of the remarkable revue *Beyond the Fringe* in the early sixties, he directed a one-act play by John Osborne at the Royal Court Theatre. Almost two years later he staged his friend Robert Lowell's *The Old Glory* in New York largely because no one else wanted to do it. It was not until several years after his considerable success with this play and after his television accomplishments that he decided "it would be nice to do some theatre properly"—all the while maintaining professional ties with medicine. First at Nottingham and then with a student company from Oxford and Cambridge, he began that series of Shakespearean productions that earned him an invitation to the National Theatre. There his production of *The Merchant of Venice* in 1970 saved a bad season and was the occasion for the return of Sir Laurence Olivier in a new, major Shakespearean role. Since then Miller has offered a Shakespearean staging almost every season, either at the National Theatre or at the Chichester Festival—or more recently at the Greenwich Theatre.

Miller confesses, "I'm not really a man of the theatre. I don't go to very many productions. I'm not really interested in *the* theatre." What interests him are ideas. "As far as I'm concerned, theatre, television, films are simply media which can be used to put across certain ideas." But how Miller stages Shakespeare to "put across ideas" bears little resemblance to the usual simplistic or tendentious interpretations of today's

directors. What Miller means by "ideas" is all that is in the head, especially *his* extraordinary head, which has been described by one critic as "a turmoil of sizzling wires, connecting drama with anthropology, literature with quantum physics, linguistics with genetic theory."

What, for example, was in Miller's head when he started his production of *The Merchant of Venice?*

"I start with a vague image of some sort. It may be a picture taken from some painting. It very often is. That picture is chosen because it suggests some sort of atmosphere which is at least congruent with the text. For *The Merchant of Venice* I knew that the scene was to look rather like some photographs of Milan and Turin in the 1880s I had spent a long time looking at a year before without having *The Merchant* in mind at all. When I was asked to do the production, these photographs and the play sort of took off of each other. And I knew it had to be like that.

"Sometimes I have a series of rather vague, novelistic notions of what the characters must be like. I knew, for example, that Bassanio and Antonio were rather like Oscar Wilde and Lord Alfred Douglas. I also knew that the overall tone was to some extent rather like the novels of Svevo, like the *Confessions of Zeno.* And there were bits and pieces of Henry James and *The Portrait of a Lady.*

"Sometimes I start with some particular social or philosophical notion which I get from the text." For *The Merchant of Venice* there were resonances from the punning on the word "kind," used for compassion and for kin, and implications about the choices people make in the casket rite. As a Jew, Miller was especially interested in Shylock and how the Jew has been portrayed on the stage. "It's a mistake to have the actor playing in ringlets, beard, or greasy mitten in the pantomine tradition," he has said, even if that was the image of the Jew Shakespeare's audience may have known, a kind of fantasy figure of the myths of the middle ages. Miller sees antisemitic myths as occurring when two ethnic groups meet and, repelled by each other, "begin to look for appearances which will substantiate their prejudices." His Jew is a product of modern anti-semitism, which scholars like Hannah Arendt relate to nineteenth-century capitalism and politics rather than to biblical theories about the death of Christ. His Shylock, "corpulent, toothy, uneasily sociable, affected," is seen in the era of economic expansion, the era of the Rothchilds' banking house. The play thus becomes, as one reviewer in London said, "an investigation of the contrasts and similarities between Christians and Jews in a mercenary world."

"All these bits and pieces," says Miller, "Wilde, James, Svevo, the photographs—all spin around in a sort of bouillabaisse of ideas. I dip the actors into and out of the bouillabaisse until we all become part of it." This is Miller's description of his production process. While critics picture him playing the Cambridge don lecturing his actors, Miller is actually busily stirring his creative bouillabaisse of images and ideas. He does not work out the production before rehearsals. He gets the actors to read the play and to start moving around. Their action "will start a series of suggestions in my mind," says Miller, "that spreads outwards from the center, like dropping crystals into a supersaturated solution." He does not care much about accumulated theatrical traditions or make use of what other directors and actors have said or done. "I read a lot about Shakespeare, but usually literary criticism," and the names of Frank Kermode, Wyndham

Lewis, G. Wilson Knight, and William Empson crop up as he talks.

For Miller directing is like storytelling. "One is a mythagog. That's really what one is if one's a good director. You're telling the story of the play in a different tone of voice, and you are hoping in doing this that the actors will do as children do, that is, start to ask questions. 'What's next?' and 'Oh, I know what's next?'—and they start to contribute. It's like inviting them into your dreams. I don't think that dreams are romantic, beautiful things. What I like about a dream is that it's a free cabaret that you have every evening. I like to invite people into the dream. I suppose I like making people laugh. Even when dreams are serious, they can make people laugh. I had a marvelous dream last night I would love to incorporate into a play." (pp. 7-10)

Is there likely to be conflict between a great actor's desire to flesh out a part with his own dreams and myths and his fitting into Miller's storytelling? "Yes, there is always a conflict. Some actors become more obstinate as they get older because they rely on the fact that they are box office and one is lucky to have them in the production. On the other hand, some of them are tremendously open to you. I did a lot of horsetrading with Olivier in *The Merchant of Venice,* and he did the things I wanted him to do. In fact several of the things that he'll be remembered for in this production, I gave him. The dance that he did when he hears that Antonio's ships have gone down, for example. Just before that moment I suddenly remembered Hitler's dance at Compiegne when France surrendered. I said it would be rather a marvelous paradox or irony if in fact Shylock, as a Jew, at that moment did something that in the audience's mind would be completed by the memory of Hitler. He suddenly did it and it worked.

"The cry offstage, I told him to do that. He's very receptive. He's got extremely good theatrical horse sense. He knows when a piece of business will attract attention which will be noted down in the history books. Everyone remembers his great cry offstage in *Oedipus,* everyone remembers the great fall backwards in *Titus Andronicus;* they remember the epileptic fit in *Othello.* Well, as director, all I had to do was help think up some things that would be memorable for him. He comes up with many things of his own, of course. He has barbaric energy on stage. No matter what happens, when he comes on stage, he happens in a very spectacular way. He has that special power which is almost threatening to the audience. The audience is alarmed with great actors. They feel that something peculiar and even disastrous might happen. It's a very important ingredient, but it is sometimes very difficult to work with or to build a production around." (pp. 10-11)

He unashamedly admits that he uses the play to serve his own means. "That's my game. I'm in it for that. There are no rules, except, Is it consistent? Is it interesting? Is it nice to be in the middle of ? Each reconstruction finds the *dramatis personae* assuming different roles. Suddenly somebody relatively small in the action assumes a cardinal role, like Jessica suddenly enlarging at the end of *The Merchant of Venice.* The play is five minutes longer in my production than it is in Shakespeare's and the five minutes are taken up with something that Shakespeare never wrote, which is Jessica's slow walk alone to the sound of the Jewish prayer for the dead."

To complaints that Portia and the poetic comedy are rather left out of his conception of *The Merchant of Venice,* he

makes no denials or excuses. "It's too bad when that happens. I can imagine doing another production in which she assumes a different shape. I aim to present versions, not definitive productions. I regard plays as being the contents of memory. Each successive production for me is part of an on-going, never-ending retrieval process through which memory attempts to come into some sort of relationship with an original experience which can never actually be recaptured." (p. 13)

Helen Krich Chinoy, "The Director as Mythagog: Jonathan Miller Talks About Directing Shakespeare," in Shakespeare Quarterly, *Vol. 27, No. 1, Winter, 1976, pp. 7-14.*

Jonathan Miller   (essay date 1986)

[*In the excerpt below, Miller recreates the thought process that led him to choose late-nineteenth-century Venice as the setting for his production of* The Merchant of Venice. *Miller also describes the adjustments Olivier made in order to most effectively integrate his own conception of the character with his director's setting. Miller assisted Olivier, he states, by suggesting various stage gestures and business to accommodate directorial vision.*]

There are very great performers who are too shrewd to overlook the setting in which the director has put them, and they will adapt their performance. When, as a young director, I worked with Olivier and we put on *The Merchant of Venice* in a late nineteenth-century setting, he took note of the production. While he could have given *his* performance regardless, he realized that either he or the production could then have looked absurd. He recognized that there was something interesting in the format of the production that was consistent with the work, adapted himself, and gave a performance of a nineteenth-century character, rather than a barnstorming, Irvingish performance of what he thought the traditional Shylock should be like.

If I were to direct *The Merchant of Venice* now I would not dream of setting it in the nineteenth century but, in 1970, when Olivier offered me the job at the Old Vic it seemed appropriate. It is difficult to explain precisely why I chose that setting, and it certainly did not start with the thought of how interesting it would be to move the play to that century. I think it came out of my hearing certain speeches, in my mind's ear, delivered in a way that was incompatible with a sixteenth-century setting. As a director I often respond negatively to a precedent and, in this case, I recoiled from the sentimental radiance that actresses bring to Portia's famous mercy speech. I could imagine the speech being delivered in a much more argumentative and impatient way, in response to the apparent stupidity of Shylock's enquiry when he asks, *'On what compulsion must I? tell me that'* [IV. i. 183]. In my mind's eye I saw Portia leaning impatiently across the table to say, *'The quality of mercy is not* strained' [IV. i. 184] as if having laboriously to explain what should have been self-evident to someone too stupid to understand. This dispute was too ugly to be argued out in public. The courtroom disappeared and was replaced in my mind by a rather drab Justice's Chambers. When I reached this point, I began to realize that it would be an impossible location for the sixteenth century, but I did not want to set it in a modern era where all the twentieth-century notions of anti-Semitism would overwhelm the play.

I began, then, to think about other themes of the play which might themselves suggest an appropriate setting. The relationship between Bassanio and Antonio made me think of the relationship between Oscar Wilde and Bosie where a sad old queen regrets the opportunistic heterosexual love of a person whom he adored. Again, this echo of a relationship seemed appropriate to the nineteenth century. But the production had to acknowledge Venice as its location, and so I looked at late nineteenth-century photographs of that city taken by the Count de Primoli who also recorded Trieste, and the trading cities of northern Italy. I imagined the rather dull, Adriatic mercantile life that Italo Svevo re-creates in his novels, and the footling young men who frequented the waterside cafés. By this time, I felt that I had the beginnings of a totally new way of staging *The Merchant of Venice,* which could bring the speeches to life in a completely different context, and yet remain consistent with Shakespeare's play. The costumes and designs were all influenced by the Count de Primoli's photographs. In many ways I regret making the production quite so richly pictorial. I would have preferred to make it resemble Svevo's Italy, and set it in a rather boring, unscenic, un-Venetian world of the kind that you find in Trieste.

It was in relation to this that Olivier adjusted his performance. He began with the idea of being a grotesque, ornamentally Jewish figure and bought himself very expensive dentures, a big hook nose and ringlets. I think he had a George Arliss view of himself, but gradually he realized the possible advantage in making himself look much more like everyone else, as it is this crucial question of difference that lies at the heart of the play. With the exception of the teeth, in which he had invested such a large amount of money that I did not feel justified in asking him to surrender them, he gradually lost the other excrescences, partly because I suspect that he could see that the production could have made him appear like a ridiculous pantomime dame in the midst of the rather ordinary nineteenth-century set. As a director, I was able to supply him with bits of business that made him feel secure enough to abandon the Arliss look. When I suggested that Shylock might enter with Jessica's dress in his arms, I simply pointed out that when she leaves the house wearing men's costume she would have left her dress behind her—like a snake shedding its skin—for Shylock to find in her absence. Shylock coming in with the dress draped in his arms has a wonderful overtone of Lear carrying Cordelia. In *King Lear,* as in *The Merchant of Venice,* a daughter who betrays her father seems, in his eyes, to die when she denies him her love. Holding the empty dress, Olivier appeared to be carrying the corpse of the departed daughter, as Shylock wishes when he says, '*I would my daughter were dead at my foot, and the jewels in her ear! would she were hearsed at my foot, and the ducats in her coffin!*' [III. i. 87-90].

There was another little gesture that pleased Olivier. At the moment when Tubal tells Shylock that Antonio's ships have gone down there is a pause for some memorable and exotic gesture. I asked Olivier if he recalled the newsreel showing Hitler in the railway carriage at Compiègne, at the surrender of France. Suddenly, the Führer was seen dancing a funny little jig of triumph, and I suggested that Olivier follow it. He was delighted with the unpredictable peculiarity of this gesture, and felt he had enough in these details to make the part stand out without needing false noses. (pp. 104-08)

Jonathan Miller, in an excerpt from his Subsequent Performances, *Faber & Faber, 1986, pp. 95-108.*

PRODUCTION:

John Barton and Patrick Stewart • Royal Shakespeare Company • 1978

BACKGROUND:

Barton's restrained, well-balanced production won the admiration of most critics. The director skillfully exploited the intimacy created by the relatively small theater, the Other Place, drawing attention to the drama's pivotal scenes. Patrick Stewart's dynamic and critically well-received interpretation of Shylock sought to strip the character of his "Jewishness." Stewart attempted to discard the caricature of Shylock, to minimize the heroic or tragic aspects of the character and thus humanize him. J. W. Lambert deemed Stewart's "educated, almost donnish" Shylock "richly characterised," and Roger Warren called it "a virtuoso performance encompassing all the variety of the part, now quietly colloquial, now impassioned." When the production moved to London the following season, Lisa Harrow replaced Marjorie Bland as Portia. In 1981 Barton reprised his original production at the Royal Shakespeare Theatre in Stratford-upon-Avon with David Suchet as Shylock and Sinead Cusack as Portia.]

COMMENTARY:

J. W. Lambert   (review date Autumn 1978)

[*Lambert finds Stewart's "educated, almost donnish" Shylock "richly characterised." Bland's Portia was uninteresting, according to the critic, and tarnished by "her sloppy speech." Lambert remarks that the director's thoughtful guidance was evident throughout the production.*]

The Merchant of Venice was given at The Other Place. . . . This small square box, with its two levels of seats, puts the plays under a microscope. John Barton again directed, and the sense of a governing intelligence was again strong, evidently working closely with Patrick Stewart's powerful characteristics as an actor—the athletic frame, the piercing eye, the finely focussed dark, bronze voice. Sharply focussed, dark and bronzed, that is, at its best; but this excellent actor does tend to rev it up, if I'm allowed the phrase, into a prolonged howl, this year's only example—particularly noticeable, sometimes physically painful, in such a small space—of what I call the 'Stratford overdrive', rife in last year's Histories. Nevertheless his educated, almost donnish Jew was richly characterised. First came the distant, almost playful, relation with the gentiles he knew despised him. Then, very nastily, the domestic portrait of a man who, possibly because he had lost a beloved wife, had turned his whole attention to business, behaving with brutal harshness to his daughter, whom he clearly regards as just another possession; the only real grief, as opposed to mortification, he feels after her flight springs from the fact that she has taken the ring his wife gave him before they were married. Then, in the courtroom (a very relaxed courtroom—I was surprised to see Antonio calm his nerves by lighting up a cigarette) his satisfaction thwarted, he falls back like Katherina on a submission which is no submission, invoking the ritual gestures of his Faith in a most impressive and far from reassuring exit. I could find little of interest in Marjorie Bland's Portia; but perhaps that is because I was put off by her sloppy speech ('Yeeoo must chee-uese'). What the small theatre helped most, I think, was the toing and froing of the Venetian gentlemen. Solanio and Salerio sitting chatting at a café table—we're in more or less modern dress again—were no longer two chaps churning out some introductory explanations but real people gossiping. John Nettles' Bassanio was no longer a mere rather wet playboy figure, but a living man, of not very admirable character certainly, still initially after Portia as a lady richly dight—yet, in conditions of such intimacy with the audience, offering, in such quiet playing, the possibility that he might come to deserve the good fortune he has sought as yet another fortune-hunter; and that Portia's instant submission, more complete than Katherina's (how that lady begins to haunt the scene) and more sincere than Shylock's, may not after all be misplaced, as in too many productions of this play one has gloomily felt that it must be. (pp. 15-16)

J. W. Lambert, "Shakespeare for Pleasure," in Drama, *London, No. 130, Autumn, 1978, pp. 11-17.*

S. Schoenbaum   (review date 27 October 1978)

[*Schoenbaum avers that "Barton's* Merchant *deserves the tumultous ovation which greeted it." The critic deems Stewart's dynamic Shylock riveting, although he finds at least one bit of his stage business—striking Jessica—questionable.*]

The play [*The Merchant of Venice*] gives us Shylock as the Devil Jew: the usurer and paternal despot, his name synonymous with antisemitic opprobrium. Yet Shakespeare allows him ample scope to state his case, which he does with an intelligence and eloquence that only Portia, of the gentiles, can command. Scapegoat and outcast, Shylock is spat upon and spurned like a dog by the otherwise tender-hearted Antonio. His own daughter rejects his faith, steals his gold, and casually exchanges for a monkey the ring Leah gave him when, as a bachelor, he came courting. In that most purple of passages, when Shylock asks his Christian persecutors whether a Jew has not the same senses, affections, and passions as they, contradictory voices co-exist side by side. The speech that so movingly affirms the humanity of which we all partake serves, in the last resort, to justify an inhuman purpose: "The villainy you teach me I will execute", Shylock warns Antonio's friends; "and it shall go hard but I will better the instruction" [III. i. 71-3].

After the holocaust and the history of European Jewry in this century, what is the producer—conscious that he too partakes of common humanity—to do? Some, especially in the United States, will decide to leave well enough alone, and join the school administrators who have banished *The Merchant of Venice* from the classroom. When the play is performed, the director usually takes the easier option of harkening to the opposing voice. In the Jonathan Miller production, which was deemed sufficiently innocuous to be taped for the box and viewed by the impressionable millions, Olivier wore no beard for Antonio to void his rheum on, nor did he murderously whet his knife in the Court of Justice. Offstage, after his final exit, he harrowed his audience with a great Kaddish wail of suffering: that we should not forget Shylock in the tranquillity of Belmont, Antonio and Jessica exchanged meaningful glances when left alone on stage at the end. All things considered, it was a sentimental *Merchant*. Barton, on the other

hand, has had the courage to be faithful to the main thrust of the play.

Shylock may not be one of Olivier's great parts, but Patrick Stewart riveted us in the role at The Other Place. He wants us to see Shylock not as a despicable Jew but as a despicable person, so he avoids stereotypically semitic features: no ringlets or prayer shawl or stage nose. This strategy cannot, of course, fully succeed, for the script makes Shylock's Jewishness part and parcel of his villainy. But Stewart takes advantage of such opportunities as come his way. Shylock smokes hand-rolled cigarettes—the setting is Edwardian—and saves the ends in his case: a practice that at once illustrates his meanness and distances him from even his fellow Jew Tubal, who puffs a cigar. We see Shylock weighing his gold on the same scale that is later set forth for Antonio's flesh. At home, in Shylock's only private scene, we are given Jessica's view of their domesticity: "Our house is hell" [II. iii. 2]. In the most questionable bit of business in this production, Shylock slaps his daughter after handing over his keys to her. Why? Shylock has caught the flicker of rebellion in her eyes—she is about to elope—and chastises her for it. Thus Stewart explicates. But nothing in the dialogue explains or supports the gesture, and a theatre, unlike a cinema audience, cannot read the expression in Jessica's eyes. Shylock's only overtly violent act comes across as capricious tyranny.

In public he runs the gamut of emotion. He weeps, he laughs; hands and body are energetically expressive. At one point Stewart pops a couple of pills in his mouth; tranquillizers, I thought, to bring him down a peg. With Tubal he dramatically exhibits the knife he plans to use, while his friend, who has goaded him on, shakes his head disapprovingly. In the great scene of reckoning, which I have never seen more excitingly realized, Shylock removes his boot and, ostentatiously raising it, whets his blade on the sole so all may shudder. At first he is wary of Portia—he knows, from experience, the cunning of these Christians—but, like everybody else, he is mesmerized by her rhetoric, and drops his guard. When she reminds him of his alien status, Shylock knows he is done for. He grovels on hands and knees for mercy; he throws off his yarmulka, embraces his enemy (how Christian can you get?), even laughs at Gratiano's taunting joke. He will survive. As for the Venetians, they have behaved fairly by their own standards, but it is appalling to see the power of the state extort such abject submission.

All through the performance one might hear the proverbial pin drop; so rapt were we. Unfortunately, silence also greeted the Gobbo routines. With his curly hair and battered hat, Hilton McRae intended (I suppose) to remind us of Harpo Marx, and he even had Harpo's horn, which now and then he squeezed. But his noisy efforts proved strenuously unfunny; this company is weakest when it comes to the clowns. The patronizing notion that it is hilarious for an actor merely to bob up and down and scamper about dies hard, despite the fact that such antics, employed for any other playwright, would be hooted off the stage. The Edwardian setting made an anachronistic hash of Shylock's point about the Venetians using purchased slaves but otherwise did not unduly distract. These are mere details; Barton's *Merchant* deserves the tumultuous ovation which greeted it. He is this season's hero. (pp. 1262-63)

S. Schoenbaum, "Alternative Shakespeare," in The Times Literary Supplement, *No. 3995, October 27, 1978, pp. 1262-63.*

Ann Jennalie Cook (review date Spring 1979)

[*Cook argues that Barton's restrained, well-balanced production was extremely effective. She commends Stewart's efforts to "strip away centuries of interpretation and get back to the human being represented in the text," abandoning the "Jewish trappings" associated with the role. The result, according to Cook, was "a powerful, subtle, credible Shylock."*]

Certain actors of the Royal Shakespeare Company hold a special interest for Shakespearean scholars. One of these is Patrick Stewart. In such roles as Oberon, Aufidius, and Enobarbus, his acting alone would command serious attention. But Mr. Stewart has stepped beyond the confines of the stage to take a principal part in the growing dialogue between scholars and theatre professionals. As a leader in the Actors-in-Residence (AIR) program organized and directed by Homer Swander, Patrick Stewart has for several years traveled to college campuses in the United States, working with students and faculty, performing, and discussing his craft. With Tony Church and Lisa Harrow, he appeared in New Orleans before the annual meeting of the Shakespeare Association of America in 1977. And in 1978 he spoke to the International Shakespeare Conference at Stratford on a panel that also included David Suchet and Maurice Daniels. Patrick Stewart's appearance as Shylock in *The Merchant of Venice* at The Other Place was therefore no ordinary event for many of the academics who comprised the audience at a Thursday matinee last August.

For members of the Royal Shakespeare Company, the scholars who attend the biannual meetings of the International Shakespeare Conference always pose a formidable body of critics. Even in the big theatre, where they are absorbed into the mass of a large audience, academics can noticeably change the atmosphere—at least according to the actors on-stage, who sense a more subdued response.

The intimate relationship between actors and audience dictated by the restricted dimensions of The Other Place makes it impossible for actors to perform there without full awareness of the spectators' responses, almost on an individual basis. At the interval, the cast of *Merchant* felt that the house was cool, uninvolved, not emotionally responsive to the play. They wondered what more they could do to break through the reserve. Without knowing it, the actors had long since won over the audience. What seemed detachment was intense, thoughtful concentration. At the end of the play, virtually the entire house rose at once, in the warmest, most spontaneous applause I have ever seen.

Stewart himself deserves much of the credit. Without false nose or earlocks or any of the other Jewish trappings he deliberately decided to abandon, he created a powerful, subtle, credible Shylock. He tried to strip away centuries of interpretation and get back to the human being represented in the text, and he succeeded to an extraordinary degree. He was disturbing but not tragic, moving but not pathetic. Whether desperate or despicable, Stewart's Shylock remained a man whose greed and meanness of spirit set him athwart the liberal generosity and love of the other characters. A dozen minor details contributed to the overall portrait. He narrowed his eyes, as if frugal even of his sight, ever sizing up a bargain. His stained, frayed clothes, barely on this side of respectability, persuaded us of his stinginess long before Launcelot Gobbo's complaint of starvation and Shylock's counter-complaint of the servant's great feeding. From a small tin box, Stewart repeatedly extracted a thread-thin cigarette,

thriftily extinguishing what remained and returning it to the box for future use. In the daughter-ducats lament, there was no doubt that the loss of the ducats outweighed the loss of the daughter.

The two points of controversy in Stewart's portrayal of Shylock occurred in his scene with Jessica (Avril Carson) and in the trial scene. In the former he gave his daughter an unscripted slap before leaving her in charge of his house and money while he went to dine with the Christians. Though it helped explain why Shylock's home was "hell" to Jessica, this slap nonetheless came across as shocking, gratuitous cruelty. Stewart himself explained that Shylock saw some sign of rebellion in Jessica's eyes (attributable to the impending elopement) which required harsh discipline, but he acknowledged that the emotional interchange was not being communicated effectively.

The trial scene—always potentially unbalancing to the play—remained disturbing to several in the audience. Stewart's Shylock prostrated himself before his judges, groveling in obsequious acceptance of his enforced baptism. To those who would prefer a Shylock irreparably injured by an unjust Christian sentence, Stewart disappointed. To others, myself included, who see Shylock's acceptance of baptism as a logical response to the offer of continued use of his money, Stewart succeeded brilliantly. (Money and revenge are the sole passions in Shylock's life; bereft of revenge, he will do anything to retain his money.) Indeed, Stewart's portrayal was the first I have ever seen that suggested any sense of mercy extended to or apprehended by Shylock. (If Shylock's fawning gratitude for life and lucre mark him as mean, so do the other events of the play.)

Somewhat surprisingly, Patrick Stewart's Shylock did not unbalance the play. Indeed, one of the great virtues of *Merchant of Venice* at The Other Place was its evenness. The restrained nineteenth-century setting gave point to Antonio's languid melancholy in a male mercantile world of clubs, cigars, and brandy, even as it translated effectively into Portia and Nerissa's black moiré mourning dresses. The costumes and set were far too economical to intrude on the text of the play. The cast, functioning as an ensemble, offered a true reading of the comedy at both surface and subsurface levels—no gimmicks, no strained interpretations, no quest for novelty or relevance. With the possible exception of Launcelot (Hilton McRae), who appeared as a Harpo Marx music man, the actors played in such harmony with one another that individual performers did not divert the audience's attention from the production as a whole. For such superb actors as Stewart, Marjorie Bland (who portrayed Portia), or David Bradley (as Antonio), this restrained exercise of craft was uncommonly effective. The audience saw *The Merchant of Venice,* not Shylock and Company, as is so often the case. (pp. 158-60)

Ann Jennalie Cook, " 'The Merchant of Venice' at the Other Place," in Shakespeare Quarterly, *Vol. 30, No. 2, Spring, 1979, pp. 158-60.*

Benedict Nightingale (review date 4 May 1979)

[*Nightingale affirms that in avoiding sentimentality, Barton treated "his combatants with equal scepticism." The critic lauds the "intelligence and balance" of the production, and asserts that Stewart's portrayal "has done as much to illumine the causes and consequences of racial bigotry as any Shylock I can recall.'*]

There are, or were, two main varieties of *Merchant:* the tale of a fanged and ferocious Semite muzzled by the agility of Portia, Nerissa, et al; and the tale of a dignified Rothschild baited past decency and endurance by Christian curs. Macklin set the first tradition in motion back in 1753: Olivier, in 1971, best represents the style that continues slowly to replace it. John Barton avoids both sorts of sentimentality by the simple expedient of treating his combatants with equal scepticism. The Christians are, on the whole, a spoiled, boorish bunch, much given to throwing bread-rolls, shooting off cap-pistols, and other types of horseplay; and the shock provoked by their deep, instinctive prejudice is the shock of recognition, because they wear the suits some of our generation's grandfathers wore at public school or Oxbridge. The upper-crust yob Gratiano, whose pet idiocy is dog-imitations, represents this faction at its most gruesome. And yet behind the witty, teasing front displayed by Patrick Stewart's Shylock, there festers a no less nasty temperament. The droopy, do-it-yourself fags he stingily smokes are a tiny symptom. The contemptuous slap he gives a hunched, browbeaten Jessica is a more substantial one. Here's a sour, loveless man, corroded by avarice, mutilated by money. Even his friend Tubal finds him faintly appalling.

Mr Stewart is no simple villain. Witness his discomforting blend of fury and laughter, the half-hilarious disbelief and outrage of his 'Hath not a Jew eyes?' [III. i. 59], and, especially, his handling of humiliation. Realising that the Christians have found a loophole in the law, and will win as they always do, he nods and smiles in cynical admiration. Threatened with penury, he loses all self-respect, grovels before the Duke, bobs and bows to Antonio. So some German Jews of our own era must have degraded, ridiculed and ingratiated themselves in hopes of avoiding the gas chambers. By the time Mr Stewart has bumbled offstage chuckling to himself, a dazed, cracked, broken figure, he has done as much to illumine the causes and consequences of racial bigotry as any Shylock I can recall: proof in itself of the intelligence and balance of a production only one of whose other excellences I have space to celebrate. Lisa Harrow is the first Portia I've seen who is actually breathless with fear that someone other than Bassanio may plump for the correct casket and oblige her to marry him. In fact, she looks as if she might throw up. Isn't this a blow for truth? (pp. 656-57)

Benedict Nightingale, "All Bull," in New Statesman, *Vol. 97, No. 2511, May 4, 1979, pp. 656-57.*

Roger Warren   (review date 1979)

[*Warren claims that Barton's skillful use of the intimacy created by the Other Place to draw attention to the play's pivotal scenes constituted the production's greatest strength. Warren also admires Stewart's Shylock, "a virtuoso performance encompassing all the variety of the part, now quietly colloquial, now impassioned."*]

Christopher Morley's designs for John Barton's *Merchant of Venice* at the Other Place were late nineteenth-century, rather Chekovian in feel, especially the *Three Sisters*-like severe black mourning dresses for Portia and Nerissa, with buttoned-up necks and mutton-chop sleeves. Shylock was shabby, almost miserly, carefully preserving the stubs of the home-rolled cigarettes which constantly drooped from the side of his mouth. He contrasted sharply with Tubal, who dressed impeccably and smoked cigars, like the smart Venetians-about-town. At home, Shylock worked at a Dickensian stand-up desk, with a large pair of scales, which he subsequently brought into court. Launcelot Gobbo was a music-hall comedian, armed with concertina and klaxon horn to accompany the voices of Conscience and Fiend; these sorted oddly with a lute, on which he accompanied speeches later on: the effect was muddled, the character as ineffective as ever.

The change of period did not seem to have any such interpretive purpose as the revelation of a superficial society in Mr Barton's British Raj *Much Ado,* beyond establishing a world which simply took it for granted that the Jews should be set apart, and even, as Antonio's offhand reply to Shylock put it, spat on. But the Jew-baiting was not over-emphasised; neither the production nor the adequate but undistinguished supporting playing distorted (or clarified) the studied ambiguity of Shakespeare's presentation of the Christians.

The real strength of the production lay in Mr Barton's masterly exploitation of the intimacy of the Other Place to present the play in the round, and thereby to concentrate maximum attention on crucial events taking place dead centre, especially Bassanio's choice, the trial, and the finale. The caskets were placed centre, simply set out on a small cane table, emphasised by a spotlight pointing down on them; Bassanio nervously circled them while Portia herself sang 'Tell me where is fancy bred' [III. ii. 63], built up into a powerful, evocative ensemble when the others, grouped at the edges of the circle, joined in with 'Ding dong bell' [III. ii. 72]. There was no crude suggestion that Portia gave the game away by stressing the 'ed' rhymes to hint at 'lead', but there was the oblique hint at the emptiness of outward show, seized on by Bassanio at '*So* may the outward shows be least themselves' [III. ii. 73]: the formality, the music, the circling movement built up to a tremendous climax: 'here choose I' [III. ii. 107] was electric. The caskets were then removed and the stage cleared for Portia's and Bassanio's elaborate vows, the crucial ring held up in the hot-spot at the centre; it was similarly held up there when Portia claimed it at the end of the trial scene, the cross-reference helping to begin the transfer back to Belmont.

The trial was laid out with similar formality, heavy dark chairs and judgement table replacing the cane furniture: Shylock and Antonio sat facing one another, the Duke facing a black-draped chair to which Antonio was subsequently strapped. This created a central debating-area which became a combat-area; and by grouping everyone else around the edges, Mr Barton stressed that this is essentially a duel between Shylock and Portia, not primarily about abstract issues like Justice and Mercy, but arising out of a particular situation. Portia started 'the quality of mercy' [IV. i. 184] seated at the edge; then, warming to her task, she moved to the centre to dispute with Shylock: he brought the debate back to judicial relevance with an insistent 'I crave the law' [IV. i. 206]. Thereafter Marjorie Bland and Mr Barton emphasised the vital point that Portia, having given Shylock every chance to show a mercy outside the rigid terms of 'the law', then insists equally rigidly on the enforcement of that law, including its penalties. But when Shylock, after grovelling before the Duke and shaking Antonio's hands in abject gratitude for his mercy, fumbled for his cigarette tin, dropped it, and spilled the contents, it was Portia who picked it up for him: 'give me leave to go from hence' [IV. i. 395] was spoken directly to her. And his response to Gratiano's ferocious gibe about the gallows not the font was to break into the laughter with which he had shared jokes with the Christians earlier.

Patrick Stewart's Shylock was a virtuoso performance encompassing all the variety of the part, now quietly colloquial, now impassioned. Genial in public (even mocking Bassanio's 'be *assured* you may' [I. iii. 28] by the way he pronounced the word), he was sober in private, even giving Jessica a quite gratuitous slap in the face before leaving for supper. He caught all the changes of mood in the Tubal scene, the quiet passion of 'no sighs but o' *my breathing; no tears but o' my shedding*' [III. i. 95-6], switching from the ecstatic 'Good news!' of Antonio's fate to despair both over Jessica's profligacy and Tubal's expenses, which he scrupulously paid out there and then with soiled notes from a pocket book in which he had calculated the 'rate' of Bassanio's loan. After a pause to light the inevitable drooping cigarette, he was struck with the idea of paying Tubal (more notes) to 'fee me an officer' [III. i. 126], answering Tubal's surprise that he should actually pursue the bond with a sharp, quiet, edged 'were he out of Venice, I can make what merchandise I will' [III. i. 127-29], a commercial motive duly appreciated by Tubal.

Mr Barton balanced the complex variety of this Shylock by encouraging Marjorie Bland to bring out the variety of Portia too, pinpointing her anxieties and ecstasies in the casket scenes: 'I would / not / lose / you' [III. ii. 5], was intensely emphatic. I particularly admired her refusal to soften Portia's unsentimental hardness and sententiousness: 'To offend and judge are distinct offices' [II. ix. 61] was a tart rebuke to a brisk Prussian officer of an Arragon, complete with iron cross, who, after pawing her with barely restrained desire, had complained with furious wounded pride and no trace of humour, 'Did I deserve no more than a fool's head?' [II. ix. 59].

John Nettles's Bassanio was almost as striking, developing from nervy eloquence to a thoughtful power in response to Portia. The final sense of harmony, of the music of the spheres even, was secured partly by music and formality, the cast sitting in a circle for *al fresco* drinks, a ring of harmony broken by argument and re-formed again as Antonio restored the ring to Bassanio (again catching it in that central spot), but still more by the strength of feeling in this Portia and Bassanio.

The Merchant is much less fashionable than it was, especially in academic estimation. While this production absolutely justified earlier esteem for it, making you marvel afresh at Shakespeare's subtleties and complexities in the Shylock / Portia scenes, it also reinforced another older view that those powerful peaks make the scenes in which neither appears seem somewhat wan. (pp. 204-05)

> *Roger Warren, "A Year of Comedies: Stratford 1978," in* Shakespeare Survey: An Annual Survey of Shakespearian Study and Production, *Vol. 32, 1979, pp. 201-10.*

Patrick Stewart   (essay date 1985)

[*Stewart relates his experience playing Shylock and the process through which he came to understand the character. Stewart describes the motives behind his intention to divest Shylock of his "Jewishness": to minimize the heroic or tragic, and poten-*

tially symbolic, aspects of the character in order to humanize him, as "a small, complex, real and recognizable human being, part of us all."]

'Shylock, in *The Merchant of Venice,* can be played as a wolfish villain, sadistically lusting for the blood of a Christian he hates. Or, he can be interpreted as a dignified symbol of an oppressed people intellectually and morally superior to the Christians who taunt and abuse him.' So began one review of John Barton's production of *The Merchant of Venice* when it opened in London in May 1979. The production was then a year old, having opened in Stratford in the previous spring, and I had been playing Shylock almost continuously since then. At the time, the depressing narrowness of this critic's view of the role appalled me, but had I been more objective, I might have recalled there had been a time when I would have shared this blinkered view.

The prospect of rehearsing Shylock had not excited me. On the day the part was offered I had felt an irritable disappointment that my principal role in the 1978 season might only be Shylock in *The Merchant of Venice,* rather than a challenging role in a greater play. I had played the part thirteen years earlier. That experience, and other later contacts with the play, had soured my feelings in such a way that I too could only see Shylock as a racial symbol, serving the play with either of these two clichéd faces; inhibited by gentile timidity, and uneasy and ambivalent feelings about the alleged racist nature of the *Merchant,* only the sentimental interpretation would seem to be tolerable; and that prospect was only marginally more tiresome than the melodramatic alternative. Not an appealing prospect, to be trapped in the straitjacket of a rigid and predetermined characterization, suspecting that the part could only be made distinctive and vivid through effects, and faced with all that 'my daughter and my ducats' acting; not 'owning' the play, nor dominating it. Shylock is a curious role, in that its fame and reputation are quite out of proportion with his share of the lines. He appears in only five scenes and two of these are very brief. There have been occasions when producers and actor-managers, reacting perhaps to the feeling that the part needed 'expanding', have added a sixth scene. The scene which might be called 'Shylock's return' was played after Act 2, Scene 6 and shows Shylock arriving home to find his house bereft of daughter, jewels and ducats. Past productions have developed this scene in different ways. Irving played it very tastefully. A solitary figure crossing a bridge, reaching the door of his house, knocking and waiting in lonely silence as the curtain falls. Thirty years later Herbert Beerbohm Tree had a livelier approach. As Toby Lelyveld reports [in his *Shylock on the Stage,* 1961]:

> When Shylock returns home, to find Jessica and his money gone, he bursts in to the house, rages through its rooms and appearing now at this window and now at that, cries out the name of his daughter in a crescendo, until he at last collapses. [Then he came] dashing out of doors; he flung himself on the ground, and tore his garments and sprinkled ashes on his head.

Shylock's role is also diminished by his having no appearance in Act 5 and some have resolved this by ending the play with his exit from the trial.

One of the intriguing pleasures of performing a long role, particularly in Shakespeare, is to feel oneself as the heartbeat of the play; not only caught up in the rhythmic surging movement of the play's energy, but to be the energy itself, the pulse. Like riding a powerful horse, in performance the actor feels the reins of the play, holding in or giving head as the story moves forward, and the control never being applied in quite the same way twice. For the actor playing Shylock this control is never possible as he spends more time waiting his turn to mount than actually riding in the saddle.

However, it was not Shylock's limited share of the play and his stereotyped function that were discouraging for an actor looking for rich, human complexities; there is even a stereotyped image that goes with the part—swarthy, foreign features (invariably incorporating a prominent hooked nose), ringlets, eastern robes (rich or shabby to taste) and clutching either the famous scales or the murderous knife. So strong is this image of the Jew with the raised weapon that in rehearsals I had to resist the impulse to menace Antonio in this way, and throughout the life of the production I felt secretly guilty that I was denying the audience their right to see this traditional tableau. I think it was this sense of so much tradition attached to the role that was uninspiring, and the fear of finding oneself trundling along tramlines, trapped in a lifeless mould. Nevertheless, actor's curiosity, the mysterious reputation of the role and the appeal of Shakespeare in the small space of The Other Place was finally sufficient reason for accepting the part. And so I found myself on the threshold of an experience that was for two years to be entirely fascinating and very rewarding.

At my first meeting with the play's director, John Barton, he spoke briefly of his feelings about the play and its characters but he said it was a 'cool' play, a fairy story, and he talked of a sense of melancholy threaded through it. Music would be very important, he said (James Walker's lovely score was a marvellous unifier of the play). He and the designer, Christopher Morley, had decided to adapt the auditorium of The Other Place into a 'theatre in the round', thus making a set unnecessary and destroying, at a stroke, one *Merchant of Venice* cliché, the bridge and gondola backdrop. As for Shylock, his brief was very simple—he must be a monster. At my first reading I had been delighted to discover how marvellously witty Shylock was, particularly in the early part of the play, and so suggested he might be an entertaining monster, and so we 'shook hands and a bargain'. Finally, and with some firmness, John Barton said that he felt that the play had for too long belonged to Shylock (so much for all the above), and that this production should restore an equal balance between Bassanio, Shylock and Portia.

My homework begins with reading the play—contriving an innocence if the play is familiar—setting my imagination free to react intuitively and simply to whatever the reading suggests. After a long rehearsal period, when the play has been so dismantled and probed that the simple elements, such as the story-line, or the bold outlines of a character or of a relationship, have become blurred or submerged with elaboration

Patrick Stewart as Shylock.

and detail, it is valuable to remind oneself of those first un-complicated responses.

In 1.3 Shylock jokes with Bassanio and lightens their opening discussion with a series of puns—though rather bad ones.

> SHYLOCK   Antonio is a good man.
> BASSANIO   Have you heard any imputation to
>   the contrary?
> SHYLOCK   Ho, no, no, no, no! My meaning in
>   saying he is a good man is to have
>   you understand me that he is suf-
>   ficient.
>
> [I. iii. 12-17]

Like an experienced comic Shylock sets up Bassanio with his 'good man' and Bassanio will indignantly rise to the bait, only for Shylock to prick his pompous bubble with innocent laughter, and his explanation of his commercial use of 'good'. Then again, Shylock plays on words in, 'There be land rats . . . pirates' [I. iii. 22-4], and in his reply to Bassanio's 'Be assured you may'—'I will be assured I may' [I. iii. 28-9]. His highly tuned, ironic sense of double meanings, his use of language as a weapon or a smoke-screen or an analgesic, pres-ent an insight into his character. Possibly his wit provides a way of ingratiating himself with the Christian businessmen, and the irony protects him from the humiliation of being an alien, without losing his self-respect. Does it also suggest this could be someone speaking in a language which is not his own but which he has so carefully assimilated that, like many nat-uralized foreigners, he uses it better than the natives? He cer-tainly employs a colourful and at times bizarre turn of phrase—particularly the Jacob/Laban speech in 1.3—and this persuaded me not to use a 'foreign' accent, as it seemed that the nature of his language itself set him apart. Shylock's good humour is still present after Antonio has entered in 1.3:

> ANTONIO Was this inserted to make interest good?
>   Or is your gold and silver ewes and rams?
> SHYLOCK I cannot tell, I make it breed as fast.
>
> [I. iii. 94-6]

And in the speech where Shylock describes Antonio's treat-ment of him, from 'what should I say to you', Shylock, with delicious mockery, is turning Antonio's insults back on him.

During my early work on the play I was strongly influenced by a theme that runs throughout but is particularly marked in the early scenes. Images of money, commerce and posses-sions abound, and even people seem to have a price. The value of assets and possessions always seems to dominate and colour relationships. This theme, where it touches Shylock, appears as a series of alternatives for comparison. People, feeling, religion and race versus commerce and material se-curity. Shylock's choices are surprising but—with one excep-tion—consistent. This evidence, and what it seemed to indi-cate about his personality, became the foundation for my characterization of Shylock. The principal moments of choice were these, in 1.3:

> I hate him for he is a Christian;
> But more, for that in low simplicity
> He lends out money gratis and brings down
> The rate of usance here with us in Venice . . .
> He hates our sacred nation and he rails
> Even there where merchants most do congregate
> On me, my bargains, and my well won thrift,
> Which he calls interest.
>
> [I. iii. 42-51]

Then in 3.1 where Shylock, who has been discussing the loss of his daughter, hears of Antonio's commercial loss, and lumps the two together as 'another bad match':

> He hath disgraced me and hindered me half a mil-
> lion, laughed at my losses, mocked at my gains,
> scorned my nation, thwarted my bargains, cooled
> my friends, heated mine enemies; and what's his
> reason?
>
> [III. i. 54-8]

Only one point in Shylock's list of Antonio's wrongs touches on race and religion. The rest is business.

> TUBAL I often came where I did hear of her but
> cannot find her.
> SHYLOCK Why, there, there, there, there! A dia-
> mond gone, cost me two thousand ducats in
> Frankfort!
>
> [III. i. 81-5]

Shylock is mourning not for the lost daughter, but for the lost diamond:

> I would my daughter were dead at my foot, and the
> jewels in her ear. Would she were hears'd at my
> foot, and the ducats in her coffin!
>
> [III. i. 87-90]

Shylock's wish to punish his daughter and to remove her shame by having her dead is at one with the return of his valuables:

> I will have the heart of him if he forfeit, for were
> he out of Venice I can make what merchandise I
> will.
>
> [III. i. 127-29]

Shylock's justification of Antonio's death is solely and ruth-lessly commercial:

> You take my life
> When you do take the means whereby I live.
>
> [IV. i. 376-77]

With three simple words—'I am content' [IV. i. 394]—Shylock agrees that half his fortune should be put in trust for Jessica and Lorenzo, that he should bequeath his estate to them at his death, and that he should at once become a Chris-tian.

A picture emerges of a man in whose life there is an imbal-ance, an obsession with the retention and acquisition of wealth which is so fixated that it displaces the love and pater-nal feelings of father for daughter. It transcends race and reli-gion and is felt to be as important as life itself. It inhibits warm, affectionate responses and isolates him from his fellow man. There is a bleak and terrible loneliness in Shylock which I suspect is the cause of much of his anger and bitterness. This sense of loneliness and how he copes with it became increas-ingly important to me throughout the life of this production. Indeed, there were occasions when its presence became al-most dangerously overwhelming. Of course, it is not loneli-ness that the actor *shows*, but its compensating aspects: false gregariousness, ingratiating humour, violence and arrogance. Whatever the circumstance of his situation, scene by scene Shylock always stands in isolation. Until, that is, in 4.1 when a young doctor from Rome stands with him and seems to take his part. Shylock trusts this support and suffers for it. But if Shylock's nature is distorted by avarice, what is the cause? A man does not spring into the world unhappy, cruel and mean. It is his experience of the world, its treatment of him and his attempts to cope, that shape and form or bend and warp him. Shylock and his kind are outsiders, strangers, feared and hated for being different. They belong to the world's minorities. They are, as the laws of Venice state, alien, stamped by that world to be always vulnerable and at risk; therefore survival is paramount. Shylock is a survivor. He has clung to life in Venice and he has prospered. The alien's methods of survival in a suspicious and hostile environment are many. He can go underground and disappear. He can establish a bold and confident public reputation—a dangerous method. He can abandon all aspects of himself that set him apart and develop a new and conforming identity. Shylock, I believe, has found a way of merging with his surroundings, shabby and unmemorable, and, if he attracts attention at all, appearing as an eccentric and harmless clown. Only Antonio, his competitor in business whose senses are sharpened by commerce, smells the contempt that hides behind Shylock's jokes.

A further aid to survival is money. It will purchase favours and friends, build a wall of protection, buy silence and, in the hardest times, help to maintain a grip on life. It can also create a multitude of dependencies which, being impossible to unravel, will prove a true security. In the twelfth century the Jews in England were extremely useful in the economic scheme. Lelyveld says:

> [They] paid one half of King Richard's 100,000 marks ransom, while the entire city of London was assessed only 1,500 marks. In order to finance the Third Crusade, the Jews . . . were taxed to the extent of one-fourth of their movable property, while the remainder of the population paid one-tenth. Although the Jews constituted only one quarter of one per-cent of the total population . . . they contributed eight per-cent of the total income of the treasury.

Shylock has perhaps known the vulnerability of poverty—maybe the memory of Leah is linked with it—and from that experience has grown the determination to forge a material security which has, through years of bitter compromise and humiliation, grown into the wretched obsession that possesses Shylock at the start of the play. A feature of this obsession could be excessive meanness. Lancelot claims that he is famished in Shylock's service and in this production he might be believed, as he appeared severely undernourished. Shylock's notion of gourmandizing might be merely the satisfying of youthful appetite. In 2.5, which was set inside Shylock's house, the lighting was so dim as to suggest that most of the lightbulbs, or rather candles, had been removed. As this production was set towards the end of the nineteenth century it allowed the use of modern props to help establish location, create mood and define character—playing-cards, toy pistols, champagne, cigars and cigarettes. Antonio smoked cheroots, Tubal a havana, and Shylock his mean little hand-rolled cigarettes, whose butt-ends were safely stored away for future use. This meanness was carried over into Shylock's appearance which showed an almost studied contempt for neatness or even cleanliness. A shabby black frock coat, torn at the hem and stained, a waistcoat dusted with cigarette ash, baggy black trousers, short in the leg, exposing down-at-heel old boots, and a collarless shirt yellowing with age. Apart from the yarmulke, the only other distinctive garment was a yellow sash, twisted round the waist and only just visible beneath the waistcoat. This ritual-like garment and its wearing was an invention of the designer's, though based on photographs of

Russian Jews in the nineteenth century, who wore a yellow sash over a long frock coat. We wanted to avoid any excessive sense of Jewishness or foreignness in appearance but this detail, almost unnoticeable in the earlier scenes could, in the court, be boldly worn over the frock coat as a proud demonstration of Shylock's racial difference.

In the early scenes, however, I was anxious to minimize the impression of Shylock's Jewishness. Whenever I had seen either a very ethnic or detailedly Jewish Shylock I felt that something was lost. Jewishness could become a smoke-screen which might conceal both the particular and the universal in the role. See him as a Jew first and foremost and he is in danger of becoming only a symbol, although a symbol that has changed over the centuries as society's attitudes have changed.

Toby Lelyveld traces the role through from the beginning. For the Elizabethans Shylock's outrageous behaviour came as no shock, and for many years he was played 'in the vein of the lowest comedy'. After the 'stormy and diabolical Shylock' of Macklin, Kean broke tradition 'and recreated the character as a persecuted martyr, forced by circumstance to become an avenger'. Irving's Shylock was marked by 'intense pathos and a keen sense of injury', and the role began to assume its tragic intensity. Over the years, however, Irving's 'early humanitarian treatment coarsened', and the obsessive, sneering avenger returned to the stage. In the nineteen-twenties and thirties, *The Merchant* was produced three times at the Old Vic and on each occasion an attempt was made to focus attention away from Shylock, the bond-plot subordinated to the fairy tale. In 1932 Malcolm Keen's 'realistic and powerful' Shylock was 'not allowed to dominate the action'. And when John Gielgud, who had directed Keen, played the part himself in 1938, he showed himself still determined 'to keep the play from becoming the tragedy of the Jew'.

Because of the Nazis' Final Solution and six million deaths, those passages of anti-semitic expression in *The Merchant* will reverberate powerfully for any audience in this second half of the twentieth century. Actor and director will not need to emphasize them, nor must they be avoided. An audience must witness the intolerance of Antonio, the shallowness of Bassanio, the boorishness of Gratiano and the cynicism of Lorenzo. The unease we feel at these characterizations is important. It complicates these men who are at the heart of the romantic story of *The Merchant,* makes us less happy to accept them or not question their motives. Indeed there is an ambivalence in every corner of the play, so that no matter how well a director may bathe Act 5 in the lyrical wash of romance and fairy tale, the memories of cruelty, dishonesty and selfishness will cast troubling shadows across the Belmont dawn. But however important Jewishness and anti-semitism are in the play they are secondary to the consideration of Shylock, the man: unhappy, unloved, lonely, frightened and angry. And no matter how monstrous his cold-blooded attempt on Antonio's life, it is the brave, insane solitary act of a man who will defer no more, compromise no more. Taking Antonio's life is his line of no retreat and, although justified on commercial grounds, this murder is also, therefore, symbolic. Perhaps this makes of Shylock a revolutionary in modern terms. Certainly, when as Shylock I stood in the court and said 'my deeds upon my head' [IV. i. 206], I felt closer to *all* those oppressed and abused who stand up in the face of a hostile and powerful enemy. This was not one

Jew, but all victims who turn on their persecutors. It is in this sense that it seems Shakespeare created a portrait of an outsider who happened to be a Jew. But of course Shylock does step back from the line, he does compromise, he settles for a deal, and the patient shrug once more copes with humiliation. In the humble compliance of 'I am content' and 'send the deed after me and I will sign it' [IV. i. 396-97], Shakespeare's massive understanding touches the harsh, unsentimental facts of survival. However, this is at the end of the Shylock story, and I would like now to look at that story in more detail, noting the major objectives, the motivations, thought processes and imaginative associations that lay behind one actor's interpretation.

Shylock appears in five scenes. Each scene has a quite distinctive quality. One approach would be to blend these qualities in such a way as to present a regular and consistent picture at all appearances. On the other hand, the particular characteristics of each scene can be isolated and individually played without reference to other scenes. This approach relies on the conviction that it will not be until the moment of his final exit that the last piece will be added to the puzzle that is Shylock, and the picture completed and truly consistent. I have said that the first scene is rich in humour. There is an extravert energy in Shylock. He is garrulous, friendly and entirely reasonable. Even before the scene begins, however, Shylock's arrival is anticipated, almost ominously, by Portia's last words at the end of the preceding scene. 'Whiles we shut the gates upon one wooer, another knocks at the door' [I. ii. 133-34]. Shylock is not a wooer but Portia's apprehension is well-founded, as the next person we shall see will be the play's villain. Perhaps there lies in 'knocks at the door' a suggestion as to how '3,000 ducats' should be said. It seems probable that in the offstage dialogue Bassanio has explained the details of the loan and now Shylock is having him repeat it over, giving no answer but teasing him with each repeated 'well'. There is too a sense of surprise and pleasure in being approached by Bassanio and Antonio, though this is certainly a pretence.

But the speech about Antonio's sufficiency must impress Bassanio with Shylock's knowledge of the merchant's business and the risks involved in maritime trading. This speech is also an opportunity to demonstrate Shylock's quickness of thought and agility with language. He picks up his cues eagerly, often impatient for the other character to finish. It is an indicator of his bright intelligence. I saw no sign in the text that he is deliberate, pedantic or ponderous in his speech. Everything points to speed and liveliness. There is more humour in the 'pork' speech. A joke about 'the Nazarites' and a polite little lecture about the dietary and religious laws of the Jews. This speech is often played as hostile and aggressive, but why risk antagonizing Bassanio when there are so many intriguing possibilities behind this encounter? Antonio arrives and we move from prose to verse. The contenders are face to face; the tone of the scene shifts and becomes more tense. Verse is needed now, and the change of rhythm must be apparent in Shylock's aside. Here are no games, no jokes, but bitterness and resentment. It is a speech to the audience, therefore the truth, and they should be shocked to see this change. Shakespeare permits the audience to taste Shylock's real feelings so that they will see through the play-acting that is to follow. It is interesting that Antonio begins by justifying his involvement in this deal. It is for a friend, but he is clearly embarrassed. This makes him vulnerable and Shylock knows it. So the teasing and the mockery begin. The Jacob speech is very

characteristic of Shylock. A colourful and witty justification of thrift and sharp dealing. Shylock also plays the 'amusing story-teller' but Antonio is not amused. His response is crude and insulting. Has Shylock merited 'devil', 'evil soul', 'villain', 'rotten at the heart' and 'falsehood'? Here is a sure sign of Antonio's discomfort and embarrassment. How does Shylock react? He tells us in the next speech. A patient shrug and back to the matter in hand. But Shylock's passive acceptance is a goad to Antonio and he angrily demands an answer. Shylock's response is a masterly piece of controlled and brilliant irony. He is saying: 'Signor Antonio, I am puzzled. You abuse me for the way I make my living and I understand that, and can put up with it. But now I am confused because you want my professional help and I don't know how I should react to you. Please tell me what is right, what I should do.' Antonio cannot live with that level of complexity and he clubs his way back to a simple hostility that makes him feel secure. Shylock, still sympathetic, talks of friendship and love, but baits his hook with mention of an interest-free loan. And still the puns continue: 'This is kind I offer' [I. iii. 142]. Bassanio, quick to sense something for nothing, bites. And Shylock, in one swiftly flowing, innocently spontaneous sentence, delivers the final mock of the flesh bond. And mockery is all it is. Shylock, knowing the extent of Antonio's wealth, could not dream that he would fail so dramatically. He will help his enemy but his hatred will publicly show itself in the humiliating clause of the pound of flesh. Shylock teases them about their suspicions and daringly inserts a final mock about the flesh of muttons, beefs and goats being more estimable than Antonio's. For most of the scene the audience should have enjoyed watching him enjoying himself. Here is an entertaining eccentric we look forward to seeing again. Before his exit a private shadow passes across Shylock as he mentions his house and this shadow will soon blot out the cheeriness of 1.3.

2.5 is Shylock's most private scene. The others are public, and as such, Shylock is on show, conscious of onlookers and the effect he is having. In 2.5 there is no need for a public face and the unrestrained man will emerge. There are only two references to life in Shylock's house, and though they come from different people they are complementary, and present an appalling picture: 'The Jew my master is a kind of devil' [II. ii. 23-4], 'The very devil incarnation' [II. ii. 27], 'I am famished in his service' [II. ii. 106]. Jessica says simply and bleakly 'Our house is hell' [II. iii. 2]. This, I felt, is the description that 2.5 has to live up to. It is not the hell of poverty or meanness or even cruelty, but the hell of a house from which love has been withdrawn. This is the hell that Jessica flees from to give herself to the (questionable) love of Lorenzo. Young Gobbo is leaving to work for Bassanio and is sneered and snarled at while Jessica is called with an impatience that grows dangerous. Jessica is treated like an incompetent servant, and the mention of masques releases Shylock's suppressed, sour anger, the anger of resentment—resentments of a lifetime that each day grow more bitter. Only within the walls of his home can this anger be released. The joker of 1.3 is here appalled at the thought of the drum and the fife, and in 5.1 Lorenzo tells Jessica that

> The man that hath no music in himself,
> Nor is not moved with concord of sweet sounds,
> Is fit for treasons, stratagems and spoils;
> The motions of his spirit are dull as night,
> And his affections dark as Erebus:

Let no such man be trusted.

[V. i. 83-8]

There is violence in Shylock as well as anger, and it ripples below the surface of this domestic scene. Perhaps Shylock sees in Jessica's eyes something of her inexplicable defiance and her intended escape. I saw it and struck at her face in anger and frustration—painful and humiliating for her and for Shylock. 'Perhaps I will return immediately' [II. v. 52] may be a kind of apology—Shylock's hopeless attempt to play the father, but Jessica is no longer his daughter, and his farewell is a wretched cliché. This was consistently the most satisfying scene to play.

When Shylock arrives at the great scene of 3.1 Shakespeare has prepared the audience for his condition and has done half the actor's work for him with Solanio's description in 2.8 of his outrageous and uncontrolled passion at the loss of daughter and ducats. The intensity of this passion cannot be sustained and Shylock must be exhausted by his experience and very vulnerable. There is a plaintive, complaining tone about his first speeches and little threat in the repeated 'Let him look to his bond' [III. i. 47]. To Salerio's question 'Why, I am sure, if he forfeit, thou wilt not take his flesh. What's that good for?', Shylock can only impotently howl, 'To bait fish withal' [III. i. 51-3]. But from this cry of frustration grows Shylock's most famous speech. In rehearsals its reputation inhibited me. I stumbled unhappily through that quicksand of famous lines, memories of other actors' voices and rhythms in my head, and what proved to be a mistaken notion of what the speech was about: injustice, compassion, racial tolerance, equality and the evils of bad example. Interpreted this way the speech seemed to come from another play and had little connection with the Shylock of the earlier scenes. This reading, though fitting in parts, did not seem to be serving Shakespeare and made me very dissatisfied. At this point two things happened. I began to pay more attention to that word 're-venge', appearing in the speech like a recurring major chord. And I was lucky enough to see a paper ["The Elizabethan Stage Jew"] by Professor Alan C. Dessen of the University of North Carolina which dealt with the very heart of the problem. Towards the end of his discussion of earlier plays about money-lenders, Dessen asks:

> What then are we to conclude about the stage Jew as presented by Wilson, Marlowe, and Shake-speare? Although initially the three plays seem to have little in common, in each the same distinctive stage figure has served a comparable function—not merely to vilify Jews and Judaism but to challenge the professions of supposedly Christian London or Malta or Venice . . . By viewing Gerontus, Bara-bas, and Shylock as dramatic kinsmen, the modern reader can grasp the convention that stands behind them and informs them. In morality play, tragedy, or comedy, the stage Jew could function as a dramatic scalpel with which the Elizabethan dramatist could anatomize the inner reality of a society Christian in name but not necessarily in deed. The fact remains that Shakespeare *did* choose as his villain what seems to us an objectionable stereotype, but by recognizing the stage Jew as a potential theatrical device (and not a direct expression of authorial bigotry) we may be able to sidestep Shakespeare's alleged anti-semitism and instead appreciate the artistry with which he has incorporated such a stock figure into the world of romantic comedy.

Here was the insight that transformed that speech from a muddled and sentimental bit of humanism to a vigorous justification of revenge by Christian example. And yet all this is only rhetoric, as Shylock has yet to hear the confirmation of Antonio's failure.

Tubal has not found Jessica in Genoa and in his grief and loss Shylock pitifully blurs the distinction between daughter and ducats, and wretchedly complains about the cost of searching for her. (At 'And I know not what's spent in the search' [III. i. 92], Tubal presented his bill of expenses which included, in writing just too small for the audience to read, a huge bar and restaurant bill for two nights at the Genoa Hilton.) Shylock becomes almost hysterical as he crashes from deep despair to wild elation at the alternating news of Jessica's profligacy and Antonio's losses, until he hears of the exchange of Leah's ring for a monkey. Here is something that cannot be priced, that 'a wilderness of monkeys' [III. i. 122-23] cannot equal, beyond value. A simple gift, possibly a betrothal ring, from a woman to her lover: 'I had it of Leah when I was a bachelor' [III. i. 121-22]. That word shatters our image of this man Shylock and we see the man that once was, a bachelor, with all the association of youth, innocence and love that is to come. Shakespeare doesn't need to write a pre-history of Shy-lock. Those two lines say it all. At this deepest moment of sorrow Tubal confirms that Antonio is utterly vulnerable, and *now* Shylock decides to kill him. No single incident or word is entirely responsible, but it is certainly Leah's ring and Shy-lock's confusion of love and grief that is the trigger. Shake-speare's choice of a name for Shylock's wife is interesting—John Russell Brown in the Arden Shakesepeare points out that in Hebrew Leah means 'painful' or 'wearied'. Shylock and Tubal will meet at the synagogue and it is there that the 'oath in Heaven' will presumably be made. When we next see Shylock, the oath and the bond are public knowledge and, al-most revelling in the general condemnation, Shylock chants and howls his murderous intention abroad. I felt there was a wildness about Shylock here, shown by the repetition of 'I'll have my bond', and the refusal to let Antonio speak, as if the anticipation of his deed has made him mad. This is the man that the unsuspecting Portia is preparing to meet.

Act 4, Scene 1 is often referred to as the trial scene or court scene. In fact it is neither. No one is on trial and there is no formal court—in the legal sense. It seems to be much closer to a hearing in chambers or a final, private appeal before the highest authority, the Duke. There is no judge and Portia is there as a legal expert, to advise the Duke and pronounce on law. Only those characters necessary to the action need be present. (In Charles Kean's production in the 1850s this scene had no fewer than twenty-six judges and forty sena-tors.)

What a change there is in Shylock from the previous scene. He listens calmly without interruption to the Duke's speech, although it is not without provocation, and waits until he is invited to speak. In John Barton's production this mood of calm politeness and restraint was emphasized by the Duke himself serving Shylock with coffee. When at last he speaks, he is once more the controlled, articulate, witty man of 1.3. His words are almost apologetic at first, though quickly growing firmer. The speech becomes mockingly rhetorical, however, when he calls the cutting of Antonio's flesh a whim, and will not justify himself more than one would need over a troublesome rat, a gaping pig, a cat or a bagpipe. It's just a simple impulse, he says, like urinating. So this man is going to be killed, but his murder needed no justification, except, perhaps, that he is hated and loathed. Shylock is not going to waste this hour of triumph. The knife will be twisted many times before it enters Antonio's body, and everyone will suffer. Bassanio takes Shylock on, but is brushed aside like a troublesome fly. Antonio alone understands what Shylock is up to, and with fearless contempt towards him, he urges the sentence. Bassanio, judging others by himself, is still convinced that Shylock has his price, waves ducats in his face, and the Duke alludes to Shylock's prospects of mercy on judgement day; but this cannot frighten him and he again cites Christian example as his security. In this speech there is marvellous evidence of why Shylock is such a troubling character for an audience; deeply critical of society's cruelty, he uses a truly humanist argument to justify more wickedness. The speech returns to judgement at the end, but this time of the 'here and now' variety. The Duke threatens to dismiss the court and Shylock is alert at once. He will, of course, expect the Christians to trick him or slip out of their responsibility and he must watch their every move.

Shylock sharpening his knife is the black humorist at work again. Antonio is being stoical and noble, and Shylock's response is the crude reality of cold steel. It's just possible that it is also meant to frighten the young clerk (Nerissa). Gratiano thinks it will help to call Shylock an inexecrable dog and talk of his unhallowed dam, but Shylock politely refuses to be provoked. Instead he gives all his attention to Bellario's letter and the news of a 'young and learned doctor' [IV. i. 144]. This could be the Christians' trick. Portia appears and Shylock becomes withdrawn and defensive. He gives nothing but his name and when again mercy is proposed Shylock tests this young doctor's quality with a simple 'Why?' Her answer is well known and it is a good speech, but I am convinced that what makes it remarkable in performance is that it is pure improvisation. Any interpretation that is at all predetermined will turn it into a tract. Portia proposes mercy because her upbringing and nature cannot conceive of any other response to someone in such difficulty. She has never imagined that anyone could ask 'why mercy?' or that such a person could exist. She is invited to justify something which is as natural to her as breathing and it is the shock of that which motivates 'The quality of mercy is not strained' [IV. i. 184], and we are moved as we hear her articulate her faith, perhaps for the first time. I believe that Shylock too is moved by her words and that is why he has to dredge up the terrible oath, 'My deeds upon my head' [IV. i. 206]. Bassanio is still offering more money (Portia's presumably) and bits of himself he is never likely to have to pay; but when he begs the Duke to twist the law, 'to do a great right, do a little wrong' [IV. i. 216], we see the real slippery opportunist at work. This is what Shylock has been expecting, though perhaps not quite so crudely proposed. Portia's response, therefore, is utterly unexpected. Suddenly she is standing by his side supporting him. The Venetians' legal lackey turns out to be honest. Shylock is euphoric and for the first time in the scene he loses control. He stops thinking, watching and listening and his defences drop. Had he continued to think he would have known this 'honest' person would not let him take a man's life. Had he truly listened he would have heard her continue to urge mercy as before, and had he watched her face, he would have seen her struggling to save him from the blows that are to come. She even allows Shylock a glimpse of her trump card—the blood clause—by indicating that Antonio may bleed to death; but at last she hardens her heart against Shylock when he refuses to provide a surgeon to stop Antonio's wounds. Shylock has set himself up and the thunderbolts are about to fall.

Bassanio and Gratiano would see their wives dead if it could save Antonio's life. Hollow words again, but interesting for Portia and Nerissa to hear. The sentence is given and Shylock moves in to carry it out and the trap closes. In the past I had been puzzled by the speed at which Shylock slams into reverse, from 'A sentence, come prepare' to 'I take this offer then' [IV. i. 304, 318]. If the interpretation is heroic or sentimental I don't know how the actor does it. If it's pragmatic, then it's easy. Shylock is told he will lose his lands and his goods. Portia plays the blood card. Shylock immediately sees the (expected) trap he has walked into, considers for a moment that he will lose, checks the law, and knows at once that he must back off. What is delightful about Shylock at this moment is that, though under threat, he still tries to make off with three times the value of the bond. Portia is stubborn and Shylock, not really understanding her, and thinking himself back in the market place, tries to bargain with her. He will settle for his principal. Now, however, the experienced survivor begins to smell real danger and he knows he must put distance between himself and this place; but the ground is opening up beneath him and when the word 'alien' hits his ears he knows he is to be finished off. Once again he is an outsider, without rights and utterly vulnerable. This is no place for pride or heroics. Shylock knows if he wants to survive he must get down in the dirt and grovel. So his life is spared. He howls and whines and he gets back half his fortune. They want him to become a Christian and bequeath his estate to Lorenzo and Jessica and he is content because he has saved something when moments before he had nothing. Now he must get away before they change their minds or think up further punishment. Illness is a good excuse and he leaves them with the assurance that the deed *will* be signed.

Every actor playing Shylock looks for an effective way to 'get off'. Kean apparently went through a startling physical change on his exit. Edwin Booth invented an elaborate and melodramatic mime. Irving was still and tragically defeated, letting out a long sigh as he left; and recently, Laurence Olivier left his effect for offstage when, after a moment of silence, the audience heard a despairing howl of grief and rage. Here Gratiano provided the clue. He makes a cruel joke out of Shylock's christening, and the person who must laugh most is, of course, Shylock. And so he leaves. It saddened me that people were upset by the squalor of Shylock's ending, rather than angry that it should be necessary and moved by the tragedy of 'You take my life / When you do take the means whereby I live' [IV. i. 376-77], and the humiliation of 'I am content.' Shylock is a great role and in its way a tragic one. Its power over actors and audiences alike may be in part because he is not a king or tyrant or great lover, but a small, complex, real and recognizable human being, part of us all. The role took me by surprise and I learned again the important lesson on the foolishness of coming to Shakespeare with preconceived ideas. Everything I once felt about the part was turned upside down and where there had been indifference I became a passionate enthusiast. I know that I was lucky, too. This was a perfect instance of that rare and blessed identification with a character, which an actor cannot manufacture, but which will, at the most unexpected moment, pounce, grab him by the throat and invade his heart. It is said that an actor must love the character he plays—however unpleasant. I loved Shylock and know that it was a privilege to be given an insight into such a life. (pp. 11-28)

Patrick Stewart, "Shylock in 'The Merchant of Venice'," in Players of Shakespeare: Essays in Shakespearean performance by twelve players with the Royal Shakespeare Company, *edited by Philip Brockbank, Cambridge University Press, 1985, pp. 11-28.*

Sinead Cusack   (essay date 1985)

[*Deeming her portrayal of Portia a failure, Cusack describes her experience interpreting and developing the role through rehearsals and consultations with the director and cast members. Cusack also reveals how aspects of her characterization of Portia and of the production in general evolved during its run. As for her confessed failure in the role, Cusack speculates that she may have appeared too dour or solemn for a Shakespearean comic heroine.*]

I failed when I played Portia. By which I mean that when I do it again—if I do—I'll do it differently. Let me say a little about the history of Portia and myself. I read *The Merchant of Venice* for the first time, as most of us probably did, at about the age of fourteen, and I delighted in it. Although I had read quite a few of the plays at that time—my father being an actor, and ours being a very theatrical household—it was Portia who captured my imagination more than any other Shakespearean character. I liked what I saw in her on that first reading—warmth and humanity, together with wit and a shining intelligence. I have since, over the years, seen maybe three or four productions, and I have to say that on all occasions I left the theatre not liking Portia very much, and I couldn't understand why. I finally worked out that the great problem for the actress playing the role is to reconcile the girl at home in Belmont early in the play with the one who plays a Daniel come to judgement in the Venetian court. I couldn't understand why Shakespeare makes her so unsympathetic in those early scenes—the spoilt little rich girl dismissing suitor after suitor in very witty and derisory fashion. The girl who does that, I thought, is not the woman to deliver the 'quality of mercy' speech. I knew that was a problem.

Although all my life I had wanted, more than any other part, to play Portia, when I was finally asked to do so, by John Barton, in December 1980, I said no. I look back astounded at the arrogance of that reaction, but at the time it seemed right and proper. John had already done a small-theatre production at The Other Place in 1978 and had transferred it to the Warehouse in the season following. The production had had two Portias—Marjorie Bland in Stratford and Lisa Harrow in London. I had not seen it, but I thought John's ideas would probably be very fully formed, and that I might be straitjacketed into a performance not my own. The role would have been worked out with other players, and I feared I would not be allowed to grow into it in my own way. On two previous occasions I had taken over roles from other actresses and the experience had left me jaundiced. I said no, and it was a distressing moment of my life. However, it took a couple of dinners out, we discussed it, and John persuaded me.

I remember a professional tip that my father once gave me—'Always look for the comedy in tragedy, and for the tragedy in comedy.' I set out to find a distinctly tragic Portia, and I was glad to learn that John was ready to encourage me. It turned out that, while we differed here and there about the play, our ideas about Portia were very close. He also saw her as a passionate, human and loving girl, and, unlike many directors, he took her to be the centre of the play. Our biggest area of disagreement as we talked about the play concerned its last scene, which I like to think of as yet another trial

scene. Bassanio is on trial when he makes choice of the caskets, Shylock is on trial in the court scene, and Bassanio on trial again when he returns to Belmont after betraying a trust. The final scene, I argued, should not be played as a mischievous little game; it was not comic. John in his wisdom said, 'You can combine the two, Sinead. There is room for the important issues of love and the betrayal of love within a comedic framework.' And so we agreed, and moved on to other topics.

I was, of course, eager to know the rest of the cast, and the first question that comes to every Portia's mind is 'Who is playing Shylock?' It is strange, for Portia and Shylock have only one scene together while she and Bassanio have many. I was delighted to hear that it was David Suchet, for he is a consummate actor and I love playing with him. Portia's relationship with Shylock is brief but it forms the climax of the play and I looked forward to working it out with David, who was also coming new to the production. Rehearsals started in January.

All directors have their different systems of working, and John's is extraordinary in that he does not believe in the preliminary 'read-through' and he does believe in the 'solo-call'. The cast never assemble to discuss the play as a whole, and they are likely to be called on to rehearse separately, in isolation from the scene and from most of, or all of, the other players. Sometimes you find this useful, because you are not intimidated by other actors, don't have to give them something, and feel more free to explore the part. On the other hand, it can make you form ideas in a vacuum, and when the time comes to respond to your fellow actors you find you are not doing it at all. I think this a drawback in John's rehearsal pro-

Sinead Cusack as Portia.

cess. He does tend to isolate his actors from one another—an effect very apparent in his production of *Hamlet*. I don't like the system, and both David Suchet and I fought against it very strongly. However, I had enjoyed the unusual privilege of talking with the director about the nature of the play, and in practice we rehearsed many scenes in pairs, the first call being upon Corrina Seddon and myself, with an invitation to look through all the Portia/Nerissa scenes in the play.

We sat around a table, over endless cups of coffee and cigarettes, and discussed our impressions of that immensely important first scene in Belmont. We felt that if we got that scene right for Portia, everything else would follow. We concentrated first on her youth, for it seemed to me that she is, at the beginning of the play, very young. She moves from despair to laughter, from anger to filial obedience, and I found myself likening her mercurial moods to those of my nineteen-year-old sister. John saw Nerissa as the older and more worldly of the two, loving Portia, but forever cheering her up, joking with her and reasoning with her. Corinna (six years younger than I am) felt that the age-difference was unimportant and was content to concentrate on the friendship, but John insisted on Nerissa's sophistication and dressed her in bright pink in his production, which otherwise presented a sombre Belmont.

John's idea was to set the scene in autumnal gloom, with Portia seated on a bench contemplating the caskets in a mood of despair and misery when Nerissa enters. I liked the idea of carrying the caskets around with me wherever I went, to remind me of my horrible dilemma. Portia is bound by a promise given to her father on his deathbed to abide by his will, and to marry only the man who chooses the correct casket. She chafes against the restriction that curbs 'the will of a living daughter' [I. ii. 24] by 'the will of a dead father' [I. ii. 25]. Yet she is adamant in her resolve to honour her father's conditions. When Nerissa tentatively suggests to her that she might be won 'by some other sort than your father's imposition' [I. ii. 104-05], Portia responds uncompromisingly, 'If I live to be as old as Sibylla, I will die as chaste as Diana, unless I be obtained by the manner of my father's will' [I. ii. 106-08]. Taking her predicament seriously, I decided to play Portia's words 'my little body is aweary of this great world' [I. ii. 2], not in the bored voice of a child who has too much of everything, but as a cry of anguish from one who finds the whole business of the caskets very painful. But I did not feel that Portia submits merely from filial obedience. There is something in her nature that is attracted by the idea of 'a test'. Marriage is not to be embarked on easily and thoughtlessly, and that, I thought, is why Bassanio's betrayal of her later in the play will cause her such distress.

Portia's mood switches from one extreme to another as she takes comfort from Nerissa's reassurances about her father's lottery—'holy men at their death have good inspirations' [I. ii. 28], and accepts the suggestion that they run through the list of suitors. We agreed that at this point Nerissa may well be prompting Portia to laugh in spite of her tears. I liked this idea very much and worked hard at it. But it is a difficult moment for the players of both Portia and Nerissa. For Nerissa the problem is to give colour and shape to that interminable list, and for Portia it is to escape the effect of a spoilt brat maliciously destroying her suitors. Both in rehearsal and in performance this scene caused me more trouble than any other. I think we finally made it work, although it was at the price of cutting out the Scotsman, and perhaps one or two others.

We decided early in rehearsal that neither Portia nor Nerissa knew the contents of the caskets, and that Portia's suggestion that Nerissa set a glass of Rhenish wine 'on the contrary casket' [I. ii. 96] was no more than an inconsequential joke. We also decided that no suitor had yet undergone the ritual of choice. Both decisions made good theatrical sense, heightening the tensions of expectation and highlighting the horror of both Portia's predicament and that of her unfortunate wooers (under oath 'never to woo a lady afterward in way of marriage' [II. i. 41-2]).

From John's original production at The Other Place I inherited an old raincoat. When he first revived the idea I said, 'I don't want a raincoat', and he said, 'I think that Portia misses her father so much she wears his coat.' Indeed he lent me his bearskin and I used to love playing in John's mouldy old coat (you discovered the most revolting things in his pocket). I was pleased by the idea that Portia didn't care how she looked. It fitted well with my conviction that she is unschooled in the social ways of men and the world, and awkward in her relationship with Bassanio. That shabby raincoat related Portia to the distant world of her father, the wise and 'ever virtuous' old man who understood the law and money and marriage. She has no idea of her own attractiveness, her own appeal. At Belmont she lives in a woman's world, and John accentuated the idea by casting Balthazar, one of her manservants, as a woman—we called her Betty Balthazar. John gave no reason (he never gives reasons) but I suppose he liked the idea of three girls in the household with no men, leaving them tender and vulnerable, with all those suitors coming at them.

We played the suitor scenes for their grim, rather than their comic, qualities. I sat in a chair with the caskets in front of me, Nerissa and Betty on either side, while Morocco and Arragon circled us like animals getting ready to pounce, one might say, upon their pound of flesh. Again, this way of playing the scene underscored the pathos of Portia's predicament ('I stand for sacrifice' [III. ii. 57], as she puts it later to Bassanio) and her courage in abiding by her father's harsh dictates. Yet this effect may be a little at odds with her interest in, and perhaps her confidence in, the 'good inspiration' of the lottery test.

John had me roped as part of the ritual. One day at rehearsal he said to me 'Sinead, I had a great idea in my bath. What about your being tied up?' Obviously he had seen *The Maid's Tragedy* in which I played the king's mistress and tied him up before killing him. I fought against my bondage for a while, but he was wedded to the idea and roped I was. (Unknown to John, I managed to lose the rope somewhere between Stratford and London.) The rope was made of silver, gold and lead, and placed ritualistically over my lap—I wasn't actually tied up. It was meant to highlight the idea that I was a sort of sacrificial victim. And yet I had to keep my confidence in my father and in the test he had devised. Much depended, therefore, on my expectations of Bassanio. For, while Shylock's role is important for Portia, Bassanio's is much more so. In early rehearsals we spent a lot of time speculating on the relationship between Portia and Bassanio before the play begins. Bassanio talks to Antonio of the fair speechless messages he received from her when he formerly visited Belmont, and Portia in her first scene with Nerissa recalled Bassanio the 'scholar and soldier' [I. ii. 113] who came to Belmont in the company of the Marquis of Montferrat. The discussion was never really resolved, but I felt sure that, however brief and mute their meeting, the effect on Portia had been overwhelming. I therefore played the first mention of him, not as a vague and distant recollection, but as a poignant memory of one I had loved, in however young and adolescent a fashion, from the first moment I had set eyes on him.

For Jonathan Hyde, playing Bassanio, the choice was much more difficult. He speaks of her as

> a lady richly left,
> And she is fair and, fairer than that word,
> Of wondrous virtues.
>
> [I. i. 161-63]

The precedence given to the riches made such an impression that Jonathan (and John Barton) decided that Bassanio in his first scene with Portia should concentrate on making the right choice of casket rather than on wooing the lady. This produced some memorable moments in rehearsal—Jonathan circling the caskets while I followed him around and addressed the whole of the 'I pray you tarry' [III. ii. 1] speech to his retreating back. On one occasion, at the end of that speech Jonathan turned and said 'Sinead, what were you saying just now?' I explained that I was painfully telling him that I loved him and that I couldn't bear the idea of his going through the ritual in case he made the wrong choice. He nodded, thanked me, and said he thought he ought to start listening to the speech in future and maybe 'looking at you now and again'. Until then he had seemed unaware of my presence.

Now, in retrospect, I see that I approached both the first and the climactic scenes with Bassanio in the wrong spirit. In my early days of playing Shakespeare I never smiled. My Desdemona was dour and my Juliet joyless. I learnt to smile and laugh in Shakespeare only when I played Celia in *As You Like It,* realizing that the delight and fun of comedy were of a piece with its seriousness. I forgot this, for me, momentous discovery, when I performed the 'I pray you tarry' speech for its desperation and not its love. Now I see that there is pain in it, but that her protest against the restraint imposed on her by her father's will is overlaid with a playful and affectionate awareness that her own distress must not be pressed upon Bassanio. The punctuation of the speech shows how hard she is trying not to say too much:

> One half of me is yours, the other half yours—
> Mine own, I would say.
>
> [III. ii. 16-17]

She stops, she starts, she says one thing and contradicts herself with another. She begins by saying merely that the wrong choice on his part will deprive her of his company, but she ends by proclaiming herself all Bassanio's and to hell with the consequences. I didn't get that mixture of humour and despair right for many months, merely because I stupidly thought that declarations of love should always be worthy and earnest, untouched with comedy and an awareness of one's own idiocy.

The staging of the scene's first movement altered from day to day, and was not satisfactorily resolved until we took the play to London. But the staging of Bassanio's choice and of Portia's response was decided early in rehearsal. John wanted Portia isolated centre-stage, under a spotlight, from the moment when she bids 'Nerissa and the rest stand all aloof' [III. ii. 42]. Bassanio was to circle about her in the shadows throughout her speech likening him to Hercules and herself

to 'the tribute paid by howling Troy to the sea monster' [III. ii. 56-7]. At the end of this magnificent speech (again with its touch of comedy and wry objectivity—'with much, much more dismay / I view the fight than thou that mak'st the fray' [III. ii. 61-2]) comes the song.

Now, the text does not specify the singer of the song. Traditionally it is given to Nerissa or to a special singer for the occasion but John was determined, stubborn, obdurate and intractable—that Portia should sing it. His reason was valid: Portia is telling Bassanio that appearance is not everything. But my reaction as an actress was horror. I cannot sing and the idea of singing after such a long and difficult speech appalled me (the more so, perhaps, because Jonathan Hyde is married to a great opera singer). I felt that a musical number would be out of keeping, but John insisted that Portia was dredging up the song from childhood memories and found it apt for that occasion. I have to admit that after playing it for so long and listening to audience reactions I have come to agree. I still find it hard to do and my voice cracks on the top note, but I think the effect wonderfully theatrical; and it also makes sense that Portia should use every means at her disposal, without dishonouring her oath, to point Bassanio in the right direction. Early in rehearsal I discounted, as too cheap or trite on either Shakespeare's or Portia's part, the idea that the three rhymes ('bread', 'head', 'nourished') invited the fourth rhyme 'lead'. The wonder of that moment of choice hits me anew every time I play it. Portia cries to love to moderate and allay her ecstasy, remembers all she had had to endure in obedience to her father's will—'As doubtful thoughts, and rash embraced despair' [III. ii. 109-10]—and bids them all a glad farewell. She breaks out of the terrible prison her father's love has built for her. Every time I speak that speech I salute Portia's courage and endurance, and it is these qualities that she later takes into the courtroom in Venice.

Bassanio looks to Portia for her signature and ratification of his choice and at this point we took a little licence, not with the text perhaps but with its performance. I look from Bassanio to the caskets and then in joyful abandon I pick up those wretched boxes, which have threatened me for so long, and I fling them violently across the room. Again, it is an unashamedly theatrical moment, but it serves as a release of tension both for the audience and for the actress playing Portia. It provides too a springboard for the speech 'You see me, Lord Bassanio, where I stand' [III. ii. 149] which has as much to do with release as with commitment. Her commitment nevertheless is total and passionate. He takes the ring in the same spirit and vows that only death will part him from it. At this point Venice casts its grim shadow over magical Belmont, as Bassanio receives news of Antonio's predicament. Portia, liberated and married, has come of age and is ready now to move in a larger world.

I like to think that both Bassanio and Portia grow wiser and more mature in the course of the play, and particularly in the casket 'trial'. Bassanio begins as a feckless ne'er-do-well and opportunist but it must be love of Portia that moves him to make the right choice. Jonathan found it hard to believe that he fell in love with Portia in the course of making his choice, and preferred to think that they had been together for some weeks. However, my speech 'I pray you tarry' made that impossible. Bassanio has to rise to the occasion to pass the test, to win both Portia and the gold by making the humble choice of lead. The choice is liberating for them both, for by making it he proves his worth.

Owing to John's way of working and rehearsing, however, Bassanio's relationship with Antonio in Venice was kept from me until a very late stage in rehearsal. David Suchet and I had worked in isolation through the courtroom scene, but when the time came to put it all together we were in for some surprises. We had been directed to look at each other, but out of the corners of our eyes we noticed that there was an undressing process going on downstage right, between Antonio and Bassanio, which was riveting in its detail. Collar studs and buttons were being undone, all in mime of course, and there was a lot of kissing. Finally David (I didn't have the courage) asked what was going on. Tom Wilkinson playing Antonio said 'I am getting ready for the moment when I bare my chest.' When David protested 'This is the focus of the scene, not that', Tom said 'Well, look, you have got all the text.' It is true that to distract focus on stage you do not have to say anything. There is a famous story about the Lunts. She had a great soliloquy to deliver down front, and he was upstage, sitting behind a table, smoking a cigarette. About half way through her soliloquy she noticed that the whole focus of attention had shifted from her to her husband. She thought 'What's he doing?' and turned and looked, but he was sitting there, no movement at all, just smoking. The audience had left her entirely and she finished up very lamely. That went on for three nights—she would check him, and he was doing nothing. She finally discovered he had put a hair-grip through his cigarette so that his ash didn't drop off. So it was with Antonio and Bassanio downstage—we didn't have a chance. We did compromise in the end, but Antonio continued to undress a lot, and the *Sunday Times* critic, James Fenton, spent a lot of space on the matter. In spite of the setback I felt that David and I found a convincing way of playing the courtroom scene. The nature of the rehearsals encouraged the two of us to form a very strong theatrical relationship that excluded the rest of the world and the court. Shylock and Portia are head and shoulders above the rest of the group and are fighting a battle there, just the two of them. I decided that when I entered the courtroom I knew exactly how to save Antonio; my cousin had shown me that loophole in the law which would save him from his bond. A lot of people ask why then does Portia put everyone through all that misery and why does she play cat-and-mouse with Shylock. The reason is that she doesn't go into the courtroom to save Antonio (that's easy) but to save Shylock, to redeem him—she is passionate to do that. She gives him opportunity after opportunity to relent and to exercise his humanity. She proposes mercy and charity but he still craves the law. She offers him thrice his money but he sticks to his oath. It is only when he shows himself totally ruthless and intractable (refusing even to allow a surgeon to stand by) that she offers him more justice than he desires.

I was satisfied with the Portia/Shylock relationship and I think David was too. But the courtroom scene also initiates the ring-play which is so important in the last act. When Bassanio tells Antonio that he is married to a wife 'as dear to him as life itself' [IV. i. 283] and that he 'would sacrifice wife, life, and world to save him', Shakespeare gives Portia one of her big laugh-lines: 'Your wife would give you little thanks for that' [IV. i. 288]. I found the laugh difficult to accept (although I had to accept it) because I believed that Bassanio's willingness to part with the ring must have been very hurtful to Portia. Now I begin to change my mind. From the start I took the last scene to be another painful trial scene and I tried to play it that way. Now I see more clearly that it is, after all, Portia herself who wins the ring back from Bassanio. She wins both ways, and is in a wonderful position to know

the whole truth about Bassanio in the courtroom, and is therefore in a position to show him something as well as to forgive him.

There is a big difference too between life in Venice and life in Belmont, to which we return at the end of the play, but this wasn't always made clear in the production. John made it rather a gloomy place, and not very far away in mood and style from Venice. Perhaps because the production began in The Other Place, the cast was very small, and I should have been glad of more people about in Venice, particularly in the courtroom. There should be something fabulous about Belmont where 'patines of bright gold' [V. i. 59] and 'the sweet power of music' [V. i. 79] can change our nature, if only 'for a time'. Some details of costume and design didn't help either. Jonathan Hyde, for example, persuaded the designer Christopher Morley to make a swinging Byronic cloak for Bassanio in Venice; but there is no justification whatever for him turning up at Portia's in the same coat—what did he do with the three thousand ducats he got to furnish him for Belmont?

If I return to the play I shall give fresh thought to Portia and Bassanio. Perhaps she changes him. She gives him the ring, wins it back from him, and gives it to him again. She teaches him 'doubly to see himself' [V. i. 244]. Perhaps I wasn't quite witty enough, nor sure or light enough in touch in these last scenes—and that is why I failed when I played Portia. (pp. 29-40)

> Sinead Cusack, "Portia in 'The Merchant of Venice'," in Players of Shakespeare: Essays in Shakespearean performance by twelve players with the Royal Shakespeare Company, *edited by Philip Brockbank, Cambridge University Press, 1985, pp. 29-40.*

COMPARISONS AND OVERVIEWS

Richard Foulkes (essay date 1977)

> [*Foulkes contrasts Helen Faucit's intelligent, dignified, and aristocratic conception of Portia with Ellen Terry's interpretation, in which "beauty was paramount." The critic argues that both conceptions had drawbacks; whereas Faucit's sense of command was just right in the trial scene, she lacked a lighter touch necessary for the comic scenes. Terry exhibited ideal beauty and a keen sense of comedy, but lacked Faucit's presence in the trial scene. "An ideal Portia," Foulkes affirms, "would succeed in combining certain aspects of both interpretations, Helen Faucit's dignity and intelligence, especially in the trial scene, with Ellen Terry's beauty and sense of comedy."*]

Portia in *The Merchant of Venice* was a role with which the two pre-eminent actresses of the Victorian period, Helen Faucit (1815-98) and Ellen Terry (1847-1928) were associated for much of their lengthy stage careers. Helen Faucit first played Portia in 1836 with Charles Kemble as Shylock; again in 1839 with Macready as Shylock; in Glasgow in 1857 and Edinburgh in 1869; and finally in a series of readings culminating in one at Llangollen Public Library near to her home at Brystysilio in August 1888. Ellen Terry played Portia for the Bancrofts in 1875, and repeated it numerous times during her long partnership with Henry Irving at the Lyceum Theatre, appearing with him in an all-star performance of *The Merchant of Venice* in aid of the Actors' Benevolent Fund at Drury Lane in July 1903. Helen Faucit and Ellen Terry were very different personalities, Helen Faucit after her marriage to Theodore Martin in 1851 became a pillar of establishment society; Ellen Terry, thrice married and mother of two illegitimate childeren, although created DBE in 1925, never completely forsook the role of the wayward non-conformer. Like all great acting parts Portia embodies a range of interpretative possibilities, which became crystallized to a remarkable extent in the contrasting performances and written views of these two Victorian actresses.

An extensive review of the Lyceum *The Merchant of Venice* appeared in *Blackwood's Edinburgh Magazine* in December 1879. The author of the review, to which Ellen Terry referred as "the unkind *Blackwood* article" [in her *The Story of My Life*], was ostensibly anonymous, but was generally recognized as Helen Faucit's husband Theodore Martin. Irving's biographer Austin Brereton wrote [in his *The Life of Henry Irving*]: "In the December number, 'The Merchant of Venice' came in for severe handling by a writer who apparently sought to belittle the players of the day by the process of exalting a certain admirable actress, but one whose career had closed. He described, in language which now seems strange, so wanting was it in judgement, Sarah Bernhardt as well as Miss Terry".

Within a year of the publication of the *Blackwood's* article Helen Faucit composed her "Letter on Portia" to her ailing friend Miss Jewsbury who wrote on 27 August 1880: "Many thanks for writing and sending me *Ophelia . . .* please do another. Portia is one of my great heroines. How came you to your silent play in the casket scene?" The "Letter on Portia" was published privately that autumn and reproduced in *On Some of Shakespeare's Female Characters* published by none other than William Blackwood and Sons, in 1885. Clearly husband and wife devoted much thought to Portia during 1879-80 and their written comments show a striking concurrence, which often extends beyond the views expressed to the style in which they are expressed. Furthermore their written views can be related to Helen Faucit's performance of Portia 40 years earlier, a part which she repeated on 27 February 1878 when she gave one of her drawing-room readings before a select, invited audience: "The play was again *The Merchant of Venice,* with Irving as Shylock" [Theodore Martin, in his *Helena Faucit*]. History does not record Irving's impressions of his two contrasting Portias and whilst he may have been prepared to indulge the Martins' view that "Portia, and not Shylock, is the central object of interest in the play" in a private drawing-room, he was hardly likely to countenance it on his own stage at the Lyceum Theatre.

The Martins were at one in their high regard for Portia: "To present Portia, as she was revealed by an independent study of Shakespeare's text, unwarped by any thought of what others had conceived, was the aim of my wife. In her hands, accordingly, Portia was not merely the lady, 'richly left', living in almost regal state, and worthy to be wooed by princely lovers, but a woman of strong character and high intellectual culture". Helen Faucit saw Portia as Bellario's long-standing pupil and stressed her "wit and insight . . . her cultivated and bright intelligence" [in her *On Some of Shakespeare's Female Characters*] as did her husband in the *Blackwood's* article: "She is the ideal of high-born woman, gloriously endowed in body and in mind, and with her intellect cultivated

to the highest point to which female culture can be brought". The Martins' emphasis on the intellect contrasts markedly with Ellen Terry's view [in her *Four Lectures on Shakespeare*]: "But from my point of view, no interpretation entailing a sacrifice of beauty, whether to mirth or realism can ever be satisfactory. Portia is the fruit of the Renaissance, the child of the period of beautiful clothes, beautiful cities, beautiful houses, beautiful ideas. Wreck that beauty and the part goes to pieces".

The beauty of Ellen Terry or that of her Portia, if indeed they were separable, won over most hearts: "One could say the entire house fell head over ears in love with her as soon as she put her foot upon the stage. A more adorable Portia it would be hard to conceive", wrote one American devotee [in *Mr Henry Irving and Miss Ellen Terry in America: Opinions of the Press*], but at least one English heart remained unmoved: "She turns the whole character to 'favour and prettiness', but she does not even aim at the distinction and dignity which essentially belongs to it" [*Blackwood's Magazine,* December 1879]. How much dignity could there be in a Portia who "lounges idly on the sofa as Nerissa describes her lovers" [Clement Scott, in his *From "The Bells" to "King Arthur."*] in her opening scene (Act I, scene ii). For Ellen Terry her scene with Nerissa (her sister Florence, described as a "soubrette" by Martin) provided an opportunity to establish the beauty, wit and charm of a character who was never to stray far from the realms of comedy. Her father's will was not allowed to loom oppressively large, for after all as F. A. Marshall wrote in his Introduction to *The Merchant of Venice* in *The Henry Irving Shakespeare:* "when one considers the fearlessness and promptitude of action which Portia displays, one cannot help thinking that, if her father's absurd legacy of the caskets had resulted in the choice of an uncongenial husband, Portia would not have found it difficult to set aside the parental injunction in spirit if not in letter. At any rate we may safely prophecy that an unacceptable husband would not have had it all his own way". Ellen Terry's sympathy with such a liberated viewpoint is indicated in the manuscript of her lecture "The Triumphant Women" in which she wrote: "I feel that had they (Portia, Beatrice and Rosalind) been disappointed in love they would have arisen and set about making another life in their own masterful way". By 1879 Ellen Terry had already disposed of one "uncongenial husband" and was to deal similarly with two more. In contrast Helen Faucit's high regard for family loyalty is expressed in her views on the binding nature of Portia's father's will: "She (Portia) feels this (the will) to be hard; but so deep is her reverence for her father, that she has schooled herself to bow implicitly to his will". Of her performances in 1836 and 1839 it is not surprising to read: "She played the first scenes without much effect" [*The Morning Post,* 26 September 1836]; and "Miss Faucit became the gravity of the learned doctor better than the gaiety of Portia; her sprightly sallies at the expense of her suitors were forced, and her modest sweetness was not wholly free from the reproach of affectation" [*The Spectator,* 12 October 1839].

Of Portia's two unacceptable suitors Ellen Terry was spared Arragon, who disappeared from Irving's inevitably abbreviated text. Of her encounter with Morocco, Clement Scott wrote she "nervously trembles when the Prince of Morocco chooses from the caskets" (Act II, scene vii). Helen Faucit conceded that "Portia cannot have been an unmoved spectator of these scenes (Arragon and Morocco)", but her husband found Ellen Terry guilty of "forgetfulness of what the truth to the character and the situation demands while the Prince of Morocco is making choice among the caskets", which was "visible in the far too marked demonstrativeness with which Miss Terry follows his movements from casket to casket. . . . It requires subtler touches than this lady seems to have at command, to indicate, without exaggerating, the emotion proper to a nature disciplined to self-command".

The discipline of self-control in matters of the heart was not particularly prominent in Ellen Terry's life and certainly not in her playing of the Bassanio casket scene (Act III, scene ii). "She (Ellen Terry) fails especially to suggest the Portia that, as Shakespeare most carefully makes us aware, would have sacrificed even her love for Bassanio, deep as it is, had he failed to win her by the process appointed by her father". Martin found "too much of what Rosalind calls 'a coming-on disposition' in Miss Terry's bearing towards her love" and had a powerful ally in Henry James [in his *The Scenic Art*]: "Miss Terry's mistress of Belmont giggles too much, plays too much with her fingers, is too free and familiar, too osculatory in her relations with Bassanio". Other critics observed the unambivalent presentation of Portia's love for Bassanio, but were less censorious: "The exquisite tenderness of her manner with Bassanio over the casket, when her love almost tempts her to be forsworn and her fear lest he should choose wrong, drives her hard to disobey her father's will" and "the eager surging love that ever and anon would vent itself in ejaculations more eloquent than words, was exquisitely expressed" [*The Referee*, 3 November 1879]. Ellen Terry's own awareness of the need for some restraint is indicated in her prompt-book note to "O love, be moderate" [III. ii. 111]— "Keep low in pitch!" It was Helen Faucit's "silent play in the casket scene" which prompted Miss Jewsbury to request the "Letter on Portia" in which the actress was to write: "Throughout the early part of the last of the casket scenes what tortures of suspense must Portia have endured, for by this time her heart has made its choice". Although Helen Faucit shared Ellen Terry's conviction of Portia's love for Bassanio she considered that Portia "must try to rest her faith in her father's love". The possibility of any hint to Bassanio is totally rejected: "Hard it is for her to know the right casket and yet to give no hint (and) . . . to ensure that no accident shall unintentionally on the part of the bystander, direct Bassanio's choice". The choice made a "final gleam of joy . . . lighted her countenance as her love chose rightly. . . . Subdued, yet intensely happy, she rose from her seat and awaited the approach of him who is now 'her love, her governor, her king' " [*Blackwood's Magazine*, December 1885]. In fairness to Ellen Terry it must be admitted that no critic accused her of giving Bassanio a hint, though Christopher St John noted [in *Ellen Terry's Memoirs with Preface, Notes, and Additional Biographical Chapters*, by Edith Craig and Christopher St John]: "I have found a cutting from an Italian essay on 'The Merchant of Venice', dated 1903, with comments in her writing. . . . The writer of the article made the ingenious suggestion that the song in the casket scene: 'Tell me where is fancy bred' had been deliberately selected by Portia in order to guide Bassanio to the choice of the right casket. 'I like the idea', writes Ellen Terry. 'And why shouldn't Portia sing the song herself? She could make the four rhymes, "bred, head, nourished, fed" set the word "lead" ringing in Bassanio's ears. A woman of Portia's sort couldn't possibly remain passive in such a crisis in her life'."

The choice made, Portia and Bassanio are soon confronted by Antonio's predicament, and of his letter to Bassanio, Ellen

Terry wrote [in *The Atlantic Monthly*, 1921]: "To my mind, in this letter human love at its greatest finds expression". Next Lorenzo and Jessica come forward and for once the two actresses agreed on their sympathetic reception of the Jew's daughter, who in Henry Irving's opinion was a "friend of Portia" [J. Hattan, in his *Henry Irving's Impressions of America*]. It is, of course, Antonio's letter to Bassanio which prompts Portia to go to Bellario, but the spirit in which she goes is open to interpretation. Here Helen Faucit's emphasis on Portia's intellect came to the fore: "Then having read the letter herself, and having despatched Bassanio, with full means, to his friend's assistance, Portia's quick intellect, as Lady Martin believes, discovers a loophole in the wording of the bond". The text does not indicate that Portia knows the exact wording of the bond at this juncture, but it is fair to assume that she would obtain that information before going to Bellario. The great advantage of Helen Faucit's interpretation was that it made Portia's decidedly light-hearted mood as she set off to Bellario (Act III, scene iv) convincing, since she thought she had found the loophole and was going to obtain confirmation of her opinion. In contrast Ellen Terry thought Portia's plan was proof that she retained "her independence of thought and action", but she was open to the criticism that "her sally to Antonio's rescue is not an heroic enterprise but a girlish freak; and in this way the character is diminished and a little dulled, while the chief situation of the play is robbed of some of its gravity and some of its point" [*Pall Mall Gazette*, 4 November 1879]. Without the conviction that the loophole existed Ellen Terry's Portia's buoyancy of spirit must indeed have appeared ill-justified.

The contrast is exemplified in the trial scene (Act IV, scene i) in which Portia appears in male disguise and Ellen Terry's reliance upon her beauty, "prettier fellow" though she undoubtedly proved, became less appropriate (the part was, of course, first played by a boy-actor). The dilemma confronting actresses in disguise scenes is the extent to which they are to enlist the audience's complicity in the disguise for the sake of comic irony. Whereas it may be legitimate to do this in the Rosalind and Orlando wooing scene in *As You Like It*, it is more doubtful whether it should be done in the trial scene in which the humour arising out of Portia's disguise must be secondary to her role as earnest and convincing advocate. Helen Faucit made little concession to Portia's underlying *femininity:* "She looked the 'learned Doctor' very well" [*The Morning Post*, 22 September 1836] and "appeared, not like a masquerader who assumes the manners of a barrister, but as a youth who never for one instant lost her tone of high breeding and earnest sense of the serious nature of the work in hand"; "in the trial scene, the comic mask is for the time, almost completely laid aside by all that take part in it, and by Portia especially" [*Blackwood's*, December 1885]. At the Lyceum, Ellen Terry was greeted with tumultuous applause as she entered "radiant in her rose-coloured lawyer's gown, with her face wreathed in smiles" [Sir Seymour Hicks, in his *Hail Fellow Well Met*]. Theodore Martin claimed that "even those who have racked the language of panegyric in its (Ellen Terry's performance) praise have shrunk from claiming unqualified admiration for her in the trial scene". This was true of her Bassanio, J. H. Barnes, who wrote [in his *Forty Years on the Stage*]: "Miss Terry's Portia was bewitching and artistic in all the scenes at Belmont. Her final scene was less convincing." Ellen Terry maintained that: "The impenetrableness of a disguise is a dramatic convention" but it was a convention into which some of her critics were not prepared to enter: "As a boy, Miss Terry is by no means a success. . . .

When Miss Terry appears disguised as a young advocate, her acting is very spotty indeed, to tell the truth, it is bad. She does not look the part, and she has disguised herself so badly that her husband and anyone else must, unless they were blind, have seen in a moment who she is" [*Truth,* 6 November 1879]. Another critic [*The Theatre,* 1 January 1880], albeit offering praise, indicated how far the balance of the part had strayed in the direction of comedy: "How archly, in self-preservation, she shields her face from her husband". In fact the lines which give most justification for the suspension of Portia's disguise: "Your wife would give you little thanks for that . . . " [IV. i. 288] were cut, presumably at Irving's direction, since in the trial scene his tragic Shylock shunned such levity. However, of the prevailing tone of Ellen Terry's Portia, Martin wrote: "at no one point in it does she appreciate her situation, or how it should be treated. The words are spoken, but so spoken that one marvels why they should issue from the lips of one who looks so little in earnest, who takes so little notice of Shylock, or Antonio, or the Doge, and of the Court."

In the view of Helen Faucit, shared by her husband, Portia's intellectual qualities predominated. She arrived at the Court with her opinion about the flaw confirmed by Bellario and therefore quietly confident of her ability to rescue Antonio: "The 'something else' is kept in the background until every other argument has failed" or, as Sir Theodore Martin put it using almost the same words, Portia has "the noble forbearance of a Christian woman, to keep in the background her weapon for discomfiting the Jew, until she had found that every appeal to his heart or to his avarice was of no avail". In her performance Helen Faucit's appeals to Shylock's better nature were made forcefully and compassionately from a position of strength and were apparently not without their effect on Macready's Shylock of whom one critic wrote [*The Spectator,* 12 December 1839]: "one almost suspected he would have relented, and instead of his slice of flesh, taken the money".

Ellen Terry's Portia arrived at the Court with no such confidence. In her account "the learned Bellario told Portia at once that the law could not help Antonio. He advised her to try to appeal to Shylock's mercy, and as that failed, well then I fancy the learned Bellario may have suggested trying a threat. Let the Jew be warned of the consequences of exacting his pound of flesh. To my mind, and I have always tried to show this in the trial scene, Portia is acting on a preconceived plan up to the moment of pronouncing sentence: then she has an inspiration, and acts on that. Hence her 'Tarry a little; there is something else' [IV. i. 305]" In fact in a passage in the lecture manuscript, which was excised from the printed version (presumably by Christopher St John) Ellen Terry conceded that it might be "difficult to take up the continuation of the part after the words—'Thyself shall see the act, for as thou urgest justice be assured thou shalt have justice more than thou desirest it' [IV. i. 314-16]", presumably on the grounds that if Portia's inspiration only came to her at "Tarry a little" [IV. i. 305] she had little time (nine lines) to look up the chapter and verse in the law books. Helen Faucit's interpretation, of course, avoided any such inconsistency, but it is an indication of Ellen Terry's critical asperity that she was aware of this fine point. One of the few moments in Ellen Terry's performance of which Theodore Martin approved occurred at line [348], "It is enacted in the laws of Venice", which Portia quoted from a volume of the Venetian Statutes, a piece of business which Helen Faucit had originat-

ed. However, that apart, the two actresses played the all-important trial scene along very different lines and in place of Helen Faucit's legally well-informed preconceived plan, Ellen Terry depended upon a series of increasingly desperate appeals to the Jew. This approach should have given a greater tension to the scene and indeed Irving's prompt book is interspersed with directions for reactions from the onlookers at points of particular stress. One critic wrote: "Her serious speeches here seemed over-studied and altogether lack the spontaneity that lends such airiness and grace to her comedy. I should say that she had rehearsed them so much as to miss the effect she sought to arrive at. The only thing I cared for in any of them—the famous 'mercy' speech included—was a very natural trick of hesitating now and then for a word." The distinction between an over-rehearsed Ellen Terry and an over-rehearsed Portia may be fine, but the implication is that the actress was happiest when the character was apparently prompted by impulse, as in the escapade to Bellario's.

Having arrived at the "flaw" by their different routes, Helen Faucit and Ellen Terry adopted very different attitudes to the now humbled Shylock. Helen Faucit found that her "desire to find extenuation for Shylock's race and for himself" left her and her heart grew "almost as stony as his own," though she did not think that Portia would subscribe to what she considered to be a harsh sentence by the Doge. In contrast Ellen Terry considered that: "From this point in the trial the sympathies of a modern audience are with Shylock" as of course they were in Henry Irving's romanticized interpretation of the Jew. Such a viewpoint harmonized with Irving's view of his part, but Ellen Terry's ability to adopt a critical attitude towards the character she played is indicated in a passage in the manuscript, suppressed in the printed version, which reads: "However one looks at it one cannot admire it (the 'quibble' as she called it). It has an unattractive element of moral deceit—of the dangerous doctrine that the means is justified by the end." That Ellen Terry's distaste for the "quibble" filtered through in her performance is indicated by W. Graham Robertson's recollection of her [in his *Time Was*] as "the Lady Beauty"; "How small and mean sounded her quibbling tricky speeches when addressed to a being who united the soul of Savonarola and the bearing of Charles the First, with a touch of Lord Beaconsfield that made for mystery. . . . I left the theatre with the profoundest sympathy for the noble, ill used Jew." In spite of that Ellen Terry did not think the Doge's sentence particularly harsh, claiming that far more violent actions against the Jewish race had been displayed more recently.

Although the fact that the latter part of the play is devoted to Portia rather than Shylock was cited by the Martins as justification for their assertion that she was the central character, Helen Faucit counselled restraint in the reassertion of the comic spirit: "The 'marriage-bells', which for the first time ring in her heart must not yet be heard by others. She must keep up and carry out her self-imposed character to the end." Thus in the "ring-scene" she maintained her disguise fully and affected "to be slightly indignant". Ellen Terry in contrast was "inimitably coquettish, with secret touches of wifely delight" [*The Theatre,* 1 January 1880] in her interview with Bassanio, and left the court with a swagger and "archness that was irresistable". Edward Gordon Craig [in his *Ellen Terry and her Secret Self*] considered that her "unforgettable action at the end of the trial scene of 'The Merchant of Venice' . . . drew us all together silently, immediately".

Although Irving cut Act V in some performances it was generally retained, and with the aid of sensitive lighting the production ended on a note of harmony and enchantment, with the famous Ellen Terry charm coming indisputably into its own. Far from cutting the play short Helen Faucit was disposed to give Portia and Shylock a life beyond it, in which she visited him with gifts of wine and oil and her former antagonist found comfort in her likeness to his beautiful Leah.

Actresses playing Portia have to make certain fundamental interpretative decisions. These decisions include Portia's attitude to her father's will (does she regard it as absolutely binding?); the strength of her feelings for Bassanio (is there any question of a hint in the song?); the mood in which she leaves Belmont with Nerissa; and perhaps most important of all her conduct in the trial scene (is it Portia who spots the "flaw" and if so at what point?). How much comedy should she introduce, and should she act within her disguise throughout? Much of the interest in Portia as a stage character lies in the interpretation of these ambiguities. The extent of this interpretative freedom becomes evident in the contrasting performances of Helen Faucit and Ellen Terry, but it must be remembered that, Victorians though they both were, they acted in a period during which acting styles and theatre practice changed significantly. Furthermore, both actresses played Portia for many years, and what was accepted as "natural" in Helen Faucit's 1836 performance, at the age of 21, was evidently becoming less acceptable by 1869, when at the age of 54 she prompted *The North British Daily Mail* [20 November 1869] to write: "The elocution throughout (the trial scene) was too laboured—sometimes painfully so. Whole sentences were given in a slow 'staccato' style that was, to speak the truth, somewhat tedious and strikingly unnatural." This may in part account for Theodore Martin's hostility towards Ellen Terry, who was over 30 years his wife's junior and whose performance as Portia at the Lyceum took place eight years after Helen Faucit's final stage performance (as opposed to reading) in the part at the Theatre Royal, Manchester, on Saturday 25 November 1871. Martin's personal allegiance to his wife may have allied him to what was becoming an outmoded style of acting and rendered him unreceptive to a new, less formal approach. A further distinction was that Helen Faucit never had a regular partner as Shylock, but played her independently conceived Portia to many Shylocks both in London and in provincial stock companies. Ellen Terry's Portia on the other hand was associated with Irving's very powerful and individual Shylock for nearly a quarter of a century, which necessitated some adjustment in her interpretation and should have facilitated a greater degree of ensemble orchestration. However, developments in theatrical companies and acting styles apart, the Portias of Helen Faucit and Ellen Terry do represent significantly different responses to the part, and both performances were accounted successes by the majority of those who saw them. In April 1879, just a few months before the Lyceum *Merchant of Venice,* Irving and Ellen Terry appeared in a revival of Bulwer-Lytton's *The Lady of Lyons,* in which Helen Faucit and Macready had appeared in 1838, the year before their joint appearance in *The Merchant of Venice.* Helen Faucit wrote to Irving referring to "real, natural acting" and "different types of reality: there is the reality which is natural to the noble nature and the reality of the commonplace one. The situation may be the same, the words spoken may [be] the same—the tone and manner will signify the difference."

In *The Merchant of Venice* the situations in which Helen Fau-cit's and Ellen Terry's Portias found themselves were indeed the same, as were the words which they spoke; the difference lay in "the tone and manner" in which they played the part. Helen Faucit based her characterization on Portia's breeding and intellect and sought to anchor each scene in its underlying reality. She succeeded best in the trial scene, whereas in the opening scene with Nerissa the comic exuberance was missing. For Ellen Terry Portia's beauty was paramount to the extent that even in her disguise her audience, on the whole willingly, remained conscious of her charm and femininity. Her performance belonged to the realm of comedy. It is invidious and difficult to compare these two outstanding Portias, both of which have stood the test of time by living in the annals of theatre history. An ideal Portia would succeed in combining certain aspects of both interpretations, Helen Faucit's dignity and intelligence, especially in the trial scene, with Ellen Terry's beauty and sense of comedy. Nevertheless it is through performances of the calibre of Miss Faucit's and Miss Terry's that we can increase our understanding of the enduring qualities of Portia, "nothing undervalued to Cato's daughter, Brutus' Portia" [I. i. 165-66] (pp. 27-36).

> *Richard Foulkes, "Helen Faucit and Ellen Terry as Portia," in* Theatre Notebook, *Vol. XXXI, No. 3, 1977, pp. 27-37.*

STAGING ISSUES

William Poel   (lecture date June 1887)

[*Poel, an English actor and manager, was the founder of the Elizabethan Stage Society, an organization devoted to producing Shakespeare's plays in accordance with the stage conventions of the poet's age. Although financially unsuccessful, surviving only from 1894 to 1905, the Elizabethan Stage Society had an enormous impact on subsequent stagings. In the excerpt below, taken from a lecture delivered to the New Shakspere Society in 1887, Poel provides a plot synopsis of* The Merchant of Venice *with an interwoven discussion of staging issues. Poel, whose subsequent staging of the play militated against the nineteenth-century tendency to sentimentalize Shylock, provides a "dramatic purpose" for many of the play's crucial scenes.*]

The story of this play is as follows. In the opening scene, the words of Antonio to Bassanio—

> Well, tell me now, what lady is the same
> To whom you swore a secret pilgrimage,
> That you *to-day* promised to tell me of?
>
> [I. i. 119-21]

And Lorenzo's apology for withdrawing—

> My lord Bassanio, since you have *found* Antonio
> We two will leave you:
>
> [I. i. 69-70]

and that of Salarino—

> We'll make our leisures to attend on *yours*—
>
> [I. i. 68]

lead us to suppose that Bassanio has come by appointment to meet Antonio, and that Antonio should be represented on his entrance as somewhat anxiously expecting his friend, and

we may further presume from Solanio's words to Salarino in
Act II., Scene 8 [l. 50]—

I think he only loves the world for *him*—

that there is a special cause for Antonio's sadness, beyond
what he chooses to admit to his companions, and that is the
knowledge that he is about to lose Bassanio's society.

With regard to Bassanio, we learn, in this first scene, that he
is already indebted to Antonio, that he desires to borrow
more money from his friend, to free himself from debt, before
seeking the hand of Portia, a rich heiress, and that Portia has
herself encouraged him to woo her. In fact, we are at once
deterred from associating purely sordid motives with Bassanio's courtship by his glowing description of her virtues
and beauty, as also by Antonio's high opinion of Bassanio's
character.

Antonio, however, has not the money at hand, and it is arranged that Bassanio is to borrow the required sum on Antonio's security. The entrance of Gratiano is skilfully timed to
dispel the feeling of depression that Antonio's sadness would
otherwise leave upon the audience, and to give the proper
comedy tone to the opening scene of a play of comedy.

In Scene 2 we are introduced to the heroine and her attendant, and learn, what probably Bassanio did not know, that
Portia by her father's will is powerless to bestow her hand on
the man of her choice, the stratagem, as Nerissa supposes,
being devised to insure Portia's obtaining "one that shall
rightly love" [I. ii. 33]. This we may call the first or casket-
complication. Portia's strong sense of humour is revealed to
us in her description of the suitors "that are already come"
[I. ii. 35], and her moral beauty in her determination to respect her father's wishes. "If I live to be as old as Sibylla, I
will die as chaste as Diana, unless I be obtained by the manner of my father's will" [I. ii. 106-08]. The action of the play
is not, however, continued till Nerissa questions Portia about
Bassanio, in a passage that links this scene to the last, and
confirms, in the minds of the audience, the truth of the lover's
statement—

> Sometimes from her eyes
> I did receive fair speechless messages.
> [I. i. 163-64]

A servant enters to announce the leave-taking of four of the
suitors, who care not to submit to the conditions of the will,
and to herald the arrival of a fifth, the Prince of Morocco.

We now come to the third scene of the play. Bassanio enters
conversing with one, of whom no previous mention has been
made but whose first utterance tells us he is the man of whom
the required loan is demanded, and before the scene has
ended, we discover further that he is to be the chief agent in
bringing about the second, or pound-of-flesh-complication.
There are no indications given us of Shylock's personal appearance, except that he has been dubbed "old Shylock,"
which is, perhaps, more an expression of contempt than of
age, for he is never spoken of as old man, or old Jew, and is
chiefly addressed simply as Shylock or Jew; but the epithet
is one recognized widely enough for Shylock himself to
quote—

> Well, thou shalt see, thy eyes shall be thy judge,
> The difference of *old Shylock* and Bassanio:
> [II. v. 1-2]

as also does the Duke—

> Antonio and *old Shylock* both stand forth.
> [IV. i. 175]

So was it with Silas Marner. George Eliot writes: "He was
so withered and yellow that though he was not yet forty the
children always called him 'old master Marner.'" However,
the language that Shakespeare has put into the mouth of Shylock does not impress us as being that of a man whose physical and mental faculties are in the least impaired by age; so
vigorous is it at times that Shylock might be pictured as being
an Edmund Kean-like figure, with piercing black eyes and an
elastic step. From Shylock's expression, "the *ancient* grudge
I bear him" [I. iii. 47], and Antonio's abrupt manner towards
Shylock, we may conclude that the two men are avowed enemies, and have been so for some time previous to the opening
of the play. This fact should, from the very first, be made evident to the audience by the emphasis Shylock gives to Antonio's name, an emphasis that is repeated every time the name
occurs till he has made sure there is no doubt about who the
man is that shall become bound.

The dramatic purpose of this scene is to show us Shylock directly plotting to take the life of Antonio, and the means he
employs to this end are contrived with much skill. Shylock,
in his opening soliloquy, discloses his intention to the audience, and at once deprives himself of its sympathy by admitting that his motives are guided more by personal considerations than by religious convictions—

> I hate him for he is a Christian,
> But *more* for that in low simplicity
> He lends out money gratis and brings down
> The rate of usance here with us in Venice.
> [I. iii. 42-5]

The three first scenes should be so acted on the stage as to
accentuate in the minds of the audience (1) that Bassanio is
the very dear friend of Antonio; (2) that Portia and Bassanio
are in love with each other; (3) that Antonio and Shylock are
avowed enemies; (4) that Shylock conspires against Antonio's life with full intent to take it should the bond become
forfeit.

We are again at Belmont and witness the entrance of the
Prince of Morocco, and the whole scene has a poetic dignity
and repose which form a striking contrast to the preceding
one. We get in the character of the Prince of Morocco a preliminary sketch of Shakespeare's Othello, and certainly the
actor, to do justice to the part, should have the voice and
presence of a Salvini. The second scene shows us the Jew's
man about to leave his rich master to become the follower of
Bassanio, and the latter, now possessed of Shylock's money,
preparing his outfit for the journey to Belmont, whither Gratiano also is bent on going. There is, besides, some talk of
merrymaking at night-time, which fitly leads up to our introduction to Jessica in the next scene, and prepares us to hear
of her intrigue with Lorenzo. Jessica is the third female character in the play, and the dramatist intends her to appear, in
contrast to Portia and Nerissa, as a tragic figure, dark, pale,
melancholy, demure, yet chaste in thought and in action, and
with a heart susceptible of tender and devoted love. She plans
her elopement with the same fixedness of purpose as the father pursues his revenge. In Scene 4 the elopement incident
is advanced a step by Lorenzo receiving Jessica's directions
"how to take her from her father's house" [II. iv. 30], and a
little further in the next scene, by Shylock being got out of

the way, when we hear Jessica's final adieu. It is worth noting in this scene that, at a moment when we are ready to sympathize with Shylock, who is about to lose his daughter, the dramatist denies us that privilege by further illustrating the malignancy of the man's character. He has had an unlucky dream; he anticipates trouble falling upon his house; he is warned by Launcelot that there are to be masques at night; he admits that he is not invited to Bassanio's feast out of love, but out of flattery, and still he can say—

But yet I'll go in hate, to feed upon
The prodigal Christian,

[II. v. 14-15]

No personal inconvenience must hinder the acceleration of Antonio's downfall.

In Scene 6 the elopement takes place, but is almost prevented by the entrance of Antonio, whose solemn voice ringing clear on the stillness of the night is a fine dramatic contrast to the whispering of the lovers.

Shakespeare now thinks it time to return to Belmont, and we are shown the Prince of Morocco making his choice of the caskets, and we learn his fate. But he bears his disappointment like a hero, and his dignified retreat moves Portia to exclaim: "A *gentle* riddance!" [II. vii. 78].

Scene 8 is one of narration only, but the speakers are in an excited frame of mind. The opening lines are intended to show that Antonio was not concerned in the flight of Jessica, and our interest in his character is further strengthened by the touching description of his farewell to Bassanio.

Scene 9 disposes of the second of Portia's remaining suitors, and, being comic in character, is inserted with good effect between two tragic scenes. The keynote to its action is to be found in Portia's words: "O, these *deliberate* fools!" [II. ix. 80]. The Prince of Morocco was a warrior, heroic to the tips of his fingers; the Prince of Arragon is a fop, an affected ass, a man "full of wise saws and modern instances" [*As You Like It*, II. vii. 156], and the audience should be prepared for a highly amusing scene by the liveliness with which Nerissa announces his approach. His mannerism is indicated to us in such expressions as "Ha! let me see," and "Well, but to my choice" [II. ix. 23, 49]. He should walk deliberately, speak deliberately, pause deliberately, and when he becomes sentimental, "pose." Highly conscious of his own superiority, and unwilling to "jump with *common* spirits" and "rank me with the *barbarous* multitudes" [II. ix. 32, 33], he assumes superiority, and gets his reward in the shape of a portrait of a blinking idiot. In fact, the whims of this Malvolio are intended to put everyone on and off the stage into high spirits, and even Portia is carried away by the fun as she mimics the retiring suitor in her exclamation to the servant. The scene ends with the announcement that Bassanio, "Lord Love," is on his way to Belmont, and we go on at once to Act III., Scene 1, which, I take it, is a continuation of Act II., Scene 8, and which, therefore, should not form part of another act.

The scene opens with Salarino and Solanio hurrying on the stage anxiously questioning each other about Antonio's rumoured loss at sea. Shylock follows almost immediately, to whom they at once turn in the hope of hearing news. It is usual on the stage to omit the entrance of Antonio's man, but apart from the dramatic effect produced by a follower of Antonio coming on to the stage at that moment, his appearance puts an end to the controversy, which otherwise would prob-

ably continue. Salarino and Solanio leave the stage awed almost to breathlessness, and Tubal enters. Then follows a piteous scene as we see Shylock's outbursts of grief, rage, and despair over the loss of his gold; yet is his anguish aggravated by the one from whom of all others he had a right to expect sympathy. But Shylock, after Tubal's words, "But Antonio is certainly undone," mutters, "Nay, that's true, that's very true" [III. i. 124-25], and takes from his purse a coin, and with a countenance and gesture expressive of indomitable purpose, continues: "*Go*, Tubal, fee me an officer; bespeak him a *fortnight* before. I will have the *heart* of him if he forfeit. . . . *Go*, Tubal, and meet me at our synagogue. *Go*, good Tubal; at our synagogue, Tubal" [III. i. 125-30].

Shylock's misfortunes in this scene would arouse sympathy were it not for the damning confession to Tubal of his motive for hating Antonio "for were he out of Venice I can make what merchandise I will" [III. i. 127-29]. Words that Jessica's lines prove are not idle ones.

When I was with him I have heard him swear
To Tubal and to Chus, his countrymen,
That he would rather have Antonio's flesh
Than twenty times the value of the sum
That he did owe him.

[III. ii. 284-88]

Act III., Scene 2, brings us to the last stage of the casket complication, and here Shakespeare, to avoid sameness, directs that a song shall be sung while Bassanio is occupied in deciding his fate; so that his long speech is spoken after the choice has been made, the leaden casket being then in his hands, and his words merely used to justify his decision. That Bassanio must win Portia is realized from the first. Moreover, his success, after Shylock's threats in the last scene, has become a dramatic necessity, and is thus saved from an appearance of unreality, so that his love adventure develops naturally. His good fortune is Gratiano's; then news is brought of Antonio's bankruptcy and Bassanio is sent to his friend's relief. Scene 3 does no more than show in action what was previously narrated by Solanio in the preceding one, for the Elizabethan dramatists, differing in their methods from the Greeks, rarely allowed narration to take the place of action on the stage. Perhaps this was on account of the mixed character of the audience, the "groundlings" being too busy cracking nuts to take in an important situation merely from its narration. To them Antonio's danger would not become a fact till they actually saw the man in irons and the jailor by his side. In the fourth scene we go back to Belmont to hear that Portia and Nerissa are to be present at the trial, though with what object we are not told. We hear, also, of Portia's admiration for Antonio, whose character she compares with that of her husband. Scene 5 being comic, well serves its purpose as a contrast to the tragic intensity displayed in the scene which follows. Here, too, Portia and Bassanio win golden opinions from Jessica:

It is very meet,
The Lord Bassanio live an upright life;
For having such a blessing in his lady,
He finds the joys of heaven here on earth; . . .
Why, if two gods should play some heavenly match,
And on the wager lay two earthly women,
And Portia one, there must be something else
Pawn'd with the other, for the poor rude world
Hath not her fellow.

[III. v. 73-83]

The trial scene is so well known that I shall not dwell upon it except to mention that I think the dramatist intended the scene to be acted with more vigour and earnestness on the part of all the characters than is represented on the modern stage, and with more vehemence on the part of Shylock. Conscious of his lawful right, he defies the duke and council in language not at all respectful,

> What if my house be troubled with a rat,
> And I be pleased to give *ten* thousand ducats
> To have it baned?
>
> [IV. i. 44-6]

When Shylock is worsted the traditional business is for him to leave the stage with the air of a martyr going to his execution, and thus produce a tragic climax where none is wanted. We seem to get an indication of what should be Shylock's behaviour in his hour of adversity by reading the Italian version of the story, with which Shakespeare was familiar. "Everyone present was greatly pleased and deriding the Jew said: 'He who laid traps for others, is caught himself.' The Jew seeing he could gain nothing, tore in pieces the bond *in a great rage.*" Indeed, Shylock's words,

> Why, then the devil give him good of it!
> I'll stay no longer question,
>
> [IV. i. 345-46]

are exactly suited to the action of tearing up the bond. Certain it is that only by Shylock being "in a great rage," as he rushes off the stage, can the audience be greatly pleased, and in a fit humour to be interested in the further doings of Portia. Scene 2 of this act is generally omitted on the stage, though it seems to me necessary in order to show how Nerissa gets possession of Gratiano's ring; it also affords an opportunity for some excellent business on the part of Nerissa, who walks off arm in arm with her husband, unknown to him.

The last act is the shortest fifth act in the Globe edition, and if deficient in action Shakespeare gives it another interest by the wealth and music of its poetry, a device more than once made use of by him to strengthen undramatic material. Shakespeare's knowledge of the value of sound, in dramatic effect, is shown by Launcelot interrupting the whispering of the lovers, and profaning the stillness of the night with his halloas, which have a similar effect to the nurse's calls in the balcony scene of *Romeo and Juliet;* it is also shown by the music, and in the tucket sound; while the picture brought to the imagination, by allusion to the light burning in Portia's hall, gives reality to the scene. (pp. 123-33)

> *William Poel, "The Merchant of Venice," in his*
> Shakespeare in the Theatre, *Sidgwick and Jackson,*
> *Ltd., 1913, pp. 123-33.*

Ellen Terry   (lecture date 1911-21)

[*In the excerpt below, taken from a lecture she delivered in various places in Great Britain, America, Australia, and New Zealand over a period of about ten years, Terry describes her interpretation of Portia, explaining that the character is first and foremost an Italian Renaissance lady who must embody and radiate the beauty of the culture she represents. In addition, Terry addresses certain critical issues pertaining to Portia, including the character's relationship with Bassanio and the origin of her defense of Antonio in the trial scene.*]

No one can tell us how Shakespeare got what we call 'local colour'. He may have been to Italy. He may not. It is 'as you like it'. His Venetian topography is amazingly accurate, but that proves nothing. He could have got it out of a book, or picked it up from an Italian traveller he met in a coffee-house in London. It does not matter. What does matter is that the genius of the man enabled him in *The Merchant of Venice* to give the very echo to the place where the Adriatic is enthroned. This is why I believe in representing Portia as a Venetian lady. There are many different ways of playing the part. I have tried five or six ways myself, but I have always come back to the Italian way, the Renaissance way. In Germany, and allow me here to pay my tribute to Germany—yes I must, although you don't want me to, I can see—for honouring Shakespeare worthily by frequent performances of his plays—in Germany there is a tradition that Portia is a low comedy part. The German Portia is compelled by this tradition (or was when I was last in Germany. Things may have altered) to appear in the Trial Scene in an eighteenth-century wig, horn spectacles, a barrister's cravat, and a fierce moustache. Well, there is something to be said for it. As Sancho Panza remarks, 'an ounce of laughter is better than a pound of care'. Besides, the prodigious wealth of implication in Shakespeare's plays, which makes them all As You Like Its, allows of a great variety of interpretations. But from my point of view, no interpretation entailing a sacrifice of beauty, whether to mirth or to realism, can ever be satisfactory. Portia is the fruit of the Renaissance, the child of a period of beautiful clothes, beautiful cities, beautiful houses, beautiful ideas. She speaks the beautiful language of inspired poetry. Wreck that beauty, and the part goes to pieces.

I think Georg Brandes, the Shakespearean commentator I have found of most use to me as an actress, sums up Portia's character as well as it can be done, when he writes that 'in spite of her self-surrender in love there is something independent, almost masculine in her attitude towards life. This orphan heiress has been in a position of authority from childhood. She is used to acting on her own responsibility, without seeking advice first.' It makes me rather impatient when I am told that it is strange that a woman of this type, in the habit of directing herself and directing others, should be willing to be directed by a man so manifestly inferior to her as Bassanio. I think if we take the trouble to enquire into the motives at the back of the famous speech of surrender, it will not strike us as either strange or repellent.

Remember that Portia so far has had everything given to her. She is the spoiled child of fortune, or would be if she were not so generous. It is this excessive generosity which partly explains her offering with herself all she has to the man she loves. We have to take into account too that she is a great lady. 'Noblesse oblige' was not an empty phrase in her day. Even in our own day a well-bred person who is rich is always anxious not to wound anyone who is poor by even a breath of patronage. When I have added that the first-fruit of love is humility, I need say no more in explanation of Portia's attitude to Bassanio. It seems quite natural that she should assure him that her spirit

> Commits itself to yours to be directed,
> As from her lord, her governor, her king.
> Myself and what is mine to you and yours
> Is now converted: but now I was the lord
> Of this fair mansion, master of my servants,
> Queen o'er myself; and even now, but now,
> This house, these servants, and this same myself
> Are yours, my lord.
>
> [III. ii. 164-71]

If the speech jars on you—surely such heavenly word-music cannot jar, on the ear at any rate—it is because you take it too literally. I don't mean that Portia is not in earnest. A Cardinal is in earnest when he washes the beggar's feet, but he does not commit himself by this gesture of humility to making a practice of it! It is clear that Portia's gracious surrender is a 'beau geste', and little more. The proof is that she retains her independence of thought and action. The first thing she does after her marriage is to lay her own plans for saving Antonio's life, without so much as a 'with your leave or by your leave' to her lord and master!

The general opinion of Bassanio is unflattering. I don't know why he is considered such a poor specimen of manhood. My impression is that he has great charm. His loyalty to Antonio is in his favour. He does not let his friend down when he is in trouble. What reason is there to suppose that he will let Portia down, and that she will bitterly regret her marriage? We must not infer that he is stupid because of his failure to recognise Portia in her lawyer's robe at the trial. The impenetrableness of a disguise is a dramatic convention. Shakespeare employs it over and over again.

I have often been asked whether I think Portia's line of pleading in the Court is her own. Was the quibble by which she destroys Shylock's case, and so saves Antonio, her own idea, or did it originate with the learned Bellario? This question interests me more than the one whether the quibble was justified. The answer to this second question is simple. Desperate evils demand desperate remedies. I am driven to think we are dreadfully sentimental nowadays when I hear people say Shylock was infamously treated. He had laid a trap for Antonio, and there was nothing unjust in laying a trap for him. If we regard the Duke's sentence as harsh, especially that clause about Shylock's presently becoming a Christian, we ought to remember that in our own day far more violent animus against the Jewish race has been displayed than in this Venetian Court centuries ago.

But to go back to the question: Who thought of the trap in which Shylock was caught? It is my belief that it was not a man! I have an idea that the learned Bellario told Portia at once that the law could not help Antonio. If he turned o'er many books with her (as he says in his letter to the Duke) it was to instruct her in the statutes by which Shylock, in any event, could be punished, not in the hope of proving the bond invalid. He advised her to try an appeal to Shylock's mercy, and if that failed, to try another to his cupidity. If *that* failed, well then I fancy the learned Bellario may have suggested trying a threat. Let the Jew be warned of the consequences of exacting his pound of flesh. To my mind, and I have always tried to show this in the trial scene, Portia is acting on a preconcerted plan up to the moment of pronouncing sentence: then she has an inspiration, and acts on that. Hence her 'Tarry a little; there is something else' [IV. i. 305].

There has flashed through her brain suddenly the thought that a pound of flesh is not quite the same thing as a pound of flesh and blood. (We know how careful lawyers have to be when drawing up legal documents, to specify *exactly* what is meant. That is why they are so terribly long.) She tries to disguise her apprehension that this may be a distinction without a difference, and says firmly:

> This bond doth give thee here no jot of blood.
>
> [IV. i. 306]

I am convinced that this bit of casuistry was not conceived

by Shakespeare as being carefully planned. It strikes me as a lightning-like inspiration—just such an inspiration as a woman might have when she is at her wit's end, and is willing to try anything to avoid defeat. Well, whatever view one takes of it, it is impossible to admire it, although it may be defended on the ground that the end justifies the means. From this point in the trial scene the sympathies of a modern audience are with Shylock. Portia's moment is when she appeals to him for mercy.

That famous mercy speech! To me it will always be a thing 'ensky'd and sainted' [*Measure For Measure*, I. iv. 34]. I often pray that to the end of my life I may be able to do *some* justice to these inspired words, written I feel sure to the glory of God, with faith and adoration. The speech is a noble kinsman to the Lord's Prayer, on which indeed it is modelled. It urges with the same beautiful simplicity the same beautiful ideal of justice: 'And forgive us our trespasses as we forgive them that tresspass against us.'

> *Portia*
>   Then must the Jew be merciful.
>
> *Shylock*
>   On what compulsion must I? tell me that.
>
> *Portia*
>   The quality of mercy is not strain'd,
>   It droppeth as the gentle rain from heaven
>   Upon the place beneath: it is twice blest;
>   It blesseth him that gives and him that takes:
>   'Tis mightiest in the mightiest; it becomes
>   The throned monarch better than his crown;
>   His sceptre shows the force of temporal power,
>   The attribute to awe and majesty,
>   Wherein doth sit the dread and fear of kings;
>   But mercy is above this sceptred sway;
>   It is enthroned in the hearts of kings,
>   It is an attribute to God himself;
>   And earthly power doth then show likest God's
>   When mercy seasons justice. Therefore, Jew,
>   Though justice be thy pleas, consider this,
>   That, in the course of justice, none of us
>   Should see salvation: we do pray for mercy;
>   And that same prayer doth teach us all to render
>   The deeds of mercy.
>
>   [IV. i. 182-202]

I have done. I want you to go away with those words in your ears, and to try and make them a living force in your hearts. (pp. 115-22)

Ellen Terry, "The Triumphant Women," in her Four Lectures on Shakespeare, *edited by Christopher St. John, 1932. Reprint by Benjamin Blom, 1969, pp. 79-122.*

Harley Granville-Barker   (essay date 1930)

[Granville-Barker was a noted actor, playwright, director, and critic. His Shakespearean criticism is informed by his experience on the stage, for he treats Shakespeare's plays not as literature better understood divorced from the theater, but as pieces intended for actual production. As a director, Barker emphasized simplicity in staging, set design, and costuming, believing that elaborate scenery obscures the poetry which is of central importance to Shakespeare's plays. He also eschewed the approach of directors who mount productions that scrupulously employ Elizabethan stage techniques, maintaining that this, too, detracts from the play's meaning. In the excerpt below

*from his preface to the work, Barker pronounces The Mer-
chant of Venice "a fairy tale," a dictum that influenced many
twentieth-century productions of the play. Barker asserts that
the play, as written, is well-balanced between the two plots and
flows smoothly, provided "we do not bedevil it with sophistries."
In addition, Barker comments on plausible act divisions of the
play, arguing that the fewer pauses or breaks in a performance
the stronger the production.]*

The Merchant of Venice is a fairy tale. There is no more reality in Shylock's bond and The Lord of Belmont's will than in
Jack and the Beanstalk.

Shakespeare, it is true, did not leave the fables as he found
them. This would not have done; things that pass muster on
the printed page may become quite incredible when acted by
human beings, and the unlikelier the story, the likelier must
the mechanism of its acting be made. Besides, when his own
creative impulse was quickened, he could not help giving life
to a character; he could no more help it than the sun can help
shining. So Shylock is real, while his story remains fabulous;
and Portia and Bassanio become human, though, truly, they
never quite emerge from the enchanted thicket of fancy into
the common light of day. Æsthetic logic may demand that
a story and its characters should move consistently upon one
plane or another, be it fantastic or real. But Shakespeare's
practical business, once he had chosen these two stories for
his play, was simply so to charge them with humanity that
they did not betray belief in the human beings presenting
them, yet not so uncompromisingly that the stories themselves became ridiculous.

What the producer of the play must first set himself to ascertain is the way in which he did this, the nice course that—by
reason or instinct—he steered. Find it and follow it, and there
need be no running on the rocks. But logic may land us anywhere. It can turn Bassanio into a heartless adventurer. Test
the clock of the action by Greenwich time, it will either be
going too fast or too slow. And as to Portia's disguise and Bellario's law, would the village policeman be taken in by either?
But the actor will find that he simply cannot play Bassanio
as a humbug, for Shakespeare does not mean him to. Portias
and Nerissas have been eclipsed by wigs and spectacles. This
is senseless tomfoolery; but how make a wiseacre producer
see that if he does not already know? And if, while Shylock
stands with his knife ready and Antonio with his bared
breast, the wise young judge lifting a magical finger between
them, we sit questioning Bellario's law—why, no one concerned, actors or audience, is for this fairyland, that is clear.

The Merchant of Venice is the simplest of plays, so long as
we do not bedevil it with sophistries. Further, it is—for what
it is!—as smoothly and completely successful, its means being
as well fitted to its end, as anything Shakespeare wrote. He
was happy in his choice of the Portia story; his verse, which
has lost glitter to gain a mellower beauty and an easier flow,
is now well attuned to such romance. The story of Shylock's
bond is good contrast and complement both; and he can now
project character upon the stage, uncompromising and complete. Yet this Shylock does not overwhelm the play, as at a
later birth he might well have done—it is a near thing,
though! Lastly, Shakespeare is now enough of the skilled
playwright to be able to adjust and blend the two themes with
fruitful economy. (pp. 67-9)

However well the First Folio's five-act rule may fit other
plays, and whatever, in Elizabethan stage practice, division
into five acts implied, there is ample evidence that *The Mer-*

chant of Venice was meant to be played without an effective
break. The scenes, and the padding in them, that give time
for Portia and Nerissa to change clothes are one sign of it.
The first of these is padding unalloyed, and very poor padding
at that. For the second, Shakespeare finds better and plea-
santer excuse; but in part, at least, we owe that charming duet
between Lorenzo and Jessica to this practical need.

A case of a sort can be made out for the division in the Folio.
Granted five acts, this fourth and fifth are manifest; the beginnings and finishings of the first three make useful milestones
in the story, but others every bit as useful could be set up. It
is worth noting that this act division does nothing to elucidate
the complex time-scheme of our anxious editors; but the
Folio's expert playdivider would be no more bothered by that
problem than Shakespeare had been. Nor was he concerned
to end his acts memorably; the second leaves Aragon in our
minds and the third ends with Jessica and Lorenzo's and the
play's worst scene. There might, however, be good enough
reason in the Elizabethan theatre for making an act's first
scene arresting and for letting its last tail away; for they had,
of course, no curtain to lower upon a climax, and after an interval interest would need quick re-kindling. No producer today, one hopes, will want to lower a picture-stage curtain at
such points. Nor, if he is wise, while his stories are working
to their joint climax will he give us pause to think by what
strange leaps in time and space they travel.

But surely there are many signs that—however, for convenience sake, it is to be acted, with or without pause—
Shakespeare has conceived and constructed the play indivisi-
bly. There is the alternating between Venice and Belmont, and
the spinning out of the Portia story to fit with the other;
neither device gains by or countenances act division. There
is the unhesitating sweep of the action up to the Trial scene,
and indeed beyond it. One can parcel it up in various ways—
the Folio's and half a dozen others—and on various pleas; but
will any one of them make the story clearer; will it not, on
the contrary, do something to disclose its confusions? Prose
and blank verse, rhymed couplets and a quatrain are used indifferently for tags; so these form no consistent punctuation.
There is no scene, not even the Trial scene, that ends with a
full close, until the play ends. There is, in fact, no inherent,
no dramatic pause in the action at all; nor can any be made
which will not be rather hindrance than help to a performance.

Well-paced acting will take the play straight through in the
traditional, vague two hours. But if, for the weakness of the
flesh, there must be pauses, division into three parts will be
a little less awkward than into two. If you do not stop before
the Trial scene you cannot, of course, stop at all; the play will
be virtually over. You may reasonably pause at the end of the
Folio's Act III. This alone, though, will make very unequal
division. For an earlier pause, the moment of Bassanio's departure from Venice will serve. This splits the first three acts
of the Folio all but exactly in two. Delay the pause another
scene and we shall have done with Morocco. The second part
would then begin with the tale of how Shylock took his loss
and our first news of Antonio's losses, and would develop this
interest till the eve of the trial. Incidentally it would hold all
the inordinate time-telescoping; a helpful quickening, this, to
its pulse. But these divisions and the choice of them have no
other validity than convenience; the play must be thought of
as an integral whole.

Needless to say that the confusion of scene-divisions in most modern editions (a very riot of it when Jessica is eloping) is not Shakespeare's; nor is the expert of the Folio responsible, nor even Rowe, who contents himself with marking the moves from Venice to Belmont and back. For a century editors disputed as to when 'Venice, a street,' shifted to 'A room in Shylock's House,' or to 'Another Street,' or to 'Before Shylock's House,' and chopped up the action and checked its impetus, when one glance at Shakespeare's stage, its doors and balcony and traverses, shows with what swift unity the play and its playing flow on. And whatever picturing of Venice and Belmont a producer may design, this swift-flowing unity he must on no account obstruct. Let that be clear.

But there is little difficulty in the play's production, once its form is recognised, its temper felt, the tune of its verse and the rhythm of its prose rightly caught. The text is very free from errors, there are no puzzles in the actual stagecraft. The music may come from Elizabethan stock, and the costuming is obvious. Nothing is needed but perception and good taste, and from the actors, acting. (pp. 107-10)

> Harley Granville-Barker, "The Merchant of Venice," in his Prefaces to Shakespeare, Second Series, Sidgwick & Jackson, Ltd., 1930, pp. 67-110.

G. Wilson Knight   (essay date 1936)

[Knight was a British scholar, author, Shakespearean actor, and producer, who argued that the true test of a reading of a play is to adapt that interpretation to a stage production. His works include The Wheel of Fire: Essays on the Interpretation of Shakespeare's Sombre Tragedies (1930), The Imperial Theme: Further Interpretations of Shakespeare's Tragedies Including the Roman Plays (1931), The Shakespearian Tempest, with a Chart of Shakespeare's Dramatic Universe (1932), Principles of Shakespearian Production, With Special Reference to the Tragedies (1936), The Crown of Life: Essays in Interpretation of Shakespeare's Final Plays (1947), and The Mutual Flame: on Shakespeare's Sonnets and "The Phoenix and the Turtle" (1955). In the excerpt below, Knight offers suggestions for staging The Merchant of Venice. He affirms that "at the heart of this play is the idea of riches: false and true wealth," and many of his directions, such as dominant caskets, seek to amplify this theme.]

The meaning of The Merchant of Venice is never sufficiently brought out. You will say that it has no 'meaning': but if you do, I maintain strongly that you are wrong. We must take the play seriously. Its deeper significances do not, it is true, correspond at every point with a surface realism as they do in Macbeth. But for this very reason we must take care to bring the inherent meanings out as harmoniously and as naturally, yet powerfully, as we can.

This play presents two contrasted worlds: Venice and Belmont. The one is a world of business competition, usury, melancholy, and tragic sea-disaster; the other, a spelled land of riches, music and romance . . . I know many of our Venetian scenes are comparatively jovial: but Gratiano is scarcely a pleasant man. Venice has romantic associations: but here it is darkly toned. The supposedly pleasant people are not all they might be. Antonio is cruel to Shylock, Bassanio a spendthrift, Gratiano vulgar, and honesty certainly not the strongest point of Lorenzo and Jessica. Shylock towers over the rest, grand, it is true, but scarcely amiable. Observe that the tragedy depends on sea-wreck, tempests, and such like: Shakespeare's usual tragedy associations. But at Belmont all this is changed. All the people become noble as soon as they

arrive there: Bassanio is the loyal friend, Lorenzo the perfect lover, Gratiano is, comparatively, subdued. The name Belmont suggests a height overlooking the water-logged world of Venetian rivalry and pettiness. At Belmont we have music continually: at Venice, none. The projected Masque we may observe does not, as far as our persons are concerned, come off after all [II. iv. 64]; but it serves for Shylock's significant lines about the 'vile squealing of the wry-neck'd fife' [II. v. 30], which might be compared with his even less pretty 'bagpipe' reference later. Certainly, Venice is not here a place of romantic music. Belmont is. And the Belmont world is dominated by Portia; expressly Christian, as against Shylock, her only rival in dramatic importance; and of infinite wealth as against the penurious Bassanio and thieving Lorenzo. Everyone in Venice is in money difficulties of some sort, even the rich ones. Antonio's fortune is all at sea. Shylock has to borrow from Tubal, and later loses great part of his wealth with his daughter, and bemoans his lost ducats in the street. But Portia is infinitely rich. Her riches hold, dramatically, an almost spiritual quality.

Our permanent set must help to mark out these contrasted worlds. I suggest dividing the stage into two levels, the rise making a straight diagonal from up L to down R. The higher level is thus mainly on stage right. Half-way along this diagonal steps can be used to lead from one level to the other. Venetian scenes will concentrate on the lower, Belmont on the higher, level. I do not mean that no Venetian in Venice should ascend the higher: merely that the Venetian action should always focus on the lower with a force proportional to the particular significance. And certainly in the Belmont scenes, the lower space must never be quite empty, which would tend to rob the figures above of any dignity their raised position gives them. . . . We can arrange a background that gives a wide and variable range of tones according to the lights: this will help. For the casket scenes the suitors enter down R or down L and ascend the steps ceremoniously. Nothing must seem too rigid, however. Portia, standing aside during Bassanio's meditations, would probably come down L on the lower level; and later meet him as he descends the steps, an action which suits the submissive femininity of her speech, and his victorious choice.

The three caskets will be large and solid-looking, and must be allowed to dominate. Perhaps they should even be evident throughout the action. At the heart of this play is the idea of riches: false and true wealth. Jesus' parables are suggested. Venice is lost in the varied complexities of the false. Portia possesses the true. Not only is love and beauty continually in Shakespeare metaphorically a matter of riches, but Portia is vitally associated with Christianity, and is, moreover, an heiress with an infinite bank-balance. In this play of greed her serene disregard of exact sums has something supernal about it:

> PORTIA: What sum owes he the Jew?
> BASSANIO: For me three thousand ducats.
> PORTIA: What, no more?
> Pay him six thousand, and deface the bond;
> Double six thousand, and then treble that . . .
>   [III. ii. 297-300]

He shall have gold 'to pay the petty debt twenty times over' [III. ii. 307]. We must note further that Portia's office in the play is to demonstrate the futility, as a final resort, of business and legal exactitudes. The action drives home the truth that money is only an aspect of life, and that life itself must come before money and the laws of money. The contrast is exquisitely pointed by the situation of a man giving a pound of flesh as security. Everyone wants to save his life, but there seems no loophole. His life is now subject to laws made only for money. Observe how Portia deals with the absurd situation. She dispels the clouding precisions and intellectualities of the law court by a serene common-sense. This is something very like the common-sense of Jesus. Her Mercy speech exactly reflects His teaching. Moreover, the white beam of her intuition shows, as genius has a way of showing, as Jesus' teaching so often shows, that the academic intelligence is itself vulnerable at every point by its own weapons. Shylock's worst danger is to be allowed the rights he fights for:

> The words expressly are 'a pound of flesh':
> Take then thy bond; take thou thy pound of flesh;
> But, in the cutting it, if thou dost shed
> One drop of Christian blood . . .
>
> [IV. i. 307-10]

This is what comes of not distinguishing between the counters of finance and the bread and wine, the silver flesh and golden blood, of life itself. The serene wisdom of life works always by refusing validity to false abstractions. You can cut money into bits, but not life; there any piece involves the whole. Such are the lines of Portia's reasoning; it is fundamentally a poetic and holistic reasoning. And as soon as you begin to think in such poetic and holistic terms there are always certain supposed exactitudes that lose all meaning: so next Portia supports her first argument by insisting that poor Shylock shall take exactly a pound of flesh, neither less nor more by the weight of a hair. His whole position crumbles.

Clearly then the caskets, gold, silver and lead, containing respectively death, folly and infinite love and wealth, must be solid and dominating. This play is not all so silly as many a modern critic would have it and many a modern production makes it.

So Venice and Belmont alternate. The play works up to the climax of the Trial Scene, where the protagonists of the two worlds, Portia and Shylock, meet for the first time. Portia descends from Belmont almost as a divine being: her office is, anyway, that of a *dea ex machina*. I would have the court sitting on the high level R, some using the level itself for a seat. The Duke's chair will be half-way along. Bassanio and Antonio are down R; Shylock moves between up L, L, and C. Some spectators can edge in down L and Gratiano stand L between them and Shylock, coming forward for his big speeches.

Portia enters down R, circles up-stage to the steps, and ascends the higher level, standing beside the Duke. Her doctor's gown is better neither black nor red. Her doctorate is one of serene Christian wisdom and feminine intuition. She never gained it at Padua. Let her therefore wear a correctly cut doctor-of-laws gown of *spotless white*. She is high and central, dominating the whole court. The light should be intensified on her white gown and golden hair just showing under her cap as she speaks her Mercy speech. But, as the situation ripens, she descends: observe how this movement uses our levels to capture the essence of her arrival in Venice to render assistance, her *descent* from the happier world of her home. She comes nearly, but not quite, down the steps at: 'I pray you, let me look upon the bond' [IV. i. 225], Shylock gives it her. She warns him: 'Shylock, there's thrice thy money offered thee' [IV. i. 227]. She is kind, is meeting these people

on their own terms, descending to their level. But Shylock will have none of it. She tries again. He returns to his corner, talking to Tubal, adamant. Portia, on the steps, begins to prepare judgment. She addresses Antonio, asks for balances and a surgeon. Antonio says his farewell. Now, swaying slightly, she pronounces judgment, the speed gathers as the whirl of her repetition gains force, the whirl of a lasso:

> The court awards it and the law doth give it,
>
> [IV. i. 300]

and

> The law allows it and the court awards it.
>
> [IV. i. 303]

Shylock, in ecstasy of hatred, cries 'A sentence! Come, prepare!' [IV. i. 304]. Unleashed, he springs down-stage. Bassanio shields Antonio. The Duke stands. The crowds murmur. But at this instant Portia takes the last step down to the lower level and cuts off Shylock's attack with a raised hand. 'Tarry a little'. There is silence. In a quiet voice she continues:

> . . . there is something else.
> This bond doth give thee here no jot of blood . . .
>
> [IV. i. 305-06]

The terrible judgment of a fathomless simplicity and divine common-sense.

It is, of course, an amazing scene, and its tremendous dramatic impact derives from the clash of the two dominating forces in the play, Shylock and Portia, and all that they stand for. Our set of two levels with Portia's descent will assist; so will her white gown, and her significant barring of Shylock's attack at the crucial moment, which must be given expressive action. We must work always from the profound issues implicit in the dramatic thrill if it is to have full power. Portia's standing on the same steps where previously we have seen her meet her suitors, with the caskets behind, priestess of the knowledge of true and false wealth, clearly helps this scene. We are aware of her bringing her own world, and all it symbolises, into the new context.

For the rest of the scene do not be afraid of an anticlimax. Portia must be firm and not too pitiful. Shylock's exit, C to down L through the crowd, can be as pathetic as you will, but not too long delayed. The play shows a Christian, romantic, and expressly feminine Portia against a down-trodden, vengeful, racially grand, usurious Jew. I do not claim that all the difficulties inherent in this opposition are finally settled in our play: but I do claim that this dramatic opposition is a profound one. You must not suppose that since Portia has all our sympathy Shylock can have none: poetic drama can be paradoxical. Portia stands serene in white purity, symbol of Christian romance. But Shylock, saying he is ill, picks up his cloak and goes out robed in purple: the purple of tragedy. Two tremendous imaginative issues conflict: the romantic dream and tragic realism. Later Shakespeare is to reconcile them. Here the opposition must be stark: neither must be watered down.

The last scene at Belmont acts itself easily: but I object to so unfortunate a back-cloth as one with *waves* painted on it, for obvious reasons. Our set here might for the first time dispose of the change in level. The action's dualism may not have been perfectly unified: but you certainly are not supposed now to be worrying about it. Or again, you might keep it: and get highly significant comedy out of the lovers chasing each other—as they usually do—about from one level to the other. On second thoughts, I think this best. It would have meaning. Lorenzo and Jessica would be comfortably placed on the steps at the beginning. (pp. 185-93)

G. Wilson Knight, "The Ideal Production," in his Principles of Shakespearian Production with Especial Reference to the Tragedies, *Faber & Faber Limited*, 1936, pp. 183-216.

Hugh Hunt   (essay date 1954)

[*Hunt provides an introduction to the Old Vic production he directed in 1953, which featured Paul Rogers as Shylock and Claire Bloom as Portia. Hunt reveals his indebtedness to Granville-Barker's notion of the play as a "fairy-tale," and describes his attempts to translate this idea to the stage, through scenery, costume, and characterization. The director addresses various critical and staging issues, including the primary task of reconciling the fairy-tale elements with the realistic figure of Shylock.*]

Granville Barker called *The Merchant of Venice* a fairy tale. It is in fact two fairy tales; the tale of the Princess destined to be won by the lover who solves the riddle of the caskets, and the tale of the wicked Oriental money-lender who tries to encompass the death of the honest merchant. These two stories are eventually amalgamated by an exciting, if rather improbable, trial scene in which the Princess and her maid disguise themselves as men, and the whole rounded off with a lyrical ending, in which the merchant is rescued and the lovers united. Like all fairy stories *The Merchant of Venice* contains much that, if looked at too closely, seems improbable; such as the business of the caskets and the disguise of Portia and Nerissa as a lawyer and his clerk. Indeed, critics, scornful of its ingenuosity, have marvelled at its popularity. Some of these critics find Portia priggish and pedantic, others accuse Bassanio of being a calculating fortune-hunter, others maintain that the jingoism and intolerance of the Christians destroy the play's equilibrium, turning it from a comedy into an intolerable melodrama of Jew-baiting.

The truth lies in the fact that the play is a fairy tale, and in the acting of it we must hold fast to the principles upon which fairy tales are founded. These principles have little to do with material probabilities, with psychological complexes, or with introvert personalities, which are the stock-in-trade of naturalistic playwrights.

A fairy tale demands firstly, the telling of a plain, unvarnished tale and secondly, the simple, epic type of characterization which divides the world between the good and the bad without any attempt to linger over probability or motivation. To tell a plain, unvarnished tale upon the stage we need speed, clarity and dramatic tension. We must not try to embellish the action by extraneous effects nor ponder too much over the thought-process of the personalities. What matters is the story and the atmosphere of the play, not the subtleties of characterization and behaviour. The apparent difficulty of accepting the naïve simplicity of this story has led some producers and players to find new meanings behind the motivation of the characters; to suggest that Antonio is degenerate or that Bassanio is only out to win a fortune, to twist the sympathy of the play on to Shylock, to show Jessica and Lorenzo as a couple of unscrupulous thieves or to vilify Gratiano and the Venetians. Such attempts to impose psychological motivation on the characters and to create dramatic situations

which the play does not possess make nonsense of the love story, destroy the poetry and render the last scene—perhaps one of the most lyrical in the English language—a mockery of itself.

I do not propose that we should load this production with realistic scenery. Our task is to give the play the lightness and magic of a fairy tale and not to move ponderously round the ghetto of Venice and the cypress groves of Belmont. Nor do I think we should clothe it in some vague quatro-cento convention about which Shakespeare knew nothing at all. A modern audience has a certain idea of Venice derived principally from the painters Canaletto and Guardi, and the simplest way to indicate Venice to an audience is to follow in the spirit of these two masters, but without deliberate imitation. Critics will no doubt pride themselves on their historical knowledge by pointing out that the play is costumed at least a hundred years later than the Elizabethan age. What a time they would have had at the Globe with the players of Macbeth, and Antony and Cleopatra in ruffs and farthingales, or with Garrick as Lear in baroque finery! Our object will be to establish Venice by the quickest and most easily acceptable means. The principal scene will be a piazza in Venice, presented in the manner of the perspective paintings of the Venetian school without realistic details or embroideries. The problem of alternating Venice and Belmont is considerable, for since we no longer possess the bare platform of the Globe, we are forced to give some kind of visual illusion to our scenery, and visual illusion to these two alternating locations means scene-change and the evil of stage waits.

My object is, as I have said, to endow the play with the magic of the fairy story and Belmont of all places must possess a magic quality. It will therefore be represented by a little white pavilion—the pavilion of the caskets—which will rise up from the floor of the stage on a lift. By this means, and without further alterations of scenery, one scene will follow on the other without interruption and we shall not disturb the flow of the play by chopping it up with ponderous scene changes. This continuous flow of scene into scene is the essential unity of action which is no less a rule of Shakespeare's theatre, than are the famous unities of time and place postulated by Boileau for the seventeenth-century neo-classical theatre. This simple device will be our setting, and all we need beyond it will be a vague stone background for the court scene.

But there is a major problem in the handling of this fairy tale which cannot be easily overcome—it is Shylock. Shakespeare was a playwright first and a story-teller second. As a playwright he gave birth to people rather than to stories, and once you start giving birth to people you cannot control the result. Milton wrote *Paradise Lost* with the pious intention of glorifying God and the good angels and vilifying Satan and the rebel angels, but the most vital character in *Paradise Lost* is Satan. From the time of the earliest mystery plays the audience's interest was aroused more by the devils issuing from the fiery mouth of hell, than by the saintly creatures walking in the gardens of paradise; and Judas on the stage is not without our sympathy. For this reason, consciously or unconsciously, Shakespeare has kept the Portia story separate from the Shylock story, and Belmont from Venice. The two stories are only brought together when the opportunity arises for a scene in which Portia can meet and defeat the Jew.

Shakespeare took his character of Shylock from an Italian Renaissance source, a source which painted this figure of the Jew in the blackest possible colours. As an Englishman of his epoch he accepted the evilness of the Jew and he set out to please the groundlings by baiting him. The choice of subject was apt enough, for in 1594 public sentiment in London had been roused by one of those traditional outbreaks of anti-Zionism which recur throughout history. Shylock was conceived as a villain, and, in the simple tradition of the fairy story, he is recognizable as such from his first entrance. 'Three thousand ducats; well . . . ' 'For three months; well . . . ' 'Antonio shall become bound; well . . . ' [I. iii. 1, 3, 6]. This repetition of the word 'well' has the same effect as the 'Ha! Ha!' of the pantomime demon-king. The tradition of pantomime demands that the demon-king should make his first entrance on the left side of the stage, whereas the fairy-queen enters on the right. Once the villain has exposed his evil intention—be it to kill Aladdin or to ruin Cinderella—the fairy-queen must change her wand from her right hand to her left so as to protect her heart from evil and place herself in a position to protect her protégées. But in the process of creating this demon-king, at the moment when inspiration took over from the simple act of story-telling, Shylock inconveniently started writing Shakespeare, instead of Shakespeare writing Shylock.

This Jew whom Shakespeare recognized as the typical bugbear of his age became a human being instead of a monster. The character grew in roundness and in dignity; his wicked imprecations against Christians became the haunted, homeless call of the outcast. Indeed he might have crossed over the stage and the fairy-queen with her wand might have been forced to retire, had not Shakespeare kept the two stories separate. No doubt the actors of the Globe, in search of a popular theme, confided to their resident dramatist the task of writing a play about the universally unpopular Jew, but they overlooked the fact that they were giving this task to a man who created characters as a mother creates a child, and that once the act of generation had begun the results were not always as predictable as the device employed by Jacob for producing parti-coloured lambs.

Shakespeare, like Milton, fashioned his villain without being fully conscious of what sort of animal he was creating, and Shylock, like Satan, refused to be restricted by the conventions of popular belief and prejudice. Even if Shakespeare and Milton shared with their contemporaries certain articles of belief and certain prejudices of their times—beliefs and prejudices which they would naturally express in their outer lives; in their inner lives, by virtue of which they were artists, they tuned-in to the inner truth about Satan and Shylock and caught the pity, the pride, the heartbreak and the loneliness which lie behind the bitterness, the evil and the cunning of the popular villain.

Thus Shylock enters *The Merchant of Venice* as a creation of Shakespeare, the Renaissance Englishman, and leaves it as the creation of Shakespeare, the artist. Our task is to reconcile the simple fairy story of *The Merchant of Venice*, in which probability and psychological truth are discarded in favour of 'magic casements opening on a sea of fairy-lands forlorn', with this realistic figure of the outcast of the ages, so close to our own experience and so demanding of our sympathy.

Without this reconciliation we cannot hope to preserve the equilibrium of the play and the fairy story will turn into callous Jew-baiting. Our task will be to observe a strict balance of the black and white elements of the characterization without denying the Jew his humanity. This can be done if we pre-serve the fairy story and do not try to embellish it with realism. The lovers must be kept simple and likeable and the villain must not be allowed to step out of the frame and knock pitifully at Jessica's door, nor pass like a shadow across the moon-lit lawns of Belmont, as has been done in some productions. Let us, therefore, be content with what Shakespeare has written. It is fine enough, and there is no need to embellish it by trying to turn it into propaganda for anti- or pro-Zionism.

Now to preserve this balance look first of all at the characters of the lovers and accept them at their simple face value. Bassanio is a gentleman by birth and in a fairy story a gentleman must be a little too liberal of his purse, a little too free in his outlook on life, as well as being loyal to his friends and genuine in his love of his mistress. That is Shakespeare's Bassanio, and the play is jeopardized if we attempt to embellish his character with deeper motives or sinister intents. Portia is rich and in the tradition of fairy stories a lady born in the purple must have a ready wit and prove her worth in the world; she must not win her spurs by a shabby trick played on a lonely, pathetic outcast. Lorenzo and Jessica elope because they are in love, not because Lorenzo is trying to steal Shylock's ducats. Gratiano and Nerissa, being lesser-born copies of Bassanio and Portia, are permitted to be broader in their outlook and behaviour than the principals, but they must remain fundamentally happy, simple people. In the behaviour of all these people we see the familiar pattern of Shakespeare's comedy. I do not mean that these people are merely replicas of similar figures in other comedies, but in Shakespeare's comedy the lovers work to a pattern and that pattern is a love-dance or mating masquerade in which Beatrice and Benedick, Berowne and Rosaline, Helena and Demeterius, Rosalind and Orlando, Katherine and Petruchio, all dance to a measure. The pattern of this dance must be kept. And so the advice I want you to follow is to keep the pattern, dance the measure, tell the story, and to do so simply and clearly. Remember what is required is style acting, not naturalistic acting. Let Shakespeare make the characters; do not try to embellish them with fancies of your own. So much for the white personalities. Now for the black.

Like Malvolio, Shylock is fundamentally a butt for the mockery of these dancing figures. Malvolio and Shylock may nearly cause our tears as well as our mockery, but they must not lose their place in the dance. Shylock will, of course, emerge as a real person; for the heart that beats beneath his Jewish gaberdine is uncompromisingly human and his words, vital and bitter as they may have been when Shakespeare wrote them, are far more so now through circumstances which have nothing whatsoever to do with *The Merchant of Venice*. These modern circumstances, however, and the pity that mixed itself with Shakespeare's ink as he drew the portrait, are no reason for sentimentalizing Shylock. The Jew is neither tragic nor comic, he is the villain, and although we may shed a tear as he walks alone and broken from the court, we must not lose sight of his villainy, nor must the fairy story lose its balance through him.

Why is Antonio sad? The problem has been left unresolved by Shakespeare, nor is it necessary to the action to know the psychological cause of it, any more than to know the psychological cause of Leontes's jealousy which opens, equally abruptly, *The Winter's Tale*. This sadness of Antonio has the elements of the beginning of a fairy story—'Once upon a time there was a merchant who was sad.' Although we must accept this situation in the fairy story way, just as we accept the fact that 'old King Cole was a merry old soul', I will here agree that the actor has need of some excuse on which to found his sadness, for though merriness is acceptable without reason, sadness is not. Is Antonio sad because he has a sub-conscious fore-knowledge of the trouble ahead? It seems most unlikely, since his affairs are going well. We know he is not in love, nor preoccupied with business. We know also that his close friend, Bassanio, has promised to tell him about a secret pilgrimage to a certain lady; that is the only known fact about his immediate mood, happy or sad, at the beginning of the play. The first question he addresses to Bassanio, as soon as the two are left alone, is 'Well, tell me now, what lady is the same to whom you swore a secret pilgrimage' [I. i. 119-20]. It is a direct question requiring a direct answer. But why should Antonio be sad that his friend has a love affair on hand? I don't know for certain, nor do I think a certain an-swer can be found, but I think we can agree without miscon-struing the friendship of Antonio and Bassanio that their friendship depends more on emotional attraction than on common interest, for Antonio is a merchant and Bassanio is a gentleman. The sad, industrious Antonio is attracted by this gay young spendthrift. This does not mean that he is jealous of his friend's love affair, indeed the signs are against such a conclusion, considering that Antonio furnishes Bassanio for the expedition to Belmont at peril of his own life. There is perhaps a clue to this sadness worth consideration. When Bassanio hints to Antonio of a plan he has in mind for im-proving his fortune, Antonio says:

I pray you, good Bassanio, let me know it;
And if it stand, as you yourself still do,
Within the eye of honour, be assured,
My purse, my person, my extremest means,
Lie all unlock'd to your occasions.

[I. i. 135-39]

Antonio is asking if Bassanio's plan to woo Portia is a strictly honourable affair. Portia's wealth is well known; suitors from all parts of the world travel to Belmont to gain possession of her fortunes. Antonio knows that his friend's fortunes are at a low ebb, that he has an easy way with money. Bassanio has just admitted as much to him. Is Bassanio joining up with the other adventurers with the sole object of enriching himself. Is he wooing Portia only for her fabulous fortune which is what later critics have accused him of doing? This is, I think, Antonio's fear and causes his melancholy, for he loves Bas-sanio and he would like to see him happily married. He would like to befriend him as an older and wiser man, who has no son of his own, and these Elizabethan gallants were attrac-tive, feckless individuals as Shakespeare knew in his early sonnets. Then Bassanio tells this tale:

In Belmont is a lady richly left,
And she is fair, and fairer than that word,
Of wondrous virtues; sometimes from her eyes
I did receive fair speechless messages:
Her name is Portia . . .

[I. i. 161-65]

And with these words, Antonio's sadness leaves him. Bas-sanio wants to go to Belmont because he has fallen in love; how deeply he probably does not yet know, but the glimpse of Portia that he has already caught in her father's time has remained fresh in his heart as her first glimpse of him has in hers. Antonio accepts the genuineness of Bassanio's passion and is prepared to do everything that lies within his power

to help him. Perhaps Shakespeare felt the same melancholy about Mr. W. H.

Are they Salerio and Solanio, or Salanio and Salarino, these two gentlemen who accompany Antonio and endeavour to find out the cause of his sadness? Not only are their names indeterminate—the Quarto has one version and the Folio an-other—but they seem somewhat indeterminate as people, to whom actors have given the derogatory name of the Salads. Traditionally they are played by the youngest and worst ac-tors in the company. I know, because I once played one of them myself and was chosen to do so because as well as being bad I was thought, erroneously, to be a well-to-do actor who wouldn't want a salary. This was, of course, before the days of Equity.

Traditionally, too, and perhaps as a result of the way they are so often cast, these parts are extensively cut. Who are these walking gentlemen who talk so much and appear to provide no more than a necessary cover-up for a scene change? Have they any character and what is their purpose? If we look at what they say we are most likely to hit upon the answer. So first let us close our eyes to the young Salads, with their tights in folds and their wigs askew, and listen to their words. In the first scene, there appears, to me at any rate, to be a differ-ence of character between them; for whereas Salarino, alias Salerio, is garrulous and rather futile, Salanio, alias Solanio, is both sober and restrained. It may be fancy but I cannot ac-cept them as young sparks, nor do I think that Antonio, a wise and royal merchant, would walk round Venice with two young gabbling puppies. I believe them to be merchants like Antonio, though not so prosperous. Perhaps their trade is confined to Venice, whereas we know Antonio is engaged in the import-export business. I find the words they speak to be more consistent with the sort of elderly merchants who stroll round the piazza of Venice or sit upon 'Change, than with young Elizabethan gallants. Moreover, I believe the Vene-tians in this play belong to two social classes: the merchant class of Antonio, and the gentleman class of Bassanio. If Bas-sanio has his Gratiano and Lorenzo to represent the compan-ions with whom a gentleman associates, surely Antonio is en-titled to a merchant's companions? And I believe this class grouping is important. The sympathy of an Elizabethan audi-ence for Bassanio is enhanced by the fact that he, a gentle-man, rushes to the aid of his friend, a merchant. Moreover, when Bassanio and his gentlemen companions go to Belmont and Antonio has been imprisoned by Shylock, we must feel that the merchant has been deserted by these powerful friends, but if Antonio is being followed round in the scene with Shylock and the gaoler (Act III, Sc. 3) by a gaily-dressed young gallant, the effect of his aloneness is lost; so, too, is the effect of the return of Bassanio and Gratiano. The purpose of the Salads is, I believe, to emphasize the position in the play of the merchant of Venice. But it is also more than that; what we said about the use of these two figures to pad out the play is also relevant, though for a different reason than mere-ly to give time for a scene change. Their job is to build up the situations and prepare us for the action that is to follow. In Act II, Sc. 8 they inform us of the successful elopement of Jessica and Lorenzo; in this and in Act III, Sc. 1, they prepare us for Antonio's disaster, and build up Shylock's rage at the loss of his daughter and his ducats in such a way as to make us laugh at Shylock. Perhaps Shakespeare knew the danger of Shylock winning our sympathy by the discovery of Jessi-ca's flight if he were allowed to play the scene of his return from the banquet on the stage. Henry Irving spotted the plum that Shakespeare had deliberately avoided, and like the great old actor he was, played the scene that was not written and cut the scene that was. So these despised Salads act as a chorus to the play as well as emphasizing and strengthening the merchant class against the Jews; and what is more right in *The Merchant of Venice* than to have merchants as a chorus.

Now let us take ship to Belmont and to the story of the caskets—a story which has often been declared intolerably boring. The mistress of this magic island is young, she says so; she is rich, we are told so; she is witty, we know her to be so. Her wit, like all good wit, can be mischievous. Portia enjoys mocking at the peculiarities of her suitors and deliberately invites Nerissa to 'over-name' them, so that she can amuse herself by recounting their eccentricities. For all her success as a doctor of law she is supremely feminine in this, as well as in her teasing of Bassanio over the lost ring. What are we to make of her character? A young, beautiful, witty girl, who must live in perpetual fear of being married to a Neapolitan prince who resembles a horse, a weeping Palatine count, a simpering French lord, a dolt of an Englishman, a quarrelling Scotsman, a drunken German, a black-a-moor Moroccan, or a really quite impossible gentleman from Arragon. Is this witty and cultured heiress really prepared to accept a husband whose sole claim to her heart is the fact that he chooses a lead casket? Has this woman, who is capable of outwitting the cunning Jew, no will of her own? Does she, perhaps, load the dice by hinting which casket her suitors should choose? To do so would be to suspect her honesty, for she swears she will die as chaste as Diana unless she be obtained by the manner of her father's will. And her father has decreed that only he who chooses the right casket shall inherit his daughter and her fabulous fortune.

The critics who declare this story of the caskets to be boring argue that everyone in the audience knows that Bassanio will choose the lead casket, and therefore the casket scenes lack dramatic tension. I can only reply that everyone in the audience knows that Cinderella's foot will fit the glass slipper. The producers who introduce such tricks as turning the song 'Tell me where is fancy bred' [III. ii. 63] into a subtle innuendo that 'lead' which rhymes with 'bred' is the right choice, or who introduce various oglings and pointings from Nerissa and Portia to indicate to Bassanio which casket he should choose, show a complete ignorance of the simplicity of a fairy story and forget how we can still be charmed by a land of make-belief. Let us please not destroy the poetry of the casket scenes by sniggerings and hints in a futile attempt to make the story naturalistic. The magic of the theatre does not depend only on suspense, and there is as much good theatre in a pantomime as there is in Ibsen. Belmont is and must remain a land where fancy is bred. Let us make it a fairy tale country with its sweet music, its moonlit banks, its ceremonious processions of suitors to Portia's hand and its simple but moving tale of the caskets. What of the outlandish suitors who come to make their choice? Morocco is often represented as a comic figure, but I think this is unfair to him and to Shakespeare's verse. As with the Shylock-Antonio situation, we have in the wooing of Portia by Morocco another form of the racial problem. Shakespeare was clearly concerned with the question of mixed marriage and dealt with it at greater length in *Othello,* but whereas he is prepared to vilify the Jew he seems to be sympathetic to the question of the coloured races. Nothing is more indicative of character than reaction to failure, and in the true English style Shakespeare shows his char-

acters' temper by the way they behave when they fail. Morocco takes the umpire's decision like a good cricketer:

> Portia, adieu. I have too grieved a heart
> To take a tedious leave: thus lovers part.
>
> [II. vii. 76-7]

We must conclude from his courteous behaviour and the majesty of his lines that the Prince of Morocco is a gentleman. With Arragon it is different; when he loses he shows bad temper, or at least petulance:

> Still more fool I shall appear
> By the time I linger here:
> With one fool's head I came to woo,
> But I go away with two.
> Sweet, adieu: I'll keep my oath
> Patiently to bear my wroth.
>
> [II. ix. 73-8]

We have, therefore, a right to regard Arragon as a pompous, self-satisfied prig, thoroughly deserving his reward—the portrait of a blinking idiot.

I would like to say one word about Portia's servants. Balthasar is responsible for arranging Portia's flight and seems to be her steward. As such I want him played with something of the mannered courtesy which will warrant Portia's remark to him—'What would my lord?' [II. ix. 85]. As her steward he is responsible for the ceremonious arrangements for the choosing of the caskets. Stephano is ordered to bring his music forth into the air, so we must presume him to be responsible for the music in Portia's household. I propose to make him into a zany, the sort of half-witted plaything who follows his mistress around like a dog, only half comprehending what is being said to her, but intensely conscious of her moods, rejoicing in her happiness with Bassanio, terrified of Morocco and Arragon. In this way he will reflect Portia's anxiety over the choice of the caskets and will help to build up the Arcadian atmosphere of the fairy tale island.

Although we have examined Shylock's position in the play, there remains the question of his background and family life which is important, in that it concerns his daughter's elopement and his own determination to press for his revenge. We have seen how the Venetians are divided into the social groups of merchants and gentlemen; equally we must consider the racial grouping of Shylock, Tubal and Jessica. To-day the Jewish communities outside Israel have on the surface been largely absorbed into the customs and habits of their adopted countries, but in the Renaissance age they remained a distinctive community preserving not only their religious and social apartness, but also their native habits and costume. The Jews are Orientals, rather than Occidentals, and lean more to the East than to the Roman world. So we would expect to find Shylock, Jessica and Tubal dressed in a fashion which is nearer to Persia than to London. By making this distinction of dress we are able to bring about a complete change in Jessica when she goes over to the Christian way of life, and emphasize that, when Shylock is instructed to turn Christian, he is in fact not only required to change his religion, but to change his clothes, and with them his behaviour and his whole way of living. The Orientalism of the Jews is emphasized by two scenes in the text: firstly, the scene in which Shylock shows his patriarchal attitude towards Jessica, bidding her lock herself close within the house (Act II, Sc. 5); secondly, the scene between Tubal and Shylock (Act III, Sc. 1) where Tubal appears to be deliberately provoking his fellow-countryman to madness. In fact, Tubal is a rival money-lender and however sympathetic he may feel towards the misfortunes of Shylock, he cannot resist the Oriental pleasure of seeing Shylock writhe beneath the whip of misfortune, nor can he forgo the pleasure of driving Shylock onwards as an instrument of racial revenge. Both Tubal and Shylock are professional money-lenders, and to the Jew as to the Oriental money-lending is a legitimate trade, sanctioned in the Jewish case by biblical authority. Thus for both of them Antonio, by his practice of lending out money gratis, is deliberately and wrongfully undermining their trade. It is an integral part of the Jewish way of life to make money and to thrive through cunning; this is no less true of other Oriental races such as the Egyptians and the Persians. To undermine usury is to undermine religion: 'You take my house when you do take the prop that doth sustain my house; you take my life when you do take the means whereby I live' [IV. i. 375-77]. It is not just the taking of his money from him that hurts, but the injustice of imposing upon one race the morality and customs of another. This distinction of cultures can be emphasized by providing Shylock, Jessica and Tubal with the sort of Oriental costume which separates them from the Europeans.

The last of the social groups which make up the characters of the play is that of the Gobbos, father and son. These are the low comedy elements which Shakespeare provides to contrast with the high comedy elements of his lovers. Launcelot is, as we know, Shylock's servant; as such his place in the early part of the play is to keep that dangerously human villain in his place as a villain. Shylock seen by us through Launcelot is a miserly and thoroughly unattractive master—'the very devil himself' [II. ii. 26]—from whose service Launcelot is justified in escaping. Launcelot's sole regret at leaving Shylock is that he has to part from the Jew's beautiful daughter, with whom he has a sympathy bred of mutual suffering. Thus beyond Launcelot's task of providing low comedy relief, there is the secondary, but no less important task, of enhancing Jessica's reputation and of condemning her cruel and tyrannical father. Once his task as a pillar of the play's construction is finished, Shakespeare wisely exiles him to Belmont, where his cheerful fooling can do no harm to the serious business of the trial.

This is the serious business of the fairy story. I have emphasized that the lovers are fairy story people, because they have so often been mistaken for the contrary, but every fairy story must have its drama and *The Merchant* is no exception. The trial scene is too well known to require much analysis, but I would draw your attention to two things; firstly, the skill with which Portia conducts her case, and secondly, the dramatic coup-de-théâtre with which she wins it.

Portia comes to the court uncertain of the outcome. There must be no suggestion, if we are to maintain the tension of the scene, that she knows she is going to win. She has learned from the lawyer, Bellario, certain scraps of Venetian law relative to aliens and citizens—such as the fact that if an alien seeks the life of a Venetian, his goods are confiscate—she has also learned that a bond legally entered into cannot be broken by any power in Venice. Legally, therefore, the Jew can claim his pound of flesh:

> Why this bond is forfeit,
> And lawfully by this the Jew may claim
> A pound of flesh . . .
>
> [IV. i. 230-32]

Bellario has told her the only hopes of saving Antonio depend, firstly, on the faint possibility that the bond has been badly drawn up—has any allowance been made for shedding human blood? And, secondly, on the possibility that Shylock himself has overstepped the law. If, for instance, Shylock has brought, or is prepared to bring, a surgeon into the court—however useless that individual would be under the circumstances—then Shylock cannot be accused of a deliberate attempt on a Venetian's life. If he has failed to do so, then he is guilty of attempted murder and the law can penalize him. But it would be extremely unwise for Portia to count on either of these possibilities. Every means must first be explored before testing such possible chinks. Portia starts her case by asking if Antonio confesses the bond. He replies that he does. Legally, therefore, the case is lost. There remains the possibility of an infringement by Shylock or a badly drawn up agreement. She appeals to the Jew for mercy, not that she expects him to comply, but because she must have time to assess her opponent, and since her case now rests on possible, but improbable, circumstances, she must first try every means open to her, other than the law. Lastly, she will try to draw the sympathy of the court to her client and against Shylock. If he refuses to show mercy then he, at least, cannot expect to receive a sympathetic hearing even if his case is sound. Next she tries to induce him to give up his case by playing on his well-known greed for money. Having tried these two methods of conciliation and having failed, Portia realizes that she must have recourse to the faint possibility that a mistake has been made by the notary who drew up the agreement. She asks to see the bond. Having read it, she suddenly realizes that in his haste for revenge the Jew has overlooked the details. There is no mention of blood. Now she knows Antonio to be safe, she can proceed to test the second possibility which, if it turns out to be true, will turn Shylock into a criminal. She makes an appeal to Shylock to show mercy by asking him to have by some surgeon to stop the flow of blood. When Shylock refuses this and when the knife is poised over Antonio's breast, Portia suddenly turns the tables on the Jew. He can have the flesh, but not a drop of blood. The scraps of Venetian law she has gleaned from Bellario fall into place: the law insists that to attempt to take a Venetian's life is a crime; had Shylock agreed to the presence of a surgeon and to taking all reasonable precautions to prevent Antonio's death, he would have left the court a free man, but his greedy desire for revenge has lost him more than his case. Why then does Portia delay the point and allow Antonio and Bassanio the agony of their final farewell? Because she must wait until the knife is actually poised over Antonio before she can claim that this alien is intending to kill a Venetian. Only when that act is undeniably proved is Shylock guilty of a crime against the state. During these last few minutes, between the realization of her success and the raising of the knife, Portia can afford to relax and be amused over Bassanio's offer to give up his wife to save Antonio's life.

This sudden realization by Portia of how to defeat Shylock is not only important theatrically, but also from the point of view of Portia's integrity; for if Portia is to come into court knowing from the beginning that she can save Antonio, then how can we regard her as other than a sadistic young lady who deliberately prolongs the agony of her husband's friend in order to win personal renown.

Of course we must agree that there is a fairy tale element about all this, otherwise how do Bassanio and Gratiano fail to recognize Portia and Nerissa when they are dressed as men? I don't think there is any need for desperate attempts to disguise Portia and her maid, other than by their male costume, for this make-believe atmosphere adds its own touch of lightness to an otherwise purely dramatic scene, helping to keep the play within the realms of 'once upon a time'.

To finish the fairy story we are led back to Belmont for the last scene. The villain has been defeated, the honest merchant rescued, and it remains only to round off this tale by uniting the lovers. After the grim story of the pound of flesh and the degrading sight of the cringing Jew, here is magic itself. The little pavilion rises, the lights change to darkness and shadows, above us are the stars. There standing in a shaft of moonlight are Jessica and Lorenzo gazing out in wonder at the splendour of the night:

> In such a night as this,
> When the sweet wind did gently kiss the trees,
> And they did make no noise . . .
>
> [V. i. 1-3]

and then come Portia and Nerissa to lean against the pillars and listen to the hymn to Diana; then their lovers, and by the light of the moon the raillery of the ring scene seems like the mating-dance of peacocks or the midnight gambols of March hares in the season of wooing. The females pirouette and decline the advances of the males, but at last they give way. As the first perfumes of the morning air rise, the little procession of lovers with Antonio moves off to answer all things faithfully. So the cover of the story book is closed and we creep upstairs to bed with the music and the poetry of this last scene lingering in our ears, forgetting if we can the lonely shadow of the broken outcast creeping back to his empty home. (pp. 149-66)

Hugh Hunt, "The Merchant of Venice," in his Old Vic Prefaces: Shakespeare and the Producer, *Routledge & Kegan Paul, 1954, pp. 147-66.*

Walter Kerr (essay date 1960)

[*Kerr proposes that the only way to resolve the critical conundrums raised by* The Merchant of Venice *and the proper portrayal of Shylock is to postulate that Shakespeare intended the character to be played as "a true comic giant." Kerr notes the tendency of productions to adopt one of two alternatives in the production of the play, neither of which leaves a flattering impression of the playwright: either Shylock is depicted as a stage villain, which leaves Shakespeare open to charges of anti-Semitism, or Shylock is portrayed as a tragic victim of race persecution, an interpretation that confounds the Belmont plot and suggests that the playwright "lost command of his craft." Kerr offers a third alternative, that Shylock is based on the traditional comic figure Pantalone, and was in fact represented as a comic character until Charles Macklin revolutionized the role in 1741.*]

Shakespeare is honored in many ways, but the most striking tribute we pay him today is in continuing to produce *The Merchant of Venice*.

Each production is, really, an act of faith, made in the face of the evidence. Every time anyone decides to mount the play he is saying, in effect, that Shakespeare cannot possibly have meant what he seems to mean, that the humane and penetrating intelligence we have come to know so well through thirty-six other plays could never have been capable of the unthinking, unfeeling anti-Semitism that poisons the portrait of Shylock.

The evidence to the contrary is formidable, both inside and outside the play. Within the fairy-tale structure of the piece, Shylock is most certainly the villain, a scoundrel whose harsh terms and ready knife constitute the only threat to the happiness of some of the nicest people who never lived. Shylock starves his servants, loves his ducats more than his daughter, and is altogether incapable of mercy. In addition to what Shakespeare has written there is the atmosphere in which he wrote: We know that the Jewish physician Lopez had just been executed for treason, that Marlowe's monstrous *Jew of Malta* had been making money in a rival playhouse, that the mood of the moment may very well have equated Jewishness with villainy. Shakespeare, great as he was, was also a man of his time: How can we be sure that *The Merchant of Venice* isn't an unconscious lapse on the part of a first-rate mind brought about by an error that was simply in the air, too much a commonplace to be questioned?

Stubbornly, and with a dogged intuition that there must *somewhere* be an explanation that will confound the plot of the play and the facts of Elizabethan life, we keep plunging into the embarrassments of the work in the hope that, one time or another, an actor's or director's inspiration will penetrate the mystery at its heart. There are clues that actors and directors have made much of. The "Hath not a Jew eyes?" [III. i. 59] speech stands there, a sudden and puzzling invitation to sympathy. This hated Jew may yet be a man. Shylock, mourning the theft of his turquoise, pauses to remember that "I had it of Leah when I was a bachelor" [III. i. 122]. This widower is clearly no monster. And, technically speaking, is Shylock ever wholly in the wrong? Antonio has understood and accepted the terms of the bond; no one has deceived him. Shylock never demands more than the terms of the bond; he is within his rights. The defeat of Shylock is not accomplished by strict justice, but by a trick. Isn't the Jew more sinned against than sinning?

The possibility that Shylock is as much a victim of Venetian society as certain improvident Venetians are the victims of his malice is the hint that has been most exhaustively explored in our time. The text has been all but X-rayed in the search for lines, phrases, hitherto unimagined attitudes that might help to justify Shylock and so acquit Shakespeare of the charge that is implicitly brought against him. In performance, all such lines, phrases, and attitudes have been carefully stressed; perhaps our commonest experience of the play in the theater is that of watching an edgy actor approach an uncomfortable passage with the thought, "How am I going to twist *this* scene so as to avoid offense and gain a little respect?" plainly written on his face. The other principals have been freshly re-examined. How admirable is this Antonio, who can barely refrain from spitting on a Jew while arrogantly taking his money? What sort of sponging fortune hunter is Bassanio, anyway? Can a more cold-blooded package than Jessica be imagined—a girl who abandons her father, steals his treasure, and turns Christian on demand?

From so much earnest inquiry has emerged a by now familiar Shylock: a man who is at the very least a dignified representative of an oppressed race and whose vigorous insistence upon his pound of flesh is the direct result of renewed insult, evasion, and betrayal by the Christian community; and a man who may, in the hands of a genuinely gifted actor, acquire something of the stature of a tragic hero, moving us to compassion and benediction as he stumbles brokenly from the courtroom.

Around him, the Venetian butterflies who pass their time in planning masked revels, marriages by guessing games, gay boy-girl disguises, and coy exchanges of rings, dance out their ephemeral lives under varying shades of light. In one production they become a tinseled, irresponsibly charming counterpoint to the main, more sober business of the evening. In another, they become a faintly melancholy echo of a romantic world that is vanishing under the burden of Venetian commerce and business-by-bond. In the production that may have brought every facet of our contemporary reinterpretation of the play into an ultimate balance—Tyrone Guthrie's staging for star Frederick Valk at Stratford, Ontario, in 1955—the sporting bloods of the Rialto were, for the most part, decadent bigots; Antonio and Bassanio were latent homosexuals, Belmont was peopled with opportunists, and the entire company joined forces in hissing, hooting, and spitting a stricken woolly bear of a Shylock out of the play. If this last series of images seems in any way excessive, it must also be said that Mr. Guthrie has given us the only recent mounting of the play that treated the play as though it were all of a piece. If Shylock is the hero, then the Venetians must be villains. And so they were.

But we are confronted now with the most disturbing evidence of all: that the persistent, humane effort to read sentiment into Shylock, even when that sentiment is actually achieved, does nothing to stabilize or illuminate the play as a whole; it merely succeeds in turning it upside down.

The late Frederick Valk, for instance, created a moneylender who was expansive, genial, even generous, and he was both believable and moving so long as the rest of Tyrone Guthrie's Venice was plainly in the wrong. The fact that Antonio, Bassanio, Portia, Lorenzo, and Jessica were in the wrong, however, effectively robbed us of any interest in their love affairs. Having watched them revile a decent man and drive him sobbing from the stage, we were disinclined to indulge them their lyrical fifth act; little patience was left for polite prattle about starry nights, forfeited rings, and the conjugal bed. Shylock appears in only five of the play's twenty scenes, with a sixth devoted exclusively to conversation about him. Three-fourths of the evening, then, and all of the major characters but one, had turned slightly sour.

This new, nervous imbalance—both of structure and of sympathy for the people at hand—is not always so marked as it was in Guthrie's uncompromising production. Most productions compromise, straining for the maximum dignity and tragic emotion in Shylock while straining for the maximum gaiety in the revels of his enemies. The effect, and we have been able to see at least six such *Merchants* in the past five or six years, is always disturbing. Shylock may have seemed dignified indeed in his exchange with the judge, only to flounder miserably, immediately thereafter, in the necessary but extremely undignified business of whetting his knife on his shoe. The line "I had it of Leah . . ." may have bolted from its context with stunning sentiment; but we are fretfully aware that the line has been isolated from its context, that the actor has most carefully suppressed the frighteningly comic touches on either side of it. Even in his own scenes, quite apart from his relationship to the light nonsense at Belmont, Shylock is inconsistent, unsettling. We come away complaining of one thing or another: the actor has not been able to sustain Shylock's tragic greatness, the other players have not been adroit enough to hoist the light scenes into the air, the director has failed to pull the "two tones" of the play into sat-

isfactory balance. After three, or six, or a dozen such productions, we reluctantly come to one of two possible conclusions: either Shakespeare never meant Shylock to be played so sympathetically, in which case he probably *was* anti-Semitic; or he did mean him to be sympathetic in the midst of all this foolery, in which case he was quite a clumsy playwright.

Both views, in effect, abandon the play. Those who come to the former conclusion simply refuse it performance, as certain high school and community theaters have done in recent years. Those who arrive at the latter conclusion go on patiently waiting for the superbly serious Shylock who is sure to come, while granting that, in the over-all management of the play, Shakespeare had temporarily lost command of his craft.

Since most of us are not quite willing to surrender the work, since there is so much in it that is irresistibly appealing, since Shylock himself will never stop teasing us, it is surprising that we have not had the energy to cast about for still another alternative—especially since one exists. There is always the hypothetical possibility that Shakespeare knew what he was doing, that what he was doing was writing a true comedy, and that he was able to sustain his single tone perfectly because in Shylock he had drawn neither a melodramatic villain nor a tragic hero but a true comic giant.

That the alternative exists, and ought to tempt us to experimentation, is plain enough. The play has always been called a comedy: it is so listed in the First Folio and in Francis Meres's catalogue of 1598. It was written circa 1596, not during the later period that produced the mixed tone of the "dark comedies," but somewhere between *A Midsummer Night's Dream* and *Much Ado About Nothing*. The oldest acting tradition has always held that, as John Munro reminds us in *The London Shakespeare*, "Shylock was apparently meant originally to be a ludicrous figure with a large nose and odd gestures which were mimicked by Launcelot." The tradition extended beyond Shakespeare's time: in his *Comic Characters of Shakespeare*, John Palmer insists that "Shylock as a comic character held the stage for over a century." The first known production after the Restoration, in 1701, featured the best-known comedian of the day, Thomas Doggett, in the role.

Indeed, there is no indication that Shylock was ever imagined as other than a comic figure until the revolutionary performance given by Charles Macklin in 1741. Whether Macklin made him a bloodcurdling villain (during the knife-whetting scene, reported a member of the audience, "Mr. Macklin was so highly characteristic in the part, that a young man who was in the pit fainted away") or a mixture of melodrama and pathos ("This is the Jew / That Shakespeare drew" enthused Pope) is not certain. What is certain is that Macklin shattered the earlier tradition and paved the way for the somber, or at least sober, Shylock we elaborate today. Macklin "rescued Shylock from the crudities of the low comedian" is Phyllis Hartnoll's verdict in *The Oxford Companion to the Theatre*.

Perhaps so. But there is something faulty in the rescue work: both character and play continue to prove troublesome and unresolved. Is it possible that the way Shylock was played in Shakespeare's time, and for nearly one hundred and fifty years thereafter, is the right way, the only practical way if the piece as a whole is to prove satisfying?

The thought horrifies us. Are we going to make Shylock a villain again and poke crude fun at him besides? Are we really prepared to double the offense we may give to Jews in the audience, while we confirm, in spades, Shakespeare's suspected anti-Semitism? The promised spectacle of a "ludicrous figure with a large nose" dancing grotesquely about the stage so that Portia and Antonio can go scot-free and the play become a unified piece of comic writing, so revolts us that we avert our eyes and cut our contemplation short.

But we have, in our quick dismay, neglected to ask certain obvious questions. What makes us think that the original comedy performance was a *low* comedy performance? Who played the part?

Not one of the low comedians, if the conjectural cast lists worked out by T. W. Baldwin can be accepted as reasonably accurate. The company's principal clowns—Kemp and Cowley—were occupied elsewhere: Kemp as Launcelot, Cowley as Old Gobbo. What sort of actor was left, then, for a funny Shylock? Apparently our Jew was the property of one Thomas Pope, creator of a quite different species of fool: Falstaff, Sir Toby Belch, Jaques, Benedick, Mercutio.

The line of parts is interesting. Thomas Pope would seem, on the face of it, to have been a comedian, most probably a superb one; and his particular humorous vein must have been capable of absorbing some fascinating complexities: a streak of knavery, a streak of melancholy, a flash of fire. One other quality leaps out of the line: the parts are one and all, no matter what skulduggery they may embrace, sympathetic. In these hands Shylock is not likely ever to have been a simple, despicable buffoon.

Even so, the likelihood that Shylock was once one of a certain brotherhood of outsize, attractive rogues does not wholly clarify the man for us. Neither Falstaff nor Jaques is really Shylock; we still lack a precise, practical, playable image, the sort of image that might have come into Shakespeare's head through a hint in his sources or in one or another comic convention of the Elizabethan stage.

The supposed sources for the play suggest very little along this line. The story of the bond appears in very early folklore, when the holder of the bond was not yet a Jew, but the atmosphere of the legends is essentially melodramatic. The Jew, the bond, the passionate love for a lady of Belmont, the lady's disguise in a court of law, and the forfeited betrothal ring are found in combination as early as 1378, in Fiorentino's *Il Pecorone;* but a translation of this work was probably not available to Shakespeare, and he is thought to have picked up the outline by hearsay, without a specific tone attached. The commercial popularity of Marlowe's *Jew of Malta* may have induced Shakespeare to write his play; but the play he wrote and the Jew he created bear only the most superficial resemblance to Marlowe's savage inventions.

These sources, which Shakespeare may have carved up and recombined in his characteristic fashion, might very well lead us to a violent Jew, a voracious Jew—but not to any comic Jew that Thomas Pope is apt to have played. Was there *no* familiar image, no elderly, moneygrubbing, fantastically funny fellow, *anywhere* in the Elizabethan storehouse to help set Shakespeare in motion and the rest of us on a likely scent?

There was such an image, just such a fellow. His name was Pantalone, and he appeared endlessly, with many droll variations but with a few indispensable comic trade-marks, in the improvised performances of the Italian *commedia dell' arte.* (The players improvised from standard scenarios, many of which survive.) That Shakespeare and his associates knew Pantalone and his retinue is quite clear. *Commedia* troupes

began visiting London as early as 1574. Companies returned at intervals thereafter; one is thought to have spent the entire season in London during the year of Shakespeare's arrival from Stratford. Playwrights Thomas Heywood, Thomas Kyd, and Ben Jonson all mention these *farceurs,* with their repertory of Harlequins, Dottores, and—in the Anglicized spelling—Pantaloons. Among the papers left by Burbage's greatest actor-rival, Edward Alleyn, were four *commedia* scenarios, in the oldest of which *Panteloun* appears. Shakespeare himself, of course, made reference to this salty, drooling, somehow venerable figure in *As You Like It,* and elsewhere came to call his own fools "zanies," after the *zanni* of the Italian travelers. Pantalone was, as a suggestive theatrical image, available.

Who was he, what was he like? To begin with, he was a merchant of Venice. He was old, wealthy, and had his fortune tied up in shipping. When one of his cargoes was destroyed by storm or pirates, he tore his beard and spat into the sea in impotent rage. He was a miser.

"All his life long," as Pierre Louis Duchartre reconstructs him for us, "he has been engaged in trade, and he has become so sensitive to the value of money that he is an abject slave to it." His precious ducats are eternally on his mind. He is swiftly suspicious, sure that someone is going to swindle him. To help save ducats, he starves his servants. His hungry valet frequently threatens to leave him. The old father of the hungry valet sometimes comes to intercede for his son. The valet invariably mimics his master's speech, behind his back.

Pantalone has a daughter, with whom he is severe. She is an ingénue in love, eager for marriage, more eager still to be out of her father's tyrannically run household. Secretly she makes arrangements to meet her lover, usually by means of letters smuggled out by the friendly, conniving servant. When the chance comes, she elopes, often taking a supply of ducats along with her. Pantalone boils in rage, driven nearly out of his wits by his daughter's behavior. Others are delighted to see him so beset, he is such a "skinflint" and "calamity-howler."

At the last, Pantalone is the butt of the joke—robbed of his ducats, deceived by his daughter, the sputtering, breast-beating, hair-tearing victim of his own greed.

He carries, of course, a large purse at his belt. He also carries a sizable dagger. He is quick to draw and brandish the dagger when outraged, which is rather often; somehow or other, though, he is never permitted to use it. Vocally, to take a cue directly from Shakespeare, "his big manly voice, turning again toward childish treble, pipes and whistles in his sound" [II. vii. 161-63]. This shrill, shuffling, furiously gesticulating patriarch is only an inch or two shy of senility. For clothing, he wears a long black cloak, a rounded black cap, and either soft slippers or Turkish sandals. He has a prominent hooked nose.

In the *commedia* scenarios and eyewitness reports that survive, Pantalone has still other characteristics. Sometimes, for instance, he is an amorous old fool bent on marrying again, a trait that Molière took hold of and elaborated brilliantly in several of his finest comedies. In the process of making varied use of the Pantalone figure, however, Molière did not neglect the particular bundle of crotchets, nor the precise story line, we have just been describing. One of his masterpieces, *The Miser,* presents us with a greedy, near-senile Pantalone (Harpagon) whose daughter deceives him, whose servants groan over the food allotted them and helpfully conspire with the daughter, whose money is stolen, and whose comeuppance is the result of his own greed. No one questions the derivation of Harpagon from Pantalone; we have simply neglected, I think, to draw the same conclusions from the same materials in the case of Shylock.

While it is unlikely now that anyone will ever be able to *prove* that Shakespeare took his Shylock from his memory of Pantalone, the catalogue of similarities is too striking to be dismissed. As will be obvious, each item in the catalogue appears—with a surprising minimum of alteration—in *The Merchant of Venice*. Nor do the resemblances end with the character of Shylock; through Jessica, Launcelot, Old Gobbo, and possibly Tubal, they extend to the general personnel, the incidental comic episodes, and the romantic story line of the play. When bound with the casket sequences and the lyric fifth act, these touches become part of consistent light-comedy pattern, notes struck in a single true chord.

We might add, speculatively, that the chord itself— Shakespeare's image of Venice and all that might pass in it— may have come from his experience of watching the Italian troupes play; these *were* Italian, they *knew* Venice, they exuded its spirit in a style that was both mocking and accurate; they constituted Shakespeare's most intimate, direct, and reliable sense of the atmosphere of the Rialto.

Pantalone does suggest Shylock, just as the standard *commedia* story of a charming ingénue who outwits her foolish, niggardly father suggests at least one of the plot lines and much of the atmosphere of the play as a whole. But does Shylock suggest Pantalone? Going back to the text with these performance images in mind, does Shylock *read* as a comic, garrulous, sputtering, excitable, stingy old goat?

We have tried so hard to read the lines in every other conceivable way that fresh hearing, uncluttered by prejudicial associations, is next to impossible. But let's make the effort. Shylock is introduced this way:

> *Shylock.* Three thousand ducats: well.
> *Bassanio.* Ay, sir, for three months.
> *Shylock.* For three months: well.
> *Bassanio.* For the which, as I told you, Antonio shall be
>   bound.
> *Shylock.* Antonio shall become bound: well.
>
> [I. iii. 1-6]

What are those repetitions all about? What is that rhythmic "well" doing there? Don't they sound, on quick acquaintance, like the mumbling, lip-smacking, beard-moistening reiterations of the amusingly aged? Abstracted from their context they might do as a pattern for a vaudeville routine, that familiar one in which the blear-eyed comic gropingly reiterates the instructions his straight-man is giving him until he is ready for the surprise switch. In the context of the play, they create precisely the kind of comic rhythm that lends itself to burlesque imitation by one of the secondary fools— which, of course, is what Launcelot Gobbo takes advantage of a little later in the evening. Indeed, if Launcelot's mimicry is to be effective, the initial rhythm—and the actor's management of it—must be inherently funny.

The longer speeches into which Shylock soon plunges are marked by absurd pedantry (he is constantly explaining what is already clear), further chatterbox repetition, and the device of a long list of negatives swiftly followed by a simple, complacent positive. The devices are all stock equipment for the comedian. Shylock has, in addition, a leering sense of humor of his own; he rather fancies himself as a jokester, doing his best to make a merry jest of the bond itself and indulging himself in casual throwaways (asked if his money has the potency of ewes and rams, he murmurs "I cannot tell. I make it breed as fast" [I. iii. 96]). It is not difficult, here, to recognize the bland, obsequious humor of the man who thinks himself cleverer than anyone else, who rubs his palms and chuckles happily as he spreads molasses for the flies and thinks lovingly of the future; he is at once crafty and transparent, a combination calculated to make him comic.

The next we hear of Shylock we hear from his hungry servant Launcelot ("I am famished in his service. You may tell every finger I have with my ribs" [II. ii. 106-07]) and from his put-upon daughter ("Our house is hell" [II. iii. 2]). The material is unmistakably giddy, topped by a romantic letter secretly delivered by the conniving servant; Shylock's household is established by a stand-up clown improvising pure nonsense.

When Shylock himself appears a scene later, the Pantalone-like stinginess recurs as he washes his hands of his servant (who was "a huge feeder" [II. v. 46]), the senile pedantry returns as he gives Jessica instructions for the night ("stop my house's ears, I mean my casements" [II. v. 34]). The phrase "I did dream of money-bags tonight" [II. v. 18] is so blatantly grotesque in its wording that it cannot be anything other than a cartoon of avarice. There are also three basic comedy bits in the scene: the business of Shylock's being of two minds, shouting for Jessica below a window and pursuing a completely different thought at the same time; the business of the shout being echoed, unexpectedly, by a too-helpful servant, startling Shylock and causing him to turn on the servant; the business of Shylock's not quite hearing a sly exchange between the servant and his daughter, leading Shylock to ask what was said and Jessica to misreport it. Add to this the fact that Launcelot and Jessica are, throughout the scene, playing *against* Shylock's abstracted, slightly frantic mood, punctuating his scattered instructions with puns, irrelevancies, malapropisms, and—we may suppose—sly winks.

Once Jessica and the ducats are gone, we do not immediately see Shylock in his anguish. The anguish is reported to us—in itself a suggestion that it is going to be humorously handled— and reported to us not by fellow Jews who might view Shylock's plight sympathetically but by friends of Bassanio's who can only view it with comic relish. Is the report truly comic? Why does it not strike all actors—as it does almost all audiences—that "my ducats, and my daughter!" [II. viii. 17] is a roaring incongruity, a pairing of values so mismatched that their juxtaposition seems the very soul of comedy? If one or another value gains a little edge in importance as the harangue goes on, it is the ducats and not the daughter—the scales fall not toward sentiment but toward the absurd. And the incongruity is stressed in that splendid burst of incoherence, "O my Christian ducats!" [II. viii. 16]. As Solanio says of it, "I never heard a passion so confused" [II. viii. 12].

What of the scene in which we *do* meet the ravaged Shylock? Its structure, after the introductory exchange between Shylock and Bassanio's friends, is completely, explicitly comic. Even the introductory passage has its familiar echoes, the obtuse and literal overexplanation ("I say, my daughter is my flesh and my blood" [III. i. 37]), the monomaniac repetitions ("Let him look to his bond" [III. i. 47]); even the "Hath not a Jew eyes?" speech begins with one of Shylock's snappish jokes (asked what Antonio's flesh is good for, he raps out "To bait fish withal" [III. i. 53]). But here is what happens in the scene proper. Tubal informs Shylock that Jessica cannot be found. Shylock is at once in the abyss, wallowing in those same comic incongruities Solanio found so "outrageous" ("I would my daughter were dead at my foot, and the jewels in her ear!" [III. i. 87-9]). Tubal next reports that Antonio has had ill luck. Shylock ("What, what, what?" [III. i. 99]) is swiftly transported to seventh heaven ("Good news, good news! Ha, ha!" [III. i. 106-07]). Tubal mentions that Jessica is thought to have spent fourscore ducats in one night. Shylock dives to despair. Tubal speaks of Antonio's creditors. Shylock soars. Tubal speaks of a ring Jessica has traded for a monkey. Shylock writhes in torment. Tubal remarks that Antonio is undone. Shylock bursts into a fever of delighted activity.

Up down, up down, with the sentences growing tighter, the exhilaration and the agony coming closer together, Shylock is alternately sobbing and gleeful in ever faster reversals until he is all but spun off the stage. The trick remains, of course, standard property among comedians today.

As we move toward the courtroom, Shylock's frenzied bout with Antonio and his jailer is a kind of popped-corn rehash of all the repetitions, rationalizations, and caterwaulings we've by now become accustomed to. And, in briefly renewing our acquaintance with Jessica, we are given a significant scene which is now most often omitted in production: a lively, witty, playful, extraordinarily candid passage in which the entire Jewish-Christian theme is made light-hearted sport of ("This making of Christians will raise the price of hogs" [III. v. 23-4]). The scene is delightfully in keeping so long as the play is regarded as a thoroughgoing comedy; it is normally abandoned in our own mountings, I suppose, because the mountings themselves make it inexplicable.

In the courtroom Shylock is impudent to the judge, fawning with Portia, shrill in his glee over "A Daniel come to judgment" [IV. i. 223], filled with a wonderfully pious righteousness ("Shall I lay perjury upon my soul? No, not for Venice" [IV. i. 229-30]), whimpering when defeated ("Shall I not have barely my principal?" [IV. i. 342]), and protected in tone at every turn by Portia's own little jokes and Gratiano's ebullience. Through it all, he whets his knife on his shoe, gleefully anticipating the victory to come, sassing the Duke who bids him to desist. That this business is irretrievably funny may be best attested to by every actor who has tried to play it as though it were not. The image is, simply as an image, outrageously, preposterously ludicrous; in ever so sober a production the snickers cannot be stilled. It is possible that Shakespeare, who knew a comedy bit when he saw one, did not intend embarrassed snickers but wholehearted belly laughs.

These are the devices that the part and the play are made of, the comic carpentry on which both structures rest. Let us suppose that Shylock *could* be played as a delightful dervish of a Pantalone, and that the comedy as a whole would profit by the vision. Clearly, we have not yet accounted for everything. Though the "Hath not a Jew eyes?" passage begins in a joke, it moves on to something else; to a quite firm defense of Jewishness and the common humanity of Jews and Christians. Though the "Leah" line is surrounded by comic images, it is in itself instantly moving, a catch of breath in the middle of a laugh. If Shylock is the English cousin of an Italian vaudevillian, where does that pathos come from? Precisely where it has always come from, I think: from that unex-

pected stab of sorrow that so often accompanies the comic image when it is raised to its highest power.

The likelihood that pathos will emerge from the most outlandishly, even grotesquely, conceived cartoon stems from a very simple principle: all truly funny figures are necessarily sympathetic figures. If a man makes us laugh, we like him. He may do quite terrible things in pursuit of the objects of his lust, his avarice, or his spite; because he delights us in his outlandishness, in his methods, in his mania—and because we are quite sure he is going to be as delightfully discomfited—we feel no emotional revulsion for the things he does, or for his person. We secretly admire him; we look forward eagerly to his next appearance on stage; in an oddly inverted but very understanding way, we feel for him. And because we feel for this enchanted buffoon, we can always be, delicately, touched by him. It is perfectly clear to us that Chaplin can kick a child at one moment and involve us emotionally at the next. (I recently took my wife to a revival of an early Chaplin film; her response at the end was "Why do you say it's funny? *I* cried!") Yet the dominant Chaplin image is funny; the pathos wouldn't stir if it weren't.

A considerable complexity is required of any comic figure if so sobering a note is to be embraced, and to be embraced without destroying the dominant image. That the original Pantalone is capable of nearly infinite extension and very rich variation is amply demonstrated by Molière; we do not have to look to Shakespeare alone to find it. Molière's Harpagon (*The Miser*) and Arnolphe (*The School for Wives*) are both Pantalones, closely derived from the *commedia* form; and they are both, in Molière's hands, men of vast stature and psychological subtlety. Nor can any villainy they may do force us to despise them. Indeed Arnolphe comes at last, in *his* up-and-down torment between raging anger and tender devotion, to a note of brokenhearted submission:

> You want to see me weep? And beat my breast?
> You want to have me tear out half my hair?
> Or shall I kill myself? Is that what you want?
> Oh, cruel girl, I'm ready to prove it so.

That last line is no longer quite comedy; it is Arnolphe's way of saying "Hath not an old, ugly man the power to love?" But Molière pulls him back quickly from this hint of a heart; the note is only faintly struck; Molière's characteristic tone, even when his characters are at their most complex, is one of detachment.

Not so Shakespeare's. Shakespeare is at his most characteristic, in dealing with outsize buffoons, in his management of Falstaff. Falstaff is a coward, a bully, a liar, a lecher, a tosspot. And he can be hurt, hurt so badly that it hastens his death. When we at last ask what was the special contribution of Shakespeare's genius to the tangle of sources that might have given birth to any such character, we can answer: the power of introducing strong feeling into the most Rabelaisian of rogues without breaking the mold that made him essentially merry. There is no reason to suppose that he might not have been able to do the same thing, with the assistance of the same actor, for Shylock.

If we are to imagine Pantalone as a playing model for Shylock, then we are not obliged to stop at the simple, playful level of senile rhythms and servant-slapping horseplay; we are free to imagine Pantalone risen to the complex comic stature and psychological brilliance of the best worst man in Molière; and we are further free to see in him the levels of sentiment that Shakespeare divined in the biggest boozers and most brazen scalawags he knew. It's a tall order, and one that has not been delivered in more than two hundred years. Ralph Richardson might bring it off. The Bert Lahr of *Waiting for Godot* might just possibly make it stick.

What of the Jewishness? Pantalone, with his black cloak, black cap, and exceedingly prominent nose, was not Jewish. In the process of dovetailing sources, Shakespeare can have taken the Jewishness from the *Il Pecorone* tradition, from the commercial popularity of Marlowe's play, from the talk current in London after Lopez's execution. Wherever he took it, what he took was a stereotype: the medieval stereotype of the Jew as avaricious. He took it *as* a stereotype; there were too few Jews then living in England for Shakespeare to have had extensive personal knowledge of the race. Insofar as he borrowed the stereotype at all, and he probably borrowed it for commercial reasons, he cannot be absolved of a certain opportunism, of having lent himself to the exploitation and perpetuation of a disparaging legend. (He behaved even more badly, and for just as poor reasons, toward Richard III.) The fact in itself is unpleasant, and we will have to live with it.

We had best, however, not be smug about the matter. It should first be remembered that Shakespeare would have employed the stereotype as matter-of-factly, and with as little malice, as an American playwright of the early twentieth century making uncritical and even affectionate use of those other stereotypes, the superstitious Negro and the drunken Irishman. Furthermore, Shakespeare might have treated his borrowed equation in one of two ways. He might have made the Jew a bloodcurdling melodramatic villain, as most of his sources had done. Or he might have taken the kinder course and made him comic, which is what I think he did do. In the public mind, the progress of social adjustment moves something like this: from the alien as menace to the alien as buffoon to the alien as human being. It is quite conceivable that Shakespeare actually furthered understanding by nudging this process into its second stage. I do not say that he did this deliberately; but he had noticed that a Jew—and especially a funny Jew—had eyes. If we can imagine an accepted stereotype slowly and mysteriously taking on, under its manipulator's instincts, a broad and rather affectionate grin—as the superstitious Negro did when Mark Twain got around to Nigger Jim, or, more pertinently, as the drunken Irishman did when Sean O'Casey decided to make us fond of the loutish Captain Boyle—we may have come closer to measuring Shakespeare's peculiar achievement, and to the image in his mind as well. The Shylock we find on our stages is ambiguous, nervous, not very attractive in spite of his tears; Shakespeare's Shylock—if he was as funny as the earliest tradition tells us he was and as Thomas Pope might well have made him—may easily have been more likable. (pp. 90-6)

Walter Kerr, "In Search of Shylock," in Horizon, *Alabama, Vol. II, No. 3, January, 1960, pp. 89-96.*

Tyrone Guthrie   (essay date 1965)

[*Guthrie, who successfully staged his own production of* The Merchant of Venice *at Stratford, Ontario, in 1955, here identifies Antonio as the pivot of the play's plot, although for a number of reasons, which he enumerates, "it is almost impossible to make Antonio dominate the play." Nonetheless, a successful production, according to Guthrie, will find a way to focus on the eponymous merchant, while presenting "a fantasia on the twin themes of mercy and justice, in which none of the charac-*

ters fully exemplify either, [and] in which none of the characters is either wholly good or wholly evil."]

Who is the Merchant of Venice? Shylock's part is the most striking and effective, and he is arguably *a* merchant. However, he is absolutely not a Venetian. I think Shakespeare referred in the title not to Shylock but to Antonio. He is the pivot of the story; his kindness enables Bassanio to woo Portia; to make the loan to Bassanio he puts himself in the power of Shylock; he is an example of gentleness and unselfishness, in striking contrast to all the other principal masculine characters. But even Antonio's gentleness does not extend itself to Shylock, the Jew. Like all the other Venetians in the play, not excluding the Duke at the extremely irregular trial, he shows marked anti-Semitic prejudice.

On this account it has been argued that the play is an anti-Semitic document. But surely, to conclude that the attitude of his Venetians represents Shakespeare's own attitude is as wild as to assume that, because he wrote *Macbeth, Hamlet* or *Richard the Third,* he condoned regicide. The Venetian attitude in this respect is stressed to show the moral climate in which Shylock had to live; it explains, and to a great extent excuses, both his and Jessica's conduct.

Several factors, although his is the title role, combine to put Antonio in the shade. First, Shylock is a much better part—a highly colored portrait in Shakespeare's most exciting vein. Second, the relation between Antonio and Bassanio is not meant to suggest that of uncle and nephew, or just two friends, but that Antonio is in love with the younger man. I will argue this case more fully in a moment, but, granting it temporarily, it is obvious that the idea is expressed between the lines, not baldly and explicitly. In epochs when conventional respectability was of great importance—the nineteenth century, for example—the hint of an "irregular" relationship will have been studiously ignored. Thus this theme will have been omitted from the play and the character of Antonio will therefore have been rendered more simple. He just becomes an entirely uninteresting, "good" man.

The third reason why Antonio, from reading the text, does not seem a very important or interesting character is that in two of the play's important scenes, though he is absolutely central to the meaning of both, he hardly speaks: I refer to the trial scene and the finale.

When you read the trial scene it is the duel between Shylock and Portia that almost exclusively occupies the attention. Gratiano and Bassanio have "moments." The Duke, as the president of the court, must be accorded a certain prominence. But what of the prisoner?

Frequently, even in the theatre, the prisoner passes almost unnoticed. Very often, I think, the set-up and opening moments of the scene are mishandled. The Duke's entrance is importantly arranged, and when he has reached his place he speaks the appointed line: "What, is Antonio here?" Antonio, already in place (and usually a rather inconspicuous place since the most effective acting positions are held in reserve for Shylock and Portia) answers, "Ready, so please your Grace" [IV. i. 1-2].

I believe that it is not only Shakespeare's intention, but also theatrical common sense, that, since this is Antonio's trial, he should be, if not the principal figure, at least one of the focal points of interest. Shylock and Portia have well-prepared, effective entrances. Common sense dictates this, but it is also apparent from the text.

Antonio, I contend, should also have an important entrance. This is less apparent from the text, but it can very easily be contrived and with no detriment to the entrance of the Duke. The Duke must, of course, have a pompous entrance with procession, fanfare and so on, to the limits of the production's budget. He has to represent the pomp, might, majesty, dominion and power of Venice at the height of her greatness. Besides, the more his entrance is built up, the better by contrast will be that of Antonio, provided that it comes later than that of the Duke. Let the Duke enter with all the theatrical pomp which can be contrived. Let him ask, "What, is Antonio here?" Then let a small and dismal door open from the cells, possibly a trap-door from below, and let Antonio appear between officers—in prison dress, pale, nervous, the very antithesis of the sleek, prosperous merchant we knew before his ruin. Then let him be conducted to a dock, so placed that constantly throughout the scene the focus may be thrown on his reactions to proceedings that are to him literally of vital importance.

The trial scene then becomes an important acting scene for Antonio, and when his turn comes to speak, it is not an interpolation by a half-forgotten personage, but an utterance for which the audience is waiting.

Antonio's speech, when it comes, seems at first glance to be disappointing. It is, to use professional jargon, emphatically "cued-in" by Portia: "You, merchant" ("merchant," note, apropos of the title), "have you anything to say?" [IV. i. 263]. One expects a tirade of some kind, a burning self-justification, a thrilling defiance of Shylock, even a monumental farewell like Cardinal Wolsey's in *Henry VIII*. But no. At first glance, and even at second, the speech seems strangely lacking in dramatic impact.

What is the explanation? Did Homer nod? Did Shakespeare try, and fail, to write a movingly eloquent speech? Is the speech—this, I think, is the customary interpretation—a deliberately dull utterance to suggest a dull character? I cannot see what possible advantage Shakespeare could have had in making Antonio a bore. Nor is he so in other parts of the play. Nor, were he intended as a bore, would the play's title be what it is. It would be called *Shylock* or *Portia*—on the analogy that in all the others of Shakespeare's plays that bear the name of a character, the title-part is the central figure.

What then?

I think the significance lies in the fact that Antonio's last words are addressed to Bassanio and in open court. Bassanio is the person who means most to him in the life he is just about to forfeit. He is in no position to pour out intimate, passionate thoughts and feelings. It is a constrained, stiff-upper-lip speech, but nevertheless a final protestation of love, ending with a gallant little attempt at a joke. If an actor playing Antonio keeps this in mind, I believe that the effect can be moving, and the more constrained and embarrassed the manner of delivery, the more moving the speech can be.

I am sure that the intention of the speech is to be moving from the fact that Bassanio's answering protest draws from Portia an "aside" which is undoubtedly meant to make the audience laugh. The theatrical structure is a poignant tension broken by a laugh, and any experienced comedian will confirm that

the laugh will come only if the preceding tension has been achieved.

It was consideration of this speech which convinced me that Antonio's relation to Bassanio is what our grandparents called a "tender" one. Granted this, his loan of the money for Bassanio to go to woo the heiress of Belmont becomes much more than the rather easy gesture of a very rich man. And it is ironic that it is his very generosity that brings about his downfall.

Further, it gives infinitely more point to the final scene. Instead of being just a frolic, in verse of incomparable elegance, by the four young people, it is immensely enriched by the presence of the solitary figure of the older man. Not only Bassanio but, on the evidence of the aside in the trial scene, Portia, too, is aware that he loves Bassanio.

I have seen an effectively contrived ending to the play, when the lovers went in to bed, with their jokes and rhymes and laughter still echoing in the garden, where Antonio is left solitary, the papers which confirm the safety of his argosies in his hand. As the lights faded, he slowly let the papers fall at his feet.

Nevertheless, when all is said and done, in the theatre it is almost impossible to make Antonio dominate the play. Although he is the pivot of its plot, and although theoretically it seems to be planned as a conflict between justice and mercy, of which the two protagonists are Shylock and Antonio, it does not work out that way. In the culminating scene of the trial, it is Portia, not Antonio, who is the advocate of mercy; Antonio is relegated to the passive role of Shylock's victim.

It is not generally realized what a long part Portia is. She is in more scenes than any of the other characters and must dominate each scene she plays. I had not realized how important the part was until I directed a production in which Portia was entirely miscast—a sweet, motherly young woman, the epitome of middle-class respectability. The more we stuck her with jewels and decked her up in pink satin, the more she resembled the Railway Queen of some remote junction; the harder she tried to be witty and sophisticated, the more she sounded like a hospital nurse reading a script prepared for somebody else. At the other end of the scale is the star actress who brings a battery of accomplishments to bear and suddenly turns Portia into a wily mantrap, mangling poor Bassanio in her rusty jaws, while, in the trial scene, everyone's sympathy instinctively transfers itself to Shylock as he gets hell beaten out of him by the most formidable female advocate of all time.

The truth is that the part was written for a boy, and exploits both the attributes and the limitations of a gifted boy-player. The companies with which Shakespeare was associated trained youngsters for the stage from a very early age. And the best evidence to their capacity is the fact that Shakespeare was willing to write Viola, Imogen, Rosalind and Portia, knowing that there would be boys fit to interpret them.

The masquerade of Portia and Nerissa in the trial scene really makes sense only when the girls are played by boys. Two boys are no more, and no less, convincing as Doctor and Doctor's Clerk than as Portia and Nerissa; whereas in the modern theatre, two actresses, who seemed credible as Portia and Nerissa, appear at the trial disguised in a manner which makes us feel either that the play has suddenly changed into operetta, or else that the Duke must be a dim old personage indeed not to see that they are a pair of young ladies and have them arrested for contempt of court.

Shylock has been the subject of so much comment and controversy that little more need be added here. It is my view that Shakespeare's portrait is not anti-Semitic, that the pound-of-flesh wager was entered upon as a jest and only turns to vengeance after Shylock has been robbed and his daughter abducted by young Venetians of Antonio's set. In fact, after the trial, and after Portia's great invocation of mercy, it is the Christians who lack all mercy toward their enemy. The sadistic vengeance taken upon Shylock is as offensive to Christianity as it is legally outrageous. To say this to Jews in the present epoch is as useless as to beg the rain not to fall. There is a rooted tradition among Jews that the play is an anti-Semitic document, and it is indeed true that many Jewish boys at school have, through generations, been taunted and execrated as "Shylock." This is to the shame of all humanity. But the remedy is not, I sincerely believe, to boycott Shakespeare's play, and pretend that it does not exist, but to interpret it so that it becomes, as its author intended, a fantasia on the twin themes of mercy and justice, in which none of the characters fully exemplify either, in which none of the characters is either wholly good or wholly evil, and in which his rightful place is accorded to the Merchant of Venice. (pp. 97-103)

> *Tyrone Guthrie, "Hidden Motives in Five Shakespearean Plays," in his* In Various Directions: A View of Theatre, *The Macmillan Company, 1965, pp. 72-109.*

B. Iden Payne   (essay date 1967)

[*Payne, an actor and director who staged over one hundred productions of Shakespeare and served as General Director at Stratford-upon-Avon from 1935-43, describes a performance of* The Merchant of Venice *as it might have appeared on an Elizabethan stage. Payne argues that because Shakespeare's plays were composed with a specific stage in mind, it is essential for a successful production of a play and a full understanding of the author's meaning to approximate as closely as possible the stage conditions in which the play was originally produced.*]

It is not my present purpose to give an account of all that can be gathered or surmised about Shakespeare at work but only of one aspect of it, namely, the consideration of whether, in constructing his plays, he held in mind and made use of the facilities of the theatre in which they were to be performed. There is a practical value in this. Long experience in various kinds of Shakespearean production has convinced me that something approximating to the main features of the Elizabethan theatre (as usually understood) is not only the most suitable but is even essential if the desire of the director is not self-exploitation but an honest determination to make the plays come to life for a modern audience.

The "something approximating" is what I have called Modified Elizabethan Production.

The flexibility of the Elizabethan stage is a commonplace; and it is frequently recognized that some means ought to be found for achieving the continuity of acting. But, generally speaking, it is not fully recognized that continuity must be, to use a musical analogy, as absolute as the playing of a piece of music from beginning to end. The movement of screens or similar devices makes the action jerky and so destroys that unbroken flow of action which can only be described as

Shakespeare's melodic line of scene development. Even the drawing of curtains across the stage near the proscenium is fatal to the flow of action because that movement is subconsciously associated with a feeling of finality—the feeling that something has been finished and something new is about to begin. Even in theatre-in-the-round—not good for Shakespeare anyhow for his plays require a background—there is a detrimental break in the action when furniture is changed.

But it is a curious psychological fact that if there is an open space between each column of the penthouse and the nearest door (as on the Elizabethan stage) then, provided a new group of characters enters while the curtains are closing, the spectator feels that the sequence of scenes brings no interruption to the action, one scene flows into another.

I learnt gradually. It was the hard school of experience which taught me that the modified method of Shakespearean production is the best, if not the only way of bringing a Shakespeare play into harmonious concord with any audience. At the end of the nineteenth century it was not unusual for a young man who had decided upon acting as his career to go straight upon the stage without preliminary training. It was easy to get an engagement in touring companies for the demand was greater than the supply. In my own case an early love of Shakespeare made me feel fortunate when I had the opportunity to join the best Shakespearean company on the road in England at that time. It was under the management of its leading actor, F. R. Benson, afterwards Sir Frank Benson. He had a fine company, but for the mounting and style of production of the plays he followed the firmly fixed conventions of the time; naturally enough, for they were regarded as the right and proper way. It was taken for granted that every scene shown to the audience had to be realistically presented. Consequently, as in a sort of Procrustean bed, scenes were freely transposed or omitted. Also at any great climactic moment even if it was in the middle of a scene (such as Claudius stopping the play-within-the-play in *Hamlet*) the act drop was lowered with a storm of applause and curtain after curtain followed as prelude to an intermission. All this resulted in blatant distortion of the text. But of this, like nearly everybody else, I was unaware.

Before long my principal interest in the theatre shifted to what was then regarded as the "new drama" and for the time being Shakespeare was in abeyance in my regard. But in 1907 when, in spite of my youth (I was twenty-six at the time), I was chosen to take in hand the foundation of Miss A. E. F. Horniman's Company at the Gaiety Theatre in Manchester—the first modern repertory theatre in England—I was anxious to bring any sincere theatrical novelty to the attention of the public. I had heard vaguely about the Elizabethan Stage Society, just enough to know that its work would probably help my purpose, so I approached its founder and leading spirit, William Poel. With some difficulty, for he did not care to work with seasoned professional actors thinking they would be too set in their technique and he had peculiar views about the speaking of verse which he feared they would resist, I persuaded him to produce *Measure for Measure* bringing with him the Elizabethan Stage Society's setting and costumes. It seems astonishing to me now (partly no doubt because at that time I was immersed in the performance of my own part, Lucio, for which Mr. Poel cast me, thus not being able to see the production as a whole clearly), but I thought about the production as being interesting and as a curiosity; as one newspaper critic put it, no more than a "museum piece." Naturally, therefore, when a year later I ventured upon my own Shakespearean production at the Gaiety Theatre, I mounted it in the conventional Victorian manner that I had learnt with Benson but making the representational scenery as simple as possible.

However, my interest was more and more swinging back to Shakespeare, and beginning in 1916 it became customary for me to undertake an annual spring production of a Shakespeare play at Carnegie Institute of Technology. My mind went back to *Measure for Measure* at the Gaiety and a nagging feeling grew that I might have missed something. I was against the idea of trying to make a reproduction of an Elizabethan performance—I thought that would be a barren academic exercise—but I wished to find some intermediate form which would make it possible to present Shakespeare's text unadulterated. I finally found in what I have called the Modified Form of Elizabethan production what I believe to be a satisfactory solution.

The modifications are few but trenchant. The use of symbolic or even representational scenery both before, within, and behind the inner stages; sometimes of both. Curtains to the penthouse hide the changes of scenery and properties from the audience. They are closed and opened by curtain boys dressed in clothes of the period depicted in the production. The only additional modification from Elizabethan practice is the free use of modern lighting effects.

It was not, however, until 1926 when I became the chairman of the drama department that I had a full opportunity to put the modifications into operation. When I did so I had some startling experiences. I found that by imagining oneself to be Shakespeare himself producing one of his own plays in the Globe Theatre, instance after instance was disclosed where his practical dramaturgy was seen to be at work, especially in the allocation of the different portions of the stage to the scenes as they unfold—the zones of interest as I call them. In this his skill and artistry is revealed in a sphere to which little, if any, attention has been given. Shakespeare, of course, sometimes wrote plays—*Love's Labors Lost* is the earliest of them—for production primarily in places where the theatre facilities were absent. But with these I am not now concerned. My present purpose is to show Shakespeare at work in the theatre on one of the plays obviously written with the Globe Theatre in mind. For no other reason than that it is so well-known I have selected The *Merchant of Venice*.

Whether or not Shakespeare had before him an earlier play on the same subject (as is highly probable), his problem in arranging the fable of the *Merchant of Venice* for the stage was that he had to integrate two diverse themes—that of Shylock and the "merry bond" and that of Portia and the caskets. Let me briefly recall the material as Shakespeare arranged it. Bassanio, a young aristocrat of Venice, is in love with Portia and eager to undertake the hazard of the casket choice. His friend Antonio offers the use of his credit to raise money to equip him for his voyage to Belmont. Antonio signs a bond with Shylock which stipulates that if he fails to repay the debt by a certain date he will forfeit a pound of flesh. Other suitors fail, but Bassanio guesses correctly and so wins Portia. But Antonio, unable to meet the due date of the bond, is arrested. When the case comes up for trial, Shylock, infuriated because his daughter Jessica has eloped with a young Christian called Lorenzo, is inexorable though offered three times the value of his bond. Portia disguised as a judge confounds Shylock by proving that his own life will be forfeited if blood is shed

in the cutting of the pound of flesh. Portia, in lieu of her fee, asks for the ring she had given to Bassanio as an eternal bond of love. Bassanio reluctantly surrenders the ring, and Nerissa, Portia's lady-in-waiting, likewise secures a ring that she had given to Gratiano, her newly wed husband and Bassanio's friend. The play ends in reconciliation between the two couples after a scene of pretended indignation by Portia and Nerissa against their husbands for having parted with the rings.

To blend the diverse themes it is necessary for the action to oscillate between Venice and Belmont. The play begins in Venice, and Antonio agrees to raise the money not having the cash in hand. The scene is expository of the Shylock theme and it is more than likely that, as in the majority of the plays, this exposition was presented by the actors on the forestage in order to be in the closest possible contact with every member of the audience. (The forestage was also used when a group of characters was on the way somewhere, for processions, and for low-comedy scenes which were not integrated into more important scenes. Such scenes were frequently necessary to give the audience the feeling that time passes.)

In the next scene the spectator is introduced to Portia in Belmont and the zone of interest moves back to the middle stage, the space under the penthouse. The change of locale was further indicated by opening the curtains to the lower stage behind which the caskets were exposed to the audience. That the caskets were shown in this way is proved by the fact that Nerissa speaks of them not as *the* three caskets but as "*these* three caskets," a clear indication that they were revealed to the audience, obviously in the Inner Below.

The use of the caskets having been established, the curtains to the inner stage were closed and the audience found themselves back in Venice for the scene where Antonio agrees to sign the merry bond. Now scenes are to follow later where the doorway of Shylock's house is shown to the audience. The side doors are too generalized in action for anything so particular as an individual house. What is more likely, then, that Shakespeare settled its place for the spectator at this point? I do not think it is a far-fetched assumption to conclude that it is probable that in the preceding scene Portia and Nerissa moved downstage at the entrance of the Servant (later to be known as Balthazar) while the caskets were removed and a doorway was placed between the curtains of the partially open Inner Below to be used as that of Shylock's house. At any rate, it is very effective in the modified production to take advantage of having the penthouse curtains by closing them at the point just mentioned and to re-open them to begin the next scene with Shylock in his doorway and Bassanio standing by and explaining the reason he had come to see him. In any case, the scene is unquestionably an exterior, for Antonio is later seen to be approaching from a distance.

The action then returns to Belmont. The scene deals with the arrival of one of Portia's suitors, the Prince of Morocco. But the caskets are not visible this time for he asks to be led to them, a request which Portia postpones until after dinner. It seems that Shakespeare was not ready to let Morocco make his choice, but the scene was necessary to give the feeling of the passage of time and Shakespeare used it to remind the audience about the casket theme; therefore Morocco is merely "on the way" to the caskets.

In the next scene (II, ii) there is no question about the necessity of the door to Shylock's house for it begins with Launcelot

Gobbo slipping out of it to tell us that he is tempted to break the law by running away from his indentured service but he learns that Bassanio has already arranged with Shylock to accept him as a member of his retinue.

The next scene is still in Venice and consists of a few lines only. Jessica bids Launcelot farewell and gives him a letter to deliver secretly to her lover, Lorenzo. Later in the play Jessica is to appear at the window of her room just before her elopement. It seems highly probably that Shakespeare, the cunning artificer, here made use of a necessary expository passage to shift the attention to a new zone of interest which will be necessary later by having this short scene played in the window above the door of the house. Here is necessary matter discussed and, simultaneously, an interesting shift to a new zone of interest! One can imagine Shakespeare feeling rather pleased when he thought of this device.

The next scene (II, iv) is a forestage scene: there can be no doubt about that. It is both "on the way" and serves to indicate the passage of time. Plotwise it gives Launcelot an opportunity to deliver Jessica's letter to Lorenzo and to forward our knowledge of the coming elopement.

Act II, v and vi, are continuous, both laid before Shylock's house. In the first he bids farewell to Jessica on setting out to Bassanio's feast and the second is the elopement. The text at the end of the latter scene is rather odd. Jessica greets Lorenzo from the window and comes down. Lorenzo and his friends carry out their purpose by running off with her, and Shakespeare indicates the end of a scene with the customary rhymed couplet. Why, then, one asks, did he tack on to it, apparently for no reason, eight unnecessary lines? Antonio needlessly tells Gratiano who is to accompany Bassanio that he is being waited for at the ship. That is all. But the next scene takes us back to Belmont, this time to bring the caskets into service. The extra lines are explained! They are, in effect, a separate little scene, ending again in a rhymed couplet, during which the inner curtains were closed and the caskets put behind them in readiness for Portia's "Go, draw aside the curtains, and discover the several caskets to this noble prince" [II. vii. 1-2].

Another passage-of-time scene follows on the forestage in which we are told that Antonio has lost some of his ships at sea and that his position is dangerous if the bond is not paid in time. In the following scene we are again in Belmont for the Prince of Aragon to lose Portia by making his wrong selection of the silver casket. Then—the action is swift here—there is another switch to Venice where in an obvious forestage scene we hear about Antonio's danger and witness Shylock's hysterical outbreak at the loss of his daughter and his jewels. After this we once more find ourselves in Belmont for the crucial scene where Bassanio wins Portia by his right choice and Portia sends him back to Venice to save his friend.

There follows a short street scene on the forestage inserted to depict Shylock as being now wholly set upon revenge. We then move our attention to the middle stage, the zone of action being again in Belmont—this time without the caskets—in which Portia tells Nerissa about her plan for them to assume male disguises and for her, Portia, to act as judge when Antonio is brought to trial.

The next scene—still in Belmont—appears to be quite unnecessary from the literary point of view, but when its purpose is understood its presence is shown as an interesting example of where Shakespeare can be seen at work. The attention

comes back to the forestage. Lorenzo and Jessica, in charge of Portia's house, jest with Launcelot about Jessica's conversion to Christianity increasing the price of pork. Well, the court room had to be set, of course, and the feeling of time passing again established. But why does the prose scene appear to be unnecessarily lengthened by verse passage which in no way helps the plot and which contains eight lines praising Portia as a fine woman, a fact with which we are already familiar and sympathetic enough? This at first appears to be so much dead wood. But the anomoly is explained if one concludes that in rehearsal it was found that the boys who played Portia and Nerissa took longer to change from feminine to masculine attire than had been anticipated!

For the trial scene I have found that a setting with the Duke of Venice on his throne on a raised platform, with his magnificos on each side of him on a lower elevation, and two long narrow tables with a space between them set below at which sit the Clerk of the Court and other lawyers and with places reserved for Portia and Nerissa, is so effective and so strikingly convenient to the action that one cannot but wonder whether it was not the very way in which it was originally played.

After Portia's triumph in the trial scene the story line provides a short forestage scene wherein Gratiano catches up with Portia in the street to receive Bassanio's ring and to make it clear that Nerissa will get her own. This serves as preparation for the complete change in the tone of the play for the final scene. Shakespeare had one final technical problem to meet and he overcame it magnificently. Literary critics may be shocked, but it is the fact that we owe the lovely night scene between Jessica and Lorenzo and the passage in praise of music to the fact that Portia and Nerissa again required time to change back, this time from masculine to feminine clothing. Shakespeare made a magnificent virtue of a necessity by taking the opportunity to express his own love of music and his conviction that it was a powerful agent in developing the soul of man. But indeed he manages to transfuse into the whole of the act, even the comedy about the ring, a deep feeling of the calm and peace of a summer's night.

This summary of the masterly manner in which Shakespeare articulated the arrangement of scenes in his plays should, I hope, convince the reader that the director working in the modified Elizabethan form has great satisfaction in feeling at close quarters with Shakespeare while at work. The warm response of the audience is the final source of gratification. (pp. 327-32)

B. Iden Payne, "Shakespeare at Work in His Theatre," in Educational Theatre Journal, Vol. XIX, No. 3, October, 1967, pp. 327-32.

FURTHER READING

Reviews and Retrospective Accounts:

Atkinson, Brooks. "First Night at the Theatre." *The New York Times* (5 March 1953): 20.
    Contends that in skirting the "unpalatable elements in the char-

acter," Luther Adler's "dignified, thoroughly modern interpretation" of Shylock "leaves the play listless."

―――. "*Merchant of Venice* is Revived Uptown." *The New York Times* (23 February 1955): 23.
   Declares that this Shakespearewrights' production, staged by Marjorie Hildreth, was "youthful," as evident in the vitality of the performances. Earle Hyman's portrayal of the Prince of Morocco stands out among a generally strong cast, which included Thomas Barbour as Shylock and Laurinda Barrett as Portia.

―――. "They Have a Style: Two Shakespeare Comedies Well Staged at the Festival in Connecticut." *The New York Times* (18 August 1957).
   Identifies two highlights of Jack Landau's American Shakespeare Festival production of *The Merchant of Venice*: Rouben Ter-Arutunian's "beautiful and vibrant" sets, and Morris Carnovsky's complex, realistic, and deeply human Shylock.

Barbour, Thomas. Review of *The Merchant of Venice*. *The Hudson Review* VI, No. 2 (Summer 1953): 278-86.
   Argues that Luther Adler's sympathetic portrayal of Shylock, whatever its individual merits, nevertheless transformed the play "from a light-hearted comedy into an angry sociological treatise," because the villainy Shakespeare intended to portray in Shylock was thrust back onto the play's romantic characters.

Barnes, Clive. "Shylock and the Anti-Semites." *Plays and Players* 10, No. 3 (December 1962): 52-3.
   Argues that Michael Elliott's Old Vic production was original and stimulating in its portrait of Venice and its avarice, but was nevertheless at odds with the spirit of the play. Lee Montague played a dignified Shylock; however Sheila Allen's Portia often seemed "diametrically opposed to Shakespeare's."

―――. "Theater: Another Look at *Merchant*." *The New York Times* (10 June 1970): 39.
   Affirms that a sympathetic portrayal of Shylock, such as that presented by the Stratford, Ontario, Shakespeare Festival and directed by Jean Gascon, is ultimately contrary to Shakespeare's design and the romantic, fairy-tale scheme of the play. Donald Davis played a noble Shylock and Maureen O'Brien was a "spirited and girlish" Portia. Given the play's "racist overtones," the critic speculates that *The Merchant of Venice* may not be stageable in the modern theater.

―――. "Stage: Modern *Venice*." *The New York Times* (5 March 1973): 23.
   Asserts that Rosemary Harris's thoughtfully conceived Portia was the highlight of this production at Lincoln Center. Although director Ellis Rabb took considerable liberties with the text and fashioned a Shylock, played ably by Sydney Walker, that was somewhat at odds with Shakespeare, it was a handsome, entertaining production, according to Barnes.

Beckerman, Bernard. "The Season at Stratford, Connecticut." *Shakespeare Quarterly* XVIII, No. 4 (Autumn 1967): 405-08.
   Maintains that Morris Carnovsky's Shylock far exceeded all other performances in this American Shakespeare Festival production, with Barbara Baxley as Portia, and staged by Michael Kahn.

Bernard, John. *Retrospections of the Stage*, Vol. 1. Boston: Carter and Hendee, 1832, 235p.
   Recalls, in Chapter 4, Charles Macklin's Shylock. Bernard writes, "I consider it to have been a chef d'oeuvre, that must be classed with the Lear of Garrick, . . . and the Coriolanus of John Kemble."

Biggs, Murray. "A Neurotic Portia." *Shakespeare Survey* 25 (1972): 153-59.
   Contends that Terry Hands's 1971 Stratford production of *The Merchant of Venice* depicted a Portia, played by Judy Dench,

who was far too troubled and threatened by Bassanio's and Antonio's friendship. According to Biggs, Hands's interpretation was antithetical to Portia's character and overlooked her powers of forgiveness and her ability to dissociate symbols, the ring, from meanings, Bassanio's fidelity.

Billington, Michael. Review of *The Merchant of Venice*. *Guardian* (6 February 1989).
   Deems Peter Hall's romantic comedy "fleet, agile, and well-spoken." Dustin Hoffman's subdued, sardonic Shylock achieved some measure of pathos but also meant a loss of the tragic dimension." Geraldine James played Portia "excellently, as a woman of strength and poise."

Bingham, Madeleine. *"The Great Lover": The Life and Art of Herbert Beerbohm Tree*. New York: Atheneum, 1979, 293 p.
   Includes a brief account of Tree's 1908 appearance as Shylock.

Boaden, James. *Memoirs of the Life of John Philip Kemble*, Vol. 1. London: Longman, Hurst, 1825, 477 p.
   Book II, Chapter 2 includes a description of Macklin's straightforward, emphatic acting style and the considerable impact he made with his decidedly uncomic portrayal of Shylock.

Brahms, Caryl. "The Taste of Raisins." *Plays and Players* 8, No. 10 (July 1961): 8-9.
   Assesses an Old Vic production of *The Merchant of Venice*, directed by Peter Potter and featuring Robert Harris as a convincing, if not tragically towering, Shylock, and Barbara Leigh-Hunt as "a witty and sympathetic Portia."

Brown, John Russell. "Shakespeare Festivals in Britain, 1956." *Shakespeare Quarterly* VII, No. 4 (Autumn 1956): 407-10.
   Brief notice of the Margaret Webster production at Stratford, featuring Emlyn Williams as Shylock and Margaret Johnston as Portia.

―――. "The Royal Shakespeare Company 1965." *Shakespeare Survey* 19 (1966): 111-18.
   Surveys the 1965 Stratford season, including a production of *The Merchant of Venice* directed by Clifford Williams and featuring Eric Porter as Shylock.

―――. "Free Shakespeare." *Shakespeare Survey* 24 (1971): 127-35.
   Surveys British Shakespearean productions of 1970, including the National Theatre's production of *The Merchant of Venice*, directed by Jonathan Miller.

Byrne, Muriel St. Clare. "The Shakespeare Season at the Old Vic, 1956-57 and Stratford-upon-Avon, 1957." *Shakespeare Quarterly* VIII, No. 4 (Autumn 1957): 461-92.
   Discerns little vitality in Michael Benthall's production of *The Merchant of Venice*. Barbara Jefford's Portia appeared languorous, and Robert Helpmann's Shylock lacked variety of expression.

Clurman, Harold. Review of *The Merchant of Venice*. *The Nation* 176, No. 12 (21 March 1953): 253-54.
   Argues that Luther Adler's original, sympathetic Shylock was compelling and "well conceived," but that ultimately the performance, staged by Albert Marre, was "emotionally thin" and "small." In addition, maintains the critic, little else in this production supported Adler's novel interpretation.

―――. Review of *The Merchant of Venice*. *The Nation* 185, No. 3 (3 August 1957): 58-9.
   Avers that the American Shakespeare Festival's production was visually pleasing, but lacked a coherent, interpretive focus. Morris Carnovsky, according to Clurman, played a traditional but nonetheless captivating Shylock, and Katharine Hepburn played Portia.

―――. Review of *The Merchant of Venice*. *The Nation* 216, No. 12 (19 March 1973): 380.
   Lauds director Ellis Rabb's deliberate staging through which

the play's dominant theme clearly emerged: "a 'parable' of the corruption of a society that founds its chief values on money." The clarity of the "message" compensated for the poetry lost in Rabb's subdued, slow-paced direction. Sidney Walker played a dignified Shylock, and Rosemary Harris performed impressively as Portia.

Colin, Saul. Review of *The Merchant of Venice. Plays and Players* 4, No. 12 (September 1957): 16-17.

Pronounces Katharine Hepburn's Portia "one of the best ever performed." Colin also commends Morris Carnovsky's Shylock and Jack Landau's staging of this American Shakespeare Festival production.

Cook, Dutton. "The Merchant of Venice." In his *Nights at the Play*, pp. 279-82. London: Chatto and Windus, Piccadilly, 1883.

Praises Ellen Terry's Portia and the impressive sets of this 1879 production staged by the Bancrofts at the Prince of Wales Theatre. So captivating was Terry's Portia, and so weak was Mr. Coghlan's Shylock that "probably for the first time, the portions of the play that relate to the loves of Portia and Bassanio became of more importance and interest than the scenes in which Shylock appears," according to Cook.

David, Richard. "Of an Age and for All Times: Shakespeare at Stratford." *Shakespeare Survey* 25 (1972): 161-70.

Maintains that behind the deficient sets and costumes of Terry Hands, the 1971 Stratford production of *The Merchant of Venice* was a strongly conceived, well-balanced and executed performance.

Denham, Reginald. *Stars in My Hair*. New York: Crown Publishers, 1958, 256 p.

Recalls the author-actor's appearance as Salanio in Bernard Fagan's production of *The Merchant of Venice* at the Court Theatre. The Dutch actor Louis Bouwmeester played Shylock in his native language while the rest of the cast spoke in English, yet, as Denham relates, his powerful performance "overflowed the stage. We were merely 'props.' "

Edinborough, Arnold. "Shakespeare Confirmed: At Canadian Stratford." *Shakespeare Quarterly* VI, No. 4 (Autumn 1955): 435-40.

Praises director Tyrone Guthrie's skillful balancing of the tragic and comic elements in *The Merchant of Venice*. In addition, Frederick Valk's powerful performance as Shylock simultaneously repelled and attracted sympathy. Edinborough also lauds Frances Hyland's Portia.

————. "A Gallic Romp Through Shakespeare: An Account of the 1970 Season at Ontario's Stratford Festival." *Shakespeare Quarterly* XXI, No. 4 (Autumn 1970): 457-59.

Affirms that in divesting Donald Davis's Shylock of his essential Jewishness director Jean Gascon sacrificed the play's pathos. The critic praises the production's scenic elements.

Edwards, Christopher. Review of *The Merchant of Venice. The Spectator* (6 October 1989).

Deems Peter Hall's production "accomplished and beautiful to look at," providing an "illusion of balance and smooth transition in a play that . . . lacks anything of the kind." Dustin Hoffman's Shylock was subdued and sardonic, rather than heroic, to the critic's enjoyment, and the rest of the cast, featuring Geraldine James, was excellent.

Esslin, Martin. Review of *The Merchant of Venice. Plays and Players* 19, No. 11 (August 1972): 44-5.

Assesses Terry Hand's "simple and straightforward" production of *The Merchant of Venice* at the Aldwych theater by the Royal Shakespeare Company, featuring strong, well-balanced performances by much of the cast, including Emrys James as Shylock.

Farjeon, Herbert. "Is Shylock a Bore?" and *"The Merchant of Ven-*

ice." In his *The Shakespearean Scene: Dramatic Criticisms,* pp. 54-5, 55-6. London: Hutchinson & Co, 1949.

Rates John Gielgud's portrayal of Shylock "the finest he has done since his Old Vic days." The performance was remarkable, according to Farjeon, for its subtle evocation of sympathy through a reliance on the text rather than overt gestures. Peggy Ashcroft made a striking Portia, the critic states, but she lacked a commanding presence. In the second essay, Farjeon affirms that Frederick Valk's 1943 performance of Shylock at the New Theatre was "a tower of excellence." Nothing else in the production, including Kay Bannerman's featherweight Portia, could match Valk's commanding presence.

Findlater, Richard. "Shylock, Lear and Antony (1953)." In his *Michael Redgrave: Actor,* pp. 118-32. New York: Theatre Arts Books, 1956.

Describes Redgrave's preparation through historical research for the part of Shylock and traces critical response to his powerful, unsentimental, villainous portrayal.

French, Philip. "Anti-Semitism." *The New Statesman* 74, No. 1905 (15 September 1967): 331-32.

Expresses disappointment at Ralph Richardson's sinister depiction of Shylock at the Haymarket Theater. In this vein, according to the critic, the production, whether intentional or not, appeared anti-Semitic.

Gardiner, William. "Oratory." In his *The Music of Nature,* pp. 57-8. Boston: Oliver Ditson & Co., 1838?

Analyzes the vocal qualities of Edmund Kean's performances, including his Shylock, by transcribing some of Kean's lines into musical notation.

Gelb, Barbara. "Great Scott!" *The New York Times Magazine* (23 January 1977): 10-12, 35, 38, 40-1.

Relates the course of the actor George C. Scott's career with reference to his critically acclaimed Shylock.

Gibbs, Wolcott. "Tract for the Times." *The New Yorker* XXIX, No. 4 (14 March 1953): 61.

Admires Luther Adler's subdued portrayal of Shylock, but notes that, consequently, some of the power of the famous speeches was lost. The critic protests that the performances of the balance of the cast were "hardly more than adequate."

Gilder, Rosamond. Review of *The Merchant of Venice. Shakespeare Survey* 7 (1954): 116-17.

Avers that in Luther Adler's "deliberately quiet, almost evasive interpretation" of Shylock the poetry is sacrificed and the passion is absent.

Gill, Brendan. "And Still Champion." *The New Yorker* XLIX, No. 3 (10 March 1973): 102, 104.

Argues that the true champion of this Lincoln Center production of *The Merchant of Venice* was Shakespeare's text, which endured the intrusions of director Ellis Rabb and still sparkled. Sidney Walker acted Shylock, and Rosemary Harris, "beautiful but, alas, too old" played Portia.

Goldman, Frederick. "When Lear Spoke Yiddish: 100 Years of Jewish Theater." *The New York Times* (19 September 1982):

Recalls the career of Jacob Adler and his widely successful appearance as a proud and passionate Shylock.

Greenwald, Michael L. " 'The Owl and the Cuckoo'." In his *Directions by Indirections,* pp. 81-114. Newark: University of Delaware Press, 1985.

Describes John Barton's 1979 and 1981 Royal Shakespeare Company productions of *The Merchant of Venice,* with Patrick Stewart and David Suchet playing Shylock and Sinead Cusack as Portia. Greenwald includes numerous critical references attesting to the popularity of these productions.

Halio, Jay L. " 'This Wide and Universal Stage': Shakespeare's Plays as Plays." In *Teaching Shakespeare,* edited by Walter Edens et. al., pp. 273-89. Princeton: Princeton University Press, 1977.

Examines the 1970 Jonathan Miller-Laurence Olivier production of *The Merchant of Venice,* particularly its mid-Victorian setting, as a means of investigating the legitimacy of adapting Shakespeare to modern settings. Using the Miller-Olivier production as his example, Halio argues that the reading of Shakespeare must be complemented by attending an actual performance which, when well conceived and performed, will enhance the meaning of the text.

Hawkins, F. W. "The Idol of the People." In his *The Life of Edmund Kean,* Vol. I, pp. 125-53. London: Tinsley Brothers, 1869.

Recounts Kean's debut as Shylock on 26 January 1814 at Drury Lane. Hawkins relates in somewhat anecdotal fashion Kean's innovative performance and the warm reception he received.

Hayes, Richard. Review of *The Merchant of Venice. Commonweal* LXII, No. 6 (13 May 1955): 149-50.

Commends the unity and overall conception of this production, directed by Marjorie Hildreth and featuring Thomas Barbour's "ideal Shylock": "smarmy and rapacious, supremely picturesque, a pointed finger of malice."

Hazlitt, William. *A View of the English Stage.* Edited by W. Spencer Jackson. London: George Bell and Sons, 1906, 358 p.

Contains two Hazlitt reviews of Edmund Kean's definitive performance of Shylock, in 1814 and 1816, originally printed in the *Morning Chronicle* and the *Examiner.*

Hewes, Henry. "Shylock vs. Shakespeare." *Saturday Review,* New York XXXVI, No. 12 (21 March 1953): 28.

Avers that the balance of the cast, as well as the "dramatic structure and elevated language," was sacrificed to Luther Adler's conception of Shylock, whom the actor portrayed as a dignified, reasonable, compassionate family man.

———. Review of *The Merchant of Venice. Saturday Review,* New York L, No. 30 (29 July 1967): 34.

Affirms that the balance between comedy and tragedy realized by director Michael Kahn in his American Shakespeare Festival production yielded "a sunny and leisurely pleasant performance." Morris Carnovsky performed admirably as Shylock, as did Barbara Bixley as Portia.

Hirsch, Foster. Review of *The Merchant of Venice. Educational Theatre Journal* 25, No. 4 (December 1973): 511-13.

Asserts that Ellis Rabb's "Felliniesque" modern-dress, contemporary interpretation of the play illuminated rather than betrayed the essence of Shakespeare's text. The cast included Sydney Walker as Shylock and Rosemary Harris as Portia.

Hope-Wallace, Philip. Review of *The Merchant of Venice. Time and Tide* 37, No. 17 (28 April 1956): 484-85.

Affirms that Margaret Webster's Stratford direction emphasized visual effects at the expense of poetry and characterization. However, Margaret Johnston's Portia was pleasing, and the audience appeared captivated. The critic claims Emlyn Williams's Shylock lacked passion and intensity.

Hughes, Alan. "Henry Irving's Tragedy of Shylock." *Educational Theatre Journal* 24, No. 3 (October 1972): 249-68.

Provides a thorough scene-by-scene description and analysis of Irving's Lyceum production, featuring Ellen Terry as Portia. Hughes makes extensive use of period reviews in order to portray Irving's Shylock and characterize the critical reception to his successful performance and production.

———. *"The Merchant of Venice,* 1 November 1879." In his *Henry Irving, Shakespearean,* pp. 224-41. Cambridge: Cambridge University Press, 1981.

Provides an extensive analysis of Irving's sympathetic portrayal of Shylock and his long-running production of *The Merchant of Venice* at the Lyceum. The essay includes a discussion of the

"theatrical context," Irving's treatment of the text itself, and the actual performance, replete with contemporary critical references.

Keown, Eric. Review of *The Merchant of Venice. Punch* CCXXIV, No. 5869 (1 April 1953): 418.

Contends that some of the effect of Michael Redgrave's "sinister, powerful" Shylock was "lost in excess." Keown deems Peggy Ashcroft's Portia "exquisite." Denis Carey directed this Stratford production, in which Harry Andrews played Antonio.

Kleb, William E. "Shakespeare in Tottenham-Street: An 'Atheistic' *Merchant of Venice." Theatre Survey* XVI, No. 2 (November 1975): 97-121.

Analyzes the Bancrofts' 1875 *Merchant of Venice,* arguing that the production represents and is emblematic of a transitional period in theater history when two ideals were in conflict: the desire for strict realism and historical accuracy versus an emerging scenic or aesthetic style of production. The Bancroft production is also noteworthy for casting Ellen Terry as Portia, a role that helped establish her reputation as one of the finest artists of her time.

———. "E. W. Godwin and the Bancrofts." *Theatre Notebook* XXX, No. 3 (1976): 122-32.

Examines the role played by E. W. Godwin, a mid-Victorian architect, in the Bancrofts' 1875 experimental version of *The Merchant of Venice.* Kleb argues that Godwin served at most as an occasional adviser rather than as the production's principal designer.

Kroll, Jack. "Money Lust in Venice." *Newsweek* LXXXI, No. 12 (19 March 1973): 86.

Commends Ellis Rabb's well-paced production of *The Merchant of Venice* at Lincoln Center, which starred Sidney Walker as Shylock and Rosemary Harris as Portia.

Lambert, J. W. Review of *The Merchant of Venice. Drama,* no. 87 (Winter 1967): 18.

Objects that Glen Byam Shaw's production at the Haymarket, featuring Ralph Richardson as Shylock and Angela Thorne as Portia, appeared lifeless and lacked intensity, though the lines were well-spoken and the sets well-designed.

———. Review of *The Merchant of Venice. Drama,* no. 97 (Summer 1970): 24-7.

Reviews Jonathan Miller's National Theatre production. Lambert admires some of the production's innovations, but confesses, "I can't, after all, wholeheartedly endorse Mr. Miller's thoughtful deformation of the text."

Leech, Clifford. "Stratford 1953." *Shakespeare Quarterly* IV, No. 4 (October 1953): 462-63.

Assesses Denis Carey's production at Stratford-upon-Avon, featuring strong performances from Michael Redgrave as Shylock, Peggy Ashcroft as Portia, and Harry Andrews as Antonio.

Lewes, George Henry. *On Actors and the Art of Acting.* New York: Grove Press, 1875, 237 p.

Refers to the Shylocks of two prominent nineteenth-century actors, Edmund Kean and W. C. Macready. Lewes asserts that Shylock was one of Kean's greatest roles, in which his rendering of "Hath not a Jew eyes?" (III. i. 59 ff.) attained an unprecedented level of pathos.

MacCarthy, Desmond. "Shylocks Past and Present." In his *Humanities,* pp. 49-53. London: MacGibbon & Kee, 1953.

Recalls Maurice Moscovitch's realistic conception of Shylock, characterized by dignity and controlled passion. Yet despite the apt picturesqueness of Moscovitch's Shylock, the critic concedes that a realistic conception of the character may be at odds with an ideal production of *The Merchant of Venice.*

Macqueen-Pope, W. J. *Theatre Royal, Drury Lane.* London: W. H. Allen, 1945, 350 p.

> Describes Edmund Kean's debut as Shylock at Drury Lane in 1814. According to Pope, Kean's innovative Shylock was a momentous triumph in the face of considerable opposition from the conservative directors of the theater, the cast, the crew, and initially, the audience.

Macready, W. C. *Macready's Reminiscences,* edited by Frederick Pollock. New York: Macmillan and Co., 1875, 750 p.

> Provides diary entries in which the prominent nineteenth-century actor recorded his impressions of Shylock and his own performance in the role.

Manvell, Roger. *Ellen Terry.* New York: G. P. Putman's Sons, 1968, 390 p.

> Recounts Terry's critically acclaimed performance as Portia in the Bancrofts' experimental, aesthetic production of *The Merchant of Venice* of 1875. Manvell also describes Terry's well-received Portia in Henry Irving's 1879 production and her response to the lone critical dissenter, Theodore Martin, husband of Helen Faucit, who was Terry's principal rival on the stage.

Marker, Lise-Lone. "Shakespeare and Naturalism: David Belasco Produces *The Merchant of Venice. Theatre Research* X, No. 1 (1969): 17-32.

> Examines the lavish 1922-23 Broadway production of David Belasco, an American exponent of theatrical naturalism. In the heritage of Henry Irving and Herbert Beerbohm Tree, Belasco sought pictorial veracity: "to approximate nature and to create as real a scenic milieu as possible."

Marowitz, Charles. "Yankee Go Home! You're Ruining Our Shakespeare." *The New York Times* (4 July 1971): 1, 4.

> Avers that Terry Hands's Stratford production of *The Merchant of Venice* lacked a unifying, "coherent concept," or context, necessary to integrate the individual performances.

Matthews, Harold. "*Hamlet, The Merchant* and *Othello.*" *Theatre World* LII, No. 378 (July 1956): 14-15, 35.

> Avers that Belmont, and particularly Margaret Johnston's Portia, dominated Margaret Webster's pleasing Stratford production, overshadowing Emlyn Williams's otherwise sound performance as Shylock.

——. Review of *The Merchant of Venice. Theatre World* LXI, No. 484 (May 1965): 22.

> Reviews the Royal Shakespeare Company's realistic interpretation of *The Merchant of Venice* at Stratford, directed by Clifford Williams, with Eric Porter as Shylock and Janet Suzman as Portia.

Merchant, W. Moelwyn. "On Looking at *The Merchant of Venice.*" In *Essays on Nineteenth Century British Theatre,* edited by Kenneth Richards and Peter Thomson, pp. 171-78. Methuen & Co., 1971.

> Examines the lavish stage decor and settings proposed for a staging of *The Merchant of Venice* by the architectural historian, E. W. Godwin. Godwin derived his detailed designs from a study of Shakespeare's text and sources. According to Merchant, Godwin's settings were implemented by Squire Bancroft in a production that debuted at the Prince of Wales Theatre, 17 April 1895.

Review of *The Merchant of Venice. Newsweek* LX, No. 1 (2 July 1962): 52.

> Relates the popularity of Joseph Papp's New York Shakespeare Festival production and includes a brief interview with Papp's Shylock, George C. Scott.

Novick, Julius. "New Look for Shakespeare." *The New York Times* (11 March 1973): II 1, 5.

> Asserts that Ellis Rabb's production was "not really a production of *The Merchant of Venice* at all, but an original work of Mr. Rabb's, ingeniously superimposed upon Shakespeare's text." Sydney Walker's Shylock became the hero in Rabb's play, and in the process, according to the critic, the comic-romantic aspects of Shakespeare's play were lost.

Perret, Marion D. "Shakespeare and Anti-Semitism: Two Television Versions of *The Merchant of Venice.*" *Mosaic* XVI, Nos. 1-2 (Winter-Spring 1983): 145-63.

> Analyzes two television adaptations of *The Merchant of Venice:* the Laurence Olivier-Jonathan Miller National Theatre production which was telecast in the United States in 1974, and a 1981 BBC production, featuring Warren Mitchell as Shylock, and also produced by Miller. Perret focuses on the strategies these productions employed to render the play's apparent anti-Semitism more palatable to modern audiences.

Pettigrew, John. "Two Comments on the Stratford Season—I: Stratford's Festival Theatre, 1970." *Journal of Canadian Studies* V, No. 4 (November 1970): 11-18.

> Characterizes director Jean Gascon's production at Stratford, Ontario, as "a solid, straight-forward, clean and intelligent production with few cuts and gimmicks." Maureen O'Brien was a "merely competent Portia," and Donald Davis played Shylock as "a sympathetic figure verging on the tragic," at times effective but ultimately detrimental to the romantic spirit of the play.

Review of *The Merchant of Venice. Plays and Players* 3, No. 8 (May 1956): 24-5.

> Reviews Margaret Webster's "straightforward," engaging production at the Shakespeare Memorial Theatre. Emlyn Williams's performance as Shylock was technically strong but unmoving. Harry Andrews played Antonio, and Margaret Johnston was a fine Portia.

Roberts, Peter. Review of *The Merchant of Venice. Plays and Players* 18, No. 212 (May 1971): 34-5.

> Assesses the Royal Shakespeare Company's presentation of *The Merchant of Venice,* directed by Terry Hands and featuring Emrys James, a "rather Welsh-sounding Shylock," and Judi Dench's "sympathetic but quick-witted Portia."

Rosenfeld, Lulla. "The Yiddish Idol." *The New York Times Magazine* (12 June 1977): 32-51.

> Chronicles the career of Jacob Adler, who first appeared as Shylock in a Yiddish production at the People's Theater in New York in 1901. He was later induced to reprise his widely acclaimed performance on Broadway.

Schlueter, June. "Trivial Pursuit: The Casket Plot in the Miller/Olivier *Merchant.*" In *Shakespeare on Television,* edited by J. C. Bulman and H. R. Coursen, pp. 169-74. Hanover, N. H.: University Press of New England, 1988.

> Contends that the National Theatre production directed by Jonathan Miller and featuring Laurence Olivier shifted the focus of the play away from Portia and Bassanio and trivialized the casket plot. With the elevation of Shylock's status, the critic argues, the play was deprived of its romantic-comedy elements.

Simon, John. Review of *The Merchant of Venice. The Hudson Review* XXVI, No. 2 (Summer 1973): 337-47.

> Cursorily dismisses Ellis Rabb's "intolerable" staging of *The Merchant of Venice* in modern dress, featuring Rosemary Harris as Portia and Sydney Walker as Shylock.

Speaight, Robert. "Shylock and Samson." In his *William Poel and the Elizabethan Revival,* pp. 132-60. London: William Heinemann, 1954.

> Attempts to place William Poel's villainous conception of Shylock in the context of the stage history of *The Merchant of Venice.* According to Speaight, Poel felt the play was intended as a romantic comedy, rather than a tragedy featuring a sentimentalized Shylock. Although Poel went too far toward the other extreme in emphasizing Shylock's villainy, the critic argues, he

helped restore a more balanced conception of the character following Henry Irving's overly sentimentalized portrayal.

——. "Shakespeare in Britain." *Shakespeare Quarterly* XVI, No. 4 (Autumn 1965): 313-24.

Declares that Eric Porter's tragic, but not sentimentalized, portrayal of Shylock was "a performance that could outbid any challenge from the past." Speaight protests that the abstractionist sets for this Royal Shakespeare Company production, staged by Clifford Williams, failed to adequately convey the romantic, fairy-tale aura of the play.

——. "Shakespeare in Britain." *Shakespeare Quarterly* XXII, No. 4 (Autumn 1971): 359-64.

Deems Emrys James's Shylock—"a fussy, wisecracking little usurer"—the most successful element in an otherwise lackluster Stratford production staged by Terry Hands and featuring Judy Dench as Portia.

Sprague, Arthur Colby. "Shakespeare on the New York Stage, 1954-1955." *Shakespeare Quarterly* VI, No. 4 (Autumn 1955): 423-27.

Deems Marjorie Hildreth's production "well cast and well spoken." Thomas Barbour played a convincing Shylock.

Stoker, Bram. "Shakespeare's Plays—1." In his *Personal Reminiscences of Henry Irving*, Vol. 1, pp. 83-6. London: Macmillan Co., 1906.

Recounts Irving's decision to mount *The Merchant of Venice*, his inspiration for the play, his conception of Shylock, and the hasty preparations for the opening, all of which yielded one of his most popular productions.

Sullivan, Dan. "Theater: At Stratford." *The New York Times* (22 June 1967): 46.

Contends that director Michael Kahn ignored the conventional comedy-tragedy dichotomy that often underlies productions of *The Merchant of Venice* and sought, in his American Shakespeare Festival production, to create a "devastating universal satire," unsupported by the text. The result was disappointing, and squandered the appearance of Morris Carnovsky as Shylock.

Taylor, John Russell. Review of *The Merchant of Venice*. *Drama* No. 142 (Winter 1981): 29-34.

Deems John Barton's production at the Aldwych theater "more than a little dull." David Suchet played Shylock, and Sinead Cusack appeared "oddly subdued" as Portia.

Review of *The Merchant of Venice*. *The Times* (17 February 1943): 6.

Reviews Frederick Valk's "intensely realistic" depiction of Shylock at the New Theatre, staged by Esme Church. The cast, including Kay Bannerman as Portia, appeared markedly youthful—a source of both the strengths and weaknesses of the production.

Review of *The Merchant of Venice*. *The Times* (18 April 1956): 3.

Admires director Margaret Webster's smooth transitions from the realistic depiction of Venice to the fairy-tale world of Belmont. The critic also praises Margaret Johnston's versatile performance as Portia but finds Emlyn Williams's Shylock slightly hampered by the actor's "showmanship."

Review of *The Merchant of Venice*. *Time* LXXIX, No. 26 (29 June 1962): 32.

Commends the "raspingly effective performance of George C. Scott as Shylock" and Nan Martin's Portia, but avers that this New York Shakespeare Festival production was "not up to the usual Papp standard."

Trewin, J. C. "Coming of Age." *The Illustrated London News* 222 (4 April 1953): 540.

Remarks that Denis Carey's production of *The Merchant of Venice* at the Shakespeare Memorial Theatre features two very

strong performances: Peggy Ashcroft's Portia and Michael Redgrave's Shylock.

——. "Six at the Vic." In *Theatre Programme*, edited by J. C. Trewin, pp. 131-58. London: Frederick Muller, 1954.

Deems Paul Rogers's Shylock "intelligently conceived but executed almost too carefully" while Irene Worth's Portia appeared "too self-consciously gay." Hugh Hunt directed this Old Vic production.

——. "Show-Pieces." *The Illustrated London News* 238, No. 6358 (10 June 1961): 994.

Commends "the visual pleasure" of Peter Potter's production at the Old Vic, as well as the strong, versatile performance of Barbara Leigh-Hunt as Portia and Robert Harris as "a proud, fierce Shylock, stricken to the heart."

——. "Past Terror and Present Laughter." *The Illustrated London News* 246, No. 6561 (1 May 1965): 30-1.

Reviews an uninspiring Stratford production staged by Clifford Williams and hampered by "too meagre decorations." Eric Porter played Shylock and Janet Suzman acted Portia.

——. "Restoring the Merchant." *The Illustrated London News* 258, No. 6871 (10 April 1971): 29.

Applauds Terry Hands's exciting Stratford production of *The Merchant of Venice*, praising the "romantic glow" that engulfed Judy Dench's Portia and Michael Williams's Bassanio. In regard to Emrys James's Shylock, Trewin avers that "one is too conscious of the actor behind the man," although not to the detriment of the dramatic action.

Wardle, Irving. "Harmony that Hides Discordant Writing." *The Times* (23 June 1972): 9.

Praises director Terry Hands skillful balancing of romantic and tragic elements in this Royal Shakespeare Company production at the Aldwych theater. Although the production suffered somewhat from the loss of the glamorous sets employed during the previous season at Stratford, the strength of the performances, especially Emrys James's inventive, villainous Shylock, as well as the director's unified conception, helped compensate.

Wilds, Lillian. "Shakespeare in Southern California." *Shakespeare Quarterly* 33, No. 3 (Autumn 1982): 380-93.

Reviews a production of *The Merchant of Venice* presented by the Shakespeare Society of America at the Globe Playhouse, Los Angeles. Directed by Simon MacCorkindale and Robert Machray, the cast included J. P. Burns as Shylock and Linda Purl as Portia.

Williams, Clifford. "Two Jews at Stratford." *Plays and Players* 12, No. 8 (May 1965): 10-11.

Interview with Clifford Williams who directed the Royal Shakespeare Company production featuring Eric Porter as Shylock and Janet Suzman as Portia. Williams also produced Christopher Marlowe's *The Jew of Malta*, presented in conjunction with *The Merchant of Venice*.

Williams, Gary Jay. "The Merchant of Narcissus." *National Review* XXV, No. 15 (13 April 1973): 422.

Derides Ellis Rabb's "humorless" 1973 production of *The Merchant of Venice* for making Antonio's and Bassanio's homosexual relationship a focal point of the play and "a noble alternative to a world of avarice and indolence." Sidney Walker's "well-mannered" Shylock likewise deviated from Shakespeare's portrait, according to the critic.

Williamson, Audrey. "West End Interlude (1941-44)." In her *Old Vic Drama*, pp. 147-71. London: Rockliff Publishing, 1948.

Praises Frederick Valk's 1943 Shylock at the New Theatre for an unsentimental yet deeply moving portrayal. The remainder of the cast, including Kay Bannerman as Portia, "seemed merely competent."

———. "Classic Experiment: Gielgud at the Queen's." In her *Theatre of Two Decades,* pp. 53-62. London: Rockliff, 1951.

Asserts that Belmont, rather than Venice or Shylock, was the dominant feature of John Gielgud's 1938 production at the Queen's theater. As Shylock, Gielgud tended "to get lost in the shimmering landscapes." According to Williamson, Gielgud's interpretation of Shylock as a rancorous, self-loathing denizen of the ghetto was excellent, "within its limits." Peggy Ashcroft appeared more comfortable in Belmont than in the Venetian courtroom, Williamson maintains, while Leon Quartermaine as Antonio and Angela Baddeley as Nerissa provided some of the production's best moments.

———. "Hugh Hunt's Last Season (1952-1953)." In her *Old Vic Drama 2,* pp. 105-09. London: Rockliff Publishing, 1957.

Declares Paul Rogers's Shylock, in Hugh Hunt's production, a triumph that established his stardom. Williamson employs a variety of critical references to characterize the favorable reception of the performances, especially Irene Worth's "fresh-minted" Portia.

Wills, Garry. "Shylock without Usury." *The New York Review of Books* Nos. 21 & 22 (18 January 1990): 22-5.

Evaluates Peter Hall's *Merchant* from an historical perspective, mindful of Renaissance attitudes toward usury and usurers. Wills objects that, "By making the focus religion instead of money, Hall loses all the poetry and plot material that turns on love's risks, ventures, hazards." Furthermore, Wills contends, Dustin Hoffman's Shylock appeared too restrained, subdued, and pitiable.

Worsley, T. C. "From Stratford to Bristol." *The New Statesman and Nation* LI, No. 1311 (28 April 1956): 448.

Praises Margaret Webster's staging of *The Merchant of Venice* at Stratford as well as the strong performances of Margaret Johnston as Portia and Emlyn Williams as Shylock.

Wyatt, Euphemia Van Rensselaer. Review of *The Merchant of Venice. The Catholic World* 181, No. 1082 (May 1955): 149.

Brief notice of the Shakespearewrights' production featuring Thomas Barbour's "wily and vengeful" Shylock and Laurinda Barrett's "graceful and lively" Portia.

COMPARISONS AND OVERVIEWS:

Brown, John Russell. "Creating a Role: Shylock." In his *Shakespeare's Plays in Performance,* pp. 71-90. New York: St. Martin's Press, 1967.

Begins by contrasting various prominent Shylocks throughout *The Merchant of Venice*'s stage history. Brown then offers his own analysis of the role of Shylock, focusing on the question of whether the character ought to dominate the play as he has so often.

Coleman, William S. E. "Post-Restoration Shylocks prior to Macklin." *Theatre Survey* VIII, No. 1 (May 1967): 17-36.

Examines six actors who portrayed Shylock following the Restoration and prior to Charles Macklin, who restored Shakespeare's text in 1741. Coleman also investigates the period's attitude towards English Jews in order to address the common critical assumption that Shylocks prior to Macklin adopted a comic interpretation of the role.

Conolly, L. W. "*The Merchant of Venice* and the Jew Bill of 1753." *Shakespeare Quarterly* XXV, No. 1 (Winter 1974): 125-27.

Investigates the effect of liberal legislation, intended to grant freedoms to English Jews, on the stage history of *The Merchant of Venice.* Conolly argues that theater managers rather than liberal politicians, who were fearful that a sinister portrayal of Shylock would foster public antipathy toward Jews, were responsible for the absence of productions of *The Merchant of Venice* during the period when the bill was debated in Parliament.

Foulkes, Richard. "Henry Irving and Laurence Olivier as Shylock." *Theatre Notebook* XXVII, No. 1 (Autumn 1972): 26-36.

Compares the acclaimed Shylocks of Irving and Olivier, discerning numerous similarities that the critic attributes to their common, realistic approach to acting.

Friedman, Lester. "The Conversion of the Jews." *Film Comment* 17, No. 4 (July-August 1981): 39-48.

Cites five film versions of *The Merchant of Venice,* made between 1908-14, all of which depict Shylock as a malevolent figure.

Furness, H. H. In an appendix to *The Merchant of Venice,* by William Shakespeare, pp. 370-94. Philadelphia: J. B. Lippincott Co., 1888.

Provides critical excerpts describing famous actors' performances of Shylock, such as Macklin, Kean, and Irving, as well as critical commentary on costumes and scenery for various productions *The Merchant of Venice.*

Hogan, Charles Beecher. *Shakespeare in the Theatre: 1701-1800.* Oxford: Clarendon Press, 1957, 798 p.

Provides a comprehensive record of cast lists for all Shakespeare performances in London theaters during the eighteenth century.

McClellan, Kenneth. *Whatever Happened to Shakespeare?* New York: Barnes & Noble, 1978, 230 p.

Documents the range of liberties actors, directors, and adapters have taken with *The Merchant of Venice* and other Shakespeare plays.

Sprague, Arthur Colby. "The Comedies." In his *Shakespeare and the Actors: The Stage Business in His Plays (1660-1905),* pp. 3-75. Cambridge, Mass: Harvard University Press, 1944.

Records innovative stage business introduced by various prominent actors in their versions of *The Merchant of Venice.*

Wingate, Charles E. L. "Shylock." In his *Shakespeare's Heroes on the Stage,* pp. 105-55. New York: Thomas Y. Crowell & Co., 1896.

Surveys the interpretations and performances of a number of eighteenth- and nineteenth-century Shylocks, including Thomas Dogget, Charles Macklin, George Frederick Cooke, Edmund Kean, Charles Kean, and Henry Irving.

Winter, William. *The Merchant of Venice.* In his *Shakespeare on the Stage,* pp. 129-231. New York: Moffat, Yard and Co., 1911.

Presents a stage history of *Merchant,* providing commentary on Lansdowne's adaptation and the performances of Charles Macklin, John Henderson, George Frederick Cooke, Edmund Kean, Junius Brutus Booth, W. C. Macready, Charles Kean, Edwin Booth, Henry Irving, and Ellen Terry, among others.

STAGING ISSUES:

Coghill, Nevill. "*Macbeth* at The Globe, 1606-1616(?): Three Questions." In *The Triple Bond: Plays, Mainly Shakespearean, in Performance,* pp. 223-239. University Park: Pennsylvania State University Press, 1975.

Speculates how the entries and exits of the last act of *The Merchant of Venice* were conducted in the Elizabethan theater. Coghill's theories are based on a comparison of the text with Dewitt's drawing of the Swan Theatre.

Dessen, Alan C. "The Elizabethan Stage Jew and Christian Example: Gerontus, Barrabas, and Shylock." *Modern Language Quarterly* 35, No. 3 (September 1974): 231-45.

Examines the dramatic function of Shylock's villainy in *The*

Merchant of Venice in relation to Shakespeare's alleged anti-Semitism. Dessen argues that Shylock is an example of an Elizabethan stage convention, the stock villain, intended to illuminate the hypocrisy of the Christians, rather than a representative of a particular ethnicity presented for the audience's ridicule.

Faucit, Helena, Lady Martin. "Portia." In her *On Some of Shakespeare's Female Characters,* pp. 23-44. Edinburgh: William Blackwood and Sons, 1885.

Relates the author's conception of Portia. Faucit was a prominent nineteenth-century actor who played many Shakespearean roles. She describes Portia as "a perfect piece of Nature's handiwork."

Oman, Julia Trevelyan. *"The Merchant of Venice."* In *Introductions to Shakespeare,* edited by Charles Ede, pp. 80-91. London: Michael Joseph, 1978.

Recounts the research conducted by set designer Oman as she prepared to devise the scenery and costumes for Jonathan Miller's 1970 National Theatre production.

Strasberg, Lee. "Past Performances." *Theatre Arts* XXXIV, No. 5 (May 1950): 39-42.

Comments on the nature of acting and the pursuit of the ideal performance through a study of theatrical history, citing Edmund Kean's portrayal of Shylock as an example of a definitive performance. According to Strasberg, although the full dimensions of a long past performance, such as Kean's, may be lost, it is worth studying the surviving accounts to uncover the novelty of the actor's approach and the essence of his performance.

Traci, Philip. "Christian and Jew in *The Merchant of Venice.*" *Drama Critique* X, No. 3 (Fall 1967): 154-56.

Argues, in response to director Michael Kahn's American Shakespeare Festival production, that both Christians and Jews are satirized in Shakespeare's text.

Ventimiglia, Peter James. "Shakespeare's Comedies on the Nineteenth-Century New York Stage: A Promptbook Analysis." *The Papers of the Bibliographical Society of America* 71, No. 4 (1977): 415-41.

Identifies the deletions of acts, scenes, and lines, and the additions made to acting versions of *The Merchant of Venice* as produced in New York in the nineteenth-century. Consulting four period promptbooks, the critic discovers that the general tendency in these productions was to focus on Shylock, either by adding lines to his role, or by diminishing the Portia-Bassanio casket plot, or both.

A MIDSUMMER NIGHT'S DREAM

Throughout the stage history of *A Midsummer Night's Dream,* a crucial concern of actors and directors has been how to meet the disparate demands of this, perhaps Shakespeare's most ethereal, play. A celebration of marriage and a lighthearted fairy tale, *A Midsummer Night's Dream* is also a play about the human imagination and its power to create illusion and reality through dreams, through love, and through theater itself. It is filled with music and dance, infused with lyrical poetry, peopled by fantastic creatures, and crowned with a theatrical set-piece, the Pyramus and Thisbe play. It is not surprising, therefore, that critics and commentators long questioned whether the *Dream* may be successfully staged. In the seventeenth and eighteenth centuries, actors and producers often did not even attempt to present the complete comedy; instead, they extracted one of the several plots to form such new pieces as *Bottom the Weaver* or *The Fairies.* Others regarded the varied elements in *A Midsummer Night's Dream* as invitations to adorn the stage with spectacle and lavish display.

Scholars generally agree that Shakespeare composed *A Midsummer Night's Dream* around 1594-95 as a private entertainment for a wedding celebration and that the play had its first performance in the great hall of a manor house. By the time of its first printing, however, the play had clearly been acted on a public stage. The title page of the first QUARTO edition of *A Midsummer Night's Dream* (1600) indicates that it had "beene sundry times publickely acted" by the LORD CHAMBERLAIN'S MEN. In addition, records of the royal household indicate that the comedy was performed at Court on New Year's night 1604. No further evidence survives of performances of the *Dream* during Shakespeare's lifetime, or, indeed, until the Restoration period in the latter half of the seventeenth century. However, John Gee's reference to *The Comedy of Pyramus and Thisbe* in his 1624 work *New Shreds of Old Snares* suggests that the mechanicals' play had been extracted from Shakespeare's comedy and presented separately. Another piece, the comic "droll" entitled the *Merry Conceited Humours of Bottom the Weaver* (1646), was also derived from *A Midsummer Night's Dream* and frequently performed at festivals and fairs in the period when the theaters were closed.

Not until 1662 was *A Midsummer Night's Dream* again staged in its entirety. In that year, it was revived by Thomas Killigrew and his company, the King's Servants. Samuel Pepys, who witnessed this production, admired the dancing, but considered the comedy "the most insipid ridiculous play that ever I saw in my life." Thirty years later, Thomas Betterton staged the first of many operatic versions of *A Midsummer Night's Dream.* This adaptation, *The Fairy Queen,* featured music by Henry Purcell and contained elaborate pageants that necessitated severe cuts of Shakespeare's text. John Downes, the bookkeeper of Betterton's company, reported that although audiences were enthusiastic in their appreciation of the opulent spectacle, the production was so expensive to mount that "the Company got very little by it." The illustrious actor-manager David Garrick also staged an operatic

Dream. His 1755 production *The Fairies* contained three acts and featured twenty-eight songs, with lyrics derived not only from *A Midsummer Night's Dream,* but from other Shakespearean plays and the works of other authors as well. Eight years following this first, moderately successful, adaptation, Garrick staged a five-act version of *A Midsummer Night's Dream* with a total of thirty-three songs. Although a more complete version of Shakespeare's comedy than Garrick's earlier presentation, this production was also marked by numerous cuts, including the excision of most of the Pyramus and Thisbe section. This adaptation was an utter failure, lasting only a single performance. Within days of the debacle, however, Garrick's collaborator George Colman had condensed the work into a two-act interlude called *A Fairy Tale,* a piece which met with some success and was revived several times over the next fourteen years. The final production in this series of derivatives was Frederick Reynolds's 1816 opera of *A Midsummer Night's Dream.* In this Covent Garden presentation, Reynolds continued the tradition of scenic splendor, including settings depicting ancient Athens and a fifth-act pageant entitled "The Triumphs of Theseus," based on various tales of the legendary king. It met with the approval of audiences and most critics. The eminent scholar and commentator William Hazlitt, however, after witnessing this production, was moved to conclude that *A Midsummer Night's Dream* is unsuited to actual performance. Although Hazlitt admired the scenery of this production, he found the physical representation of fanciful characters disappointing. Maintaining that "poetry and the stage do not agree together," he argued that what is "merely an airy shape, a dream, a passing thought" in the mind "immediately becomes an unmanageable reality" on stage. Hazlitt's comments have had a great influence on subsequent theatrical critics of *A Midsummer Night's Dream* and have served as a starting point for others who have questioned whether the play is stageable.

The middle third of the nineteenth century saw the return to the stage of *A Midsummer Night's Dream* in a form much closer to Shakespeare's original. Although the comedy continued to be embellished by music, dance, and spectacle, producers of this era restored much of the play's textual integrity. The first major nineteenth-century production in this vein was Madame Vestris's 1840 Covent Garden revival. As the reviewer for the *Athenaeum* asserted, this representation of the play transcended all previous stagings. Although no less lavish than its predecessors, and still incorporating elements of opera and ballet, Vestris's version excised traditional, non-Shakespearean interpolations, and its spectacles were directly tied to the play. In addition, all but four hundred lines of Shakespeare's text were employed, a far greater adherence to the original play than in any production since the Restoration. Vestris's gauzy fairies, carrying colored lanterns, and her own portrayal of Oberon established new traditions for staging *A Midsummer Night's Dream* throughout the Victorian period. As early as the following year, the Park Theatre in New York mounted a production of the play that was strongly influenced by Vestris's. Pageantry was essential to Ludwig Tieck's 1843 revival as well. Having received a royal commission to stage *A Midsummer Night's Dream* at the Potsdam Court Theatre, this noted German Shakespearean scholar collaborated with composer Felix Mendelssohn, who had earlier written an overture for the comedy. Mendelssohn's score has been considered the finest music ever composed for a Shakespearean work, and it became a standard feature of productions of the *Dream* well into the twentieth century. It is still occasionally employed in opulent, romantic stagings of the comedy.

Perhaps the finest Victorian presentation of *A Midsummer Night's Dream* was the 1853 production mounted by Samuel Phelps at Sadler's Wells Theatre. Phelps's use of shifting dioramas, gauze screens during the fairy sequences, and special lighting effects enthralled both audiences and critics, who found this staging truly evocative of the magical quality of Shakespeare's play. Moreover, Phelps's portrayal of Bottom was deemed brilliant and became one of his most famous roles. The intelligence and sensitivity with which Shakespeare's text was handled also garnered praise; as the noted critic Henry Morley observed, "it is very doubtful whether the *Midsummer Night's Dream* has ever yet, since it was first written, been put upon the stage with so nice an interpretation of its meaning." An even greater popular success was achieved three years later by Charles Kean with his Princess's Theatre revival of 1856, which enjoyed a run of 150 performances. The scenic aspects of this production were particularly spectacular, even by Victorian standards. They included pictorial representations of ancient Athens based on the latest archaeological research and a Puck—played by a very young Ellen Terry—who emerged from beneath the stage floor seated on a mushroom. The presentation of spectacle required major excisions of Shakespeare's text, a trend which was to continue throughout the remainder of the Victorian period.

Lavish ornamentation of *A Midsummer Night's Dream* characterized all three of Augustin Daly's late nineteenth-century productions of the play, and reached its pinnacle in the opening years of the twentieth century with Herbert Beerbohm Tree's extravagant stagings in 1900 and 1911. Daly first staged *A Midsummer Night's Dream* in 1873 at New York's Grand Opera House, revived it again at his own theater fifteen years later, and finally toured with it to London and throughout the United States in 1895-96. Daly's productions of the *Dream* were principally known for their striking visual effects, which included twinkling fireflies powered by batteries and magically disappearing fairies. In the words of the *New York Times* reviewer, the "sumptuous magnificence in the pictorial features" of Daly's presentations enchanted American audiences. British critics, however, were much harsher in their judgments. Bernard Shaw, for example, in his assessment of an 1895 London performance, scoffed at the firefly lights which the actors switched on and off "from time to time, like children with a new toy." Shaw and others also condemned Daly's cutting of Shakespeare's text; as William Archer observed, *"Daly* is fatally suggestive of *Dele."* Herbert Beerbohm Tree's productions were even more renowned for their scenic splendor and "realism." Tree's introduction of live rabbits into his 1911 revival of *A Midsummer Night's Dream* has come to be regarded as an extreme in Victorian staging of the play. Audiences and critics of the time, however, were enthusiastic. The *Athenaeum* reviewer of Tree's 1900 production maintained that "no spectacle equally artistic has been seen on the English stage," and the *Times* critic said of

the later revival that it was "as near to fairyland as the stage will ever make it."

Just three years after Tree's second revival, Harley Granville-Barker attempted a complete break from the very theatrical traditions that Tree represented. In his 1914 Savoy Theatre production of *A Midsummer Night's Dream,* Barker rejected scenic realism—detailed Athenian vistas, leafy woodlands, fairies that actually "fly"—for a highly stylized, otherworldly effect with gilded fairies, decorated curtains merely suggestive of a sylvan locale, and great columns to indicate Theseus's palace. In addition, Barker restored virtually all of Shakespeare's text and replaced Mendelssohn's romantic score with one based on English folk-songs. Critics of this production were sharply divided. Some, like the *Athenaeum* reviewer found it "rich, graceful, and authentic as a work of art"; others, most notably William Winter, were virulently hostile. Winter judged Barker's *Dream* a "desecration" of Shakespeare and a "nauseous admixture of mental decadence and crotchety humbug." Many were simply puzzled. The reviewer for the *Illustrated London News* observed that this staging seemed the result of "calculated eccentricity, and the resolve to do something new at all costs."

Romanticism in the staging of *A Midsummer Night's Dream* was not dead, however; in the first half of the twentieth century, Max Reinhardt, W. Bridges-Adams, Tyrone Guthrie, and others offered sumptuous productions of the play. From 1905 to 1939 the German director Reinhardt mounted a series of revivals throughout Europe and America under a variety of conditions, from open-air settings to a Hollywood film. Throughout this period, he continually developed his interpretation, which stressed the play's fantastic qualities. As the *Times* observed in its review of a 1933 outdoor performance with the Oxford University Dramatic Society, Reinhardt's version of *A Midsummer Night's Dream* changed "the customary emphasis of the play. . . . No longer is it a story of mortals in this world behind whom an enchantment has arisen; it is a tale of sprites and goblins pursuing the natural life of their own dwelling-place, into which men and women have blindly wandered." Even the unusual casting of such Hollywood actors as Mickey Rooney as Puck and James Cagney as Bottom in the screen adaptation did not destroy this effect. As Roger Manvell later noted, the film is "strangely effective in its own particular right." Both of Bridges-Adams's productions of *A Midsummer Night's Dream* at the Shakespeare Memorial Theatre, in 1920 and 1932, were noted for their scenic splendor and use of Mendelssohn's score. Guthrie, in his successful productions at the Old Vic in 1937 and 1957, consciously reverted to a gauzy Victorian-influenced presentation that included elements of ballet.

Opposing these romantic versions of the *Dream* were productions demonstrating the influence of Barker, including Harcourt Williams's 1929 and 1931 stagings at the Old Vic. In these revivals, Williams adopted Barker's method of speaking the verse rapidly, and he employed the score Cecil Sharp had composed for Barker's production. George Devine's 1954 Shakespeare Memorial Theatre presentation of *A Midsummer Night's Dream* featured metallic trees, fairies that resembled birds, and a Puck with ape-like movements. This production found little favor with critics, and the second of Guthrie's three Old Vic stagings of the comedy was similarly received. The 1951 presentation was set on a simplified stage that audiences found drab and depressing. Nevertheless, Paul

Rogers was highly praised for his performance as Bottom, a role he reprised in several later productions.

Several revivals of *A Midsummer Night's Dream* in the late 1950s and early 1960s, including productions at all three Stratfords—England, the United States, and Canada—emphasized the play's comedic aspects. The most significant of these was Peter Hall's series of stagings with the Shakespeare Memorial Theatre company from 1958 to 1963 and a screen adaptation in 1968. Broad physical humor, in the depiction of the four young lovers no less than in the portrayals of the mechanicals, was a cornerstone of Hall's conception. Reviewers of the 1958 production were not amused by this innovation, however. The influential critic John Russell Brown deemed this staging an "adaptation" of *A Midsummer Night's Dream,* insisting that Hall's "clownish" young lovers burlesqued Shakespeare's characters. Another significant aspect of this production was the stage design, suggestive of the great hall of an English manor house, a location in keeping with scholarly theories about the site of the first enactment of *A Midsummer Night's Dream.* This too was censured by reviewers, who judged the sets clumsy and poorly designed. Nevertheless, as Hall refined both the scenery and his conception of the play in subsequent revivals, the director and his company achieved greater critical esteem. J. C. Trewin considered the 1962 presentation a "happy surprise," given the poor quality of the earlier staging, and Kenneth Tynan claimed that the second staging "achieved levitation in a matter of minutes and thereafter never looked earthward." Although the film also stressed broad humor and featured Paul Rogers as Bottom, it initally met with little critical approbation. Reviewers judged its accelerated pace and fast cuts—often involving several changes of location in the course of a single speech—disconcerting and distracting. More recent commentators, however, have been more favorable in their appraisals of the film.

Jan Kott's essay on *A Midsummer Night's Dream* in his 1964 work *Shakespeare, Our Contemporary* had a significant impact on theatrical presentations of the comedy. In "Titania and the Ass's Head," Kott argued that elements of violence, sexuality, and cruelty appear throughout the *Dream.* Both John Hancock's Theatre de Lys revival of 1967 and John Hirsh's staging for the Stratford Festival in Ontario the following year revealed the influence of Kott's essay. The most significant production to incorporate elements of sexuality, and one of the most important revivals of *A Midsummer Night's Dream* for a host of reasons, was Peter Brook's 1970 presentation with the Royal Shakespeare Company. Like Barker's earlier in the century, Brook's *Dream* was intended as a complete break from the theatrical traditions surrounding the play. Emphasizing the erotic nature of the encounter between Bottom and Titania and the cruelty behind Oberon's arrangement of this affair, Brook broke decidedly from the gauzy romanticism of past productions. Even the music of Mendelssohn was reduced to a brief passage from the Wedding March erupting from a loudspeaker. Substituting exuberance for sentiment, Brook set this production in a white box surrounded by catwalks and hung with trapezes, suggesting both a gymnasium and a circus. Sexuality and play freely mingled in this open, undefined space, which, reviewers observed, made anything seem possible, from fairies to "translations." Many critics noted that the action took place in midair as much as it did on the stage. This scheme, Irving Wardle claimed, removed "the sense of being earthbound: it is natural here for characters to fly." Circus tricks and acro-

batics also emphasized the self-conscious theatricality of the production, which stimulated the creative participation of audiences. With the comedy "uncluttered by romantic 'scenic' tradition," Helen Dawson maintained, the audience "goes through an additional experience: propelled by the play, the imagination begins to race." Performances of this *Midsummer Night's Dream* concluded with the cast members going out into the audience to exchange warm handshakes.

Deliberate experimentation and tradition were intermingled in post-Brook stagings of *A Midsummer Night's Dream.* In 1975, the Yale Repertory Theater mounted a well-received revival in which slithery and sinister fairies were melded with Henry Purcell's seventeenth-century operatic version of the play. Two years later, in the first RSC production of *A Midsummer Night's Dream* since Brook's, John Barton offered an interpretation of the comedy in which conventional, realistic settings were peopled by an aggressive, tyrannical Oberon and nightmarish, half-human, half-animal fairies that metamorphosed into rocks, trees, and other objects. Although critics like John Elsom considered it too traditional and censured its failure to "show us anything different from our normal expectations," others, like Roger Warren, claimed that this revival "beautifully reconciled" the contrasting "combination of courtly formality and rich, vivid evocation of the British countryside" in *A Midsummer Night's Dream.* In his 1981 production, director Ron Daniels placed the play amid the props and paraphernalia of an opulent Victorian stage set. The emphasis on conscious artifice in this revival extended to the presentation of the fairies, which were grotesque and menacing puppets. Bill Bryden, too, experimented with theatrical traditions by merging Elizabethan, Victorian, and Edwardian elements in his National Theatre staging of *A Midsummer Night's Dream* the following year.

It is, perhaps, just such "experimentation" that most aptly characterizes the stage history of *A Midsummer Night's Dream.* From the lavish spectacle of Purcell's opera to Barker's gilt and bronze, from Brook's gymnastics to the loutish schoolboy fairies of the RSC's 1989 production, actors, directors, and producers have attempted to represent on stage the unique, elusive magic of *A Midsummer Night's Dream*—to make poetry and the stage "agree together."

REVIEWS AND RETROSPECTIVE ACCOUNTS OF SELECTED PRODUCTIONS

PRODUCTION:

Thomas Killigrew • The King's Servants • 1662

BACKGROUND:

The early stage history of *A Midsummer Night's Dream* is one of numerous adaptations; during the seventeenth century several farces or "drolls" extracted from the play were often produced. In 1662, however, Thomas Killigrew and his company, The King's Servants, staged what is believed to be one of the first complete performances of *A Midsummer Night's Dream* since Shakespeare's day.

Details of this revival are scanty; some scholars postulate that it may have been augmented by elaborate music and dance pieces.

COMMENTARY:

Samuel Pepys   (diary date 29 September 1662)

[*A diversified background of travel, intellectual pursuits, and public office gave Pepys the opportunity to be a close observer of his society. His unique* Diary *is an unreserved study of the affairs and customs of his time. His personal revelations create a document of unusual psychological interest as well as providing a history of the Restoration theater. In the following diary entry, Pepys briefly evaluates Killigrew's production of* A Midsummer Night's Dream. *His judgment, that it was "the most insipid ridiculous play that ever I saw in my life," has frequently been quoted by subsequent critics of the play.*]

Michaelmas day. This day my oaths for drinking of wine and going to plays are out, and so I do resolve to take a liberty today and then to fall to them again. . . . I sent for some dinner and . . . dined (Mrs. Margt Pen being by, to whom I had spoke to go along with us to a play this afternoon) and then to the King's Theatre, where we saw *Midsummers nights dreame,* which I have never seen before, nor shall ever again, for it is the most insipid ridiculous play that ever I saw in my life. I saw, I confess, some good dancing and some handsome women, which was all my pleasure. (pp. 207-08)

> *Samuel Pepys, in a diary entry on September 29, 1662, in his* The Diary of Samuel Pepys, 1662, Vol. III, *edited by Robert Latham and William Matthews, University of California Press, 1970, pp. 207-08.*

PRODUCTION:

Thomas Betterton • *The Fairy Queen* • 1692

BACKGROUND:

Betterton was the foremost actor of the Restoration period. In 1692 at the Dorset Garden Theatre, his company staged *The Fairy Queen,* an operatic version of *A Midsummer Night's Dream* with music by Henry Purcell. Although it is not known with certainty who adapted Shakespeare's work for this production, some scholars suggest that it was done by Elkanah Settle. *The Fairy Queen* is noted for its lavish pageantry, extended musical interludes, and free cutting of Shakespeare's text. This production is commonly regarded as inaugurating a long tradition of spectacular stagings of *A Midsummer Night's Dream.*

COMMENTARY:

John Downes   (essay date 1708)

[*Downes described himself as the "Book-keeper and Prompter" of The Duke's Servants, a theatrical company whose principal player was Thomas Betterton. In 1708 Downes published* Ros-

cius Anglicanus, *a miscellany of anecdotes, cast lists, and other observations regarding the plays staged by the company during his tenure. Despite its admitted inaccuracies, the work remains a valuable source of information on the Restoration theater. In the following excerpt, Downes recalls the elaborate staging of* The Fairy Queen *and observes that despite the favorable reception it received from audiences, "the Expences in setting out being so great, the Company got very little by it."*]

About this time [1685], there were several other new Plays Acted. . . .

King Arthur an Opera, wrote by Mr. *Dryden;* it was Excellently Adorn'd with Scenes and Machines: The Musical Part set by Famous Mr. *Henry Purcel;* and Dances made by Mr. *Fo. Priest:* The Play and Musick pleas'd the Court and City, and being well perform'd, twas very Gainful to the Company.

The *Prophets,* or *Dioclesian* an Opera, wrote by Mr. *Betterton;* being set out with Coastly Scenes, Machines and Cloaths: The Vocal and Instrumental Musick, done by Mr. *Purcel;* and Dances by Mr. *Priest;* it gratify'd the Expectation of Court and City; and got the Author great Reputation.

The Fairy Queen, made into an Opera, from a Comedy of Mr. *Shakespears:* This in Ornaments was Superior to the other Two; especially in Cloaths, for all the Singers and Dancers, Scenes, Machines and Decorations, all most profusely set off; and excellently perform'd, chiefly the Instrumental and Vocal part Compos'd by the said Mr. *Purcel,* and Dances by Mr. *Priest.* The Court and Town were wonderfully satisfy'd with it; but the Expences in setting it out being so great, the Company got very little by it. (pp. 41-3)

> *John Downes, in an excerpt in his* Roscius Anglicanus, 1708. *Reprint by University of California, 1969, pp. 41-3.*

George C. D. Odell   (essay date 1920)

[*In the excerpt below, Odell describes the staging of* The Fairy Queen, *devoting special attention to the entr'-act spectacles.*]

The *Fairy Queen* was produced anonymously at the Queen's Theatre, as Dorset Garden had been called after the accession of James II in 1685. This theatre, since the union of the companies, was used occasionally for spectacular shows and operas requiring much stage room. And spectacular and operatic the production notoriously was. At the end of each act is a most elaborate entry. The music was by the famous Purcell. Much stress was laid on the operatic aspects of the show. The preface speaks of the great success of opera in Italy and France, with the "machines" employed; and asserts that *The Siege of Rhodes* was a perfect opera, though it lacked the ornament of "machines."

In the story not many changes occur. The character of Hippolyta is omitted, but otherwise things run on much as in the original play, except for the ultra-elaborate "entries" at the end of acts. According to the practice of Tate and Crowne, the lines are robbed of all poetry. I cannot refrain from showing Shakespeare's much-quoted

> For ought that euer I could read,
> Could euer heare by tale or historie,
> The course of true loue neuer did run smooth,
>
> [I. i. 132-34]

as "improved" in 1692:

> O my true Hermia! I have never found
> By observation, nor by History
> That lovers run a smooth and even course.

Every time I come on one of these alterations . . . I try by every process of historical readjustment to understand what the adapter thought he was doing for Shakespeare; invariably I am forced to give up the problem.

One change that should be recorded is that of having the mock-play of Pyramus and Thisbe performed in the third act, just before the transformation of Bottom. This transposing gives more room for the unusually elaborate and gorgeous "entry" at the end of the fifth act. (pp. 71-2)

                              . . . . .

According to all I have read, [*The Fairy Queen*] was about the most splendid of the "operas" produced during the fifty years of Betterton. The play part, with variations, is practically Shakespeare's *Midsummer Night's Dream,* but at the end of each act, except the first, in style of opera or Italian *intermedii,* is a gorgeous conglomeration of scenery, machines, singing, dancing, spectacle, transformation, such as the stage probably had not seen up to that time. I shall confine my account to these act-endings. In Act II, the scene, a "wood by moonlight," changes to "a prospect of Grotto's, Arbors, and delightful Walks: the Arbors are adorned with all variety of Flowers, the Grottos supported by Terms, these lead to two Arbors on either side of the scene, of a great length whose prospect runs toward the two Angles of the House. Between these two Arbors is a great Grotto, which is continued by several Arches, to the further end of the House." There are songs, followed by a Masque, involving Night, Mystery, Secresie and Sleep and their attendances. A dance of the Followers of Night concludes all.

At the end of Act III, "the Scene changes to a Great Wood; a long row of Trees on each side: a river in the middle: Two rows of lesser Trees of a different kind just on the side of the River, which meet in the middle, and make so many Arches: Two great Dragons make a Bridge over the River; their Bodies form two Arches, through which two Swans are seen in the River at a great Distance. Enter a Troop of Fauns, Dryades, and Naides," and indulge in a song in two parts. . . . . . ."While a Symphony's playing, the two Swans come swimming on through the Arches to the Bank of the River, as if they would Land; there turn themselves into Fairies and Dance; at the same time the Bridge vanishes, and the Trees that were Arch'd, raise themselves upright. Four Savages Enter, fright the Fairies away, and Dance an Entry." As if we had not yet had sufficient mixture of elements, Coridon and Mopsa enter and contribute a genuine pastoral song; and, for good measure, the act ends with a Song by a Nymph and a Dance of Hay Makers. I defy any one to name, offhand, another thing that could have been added to make the mixture more incongruous.

At the end of Act IV, "the Scene changes to a Garden of Fountains. A Sonata plays while the Sun rises, it appears red through the mist [in 1692, mark you!], as it ascends it dissipates the Vapours, and is seen in its full lustre: then the Scene is perfectly discovered, the Fountains enrich'd with gilding, and adorn'd with Statues: The View is terminated by a Walk of Cypress Trees which lead to a delightful Bower. Before the Trees stand rows of Marble Columns, which support many Walks which rise by stairs to the Top of the House; the Stairs are adorn'd with Figures on Pedestals, and Rails and Balasters on each side of 'em. Near the top, vast Quantities of Water break out of the Hills, and fall in mighty Cascades to the bottom of the Scene, to feed the Fountains, which are on each side. In the middle of the Stage is a very large Fountain, where the Water rises about twelve Foot. Then the 4 Seasons enter, with their several Attendants." After a song, "a Machine appears, the Clouds break from before it, and Phœbus appears in a Chariot drawn by four Horses." He sings; there is a song by the four Seasons, and a dance by them. Is not this remarkable stage spectacle for a theatre lighted by wax (I suppose) in 1692?

The grand finale of the fifth act is the climax of such shows. Juno appears in a Machine drawn by Peacocks. "While a Symphony plays, the Machine moves forward, and the Peacocks spread their tails, and fill the middle of the Theater [stage]. Juno sings; the Machine ascends. While the Scene is darken'd, a single entry is danc'd; Then a Symphony is play'd; after that the Scene is Suddainly Illuminated, and discovers a transparent Prospect of a Chinese Garden; the Architecture, the Trees, the Plants, the Fruit, the Birds, the Beasts [a somewhat crowded garden?] quite different from what we have in this part of the World [undoubtedly, but were they Chinese?]. It is terminated by an Arch, through which is seen other Arches, with close Arbors, and a row of Trees to the end of the View. Over it is a hanging Garden, which rises by several ascents to the Top of the House [stage]; it is bounded on either side by pleasant Bowers, various Trees, and numbers of strange Birds flying in the Air, on the Top of a Platform is a Fountain, throwing up Water, which falls into a large Basin."

Into this not uncrowded scene come, first, a "Chinese" who sings, and then a Chinese woman, who also indulges in song. "Six Monkeys come from between the Trees, and Dance." The wonder grows: "Six Pedestals of China-work rise from under the Stage; they support six large Vases of Porcelain, in which are six China-Orange Trees . . . . . . The Pedestals move toward the Front of the Stage, and the Grand Dance begins of Twenty-four Persons; then Hymen and the Two Women sing together." The grand dance, according to the information supplied in general directions, prefixed to the play, is by "twenty-four Chineses," a pleasing way of putting it. Another grand dance ends the show, music for which was written by Purcell; who, I wonder, designed the scenes?

If I were asked what all this Chinese mummery had to do with *A Midsummer Night's Dream,* I could only answer, "Nothing at all." If as stage-entertainment, I could say it was a tremendous success for people who wanted spectacle, song and dance. Downes [in his *Roscius Anglicanus*] and Gildon (in his *Two Stages Compared*) both join it with Dryden's opera King Arthur and Betterton's alteration of Fletcher's *Prophetess* as the "most excellently adorn'd with Scenes and Machines" known up to that time. But of *The Fairy Queen* Downes continues: "This in Ornaments was Superior to the other Two; especially in Cloaths, for all the Singers and Dancers, Scenes, Machines and Decorations, all most profusely set off; and excellently perform'd, chiefly the Instrumental and Vocal part Composed by the said Mr. *Purcel,* and Dances by Mr. *Priest.* The Court and Town were wonderfully satisfy'd with it; but the Expences in setting it out being so great, the Company got very little by it."

Perhaps the expense was the reason for the discontinuance

of the operatic spectacle, before a public mad for such entertainment and largely fed on it by Betterton. (pp. 192-95)

George C. D. Odell, "Acting Versions of the Plays" and "Scenery: Particular Performances," in his Shakespeare: From Betterton to Irving, Vol. I, *1920. Reprint by Benjamin Blom, Inc., 1963, pp. 22-89, 166-201.*

PRODUCTIONS:

David Garrick • Drury Lane • 1755 and 1763

BACKGROUND:

David Garrick was the preeminent actor and theatrical manager of the eighteenth century. His numerous productions and adaptations of Shakespeare's works exerted an influence far outlasting his tenure at Drury Lane Theatre from 1747 to 1776. Two treatments of *A Midsummer Night's Dream* have been attributed to him. In 1755 he produced *The Fairies,* a three-act operatic version of Shakespeare's work with music by John Christopher Smith. This version contained twenty-eight songs, with lyrics derived from several of Shakespeare's plays as well as from works of Dryden, Milton, and others. Although moderately successful in its time, later critics have been harsh in their condemnation of *The Fairies.* Eight years later, Garrick staged a five-act version of *A Midsummer Night's Dream* that contained a total of thirty-three songs. Although more of Shakespeare's text survives in this version than in *The Fairies,* the 1763 play is marked by extensive cuts, including most of the Pyramus and Thisbe play. It was an utter failure, lasting through only one performance, on 23 November. Within three days, however, Garrick's collaborator George Coleman had condensed the work into a two-act afterpiece called *A Fairy Tale.* This was fairly well received, and was revived several times over the next fourteen years.

COMMENTARY:

George C. D. Odell (essay date 1920)

[*In the following excerpt, Odell discusses Garrick's treatments of* A Midsummer Night's Dream. *Regarding* The Fairies, *Odell observes that it was likely an "attractive entertainment in its day," and he commends Garrick's preservation of the "original purity" of the Shakespearean verse he did retain.*]

[*The Fairies* was] produced at Drury Lane on February 3, 1755. *A Midsummer Night's Dream,* alas! was never long free from the hand of the depredator, and *The Fairies* was about due, at the time of its arrival. Leveridge's *Pyramus and Thisbe,* of 1716, and Lampe's, of 1745, were ready for a successor when *The Fairies* appeared.

The Fairies, unlike these two farcical operas founded on Shakespeare's tragical mirth, omits all the episodes of the hard-handed men of Athens and the play of Pyramus and Thisbe; it deals only with the fairy scenes and the crossed loves of the quartette of young people for whom first a father's implacable will, and afterwards Oberon's magic flower,

create so much trouble and dismay. There being no Bottom the weaver among the *dramatis personœ,* we learn of Titania's infatuation for a "patched fool" only from Puck's narration to Oberon. As we never see the "patched" weakling aforesaid, the episode has no dramatic value. The character of Hippolyta, also, is reduced to the palest of nonentities; she becomes literally a walking—not a talking—lady. The whole thing is really an opera; twenty-seven songs are introduced, including some from the original play, also Puck's filching of Ariel's "Where the bee sucks, there lurk [*sic*] I" [*The Tempest,* V. i. 88-94], and Oberon's calm appropriation unto himself of "Sigh no more, ladies, sigh no more," from *Much Ado about Nothing* [II. iii. 61-74].

But Dryden, Lansdowne and Waller also contribute lyrics; and Milton as well—two stanzas from L'Allegro. The fact that Signor Curioni sang Lysander, and Signora Passerini Hermia, shows how operatically un-English the whole thing must have been. Let us finish with one or two examples of the feast.

Hermia's rebellion against her father's marriage plan for her is thus "voiced":

> So will I grow, so live, so die, my Lord,
> Ere I will yield my virgin patient (*sic*) up
> Unto his Lordship, to whose unwish'd yoke
> My soul consents not to give sovereignty.

AIR

> With mean disguise, let other natures hide,
> And mimick virtue with the paint of art:
> I scorn the cheat, of reason's foolish pride,
> And boast the graceful weakness of my heart, etc.

Is't not pretty? Soon Helena enters.

> *Hermia.* Good speed, fair *Helena,* whither away?
> *Helena.* Call you me fair? That fair again unsay,
>   *Demetrius* loves you.

AIR

> O Hermia fair, O happy, happy fair,
> Your eyes are load-stars, and your tongue's sweet air;
> More tuneable than lark to shepherd's ear, etc.

Nevertheless, I should not be surprised if *The Fairies* was rather attractive entertainment in its day. A good deal of Shakespeare's poetry is retained intact. Garrick was no Tate; he at least left in their original purity the Shakespearian verses he used—he merely omitted or put in—but in either case it was solid blocks that went or stayed. (pp. 358-59)

. . . . .

Garrick set out in September, 1763, for the Continent; he did not reappear on the stage of Drury Lane for two years. He left the management in charge of George Colman, the elder, with strong advice to lay stress on musical and spectacular productions. *A Midsummer Night's Dream* was produced as an opera on November 23rd, and enjoyed exactly one performance, a record of the time asserting that the audience were all asleep as soundly as some of the characters on the stage. This is Shakespeare's play, in five acts, turned into an opera, with thirty-three songs. The dialogue is curtailed, and much of the mock-play is omitted. Colman drew a kind of victory from defeat, and three nights later brought out *A Fairy Tale,* as an afterpiece, employing, no doubt, whatever scenes and

costumes the management had been at the expense to produce. This *Fairy Tale,* unlike *The Fairies,* of 1755, employed
the episodes of the hard-handed men, including the tragedy
of Pyramus and Thisbe, and also the Oberon-Titania-Puck
material; the quartette of lovers and Theseus and Hippolyta
are omitted. In 1755 these characters were retained, and the
hard-handed men were omitted. Variety at least was sub-
served in these successive arrangements, whatever one may
say of reverence for Shakespeare. The failure of the *Midsummer Night's Dream* galled Garrick, as his correspondence
shows, and Colman always resented the imputation of having
had a hand in the production; at best, he says, he was but godfather (which I take to mean stage-manager) to it. *A Fairy
Tale* had only a brief, uneventful career. When managers thus
could fall out over the failure of one of these perversions of
Shakespeare, one could suspect that the end of the day of
such atrocities was in sight. And so it proved; there are but
few more to record for many a long day. (p. 376)

> *George C. D. Odell, "The Plays," in his* Shake-
> speare: From Betterton to Irving, Vol. I, *1920. Re-
> print by Benjamin Blom, Inc., 1963, pp. 336-90.*

George Winchester Stone, Jr.   (essay date 1939)

[*In the following excerpt, Stone examines Garrick's versions of*
A Midsummer Night's Dream. *He defends these treatments
as attempts to provide the "sort of entertainment the public
wished" in the mid-eighteenth century.*]

By 1755 English dramatic audiences as well as English dramatic critics were less concerned with faults in the construction of Shakespeare's plays then they had been twenty years
earlier. Largely because of Garrick's excellent acting, the
focal point of Shakespearian criticism was shifting from consideration of plot structure to consideration of character delineation. But even though advance was being made in the
new criticism as well as in the growth of Shakespeare idolatry, such a varied mixture of realistic material, classical mythology, and fairy lore as Shakespeare used in *A Midsummer
Night's Dream* was bound to fail in presentation. Pepys, nearly one hundred years earlier (September 29, 1662), had seen
the play and had remarked that it was the most insipid and
ridiculous one he had ever witnessed in his life. In 1716 Richard Leveridge presented his *Comick Masque of Pyramus and
Thisbe* at Lincoln's Inn Fields, where it had nine performances (from April 11 of that year until September 9, 1723).
As the title suggests, it was a brief handling of Bottom's playing artisans—a mere fragment of Shakespeare's play. On January 21, 1745 an anonymous Mock Opera, *Pyramus and
Thisbe,* appeared at Covent Garden and enjoyed some twenty-two performances until April 13, 1748. The music was
composed by John Frederick Lampe, and the play was slightly longer than Leveridge's. No other performance of *A Midsummer Night's Dream* in any of its parts is recorded until
1755 when Garrick made his first attempt to give his audiences some more of the material of the play. He was wise, as
subsequent events proved, not to try to present it at that time
in its entirety. Yet he was vitally interested in the whole of
the play and joined eight years later with his friend George
Colman in an attempt to produce it in its Shakespearian
form.

The story of this attempt has been confused; and mistaken
conjecture, because of lack of evidence, has guided former
writers on the subject with the result that misunderstanding

has arisen concerning the share of each manager in the production, as well as of the quality of sympathetic understanding each had of Shakespeare. I wish to tell the story of the
handling of *A Midsummer Night's Dream* by Garrick and
Colman from the beginning, and to clear up the points of mis-
information and misunderstanding. It will be necessary, in
doing this, to start with a word concerning the tendencies in
the London theatres at the midpoint of the eighteenth century.

The decade 1750-60 was marked in the history of the English
stage by the growth of pantomimes, pageants, and operas.
The great exponent of these spectacle shows was John Rich,
manager of Covent Garden, who himself, as Mr. Lun, was
a remarkable pantomimic actor and a master of elaborate
stage devices. His efforts in this type of drama had caused
considerable embarrassment to Wilks, Booth, and Cibber in
their dramatic attempts earlier in the century. After a lull in
his activities—from 1741 to 1747 when Quin, and for a while
Garrick, filled his house and treasury, and when Harlequin's
wand contributed little or nothing—he again exerted himself
in the fifties. Garrick naturally had to compete with him in
this field; so he enlisted the aid of Henry Woodward, who as
a pantomimic artist was second only to Rich. Annually from
1750 to 1756 Woodward produced a new pantomime and
each met with overwhelming success. That his *Queen Mab,
Harlequin Ranger, The Genii, Fortunatus, Proteus, or Harlequin in China,* and *Mercury Harlequin* proved popular
enough to satisfy the desires of the managers and entertaining
enough to draw crowds of people is indicated by the box receipts, by the long runs they enjoyed at Drury Lane, and by
the fact that they were kept in the repertoire of the theatre
for years afterwards. Yet that Garrick was dissatisfied with
this Harlequinade is evidenced in the ironical closing lines of
his Epilogue to *Barbarossa:*

> I therefore now propose, by your command,
> That tragedies no more shall cloud the land;
> Send o'er your Shakespeare to the sons of France,
> Let *them* grow grave—let us begin to dance!
> Banish your gloomy scenes to foreign climes,
> Reserve alone to bless these golden times,
> A farce or two—and Woodward's pantomimes!

In response to the popular demand, however, on February 3,
1755, Garrick tried his hand at opera and produced *The
Fairies,* "an English opera taken from Shakespear's Midsummer Night's dream & set to music by Mr. Smith pupil to Mr.
Handel . . . ," as Richard Cross remarks in his *Diary.* It was
new enough and spectacular enough to be played without an
afterpiece and went off "with great applause." Its first night
brought the managers #200, and the next ten performances
stretching until November 7, 1755, brought in #1520. Since
it was to be an opera and its emphasis therefore was to be
upon its musical quality, Garrick procured the aid of two
Italian singers. To care for the spectacle of the fairy dances
he hired a troop of well-trained boys. "Besides our own singers," writes Cross, "we had Signor Guidani, Signora
Passerini; Miss Potier & Savages's Boys . . . "

Subsequent critics, such as Genest [in his *Some Account of the
English Stage*], have sneered at this engaging of foreigners:—
"Midsummer Night's Dream turned into an Opera and assisted by two foreigners, must have been a blessed exhibition,
and highly to the credit of Garrick, who talked so much of
his zeal for Shakespeare." But as usual the only reactions
given by contemporaries, though written after the event, are

favorable. Tate Wilkinson [in his *Memoirs of His Own Life*] wrote: "It was well performed and with good success, aided not a little by an excellent prologue and as excellently spoken by Mr. Garrick—Giordani [sic] and Passerini were great additional service as Lysander and Hermia." Murphy wrote [in his *Life of David Garrick*]: "The aerial beings, of which Shakespeare was the father, could not, it must be acknowledged, be rendered more fit for representation by any other contrivance."

The story presented in the opera is extremely slight. It is made up from the first four acts only, of Shakespeare's play. From those acts are taken only the portions dealing with the crossed loves of Lysander, Hermia, Demetrius and Helena, and the domestic quarrel in the fairy household over the possession of the Indian boy, set in a thin framework of Theseus' wedding with Hippolita. Some 840 lines are excised from the speeches of these participants, and all reference to Bottom and his troop of artisans is cut from the play. Garrick in his advertisement to the printed edition of 1755 speaks on this head as follows: "Many passages of the first merit and some whole scenes are omitted . . . it was feared that even the best poetry would appear tedious when only supported by Recitative."

Garrick was under the necessity of altering some lines and of adding a few to bind the fragments into a new whole. But there are remarkably few instances of this sort of tampering. Professor Odell, who has reviewed the opera, writes [in his *Shakespeare from Betterton to Irving*], "Garrick was no Tate: he at least left in their original purity the Shakespearian verses he used—he merely omitted or put in—but in either case it was solid blocks that went or stayed." Much of Shakespeare's dreamy fancy and precious music is lost in Garrick's version, however, as Dr. Hedgcock is quick to point out [in his *David Garrick and his French Friends*]. We miss such passages as, "I know a bank where the wild thyme blows" [II. i. 249]. Yet the attempt in the opera was undoubtedly to get musical effects from the school of Handel rather than from Shakespeare, and I am inclined to believe, especially in the light of Garrick's denial of authorship, that Mr. Smith had more of a determining hand in it than is generally believed.

Critics, however, have damned Garrick less for his omissions and for his occasional rewordings than for the addition of twenty-eight songs to to the text. But condemnation on this point seems quite academic for, though some of the songs are flat as poetry, they must have been well received as sung to Smith's music. Seven of them are from Shakespeare's play itself: four recognized as songs by the dramatist, Puck's "Up and down, up and down" [III. ii. 396ff.], and "Now until the break of day" [V. i. 401ff.]; Oberon's "Flower of this purple dye" [III. ii. 102ff.]; and the Fairies' "Ye spotted snakes with double tongue" [II. ii. 9ff.]; and three taken almost verbatim from the text, but put to musical accompaniment, Helena's "O happy fair, your eyes are loadstars and your tongue's sweet air More tuneable than lark to shepherd's ear" [I. i. 182ff.], etc., her "Love looks not with the eyes but with the mind" [I. i. 234ff.], and Hermia's "Before the time I did Lysander see Seem'd Athens like a paradise to me" [I. i. 204ff.], etc. Shakespeare contributed four more songs to the opera, for Puck appropriates Ariel's song from the *Tempest*, with a word changed, "Where the bee sucks there *lurk* I" [V. i. 88ff.], Oberon appropriates "Sigh no more Ladies, sigh no more" from *Much Ado* [II. iii. 62ff.], Titania brings "Orpheus with his lute made trees . . ." from *Henry VIII* [III. i. 3ff.],

and Lysander takes half a dozen lines from Dumain's ode in *Love's Labors Lost*, "Do not call it sin in me . . . " [IV. iii. 99ff.]. A song of two stanzas is made up from Milton's *L'Allegro* and sung by Lysander, "When that gay season did us lead To the tann'd haycock in the mead." Landsdowne contributed a stanza to the final chorus, "Hail to love and welcome joy, Hail to the delicious boy," from *The British Enchanters*. Lysander is made to sing to Helena the first stanza of Waller's song "Say lovely dream, where couldst thou find Shades to counterfeit that face." From James Hammond, the love elegist, came the song "With mean disguise let others nature hide . . . " Dryden is said to have furnished still another. But what of the remaining ones Garrick composed cannot be proved. We must always remember, however, that these songs were heard and not read, and that, as in most similar cases, the words though appropriate to the action were really vehicles for the music. Wagner's "Pilgrim's Chorus" is not a great poem.

Dr. Hedgcock after comparing the flatness of Hammond's song, and the unidentified one "Joy alone shall employ us," with the musical and poetic lines from Shakespeare, "I know a bank where the wild thyme blows," concludes:

> In a word, all the dreamy fancy and all the rich playfulness of the charming pastoral are suppressed; and in that lies the importance to the literary historian of Garrick's alterations of Shakespeare; they mark French influence at its high tide, just before the turn. The French mind, positive, realist, and intellectual has never shown much sympathy for the visionary creations, so unlike anything in heaven or on earth, of our romantic imaginative poets. Now Garrick's was a French mind, formed in what may be called a French century. . . .

I hold no brief for the poetic quality of the songs he quotes, nor for the Shakespearian quality of the opera as a whole, save that it pleased Garrick's contemporaries. What I object to in Dr. Hedgcock's statement is the conclusion to which he jumps and the generalization which he makes upon thin evidence that all Garrick's alterations are similar, and that his mind, a French one, was deficient in sympathy for or understanding of the visionary creations and rich fancy of Shakespeare. For Dr. Hedgcock has told but half the story in his treatment of Garrick's handling of *A Midsummer Night's Dream*. That Garrick was interested in a fuller presentation of the play which included all of the visionary and poetic passages cited by Dr. Hedgcock,—and more,—is evidenced by the production of the play eight years later, on November 23, 1763. To this production he refers merely in a footnote, as the "Fairies . . . revived in a slightly different version."

It was not the *Fairies* revived, but *A Midsummer Night's Dream* revived, and it failed about as completely as any play ever did on the eighteenth-century stage. It was printed in the same year, and ever since then critics who have been interested in it at all have damned Garrick for it even more, possibly, than for the opera. Genest writes:

> This piece was in five acts—it was acted but one night—it is a bad alteration of the original—nearly the whole of the Mock Play is omitted, and Shakespeare's piece is turned into a sort of Opera with thirty-three songs—the dialogue is in general judiciously curtailed, but some few lines of the original, which are omitted should have been retained—Shakespeare makes his Athenians talk of Diana's

nuns and of going a Maying—it is strange that the person who altered this play should not have omitted two such palpable absurdities—the alteration was attributed originally to Colman, but it seems that it was made by Garrick and that Colman only superintended the rehearsals at his desire.

But guesswork and conjectural criticism with reference to the play should now come to an end, for Garrick's own copy,—the Tonson duodecimo of 1734 upon which he based his alteration,—has come to light in the Folger Shakespeare Library, a copy containing notes, emendations, and directions for cutting in Garrick's own hand. Comparison of this copy with the play as printed anonymously in 1763—"with alterations and additions and several new songs as it is performed at the Theatre Royal in Drury Lane"—shows vast differences, and proves beyond a doubt that the printed version, the one for which Garrick has been criticised, should be fathered upon George Colman.

Let us proceed with the story in order. Garrick undertook the task of fitting *A Midsummer Night's Dream* for the stage sometime before September 1763,—or possibly he and Colman undertook it together. But discouraged with the attacks made upon him in the Fitzpatrick riots, and ill in health he sought escape and rest on the continent. He left England on the fifteenth of that month for an extended tour of France, Italy, and Germany, and took with him, as his biographer Fitzgerald states [in his *Life of Garrick*], the resolution of never appearing on the stage again unless a two-years' absence should prove a remedy for his unpopularity. He left George Colman to supervise rehearsals and to plan casts, and advised him, says Professor Odell, to give audiences plenty of musical entertainments. Colman also had a copy of Garrick's alteration of *A Midsummer Night's Dream*.

Garrick was interested in the success of the piece and wrote Colman from Paris on October 8, " . . . as for Midsummer Night's &c I think my presence will be necessary to get it up as it ought—however if you want it, do for the best & I'll Ensure Its Success." But Colman worked at the piece after his own fashion and rather completely revised it. The best short account of his actions as well as of the failure of the play when presented is given in the following unpublished note in [William] Hopkins' *Diary*.

> The piece was greatly Cut & Alter'd: the 5th Act Entirely left out & many Airs interspers'd all through; got up with a vast deal of trouble to everybody concern'd in it but *particularly to Mr. Coleman, who attended every Rehearsal & had alterations innumerable to make.* Upon the whole, never was anything so murder'd in the Speaking. Mr. W. Palmer & Mrs. Vincent were beyond description bad; & had it not been for the Children's excellent performance (& particularly Miss Wright who Sung delightfully), the Audience would not have Suffer'd 'em to have gone half thro' it. The Sleeping Scene particularly displeas'd. Next day it was reported the Performers first Sung the Audience to Sleep, & then went to Sleep themselves. Fairies pleas'd—Serious parts displeas'd—Comic between both.

The "alterations innumerable" that Colman made, appear in the cutting of 561 lines which Garrick had indicated should remain in the text, and the extension of some scenes which Garrick had not indicated. The largest excision by Colman was the omission of the fifth act with the play of Pyramus and

Thisbe, all of which Garrick apparently kept with the excision of only eighteen lines and of the final song of Puck, "Now the hungry lion roars . . . " [V. i. 371ff.]. At the end of Act I, to the scene in which the artisans gather for the assignment of parts, Colman added seventeen lines of dialogue and a song of four stanzas. The addition has been credited to Garrick in the *Variorum* [edition of *A Midsummer Night's Dream,* by Horace Howard Furness], but is not indicated in his annotated copy. By this addition Colman turns the first meeting of Bottom and his fellows into a glee club rehearsal.

Colman abridged nearly all the speeches of the play, cutting sometimes only half a line, but more often two or as many as eight lines. (pp. 467-75)

In Colman's version the separation of Demetrius and Lysander in their attempted duel is accomplished by Oberon. In Garrick's version which follows the Shakespearian text, it is done by Puck in a pleasant scene of thirty-two lines. Colman trimmed the number to nineteen and transferred Puck's lines to the Fairy King. The following scene in which Puck is supposed to put Hermia to sleep and to arrange for a reconciliation, Colman trimmed likewise of four of its lines, and gave all of Puck's words to Oberon and another fairy. Puck's part, of which Garrick was interested in keeping as much as possible, loses significance in the Colman version. I see no evidence here of the positivistic French mind exerting itself in Garrick.

Accompanying Garrick's annotated copy of the play there is, in the Folger Library, a most interesting and valuable sheaf of notes composed of two tentative cast lists, both differing from the cast printed in the 1763 edition, several diagrams of the prompter's disposition of the various characters on each side of the stage, and one page dealing with the songs which Garrick intended to use in the play. This page explains what he meant when, in the text, he merely inserted at various points a cross and wrote the word *Song* in the margin beside it. "Page 1st," he writes, "begin with Chorus,"—

Song	5th	Herm: With Mean Disguise . . . &c . . .	Smith
Page	7	Lys: When the Gay Season . . .	Do
Page	8	Hel: O Hermia Fair . . .	Do
Page	8	Herm: Before the time . . .	Do
Page	9	Hel: New	
Page	12	Comic Chorus Epilogue	
		Act 2d	
Page	12	Fairy should sing Where the Bee sucks . . .	
			Arne
Page	16	Fairy Queen	
		Duet: Away away . . .	
		Fairy King	

And so he continues throughout the play. At most he has only indicated twenty-seven songs and an opening and closing chorus. Fifteen come from the opera *The Fairies,* six are unidentified being marked only as *New,* the others are formed from lines of Shakespeare's text set to music. The printed version of the play contains thirty-three songs. Colman apparently added more than Garrick intended and cut out some which Garrick had suggested for, where Garrick in the above notes called for "Where the Bee sucks. . . . " Colman has substituted a new one, "Kingcup, Daffodil and Rose. . . . "

But more important than these items, even, is a four and one-half page running comment upon Garrick's altered text, keyed to the 1734 Tonson edition, written by George Colman, and dated by him June 18, 1763. Garrick apparently sent Colman his first draft of the alteration, and Colman returned it with his list of suggestions for further changes. Some of these Garrick agreed with and marked accordingly in his text. Others he rejected. Colman seemed to be obsessed with the idea that Shakespeare's rime in certain of the love scenes was unfit for an eighteenth-century audience. Three of his suggestions on the subject are as follows:

> P 7, 8, 9. All may be easily cut & put out of rhime, wch is very uncouth—I have marked them a little with that view see the crochets [ ]. . . . "

> P 22, 23. These pages shd be thrown out of rhime into plain blank verse—It may be easily done, & will have a much better effect. . . . "

> P 30 Scene v.—This scene, and indeed all the others except those between the Fairies, shd be thrown out of rhime. It will also make the Fairy-scenes appear more characteristically distinguished. It is the more necessary to do this because a good deal of the writing in this act is uncouth & wants alteration—vide scenes vi, vii, viii.—

Colman suggested some alterations by bracketing lines and words for omission or change. Examination of the text shows that Garrick accepted only a few. He was, as usual, interested in keeping Shakespeare's text in as pure a state as possible, nor apparently did he think the speeches so uncouth as to require the wholesale changes suggested by his colleague. In the printed version of 1763 however, Colman with a free hand reduced the "jingle." In one speech of Hermia's, for instance, which Garrick keeps as Shakespeare wrote it, the rimes are as follows:—best, breast, here, fear, away, pray, Lord, word, hear, fear. But in Colman's version five emendations occur so that the "jingle" may be avoided:—best, *bosom,* here, *horror,* away, *Lysander,* Lord, *sight, me,* fear. Garrick had indicated that the final scene of the play should be cut and that the play should end with Theseus' speech to the actors, "No Epilogue, I pray you, for your play needs no excuse . . . " [V. i. 355-56]. From the Pyramus and Thisbe play he marked only twenty-two lines for omission, fourteen of which were comments of Theseus and Demetrius upon the action. On June 18 Colman wrote of this act:

> The palpable gross play of Pyramus & Thisbe, as well as the interlocutory Dialogue of the other characters, must be shortened as much as possible—if the Comi-Tragedy cd be enlivened with 2 or 3 odd songs I think it wd be safer. I think it very ill judged to attempt to cut out the concluding Fairy scene.—Restore it with Songs Dances &c at all events. On the whole I think it may with care and attention be made a most *novelle* and elegant entertainment—but may tumble for want of amending a few absurdities, and altering some trifling circumstances wch make it uncouth and unsuitable to the taste of the present times—I live in hopes of seeing it a favorite entertainment of next winter.

But by the time he was ready to produce the play in November, he had cut not only the final fairy scene but also "the palpable gross play of Pyramus and Thisbe." In fact he retained from Shakespeare's fifth act only the first eighteen lines of Theseus' speech on the "lunatic, the lover and the poet" [V. i. 7].

Whether Garrick's longer play, even with its more faithful following of the Shakespearian text, would have succeeded is doubtful considering the review of Colman's shorter one which appeared in the St. James Chronicle, for November 24, 1763:

I was last night at Drury Lane Theatre, to see the Revival of Shakespeare's *Midsummer Night's Dream,* an odd romantick Performance, more like a masque than a Play, and presenting a lively picture of the ungoverned imagination of that great Poet. The Fairy part is most transcendently beautiful, and is, in poetical geography, a kind of Dramatic Map of Fairy Land; but the Love-Story wound up with it, and the Celebration of the Marriage of Theseus is very flat and uninteresting; even the very fine Speeches of Theseus, towards the conclusion of the Piece, are fitter for the Closet than the Stage, where they receive no great Addition by coming from the deep mouth of our old friend Mr. Bransby. I never at one time saw at the Playhouse so much good and so much bad acting. The Children were admirable, most of the *Grown Gentlemen* and *Ladies* execrable. Three of the four vocal Performers plainly shewed themselves incapable of delivering a Blank Verse, except in Recitative. It is a thousand pities that such sweet Children should be thus overlaid. A friend of mine who was with me in the Pit, seeing the poor Infants endeavoring to struggle under such a Heap of Rubbish, threw out the following Impromptu with which I shall conclude these observations:

Similie addressed to the Children on the Representation of the Midsummer Night's Dream

Did you ne'er see, across the Tide
By Fishermen near Town,
A mighty Net, both large and wide
In Thames fair Bosom thrown?

One end, weigh'd down with Lead, would quite
Unto the bottom drop,
But that with numerous Corks made light
The other floats at top.

Thus, pretty Dears, the lively Scene
You fill with Sense and Spirit;
Help the grown Gentlemen's dull Vein
And give the Piece some merit.

Yet you like living Bodies seem,
Coupled to Bodies dead:
You swim like Cork upon the Stream
But can't keep up *their* Lead.

But Garrick's interest in all parts of this Shakespearian play cannot, now that we can see his acting copy, be doubted.

He wrote Colman from Naples, December 24, 1763:—" . . . the poor Mids Night's Dream I find has failed by a letter in ye chronle. I know ye author & love him tho he abuses the *Grown* Gentlemen & Ladies. . . . " So Colman wishing to capitalize upon some part of this failure seemed to take a hint from Hopkins' observations, "Fairies pleased—Serious parts displeas'd—Comic between both," and three days later produced *A Fairy Tale* as the after piece to his *Jealous Wife*. This piece is composed of two short acts centering about the Oberon-Titania dispute over the possession of the Indian boy. However, it brings in those scenes in which Bottom and his fellows prepare their play and come in contact with the fairy world. But the scenes are not taken complete from Shakespeare. There is great abridgment and the play ends quickly before the Artisans have time to perform their "most lamentable comedy," for, when Titania has been sufficiently punished, and when Oberon succeeds in obtaining the Indian boy, he restores his queen to her right mind and commands:

Silence awhile. Robin remove the man
And you meanwhile, Titania, music call,
And strike more dead than common sleep his senses.

Music is brought, two fairies sing "Orpheus with his lute made trees. . . ." from *Henry VIII,* and after Oberon and Titania have joined hands they sing "Sigh no more, Ladies . . . " from *Much Ado.* A lark sings and as the fairies give a final dance Titania and Oberon exit with:

Come, my lord, and in our flight
Tell me, how it came this night,
That I sleeping here was found,
With yon mortal on the ground.

One new song has been added by Colman in which a Fairy, with an echo or two from *Macbeth,* sings of the power of the "little western flower."

Hopkins in his *Diary* makes two notes upon this afterpiece: ". . . [it] is a very pleasing Farce, & well receiv'd by the Audience." "November 28, *Careless Husband & Fairy Tale.* After the play on Saturday Night Mr. Yates sent me the part of Bottom in the Fairy Tale & said he would play it no more. The part was given to Mr. Baddeley & he play'd it tonight." But despite Yates' displeasure with his part the piece was played about seventeen more times that season. Garrick wrote to his brother George from Naples, January 31, 1764:—". . . tell Colman I love him more and more & thank him most cordially for his Fairy Tale—it puzzl'd me much for I saw it in ye papers before I rec'd his letter about it. . . ."

All in all, then, four plays must be considered,—*The Fairies,* Colman's *Midsummer Night's Dream,* Garrick's acting copy of the same, and Colman's *Fairy Tale,*—for a full treatment of the fate of Shakespeare's *Midsummer Night's Dream* in the mid-eighteenth century. And such a treatment is not without value in showing what sort of entertainment the public wished at the time, and in demonstrating the truth of the lines in Dr. Johnson's Prologue, written for Garrick at the opening of the theatre in 1747:—

The drama's laws the drama's patrons give,
For we, that live to please, must please to live.

This should be clearly kept in mind when judgment is passed upon Garrick for his participation in *The Fairies,* and in *A Midsummer Night's Dream.* Just as clearly should be kept in mind, however, what the discovery of Garrick's acting copy reveals as to his appreciation of the imaginative flights and the romantic juxtapositions of Shakespeare. (pp. 477-82)

George Winchester Stone, Jr., " 'A Midsummer Night's Dream' in the Hands of Garrick and Colman," in PMLA, Vol. LIV, No. 2, June, 1939, pp. 467-82.

PRODUCTION:

Frederick Reynolds • Covent Garden • 1816

BACKGROUND:

The first significant revival of *A Midsummer Night's Dream* in the nineteenth century was an 1816 Covent Gar-

den operatic version, adapted by Frederick Reynolds. Many of the lyrics of Garrick's version were retained, but were set to new music. The earlier tradition of scenic splendor was continued as well, with the addition of a fifth-act pageant entitled "The Triumphs of Theseus," derived from various tales concerning the legendary king. This production also inaugurated a tradition of setting the performance amid scenes of ancient Athens and costuming the actors in Greek attire.

COMMENTARY:

The Times, London   (review date 18 January 1816)

[*In the excerpt below the reviewer praises the acting, singing, and setting of the Covent Garden production, but judges the revisions of and additions to Shakespeare's text lamentable, particularly the newly composed lyrics.*]

We went last night to attend the theatrical revival of the *"Midsummer Night's Dream."* The stage history informs us, that a similar attempt was made by GARRICK, who, after sundry transpositions and other alterations in the scenes and language of his patron bard, entirely failed in reconciling the public to what may doubtless be considered a most arduous enterprise, viz. the adaptation of this pure work of fancy to the eyes and ears of a promiscuous audience. We did not anticipate a greater degree of success from the undertaking of last night, than attended the preceding one between fifty and sixty years ago; because we neither gave credit to the dramatic conductors of the present day for more ability than was exercised by GARRICK, nor to the existing generation, at least that portion of it who frequent the playhouse, for a much greater quantity of taste, of intellectual refinement, or genius, or imagination, than their ancestors. Of all the productions of SHAKESPEARE, the *Midsummer Night's Dream,* perhaps, is liable to the most opposite judgments, according to the light in which it be viewed, as a dramatic composition; or an undefined effusion of poetical power. It seems to be less wrought out by the efforts of SHAKESPEARE's intellect, than thrown off from his fancy in a sportive mood; as if he had entered accidentally into the wardrobe of his imagination, and heaped together with a careless hand some of its looser ornaments as they lay before him. Story there is none—it almost looks as if the author had grudged labour enough on the occasion to construct a consistent plot—but of invention, of imagery, and eloquence of the highest order, there is enough to beautify the materials of an hundred plays. It is natural to conjecture that the *"Fairy Queen"* had some influence in turning our Poet's mind to a field which the profuse and luxuriant spirit of SPENSER had enriched rather than exhausted by his recent and successful cultivation, and that this wild offspring of the brain of SHAKESPEARE was indeed the fruit of an excursion of the fancy indulged in an hour when sleep had reassembled the images, that suspended memory had set free. All this is delicious to a man of poetical feeling in his closet. But there is no interest to excite the passions—no event to rouse the curiosity—no character to attract the observation of that vulgar and chance medley multitude who crowd together within the walls of a theatre. The bad judgment of bringing forward such a play at all cannot be cured by any subsequent or collateral attention to points of secondary importance. The evil might be palliated by shewing a sacred regard to SHAKESPEARE's memory—by leaving his faults to seek their pardon through the medium of his proper beauties;

and let his irregularites and indiscretions bear only upon their author for forgiveness. Even this praise has not been merited in the present instance; for SHAKESPEAR's words have been superseded by more foolish words, and his absurdities have been disgraced by comparisons more absurd than they are. This offence has been committed more glaringly in the songs than elsewhere; the trash that has been obtruded upon us in this way being altogether insupportable. The passages of the *Midsummer Night's Dream,* which were originally set to music, contain some most exquisite touches of true and tender poetry. Our readers may recollect one of the earlier interpolations, commencing thus, "Sweet soothing hope, &c." allotted to *Hermia*—to prove the advancement of the art of song-writing within the last half century, we shall introduce a specimen of the present amended version—To the tune, no doubt, of *"Goosey Gander!"*—

> Whither dost thou wander?
> Lysander, Lysander—
> He hears not!
> Appears not!
> Lysander, Lysander!!

We verily believe that SHAKESPEARE might have "cudgelled his brains," to the present year, 1816, of the Christian era, without ever being able to accomplish five such lines as these: as to every branch of the management, save only the poetical, we are ready and desirous to offer our tribute of applause to the style in which this play has been got up. The characters were extremely well performed; from the *Theseus* of Mr. CONWAY down to the *"Wall* and *Moonshine"* of Messrs BLANCHARD and MENAGE—LISTON was one of the most agreeable "Asses" we ever met with. The songs were most of them exquisitely sung by Miss STEPHENS, Mr. SINCLAIR, &c. The concluding very difficult *bravura* "Now Pleasure's Voice," was a grand exhibition of vocal power. Miss BOOTH was lively and spirited in *Puck;* for which, however, the roundness of her figure contributed in some small degree to disqualify her. The scenery was new and well executed; and the final procession, descriptive of the exploits of *Theseus,* splendid and appropriate to the time. The house was crowded beyond any thing we have lately seen, and we shall be most happy to find by the future success of this revival, that others are not likely to participate the sensations of weariness which now and then threatened to steal upon us during the performance.

> *A review of "A Midsummer Night's Dream," in* The Times, *London, January 18, 1816, p. 2.*

William Hazlitt   (review date 21 January 1816)

[*Hazlitt was an eminent English essayist and critic whose work, typically focusing on characterization, reflects the influence of Romanticism. One of the first great dramatic critics, his reviews were published in the* Examiner, *the* Morning Chronicle, *the* Champion, *the* London Magazine, *and the* Times. *Some of these were subsequently collected in his* Round Table (1817) *and* A View of the English Stage (1818). *The following review is perhaps the most famous commentary on the staging of* A Midsummer Night's Dream. *After viewing the 1816 Covent Garden production, which he found a "dull pantomime," Hazlitt concludes that this play cannot be satisfactorily presented in the theater. "Poetry and the stage do not agree together," he maintains, and attempts to present such a fanciful work are disappointing and ultimately futile.*]

We hope we have not been accessory to murder, in recommending a delightful poem to be converted into a dull pantomime; for such is the fate of the *Midsummer Night's Dream.* We have found to our cost, once for all, that the regions of fancy and the boards of Covent-Garden are not the same thing. All that is fine in the play, was lost in the representation. The spirit was evaporated, the genius was fled; but the spectacle was fine. It was that which saved the play.—Oh, ye scene-shifters, ye scene-painters, ye machinists and dressmakers, ye manufacturers of moon and stars that give no light, ye musical composers, ye men in the orchestra, fiddlers and trumpeters and players on the double drum and loud bassoon, rejoice! This is your triumph; it is not ours: and ye full-grown, well-fed, substantial, real fairies, Messieurs TREBY and TRUMAN and ATKINS, and Misses MATTHEWS, CAREW, BURRELL, and MAC ALPINE, we shall remember you: we shall believe no more in the existence of your fantastic tribe. *Flute,* the bellows-mender, *Snug* the joiner, *Starveling* the tailor, farewell; you have lost the charm of your names; but thou, *Nic. Bottom,* thou valiant *Bottom,* what shall we say to thee? Thou didst console us much; thou didst perform a good part well; thou didst top the part of *Bottom* the weaver! He comes out of thy hands as clean and clever a fellow as ever. Thou art a person of exquisite whim and humour; and thou didst hector over thy companions well, and fall down flat before the *Duke,* like other bullies, well; and thou didst sing the song of the Black Ousel well; but chief, thou didst noddle thy ass's head, which had been put upon thee, well; and didst seem to say, significantly, to thy new attendants, *Peaseblossom, Cobweb, Moth,* and *Mustardseed,* "Gentlemen, I can present you equally to my friends and to my enemies!"—All that was good in this piece (except the scenery) was Mr. LISTON's *Bottom,* which was an admirable and judicious piece of acting.—Mr. CONWAY was *Theseus.* Who would ever have taken this gentleman for the friend and companion of Hercules?—Miss STEPHENS played the part of *Hermia,* and sang several songs very delightfully, which however by no means assisted the progress or interest of the story—Miss FOOTE played *Helena.* She is a very sweet girl, and not at all a bad actress; yet did any one feel or even hear her address to *Hermia?* To shew how far asunder the closet and the stage are, we give it here once more entire:—

> Injurious Hermia, most ungrateful maid,
> Have you conspired, have you with these contriv'd
> To bait me with this foul derision?
> Is all the counsel that we two have shar'd,
> The sisters' vows, the hours that we have spent,
> When we have chid the hasty-footed time
> For parting us—Oh! and is all forgot?
> All school-days' friendship, childhood innocence?
> We, Hermia, like two artificial Gods,
> Created with our needles both one flower,
> Both on one sampler, sitting on one cushion;
> Both warbling of one song, both in one key;
> As if our hands, our sides, voices and minds,
> Had been incorporate. So we grew together,
> Like to a double cherry, seeming parted,
> But yet an union in partition.
> And will you rend our ancient love asunder,
> And join with men in scorning your poor friend?
> It is not friendly, 'tis not maidenly:
> Our sex as well as I may chide you for it,
> Though I alone do feel the injury.

In turning to SHAKESPEARE to look for this passage, the book opened at the *Midsummer Night's Dream,* the title of which half gave us back our old feeling; and in reading this one speech twice over, we have completely forgot all the noise we have heard and the sights we have seen. Poetry and the stage do not agree together. The attempt to reconcile them fails not only of effect, but of decorum. The ideal has no place upon the stage, which is a picture without perspective; every thing there is in the foreground. That which is merely an airy shape, a dream, a passing thought, immediately becomes an unmanageable reality. Where all is left to the imagination, every circumstance has an equal chance of being kept in mind, and tells according to the mixed impression of all that has been suggested. But the imagination cannot sufficiently qualify the impressions of the senses. Any offence given to the eye is not to be got rid of by explanation. Thus *Bottom's* head in the play is a fantastic illusion, produced by magic spells: on the stage it is an ass's head, and nothing more; certainly a very strange costume for a gentleman to appear in. Fancy cannot be represented any more than a simile can be represented; and it is as idle to attempt it as to personate Wall or Moonshine. Fairies are not incredible, but fairies six feet high are so. Monsters are not shocking, if they are seen at a proper distance. When ghosts appear in midday, when apparitions stalk along Cheapside, then may the *Midsummer Night's Dream* be represented at Covent-Garden or at Drury-lane; for we hear that it is to be brought out there also, and that we have to undergo another crucifixion.

Mrs. FAUCITT played the part of *Titania* very well, but for one circumstance, that she is a woman. The only glimpse which we caught of the possibility of acting the imaginary scenes properly, was from the little girl who dances before the fairies (we do not know her name), which seemed to shew that the whole might be carried off in the same manner—by a miracle. (pp. 41-2)

> *William Hazlitt, in a review of "A Midsummer Night's Dream," in* The Examiner, *No. 421, January 21, 1816, pp. 44-5.*

Henry Crabb Robinson (diary date 7 February 1816)

[*In the excerpt below from Robinson's diary, the writer judges the Covent Garden production favorably, despite its alterations of Shakespeare's text and the actors' poor delivery of the verse.*]

I saw [at Covent Garden] *Midsummer Night's Dream* and though much altered from Shakespeare I still enjoyed the performance very much. The principal attraction certainly is Liston as Bottom and he was respectably supported in the burlesque scenes—Shakespeare's powerful and significant verse is delightful even when ill recited and the piece abounds in poetical beauties. . . . Mrs. Faucit formerly of the Norwich Theatre pleased me on account of her countenance which has a pleasing expression. . . .

> *Henry Crabb Robinson, in a diary entry on February 7, 1816, in his* The London Theatre: 1811-1866, *edited by Eluned Brown, The Society for Theatre Research, 1966, p. 69.*

Gary Jay Williams (essay date 1973)

[*Williams provides an overview of the 1816 Covent Garden revival of* A Midsummer Night's Dream, *paying particular attention to the music of this production.*]

The version [of *A Midsummer Night's Dream*] of 1816 was by Frederic Reynolds, a brash adapter and opera-maker of six other of Shakespeare's comedies who found himself at odds with contemporary critics over such treatments. Reynolds' three act version may be said to be an attempt at producing all of the play, comparatively, and, as the defensive Reynolds was glad to point out in his autobiography, his version did manage more success than Garrick's, with some eighteen performances. But the text of the "divine drama" which Reynolds says he was "compelled to alter," was badly cut and shuffled. In the first act, even basic exposition was cut, with Helena never being brought on in the act to be told of Hermia's elopement plans; thus her appearance with Demetrius in the forest in pursuit of Lysander and Hermia goes unexplained. There were also deep cuts in the poetry. If all this did not disturb Reynolds, it did Hazlitt (to whom we shall return). More important to Reynolds were the attractions he could provide London audiences in the way of additional songs and of scenic spectacles, accompanied by instrumental music. Oberon and Titania entered, each in a car, to begin their quarrel. To the accompaniment of the orchestra, a fairy on a descending cloud showed audiences Titania's galley in full sail from India to bring to Oberon the Indian boy who then ran onto the stage to the waiting Oberon and a chorus which sang, "Pierce the air with sounds of joy! / Hail Titania's treasur'd Boy!"—a song which had appeared in both the 1755 and the 1763 operas [by Garrick]. At the end of the play, as was the case with Purcell [in *The Fairy Queen,* 1692], Theseus was not to be entertained by Quince and company. In 1816, the entertainment given for Theseus' court and London audiences in the vast Covent Garden Theatre was, according to the playbill, "A Grand Pageant commemorative of the Triumphs of Theseus, Over the Cretans—The Thebans—The Amazons—The Minotaur—Ariadne in the Labyrinth, the Mysterious Peplum or the Veil of Minerva, the Ship Argo—and the Golden Fleece." (In 1960 critics were upset when a manacled Hippolyta appeared under guard as Theseus' captive in an Old Vic production.) Quince and company perform their play in the forest where Reynolds, with unabashed clumsiness, has Theseus call for his revels and then observe a run-through of *Pyramus and Thisbe* from behind a tree. Bottom, played by John Liston—one of the most praised Bottoms of the nineteenth century, fainted when the king was disclosed.

The composer-arranger for Reynolds' adaptation was Sir Henry Rowley Bishop, prolific composer of popular theatre music who provided much incidental music for Shakespeare in this period, including the scores for Reynolds' other adaptations of Shakespeare's comedies. There would have been twenty-four vocal pieces in this opera (counting one for each separate lyric in the libretto), with an overture by Bishop and miscellaneous incidental cues. From the list of composers at the top of the playbill, from the partial but not too accurate composer credits given in the libretto, and from what we know of previous scores, there seem to have been some sixteen or seventeen song-settings that were new with this production. Many of the lyrics Reynolds used had been set to music in the 1763 *A Midsummer Night's Dream*—some seventeen in all. According to the libretto credits, Bishop provided ten new songs and on two more collaborated with Thomas Simpson Cooke, well known composer of light operas and theatre music. Other selections, according to the libretto, came from G. F. Handel (1), Richard Stevens (1), and "Arne" (1). Some seven other song-settings are not credited in the libretto. Among the Shakespearean words set to music were (in the tradition of Smith), eight lines from the fairy blessing, used now to end the forest sequence. Oberon sang, "To the best bride bed will we / Which by us shall blessed be" [V. i. 403-04], and the fairy chorus of about thirty replied singing the four altered lines beginning, "In Theseus house give glimmering light" [cf. V. i. 391]. A new song, the first song of the opera, set six lines of Hermia's vow to elope with Lysander, beginning "By the simplicity of Venus's doves" [I. i. 171ff.]. Other Shakespearean lyrics included Oberon's "Be as thou was wont to be" [IV. i. 71ff.] (by Burney?), and "Flower of this purple dye" [III. ii. 102ff.] (Smith). Puck sang his, "Up and down, up and down" [III. ii. 396ff.] (Smith?), and the fairies sang two quartets with original text, one written by Stevens for the lullaby sung to Titania and one by Bishop and Cooke using altered lines, "Trip away, trip away." The song which Colman had given the artisans, "Most noble Duke, be kind," was used again by Reynolds. Among the mortal lovers' songs were Demetrius' "Sweet cheering hope whose magic art" (Bishop), and Hermia's song by Handel, "Hush ye pretty warbling choir," addressed to the "sylvan songsters" which Bishop's orchestra rendered on a cue marked "bird symphony." Hermia also is asked by Theseus at the end to sing a welcome to the triumphal pageant. This role was played by one pretty Kitty Stephens who with tenor John Sinclair, the Demetrius, carried the music for the young lovers. Consistent with the cutting of Helena's role mentioned above, Helena was assigned no solos and Lysander had none. One suspects that the planning of the music and the cutting of the text in these adaptations was in part determined by the musical talent at hand. It was, then, of the Reynolds-Bishop musical spectacle that William Hazlitt wrote his famous Ben Jonson-like protest:

> Oh ye scene shifters, ye scene-painters, ye machinists and dressmakers, ye manufacturers of moon and stars that give no light, ye musical composers, ye men in the orchestra, fiddlers, and trumpeters and players on the double drum and loud basson, rejoice! This is your triumph, it is not ours: and ye full grown, well fed, substantial fairies . . . we shall believe no more in the existence of your fantastic tribe [*The Examiner*, 21 January 1816].

Even to our own day, theatre critics would evoke Hazlitt's name and conclude what he did from Reynolds' opera: "Poetry and the stage do not agree together." Reynolds' opera had more life in it yet; it was revived in 1817 with three fewer songs. Some of its songs turned up in a Covent Garden pastiche of *All's Well That Ends Well* in 1832 which included a masque called "Oberon and Robin Goodfellow." And it was almost certainly Reynolds' opera which was produced in 1826 in New York at the Park Theatre and was the first production of *A Midsummer Night's Dream* to be seen in America. (pp. 48-51)

> Gary Jay Williams, " 'The Concord of this Discord': Music in the Stage History of 'A Midsummer Night's Dream'," in yale/theatre, *Vol. 4, No. 3, Summer, 1973, pp. 40-68.*

PRODUCTIONS:

Edmund Simpson • Park Theatre • 1826 and 1841

BACKGROUND:

The first productions of *A Midsummer Night's Dream* in

America took place in 1826 and 1841 at the Park Theatre in New York. Two performances of the play were given in the earlier year, on 8 and 24 November, the first being a benefit for the actress Ellen Hilson. The comedy was not staged again in this country until fifteen years later, when a staging strongly influenced by Madame Vestris's London presentation of 1840 received a week's run at the Park. Aside from its historical interest, the 1841 Park production is noteworthy for its Oberon, played by Charlotte Cushman, who was later to become one of the premier actresses of her time.

COMMENTARY:

The Spirit of the Times   (review date 4 September 1841)

[*In the following review, the anonymous critic offers qualified approval of the 1841 Park Theatre production of* A Midsummer Night's Dream, *despite its numerous revisions of Shakespeare's text.*]

The old house was re-opened on Monday last with *"Midsummer-Night's Dream,"* one of the most extraordinary creations of Shakespeare's genius. When we learned that Madame Vestris proposed to bring it upon the stage last season at Covent Garden, we were struck by the audacity of the attempt; we were still more surprised by the profitable "run" which the play made, in these declining days of the drama. An English author informs us that the play was revived by Garrick about one hundred and fifty years after Shakespeare's death, but only survived one night. Fifty years afterwards, another attempt was made at Covent Garden, which failed. Madame Vestris was the first to put the play on the stage with success. To be sure, the critics condemned it all the while, but it drew money to the house, thus answering the end in view.

We have now about the same story to tell of this wondrous "Dream" in New York. If it had been condemned by the London critics, when it was "got up" with the most lavish expense, and under the direction of the best manager living,— we scarce dared to hope that it would find any favor, where the appliances and means are so inferior to give it effect. Nevertheless it has drawn well; the first two nights, the house was crowded—it was fairly filled the third night, and on the fourth was yet better. We heartily congratulate the manager upon this result.

"Midsummer-Night's Dream," we confess, gives us far more pleasure in the quiet of our room, than it is possible to derive from it with the *aid* (?) of stage accessories. We prayed only that it might not be utterly spoiled of its charms in the hands of the actors, that we might hear the text of the author and close our eyes at any incongruities in the personation of Puck or Oberon, of Titania and her attendant fairies. We were agreeably disappointed, however, with the experiment at the Park. The order of the scenes as arranged by the poet were altered, some even were left out which are most important for the elucidation of the intricacies of the plot, and the whole was much abridged to the entire loss of many of the most delicious passages in the play; nevertheless it went off quite satisfactorily, if the applause bestowed be considered the test.

The remarks we wished to offer on the individuals in the cast are crowded out by our extracts from London journals in regard to Mr. Placide—far more interesting than anything we could say of a play of Shakespeare; but we must find room to speak of a few prominent individuals. Miss CUSHMAN appeared as the King of the Fairies, and was, as she should be, quite the star of the evening—receiving, by the way, the most cordial welcome upon her return to the boards she has hitherto trod so successfully. In paying her the compliment of saying that in reciting the text of her author, she displayed the best taste, giving it with the clearest enunciation and an appreciation of its most delicate beauties, we may as well include her sister Miss S. Cushman. Both these ladies possess great cleverness, and in *Helena,* the younger played with a taste and genuine poetical feeling for which we were quite unprepared. Our own opinion is that on Tuesday evening Miss S. Cushman's was decidedly the most effective personation in the whole cast.—We are again reminded by the compositor that he has no more room for us to-day, but we trespass upon him, if only to enumerate those who were engaged with credit to themselves in "Midsummer-Night's Dream." Miss TAYLOR, who sings and looks so well, is becoming a favorite, and has gained much by her perspicuous delivery of the poetry of *Titania;* (we follow no other method in our enumeration than that suggested by the most cursory recollection.) To Mr. WHEATLEY in the character of *Lysander,* we would next award our praise; if he will but correct one or two faults of mere mannerism, this gentleman need fear no rival in his line; the faults to which we allude—trifling in themselves—yet vastly injurious to the effects which the actor would produce—are an unmeaning shaking of his head, and a certain grimace which conceals the expression of his fine countenance whenever he would wish it be particularly expressive.—Miss BULOID was much applauded on Monday, but less on Tuesday, when for some reason she appeared agitated and flurried, and was of course not understood and not applauded. We are among the admirers of this lady, and hope to see her realize some prognostications of her success which we made last season.

Mr. FREDERICKS was never a favorite with the New Yorkers, but for one thing he deserves great credit—he recites poetry as if he felt all its meaning, and certainly gives you the language of the author, if you are content to be satisfied with that. As we said before, the highest merit we ask for in a play like this comedy of Shakespeare, is a distinct and becoming reading of the parts.

In the scenes in which the "hard-handed men of Athens" [V. i. 72] figure, there is little to condemn, though here again, the grossness and extravagance which delight you in the closet, disappoint, if they do not disgust, you on the stage. WILLIAMS as *Bottom,* was very much applauded, as was Mr. FISHER in *Peter Quince, the carpenter.* KING had little to say as *the tailor,* but without over-acting, he brought down the house once or twice. We can spare not a line further for these most lamentable notes upon this representation of one of Shakespeare's most fantastic but most delicious of creations.

A review of "A Midsummer Night's Dream," in The Spirit of the Times, *Vol. XI, No. 27, September 4, 1841, p. 324.*

George C. D. Odell   (essay date 1916)

[*Odell assembles the available information regarding the two Park Theatre productions of* A Midsummer Night's Dream, *providing an overview of these earliest American stagings of the play.*]

The first performance in America of something resembling

Shakspere's comedy was thus quietly advertised in the *Times* newspaper:

PARK THEATER

MRS. HILSON'S BENEFIT

THIS EVENING, NOVEMBER 8, 1826, WILL BE PRESENTED FOR THE

FIRST TIME IN AMERICA THE OPERATIC COMEDY OF A

MIDSUMMER NIGHT'S DREAM

Mortals—Theseus, Mr. Lee; Egeus, Mr. Foot; Lysander, Mr. Woodhull; Demetrius, Mr. Denman; Snout, the Tinker, Mr. Placide; Starveling, the Tailor, Mr. Nexsen; Bottom, the Weaver, Mr. Hilson; Hyppolita (*sic*), Mrs. Stickney; Hermia, Mrs. Hackett; Helena, Mrs. Brundage; *Immortals*—Oberon, Mr. Richings; Titania, Mrs. Sharpe; Puck, or Robin Goodfellow, Mrs. Hilson.

"after which," the announcement goes on to promise, "the petit comedy of 'Maid or Wife, or the Deceiver Deceived,' and the melo-drama of the 'Lady of the Rock,' " a liberal evening's entertainment; but, as the announcement reads further that "performances in future will commence at one quarter before seven o'clock" and as any one could presumably depart at will, a good time was no doubt had by all.

I should like to remark that this is perhaps the first time since 1826 that so much of the original cast has been printed. Ireland, whose invaluable 'Records of the New York Stage' have since been invariably quoted, confesses that he had but a "mutilated copy of the bill" for the occasion, and could furnish only an incomplete distribution of the chief parts. The allotment of the characters of Theseus, Bottom, Snout, Oberon, Puck, Titania, Hyppolita (*sic*) and Hermia is all he reports; I suspect his "mutilated bill" may have been an advertisement in an old newspaper, for these are the only parts and actors advertised in some of the papers of the time—the New York *Evening Post* of November 3rd, for instance. Whatever the service may be worth, I would claim the distinction of having saved the rest from oblivion; they will live now just as long as my article lives!

A second thought suggested by a search in old news files concerns itself with the extreme lack of excitement that attended this occasion, which seems to us, ninety years later, so highly interesting. The first performance of a Shaksperian play in America! think what our Sunday supplement would make of such an event! But in 1826, it was just as if you offered the stolid householders who were theater-goers, a large comfortable cabbage; evidently much blood of Holland still coursed imperturbably through their veins. There was no preliminary notice except what the theater paid for in advertising columns, and the following constitute the entire after-glow of criticism, so far as I can discover it in old periodicals.

The *Evening Post* of Friday, November 10, 1826, thus chronicles its experiences at Mrs. Hilson's benefit:

Midsummer Night's Dream. This play of Shakspere's, transformed by modern ingenuity into a comic opera, but not so transformed as wholly to lose the beauty and humor of the original, was performed last evening at the Park Theater. The more serious parts of it went off heavily enough, and would have been hardly endurable, but for the singing. The whole fairy machinery is too light, changing and ethereal for actors of flesh and blood, and the clumsy contrivances of the stage. Richings is a stout, heavy, fairy king and Mrs. Sharpe a substantial fairy queen. Richings has much improved lately, but he should not mangle Shakspere as he does. For instance, where Shakspere says

At a fair vestal, throned by the west,

[II. i. 158]

Mr. Richings should not say

At a vestal throned by the west.

And where Shakspere says
　　Yet marked I where the bolt of Cupid fell:
　　It fell upon a little western flower,
　　Before milk-white, now purple with Love's wound;

[II. i. 165-67]

Mr. Richings should not change the last word in these lines to *wounds,* for this simple reason, that it makes nonsense of the passage.

> The comic parts of the piece which form a large proportion of it went off quite well and the audience were exceedingly delighted. Those who were inclined to laugh, indulged themselves without scruple, because the wit was Shakspere's; those who were not, sometimes found themselves compelled to it, and we saw many a grave face wrinkling with laughter in spite of itself. Hilson made an excellent Nick Bottom, but it is a pity that he should let the audience see him put his hand behind him to pull the string that moved his asses (*sic*) ears.

The Truth Teller, a weekly, is even less informing in its notice of November 11th:

> *Park Theater.* Shakspere's operatic comedy of A Midsummer Night's Dream was presented for the first time in America to a crowded and respectable audience, on Thursday evening, with music, dances, etc., incidental to the piece, being for the benefit of Mrs. Hilson. Of the performance little need be said (*sic*) than the characters were ably cast; Mr. Hilson as *Bottom* and Mr. Placide as *Snout,* played as well as they play anything; that is, they never fail to make the most of their characters, to the great amusement of the audience. The piece met with a brilliant reception, and affords a rich treat to the lovers of comedy.

These are the records, and difficult enough it is to reconstruct from them the actual performances in the fashionable old Park Theater so far down town, with its lamp-light, its inartistic furnishings, its provincial air. The play was repeated on November 24th, but not again before the close of the year, and perhaps for the entire season. What was it like? I do not know, but I hazard the guess that it was founded on the version used at Covent Garden in 1816, and still accessible in the copy printed in the same year "for John Miller, 25, Bow Street, Covent Garden." This is the peccant thing so contemptuously treated by Genest. Obviously, there was some little effort to live up to the opportunity offered. The earlier advertisement in the *Evening Post,* referred to above, stresses the fact (1) that the play—"an operatic comedy—is to be presented for the first time in America"; (2) "as performed in London with unbounded applause"; and (3) "with music, dancing, and various scenic displays, incidental to the piece." All this seems to point with a considerable degree of probability to the Covent Garden "hit" of ten years before; Genest

records no performance thereafter in any of the theaters-royal.

And what was that 1816 'Midsummer Night's Dream'? Well, a Shaksperian of this day will shudder with disgust, as did Genest and Hazlitt at the mere recital of the violence done to the work of the gentle bard. The "opera" is divided into three acts of three, five and four scenes, respectively. The stage directions, as printed, call for such effects as "A Grand Doric Colonnade appertaining to Duke Theseus' Palace"; "a Wood. Moonlight"; "Another part of the Wood. Titania's Bower, decorated with flowers. In the center, the Duke's Oak." Incidental to the second set instanced above there was: "A March. *Enter, in procession,* OBERON, *King of the Fairies, at one wing, with his Train, and the Queen at another, with hers.* TITANIA *is in a Car.*—OBERON *in another Car.*" At the end of the play was performed a grand pageant, commemorative of the triumphs of Theseus. Evidently the Londoners in 1816 were treated to some considerable spectacle; how much did the New Yorkers of 1826 get?

But the greatest liberties were taken with the text. I shall cite the most notable. (1) The entire scene with *Helena* is omitted in Act I, making it rather difficult for the audience to know how Demetrius has come (in Act II) into the knowledge of the proposed flight of Lysander and Hermia. Against this excision Hazlitt and Genest both inveigh. (2) Much of the dialog of the four lovers is mercilessly curtailed throughout the play. (3) The scene of the acting of 'Pyramus and Thisbe' is transferred to the wood, Theseus and Philostrate observing from behind a tree.

This transposition is effected, in order to allow at the end of the play of the grand pageant of Theseus' triumphs. Shakspere's final scene with the fairies is omitted. All these changes were made necessary by the great number of musical numbers interspersed wherever possible. These are by Bishop, Arne and Smith. All the opportunities for singing offered by Shakspere are seized upon; but everywhere we get gems like this, sung by Demetrius just as he flies Helena to hide in the brake:

> Recall the minutes that are fled,
> 　　Forbid fleet time to move;
> To new life wake the sleeping dead,
> 　　But ne'er recall my love.

> Forbid the stormy waves to roar,
> 　　The playful winds to rove,
> Revive the sun at midnight hour,
> 　　But ne'er recall my love.

And while at the close Theseus, with the rest, modestly reviews his own deeds, Hermia sings, having been royally bidden thereto by these interpolated lines:

> Hark, they approach!
> My hardy veterans!
> My grave companions in the toils of war!—
> And since ourselves, we boast not of the pow'r
> To welcome them in aught, save the plain
> Rough language of a soldier,
> Hermia, stand forth, and with thy dulcet tones,
> Give, give to all, harmonious greeting.

Hermia, apparently nothing loth, warbles a martial lay by Bishop, beginning (after recitative),

> Now Pleasure's voice be heard around!
> And sweetly lute and lyre resound!

From two bones, construct the monster. When timid students quote Hazlitt as saying that he preferred Shakspere in the library to Shakspere on the stage, let them remember that it was of this very performance of "A Midsummer Night's Dream" that he was writing. His evidence is worth just what that fact implies. Other comedies of the great dramatist were treated in exactly the same way.

And what was the performance in New York like, in 1826? From the data arrayed above, can you not guess? It was doubtless a feeble attempt to reproduce what, for the thing it attempted, was very well done in London ten years before. One thing I bid you note; Oberon was played by a man, as in 1816 at Covent Garden; the part was not so played again in this city till 1906, at the Astor Theater. Mme. Vestris's Oberon, in 1840, apparently set the fashion of female Fairy Kings for all that length of time.

This fashion was followed in the performance which opened the season at the Park Theater in New York, August 30, 1841. Perhaps the most amusing, if not the most interesting document connected with that revival is to be found in the issue of the semi-weekly *American,* under date of August 31st:

> The Park Theater opened last night to a very full, and, in part, a somewhat disorderly house. More than once were the performers interfered with by the interruption of the upper tiers. This should be prevented for the future. The 'Midsummer Night's Dream' was produced in a handsome style, and, barring a few exceptions, with effect. A repetition of the piece will render the performers more familiar with their parts.

The review ends with an account of a fight between Moonshine's dog ("an ugly-looking bull") and the Lion, at which part of the audience was manifestly delighted, and tried to encourage the row. And that was dramatic criticism in this city in 1841! and for the second revival in America of one of the great Shaksperian comedies! The *Herald* of the same date is more flowery, without being more informing:

> PARK THEATER. Long before the curtain drew up, last night, there were symptoms of a very full, if not a very fashionable audience. After the national airs had been performed by the orchestra, and duly honored by the house, that rare conceit, 'A Midsummer Night's Dream,' was introduced to the American stage. This play, abounding as it does with the most poetical imagery and overflowing with the most subtle wit, is yet deficient in that essential for dramatic success—interest to keep the audience alive. In the closet, the devotees of the bard of Avon pore over its beauties, and revel in the glorious poetry of its author; but on the stage it is quite another affair, and we saw numbers almost ready to yawn, who would have been ashamed to confess themselves insensible to its merits as a poem.
>
> Of the performers we have but little room to speak now. They all did their best for their several parts, and were received with a fervor of applause which speaks well for the future popularity of the management. . . . There was about $1100 in the house.

The play ran only one week, yet, according to Ireland, it was produced with great care; the *Herald,* of August 30th (the day of the performance), announced that the cast includes some old favorites, as well as new candidates for public favor, and "great expense, we are told, has been lavished on the getting up by the manager." The actors "featured" by the directorate in preliminary notices were Mrs. Knight (Puck), Mr. W. H. Williams (Bottom), and Miss Cushman (Oberon). This seems, to later fancy, an astonishing rôle in which to find Charlotte Cushman; her fame, however, was then in the making. Other well-known players (well-known in later days, at least) were William Wheatley (Lysander), C. W. Clarke (Demetrius), Susan Cushman (Helena), Mary Taylor (Titania). The comedy, according to Ireland, did not prove attractive. "Mrs. Knight was too substantial in appearance for the frolicsome sprite, a part that would have suited Miss Taylor perfectly, although the management had not penetration enough to know it."

Curiously enough, we can discover less about this production than about that of fifteen years before at the same theater. The above data are all I could collect. But from Macready's 'Reminiscences' we learn that the directors of the Park were in the habit of crossing annually to London in search of novelties, especially in actors. Now the season before, 1840-1841, Mme. Vestris had played in this piece fifty-nine times at Covent Garden; she reproduced it at the opening of the season in 1841. What could be more natural than the assumption that Simpson, then in sole charge, saw the Vestris performance and decided to imitate it on the stage of the New York house? The fact that Oberon was given to a woman confirms this guess to a considerable degree. It was put on "with new music (Mendelssohn's?), scenery and machinery." No doubt, the American mounting lagged far behind, but let us hope that the play at least was Shakspere's and not something like Reynolds's. The critic of the *Sunday Courier,* reviewing, in 1854, the Burton revival, says, justifying his use of the term "unacted,"

> We use the term 'unacted', because this comedy has never been performed before entire, according to the text of Shakspere, and only occasionally in any shape. It was produced at the Park Theater a good many years since, under the supervision of Mr. Barry, in something approximating to a complete form, but was got up in haste and without any labored attempt at scenic display or strictness and splendor of costume, and fell completely lifeless.
>
> (pp. 121-28)

I cannot think New York had anything like [Vestris's] magnificence, but obviously our manager hoped for something of the same success. After a week, however, the play was shelved for another thirteen years or more.

Meantime, of Mme. Vestris's revival we can repeat (1) that it brought back to the stage Shakspere himself; (2) that it set the fashion of assigning Oberon to a female performer, though this had prevailed to some extent . . . in the eighteenth century; (3) that it introduced the habit of the panorama or sliding scene . . . ;(4) that it was the first to use some, at least, of Mendelssohn's music; and, (5) that it made the production of 'A Midsummer Night's Dream' the desire of every great manager of the future. (p. 129)

George Clinton Densmore Odell, " 'A Midsummer Night's Dream' on the New York Stage," in Shaksperian Studies, *edited by Brander Matthews and Ashley Horace Thorndike, 1916. Reprint by Russell & Russell, Inc., 1962, pp. 119-29.*

PRODUCTION:

Madame Vestris • Covent Garden • 1840

BACKGROUND:

Vestris's was one of the most significant revivals of *A Midsummer Night's Dream* in the nineteenth century. Prior to this production, virtually every staging of the play since the Restoration had been an operatic adaptation, embellished by elaborate scenery and dancing and involving heavy revision of Shakespeare's text. While Vestris adhered to the tradition of lavish spectacle, she restored much of Shakespeare's verse and eliminated all the songs with lyrics not original to this play, which had become fixtures of the comedy since the time of Garrick. Vestris herself portrayed the fairy king, thereby initiating a long tradition of female Oberons. Although some later critics have tended to regard this production as an example of Victorian extravagance, it was critically and popularly successful in its time and became the basis for numerous revivals well into the twentieth century.

COMMENTARY:

The Times, London   (review date 17 November 1840)

[*After noting various obstacles to the successful presentation of* A Midsummer Night's Dream, *the anonymous reviewer claims that "as far as theatrical representation of this ethereal drama is possible, it was achieved" in Vestris's production.*]

In the production of Shakspeare's *Midsummer Night's Dream* two great difficulties present themselves—the very fanciful nature of the characters, and the great want of dramatic interest. Children of every gradation of littleness, with voices of every variation of squeak, may be brought on the stage, but those minute beings—minute both with respect to space and time—who can hang drops in a cowslip's ear, and value the third part of a minute as no short period, cannot be realized. To the reader they may appear and flit before him with more or less vividness according to the force of his imagination, but give these "airy nothings" literally a local habitation, and they are but earthy symbols of the purest creations of fancy. The want of dramatic interest presents a still greater obstacle. The whole of the plot, if so it may be called, lies in the third act, or rather the whole is but a collection of episodes lightly connected. To the reader it is one gorgeous dream of poetry. The creatures of fancy, and the ideality of tenderness as appearing in Hermia and Helena being equally charming, his mind can follow at ease where the poet leads him. With the pauses incident to theatrical production, and the necessity of fixing the attention of an audience by stronger means than those that are required to secure a reader, the representation of *Midsummer Night's Dream,* so as to charm a London public, becomes a most arduous undertaking.

As far as theatrical representation of this ethereal drama is possible, it was achieved last night, and a gorgeous spectacle was produced. The beings of a moment could not be portrayed, little Messrs. Cobweb, Moth, and Mustardseed, with their shrill trumpet voices, were but inadequate likenesses of their shadowy originals; but in the conception of the whole,

a fine poetical feeling was apparent, a consciousness of the difficulties with which the struggle was to be made, and a resolution to conquer them if possible. If the minute elves could not be obtained, it was still left to give a shadowy unreal character to the scenery; if the individuals could not be realized, it was still possible to give a fairy grace to the groups, and impart to the whole *tableau,* what could not be bestowed on its parts. In the Oberon of Madame Vestris there was a dignified grace worthy of the King of fairy land, and as she stood with her glittering armour and fantastic helmet on an eminence, with a blue-tinted wood gliding by her in the back-ground, presenting different aspects of the same sylvan scenery, the effect was little short of supernatural. Madame Vestris evidently understood the value of the effect to be produced by distance, and by generally remaining as the marked out but remote figure on a dark ground, or shone upon by some artificial light, a supernatural appearance was generally given to Oberon. In another wood scene where there is a declivity which the actors really descend, and which allows them to be dispersed about in a manner quite new, the dreamy character is still kept up. The vanishing of the theatre in which the clowns act their tragedy, and discovery of the interior of the palace, with fairies crowded in every part, gliding along galleries, ascending and descending steps, soaring in the air with blue and yellow torches, which produce a curious light, is one of the most beautiful and highly wrought fairy scenes ever introduced on the stage. The music also, with the singing of Madame Vestris and Miss Rainforth, contributes much to this part of the drama.

The mortal part of the poetry is not so good as the supernatural. Mrs. Nisbett as Hermia was not in her element. The beautiful lines she uttered neither awoke nor expressed feeling. Without the greatest tenderness and delicacy of expression, the character of Hermia on the stage gives no idea of its real beauty. Mrs. Nisbett's manner and her appearance were, however, extremely beautiful as she reclined on the couch and listened to the Clown's tragedy. Her laugh at their blunders was most genuine, as if she again found herself in her own sphere. The Demetrius and Lysander of Vining and Brindal were prosaic personages. Of the quartet of lovers Miss Cooper bore the palm; her manner was constrained and artificial, but still there was that evident desire to give the words their meaning, that evident knowledge of the feeling that the part required, that, although the expression was not always attained, the audience could not refrain from giving her hearty applause.

The clowns were very strongly filled by Harley (Bottom), Keely, Meadows, F. Matthews, Bartley, and Payne. There was much amusing caricature in Harley, but the real humour was in Keely as Flute. He had a lack-a-daisical look of innocent stupidity, objected to the part of Thisbe with a slight fretfulness that at once subsided into a meek tolerance, and, utterly unable to originate a thought in his own brain, allowed his countenance to be lit up at hearing another's bright idea. He shared in the general joy and sorrow like one whose obtuse intellect apprehended it the last, but whose good-natured heart felt it the most. The tragedy of these clowns was performed on a theatre constructed after the antique, and the whole burlesque was produced with the greatest care.

Besides the fairy scenes mentioned above, there was a fine view of Athens, which opened the piece. The painters are the Messrs. Grieve. The dresses, particularly that of Hippolyta

(Mrs. Brougham), who wears a gold tunic descending only to the knee, are splendid.

At the descent of the curtain the audience burst into the loudest applause, and Madame Vestris being called for, announced *Midsummer Night's Dream* for repetition four times a week.

A review of "A Midsummer Night's Dream," in The Times, *London, November 17, 1840, p. 4.*

The Athenaeum   (review date 21 November 1840)

[*In the following excerpt, the reviewer finds Vestris's production faulty in several respects, notably in the verse speaking, but he admires its scenic aspects. He judges that this representation of* A Midsummer Night's Dream *transcended any previous one.*]

COVENT GARDEN.——All that a tasteful and liberal application of stage resources could accomplish has been done at this theatre, towards embodying that most beautiful fairy romance 'A Midsummer Night's Dream;' and the classic elegance of the scenery, costumes, the mechanical ingenuity of the scenic transformations, the musical accompaniment, altogether form a graceful and fanciful, as well as brilliant spectacle. But the exquisite poetry of Shakspeare loses its charm, if not its meaning, when uttered with those imperfections of speech, inseparable from the formal declamation of actors labouring to fill an area too large to allow a complete governance of the voice; and it is needless to say that the idea of personating the Fairy Elves is hopeless, and the material attractions of a pageant, however gorgeous, are no substitute for the spiritual essence; nevertheless, as a masque of Shakspeare's imagining is better than any other, and as this representation of it transcends any previous one, it merits the popular applause which it received on the first night. The scenes in the wood are fitting haunts for fairies, and Madame Vestris as *Oberon,* in her knightly panoply, is a very acceptable representative of an elfin warrior, though why the king of fairy land should be in arms, when his quarrel is only a matrimonial one, does not appear. Miss Marshall is an active and sprightly *Puck,* and Miss Cooper takes pains to make the plaints of *Helena* audible and touching: Mrs. Nesbitt as *Hermia* is out of her element. The lovers, and *Theseus* and *Hippolita,* are only to be admired for the sumptuous taste of their Greek costumes. Harley, as *Bottom,* the Weaver, merely buffoons the part, as is his custom: "sweet Bully Bottom" is a character so plainly written that it requires an effort to spoil it, and this effort Mr. Harley makes with great labour and success. Keeley, as *Flute,* the Bellows-mender, is the true clown; dense, uncouth, and most ludicrous when he tries hardest to act. The dressing of *Wall* and *Moonshine* was too fine for the occasion; the burlesque play, however, goes admirably, but would be none the worse for the omission of a gratuitous piece of indelicacy at the end. The concluding scene with the fairy troops running through the house of Theseus with blazing torches, filling the halls with lights of various hue, is very much applauded; but the opening view of Athens and the moonlit groves are of more refined beauty.

A review of "A Midsummer Night's Dream," in The Athenaeum, *No. 682, November 21, 1840, p. 930.*

The Literary Gazette   (review date 21 November 1840)

[*In the mixed review excerpted below, the critic considers* A Midsummer Night's Dream *ill-suited to the stage, maintaining that "but for the music, in aid of the decorations and scenery, the three hours and a half occupied in the performance would be a wearisome dream indeed." The reviewer does, however, admire this production's scenery and theatrical effects.*]

COVENT GARDEN.——On Monday, the *Midsummer Night's Dream* was revived here with most beautiful and splendid scenery, and all the accessories of fairy costume, and lights and flights of a dazzling description. Messrs. Grieves have surpassed themselves in several of the supernatural landscapes; and especially in one where a striking tree in the centre is illumed by a bluish light; and another where the Morning descends in pearls among the waving foliage of a forest. The *finale,* with sprites running through fine architectural galleries, and floating in the air with censers of coloured flames, is also magnificent. With respect to this glorious poem as an acting play, it is impossible for us to speak in terms of admiration. It is too exquisite for the stage—too subtle for representation. There is too much of action to admit of its being made an efficient spectacle; and too little of interest in the plot and characters to allow of its producing any powerful dramatic effects. From the first to the last we care not one iota for either mortal or fairy engaged in it; and but for the music, in aid of the decorations and scenery, the three hours and a half occupied in the performance would be a wearisome dream indeed. As it is, it is dull enough, in despite of the vocal exertions of Vestris, Rainforth, and Miss Grant, and the comic humours of the hard-handed men of Athens—*Peter Quince, Bully Bottom, Flute, Starveling, Snug,* and *Snout,* drolly enacted by Bartley, Harley, Keeley, W. II. Payne, F. Mathews, and Meadows. Of these, Harley and Keeley, as *Pyramus* and *Thisbe,* had most to do; and the boisterous burlesque of the one, and the ineffable quiet of the other (except in a very unseemly tumble to please the vulgar groundlings), not only contrasted happily, but furnished the only food for laughter during the night. We cannot say that much was made of the many passages of delicious poetry with which the play abounds. With the exception of *Helena's* (Miss Cooper's) touching appeal to the youthful friendship of her "parted cherry" *Hermia* (Mrs. Nisbett), and, in a lesser degree, *Titania's* (Mrs. Walter Lacy's) reasons for refusing to surrender to *Oberon* the child of her Indian votary, all the rest fell flatly and unimpressibly upon the ear. We have only to add that there was a pretty dance; that the curtain descended to shouts of applause from a very full house; and that the fair manageress was called, and announced the piece for repetition four times (too often) a-week.

A review of "A Midsummer Night's Dream," in The Literary Gazette, *No. 1244, November 21, 1840, p. 756.*

The Theatrical Journal   (review date 23 January 1841)

[*The following excerpt is from a brief appreciation of Vestris's "superb effort" in* A Midsummer Night's Dream.]

It is not the easiest thing in the world to get to the theatre this weather and when one is there, it is about the most difficult thing to get away; for the house is so warm and comfortable, so crowded with happy and merry faces, and the *Midsummer Night's Dream* so delightful a vision, as to produce feelings of forgetfulness to the storms and winds of winter's

Madame Vestris as Oberon.

nights. Having so often noticed this superb effort of the management, which has stood the test of approbation of many thousand voices, what further praise is necessary? Madame Vestris still sings beautifully: her Love in Idleness is truly rich in melody; and the duet, I know a bank, is like "bells upon the wind," true and faultless harmony. We have great pleasure in noticing the excellent delivery of Miss Marshall, her every word is heard, and the public do well in appreciating, by their applause, the advancement of this young actress. Some children enquired of us, whether little Miss Payne was not imported from 'Fairy Land;' we consider this a great compliment to the little girl.

A review of "A Midsummer Night's Dream," in The Theatrical Journal and Stranger's Guide, Vol. 2, No. 58, January 23, 1841, p. 26.

The Theatrical Journal (review date 1 May 1841)

[*In the following review, signed only with the intials E. R. W., the critic is effusive in his praise of Vestris's production of* A Midsummer Night's Dream, *asserting that "a happier revival never took place on the stage."*]

It was with no common feeling of pleasure, that I read the announcement of this beautiful poem [*A Midsummer Night's Dream*] being revived at the only royal theatre; especially as it would be presented to the public, under the unerring taste of the most fascinating woman of her day; I had a presentiment as to the effect which would be attempted, and rejoiced most heartily at the universal praise bestowed upon its "first night" by the press; yet so fearful was I lest it might not be

exactly as my fancy pictured; I, child-like, reserved my visit, not wishing to dispel the illusion, till unable longer to repress my curiosity I entered the theatre; many readers may smile at this last remark, they will not on deliberation, for be assured, no pleasure on earth is equal to anticipation, it is the finest feeling of childhood, and clings to us all with equal tenacity of life. The curtain drew up: Athens as it stood in its palmy days was before me, the eye ranged over those magnificent buildings whose ruins are the wonder and the standard of taste to all succeeding times; I was electrified with delight, and most cordially thanked the Messrs. Grieves for availing themselves of the print lately published of "Athens as it was;" the very scene so calculated to raise one to a contemplation of the finer portion of the mind, was the prologue, or rather the stepping-stone to creation's realm; I was on classic ground; my step was among the habitations of the Gods; my thoughts already soared beyond the dull routine of mortality; the wand was waved, a fluttering and a buzz rang in my ear, and I almost saw the fairies; the characters entered;—what a Theseus! he the prototype of the deified! but stay, it is not in mortal's power to put on the semblance of divinity, so let him pass; to make amends for this, we had the Amazonian Hippolyta; truly a queen, whose very step bespoke the royalty of her heart; the lovers, I did not like, and truly pitied the beauteous damsels their probation with two such cool passioned beings: Hermia, the Greek girl, whose birth place seems writ on her fair form, and no less to be admired Helena; all dressed in the becoming style of the age, all true Athenians well mated to the scene; what a remembrance to the well stored mind, to see the glories of this city of the world called up upon his imagination, to be among them, to share their feelings, to be for awhile Greek in heart and hand.

Now comes a different scene, the cottage of a mechanic, the would be player, Bottom, and most inimitably played; Quince, Flute, Snout, also well enacted; Snug, Starveling, hit off to the life with all their humorous conceits, and so ends the act: our impatience is at last set at rest, the act drop rises; a translucid lake hemmed round with trees, with here and there a break in the woody ring, thro' which you gaze on some grassy spot where tiny elves keep up their midnight gambols, or shelving banks velvetted over with nature's softest greens, fit couches for the fairest forms to lay in dalliance sweet and lisp the amorous song, while above, the star bespangled sky shoots out its myriad lights, and the pale moon pours down her silver flood in a glittering hail on the water, and sleeps the charmed spot in so soft and mellowed a tone, that the mortal sense overcome with her spirit's influence, parts with its grosser self, gives loose to nature's love, and feels at home once more in Eden's garden; the most imaginative of all creative forms, mischievious Puck, shoots up from the earth, other spirits come,—the mighty Oberon, Titania, and all their beauteous court, till so life-like all becomes, that we are in the fairy land, and mate with forms whose essence, light as the air, sport about in fantastic revelry, as leaves whirled round and round when caught by the summer's wind; the action of the poem goes on, the fairy quarrel is continued, the mortals love, and the fairy influence over it; Puck flies away; Oberon, waving his wand, melts with the scene from our sight, and leaves a forest glade with its carpet of green and line of trees, whose overspreading branches entwined one over the other, over arched the earth and jealously guards the fairies' sleeping haunts from the rude gaze of the surrounding sky; truly, these two scenes are the most beautiful of their kind ever seen on the stage; it seems as if the poet had descended from high Olympus, and throwing his own essence into the painter's pencil, re-writ in colours the words that once sprang from his pen, they are his own as much as the poem; the people, the fairies, seem to have risen with each stroke of his pencil, they bear his own impress, have the pallas stamp born of his brain; are so mingled with the scenic effect as to appear one harmonious whole.

The actors, the fairy mistake, the humorous transformation, quickly follow out the plot, till drawing towards the climax; we have another wood scene, this is at the outskirts, a lake with the distant country, hedged on one side with trees, by the side of which, a path winds its way far into the adjoining wood; a soft twilight overspreads the whole, and prepares the mind for the coming change; the plot is at its height, the turn to happiness has begun, night thickens, and as the actions begin to change, morning breaks from his couch, the sun pours out his warmth and light, the lovers are made happy and the fairy quarrel is at an end; this is another felicitous effort, and as far as can be effected in representing the atmospheric changes is here done; the poetry of the nation deserves high commendation, and we can but regret, the feeling cannot be more happily carried out. Now comes the play; then the last scene, a hall in Theseus's house; one of those rich architectural compositions with galleries and flights of stairs, that have a most impressive effect on the stage; here assemble the entire body of fairies making merry over the triple nuptials, darting from side to side, flying round and round, now here, now there, on the ground, in the air, waving their tiny lamps till the entire place seems sparkling with the countless hues of light, and the delighted eye passing its thrill of pleasure to the tongue, one exclamation of delight springs simultaneously from the beholders as down falls the curtain. Take it all together, I do believe a happier revival never took place on the stage, than in the *Midsummer Night's Dream;* the spirit of poetry seems to have actuated all concerned, and right merry am I, that the public has with a profuse hand tended their thanks to Madame for so dainty a fare: I do hope it will not for some time be set aside, and that a night at least per week will still be devoted to its use, and if the public think as I think, they will visit the theatre night after night with the same thirst and veneration, as the poor Jew journeys to the Holy Land; for Shakespear re-lives, and calls for the homage, nations declare to be justly his. (pp. 137-39)

> *E. R. W., in a review of "A Midsummer Night's Dream," in* The Theatrical Journal and Stranger's Guide, *Vol. 2, No. 72, May 1, 1841, pp. 137-39.*

Gary Jay Williams   (essay date 1977)

[*Williams provides a comprehensive analysis of Madame Vestris's 1840 presentation of* A Midsummer Night's Dream, *stressing its relationship to previous productions and its influence on subsequent ones.*]

The long stage life of *A Midsummer Night's Dream* as a leafy Victorian valentine, with all the traditions our era has so strained to be rid of, is all but gone—with few questions ever having been asked about its origins and development. That Victorian stage image of the play, still familiar to us, owes the most to the production of the remarkable Madame Lucia Elizabeth Vestris. Her *A Midsummer Night's Dream* opened on 16 November 1840, in the second of her three season management of Covent Garden with her new husband and lessee, Charles James Mathews. As well as restoring the text, for which Odell duly credited her [in his *Shakespeare from Bet-*

terton to Irving], Vestris set many precedents in staging, casting, costuming, and music. Her production has never been studied in detail, either for itself or its considerable influence. I am interested in both here; I shall be reconstructing it, surveying the critical and popular responses to it, and showing its part in the development of Victorian stage traditions for the play. We shall see among other things, for example, that Charles Kean's spectacular 1856 production, well-known through its watercolor record, is deeply indebted to Vestris' staging.

To show where Vestris departed from her predecessors and also what debts she has to them, it will be helpful to begin with a very brief review of the texts and staging features of major productions from the Restoration to 1833. Her innovations far outweighed her debts, but Vestris was somewhat indebted, visually and musically, to an 1816 operatic version of the play at Covent Garden.

From the Restoration to Vestris, the play was seen in England and America only in the form of one opera adaptation or another. In Purcell's *The Fairy Queen* of 1692, the play was altered into an elaborate vehicle for the Baroque music and spectacle of four, exotic intermezzo-like pieces introduced at the ends of Acts II through V. The play seems likely to have been overwhelmed, more than the published text indicates. The score, Purcell's longest, accompanied the soloists, chorus, dancers, machines, and *a vista* transformations at the ends of the acts.

The eighteenth century saw the play only in operatic adaptations, each of which—save one—dismantled the text and used only portions of it. One finds the young lovers without the clowns, the fairies and lovers combined but without the clowns, the clowns without the fairies or lovers, and the fairies and clowns without the lovers. "Pyramus and Thisbe" was excerpted in 1716 and 1745 for one-act spoofs on the faddish Italian opera. *The Fairies* that Garrick produced in 1755 used only the young lovers and the fairies; they spoke some 560 lines of the original play and sang a score of twenty-eight songs by John Christopher Smith, Handel's amanuensis. A later attempt at a relatively fuller version was far less successful. Brought out under the original title at Drury Lane in 1763, this version omitted "Pyramus and Thisbe" and the original fairy finale, and it had a score of no less than thirty-three songs. It lasted one performance. Prompter William Hopkins wrote, "The Sleeping Scene particularly displeas'd. Next day it was reported. The Performers first Sung the audience to Sleep, and then went to sleep themselves." Another critic [in the *St. James Chronicle,* 24 November 1763] found it "an odd romantic performance," that gave "a lively picture of the ungoverned imagination of that great poet." Even with well-ordered music, eighteenth-century audiences found no unity, no coherence in the play, clearly having little interest or faith in "such shaping fantasies that apprehend more than cool reason ever comprehends" [V. i. 5-6]. By the time Vestris restored the text and embellished it with fourteen songs, the play had had a century-and-a-half of operatic treatment.

Romanticism brought a fuller literary comprehension of the play, but this was not realized upon the stage until mid-century. The nineteenth century's first major production of the play was yet another operatic adaptation, though one to which the Victorian tradition is indebted. Produced at Covent Garden in 1816, this was a popular and successful version by Frederic Reynolds, who went on to turn five more of Shakespeare's plays into operas. The chief composer and arranger was Sir Henry Rowley Bishop. Reynolds' three-act version re-shaped the play for musical and scenic grandeur. Twenty-four songs were interpolated (the lyrics of some seventeen of which were brought over from the 1763 opera). Oberon and Titania entered for their moonlight meeting in cars from opposite sides of the vast stage and, at the end of Act II, the audience was given a view of Titania's fleet of galleys bringing the cherished Indian boy to Oberon. "From India's shores her gallies sail," sang a fairy from hovering clouds which then ascended to reveal a seascape and a fairy palace. As had been the case in the Purcell opera, such splendor was not to be ended with "Pyramus and Thisbe" or Shakespeare's delicate fairy blessing. These were shifted to positions earlier in the opera, and Reynolds concluded the evening, the playbill tells us, with "A GRAND PAGEANT, commemorative of The Triumphs of Theseus, Over the Cretans, the Thebans, the Amazons, the Centaurs, the Minotaur, Ariadne in the Labyrinth, the Mysterious Peplum, or Veil of Minerva, the Ship Argo, and the Golden Fleece." It is here, with the Reynolds opera, produced in the last years of the Kemble regime, that *A Midsummer Night's Dream* began its long association with pictorialism and antiquarian spectacle. Vestris was to be quite directly indebted to it. It was in the face of Reynolds' version that Hazlitt [in the *Examiner*, 20 January 1816] despaired of the ability of the stage ever to represent Shakespeare's fairy regions:

> This spirit was evaporated, the genius was fled; but the spectacle was fine: it was that which saved the play. Oh ye scene-shifters, ye scene painters, ye machinists and dress-makers, ye manufacturers of moon and stars that give no light, ye musical composers, ye men in the orchestra, fiddlers and trumpeters and players on the double drum and loud bassoon, rejoice! This is your triumph, it is not ours: and ye full grown, well-fed substantial, real fairies . . . we shall believe no more in the existence of your fantastic tribe.

But it was successful, and for two more decades it was Reynolds' opera (or variations on it) that was offered under the title *A Midsummer Night's Dream*. Reynolds' text was almost certainly the basis of the first American production of the play, done at the Park Theatre in 1826. Sources are sparse, but managers Stephen Price and Edmund Simpson advertised the play that season as an "operatic comedy" with "Music, Dances, and various Scenic Displays," claiming it had been "Performed in London with unbounded applause." Then, in 1841, Simpson hastily mounted the play again, and there are clues that again he used the Reynolds version. The reviews indicate the scenes had been rearranged and that in Act I the adapter had failed to include the scene wherein Hermia and Lysander confide to Helena their plans to elope. This makes the later appearance of Helena and Demetrius in the forest a bit puzzling and is a distinctive mark of Reynolds' botched text. Simpson may have been trying in 1841 to capitalize on the success of Vestris' London production the season before (he also cast a woman as Oberon—Charlotte Cushman), but his text probably resembled Reynolds' more than Vestris', contrary to Odell's surmise.

London saw one more alteration of the play between Reynolds and Vestris. Alfred Bunn opened *A Midsummer Night's Dream* "Compressed into Two Acts," at Drury Lane on 30 November 1833. For his text, the not-too-discriminating Bunn further cut and reshuffled Reynolds' version. His promptbook (previously unanalyzed) is comprised of pages from the 1816 edition of the opera with twelve full pages of Reynolds' text deleted. Fourteen of the original twenty-four songs were used, Helena was still missing from Act I, Titania's galleys did not sail, and the pageant of Theseus' triumphs was cut. Bunn can be credited, however, with being the first to use "Mindelssohn's [*sic*] Celebrated Overture" with a production of the play.

Vestris' text of 1840 was relatively whole. To be sure, the play was still musically much embellished, and its production in the vast Covent Garden assured at least as much emphasis upon spectacle and music as upon poetry. Still, it is one of the more judicious handlings of the text on the nineteenth-century stage.

The nearest we can come to her promptbook is a little known acting edition of the play, undated, bearing the following interesting claim on its title page:

> As Revived at the Theatre Royal, Covent Garden, November 16, 1840, correctly printed from the prompt copy, with exits, entrances, etc. And, (for the First time that any Dramatic Work has possessed the same advantages in publication,) Plots of the Scenery, Properties, Calls, copy of the original bill, incidents, etc.

It was published in London by James Pattie, evidently *circa* 1840-1841. Its detailed stage directions seem, at critical points, to be confirmed by the reviews of 1840. There exists another text in *Lacy's Acting Plays* (volume XXVIII), accompanied by a fuller Vestris playbill above which is the claim "As performed at . . . Covent Garden . . . November 16, 1840." But Lacy's volume was issued *circa* 1856 and includes a few stage directions that reflect unmistakably the Charles Kean production of that year. Lacy's text, however, is not Kean's cutting, as a comparison with Kean's own acting edition quickly shows. Lacy's is a conflation in which most of the stage directions are almost certainly derived from the Pattie edition with which they agree almost to the word. (Lacy's wife, Fanny Cooper, was Vestris' and later Phelps's Helena.) This would have been a quite suitable catchpenny edition to issue after Kean's revival; as we shall see, Kean is so directly indebted to Vestris that the stage directions in his own acting edition are often nearly identical to those in the Pattie edition.

As to the text, however, Lacy has given Vestris credit for more of Shakespeare's text than Pattie has. The Lacy edition shows only about 261 lines missing; the Pattie edition shows she cut some 358 lines from the play. But apparently Pattie was not above flattering the producer either. For example, J. O. Halliwell, who saw Vestris' production, commented [in his *An Introduction to Shakespeare's Midsummer Night's Dream*] specifically on two omissions not recorded in either edition— the prologue to "Pyramus and Thisbe" (25 lines), and Hermia's speech upon awakening alone in the forest (6 lines). This final figure of 392 lines cut (or about eighteen percent of the text) is as near the truth as we are likely to get.

Vestris' text compares well with six other major stage texts of the nineteenth century. Samuel Phelps cut 372 lines for his 1853 production, perhaps the nineteenth century's most artistically satisfying staging. (Phelps was the first English producer to use musical settings only for those passages of text that require them.) William Burton, for his 1854 New York production, omitted 366 lines. In 1856, Charles Kean cut 828 lines—almost forty percent of the play's 2134 lines of dialogue—for the staging that was one of the highwater marks of the century's scenic illustration of Shakespeare. Laura Keene took Kean's acting edition as the base for her 1859 New York production, and the final sum of her omitted lines was ten more than Kean's. The promptbook for Augustin Daly's 1888 revival shows 558 lines were cut by William Winter, the editor for all Daly's Shakespearean productions. Sir Herbert Beerbohm Tree's production—so often our end-of-the-century reference point—omitted 410 lines. In sum, from the best evidence available to us, it appears that in Victorian productions of this play the textual omissions ranged from roughly 370 to 410 lines (seventeen to nineteen percent) with crests such as Daly's 558 or Charles Kean's 828 lines (twenty-six to forty percent). (The uncut text reached the stage in Harley Granville Barker's 1914 production in which he omitted fewer than three lines and slightly altered five words.)

Vestris' version retained musical settings for portions of the text, but some of the play's best poetry was more intact than it will be in later productions, a matter that sheer numbers do not reveal. In relative completeness, for example, were such passages as Titania's "forgeries of jealousy" [II. i. 81] speech; Helena's lines on her childhood with Hermia; Theseus' observations on the lunatic, the lover, and the poet; Oberon's final lines beginning "Now until the break of day" [V. i. 401]; and Puck's epilogue. None of these may be taken for granted hereafter. Phelps, for example, cut thirty of the thirty-seven lines of Titania's speech as did Burton and Daly; Kean left only three lines of it. Oberon's last lines were entirely cut by Phelps, Burton, Kean, and Daly.

Vestris' cutting became the Victorian pattern: shorten and soften the lovers' wrangles in the forest, remove arcane references, shorten lyrical elaborations that do not move the plot, omit any shade of the suggestive and any shadow of the unpleasant. To illustrate quickly the latter two, Vestris cut three lines in which Titania describes how she and the then pregnant mother of her Indian boy had "laughed to see the sails conceive / And grow big bellied with the wanton wind" [II.i. 128-29]. Puck, in his "Now the hungry lion roars" [V.i. 370-90], loses all references to screech owls, shrouds, Hecate's team, and gaping graves. Managers take increasing pains to be wholesome as the century progresses. In 1840, Hermia was allowed to speak of her "virgin patent" [I.i. 80], but for Daly and Tree near the close of the century, she spoke of her "maiden heart." In 1840, Theseus could say "Lovers, to bed," but for Kean it was "Lovers, away" [V.i. 368].

It was almost certainly the clever hand of James Robinson Planché that we see in the editing of Vestris' text. He had been her producing associate at the Olympic Theatre, especially for its fairy extravaganzas and pantomimes. Among his other achievements was the libretto for Carl Maria von Weber's *Oberon* which premiered at Covent Garden in 1826. At Covent Garden, he was Vestris' play-reader, and scenic and costume supervisor; it was he who staged the fairy finale of this production. J. O. Halliwell credited Planché with the Vestris text: "The alterations from the original version of the play are few and made with that good judgment which characterizes everything that Mr. Planché undertakes."

Given the large theatre and her own musical abilities, it was in Vestris' interest to embellish the text with fourteen songs. This brought some criticism in 1840, but only Shakespeare's lines were set to music, a nicety never observed before. Also, they were turned to some intrinsic dramatic purpose; all fourteen were given to the fairies in an attempt to set them further apart from the mortals. It is understandable that with these

songs, delivered as featured numbers, plus the fuller text (not to mention the scenic efforts), the production ran three and one-half hours. This length was complained of. . . .

Mendelssohn's overture raised the curtain, and all the music thereafter was "composed and selected" by Thomas Simpson Cooke, who had collaborated with Henry Rowley Bishop on the Reynolds opera of 1816. (Bishop had been Vestris' music director for *Love's Labor's Lost* and *The Fortunate Isles* the previous season.) Vestris is indebted to that opera for several of her songs, including "Over hill, over dale," the fairy lullaby to Titania, and the music for the final fairy blessing and ballet. Vestris (as Oberon) and Elizabeth Rainforth (as the first fairy) sang the lines beginning "I know a bank where the wild thyme grows" [II.i. 249], and this brought a sharp complaint from the *John Bull* critic:

> . . . now if these are not set to music by the poet himself, then there is no music in poetry. Yet instead of Vestris delivering them with the accompaniment of her own rich speaking voice, you hear irreverent fiddlers preludizing to the butchery, and she and Miss Rainforth quaver of "the nodding, nodding vi-o-o-lets" til you are tempted to forswear Christendom and become Turk [21 November 1840].

But this song was given encores that evening and appears in the play over and over again throughout the century, prevailing over a long line of critics. The melody had been written in 1830 by Charles Edward Horn, music director for Vestris' first season at the Olympic.

At center stage for nine of the songs was Vestris herself in the role of Oberon, a major factor in the production's popular appeal. *The Town* [21 November 1840] reported that the airs and duets she sang "were rapturously applauded," and the *Theatrical Journal*, which reported on the production at intervals throughout the season, said in January, "Madame still sings beautifully," and praised her "Love in Idleness," and "I know a bank" [23 January 1841]. The breeches role was still a foil for the femininity of the forty-three-year-old actress who had been the light-opera darling of London and a bewitching figure on and off stage. She wore a translucent, star-flecked dress of yellow and gold descending only to the knee, tightly belted at the waist, and pinned at the shoulders, exposing arms and neck. Her large eyes were framed by a plumed Grecian helmet with moth-like wings appended, and she carried a gold spear topped with a butterfly. The *Times* [17 November 1840] spoke of her dignity and grace and remembered her

> as she stood with her glittering armour and fantastic helmet on an eminence, with a blue tinted wood gliding by her in the background, presenting different aspects of the same sylvan scenery . . . the marked out but remote figure on a dark ground . . . shone on by some artificial light . . . a supernatural appearance.

The play was a happy Shakespearean choice in which the actress-manager could capitalize upon her own powers as well as upon scenic spectacle. After Vestris' conspicuous success as Oberon, the role of the fairy king was played by a woman in every major English and American production of the play in the century, save one. An attractive brunette contralto, like Vestris, would play Oberon to a blond soprano as Titania—the love quarrel notwithstanding. For Victorians, a female fairy king was just that much less mortal. By the end of the century, one critic [in the *Pall Mall Gazette,* 11 January 1900] could write of Beerbohm Tree's Oberon, Julia Neilson: "Her Oberon is truly regal, while the mere fact of her being woman just differentiates it from humanity." The tradition was effectively ended with Granville Barker's Oberon, Dennis Neilson-Terry.

Vestris' choice of this play may seem, in retrospect, an obvious one given her past successes with the Olympic fairy pantomimes and her breeches roles, a more obvious Shakespearean choice than *Love's Labor's Lost* with which she had launched her management the previous season. But since the Restoration there had been no stage attempt to grasp *A Midsummer Night's Dream* as an organic and integrated whole. In the fragmented stage versions, the play had been pillaged and patched like an abandoned shrine of some forgotten faith, its parts pressed into other service. Its mythological Athenians had served for neoclassical invocations of an heroic age; its young lovers had become operatic songsters warbling through far more than Shakespeare's woodnotes wild; the mechanicals and their play had been excerpted for spoofs on the opera; and its fairies had been no more than utter fancy and never "the forms of things unknown" [V.i. 15] behind daylight surfaces. There had been no theatrical conception of Shakespeare's sanguine vision of all these elements moving in a mysterious, whimsical, reciprocal accord. Credit for the first attempt at this belongs to Vestris and Planché. If Romanticism made the play comprehensible, their experience with fairy pantomime, opera, and the pictorial stage made it practicable. It could appeal to both popular and genteel tastes, and the opportunity of restoring a Shakespearean text would have been attractive to Vestris given Macready's precedents at Covent Garden and her own quest for better quality audiences.

Her reputation as a resourceful and meticulous manager is well confirmed in this production. She had brought to Covent Garden three of the period's finest scenic artists. John Grieve, who had painted for the Reynolds opera in this theatre in 1816, now returned with his two sons, Thomas and William, to paint for Vestris' restored version of the play. At this point the web of tradition extends considerably. In 1856, Thomas Grieve had become the leading scene painter for the Charles Kean production, the settings of which survive in the watercolors in the Victoria and Albert Museum and also in the smaller watercolors bound into the Kean promptbook in the Harvard Theatre Collection. Then, in 1865, Thomas Grieve and his son, Walford, provided the scenery for Charles Calvert's production of the play in Manchester, a production for which Calvert also used the Vestris-influenced Kean acting edition. In this alone, we have a remarkable chain of traditions from 1816 to 1865. To it we may add that Vestris also employed her former machinist and decorator at the Olympic, E. W. Bradwell, the man who had been responsible for the "decorations" for the Reynolds opera. Bradwell had just engineered the flying fairies for Planché's extravaganza, *The Sleeping Beauty*. Finally, over all there was Planché who was, as he tells us in his autobiography [*Recollections and Reflections*], the "Superintendent of the Decorative Department."

> I had the pleasure of continuing my reforms of the costume of the national drama which I had commenced at this theatre with the additional advantage of the great taste and unbounded liberality of the manageress, whose heart was thoroughly in the cause, and spared neither time, trouble, nor money in the promotion of it.

The intent of such a policy had been expressed by Vestris in the prologue she delivered on the opening night of her Covent Garden management. Not long before this production, Planché would have contributed his notes on ancient Grecian costume to accompany the play in Charles Knight's edition of Shakespeare: "We must look to the frieze of the Parthenon," he begins.

Antiquarian spectacle had first attached itself to the Athens of *A Midsummer Night's Dream* in the 1816 Reynolds opera. For the first act, it had had its "Grand Doric Colonnade appertaining to Duke Theseus' Palace." A surviving engraving from the production shows Reynolds' Oberon, John Duruset, as a Grecian soldier-king in belted tunic, mantle, sandals, and with spear in hand. In 1840, Vestris' first picture was a "hall in the Palace of Theseus—with distant view of Athens," which the *Spectator* [21 November 1840] described as "a view of Athens looking up a long perspective of fanes to the Acropolis towering in the distance, the polychrome decorations of the Greek architecture being visible in the foreground." Just such a romantic rendering of classical wonders—so edifying to the Victorians—survives in the idealized watercolors of the Kean production. It is the watercolor of a backdrop by William Gordon for Kean's first setting, described in his acting edition as "A Terrace adjoining the palace of Theseus, Overlooking the City of Athens." Vestris' next scene, in which the mechanicals cast their play, would have been a carpenter scene, played before a downstage drop of a "Room in Quince's House." Vestris and Planché did not yet create Kean's authentic workshop for Quince furnished with "tools copied from discoveries at Herculaneum." But Planché's costumes for the Athenian court call for tunics with Grecian borders, mantles, laurel wreaths, and sandals.

With the forest scenes of acts two, three and four, Vestris marries the play to the pictorial stage. The full stage forest settings of the Grieves underwent a gliding sequence of transformations with the aid of a panorama. In the first such change, after the moonlight meeting of Oberon and Titania, Oberon—the manager herself—waved her wand and the "blue-tinted wood" glided behind her to change to Titania's bower, formed by the overhanging branches and foliage of moon-illumined trees. She then ascended and was flown off as Titania's fairies danced on. The third act brought a more complex sequence of changes using the panorama, gauzes, and special lighting effects. The *Spectator* describes the sequence somewhat impressionistically:

> The next change shows a stream with a raised bank in a sequestered spot, where the lovers meet: the moon, half veiled in mist, sinks after awhile, its reflection in the stream vanishes, and all is dusky gray: but presently the dawn converts the twilight . . . into the glowing sunlight of morning: mists and gathering clouds succeed for a brief space, but soon vanish. . . .

The Pattie edition gives the setting as follows: "Moonlight—transparent wood—platform, coloured as rising ground, crossing from the back R.—water piece joining it, and running off, L.—large tree in center." Then, near the end of this act, with the climax of the charmed confusion of the pairs of young lovers, Oberon gives Puck his instructions and with music, "Puck waves his hand and a thick fog pervades the scene (gauzes 2nd and 3rd entrances)." Behind these gauzes, Lysander and Demetrius vaunt their challenges by the light of a sinking moon. Puck imitates them, leads them off the stage confused, and "the mist clears off and discovers another part of the forest." The gauzes have ascended, the scenery has been in motion again, and Vestris has, in effect, moved her audience cinematically to another part of the forest where we discover the lovers sleeping, exhausted after their chase. A fairy dance and tableau around them ends the third act. Thus we see a literal, pictorial delineation in which each forest scene has its distinct locale; the lovers' chase takes them deeper into the forest and to parts distinct from the bower. This pictorial effort can be traced back to the simpler forest settings for the Reynolds opera (and a simple gauze mist, parent to those in Vestris' staging may be found there, too). But with the restored text a structural change in the play now becomes necessary. In Shakespeare, all four of the exhausted lovers re-enter and fall asleep. Titania and Bottom then enter and fall asleep. Oberon wakes Titania, releases her from her spell, and they exit. Theseus and the court hunting party then enter to discover the sleeping young lovers. After all have exited, Bottom awakes. Since Vestris has Titania, Bottom, and Oberon in one part of the forest and the lovers in another, she must go back to the bower, which she does at the opening of Act IV, and have Bottom awake after Oberon and Titania exit. Bottom's awakening she then follows with his reunion with his friends at Quince's house—played before a downstage drop in IV.ii. This sequence allows the change back to the full-stage forest setting where the lovers lie asleep. The result is awkward, of course, for it means that the excited exit of Bottom and his friends to perform at the court wedding feast ("Our play is preferred" [IV.ii. 39]), comes before the discovery of the sleeping lovers by Theseus and the exit of the court to prepare the wedding feast. But Charles Kean and the Grieves used precisely this sequence in 1856, and most Victorian managers thereafter altered the original sequence of action at this point for similar scenic reasons.

We may turn now to Vestris' final act. The curtain went up on more Periclean splendour—Theseus' "Hall of Statues, with raised stage in the centre, hung at the back with curtains." The *Spectator* spoke of "the severe forms of the marble Caryatides relieved by the chaste richness of antique draperies and classic costumes conveying a lively idea of the 'pomp of elder days.' " The quartet of lovers entered in bridal attire to a court peopled with "lords and ladies" in Athenian attire. Theseus and Hippolyta reclined on a couch to watch "Pyramus and Thisbe." Pyramus wore a red mantle over his white tunic and Thisbe (Flute) wore a white robe and veil. Moonshine (Starveling) wore a silvered gown and a mask, his dog was a real dog, and he carried his lantern on a pitchfork. Snout's long gown was painted as a stone wall, and he was masked. After the performance on the little raised stage and the exit of the court to nuptial beds, the setting was transformed to "another part of the palace." For both of these settings, the Pattie stage directions and the reviewers suggest pictures that seem very near the images of the Kean watercolors for this act. Pattie's stage directions (with some interpolated phrases from his list of scenes and properties) read as follows:

> The Scene glides away, part of it ascending, other parts descending and going off R.2.E. The [raised] Stage forms a flight of steps [and a platform center]—large flights of steps, R. and L.—platform and gallery [running along the back] from R. to L. Fairies all discovered with Torches of various coloured fires.

The *Times* described this transformation:

> The vanishing of the theatre in which the clowns act their tragedy, and discovery of the interior of the palace, with fairies crowded in every part, gliding along galleries, ascending and descending steps, soaring in the air with blue and yellow torches, which produce a curious light, is one of the most beautiful and highly wrought fairy scenes ever introduced on the stage.

Planché, in his autobiography thirty years later, proudly recalled devising this scene with the Grieves, inspired by Oberon's command, "Through this house give glimmering light."

Overall, London's critics came away impressed with the lavish scenic splendor, the high finish on the production, and with Vestris herself. Some of these opinions we have sampled. In addition, for scenic lavishness the production was compared with Macready's *The Tempest*. Athens and the forests often inspired long descriptions. The opening scene, the *Theatrical Journal* [1 May 1841] said, was "calculated to raise one to a contemplation of the finer portion of the mind . . . I was on classic ground . . . what a remembrance to a well-stored mind to see the glories of this city . . . to be for awhile Greek in heart and hand." *John Bull* [21 November 1840] conceded that the staging would "satisfy the most fastidious voluptuary in scenic effect." The *Spectator* said of the forest sequences, "all is sylvan and visionary; the wood scenes change like the phases of a dream."

But if this first attempt to realize the whole play on the stage was impressive, it seems not to have been entirely persuasive. The *Athenaeum* [21 November 1840] said:

> The material attractions of a pageant, however gorgeous, are no substitute for spiritual essence; nevertheless, as a masque of Shakespeare's imagining it is better than any other, and as this representation of it transcends any previous one, it merits the popular applause.

The *Times* struck the same note, although more charitably.

> As far as theatrical representation of this ethereal drama is possible, it was achieved last night, and a gorgeous spectacle was produced . . . Cobweb, Moth, and Mustardseed, with their shrill trumpet voices, were but inadequate likenesses of their shadowy originals; but in the conception of the whole, a fine poetical feeling was apparent, a consciousness of the difficulties with which the struggle was to be made, and a resolution to conquer them if possible. If the minute elves could not be obtained, it was still left to give a shadowy unreal character to the scenery; if the individuals could not be realized, it was still possible to give a fairy grace to the troups and impart to the whole tableau what could not be bestowed on its parts.

One will seek in vain for such dream-struck critics as those who saw Phelp's subtly integrated production. A major problem here was that in the vast Covent Garden spaces, so inimical to the dream spell, the scenery, music, and ballet carried further than the poetry, and the restored text counted for less than we count the achievement historically. The *Anthenaeum,* like the *Times,* began by saying, "all that a tasteful and liberal application of stage resources could accomplish has been done at this theatre . . ." but, it immediately continued, "the exquisite poetry of Shakespeare loses its charm, if not its meaning, when uttered with those imperfections of speech, inseparable from the formal declamation of actors labouring to fill an area too large to allow a complete governance of the voice." Thus we hear that John Cooper, as Theseus, was too formal and didactic a declaimer, counting his imaginary hounds with a demonstrative forefinger. The *Spectator,* too, said, "the performance falls short of the pageant, and the poetry is marred in the delivery." It found only Vestris distinct and musical; Miss Marshall (Puck) was distinct, but her voice was "too much taxed in order to speak loud to enable her to control its intonation." Miss Cooper played Helena with earnest feeling but could not conceal the appearance of effort in projection, and "Mrs. Walter Lacy as Titania mouths and emphasizes too much." The embellishment of the text with songs may have been an attempt to fill the vast theatre with the delicate play, but the poetry could not work its spell.

Vestris' cast seems not to have been entirely uniform in abilities and style, though this is not unique to her production in the century. Halliwell and others found only Helena strongly played among the quartet of young lovers. The Bottom of John Harley—who was later to play the role for Kean—amused audiences, but he was "a lively buffoon making fun of the character," said the *Spectator.* There was more art in the Flute of Robert Keeley, who was described as a man who "shared in the general joy and sorrow like one whose obtuse intellect apprehended it the last, but whose good-natured heart felt it the most."

Certainly Vestris pleased her audiences; she was called before the curtain on opening night, and the production enjoyed the extraordinary number of fifty-nine performances that season and eleven the next. However, some poignant evidence of the expense of such productions remains. Charles Mathews, writing in his autobiography [*The Life of Charles James Mathews, Chiefly Autobiographical*] of the hopelessness of meeting the accumulating debts of the three seasons at Covent Garden, provided a sample page from his ledgers quite relevant here. In the week ending 26 December 1840, during which *A Midsummer Night's Dream, The Merry Wives of Windsor,* and a pantomime were running, Mathews was struggling to meet the salaries of 684 persons. Among them were 199 in the scenic department and 116 in wardrobe. The playbill cast list for *A Midsummer Night's Dream* totals ninety-two, including the fifty-two supernumerary fairies who are an item on the ledger page. A report in *The Lyre, Musical and Theatrical Gazette* [21 May 1842] showed Vestris and Mathews operating at an average loss of ten pounds a night for the 221 nights, in that 1840-1841 season, though it was, with *A Midsummer Night's Dream* and *London Assurance,* the most financially successful of their three seasons at Covent Garden.

It remains only to note the wealth of minor staging traditions that grow out of the Vestris production, especially out of the Grieve-Vestris fairy forest. Phelps's forest was a less literal one, but his tools were very similar—a diorama instead of a panorama, with the addition of a green gauze stretched across the entire forest picture for Acts II through IV. For William Burton's 1854 production, John Moore instructed in his promptbook: "In all the Wood scenes the same backing may be continued merely by moving it towards L. H. as a Panorama, and all the Cut Woods & c.—should go the same way—to convey the idea that the characters have advanced farther into the same wood." It is clear from other of his promptbook entries that Moore was witness to Vestris' production. Burton's lovers, too, lost their way in a mist of descending gauzes. Thomas Barry opened a glittery production to rival Burton's the same month, and its chief feature was

a panorama of a moonlit fairyland that passed behind Oberon as he sat in a swan-drawn car. Once again the lovers were led by Puck through a labyrinth of gauzes under a darkening moon, and the chase ended with the fairies ascending in a car above the sleeping lovers. Barry produced the play in Boston two years later with many of the same features, including a "Giant Moving Double Panorama," a "Transparent Mist," and the "Break of Day." The Grieves then brought the Vestris model to Kean's 1856 staging, including the unwinding panorama supervised by Oberon, the gauzes, the transposed scene of Bottom's reunion with his friends, and the dawn. We have a record in miniature of this panorama in a fold-out watercolor (16 ½ x 5 ½ inches) in the Kean promptbook in the Harvard Theatre Collection. In 1859, Laura Keene's column-long advertisements boasted of the same features, but a new American wrinkle was added a few years later by Joseph Jefferson. He brought from London a panorama painted by William Telbin (the elder) that was used in a production of the play at the Olympic Theatre in New York in 1867. This panorama was used to illustrate the passage of Theseus, the hunting party, and the lovers out of the forest and back to the city of Athens. Augustin Daly used the obligatory panorama in its usual place in his 1873 production but in 1888, Daly adapted Jefferson's placement of the panorama. Daly had a Grecian galley (dating back to the ship Argo in the Reynolds opera) sail from the forest back to Athens carrying Theseus' hunting party and the young lovers, Ada Rehan and John Drew among them. This panorama—actually a diorama—voyage is preserved in a sequence of photographs in Rehan's souvenir album in the New York Public Library Theatre Collection. (Daly's galley had its immediate ancestors in those with which Burton and Barry furnished the Argonaut Theseus for his first act entrance. As the curtain rose, the ship docked, and Theseus and his captive bride disembarked.) The sunrise the Grieves arranged for Vestris was remembered by John Moore, who recorded it in his promptbook for Burton's production: "The back scene was a drop painted entirely on linen—a large opaque tree C. which was supposed to hide the sun itself—but made a magnificent contrast to the rest of the scene which was pervaded by a powerful white Sunlight. Sunlight mediums—yellow silk." "The morning descends in pearls among the waving foliage of a forest," said one critic [in the *Literary Gazette,* 21 November 1840], and such dawns dawn hereafter at this point in every major production in the century, including those of Phelps, Burton, Barry, Kean, Daly, and Tree.

Vestris' Puck rose up center stage seated on a mushroom just as Ellen Terry would do in Kean's production. Titania's fairies carried her and Bottom off in a floral car reminiscent of the fairy cars of the 1816 opera, and fairy vehicles proliferate through the century. Burton's Oberon entered in a dragonfly car and Barry's Oberon rode a swan-drawn car while Titania used a dolphin-drawn car and Puck a peacock car. At the Olympic in 1867, Oberon and his queen entered in golden chariots "beswarmed by bullfrogs"; and in 1888, Daly's Puck put her girdle around the earth in an airborne floral car.

As the fairy king, Vestris was costumed as a diminutive Grecian warrior, as we have seen. The fairies of her train and Titania's followed the romantic ballet pattern of *La Sylphide* (1832) and Marie Taglioni—dressed in white gauze dresses with spangles of silver, white silk stockings, chaplets of flowers, and not very aerodynamic wings. Oberon's fairies were identifiable by their blue neck scarves, Titania's by their yellow ones. The dances of fairies around Titania and Bottom and around the sleeping lovers began a romantic ballet tradition that would subsume the play itself. Vestris' dances were arranged by Oscar Byrne, who came from her Olympic staff and who went on to choreograph Kean's production in 1856. Kean had the ballet of fairies climax with a Maypole dance using garlands streaming from a palm tree sprung from beneath the stage. Kean dressed Oberon's fairies in golden classical armour, with red wings appended, to mirror their fairy king and differentiate the two camps. To Vestris' gauzy fairies, Planché added fauns in goat skins and satyrs in fur; Puck was an elfish creature in a light brown plush shirt, with long ears and bare arms and legs, similar to the Puck of Weber's *Oberon*. The eighteenth century had seen boys in the role of Puck, but in the Reynolds opera and Vestris' production, adult women played the role—the more common practice hereafter in the century, although boys and girls were used. Children seem to have usually played the roles of Peaseblossom, Cobweb, Moth, and Mustardseed, while the rest of the fairy band varied from the adults used frequently through mid-century (such as are seen in the Kean watercolors), to the children increasingly used toward the end of the century (as in the photographs of the Tree production). For species of flying fairies, one early pictorial record is notable. The watercolor of the meeting of Oberon and Titania in Kean's production shows six fairies hovering overhead; that they are not an illustrator's afterthought nor painted figures on a gauze is confirmed by the promptbook entrance warning for "6 flying fairies" and explicit directions for their flight back and forth above the stage. A dummy was substituted for Ellen Terry in Puck's flight, but Sir Frank Benson, in a Christmas production of 1889, had a child fairy deliver Puck's epilogue in suspense twenty feet above the stage. Fireflies are on the property lists from Vestris to Tree and ranged in variety from Daly's electric ones to Max Reinhardt's real ones in his Boboli Gardens production in 1933.

There were managers after Madame Vestris who were more successful in weaving the dream spell, notably Phelps, but Vestris set the pattern for the century. The elements of her 1840 production reappeared in varying proportions and combinations, with varying tastes and abilities behind them, throughout the Victorian life of the play. Charles Kean's debt to Vestris is the deepest and most direct. It is almost as extensive as his debt to Macready's *King John,* pointed out by Charles Shattuck [in his *William Charles Macready's King John*], although if *A Midsummer Night's Dream's* stage history is any indication, generous borrowing was not unusual in the century. Vestris' production was an important achievement in its era, interesting for its influence and as a study of the making of Victorian stage traditions. (pp. 1-19)

> *Gary Jay Williams, "Madame Vestris' 'A Midsummer Night's Dream' and the Web of Victorian Tradition," in* Theatre Survey, *Vol. XVIII, No. 2, November, 1977, pp. 1-22.*

PRODUCTION:

Ludwig Tieck and Felix Mendelssohn • Potsdam Court Theatre • 1843

BACKGROUND:

Tieck was a noted German Romantic critic, poet, dramatist, and Elizabethan scholar. His completion of August Wilhelm Schlegel's unfinished translation of Shakespeare's plays resulted in a definitive German version of these works. In 1843 he received a royal commission from Friedrich Wilhelm IV to stage *A Midsummer Night's Dream*. The music was composed by Felix Mendelssohn, who had written an overture for the comedy in 1826. Mendelssohn's score has been considered the finest music ever composed for a Shakespearean work, and it became a standard feature of stagings of the play well into the twentieth century. Still occasionally used in stagings, Mendelssohn's music is closely associated with lush, romantic stagings of *A Midsummer Night's Dream*.

COMMENTARY:

Feodor Wehl   (essay date 1867)

[*The excerpt below is taken from a translation of Wehl's* Didaskalien, *which was first published in German in 1867. Wehl here recounts the events surrounding Tieck's production of* The Summernight's Dream, *as Shakespeare's play is known in Germany.*]

When Tieck, in the hey-day of his life, was in Dresden, he pleaded enthusiastically for a performance of the 'Summernight's Dream.' But actors, managers, and theatre-goers shook their heads. 'The thing is impossible,' said the knowing ones. 'The idea is a chimera,—a dream of Queen Mab,—it can never be realised.'

Tieck flung himself angrily back in his chair, and held his peace.

Years passed by.

At last Tieck was summoned to Berlin, to the Court of Friedrich Wilhelm the Fourth, and among the pieces of poetry which he there read to attentive ears was Shakespeare's 'Summernight's Dream.' At the conclusion of the reading, which had given the keenest delight to the illustrious audience, the King asked: 'Is it really a fact that this piece cannot be performed on the stage?'

Tieck, as he himself often afterwards humourously related, was thunderstruck. He felt his heart beat to the very tip of his tongue, and for a minute language failed him. For more than twenty years, almost a lifetime, his cherished idea had been repelled with cold opposition, prosaic arguments, or sympathetic shrugs. And now a monarch, intellectual and powerful, had asked if the play could not be performed! Tieck's head swam; before his eyes floated the vision of a fulfillment, at the close of his life, of one of the dearest wishes of his heart. 'Your majesty!' he cried at last, 'Your majesty! If I only had permission and the means, it would make the most enchanting performance on earth!'

'Good then, set to work, Master Ludovico,' replied Friedrich Wilhelm, in his pleasant, jesting way. 'I give you full power, and will order Kuestner (the Superintendent at that time of the Royal Theatre) to place the theatre and all his soupes (actors) at your disposal.'

It was the happiest day of Ludwig Tieck's life! The aged poet, crippled with rheumatism, reached his home, intoxicated with joy. The whole night he was thinking, pondering, ruminating, scene-shifting. The next day he arranged the Comedy, read it to the actors who were to take part in it, and consulted with FELIX MENDELSOHN BARTHOLDY about the needful music.

The aged Master Ludwig was rejuvenated; vanished were his years, his feebleness, his valetudinarianism. Day after day he wrote, he spoke, he drove hither and thither,—his whole soul was in the work which he was now to make alive.

At last the day came which was to reveal it to the doubting and astonished eyes of the public. And what a public! All that Berlin could show of celebrities in Science, in Art, in intellect, in acknowledged or in struggling Authorship, in talent, in genius, in beauty, and grace,—all were invited to the royal palace at Potsdam, where the first representation was to take place.

The present writer was so fortunate as to be one of the invited guests, and never can he forget the impression then made on him.

The stage was set as far as possible in the Old English style, only, as was natural, it was furnished in the most beautiful and tasteful way. In the Orchestra stood Mendelssohn, beaming with joy, behind him sat Tieck, with kindling looks, handsome, and transfigured like a god. Around was gathered the glittering court, and in the rear the rising rows of invited guests.

What an assemblage! There sat the great Humboldt, the learned Boekh, Bachmann, the historians Raumer and Ranke, all the Professors of the University, the poets Kopisch, Kugler, Bettina von Arnim, Paalzow, Theodor Mundt, Willibad Alexis, Rellstab, Crelinger, Varnhagen von Ense, and the numberless host of the other guests.

It was a time when all the world was enthusiastic over Friedrich Wilhelm the Fourth. His gift as a public speaker, his wit, his love and knowledge of Art had charmed all classes, and filled them with hope. All hearts went out to meet him as he entered, gay, joyous, smiling, and took his place among the guests.

Verily, we seemed transported to the age of Versailles in the days of the Louises. It was a gala-day for the realm, fairer and more brilliant than any hitherto in its history.

What pleasure shone in all faces, what anticipation, what suspense! An eventful moment was it when the King took his seat, and the beaming Tieck nodded to his joyous friend in the Orchestra, and the music began, that charming, original, bewitching music which clung so closely to the innermost meaning of the poetry and to the suggestions of Tieck. The Wedding March has become a popular, an immortal composition; but how lovely, how delicious, how exquisite, and here and there so full of frolic, is all the rest of it! With a master's power, which cannot be too much admired, Mendelssohn has given expression in one continuous harmony to the soft whisperings of elves, to the rustlings and flutterings of a moonlit night, to all the enchantment of love, to the clumsy nonsense of the rude mechanicals, and to the whizzings and buzzings of the mad Puck.

How it then caught the fancy of that select audience! They listened, they marvelled, they were in a dream!

And when at last the play fairly began, how like a holy bene-

diction it fell upon all, no one stirred, no one moved, as though spellbound all sat to the very last, and then an indescribable enthusiasm burst forth, every one, from the King down to the smallest authorkin, applauded and clapped, and clapped again.

Take it for all in all, it was a day never to be forgotten, it was a day when before the eyes of an art-loving monarch, a poet revealed the miracle of a representation, and superbly proved that it was no impossibility to those who were devoted to art. In this 'Summernight's Dream' the elfin world seemed again to live; elves sprang up from the ground, from the air, from the trees, from the flowers! they fluttered in the beams of the moon! Light, shade, sound, echo, leaves and blooms, sighings and singings, and shoutings for joy! everything helped to make the wonder true and living!

Not for a second time can the like be seen.

It was the highest pinnacle of the reign of Friedrich Wilhelm the Fourth. Who could have dreamt that behind this glittering play of poetic fancy there stood dark and bloody Revolution, and fateful Death? Yet it was even so! (pp. 329-30)

> Feodor Wehl, *"Appendix: Notable Performances,"* translated by Horace Howard Furness, in A New Variorum Edition of Shakespeare: "A Midsummer Night's Dream", *edited by Horace Howard Furness, 1895. Reprint by Dover Publications, Inc., 1963, pp. 329-32.*

Simon Williams   (essay date 1986)

[*In the following excerpt, Williams discusses the 1843 production of* A Midsummer Night's Dream *as it relates to Tieck's belief in staging Shakespeare on a bare stage. Although this production was successful, he observes, "it did not fulfill to the letter Tieck's ambition to reproduce a staging as sparse as he considered that of the Elizabethans to be."*]

[Ludwig Tieck] from the early 1790s through to his death in 1853, published regularly editions of Elizabethan plays and essays on them that argued consistently for a return to the original performance conditions as a prerequisite for successful production. For Tieck, Shakespeare's plays were remarkable because of the playwright's ability to summon up a world of fantasy that the audience experienced as if it were in a dream. In an early essay, which introduced his translation of *The Tempest*, 'Shakespeares Behandlung des Wunderbaren' ('Shakespeare's Treatment of the Marvellous', 1793), Tieck demonstrated a broader, more generous view of the potential of the theatre than Goethe would do later, finding Shakespeare above all other dramatists fulfilling this potential. 'Perhaps no other writer', he wrote, 'has so well calculated theatrical effect in his works of art as Shakespeare, without resorting to empty *coups-de-théâtres* or providing entertainment through wretched surprises'. Especially remarkable for Tieck was the completeness of Shakespeare's fantasy world. This challenged the performer to maintain entire the illusion, 'so that the mind [of the spectator] is never transferred to the normal world and the illusion broken'. Tieck considered the conventional theatre of his time—and he was particularly antagonistic towards the arch-illusionist, August Iffland—to be inadequate. Its actors were too precise and dry, while its concern with impressive spectacle stood between the audience and the play. So that Shakespeare's plays could be performed in a manner that allowed the audience to participate fully in their world, Tieck argued for a stage that allowed the actors closer proximity to the audience than was possible in the early nineteenth-century theatre with its broad orchestra pit. Furthermore, their stage should not be encumbered with heavy, realistic scenery, but should be arranged so as to allow for swift transitions from one scene to the other. This non-scenic stage would, by its very nature, not presuppose the unity of tone implied by the conventional perspective stage, but would be an ideal environment for the 'variety, episodes, and juxtapositions of the comic with the tragic' characteristic of Shakespearean drama. Naturally, the Elizabethan theatre provided a model for this stage, and Tieck did much pioneering research into the conditions in which Shakespeare's plays were first performed. In addition to several publications on the Elizabethan dramatists and their theatre, in 1836 he completed, with the help of the architect Gottfried Semper, a reconstruction of the Fortune Theatre. This was not entirely accurate. Instead of the stage thrust out into the audience, indicated by the Henslowe contract, he provided a broad, shallow, relief stage, and from this he had two conspicuous flights of stairs leading up to a substantial balcony stage. But, despite its inaccuracies, this reconstruction demonstrated the possibility of staging Shakespeare in an alternative way to that of the illusionist stage. (pp. 211-12)

[In 1841 Tieck] received a summons to join the Berlin Royal Theatre as dramaturg. His first experiment in presenting a play in a style approximating its original performance conditions was with Sophocles' *Antigone;* but in 1843, with the aid of the stage designer J. C. Gerst, he produced *A Midsummer Night's Dream.* . . . Tieck did not attempt to reconstruct precisely the Elizabethan stage, though in the context of the proscenium stages first of the Potsdam Court Theatre, then of the Berlin Royal Theatre, he incorporated some of its principles, especially in the use of vertical space. This he had already exaggerated in his reconstruction of the Fortune. Gerst's permanent set consisted of three storeys that included 'visible flights of stairs and several playing areas, a forestage and side-steps behind the proscenium, covered by carpets'. The multiple playing areas enabled Tieck to present the action with a fluidity unique to the time. But the popularity of this production—it was given more than forty times, a considerable number for those days—must have been dependent partially upon substantial concessions being made to audience taste for realistic illusion and spectacle. The galleries at the back were so constructed as to allow realistic backdrops to be lowered into each partitioned space. In this way, a particular area at a particular point in the action was localised. Moreover, the workshop of the mechanicals, which could not be accommodated in one area of the permanent stage was realised through lowering, in front of the galleries, a realistic backdrop as specific as anything in the conventional theatre. Also, this was the production for which Mendelssohn wrote his popular incidental music to *A Midsummer Night's Dream,* which meant that considerable portions of the performance included ballet, performed among attractively designed woodland scenery lowered from the flies. This served to disguise the architectural nature of the permanent set. . . . Tieck settled for a compromise between conventional theatre and the non-illusionism of the Elizabethan stage. While this was a highly successful venture (especially as the audience, helped by Mendelssohn's music, became deeply involved in Shakespeare's fantasy world), it did not fulfil to the letter Tieck's ambition to reproduce a staging as sparse as he considered that of the Elizabethans to be. (pp. 214-15)

Simon Williams, "The 'Shakespeare-Stage' in Nine-

teenth-Century Germany," in Shakespeare and the Victorian Stage, *edited by Richard Foulkes, Cambridge University Press, 1986, pp. 210-22.*

PRODUCTION

Samuel Phelps • Sadler's Wells • 1853

BACKGROUND:

Between the time he became manager of Sadler's Wells Theatre in 1844 and his retirement in 1862, Phelps staged all but four of Shakespeare's plays there, including many which had not been seen in London for decades. His 1853 production of *A Midsummer Night's Dream* has been judged his greatest success at Sadler's Wells and is still regarded as perhaps the finest staging of the play in the nineteenth century. Critics and audiences found the use of gauze screens in the fairy scenes, special lighting effects, and shifting dioramas truly evocative of the enchanted quality of Shakespeare's play. Moreover, Phelp's portrayal of Bottom was considered brilliant, and it became one of his most famous roles.

COMMENTARY:

Henry Morley   (review date 15 October 1853)

[*Morley was a nineteenth-century English scholar, editor, and dramatic critic whose writings often focused on the various relations between literature and the stage. As a member of the School for Dramatic Art, his chief goal was to raise the standard of the acting and drama of his day. Morley also contributed essays and reviews to the* Examiner *from 1850 to 1864. Many of his dramatic criticisms were collected and published in 1891 as* The Journal of a London Playgoer. *In the originally unsigned review below, Morley extols Phelps's production, maintaining that "it is very doubtful whether the* Midsummer Night's Dream *has ever yet, since it was first written, been put upon the stage with so nice an interpretation of its meaning." The critic particularly admires Phelps's innovative portrayal of Bottom, in which the initially excitable weaver became dreamily quiet once he was "translated."*]

Every reader of Shakespeare is disposed to regard the *Midsummer Night's Dream* as the most essentially unactable of all his plays. It is a dramatic poem of the utmost grace and delicacy, its characters are creatures of the poet's fancy that no flesh and blood can properly present—fairies that "creep into acorn cups" [II. i. 31], or mortals that are but dim abstractions, persons of a dream. The words they speak are so completely spiritual that they are best felt when they are not spoken. Their exquisite beauty is like that of sunset-colours which no mortal artist can interpret faithfully. The device of the clowns in the play to present moonshine, has seemed to us hitherto but a fair expression of the kind of success that might be achieved by the best actors who should attempt to present the *Midsummer Night's Dream* on the stage. We have thought it, therefore, properly avoided by managers as lying beside and above their art, nor did we feel that there was reason to be disappointed when the play some years ago furnished Madame Vestris with a spectacle that altogether wanted the Shakespearean spirit.

In some measure we have found reason to modify our opinion on these matters, since we have seen the *Midsummer Night's Dream* as produced by Mr Phelps. Though stage fairies cannot ride on bluebells, and the members of no theatrical company now in existence can speak such poetry as that of the *Midsummer Night's Dream* otherwise than most imperfectly, yet it is proved that there remains in the power of the manager who goes with pure taste and right feeling to his work, enough for the establishment of this play as a most charming entertainment of the stage.

Mr Phelps has never for a minute lost sight of the main idea which governs the whole play, and this is the great secret of his success in the presentation of it. He knew that he was to present merely shadows; that spectators, as *Puck* reminds them in the epilogue, are to think they have slumbered in their seats, and that what appeared before them have been visions. Everything has been subdued as far as possible at SADLER'S WELLS to this ruling idea. The scenery is very beautiful, but wholly free from the meretricious glitter now in favour; it is not so remarkable for costliness as for the pure taste in which it and all the stage arrangements have been planned. There is no ordinary scene-shifting; but as in dreams, one scene is made to glide insensibly into another. We follow the lovers and the fairies through the wood from glade to glade, now among trees, now with a broad view of the sea and Athens in the distance, carefully but not at all obtrusively set forth. And not only do the scenes melt dream-like one into another, but over all the fairy portion of the play there is a haze thrown by a curtain of green gauze placed between the actors and the audience, and maintained there during the whole of the second, third, and fourth acts. This gauze curtain is so well spread that there are very few parts of the house from which its presence can be detected, but its influence is everywhere felt; it subdues the flesh and blood of the actors into something more nearly resembling dream-figures, and incorporates more completely the actors with the scenes, throwing the same green fairy tinge, and the same mist, over all. A like idea had also dictated certain contrivances of dress, especially in the case of the fairies.

Nor should we fail to remark upon the very perfect taste shown in the establishment of a harmony between the scenery and the poem. The main feature—the Midsummer Night—was marked by one scene so elaborated as to impress it upon all as the central picture of the group. The moon was just so much exaggerated as to give it the required prominence. The change, again, of this Midsummer Night into morning, when Theseus and Hippolyta come to the wood with horn and hound, was exquisitely presented. And in the last scene, when the fairies coming at night into the hall of Theseus "each several chambers bless" [V. i. 417], the Midsummer Moon is again seen shining on the palace as the curtains are drawn that admit the fairy throng. Ten times as much money might have been spent on an infinitely worse setting of the *Midsummer Night's Dream*. It is the poetical feeling prompting a judicious, but not extravagant outlay, by aid of which Mr Phelps has produced a stage-spectacle more refined and intellectual, and far more absolutely satisfactory, than anything we can remember to have seen since Mr Macready was a manager. Even now we cannot quit this topic of the scenery without reverting to the stage effect produced as Robin is bidden

Overcast the night—

The starry welkin cover thou anon
With drooping fog as black as Acheron

[III. ii. 355-57]

when the gathering of mists about the stage was presented with perfect illusion by a singularly dextrous use of painted gauzes.

That the flesh and blood presentments of the dream-figures which constitute the persons of the play, should be always in harmony with this true feeling, was scarcely to be expected. A great deal of the poetry is injured in the speaking. Unless each actor were a man who combined with elocutionary power a very high degree of sensibility and genius, it could hardly be otherwise. Yet we cannot say even here that the poet's effects entirely failed. The *Midsummer Night's Dream* abounds in the most delicate and choicest passages of Shakespeare's verse; the SADLER'S WELLS pit has a keen enjoyment for them; and pit and gallery were crowded to the farthest wall on Saturday night with a most earnest audience, among whom many a subdued hush arose, not during, but just before, the delivery of the most charming passages. If the crowd at DRURY LANE is a gross discredit to the public taste, the crowd at SADLER'S WELLS more than neutralises any ill opinion that may on that score be formed of the playgoers. The SADLER'S WELLS gallery, indeed, appeared to be not wholly unconscious of the contrast, for when *Bottom* volunteered to roar high or roar low, a voice from the gallery desired to know whether he could "roar like Brooke." Even the gallery at this theatre, however, resents an interruption, and the unexpected sally was not well received.

A remarkably quick-witted little boy, Master F. Artis, plays *Puck,* and really plays it with faithfulness and spirit as it has been conceived for him by Mr Phelps. His training has evidently been most elaborate. We see at once that his acts and gestures are too perfect and mature to be his own imaginings, but he has been quickwitted enough to adopt them as his own, and give them not a little of the charm of independent and spontaneous production. By this thoughtfulness there is secured for the character on the stage something of the same prominence that it has in the mind of the closet-readers of the play.

Of Miss Cooper's *Helena* we cannot honestly say very much. In that as in most of the other characters the spirit of the play was missed, because the arguing and quarrelling and blundering that should have been playful, dreamlike, and poetical, was much too loud and real. The men and women could not fancy themselves shadows. Were it possible so far to subdue the energy of the whole body of actors as to soften the tone of the scenes between *Theseus, Hippolyta, Lysander, Demetrius, Hermia,* and *Helena,* the latter character even on the stage might surely have something of the effect intended by the poem. It is an exquisite abstraction, a pitiful and moving picture of a gentle maid forlorn, playfully developed as beseems the fantastic texture of the poem, but not at all meant to excite mirth; and there was a very great mistake made when the dream was so worked out into hard literalness as to create constant laughter during those scenes in which *Helena,* bewildered by the change of mood among the lovers, shrinks and complains "Wherefore was I to this keen mockery born?" [II. ii. 123]. The merriment which Shakespeare connected with those scenes was but a little of the poet's sunlight meant to glitter among tears.

It remains for us only to speak of the success of Mr Phelps

as *Bottom,* which he presented from the first, with remarkable subtlety and spirit, as a man seen in a dream. In his first scene, before we know what his conception is, or in what spirit he means the whole play to be received, we are puzzled by it. We miss the humour, and we get a strange, elaborate, and uncouth dream-figure, a clown restless with vanity, marked by a score of little movements, and speaking ponderously with the uncouth gesticulation of an unreal thing, a grotesque night-mare character. But that, we find, is precisely what the actor had intended to present, and we soon perceive that he was right. Throughout the fairy scenes there is a mist thrown over *Bottom* by the actor's art. The violent gesticulation becomes stillness, and the hands are fixed on the breast. They are busy with the unperceived business of managing the movement of the ass's head, but it is not for that reason they are so perfectly still. The change in manner is a part of the conception. The dream figure is dreaming, there is dream within dream, *Bottom* is quiet, his humour becomes more unctuous, but *Bottom* is translated. He accepts all that happens quietly, as dreamers do; and the ass's head we also accept quietly, for we too are in the middle of a dream, and it does not create surprise. Not a touch of comedy was missed in this capital piece of acting, yet *Bottom* was completely incorporated with the Midsummer Night's Dream, made an essential part of it, as unsubstantial, as airy and refined as all the rest. Quite masterly was the delivery by Mr Phelps of the speech of *Bottom* on awakening. He was still a man subdued, but subdued by the sudden plunge into a state of an unfathomable wonder. His dream clings about him, he cannot sever the real from the unreal, and still we are made to feel that his reality itself is but a fiction. The pre-occupation continues to be manifest during his next scene with the players, and his parting "No more words; away; go away" [IV. ii. 45], was in the tone of a man who had lived with spirits and was not yet perfectly returned into the flesh. Nor did the refinement of this conception, if we except the first scene, abate a jot of the laughter that the character of *Bottom* was intended to excite. The mock play at the end was intensely ludicrous in the presentment, yet nowhere farcical. It was the dream. *Bottom* as *Pyramus* was more perfectly a dream-figure than ever. The contrast between the shadowy actor and his part, between *Bottom* and *Pyramus,* was marked intensely; and the result was as quaint a phantom as could easily be figured by real flesh. Mr Ray's *Quince* was very good indeed, and all the other clowns were reasonably well presented.

We have said a great deal of this revival, for it is very doubtful whether the *Midsummer Night's Dream* has ever yet, since it was first written, been put upon the stage with so nice an interpretation of its meaning. It has pleased us beyond measure to think that an entertainment so refined can draw such a throng of playgoers as we saw last Saturday sitting before it silent and reverent at SADLER'S WELLS. (pp. 661-62)

> *Henry Morley, in an originally unsigned review of "A Midsummer Night's Dream," in* The Examiner, *No. 2385, October 15, 1853, pp. 661-62.*

The Illustrated London News   (review date 15 October 1853)

[*In the following review, the critic praises Phelps's entire production highly and claims that in his depiction of Bottom, "Mr. Phelps evinced decided genius."*]

The revival of the season was produced on Saturday, in the

shape of "A Midsummer Night's Dream," in which the fancy of Shakespeare is so playfully manifested in the field of the supernatural. The graceful manner in which the poet sports with his subject is within the apprehension of all. The play is seldom performed; not because, as it is vulgarly supposed, of its being too poetical, but on account of its requiring too extensive an interpretation. It demands a large company, and a variety of talent, to give it with grace and effect. The *dramatis personae,* on this occasion, have been very efficiently provided for: Miss Cooper's *Helena* being excellent, and Mr. Phelps's *Bottom* equally original and admirable. The latter, indeed, is one of those singular eccentric assumptions in which the manager of this suburban theatre has occasionally indulged, to the gratification of the select audiences that visit this well-conducted house. There is nothing conventional in Mr. Phelps's performance of this part, but he has evidently conceived for himself both the idea and fashion of its embodiment. The nervous temperament of the sedentary weaver, and his anxious eagerness to enter into a new world of activity, with the sense of the importance attached to the adventure in which he and his fellow-mechanics are engaged, were all most artistically indicated. A certain angular and fidgetty motion of the arms aided the impersonation. The perplexity into which he was thrown by his dream, and the acting of the tragical comedy, were delineated and illustrated with first-rate histrionic skill. In such creations Mr. Phelps evinces decided genius. The appointments of the play were excellent. The whole had, indeed, a gorgeous and faëry-like effect; and the scenery—some of which was moving—does great credit to the painter, Mr. Fenton. The house was crowded, and the plaudits were frequent and well-merited.

> *A review of "A Midsummer Night's Dream," in* The Illustrated London News, *Vol. XXIII, No. 649, October 15, 1853, p. 326.*

Punch   (review date 15 October 1853)

[*In the excerpt below, the reviewer, despite his frequently facetious tone, greatly admires Phelps's portrayal of Bottom, stating that, in this production Bottom was "translated by* MR. PHELPS *from dull tradition into purest, airiest* SHAKESPEARE.*"*]

Bully *Bottom* is, in truth, "translated" by MR. PHELPS. Translated from matter-of-fact into poetic humour—translated from the commonplace tradition of the playhouse to a thing subtly grotesque—rarely, and heroically whimsical. A bully *Bottom* of the old, allowed sort, makes up his face—even as the rustic wag of a horse-collar—to goggle and grin; and is as like to the sweet bully of PHELPS—bears the same relation in art to the *Bottom* of Sadler's Wells—as the sign-post portrait on the village green to a head, vital by a few marvellous dots and touches of RICHARD DOYLE. In these days we know of no such translation! Translate a starveling Welsh curate into a Bishop of London, and PHELPS's translation of *Bottom* the weaver shall still remain a work of finer art, and—certainly to all humanising intents of man-solacing humour—of far richer value. We have had, plentiful as French eggs, translations of facile, delicate French, into clumsy, hobbling British; and now, as some amends, we have *Bottom* translated by PHELPS from dull tradition into purest, airiest SHAKESPEARE. MR. PHELPS has not painted, dabbed, we should say, the sweet bully with the old player's old hare's-foot; but has taken the finest pencil, and, with a clean, sharp, fantastic touch, has rendered *Bottom* a living weaver—a weaver whose brain is marvellously woven, knitted up, with self-opinion.

Now this, we take to be the true, breathing notion of SHAKE-SPEARE, and this notion has entered the belief of the actor, and become a living thing. *Bottom* is of conceit all-compact. Conceit flows in his veins—is ever swelling, more or less, in his heart; covers him from scalp to toes, like his skin. And it is this beautiful, this most profitable quality—this human coin, self-opinion, which, however cracked, and thin, and base, may be put off as the real thing by the unfailing heroism of the utterer—it is this conceit that saves *Bottom* from a world of wonderment when he finds himself the leman dear, clipp'd by the Queen of Faery. *Bottom* takes the love—the doting of *Titania*—as he would take the commanded honey-bag of the red-lipped humble-bee—as something sweet and pleasant, but nought to rave about. He is fortified by his conceit against any surprise of the most bountiful fortune: self-opinion turns fairy treasures into rightful wages. And are there not such *Bottoms*—not writ upon the paper Athens of the poet; not swaggering in a wood watered of ink-drops—but such sweet bullies in brick and mortar London—*Bottoms* of Fortune, that for sport's sake play *Puck?* The ingenuous *Bottom* of the play has this distinction from the *Bottoms* of the real, human world—he, for the time, wears his ass's head with a difference; that is, he shows the honest length of his ears, and does not, and cannot abate the show of a single hair. His head is outwardly all ass: there is with him no reservation soever.

MR. PHELPS has the fullest and the deepest sense of the asinine qualities of *Bottom* from the beginning. For *Bottom* wants not the ass's head to mark him ass: the ass is in *Bottom's* blood and brain; *Puck* merely fixes the outward, vulgar type significant of the inward creature. When *Bottom* in the first scene desires to be *Wall,* and *Moonshine,* and *Lion,* his conceit brays aloud, but brays with undeveloped ears. But herein is the genius of our actor. The traditional bully *Bottom* is a dull, stupid, mouthing ass, with no force save in his dullness. *Bottom,* as played by MR. PHELPS, is an ass with a vehemence, a will, a vigour in his conceit, but still an ass. An ass that fantastically kicks his heels to the right and left, but still ass. An ass that has the most prolonged variations of his utterance—nevertheless, it is braying, and nothing better. And there is great variety in braying. We never heard two asses bray alike. Listen—it may be the season of blossoming hawthorns—and asses salute asses. In very different tones, with very different cadence, will every ass make known the yearning, the aspiration that is within him. We speak not frivolously, ignorantly, on this theme; for in our time we have heard very many asses. And so return we to the *Bottom* of merry Islington—to the Golden Ass of Sadler's Wells.

That ass has opened the playhouse season of 1853-4 very musically—would we could think hopefully, and with prophetic promise. At present, however, *Bottom* is the master-spirit: and, in these days of dramatic *pardonnez-mois,* it is a little comforting—not that we are given to the sanguine mood in things theatrical—to know that folks are found ready to make jocund pilgrimage to Sadler's Wells, where a man with a real vital love for his art has now for many seasons made his theatre a school; and more, has never wanted attentive, reverent, grateful scholars. In this, MR. PHELPS has been a national school-master; and—far away from the sustaining, fructifying beams of the Court—for hitherto our ELIZABETH has not visited our BURBIDGE—has popularly taught the les-

sons left to England by SHAKESPEARE—legacies everlasting as her cliffs.

As yet, HER MAJESTY has not journied to the Wells. But who knows, how soon that "great fairy" may travel thither, to do grace to bully *Bottom!* If so, let MR. PHELPS—if he can—still heighten his manner on his awakening from that dream. Let him—if he can—more subtly mingle wonderment with struggling reason, reason wrestling with wonder to get the better of the mystery!

> I have had a dream—past the wit of man to say what dream it truly was!—Man is but an ass, if he go about to expound this dream. Methought I was—there is no man can tell what! Methought I was, and methought I had.—The eye of man hath not heard, the ear of man hath not seen, man's hand is not able to taste, his tongue to conceive, nor his heart to report, what my dream was
>
> [IV. i. 205-09, 211-14].

We do not think it in the wit or power of MR. PHELPS—under any newer inspiration, to give a deeper, finer meaning to this than he has done. But, if HER MAJESTY command the play, as a loyal subject, he will doubtless make the essay. In these words, *Bottom*—as rendered by the actor—is taken away from the ludicrous; he is elevated by the mystery that possesses him, and he affects our more serious sympathies, whilst he forbids our laughter. One of the very, very few precious things of the stage—of this starved time—is an Ass's head, as worn by the manager of merrie Islington.

We hope, at least, the QUEEN will command that head to be brought—with due solemnity—to Windsor Castle. Let *Bottom* be made to roar again before HER MAJESTY, the PRINCE, the heir-apparent, and all the smaller childhood royalties. Let *Bottom* be confronted with the picked of the Cabinet—the elect of Privy Councillors. And—as we have Orders of Eagles and Elephants, why not the ingenous outspeaking significance, the Order of the Ass? As a timid beginning, we have the Thistle—wherefore not the Ass himself?

In which case, the Order established, the *Bottom* of Sadler's Wells ought rightfully to be the Chancellor thereof.

"Bully Bottom," in Punch, *Vol. XXV, No. 640, October 15, 1853, p. 165.*

Richard Foulkes   (essay date 1969)

[*In the following excerpt, Foulkes assesses the impact of the Sadler's Wells production of* A Midsummer Night's Dream, *both on its immediate audience and on subsequent revivals of the play.*]

Samuel Phelps was involved in three London revivals of *A Midsummer Night's Dream*—at Sadler's Wells (8th October, 1853), at the Queen's Theatre (17th September, 1870) and at the Gaiety (15th February, 1875). Of these the first was perhaps the finest achievement of Phelps's eighteen years management at Sadler's Wells. Prior to this production *A Midsummer Night's Dream* had had an unfortunate history on the stage; during the eighteenth century it had been the victim of several, mostly musical, adaptors; and it was not until Madame Vestris turned her attention to it, at Covent Garden on November 16th, 1840, aided by Planché and Mendelssohn, that the play received anything like worthy treatment.

Against this background the impact of Phelps's production

in 1853, was all the more powerful; and it was natural that the critics should concern themselves with what had been the hitherto insurmountable barriers to a successful staging of *A Midsummer Night's Dream*. The first of these was considered to be the impossibility of giving visual expression to the poetic images of the play, for, as Henry Morley wrote in his review of the 1853 production in *The Journal of A London Playgoer from 1851 to 1866*.

> Every reader of Shakespeare is disposed to regard the *Midsummer Night's Dream* as the most essentially unactable of all his plays. It is a dramatic poem of the utmost grace and delicacy; its characters are creatures of the poet's fancy that no flesh and blood can properly present—fairies who "creep into acorn cups", or mortals who are but dim abstractions, persons in a dream. The words they speak are so completely spiritual that they are best felt when they are not spoken. Their exquisite beauty is like that of sunset colours which no mortal artist can interpret faithfully.

The Illustrated London News (15th October, 1853), somewhat rudely, cast aside this barrier, only to substitute another in its place—

> The play is seldom performed; not because, as it is vulgarly supposed, of its being too poetical, but on account of its requiring too extensive an interpretation. It demands a large company, and a variety of talent, to give it with grace and effect.

Phelps did have a large company (over seventy actors performed in his 1853 staging), and he succeeded in achieving a unity of conception and execution from every part of it.

The full range of artistic ability, which went to make up the production, is indicated in the play-bill of its performance—"Scenery—F. Fenton. Costumes—Miss Bailey. Decorations—Mr. Harvey. Music—W. Montgomery. Dances—Mr. Frampton. Machinery—Mr. Cawdery." That Phelps succeeded in co-ordinating these various theatre arts is evident from Henry Morley's review—

> Mr. Phelps has never for a minute lost sight of the main idea which governs the whole play, and this is the great secret of his success in the presentation of it. He knew that he was to present merely shadows; that spectators, as Puck reminds them in the epilogue, are to think they have slumbered on their seats, and that what appeared before them have been visions. Everything has been subdued as far as possible at Sadler's Wells to this ruling idea.

It is indicative of Phelps's attitude towards the theatre, that he is best remembered, as an actor, for his impersonation of Bottom. Bottom is the most interesting character in *A Midsummer Night's Dream*, but it is not a star-personality role as were those essayed by Irving and Tree; and in Phelps's presentation it was harmonised into the play as a whole. Phelps's characterisation of Bottom was innovatory, and, to quote Clement Scott (*The Drama of Yesterday and Today*)—"different from all previous concepts of the character". Of such "previous concepts" Douglas Jerrold wrote (*Punch*, 15th October, 1853)—"a bully Bottom of the old allowed sort makes up his face . . . to goggle and grin"; unlike these earlier impersonations, Phelps's did not rely on exterior comic trappings, but derived its humour from Bottom's character, in particular his conceit.

Jerrold wrote of "a weaver whose brain is marvellously woven, knitted up, with self-opinion", and continued—

> Now we take this to be the true, breathing notion of Shakespeare, and this notion has entered the belief of the actor, and become a living thing. Bottom is of conceit all compact. Conceit flows in his veins . . . covers him from scalp to toe like his skin . . . it is this conceit that saves Bottom from a world of wonderment . . . Bottom takes the love . . . of Titania. . . . as something sweet and pleasant, but nought to rave about. He is fortified by his conceit against any surprise of the most bountiful fortune, self-opinion turns fairy treasures into rightful wages.

Westland Marston (*Our Recent Actors*) found this same quality of conceit in Phelps's Bottom and examined its comic implications—

> The calm self-conceit of his Bottom, who finds so many things within his range, because his ignorance conceals their difficulties, was far more humorous, than if his vanity had been made broader and more boisterous. His absolute insensibility to the ridiculous was more mirth-moving than the most grotesque means by which inferior actors would have italicised the absurd conceit of the character. His quiet matter-of-course belief that the parts of Thisbe and the Lion are equally within his grasp . . . was more telling than would have been a highly-coloured expression of his self-complacency. In all this, the sense of acquiescence in the absurd was far more ludicrous than extreme wonder would have been. As a picture of intense self-conceit, expressed generally rather by signs of inward relish of his acuteness than by more open display—of ridiculous fastidiousness and equally ridiculous devices to satisfy it—as a parody of sense and ingenuity by a shallow brain—Bottom must be ranked as one of this actor's most original conceptions.

Henry Morley links what Westland Marston referred to as "the sense of aquiescence in the absurd" to the dreamlike quality, which pervades the whole play. He writes "He [Bottom] accepts all that happens, quietly as dreamers do". This being so, one is not surprised to find that Bottom's awakening from his dream was one of the most celebrated passages in Phelps's performance. John A. Heraud writing in the *Athenaeum* (15th October, 1853) described this scene in interesting detail—

> When relieved from this skull cap [the ass's head], and endeavouring to recollect his dream, Bottom in the hands of Mr. Phelps becomes a remarkable artistic presentment. His perplexity, as he endeavoured to retrace his vision, was elaborately delineated; and this was succeeded by some admirable byplay, in which, without a word spoken, the pantomimic action was suggestive of an entire soliloquy concerning the mysterious loss of the long ears and the beard so recently worn. As he makes his exit, we see clearly enough that Bottom gives up the whole as an insoluble problem.

The Introduction to *A Midsummer Night's Dream*, in the edition of Shakespeare published by Willoughby's in 1854, "Under the immediate and personal supervision of Samuel Phelps esq.", quotes Coleridge—"I am convinced that Shakespeare availed himself of the title of the play in his own mind, and worked upon it as a dream throughout". Coleridge then goes on to quote Puck's

> If we shadows have offended,
> Think but this, and all is mended:
> That you have but slumbered here
> While these visions did appear.

[V. i. 423-26]

That this was achieved is indicated by Douglas Jerrold writing in *Lloyd's Weekly London News*—

> The best way to enjoy it is, to half-close your eyes, and to resign yourself completely to the influence of the scene. It is our firm belief, from the silence that reigns at times through the house, that one-half the spectators are dreaming without knowing it, and that they only wake up when the curtain drops, and are surprised to find that they have a playbill in their hand . . . you dream quite unconsciously, lost one minute in a beautiful wood flooded with moonlight, through which you wade as refreshingly as through a summer stream . . . You feel quite disconcerted when you rub your eyes, and discover that there is a chandelier instead of the stars shining above you . . . the illusion is pulled like a common cotton night-cap, from off your brow; and the ideal trance, in which you have been plunged for the last three hours is followed by an awaking conviction that you have been fooled during that time not less completely than Bottom himself.

Much of the dream-like effect of the production was derived from the scenery. This was achieved mainly by two effects; both of which are explained by Frederick Fenton, Phelps's scenic designer, in the introduction to an edition of *A Midsummer Night's Dream,* edited and illustrated by J. Moyr Smith in 1892. First of all he refers to the lighting—"I obtained permission for the gas to be supplied as a permanent lighting for the theatre, and it was used for the first time in *A Midsummer Night's Dream.*" Fenton proceeds to explain his first scenic device—that of a diorama:

> By various ingenious devices the moon was seen to rise, to shine between the boles of the trees, to be partly obscured by passing clouds, and then to swim as it were, over and through the trees. This effect of movement was given by a diorama—that is two sets of scenes moving simultaneously. These had cuts and shapings to represent, in the front sets, openings of the woods, spaces between stumps of trees, and the light parts between the foliage. The back set of the diorama was similarly treated to produce various cloud effects. In the scene representing Titania's bower the flowers arose and descended, so as to disclose or conceal the fairy queen as occasion demanded.

The success of the diorama is testified by eye-witnesses. Douglas Jerrold in *Lloyd's Weekly London News* wrote—

> The scenery was quiet and subdued, as sylvan scenery at night should be. The different views of the wood were deliciously refreshing—just the cool retired spots that fairies would delight to dance in, on a warm midsummer's evening. There was no grand effect produced, but everything was natural and simple, and yet beautiful; precisely the impressive simplicity one meets with in nature. The views also were made to *melt, dream-like into one another;* and all was done noiselessly, as though there were

a secret feeling in the breasts of all, that the smallest sound would have broken the spirit of the dream. There are not more than three or four scenes in the whole play, and yet so artistically are the different changes of moonlight, fog, and sunrise produced, that you imagine you have been wandering through an entire forest, with a fresh prospect meeting you unexpectedly at every turn.

Henry Morley concurs with Jerrold, to the extent of coining the same phrases at times—

> The scenery is very beautiful, but wholly free from the meretricious glitter now in favour; it is not so remarkable for costliness as the pure taste in which it and all the stage arrangements have been planned. This is no ordinary scene-shifting; but, as in dreams, one scene is made to glide insensibly into another. We follow the lovers and fairies through the wood from glade to glade, now among trees, now with a broad view of the sea and Athens in the distance, carefully but not at all obtrusively set forth . . . *The scenes melt dream-like one into another.*

Fenton's second scenic device was that of a piece of gauze let down in front of the stage. He recounts—

> For the first time used, to give a kind of mist, I sent to Glasgow expressly for a piece of blue nett the same size as the act drop, without a seam. This, after the first act, was kept down for the whole of the performance of the Dream, light being on the stage sufficient to illuminate the actors acting behind it. The gauze ascended when Oberon and Titania made their exeunt in the fourth act.

In spite of what Fenton claims the gauze device was not entirely original. Phelps himself had used it in his production of *Macbeth* (at Sadler's Wells, 27th September, 1847), as described by Jones Levy in *Lloyd's Weekly London News*—

> The stage was darkened to a much greater degree than usual, so much so that but the imperfect outlines of the weird sisters were visible. In front only a dim lurid light played, and as the hags stepped backwards, the darkness aided by a combination of gauze screens, procured one of the most perfect effects of vanishing we ever saw.

However original or not, Fenton's gauze was a great success. Henry Morley describes it—

> Over all the fairy portion of the play there is a haze thrown by a green gauze placed between the actors and the audience, and maintained there during the whole of the second, third and fourth acts. This gauze is so well spread that there are few parts of the house from which its presence can be detected, but its influence is everywhere felt; it subdues the flesh and blood of the actors into something more nearly resembling dream-like figures, and *incorporates more completely the actors with the scenes, throwing the same fairy tinge,* and the same mist over all.

Morley goes on to remark on the harmony of the costumes—"A like idea dictated certain contrivances of dress, especially in the case of the fairies"; a point noted too by Douglas Jerrold, who wrote in *Lloyd's Weekly London News*—"The living figures are so dressed as to harmonise with the scenery". One must note that Morley described the gauze as green, whereas Fenton described it as blue. The scenes in which it was used take place in the forest (green), at night (blue), and this may partly explain the dichotomy. Or it may be that the gauze was blue, but when subjected to the lighting used became more green.

Not all the scenes in *A Midsummer Night's Dream* take place in the woodlands; and writing at a time of great historical accuracy (1892) in scenic design, Moyr Smith had some qualms about Phelps's production in which "the architecture represented was more closely allied to the age of Pericles than to that of the more primitive Theseus". Now-a-days we are not very inclined to share Mr. Smith's qualms, but we can benefit from his description of Fenton's scenery.

> The architectural scenes were, of course, those of Acts I and V. The first scene of Act I represented the palace of Theseus, with a view of the Acropolis of Athens behind. The second scene represented the workshop in which the clowns apportionate the characters of their play; it was divided by a pier and heavy beam; through an opening in the left hand compartment a glimpse was caught of the open sky and the trees of a suburban garden. The fifth act showed first a columned hall, with a background of closed curtains, the stage being lighted by Greek candelabra. When the clowns finished their play and Theseus and his train retired, servants came in and put out the lights, and simultaneously the curtains opened. The fluted columns of the hall were partly 'made out' and covered with linen; inside the columns were lengths of gas jets, kept turned down till the curtains opened and the moonlight streamed into the hall; then the gas within the columns was turned up, and the columns had the appearance of being illuminated by the moonlight. The opening of the curtains disclosed a terraced garden overlooking Athens. Down the steps and along the terraces trooped Oberon and Titania with their fairy band, all carrying glimmering lights. The fairy song and dance were given, and the curtain fell on the moonlighted palace of Theseus with the slumbering city behind, on the picturesque groups of the fairies arranged on the terraces behind, and on the graceful figures of Oberon, Titania and Puck in front.

From an examination of Phelps's *A Midsummer Night's Dream* one can see that he succeeded in overcoming both of the barriers, which contemporary critics saw as the reasons for the play's lack of success in previous stagings. He gave visual expression to the play's poetic images, and to do this he used a large company, every part of which was fused with the same concept of the play (its dreamlike quality). From the point of view of acting "the dramatic personae", as the *Illustrated London News* critic wrote (15th October, 1853), were "very efficiently provided for". Of the twenty-one named parts, Phelps's Bottom was undoubtedly the crown; but there were fifty other actors on the stage, and their integration into the whole, which has already been hinted at in Moyr Smith's description of the last scene, is evidenced by John A. Heraud, who wrote in the *Athenaeum* (15th October, 1853) that "the grouping was highly picturesque". Frederick Fenton was clearly helped in his scenery by the innovation of gas-lighting, which lent power to his illusionist's elbow; but Fenton was not heavy-handed and did not seek to steal the 'lime-light'. He evidently collaborated with the Miss Bailey whose costumes harmonised so well with his settings. Miss Bailey herself probably benefited from the advice of Mr. Cawdery, who was in charge of machinery, in creating for Phelps an ass's head which could be manipulated by a mechanism at the actor's breast.

Certainly not before, and probably not since has *A Midsummer Night's Dream* received such a fine and appropriate staging as that by Samuel Phelps at Sadler's Wells in 1853. The production is important in that respect; but its even greater importance lies elsewhere, in that it was the product of a certain method of production, in which all the theatre's arts are harmonised into a whole. This is still the aim of directors today, whether they aspire to embodying all the theatre's arts in themselves (as Craig would have them do), or whether they accept the role of co-ordinator as Phelps did. (pp. 55-60)

> *Richard Foulkes, "Samuel Phelps's 'A Midsummer Night's Dream',"* in Theatre Notebook, *Vol. XXIII, No. 2, Winter, 1968-69, pp. 55-60.*

Shirley S. Allen   (essay date 1971)

[*Allen examines this production of* A Midsummer Night's Dream *in the context of Phelps's career as manager of Sadler's Wells and as a theater craftsman.*]

Phelps . . . opened his season of 1853-1854 with a production of *Macbeth,* but he could not compete with the interest generated by [Charles] Kean's elaborate production [at the Princess's Theatre]. Although he had engaged three new actors (Lunt from Liverpool, Josephs from Edinburgh, and Rousby from Norwich), he could not compensate for the draining off of his actors to West End theatres. Mellon and Graham had gone to the Princess's, Robinson and Williams to the Lyceum, George Bennett and Miss Vining to Drury Lane. The *Theatrical Journal* described the remnant as "the ghost of a company" compared with former seasons.

Phelps immediately turned to comedy, taking for himself the role of Sir Peter Teazle in *The School for Scandal,* which had been Bennett's, and making it so much his own that he played it until the end of his career. He then put on four almost forgotten comedies: Cibber's *Love Makes a Man,* Bickerstaffe's *The Hypocrite,* Fielding's *The Miser,* and O'Keeffe's *Wild Oats.* For the major production of the season he chose another rarely acted comedy, Shakespeare's *A Midsummer Night's Dream,* which had been seen on the nineteenth-century stage only in versions that emphasized music, ballet, and spectacle. Phelps's production combined his talent for stage design, now fully developed by years of practice, his ability to direct his company with their fullest cooperation, and his own gift for comic characterization (in the role of Bottom). He never had a greater success. He won approval from spectators, critics, and even from his rival manager, Charles Kean, who imitated the production in his own fashion three years later. *Punch* (October 15, 1853) called upon the Queen to journey to Sadler's Wells, "for hitherto our Elizabeth has not visited our Burbidge." Other reviewers urged all London playgoers to see *A Midsummer Night's Dream* at Sadler's Wells.

Apparently Islingtonians needed no urging to attend a major production at Sadler's Wells. During the first week the house was so full of regular patrons that those less experienced in the methods of gaining entrance found no way to get in. *Lloyd's Weekly* apologized on October 16 for the lack of a review and gave the reason that no boxes had been available, the pit had been packed, and the steep staircase to the gallery had been full of those descending after unsuccessful attempts to find space. Comments upon the reaction of the audience to *A Midsummer Night's Dream* are interesting not only for information about the performance but also for a glimpse into the character of this unusual congregation of playgoers. Their silence impressed the reviewer of *Lloyd's Weekly* when he finally got into the theatre:

> It is our firm belief, from the hushed stillness that reigns at times through the house, that one-half the spectators are dreaming without knowing it, and that they only wake up when the curtain drops, and are surprised to find they have a play-bill in their hand. The belief is strengthened by the fact of the unusual sparingness of the applause. All motion, all action, seems to be involuntarily suspended. Occasionally a loud laugh bursts out, but it is quickly succeeded by a deep stillness, as of midnight sleep. This feeling is something more than the mere reverence of attention. You would suppose from the silence that closes you in like a dark room, that you were all alone, with your senses far away, wandering you knew not where, but watching intently some strange illusion of a man with an ass's head being kissed by a Fairy Queen.

[Henry Morley, in the] *Examiner* (October 15, 1853) noted that the behavior of the audience revealed not only a discriminating appreciation but also knowledge of the text of the play.

> The *Midsummer Night's Dream* abounds in the most delicate passages of Shakespeare's verse. The Sadler's Wells pit has a keen enjoyment for them; the pit and gallery were crowded to the farthest wall on Saturday night with a most earnest audience, among whom many a subdued hush arose, not during, but just before, the delivery of the most charming passages.

That the audience was composed of regular patrons, fiercely loyal to Phelps's management and jealous of his reputation in London, is clear from an incident recorded by the same reviewer:

> When Bottom volunteered to roar high or roar low, a voice from the gallery desired to know whether he could "roar like Brooke." Even the gallery at this theatre, however, resents an interruption, and the unexpected sally was not well received.

G. V. Brooke was at this time starring at Drury Lane, where his vehement acting was delighting boisterous audiences described as "a gross discredit to the public taste."

The warm partisanship of the local audience at Sadler's Wells led some stray visitors to mistake its nature. A writer in the *Theatrical Journal* (February 28, 1850) complained that they were indiscriminate:

> Once bring a man to the footlights, and set the gallery going, and stop them who can—the second man then the third, and on they go calling for every body, almost down to the supernumeraries, dead stock and live stock, talent and mediocrity.

This correspondent had perhaps strayed into the theatre on the opening night of a season or on a Saturday night when the audience was in a holiday mood. It is not unlikely that on some occasions, like the opening night of a season when the theatre had been redecorated over the summer, that they applauded the dead stock as well as the live stock.

The *esprit de corps* of the audience and its unusual character emphasized the widening gulf between Sadler's Wells and the theatres of central London. Its taste for the now old-fashioned "legitimate" drama and its status as lower class combined to make Sadler's Wells a backwater, cut off from the main current of the English theatrical world. *Punch,* in its review of *A Midsummer Night's Dream,* called Phelps a national schoolmaster, meaning to emphasize the excellence of his interpretations of England's greatest poet (and also to contrast his repertory with the predominantly French fare at fashionable theatres), but many writers regarded Phelps primarily as an educator of the underprivileged, as if his greatest achievement was an increase in the cultural level of his audience. A patronizing attitude toward the audience is evident even in laudatory descriptions of its behavior, as in this one by Henry Morley in 1857:

> The aspect and behaviour of the pit and gallery at Sadler's Wells during the performance of one of Shakespeare's plays cannot fail to impress most strongly every visitor who is unaccustomed to the place. There sit our working classes in a happy crowd, as orderly and reverent as if they were at church, and yet as unrestrained in their enjoyment as if listening to stories told them by their own firesides [*The Journal of a London Playgoer*]. (pp. 136-39)

. . . . .

In *A Midsummer Night's Dream* Phelps's portrayal of Bottom was an expression of his interpretation of the whole play—a poetic fantasy with the atmosphere of an actual dream. In the opening scenes he was the conceited and nervous weaver, with red nose, shaggy hair, and a look of sottish stupidity, revealing his restlessness by constant gesticulation and the angularity of his movements, and showing self-importance by an equal emphasis upon all his words. *Punch* (October 15, 1853) said that Phelps caught the asinine qualities of Bottom so well that the ass's head was not needed to mark him as an ass:

> When Bottom, in the first scene, desires to be Wall, and Moonshine, and Lion, his conceit brays aloud, but brays with undeveloped ears. But herein is the genius of our actor. The traditional bully Bottom is a dull, stupid, mouthing ass, with no force save in his dullness. Bottom, as played by Mr. Phelps, is an ass with a vehemence, a will, a vigour in his conceit, but still an ass. An ass that fantastically kicks his heels to the right and left, but still an ass. An ass that has the most prolonged variations of his utterance—nevertheless it is braying, and nothing better.

One reviewer saw him as a "despot of low life who has gained a character for intellect among his companions by force of mere dogmatism." Marston speaks of the calmness of his self-conceit, expressed rather by signs of inward relish of his own ability than by boisterous display; to Morley he seemed "a strange, elaborate, and uncouth dream-figure," as grotesque as a man seen in a nightmare. In the fairy scenes Bottom was subtly changed, as if a mist had also been thrown over his character. Morley carefully describes the difference:

> The violent gesticulations become stillness, and the hands are fixed on the breast. They are busy with unperceived business of managing the movements of the ass's head, but it is not for that reason they are so perfectly still. The change of manner is a part of the conception. The dream-figure is dreaming, there is dream within dream; Bottom is quiet; his

humour becomes more unctuous, but Bottom is translated. He accepts all that happens, quietly, as dreamers do; and the ass's head we also accept quietly, for we too are in the middle of our dream, and it does not create surprise. Not a touch of comedy was missed in this capital piece of acting, yet Bottom was completely incorporated with the Midsummer Night's Dream, made an essential part of it, as unsubstantial, as airy and refined as all the rest. Quite masterly was the delivery by Mr. Phelps of the speech of Bottom on awakening. He was still a man subdued, but subdued by the sudden plunge into a state of an unfathomable wonder. His dream clings about him, he cannot sever the real from the unreal, and still we are made to feel that his reality itself is but a fiction. The preoccupation continues to be manifest during his next scene with the players, and his parting, "No more words; away; go away," was in the tone of a man who had lived with spirits and was not yet perfectly returned into the flesh.

Phelps had given special attention to designing the ass's head so that it would carry out his interpretation. The ears and features were controlled by strings, which Phelps worked invisibly with his fingers. The movements of the head were not used to provoke laughter, but only to aid in the actor's expression of the character. In a letter to his wife written in 1867 when he was playing Bottom in Liverpool, he contrasts the ass's head of the local theatre with his own:

I am very glad I have brought the Donkey's head, for though they have a new one it is not good. It is a most *impudent* looking ass instead of the *stupid* sleek thing it should be for Bottom. It looks impossible that it should *sleep*. I should be dreadfully annoyed if I had to wear it.

Phelps's success in realizing Shakespeare's character on the stage is indicated both by the enthusiasm of a large and diverse group of critics and by the similarity of their reactions. They grasped the essence of his interpretation and approved of it as thoroughly Shakespearean while praising his portrayal as one of the great achievements of the English stage. *Punch's* review began with the statement that bully Bottom had been "translated" by Phelps, "translated from matter-of-fact into poetic humor; translated from the commonplace tradition of the play-house to a thing subtly grotesque—rarely, and heroically whimsical . . . from dull tradition to purest, airiest Shakespeare." (pp. 183-85)

. . . . .

Phelps's most important textual restoration in the field of comedy was *A Midsummer Night's Dream*. The few performances of this play during the nineteenth century had tended toward the operatic, with emphasis on interpolated songs and dances set to Mendelssohn's music. A production at Covent Garden in 1840 featured beautiful staging and the singing and dancing of Mme. Vestris. Shakespeare's play, unadorned, had seldom tempted actors, and it was generally considered too poetic and imaginative a work for actual representation. Hazlitt's disappointment with a performance in 1816 led him to the conclusion that it was as idle to attempt to embody the fancy of it as to personate Wall or Moonshine.

Phelps, however, set out to embody the fancy of it, and his first principle was reliance on Shakespeare's text. Without the songs and dances he had time for all but 300 lines of the original, and he reconverted the play of Pyramus and Thisbe from

opera to spoken dialogue. The result was one of the greatest triumphs of his management, and no critic complained that the text was too long. (pp. 223-24)

. . . . .

In *A Midsummer Night's Dream,* Phelps fully expressed his concept of staging as interpretation. Giving up the usual tinsel wings, white muslin, glittering light, music, dancing, and stage machinery, he tried to create the poetic fantasy of Shakespeare's *Dream*. In the settings he sought the fluidity, insubstantiality, and silence of a dream. He avoided breaks between scenes by using a diorama and movable flats. In the fairy scenes he had a thin green gauze drawn up to mask the entire playing area of the stage from the floor to the borders and from the flat on one side to the flat on the other. The effect of these devices is described by Henry Morley in a well-known review:

There is no ordinary scene-shifting; but, as in dreams, one scene is made to glide insensibly into another. We follow the lovers and the fairies through the wood from glade to glade, now among trees, now with a broad view of the sea and Athens in the distance, carefully but not at all obtrusively set forth. And not only do the scenes melt dreamlike into one another, but over all the fairy portion of the play there is a haze thrown by a curtain of green gauze placed between the actors and audience, and maintained there during the whole of the second, third, and fourth acts. This gauze curtain is so well spread that there are very few parts of the house from which its presence can be detected, but its influence is everywhere felt; it subdues the flesh and blood of the actors into something more nearly resembling dream-figures, and incorporates more completely the actors with the scenes, throwing the same green fairy tinge, and the same mist over all.

When the flats were changed during the performance, the movement was accomplished without sound, using the system of grooves in the floor. But the scenery had a simplicity that was designed to obviate the necessity of change. The views of the wood which had been painted on the moving back cloth were closely related, as if portraying the same area from different vantage points, and the flats which represented tree and foliage blended into the background even as it changed.

Light was also used to give variety to the scene, both by the use of mediums and by changes of intensity which suggested the progress of night and day during the action. The principles of camouflage were used in the costumes of the fairies, relating colors and design to the scenery. The invisible veil of gauze and the green light helped to blur definite outlines of the flats and to blend the actors more completely into the scenery. *Lloyd's Weekly* (October 23, 1853) described the setting thus:

There is a misty transparency about the figures that gives them the appearance of flitting shadows more than of human beings. You fancy you can see the moon shining through them. . . . The different views of the wood were deliciously refreshing—just the cool, retired spots that the fairies would delight to dance in, on a warm midsummer's evening. There was no grand effect produced, but everything was natural and simple, and yet beautiful; precisely the impressive simplicity that one meets with in nature. . . . There are not more than three or four scenes in the whole play, and yet so artistically are the different changes of moonlight, fog, and sunrise produced, that you imagine you have been wandering through an entire forest, with a fresh prospect meeting you unexpectedly at every turn. The living figures are so dressed as to harmonize with the scenery, looking as if they were inseparable parts of the same picture; thus, the fairies, as they glide in and out of the trees and foliage, give you a notion that they have actually stepped out of them, as though the trunks and flowers were their natural abiding-places.

Staging, clearly, was an important aspect of this production. Many of the techniques, such as colored mediums, the gauze curtain, and costumes that blended with the scenery, had rarely been used before. Others, such as the diorama and variations of light, were employed in new ways. But . . . , the innovations are less remarkable than the new concept of stage decoration which the production expressed. As in the *Macbeth* of 1847, the staging was used to define the underlying theme of the play and to create a mood which helped to interpret its meaning. The diorama did not call attention to itself, as it had in Macready's settings, but was used wholly for dramatic purposes: to give dreamlike fluidity and silence and to emphasize the theme of man's relation to nature which runs through the play.

In the acting of *A Midsummer Night's Dream* Phelps sought to convey the same atmosphere of dream and fantasy established by the setting. In the fairy scenes the poetry of the dialogue was given full prominence by skillful and unhurried reading, aided by the absence of all other sound and any distracting movement. When the lovers entered this natural fairyland, its mood infected them, as the gauze and green light blurred their physical outlines. Morley complained that the mood was broken by overly loud and comic acting in the parts of the quarreling lovers, particularly by Miss Cooper's Helena. It is possible that Fanny Cooper, who had played the role on the great stage of Covent Garden, did not wholly submit to Phelps's direction. She was at this time the most famous actress in the depleted company and immensely popular with the audience. In general the acting was not distinguished, since many of the actors were too young and untrained to create their individual parts with assurance and skill, but they had learned to read the poetry and to carry out the interpretation Phelps intended.

For the role of Puck, Phelps had carefully instructed a young boy, coaching him in speech and gestures so that he expressed Phelps's view of the role. Apparently Master F. Artis was able to add something of spontaneity to his memorized lesson, since Morley felt that he "secured for the character on the stage something of the same prominence that it has in the mind of closet readers of the play." In a later production Phelps had his boy Puck wear an outsize head—a grotesquerie that further emphasized the elfin quality and set him apart from the other fairies, while it drew a parallel with the ass's head. Phelps's interpretation of the play brought out the importance of Puck as a fairy who impinges upon the human world just as Bottom the Weaver invades the fairy world.

In his own acting of Bottom Phelps brought out the grotesque and dreamlike, subduing the human flesh in the fairy scenes and showing the remnants of the dream clinging to the workaday weaver as he puzzled over his recent experience:

> I have had a dream, past the wit of man to say what dream

it was. Man is but an ass if he go about to expound this dream. Methought I was . . . [IV. i. 205-08]

(pp. 236-38)

. . . . .

After Easter, 1867, Phelps played a two-week engagement in Liverpool at the new Alexandra Theatre. Since Mrs. Phelps was too ill to accompany him on this trip, he wrote her daily of his experiences. The letters are interesting for their revelations of an old actor's reaction to a new kind of theatre and audience. His first impression was highly favorable: the theatre was beautiful and the stage amazingly well equipped. But he found the settings for *A Midsummer Night's Dream* gaudy and inappropriate to his poetic interpretation of the play. Over Easter weekend he worked hard at rehearsals to adjust the setting and give unity to the acting. On the opening night he had his first experience of a theatre without a pit. The orchestra was occupied by stalls (reserved seats) in which sat the upper-class audience he had been used to see only in the boxes. He found them stiff and unresponsive compared to the usual pit audience.

> Well, my darling Wife, I have got the first night over. The house was very full—all rank and fashion, notwithstanding it was Easter Monday, and a wet night. It certainly looked splendid, but the audience are so infernally genteel that they seem to think it must be vulgar to laugh or applaud in the stalls (which is *all* the pit) and boxes—and the pit (which is above the boxes) and gallery people seem so overawed by the grandeur that they are dumb too. It was very depressing to me after what my "Bottom" has been used to. Still the managers tell me it was an uproarious audience to what they generally are. They certainly did smile a little in the last act—but altogether it put me in mind of Windsor Castle. Between the acts all the grandees go out to promenade in the magnificent crush room or go down to the refreshment department for coffee, etc. Five minutes before the acts commence the prompter strikes an electric apparatus which rings a bell in all the different rooms at once and that brings the swells back to their places. I fancy I shall be able to put a little life into them in a night or two as the managers tell me they were wonderfully pleased. The papers are loud in their praises . . . but they are "bosh."

The next day he wrote that "the audience were a *little* more lively. They even managed to get up a call at the end of one act and again at the finish." On Thursday he reported, "We had a great house last night and the audience *woke up* astonishingly." By Friday he was able to assure his wife of the success of his engagement:

> We had a splendid house last night and *every seat* in the boxes and stalls is taken for to-night. The ladies dress so well that from the stage the house looks magnificent.

(pp. 300-01)

Shirley S. Allen, in her Samuel Phelps and Sadler's Wells Theatre, *Wesleyan University Press, 1971, 354 p.*

PRODUCTIONS:

Rival productions • The Broadway and Burton's Theaters • 1854

BACKGROUND:

In 1854 two New York playhouses simultaneously offered revivals of *A Midsummer Night's Dream*. William Burton presented the play at his theater from 3 February to 6 March, and E. A. Marshall staged it at the Broadway from 6 February to 11 March. Both productions were characterized by opulence and pageantry, but contemporary critics were divided as to which was superior. Some reviewers found Burton's the better-acted performance, while others argued that the much larger Broadway playhouse was far better suited to the spectacle and lavish stage effects.

COMMENTARY:

The New York Daily Tribune   (review date 4 February 1854)

[*The following excerpt is drawn from a review of the opening night performance of* A Midsummer Night's Dream *at Burton's Theatre. The critic considers this production "one of the best representations in regard to stage-effect and appointments, if not the best, that we have yet had in this City."*]

The representation of the *Midsummer Night's Dream* at Burton's Theatre last night may be signalized as one of the best representations in regard to stage-effect and appointments, if not the best, that we have yet had in this City. The Theatre itself is a miniature affair, and the stage incompetent as to depth or breadth for the right setting forth of the dainty imaginations of the great poet; but viewing it not as a great but as a neat affair, the whole is deserving of emphatic approval. The house was over-crowded, and the audience manifested the deepest attention, and the droll portions were greeted with much laughter.

The parts were well cast, and the whole passed off with extraordinary smoothness. There were some fifty people, first and last, on the stage; and when we say that every one was appropriately dressed, most of the costumes being rich and beautiful, and that there were throughout new scenes, the public may have an idea of the care Mr. Burton has taken and the expense he has undergone to render the piece worthy of acceptance. A few years ago such a mode of presenting Shakspere would have made the town ring; but the public has ceased to be surprised at anything, and to take whatever splendors that are presented to it in an artistic way with greater coolness and less criticism than any European nation would credit.

Mr. Burton's very full advertisement relieves us from naming much in the way of giving names and mere details. Sufficient to say that all the principals were well posted up in their parts—and among the chief, Mr. Burton himself as *Bottom*. We may also instance Master C. Parsloe as *Robin Goodfellow* as very clever acting. The chief scenery, a court-yard in the Palace of Theseus, the wood by moonlight, Titania's Bower, a Port and a grand Hall, may be specially noticed for freshness and brilliancy.

The performance of *Pyramus and Thisbe* in the presence of the Court was one of the most laughable things we have seen for a long time. Mr. Burton after killing himself and rolling off the platform and then gathering himself on again, was eminently Burtonian. His power over the muscles of the ass's head in the transformation scene convulsed the auditory.

The celebrated music of Mendelssohn was given entire, and we may specially note the horn player for the elegance with which he rendered the sylvan delineations of the composer. The overture, which we prefer to any subsequent works of the same hand, may be cited as a noble piece of dramatic painting, expressing in idea and orchestration what is needed. The mock death of Pyramus, as rendered by the music is a most felicitous hit. The wedding march needs—as indeed all the music—more resource in the orchestra than it is possible to command in a small theater. But the value of dramatic music, ordinarily given independently of the action, comes forth with additional clearness when we see it connected with the action. The grotesque, the sylvan, the grandiose, may be easily divined when so interlinked with scenes and characters.

It would be ungrateful on the part of the public not to support such a rendering of Shakspere as Mr. Burton has given us, faithful in text, excellent in cast, brilliant in mounting, and conscientious throughout, illustrated, too, with consonant music.

A review of "A Midsummer Night's Dream," in The New York Daily Tribune, *February 4, 1854, p. 7.*

The New York Herald   (review date 8 February 1854)

[*In the excerpt below from a review of the Broadway production of* A Midsummer Night's Dream, *the critic disparages the play as tedious and boring. He admits, however, that some of the scenic effects were beautiful and observes that the audience was generally receptive.*]

We seldom have two Shakspearean revivals in a week to notice. Thanks to the enterprise which rivalry is inspiring in our managers, the last week has witnessed the production of "The Midsummer Night's Dream" at two of the most popular houses in the city; and that in a style which we may safely say has seldom if ever been surpassed. The play was performed once before in New York, at the Old Park theatre in 1841. It was the means of saving the drooping fortunes of the manager of that day, Mr. Simpson. His audiences had been falling off for some time, and ruin stared him in the face, when Mr. Barry, the present stage manager of the Broadway, proposed the very bold step of attempting this old comedy. Mr. Simpson demurred at first, fearing that the experiment might prove a failure; but his more courageous lieutenant overcame his apprehensions, the play was produced, and drew on the first night a house worth $1,400. We trust it will prove an equally profitable card to the Broadway. The following were the casts of Monday evening and of 1841:—

Personages.	Actors, 1841.	Actors, 1854.
Theseus	Mr. Fredericks	Mr. Conway.
Titania	Miss M. Taylor	Mrs. Abbot.
Lysander	Mr. Wheatley	Mr. Lanergan.
Bottom	Mr. Williams	Mr. Davidge.
Oberon	Miss C. Cushman	M'de Ponisi.
Helena	Miss S. Cushman	Miss A. Gougenheim.
Quince	Mr. Fisher	Mr. Howard.
Puck	Mrs. Knight	Viola.
Hermia	Miss Buloloi	Mrs. Nagle.

As the "Midsummer Night's Dream" has already succeeded once in this city, and is now again put upon the stage in preference to novelties by two of our most experienced managers, it may seem rash to hazard a criticism on the wisdom of its exhumation. It has great beauties, doubtless. Many of our household words are taken from it; the characters have been familiar to us all from childhood. Shakspeare's imaginative vein was never happier. Add to this that the whole of Mendelssohn's music was given last evening at the Broadway, and a formidable array of arguments in its favor will be presented. Still we cannot rejoice over its production as we would over a treasure that has been lost and is found. We cannot go into ecstacies over any act or any scene. We cannot take an interest in the plot, for there is none. Bottom tires us at best; even Puck is wearisome before the close, and Theseus, Hippolyta and the two other brace of lovers are positive bores. We have picked the diamonds out long before the actors have waded through the trash. We want to go home when Lysander is talking gabble to Hermia, and Theseus is declaiming about Thebes. Who on earth cares about any of them? To those lovers of Shakspeare who talk of his works in the same breath with the Bible, this will seem positive profanity; but let it pass. So far we have no reason to believe that our doubts are shared by the public. The Broadway was crowded from gallery to orchestra on Monday evening; and though we noticed few displays of enthusiasm, the old comedy was received with something very like a welcome.

To pursue to the end our ungracious task as critics, we demur to the music. The orchestra at the Broadway does not understand Mendelssohn, or the overture would have been rendered very differently. The march was a jingle, and "Ye spotted snakes" reflected very little credit on the singing fairies. The only exception to the rule in the matter of music was the duet, "I know a bank," which was very prettily sung.

Most of the characters in the "Midsummer Night's Dream" are so flat, that an actor has little chance to gain either glory or disgrace. This was fortunate for Messrs. Lanergan and Grosvenor, who have not made much progress since we saw them last. Mr. Conway is a little too energetic for Theseus; what has persuaded him to model himself on Anderson? Mdes. Ponisi and Abbott managed Oberon and Titania passably. In the comic underplot, the great character as every one knows, is Bottom the weaver. It was taken by Davidge on Monday, and a great deal of talent displayed in the rendering. Still, it is impossible to endorse him as Bottom until first, he learns his part thoroughly, and secondly, his grotesque action and comic exclamations approach a little nearer to nature. Fisk made a capital Snug, and Starveling was excellently rendered by Cutter. But the great "star" of the night was a beautiful child who, under the name of "La Petite Viola," played Puck in a truly fairylike way. Such aplomb, such confidences, such accuracy of tone and gesture, combined with visible symptoms of real youth and infantile attractions, are likely to make little Viola one of the greatest favorites of the day.

The dancing and "spectacle" generally were as good as such things are when Leader leads the way. The scenery, by M. Heister, has certainly never been excelled in this city. Loud bursts of genuine applause greeted the panorama with which the first act ended; and for our part, we will add, that we doubt whether a more perfect triumph in the way of decorations is ever achieved in any of the theatres of Europe. To see that panorama and La Petite Viola, is well worth a visit to the Broadway.

A review of "A Midsummer Night's Dream," in The New York Herald, *February 8, 1854, p. 4.*

George C. D. Odell (essay date 1916)

[*Odell provides an overview and comparison of the two New York productions of* A Midsummer Night's Dream.]

No event in our mid-century theatrical history is more interesting than the double production of 'A Midsummer Night's Dream' brought about by managerial rivalry in 1854. I have no doubt that it was inspired by the success of Samuel Phelps at Sadler's Wells, in 1853, but I have been forced to give up my original suspicion that either of these or any of the revivals in New York except that of 1867 employed scenery imported from an English rendering of the drama. At Burton's and the Broadway we have assurance that the painting was by the artists connected with the theaters involved. It is extraordinary that a play acted but twice before in the city should thus emerge simultaneously at two houses. W. E. Burton, at that time perhaps the most popular of New York comedians had, at his theater, one of the best companies of actors in the English-speaking world; old comedies and new were presented on his stage with incomparable art. He was turning more and more to Shakspere, and had given or was shortly to give memorable performances of 'Twelfth Night,' the 'Winter's Tale,' and the 'Tempest.' One might say that this revival was his, by right of service; besides he was a thor-

William Burton as Bottom.

ough Shaksperian scholar. But the Broadway Theater, near Anthony Street, was a house of no settled policy; it was a huge affair, seating, we are told, about 4,000 people, and had been built as a speculation. It was never a success, and obviously the performance of our comedy about to be discussed was purely a commercial inspiration. Nevertheless, it was beautifully done, and rather eclipsed, scenically, the production in Burton's small, more intimate theater.

One thought impresses as we look about for records of these rival attractions; the newspapers were now awake, and advertisements and criticisms throw ample light on the methods of staging. The press, as well as the theater, had made enormous strides in the years between 1841 and 1854; it is little short of marvellous. Let me illustrate by placing in parallel columns the announcements of the competing establishments:

> The advertisement for Burton's, *The Daily Tribune,* Feb. 3, 1854
>
> Produced from original Text, with but few curtailments, and graced for the first time on any stage with
>
> *MENDELSSOHN'S MUSIC!*
>
> Entirely New Scenery, of the most beautiful description, painted by Mr. Heilge. Gorgeous new costumes by Mr. Keyser and assistants. The Classical Dresses are from the first authorities—The Fairy Habiliments, Decorations and Accessories are of the very best and richest construction. Extensive machinery by Mr. William Foudray and assistants. Costly Properties by Mr. T. Cross. The Fairy Dances and Groupings, arranged by Mons. Frederic, Ballet Master. The Comedy produced under the immediate direction of Mr. Burton, materially assisted by Mr J. Moore, Stage Director.
>
> The advertisement for the Broadway, *The Daily Tribune,* Feb. 6, 1854
>
> The whole of Mendelssohn's beautiful vocal and instrumental music. The scenic illustrations entirely new, painted by Mr. Heister and his assistants; the costumes by Mrs. Wallis; the decorations, banners and appointments by Mr. Wallis; the machinery by Mr. John Furze; the ballet produced under the direction of Mlle. Leader; the music arranged and adapted by Mr. Jo. Mayer, produced under the direction of Mr. Roberts.

The casts at the two houses have always been thus opposingly grouped in subsequent records, and I follow the invariable custom in so doing. Unlike the Park Theater cast of 1841, these two are worth repeating almost in full:

	Burton's	Broadway
Theseus	Charles Fisher	F. B. Conway
Lysander	George Jordan	Lanergan
Demetrius	J. Norton	Grosvenor
Bottom	Wm. E. Burton	William Davidge
Quince	T. Johnston	Howard
Flute	George Barrett	Whiting
Puck	Master C. Parsloe	Little Viola Crocker
Oberon	Miss E. Raymond	Mme. Ponisi
Titania	Mrs. Burton	Mrs. Abbott
Hippolyta	Miss J. Cooke	Mrs. Warren
Hermia	Miss Lottie Hough	Mrs. Nagle
Helena	Mrs. Buckland (Kate Horn)	Miss A. Gougenheim

Ireland, in speaking of the performance at the Broadway, remarks, "it had already been produced (though not with quite equal magnificence) at Burton's." Col. T. Alston Brown, in his 'History of the New York Stage' agrees: "The play," he says "at Burton's ran until March 6, and at the Broadway until March 11. In effectiveness of stage setting, and in the costuming, the comedy had an infinitely more brilliant showing here than at Burton's; in the acting, there was little left for critical cavil in the performance at either house."

Actual contemporary criticism gives the same impression. The New York *Tribune,* February 4, 1854, became enthusiastic over Burton's spectacle: "The representation of the Midsummer Night's Dream at Burton's Theater last night may be signalized as one of the best representations, in regard to stage effects and appointments, if not the best, that we have yet had in this city. The theater itself is a miniature affair and the stage incompetent as to depth and breadth for the right setting-forth of the dainty imaginations of the great poet; but viewing it not as a great affair, but as a neat affair, the whole is deserving of emphatic approval." The *Herald* of February 8, however, shows the superiority scenically, of the other production: "The dancing and spectacle were as good as such things usually are when Leader leads the way. The scenery, by Mr. Heister, has certainly never been excelled in this city. Loud bursts of genuine applause greeted the panorama with which the first act ended; and for our part we will add that we doubt whether a more perfect triumph in the way of decorations is ever achieved at any of the theaters of Europe. To see that panorama . . . is well worth a visit to the Broadway." (pp. 129-32)

Since the two theaters mentioned in this section thus pitted forces against each other, why should not we, taking the hint from them, end by placing side by side two literary estimates made by famous theater-goers of that day? At least the connection will show that each production had its following of enthusiastic youth:

Says W. L. Keese, in his 'Life of Burton':

> A Midsummer Night's Dream was produced at Burton's in 1854, and the manager played *Bottom.* We well remember with what delight the play was received, and what a marked sensation was created by the scenery and stage effect. The public wondered how so much could be presented on so small a stage. . . . The fairy element was made a beautiful feature, and the spirit of poetry brooded over the whole production. The unanimity of the press in its encomiums was remarkable. . . .
>
> As we think of it now, it seems to us that Burton's idea of Bottom was the true one. . . . We remember his acting in the scene where the artisans meet—how striking it was in sustained individuality, and how finely exemplified was the potential vanity of Bottom—He was capital, too, in the scene of the rehearsal, and of his translation. . . . What pleased us greatly was the vein of engaging raillery which ran through his delivery of the speeches to the fairies, Cobweb, Peas-Blossom and Mustard-Seed. It goes without saying, that as *Pyramus* in the tragedy, Burton created unbounded amusement. . . .

And Laurence Hutton, in 'Plays and Players', New York, 1875:

> Mr. Burton was anxious to match his reputation

with that of Mr. Davidge as Bottom. . . . In our humble estimation, however, the presentation of the part of Bottom by Mr. Davidge has had no equal before or since. . . . Public interest was now excited and full houses the result. At the Broadway the entertainment was well worthy its popularity and success.

We have seen lately in print articles on the splendor of theatrical representations of the present, that ignore the magnificence of the scenic effects of other days, but we have had on our stage nothing more gorgeous in late years than the setting of the "Midsummer Night's Dream" at the Broadway. . . . Particularly fine, as we remember it, was the panorama of fairyland, done by the "compounding of flats" and the artistic adjustment of lights. George Heister, the scenic artist of the Broadway, may have been wanting in some of the improvements and inventions of modern stage craft, but his taste was then . . . artistic and correct in its judgment of effects. . . . The piece as a whole is recalled by old theatre-goers as one of those bright particular productions where master, art, artist, and public were in perfect accord. . . . William Davidge . . . alone of the present school has fully comprehended the part (of Bottom).

To a reader familiar with mid-century methods of production, it will be apparent that these two simultaneous revivals were unique in our history; probably no play had ever before in this city been so carefully and so sumptuously mounted. If I were to weigh evidence, I should guess that Burton gave the more scholarly, and Marshall of the Broadway the more spectacular presentation. The men of the cast at Burton's were far better than those at the Broadway; but the pulchritude of the ladies at the latter theater quite eclipsed that of the *routinières* of Burton's company. Adelaide Gougenheim and Mrs. Nagle, the Helena and Hermia at the Broadway, were two of the most beautiful actresses of their time; Mme. Ponisi, the Oberon, was for years the only Lady Macbeth (Charlotte Cushman excepted) that New York would hear of. It is to be observed that now, for the first time in America, Puck, in both these productions, is played by a child, by a boy at Burton's, at the Broadway, by la Petite Viola (later briefly on the stage as Viola Crocker—a sister of two famed actresses, Mrs. F. B. Conway and Mrs. D. P. Bowers). Little Viola by her beauty and cleverness made quite the hit of the piece. It will be seen, then, that in every way extreme care had been exercised in each theater; I feel justified in repeating that the twin production marked an epoch in New York staging. Every new Shaksperian revival (apart from the hack repertory) had to model itself satisfactorily to the memories of those who had passed excitedly from Burton's to the Broadway in 1854, taking sides and arguing, no doubt to the swelling of the box-office receipts. (pp. 137-39)

George Clinton Densmore Odell, " 'A Midsummer Night's Dream' on the New York Stage," in Shaksperian Studies, edited by Brander Matthews and Ashley Horace Thorndike, 1916. Reprint by Russell & Russell, Inc., 1962, pp. 129-39.

PRODUCTION:

Charles Kean • Princess's Theatre • 1856

BACKGROUND:

Kean's production of *A Midsummer Night's Dream* at the Princess's Theatre was one of the nineteenth century's most popularly successful revivals of the play, lasting through 150 performances. The scenic aspects of this production were particularly spectacular, even by Victorian standards, and included a diorama and pictorial representations of Athens based on the latest archaeological research. Puck, played by a very young Ellen Terry, first appeared on a mushroom that emerged from beneath the stage floor.

COMMENTARY:

The Athenaeum   (review date 18 October 1856)

[*In the following review, the critic admires Kean's numerous elaborations of* A Midsummer Night's Dream, *extolling his method of "not parsimoniously adhering to the usual stage-directions, but suffering his own fancy to disport itself in adding new beauties wherever he can find opportunity."*]

On Wednesday, Mr. Kean redeemed his promise of producing 'A Midsummer Night's Dream' with appropriate illustrations. The scenery is certainly exquisite, and the costumes are pictorial. The opening scene presents us with a view of Athens, such as it was in the days of its glory, long subsequent to Theseus,—an anachronism for which Mr. Kean may be pardoned, and which did not require the apology he tenders. The workshop of *Quince the Carpenter* is also a curiosity in its way, and the introduction of furniture and tools copied from the discoveries of Herculaneum shows the diligence that has been exercised to impart historical accuracy, where possible, to the scene.—The moonlight and forest scenes are all excellent,—that in which *Titania's* shadow-dance was presented is something more. The magic circle formed by the moon's rays, and the shadows of the Faëry-dancers thrown on the verdure, are as poetic in conception as delightful in execution. In such inventions, Mr. Kean brings an imagination to the poet's aid which proves him to be of a kindred spirit. There is also a faëry-dance in the wood at the end of the fourth act, during the sleep of the lovers, which is entitled to the like commendation for the like reasons. Mr. Kean takes the drama, not parsimoniously adhering to the usual stage-directions, but suffering his own fancy to disport itself in adding new beauties wherever he can find opportunity.—It is still more gratifying to be able to add, that the play throughout was beautifully acted. Mr. Ryder and Miss Murray as *Theseus* and *Hippolyta* were the perfection of such heroic representatives. *Oberon*, by Miss F. Ternan, and *Titania*, by Miss Carlotta Leelereq, were as faëry-like as could be desired. *Helena*, by Miss Heath, was excellent; and *Hermia*, by Miss Bufton, a new actress, was very good. We somewhat object to Mr. T. F. Cathcart's *Lysander;* he showed a tendency to rant, and we recommend more moderation to him in future. The main part of the evening, however, was the *Bottom* of Mr. Harley. He played it as we have seen him play it years ago, "when George the Third was King." It is, as it was, a thing of peculiarities—an eccentric piece of mannerism rather than a character; and carried us back to "the palmy days," as they are called, of the Drama.

Thus much concerning the acting, scenery, and costumes of this revival. But the 'Midsummer Night's Dream' has, of late years, been also musically illustrated whenever it has been brought forward; nor did ever play lend itself more charmingly to such aid and adornment, even though Shakspeare gave to his own verse a melody which would seem, at first glance, incapable of enhancement,—and which would not only seem, but *be* so, could interpreters be found as musical as the delicious poetry which they have to speak.—It has chanced that a poet in one art has here lovingly bent himself to do homage to a greater poet in another. When a Handel sets 'L'Allegro,'—when a Mendelssohn deals with a

roundel and a faëry song

[II. ii. 1]

by Shakspeare, it is not in the spirit of a painter obliged to History or Fancy for his subject, but in that of a fellow-worker or fellow-creator. The cases of such possible or permissible co-operation are few and far between as "angels' visits." The jewels with which Mendelssohn decked (not over-hung) the poetry of Shakspeare's delicious play furnish the most exquisite example of music applied to an already existing stage work in our knowledge.—They could hardly have been fashioned, let it be added, had not the commission to fashion them been a Court commission, had not the play been a Court play,—in which the best of orchestras and the choicest of singers could be procured to do work to which best orchestras and best singers lend themselves unwillingly. The difficulty of the music is extreme; hence (to come to our point), we cannot hope to see Shakspeare with Mendelssohn adequately worked out in any average theatre,—and Mr. Kean is rather commendable because so much of Mendelssohn's music was given by him, than to be complained of because that which he gave was insufficiently performed. The interpolations are another affair. Bits from Beethoven, bits by some *Anonymous,* (not bad of their commonplace kind) mixed with Mendelssohn's faëry work, must offend every one with a musical sense—as much as lines from 'Samson Agonistes' interpolated into a Shakspearian tragedy, or from Haynes Bayly *sandwiched* into 'Sir Eustace Grey,' would afflict a poetical ear. We cannot expect a point-device execution of such exquisite music in a theatre not musical,—but we cannot acquiesce in seeing Brabant lace patched with Broussa silk or Yorkshire worsted.—As an illustrating manager, Mr. Kean, with all his picturesqueness and liberality, will do harm rather than good, if to please his public he outrages any one art (be it accessory) for the sake of another. Meanwhile, the effect of the faëry *intermezzo*—of the two-part song—(though weakened by the long interpolated dance before it),—of the gorgeous wedding march—of the absurd music to the mechanics' play, and of the beginning of the *final* chorus (which some stupid hand had been allowed to eke out) were so delicious as to make us wish that in this case Mr. Kean had been contented to let well alone, and to adorn his tasteful and fantastic revival with the entire "suit of musical trimming" of the great German Shakspearian, unaltered and untampered with. (pp. 1280-81)

A review of "A Midsummer Night's Dream," in The Athenaeum, *No. 1512, October 18, 1856, pp. 1280-81.*

Henry Morley   (review date 25 October 1856)

[*In the originally unsigned review excerpted below, Morley focuses upon the spectacle of Kean's production, finding it excessive and claiming that the scenery overwhelmed Shakespeare's poetry.*]

The beautiful mounting of the *Midsummer Night's Dream* at [the Princess's Theatre] attracts and will attract for a long time crowded audiences. The words of the play are spoken agreeably, some of the sweetest passages charmingly, and much of Shakespeare's delicate pleasantry is made to tell with good effect upon its bearers. The *Midsummer Night's Dream* is full of passages that have only to be reasonably well uttered to be enjoyed even by the dull, and with so fair a *Hermia* as Miss Bufton, so whimsical a *Bottom* as Mr Harley, who seems to have no particular conception of the part, but nevertheless makes it highly amusing,—with a generally good delivery of words and songs, the play speaks for itself in a great measure.

The one defect in the mounting of the *Midsummer Night's Dream* is that which has lessened the value of many former efforts made at this house to produce Shakespeare with every accessory of scenic decoration. We do not think money ill spent upon stage furniture, and certainly we can only admire the exquisite scenery of the play now being presented at the Princess's, but there may be a defect of taste that mars the effect of the richest ornament, as we can best show by one or two examples.

Shakespeare's direction for the opening scene of the *Midsummer Night's Dream* is "Athens, a Room in the Palace of Theseus." For this, is read at the Princess's theatre, "A Terrace adjoining the Palace of Theseus, overlooking the City of Athens," and there is presented an elaborate and undoubtedly most beautiful bird's eye view of Athens as it was in the time of Pericles. A great scenic effect is obtained, but it is as far as it goes damaging to the poem. Shakespeare took for his mortals people of heroic times, "Duke Theseus and Hippolyta," and it suited his romance to call them Athenians, but the feeling of the play is marred when out of this suggestion of the antique mingled with the fairy world the scene-painter finds opportunity to bring into hard and jarring contrast the Athens of Pericles and our own world of Robin Goodfellow and all the woodland elves. "A Room in the House of Theseus," left that question of the where or when of the whole story to be touched as lightly as a poet might desire, the poetry was missed entirely by the painting of the scene, beautiful as it is, which illustrates the first set of the *Midsummer Night's Dream* at the Princess's.

We shall not dwell more on this subject than is requisite to show good reason for our criticism. In the second set there is a dream-like moving of the wood beautifully managed and spoilt in effect by a trifling mistake easily corrected. *Oberon* stands before the scene waving his wand as if he were exhibitor of the diorama, or a fairy conjuror causing the rocks and trees to move. Nobody, we believe, ever attributed to fairies any power of that sort. *Oberon* should either be off the stage or on it still as death, and it should be left for the spectators to feel the dreamy influence of wood and water slipping by their eyes unhindered and undistracted. This change leads to the disclosure of a fairy ring, a beautiful scenic effect, and what is called in large letters upon the play bills *Titania's Shadow Dance.* Of all things in the world a shadow dance of fairies! If any thing in the way of an effect of light was especially desirable, it would have been such an arrangement as would have made the fairies appear to be dancing in a light so managed as to cast no shadow and give them the true spiritual attribute. Elaborately to produce and present, as an especial attraction, fairies of large size casting shadows made as black and distinct as possible, and offering in dance to pick

Fairy pageant from Kean's production.

them up as if even they also were solid, is as great a sacrifice of Shakespeare to the purposes of the ballet master as the view of Athens in its glory was a sacrifice of poetry to the scene-painter. We have said enough to show the direction in which alone we think improvement necessary to make the stage ornament at the Princess's theatre as perfect as it is beautiful. The *Puck* is a pretty little girl belted and garlanded with flowers! From the third act we miss a portion of the poem most essential to its right effect—the quarrel between *Hermia* and *Helena*—but we get at the end a ballet of fairies round a maypole that shoots up out of an aloe, after the way of a transformation in a pantomime and rains down garlands. Fairies, not airy beings of the colour of the greenwood, or the sky, or robed in misty white, but glittering in the most brilliant dresses, with a crust of bullion about their legs, cause the curtain to fall on a splendid ballet, and it is evidence enough of the depreciated taste of the audience to say that the ballet is encored.

We have made these comments in no censorious mood. It has given us great pleasure to see Shakespeare enjoyed by the large number of persons who are attracted to the Princess's Theatre by the splendours for which it is famous. We do not wish the splendour less, or its attraction less, we only ask for more heed to the securing of a perfect harmony between the conception of the decorator and those of the poet. We need hardly add that the presentment of the *Midsummer Night's Dream* here discussed is well worth seeing, apart from the po-

etry, and well worth hearing apart from the scenery, while there are portions of the play and not a few in which the scenery and the poetry harmonise in the most exquisite manner. (pp. 28-9)

> *Henry Morley, in an originally unsigned review of "A Midsummer Night's Dream," in* The Examiner, *October 25, 1856, pp. 28-9.*

Charles Kean (essay date 1856)

[*The excerpt below is drawn from Kean's Preface to the published edition of his version of* A Midsummer Night's Dream. *He here explains the historical and aesthetic considerations that went into his stage designs, which depicted Athens during the period of its "pride and glory" rather than the much more primitive and "rude" city of Theseus's own time.*]

A Midsummer-Night's Dream was, according to the best authorities, written by Shakespeare, at a period of life when his creative mind "glowed with all the warmth of a youthful and lively imagination." The poet did not search into history or tradition for the story, but, relying solely on his own exquisite genius, bequeathed to posterity one of "those unparalleled compositions which have rendered him the delight and wonder of successive ages."

Apart from the supernatural agencies, which relate to the quarrels of Oberon, the Fairy Monarch, and his Queen Titania, the classical figures of Theseus and Hippolyta stand forward as the chief human personages of this most harmonious of dramas. Nevertheless, the general character of the play is so far from historical, that while I have made Athens and its neighbourhood the subject of illustration, I have held myself unfettered with regard to chronology. Indeed, sufficient is not known of the details of Greek life and architecture in the time of Theseus to render complete (or proximate) accuracy possible, even if a theatrical representation of the period were attempted.

It may be added, that the buildings existing in Athens during that early age (twelve hundred years before the Christian era), were most probably rude in construction, were formed of the simplest materials, and retained the Egyptian features introduced by Cecrops, the mythical founder of the city. Such edifices could have nothing in common with the impressions of Greek civilization that exist in every educated mind.

Influenced by these considerations, I have selected a later period, in the hope of conveying an idea of Athens as it would have appeared to one of its own inhabitants, at a time when it had attained its greatest splendour in literature and in art—when it stood in its pride and glory, ennobled by a race of illustrious men, and containing the most beautiful objects the world had ever seen.

The Acropolis, on its rocky eminence, surrounded by marble Temples, has been restored, together with the Theatre of Bacchus, wherein multitudes once thronged to listen to the majestic poetry of Æschylus, Sophocles, and Euripides; and near which stands that memorable hill from whence the words of sacred truth were first promulgated to the Athenian citizens by apostolic inspiration.

A portion of the music, hitherto introduced in the *"Midsummer-Night's Dream,"* will be retained (under the direction of Mr. J. L. Hatton), with the addition of the overtures, *entr' actes,* and airs composed expressly for this play by the late Dr. Felix Mendelssohn Bartholdy, and pronounced to be amongst the most successful efforts of that celebrated master. (pp. v-vi)

> *Charles Kean, in a preface to* A Midsummer Night's Dream *by William Shakespeare, arranged for representation at the Princess's Theatre, 1856. Reprint by Cornmarket Press, 1970, pp. v-vi.*

John William Cole   (essay date 1859)

[*In the following excerpt from his biography of Kean, Cole lauds the 1856 production of* A Midsummer Night's Dream, *maintaining that the "skillfully-blended, pictorial, mechanical, and musical effects overpowered the faculties of the spectators with the influence of an enchanting vision."*]

On the 15th of October, 1856, before the attraction of *Pizarro* had begun to wane, *A Midsummer Night's Dream,* was produced. This beautiful emanation of Shakespeare's fancy may be considered, perhaps, the most exquisite specimen of graceful, imaginative, and harmonious composition that the mind of a great poet has ever conceived, or his pen transmitted to posterity. The prying investigation of commentators has tortured itself in vain attempts to discover any direct source or popular story from whence Shakespeare derived or constructed his drama. All that they have been able to burrow out amounts to the coincidence of a few names which have been met with before, and a very slight similarity between his

fairies and those introduced in Michael Drayton's fantastical poem of "Nymphidia." These frivolous disparagements have been hypercritically set forward to detract from the original conception of the most universal and discursive genius ever enclosed within a human form; a genius which, with the swiftness of thought, could traverse and surpass the boundaries of the universe, control space and time, and in the words of his own *Puck,* "put a girdle round about the earth in forty minutes" [II. i. 175-76]. When Shakespeare wrote for the emergencies of the theatre, he borrowed his subjects from familiar tales, legends, or chronicles; when he composed from pure inspiration and poetic impulse, he drew upon his own exhaustless invention.

Garrick, when he revived *A Midsummer Night's Dream* at Drury Lane, in 1763, omitted many of the most poetical passages, which are so profusely scattered through the play that they supply more standard quotations than almost any other single production of the same author. The manager also supposed that as fairies are generally associated with the idea of tiny, diminutive elves, it would be a happy thought to have *Oberon, Titania,* and their attendant courts and familiars, represented by small children. The conception was a mistake, and the experiment a failure. The piece, thus metamorphosed, was acted only once, to a thin November audience who were cold and drowsy. Respect for Shakespeare kept them silent, but that silence also induced them to follow the example of the four lovers, who in one scene are all discovered lying fast asleep on the stage. Shakespeare has endowed the fairy monarch and his queen with the language, feelings, sentiments, passions, and jealousies of matured humanity. They speak, think, and act like real men and women, reminding us of Cupid, no longer the mythological infant, but the lover and husband of Psyche. None of the attributes given to them could be adequately conveyed through the puerile organs of childhood. Consistency might to a certain extent be imparted to the eye, but it was lost to the intelligence. Shakespeare's fairies delight in the moonlight revel on the noiseless grass; they are shadowy, etherial, bright, elastic essences, gifted with supernatural power and refinement, continually mixing themselves up with the affairs of mortals; but we cannot figure them to our minds as bearing any resemblance to the lilliputian, household imps, so inseparably connected with our nursery fables and recollections.

It has been said, too, that the play is deficient in dramatic interest; that the lovers are tame, and that *Theseus* and *Hippolyta* do nothing. Assuredly it is not intended to embody a history of deep, concentrated passion. There is no design of harrowing up the soul, and of conveying the fearful lessons which are taught by *Othello, Macbeth,* or *Lear.* To look for violent, conflicting action, and collision of opposite character, where the scene passes the boundaries of common nature, and the chief actors are etherialized beings, flitting through boundless space, is to expect them where they can never be found, except in the incongruous tales of eastern enchantment. The interest and incidents of Shakespeare's play amply suffice for the purpose in view, and he has combined them with the hand of a great master, and with skilful variety to produce what he designed,—a fairy drama, *A Midsummer Night's Dream.* If the mortals introduced had been rendered more prominent than the mythological agents, the entire construction and object of the play would have been subverted. Shakespeare knew better than his critics when, where, and how to bring his resources together, and to balance them so as to preserve that just harmony of proportion, which marks one of the most delicate distinctions between ordinary ability and exalted genius.

Very few of Shakespeare's immortalities have been so unmercifully subjected to the transmuting process of the crucible as the *Midsummer Night's Dream*. As far back as the return of Charles II. (in 1661), a comic actor named Cox, celebrated for a peculiar class of drolls and farces, added this magnificent conception to the list of his mummeries, or rather a part of it, under the title of the *Humours of Bottom the Weaver*. About thirty years later (1692) it became an opera, and was called the *Fairy Queen*. In 1716, a drunken bass singer, Leveridge by name, changed it into a masque, entitled, *Pyramus and Thisbe*, from which it became a mock opera in 1745, the music being supplied by a composer named Lampe. Ten years later, Garrick produced it as *The Fairies*, with Italian singers. Colman repeated a similar experiment in 1777; and, in 1816, it was presented as a musical play at Covent Garden, with alterations and additions by Frederic Reynolds. The interpolations of the last-named writer wound up with a grand pageant, commemorative of the triumphs of *Theseus;* which same triumphs have no more connexion with the incidents and progress of the original drama, than a panorama of the battle of Waterloo. *Theseus* himself is only a subordinate pivot, or indicated point to connect the story. During Madame Vestris's management at Covent Garden, the true Shakespearean version was restored, proving one of her most attractive cards. Mr. Phelps also included it in his list at Sadler's Wells. The two latter restorations deserve to be mentioned in terms of the highest praise; they were steps in the right direction, although the palm of superiority must be assigned to the still more recent revival by Mr. Kean, of which we are now speaking.

In the *"Midsummer Night's Dream,"* which is almost exclusively a creation of fancy, there is scarcely any scope for that illustrative and historical accuracy, or for that classical research, so peculiarly identified with Mr. Kean's system of management, and with which his name had now become almost synonymous: nevertheless, he availed himself of the few opportunities afforded by the subject, of carrying out his favourite plan. So little is known of Greek manners and architecture in the time of Theseus, twelve hundred years before the Christian era, and so probable is it that the buildings were of the rudest form, that any attempt to represent them on the stage would have failed in the intended object of profitable instruction. Holding himself, for these reasons, "unfettered with regard to chronology," Mr. Kean presented ancient Athens to us, in the opening scene, at the culminating period of its magnificence, "as it would have appeared to one of its own inhabitants at a time when it had attained its greatest splendour in literature and art." His scholastic taste took advantage of the specified scene of action, to place before the eyes of the spectators, on the rising of the curtain, a restored view of that famous city, "standing in its pride and glory," which excited the spontaneous sympathy, and called up some of the earliest and deepest impressions of every educated mind. We saw, on the hill of the Acropolis, the far-famed Parthenon, the Erichtheum, and the statue of the tutelary goddess Minerva, or Athena; by its side the theatre of Bacchus; in advance, the temple of Jupiter Olympus, partially hiding the hall of the Museum; and on the right, the temple of Theseus. The view also included the summit of that memorable eminence, "from whence the words of sacred truth were first promulgated to the Athenian citizens by apostolic inspiration."

Nothing could exceed the consistent harmony with which all the varied elements of the play were blended together. The introduction to the haunt of the supernatural beings; the first appearance of *Oberon* and *Titania,* with their attendant trains; the noiseless footsteps of the dance on the moonlit greensward, with the shadowed reflection of every rapid and graceful movement; the wood peopled with its innumerable fairy legions, whose voices lull their queen to sleep upon a bank of flowers; the melodious music composed by Mendelssohn to the words of the author, in a strain and tone of feeling in intimate sympathy with the subject; the perpetual change of scene and incident; the shifting diorama; the beams of the rising sun glittering on the leaves; the gradual dispersion of the mist, discovering the fairy guardians, light and brilliant as gossamer, grouped around the unconsciously sleeping mortals; the dazzling magnificence of the palace of Theseus at the close, thronged on every staircase, balustrade and corridor, with myriads of aerial beings, who join in an unseen and unheard epithalamium on the mortal inmates who have retired to rest;—these, in an endless succession of skilfully-blended, pictorial, mechanical, and musical effects, overpowered the faculties of the spectators with the influence of an enchanting vision. Written description can convey but a faint idea of the glowing, animated reality. The monotonous feelings of every-day life were forgotten, and we woke after a three hours' journey into another world, as if from the recollection of a delicious dream. What more convincing evidence could be given of the potency of the spell than a mention of the fact that *A Midsummer Night's Dream* was repeated for one hundred and fifty nights during this and the following season.

The actors ought not to be forgotten. The play contains no character suited to the abilities of Mr. and Mrs. C. Kean. *Theseus* of Athens, and *Hippolyta,* his Amazonian queen, take the lead amongst the human personages. *Hippolyta* says little, while *Theseus* has only to look heroic, and speak some fine passages of poetry, never omitted in selections from the "beauties of Shakespeare." Both were splendidly impersonated by Miss Murray and Mr. Ryder. Miss Heath and Miss Bufton, as *Helena,* and *Hermia,* were beautiful to gaze upon. Miss Fanny Ternan made a highly successful first appearance as *Oberon,* and Miss Carlotta Leclercq acquitted herself with bewitching grace as *Titania,* the Fairy Queen. The progress of this young lady may be quoted as a remarkable evidence of the excellent training of the Princess's Theatre. In six years, from a member of the corps de ballet, she became one of the most accomplished and versatile comic actresses of the present day. Another presented itself in the precocious talent of Miss Ellen Terry, a child of eight years of age, who played the merry goblin, *Puck,* a part that requires an old head on young shoulders, with restless elfish animation, and an evident enjoyment of her own mischievous pranks. For *Bottom* and his brother operatives, the "hard-handed" men of Athens, who gratify their own vanity and amuse their superiors with the tragic mirth of "Pyramus and Thisbe," we had Harley, F. Matthews, Meadows, Saker, and F. Cooke. These rich comedians carried off the underplot and relief of the play with exquisite fooling. Harley in particular, presented a variety in the line of originals in which that worthy scion of the old school had long been without a rival. His acting was, in fact, a school of itself which baffled imitation and died with its master. (pp. 194-200)

John William Cole, "Chapter IX," in his The Life and Theatrical Times of Charles Kean, F. S. A.,

Vol. I, *second edition, Richard Bentley, 1859, pp. 184-201.*

Ellen Terry (essay date 1908)

[*Terry was one of the preeminent actresses of the Victorian era. At the age of nine, she played Puck in Kean's revival of* A Midsummer Night's Dream. *In the following excerpt from her* Story of My Life *(1908), she recalls her experiences in that production.*]

From April 1856 until 1859 I acted constantly at the Princess's Theatre with the Keans, spending the summer holidays in acting at Ryde. My whole life was the theatre, and naturally all my early memories are connected with it. At breakfast father would begin the day's "coaching." Often I had to lay down my fork and say my lines. He would conduct these extra rehearsals anywhere—in the street, the 'bus—we were never safe! I remember vividly going into a chemist's shop and being stood upon a stool to say my part to the chemist! Such leisure as I had from my profession was spent in "minding" the younger children—an occupation in which I delighted. They all had very pretty hair, and I used to wash it and comb it out until it looked as fine and bright as floss silk.

It is argued now that stage life is bad for a young child, and children are not allowed by law to go on the stage until they are ten years old—quite a mature age in my young days! I cannot discuss the whole question here, and must content myself with saying that during my three years at the Prin-

Ellen Terry as Puck.

cess's I was a very strong, happy, and healthy child. I was never out of the bill except during the run of "A Midsummer Night's Dream," when, through an unfortunate accident, I broke my toe. I was playing Puck, my second part on any stage, and had come up through a trap at the end of the last act to give the final speech. My sister Kate was playing Titania that night as understudy to Carlotta Leclercq. Up I came—but not quite up, for the man shut the trap-door too soon and caught my toe. I screamed. Kate rushed to me and banged her foot on the stage, but the man only closed the trap tighter, mistaking the signal.

"Oh, Katie! Katie!" I cried. "Oh, Nelly! Nelly!" said poor Kate helplessly. Then Mrs. Kean came rushing on and made them open the trap and release my poor foot.

"Finish the play, dear," she whispered excitedly, "and I'll double your salary!" There was Kate holding me up on one side and Mrs. Kean on the other. Well, I did finish the play in a fashion. The text ran something like this [V. i. 423-30]—

> If we shadows have offended (Oh, Katie, Katie!)
> Think but this, and all is mended, (Oh, my toe!)
> That you have but slumbered here,
> While these visions did appear. (I can't, I can't!)
> And this weak and idle theme,
> No more yielding but a dream, (Oh, dear! oh, dear!)
> Gentles, do not reprehend; (A big sob)
> If you pardon, we will mend. (Oh, Mrs. Kean!)

How I got through it, I don't know! But my salary was doubled—it had been fifteen shillings, and it was raised to thirty—and Mr. Skey, President of St. Bartholomew's Hospital, who chanced to be in a stall that very evening, came round behind the scenes and put my toe right. He remained my friend for life.

I was not chosen for Puck because I had played Mamilius [in *The Winter's Tale*] with some credit. The same examination was gone through, and again I came out first. During the rehearsals Mrs. Kean taught me to draw my breath in through my nose and begin a laugh—a very valuable accomplishment! She was also indefatigable in her lessons in clear enunciation, and I can hear her now lecturing the ladies of the company on their vowels. "A, E, I, O, U, my dear," she used to say, "are five distinct vowels, so don't mix them all up together as if you were making a pudding. If you want to say, 'I am going on the river,' say it plainly and don't tell us you are going on the 'riv*ah*!' You must say *her*, not *har*; it's *God*, not *Gud*: rem*on*strance, not rem*un*strance," and so forth. No one ever had a sharper tongue or a kinder heart than Mrs. Kean. Beginning with her, I have always loved women with a somewhat hard manner! I have never believed in their hardness, and have proved them tender and generous in the extreme.

Actor-managers are very proud of their long runs nowadays, but in Shakespeare, at any rate, they do not often eclipse Charles Kean's two hundred and fifty nights of "A Midsummer Night's Dream" at the Princess's. It was certainly a very fascinating production, and many of the effects were beautiful. I, by the way, had my share in marring one of these during the run. When Puck was told to put a girdle round the earth in forty minutes, I had to fly off the stage as swiftly as I could, and a dummy Puck was whirled through the air from the point where I disappeared. One night the dummy, while in full flying action, fell on the stage, whereupon, in great concern for its safety, I ran on, picked it up in my arms, and ran off with it amid roars of laughter! Neither of the Keans was acting in this production, but there was some one in authority to give me a sound cuff. Yet I had such excellent intentions. 'Tis ever thus!

I revelled in Puck and his impish pranks, and unconsciously realised that it was a part in which the imagination could run riot. I believe I played it well, but I did not *look* well, and I must contradict emphatically the kind assumption that I must have been a "delightful little fairy." As Mamilius I was really a sweet little thing, but while I was playing Puck I grew very gawky—not to say ugly! My hair had been cut short, and my red cheeks stuck out too much. I was a sight! (pp. 16-19)

> Ellen Terry, *"A Child of the Stage, 1848-56: Training in Shakespeare, 1856-59,"* in her The Story of My Life, *second edition, Hutchinson & Co., 1922, pp. 16-29.*

Stanley Wells (essay date 1970)

[*Wells provides a general survey of Kean's revival of* A Midsummer Night's Dream, *with special attention to the scenery and revisions of Shakespeare's original.*]

Charles Kean's Shakespeare performances at the Princess's Theatre, London, belong to a period when most of the adaptations and revisions made during the Restoration and the eighteenth century were at last being abandoned. Shakespeare was being restored; but by no means completely. *A Midsummer Night's Dream* had been frequently altered, but in 1840 Madame Vestris and Charles Mathews presented an abbreviated but wholly Shakespearian version at Covent Garden, and in 1853 at Sadler's Wells Samuel Phelps gave what was probably the most genuinely Shakespearian version for two hundred years. Kean's production, first performed in October 1856, represented something of a retrograde step.

Charles Kean (1811?-1868), an enthusiastic antiquarian, delighted in presenting Shakespeare's plays with scenery, costumes, and properties appropriate to the historical setting of the action. His Preface [1856] explains some of the problems encountered in applying his method to this play, and describes the steps he took to overcome them. It seems unlikely that the mechanicals' scenes were much enhanced by the use of 'Furniture and Tools . . . copied from discoveries at Herculaneum'. Kean's didacticism is reflected too in his other annotations and comments. The production's great emphasis on spectacle is only barely discernible in the printed stage directions. Kean's official biographer, J. W. Cole, eulogizes the splendours: 'these, in an endless succession of skilfully-blended, pictorial, mechanical, and musical effects, overpowered the faculties of the spectators with the influence of an enchanting vision' [*The Life and Theatrical Times of Charles Kean*]. Not everyone agreed. Henry Morley found that 'Titania's Shadow Dance' was 'as great a sacrifice of Shakespeare to the purposes of the ballet-master, as the view of Athens in its glory was a sacrifice of poetry to the scene-painter . . . we get, at the end, a ballet of fairies round a maypole that shoots up out of an aloe, after the way of a transformation in a pantomime, and rains down garlands. Fairies, not airy beings of the colour of the greenwood, or the sky, or robed in misty white, but glittering in the most brilliant dresses, with a crust of bullion about their legs, cause the curtain to fall on a splendid ballet; and it is evidence enough of the depraved taste of the audience to say that the ballet is encored' [*The Examiner*, 25 October 1856]. So depraved were the audiences that, in two seasons, the production was given 150 times.

Spectacle was achieved at the sacrifice of the text. Roughly, Kean omits 830 of 2200 lines. As usual, the episodes involving the young lovers suffer most. Some passages intended to be spoken are sung, as at the beginning of II.1, where Puck's earlier lines are given to a fairy, permitting Puck's later entry 'on a mushroom'. Puck's role is considerably shortened, perhaps because he was played by a little girl. There are some bowdlerizations. Some of the more obviously 'poetical' passages suffer (Titania is allowed only 5 of the 37 lines of 'These are the forgeries of jealousy' [II. i. 81ff.]), and so do some of the more thoughtful ones. The severest cuts are in III.2 (Kean's III.1). There are some transpositions, notably the awakening of the lovers, which is moved from IV.1 to make IV.3. The play scene is severely abbreviated, and so is the end of the play, where again lines meant to be spoken are sung.

Neither Kean nor his wife acted in the play. Oberon was played by a woman (a longstanding practice), and Puck by the nine-year-old Ellen Terry. Her autobiography [*The Story of My Life*] includes some charming anecdotes about the production. C. H. Shattuck records [in *The Shakespeare Promptbooks*] in the Folger Shakespeare Library a copy of the stage manager's workbook; the timing is given as 2 hours, 40 minutes. (pp. iii-vi)

> Stanley Wells, in an introduction to A Midsummer Night's Dream *by William Shakespeare, arranged for representation at the Princess's Theatre, Cornmarket Press, 1970, pp. iii-vii.*

PRODUCTION:

Augustin Daly • Daly's Theatre • 1888

BACKGROUND:

Daly staged several revivals of *A Midsummer Night's Dream* in New York, London, and elsewhere. He first produced the play in 1873 at the Grand Opera House, staged it again at his own theater fifteen years later, and finally took it on tour to London and afterward throughout the United States in 1895-96. These productions were principally known for their striking visual effects—including twinkling fireflies powered by batteries and magically disappearing characters—and severe cutting of Shakespeare's text. Generally, New York audiences and critics were enthralled by Daly's presentations, while London reviewers, including Bernard Shaw, were scandalized by his cavalier treatment of Shakespeare's drama, which, they argued, was sacrificed for the sake of sensationalism.

COMMENTARY:

The New York Times (review date 20 August 1873)

[*The excerpt below is from a review of Daly's 1873 production of* A Midsummer Night's Dream *at the Grand Opera House in New York. The critic offers a generally favorable assessment, particularly admiring G. L. Fox's portrayal of Bottom, but he disparages the execution of Shakespeare's verse and Mendelssohn's score.*]

The Fall and Winter season was entered upon at the Grand

Opera house last evening, with a performance of Shakespeare's "Midsummer Night's Dream." We hardly think this exquisite poem susceptible of adequate illustration by the methods resorted to for the representation of ordinary stageplay; but inasmuch as "A Midsummer Night's Dream" was acted for many successive nights, some years since, at the Olympic Theatre; and, furthermore, as it has been given time and again abroad, it is to be supposed that the public are wellcontent to have it removed from the closet to the boards. Yesterday's revival of the piece—for it is a revival only, after all—offered convincing proof that Mr. Daly has striven to realize, by all the means at the command of labor, money, and taste, the ideal of most spectators. There is much good acting in "A Midsummer Night's Dream," as its pictures are successively disclosed at the Grand Opera-house; there are several brilliant and not inappropriate pageants, and the scenery shown is admirable. The delicate love-passages of the story are, of course, those which suffer particularly in their interpretation. If actors in the past have possessed the secret of endowing the dainty words of Shakespeare's dialogue with the charm and eloquence so clear to the most careless reader, their successors in the present have surely not inherited it; and we can expect an intelligent reading of the lines, and nothing more. . . . Mr. G. L. Fox's personation of *Bottom*—a familiar one—is first in order. It is, as may be imagined, a highly entertaining effort. Mr. Fox is not a great comedian, for we are not aware that he has ever elaborated a character; but he has a keen appreciation of humor; the most comical and expressive face now looking upon American audiences, and vast experience. These traits are apparent in *Bottom* as they were in *Humpty Dumpty,* and they are quite as effective. It is impossible not to laugh heartily over the speeches of the weaver as one glances at them in the book, and they are twice as droll when they are delivered, with a countenance and an attire provocative of the wildest mirth, but with an imperturbable gravity, by the performer we write of. Mr. Fox diffused merriment throughout the entertainment and bore off, as was anticipated, the largest share of the honors. A remarkably intelligent personation of *Puck* by little May Templeton, is to be mentioned with Mr. Fox's work as deserving of compliment, and Miss Nina Varian's progress ought not to go unnoticed. Of the pageants, the children's ballet, occurring in the third act, was most conspicuous. The fifty children who disport themselves under the direction of Mme. Lanner present some very pretty groupings, and although their labors should be called evolutions rather than dances—as *ballerine* do not as a rule dance on their heels— they are a pretty sight. The scenery is superb. Every set is not only grateful to the eye, but extremely artistic. A deliciously cool wood in act the second from the brush of Mr. Heister, and a fine panorama unrolled soon after, were greeted with loud applause. As illustrated under Mr. Daly's administration, "A Midsummer Night's Dream" deserves better music, or rather the better execution of that selected; for, if properly rendered, none sweeter could be wished than Mendelssohn's score. M. Predigam, however, needs a stronger force to cope with it. As for the vocal selections, those assigned to Mrs. Bowler received ample justice; the California quartet, in our judgment, might advantageously have been left in California. To the foregoing there is little to add, beyond a record that plaudits were liberally bestowed on artists and pictures, and that Mr. Fox, on his appearance, was the object of a most cordial reception.

A review of "A Midsummer Night's Dream," in The New York Times, *August 20, 1873, p. 5.*

The New York Times (review date 1 February 1888)

[*The anonymous reviewer of Daly's 1888 New York revival asserts that the production of* A Midsummer Night's Dream *was effected by Mr. Daly with "loving reverence for the poet, with scrupulous care in the treatment of the text and the expression of its meaning, with delicacy, refinement, and sumptuous magnificence in the pictorial features."*]

The best in this kind are but shadows.

[V. i. 211].

The dreamland of Shakespeare was pictured on the stage of Daly's Theatre last night; Duke Theseus wedded his amazon queen, Hippolita, and two Athenian maidens, wandering in the moonlight in an "intricate wildwood" with two Athenian youths were sadly perplexed by the pranks of the gentle fairies who held sway there. The dull mechanicals rehearsing their play in the wood were put to flight by Nick Bottom's unaccountable translation. The Queen of the fairies, rebelling against the sway of her lord, was punished for it when, under the spell of his magic, she awoke from her slumbers and "straightway loved an ass." [III. ii. 34]. The antics of Puck were shown in action, and the wildwood teemed with invisible life, and strains of melody were heard in its leafy recesses.

The production of "A Midsummer Night's Dream" has been effected by Mr. Daly with loving reverence for the poet, with scrupulous care in the treatment of the text and the expression of its meaning, with delicacy, refinement, and sumptuous magnificence in the pictorial features. The comedy, perhaps the most difficult of all Shakespeare's plays to render on the stage because of its delicate beauty, its fanciful theme, and the wealth of imagination that its poetry contains, has never before received a performance so nearly perfect as this. The best that can be done, even with all the resources of the modern stage, does not often satisfy the imaginative reader of the poet when an effort is made to give substance, form, and motion to such a creation. A significant fact concerning this revival is that, with all the expenditure of money and thought and time the manager has given to it, he has ever borne in mind that the poetry of Shakespeare, intelligently spoken, conveys more than the use of painted pictures, ingenious grouping, rich dresses, and clever mechanism can possibly convey. The comedy of Shakespeare is presented by actors competent, by reason of their artistic skill and their personal grace, to interpret its meaning: the pageantry is all subordinate to the drama. The stage pictures are all beautiful, however, and many of them are novel and even startling. The falling mists in the wood near Athens, shrouding the scene in darkness, and the assembling of the goblins and fairies by the light of fireflies to sing their melodies around the sleeping lovers form a wonderful piece of stage illusion.

There are many incidents of this memorable first night worthy of description, but there are only a few that can be treated of this morning. The performance was watched with close attention and with constant delight by a house full of spectators. From the opening of the play the favor of the audience was securely held, and there was not at any time a doubt of the success of Mr. Daly's latest venture. Some of the machinery did not work quite as well as it will hereafter, a failing that it is impossible to provide against on the first night of so elaborate a production. But the story was carried forward smoothly and with all needful briskness. The sentiment of the play was expressed with delightful effect. "The pert and nimble spirit of mirth" [I. i. 13] was never lacking. It was no surprise to anybody in the auditorium that the actors should acquit themselves so well in the poetic drama. They were acting in the presence of friends who retained pleasant memories of their triumph in "The Taming of the Shrew." Miss Rehan, as might have been expected, was charming to look upon as Helena, that younger Helena of the poet, whose experience, though told in a sportive vein, is so like that of the Helena of his later years [in *All's Well that Ends Well*]. This was a beautiful portrayal in all its moods—of yearning love, of sorrow and dejection, of childish pettishness, of happy merriment. Miss Dreher, too, was a lovely Hermia, giving abundant spirit to her scene of ill-temper and pique, and sweetly communicating the tenderness of the maiden. Mr. Drew and Mr. Skinner as Demetrius and Lysander were both graceful, ardent, and gallant. And Mr. Lewis as Nick Bottom gave expression to the rich humor of this famous personage with masterly effect. But before we give further attention to the players let us briefly consider the play itself as Mr. Daly has arranged it for his stage.

The arrangement of the play for performance on the stage was newly made for this production, and it need not be said that the traditions of the theatre were not servilely followed in its making. It is an entirely new rendering of Shakespeare's work, and it adheres more closely to the text of the poet than any other existing prompt book of "A Midsummer Night's Dream." There is little of the coarseness that was tolerated in the Elizabethan age in this play, and what little there is has been properly expunged. Very few changes have been made merely to suit the conditions of the present performance, and those in no way mar the melody of the verse or cloud its meaning. The allusions to Hermia's short stature are of course omitted, and some of the sharp words that fair Athenian maid uses in her quarrel with Helena have also been dispensed with. All the best remembered lines of the text are spoken on the stage, and the elusions in the dialogue have all been made with absolute fidelity to the spirit of the work. Shakespeare's play contains 2,174 lines, and less than 400 of these have been discarded.

It is the opinion of most Shakespearian students that "A Midsummer Night's Dream" is one of the poet's early works. One of the ablest of the commentators thinks that in it we find for the first time "Shakespeare's genius in the full glow of fancy and delightful fun." Mr. Furnivall places it even before "The Two Gentlemen of Verona," and Prof. Dowden places it in his list next after that play. It contains an uncommonly large proportion of rhyming lines, and bears other evidence, in the opinion of these and other sagacious critics, of the poet's immaturity. But these speculations scarcely concern the stage representation.

The first act of Mr. Daly's version comprises the first scene of the original, with less than 25 lines omitted. The second act begins with the meeting of the hard-handed men of Athens at the house of Peter Quince, and the "cuts" are slight and of no importance. The wood near Athens is then revealed, and in this scene the longest "cut" of the play is made, 30 lines being omitted after Titania's speech beginning:

These are the forgeries of jealousy.

[II. i. 81]

The first transposition of incidents occurs here, the episode involving the wandering lovers being carried forward without a break, to close the act with the revels of Titania and her train, and the vision of Oberon placing his spell upon the fairy queen's eyes. Act III. closely adheres to Shakespeare's text,

with one slight transportation, and remarkably few elisions. The transposition of incidents in Act IV. for the sake of pictorial effect, in no way disturb the sequence of incidents, and the last act is as Shakespeare wrote it, except that Demetrius reads to Theseus the list of promised entertainments and the dialogue is somewhat condensed. These facts are dwelt upon to indicate how reverently the poet has been treated in this production.

There will be plenty of time in the future to review the acting in "A Midsummer Night's Dream;" to do justice to the actors who act all their parts so well; to speak at length of Mr. Fisher's impressive sketch of old Egeus; of Mr. Joseph Holland's successful embodiment of the dignity and gentleness of Theseus; of Miss Russell's queenly Hippolita; of the drollery of the mimic play before the Duke, of the exquisite grace of the scenes of fairyland. Miss Shannon is Titania, Miss Alice Hood Oberon, Miss Bijou Fernandez Puck. The pageantry includes a panoramic view of the passage of the barge of Theseus through the wood to the piers of Athens. This is a striking picture, and the spectators cheered it lustily.

The atmosphere of dreamland pervades the work, and as an interpretation of poetry it has never been surpassed on our stage. It will be on view for the remainder of the Winter, everybody will see it, and everybody will praise it.

A review of "A Midsummer Night's Dream," in The New York Times, *February 1, 1888, p. 5.*

The New York Times   (review date 5 February 1888)

[*In the excerpt below, the reviewer judges the settings and costumes of Daly's production ideally suited to Shakespeare's conception of the locations and characters in* A Midsummer Night's Dream.]

The deftness and ingenuity with which the fantastical element in Shakespeare's fairy play is managed in the present valuable revival at Daly's Theatre deserve all the commendation they have received; but in the acting lies the substantial worth of the representation.

The loveliness of the scenic pictures is not to be denied. The Grecian architecture in the views of the palace; the vast and antique wood through which in the moonlight "a maze of light and life and motion is woven;" the passage of the royal barge among the islets to the stone and marble city with stately Mount Hymettus rising in the distance; the falling mists; the revels of the fairies by the fireflies' light; the visions of dreamland revealed as the estranged lovers sleep on their soft couches in the forest: the rising of the young moon "like to a silver bow, new bent in the heavens" [I. i. 9-10], as Titania rests and piqued Oberon places his spell upon her—all these enchant the eye and justly convey a sense of the mystery and beauty of the subject. The dresses are tasteful and accurate in the true sense of that word, as applied to the appointments of a play. What kind of clothes the aboriginal Greeks may have worn in the thirteenth century before the Christian era it would puzzle the most diligent archaeologist to determine: probably they wore very little of anything worth mentioning. Shakespeare undoubtedly had in mind the regal splendor of Athens in the historic age; but his fantasy belongs to no particular era: the hobbledehoys of his Athens are rustics of the poet's own Warwickshire; the "musical discord" Hippolita heard in Sparta came from the sturdy throats of English hounds, and Shakespeare himself had often seen the pack Theseus describes—

With ears that sweep away the morning dew.

[IV. i. 121]

The fairies belong to the poet's own imagination; they originated with him. Oberon and Titania when they meet in the wood have just journeyed from the India of the Elizabethan age—dimly known as a region of mystery and barbaric splendor—when Drake circumnavigated the globe and voyager Thomas Stephens's glowing epistles to his father in London gave birth to the enthusiasm that led to the formation of the great East India Company. They are the first fairies of their own whimsical kind in English literature; they are creatures of the lanes and groves of old England so often contemplated by the poet, and the most exquisite lines spoken by their King relate to the virginity of Elizabeth. So the fantasy cannot be given an exact historical setting. Theseus and his Queen are suitably attired in garments such as Pericles and his court might have worn, and all the dresses are Grecian; the chiton, himation, diploidion, and the fillet have all been either simulated or suggested in the designs of the costumer. The architecture suggests that of the golden age of art in Greece. The tones of color are harmonious; the materials of the dresses are rich and costly. The attire of the principal fairies, of beautiful fabrics, is purposely made after purely conventional patterns, the important fact being realized by Mr. Daly that these personages must talk and act, love and suffer the pangs of jealousy like human beings, and that any attempt to make them look like ethereal spirits, dim, shadowy, and grotesque, would inevitably destroy the meaning of the episodes in which they figure. Puck is a merry, knowing child clad like a little forester. But the goblin element is not lacking, for the little imps that attend on Titania are eerie figures, exactly in keeping with the spirit of the scenes in which they appear. These goblins are worthy of the pencil of Doré. The music, selected partly from Mendelssohn's delightful "Sommernachtstraum" and partly from various English composers, is rendered in a manner that increases the charm of the performance.

But all these things are merely accessories, and subordinate to the acting. The prominence gained by Mr. Daly for his theatre is due to his skill in choosing actors and his ability to train them to work harmoniously together. He now has the best comedy company of the English stage, and he has put forward this play, without dwelling in the announcements

Theseus is the most august person in the play if the dramatic value of the part is not great, and Mr. Joseph Holland reads the beautiful lines of the text with nice appreciation and fills the idea of Shakespeare's Theseus, who was not much like the Theseus of other poets, the kinsman of Megara and Herakles, the abductor of the amazon, the husband of Phædra and the father of Hippolitus. The learning, the politeness, the gentleness of an English gentleman like Raleigh or Southampton, the poet's patrons, belong to this Prince. His heart is full of kindness; he has sympathy with the meanest of his fellow-men; he is a philosopher as well as a soldier; he knows poetry and understands poets. Miss Phoebe Russell, as Hippolita, is a fitting consort to the kingly Theseus of Mr. Holland, and she too delivers the text with uncommon intelligence. This Prince and Princess Shakespeare got from Chaucer, and they reappear in the same epoch of their lives in "The Two Noble Kinsmen," where, in the best judgment of recent critics, Shakespeare put them. Another fine figure in this revival is

the aged Egeus of Mr. Fisher, wonderfully picturesque, firm, strong, and true, and essentially Shakespearean.

The quartet of perplexed lovers exactly reflect the grace, the ardor, and the bewilderment expressed in the love scenes of the play. Mr. Drew gets further away from himself than ever before in depicting the "spotted and inconstant" Demetrius: there is nothing modern in his action, and both he and Mr. Skinner read verse fluently and with understanding, as was shown in "The Taming of the Shrew." If Miss Dreher's Hermia is not a "little vixen," she is what Shakespeare's Hermia surely should be, a loving and lovable woman, and Miss Rehan's Helena will be held in memory as one of her sweetest and most delightful portrayals. The plastic grace and the perfect sincerity of this embodiment are its distinguishing characteristics. The part does not admit of the revelation of emotional power, and its touches of humor are delicate and elusive. Helena is a gentle, simple-minded woman absorbed by love, and in the dreamland she follows her inconstant lover bodily, as in the practical world such a woman would ever keep her lover in her thoughts. Helena is merely the poetic counterpart of Laura Pendennis, and she is the direct predecessor in Shakespeare of the other Helena, whose experience had more of shadow in it, as her nature was deeper and stronger—the heroine of "All's Well That Ends Well." Both are types of womanly faith and devotion. While the part has not the piquancy or force of Katharine [in *The Taming of the Shrew*], Miss Rehan's acting in Helena is as fine and true as her treatment of the shrew. She has made a splendid beginning in Shakespearean comedy and her future work in that direction would not be hard to predict. The scenes of perplexity in the forest are admirably treated by all four of these players, and in them the greatest worth of this revival may be found.

As they become used to their parts the representatives of the principal fairies will constantly gain in facility. The fairy scenes are difficult; it has, indeed, been thought impossible to put them on the stage, but the play was written for the stage and was acted with crude accessories. Miss Effie Shannon has the litheness of figure and the delicate prettiness needful for Titania, and she has a clear conception of all the dramatic possibilities of the part, which, after all, are not great. A handsome fairy King and a cunninger Puck could not be found than Miss Alice Hood and Miss Fernandez, and both are now free from the nervousness that somewhat hampered them on the first night. The subordinate fairies are all pretty and their antics are fairylike, and Miss St. Quinten's roguish manner and sweet singing voice are well utilized in the fantastic episodes.

And now for the crew of patches, who, like the Roman citizens of "Julius Caesar," the roystering Illyrian cavaliers, and the Veronese clowns, are clear reproductions of the droll louts of Stratford and the country about it. All of the hardhanded men are happily represented—Mr. Leclercq, Mr. Bond, a comic actor of remarkable versatility; Mr. Wood, and Mr. Wilks lacking nothing in the way of inherent humor or artistic skill. But they are not likely to lack their full share of appreciation either. Mr. Lewis's performance of Bully Bottom is the only subject of dispute. This is one of the richest bits of low comedy our stage has ever known. It has been received every night since last Tuesday with shouts of laughter. The stupidity, the self-sufficiency, the unconscious humor of this weaver of Athens have provoked uncontrollable mirth. The salient characteristics of Nick Bottom are those of a don-

Theseus's barge, Act V, Daly's production.

key, and Mr. Lewis has made them perfectly plain; the transformation only changes his physical aspect. The portrayal is remarkably well poised, is free from exaggeration and vulgarity, is crisp and distinct in execution. But Burton acted Bottom, and there are lots of persons alive who know that Burton was a large, stout man, with a heavy voice. The opinion has been frequently expressed lately that Bottom should be stolid and unctuous—not nimble and quaint. But many stupid persons are nimble and quaint, and, moreover, there is a good deal of shrewd cunning in this amateur actor of Athens. Traditions of the stage are hard to overcome. Burton used to do Dogberry as well as Bottom, and when he acted the foolish officer of "Much Ado" the gray-haired playgoers of that time used to shake their heads and exclaim: "Funny, to be sure, but not the character at all; Dogberry ought to be a small, dry man; you ought to have seen Barnes!" Barnes then was only a memory. He was the reigning comic actor of an earlier day, and he was a small, dry man. Hence Dogberry should be small and dry. No low comedian of any age ever had a more amusing personality, a keener sense of dramatic effect, a better knowledge of human nature than James Lewis. We predict that his portrayal of Nick Bottom will be remembered in the twentieth century to the detriment of some plump actor with a deep voice and slow locomotive power. For the present he is the living embodiment of fun, and the doleful tragedy of "Pyramus and Thisbe," done before the Duke, makes all the old folks who go to Daly's forget their ills and their Burton. (pp. 4-5)

A review of "A Midsummer Night's Dream," in The New York Times, *February 5, 1888, pp. 4-5.*

William Winter   (review date 18 February 1888)

[*Winter was a conservative American dramatic critic who es-*

chewed innovation, theatrical realism, and non-Anglo-American actors. He served as dramatic critic for the New York Tribune *from 1865 to 1909 and wrote several theatrical biographies. In the excerpt below from his review of Daly's 1888 staging of* A Midsummer Night's Dream, *Winter praises the "delicacy and splendor" of its "scenic embellishments" and the performances of its "almost faultless cast."*]

It is the involuntary action of a poet's mind which imparts to his writings the crowning glory of inspiration. He may impress and satisfy the judgment by virtue of his preconceived purpose; he arouses the imagination and touches the heart only through the spontaneous volition of his genius. This is a good truth to remember when reading SHAKESPEARE, with whose great name the dull wit of detraction is often busy. SHAKESPEARE's plays, it is urged, had their origin in necessity and thrift; any other view of the subject is ideal, and therefore foolish; SHAKESPEARE wrote for the stage because he wanted money, and precisely as any hack dramatist of the present day writes for it. The late RICHARD GRANT WHITE entertained that opinion, and he stated it well. It is one thing, however, to declare, and another thing to convince; and a man may have profound scholarship without comprehending the soul of SHAKESPEARE. Many actors, although in a different spirit, are prone to assign specific limits to that illimitable genius, fondly and not unnaturally claiming that SHAKESPEARE wrote solely and exclusively for them, and some of them seem to think that but for the stage he would not have written at all.

Such reasoning is seen to be fallacious the moment it is viewed in the intrinsic light of his works, and tested by the ascertained laws which govern the operation of the human intellect. SHAKESPEARE, without doubt, got money for writing plays, and was pleased to get it; and equally, without doubt SHAKESPEARE was influenced by that potent dramatic movement—ancient in Italy, youthful in England, and then as yet unfelt in France—which made the dominant drift of literature in his time. But the ability to express and interpret human nature in dramatic forms is not created by the existence of a public demand for plays. There is a most opulent and eager "market" for a SHAKESPEARE now, but it does not produce him. Furthermore, each of SHAKESPEARE'S greater plays abounds with inspired passages, such as not the promise of all the gold in Ophir's mountain could have extorted from the mere mercenary hack. The requirements of the stage, even in our time of profuse and complex mechanical contrivance, are much more than fulfilled by SHAKESPEARE'S plays. Every one of them has to be shortened and altered before it can be acted. He did indeed write for the stage, but it happens that his works transcend every stage, and are superior to all actors and quite independent of the theatre; their greatness, their puissant vitality, and their charm consisting in their quality of inspiration. It manifestly was his nature to write in the dramatic vein, to express at once the form, the picture, and the movement of human life, and he would have uttered himself in this vein even had there been no Globe Theatre and no BURBAGE. The impulse arose in the depth of his own soul; it was not derived from his circumstances. All true art springs from an elemental source, and that source is not a money-bag.

The beautiful production of *A Midsummer Night's Dream* that Mr. AUGUSTIN DALY has made at his theatre, since it serves to turn the public attention again and specially upon SHAKESPEARE'S poetry, will serve a good purpose at this time in teaching this lesson. No happier illustration of SHAKESPEARE'S method illumined by SHAKESPEARE'S inspiration could readily be found than is provided in this ethereal and lovely comedy. This piece, according to an accepted tradition, was written by him with special reference to an occasion—to the nuptials of the Earl of Southampton and ELIZABETH VERNON. Here was the preconceived purpose to produce a play which would fit and satisfy the need of the hour; but here also was the inspiration of poetic genius, the involuntary golden tide of imagination and feeling, back of the purpose, and certain to irradiate it; so that when at length SHAKESPEARE had wrought out his plan, and the comedy was finished, he had created a drama so aerial in its grotesque fancy, so subtle and elusive in its poetic loveliness, that it has caused many a commentator to become entangled with his own ears, and generally has perplexed and baffled the players, for wellnigh three centuries. SPENSER had made fairies familiar to the readers of poetry, but never before had fairies been introduced into a play, and made in that manner participant in mortal affairs. SHAKESPEARE'S plan, it is easy to perceive, was redolent of his subject. The scene is Athens, in order that the tone may be chaste and fine, the architecture stately, the landscape luxuriant, the attire beautiful. Theseus and Hippolyte are to be wedded after the lapse of four days. How shall this "gap of time" be made populous and active? The theme shall be love. The argument shall be the perplexities of mating lovers, who at first are playfully perplexed, but finally are harmonized and rewarded, by the operation of fairy magic. Oberon and Titania, the fairy king and queen, attended by their sprites, shall hover about the imperial pair, and ultimately unite to prosper and bless them. Common life, with a comic strain in it, shall be intertwined with this fantastic web of fancy. The action shall mostly pass in a woodland region of phantasy and dream. And at last shall come a splendid and jubilant revel at the fulfilment of youthful hopes and the coronation of happy love. So much, no doubt, was involved and forecast in the poet's plan; but the floods of felicitous thought, noble imagery, and poetic eloquence that pour themselves through his execution of it are too affluent not to be spontaneous. The lines on marriage and "single blessedness" [I. i. 78]; on "the course of true love" [I. i. 134]; on the tempestuous English summer (of 1594); on the "fair vestal" and "Cupid all armed" [II. i. 158, 157]; on imagination as shown in lover, madman, and poet; on the friendships of youth; on the music of the hounds, "matched in mouth like bells, each under each" [IV. i. 123-24]—what are these but the excess of richness with which the spirit of SHAKESPEARE continually overflowed?

A Midsummer Night's Dream has seldom been acted. GARRICK produced unsuccessfully a version of it, made by himself in 1763 at Drury Lane; CHARLES KEAN accomplished a sumptuous revival of it at the Princess's Theatre, London, about forty years ago; SAMUEL PHELPS subsequently gave a scholar-like production of it at Sadler's Wells. Its first presentation in America was made on November 9, 1826, at the old Park Theatre. The most important revival of it prior to that now effected by Mr. DALY was that offered by W. E. BURTON on February 6, 1854, at Burton's Theatre, when that great comedian himself enacted Bottom. It had a run of one hundred nights at the New York Olympic in 1867, with the late G. L. FOX as Bottom, and with a panorama by TELBIN. Mr. DALY himself presented it at the Grand Opera-house in 1873, and he now brings it forward again after fifteen years of disuse. This time it is adorned with scenic embellishments of a delicacy and splendor quite compatible with its own, besides having the advantage of an almost faultless cast. Miss ADA REHAN plays Helena; Miss VIRGINIA DREHER, Hermia; Mr. JOHN DREW, Demetrius; Mr. OTIS SKINNER, Lysander; Mr. CHARLES FISHER, Ægeus; Mr. JAMES LEWIS, Bottom; Mr. JOSEPH HOLLAND, Theseus. And all these parts are well played. Mr. LEWIS has caused some little controversy among critical observers by investing Bottom with a lively temperament and a rapid manner instead of the dull, ruminant mood and slow demeanor with which it has been customary to embody it. The essential fact about Bottom is that he is a most consummate ass without ever knowing it, though once he becomes comically amazed at having dreamed of it. So long as the colossal self-conceit is maintained, and the delineation remains unconsciously humorous, it surely matters not whether the manner be sluggish or alert. The danger of the brisk manner is display of too much intelligence. Mr. Lewis gives a studied, symmetrical, and very comical performance.

There is some weakness, where it might be expected, in the fairy realm; for the Oberon is defective in elocution, the Titania, though a feast to the eye, is modern and conventional, and the painful precocity of the Puck creates a sense of weariness. Nevertheless, the management of the fairy scenes is marked by perfect sympathy with the spirit of the piece and by a most pleasing and convincing grace. There is a scene in which Titania is lulled to sleep by the songs of her fairies; and then the fire-flies flash through the mist, and sounds are audible such as haunt the woods by night, and the dark boughs seem to shimmer under the faint light of stars, and presently the moon rises and half illumines the green and fragrant dells, though only to deepen their charm of romantic mystery. No scenic pageant more lovely than this, or more deftly handled, has been shown upon the American stage. Toward the close of the piece a barge is presented, wherein Theseus and the other chief mortals of the story—all the bewilderments of the haunted woodland being now over—are seen sailing down to Athens; and here is displayed, after the precedent indicated in TELBIN'S work, a gorgeous panorama, showing the riverbanks and the contiguous landscape as seen from the barge or from a distant eminence commanding the whole prospect. It is a feast of color and truly a marvel of illusion; and as you gaze upon it your senses are bewitched by the enchanting music of MENDELSSOHN, and you realize indeed the ecstasy of a happy dream.

William Winter, "Mr. Daly's Latest Revival," in
Harper's Weekly, *Vol. XXXII, No. 1626, February
18, 1888, p. 115.*

Bernard Shaw   (review date 13 July 1895)

[*Shaw, an Irish dramatist and critic, was the major English playwright of his generation. His hostility toward Shakespeare, evident in his criticism of the poet's work, was based in large measure on his belief that Shakespeare's reputation as a dramatist was inflated and that his plays interfered with the acceptance of Henrik Ibsen and the new social theater he so strongly advocated. Shaw served as theater critic for the* Saturday Review *from 1895 to 1898. The following excerpt is from his* Saturday Review *assessment of Daly's production when it was offered in London in 1895. Shaw is contemptuous of the scenic aspects of this staging, but greatly admires Ada Rehan's performance as Helena.*]

"The Two Gentlemen of Verona" has been succeeded at Daly's Theatre by "A Midsummer Night's Dream." Mr. Daly is in great form. In my last article I was rash enough to hint that he had not quite realized what could be done with electric lighting on the stage. He triumphantly answers me by fitting up all his fairies with portable batteries and incandescent lights, which they switch on and off from time to time, like children with a new toy. He has trained Miss Lillian Swain in the part of Puck until it is safe to say that she does not take one step, strike one attitude, or modify her voice by a single inflexion that is not violently, wantonly, and ridiculously wrong and absurd. Instead of being mercurial, she poses academically, like a cheap Italian statuette; instead of being impish and childish, she is elegant and affected; she laughs a solemn, measured laugh, like a heavy German Zamiel; she announces her ability to girdle the earth in forty minutes in the attitude of a professional skater, and then begins the journey awkwardly in a swing, which takes her in the opposite direction to that in which she indicated her intention of going: in short, she illustrates every folly and superstition that still clings round what Mr. Daly no doubt calls "the legitimate." Another stroke of his is to make Oberon a woman. It must not be supposed that he does this solely because it is wrong, though there is no other reason apparent. He does it partly because he was brought up to do such things, and partly because they seem to him to be a tribute to Shakespeare's greatness, which, being uncommon, ought not to be interpreted according to the dictates of common sense. A female Oberon and a Puck who behaves like a page-boy earnestly training himself for the post of footman recommend themselves to him because they totally destroy the naturalness of the representation, and so accord with his conception of the Shakespearean drama as the most artificial of all forms of stage entertainment. That is how you find out the man who is not an artist. Verse, music, the beauties of dress, gesture, and movement are to him interesting aberrations instead of

being the natural expression which human feeling seeks at a certain degree of delicacy and intensity. He regards art as a quaint and costly ring in the nose of Nature. I am loth to say that Mr. Daly is such a man; but after studying all his Shakespearean revivals with the thirstiest desire to find as much art as possible in them, I must mournfully confess that the only idea I can see in them is the idea of titivation. As to his slaughterings of the text, how can one help feeling them acutely in a play like "A Midsummer Night's Dream," in which Shakespeare, having to bring Nature in its most enchanting aspect before an audience without the help of theatrical scenery, used all his power of description and expression in verse with such effect that the utmost any scene-painter can hope for is to produce a picture that shall not bitterly disappoint the spectator who has read the play beforehand? Mr. Daly is, I should say, one of those people who are unable to conceive that there could have been any illusion at all about the play before scenery was introduced. He certainly has no suspicion of the fact that every accessory he employs is brought in at the deadliest risk of destroying the magic spell woven by the poet. He swings Puck away on a clumsy trapeze with a ridiculous clash of the cymbals in the orchestra, in the fullest belief that he is thereby completing instead of destroying the effect of Puck's lines. His "panoramic illusion of the passage of Theseus's barge to Athens" is more absurd than anything that occurs in the tragedy of Pyramus and Thisbe in the last act. The stage management blunders again and again through feeble imaginative realization of the circumstances of the drama. In the first act it should be clear to any stage manager that Lysander's speech, beginning "I am, my lord, as well derived as he" [I. i. 99], should be spoken privately and not publicly to Theseus. In the rehearsal scene in the wood, Titania should not be conspicuously exhibited under a limelight in the very centre of the stage, where the clowns have, in defiance of all common sanity, to pretend not to see her. We are expected, no doubt, to assume that she is invisible because she is a fairy, though Bottom's conversation with her when she wakes and addresses him flatly contradicts that hypothesis. In the fourth act, Theseus has to enter from his barge down a bank, picking his way through the sleeping Lysander and Hermia, Demetrius and Helena. The four lions in Trafalgar Square are not more conspicuous and unoverlookable than these four figures are. Yet Theseus has to make all his hunting speeches in an impossible unconsciousness of them, and then to look at them amazedly and exclaim, "But soft, what nymphs are these?" [IV. i. 127] as if he could in any extremity of absence of mind have missed seeing them all along. Most of these absurdities are part of a systematic policy of sacrificing the credibility of the play to the chance of exhibiting an effective "living picture."

I very soon gave up the attempt to keep a record of the outrages practised by Mr. Daly on the text. Everyone knows the lines:

> I swear to thee by Cupid's strongest bow,
> By his best arrow with the golden head,
> By the simplicity of Venus' doves,
> By that which knitteth souls and prospers loves, &c.
>
> [I. i. 169-72]

Mr. Daly's powerful mind perceived at a glance that the second and third lines are superfluous, as their omission does not destroy the sense of the passage. He accordingly omitted them. In the same scene, Shakespeare makes the two star-crossed lovers speak in alternate lines with an effect which sets the whole scene throbbing with their absorption in one another:

LYSANDER: The course of true love never did run
      smooth.
      But either it was different in blood—
HERMIA: O cross! too high to be enthralled to low!
LYSANDER: Or else misgraffed in respect of years,
HERMIA: O spite! too old to be engaged to young!
LYSANDER: Or else it stood upon the choice of friends,
HERMIA: O hell! to choose love by another's eye!
LYSANDER: Or if there were a sympathy in choice,
      War, death, or sickness did lay siege to it, &c.

[I. i. 134-42]

With a Hermia who knew how to breathe out these parentheses, the duet would be an exquisite one; but Mr. Daly, shocked, as an American and an Irishman, at a young lady using such an expression as "Oh hell!" cuts out the whole antiphony, and leaves Lysander to deliver a long lecture without interruption from the lady. At such moments, the episode of the ass's head rises to the dignity of allegory. From any other manager I should accept the excuse that the effects of verse for which I am pleading require a virtuosity of delivery on the part of the actor which is practically not to be had at present. But Mr. Daly has Miss Rehan, who is specially famous for just this virtuosity of speech; and yet her lines are treated just as the others are. The fact is, beautiful elocution is rare because the managers have no ears.

The play, though of course very poorly spoken in comparison with how it ought to be spoken, is tolerably acted. Mr. George Clarke, clad in the armour of Alcibiades and the red silk gown of Charlie's Aunt, articulates most industriously, and waves his arms and flexes his wrists in strict accordance, not for a moment with the poetry, but with those laws of dramatic elocution and gesture which veteran actors are always willing to impart to novices at a reasonable price per dozen lessons. Mr. Lewis as Bottom is not as funny as his part, whereas in modern plays he is always funnier than his part. He seemed to me to miss the stolid, obstinate, self-sufficient temperament of Bottom altogether. There is a definite conception of some particular sort of man at the back of all Shakespeare's characters. The quantity of fun to be got out of Bottom and Autolycus [in *The Winter's Tale*], for instance, is about the same; but underneath the fun there are two widely different persons, of types still extant and familiar. Mr. Lewis would be as funny in Autolycus as he is in Bottom; but he would be exactly the same man in both parts.

As to Miss Rehan, her scenes in the wood with Demetrius were very fine, although, in the passage where Hermia frightens her, she condescended to arrant clowning. Her treatment of Shakespearean verse is delightful after the mechanical intoning of Sarah Bernhardt. She gives us beauty of tone, grace of measure, delicacy of articulation: in short, all the technical qualities of verse music, along with the rich feeling and fine intelligence without which those technical qualities would soon become monotonous. When she is at her best, the music melts in the caress of the emotion it expresses, and thus completes the conditions necessary for obtaining Shakespeare's effects in Shakespeare's way. When she is on the stage, the play asserts its full charm; and when she is gone, and the stage carpenters and the orchestra are doing their best to pull the entertainment through in Mr. Daly's way, down drops the whole affair into mild tedium. But it is impossible to watch the most recent developments of Miss Rehan's style without some uneasiness. I wonder whether she is old enough to re-

member the late Barry Sullivan when he was still in his physical prime. Those who do will recall, not an obsolete provincial tragedian, trading on the wreck of an unaccountable reputation, but an actor who possessed in an extraordinary degree just the imposing grace, the sensitive personal dignity of style, the force and self-reliance into which Miss Rehan's style is settling. Miss Rehan's exit in the second act of "A Midsummer Night's Dream," with the couplet,

I'll follow thee, and make a heaven of hell
To die upon the hand I love so well.

[II. i. 243-44]

is an exact reproduction of the Barry Sullivan exit. Again, in the first act, when Miss Rehan, prone on a couch, raises herself on her left hand, and, with her right raised "to heaven," solemnly declaims the lines:

For ere Demetrius look'd on Hermia's eyne He hailed down oaths, that he was only mine; And when this hail some heat from Hermia felt, So he dissolved, and showers of oaths did melt,

[I. i. 242-45]

you are, once more, not forward with Duse, but back with Barry Sullivan, who would in just the same way, when led into it by a touch of stateliness and sonority in the lines, abandon his part, and become for the moment a sort of majestic incarnation of abstract solemnity and magnificence. His skill and intense belief in himself gave him the dangerous power of doing so without making himself ridiculous; and it was by this power, and by the fascination, the grace, and the force which are implied by it, that he gave life to old-fashioned and mutilated representations of Shakespeare's plays, poorly acted and ignorantly mounted. This was all very well whilst the fascination lasted; but when his voice lost its tone, his figure its resilience and grace, and his force its spontaneity and natural dignity, there was nothing left but a mannered, elderly, truculent, and, except to his old admirers, rather absurd tragedian of the palmy school. As I was a small boy when I first saw Barry Sullivan, and as I lost sight of him before his waning charm had quite vanished, I remember him, not as he is remembered by those who saw him only in the last ten years of his life, but as an actor who was in his day much further superior in pictorial, vocal, and rhetorical qualities to his next best rival than any actor or actress can easily be nowadays. And it strikes me forcibly that unless Miss Rehan takes to playing Imogen [in *Cymbeline*] instead of such comparatively childish stuff as Julia [in *The Two Gentlemen of Verona*] or even Helena, and unless she throws herself into sympathy with the contemporary movement by identifying herself with characteristically modern parts of the Magda or Nora type, she may find herself left behind in the race by competitors of much less physical genius, just as Barry Sullivan did. Miss Rehan is clearly absolute mistress of the situation at Daly's Theatre: nobody can persuade me that if she says "Cymbeline," Mr. Daly can say "The Two Gentlemen of Verona," or that if she says Sudermann or Ibsen, Mr. Daly can insist on the author of "Dollars and Cents." But the self-culture which has produced her superb graces of manner and diction seems to have isolated her instead of quickening her sympathy and drawing closer her contact with the world. Every woman who sees Duse play Magda feels that Duse is acting and speaking for her and for all women as they are hardly ever able to speak and act for themselves. The same may be said of Miss Achurch as Nora. But no woman has ever had the very faintest sensation of that kind about any part that Miss Rehan has yet played. We admire, not what she is doing, but the charm with which she does it. That sort of admiration will not last. Miss Rehan's voice is not henceforth going to grow fresher, nor her dignity less conscious, nor her grace of gesture less studied and mannered, nor her movements swifter and more spontaneous. Already I find that young people who see her for the first time cannot quite agree that our raptures about her Katharine [in *The Taming of the Shrew*] and her Rosalind [in *As You Like It*] are borne out by her Julia and Helena. Five years hence she will be still more rhetorical and less real: further ahead I dare not look with Barry Sullivan in my mind. There is only one way to defy Time; and that is to have young ideas, which may always be trusted to find youthful and vivid expression. I am afraid this means avoiding the company of Mr. Daly; but it is useless to blink the fact that unless a modern actress can and will force her manager, in spite of his manly prejudices, to produce plays with real women's parts in them, she had better, at all hazards, make shift to manage for herself. With Grandfather Daly to choose her plays for her, there is no future for Ada Rehan. (pp. 43-5)

Bernard Shaw, "Toujours Daly," in The Saturday Review, *London, Vol. 80, No. 2072, July 13, 1895, pp. 43-5.*

William Archer   (review date 17 July 1895)

[*Archer offers a lukewarm review of a 17 July 1895 perfor-*

Ada Rehan as Helena.

mance of Daly's A Midsummer Night's Dream. *He finds particular fault with Daly's cutting of Shakespeare's text, observing that* "Daly *is fatally suggestive of* Dele."]

Pleasure first, duty afterwards; it is a pleasure to thank Mr. Daly for what he has done, before remonstrating with him for what he has left undone. There is much—very much—to enjoy in his revival of *A Midsummer Night's Dream*. I have seen it twice, and I enjoyed it more the second time than the first—probably because I was prepared in advance for the inadequacies and stupidities of the performance, and was therefore able to concentrate my attention on its beauties. No doubt, too, the delight of my companion on the second occasion—a boy of ten—was in some degree contagious. It was better than a pantomime to him; and this I say without any sort of sneer. It was better because it was fundamentally beautiful. Had the poem been simply vulgarised, I should have been very careful not to let him see it. He clearly felt, though he could not have explained, the difference between this harmoniously-developed fable and the travestied nurserytales of Christmastide, between these exquisite verses (some of them beautifully spoken) and the doggerel patter of the pantomime librettist. What was vulgar and pantomimic in the production pleased him less than the rest, or not at all. Mr. Clarke's Theseus he could not away with; the pantomime mask which Mr. Daly has substituted for the elfin Mustardseed simply puzzled him in its incongruity; and his remark on the famous "panoramic illusion" was, "It only makes you dizzy." Now the public, I take it, is in these matters simply a child of larger growth: it feels a great deal that it cannot explain or express, even to itself. Mr. Daly regards us critics as a set of visionary, if not malicious, pedants, because we worry over his cuts and transpositions, and are careful and cumbered about syllables and accents. "What does the public know or care about these things?" he asks. "If I cut half-a-dozen lines here and there, who misses them? Not one person in a hundred. And if a syllable or two is omitted or inserted in a blank verse line, do you suppose that the public notices it?" In these cases, it is true, only a small percentage of any given audience knows what is wrong, or is even clearly conscious that there is anything wrong at all; but it does not therefore follow that, even from the practical, managerial, dollars-and-cents point of view, the errors are not worth putting right. The manager's aim is, and must be, to give the largest possible sum of pleasure to his audience; and if he cuts or maltreats a beautiful passage which would have given pleasure, he in so far diminishes that sum, even though not one of his audience may distinctly realise the loss. The resultant impression of such a performance is made up of an innumerable host of small sensations. Every line, to carry the analysis no further, may, or rather must, produce in the hearer one of three conditions: satisfaction, indifference, or dissatisfaction. Now, Mr. Daly will surely admit that a line spoken as Shakespeare wrote it has a better chance of making the needle veer towards "Satisfaction" than one stupidly or carelessly misspoken. If it be delivered with grace and feeling, it will send the mental indicator of those who are sensitive to these things flying to the extreme of "Satisfaction"—to delight— and it will give a vague pleasure even to the unskilful. Misspoken, on the other hand, it will at best leave the indicator at "Indifference" in the unskilful, while in those who know (and, after all, there are *some* people with an ear for verse in every audience) it will deflect the needle more or less violently on the side of "Dissatisfaction," not to say disgust. This is not a matter in which, by pleasing the few, you run the risk of displeasing the many. No one actively prefers a bad line to a good, though many may not see the difference or may be unable to explain it. For instance, when Mr. Daly suffers Mr. George Clarke to say, "The poet's eye, in fine frenzy rolling" [cf. V. i. 12], not a soul in the audience is pleased, while many are tortured, by the omission of the single letter "a." For my part, it makes my hand steal towards my pistol-pocket; for I feel that, unlike the musician at whom the Western audience was requested not to shoot, the actor is *not* "doing his best." If he does not know the difference between verse and prose, he might at least mechanically memorise the plain words of his part. And let not Mr. Daly think this a trifling matter. That single inexcusable blunder might quite well prove the last straw to a sensitive playgoer, and send him away with a general impression of dissatisfaction which, spreading among his friends and acquaintances, would keep out of the treasury an indefinite number of half-crowns and half-sovereigns.

On the whole, Mr. Daly has dealt not ungently with *A Midsummer Night's Dream*. His transpositions are inessential, and his excisions are not so inhuman as they are apt to be. In the main, he lets Shakespeare tell his story in his own way; and that is all we ask. But though Mr. Daly has not been so truculent in his slashing as he sometimes is, many priceless lines and passages have fallen before his blue pencil. There is much in a name, and *Daly* is fatally suggestive of *Dele*. How could he find it in his heart, for instance, to mutilate this passage:

Lysander.	Ah, me! for ought that ever I could read,
	Could ever hear by tale or history,
	The course of true love never did run smooth:
	But, either it was different in blood;
Hermia.	O cross! too high to be enthrall'd to low!
Lys.	Or else misgraffed, in respect of years;
Her.	O spite! too old to be engag'd to young!
Lys.	Or else it stood upon the choice of friends:
Her.	O hell! to choose love by another's eye!
Lys.	Or, if there were a sympathy in choice,
	War, death, or sickness did lay siege to it.

[I. i. 132-42]

Will it be believed that Mr. Daly cuts all these silver-sweet antiphonies, making Lysander say, "The course of true love never did run smooth. For, if there were a sympathy in choice," etc.? A little further on Hermia is robbed of the lines printed in inverted commas:

I swear to thee by Cupid's strongest bow;
'By his best arrow with the golden head;
'By the simplicity of Venus' doves;'
By that which knitteth souls, and prospers loves;
'And by that fire which burn'd the Carthage queen,
'When the false Troyan under sail was seen.'

[I. i. 169-74]

I presume it is from motives of delicacy that this speech of Oberon's is docked of its last four lines, the most magnificent in the whole play:

How canst thou thus, for shame, Titania,
Glance at my credit with Hippolyta,
Knowing I know thy love to Theseus?
Didst thou not lead him through the glimmering night
From Perigenia, whom he ravishëd?
And make him with fair Ægle break his faith,
With Ariadne, and Antiopa?

[II. i. 74-80]

Immediately after, the whole of Titania's description of the rains and floods disappears without a trace—an excrescence on the play, no doubt, but a curious and beautiful one. True, it would have needed an actress to speak it. There is more justification for some (but not for all) of the deletions in the lovers' quarrelling scenes. Passages so "conceited" in style as to baffle the comprehension of a modern audience may fairly be omitted; but this principle does not apply to Helena's

We, Hermia, like to artificial gods,
Have with our needs created both one flower,
Both on one sampler, sitting on one cushion, etc.

[III. ii. 203-05]

At a low estimate, I should say that two-thirds of Mr. Daly's cuts are quite unnecessary, while of these, again, a full third is positively detrimental. In several briefer passages, he makes unaccountable havoc of the text. For instance, where Shakespeare wrote:

Were the world mine, Demetrius being bated,
The rest I'd give to be to you translated,

[I. i. 190-91]

Mr. Daly makes Miss Rehan say:

Were the world mine, it would I give
To be to you transformed.

Where the original texts mar the metre, Mr. Daly at once becomes a purist. He will have Oberon say, "Quite overcanopied with *luscious* woodbine" [II. i. 251], rejecting [the eighteenth-century editor Lewis] Theobald's obvious and beautiful conjecture of *lush*. Countless are the places in which he suffers his actors to ignore the accentuation obviously demanded by the measure. For instance: *Hermia*. "It stands as an édict in destiny" [I. i. 151] (it should, of course, be "edíct"). *Puck*. "She never had so sweet a chanjling" [II. i. 23] (instead of the trisyllable, "changëling"). *Hermia*. "Lysander! What! removëd! Lysander! Lord!" [II. ii. 151] (instead of "remov'd"—as, indeed, it is printed in the Folio). In both places where the name of Philostrate occurs, the metre makes it abundantly evident that Shakespeare pronounced it *Phílostrait;* in both places Mr. Daly must needs have it *Philóstratee*. Lysander says to Helena, "Farewell, sweet playfellow; pray thou *for* us," thus ruining the line and disguising the rhyme with the following line, "And good luck grant thee thy Demetrius" [I. i. 220-21]. Even in the "tedious brief scene" [V. i. 56] of *Pyramus and Thisbe* it would surely be worth while to let Wall say, what Shakespeare indisputably intended:

And this the cranny is, right and siníster,
Through which the fearful lovers are to whisper,

[V. i. 163-64]

instead of accenting "sinister" on the first syllable, according to modern usage. These, to be sure, are small matters; but it is as easy to be right as wrong, and every wrong accentuation, while it gives no satisfaction to any one, inflicts on many a very appreciable dissatisfaction. And in no case, observe, have I noted a mere momentary slip of the tongue on the actor's part. These are all, so to speak, rehearsed errors, for which Mr. Daly is responsible. I am willing to believe that it was by a slip of the tongue that Mr. Clarke, the other night, said, "The lover, the lunatic, and the poet," instead of "The lunatic, the lover," etc. [V. i. 7]; but such slips would be impossible to any one with the slightest ear for verse.

With the exception of the "panoramic illusion of the passage of the Barge of Theseus to Athens," the mounting was passable. The Pompeiian interior of the first act was a trifle garish, and the caryatids of the last act seemed somewhat elephantine; but the forest scene was really pretty and tasteful. The "panoramic illusion" was justly jeered at by the first-night gallery. An ambidextrous barge (propelled, that is to say, by a motionless steering-oar at bow and stern alike) was seen threading its way, obviously on dry land, through an epileptic forest, jerked spasmodically along like a freight-train in the act of shunting. And for the sake of this childish and contemptible effect, Theseus and Hippolyta were made to perform a sort of egg-dance among the sleeping lovers, pretending not to see them until the cue came for recovering their eyesight. Mr. Daly is the only person illuded by this "panoramic illusion." In the fairy-scenes, again, the disorderly and meaningless flashing and fading of the electric lamps in the fairies' wands and hair seemed to me far more disturbing than pretty. Surely these scintillations should be subjected to some rule, however fantastic or conventional. We instinctively look for some "natural law in the spiritual world." Beings who have this faculty of luminance must be conceived to employ it to some end, probably of emotional expression. Either the jewels should glow continuously, or, if they flash and fade, they should do so, not higgledy-piggledy, but with meaning and appropriateness—pulsing, not merely fluttering. As it is, when Oberon says, "I am invisible" [II. i. 186], he seizes the opportunity to blaze forth like the Eddystone light. If the trick had been reversed—if the Faery King had been radiant throughout the scene, and then suddenly eclipsed his fires—one could have applauded Mr. Daly's ingenuity. At the very least, when the fairies are singing Titania's lullaby, their phosphorescence might surely follow the rhythm of the song instead of flitting and flickering in chaotic discordance.

Where Mr. Daly gives her unmutilated lines to speak, Miss Rehan, as Helena, croons her verses very beautifully. She makes a noble and memorable figure. The one thing I regret in her performance is a sudden lapse into schoolgirl Americanism at the line, "Nor longer stay in your curst company" [III. ii. 341]. Miss Maxine Elliott, too, as Hermia, looks singularly handsome, and speaks with intelligence and feeling. Mr. Frank Worthing and Mr. John Craig play Demetrius and Lysander quite creditably, though Mr. Worthing is a little careless of his words. It is really cruel of Mr. Daly to cast Mr. George Clarke for Theseus. He was ludicrous enough as Richard Cœur de Lion; under the huge helmet and in the cherry-coloured cloak of Theseus he is simply grotesque. Of his treatment of the text I have already given some specimens. Mr. Tyrone Power is good as Egeus, in spite of his Father-Christmas-like make-up. Miss Sibyl Carlisle makes a graceful and fairly intelligent Oberon; but Titania and Hippolyta simply cease to exist in the hands of Miss Percy Haswell and Miss Leontine. Miss Lillian Swain, as Puck, is conventional and nothing more. The clowning of the Athenian amateurs has at least the merit of being irresistibly funny. Mr. James Lewis as Bottom is mercurial rather than stolid; but, after all, there is nothing in the text to exclude this reading of the character. Nevertheless, I cannot think him so consummate in this part as he was in Sir Toby Belch [in *Twelfth Night*]. (pp. 243-53)

> William Archer, "A Midsummer Night's Dream,"
> in his The Theatrical "World" of 1895, *Walter
> Scott, Ltd., 1896, pp. 243-53.*

John Rankin Towse   (essay date 1913)

[*Towse was born and educated in England before emigrating to the United States in 1869. Five years later, he became dramatic critic for the* New York Post, *a position he held until his retirement in 1927. His theatrical memoirs, which reflect his disdain for much of modern theatre, are collected in the volume entitled* Sixty Years of the Theatre *(1913). In the following excerpt from that work, Towse briefly recalls Daly's presentation of* A Midsummer Night's Dream, *remembering it as a visually beautiful but poorly acted production.*]

Mr. Daly's revival of "A Midsummer Night's Dream," in 1888, was chiefly remarkable for its beautiful pictures, especially in the woodland and fairy scenes, and an excellently painted panorama showing the passage of Theseus in his barge to Athens. A most felicitous use of little electric lights was made in the fairy episodes, and the management of the elfin troops themselves was eminently imaginative and picturesque. A more exquisite or delicate setting of this lovely poetic fantasy could not reasonably be desired, but the performance itself was far from satisfactory and calls for no prolonged comment. The poetry suffered severely in its delivery by unaccustomed lips, and most of the impersonations were laboriously feeble.

Ada Rehan was a charming Helena to the eye, but was unimpressive in the serious passages, while her reading of the blank verse was monotonous. It was not until her quarrel with Hermia that she did herself justice. This she made delicious with a dash of her characteristic comedy. Otis Skinner imparted a welcome spirit to his Lysander. John Drew was not at all at ease as Demetrius, but avoided positive failure. James Lewis was exceedingly comical as Bottom, and was rewarded with abundant laughter, but exhibited no comprehension of the character. He was a clever mime striving to make himself ridiculous, not a stupid man ridiculous in spite of himself. His burlesque tragedy, however, set the audience in a roar. . . .   (pp. 349-50)

> *John Ranken Towse, "Augustin Daly's Company,"
> in his* Sixty Years of the Theater: An Old Critic's
> Memories, *Funk & Wagnalls Company, 1916, pp.
> 341-57.*

Marvin Felheim   (essay date 1956)

[*In the excerpt below from his* Theater of Augustin Daly *(1956), Felheim pays particular attention to Daly's revisions of Shakespeare's text in his production of* A Midsummer Night's Dream.]

Daly's production of *The Taming of the Shrew,* whatever reservations one may entertain about it, was an eminently successful revival, mainly because its humor was suited to the tenor and methods of the Daly company. Its farcical elements in particular were cakes and ale to these actors. On the other hand, *A Midsummer Night's Dream,* which was to follow as the next revival, presented an entirely different problem. Neither Daly nor his actors had the talent or the imaginative grasp to convey either the poetry or the spirit of the fairy play. In Daly's hands, *A Midsummer Night's Dream* became a spectacle, not a play at all. Evidently, Daly shared the opinion, first enunciated by Hazlitt, that the piece was incapable of being performed; so he "staged" it. The critics were almost unanimous in their condemnations. Even Winter treated it sparingly.

Daly's revisions were typical. Since the plot of *A Midsummer Night's Dream* is fundamentally meager, he could not afford to eliminate any parts of it; consequently, his excisions were ruthless cuts of many well-known and much loved poetic passages. It was in connection with *A Midsummer Night's Dream* that Archer pointed out the fatal resemblance between *Daly* and *Dele*. For example, he eliminated the description of Robin Goodfellow and Titania's speech on the wind, the rains, and the floods, and cut some of the most charming lines from Lysander and Hermia's wonderful love duet in [Act I, Scene i]. Archer estimated that "two-thirds of Mr. Daly's cuts are quite unnecessary, while . . . a full third is positively detrimental." For some blunders there is no accounting; where Shakespeare wrote,

> Were the world mine, Demetrius being bated,
> The rest I'ld give to be to you translated,
>
> [I. i. 190-91]

Daly had Miss Rehan say

> Were the world mine, it would I give
> To be to you transformed.

The only explanation one can offer is that Daly somehow confused "bated" with "baited," which had disagreeable or inelegant overtones. Certainly it was such prudery that prompted him to change "virgin patent" [I. i. 80] to "maiden heart and vow," "from her bum" [II. i. 53] to "from beneath," and "lovers, to bed" [V. i. 364] to "lovers, now list."

Again Daly has rearranged lines in order to project Helena, played by Ada Rehan, into a more important part than Shakespeare envisaged for her. To accomplish this, he eliminated scene ii from his Act I in order to allow Helena the curtain speech; in Act III, he rearranged the lines to permit Helena to enter last and thus assume a more effective position; finally, in Act IV, he transferred lines from Demetrius to Helena. His reordering of the concluding lines of the play was simply arbitrary and pointless. To Oberon he gave Robin Goodfellow's lines, and then ended with Titania reciting parts of Oberon's concluding speech. In general, however, *A Midsummer Night's Dream* is notable among Daly's Shakespearean adaptations because, except for the complete omission of [Act IV, Scene ii], he did preserve the ordering of the scenes throughout.

The most distressing elements in the production were connected with the staging. The scenes were much too garish, especially the panoramic illusion of Act IV, which Archer says was "justly jeered at by the first night gallery." As a consequence of their peculiar entrance from a "spasmodically jerking" barge moving through "an epileptic forest," Theseus and Hippolyta, according to Shaw [in the *Saturday Review*, 13 July 1895], "were made to perform a sort of egg-dance among the sleeping lovers, pretending not to see them until the cue came for recovering their eyesight . . . The four lions in Trafalgar Square are not more conspicuous."

But the most outrageous effect was the installation of blinking electric lights in the hair and wands of the fairies. "Surely these scintillations should be subjected to some rule, however fantastic or conventional," complained Archer. "As it was, when Oberon says, 'I am invisible,' he seizes the opportunity to blaze forth like the Eddystone light." The whole effect was one of "chaotic discordance." Isadora Duncan, who was one of the dancing fairies, relates that she objected to the wings Mr. Daly made her wear. "I tried to tell Mr. Daly I could

express wings without putting on papier-mâché ones, but he was obdurate," she reports. However, on opening night, her dance was so well executed that "the public broke into spontaneous applause." Instead of pleasing Daly, this put him into a "towering rage." "This isn't a music hall!" he thundered. So the next night Miss Duncan found all the lights "turned out" when she came on to do her dance.

Discussing Daly's approach to Shakespeare on the basis of this production, Shaw has contended that the manager did these fantastic things "partly because he was brought up to do such things, and partly because they seem to him to be a tribute to Shakespeare's greatness, which, being uncommon, ought not to be interpreted according to the dictates of common sense." Such a man as Daly, a man who is not an artist, continued Shaw, "regards art as a quaint and costly ring in the nose of Nature."

The utter incapability of Daly's comedians properly to pronounce Shakespeare's verse was the final charge against the production. Not only the English critics but also the Americans complained of this defect. "The poetry suffered severely in its delivery by unaccustomed lips," wrote Towse [in his *Sixty Years of the Theatre*], and Montgomery, whose review shilly-shallied between praise and condemnation, had to admit that "the blank verse of this play was mangled out of its music."

Despite the complaints of the critics, *A Midsummer Night's Dream* had a run of 79 performances, from January 31 to April 17, 1888. Indeed, Daly's Theatre and the Star Theatre (featuring the visiting Irving and Ellen Terry in *Faust*) were the only ones open on the night of the memorable blizzard of March 12. The play was revived on March 5, 1890, in New York, and was presented in London at Daly's during the summer of 1895. A special company, organized by Daly and Arthur Rehan, a relative of Ada's, presented Daly's version in the smaller cities of the United States. (pp. 243-46)

> *Marvin Felheim, "Shakespeare, New Style," in his* The Theater of Augustin Daly: An Account of the Late Nineteenth Century American Stage, *Cambridge, Mass.: Harvard University Press, 1956, pp. 219-84.*

Charles H. Shattuck   (essay date 1987)

[*Shattuck provides an overview of Daly's production of* A Midsummer Night's Dream, *with special attention given to the reactions of Daly's contemporaries to the text, settings, and performances of the several revivals.*]

A Midsummer Night's Dream always invites spectacle: Daly's *Dream* was probably the most spectacular of the century. He brought it out in the winter of 1888 (January 31 to April 17), revived it in March of 1890, took it to London in the summer of 1895, and toured it throughout America in 1895-96.

William Winter called Daly's arrangement of the play "an excellent working version," and early critics flattered Daly for his "loving reverence of the poet" [*New York Herald*, 1 February 1888], declaring that he "takes the play as Shakespeare wrote it, follows the text with conscientious care" [*The New York Times*, 1 February 1888]. The fact is, he followed the text with a carving knife, eviscerating the poetry with murderous care. In the opening scene he lopped out the charming stichomythic exchanges between Hermia and Lysander that follow "The course of true love never did run smooth" [I. i.

134] (those "silver-sweet antiphonies," as William Archer called them [in *Theatrical World of 1895*]), and half of Hermia's pretty "swearings" that she will meet Lysander in the wood. He cancelled Titania's famous poem about stormy weather; large sections of bitter snip-snap between the quarreling lovers (many of these lines that Daly actually printed in his souvenir edition were penciled out by the prompter as omitted in performance); some twenty-five lines of delightful fooling when Bottom, in the arms of Titania, orders a honey-bag for breakfast (also printed but struck out by the prompter); the entire scene of Bottom's reunion with his fellows; and at least fifty lines of the fairies' verses at the end of the play. In [*The Saturday Review,* 13 July 1895] Bernard Shaw raged against such abuse of the text, and William Archer remarked grimly that "there is much in a name, and *Daly* is fatally suggestive of *Dele.*"

The modern reader will not readily recall "indecencies" in the *Dream,* but Daly and Winter did. Puck's recital of his pranks did *not* include a fat and bean-fed horse beguiling a filly foal with sexy neighing; nor did he slip a stool from an old lady's "bum," but from "beneath" her. Titania's pregnant friend did not run down the strand imitating the "big-bellied" sails of passing ships. Theseus did not order the lovers "to bed" but to "now list." Who would sniff obscenity in Thisbe's line to Wall [V. i. 190-91]: "My cherry lips have often kissed thy stones"? Daly expunged it.

The casting went somewhat askew. After Ada Rehan's storming Shrew and Virginia Dreher's mild Bianca [in *The Taming of The Shrew*], Daly reversed the assignments: that is, he gave the tiny vixen Hermia to tall Virginia Dreher and the tall but gentle Helena to less tall Ada Rehan. Miss Rehan salvaged something by her first entrance when she "came bounding on in her love mania," and she showed a flash of fire in the third act when she rounded on her "moonstruck, herb-bewitched adorers." But for the rest she had nothing to do but read poetry, and she did so rather badly. Jeannette Gilder in *The Critic* [11 February 1888] found both the actresses "floored, to speak figuratively, by the blank verse." John Ranken Towse [in his *Sixty Years of the Theatre: An Old Critic's Memories*] faulted Miss Rehan in particular for monotonous reading, and declared that throughout the company "the poetry suffered severely in its delivery by unaccustomed lips."

On the other hand, Bernard Shaw, who like most Londoners adored Miss Rehan, praised her reading without reservation. Considering the demands he usually put upon stage speakers, his tribute to her vocal skills is, to say the least, out of character.

> She gives us beauty of tone, grace of measure, delicacy of articulation; in short, all the technical qualities of verse music, along with the rich feeling and fine intelligence without which those technical qualities would soon become monotonous. When she is at her best, the music melts in the caress of the emotion it expresses, and thus completes the conditions necessary for obtaining Shakespear's effects in Shakespear's way.

When we take Shaw's passage in context, however, we find it reaching toward a darker meaning, a warning: beauty of speech and [youthful] charm are not enough to make a great actress. Unless she moves on to Shakespear's Imogen [in *Cymbeline*], Shaw said, unless like Duse and Janet Achurch she takes up Sudermann and Ibsen, her appeal will be gone when youth is gone. Just as Shaw longed to rescue Ellen Terry from Henry Irving so too he would rescue Ada Rehan from Augustin Daly: "With grandfather Daly to choose her plays for her, there is no future for Ada Rehan."

Daly's production of the *Dream* recalled almost every flashy effect and device that had accreted to the play during the past half-century. His stage manager, old John Moore, had seen Eliza Vestris's Covent Garden *Dream* in 1840, had prompted William Burton's New York *Dream* in 1854, and had recorded in his promptbook masses of information about traditional scenic arrangements and stage business: the stage history of the play with all its devices was at Daly's elbow.

As was the custom, Daly assigned the role of Oberon to a woman, thereby earning a sneer from Shaw, who seems never to have heard of the "feminized" Oberons of Mme Vestris, Fanny Ternan, Charlotte Cushman, and many another. "It must not be supposed that he does this solely because it is wrong," said Shaw, "though there is no other reason apparent. He does it partly because he was brought up to do such things, and partly because they seem to him to be a tribute to Shakespear's greatness, which, being uncommon, ought not to be interpreted according to the dictates of common sense." In Charles Kean's production, Puck (Ellen Terry, age eight) made his first entrance seated on a mushroom which sprang up through a trap. Daly did not repeat that device, but he remembered it: "*Enter a fairy plucking flowers. With her wand she switches at a mushroom growth near C. and from it Puck appears.*" Puck used to embark upon his "girdle round the earth" by flying: Daly wired up little Bijou Fernandez for that feat—though on opening night "Puck had misadventures in his early efforts to whirl about the stage, but we presume the carpenter will do better tonight."

The Indian boy that Oberon and Titania quarrel about was actually brought upon the stage and then made to disappear magically. Two bearers in Moorish dress carried in a curtained palanquin within which the boy lay on a silver couch. When Oberon begged Titania to give him the boy, she signaled the curtains to be closed. When Oberon tore the curtains open, the boy was gone. According to John Moore, one of the bearers had released a spring, and boy and couch flew upward and were concealed in the roof of the palanquin.

Sunset, darkness, moonlight, and dawn were effects that Daly could execute far better than earlier producers because by 1888 he had both electricity and calciums (gas) to work with. He could make mists rise and clear them away by manipulation of gauzes. By change of light upon gauzes he could reveal scenes or wipe them out. Thus, at the end of the first workmen's scene "the house of Peter Quince disappears as though drawn into airy nothingness," and again in the fourth act, "the glen and tangled wood appear to dissolve." One of the prettiest effects occurred at the end of the third act when the lovers one by one lay down to sleep. As the darkness thickened around them and the air was filled with music, a crowd of goblins and fairies danced about in the mist, singing and flashing tiny battery-powered lamps on their wands and in their hair. *Fireflies!* Audiences were delighted. In London, however, the effect went for nothing, for fireflies are unknown in England. Shaw scorned the business as only one more unaccountable Daly foolishness. William Archer fretted through a long paragraph at "the disorderly and meaningless flashing and fading of the electric lamps." He thought they could at least have been made to "follow the rhythm of the song instead of flitting and flickering in chaotic discordance."

To bring his fourth act to a grand climax, Daly merged two traditional elements—a moving panorama and travel by boat. In an 1867 production in New York a panorama, imported from London, exhibited scene after scene of landscape along the lovers' route as they strolled back to Athens. In two 1854 productions, despite the fact that Athens is miles from the sea, the play opened with the arrival of a Grecian galley bearing Theseus and Hippolyta to the steps of Theseus's palace.

Daly combined boat and panorama in an operation of extraordinary complexity. Just after Bottom wakes from his dream and rushed off to find his fellows,

> Daybreak begins to appear. The air is tremulous with joyous song, and the first red flare of sunlight burns down a woodland glen. . . . As the sun rises higher, as the crimson of dawn melts into the golden splendor of early morning, the mist ascends, the glen and the tangled wood appears to dissolve, and a bright open scene with a luminous river in the background bursts into view. On the bare earth lie the four lovers, locked still in slumber. . . . Suddenly, from a distance, sounds the echoing note of a huntsman's horn, and the barge of Theseus glides down the stream. [George Edgar Montgomery, in *The Cosmopolitan,* April 1888].

From upstage left the barge moves to upstage center, and Theseus, Hippolyta, and company disembark, come forward to discuss the pleasures of the hunt, and presently discover the sleeping lovers. Then the grand scenic marvel ensues. The entire party enters the barge, and while the orchestra plays Mendelssohn's music, they sail from this mile without the town to Theseus's palace.

What in fact happened was that the barge sat still in its "stream" at upstage center while the panorama behind it and the ground row on the nearer shore moved from audience right to audience left so that the barge seemed to move from audience left to right through everchanging landscape until it reached the crowd of waving welcomers at the palace steps.

Did this panoramic journey "call forth applause"? Did the spectators "cheer lustily"? Was it "a feast of color and truly a marvel of illusion; and as you gaze upon it your senses are bewitched . . . and you realize indeed the ecstasy of a happy dream"? So certain American reviewers tell us [E. A. Ditmar, in *The New York Times,* 1 February 1888; William Winter, in *Harper's Weekly,* 18 February 1888]. Or was the passage "justly jeered at by the first-night gallery"? Did the galley appear "an ambidextrous barge . . . seen threading its way, obviously on dry land, through an epileptic forest, jerked spasmodically along like a freight train in the act of shunting"? Was it "more absurd than anything that occurs in the tragedy of Pyramus and Thisbe"? Thus certain witnesses in London [William Archer and Bernard Shaw].

The New York audiences and critics were, for the most part, simply amazed at the ingenuity and beauty of Daly's stagecraft. As Maurice Minturn put it in the *Herald* [1 February 1888], "Mr. Daly may be said to have realized what Wagner taught to be the perfection of stage art, where music, scenery, poetry and prose in their highest degree should be combined, and no one branch sacrificed to the other." Minturn failed to notice that Daly was less concerned than Wagner about the libretto. He actually asserts that Daly was conscientiously faithful to the text, quite overlooking the omission of famous passages and minor violations of Shakespeare's language.

Nym Crinkle was very much aware that, triumph as it was, neither Shakespeare nor the actors had much share in it. It was a triumph, he said, of Daly and stage scenery. He called it only "a prime example of good housekeeping. Mr. Daly is the best Dame Trot of a manager that we have. And when Shakespeare is in question let us by all means give our attention to Mr. Daly's neatness, and industry, and cleanliness, and propriety" [*The Dramatic Mirror,* 4 and 11 February 1888]. Winter and Dithmar, like Minturn, were uncritically enthusiastic over this "remarkably able production of one of the great plays . . . mounted and clothed in scenery and attire as rich and beautiful as any that has ever been used to dress a play on the American stage." It meant nothing to them that Daly had a blind eye and a tin ear when it came to the uses of dramatic poetry.

One of the surprising castings was that of James Lewis as Bottom. Anyone in those days who remembered the Bottom of portly William Burton or of Ben DeBar would turn for Bottom to the Falstaffian W. F. Owen, an actor of the size and the unctuous, rubicund order that the part seems written for; but Daly chose instead—perversely or cunningly—an actor of the exact opposite mold—"thin, dry, quaint, and chirrupy." Such was Lewis, and he reveled in the part. "The manner that he imparts to Bottom is not that of slow sapience and ruminant gravity, but that of nimble and eager delight in himself and all his faculties and deeds," said Winter. "He made a separate entrance, crying 'Ready,' and he struck the keynote then of his whole impersonation. It was received from first to last with the keenest enjoyment" [*New York Tribune,* 1 February 1888]. Even Jeannette Gilder, who protested that it was "not in the least Shakespearean—is, in fact, nothing but broad burlesque without insight or significance," gave in to it, for "it is funny all over, and excites so much merriment that it would be useless to criticize it." Someone noticed that after he awoke from his dream, and approached his exit, Lewis gave a donkeyish kick that was "preposterously exuberant" [*New York Star,* 1 February 1888].

To George Odell, writing as late as the 1940s [in his *Annals of the New York Stage*], this production of the *Dream* was "the best within my experience of half a century." To the English, however, the actors, with the possible exception of Miss Rehan, seemed little above the ordinary, and as for Daly's aerial flights, trick palanquins, and panoramic barge journeys, every English Christmas or Easter pantomime offered many more and far more ingenious gimcracks. The London *Athenaeum* [13 July 1895] was scandalized by the indiscriminate scissoring and the "Transatlantic squeamishness" of the bowdlerizing, acknowledged Daly's work at best as "pretty," and dismissed the whole affair as a "triviality." (pp. 70-6)

> *Charles H. Shattuck, "Augustin Daly and the Shakespeare Comedies," in his* Shakespeare on the American Stage: From Booth and Barrett to Sothern and Marlowe, Vol. 2, *Folger Shakespeare Library, 1987, pp. 54-92.*

PRODUCTIONS:

Herbert Beerbohm Tree • Her Majesty's • 1900 / 1911

BACKGROUND:

Tree's productions of *A Midsummer Night's Dream* at Her Majesty's Theatre in the opening years of this century are often considered the apogee of the Victorian tradition of sumptuous stagings of the play. Tree was a contemporary of William Poel, Harley Granville-Barker, and others whose progressive theories of staging would soon supplant Tree's elaborate techniques as the prevailing method of producing Shakespeare. Tree's two revivals of *A Midsummer Night's Dream,* the first in 1900 and the second eleven years later in one of his annual Shakespeare festivals, have been frequently disparaged by later critics for their introduction of live rabbits to the stage. However, they were extremely popular in their time and several contemporary critics were staunch defenders of Tree's staging techniques.

COMMENTARY:

The Times, London   (review date 11 January 1900)

[*In the excerpt below, the anonymous critic offers high praise for Tree's 1900 staging of* A Midsummer Night's Dream, *particularly the sumptuous scenery. Significantly, this reviewer advocates cutting Shakespeare's text, for, he argues, "there is plenty that can be cut out without loss to the interest" of the play.*]

Mr. Beerbohm Tree is nothing if not versatile. He is none of your one-part players, actors of temperament, superimposing their own personality upon every character they are supposed to assume. If we are agreed that the business of the actor is to act, that is, to impersonate, Mr. Tree deserves the name a good deal better than some of his fellow-managers. His many-sidedness has always been his strongest point. In broad farce he was the best "Private Secretary" we have had. In drawing-room melodrama his Captain Swift is a capital performance. He has played character-parts innumerable. In the "legitimate drama" he has shown himself a capital Falstaff, a stirring, if not very subtle, Mark Antony, and lately a fair King John. For Mr. Tree, therefore, the transition from King John to Nick Bottom a not so surprising a feat. He is the only actor of leading rank who could pass from the one character to another so entirely different without exciting our wonder and perhaps our censure. Possibly he is the only actor who would have had the courage to attack both tasks so energetically and heartily as to win a good deal of success in each. For as Nick Bottom he is, if not altogether successful in drawing a broadly comic character, quite as good on the whole as he was in *King John,* and this is in itself a remarkable feat.

The part of "that most lovely gentlemanlike man" [I. ii. 87-8], Bottom, must clearly have a decided attraction for Mr. Tree. This and the opportunities which *A Midsummer Night's Dream* offers for stage spectacle must have been the reasons which led him to make choice of the play. For, in truth, full of poetry and graceful charm as it is, these are the only reasons that recommend it from the purely dramatic point of view. Without for a moment agreeing with Mr. Pepys, who dismissed it as "the most insipid, ridiculous play that ever I saw in my life," we cannot regard the loves of Theseus and Hippolyta, Lysander and Hermia, Demetrius and Helena as offering any real interest. They are not real people any more than the fairies—Oberon, Titania, and the rest—who, by the way, are not real fairies either, unless we suppose that immor-

tals are swayed by motives essentially mortal and behave exactly like human beings. The human interest of the play lies with the clowns and their famous performance of "Pyramus and Thisbe." So little hold has the plot of the *Dream* ever had that for about a century and a half it was only given in the form of an opera. Such was the production towards the end of the 17th century for which Purcell wrote music, and which included scenes so far from the original as "a Chinese garden" in which a Chinese man and woman sang, and there was a "dance of six monkeys." The credit of bringing back the play into favour as Shakespeare wrote it is due to Phelps and later to Charles Kean, whose revival in 1856 gains an added after-interest for us from the fact that Miss Ellen Terry as a very little girl played Puck. At Her Majesty's Theatre we have a performance of great beauty, a more perfect setting than the play can ever have had, and plenty of fun in the comic scenes—altogether a delightful holiday entertainment.

No scene has ever been put upon the stage more beautiful than the wood near Athens in which the fairies revel and the lovers play their game of hide-and-seek. With a carpet of thyme and wild flowers, brakes and thickets full of blossom, and a background seen through the tall trees, of the pearly dawn or the deep hues of the night sky—the picture is one of real charm and restfulness. All the scenery has been prepared with exceptional taste, but this one scene stands out from the rest. The mind in recalling it seems to dwell upon some actual beauty of nature instead of a painted arrangement of canvas and pasteboard. The fairies by whom this sweet solitude is peopled are so dainty and fairylike that they seem quite in place as its nightly habitants. They are played by troops of graceful children, who go through their dances and gambols with pretty enjoyment, and a more magnificent King of Fairies than Miss Julia Neilson as Oberon could scarce be imagined. Oberon's glorious speeches are well delivered, too, and in the songs Miss Neilson has an opportunity of using her very pleasant singing voice. Mendelssohn's delicious music is given all through, and, of course, adds very greatly to the performance. Very charming, too, is Mrs. Tree's Titania. Her every movement is light and dainty, and as she trips to and fro amid her attendant sprites she looks just such a fairy queen as we have all in childhood pictured to ourselves. Miss Louie Freear supplies the element of curiosity which is seldom lacking in any production of Mr. Tree's. She is a funny little Cockney Puck, with a true Puckish laugh and a freakishness of speech and movement that cleverly suggest the antics of Robin Goodfellow. The costumes of fairies and mortals alike are harmonious and graceful. Designed by Mr. Percy Anderson, they have been tastefully carried out by Messrs. Simmons and Miss Fisher. They largely help to make up a very pretty series of stage pictures.

Coming to the mortals we have in Mr. Lewis Waller (who was last night hampered by a bad cold) and Miss Sarah Brooke a poetical Lysander and Hermia. The part is one that gives little scope for Mr. Waller's fine powers, but he lends it dignity, looks extremely handsome, and makes the most of the little he has to do. Miss Dorothea Baird is so fascinating a Helena that it is difficult to understand Demetrius's harshness. The latter warrior is played with something more than enough energy by Mr. Gerald Lawrence; he makes a fine figure, but should moderate his transports. There could be no finer figure for Hippolyta than Miss Miriam Clements, who looks amazingly handsome, and appears duly bored, as the Queen of the Amazons would appear, when that prosy Don

Juan, Theseus, played with spirit by Mr. William Mollison, indulges his habit of speech-making in the midst of his Court.

This brings us to the clowns, who are, one and all, exceedingly comic. Mr. Tree makes Bottom unnecessarily unpleasant in appearance—he has the bibulous visage of a confirmed toper and a voice thickened with indulgence in liquor. But he presents a capital study of the conceited peasant with his fancy for playing every part in turn and his confidence is his power of playing all equally well. Especially good is his awakening in the wood after the ass's head has been taken off. His cloudy astonishment at being restored to his own shape and his dazed bewilderment as to the events of the night are very cleverly acted. Of the rest of the performers in the very droll interlude Mr. Franklin McLeay, Mr. Louis Calvert, and Mr. Robson are particularly good. The clowns' ridiculous performance is given in a splendid Duke's palace, which, as soon as the mortals have retired, is filled with the fairy throng. There they dance, and, as they wind in and out, gradually the pillared hall glows with mysterious light, every pillar a shaft of fire, with little points of light starting out here and there at the touch of Oberon's wand. Then the fairies are dismissed by their king and queen, they troop off, and slowly the hall darkens again. The glow dies away, the stage is swallowed up in gloom, the lights in the house are suddenly turned up, and the play is over. It is as if the audience were rudely awakened from a pleasing vision. A moment before they have been in darkness, watching the lighted stage and its throng of gay figures. There is a quick shifting of lights and they find themselves blinking at the curtain, wondering whether it has not really all been a dream. A fitting ending to a performance full of beauty and charm.

The reception of the play was rapturous, even though it lasted until hard upon midnight. This will, of course, be altered. There is plenty that can be cut out without loss to the interest. The second act could be sensibly reduced, for, in truth, the goings to and fro of the lovers soon become tedious. The curtain was raised again and again in acknowledgment of the applause, and Mr. Tree was able to congratulate himself upon a most successful result of all the expense and care that have been lavished upon the revival.

A review of, "A Midsummer Night's Dream," in The Times, *London, January 11, 1900, p. 4.*

The Athenaeum   (review date 20 January 1900)

[*In the following rapturous review of Tree's 1900 production of* A Midsummer Night's Dream, *the anonymous critic contends that "no spectacle equally artistic has been seen on the English stage."*]

In presenting the poetic aspects of 'A Midsummer Night's Dream' Mr. Tree has not only gone beyond precedent and record, he has reached what may, until science brings about new possibilities, be regarded as the limits of the conceivable. No spectacle equally artistic has been seen on the English stage. The glades near Athens in which the action passes are the perfection of sylvan loveliness, the palace of Theseus is a marvel of scenic illusion, the dresses are rich and tasteful as they can be, and the entire spectacle is of extraordinary beauty. What in it is best, moreover, is that the fairy revels, unlike anything previously seen, are not mere ballets of children, but seem to be spontaneous ebullitions of mirth and joyousness. Many of the children were so youthful as to be all but incapable of supporting themselves, yet all took part in

actions that seemed dictated by individual volition rather than concerted purpose. For the more important personages, elfin and human, the stateliest and most picturesque of exponents had been secured. As Oberon Miss Julia Neilson, richly clad and with an electric coronal and breastplate, moved with the splendour and state of Apollo; Mrs. Tree, in clinging robes and with willowy grace of movement, realized Titania well. The effects of twinkling lights and floating shapes were magical, and the whole, for the first time on record, merited its name, 'A Midsummer Night's Dream.' High as is this eulogy, it is fully merited—stage illusion and stage splendour being capable of nothing further. Equal raptures are not elicited in the scenes of human interest; yet there, even, it would be difficult to suggest a change in the cast that would not involve a loss. Mr. Lewis Waller as Lysander was so afflicted with cold as to be unable to speak above a whisper; but he and Mr. Gerald Lawrence, picturesque as Demetrius, bore themselves with exemplary gallantry. Miss Dorothea Baird struck exactly the right note as Helena, and Miss Sarah Brooke stood in perfect contrast as Hermia. Theseus and Hippolyta were finely presented, and the princely pageant lacked no desirable feature. In the case of the players in the interlude, Mr. Tree's allotment of the parts had been no less happy. Some satirical touches which scarcely escape the charge of modernity were introduced, but the general effect was animated, and the characters of the different "mechanicals" were as a rule admirably shown. Mr. Tree's "Bully" Bottom is one of the finest performances he has given us, and a complete realization of the part. Mr. Franklin McLeay's Quince, Mr. Calvert's Flute, and Mr. E. M. Robson's Snug were excellent, and the assortment of the entire crew was praiseworthy. The performance is, in fact, a credit to the management and to the English stage. It is scarcely too much to say that a play of Shakspeare's has never been given in equally artistic fashion, and it is but just to counsel those who prefer to study Shakspeare in the closet to make an exception for once, if only to see of what the scientific resources of the stage are capable. A strikingly pleasant feature is the restitution of passages not ordinarily spoken. It is matter for regret, however, that some of the best lines of Titania, enshrining a beautiful (and to the pure-minded a chaste) picture can no longer be spoken. The rendering of the whole of Mendelssohn's charming music added to the grace of the play. (pp. 91-2)

A review of "A Midsummer Night's Dream," in The Athenaeum, *No. 3769, January 20, 1900, pp. 91-2.*

Max Beerbohm   (review date 20 January 1900)

[*Max Beerbohm was an English theatre critic, dramatist, and the half-brother of Herbert Beerbohm Tree. Beerbohm's reviews appeared in the* Saturday Review *from 1898 to 1910. Some of these pieces were later reprinted in* Around Theatres *(1924) and other collections. In the following excerpt, Beerbohm defends the elaborate scenery of Tree's 1900 production of* A Midsummer Night's Dream *as consistent with contemporary stagecraft and audience expectations.*]

Surely, Shakespeare never achieved anything more perfect than the "Midsummer Night's Dream." He, the weaver of wonderful brocades, not even in the noblest of his designs, the most gorgeous or sombre, the most illustriously inlaid and weighed down with jewels, ever fashioned anything whose splendour one would exchange for the fragrance of this idly-woven chaplet of little wildflowers. Idly-woven! That is the secret of its charm. The great poet never so absolutely reveals himself as in those idle moments when, laying aside the grand manner, he lolls, forgets, laughs. Smaller men may assume the grand manner, cheating us with high sounds and tremendous flourishes; it is when they come out of the giant's mantle that we see how small they are. It is when Shakespeare doffs his mantle that we see the giant's limbs, the giant rejoicing in his strength, and performing prodigious feats because he cannot help performing them. Yes! The "Midsummer Night's Dream" is the most impressive of all Shakespeare's works, because it was idly done, because it was a mere overflow of genius, a parergon thrown off by Shakespeare as lightly as a modern author would write an article on International Copyright for an American magazine. It is the most impressive of all the plays, and the loveliest, and the most lovable. I do not wonder that Mr. Beerbohm Tree determined to lay hands on it.

This adventure of his was beset with many dangers, and he is to be congratulated on having evaded them. To produce "Julius Cœsar" was comparatively safe and easy. The play was full of human drama, which had but to be acted for all it was worth to please everyone. "King John" was more difficult, for it was a dull play, into which humanity had to be foisted by the actors, and it was full of voids which had to be filled up with spectacular effects. But even "King John" was an easy matter in comparison with the "Midsummer Night's Dream." Of the three separate elements in the play, the fairy element is, of course, the dominating one. The scenes of the clowns and the scenes of the lovers might be done ill without spoiling the play. But the scenes of the fairies must be done well at all costs. There must be the illusion of fairies, illusion of a true dream. And this kind of delicate illusion is hard to produce through the definite and concrete means of the stage, and may be easily destroyed by them. A poet's words, as you read them, will illude you with certain images. But those very images, materialised, may dispel all illusion. Material equivalents for the images made by words are very dangerous things to handle. They must be "prepared" very cunningly. They must be made faint and mysterious. You remember Pater's gentle rebuke to "painters who forget that the words of a poet, which only feebly present an image to the mind, must be lowered in key when translated into visible form." You remember, too, Fuseli's picture of "Titania and Bottom" in the National Gallery. That picture is a good illustration of Pater's meaning, because it is so very bad an illustration of Shakespeare's. In it all the glamour of the wood near Athens is dispelled. Even the bad light it hangs in fails to imbue it with aught of the mystery it needs. The big fairies look like pupil-teachers, and the little fairies look like freaks in a dime-museum, and Titania looks merely improper. Yet Fuseli, I think, failed less utterly than would any living painter whose work is known to me. And, if it is so hard for a painter, working in two dimensions, not to affront one's imagination, how much harder must it be for the producer of a play, working in three, with solid, live media of flesh and blood! How much greater the trouble and finer the tact, when so much more lowering and mystifying of the tone is needed! I did not suppose it possible that my imagination would not be at every turn affronted in Her Majesty's (and, since Fate has prejudiced me in Mr. Tree's favour, I was wondering how I should manage to let him down easily without being altogether dishonest to myself). But my forecast was quite wrong. The production was charming. Though now and again, of course, something or other came out of key, I found myself really and truly illuded by the Wood near Athens. All the little fairies

there gambolled in a spontaneous and elfin way; the tuition of them had been carried so far as to make us forget that they were real children, licensed by a Magistrate, and that "at break of day" they were going to meet, not Oberon, but a certificated Board School teacher. They were dressed like fairies, behaved like fairies—in fact, *were* fairies, for me. The music to which they were dancing seemed, not to have been incidentally composed by Mendelssohn, but to be the music of the birds in the enchanted wood. Oberon, too, *was* the King of the Fairies, not Miss Julia Neilson; nor did Titania strike me as being Mrs. Tree. Nor did I notice Mr. Hawes Craven lurking in the bosky shadows of the trees. The only real person who came on to disturb me was Miss Louie Freear. At other times, I have been very glad to see her; but, on this occasion, I resented her presence, especially as it entailed the absence of Puck—dear Puck, whom I really did want to see. Mr. Robert Buchanan . . . once declared himself to be a fairy, and perhaps Miss Freear will be writing to protest that she too is of that engaging race, and so had a right to be in the wood. But, fairy or no fairy, Miss Freear struck a false note whenever she appeared, and I think that Mr. Robert Buchanan would have given a far better performance of the part. He, at least, would have shown some sense of the poetry he had to speak. Miss Freear showed none. However, she was the only discordant person in the wood. The others seemed to "belong there."

I suppose that Mr. Sidney Lee would not praise the production so warmly as I. In the elaboration of the woodland scenery he would see a further pandering to the lamentable decay of the imaginative faculty in modern audiences. But the brief performance of "Pyramus and Thisbe" would be after his own heart. When Quince comes on, bearing a board with the inscription "This is a wood," Mr. Sidney Lee, I can well imagine, would cease to frown and would settle down comfortably to enjoy himself. He would see, in his mind's eye, without any effort, a lovely wood ready-grown upon the stage. Even so, according to him, could the Elizabethans see things. But could they? And, if they could, must not there have been, even in those spacious days, a certain effort, a certain strain of the visual organs, the making of which must have distracted their attention from the play? Mr. Sidney Lee appears to be distracted only by the actual sight of scenery. But why should he be? Surely, if the scenery is well done—that is, kept in the same relation to the figures of the players as real surroundings bear to persons in real life—there need be no distraction of the kind. If the play is good, and well acted, such scenery cannot be intrusive. On the other hand, bad or skimpy scenery is bound to bother one. It bothered the Elizabethans less than us, because they were accustomed to it. Doubtless, too, good modern scenery would be distracting (at first) to a resurrected Elizabethan, because he would never have seen anything like it. Hansom cabs and bicycles would also puzzle him. But it does not follow that, because modes of locomotion were few and primitive in his day, hansoms and bicycles ought to be abolished. They save us a great deal of time and trouble. Nor have they produced decay in our faculty of walking, though there are many occasions when they are more useful to us than our unaided feet. Even so the developments in modern scenery, which are but a means of quickening dramatic illusion, do not signify that the imagination of the race has been decaying. When the average Victorian reads the "Midsummer Night's Dream" he sees, I am sure, quite as much of a wood as was seen by the average Elizabethan. But reading a play and seeing it acted are two different things. In reading a play, you have to imagine the characters. When you see it acted, the characters are there, as large as life, before your very eyes. Surely, their surroundings ought to be there too. You must imagine either everything or nothing. The only justification for no scenery would be invisible mimes. If the Elizabethans were so imaginative as Mr. Lee supposes, why did they want to see their mimes? The fact that they did want to see them suggests that they did not see scenery which was not there. However, I am quite willing to believe that Mr. Lee has the faculty which he attributes to them. My contention is merely that no one else has it. And that is his contention, too. So all is well. (pp. 77-8)

Max Beerbohm, "At 'Her Majesty's'," in The Saturday Review, London, Vol. 89, No. 2308, January 20, 1900, pp. 77-8.

The Times, London   (review date 18 April 1911)

[*In the excerpt below, the reviewer faults the verse-speaking in Tree's 1911 revival, but lauds the scenery, claiming that this production was "as near to fairyland as the stage will ever make it." He also mentions the presence of live rabbits on stage, noting that one responded when Bottom called out for Peter Quince.*]

Let us get our grumbling done with first. The speaking of the verse last night was really not up to the mark. Sometimes the sense was spoiled, sometimes the rhyme, more often the rhythm. Modern players are so apt to drop syllables out of words in modern fashion that it was quite a pleasure by contrast to hear Puck boldly say "reme*die*," because it had to rhyme with "eye," and the Wall cram three or four extra syllables into "secretly," just to stretch out the line to what he conceived to be its metrical value. Indeed, only two of the players were quite impeccable in this respect—Miss Margery Maude, whose diction is a delight to listen to, and Mr. Ion Swinley. The productions at His Majesty's Theatre are sometimes so fiercely attacked on other scores that it would be worth while to be particularly without offence on this. Secondly, in this very beautiful production there is now and then just a little needless, and, therefore, disturbing, display. What is the meaning of the golden leaves that fall on the end of the first act? Why is the magic flower fitted with electric light? And when, right at the end, the fairies come and dance in Theseus's palace, could not the difference between the human splendour of Theseus's Court and the fairy splendour of Oberon's be marked without those luminous pillars, those garlands strung with electric lights? This is fairyland in the sense in which we use the word of illuminated gardens at an Exhibition. It is certainly not the fairyland of what went before.

For what went before (we have got grumbling out of the way now) was perhaps as near fairyland as the stage will ever make it. The salient merit of this production of *A Midsummer Night's Dream* is that, once it has brought us into the forest, it remains a fairy play to the very end, and at every moment. The only possible interval is during the performance of the comedy at Court; but we know that the fairies are coming there too a little later, and how long is it since Bottom was translated? But those four lovers, who have sometimes been found a little tedious, are far from that while they carry on their absurdities with little fairies peeping from behind trees, and little fairies crawling in on all fours to listen, or flying up and down and in and out on the sky behind. The whole forest is humming with little fairies; and it seemed as if the lovers

felt it, for they all four became lighter, more fantastic, less solemn and pompous than they showed signs of being in the first act. As for Puck, that little rogue fairly rolled on the ground with laughter at the mortal fools, and only grew solemn with difficulty when Oberon, a monarch who took affairs of State a thought too gravely and grandly, was looking at him. If some one would teach Master Burford Hampden to chuckle instead of shouting with laughter, he would be as good a Puck as there is ever likely to be.

Fairies—never too clearly seen—in a fairylike forest, all faint, elusive, misty lights and shadows in the moonlight—a noble Oberon, a very sweet Titania, a droll Puck—perhaps these are what given the production its chief attraction. There is more forest and less stage about it than we could have expected. It was real enough even for the real rabbits, who made themselves quite at home. One of them was clearly named Peter Quince, for when Bottom, on waking, called on the carpenter, the rabbit promptly answered the call. Needless to say Mr. Bourchier took the chance. But Mr. Bourchier took all his chances, and his Bottom combines ingenuity with robustness till his audience shake with laughter. All the clowns, indeed, are very funny. And the four lovers are all very good to look at. And we and they are seldom far from the little fairies.

The music, if we are right, is very much what it was on the first production at His Majesty's some ten years ago. It is very nearly, if not absolutely, all by Mendelssohn. Besides the *Midsummer's Night's Dream* music proper, the first movement of the Italian Symphony, the scherzo of the Scotch Symphony, and several of the "Lieder ohne Worte" are played; and "I know a bank" (which we had hoped to hear not sung but well spoken) was given, not to Horn's music, but to "Auf Flügeln des Gesanges." Miss Evelyn d'Alroy sang it very prettily, but perhaps a little nervously the first time (for it is sung more than once). Moreover, the singing of most of "Ye spotted Snakes" fell for some reason to her, and no one could regret it. Miss Maude also revealed a charming singing-voice.

A review of "A Midsummer Night's Dream," in The Times, London, April 18, 1911, p. 9.

The Athenaeum   (review date 22 April 1911)

[*In the following excerpt, the critic presents a balanced assessment of Tree's later production of* A Midsummer Night's Dream. *He particularly admires the stage setting of "typically English woodland scenery," judging this truer to the spirit of the play than a setting in ancient Athens.*]

Sir Herbert Tree made a happy choice when he decided to inaugurate his Shakespeare Festival this year with a revival of 'A Midsummer Night's Dream'; for though half-a-dozen plays at least might be enumerated in which the poet's genius took a loftier flight, this vision of fairyland and of Nature bathed in the magic of moonlight has a perfection all its own by virtue of the pure beauty of its effects, yet is characteristically English in the inspiration which has blended poetry, fantasy, and fun. Hermia and Helena and their swains may be talked of as having wandered from the Court of Athens, Nick Bottom and his fellow-yokels may act their interlude before Theseus and his queen, but after all the lanes and woods of Warwickshire are their real home, and it is in the atmosphere of an English summer night that we listen to their story, or watch the revels of Titania's fairies. Puck may boast that he can put a girdle round the earth in forty minutes, but it is the forest of Arden to which his rogueries really belong, and which should be made their setting. Rightly therefore at His Majesty's, when once we pass into the night and the open air, we are plunged into typically English woodland scenery. Silver birches lift their slender stems to the skies, clouds of bluebells spread a mist of colour across the turf, while in the background a brook trickles down a mossy bank, or we have vistas of the sea. Amid such surroundings we are in the rural England of the poets, the month being rather May, when in kindly mood, than mid-June.

It is difficult in any modern presentment of the play to keep all three elements of its scheme in due proportion. However carefully the cast may be selected, one of them is pretty sure to be subordinated to the rest. In Sir Herbert Tree's present revival the quartet of lovers whose affairs Puck so quaintly muddles suffer eclipse, and the honours of prominence are divided between the fairies and the village clowns. To say this is not to imply that the parts of Lysander and Demetrius or of their sweethearts are "let down" by their interpreters. The kittenish Hermia of Miss Laura Cowie, so ready to snuggle softly into her lover's arms, yet prepared also to scratch and spit under provocation, is a delightfully fresh reading of the character; and Mr. Swinley, a new-comer from the School of Dramatic Art, shows promise as Demetrius. The manager has been singularly fortunate, too, in his choice of the fairy king and queen. His Oberon, Miss Evelyn D'Alroy, may impart too much feminine emotion to her rhetoric, but she phrases admirably and is able to sing, being allowed, oddly enough, to render the lullaby over the sleeping Titania; moreover she contrives to convey an air of majesty as well as grace. About Miss Margery Maude's Titania there is a curious charm not easy to describe—it is made up partly of girlish ingenuousness, partly of spiritual delicacy and refinement; it is phantasmal almost; and her fairy queen fits in naturally with the dancers of her train. In sharp contrast is the Puck of little Burford Hampden, a boy of precocious talent, impish and highspirited, but rather too perky to suit the company of such a Titania and Oberon.

If to raise laughter at all costs be the function of the comedian, then may Mr. Bourchier as Bottom and the troop of drolls he leads claim to be successful indeed. This Bottom does not need to play the Lion. He roars almost unceasingly, and never so much so as when he stalks the stage in the robes of Pyramus and woos Mr. Robson's grotesquely solemn Thisbe. He is evidently a village autocrat, huge of size, overbearing, almost beyond measure noisy; well up, too, in the tricks of the ranting actor and inventive in the mispronunciation of English, thus in making an extra syllable out of the word "prologue." Mr. Bourchier's is a performance full of boisterous humour and keen self-enjoyment. (pp. 454-56)

A review of "A Midsummer Night's Dream," in The Athenaeum, *No. 4356, April 22, 1911, pp. 454-55.*

W. L. Courtney   (essay date 1917)

[*The excerpt below is drawn from a general appreciation of Tree following the actor's death. Courtney lauds Tree's* Midsummer Night's Dream, *asserting that such productions demonstrate that Tree had "the eye, the feeling, the touch of an artist."*]

What were the positive contributions of Herbert Tree to the English stage? Here, there is some room for dissent and dis-

agreement; I will only put down certain facts in the form in which they appear to me. Remember, in the first place, that he inherited a great tradition from Henry Irving, who had set a magnificent example of stage-production at the Lyceum. Tree was at first content to carry on the tradition on similar lines. He produced plays with extreme care for detail and many appeals to the eye. There was never anything slipshod either in the method of stage representation or in the attention paid to what the diplomats call "imponderabilia." Indeed, it was the care taken over the minutiæ which guaranteed the effectiveness of the whole. Thanks in especial to Irving and Tree, London stage-production reached a higher level of completeness and finish than was to be seen in foreign capitals. Sarah Bernhardt and other foreign visitors acknowledged that in this respect they did not do things better in France. Gradually Tree bettered the examples of his predecessors. His critics said he over-elaborated his effects; his friends were never tired of welcoming new grades of beauty. I take only two instances out of many which offer themselves in recollection. Probably there never was a more beautiful stage picture than Olivia's pleasaunce in *Twelfth Night.* We talk of the hanging gardens of Babylon as of something legendary and rare. Here before our eyes were to be seen Olivia's hanging gardens, a dream of exquisite and appealing beauty which seemed to bring out the more clearly by contrast the vulgarity and coarseness of Sir Toby Belch and Sir Andrew Aguecheek, while it enhanced the delicacy of Viola and Olivia herself. The other example I will take from the *Midsummer Night's Dream.* You will recall that, though the scene is supposed to be laid in the neighbourhood of Athens, the feeling, the atmosphere of the play belong essentially to Stratford and England. Accordingly, Tree gave us, alternately with some marble seats and olive trees, splendid glimpses of British forests in which the fairies ran wild and Bottom and his companions rehearsed their uncouth theatricals. Anything more restful to the eye than these glades of sylvan beauty I have never seen on any stage. I used to drop into the theatre while the play was going on just to realize once more the solemn delightful effect of the old beeches sheltering the wayward fancies of Oberon, Titania and Puck, and providing a rehearsal ground for *Pyramus and Thisbe.* I must also add something about the elaborate scene at the end of the play when the pillars of the Duke's palace glow with internal light to enable the fairies to carry on their domestic tasks of making everything clean and sweet for the mortals. It was beautiful, but perhaps too elaborate. One missed in this case the note of simplicity, the wise sobriety of an accomplished artist who would not strive "to do better than well" lest he should "confound his skill in covetousness" [*King John,* IV. ii. 28-9]. There were charming pictures, too, in the *Tempest,* little sea-fairies peeping round the edges of the rocks, while Ariel sported in the pools, which one remembers with gratitude. But, indeed, the time would fail me if I were to recount half the wonders which the magician Tree displayed before our eyes in play after play. You may call him a consummate decorator, if you like, *le Tapissier de notre Théâtre,* as Luxemburg—was it not?—was called by reason of his conquest of flags and other costly stuff, *le Tapissier de Notre-Dame.* But I maintain that he had the eye, the feeling, the touch of an artist. (pp. 260-61)

W. L. Courtney, "An Open Letter to an American Friend," in Herbert Beerbohm Tree: Some Memories of Him and of His Art, *edited by Max Beerbohm, E. P. Dutton and Company, 1920, pp. 253-66.*

Maud Tree   (essay date 1917)

[*In the excerpt below, Tree's wife discusses the 1900 production, recalling that it featured "such fairies, lighting and scenery as had never before been seen—a very Midsummer Night's Dream of loveliness and magic."*]

Herbert wanted me for Titania in *A Midsummer Night's Dream.* I have often wondered how so unlikely a mortal as I came to be cast for that fairiest of fairy parts. I think it must have been because of my great love for the words and may sense of mystery and music. At all events, it proved not the least happy bit of casting in an extraordinarily happy cast, crowned by the Oberon of Julia Neilson. This was a noble and radiant creation, a golden King of the Fairies, instinct with poetry and dignity. With what majesty of beauty and utterance she spoke the divine speeches! "And the imperial votaress passed on, In maiden meditation, fancy-free" [II. i. 163-64]—rings in my ears; as does her lovely singing of "I know a bank whereon the wild thyme grows" [II. i. 249ff.]. By the by, it was my suggestion that she should sing this to the setting of Mendelssohn's "*Auf Flügel des Gesanges.*" It must have been an entrancing production, carried on to every available atom of Mendelssohn's entrancing sounds. Music-lovers would come over and over again to see the play, arriving at a quarter to eight that they might hear the perfectly-played and interpreted overture.

Well do I remember the final dress-rehearsal two days before the production. It was one of those fiasco rehearsals such as from time to time precede a triumph or a disaster. It lasted until the small hours of the morning. The poor, tired little fairies had all been sent home at midnight, stuffed with sandwiches and stuffed into cabs. Everyone except Herbert was cross, worn-out and correspondingly despondent. He, as always, rose to the occasion; summoned a few of us to his room, and for an hour—probably from 4 to 5 a.m.—we discussed how failure was to be averted, how things were to be pulled together, what could be done to evolve order and beauty from chaos. And lo! the first night brought a performance without a hitch; such fairies, lighting and scenery as had never before been seen—a very Midsummer Night's Dream of loveliness and magic.

It ran for many happy months, being one of Herbert's greatest managerial successes. As actor, there was really no part for him in the play. Oberon is the hero, the be-all and the end-all of *A Midsummer Night's Dream.* I hated to see Herbert acting Bottom the Weaver, as I hated to see him act Caliban in *The Tempest*—I had rather have seen him as Theseus in one and as Prospero in the other—but one's opinion could not always prevail. (pp. 114-15)

Maud Tree, "Herbert and I," in Herbert Beerbohm Tree: Some Memories of Him and of His Art, *edited by Max Beerbohm, E. P. Dutton and Company, 1920, pp. 1-170.*

Ralph Berry   (essay date 1981)

[*In the excerpt below, Berry defends Tree's lush productions of* A Midsummer Night's Dream, *arguing that "Tree served his day, within the modes of that day," and also that "he served the texts of Shakespeare with discrimination and flair."*]

Beerbohm Tree's Shakespeare Festivals (1905-1913) have always been recognized as a step toward the National Theatre. They were annual, glittering, and—at least until the last

two—highly successful ventures, that placed Shakespeare firmly in a metropolitan repertory. There is no doubt that Tree was the Shakespearean standard-bearer of his day, the high Edwardian. Yet the intrinsic value of his work has always been questioned. His contemporaries saw him as a successful flâneur, obsessively addicted to overelaboration, a view which has not been much challenged since. J. C. Trewin, while alert to the positive features of Tree's work, speaks [in his *Shakespeare on the English Stage 1900-1964*] of "Decorated Shakespeare at its most ostentatious," and says "[Tree] strove in his own theatre to translate every play into a sequence of pictures, slow moving and ornate." For posterity in general, Tree is still the man who brought live rabbits into the Athenian woods, and placed an impenetrable barrier of matériel between Shakespeare and the audience. "More see Shakespeare, but was more of Shakespeare seen?" asked J. L. Styan [in his *The Shakespearean Revolution*], That was the consensus, and the penetrating critique by Wilson Knight in *Shakespearian Production* a lonely dissenting voice: "Tree was an artist and a great one." (But even Wilson Knight forebore to defend the rabbits.) In the dialectic of Styan's *The Shakespearean Revolution*, Tree—along with A. C. Bradley, "closet Shakespeare," and the Victorian stage tradition generally—is a negative historical force, destined to be overthrown by Granville Barker, William Poel, and Peter Brook. But it is inapposite to think of theatrical evolution as a struggle between good and evil. The stage is a gallimaufry of traditions, and much of it is a dialectic between the spectacular and the simple. That dialectic is embraced in the texts of Shakespeare, as Tree well knew. Lately the publication of Madeleine Bingham's popular biography [*"The Great Lover": The Life and Art of Herbert Beerbohm Tree*] has given the reviewers the chance to reassess Tree's achievement, and Irving Wardle's is an especially impressive tribute [*"The Glittering Tree," in Books and Bookmen,* April 1979]. The reviewers have been generally sympathetic, and it is clear that the time is now ripe for a reassessment of Tree's methods and aesthetics. (pp. 23-4)

[*A Midsummer Night's Dream* is] I suppose the most notorious of Tree's productions. Although it appeared in only one of his festivals (1911, in a revival of the 1900 production), it demands treatment here as a key instance of Tree's way with Shakespeare. First, genre. *A Midsummer Night's Dream* for us, whatever its high-school associations, is an adult play: we see it in part through the spectacles of Brook and Kott. There are deep, erotic structures of desire and appeasement latent in the text that today are given full weight. Currently directors are fascinated with the possibilities of doubling. Tree saw the play as family entertainment. The souvenir program for the 1900 version contains a note "FOR CHILDREN ONLY," and the Introduction takes "Fairy" as the key word. Moreover, the text has been subtly bowdlerized in places. "Now I do wish it, love it, long for it" [IV. i. 175] becomes "Now do I wish, love, long for her!" Another trace of prudery appears at the end of the lines: from "Lovers, to bed . . . " [V. i. 364] to "gait of night" [V. i. 368], only " 'tis almost fairy time" [V. i. 364] remains. "Lovers" yields to "friends." The family is the best guarantor of box-office activity.

It is, of course, Tree's rendering of events in the Athenian woods that stamps his production. Here is the stage direction for his Act II:

Curtain on last note of music. Owl hoots twice. On Introduction to song fairy child enters, looks round, sees rabbit by trees L. pulls its tale [sic], exit rabbit behind tree. Child goes and wakes other fairies who are lying about, all rise and dance and at end of dance singing fairy enters others sit in a broken ring with the singer C (ibid.)

Puck runs around to music. When Oberon and co. enter, it's *March music.*

There are *boy fairies* and *girl fairies.* The fairies are always good for business. For instance, at [II.ii.26] (exeunt fairies) *Fairies arise and exeunt. One child remains. Enter Oberon. Directs 2 elves to take off the child.* Another cameo that shows Tree's visualizing, one might say anecdotalizing imagination, occurs with Puck's business with the mechanicals in [Act III, Scene i]:

> *Puck tickles Bot's legs 3 times, he thinking it is a fly tries to catch it. Puck buzzes, all rise and try to catch it.*

Music (which included Mendelssohn), fairy lights, little boys and girls dressed up, comic business—these were major elements in Tree's formula. There were even suggestions of *Peter Pan* in the 1911 revival: "Puck and his attendant fairies wing their flight for the 'flies,' leaving Oberon and Titania ankle deep in the lovely blooms . . . " Not much to our taste, all this, nor to J. L. Styan's, who refers to "Beerbohm Tree's little sugar-cake girls with pretty wings and tutus." Still, this was an Edwardian adjustment to the Victorian version of the play; and Tree was aiming at a different audience from Granville Barker's. The genre of Tree's *Dream,* I suggest, can be thought of as Disney.

And now consider the rabbits. They are usually advanced as evidence of Tree's dogmatic "realism." . . . Tree was never a crude "realist," nor was he here. The function of the rabbits emerges clearly from the reviews:

> The hero, or heroine, of Sir Herbert Tree's revival of *A Midsummer Night's Dream* at His Majesty's last night was a rabbit. "Peter Quince!" cried Mr. Bourchier as Bottom emerged from his trance. And as if in answer to the summons a black and white rabbit went boldly up to Mr. Bourchier, with a "Did you ring, sir?" air. The crowded audience rocked with laughter
> [*The Evening News,* 18 April 1911].

And again:

> . . . the sudden answering to Bottom's cry for Quince [was] a live rabbit that ran to him as if it had been a spaniel
> [*The Morning Post,* 18 April 1911].

And again:

> They are obviously not wild rabbits, nor do they behave as such, though it is only fair to say that one proved itself quite a comedian and took its cues with Mr. Bourchier admirably
> [*The Daily Graphic,* 10 April 1911].

The rabbits were *funny!* Natural comics, they were trained and planted to steal their scenes. Even if one doesn't accept them as an anticipation of Disney techniques, the rabbits are obviously out of place in any discussion of realism. Oddly enough, one of the reviewers failed to grasp the point here:

> Of course rabbits, wild rabbits, do not do that sort of thing. But then neither are they black and white. The incident was an amusing illustration of the fal-

lacy that realism on the stage can best be secured by the employment of the genuine article . . . A sleeping sheep is better represented by a sack than by a sheep. You can be sure that the sack will not awake. What the sheep can do no man can say
[*The Evening News,* 18 April 1911].

Quite. But Tree was after different game. Comic business transforms all rules: one must talk about real horses in *Richard II* in a mode separate from real dogs (Launce's) in *The Two Gentlemen of Verona.* (It is clear from Launce's cadenza in [Act IV, Scene iv] that he is addressing a real dog, and editors customarily expand the stage direction to read *Enter Launce with his dog.*) Comic mode aside, the critical question with animals is their training, and Tree seems to have secured good discipline among his personnel. All in all, the rabbits appear to have been misconstrued in theatrical history. I am happy to restore their status, and I plead also for the reviewer who ventured suggestions for the feeding of the three rabbits lest their demise impair the run, and thought that "these rabbits are pregnant with inner meaning . . . There is, for example, the delicate symbolism by which their little natural proclivities are united with the main theme of the story, the four pairs of lovers . . . " [*The Star,* 18 April 1911].

Tree's *Dream* was not Granville Barker's, but it was magic, high Edwardian entertainment for families that even then had nostalgia in their bones: one thinks of Elgar's *Starlight Express,* Kenneth Grahame's *Dream Days* and *The Golden Age, Peter Pan.* This *Dream* was a brilliant and harmonious fantasy, a mingling of light and color and darkness. Ultimately, it appealed to those subterranean forces that Tree knew so well how to tap:

> You watch all the colour fade out into the mysterious dreaming depths of night. And then comes laughter, holding both his sides, as you think of Nick Bottom's strut and his joy when he found that his tail was not hanging down behind. Again the lights die out in the palace, again the gay procession marches out, and all is dark, and there comes a light not of this world and in flies Puck
> [*The Daily Telegraph,* 18 April 1911].

My argument has been that Tree served his day, within the modes of that day, but also that he served the texts of Shakespeare with discrimination and flair. Tree did not oppose his age. He worked with its grain. Michael Booth speaks [in his "Spectacle as Production Style on the Victorian Stage," in *Theatre Quarterly* 32, 1979] of the public "taste for the pictorial, the richly decorated image, the visual recreation of history, and the ostentation of lavish display in an ostentatious age." Tree satisfied that taste; but he tried to match it with texts apt for spectacle and ornament. (pp. 43-7)

> *Ralph Berry, "The Aesthetics of Beerbohm Tree's Shakespeare Festivals," in* Nineteenth Century Theatre Research, *Vol. 9, No. 1, Summer, 1981, pp. 23-51.*

PRODUCTIONS:

Max Reinhardt's *Midsummer Night's Dream* • 1905-1939

BACKGROUND:

Throughout the first half of the twentieth century, the renowned German director Reinhardt presented a series of productions of *A Midsummer Night's Dream* throughout Europe and America, including open-air presentations and a 1935 film version made in Hollywood. Although Reinhardt's conception of the play developed each time it was staged, each of his productions was characterized by romanticism and rich beauty.

COMMENTARY:

J. Brooks Atkinson   (review date 27 November 1927)

[Atkins favorably reviews a 1927 New York performance of Reinhardt's Dream, *asserting that this production was a work of "genius."]*

Nearly four years ago we had a sample of Dr. Reinhardt's quality in the colossal production of "The Miracle," at the Century Theatre, where he is now reestablished. That was a stupendous enterprise. Under the sweeping management of Morris Gest, Norman-Bel Geddes had transformed our largest theatre into a Gothic cathedral with an extravagance and a thoroughness never equaled on the stage before or since. By an imaginative use of processionals and mass effects Dr. Reinhardt then summoned a medieval fable to life, up and down the aisles, across the stage, with a reverent yet hysterical emotional authority. At one time or another, in one form or another, nearly every large city from Bucharest to Los Angeles has seen "The Miracle."

But perhaps "The Miracle" has given us a distorted image of Dr. Reinhardt's theatrical genius. Far from being a ringmaster, as "The Miracle" seemed to indicate, he is a versatile director, as able in staging drawing-room comedy for an intimate theatre as he is in organizing "Everyman" for an out-of-doors production in the square before Salzburg Cathedral. Somehow all his productions redound to the credit of his reputation. But those who have seen them over a period of twenty-five years insist that he does not subordinate the play to showy effects; when he employs big set-pieces he does so merely to bring the play into its highest perspective.

"Do not write out prescriptions," he says in one chapter of Oliver Sayler's "Max Reinhardt and His Theatre," "but give to the actor and his work the atmosphere in which they can breathe more freely and more deeply. Do not spare stage properties and machinery where they are needed, but do not impose them on a play that does not need them. Our standard must not be to act a play as it was acted in the days of its author. To establish such facts is the task of the learned historian and is of value only for the museum. How to make a play live in our time—that is decisive for us."

For the past week and a half we have had a chance to test him by his own formula in a splendid production of "A Midsummer Night's Dream," which closes Wednesday. Without having seen every production of that play since Shakespeare wrote it—not even the one Pepys, the London flaneur, damned as silly—one may be presumptuous enough to cite Reinhardt's as the best in design and execution. Not in diction, however, for no German translation can catch the loveliness of Shakespeare's lyrical verse. Those who dismiss all Shakespeare in translation as no Shakespeare at all are well

within their rights. Furthermore, a German correspondent writes to this department that Reinhardt's company speaks "a conglomeration of German dialects—this and that—high and low, not much like the purity of speech of the Russian players and the French of M. Gemier's band of artists." But as a production, interweaving all the synthetic arts of acting, dancing, lighting, music and costume, Dr. Reinhardt's "Dream" restores Shakespeare in our day without excrescent tricks or florid embellishment—as Theseus says:

> Such shaping phantasies, that apprehend
> More than cool reason ever comprehends.
>
> [V. i. 5-6]

There is reason to believe that Shakespeare did not write "A Midsummer Night's Dream" for the public stage, but for a nobleman's wedding, possibly for the marriage of the Earl of Derby to Elizabeth Vere at the court, and perhaps the virginal Queen Elizabeth herself was present to hear her chastity slyly celebrated by an ever-obliging dramatist—

> Thrice-blessed they that master so their blood
> To undergo such maiden pilgrimage.
>
> [I. i. 74-5]

At any rate, "A Midsummer Night's Dream" is more akin to masque than to drama. In its verse, in its elfin fripperies, in its passion for the sweets of the earth and the heavens, it cannot breathe the stale air of the playhouse. Dr. Reinhardt blesses it with limitless space. On a sloping circular platform he gives Puck and the fairies free scope for their tiptoe flourishes; and without dropping the curtain or changing scenes radically he uses the same space for the palace of Theseus. For the first and last conventional masque scenes he brings a stately candle processional from the orchestra pit to the stage, and then winding interminably, slowly, to a boundless space beyond. Keeping the stage free, keeping the background mysteriously deep, sprinkling the heavens with stars, the "Dream" is never cramped. Far up on the second balcony the orchestra blows the wood-wind measures of Mendelssohn.

When Dr. Reinhardt mounted his first, and somewhat different, "Dream" in Berlin in 1905 it was too sensationally successful to escape criticism. "Of course, he makes a pompous show of Shakespeare's comedy. That always draws," said the Brahms canaille jealously. "Really the bluff was too stupid," Maximillian Harden retorted. "Never had 'A Midsummer Night's Dream' been staged less pompously." Those who can distinguish between decoration and embellishment believe that the 1927 version of the "Dream," far from being a pompous show, subordinates its details to the fantastic mood of Shakespeare's poem. Indeed, compared with the bronze fairies, white-gauze and china-silk curtains and vari-colored electric bulbs of Granville Barker's preposterous 1915 production, Dr. Reinhardt's is vagrancy.

All such chatter of details is bickering rather than appreciation. And the genius of Dr. Reinhardt's "Dream" is not the machinery but the product, which is a mood—iridescent and sheer, "spangled starlight sheen" [II. i. 29], something "which no intelligence can understand." This, one might dogmatically assert, is the highest achievement of the theatre. To represent something which resembles our daily life concretely requires talent and ingenuity. To create an unreal mood, to create a microcosm that owes nothing to our experience, requires genius. Dr. Reinhardt does it partly by frank magic lighting, partly by a style of costuming that represents no time or place.

But chiefly by acting. Taking the tempo from Mendelssohn's round-noted score, he keeps his production all of a piece. From the initial march it progresses to the bumptious artisan scene and to the fairy revelries, interspersing ballets and puckish rogueries without treading a realistic measure. Dr. Reinhardt provides one intermission. But the production is formed so symmetrically—and simply—that it might well go unbroken to the end.

In America we are only just beginning to appreciate the supreme importance of the director,—perhaps because we are only just developing directors of commanding influence. In their excited gossip about symphonic conductors, music lovers recognize the genius of one man, like Toscanini, to freshen the interpretation of old scores and to charge the players with brilliance. In the titanic world of the theatre, which employs not one art but many, Reinhardt is the counterpart to Toscanini. Every play comes fresh through his supple imagination. "This is the strongest feature of his art," writes Arthur Kahane in the bewilderingly fat Reinhardt volume, "the directness and freshness with which he can view every drama, as if it had never been played before; and the intensity of his conception with which he intuitively feels the essential character of a drama. Only the essential character is of importance, whether it be soul, atmosphere, basic idea, leading motive. By this essential feature a dramatic work becomes an entity, a world in itself. In the true sense, every great masterpiece means the creation of a new world, an entire world in itself, strictly limited, rounded off, constructed on a great principle, for which the term 'idea' is insufficient."

No mincing of words alters the simple fact that Dr. Reinhardt is, at the age of 54, the greatest and most versatile theatrical director in the world. And to admire him one need not blink the fact that playing in a foreign tongue—whether it be German or Russian—seriously curtails the enjoyment of a drama set before American audiences. Dr. Reinhardt's brief visit gives us all an opportunity, whether we agree with his methods or not, to expand considerably our ideas of the capacities of the modern theatre.

J. Brooks Atkinson, "Drama from Across the Sea,"
in The New York Times, *November 27, 1927, p. 1.*

The Times, London (review date 16 June 1933)

[*The excerpt below is taken from a review of an open-air performance of* A Midsummer Night's Dream *staged by Reinhardt with the Oxford University Dramatic Society in 1933. In this production, the critic notes, "the customary emphasis of the play has been changed. No longer is it a story of mortals in this world behind whom an enchantment has arisen; it is a tale of sprites and goblins pursuing the natural life of their own dwelling-place, into which men and women have blindly wandered."*]

Forsaking college gardens that Professor Max Reinhardt's production may have full range, the Oxford University Dramatic Society has chosen as the setting of its play a great meadow at Southbank, Headington. At the foot of the audience a bank rises sharply for some 20 yards, set with elm and beech and may. Beyond the great trees the incline is less. The prospect widens and flattens into what appears as a vast circle of grass, set about with distant woods.

In such a theatre there is nothing the faeries may not do. Puck may mock his victims from branches above their heads or from the swift invisibility offered him by a hole in the ground; Oberon's troop and Titania's, advancing from opposite woods, may meet by sudden chance and vanish, when their encounter is over, like the legions of a dream; from far away, while the lovers in the foreground are disputing the confusions of the night, a solitary faery may come through the late dusk, come for no reason of ours and depart beyond our knowledge, having miraculous business of her own.

The customary emphasis of the play has thus been changed. No longer is it a story of mortals in this world behind whom an enchantment has arisen; it is a tale of sprites and goblins pursuing the natural life of their own dwelling-place, into which men and women have blindly wandered. That it has been Professor Reinhardt's purpose to enforce this emphasis to create an illusion of immortal intimacy becomes increasingly clear as the evening passes and his lighting, which is masterly in its restraint and its gentle use of foliage, begins to have its full effect. At first there is an inclination to be over-jealous of the text, not because Bottom and his friends are too lavish in their amendment of it, for clowns must have licence to gag, but because a passage of verse is gone that one misses, or because the virtue of Titania, and not of Titania alone, is in her movement and appearance rather than in the music of her words, and it remains conspicuously true to the end that individuals have been subordinated to the mass.

Miss Sanchia Robertson is a charming Hippolyta: Miss Mary Gaskell and Miss Joan Maude are allowed the opportunity of their quarrel; the men speak well and act lively, Mr. Felton being full of clownish invention, Mr. Hutchinson giving an unaccustomed life to old Egeus, and Mr. Arnhold discovering an unknown power and mystery in Oberon; but still it is to the mass that one returns. The only outstanding individual is Miss Nini Theilade, and she is the first faery and the chief of all the dancers.

Through her and her companions, through Mendelssohn and his music, through the meadow and its woods and the glow of the concealed lights on the underbranches of giant trees, Professor Reinhardt exercises his influence. *A Midsummer Night's Dream* has never been more lovely to the eye, nor has it ever partaken more fully of the nature of a dream. The panic of his friends at the sight of Bottom translated has a superb flash of terror in it; the advance of the faeries when the sleeping lovers await their reconciliation is a brilliant enchantment. It would be childish to cavil at a line lost or a line added. The play has not been sacrificed to mere productionism. It has been freshly seen, freshly interpreted, and performed in accordance with its woodland circumstance and an artist's dominating idea. It is not flawless; the spoken poetry is sometimes weak, and the clowns have been dangerously given their heads; but at its peaks it is a production to take the breath away.

A review of "A Midsummer Night's Dream," in The Times, *London, June 16, 1933, p. 12.*

Rupert Hart-Davis (review date 23 June 1933)

[*In his review of the Oxford production, Davis expresses disappointment with the performance, judging the acting mediocre and the outdoor setting in broad daylight destructive of any sense of enchantment.*]

Gertrude Eysoldt as Puck and Ellie Rothe as a fairy, 1905, the Neues Theater.

Professor Reinhardt is a man of the theatre, a master of it if you will. All the more surprising that he should have so far handicapped himself in this production as to allow the first two-thirds of the play to be given in broad daylight. If the performance had begun at 10 o'clock, the mediocrity of the acting and the difficulties of reaching and leaving the stage would have been masked, as they were later in the evening, by the excellence of Professor Reinhardt's lighting and arrangement.

The stage was set on a sloping bank with a small tree on each side at the back, shrubberies in the far-distant "wings," an artificial pond in the extreme foreground, and in place of backcloth a many-acred meadow bordered by trees in the distance. Twice only during the daylight hours was Professor Reinhardt able to make good use of this huge arena: once at the rustics' first meeting, when, to the music of Mendelssohn played in an adjacent thicket, they advanced literally from three of the four winds and assembled in the centre—a fine effect lasting some minutes which I have never seen equalled or attempted anywhere else; and secondly when Fraülein Nini Theilade danced on to the stage leading by the hands a tiny child dressed in white. For the rest, in a merciless light, upon parched browning grass, neither mortals nor fairies could suggest an atom of the magic or the mystery which are the essence of this play. All were pathetically and rather em-

barrassingly earthbound. Often too they were breathless, since with the wings (and presumably the dressing-rooms) some distance away, they were compelled, in order not to delay the action of the play, to make their entrances as well as their exits at the double. The ladies had seldom more than a 100 yards' sprint to negotiate—no inconsiderable feat in their elaborate dresses—but the men covered all distances up to and including the half-mile. One competitor suddenly dashed along the footlights and, much to the delight of the audience, failed to clear the water jump. Often during an intimate scene in the foreground one's eye was caught by some lonely player plodding wearily round the furthest fringe of the meadow, the last lap of the three miles cross-country. Puck must have put a girdle round about Headington in forty minutes, and Theseus' "Well run, This be" [V. i. 266] came as a tardy tribute to such athletic prowess.

After the interval, however, and with the arrival of darkness, all was changed. Now Professor Reinhardt was at his best. His lights were distributed subtly in grass and tree, his fairy dancers came out of nothing and to nothing went. Even his actors seemed to take on themselves something of the mystery of things. Points of light danced and twinkled through the trees, the music grew seemingly odd and unearthly; we were back in the Golden Age. Play and producer had come into their own.

And the acting. Do the boys carry it away? They do not. The performances (with one exception) were bad by any standard, amateur or professional, and compared with last year's production of *Romeo and Juliet* pointed a sad retrogression. The comics in particular were a disgrace. No attempt whatever was made to simulate rusticity. Bloomsbury and Oxford mingled their accents in a troupe, whose one idea of humour was to fall down. They fell backwards, forwards, sideways. They tripped each other and themselves. Half of them seemed perpetually on the ground. The President of the Club, Mr. R. F. Felton (Balliol), played Bottom. Apart from energy and a certain facial virtuosity, his performance was like a member of the staff of a highbrow weekly trying to play Nervo and Knox at the same time. Nor did he and his comrades confine themselves to the words of Shakespeare. Modern interpolations exaggerated most of their scenes into a feeble imitation of Crazy Month, and made the whole sound like what in fact it may have been, a literal translation of a modern German version of the play. The Puck of Mr. P. B. P. Glenville (Christ Church) was agile, but nimbleness and a form of semaphore are not enough for Robin Goodfellow. The ladies were beautiful to look at, and the Athenians adequate. We were reminded of the existence of poetry in the play only when Mr. P. R. E. Arnold (Balliol) was on the stage. His Oberon was finely conceived and firmly played. His appearance, movement and speaking voice were very good indeed.

It remained for Fraülein Nini Theilade, who directed the ballet and led the dancers, to supply enchantment and beauty of motion, and to run, or dance, away with the production as she would. Her entry in the moonlight, long deep-blue train held shoulder-high by following sprites, her dance between the trees and her subsequent disappearance into the darkness on the shoulder of a satyr will not easily be forgotten. Altogether a disappointing evening, redeemed towards the end by momentary flashes of beauty.

> *Rupert Hart-Davis, in a review of "A Midsummer Night's Dream," in* The Spectator, *Vol. 150, No. 5478, June 23, 1933, p. 906.*

Otis Ferguson   (review date 16 October 1935)

[*Ferguson provides an early response to Reinhardt's film adaptation of* A Midsummer Night's Dream *for Warner Brothers pictures. He judges it an uneven performance, claiming that "its worst contradiction . . . lies in the way Warners first ordered up a whole batch of foreign and high-sounding names to handle music, dances, general production—and then turned around and handed them such empty vessels as Dick Powell, Jean Muir, Victor Jory, for actors."*]

Opening at an $11 top, running well over two hours, costing more than a million and (to ensure getting this back) press-agented for months ahead as the greatest marriage that was ever married between (among) William Shakespeare, Max Reinhardt, William ("Fog Over Frisco") Dieterle, Felix Mendelssohn, Bronislava Nijinska, James Cagney and a good sprinkling of Warners' best California baked hams—being all this, the film "A Midsummer Night's Dream" demands a certain attention that will never be justified in terms of pure entertainment. At its many screenings there will be no lack of Ah's and Oh's, culture clubs will have discussions, newspaper critics will put on their Sunday adjectives; but the picture is fairly tedious, being twice the average running time, and there is going to be a powerful minority of American husbands who will get one load of the elves and pixies, and feel

betrayed away from their stocking feet and sports page, and say as much, violently.

Apart from such unconscious and partly philistine criticism, there is to be said about this version of the Shakespeare extravaganza that it is topheavy with the weight of its art departments. (You can just see the camera and property and boom men standing around and scratching themselves, balancing the impulse to guffaw against the uneasy wonder whether there may be something deep in these here Nijinska, what do you call them, esthetic dances.) Its worst contradiction, in fact, lies in the way Warners first ordered up a whole batch of foreign and high-sounding names to handle music, dances, general production—and then turned around and handed them such empty vessels as Dick Powell, Jean Muir, Victor Jory, for actors. A second major contradiction appears in the way the whole thing is approached. For a while the producers will stand outside Shakespeare, handling each line literally, with marvelment and awe. Then suddenly they will either forget the book altogether and go Hollywood, or else get inside it, improvising on it as familiarly (and justifiably) as they would with any mortal working script.

Where they have arranged to forget the original is principally in the supernatural doings of the midsummer night, where there are fairies singly and in Music Hall troops, Titania, Oberon and Puck (Mickey Rooney, too ill instructed and raucous to be given such prominence). Here situations are elaborated for all they are worth, regardless of the main play, like so many independent sideshows on a midway. Oberon's ensemble departure, for example, must take up all of ten minutes, and yet right in the middle of it is inserted, for no earthly reason, the detailed seduction of a white nymph by a black sprite, she finally on his shoulder and disappearing down a black distance, weaving away at a fire symbol with her hands, wrists and forearms—in short, a dancer with a specialty in a long vanish shot. The necessity for some such figuration in a play of this type is obvious; but there is also a need for distinguishing between fantasy and "Flying Down to Rio."

The idea of the goblin orchestra—grotesque little figures in masks—is by way of contrast a touch of what is needed. Introduced only occasionally, this effect is fresh, pleasing; it represents the imagination at work and is worth all the brute mechanics, however elaborate, of settings, costumes, parades and spangled gauze shots.

But where the film really goes along with Shakespeare is in all that play-within-a-play business of hempen homespuns, the weavers, tinkers, cobblers of the city. Here the lines are surrounded with enough business to give them a bright and plausible reality. As Bottom, Cagney is out of character but still able to give it something; and his associates in earnest buffoonery—Joe E. Brown, Hugh Herbert, etc.—are the best cast figures in the production. With their various interpolations and properties, they are made into something that can be laughed at because it is real and funny, rather than a classic thing to laugh at.

The principal difficulty is that the stage of Shakespearean comedy is not the stage today, that this business of groaning, sighing, jiggling couplets, spouting passion and still mistaking your grandmother for the girlfriend for three acts straight—this tradition in humor is a diaper that we have put away for good. The humor that really comes out in Hollywood's "Midsummer Night's Dream" is based, like the best of Shakespeare, on people; the formal comedy element is false to us and must be toned down with more subtlety than the producers of this film can muster. They could have done it far better by taking the whole less solemnly, by using people who (like Olivia de Haviland) might read the lines with some comprehension of what they were about. But they would have done still better by taking another play than this particular play, the product of a poet's exuberance and youth. Its phrases still ring like bells, there is an easy strong vigor and charmed air to the whole. But owing to circumstances and the matter of a few centuries in time, its words are beautiful as words in a book, not in the mouths of fools.

Otis Ferguson, "Shakespeare in Hollywood," in The New Republic, Vol. LXXXIV, No. 1089, October 16, 1935, p. 272.

Felix Felton   (essay date 1963)

[Felton, who played Bottom in Reinhardt's 1933 Oxford University Dramatic Society's staging of A Midsummer Night's Dream, here recounts his experiences with the German director in that production.]

Max Reinhardt's productions in [England] were all too few; but his impact was tremendous, both on those who saw them, and, even more, on those who had the exciting experience of working under his direction. It was my own good fortune to be in the cast of his last English production, A Midsummer Night's Dream, at Oxford in 1933. During the run he signed a photograph for me, with the words "Zür Errinerung"—"For Remembrance". I need hardly say that after thirty years that remembrance is still very much alive: no one who knew Max Reinhardt is likely to forget him. (p. 134)

Reinhardt's last production in this country was A Midsummer Night's Dream at Oxford, in the summer of 1933. The O.U.D.S.—The Oxford University Dramatic Society—of which I happened to be President at the time, was looking round for a producer of its summer open-air play. It was the custom in those days to invite professional producers and actresses to co-operate, and, a year or two before, the Society had presented John Gielgud's production of Romeo and Juliet, in which the late Christopher Hassall played Romeo, Peggy Ashcroft, Juliet and Edith Evans the Nurse. Even so, we felt we were being bold indeed when we sent a cable to Max Reinhardt inviting him to come and produce the Dream, and never expected him to accept. But the reply came: yes, he would be delighted.

Large, alarming wheels began to turn. Cables arrived. The Herr Professor Doktor would like "eighty extras and a lake". (He was at the time producing the play in Florence, where there were far greater resources than we could possibly offer.) And, equally disconcerting, he would like to produce the play on a hill. Hills are not two-a-penny in Oxford. For a start, this knocked out the grounds of all the Colleges, many of which were quietly but keenly competing for the honour. Eventually we obtained the use of Headington Hill, just beyond Magdalen Bridge—and a wonderful site it proved, with a foreground area of meadow, a row of sparsely placed but thick trees behind it, through which was seen a further meadow, and a wood to one side.

The stories of these weeks of preparation would make a book of their own, and there are many unsung heroes. Herr Felix Weissberger arrived, one of Reinhardt's always highly able lieutenants. The actresses were cast: Mary Gaskell as Her-

mia, Joan Maude as Helena, Oriel Ross as Titania; and, on the undergraduate side, Peter Glenville was cast as Puck, and I, to my great joy, as Bottom. I very quickly learnt two things: that rehearsals meant very hard work; I have never worked harder, even in many years on the professional stage; and, secondly, there came, as a complete revelation, Reinhardt's approach to the comic scenes. I learn from Martin Esslin, the B.B.C.'s Head of Radio Drama, that, in earlier days, Reinhardt and Bernauer had been a team which put on a satirical act in Berlin called "Die Bösen Buben"—"The Naughty Boys". Certainly the comic invention showered on the craftsmen's scenes was impish in the extreme. Bottom was, in Reinhardt's phrase, the "dilettante κατεξοχην"—the madly enthusiastic amateur. Quince, the solemn literalist, was always half-hidden behind an enormous prompt copy—even in the final scene when the play was being performed at Court. Was this a crack at English pedantry? We never knew. A running argument raged between Bottom and Quince about the correct pronunciation, Thisne or Thisbe, and this also was carried into the Court performance itself.

As for Max Reinhardt's spontaneity . . . we had abundant examples. When we were rehearsing on Headington Hill, University rules compelled us to be in our Colleges by midnight. At ten to twelve, on a signal from the stage manager, we used to break and run to our cars, leaving the great man shouting after us on the hill-top. To our great delight, this situation was used at the end of the first craftsmen scene: the craftsmen all ran off, leaving Quince yelling after them: "Meet me in the wood" [I. ii. 101], etc., purple with rage. And again, when, as Bottom, I was calling for my companions, Reinhardt discovered that, if I shouted in a certain direction, there was an echo from across the valley, and at once a double-take was added by my pulling the string attached to one of the ears of the donkey's head.

Most wonderful of all, though, was his direction of the "Methought I was, methought I had" speech [IV. i. 200ff.]. Usually this seems to go for very little. With Reinhardt, it began with a nervous groping, to see if the long snout and the long ears were still there; then a quickening of gesture, a nervous laughter; a sudden cut to silence; a fifty-yard run to the pond; a look at the reflection in the water; a scream of relief; and a jubilant dance off through the trees towards Athens. I don't know what impression this gives in print, but I can assure you that every night it held the audience like a vice. And, to repeat what others have said, although every minutest gesture and moment of timing was controlled, I felt as if it welled up naturally from deep inside me. Reinhardt never imposed an interpretation; he evoked it.

As for the pictorial side, what was so impressive from behind the scenes was the simplicity with which the most powerful effects were achieved. At the play's opening, the lords and ladies just stepped out from behind the trees where they had been hidden. The whole landscape was suddenly, effortlessly, alive. When the craftsmen first met, in the fading evening light, they started from the back of the further meadow, the jogging lights of their lanterns gradually converging, to the music that Mendelssohn wrote for them. (And a word here for Michael Scott, the Musical Director, who assembled a wonderful team of distinguished musicians, Leon Goossens among them, contributing handsomely, I believe, from his own pocket.) Then there was the moment when Puck ran across the sward, and vanished, bringing a gasp from the audience every night. He had simply jumped into a pit, banked up so as to be invisible to the audience—from which his arm now came up, like a malevolent twig, to trip each craftsman as they came into the enchanted wood. When Oberon (Philip Arnhold) climbed into a tree to overhear the lovers, he disappeared, but the tree shimmered with a mysterious magic. And anyone who saw that production will remember the end of the Nocturne, when Nini Theilade, Reinhardt's exquisite little Danish dancer, was carried off into the night by Michael Martin Harvey, a slowly narrowing spotlight following the undulation of her hands to a pinpoint of light in the darkness.

Critics spoke of the lyric unity of this production; and one said that he had seen many open-air productions of this play, but never one so much at ease in its surroundings. It was a typically generous gesture of Reinhardt's to entrust himself to a largely undergraduate and inexperienced cast; and it is good to think that, for his last production in England, he achieved what had long been his ambition, to produce a play by Shakespeare in Shakespeare's own countryside.

Zür Errinerung. (pp. 140-42)

> Felix Felton, "Max Reinhardt in England," in Theatre Research, *Vol. V, No. 3, 1963, pp. 134-42.*

Roger Manvell   (essay date 1971)

[*Manvell surveys Reinhardt's film adaptation, observing that despite the unorthodox casting of such actors as Mickey Rooney as Puck and James Cagney as Bottom and the severe cutting of the text, "much of the film is still strangely effective in its own particular right."*]

[In 1934] Max Reinhardt's celebrated stage conception of *A Midsummer Night's Dream* was produced as a film by the Warner Brothers, jointly directed by Reinhardt and William Dieterle. For Dieterle, who had emigrated in 1930 to the United States from Germany, where he had been distinguished both as actor and director, *A Midsummer Night's Dream* was to be his first film of distinction in Hollywood; in a note written for the author he says of Reinhardt:

> This remains one of my most pleasing professional memories, largely because I had, of course, been his devoted admirer ever since I had been fortunate enough to play under his direction in the Deutsche Theater as a young actor in my twenties. The *Dream,* of course, had been one of his favourite productions for decades, and I had had considerable experience of it. Contractually, we were given equal credit (he, of course, being named first), and it was clearly understood between us that he was to be concerned with dialogue and leading the actors, while I attended to all technicalities connected with the filming. Inevitably there was some overlapping but everything went without a hitch and in the most pleasant atmosphere, simply because we understood each other so very well.

The film cost $1½ million, ran for over two hours, and failed at the box-office. Nevertheless, it was by far the most spectacular attempt of the decade to present Shakespeare on the screen, rivalled only by M.G.M.'s highly pictorialized version of *Romeo and Juliet* which was to follow hard upon it.

Reinhardt's spectacular stage productions, centred on Berlin but well known elsewhere, had been a feature of the European theatre since the period preceding the First World War. Among his larger-scale presentations was *A Midsummer*

Night's Dream, in which he developed the fairy element in the play along romantic, magical lines until it dwarfed the rest with its lighting effects and choreography; he took this production, with others, to the United States in 1927-8. With the rise of Hitler he left Germany. He presented *A Midsummer Night's Dream* for the Oxford University Dramatic Society at night in a beautifully lit open-air production; later he was to produce the play again in Hollywood itself. As a result of this, Jack L. Warner ventured into setting up Reinhardt's production as a film, insuring himself at the box-office by introducing as many stars as he could into the cast—whether they were appropriate or inappropriate. They included James Cagney (Bottom), Joe E. Brown (Flute), Mickey Rooney (aged 11, Puck), Anita Louise (Titania), Victor Jory (Oberon), Dick Powell (Lysander), and Olivia de Havilland (Hermia). The choreography for the fairies was devised by Bronislava Nijinska and by Nini Theilade, who played the principal fairy. Among the team of directors of photography was Byron Haskin, head of the Special Effects department at Warner Brothers, and some twenty years later to be closely associated with George Pal in the production of outstanding science fiction films.

The choreography and special effects, in fact, make the principal value of the film, as a film. The whole nineteenth-century romantic concept of the production arises from Mendelssohn's score which, arranged by Erich Wolfgang Korngold, pervades the atmosphere; there is even a miniature orchestra of dwarfs present in the wood to assist in the performance. If one accepts Mendelssohn's interpretation of the fairy wood (as distinct from the far darker concept of Shakespeare's intentions, as understood by Jan Kott, for example, or represented in Peter Hall's stage and film productions of the play a generation later), then the commanding performance of Victor Jory as Oberon amply fulfils Reinhardt's intentions, while Mickey Rooney's urchin Puck stands somewhat left of centre—not sinister enough for Kott, not elfin enough for Mendelssohn.

An even further disparate element came with the lovers—Dick Powell, in particular, introduced a light-weight presence which, admirable in its place, could bring little which could be relevant to this Mendelssohn-Shakespearean film. Again, the hard professional clowning of Joe E. Brown established an alien atmosphere in the third element of the play, the rustics, while James Cagney, with his own form of tough sophistication, made Bully Bottom into a relatively straight character which was once more out of sympathy with the rustics as a whole. The text of the play was cut back by over half, and its order sometimes changed in the interests of visual continuity. With a running time of 140 minutes, it is the choreographic spectacle of the corps de ballet of the fairies to which Reinhardt constantly returns, with such startling effects as the absorption of the fairy train at dawn into Oberon's long, magic cloak. However much one may object to the characterization, to the truncated lines, to the speaking, or non-speaking, of Shakespeare's verse, much of the film is still strangely effective in its own particular right. Even so exacting a critic as John Russell Taylor [in *Shakespeare: a Celebration*] does not mind admitting this:

> Not, clearly, a 'serious' approach to Shakespeare at all, and yet, strange to relate, a remarkably successful film, one which even today is fresh and vivid when its more worthy, respectable contemporaries look hopelessly faded. However dubious it may all look on paper, in the cinema it nearly all works.

Victor Jory as Oberon with attendant fairies. Reinhardt's film adaptation.

The performances, if sometimes a trifle odd, are lively and interesting, and Mickey Rooney's Puck is absolutely brilliant. The fairy sequences in particular, shot through spangled gauze for the most part, distil precisely the slightly cruel, slightly sinister poetry that Shakespeare achieved in words, often by cutting the words and replacing them with visual equivalents of startling beauty. Oddly enough, Reinhardt the stage director has in his only film managed to do what most experienced film directors have hardly considered doing: he has translated Shakespeare instead of merely recording him.

(pp. 25-7)

> Roger Manvell, "The Arrival of Sound: The First
> Phase of Adaption," in his Shakespeare and the
> Film, Praeger Publishers, 1971, pp. 23-36.

J. L. Styan   (essay date 1982)

[In the excerpt below, Styan provides an overview of several of Reinhardt's productions of A Midsummer Night's Dream, stating that "the elements of baroque fantasy" in the play "were so much to Reinhardt's taste that it may be seen as his representative Shakespearian offering."]

In January 1905, Reinhardt first presented what would be-come his favourite play, A Midsummer Night's Dream. It was this play which he continued to revive for thirty-four years, a span of time in which the production suffered many changes before it finally arrived in America. The actual itinerary was: Berlin (Neues Theater, 1905), Prague (1906), Berlin (Deutsches Theater, 1907), Budapest (1908), Munich (1909), Vienna and Munich again (1910), Berlin (Deutsches Theater again, 1913), Stockholm and Christiana (1915), six cities in Switzerland (1917), Berlin (Grosses Schauspielhaus, 1921), Vienna again (1925), Salzburg and New York (1927), Berlin (Deutsches Theater again, 1930), Florence and Oxford (1933), six cities in the United States (1934), Hollywood for the film (1935) and Hollywood on the stage (1939). Nobody has attempted to trace the production changes and the vagaries of performance over this long period, but the elements of baroque fantasy in the production were so much to Reinhardt's taste that it may be seen as his representative Shakespearian offering. He displayed his A Midsummer Night's Dream like a personal banner.

In its happy acceptance of imaginative license, the production of 1905 was recognized as a new attack on the mood and style of the naturalistic movement, and the Austrian critic Rudolph Kommer named it the keystone of the director's career:

215

Reinhardt fought the royal battle against drab naturalism under the star of Shakespeare. It was not a German play that won the fight for romanticism of a new brand; it was the fanciful comedy, *A Midsummer Night's Dream*. Nothing could have suited Reinhardt's imaginative temperament better; no other play could have been more programmatic . . . It was a revelation. Berlin was jubilant. He had not added a word, he had not cut a line. And yet, it seemed a new play entirely. Full of life, colour, music and joy, it had a message that did away in one evening with all the voluptuous pessimism and sordidness of the preceding fifteen or twenty years of naturalism ["The Magic of Leopoldskron," in *Max Reinhardt and his Theatre*, ed. Oliver M. Sayler].

With others by Shakespeare, this play had previously been treated in the ponderous style with which the German theatre approached the classics. Now it was freshly seen, the director's touch was quick and light, and the production brought together again all the arts of the theatre, including, in Felix Mendelssohn's score, the element of music that the naturalistic directors had inhibited.

The *Regiebuch* of 1905 is disappointing in that it gives little hint of how Reinhardt handled the variations in the lovers' quarrel, nowadays a test of a production's insights into the play's motifs and its mode of comedy, nor of how Puck (played in the early years by actresses - Gertrud Eysoldt or Leopoldine Konstantin) teased the lovers at the end of the scene, worked with the audience in the imaginary "darkness" of the wood, and magically arranged the sleeping bodies for the best results: we learn only that Lysander and Hermia are Right and that Demetrius and Helena are Left. But the *Regiebuch* is rich in those details by which Reinhardt indicated the stage setting and the appropriate business for the immortals. These details were unashamedly fantastic.

The early sets for the "wood near Athens" were lavishly impressionistic and ingeniously managed:

> When the curtain goes up, the scene is covered with screens. Through these silver screens the moon shines palely, and slowly the light increases. The screens are raised slowly one after another in individual trails of mist. Streams trickle.
> The scene is set with tall grass and many trees overhanging a clearing among them. At the back is a view of a high wooded hill which ends backstage. On the right is seen a lake glinting between the trees. On the left is the hillside. Past the lake on the left runs a fairly narrow path to the back of the stage.
> The trees are very tall. The tops begin high up, so that the fairies appear very small. The tree-trunks must be as thick as possible. The roof of leaves is high up.
> Moonlight, which falls in patches on the grass through the leaf pattern. The lake is lit from behind.

Caverns and vistas could be discerned through the trees, and billows of smoke puffed from the ground. So it was that the first designer, Gustav Knina, was able to enhance the illusion of diminutive fairies and immense distances.

This wood was central to the performance, as Heinz Herald recognized:

> In the beginning was the wood. With the exception

of the short overture of the opening scene and the big wedding finale, it is the setting for the whole play. It is its nurse, its native soil; from it everything flows, in it everyone is hidden, runs away, is mixed up, discovered, reconciled . . . It breathes, it is alive. It seems without beginning or end. It is inexhaustible, without visible limits, and yet, to sum up, it somehow represents every wood [*Reinhardt und seine Bühne*].

Siegfried Jacobsohn [in his *Max Reinhardt*] also tried to account for the illusion of a supernatural world: "Moonlight shimmered, and dawn broke in a blaze of light. In the distance echoed earthly voices. Here and there a glowworm shone. Leaves rustled and twigs snapped."

Macgowan [in his *The Theatre of Tomorrow*] reported that in the early years the wood was "a forest of real papier-maché trees," but when Ernst Stern was the designer in 1913, the heavy, three-dimensional trunks and rolling grass gave place to a more suggestive treatment of light and shade. Washburn-Freund [in his "The evolution of Reinhardt," in Sayler] considered it an almost symbolist effect of colour and light, creating an atmosphere of "endless woods, now threatening, now sheltering, full of mysterious sounds and beings." Jacobsohn found everything very simple, but argued that "perhaps for that reason it was more evocative: when the spectator's imagination is receptive, then it is unnecessary to inflict a naturalistic production on him." By the time the production had reached Vienna in 1925, the stage was virtually bare, a playing-space in front of green curtains which merely suggested the wood. The scenic display had become less obtrusive, and the stage was given over principally to the actors. When the production came to New York in 1927, Brooks Atkinson of the *New York Times* would not accept the verdict that it was merely "a pompous show." Reinhardt, he declared [27 November 1927], "does not subordinate the play to showy effects; when he employs big set-pieces he does so merely to bring the play into its highest perspective."

The *Regiebuch* indicates that great care was also given to the fairies. Here are some of the notes on their costumes:

> A light, soft gauze covering their colours of lilac, violet, light and dark, then in all shades of green to dark green, and the same with a delicate light blue and dark blue. In the distance, an irridescent screen, rainbow-coloured, then shimmering with grey, white, gold and silver.
> Also dresses like flowers, and, for example, like green grass with dewdrops (glass).
> The children in flesh-coloured tights, and fitted with little quilted wings.
> The wings various: white, multi-coloured, transparent and shining, big and little.
> No shoes.

Stern considered the immortals to be "a delight," although he did not approve of Eysoldt as Puck with "a piece of leopard skin round her bosom"—she was "a wraith of a girl instead of a broth of a boy." But he recognized that the fairies were "no longer the depressing ballerinas of old-fashioned performances, but slim and elegant girls in close-fitting green tights and green wigs" [*My Life, My Stage*].

Everyone was impressed by the way Reinhardt made the wood come alive. Oberon was very much the central figure and the key to the play, and he first appeared apparently riding on a white stag with great antlers, and wearing a lighted crown upon his head. Then the *Regiebuch* suggests the activities of the fairy train:

> His followers are trolls, dwarfs, gnomes and pixies, and they skip along behind and jump in front of him from the grass and the hill, down left, and tumble in his path.
> Everything is alive. Everything is moving. Everyone skips, tumbles, jumps, runs and dances. A little later Titania hovers over the lake, and round her dance fairies with wings, others jump and skip in front of her. Mustardseed, Peaseblossom and Cobweb to the fore. Behind her six bigger fairies embrace in a circle.

For Jacobsohn, the constant coming and going created "a total mobility which concealed how repetitive were the movements of individual fairies." Herald found their movements entrancing: "gliding, jumping, hovering in a dance, flying over bush, stream and hillock." And he concluded, "Their motion is music, like their speech."

On the line, "Ill met by moonlight / Proud Titania" [II. i. 60], the opposing kinds of fairy joined in combat, as the *Regiebuch* suggests: "The encounter is staged as a battle of flowers. Flowers fly to and fro, and the fairies menace one another with their wands, and romp and scuffle in the grass." When they come upon Lysander asleep beside Hermia, we read this:

> A small fairy cautiously emerges from behind a tree, tiptoes gently at a distance round the sleepers with his bow, then dares to come closer, laughs and fetches a second fairy, with whom he runs forward swiftly, then back again laughing. Finally five come forward together, wind in a circle round the couple. They tickle the lovers on the nose and feet. The smallest sits astride Lysander.

All this had the effect of making the lovers more ridiculous and an extension of the fantasy. And, needless to say, the unashamed sentimentality of these scenes made them immensely popular.

If Karl Walser's costumes for the lovers were conventionally Greek, the visual aspects of the production were otherwise telling. There were brilliant processionals under a star-spangled sky, with Theseus and Hippolyta making their entrance to a candle-lit parade, and much more. The invention of comic business for the mechanicals knew no bounds. The basic joke was their proclivity for falling down, but Quince was always hidden behind a voluminous script and Bottom was played as an amateur actor of all-consuming enthusiasm. Felix Felton, who later played Bottom in Reinhardt's Oxford University Dramatic Society production in 1933, records that throughout the play and even "on the night" a running argument raged between Bottom and Quince about the correct pronunciation of "Thisbe/Thisne." As each mechanical entered the wood, he was tripped up by Puck's arm "like a malevolent twig." Best of all, however, was Bottom's "Methought I had, methought I was" [IV. i. 208-09] speech:

> Usually this seems to go for very little. With Reinhardt, it began with a nervous groping, to see if the long snout and the long ears were still there; then a quickening of gesture, a nervous laughter; a sudden cut to silence; a fifty-yard run to the pond [a feature of the open-air set at Oxford]; a look at the reflection in the water; a scream of relief; and a jubilant dance off through the trees towards Athens ["Max Reinhardt in England," *Theatre Research*, 1963].

Felton added, "I don't know what impression this gives in print, but I can assure you that every night it held the audience like a vice."

The production at Oxford revealed some of Reinhardt's characteristics as a director. In New York, Brooks Atkinson had remarked that Reinhardt blessed the play with "limitless space"; the space at Oxford appeared to have blessed him. He had already enjoyed directing an open-air production in the grounds of his Schloss Leopoldskron at Salzburg in 1932, when he cast Isadora Duncan's students as fairies flitting in the twilight across the grass and devised a way of making Puck seem to materialize against the moonlight. At Oxford he had all the space he could have wanted, because he chose, not some convenient college garden, but the great meadow at South Park, Headington Hill, just beyond Magdalen Bridge, a great sloping field set with elm and beech and may, with a line of trees behind it through which a further meadow could be seen, and a wood and bushes on either side. An apocryphal story is told that when Reinhardt caught a glimpse of the village over the hill, he cried, "That town—it must go!"

The correspondent of *The Daily Telegraph* [16 June 1933] suggested that, once out in the open, Reinhardt thought in terms "not of square feet but of acres." The production became an unique exercise in the use of space and light, with all the emphasis on the immortals (some eighty supers), and a certain athleticism demanded of the players. *The Times* [15 June 1933] approved:

> In such a theatre there is nothing the fairies may not do. Puck may mock his victims from branches above their heads or from the swift invisibility offered him by a hole in the ground; Oberon's troop and Titania's, advancing from opposite woods, may meet by sudden chance and vanish, when their encounter is over, like the legions of a dream.

But the writer saw that the play's focus was somewhat altered:

> No longer is it a story of mortals in this world behind whom an enchantment has arisen; it is a tale of sprites and goblins pursuing the natural life of their own dwelling place, into which men and women have blindly wandered. That it has been Professor Reinhardt's purpose to enforce this emphasis to create an illusion of immortal intimacy becomes increasingly clear as the evening passes.

Some loss of individual character and neglect of the text were also inevitable: the image of Titania, played by the Swedish dancer Nini Theilade, lay "in her movement and appearance rather than in the music of her words."

It was a little embarrassing to watch the actors traversing such great distances and making breathless entrances and exits at the double. Rupert Hart-Davis in the *Spectator* [23 June 1933] thought this dispelled some of the magic:

> The ladies seldom had more than 100 yards sprint to negotiate—no inconsiderable feat in their elaborate dresses—but the men covered all distances up to and including the half-mile. One competitor suddenly dashed along the footlights and, much to the delight of the audience, failed to clear the water-jump [the pond mentioned above]. Often during an intimate scene in the foreground one's eye was caught by some lonely player plodding wearily

round the furthest fringe of the meadow, the last
lap of the three-miles cross-country.

The Daily Telegraph praised Puck for running far and fast
enough to establish a good claim to a cross-country Blue, "if
he has not got one already." So the wits had their field-day,
but no one denied that the effects produced were justified.

The play had never been "more lovely to the eye, nor has it
ever partaken more fully of the nature of a dream" (*The
Times*). Concealed lights under the trees and in the grass
made it possible for fairies to appear and disappear: "Points
of light danced and twinkled through the trees, the music
grew seemingly odd and unearthly; we were back in the Golden Age." Titania made a dancing entrance from afar across
the meadow, leading a small child dressed in white, so that
even Hart-Davis was enchanted: "Her long deep-blue train
held shoulder-high by following sprites, her dance between
the trees and subsequent disappearance into the darkness on
the shoulder of a satyr will not easily be forgotten" (*Spectator*). The mechanicals approached their rendezvous in the
wood by several separate paths across the meadow, their lanterns converging in the darkness. Puck's ability to vanish
abruptly by dropping into a pit made the audience gasp. And
when he carried off a fairy into the night, Felton described
how "a slowly narrowing spotlight followed the undulations
of her hands to a pin-point of light in the darkness."

Had the play been sacrificed to the producer? *The Times* felt
not. On the contrary, "it has been freshly seen, freshly interpreted, and performed in accordance with its woodland circumstance and an artist's dominating idea . . . At its peak
it is a production to take the breath away." (pp. 54-61)

> *J. L. Styan, "Reinhardt's Shakespeare," in his* Max
> Reinhardt, *Cambridge University Press, 1982, pp.
> 51-68.*

PRODUCTION:

Harley Granville-Barker • Savoy • 1914

BACKGROUND:

Granville-Barker's production of *A Midsummer Night's
Dream* at London's Savoy Theatre in 1914 is unquestionably one of the most significant stagings of the play in the
twentieth century. Intended as a complete break from all
the theatrical traditions associated with the *Dream,* Barker's production rejected Victorian scenic "realism," restored all but six words of Shakespeare's text, and even replaced Mendelssohn's romantic score with one based on
English folk songs. The simplified sets consisted of curtains decorated to suggest a sylvan locale and large columns to indicate Theseus's palace. Perhaps the most striking innovation was the representation of the fairies, who
were completely covered in gilt and bronze and whose
movements were distinctly mechanical. While many spectators and critics hailed this production as brilliant, others
were disconcerted by its other-worldly qualities, and some
were hostile to Barker's conception. In 1915 the play was
taken to New York where it was staged at Wallack's Theater.

COMMENTARY:

The Times, London   (review date 7 February 1914)

[*In the following review, the anonymous critic admits initial
misgivings about Barker's production of* A Midsummer
Night's Dream, *but concludes that it left on the mind "a
strange new impression of the play as golden, a 'golden book
of spirit and sense'."*]

Is it Titania's "Indian boy" that has given Mr. Barker his notion of Orientalizing Shakespeare's fairies? Or is it Bakst?
Anyhow, they look like Cambodian idols and posture like Nijinsky in *Le Dieu Bleu.* But the most startling thing about
them is that they are all gold—gold hair, gold faces, gold to
the tips of their toes. A golden Oberon is flouted by a golden
Titania. Peas-Blossom and Cobweb and Moth and Mustard-
Seed are golden children—the only children among these
fairies—three in flakes of gold and the fourth in golden baggy
trousers out of *Sumurûn.* The rest are "golden lads and
lasses," who, some of them, dance old romping, obviously
English, dances, while the others, the Cambodian idols, fall
into stiff postures in corners. One with a scimitar stalks like
the black marionette, with *his* scimitar, in *Petrouchka.* Evidently the Russian ballet, which has transformed so much in
London, has transmogrified Shakespeare. The golden fairies
chase one another through the wood in single file or lie prone
on a low green mound, grouped round Titania, under great
shafts of green mounting to the sky, against a purple background. This colour-effect, the heavy mass of old gold against
the purple and the green, is wonderfully beautiful. In the end
the golden fairies play hide-and-seek round the columns of
Theseus's palace. Gradually their numbers dwindle. At last
only one, a girl, is left—the last patch of gold to fade from
the sight, and to leave on the mind the strange, new impression of the play as golden, a "golden book of spirit and sense."
Who is the magician who invented these golden fairies? Is it
Mr. Barker or Mr. Norman Wilkinson? One might perhaps
have had misgivings about the thing in advance, a fear of taw-
driness, dreadful associations with the golden image in Ken-
sington-gardens. But the thing turns out to have been an inspiration, something to strike us all with wonder and delight.
As soon as you see the thing you know that Mendelssohn
would never do. For our part, we should have welcomed Stra-
vinsky. But Mr. Cecil Sharp has given us old English folk-
music, rather dolorous, always *piano,* more quaint than tune-
ful. Well, somehow or other, as the Americans say, it "goes."
It goes quite well with the gold.

On the gold is one single patch of scarlet. This is Puck, with
a baggy wig and baggy breeches, a hobgoblin. He—Puck is
this time really a he—is Mr. Donald Calthrop, gyrating, sitting at Oberon's feet cross-legged, tumbling head over heels,
or, like a mischievous boy, putting finger to nose behind Bottom's back. A most uncanny Puck, this scarlet patch.

As for Theseus and Hippolyta and their train, we do not
know where their dresses come from. We can only make
shots. Is it from the mural decorations of Minos's palace un-
earthed in Crete? But some of them seem Byzantine and suggest a Ravenna fresco. All, men and women alike, wear "peg-
top" trousers, tight at the ankle. But in the last scene, at the
performance of Pyramus and Thisbe, they, so to speak, put
on their evening clothes—flowing Greek robes. So clad, they
recline on couches in the very front of the stage (Mr. Barker's
now familiar "apron stage") while the performance of Quince

and his fellows takes place on the palace steps in the rear. This, again, is a novel arrangement and an admirable. Quince (Mr. Whitby) is *impayable,* Bottom (Mr. Playfair) immense, Flute (Mr. Quartermaine) deliciously absurd as Thisbe. And then the "Bergamask" dance! It never came out of Bergamo, but is right Warwickshire, the acme of the clumsy grotesque with vigorous kickings in that part of the anatomy meant for kicks. Perhaps the best thing in the performance, however, was the behaviour of the audience; Theseus's courtly lead in the applause, the whispered comments of Demetrius and Lysander, the lively interest of the courtiers. It was all alive, this scene, all at the high-watermark of excitement.

As always in *A Midsummer Night,* the difficulty is with the bewitched quartet of lovers. The difficulty is that they are often in imminent danger of becoming bores. If they escape being bores, they may be said to have succeeded. We are not sure that the men did altogether escape: but the ladies, Miss McCarthy and Miss Cowie, were more lucky. Miss McCarthy hardly shows at her best in a flaxen wig, but no doubt she must needs be contrasted with Miss Cowie's *brunette.* The quarrel of the two girls gives, as always, a tremendous "lift" to this part of the play. Miss Cowie makes a surprisingly intense vixen—an anticipation of Carmen.

But it is not of these one thinks in the end. The mind goes back to the golden fairies, and one's memories of this production must always be golden memories. The golden Oberon, Mr. Dennis Neilson-Terry, is a figure of slim, noble, and Giorgionesque beauty. His movements are grace itself. His voice, with the familiar family *timbre,* is the very voice for some of the most beautiful lines Shakespeare ever wrote. This Oberon, for the first time, dominates not only the scene, but the whole play, informs it with graciousness and majesty (fairy majesty, golden majesty) and exquisite rhythmic beauty. Miss Christine Silver's Titania is a delicate, fragile pendant to the Oberon. The little golden child-fairies are delightfully childish, even in their stiff Cambodian-idol attitudes. There was a great outburst of enthusiasm—pent up in silent absorption during the evening—at the fall of the curtain. Mr. Barker, standing amid his golden fairies, seemed to be thinking that silence, too, has been said to be golden; but he was compelled, nevertheless, to utter a word of thanks. If only he can keep it up! If only he can run through all Shakespeare in the spirit of daring artistic adventure with which he has turned the fairy-land of *A Midsummer Night* into gold.

A review of "A Midsummer Night's Dream," in The Times, *London, February 7, 1914, p. 8.*

The Athenaeum   (review date 14 February 1914)

[*In the review reprinted below, the anonymous critic admires Barker's production of* A Midsummer Night's Dream *as "something in itself rich, graceful, and authentic as a work of art," but, he adds, it had only a slender relation to Shakespeare's text.*]

There is no play from which one can draw more justification than from 'A Midsummer Night's Dream' for bringing together, out of any country or time or mythology one likes, details to compose or to decorate the production. Mr. Granville Barker has availed himself gallantly of this liberty. There is hardly any idiom of pictorial art of which some trace may not be discovered in the rendering of the 'Dream' now being given at the Savoy; and so strongly are all the diverse elements suffused with the peculiar qualities of twentieth-century imagination, that, for the most part, they appear as natural in their places as stones do in some elaborately wrought setting of gold.

Gold is one of the prevailing ideas of the play: every one knows by this time that a golden Oberon and Titania reign over a population of golden fairies. There is something a little trying, especially for Titania, in the high lights that come on the shiny golden faces, and in the scene with Bottom one has almost a surfeit of gold; but the first scene in which the fairy nation appears is a triumphantly beautiful spectacle, nor can it be denied that by this device they are admirably separated from the human inhabitants of the country.

Mr. Dennis Neilson-Terry made an ideally graceful and majestic Oberon, and Miss Christine Silver's Titania was no less charming; but both alike illustrated one of the weaknesses of the production—the uneven and inadequate treatment of the verse of the play. One gets irresistibly the impression that these actors belong, by instinct, so to speak, to a school of drama so widely different from the drama of pure poetry that they are embarrassed by the very loveliness of the lines they have to speak. They have no convention to serve them, and seem to have no exact conception of their function. This weakness, apparent even amid the unfailing grace of diction in Titania and Oberon, was much more conspicuous in Puck. Puck—as being the *clou* of the play—was assimilated to the human beings in his "get-up," allowed to retain his natural complexion, and dressed in scarlet with black trimmings. Mr. Donald Calthrop worked hard, and there was no lack of happy touches, but he never seemed to hit the mark. His general appearance suggested a combination of Paderewski and Struwwelpeter, which in itself we cannot but think unfortunate. There was no touch in him of genuine, spontaneous mischievousness, or of the woodland spirit, or of rustic humour. He was nearer a clown than an elf, and despite his praiseworthy antics suggested more distinctly than did any other figure indoor life—the life of a comfortable, bourgeois interior, from which, like a naughty boy, he had run away without his hat. This jarred against the verses provided for him: these, indeed, he rendered on occasion admirably, but even more unequally than the others, and sometimes actually with heaviness—which is the more pity because the play, as a play, depends greatly on the satisfactoriness of Puck.

The night-scene, with the "bank whereon the wild thyme blows," was charming. Mr. Nigel Playfair as Bottom was great, and in general Quince (Mr. Arthur Whitby), Snug (Mr. Neville Gartside), Flute (Mr. Leon Quartermaine), Snout (Mr. Stratton Rodney), and Starveling (Mr. H. O. Nicholson) were all that could be desired. Mr. Baliol Holloway as Theseus started rather woodenly, but improved in every way as the play went on. Miss Laura Cowie's Hermia contributed the most markedly "twentieth-century" element to the whole. Her appearance was like a résumé in one person of the prettiest and most up-to-date ladies on recent posters, and her playing was delightful. Miss Lillah McCarthy gave Helena a dignity which redeemed the absurdity of the part by rendering the incongruity just faintly distressing—an effect which was excellently calculated, being nowhere over-emphasized.

The last act, where the ducal party recline on couches in front of the stage, with their backs to the auditorium, and watch 'Pyramus and Thisbe' performed on the terrace of the palace, is one of the most admirably devised and most tellingly enacted scenes of recent contrivance, and the close of the play is beautifully, if a little over-seriously imagined.

The total impression it leaves with one is that of something in itself rich, graceful, and authentic as a work of art, but having in many parts as slender a relation as is well possible to the spirit of the play as it is expressed in the text, and diverging from it chiefly in the direction of too much solemnity. (pp. 239-40)

A review of "A Midsummer Night's Dream," in The Athenaeum, *No. 4503, February 14, 1914, pp. 239-40.*

The Illustrated London News   (review date 14 February 1914)

[*While finding the verse-speaking of Barker's Savoy production admirable, the reviewer in the following excerpt nevertheless considers the fairies in this staging the result of "calculated eccentricity, and the resolve to do something new at all costs."*]

Fairies with gilt faces, crimson eyebrows, and Oriental headdresses are an innovation which it requires, to say the least, a very open mind to accept as corresponding with Shakespeare's fancy, and to conceive of as fit denizens of the forest-glades of his "Midsummer Night's Dream." Mr. Granville Barker's fairies at the Savoy look neither pretty nor poetical; they seem the invention of calculated eccentricity, and of the resolve to do something new at all costs. Not even Bakst has ever had a more grotesque idea in the way of decoration; they introduce an element of jarring modernity into an atmosphere in which hitherto lovers, "little people," and farcial mechanics have seemed to mix with perfect naturalness and harmony. This mistake of audacity in Messrs. Barker and

Norman Wilkinson's scheme is the more vexing because their new way of presenting Shakespeare provides in the latest instance so much that is gladdening and beautiful, and we are given the whole text of the play. What is more, we hear it and can savour every word. Never in any recent performance has such ample justice been done to the music of the verse. Theseus's big speech comes admirably from Mr. Baliol Holloway, who is supported, in the person of Miss Evelyn Hope, by a Hippolyta as eloquent as she is queenly. Messrs. Ion Swinley and Guy Rathbone, gallant as the men-lovers, and Miss Laura Cowie, the daintiest of Hermias in her green gown, and Miss Lillah McCarthy, given golden hair as Helena, lose not a point in their lines. The rustics, among whom Mr. Nigel Playfair figures, as a rather mild-spoken but extremely genial Bottom, bring out all the humours of the Thisbe interlude; and while neither Mr. Dennis Neilson-Terry as Oberon, nor Miss Christine Silver as Titania, can be felicitated on the dresses they have to wear, both they and Mr. Donald Calthrop, as Puck, convey the full charm of Shakespeare's poetry.

"The Playhouses," in The Illustrated London News, *Vol. CXLIV, No. 3904, February 14, 1914, p. 252.*

John Palmer   (review date 14 February 1914)

[*In the excerpt below, Palmer regards this production "more like a battlefield than a collaboration" between designer Norman Wilkinson's "unearthly vision in purple and green; Mr.*

Christine Silver as Titania, with attendant fairies.

Barker's entirely Gallic vision of Shakespeare's comic people; and Mr. Cecil Sharp's old English music. "]

Mr. Granville Barker, like Bottom in the play, has had a most rare vision. Or is it Mr. Norman Wilkinson? Someone, at any rate, has wandered into a purple-green forest—surely the forest where Keats's wretched knight, palely loitering, met La Belle Dame; and where Ondine, through the cool rain, came to Ravel as he brooded of "Gaspard de la Nuit". There we encounter fantastical shapes in gold and vermillion, and a bright red mannikin with streaming hair escaped from an old showman's box of puppets. So long as this vision passes as a mute procession of quaint spirits, we are happy to be drawn into the vistas of their strange world. But these spirits unfortunately are required to utter sweet English breath, and trip to old English measures. Occasionally Shakespeare comes breaking in; and then we remember that this is a production for which we seem to have waited years—Mr. Granville Barker's "A Midsummer Night's Dream". We remember, too, that this is the Forest of Arden (the Forest of Arden is in Shakespeare's plays a movable property transported from Athens to Verona, from Verona to Sutton Coldfield, as the author pleases); that shortly Bottom and his company will appear from yonder brake; that the primrose and nodding violet grow not far away; that an English fairyland is lurking about us on every hand.

If only I could have got Shakespeare out of my head! How different it all would have been! Having, as I insist, no taste in pictorial or plastic art, I am quite content with Mr. Norman Wilkinson. I like geometry and audacious colour. I like simple and entirely conventional pretences, as for example that a symmetrical green cone, flanked with hanging curtains of green and purple is a forest, and a bank where the wild thyme blows. Similarly when I am invited into a world of immortal sprites, I like to see them decked with spiral ornaments, beards of formal cut, and golden faces, to attest that they are no ordinary people. I would have been quite happy in Mr. Wilkinson's forest had it not been for the unfortunate coincidence that Mr. Barker's company of players were there in trying to present a play purporting to be by William Shakespeare.

When, a week or so ago, I read Mr. Barker's happy preface to "A Midsummer Night's Dream" . . . , I felt that only he and I, in all the world, really loved and understood Shakespeare as a practical dramatist writing for a stage and an audience. Now that Mr. Barker has produced the play he seemed so thoroughly to know, I realise that only one just man is left in this modern world. For the play now running at the Savoy, though it be almost everything by turns, and nothing long, is never Shakespeare's "Dream". It is the child of Mr. Barker's perfect sanity—that perfect sanity whose pitiless iron seems finally to have entered Mr. Barker's producer soul.

The producer of "A Midsummer Night's Dream" is severely tested at the start. If he can by any means successfully survive the first act, we may know that the rest is safe. If he can get into that opening scene the note of fantasy; suggest the lovely impudence and virtuosity of Shakespeare's heedless talk of wooing and death and virginity; of dread penalties never to be incurred; woes never seriously to be suffered; love never to be more than the web of an idle tale—if the producer can so present his players from the start that at once we see them with the eyes of Puck (Lord! what fools these mortals be! [III.

ii. 115]), then the rest of his task will come as easily as language to Pompilia's advocate.

Mr. Barker may counter this by saying that Shakespeare's opening scene is mere creaking machinery to get his lovers into a wood—that the play really begins with the fairies; that the opening scene simply *cannot* be produced into anything credible or true. I will answer that challenge, when and if it be made. To me that opening scene is a key to the whole play; and I instinctively knew, when Aegeus began to arraign Lysander and his daughter like a counsel for the prosecution; when Hermia pleaded for her love like a logician making points in an argument; and when Theseus put on the black cap with a solemn recommendation to mercy—I knew that Mr. Barker had failed. He had presented the scene with just that incorrigible reasonableness which the play cannot endure, and was never intended to endure. If we bring the characters of "A Midsummer Night's Dream" before that comic bar where motives are measured and weighed with due regard for the likelihood and sanity of everyday, at once they are tedious monsters. These creatures are not visible in the sunlight which Mr. Barker's intelligence has turned upon them. Was it Heine who said that the people of Shakespeare's comedies live only under the moon? Well, the moon was in snuff upon Friday last. No casement was left open for moonshine. Aegeus stood clearly forth as an unreasonable brute; Theseus as the serious exponent of a monstrous theory of parental control; and Helena, arguing out her position at the end, as an altogether perfect imbecile. We actually began seriously to ask ourselves why she should go to the trouble of putting Demetrius on the track of her rival!

Mr. Barker's terrible sanity did not stop short at Aegeus and Helena. Oberon—a rather cynical and maleficent Oberon with contemptuous eyes—brooded over the quarrels of the forest lovers as if he were the embodiment of comic sanity— symbolical of Mr. Barker's clear and penetrating intelligence, active yet, even amid the mysterious shades of Mr. Norman Wilkinson's purple and green. Puck was a shining schoolboy, momentarily bewitched as to his lower limbs, lost in the forest on his way to a county council building somewhere in Warwickshire; and the fairies curry-combed Bottom transported with the efficiency of experienced ostlers. Quince, producer and author of the tragical history of Pyramus and Thisbe, dealt with Bottom like a worried, but wary, stage-manager soothing the susceptibilities of his leading man; whereas Bottom was intellectually presented as an artist craving for opportunities of self-expression. It was quite a pleasant surprise for all of us when he condescended at last to a bergamask, his only other lapse of the evening being a call for the tongs and bones.

I imagine that even those who do not resent Shakespeare being slaughtered to make an intellectual and post-impressionist holiday will find it rather difficult to endure the dissonance of the inharmonic intervals between Mr. Norman Wilkinson's unearthly vision in purple and green; Mr. Barker's entirely Gallic vision of Shakespeare's comic people; and Mr. Cecil Sharp's old English music. The production as a whole is more like a battlefield than a collaboration. Hardly has Mr. Wilkinson succeeded in conveying to our fancy an impression of airy nothings, than Mr. Barker's players come breaking in with their cheerful daylight manners and argumentative chatter, doing their utmost to turn Shakespeare's silly play into something reasonable and watertight. Then Mr. Cecil Sharp plays a bergamask; and Mr. Barker's players escape into England for a moment. Who really wins the fight is not entirely clear; but after an exciting final round with Mr. Wilkinson, Mr. Sharp and Mr. Barker all hitting out as hard as they can, Mr. Barker has the last word with Puck before the curtain conscientiously expounding the merits of his performance. But we are forgetting Shakespeare. Shakespeare from the beginning never had a chance. Having made a few feeble attempts to survive through the first scene, he was knocked completely out with a staggering blow from Nedar's Helena. Shakespeare, after all, was only a dramatic poet; and no dramatic poet, poor fellow, could be expected to survive Miss McCarthy's carefully laid plans for a midnight picnic in the Athenian woods. The fit climax of her argument would be an order, by telephone, to the local caterer for sandwiches. Alas! that so much sterling common sense should have been so grievously wasted. Shakespeare, I fear, is in some ways a graceless fellow. Perfect sanity is merely wasted upon him. He does not repay that kind of virtue.

And now I am wondering whether Miss Lillah McCarthy is really so entirely sensible a woman as Mr. Barker's Helena would show her to be. If this be really so, I can only advise her no longer to throw herself away on the poor foolish and ungrateful parts which are all that Shakespeare has to offer. Of the acting in general, I have no room to speak. The minor clowns were best; and as I have space for not more than two names, I will mention for high praise only Mr. Neville Gartside and Mr. H. O. Nicholson. Mr. Nigel Playfair was too obviously suffering from the same complaint as his producer. Mr. Barker is suffering from brains. I know all about brains. I have had them badly myself. (pp. 202-03)

John Palmer, "Mr. Barker's Dream," in The Saturday Review, *London, Vol. 117, No. 3042, February 14, 1914, pp. 202-03.*

Punch (review date 18 February 1914)

[*In the following excerpt, the critic approves many aspects of Barker's conception and staging of* A Midsummer Night's Dream, *but contends that "there was no distance, no suggestion of the spirit-world, no sense of mystery" in this production.*]

I am not sure that Mr. GRANVILLE BARKER'S faithful followers are being quite kindly entreated by him. He happens to have a keen sense of humour and for some little while he has been trying, with a very grave face, to see how much they will swallow. This time, everybody else except the initiated can see the bulge in his cheek where his tongue comes.

The alleged faults of the old school, which the new was to correct, were (1) an over-elaboration of detail in the setting; (2) a realism which challenged reality. ("Challenge," I understand, is the catch-word they use.) Both these qualities were supposed to distract attention from the drama itself. The answer, almost too obvious to be worth stating, is that the grotesque and the eccentric are vastly more distracting than the elaborate; and that, if you only sound the loud symbol loud enough the audience has no ear left at all for the actual words. As for the "challenging" of reality the new school would argue that, as the stage is a thing of convention to start with—artificial light, no natural atmosphere or perspective, no fourth wall, and so on—all the rest should be convention too. The answer, again almost too obvious, is that, since the audience has to bear the strain of unavoidable convention, you should not wantonly add to their worry. And, anyhow, the

human figures on your stage (I leave out fairies and superhumans for the moment) are bound to challenge reality by the fact that they are alive. If Mr. BARKER wants to be consistent (and he would probably repudiate so Philistine a suggestion) his figures should be marionettes worked by strings; and for words—if you *must* have words—he might himself read the text from a corner of the top landing of his proscenium.

And the strange thing is that no one in the world has a nicer sense of the beauty of SHAKESPEARE'S verse than Mr. BARKER. Indeed he protests in his preface: "They (the fairies) must be not too startling . . . *They mustn't warp your imagination—stepping too boldly between S' spirit and yours."* (The italics are my own comment.) He is of course free, within limits, to choose his own convention about fairies, because we have never seen them, though some of us say we have. Mr. CHESTERTON naturally says they can be of any size; Mr. BARKER says they can be of any age from little *Peaseblossom* and his young friends to hoary antiques with moustaches like ram's horns and beards trickling down to their knees. And as many as like it, and are not afraid of being poisoned, may have gilt faces that make them look like Hindoo idols with the miraculous gift of perspiration. But he should please remember that the play is not his own. It is, in point of fact, SHAKESPEARE'S, and I am certain he was not properly consulted about the Orientalisation of the fairies out of his Warwickshire woodlands. You will be told that he *has* been properly consulted; that he himself makes *Titania* say that *Oberon* has "come from the furthest steppe of India," and that she too had breathed "the spiced Indian air" [II. i. 69, 124]. But on the same authority Mr. BARKER might just as well have fixed on Asia Minor or Greece as their provenance. She charges *Oberon* with knowing *Hippolyta* too well, and he accuses her of making *Theseus* break faith with a number of ladies. Clearly they were a travelling company and would never have confined themselves to the costumes of any particular clime.

Anyhow, when at His Majesty's you saw *Oberon* in sylvan dress moving lightly through a wood that looked like a wood (and so left your mind free to listen to him), you could believe in all the lovely things he had to say; but when you saw Mr. BARKER'S *Oberon* standing stark, like a painted graven image, with yellow cheeks and red eyebrows, up against a symbolic painted cloth, and telling you that he knows a bank where the wild thyme blows, you know quite well that he knows nothing of the kind; and you don't believe a word of it.

But, to leave SHAKESPEARE decently out of the question, I liked the gold dresses of the fairies enormously, so long as *Puck*—a sort of adult Struwel-Puck that got badly on my nerves—was not there, destroying every colour scheme with his shrieking scarlet suit, which went with nothing except a few vermilion eyebrows. I liked too the grace of their simple chain-dances on the green mound (English dances, you will note, and English tunes—not Indian). But in the last scene, where they interlace among the staring columns, their movements lacked space. Indeed that was the trouble all through; that, and the pitiless light that poured pointblank upon the stage from the 126 muzzles protruding from the bulwarks of the dress-circle. There was no distance, no suggestion of the spirit-world, no sense of mystery (except in regard to Mr. BARKER'S intentions).

The best scene was the haunt of *Titania,* with its background of Liberty curtains very cleverly disposed. As drapery they were excellent, but as symbols of a forest I found them a little arbitrary. I do not mind a forest being indicated, if you are short of foliage, by a couple of trees (in tubs, if you like) or even a single tree; but somehow—and the fault is probably mine—the spectacle of hanging drapery does not immediately suggest to me the idea of birds' nests. I am afraid I should be just as stupid if Mr. BARKER gave me the same convention the other way round, and showed an interior with foliage to indicate window-curtains.

The play itself, with its rather foolish figures from the Court and the easy buffoonery of its peasants, does not offer great chances of acting; and Miss LAURA COWIE was the only one in the cast who added to her reputation. Her *Hermia* was a delightful performance full of charm and piquancy and real intelligence. Miss LILLAH MCCARTHY sacrificed something of her personality to the exigences of a flaxen chevelure. Mr. HOLLOWAY's *Theseus* was wanting in kingliness, and his hunting scene was perhaps the worst thing in the play. He was not greatly helped by his *Hippolyta*, for Miss EVELYN HOPE never began to look like a leader of Amazons. Miss CHRISTINE SILVER's *Titania* had a certain domestic sweetness, but even a queen of fairies might be a little more queenly. Mr. DENNIS NEILSON-TERRY as *Oberon* was a curiously effeminate figure for those who recalled the manly bearing of his mother in the same part. Of the two bemused Athenian lovers, Mr. SWINLEY, as *Lysander,* bore himself as bravely as could be expected.

Mr. NIGEL PLAYFAIR had, of course, no difficulty with the part of *Bottom,* and Mr. ARTHUR WHITBY's *Quince* and Mr. QUARTERMAINE's *Flute* were both excellent. It is to the credit of the whole troupe of rustic players that nobody tried to force the fun.

Apart from a slight tendency to hurry, a trick that, except in swift dialogue or passionate speech, gives the effect of something learnt by heart and not spontaneous, the delivery of the lines—and some of SHAKESPEARE's most exquisite are here—was done soundly.

Finally, no one who wants to keep level with the table-talk of the day should miss this interesting and intriguing production, especially if he hasn't been to *Parsifal.* (pp. 136, 138)

> *O. S., in a review of "A Midsummer Night's Dream," in* Punch *Vol. CXLVI, No. 3789, February 18, 1914, pp. 136-38.*

Desmond MacCarthy   (review date 21 February 1914)

[*In the first part of MacCarthy's discussion of* A Midsummer Night's Dream, *which appeared in the 14 February 1914 issue of the* New Statesman, *the critic presented general views on staging the play. As he states in the following excerpt from the concluding installment, the initial part was composed after he had first seen Barker's production, which had left him disconcerted. Upon seeing it a second time, however, he is much more enthusiastic, noting that "the merits of this production come out clearer when surprise at the scenic effects, the golden fairies, and the red-puppet-box Puck has subsided."*]

Last week I wrote about the art of producing poetic drama. The reaping machine went clattering round and round, diminishing with each circuit the standing corn till it was a mere island in a shaven field, and when the game did come out, it was only a small rabbit. The only generalisation which bolted at last was that the setting of such plays should be beautiful yet undistracting, leading our fancies in the direction of the spirit of each scene, yet leaving them free. Had space permitted, I should have gone on to say of the performance of *A Midsummer Night's Dream* that I did not think Mr. Norman Wilkinson's scenery beautiful, that it was distracting and not in harmony with the spirit of the play. I should have left it at that. I am glad I had no room. I am glad I had the sense to go again before writing my criticism. I strongly recommend everyone who felt, while enjoying the performance, dissatisfied with it on such general grounds to go again. They will enjoy it a great deal more the second time. The merits of this production come out clearer when surprise at the scenic effects, the golden fairies, and the red-puppet-box Puck has subsided.

Mr. Granville Barker has said in his preface he wished people were not so easily startled. If you are among such people you ought certainly to go twice. The producer has always two choices open to him in such cases. He can employ methods which disconcert at first sight, but when familiar serve his purpose best, or others, not in the end so serviceable, which on first acquaintance are not so likely to attract disproportionate attention. Mr. Barker chose the first alternative. I am sure (the newspaper criticisms confirm this) that the majority of the audience thought as much about scenery at the Savoy Theatre as ever did an audience at His Majesty's. It was a different kind of scenery, but just as distracting to most people. When, however, your astonishment at the ormolu fairies, looking as though they had been detached from some fantastic, bristling old clock, no longer distracts, you will perceive that the very characteristics which made them at first so outlandishly arresting now contribute to making them inconspicuous. They group themselves motionless about the stage, and the lovers move past and between them as casually as though they were stocks or stones. It is without effort we believe these quaintly gorgeous, metallic creatures are invisible to human eyes. They, therefore, possess the most important quality of all from the point of view of the story and the action of the play. Dramatically, they are the most convincing fairies yet seen upon the stage. Whether their make-up is the best for making the peculiar poetry of Shakespeare's fairies felt is another question. Personally, I do not think it is. In this case, as throughout this production, Mr. Barker has chosen to bring out the dramatic quality of the scene before the poetic one. He seems to have said to himself, "I am staging a work written for the stage. It is my business to look after the drama; the poetry can look after itself." The production is primarily a dramatist's production, not a poet's. You may be thinking, remembering the stuff out of which the play is woven, that this implies a condemnation. As a reader I am with you. I have always enjoyed *A Midsummer Night's Dream* as a poem, not as a play. What is remarkable about Mr. Granville Barker's production is that it shows, as has never been shown before, how dramatic also passages and scenes are which seem to the reader to be entirely lyrical. This is a very considerable achievement. There are consequent losses, and these were what at first I felt most; on a second visit to the Savoy it was the positive achievement which impressed me.

People are always wondering whether it is true or not that first judgments of others are most trustworthy. First impressions of people often seem to tell one most, and yet one finds one is always going back on them afterwards. The truth is we are often aware of the *temperament* of anyone we meet for the first time more acutely than we are afterwards aware of it again; his character, intellect, etc., we judge of far better on closer acquaintance, so that those we liked at first we often cease to like, and *vice versa.* If a play can be said to have a temperament, and I don't see why it shouldn't, the temperament of Mr. Granville Barker's production was not one which attracted me; but on nearer acquaintance, however, as might be the case with a human being, I began to be immensely impressed by admirable qualities. I missed poetry at all sorts of points. Puck was a shock to me. I kept staring at Mr. Norman Wilkinson's arrangements in green and red and blue and gold and asking myself if each moment were a picture should I like to buy it, and answering emphatically, "No." The scene upon the stage was so absorbing that I did not think of it as a background for acting, and judged it solely on its own merits. But the second time I was not so attentive to it, and began to notice instead that it served excellently as a generalised background against which any sort of figure, Greek, gilded, or bucolic, was more or less congruous. I had ceased to wonder if there were too many silver stars on the curtain of night, or if they were cunningly placed. I had given up my Puck, a phantom born of reading, a bundle of glorious inconsistencies, and begun to wonder, since he must be materialised on the stage, if Mr. Calthrop were quite so impossible. Puck is at once will-o'-the-wisp, Oberon's jester, and a rowdy imp; he touches Nature on one side, and on the other country superstitions about poltergeists. Mr. Granville Barker has decided, with that peremptoriness which is responsible at once for the merits and the shortcomings of the whole production, that he must be either one or the other, and he has made him a buffoon-sprite. There is nothing of Nature in him, nothing of Ariel, nothing of Loki; he is a clowning bogey. Much of the poetry of Puck is therefore lost. When Puck says, "I'll put a girdle round the earth in a minute" [II. i. 175-76], Mr. Calthrop (quite consistently) pronounces these words as a piece of fantastic bombast, and off he struts extravagantly kicking out his feet in a comic swagger. It is true that Puck is a creation of English folk-lore, but he is English folk-lore transmuted by Shakespeare's imagination, and by turning him again into Robin Goodfellow we lose the effects of that wonderful alchemy. On the other hand, all in Puck that is represented in his exclamation "Lord, what fools these mortals be!" [III. ii. 115] that is to say, all that tells dramatically in such situations as the quarrel between Hermia and Helena and the rivalry between the two lovers, was admirably brought out. Whenever the presence of Puck as a spirit of unmalevolent mischief on the scene adds to the piquancy of the situation Mr. Calthrop succeeds. He was admirable in this scene, and it was also one of the very best in the performance. Hermia and Helena (Miss Cowie and Miss Lillah McCarthy) were admirable. Hermia's vindictive, suspicious fury, her gradual transformation into a spiteful little vixen, and the fluttering, frightened indignation of Helena were excellent. The acting revealed more dramatic comedy in the situation than any reader, however imaginative, is likely to feel in it. Everyone has praised Bottom and his friends. The fussy, nervous, accommodating Quince, the exuberant Bottom, poor timid old Starveling, Snout with his yokel's grin, and Flute with the meek blankness which marks him out for the lady's part, the laconic and cautious Snug—they were perfect. The performance of Pyramus and Thisbe was the great success of the production; for the first time the presence of an audience, of Theseus and his court, on the stage was a sounding-board for the fun. Mr. Dennis Neilson-Terry was a graceful and dignified Oberon. His movements, his stillness were delightful to watch. In some passages his elocution was

excellent, but his voice—a fine one in timbre—is not yet completely under his control. He fails when the passage demands rapidity of utterance (just, by the by, where Miss McCarthy as a speaker succeeds most), and there is a curious kind of expression of composed surprise in his voice which often suits the lines ill and becomes monotonous. Miss Silver was a delicious Titania. She spoke her first long speech admirably, or rather the first part of it, losing her art, it seemed to me, over the description of the floods and frosts, recovering it again in her second speech—and delivering perfectly the lines at the close

> But she, being mortal, of that boy did die;
> And for her sake do I rear up that boy,
> And for her sake I will not part with him.
>
> [II. i. 135-37]
> (pp. 629-30)

Desmond MacCarthy, in a review of "A Midsummer Night's Dream," in the New Statesman, *Vol. II, No. 46, February 21, 1914, pp. 629-30.*

Alexander Woollcott   (review date 17 February 1915)

[*Woollcott is best known as a wit and raconteur, as well as an influential pioneer of modern dramatic criticism. The excerpt below is taken from a review of Barker's presentation of* A Midsummer Night's Dream *at Wallack's Theatre in New York. Woollcott is reserved in his praise of the production, noting that there was a good deal that was "pretty to see and pleasant to hear," together with much that was "merely odd and perversely curious."*]

Granville Barker's New York season reached its second stage last evening when he presented *A Midsummer Night's Dream* at Wallack's Theatre. It is the first production of the comedy to be made on Broadway in nearly a decade, and is the same production that gave the London reviewers so much to talk and shake their heads over when it played for more than a hundred nights last Spring at the Savoy. It shows this city for the first time an unreserved application of some of the new art of the theatre to a Shakespearean text, although a few of the simpler leaves out of Gordon Craig's book were taken by Miss Anglin and Mr. Platt when the romantic comedies were brought to the Hudson Theatre last Spring.

The present production is marked by a rapid pace, by a loyalty to the sheer music of the verse, and by an unquestioning devotion to the idea of the purely decorative in investiture. It thereby achieves a fresh spirit and some moments of exceeding loveliness. The performance at Wallack's represents a brave effort to leash the irresponsibility and capture the magic of a fantastic play that will forever provide the producer with a most difficult task. Although some of the effects here are rather unhappy, some of them are surprisingly and satisfyingly successful in their invitation to the right mood. There is a good deal that is pretty to see and pleasant to hear, together with considerable that is merely odd and perversely curious. All told, Shakespeare a la Granville Barker insures at least one entertaining evening in the theatre.

Mr. Barker pays his author's text the respect of leaving it alone. It is all here—uncut, thanks to the rapidity of the performance, which is made possible by the absence of all cumbersome trappings and by the swift utterance of the lyric poetry.

First as to the appeal to the eye—for here is most of what is new. The decoration is by Norman Wilkinson, who has made full use of his great license. It is to be noted that Shakespeare's *Dream,* while it gives the producer his hardest task, gives him also his greatest liberty. He has plenty of rope. One knotty problem is the company of fairies. Here your producer knits his brows, and the product of Mr. Barker's meditations is the golden immortal, a gilded Oberon and a gilded Titania, with trains of fairies gilded from top to toe. They provide something of a shock, and it must be confessed that, out on the platform, they provoke impious memories of Gen. Sherman surveying the Plaza and of a certain gilded lady at a fountain long advertised as a convenient rendezvous.

But within the inner proscenium as these immortals weave their way about the fairy glen, the effect is charming. The scene captivates—the bank where the wild thyme blows walled in with towering green and marked as an enchanted spot. It is pretty as Titania's fairies tread their measures there at night, and lovely in the cool, early morning light as the four Athenians, aroused by the winding of the huntsmen's horn, move slowly down the path that leads to Athens. This dream scene is the test of the production, and as Mr. Barker does it, its spell is kept most potent.

Not all the rest is so happy. The last act, set for the playing of "Pyramus and Thisbe," is handsome and rich enough, but a bit too mussy and distracting. The drops that permit the free use of the fore-stage for the nondescript scenes, are mixed blessings. One may object to them as neither particularly pretty nor serviceable without thereby betraying a yearning for solid masonry or a scholarly passion for Elizabethan tapestry. The pink silk architecture is not bad, but the light foulard of the castle of Theseus is reminiscent of a foresaken ideal in wall papering, and the wildly decorative starry welkin of another occasion is as permanent and genuine a contribution to art as the "Nude Descending a Staircase." Plain curtains would be more attractive and would better serve the fine colors of the costuming.

One wonders a little whose taste decreed the curious gossamer canopy, inclosing an incredible spray of vari-colored electric bulbs which may possibly represent Titania's close and consecrated bower. One challenges the Puck, for Robin Goodfellow, that mischievous and most English of spirits, looks very German indeed as he emerges from under Mr. Wilkinson's brush. Touches like these and some other dissonances suggest an occasional ambition to be different at all costs, and a certain confusion in the effort to match the fantastic quality of *A Midsummer Night's Dream.*

The delivery represents an open and welcome rebellion against all the pomposities of Shakespearean declamation. The mood of the comedy is capitally served by the swift, rhythmic, utterance of the verse in clear, fine head-tones. The price is not small. The lines of Oberon and Helena fare well, but, while Titania's voice is lovely, her fancies are often indistinguishable and Puck is spiritedly unintelligible much of the time.

There is a nice harmony in the work of the company. Some of the individual contributions are excellent. Miss McCarthy shines as Helena. It is a most pleasing presentation of that simple and preposterous lady. The quarrel scene is very well done. Horace Braham is an excellent Oberon. Mr. Heggie is a good Quince and Mr. Cossart a capital Bottom, playing the rich humor of that immortal rustic with the greatest relish,

abetted by a most ingenious ass's head. Indeed, there can be no criticism of the zöological aspects of Mr. Barker's art.

And then there is the old English music, arranged by Cecil Sharp to take the place of Mendelssohn. Mr. Sharp's measures are delightful, but their suggestion is all of country lads and lasses dancing together down country lanes in Merrie England. They better fit the company of the clowns than the gilded folk of the glen. There is more in them of sunlight than of moonshine and, for all their charm, they are curiously out of tune with Mr. Wilkinson's conception of the never-never folk in this land that never was.

> *Alexander Woollcott, in an originally unsigned essay titled "Mr. Barker Gives Some Shakespeare," in* The New York Times, *February 17, 1915, p. 11.*

William Winter   (essay date 1916)

[*Winter was one of the harshest critics of Barker's theatrical theories in general and his production of* A Midsummer Night's Dream *in particular. In the excerpt below, Winter condemns Barker's production as a "desecration" of Shakespeare and a "nauseous admixture of mental decadence and crotchety humbug absurdly designated 'progressive' and foolishly accepted by irrational persons and by others who seek to run with every vagary of the hour."*]

On February 16, 1915, "A Midsummer Night's Dream" was presented at Wallack's Theatre by the English actor and

A gilded fairy, Savoy Theatre, 1914

manager Granville Barker in what has been loftily vaunted as the "modern" manner. As a performance of Shakespeare's lovely poetic play the presentment was a desecration, but it provided a representative example of the nauseous admixture of mental decadence and crotchety humbug absurdly designated "progressive" and foolishly accepted by irrational persons and by others who seek to run with every vagary of the hour,—fearing to protest against pretentious quackery lest they should be reprehended as "reactionary," "hidebound," and "not up to date."

The fundamental purpose of the votaries of "progress" in the Theatre,—the Max Reinhardts, Gordon Craigs, Richard Ordynskis, Granville Barkers, etc., prodigies "new hatched to the woful time" [*Macbeth*, II. iii. 59],—is, assumptively, Improvement. That, in itself, is a right and admirable purpose and one which every sensible lover of the Theatre approves. By all means let us have all the *improvement* possible: let us discard every wrong convention, every *obstructive* tradition, every curable defect that impairs the efficiency of the Stage! Many persons have sought to accomplish this result, and some were laboring for it long before any of those mushroom votaries of "reform" emerged. Examination of "modernist" methods, however, while it discloses employment (without credit) of expedients and methods that are not new,—some of them, indeed, having been old when Shakespeare was an actor!—reveals a deplorable proclivity for frivolous and fantastic innovation.

A just estimate of what the Barker presentment actually accomplished will be indicated by a sketch of the spectacle that was shown. Changes had been made in the construction of the stage and in the methods of lighting. Within the regular proscenium opening a smaller opening was formed by the use of a light framework of wood, covered with canvas or heavy linen, which was gilded. The open space thus formed was about thirty feet wide and about eighteen feet high. The two lower stage boxes had been removed and a platform had been constructed, extending forward from the stage proper and covering the musicians' pit and also, at the right and left, the spaces formerly occupied by those boxes. The top level of this platform or supplementary stage was, at the front, a little less than three feet above the floor of the auditorium, and the face of it was so close to the front row of the orchestra seats that the occupants of those seats touched it with their feet: when, at the close of the performance of the first play produced,— "The Man Who Married a Dumb Wife,"—one of the characters, a blind fiddler, came to the edge of this platform and sat upon it, his bare feet were, practically, in the lap of the spectator sitting before him. The platform stretched forward about twelve feet from the regular stage line. On about that line, or about four feet in front of the old curtain line, there were two steps, each about eight or ten inches high, extending from side to side and connecting the front platform with the level of the true stage. The whole surface of this structure was sheathed with canvas of a slate-gray hue,—the cold, flat color usually seen on the decks of our harbor ferry boats when newly painted. The spaces, right and left, which formerly had been occupied by the stage boxes, were utilized by the performers, in making entrances and exits. The proscenium opening was closed by a drop-curtain, of somewhat dingy, unbleached linen.

All footlights and side-strips had been discarded. The stage was lighted by a quadruple calcium, directed from the rear of the upper gallery, which suffused the scenes with a cold, hard, water-white light, exceedingly trying to the eyes. This calcium was supplemented with seven "bunch-lights," each comprising four yellow electric lamps of, apparently, not less than the sixty-watt capacity, each group of those lights being placed at the rear end of a short funnel. The seven funnels thus indicated were fastened to the front of the balcony, at intervals of about twenty feet, and all of them were focussed on the stage. Other light, during the performance of "A Midsummer Night's Dream," was, in some of the scenes,— notably those in the wood,—shed from above, in the flies.

The results obtained by those changes in the construction of the stage and in the methods of lighting it were bad. Illusion was destroyed. Dramatic effect was nullified. The performers, hampered by unsuitable conditions, were made to appear anxiously and uselessly laborious, and the representations were invested with an atmosphere at once amateurish and freakish. The object sought in this "advanced" method of lighting the stage I understand to be simulation of the diffused light of day. That object was not gained. Every competent artist, every close observer, knows that in the open light of day, out of doors, high lights and low lights, shadows, shadings, and minute lines become visible in the human face which ordinarily are not visible within doors or under artificial light. The open light of day, however, cannot be artificially produced, and this "diffused" lighting method totally failed, its effect being to *flatten* the faces of the performers and dissipate facial expression,—the thing imperatively essential to be shown, and to be intensified, by stage-lighting in association with make-up. In only a few instances were the players made up in such a way as to accommodate their painted faces to the quality of the light shed upon them. In most instances their faces appeared flat and almost mask-like. The notable exceptions were those of O. P. Heggie, Ian Maclaren, and Ernest Cossart.

The theatrical company that appeared in "A Midsummer Night's Dream" was a good one,—though it was seen to better advantage in other plays. The leading member of it, Lillah McCarthy (Mrs. Granville Barker), is an Irishwoman, interesting in herself and expert as an actress. Her appearance and demeanor indicate exceptional force of character and uncommon executive faculty. In person she is large and commanding; in physical type apparently a blonde, with gray eyes. She possesses a good voice and knows how to use it. Her face is somewhat immobile; her manner monotonous. She is self-possessed and authoritative, seeming to have had considerable experience. As *Helena,* though a little heavy, she looked well, in loose Grecian drapery, moved with grace, spoke sweetly,—sometimes with exceptional fluency and moving earnestness,—and cleverly simulated the ways of a lithe girl, without, however, creating illusion: fine intelligence and rightly governed feeling characterized her performance. Her leading professional associate, O. P. Heggie, while intrinsically utilitarian and destitute of personal magnetism, is a highly talented, competent performer, well trained, amply experienced, agreeably self-confident, and, in technical mechanism, exceptionally proficient. A conspicuous merit of his acting is the continuous sustainment of an assumed character: he maintains an invariable identity. . . . In "A Midsummer Night's Dream" he appeared as *Peter Quince,* a part which provides no opportunity for anything more than the perfunctory assumption of an office which *Quince* considers to be one of tremendous responsibility and importance,—that of stage-manager. The actor showed himself entirely and easily capable of acting much better parts than *Quince.* Shakespeare seems to have foreseen the "modern" producer of his plays, when he caused *Quince* and *Bottom* to discuss and arrange the "business" of the wall. "We must have a wall in the great chamber," observes the sapient *Quince,* "for *Pyramus* and *Thisby,* says the story, did talk through a wall" [III. i. 62-4]. "Some man or other," replies the omniscient *Bottom,* "must present wall; and let him have some plaster, or some loam, or some rough-cast about him, to signify wall: or let him hold his fingers thus, and through that cranny shall *Pyramus* and *Thisby* whisper" [III. i. 67-71].

The play was presented in two acts, of almost equal length. In the acting of it there was no poetic atmosphere, no suggestion of poetry, aside from that which sometimes naturally resulted from romantic situations and lovely language. The words, in general, were so spoken as about equally to annoy and disgust the listener. The performances of *Theseus* by Eric Blind, *Demetrius* by Ian Maclaren, *Lysander* by Walter Creighton, and *Hermia* by Eva Leonard-Boyne were utilitarian and commonplace. During the Interlude *Theseus, Hippolita,* and the courtiers sprawled on couches ranged across the front of the stage, with their backs to the audience, so that, practically, their speeches were inaudible except to themselves. The Interlude was played on an elevated platform of the palace room, accessible by black steps, and visible to the spectators, looking over *Theseus* and his Court. On this platform, after the Athenian "mechanicals" had ended their play and the mortals had all retired, among short, ugly pillars painted black and silver, the "fairies" of *Oberon* and *Titania* closed the melancholy exhibition by performing a saltatory exercise called "a Morris Dance,"—one by one leaving the scene.

Ernest Cossart, who appeared as *Bottom,* played with assurance and self-complacency, the display of those attributes, however, being solely personal to himself, not at all to the character that he had undertaken to represent. There was nothing interesting in himself, nothing intrinsically humorous,—every comic effect that was caused proceeding from the situations and the words, not from the actor. The ass's head was a well-made stage property, and the performer used it in an occasionally droll way,—as any child might have done who had ever seen a donkey. The "Wood" scene displayed a large, grass-covered mound, in the centre of the stage. Adjacent trees were indicated by long festoons of gray cloth, suspended from the flies, and among these eccentricities of foliage the performers walked, sometimes in front of the mound, coming down upon the extended supplementary stage (which, in fact, was only an inferior variant of the old-fashioned "apron," which still exists in a few old theatres), sometimes behind it. *Bottom,* when he went to sleep, rolled down back of this mound and so vanished. The "fairy ring" was a large circular structure, suggestive of a heavy wreath, composed, apparently, of blue celluloid, embossed with yellow and pink ornamentation. This absurd object was suspended by wires, high above the mound, and through the centre of it depended a festoon of gray gauze, in which hung a loose, irregular cluster of small electric lights of several colors, red, green, etc.: beneath this the fairies gathered and *Titania* slumbered.

The personal appearance and deportment of fairies and elves are matters of fancy and conjecture. It seems, however,—and certainly it is true for the purposes of Shakespeare's dream-play,—that as far as possible they should be represented in such a way as to suggest delicate, elusive, airy creatures, who,

while obviously they feel human emotions and act from human motives, are purged of human grossness, are transcendent of mundane materiality, are finer, more ethereal, more dainty than men and women; creatures, in short, of which the form is gossamer and the spirit poetical. That, surely, is not an irrational ideal of beings who flit and "wander everywhere,"

> Over hill, over dale,
> Thorough bush, thorough brier,
> Over park, over pale,
> Thorough flood, thorough fire,

> [II. i. 2-5]

beings who "war with rere-mice for their leathern wings" [II. ii. 4], combat with the newt, the blind-worm, the weaving spider, and the snail, dwell in "the quaint mazes in the wanton green" [II. i. 99], sport in "the spangled starlight sheen" [II. i. 29], "creep into acorn-cups and hide them there" [II. i. 31], and couch them on banks

> . . . where the wild thyme blows,
> Where ox-lips and the nodding violet grows,
> Quite over-canopied with lush woodbine,
> With sweet musk-roses and with eglantine.

> [II. i. 249-52]

In the visualization of Granville Barker's erratic fancy those evanescent creatures appeared in the persons, male and female, of children and adults, of various sizes, with "hair" made of ravelled rope and twisted tape, stiffened with glue; their bodies encased, variously, in cloth, leather, and gauze garments, and all,—clothing, shoes, sandals, "hair," faces and hands,—gilded! The effect was much as though a considerable number of steam-heat radiators, cast in human form, had become mechanically animate. The only exception among those galvanized metallic "fairies" was *Puck.* That character was assumed by Cecil Cameron, a person of medium size, considerable agility, and heavy on his feet. This *Puck* was attired in a bright red body garment and trousers reaching to the ankles: those and the upper parts of his feet were bare and he wore low slippers of red morocco leather. His face was made up with yellowish-white paint, the cheeks being reddened. He wore a wig, made, apparently, of very coarse hair or rope yarn, which had been stiffened so that the hairs stood on end, and the head presented somewhat the appearance of a huge chestnut burr, bright yellow in color, with large red berries, about the size and appearance of haws, entangled on it. In this amazing garb this performer cavorted, making most weighty and noisy thumps and bumps, as he jumped about the stage. His exertions were vigorous and he perspired freely: also, on the occasion when I saw his exhibition of "fairy" antics, he unluckily scratched one of his ankles, so that, as he pranced down to the edge of the platform, a few drops of blood were visible, trickling down the ankle, commingled with little rivulets of sweat. These are disagreeable details, but I am describing what I saw, not what I wished to see or to describe. This was the "progressive" performance of *Puck,* the "new," the "modern," the "up to date."

Horace Braham, the representative of *Oberon,* besides wearing the gilded steam-radiator raiment which I have designated, had daubed his upper eyelids with a glossy, luminous green paint, of a shade seen on certain beetles and serpents, and as he rapidly and almost continually blinked his eyes he was a most obnoxious object. This performer portrayed *Oberon,* the "king of shadows" [III. ii. 347], the beautiful figment of a poet's dream, as an effeminate and much bored automaton: anything more contemptible than the thin, inexpressive, unintelligent, and at times unintelligible delivery of the text by this wretched simulacrum of an actor, and likewise by a kindred non-entity, Miss Isabel Jeans, who spoiled the part of *Titania,* it would be impossible to conceive. There was not one touch of feeling, one glimmer of poetry, one suggestion of imagination, one hint of romance, about either of the Fairy monarchs or their subjects. Many things in Art are open to differences of rational opinion and judgment; others are mere matters of obvious fact. The visitor to any large lunatic asylum can ascertain that among the unfortunate inmates of that desolate retreat there are some who sincerely believe that their crazy illusions are sane and that the only madmen are those who differ from them. It is even so with some of the decadent followers and advocates of the vaunted "progressive stage art," and with the "Cubists" and "Futurists" of painting. It would be unjust to classify Granville Barker as actuated by such pitiful sincerity. His productions and his writings indicate him as a shrewd, sensible, calculating speculative theatrical manager, proficient in his business, able to do many things in the Theatre intelligently and well, who deems it expedient and advantageous, because profitable, to put himself "into the trick of singularity [*Twelfth Night,* II. v. 151-52], and who,—with some natural inclination toward fads,—is willing to gull "the fool multitude" [*The Merchant of Venice,* II. ix. 26] to the top of its bent. Barnum did it with great success, and if Barnum why not Barker?

The advocates of the "progressive" doctrine exemplified in this production of "A Midsummer Night's Dream" declare that such exhibitions are desirable because contributory to improvement in stage representations. When this experimental innovator began his season at Wallack's Theatre several of the public-spirited, influential citizens of New York who had generously and splendidly coöperated in founding the New Theatre,—a magnificent enterprise which ought to have succeeded and which if judiciously managed would have succeeded, with even less than the financial foundation and support which it received from its promoters,—signed and circulated a document, dated January 11, 1915, containing these remarkable words:

> In the line of their hope that they could continue to be of some service in advancing the cause of drama in New York, the founders of the New Theatre have encouraged Granville Barker to bring to New York some of his recent productions. Mr. Barker's productions have had an international importance. They have marked *a very distinct advance* in the producer's art, and *certainly have furnished the most notable contribution of the period* toward the progress of the Drama in England. . . . Mr. Barker has staged Shakespeare in a way that has created the keenest interest, both because of the spirit of the production and of the originality of the scenic conceptions."

Those statements, sanctioned by leading, representative, influential persons, are no less pitiable for their ignorance and folly than deplorable for their potentially mischievous effect. The "period" in which this wondrous service was done is not specified. The pretence that Granville Barker's productions show *any* "advance in the producer's art" is preposterous. At their best (which, in this country, has thus far been shown not in Shakespeare but in a production of G. B. Shaw's "The Doctor's Dilemma") they indicate nothing higher than a commercial purpose to profit, if possible, by ministering to a craze for "something different," merely because it *is* different. The propensity for fads and experiments explains, in large part, the failure of the New Theatre: the methods used there were not identical; the animating spirit was.

"A Midsummer Night's Dream" should be presented as a dreamlike spectacle: it should be made to move with ease and celerity through a sequence of handsome scenes, imbued with an atmosphere of poetry, charming with drollery,—never rough, obtrusive, or boisterous,—and every available means, spiritual and mechanical, should be used to create and sustain this effect. In the Barker presentment of it, since that was made by a skilful manager with the professional coöperation of experienced actors, there were a few—though only a few—features of merit; and it must not be forgotten that Shakespeare does much for *every* presentment of his plays. As a whole, however, this ostentatious and conceited exhibition of grotesque "novelty" was the very apotheosis of "parlor theatricals." Illusion was never created. The absurd scenery was destructive of all right effect. It is impossible for the mind to abandon itself to the enchantment of the acted drama and allow itself to drift with the representation, self-forgetful and delighted, when it is continually compelled to consider that trees are indicated by long festoons of gray cloth, wooded banks by wooden benches, and flitting sylphs by prancing gnomes that no more suggest fairies than so many coal-scuttles would! (pp. 281-96)

> *William Winter, "A Midsummer Night's Dream,"*
> *in his* Shakespeare on the Stage, *third series, 1916.*
> *Reprint by Benjamin Blom, 1969, pp. 232-96.*

J. L. Styan   (essay date 1977)

[*Styan draws on contemporary reviews and other documents in an assessment of Barker's artistic achievement in his production of* A Midsummer Night's Dream.]

Every student of stage history knows that Pepys found *A Midsummer Night's Dream* 'the most insipid ridiculous play' he ever saw in his life, and, for want of understanding, the 250 years that followed his unhappy experience seemed bent upon adopting any device of theatre that was vaguely admissible as reparation. As one of Shakespeare's most fantastic vehicles, the play lay open to every abuse. Until 1840 it had been treated as an operetta; Madame Vestris and Charles Kean brought back Shakespeare's lines, but dressed it for an archaeologist's Athenian holiday; Phelps advanced its popularity with the beauties of dreamy green gauze curtains which melted the actors into moonlight. By the twentieth century it had become a play of magic transformation scenes: Tree created his own scenic marvels and in 1905 and 1911 went so far as to grace his carpets of wild flowers and bosky thickets with live rabbits. The Victorian *Dream* was a thing traditionally embellished with Mendelssohn's music (which also involved the suppression of the lyrics), female Oberons, child Pucks and charming little girls for fairies. Barker departed utterly from all of this.

At the Savoy, the sense of an apron-stage structure was . . . lit from the front without footlights or side-strips against a white rectangular proscenium: the prompt-book indicates bold address to the audience from time to time, and for the court entertainment of the last act, Theseus and Hippolyta reclined on couches at the very front of the apron ('sprawled on couches ranged across the front of the stage, with their backs to the audience', according to William Winter [in his

Shakespeare on the Stage], who found them inaudible in this position). Winter complained that the front of the apron projected about 12 feet from the regular stage line and was only three feet high: it was so close to the front row that spectators could touch it with their feet. Two steps, the width of the opening, took the actor on to the original stage level, and stage boxes were replaced by entrances right and left. 'Pyramus and Thisbe' was played on a third level, an elevated platform in front of a line of 'short, ugly pillars painted black and silver'. 'The whole surface of this structure', reported Winter, 'was sheathed with canvas of a slate-gray hue,—the cold, flat colour usually seen on the decks of our harbour ferry boats when newly painted.'

Norman Wilkinson . . . designed the production, strongly contrasting the palace and woodland scenes. There were no gorgeous sets: rather, the design was thought to bear the hallmark of 'Futurism' and Barker afterwards acknowledged a debt to the thinking of Gordon Craig in trying to achieve a unity of atmosphere appropriate to the whole play. A grey painted drop was used for the first palace scene, another in pink with a painted door for Quince's house, another with shadowy green and indigo-blue trees for the first wood scene, and a starry night sky-cloth backed the pillars of the final scene. The central wood scenes were played upon a grassy knoll over which hung a wreath of flowers spangled with lights and surrounded with 'trees' of flimsy strips of green and purple sheer silk; a grey gauze served for Titania's bower. The effect was mystical and right, 'a strange and beautiful place', according to *The Observer* [8 February 1914]:

> a wood in which the English hobgoblin, Puck, is quite at home, a wood where the lovers and other human beings can pass in and out of sight among the trees; and yet a wood which is august and dream-like, and none too exact and earthy.

Realism, for both play and audience, was dispelled, and all was done by painting a curtain and hanging a few strips of gauze.

It was Barker who first seems to have recognized that one's understanding of *A Midsummer Night's Dream* is to be measured by one's perception of the fairies. Beerbohm Tree's little sugar-cake girls with pretty wings and tutus, or Max Reinhardt's diaphanous young ladies, indicate the limitations of the director's imagination and the subsequent inhibition of the spectator's vision. Barker strove to create immortals who surpassed anyone's conception and were completely liberating. He dressed and painted them in shimmering gold from top to toe. Faces were gilt and eyebrows picked out in crimson. They wore masks, and quaint Indian head-dresses, with moustachios and wigs of ravelled rope and metallic curls. They came in all sizes, all but four fully grown. They did not skip and cavort, but stood in Oriental poses and moved with a dignified, shuffling gait, making weird mechanical gestures. They were shocking, but unforgettable. According to William Winter, 'The effect was much as though a considerable number of steam-heat radiators, cast in human form, had become mechanically animated'. They were 'peroxidized pixies' or 'an odd lot of brass ornaments' or 'bronzed or brazen-faced Indians' or 'strange Cambodian deities' for some, 'magic', 'quaint and comical' for others. Harold Child in *The Times* [14 February 1914] drew a little desperately upon comparisons from Bakst, Cambodian idols, Nijinsky in *Le Dieu Bleu*, *Sûmûrun* for its baggy trousers, *Petrouchka* and the Russian

Ballet, Minos's palace in Crete, a Byzantine fresco from Ravenna and Grecian robes:

> The golden fairies chase one another through the wood in single file or lie prone on a low green mound, grouped round Titania, under great shafts of green mounting to the sky, against a purple background. This colour-effect, the heavy mass of old gold against the purple and green, is wonderfully beautiful. . . . An inspiration, something to strike us all with wonder and delight.

Other reviews reflected the uncertainty of the audience:

> Titania was most unhappy in her make-up, which not only took away all chance of facial play but whenever one of Mr. Barker's searchlights focussed her from the front of the circle tier she looked like a quaint little golden idol from an Indian temple. . . . As for the fairy attendants, being such big and burly persons, of course they could not convey the accepted notion of the 'Little People'. Moreover, being made for the most part, certainly till nearly the end, to stand rigid and motionless through Oberon's and Puck's speeches and business—all the elfin poetry evaporated. . . . It may be that [Mr. Barker] was influenced by Titania's statement that Oberon has 'come from the farthest steppe of India' [II. i. 69] [*The Referee*, 8 February 1914].

While some found the effect a 'Shakespearian nightmare' and not *The Dream* at all, others waxed lyrical as they sensed what Barker was doing:

> 'Gilded fairies' gives indeed a poor notion of these elegant creatures, not children but tall and graceful, clad in the soft metallic shimmer of their web of gold over gold armour, all of the daintiest fancy of design. We knew how right the fancy of these fairies was when we found them not clashing with the mortals—Oberon standing like an ikon unperceived in the midst of the quarrelling lovers
> [letter to the *Daily Mail*, 10 February 1914].

The Nation [14 February 1914] recognized 'A New Fairy Convention' in its headline and perceived the fairies as symbolic agents:

> It made a rich pageant when they marched across the stage in a glittering procession. It softened to the likeness of a shimmering cob-web when they danced around their knoll. It gave them an elusive unreality when they mingled, invisible, among the parti-coloured mortals. It was an original and wholly successful attempt to achieve romance without convention.

The prompt-book offers further insights into Barker's conception of the fairies. At their general entrance in [II. i. 60] ('Ill met by moonlight'), they were designated by individual characteristics: one was a soldierly leader named as 'Major', who frightened small fairies on his entrance and twisted the 'Twins' round until they spun into their places. Three were intentionally grave, being named 'Professor', 'Doctor' and 'Ecclesiastic', and there was also an 'Old man fairy'. They were a complete fairy community. Oberon's train-bearers lined up in pairs behind him. Two male and female pairs of singers entered in step, and Oberon's and Titania's trains nodded and bowed their heads in unison. To become invisible to the lovers ('I will overhear their conference' [II. i. 87]), Oberon simply stepped back; when Helena and Demetrius exited, he stepped forward; the convention was repeated in [Act III, Scene ii]. Desmond MacCarthy [in the *New States-man,* 21 February 1914] described how the fairies seemed to make themselves invisible, believing that 'the very character-istics which made them at first so outlandishly arresting' con-tributed to making them inconspicuous:

> They group themselves motionless about the stage, and the lovers move past and between them as ca-sually as though they were stocks or stones. It is without effort we believe these quaintly gorgeous metallic creatures are invisible to human eyes.

The dancers and singers of Titania's party were all in pairs for her sleep of [Act III, Scene ii], and they wove and wound a symmetrical path around her bower. Cecil Sharp arranged his English folk music and dance for the impressive and poet-ic last scene of the play, the golden fairies blessing the house by weaving through the pillars and slowly fading away until there was but one girl left: according to Harold Child, 'the last patch of gold to fade from sight'.

Against the gold was a patch of scarlet. This was Puck, played by a man for the first time. He was dressed in a red cloak, a bright, shock-headed wig covered with berries, and baggy breeches, 'somewhat in the style of Struwwelpeter', an immensely attractive elf who 'seemed to be more nearly allied to Hans Andersen's fairies than those of Shakespeare' [*The Daily Mail,* 7 February 1914]. The critic for *The Nation* again recognized the importance of the innovation:

> The really significant departure from the prettiness of Mid-Victorian convention . . . was the Puck of Mr. Donald Calthrop. Shakespeare's Puck is no ro-mantic invention like Ariel. He is a genuine rustic hobgoblin, an authentic fragment of Warwickshire folk-lore, a crude deliberate patch of ugliness in a fairy play, and in this spirit he was acted. With his yellow wig, scarlet dress, and antic motions he seemed something sinister and alien among the gol-den elves of Oberon's court, and Mr. Calthrop car-ried out this conception in his elaborately harsh elocution. . . . The play absorbed him as music absorbs discords.

With Theseus looking like a god, Hermia like a Tartar maid-en, Helena like a Grecian Gretchen with flaxen hair, and Ly-sander and Demetrius with a touch of Japanese in their cos-tume, the total visual image was unimaginable and other-worldly—which, as J. C. Trewin has recently observed [in his *Shakespeare on the English Stage 1900-1964*], was the whole idea.

'As soon as you see the thing, you know that Mendelssohn would never do. For our part, we should welcome Stravin-sky'. This was Harold Child in *The Times,* and the consensus was that the visual surprises prompted a new awareness of every word in the play and the musical pattern of the whole. In his preface to the acting-edition, Barker showed his close concern with the word-music, acknowledging Poel, who had taught that the merit of Elizabethan verse lay in 'its conso-nantal swiftness, its gradations sudden or slow into vowelled liquidity, its comic rushes and stops, with, above all, the pe-culiar beauty of its rhymes'. During the speaking of the major speeches, the prompt-book indicates, Barker again required his stage to be still: Lysander and Hermia were made to sit for their first amorous exchange, Titania and Oberon ad-dressed each other in their quarrel over the changeling boy with hardly a motion, Puck squatted at Oberon's feet to re-

ceive his instructions to find the 'little western flower' [II. i. 166]. During the lovers' quarrel Barker struck a burlesque style, as suggested by the symmetrical kneeling of the young men, an 'exact' changing of places, kissing of hands and turns to the audience. The programme carried the unusual legend, 'With the indulgence of the Audience, no calls will be taken by the Actors until the end of the Play'.

The mechanicals were not clowns but countrymen of War-wickshire, and they did not play with the customary slapstick stupidity. Their business was simple, in spite of the host of invitations to improvise nonsense that this play offers: Flute found he had Starveling's part in [Act I, Scene ii]; Bottom was granted some business with his sword and had a roaring match with Snug, Flute read his part to himself gesticulating wildly and Puck chased them away with general tripping and tumbling in [Act III, Scene i]; in [Act III, Scene ii], Bottom sneezed upon introduction to Mustardseed and introduced business with his missing ears and tail when he woke in [IV. i. 408-09] ('Methought I was,—and methought I had,—'). Altogether a modest allowance of comedy with which to ex-tend these scenes. According to *The Referee* [6 February 1914], the play-scene, 'with Theseus, Hippolyta, and all the guests reclining while the amateurs acted on the grand stair-case, was a triumph of novel stage-management'. Yet even in this scene the nonsense was restrained. One critic found Moonshine to be 'the funniest Moon of mortal memory', struggling with his superfluity of props, giggling and drying up, troubling Bottom with his dangling lantern on 'Sweet Moon, I thank thee for thy sunny beams' [V. i. 272], and upon his exit forgetting his stool and dog so that he had to stretch out an arm from behind a pillar to retrieve them. The death of Pyramus was also notable for his contest with Thisbe: the lady wanted the corpse on its back and accordingly rolled it over, but Bottom had other ideas and persisted in repeatedly rolling on his side to face the audience. *The Observer* thought that the play scene was 'never for a moment forced', and had 'never seemed so funny'.

The prompt-book contains one striking direction which re-veals the director's implicit attitude towards the play. When Oberon gave Puck his final orders to put right the mistakes of the night, Puck ended the scene by seeming to stage-manage the production himself. Two fairies opened the cur-tain, Puck came down centre and motioned for the lights to be dimmed, and then bent down as if raising the drop cloth as it ascended to bring in Demetrius and Lysander [Act III, Scene ii]. For Puck to be physically aware of the mechanics of the Savoy stage was an extra-dramatic device by which Barker's audience could be compelled to accept the mode of the play as one of conscious non-illusion. The spectator had in part become an immortal himself, granted the power to control and observe the antics of the earthly lovers. By this simple device, the theatre of Bertolt Brecht, Peter Brook and perhaps the real Shakespeare came a step closer. After the war, Barker would write, 'Upon the platform stage of the Elizabethan drama every detail of workmanship tells . . . you may turn all the lights full on if you want to, and not be ashamed to let the audience see everything just as it is. Not that the aim is to destroy illusion, but only to transfer it to the subliminal region of the actors' interpretation of the play.'

Not all were content to have their own notion of the play's illusion damaged. John Palmer, a previous supporter, thought that Barker was 'suffering from brains' and that 'Shakespeare from the beginning never had a chance' [*The*

The fairy dance, Act V, scene i. Savoy Theatre, 1914.

Saturday Review, 14 February 1914]. And in New York, William Winter asserted baldly that 'illusion was destroyed. Dramatic effect was nullified'.

> The absurd scenery was destructive of all right effect. It is impossible for the mind to abandon itself to the enchantment of the acted drama and allow itself to drift with the representation, self-forgetful and delighted, when it is continually compelled to consider that trees are indicated by long festoons of gray cloth, wooded banks by wooden benches, and flitting sylphs by prancing gnomes that no more suggest fairies than so many coal-scuttles would!

But among Barker's champions, the critic for *The Observer* claimed that the production was 'revolutionary in its attempt to get back to what the poet planned'. The play was not drama, farce, a musical or spectacle, nor all these combined, but 'the dream of a poet': 'That is what Mr Barker has tried to express, his first step being to go direct to the poet, and find out what sort of idea the poet had about the relative proportions of the elements of his play.' Barker sought, in a phrase, 'the poetic whole'. J. T. Grein, founder of the Independent Theatre in London and sponsor of the Stage Society, joined those who recognized that another Shakespeare had been revealed, and is to be quoted at length:

> As there was war in the critics' camp through the advent of Ibsen, so there will be war through the progress of Barker. . . . Is it wrong to infuse the new spirit of freedom into the interpretation of the master . . . ? Barker and his henchmen read Shakespeare as wholly human—they scorn the corset of the cathedral library, of academic solemnity, of ceremonial discomfort. As usual they overshot the mark—pioneers always do—and *The Winter's*

Tale was grotesque. Then came *Twelfth Night* and people said: 'How much more fascinating this play is than I thought, what freshness pervades it in its unforced diction; of course there are eccentricities in the adornment, but on the whole I prefer Shakespeare in this modern, vital spirit.' And now comes *The Dream,* inspired by imagination, in plasticism and in colour, the eccentricities have mellowed into a new and definite manifestation of Art. . . . When the dovetailing begins, when the fairies and some mortals laze in the forest with its mound of green, its dome of flowers and leaves twined to a wreath, its wafting trees and mysterious horizon . . . then it becomes paramount enough that one thought guided a firm hand in the production. It is an effort to bring poetry, fancy and the living into line

> [*The Sunday Times,* 8 February 1914].

With this beacon of a production came new understanding of what Shakespeare had achieved, of how he had engaged all the flexibility and licence of his medium to speak to his audience. Granville Barker's *Dream* granted the twentieth century an insight into his mode of vision as perhaps only Peter Brook's has done since. (pp. 95-104)

> *J. L. Styan, "Barker at the Savoy," in his* The Shakespeare Revolution: Criticism and Performance in the Twentieth Century, *Cambridge University Press, 1977, pp. 82-104.*

Dennis Kennedy   (essay date 1985)

[*In the following excerpt, Kennedy provides a comprehensive overview of Barker's* Midsummer Night's Dream, *including its conception, staging, and critical reception. His commentary was first published in 1985; it has been slightly revised for re-publication here.*]

Barker was preoccupied by a series of new plays and a short repertory experiment throughout 1913. Included was Arnold Bennett's dramatization of his popular novel *Buried Alive,* produced as *The Great Adventure* in March at the Kingsway with Henry Ainley in the lead. Perhaps Barker intended to bring on *Macbeth* soon after, but Bennett's play was a roaring success—it ran for almost twenty months—and Ainley was engaged as Ilam Carve the entire time. In the event Barker decided to go ahead with another comedy. He was worried about money in November 1913, when he wrote Ottoline Morrell asking for five or six thousand pounds for *Midsummer Night's Dream.* But the Kingsway success eased the tension. Financially the management was more secure than ever; it seems deliciously appropriate that *The Great Adventure* could pay for Shakespeare, and Barker was properly grateful. "I am against long runs on principle," he wrote to Bennett, "but *thank you* for this for it has enabled me to devote a lot of time to fussing about elsewhere with your rival W. S."

And "fussing about" is exactly what many reviewers thought he was doing with *A Midsummer Night's Dream.* If the reaction to *Twelfth Night* tempered Barker's usual opinion of critics, he must have felt at home again the morning after 6 February 1914. The battlefield was confused, some critics disliking what others praised, many happy with one thing and vitriolic about another. Barker converted J. T. Grein, who had been hostile to the two previous plays ("the eccentricities have mellowed into a new and definite manifestation of Art"—*Sunday Times* 8 Feb. 1914), but lost John Palmer, his staunchest supporter ("Shakespeare being slaughtered to make an intellectual and post-impressionist holiday"—*Saturday Review* 14 Feb. 1914). Desmond MacCarthy struck the best balance. Dissatisfied after his first visit, he "had the sense to go again," and recommended his readers do the same. The first time he was distracted by the setting, but then discovered that the merits of the performance were more notable when "surprise at the scenic effects" had subsided (*New Statesman* 21 Feb. 1914). He saw that the virtue of the production was Barker's success in capturing the dramatic qualities of a work usually thought of as a romantic poem or a pretext for canvas and paint. But Walkley wrote what would become the classic sentence for the occasion (*Times* 7 Feb. 1914). "The mind goes back to the golden fairies, and one's memories of this production must always be golden memories."

The fairies received much critical attention, and quite properly. They are the secret to establishing a style for the play, and their treatment exemplifies the general tone of any production. "The fairies are the producer's test," Barker wrote in the sixpenny preface, admitting that "a hope of passing that test" had partially prompted him to undertake the project. "Foolhardy one feels in facing it. But if a method of staging can compass the difficulties of *A Midsummer Night's Dream,* surely its cause is won." Using the same method of staging as before, he took the fairies to an extreme of non-illusionist portrayal. What seemed important to him was that they be instantly apprehended as beings separate from the mortals. "They must not be too startling. But one wishes people weren't so easily startled. I won't have them dowdy. They mustn't warp your imagination—stepping too boldy between Shakespeare's spirit and yours. It is a difficult problem" [*More Prefaces to Shakespeare*]. His solution—with the aid

of Norman Wilkinson again—was bound to displease many, and some of that displeasure distracted from the other values of the production. It is the risk a director runs in electing any new and distinctive style. One wishes people weren't so easily startled.

Three days before the opening he invited Arnold Bennett to "come early before all the gold has rubbed off the fairies, for it is going to be rather pretty." Most commentators did not think *pretty* was the word; *fantastic* might catch the mood better. For Desmond MacCarthy they were "ormolu fairies, looking as though they had been detached from some fantastic, bristling old clock." For Walkley they were "Cambodian idols," and others repeated the thought: Oberon "a painted graven image" (*Punch* 18 Feb. 1914), Titania "a quaint little golden idol from an Indian temple" (*Referee* 8 Feb. 1914). But gold they certainly were, from head to foot, gold and bronzed-gold. And there was indeed some danger of the gold rubbing off, for their faces and necks were also gold. A voyeuristic reporter watched Titania's preparations for the New York version and discovered the makeup was gold leaf, applied from small sheets with the fingers, at a cost of thirty-five cents per sprite (NY *World* 21 Feb. 1915). Lillah McCarthy says the cost was a shilling in England; for economy's sake the fairies had to stay gilded between matinees and evening performances. The fairy king and queen wore fantastic gold crowns and long, translucent, shimmering trains, hers an iridescent mauve, his copper-gold tinsel. Color photographs of Oberon and Titania, published while the production was still running, provide ample evidence that the visual effect was stunning. Wigs, and some beards, were of curled gold buckram looking like wood shavings or unsprung clock springs; gloves were copper; shoes, a book, a quill and scroll, a four-foot scimitar, a seven-foot scepter, were all gold.

This golden woodland was violated by one brilliant flash of color: Puck was costumed in flaming scarlet. He wore heavy rouge, exaggerated black eyebrows, and a stiffened orange wig, spotted with red berries; red ballet slippers and anklets of red berries; on his left breast, a large blue flame. "Oberon and Titania are romantic creations: sprung from Huon of Bordeaux, etc., say the commentators; come from the farthest steppe of India, says Shakespeare. But Puck," Barker insisted, "is pure English folklore." The acting of Donald Calthrop matched his physical appearance. Avoiding a lyrical portrayal, he accented the hobgoblin, the prankish side of Robin Goodfellow, which is to say that Barker followed Puck's position in the action rather than in the poetry. According to Desmond MacCarthy, he read "I'll put a girdle round about the earth in forty minutes" [II. i. 175-76] as "fantastic bombast" . . . and strutted off "extravagantly kicking out his feet in a comic swagger." Though MacCarthy thought he unnecessarily denied the other side of Puck's nature ("there is nothing of Nature in him, nothing of Ariel"), the effect was calculated to emphasize his masculinity: an important matter, for Calthrop was the first grown man on record to play the role in England.

This was systematic visual shock, but with a point. Like the white world of *Winter's Tale* or the Futurist trees of *Twelfth Night,* Barker's fairies were meant to unblinker the spectators' eyes; the audience was to see the substantial immortals that Shakespeare created, instead of the precipitate of moonlight preferred in the nineteenth century. Few items of the pre-war imagination were as trammeled by Victorian sensibility as fairies. One result was that readers believed *Midsum-*

mer Night's Dream to be the supreme example of Shakespeare's mistaken vocation; to them the work was a lyric poem, to be realized only in the mind, where the fairies had free roam over time and space. When the play was put on the stage, it tended to become a sad spectacle of the body's failure to equal the mind's dreaming. No play of Shakespeare's came with more expected trappings: Mendelssohn's music, realistic outdoor scenery (for Tree, live rabbits), hyperbolic stage illusions, children for the elfin folk, Puck and Oberon played by women, and the full-bodied plot of the rustics reduced to a series of music hall intermezzi. Ralph Berry [in his essay in *Nineteenth Century Theatre Research,* 1981] suggests that Tree's version, first produced in 1900, belonged to the same genre as Walt Disney. Barker attacked all of this, and with more force than he used in either of his previous Shakespearian plays. He indeed meant to prove his method by direct assault on the accepted way. The fairies were the golden key.

And how they came on! Not in moonlit woodland mist but in three-quarter white light, in front of the proscenium and a conventionalized forest drop, making full use of the forestage. From opposite sides in five distinct entrances the two camps moved, in a lightly choreographed and comic ceremony leading to the swift arrival of their king and queen, accompanied by trumpets. . . . [There] was no illusion there, no attempt to *"realise* these small folk who war with rere-mice for their leathern wings." Whatever they were, they were not little Victorian girls. Barker used only four children, for "Cobweb and Co.," recognizing that there is no modern equivalent of Elizabethan choir schools and thus no tradition of trained children's singing voices. The rest were adult actors, individualized as much as possible. The promptbook gives names to many: the scimitar-wearer is the Major, the book-bearer the Professor, and there were the Twins, an Old Man Fairy (with rope beard to the floor), and a Doctor. Movements were often synchronized and abstract, but strong. It was a vigorous, passionate elfland. The fantastic appearance was the distancing device.

The fairies successfully defined as separate beings, the way was clear to point out their parallels to the mortal world. So long as Oberon was an actress, attended by another actress, it was difficult to see relationships between the kingdom of Athens and the kingdom of sprites. Yet the text is at pains to establish them, marital harmony being the desired end of all the plots of the play—including what might be called the super-plot, if the work was indeed written to celebrate a great noble wedding. Julia Neilson-Terry, who impersonated Oberon in Tree's productions, could hardly have been engaged to turn in a virile performance. But her son Dennis, as irony would have it, took the role for Barker and was by most accounts a match for the Thesean virtues of Baliol Holloway. (I am obliged, however, to report that *Punch* found son Dennis "a curiously effeminate figure for those who recalled the manly bearing of his mother in the same part." Tastes differ.) Oberon's followers, almost all men, emphasized the sexual contrast further.

Barker insured that the parallels between the two kings would be evident: the ceremony of the opening scene in Theseus' palace, also held on the forestage in front of a drop, was echoed in the meeting of Titania and Oberon. Titania's mostly female band, though they shared her anger, acknowledged him as their ruler. At the end of the scene they scurried after the queen, but first each one bowed ceremoniously to the king. Later Barker wrote that in this play of transformations

only "Oberon remains master of himself . . . he is kinglier than Theseus". His authority is unchallenged within and without. Barker restored him to his rightful position, and he is now commonly played by a leading actor.

What was swept aside gave room for a new approach to the entire play. Mendelssohn's incidental music of course had to go. In its place Cecil Sharp arranged old English folk songs, claiming (in his introduction to the printed score) that they have more universality than Elizabethan music or music composed in the Elizabethan idiom. Sharp also choreographed the dancing; fairies and rustics alike stepped to traditional English tunes. The clowns, usually made farceurs, were played as simple countrymen, in accord with the text. Shakespeare discovered, Barker held, that "set down lovingly, your clown is better fun by far than mocked at". Like Toby Belch and Andrew in his *Twelfth Night,* the rustics abandoned outworn comic business for their place in the architecture of the drama. Barker had himself made the simplest of discoveries: left alone, Shakespearian comedy plays better than when mugged, hammed, or forced. "By being kept in proportion and played quite naturally," *The Observer* noted (8 Feb. 1914), the rustics "rouse roars of laughter while they are before us, and leave us longing for more of them."

The settings followed the equally simple pattern established in 1912; obviously, Barker would have no truck with rabbits. The first scene took place in front of a gray curtain with grapevine patterns. Quince's house was suggested by dropping a rose-pink curtain in front of this, with painted doors and windows and a sketch of a town's skyline. Though less than 400 lines of the play had passed, Barker took a five-minute break here, then ran the entire night in the wood uninterrupted, from act 2 through the arrival of the hunting party in act 4. The third scene of the play, the fairy meeting, was in front of the forest drop. . . . (pp. 158-64)

Titania's bower was the first full-stage set. It consisted of a green mound in the center, high over which was hung a large wreath of colored fairy lights like glow worms. A cylinder of gauze dropped inside it to the floor, to encase her while asleep. The backdrop was a semi-circle of semi-abstract woodland curtains, strips of cloth for trees, which kept the action relatively forward: the center of the mound was no more than ten feet upstage of the proscenium, to judge from the photographs. Frosted light illuminated these scenes from the dress circle, according to the promptbook, dimmer than that used for the fairy meeting, and some colored light was added from a source overhead in the flies. But the light never sought illusion; in the view of *Punch* it was a "pitiless light that poured point-blank upon the stage from the 12.6 muzzles protruding from the bulwarks of the dress circle. There was no distance, no suggestion of the spirit-world, no sense of mystery (except in regard to Mr Barker's intentions)."

Mr Barker's intentions are easier for us to discover: in such a setting stage tricks would be ridiculous and redundant. To be invisible the fairies had only to step back and observe the mortals' folly: "I am invisible," says Oberon [II. i. 186]. Despite their fantastic appearance, or perhaps because of it, the audience easily accepted the convention so important to the plot. "They group themselves motionless about the stage," Desmond MacCarthy wrote, "and the lovers move past and between them as casually as though they were stocks or stones. It is without effort we believe these quaintly gorgeous metallic creatures are invisible to human eyes." The promptbook reveals, as it does for *Twelfth Night,* that there was little movement during long verse passages in the forest. Barker held that Shakespeare's chief delight was in "the screeds of word-music" of the immortals rather than in character. Indeed in this play, as in *King Lear* and in *Antony and Cleopatra,* "Shakespeare's stagecraft is at issue with the mechanism of the modern theatre."

The four lovers, who are close to anonymous in the text, were individualized as something like a stockbroker and poet matched to a minx and a fool. The importance attached to them can be assumed from the fact that Lillah McCarthy played Helena. She would have made an obvious Titania, but Barker wanted lightness there. Lillah wore a wig of long flaxen tresses; some critics caviled that the nordic look did not suit her dark Irish features, but she appears ravishing in the color photographs. So does Laura Cowie, a thoroughly modern Hermia, "like a résumé in one person of the prettiest and most up-to-date ladies on recent posters" (*Athenaeum* 14 Feb. 1914). Her Greek dresses would have been acceptable for street wear.

The final scene of the play, which brings all the characters together in an epithalamium, deserves some attention. The night in the forest completed, Barker allowed a fifteen minute interval and provided a new set. This second full decoration used the entire depth of the Savoy stage and was dominated by seven heavy white pillars with black bands, elevated on a high platform at the rear. Behind them, silver stars on a night sky cyclorama. Seven steep white steps led down to the proscenium, occupying most of the middle stage. "These modern theatres with their electric lights, switchboards and revolving stages are all well enough but what is really needed is a great white box." So Barker spoke the following year in New York. "That's what our theatre really is. We set our scenes in a shell" (*Harper's Weekly* 30 Jan. 1915). At the Savoy the white box held black and silver costumes for the last scene that echoed the set: even the motif on the base of the pillars was repeated at the hem of attendants' tunics.

A simple but significant set change was effected during the scene. When Theseus announced that he would hear the rustics' play, four large couches were brought on by stewards and placed along the arc of the forestage extension, immediately in front of the spectators. From them the nuptial sextet watched "Pyramus and Thisbe," which was played at the top of the steps. The front lighting was concentrated on the clowns; Theseus and his court, half in shadow, blended almost imperceptibly into the paying audience behind. This novel arrangement gave the comic sketch its due—it received high and frequent praise—but also kept it fully inside its dramatic function in the larger play. Its hilarity in performance has often obscured its basic and ironic purpose, the fact that the story of star-crossed lovers is an inversion of the sexual celebration, a magnificently inappropriate wedding present. Barker's staging emphasized that Peter Quince's very tragical mirth is presented to the Court first, then to us. For the Bergomask ("it never came out of Bergamo, but is right Warwickshire . . . with vigorous kickings in that part of the anatomy meant for kicks"—*Times*), the couches were removed and positions reversed. The dance took place downstage center and the lovers were on the platform and steps watching it.

The scene had begun ceremoniously with large lighted torches; at the end formal ceremony returned. Hippolyta, Hermia, and Helena made their exit upcenter, accompanied by Amazons and bridesmaids with torches, followed by Lysander and

Demetrius. The remaining attendants, all bearing torches, ranked themselves into a guard of honor as Theseus walked up the steps alone. Then the fairies. Barker believed that a song was missing at the end and, with apology, used the nuptial verses from the opening of *The Two Noble Kinsmen,* with music and dancing by Cecil Sharp:

> All dear Nature's children sweet,
> Lie 'fore bride and bridegroom's feet,
> Blessing their sense.
>
>   [I. i. 13-15]

The dance . . . [took place] high up on the top platform. Walkley can do the honors for their final moments: "In the end the golden fairies play hide-and-seek round the columns of Theseus's palace. Gradually their numbers dwindle. At last only one, a girl, is left—the last patch of gold to fade from sight, and to leave on the mind the strange, new impression of the play as golden." The lights faded, the curtain fell. Puck spoke the epilogue in front of it and disappeared through the center in a flare of trumpets.

It was not somnolent, it was not romantic, it certainly was not insouciant. It was a clear-headed vision; in the words of *The Nation* (14 Feb. 1914), an "original and very wide-awake 'Dream.'" It was calculated to awaken the audience, to disturb old notions. What the traditionally-minded critics objected to best reveals what was new. *The Standard* (7 Feb. 1914) merits quoting at length for a condemnation of the apron stage, which

> is becoming something of an infliction. For one thing, the audience is aware constantly of the shuffle of the actors' feet on the boards. And they come up much too close to the mere spectator. One is tempted to say "Ha, ha! I can see the joining of your wig!" or even to lean over and shake hands with somebody. After all, it is best to keep the time-honoured gulf between spectator and actor. . . . The average theatre goer craves illusion.

Peter Brook would be interested in that: at the end of his famous *Dream* (1970), much the grandchild of Barker's, the actors did invade the audience to shake hands. *The Standard*'s man was not the first reviewer to feel uncomfortable with the sheer physical presence of the actors at the Savoy, and his reaction helps us to see how Barker was assaulting the conventions of the time. Illusion was, it seems, a powerful and addictive drug: "the average theatre goer craves illusion."

A writer of much greater insight, G. C. D. Odell, had a similar reaction to the New York version, one year later. Odell grew purple about the forest curtains; he was incapable of apprehending the non-illusionist premise of the production, noting three times that the scene curtains "waved, to the loss of all illusion." Like his colleague William Winter, Odell thought Barker an upstart, an artistic anarchist, whom history would pass by. In 1920, at the end of his history of Shakespearian staging [*Shakespeare from Betterton to Irving*], he expressed the hope that "this silly and vulgar way of presenting Shakespeare died with all other vain, frivolous, un-simple things burnt up in the great war-conflagration." How Barker's work could be seen as frivolous or unsimple is difficult for us to grasp, and our difficulty demonstrates that Barker's way became the way of the twentieth century. But if the great conflagration did not burn up the new method, it nonetheless brought an end to Barker's active work with Shakespeare. When the *Dream* closed in May 1914 the guns of August were already primed, and soon he would cease directing entirely. (pp. 164-69)

Dennis Kennedy, "A Wide-Awake Dream," in his Granville Barker and the Dream of Theatre, Cambridge University Press, 1985, pp. 148-69.

PRODUCTIONS:

Tyrone Guthrie • Old Vic • 1937 and 1951

BACKGROUND:

Guthrie was an influential English actor, director, producer, and administrator of the Old Vic Theatre from 1939 to 1945. He was also one of the founders of the Stratford Festival, Canada and the Guthrie Theatre in Minneapolis. Guthrie directed *A Midsummer Night's Dream* several times at the Old Vic, including a lush Victorian production with Ralph Richardson as Bottom during the 1937-38 season and a 1951-52 production with Paul Rogers as the weaver in a simple, austere staging.

COMMENTARY:

Herbert Farjeon   (review date 1938)

[*An actor, writer, and dramatic critic, Farjeon was principally known as an author and producer of small-scale revues. He compiled several editions of the works of Shakespeare and served as the editor of the* Shakespeare Journal *from 1922 to 1925. In the following review of Guthrie's first presentation of* A Midsummer Night's Dream, *Farjeon offers a generally favorable assessment, but expresses reservations about this balletic, Victorian-influenced production.*]

Here is a thing, and a very pretty thing, and whether the owner of this very pretty thing is Shakespeare or Mendelssohn or Mr. Oliver Messel or Kirby's Flying Ballet, let us not worry to inquire. This much, however, may be told at a glance—that *A Midsummer Night's Dream* at the Old Vic has gone appropriately Old Victorian. You can almost see our young Queen leaning forward in one of the boxes. And it is nice to be able to approve the transports of underlining into which she would surely have been plunged when writing up her darling diary on her return home.

Mr. Tyrone Guthrie has clearly enjoyed himself. A tendency to produce Shakespeare's comedies "just like ballets" has here developed into a full and life-size *corps de Sylphides*. These so fill the forest that it is only a small exaggeration to say you can't see the wood for the wings. When they invade the Palace of Theseus, they prove such an imposing crowd that what should seem spacious seems more than a little cramped. But that the wood is as pretty as a transformation scene, the palace as superb as pre-Victorian Inigo Jones, Mr. Messel is permitted to reveal during less congested intervals. For beauty, for humour, for the magic that is the life-stream of theatrical art, here (though it's produced all wrong!) is *the* Christmas pantomime.

Certainly, no comedian now dame-ing it at the Adelphi or the Lyceum or the Prince's succeeds in being half as funny as Mr. Ralph Richardson in the part of Bottom. But Mr. Riscoe,

Mr. Rose and Mr. Lupino may well answer, "Look at his material!" That this Bottom should drop his aitches seemed so much more Early Victorian than late Elizabethan that I found myself waiting in some alarm to hear whether he would "Beseech your *vorship's* name" [III. i. 179-80] or announce that he had had "a most rare *wision*" [IV. i. 204-05]. It was, too, a little startling to see Theseus and Hippolyta joining hands with the mechanics in their rowdy bergomask—would our young Queen quite have approved of *that?*

But the rustic rehearsals are excellently fooled, and with Miss Agnes Lauchlan—the best Helena I have seen—to liven the lovers with her plaintive wit, no one could be unhappy for long—not even those who realized that, the mistakings in the forest at an end, Helena was getting back at Lysander by stealing some of his lines. Just before this, another interesting novelty had been introduced, Hippolyta in the morning dew serving the awakened lovers with brew from a bowl with a ladle. No doubt they were glad of it, but I don't think Shakespeare's verse was.

Miss Vivien Leigh looks delicious and behaves every inch like a nice young Victorian miss playing the part of Titania. Mr. Robert Helpmann, making his first appearance in legitimate as Oberon, speaks his verse better than almost anyone else in the company—a majestic, ominous and most romantic figure. To see the part of Puck acted by a little boy is usually

Vivien Leigh as Titania.

more satisfactory than to see it acted by a little girl, but not, I submit, in a Victorian production. Miss Chattie Salaman would have been a more suitable choice than Master Gordon Miller. But then Miss Salaman would not have been able to appear as the First Fairy, which she did so entrancingly that one day she must certainly be promoted to Titania.

Altogether, a diverting evening. But it remains to be demonstrated how they did *A Midsummer Night's Dream* in periwigs, or how (if it had been written then) they would have done it in the Stone Age. (pp. 46-7)

> Herbert Farjeon, "A Dream for Queen Victoria," in
> his The Shakespearean Scene: Dramatic Criticisms,
> Hutchinson & Co. Ltd., 1949, pp. 46-7.

The Times, London   (review date 27 December 1951)

[*The reviewer in the following excerpt praises the acting in Guthrie's 1951 production of* A Midsummer Night's Dream, *He is, however, less admiring of the scenery, describing it as "charming and amusing in a rather mundane way."*]

Mr. Tyrone Guthrie in a famous production before the war showed that this play fitted well not only into the setting of Mendelssohn's music but into the dresses and decorations that it might have been asked to wear in the composer's period. His handling of the stage was exquisitely in sympathy with Mr. Oliver Messel's settings which with a lavish use of rosebuds suggested a Victorian essay in Elizabethanism; and the effect was enchanting. This second production, not unnaturally, swings to the other pole of taste. Miss Tanya Moiseiwitsch's settings seek in Athens for classical simplicity and in the wood near by for the spareness and elegance of twisted bamboo lightly decorated with flowers of silver hue. Mr. Guthrie presents the play to the intelligence, turning a somewhat inauspicious eye on sentiment. All the characters are highly individualized, and even the fairies have clever little tricks enabling us to distinguish one from the other. The effect is not enchanting. The stage never appears to be part of some lovely gliding hallucination. The effect is charming and amusing in a rather mundane way.

It is a production in which individual performers become prominent. The impression they make collectively is comparatively weak, and we come away thinking, not of the play, but of Miss Irene Worth's absurdly distracted looks as the lovelorn Helena; of the very human interest in the translated weaver taken by the Titania of Miss Jill Balcon; of Mr. Kenneth Griffith's most ungodlike fear that Oberon's potions are working unintended mischief; of the quirks of conscience that endear us to the Quince of Mr. Alan Badel, and of many lesser things. Mr. Paul Rogers is genial and forceful as Bottom, but the contraption which replaces the traditional ass's head, though no doubt more comfortable to wear, surely spoils the joke. It is no more ludicrous than the conventional Ruritanian helmet. There is a juvenile Puck in Terry Wale, and many will think this also a mistake. But the performance is consistently lively, for Mr. Guthrie has given all the players, whether mechanics, romantics, or immortals, plenty of effective things to do.

> A review of "A Midsummer Night's Dream," in The
> Times, London, December 27, 1951, p. 2.

Ivor Brown   (review date 30 December 1951)

[*Brown was a British author, dramatic critic, and editor. As a critic, he regularly contributed to such periodicals as the* Guardian, Saturday Review, Sketch, Punch, *and the* Observer. *His published works include* Shakespeare in His Time *(1960),* Shakespeare and His World *(1964), and* Shakespeare and the Actors *(1970). In his review of Guthrie's second revival of* A Midsummer Night's Dream, *Brown considers the simplified setting of this production destructive of any sense of magic or enchantment.*]

One does not expect the Old Vic to be as lavish as the Palladium, but surely a less scrubby and disenchanted forest might have been found by Tyrone Guthrie and Tanya Moiseiwitsch for *A Midsummer Night's Dream,* which is the Vic's midwinter carnival. Behind the bare-bones coppice of their choice—a thicket of canes—rises a supposedly Grecian mountain, which, despite a hinted temple or two, reminded me more of the Pennines under cloud than of Hymettus under Phoebus. I found nothing of classic loveliness or of moonshine magic in this glum prospect, and even Titania (Jill Balcon) had to be handicapped by a costume and wig which suggested that she had fluttered in from a coven of witches in the Macbeth country. Mendelssohn has been left out, which I do not regret, though many will. But surely there should be a substitute, say the Tudor airs which some have so happily employed to match the spirit of the play, and not the meagre chords offered in this case. For such a piece the great apron-stage at the Vic is awkward; it assists the scuffles and pursuits, but one needs the remoteness of the so-called peep-show stage to create a forest of fantasy. I moved my seat a long way back in order to try to catch some sense of enchantment, since distance may, as Thomas Campbell observed, indeed have that effect upon the view. But I have rarely found Shakespearean Athens further off, and glamour—in the true sense of that exquisite, much-abused word—more elusive.

For consolation there is fair quality in the clowning. Irene Worth's Helena is a captivating sprite (I say "sprite" because the mortals in this production do cast some of the spell which the immortals miss). Miss Worth has a charming petulance and pathos and consistently fascinates throughout the sometimes laborious humours of the bewildered lovers' quartette. Jane Wenham does nicely, too, as little Hermia, while Robert Shaw and Douglas Wilmer make effective contrast between the romantic Lysander and the dry Demetrius. Paul Rogers is, of course, unlikely to miss a chance, and his Bottom is a most engaging little man assuming size and might, while Alan Badel's Quince is sweetly the harassed master of the homespun revels. But why is Bottom turned only into demiass from the neck up? The fairies are played by boys, and Terry Wale's Puck indicates that a boy is better in this role without proving that he is the right boy for it.

> Ivor Brown, "Tudor and Palladian," in The Ob-
> server, December 30, 1951, p. 6.

J. C. Trewin   (review date 1952)

[*Trewin is a British dramatic critic, editor, and author whose reviews have appeared in the* Observer, *the* Illustrated London News, Sketch, *the* Birmingham Post, *the* Listener, *and the* Times Literary Supplement. *In addition, he has written numerous theatrical biographies and dramatic studies, including* The English Theatre *(1948),* Stratford-upon-Avon *(1950),* Mr. Macready: A Nineteenth-Century Tragedian *(1955),*

Shakespeare on the English Stage: 1900-1964 (1964), Shakespeare's Plays Today (with Arthur Colby Sprague, 1970), and Peter Brook: a Biography (1971). The following excerpt is taken from A Play To-Night (1952), a collection of observations on the theater, covering the years 1949 to 1952. In his consideration of Guthrie's second Old Vic production of A Midsummer Night's Dream, Trewin focuses on the performance of the Mechanicals, particularly admiring Paul Rogers's portrayal of Bottom.]

The toast, ladies and gentlemen, is Nick Bottom, the Weaver: Bottom, whom I have just met in Quince's dramatic club at Athens-by-Arden, visible now on the stage of the Old Vic. Not Arden, maybe. Athens-by-Widecombe is more reasonable, for Paul Rogers, the latest Bottom, speaks with the loamy, sunlit relish of a Phillpotts rustic. The man sends postcards from Athens to Churdles Ash down at Little Silver. I have never heard a Bottom say less plausibly: "If I tell you, I am no true Athenian" [IV. ii. 30-1]. He was never a true Athenian: merely there on a visit. We might say the same of his friends, the hard-handed men. Whenever I see and hear A Midsummer Night's Dream, a play that to the moon in wavering morrice moves, I know within twenty minutes which of the groups in the tripartite fantasy will hold my allegiance: the Mechanicals, the Romantics, or the Immortals. In this midwinter Dream in Waterloo Road, the first Tyrone Guthrie has produced since his famous attempt to "make a union between the words of Shakespeare, the music of Mendelssohn, and the architecture of the Old Vic", the Mechanicals have it—just as, more than twenty years ago, in a Harcourt Williams revival, my heart was with the Immortals: with Gielgud's Oberon which (I must hold perversely) waned in later years, Leslie French's Puck, and the Titania of Adèle Dixon, who side-slipped later into musical comedy.

Here now Bottom rules. The Weaver, as Paul Rogers knows, should never be conscious that he is a funny fellow. In fact, he has no sense of humour. He is monstrously sincere, assured that he can draw tears when he plays a lover that "kills himself most gallant for love" [I. ii. 23-4]. He is just as certain that he can play Ercles rarely, "or a part to tear a cat in, to make all split" [I. ii. 29-30]. He would have liked to try his hand at Thisby, but no one responded. And it was a pity indeed that he could not play the Lion, roaring that it would do any man's heart good to hear him. As it was, Bottom had to make do with Pyramus. He, Flute (Thisby) and Snug (Lion) were the only three Mechanicals to keep at the last the parts they were given in Quince's house. Tom Snout, who took on Wall, and Starveling, a tetchy Moonshine, forgot entirely that they had been cast for the father of Pyramus and Thisby's mother. Quince, too, never appeared as Thisby's father. We have to surmise that, between Duke's Oak and Palace, there had been some uncommonly swift cutting.

What I like about the Athenian amateurs, and especially about Bottom, is their single-mindedness. The play's the thing. Paul Rogers, at the Vic, never bangs at Nick Bottom, thwacks him around in a desperate effort to be funny. The lines are burred out in a full mid-Dartmoor accent that can warm any speech. We are sitting in the full glow of the fire. This Bottom is always in character. It was said, of two actors in another and lordlier Shakespearean part, that while the first—when he had to address a page in an undertone—would have whispered, "Go, bear these papers to my lord the Duke", the second would infallibly have said: "I want you to go out and fetch me a beer." Paul Rogers never forgets that he is Bottom. With the ass's head newly on, he has to say

something to Robin Starveling, the tailor, who is working away, still unconscious of the change. I was close enough to hear Bottom murmur, still in ripe Widecombe, "Caw! Aren't it pretty!"

The other Athenian actors are goodish. Quince (Alan Badel) seems to have an Irish tang. He is an endearing fusser; I like his hurt aloofness at the end of the tragedy before Theseus hastens to commend him and to hand over the purse of gold. In the rest of the company, Snout, the least single-minded, clearly prefers music to acting, but will drop his pipe to do a job of work as Wall; Flute is an eager boy; Snug is a grinning buffle-head; and Starveling, silver-haired, soft-voiced, short-sighted, flares into querulous rage for one moment when—after the unfortunate entry of Moonshine—he snaps out at the interrupting Lysander. They make a pleasant team, though I have known each part better done individually. We wait to know if a producer has found any fresh touches for the palpable-gross play of Pyramus and Thisby; anything new in a few pages that by now must surely have been drained of humour. Miraculously, there is always something fresh. At the Vic this time we have little word-twisting: I think "blude" and "swerd" are the only chestnuts; Wall even denies himself the traditional "whisisper". Moonshine is involved in some Guthrie-ish step-ladder rough-and-tumble, but I shall remember most two things. First, the way in which Guthrie has turned into salutes to Lysander and Helena the lines:

> Pyramus: And, like Limander, am I trusty still.
> Thisby: And I like Helen, till the Fates me kill.
>
> [V. i. 196-97]

"Helen" and "Limander" may be, of course, errors for Hero and Leander. Never mind, I prefer Guthrie's gloss.

The second surprise at the Vic is the fact that, for once, the Court party's interruptions mean something. As a rule, these are tossed off self-consciously, half-heartedly. Here, at last, are real people really listening to the piece: they cannot resist helping Quince out with the last word of that alliterative marvel:

> Whereat with blade, with bloody blameful blade,
> He bravely broached his boiling, bloody breast.
>
> [V. i. 146-47]

We can be sure, then, of the hempen homespuns and their midwinter pantomime. In the middle of the play Paul Rogers has to deal with the business of the ass's head and with the Bottom-Titania scenes. He does it all discreetly. Tanya Moiseiwitsch has supplied Bottom with a skeleton head, so that for once we can see the actor's wondering eyes; he has not to speak encased; he need not always be fumbling for the strings that work ears and jaws.

So far, good; Rogers makes excellent use of his freedom. And yet I was not altogether happy about the mask. I sighed a little for the old ass's head of tradition—no doubt in the same way that Stratford audiences, years ago, insisted on having in As You Like It the moth-eaten carcass of the stag killed long before at Charlecote. Paul Rogers appeared to be wearing a cross between a helmet and a rugby scrum-cap. It was not the "sleek, smooth head" [IV. i. 3] in which Titania stuck musk-roses. Jill Balcon can express Titania's lines; but I do not think that Guthrie has been too successful with the Immortals. Agreed, there is no prettification, no gauze and butter-muslin. Even so, Oberon need not have the semblance of a Second Murderer; his speeches demand as "dulcet and harmonious" [II. i. 151] a voice as the singing mermaid's. The Puck is no more than an agreeable schoolboy (it is ninety-five years now since a certain "pretty little girl, belted and garlanded with flowers", played this part at the old Princess's), and the rest of the Immortals clump and clatter. The music this time is not Mendelssohn's, but that of Cedric Thorpe Davie—charming, though music in the *Dream* is a secondary matter: Shakespeare distils his own. The Romantics are better than the Immortals. We get a Helena (Irene Worth), a dying duck in a thunderstorm, a breathless flitter-jill, quacking about with eyes like saucers; a fiery and compact Hermia (Jane Wenham); a serviceable Lysander and Demetrius; a Hippolyta who looks like an Amazon, and who "bayed the boar", not "bear", with Hercules and Cadmus; and a Theseus (Douglas Campbell), who has a sense of humour.

The Moiseiwitsch setting is elegantly austere: a simple arrangement of columns for the Palace; and, for the Wood, a silver-threaded circlet of twisted bamboo that can become indeed a "haunted grove"—in deep-sea lighting—and has behind it a noble, temple-bossed landscape of Greece. ("Caw! Aren't it pretty!"—not here the best word.) Early in the piece I supposed that, by letting his lovers duck and dive under imaginary boughs, Guthrie intended to repeat the dipping-and-ducking progress of the three Gentlemen in his Stratford *Henry the Eighth;* but wisely, having once suggested the tangled Wood, he left the rest to our imaginations. The revival can certainly work on the imagination, though it is a *Dream* without the fullest magic. In performance I found it successful in part only. On the next morning there remained with me a glimmer-and-gleam and a firefly-whirl; over all, a noise of laughter and the clopping of a Bergomask. The face that shines first in memory is that of Nick Bottom, the Weaver, a fellow with "simply the best wit of any handicraft man in Athens" [IV. ii. 9-10]; and the voice is that of Paul Rogers from somewhere near Widecombe-in-the-Moor. Widecombe-by-Arden-by-Athens. (pp. 153-56)

> *J. C. Trewin, "1951," in his* A Play To-Night, *Elek Books Ltd., 1952, pp. 69-156.*

Paul Rogers and Alfred Rossi   (interview date 1976)

[*Rogers played the role of Bottom the weaver in Guthrie's 1951 staging of* A Midsummer Night's Dream. *In the excerpt below, he recalls working with Guthrie on that production.*]

ALFRED ROSSI: *You played Bottom in* A Midsummer Night's Dream *the second time Guthrie directed the play. He had directed the gorgeously romantic production in the late thirties at the Vic.*

PAUL ROGERS: Yes, that's right. Of which he was deeply ashamed.

Did he tell you that?

Yes. He made it quite clear, just in conversation, not having said, 'I did such-and-such and it was terrible,' because it wasn't—it was absolutely wonderful—but, in fact, he was rather ashamed of that huge success, because it was all wrong. And he was aiming really to discover what the play was about.

He genuinely tried to really put the play on its three levels—fairies, lovers, mechanicals. Fairies and lovers got the most work out of him, because they stylistically were a greater challenge than the mechanicals. He had cast in the mechanicals a collection of favourite sons. Which doesn't mean to say that the others weren't, but it would often happen with his favourite sons particularly, often to the detriment of the production, that he would not only give us our heads but would, as you know very well, encourage us to go sometimes too far, and it was all 'lovely and delightful and most enjoyable'.

He shocked people by his fairies—little boys, in the main: scrubby little boys, who looked as though they'd crawled out from under stones.

The lovers—this is where I came across Tony [Guthrie] the great teacher of verse speaking, because he wanted to achieve—and did achieve, my God, because it was a superb quartet when he finally got it going—a matching of movement and speech and the wonderful high comedy. And this was achieved by the use of the text, the wonderful *use* of the text. And he could be merciless, as you know, particularly with actresses, on verse speaking. He could be brutal. Well, no, it was merely a matter of that marvellous tall, tall gentleman saying, 'Now little Miss So-and-So, don't be so silly.' That sort of lark, you know. And his old thing that any actor worth his salt should be able to do five sentences on a breath.

Do you recall some of the work he did with the mechanicals?

Tony had this gift for bringing things out, and then he allowed us to make a marvellous big mistake. And what was hysterical was that that mistake was perpetuated later by an admirer of the mistake, namely Peter Hall. Tony and I were talking about the ass's head, and I said, 'Wouldn't it be fun if the head was actually open—ears and sides, so that what was actually happening to the poor devil inside could be seen?' It *was* marvellous, at Cambridge, with all those undergraduates. And that was where Peter Hall, as a student, saw it. And later on at Stratford-on-Avon Peter perpetuated it.

And Guthrie obviously liked it and allowed you to do it.

Oh he loved it of course, absolutely loved it. He encouraged me, and we had the head made so that this was the case. But seeing it, in the way that actors instinctively know, one discovered it was wrong.

Why?

The essential thing was that indeed Bottom should seem to be *completely* transported. That there was no virtue in seeing the 'Bottom' inside the head. I forget at what moment it was that we decided, but we came to that conclusion very strongly, and I said to Tony, 'We were wrong.' And interestingly enough, later on, with Peter Hall directing, when I was to do the Bottom for him for the television movie with the Stratford company, Peter wanted me to wear a head like that, and I said, 'No, my darling, I know where you got *that* idea. It was my idea. Tony allowed me to do it and it was wrong, utterly wrong, and we're going to have a real ass's head. He must be turned into an ass.' This is just illustrative of Tony taking an idea from an actor, with pleasure, and encouraging him to do it in order to see what did happen. (pp. 169-70)

> *Alfred Rossi and Paul Rogers, in an interview from* Astonish Us in the Morning: Tyrone Guthrie Remembered *by Alfred Rossi, Hutchinson & Co., Ltd., 1977, pp. 169-76.*

PRODUCTION:

Jack Landau • American Shakespeare Festival • 1958

BACKGROUND:

In 1958 the American Shakespeare Festival Theater in Stratford, Connecticut—which had been established just four years earlier—presented a very successful staging of *A Midsummer Night's Dream,* directed by Jack Landau and choreographed by George Balanchine. Despite the loveliness of the costumes and sets, this production was characterized by a strong emphasis on the play's comedic aspects.

COMMENTARY:

Herbert Whittaker   (review date 23 June 1958)

[*Whittaker judges Landau's production of* A Midsummer Night's Dream *"a dream to look at and also a rip-roaring comic romp."*]

For its second entry of the season, the American Shakespeare Festival switches violently from the tragedy of "Hamlet" to a production of "A Midsummer Night's Dream" that is a dream to look at and also a rip-roaring comic romp. Everybody—lovers, clowns and fairies—is broadly, unashamedly funny all the time, on every pretext and with almost every device known to the comedy stage.

Jack Landau's production finds its balance and contrast by setting the clownish lovers, fairies and rude mechanicals against a setting by David Hays that is so delicate and so charming as to constitute a delight to the eye—from the very first moment until Puck stands in a star-shaped spot-light against a night sky hung with twinkling blue stars.

Against the Venetian-New England background, which is the Festival theater's trademark, two staircases sweep up to a minstrels' gallery. The slender pillars and vaulting which support this gallery become the trees of the wood and the mille-fleur tapestry grows into a leafy backdrop.

Gay, amusing music by Marc Blitzstein accompanies the actions of the setting as of the actors, coming from under the stage or from offstage choirs. Also, in Russell Oberlin there is a tenor of true Elizabethan pitch and sweetness.

Elizabethan, or early Jacobean, is the period Mr. Landau and his costume designer, Thea Neu, have settled on for the very elegant costumes, which make no nod to Athens.

The Duke and his Hippolyta break onto the stage—the lady played by Nancy Wickwire with the mannish stride of the young Queen Elizabeth, while Jack Bittner makes the Duke a pompous, ostentatious fellow.

Egeus, very fatly overplayed by Patrick Hines, thrusts onto the scene with his parental problem, trailed by clever Barbara Barrie as a peevish Helena, flanked by the bold, confident Lysander of John Colicos, and the tall, bemused Demetrius of James Olson. To this latter trio is added the long, blonde figure of Inga Swenson as Helena, and the quartet starts the furious wrangling that carries them through the evening.

The wrangling of Oberon and Titania is almost as violent. June Havoc transforms the Fairy Queen into a most antic

lady, giving a rich burlesque of a Shakespearean actress throughout and making you like it. Richard Waring, as Oberon, for all his sequins, is of sterner stuff, as if to show that even a fairy king can have his dignity. One of the most delightful figures of the evening is that of tall Richard Easton, who makes Puck a rather loutish sprite, very pleased with himself and stupid enough to have mixed up the famous instructions calculated to make the right pair of lovers fall in love in the Athenian wood.

Hiram Sherman naturally dominates this Athenian Little Theater group, but not unfairly. Mr. Sherman is a generous comic and has a gentleness to him that makes Bottom a very likable egotist indeed.

Morris Carnovsky, as Quince, is a director of amateur theater who has obviously trodden some boards himself. His cry of players notably includes an absent-minded Starvling by Ellis Rabb and a lugubrious Snout by Will Geer. One other character makes her mark; June Ericson as the First Fairy is a very knowing pixie, with an eye for Puck.

There is choreography by George Balanchine but you must not be alarmed, for it is kindly to the players and never overly convoluted. Mr. Landau himself has devised much ingenious business, all on the comic side. His "Midsummer Night's Dream" may well be one of the funniest on record, if the least poetical.

Herbert Whittaker, "'A Midsummer Night's Dream' at Stratford, Conn.," in the New York Herald Tribune, *June 23, 1958, p. 11.*

Brooks Atkinson   (review date 23 June 1958)

[*In the following review, Atkinson admires nearly every aspect of this "soft and rapturous production" of* A Midsummer Night's Dream.]

Since "A Midsummer Night's Dream" is more than three and a half centuries old, one must be cautious about using absolutes. But on the basis of the exuberant performance staged last Friday at the Shakespeare Festival Theatre, this column with difficulty refrains from declaring that the "Pyramus and Thisbe" interlude has never been so well acted.

Jack Landau, the director, has not tossed it into the midst of the play with a careless gesture. He has made a hilarious antic out of it by treating the country clowns as human beings with character. And Thea Neu, the costume designer, has taken pains to dress them as individual though rough-mannered members of the human race.

No one should be surprised to discover Hiram Sherman in top form as Bottom, the weaver. To his moonstruck good nature, Mr. Sherman adds innocent relish of ham acting and childlike enthusiasm for the excitement of playmaking. As Quince, Morris Carnovsky, with a putty nose, is a caricature of the stage director, fatuous about the importance of his office, humorously incompetent in solving its problems. A grinning slow-witted Snout by Will Gerr, a stumbling awkward falsetto Flute by William Hickey and a Starveling by Ellis Rabb—who is long gone in iron deficiency of the blood—complete a cast of incomparable drolls. The final performance of "Pyramus and Thisbe" before the court is uproarious because it has a frank point of view.

Nothing in the text is blurred or bungled. If Shakespeare intended "Pyramus and Thisbe" to conclude his outdoor masque with solid buffoonery, he would be gratified by this explosion of bumpkin humor. Were his own clowns—with Will Kempe at the head of them—any funnier?

As humor, the main story of "A Midsummer Night's Dream" is a little tedious today. Modern audiences are not so close to supernatural figures as the Elizabethans were. Mr. Landau might do better to concentrate on the lyricism rather than the comedy of the central plots. Excepting in the case of Richard Waring, as Oberon, the poetry is not musically or beautifully spoken.

But this is a pleasant performance on the whole. David Hays has set it with elegance. Tharon Musser has lighted it with enchantment. Marc Blitzstein has composed some tender songs that Russell Oberlin sings with Elizabethan sweetness. The lovely dance turns have been daintily staged by George Balanchine. They have all evoked a soft and rapturous production.

It is well acted. Richard Easton, who succeeds in making a plausible man out of Osric in "Hamlet," brings the same freshness of imagination to Puck in the "Dream." There is nothing precious or affected about this sprite; he is a creature of boyish delight. All the male parts are well played, especially the King's Chamberlain by Earle Hyman, whose ceremonial acting is thoroughly festive.

But the women are conspicuously delightful. June Havoc's temperamental good humor as Titania; Nancy Wickwire's cool formality as Hippolyta; Barbara Barrie's headstrong belligerence as Hermia; Inga Swenson's glowing charm and quick wit as Helena—compose a fine Shakespearean revel.

In the final scene the rustic comedians bring Shakespeare's lyric enchantment back to earth with their fumbling, excited humor. It is the purest sort of Shakespearean fooling.

> Brooks Atkinson, "Exuberant Production in Stratford, Conn.," in The New York Times, June 23, 1958, p. 19.

Harold Clurman   (review date 5 July 1958)

[*In the excerpt below, Clurman deems this Stratford, Connecticut staging of* A Midsummer Night's Dream *"the pleasantest performance I remember seeing at the festival" and considers it an encouraging sign for the young company.*]

Once during the question period of a lecture I was asked "Do you favor our having a national theatre?" I answered "Yes. Let us have one, so that we can attack it."

At the Stratford, Connecticut, American Shakespeare Festival Theatre's production of *Hamlet*, which I enjoyed much less than their *Midsummer Night's Dream*, I thought "I am glad they have this good-looking theatre devoted to Shakespeare where the actors are given the opportunity to play him so that whether we like what they do or not we can see Shakespeare this way as a preparation for the day when it may be better done."

A Midsummer Night's Dream is the pleasantest performance I remember seeing at the festival since its inception four years ago. Generally speaking the lighter Shakespeare there has fared much better than the weightier—for the demands of the latter are very heavy indeed. The *Dream* is a delightful prank, full of exquisite and easy poetry, a true fun piece, jocund,

good-humored, inconsequential. It is a play that needs no interpretation: it says what we all know: "what fools these mortals be" [III. ii. 115]—especially about love. To play it well what is needed is a youthful spirit, fancy, comic invention and a carefree mood. These the actors of this season's company supply. The director and his associates are to be congratulated.

In these instances I am shy of singling out actors, for though to the technical observer they are of varying merit, one fears doing some injury to the health of the ensemble by picking and choosing individual names. I would say only of this very wholesome company that those who represent the "proletariat"—Quince, Bottom, Starveling, etc.—are more evenly excellent than the "Middle-Class," the Athenian lovers. However, this middle group is certainly attractive, and the climactic quarrel scene is particularly well directed and well acted. The "upper classes"—the nobility and the gods—are somewhat less satisfactory. A most "democratic" scale!

This may reflect a social as well as a theatrical factor. American society nowadays does not produce distinguished manners, people whose breeding is notable for grace or a natural high-mindedness coupled with charm or refinement of bearing; and our theatre does not produce actors who can speak or feel verse with noble musicality. Most of the actors at the Connecticut festival have learned to speak clearly and one hears the words more distinctly each year; except when either rapidity or impassioned agitation is required; but the sounds, and more particularly the tone, are rarely beautiful. Still—Rome was not built in a day.

The stage of the Festival Theatre was designed for functional settings. That is a great advantage for a company committed to the playing of Shakespeare in our country, but it has its disadvantages. In *The Dream* the scenic arrangement is airy and nicely patterned—the lighting is particularly gratifying—but in *Hamlet* the stage often looks like a gymnasium. The costumes in *The Dream* are also far more successful than those in *Hamlet*.

The modern functional set was created not only because it is more practical for productions of Shakespeare than, let us say, the stuffy decoration of the Irving-Tree era, but because it is presumed to free the imagination for poetic flights permitting us to concentrate on the lovely language. Nevertheless, before leaving the subject I should like to remind producers that the functional set often takes on a wholly mechanical aspect, empty of feeling or meaning, aesthetically hideous. (pp. 19-20)

> Harold Clurman, in a review of "A Midsummer Night's Dream," in The Nation, New York, Vol. 187, No. 1, July 5, 1958, pp. 19-20.

Henry Hewes   (review date 5 July 1958)

[*Hewes offers a somewhat mixed review of Landau's production, admiring the settings, direction, and several of the performances, but claiming that this revival's virtues were "sporadic."*]

What is worse than a bad performance of "Hamlet"? An indifferent one—which is the kind the American Shakespeare Festival Theatre and Academy is giving. Accepting almost none of the play's challenges, Fritz Weaver plays the Danish Prince more as a well-intentioned boy with a weak stomach than as a tragic hero trapped between thought and action. . . .

The second ASFTA, "A Midsummer Night's Dream," is somewhat better, although its virtues are sporadic. Scene-designer David Hays stimulates our imagination with an inventive and beautiful transformation from the court of Theseus to a fairy forest. But the overly-wide stage opening and the slats and steps that fill it work against the atmosphere of the play. Hiram Sherman's Bottom is good in spots. The droll anti-nonsense he injects into "When my cue comes, call me" [IV. i. 200-01] is amusing Sherman even if it may not be what Shakespeare had in mind. Standing out among the other tradesmen is Ellis Rabb's classic characterization of Starveling, the laconic tailor, which though it is somewhat less funny than it seemed in an off-Broadway production three seasons ago is still an object lesson of how much can legitimately be made of a small part. The audience heartily enjoys the slapstick performance of "Pyramus and Thisbe," and only the cynics will object that it is really more "carrying on" than performing.

"A Midsummer Night's Dream" contains some of Shakespeare's loveliest poetry, and the ASFTA company delivers it with widely varying degrees of skill. At the low end of the scale is Jack Bittner's heavily prosaic Theseus, June Havoc's over-embroidered, silly Titania, and Richard Easton's insufferable Puck. Somewhere in the middle is Richard Waring's Oberon. And in the zone of pure delight is June Ericson's enchanting rendition of the Philomel lullaby as set to music by Marc Blitzstein.

Director Jack Landau has managed to make the mixed-up love plot a penetrating but nonetheless hilarious comment on female psychology. Inga Swenson and Barbara Barrie perform Helena and Hermia with refreshing lust and vigor. And John Colicos is a fine romantic Lysander.

> Henry Hewes, "Reform It Altogether," in The Saturday Review, *New York, Vol. XL, No. 27, July 5, 1958, p. 22.*

Claire McGlinchee   (review date Autumn 1958)

[*In the following review, McGlinchee praises the American Shakespeare Festival's production of* A Midsummer Night's Dream *as a "delightful performance" and asserts that "a better casting of the tradesmen" could "scarcely be imagined."*]

The two plays that opened the 1958 season at Stratford, Connecticut [*Hamlet and A Midsummer Night's Dream*], served to illustrate not only the infinite range of Shakespeare's genius but also the growing versatility of the cast members who have been with the Company now for several seasons. (p. 539)

A Midsummer Night's Dream offers no particularly challenging parts, but it was given a generally delightful performance.

David Hays's scenery was highly atmospheric in this play. Tharon Musser's lighting proved that Jean Rosenthal has in her a compeer, and Thea Neu's costumes, especially for the tradesmen and for Oberon, Titania, and Puck were perfect. Credit should also go to Marc Blitzstein for agreeable music if we except the anachronistic use of strings (viols) and the Leroy Anderson effect of the drops of love-in-a-mist and the restorative herb as these were applied to the eyelids of various sleeping creatures. What Mr. Blitzstein's music lacks is the perfect fairy quality of Mendelssohn's score for the play. Russell Oberlin's rendition of various lyrics was as always a pleasure to hear, and the fairy dances, directed by George Balanchine, added to the beauty and enjoyment of the play.

A better casting of the tradesmen can scarcely be imagined. Each was perfect for his part and distinctly individual. Morris Carnovsky's Peter Quince stood out, especially as Prologue to the play. He and Hiram Sherman as Bottom were superior. Ellis Rabb's Starveling the Tailor was remarkable, too, both in the rehearsal scenes and as Moonshine in the play of *Pyramus and Thisbe*.

Although picturesque in her entrance as Titania, June Havoc lacked the illusion of youth to be truly pleasing in the role. She played the Fairy Queen with evident relish but with a constant jerkiness of motion instead of the appropriate grace. A peculiarly nasal quality in her voice was distrubing. As Oberon, Richard Waring was fully satisfying in every respect. Richard Easton's Puck was a constant joy—the trusty servant to Oberon and the mischievous Robin Goodfellow, who took undisguised pleasure in the confusion he caused by squeezing the fairy potion into the wrong pair of Athenian eyes. When he replied to Oberon's injunction that he execute a command speedily: "I'll put a girdle round about the earth in forty minutes" [II. i. 175-76], we never doubted his ability to make what is still the record for this journey.

Jack Landau, who deserves much praise for this production, should have reserved the farcical business for the tradesmen. Shakespeare's romantic characters should not be confused with the comic ones. The Duke, Hippolyta, Hermia, and at times Helena, were played as if they were part of a burlesque. The quarrel between Hermia and Helena was in part distasteful rough-house, especially Barbara Barries's Hermia. One might well doubt that the fairies would bother straightening out the love quarrels of a virago. John Colicos' Lysander and James Olson's Demetrius gave a welcome vitality to these usually colorless roles. Patrick Hines's Egeus had a Polonius-like quality that did not suit the text.

Puck, Oberon, and the Tradesmen made this performance worth several times the journey to Stratford. (p. 541)

> Claire McGlinchee, "Stratford, Connecticut, Shakespeare Festival, 1958," in Shakespeare Quarterly, *Vol. IX, No. 4, Autumn, 1958, pp. 539-42.*

PRODUCTIONS:

Peter Hall • Royal Shakespeare Company • 1959-1968

BACKGROUND:

Hall mounted a series of productions of *A Midsummer Night's Dream* with the Royal Shakespeare Company, from a poorly received staging in the late 1950s to a film adaptation in 1968. It was revived for performances in 1962 and again the following year for the RSC's London season at the Aldwych. As Hall's conception developed and matured over the years, critical approval increased. The cornerstone of his productions was the presentation of the play as part of a wedding festival in the hall of a great manor house, a setting many scholars believe was the condition of the play's first performance in Shakespeare's time. In addition, Hall's stagings were noted for their emphasis on broad, fast-paced humor.

COMMENTARY:

The Times, London   (review date 3 June 1959)

[*The* Times *reviewer finds little to admire in Hall's earliest production of* A Midsummer Night's Dream, *despite the novelty of its setting.*]

Mr. Peter Hall has found a new way of treating *A Midsummer Night's Dream*. He presents it as it might have been played by well meaning amateurs at a wedding revel in a great Elizabethan house.

Novelty in staging Shakespeare is to be applauded only if it comes off and is genuinely revitalizing in its effects, but in this instance the advantages of Mr. Hall's treatment are, it would seem, mostly on the surface. He is given a perhaps plausible excuse for dispensing with the music of the verse and for attempting to capture the enchantment of the moonlit wood. We for our part are helped to smile more or less continuously a somewhat superior smile at everything and everybody connected with the comedy, as though we were Theseus and Hippolyta and their courtiers trying to take with polite seriousness the ridiculous play at which the rude mechanicals have laboured so hard. We come to feel in the end that possibly the director in an excess of imaginative energy has cut off his nose to spite his face.

At all events nothing works quite so ingeniously as it is obviously meant to work. The wooden balustraded balcony in the Elizabethan house where the play is supposed to be acted remains as a rustic bridge in the enchanted wood, but it is so big that it somehow refuses to blend into the woodscape. The lovers whose swift transferences of affection illustrate the lawlessness and absurdity of love as it appears to the comic spirit are pleasant grotesques. Miss Priscilla Morgan is dwarfish and comically shrewish, Miss Vanessa Redgrave is a tall maypole of a girl spouting tears and wrapped about with tear-bedewed timidities.

But hard as they and their partners, Mr. Albert Finney and Mr. Edward de Souza, work to be funny we are left with the impression that a more graceful dance of misunderstanding would suit the scenes a great deal better, especially if the words were made easier to follow. Mr. Robert Hardy has little of Oberon's dignity. He is simply his street urchin Puck drawn on a larger scale. His lovely verse goes for nothing. Miss Mary Ure can hardly be called a musical Titania, but at least she speaks the verse as though determined that it shall be heard. The most conspicuous advantage that Mr. Hall gains by his treatment is that the immortals for once appear wholly different from the mortals and the little fluttering fairies are delightful.

Mr. Charles Laughton has some amusing patches as Bottom, but he plays him too consistently for mere buffoonery. We miss the imaginative man naturally taking command of his feeble associates and his heartening enthusiasm for the project in hand. Mr. Laughton neither gives the weaver's innocent conviction of superiority nor the wonder and pathos of his translation. But he is great fun when "Pyramus and Thisbe" is brought to the stage and in his extraordinary unwilling-

ness to die we discover in the buffoon something of the spirit that has been absent from the earlier scenes. Mr. Ian Holm is a lively Puck and Mr. Anthony Nicholls a clear spoken Theseus.

"A Novel Staging of the 'Dream'," in The Times, *London, June 3, 1959, p. 5.*

J. C. Trewin   (review date 13 June 1959)

[*In the following review of Hall's 1959 presentation, Trewin especially faults the verse-speaking of the RSC players and the exaggeration of the play's comic elements at the expense of its romantic aspects.*]

When we left the Shakespeare Memorial Theatre after "A Midsummer Night's Dream" Stratford-upon-Avon was in profound serenity, the river curving in shadowed silver between the bridges and Holy Trinity Church. The evening soothed, and we needed soothing because we had just met a performance of the fantasy of Athens-by-Arden that had had most of the poetry stripped from it. Too many directors in the current classical theatre care little for the word. They are anxious to take an old play and, at any cost, to do something new to it. Peter Hall is a young man of high talent, but in his anxiety to equip the "Dream" with comic business—in what one has to assume is a country-house revel—and to exaggerate the racing and chasing of the lovers, he has lost all sense of the haunted night of the Athenian wood, and of the gleaming moonshine of the verse.

If it is old-fashioned to ask a director to preserve the sound of Shakespeare, and not to fuss about with a great play for the sheer sake of the décor (no "weeds of Athens" in the present costumes), and Peter Hall's inventive and sometimes superfluous charade-business, fail between them to compensate for the flatness of so much of the speaking. I except Anthony Nicholls, whose Theseus has style and a glint of humour, and the Lysander, Albert Finney, who has always managed to speak Shakespearian verse, and who is unlikely to be laughed out of the habit.

Among the rest all must be amused by the comic sense of Vanessa Redgrave, the Helena. The Mechanicals are ably enough done, though inspiration flashes only when Charles Laughton, as Nick Bottom, is recalling the wonder of the night's dream without knowing what exactly had happened to him in Titania's bower. Laughton is to act King Lear during August: he must regard his hempen homespun as a holiday exercise. Mr. Hall has cut out Mendelssohn, and his fairies, so he says with pride, are not "balletic." No complaints about that, but I do complain about the mediocre speaking of the Immortals (though Robert Hardy, who has a voice, manages a speech or two), about the cut in "The forgeries of jealousy" [II. i. 81], and, all said, about the wanton withdrawal of poetry from the loveliest fantasy in the English tongue.

J. C. Trewin, "New Lamps and Old," in The Illustrated London News, *Vol. 234, June 13, 1959, p. 1028.*

M. St. Clare Byrne   (review date Autumn 1959)

[*Byrne regards the young lovers in Hall's first production of* A Midsummer Night's Dream *"the most disappointing I have seen for a long time" and deems the settings devoid of "en-*

Michael Blakemore as Snout, Julian Glover as Snug, Peter Woodthorpe as Flute, Donald Eccles as Starveling, Charles Laughton as Bottom, and Cyril Luckham as Quince. Act I, scene ii.

chantment." But she greatly approves of much of the conduct of the fairy scenes.]

Various theories have been advanced to account for the style of [Peter Hall's] production, which suggests that it is not one of those happy inspirations "whose truth convinc'd at sight we find". One critic saw it as "a complete break with modern tradition and an attempt to get back to something like the Elizabethan original", as if performed in honor of a wedding at a great country house. Another opined that it was presented "as it might have been played by well-meaning amateurs" at such a wedding. There is nothing new, no break with tradition, in the idea that the occasion is a noble wedding in a great house, and it has frequently been played in this manner at Stratford. Possibly Mr. Hall wanted to show us what the lovers were like when the girls were played by boys, and so encouraged his actors to galumph, not unattractively but absurdly and coltishly, through their woodland confusions, *and* through the verse. If so, he ought to see more of what boys today really accomplish in these and the other female parts written for them, and think again. The 1952 Harrow School production had a delicious, fluttering creature who remains almost my favorite Helena, though I have been immensely taken, in recent years, with Diana Wynyard (1949) and Coral Browne (1958), to mention only two of our leading ladies who have presented her in the spirit of true comedy. Whatever Mr. Hall's intentions, the lovers and their

part in the play were the most disappointing I have seen for a long time. Young and very silly they may be, but they have some lovely "early Shakespeare" to speak, and we should not be deprived of this pleasure by another production gimmick. These hobbledehoys and hoydens are out of place in the concluding court scene; and the clumsiness and clowning in their behavior takes away from the discreet and well controlled fun of the mechanicals, which is played down rather more than it need be, especially with such a seasoned team, led by Charles Laughton (Bottom), Cyril Luckham (Quince) and Donald Eccles (Starveling), supported most obscenely and courageously by Peter Woodthorpe (Flute), Michael Blakemore (Snout) and Julian Glover (Snug). One of their best moments occurs when Thisbe's cloak, required by Lion for the ritual mauling, remains obstinately attached to her person. Messrs. Woodthorpe and Glover, playing it with all the conviction of a genuine stage mishap, occurring for the first time that night, make it extraordinarily funny. We could have done with a little more both of the play and the Bergomask. As for the lovers, through that enchanted woodland the music of their fanciful protestations and everlasting vows, no sooner made than broke, with their bickerings and rivalries and the squaring of the males and the jealousies and dismays of the maidens, should echo as conceitedly and delicately as the melody of youth itself—the stuff that will not endure, and yet . . . and yet . . . "forever wilt thou love and she be fair."

They are neither real nor unreal, but simply ideal; so why rob audiences, in which many may be hearing it for the first time, of this idyllic verbal music?

Bottom, of course, is growing Lear's beard. It would not be impossible (at its present stage!) to justify the speech in which he relishes the idea of the disguise-beards for playing Pyramus by adding a super-theatrical specimen to his own "on the night". But it makes nonsense of his surprise at finding himself "marvellous hairy about the face" [IV. i. 24-5] when the ass-head is only represented by a pair of excellent ass's ears—an excellent innovation, as it enables Mr. Laughton to use his own humorous and engagingly expressive countenance to real advantage in the fairy scenes, which he plays with very great charm. For once, surely, the cutting of a famous line would be in order? What I did not care for was his treatment of the awakening from his dream. It had a touch of the slyly suggestive which evokes a laugh but not the laugh asked for by the text—a little snicker and a hunch of the shoulders that spoke volumes, but the wrong ones. The words and his behavior make him an unresponsive ass to the ethereal wooing of the Queen of Elfland: there is an ineffably obtuse innocence about Bottom, his dream and his expounding thereof—a round-eyed wonder which Mr. Laughton's artistry could have caught to perfection, and therein lies its real humor. (pp. 554-55)

[The] permanent set consists of a small balcony from which a stairway leads down on either side. Underneath, a curtained-off recess, reminiscent of the Elizabethan theater's inner stage, serves well for Titania's bower. I failed to follow the intention and scenic logic of the structure. The handsomely balustraded upper halves, which might have graced a nobleman's hall, are finished off at the turn by theatrical rostrums and four steps, which even at the Bankside theaters would certainly have been masked-in for anything save a rehearsal. Similarly, the rushes might betoken "the presence strewed" or the stage of the Globe. When the wood near Athens is required, walls melt away, and in and through transparencies shadowy trees glow and glimmer, and bushes in pots and branches are brought on by the actors themselves to add a little more boskage. As a set it is simple and workable, but it diminishes the amount of useful depth and space which the Stratford stage can provide, which in this play can be so helpful for the suggestion of woodland paths and vistas and groves in which fairies can lurk. It is a tolerable wood, as woods go, but there is no enchantment about it, and the acting area is too small.

The fairies, however, were enchanting to look at, being given not, indeed, the full Inigo Jones treatment but something sufficiently similar and Jacobethan to fit in with the general style of the mortals' costuming, turning Oberon into a creditable Knight Masquer and Titania and the First Fairy and the dear little elderly fairy (Mavis Edwards) into ladies in court masquing attire. But why, oh why, the basic incongruity—or, bluntly, another inexplicable lapse of taste—which condemns these delicate creatures, wearing the most beautifully formal and elaborate costumes in the production, to appear bare-legged and bare-footed? Puck, the urchin, if you like, and Peaseblossom and Company, but not the fairy aristocracy, with their ruffs and jewels and wheel farthingales, who deserve their buskins and roses for their shoes.

Some of the fairy "business" was delightful. After putting the girdle round the earth in forty minutes Puck pops up through the down-stage trap, slightly puffed and dishevelled but tri-

umphant; and I was as delighted by the neat inventiveness of the kidnapping of Titania's little sentinel as were those members of the audience whom James Agate once described as "rapt, englamoured tots". With a miniature morion perched on his head and armed with a spear he did Palace guard-duty in front of the Fairy Queen's bower. From above, unseen, Oberon and Puck, with two full-size attendants, looked down. At a signal from Oberon the kidnappers dropped lightly and in perfect unison to the ground, seized him, turned him upside down, presented him feet first to Oberon and Puck who hauled him up to the balcony in one quick movement, and carried him off into the forest. When he eventually returned to the scene, looking slightly the worse for wear, he too emerged from the trap.

The honors for really beautiful speaking went to Anthony Nicholls as Theseus—the first Theseus I have heard for some years who gave "the lunatic, the lover and the poet" [V. i. 7] magnificently, instead of throwing it away: to Robert Hardy as Oberon, Ian Holm as Puck and Zoe Caldwell as the First Fairy. The loutish lovers did as they were told, and their lovely lines mostly went for nothing even if they were not deliberately mocked, though Albert Finney (Lysander) and Edward de Souza (Demetrius) were able to make it clear in other productions that they were both capable of good and pleasing delivery. Mary Ure was a delicately lovely Titania. This part was her happiest casting this season and in it her speaking of the verse was at its most satisfactory. The lack of feeling which was fatal to her Desdemona was a positive fairy asset. But there were too many cuts in a play which, allowing for the "business" of Pyramus and Thisbe but not for any dances, etc., or an interval, can be acted in the two hours' traffic of the stage. (pp. 555-56)

> *M. St. Clare Byrne, "The Shakespeare Season at The Old Vic, 1958-59 and Stratford-upon-Avon, 1959," in* Shakespeare Quarterly, *Vol. X, No. 4, Autumn, 1959, pp. 545-67.*

John Russell Brown (review date 1960)

[*Brown is a British scholar, dramatic critic, director, editor of several Shakespearean plays, and associate director of the British National Theatre. His published works include* Shakespeare and His Comedies (*1957*), Shakespeare's Plays in Performance (*1966*), Shakespeare's Dramatic Style (*1970*), Free Shakespeare (*1974*), Shakespeare in Performance: An Introduction through Six Major Plays (*1976*), *and* Shakespeare and His Theatre (*1982*). *In the following review of the 1959 RSC staging of* A Midsummer Night's Dream, *Brown considers this production an "adaptation" of the play, arguing that Hall's "clownish" and clumsy young lovers burlesqued Shakespeare's characters.*]

The Old Vic's production of *The Tempest: or the Enchanted Island* in June 1959 was intended to honour the tercentenary of the birth of Henry Purcell who, in 1695, composed music for this adaptation [by William Davenant and John Dryden] of Shakespeare's *Tempest*. But the revival was also timely in that, during the same month, two variously accomplished and modern adaptations of Shakespeare's plays were being presented at the Memorial Theatre, Stratford-upon-Avon [Tyrone Guthrie's *All's Well That Ends Well* and Peter Hall's *A Midsummer Night's Dream*]. So an act of reverence towards one artist, involving careful research and editing, has been the occasion for comparing the ways in which different ages have amplified, altered, and curtailed the work of another. (p. 137)

Like *The Tempest*, [*A Midsummer Night's Dream*] has always been a favourite with adapters. In the summer of 1933, for instance, Max Reinhardt produced it in the open-air at South Park, Headington, cutting the text severely, adding lines for the comics, introducing several ballets and so altering the emphasis that it was 'no longer . . . a story of mortals in this world behind whom an enchantment has arisen . . . [but] a tale of sprites and goblins pursuing the natural life of their own dwelling-place, into which men and women have blindly wandered' [*The Times*, 16 June 1933]. Six and a half years later, an adaptation [*Swingin' the Dream*] was produced in New York for which the scene was changed to New Orleans in the 1880's; the cast of two hundred included Louis Armstrong as Bottom, Maxine Sullivan as Titania and the Dandridge Sisters as three fairies; the scenery was inspired by Walt Disney and there were three bands, including the Benny Goodman Sextet.

At first sight, Peter Hall's Stratford adaptation seemed modest in comparison. His setting, by Lila de Nobili, looked very much like an illustration of 'the Elizabethan Theatre' from one of the older text-books. It was constructed of unpainted wood, and, between two inwardturning stairways, it had an "inner" and an "upper" stage. For the woodland scenes, the painted backcloth depicting an Elizabethan interior was lit from behind so that it became transparent, and a grove of saplings was visible above the steps. The costumes were conservatively Elizabethan, some of them being copied from Hilliard miniatures. Moreover, Hall made no additions to Shakespeare's text and introduced no extensive dumb-shows.

His work as an adapter centered in his treatment of the quartet of young lovers. Shakespeare has given them dramatic poetry which is verbally conceited and decorated, with occasional colloquialisms, yet musically pure and clear. All four lovers are presented as ardent and inexperienced: they have 'most rare visions' [IV. i. 204-05] of love and, in consequence, are successively (though in varying order and to varying degrees) courteous, rude, awed, foolish, presumptuous, devoted, incredulous. To the normal hazards of very young love are added those of fairy influence, but before the close of the play their amazement and struggles begin to grow towards 'something of great constancy' [V. i. 26]:

> *Demetrius.* These things seem small and undistinguishable,
>   Like far-off mountains turned into clouds.
> *Hermia.* Methinks I see these things with parted eye,
>   When every thing seems double.
> *Helena.*   So methinks.
>   And I have found Demetrius like a jewel,
>   Mine own, and not mine own.
> *Demetrius.*   Are you sure
>   That we are awake? It seems to me
>   That yet we sleep, we dream. Do you not think
>   The duke was here, and bid us follow him?
> *Hermia.* Yea, and my father.
> *Helena.*   And Hippolyta.
> *Lysander.* And he did bid us follow to the temple.
> *Demetrius.* Why, then, we are awake: let's follow him;
>   And by the way let us recount our dreams.
>
> [IV. i. 187-99]

Bottom, the weaver of Athens, also has strange dreams in the wood, yet he will not 'discourse wonders'; he has not a lover's imagination and faith, and so dares not risk ridicule.

This presentation of young love held little interest for Peter Hall: he was content to direct the quartet to be young, foolish and clumsy. In his adaptation their verse is absurdly guyed, with exaggerated, unmusical stresses and with coarse tone and high pitch. Their actions are consistently clownish: for instance, as soon as Helena enters to Demetrius in the first woodland scene, she reaches towards him, misses, and collapses on the floor; before long, she is screaming and both are sitting on the floor, legs straight before them, on the other side of the stage. All four chase up and down the stairs, lunge at each other, trip up, and spend much of the time on their backsides. When Lysander is charmed to love Helena and exclaims, with a show of reason, 'who will not change a raven for a dove?' [II. ii. 114], he lays hold of Helena and pulls her round to face him, and soon Helena is lying on the stage with Lysander crouching close over her; his desire to read 'love' stories' in her eyes (which are for him 'love's richest book' [II. ii. 122]) and his attempts to 'honour Helen and to be her knight' [II. ii. 144] lead only to horse-play, repetitive and crude. Presenting the lovers in this manner, it is no wonder that Hall cut entirely their quartet of amazement and determination as they are about to return from the wood; the strange thing is that he presumably thought the audience would prefer the continual, unrelieved and not very resourceful burlesque to a fuller rendering of the play Shakespeare wrote.

But clearly he had great faith in this kind of fooling. Anthony Nicholls, as Theseus, was encouraged to speak most of his lines musically and without intrusive comic action, yet he was given an Hippolyta who leers knowingly as she speaks to her intended husband of 'the night of our solemnities' [I. i. 10-11]. Theseus himself was occasionally given odd, schoolmasterly mannerisms; so, having said that love and 'tonguetied simplicity in least speak most', he points to himself and then adds 'in *my* capacity' [V. i. 104-05], with a sage nod of the head. Possibly a Theseus who has to countenance such young rowdies must be more than a little unsubtle in feeling.

Certainly Peter Hall did not pursue contrasts rigorously. Among the fairies, Titania was the only one to give a counterbalance to the rough and tumble. As played by Mary Ure, she is a frail, vain, thin-faced creature, speaking carefully (almost as if she were trying to be understood in some foreign language), and striving to keep her dignity and show off her glittering costume. Here, of course, the director neglected much of Shakespeare's Titania and he seemed to acknowledge this by cutting her long speech about the 'progeny of evils' [II. i. 115] which come from her 'dissensions' with Oberon:

> The ox hath therefore stretch'd his yoke in vain, . . .
> The seasons alter: hoary-headed frosts
> Fall in the fresh lap of the crimson rose, . . .
>
> [II. i. 93, 107-08]

The other fairies, in this adaptation, are like a pack of squabbling children. Oberon, the 'King of Shadows' [III. ii. 347], is scarcely distinguishable in character and manner from Puck: so, when he demands 'Why should Titania cross her Oberon?' [II. i. 119], he speaks in a mocking, wheedling voice, like one naughty child to another. The lesser fairies are, like the young lovers, played consistently for a burlesque humour: the 'First Fairy' announces that she has to 'hang a pearl in *every* cowslip's ear' [II. i. 15] as if she were some slut about to continue an endless and boring chore; and even when the fairies intend to dance 'solemnly' at Theseus' wedding, they arrive somersaulting and falling on the floor. Ian

Holm's Puck, looking and behaving curiously like a 'dirt-imp' in a detergent advertisement, hardly seems to deserve the epithets 'knavish' or 'mischievous', for the whole fairy world runs that same way.

Hall's invention did not, however, reach to the mechanicals: these amateur actors of Athens are played, as they usually are, slow in wit and clumsy in action, and straightforward in 'simpleness and duty' [V. i. 83]. Bottom, played by Charles Laughton, is a little unusual: he is a soft-hearted old codger, self-satisfied rather than ambitious or awed at his adventures in the wood; his meeting with Titania is punctuated by what is presumably meant to be the mating-call of an ass. Nevertheless, the encounter between the weaver and the Queen of Fairies did provide one of the rare moments of dramatic contrast in this adaptation, and its humour therefore had a wider range than that of the rest of the play. But Bottom, like every other character, suffers from Hall's treatment of the text; his singing to show the others that he is 'not afraid' loses its point because the wood is never mysterious enough to exact a 'distracted fear'; and the clumsy acting of Bottom and his fellows in the 'tedious, brief scene' [V. i. 56] of *Pyramus and Thisbe* is so like the burlesque 'performances' of the young lovers that its type of humour has already been devalued by constant and needless repetition.

Unlike Guthrie's and Davenant and Dryden's adaptations, *A Midsummer Night's Dream* at Stratford did not provide varied entertainment. As well as ignoring the humanity and poetry of Shakespeare's comedy, Peter Hall also missed its width of appeal (it is a play in which these three qualities are more than usually interdependent); it would seem that he pursued liveliness—or perhaps he would call it 'raciness' or 'burlesque'—too thoroughly; probably he was so bored with routine productions of this popular work that, in devising his adaptation, he became too narrowly concerned with being brightly amusing.

This adaptation, like Guthrie's, had all the attention to detail and all the expense which are customarily bestowed on productions at the Memorial Theatre, Stratford-upon-Avon. Both gave the impression that everything had been effected as their creators had wished, so that both directors have every reason to be pleased with the results, and their public will have been able to judge the value of such adaptations in the most favourable circumstances. (pp. 142-45)

John Russell Brown, "Three Adaptations," in Shakespeare Survey: An Annual Survey of Shakespearian Study and Production, *Vol. 13, 1960, pp. 137-45.*

The Times, London   (review date 18 April 1962)

[*In the following excerpt from a favorable review of Hall's 1962 revival, the critic asserts that "what Mr. Hall had seen in the play and wished to bring home to us was the beauty of life that is simple, innocent, inarticulate, like that of Bottom and his mates."*]

The feeling that something at the back of the play is the important thing about it for Mr. Peter Hall, now that he is again directing it after an interval of three years, gained ground during tonight's performance of *A Midsummer Night's Dream*. It was hard to make a confident guess at what this thing is until near the end. But after Bottom and his friends had acted their interlude and in so doing seemed to supply

a missing clue, one felt that what Mr. Hall had seen in the play and wished to bring home to us was the beauty of life that is simple, innocent, inarticulate, like that of Bottom and his mates, if not in their working hours, then in their hours of leisure.

It sounds like a contradiction in terms to praise a production of the *Dream* because in it a sense of the beauty of the inarticulate comes over as being the thing closest to the poet Shakespeare's heart. The mortal lovers do their best to straighten out their feelings by giving utterance to them both before and after the pouring on of the love juice has brought their affairs into confusion. But in giving utterance or articulate expression to their feelings, they fail to straighten them out. They get more and more into a tangle, and this one feels to be the point of their scenes as played on Mr. Hall's stage. The comedy in them is that of lost, helpless young people who find themselves mocked by each new action as they take it. Their self-confidence is steadily and ludicrously turned inside out.

Mr. Brian Murray as a brash, tactless Lysander, Miss Patricia Brake as a spitfire Hermia, and Mr. Barry MacGregor as an amusingly lethargic Demetrius play these scenes very pleasant, but there is a want of humour in Miss Diana Rigg's contralto Helena, and we are made to feel throughout the essential inadequacy of this whole batch of characters. Their very elders among the mortals, the Duke (Mr. Tony Steedman) and Hippolyta (Miss Yvonne Bonnamy), seem to be aware of this and to apologize to us for it on behalf of sophisticated humanity in general.

It is impossible to admire or find comfort in the immortals as they are here presented. They are utterly restless creatures. They have not a heart between them. Mr. Ian Holm as Puck, the only remaining member of the cast of Mr. Hall's first production of the play, has something like a mortal grossness and malice. We at least know where we are with him; but Titania (Miss Judi Dench) is, so far as her personality is concerned, elusive as a glowworm, while Mr. Ian Richardson's Oberon is all paradox, a fop in his bearing and a poet in his speaking, like a dandy such as Lytton Strachey in his book on Elizabeth I and Essex represented as being typical of the period.

All these characters, the courtiers and the immortals, are here incomplete, unhappy, or at any rate marked out for unhappiness. Bottom and his friends are not. They are content with life as they have found it. For them even the play of Pyramus and Thisbe is no great or exceptional experience, but a relaxation, a hobby, a legitimate pastime after the day's work. This is beautifully expressed in the unemphatic work of all Mr. Hall's clowns, led by Mr. Tony Church's businesslike, quietly pedantic Quince. But Mr. Paul Hardwick's performance as Bottom burns like a gentle candle flame at the centre of the whole play.

We are made to feel Bottom's enjoyment of all that happens to him, including his dream love affair with Titania, an enjoyment which is not that of a vain man but of a humble man. Also he really is something of an actor when it comes to the interlude and in particular to Pyramus's death agony. But this Bottom is most important to the production when he is quietly discovering unexpected truths about life, as when he accepts modestly but with respectful rapture the embraces of Titania and the homage of her fairy attendants.

"Beauty that Lies Deeper than Words," in The Times, *London, April 18, 1962, p. 7.*

Lila de Nobili's set for Theseus's palace (1959).

Kenneth Tynan   (review date 22 April 1962)

[*In the excerpt below, Tynan highly commends the RSC's 1962 revival of* A Midsummer Night's Dream, *stating that it "achieved levitation in a matter of minutes and thereafter never looked earthward."*]

After last year's upsets, Stratford seems to be finding its feet again. And not only its feet, its wings: Tuesday's production of *A Midsummer Night's Dream* (Royal Shakespeare Theatre) achieved levitation in a matter of minutes and thereafter never looked earthwards. The pace was easy, and the company played together like champions; and at the end, levitating of its own accord, the house rose to them.

This is a revival, extensively recast, of Peter Hall's 1959 production; as so seldom, the revival is better than the original. When Vanessa Redgrave and Albert Finney were two of the young Athenians, a good deal of excess romping went on, as if Mr. Hall had directed the love-plot with a slapstick instead of a magic wand. Now, happily, things have quieted down, with no loss of gaiety.

The two governing ideas that sustained the earlier version come across, if anything, more potently than before. One of them concerns the method of staging. The play was composed for a hymeneal celebration, and Mr. Hall presents it as such. The action begins in the great hall of a Tudor mansion, which, by a series of subtle transformations, turns into a limitless bower of greenth; the decor is by Lila de Nobili, a past-mistress of such delicate visual revels.

Mr. Hall's second notion has to do with the acting style. Mortals and immortals alike, the characters appear before us as a child, reading the text for the first time, might imagine them. The fairies are children pretending to be grown-ups, as you may guess from the fact that they wear outsize grey wigs; the latter, sprouting from their scalps like thickets of steel wool, are weirdly, inexpressibly sinister. But beneath their wigs the sprites are Barrie's Lost Boys (augmented by a Lost Girl or two); and Oberon and Titania are unmistakably Peter and Wendy. Their row is a nursery tiff, conducted with all the determined vindictiveness that that implies: Oberon deprived of his changeling behaves with the icy petulance of Pan deprived of his shadow.

Ian Richardson and Judi Dench play the royal elves superbly, and when Miss Dench delivers the "wonted liveries" speech [II. i. 81-117], the ailing cause of Shakespeare-designed-to-be-read-as-word-music receives its most powerful shot in the arm for a very long time.

From what we hear of his favourite gags (viz, spilling wine on people and pulling stools out from under old ladies), it seems clear that Puck has no sense of humour: hence my gratitude to Ian Holm for playing this capering oaf as something less than a scream. His Puck is the swot of the Never-Never Land, a smug boy scientist engaged in supernatural research, and never happier than when experimenting with some new technique for cut-rate earth-girdling.

If the fairies are tots, the lovers are not much older. Mr. Hall sees them as a quartet of intensely romantic high-school kids, whose allegiances would probably have changed anyway, even without the aid of aphrodisiac eye-drops. Rather than love, they may be said to dote. Diana Rigg and Patricia Brake are a fetching pair of room-mates; the latter's Hermia is the epitome of pink, pampered, overgrown babydom, and the fact that she has a nightmare about a snake immediately after refusing to sleep beside Lysander can be used in simultaneous corroboration of two Freudian hypotheses—dream-symbolism and infantile sexuality.

The play-within-a-play is cannily supervised by Tony Church, who, as Peter Quince, puts on the Birmingham accent that has lately grown so modish in our theatre. None of the other mummers shares it, which makes for a certain disunity; but I shall not let that deter me from praising two ripe little sketches by Ian Hewitson (Flute) and Bill Travers (Snout). Why, incidentally, do we call these clowns "rustics" when the text repeatedly insists that they are urban artisans?

As for Bottom himself: Paul Hardwick beams and is pleasantly bashful, though one misses the sense of driving, euphoric egotism. And with that I'll stop carping; for I have just remembered the Bottom he is replacing, of whose performance I wrote in 1959 that it had "nothing to do with acting, although it perfectly hits off the demeanour of a rapscallion uncle dressed up to entertain the children at a Christmas party." When I think of Charles Laughton's stage-hogging Bottom, I thank God for Mr. Hardwick's. Finally—or rather initially, since he is the first to speak—Tony Steedman's Theseus invokes the right atmosphere of golden leisure in a golden age as soon as he opens his mouth. Raymond Leppard's music is charming in the oldest sense of the word: it casts a spell.

Kenneth Tynan, "Good News for Tinkerbell," in *The Observer*, April 22, 1962, p. 23.

Roger Gellert   (review date 27 April 1962)

[*In the following review, Gellert judges Hall's 1962* Dream *"the most satisfying Shakespearean comedy production of recent years."*]

I first saw *A Midsummer Night's Dream* on a sticky August evening in Regent's Park, where squadrons of gnats droned in at scalp-level, dodging raindrops as they poised for the prang. The fairies were sweating refugees from some blitzed ballet-school, the mechanicals fruitily rude, the court all wrinkled tights and wig-join. Four indistinguishable young people tripped thorough shrub, thorough wire, while an elderly hobgoblin pranced and postured through all. I couldn't for the life of me see how this elaborate charade could ever be made magical.

Subsequent performances in more favourable conditions have partly brought the play to life, but none so triumphantly as Peter Hall's just-revived Stratford-on-Avon production, which I missed three years ago in its first outing, with Laughton as Bottom. I don't remember the reports then as being more than mildly gratified, and can only assume that the conception has ripened with age, for this *Dream* is, quite simply, marvelous: the true fairy gold. With the aid of his designer (Lila de Nobili) and composer (Raymond Leppard), Hall has found the aptest compromise between exuberance and artifice. Costumes are richly-sober Elizabethan. The girls wear plain hobble-skirts, rather Dutch-looking, with hempen

stockings and clumping, sensible shoes showing beneath. The fairies are filmily tricked out in dull rusty gold, with billowing hair like white wind; their madrigals chime sweetly, directed by a staid conductress. The elfin pages wear tiny Spanish morions, and parade as diminutively fierce as Marvell's bees. A formal archway spans the stage, supporting a balustrade and flights of steps curling to ground level. Beyond it Titania has her retiring-room. Aloft, small oaks and brushwood perfectly suggest the edge of a forest.

From a trapdoor in midstage Puck pops, snuffing the air like a vole, and I must start with Puck, for in the person of Ian Holm he haunts, chivvies and galvanizes this *Dream*. Holm, with his taut energy and total rejection of sentimentality, is as near faun as we can comfortably get. His ears are pricked, he anaesthetizes mortals with a flick and a Pfft! and I expected at any moment to see his knees alarmingly bend backwards. But he is also part vole (small twitching snout) and part lizard (darting, spitting tongue), unless these are faun-properties too. His petulant master Oberon (Ian Richardson) is cold quicksilver; but Titania (Judi Dench) is more. Like a Persian kitten turned maenad, she frisks and swoops. Her voice is by turns sad, scuttling, regal; she is formidable, and when she tells Bottom 'Out of this wood do not desire to go' [III. i. 152], the simple fellow blenches. This, he realizes with a shiver, is no lady. As he withdraws with her, you sense the old Bottom-brain seething with dumb questions. Should he speak again? And just how *does* one lie with a fairy?

The balance is unusually good, for this Bottom (Paul Hardwick) is comparatively lightweight, a pleasant red-faced giggler, and springy ass-ears make him more than a little fey. For once, he and his mechanical mates (led with touching earnestness by Tony Church's Quince) supply merely a modest if monotonous drone-base to the couplings of fairies and teenagers—and the latter are acceptable too, with a superlative Helena from Diana Rigg. Miss Rigg, who has so far specialized in stately innocents (*The Devils, The Art of Seduction*), now blossoms into the same sort of spontaneous revelation as Vanessa Redgrave's early performances. A gawky contralto, with hurt pitch-ball eyes and tawny-red hair dangling helplessly on school-girl shoulders, she is the most dynamically sad and comic maypole one could hope for, with vast reserves of angular rage and wounded dignity. She, Miss Dench and Mr Holm are the pinnacles of this most satisfying Shakespearean comedy production of recent years.

Roger Gellert, "Athens 5 Rome 1," in the New Statesman, Vol. LXIII, No. 1624, April 27, 1962, p. 612.

J. C. Trewin   (review date Autumn 1962)

[*In the excerpt below, Trewin compares Hall's 1962 revival of* A Midsummer Night's Dream *with the director's earlier RSC staging. The critic finds the new production a "happy surprise," given the poor showing in the earlier presentation.*]

[Revivals] of *A Midsummer Night's Dream* (April 17) and *The Taming of the Shrew* (April 23) confirmed that Stratford was having its best opening for several years. Time and new judgment and some fostering star had brought new life to both Athens-by-Arden and Padua, nursery of arts. Three seasons ago, when *A Midsummer Night's Dream* was staged with a cast almost entirely different, I wrote [in the *Illustrated London News*, 13 June 1959] about "the wanton withdrawal of poetry from the loveliest fantasy in the English tongue."

The revival was a happy surprise. Physically, the framework had hardly altered. We were still in the balconied, garlanded hall of an Elizabethan mansion, reminding one slightly of the set that Quiller-Couch visualized [in his introduction to the Cambridge edition of *A Midsummer Night's Dream* (1924)], but with the wood growing up round and behind the staircases and balconies. This time the scampering of the Romantics had been lessened; throughout, one was not so conscious of the racing and chasing. Oberon did not fuss with his rhyming, and Mr. Peter Hall—again the director—allowed Titania to speak the whole of "The forgeries of jealousy" [II. i. 81]. These concessions were wise. We look in *A Midsummer Night's Dream* for the glistening of moonlit sound. We had it in the speech of Mr. Ian Richardson (an Oberon with not a syllable misplaced) and of Miss Judi Dench, a Titania who looked like spun crystal. The Puck of the one survivor from 1959, Mr. Ian Holm, had improved out of knowledge: still a tough little goblin with a liking for trapdoors, but now more accurately judged. All was well, then, with the Immortals, and if only one of the lovers (Miss Diana Rigg, a Helena puzzled and bewitched) had an accurate ear for the verse, with the Mechanicals we were again on surer ground. Mr. Paul Hardwick (Bottom) was lovable and blandly tempermental, and it was a good idea not to use the traditional ass's head: we wanted to see the man's eyes in the full wonder of the dream: hooves and flapping ears served for transformation. Mr. Tony Church was a Quince with the cares of office richly on his mind; Mr. Clive Swift's Snug, the most timid lion on record—never before had the entire Court leant forward to catch a murmur of the dear man's roaring—and the Snout of Mr. Bill Travers, a fellow who gave himself time to think and seemed to forget the beginning of any sentence as soon as he approached its end. As for Mr. Ian Hewitson's tetchy Flute, it occurred to me during the interlude that this was how the Dickensian Mrs. Raddle of Lant Street might have played the part if Bob Sawyer had decided, implausibly, to get up a performance. (pp. 514-15)

J. C. Trewin, "The Old Vic and Stratford-upon-Avon: 1961-1962," in Shakespeare Quarterly, Vol. XIII, No. 4, Autumn, 1962, pp. 505-19.

The Times, London   (review date 14 June 1963)

[*The following excerpt is taken from a review of Hall's revival during its London run at the Aldwych. This production, the anonymous critic states, possessed "a richness of detail and emotional depth" that forced one to "encounter the play as if for the first time."*]

One of the healthiest features of the Royal Shakespeare regime is the policy of nursing some productions along from one season to the next so that they can develop with a fullness which the normal conditions of the British theatre do not permit. In this way *Troilus and Cressida* grew from a patchy experiment into a production of unforgettable authority. The process can now be seen at work on *A Midsummer Night's Dream,* a production that has been in and out of the Stratford Repertory since 1959 and which arrives in London with a richness of detail and emotional depth that force one to encounter the play as if for the first time.

Although it is not a production that exudes superficial business, itemizing its details would be a lengthy process. Some of them represent a deliberate reversal of the usual conventions: Flute, for instance, instead of speaking Thisbe's lines

in falsetto, retains a shamefaced baritone (doubly asserting his masculinity with a heavy pair of boots). But mainly they spring simply from the text. Other productions have left unanswered the question of how Oberon slipped past the guard on Titania's bower—Mr. Hall disposes of the matter by sending on one of Oberon's followers to cosh the sentry. Sometimes the detail stems not from the lines but simply from the atmosphere—as when Snug (John Nettleton) wanders away from the rehearsing mechanicals and starts smelling the flowers until the accusing silence of the others brings him out of his reverie.

But of course it is the context of the production that gives these moments their real strength. What gives the production its identity is the fact that each of the comedy's three levels is anchored to reality. The opening scene at Theseus's court, instead of being treated as a perfunctory flourish to the play proper, acquires a life of its own, exploiting to the full Theseus's pre-nuptial frustration and his embarrassment in the Egeus affair. The portrait of wry, magnanimous nobility Tony Steedman gives in this inconspicuous part typifies the integrity of the production.

Fairyland similarly escapes bloodless disembodiment. Ian Richardson (Oberon) in particular practises a style in which lyricism and common-sense can co-exist without contradiction. His appearance, as a gilded Elizabethan fop, and his habit of direct address ("I am invisible" [II. i. 186], with a mocking bow to the audience) in no way interfere with his exquisitely formal delivery of the enchanted poetry. The same, alas, is not true of Juliet Mills's finishing-school Titania; but Ian Holm's Puck (the only survivor of the 1959 production) is an earth spirit who can sag as well as dance.

The lovers comedy of errors goes off with zestful invention (particularly in the case of Diana Rigg's whirligig Helena), and Paul Hardwick's beamingly self-satisfied Bottom finishes off Pyramus with a crescendo of five "dies" which, in their own way, have as much impact as Lear's "nevers".

"Seeing Plays as If for the First Time," in The Times, *London, June 14, 1963, p. 6.*

Gerald Barry   (review date 26 June 1963)

[*Assessing a presentation of Hall's production of* A Midsummer Night's Dream *at the Aldwych Theatre, Barry asserts that this was "the most satisfying and spirited performance I can ever recall seeing of a play that for me ever skirts and often tresspasses on tedium."*]

Those whose Bardolatry, like mine, normally falls this side the "Dream" can nevertheless visit with complete confidence the Royal Shakespeare Company's production by Peter Hall as now brought from Stratford to the *Aldwych.* This is the most satisfying and spirited performance I can ever recall seeing of a play that for me ever skirts and often trespasses on tedium. It is played robustly for the comedy rather than the fairies, which pleases me for one; though most of the players do culpably short-change us on the poetry.

Maximum comic articulation is put into the scenes between Hermia and Helena, and between Lysander and Demetrius in the forest; and the mechanicals bring a welcome vitality and invention to their rustic routines, although on the first night Bottom (Paul Hardwick) was inclined to labour overmuch—and wasn't the play-scene just a thought too long-drawn out?

Among outstanding performances were Diana Rigg's Helena and Ian Holm's Puck. Ian Richardson's spritely, mischievous Oberon was alas ill-paired by the Titania of Juliet Mills, who managed only an un-fairylike cosmetic efficiency. But the most rewarding single item in this authoritative production is Tony Steedman's Theseus. Playing him as a knowing, slightly cynical, urbane man-of-the-world, he invests this customarily wooden part with new point and life. (p. 934)

Gerald Barry, in a review of "A Midsummer Night's Dream," in Punch, *Vol. CCXLIV, No. 6407, June 26, 1963, pp. 934-35.*

John Percival   (review date August 1963)

[*In the following excerpt, Percival judges Hall's 1963 revival "quite the funniest production of* A Midsummer Night's Dream *for years."*]

Isn't it strange what we will accept in the way of art if only we are used to it? Not many of us really believe in fairies—Shakespeare's sort, at any rate; the wedding of Theseus and Hippolyta means little to us, and we are hardly much taken by the adventures of poor Thisbe and her Pyramus. Put all these together and you have a pretty unlikely mixture. What kind of reception could a new play on these subjects hope for?

Shakespeare's magic name will make an audience swallow the mixture whole, but not necessarily happily. Peter Hall's production at the Aldwych, which has had one previous revival and a northern tour in which to settle down since first given at Stratford in 1959, wins through by one great virtue: it is quite the funniest production of *A Midsummer Night's Dream* for years. Even the opening speeches of Theseus and Hippolyta, a shameless piece of scene-setting, are given a wryly humorous twist, then in burst three of the four young lovers and we're away.

Diana Rigg's drooping, swooping Helena has the most outrageously comic invention and she makes the most of it; this girl is rapidly proving herself one of our best Shakespearean actresses. Ann Beach's dourly romantic Hermia, though, matches her nearly—neither Lysander nor Demetrius is going to know what hit him when once the nuptial celebrations are over. The scene of these four in the woods becomes (as in Britten's opera or in Balanchine's ballet on the same subject) the core of the work. They chop logic and sentiment with the same misplaced dexterity and vigour that the two men are later to show in a delightful fight in the dark. It is, incidentally, not only funnier but also more interesting to put the stress thus on the most natural characters in the play rather than the clowns or the fairies.

Not that the clowns are far-fetched in this version. Paul Hardwick's Bottom wants desperately to be admired and has a certain panache; definitely a character to be laughed *with* as well as *at*. I shall remember, too, Ian Hewitson as Flute discoursing sadly on the sixpence a day Bottom seems likely to lose by his absence, and Newton Blick makes indeed a sweet and lovely Wall.

Ian Richardson barbs every line of his snappy Oberon (with what dyspeptic glee he intones his spell 'Wake when some *vile* thing is near' [II. ii. 34]), and Michael Williams, who now al-

ternates with Ian Holm as Puck, makes his mischief with relish.

The rest of the cast fit well together despite a strange mixture of accents and manners. Only Juliet Mills as Titania disappoints, being o'er-parted where more authority and a more flexibly ringing voice are needed.

Lila de Nobili's ornately simple dresses in the Carolingian style are as attractive as the beautifully textured settings by her and Henry Bardon. John Bradley's lighting is excellent. (pp. 47-8)

John Percival, in a review of "A Midsummer Night's Dream," in Plays and Players, *Vol. 10, No. 11, August, 1963, pp. 47-8.*

Michael Mullin   (essay date 1975)

[*In the excerpt below, Mullin provides an overview of Peter Hall's 1969 film adaptation of* A Midsummer Night's Dream. *The critic praises the film's "conceptual setting" and "graceful subtleties of visual composition" and admits puzzlement at the generally poor reviews the work received when first released.*]

Peter Hall's film of *A Midsummer Night's Dream* is a problem. From the start, its strengths were clear. The text was virtually uncut. The cast was uniformly excellent, many of them having performed their parts onstage, and some, like Diana Rigg of *The Avengers,* having acted in films. The director, Peter Hall, had staged the *Dream* twice during his ten years at Stratford. Full text, skillful actors, a mature, coherent interpretation which had worked in the theatre—during the Fall of 1968 The Royal Shakespeare's Company's *Midsummer Night's Dream* was to be transmuted into film.

Yet, for all the film's apparent strengths, it also ran great risks. The full text heightened the conflict between poetic drama and cinema. So much speaking seems unnatural in a film, especially when the film, shot on location, illustrates much of what the speakers describe. It is redundant, and when the realistic picture is at odds with the poetic description, the poetry can be undercut, making it seem at times like a film of actors acting. To these difficulties, Hall added others by designing the film for both British cinema and for American television. Television's need for a large, clearly defined image meant that most of the film had to be close-up or medium shots. Not surprisingly, in trying to satisfy the demands of film, television, and theatre, Hall satisfied none very well. Film critics complained about seemingly "amateurish" techniques; television critics complained of boredom; and those who tried to assess the film as theatre often complained that Hall had robbed the play of its poetic fantasy, reducing it to

If one accepts the technical limitations of Hall's mixed media, however, his *Midsummer Night's Dream* is an extremely interesting interpretation of the play. Unlike other films, a Shakespeare film works with a well-known script within a tradition of performance. In his film of the play (1935), Max Reinhardt delighted in startling special effects: Titania's train dancing down a spiral moonbeam, Bottom's ears and snout growing long and hairy, a cobwebby tissue shimmering with glints of light through which we glimpse Oberon (Victor Jory) garbed in black and crowned with a weird nest of thorny twigs, mounted on a black steed, and flanked by a horde of batlike creatures who in the end carry off Titania and her white-robed maidens. Memorable, but, matters of film technique and film history aside, an eloquent example of

Judi Dench as Titania and Paul Rogers as Bottom, 1969 film adaptation.

how the play's flights of vivid poetic fantasy tempt those who stage or film it to make fantasy real, replacing verbal magic with visual display. This was the tradition Hall shunned.

The tradition he honored begins with Harley Granville-Barker's innovative *Midsummer Night's Dream* at the Savoy Theatre in 1914. Controversial as it was, the production nonetheless reappeared after World War I at the Kingsway Theatre in 1923. And, somewhat altered, it was again revived in 1929 by Harcourt Williams and John Gielgud at the Old Vic. Just after the War, in 1945, Gielgud staged the play again, this time as a Jacobean masque at the Haymarket Theatre. (pp. 529-30)

The film extends discoveries Hall made onstage and makes new ones. The setting develops the sense of time and place given by Lila de Nobili's "Elizabethan" stage set. Exterior shots of Compton Verney, labelled "Athens" but recognizably a rural English great house, frame the action with the solid, credible architecture of Enlightenment England, to suggest an era of rationality enduring in familiar landmarks, but distant in time, as the Athens of Duke Theseus was for Shakespeare's audience. The original stage set appears within the house as Theseus' presence chamber in the opening scene and as the theatre in the last act. There, the placement of the nobles around the players on their makeshift stage forms a theatrical metaphor for the ironies and confusions that are knit up at last. Cuts from the artisan actors to each pair of lovers underline the ironic ties between Pyramus and Thisby's tale and their own, giving at the same time a sense of the interaction between actor and audience. Developing Hall's earlier conception, in which the solid walls of the great hall shifted to reveal Titania's bower and the moonlit glade, visual magic transforms the familiar English woodland, rain-soaked, damp, and muddy, into a shape-shifting world of wood demons, washed now in hues of verdant green, now in dull crimson, now in moonlight. The substantial, everyday worlds of the great house and the forest combine to form an objective reality from which fantasy may spring.

The film extends Hall's earlier interpretations of the charac-

ters. Oberon, Titania, and Puck are more sinister green-skinned and naked than they were as aristocratic masquers. Nudity and weird camera effects link the wood demons of Elizabethan folklore with the modern vision of the play as "erotic nightmare." An Oberon with furred loin darts through the tangled copse, his face with goatish beard and satyr's horns peering between the leaves. At first spiteful of Oberon, the naked Titania wraps herself around Bottom as he lies on the ground, and then, her bestial fantasy ended, she dances in languid ecstasy with Oberon. A panting, red-mouthed Puck sniffs out the lovers. Trick shots make the fairies appear or vanish in an instant, green skin among the forest leaves rendering them invisible when they choose to be. As it must, their exact nature remains elusive.

For the lovers, mini-skirts and Carnaby-Street outfits suggest a self-conscious posturing which parodies the high-flown sentiments of their impassioned lyrics. When we see them sleeping, muddy and bedraggled in the morning light, we realize that here, dressed in strange garments and affected language, are some comfortably ordinary teenagers. The treatment of Bottom and friends as onion-chomping English workmen, clad in tweeds, moleskins, and leather, reverses the same dramatic strategy, insisting first that they are everyday blokes, then, through magic and art, revealing the extraordinary beings we can in imagination become. Theseus and Hippolyta are no mere speakers for unimaginative rationality. As Hall's attentive camera shows, Theseus's complaint at the slow old moon who lingers his desires enkindles a bright-eyed eagerness in Hippolyta, who speaks of "our solemnities" almost as if the phrase were a euphemism.

To record these subtleties, and to make the verse paramount, Hall uses the techniques of film and television documentary—his handheld camera focuses on the speakers in close-up, face front to camera, with little panning and tracking, and with vocal continuity favored over visual in the cutting. The documentary style acts as a kind of prism by which we may differentiate the play's spectrum of characters. The rude mechanicals and the Athenian nobility are comfortable with the documentary style—for opposite reasons. Unremittingly close observation favors both extreme realism and extreme artifice. Even at close range, we can imagine Bottom addressing us in his own words, and we believe the anxious faces of his mates in the reaction shots. By virtue of their name and station, on the other hand, Theseus and Hippolyta are entitled to speak as artificially as they will, since the observant camera reveals the human passions pulsing beneath the elegant talk of "solemnities" and "the anguish of a torturing hour" [V. i. 37]. And, under the minute inspection of a handheld camera a few feet or even a few inches away from the distressed speaker, the lovers' artificial speech clearly depicts artificially inflated passions. For the fairies, the cutting from one close-up to another—always a little quicker than we expect, often moving them from one part of the forest to another in the midst of a single speech—matches their otherworldly appearance and powers. Yet the tight close-up fails when exploited for a sight gag—Oberon's little henchman bopping an unsuspecting fairy with a club—or worse, when the bawdy eye of the camera looks too closely at the naked Titania in dishabille.

Because it is selective in what it sees, Hall's camera can stress the relationships between characters in several ways. In a sequence of speeches, each new speaker brings in a different point of view, as all readers know; yet onstage these different viewpoints are modulated by the presence of non-speakers who may only stand silent onstage, or who may call attention to themselves by a movement or gesture. By alternating between close-ups of the speaker and others, as in the cuts from actors to audience in the play scene, the film heightens these differences in point of view. By a close-up framing two faces, as in the shots of Lysander and Hermia, first in the house, then in a boat, and then on the lawn, the camera puts us at the same intimate distance the lovers share. And by moving another figure into the background, with the focus still on two speakers in close-up, as when Helena enters behind the feuding Lysander and Demetrius, for example, the camera makes the silent figure visually significant, reminding us, as Lysander tells Demetrius, that there is a fourth victim in this lovers' triangle.

Heightening some contrasts, the camera obliterates others, most noticeably in the long forest scene. On the stage, first Hermia and Lysander, then Bottom and Titania, fall asleep before us; as others enter, the audience remains constantly aware of the sleepers', sources of comic ironies and confusions held in suspended animation. By following each pair, the camera obscures ties between the different groups which are made by their simultaneous presence on a single stage set. The appearance of the rude mechanicals, for instance, in the same setting as the one just left by the Duke and his retinue, suggests comic parallels between the two worlds, as the contrast in the film between Theseus' presence chamber and Bottom's workshop does not.

Camera techniques can recall the recurrent imagery of the poetic text: a fairy's face thrusts itself from tangled undergrowth or from a forest pond Puck arises. Hall exploits the film's ability to show what readers or theatre-goers can only imagine. In making the forest and fairies actual through the dizzying surrealism of special effects, the camera brings us into their world, even induces something like the lovers' unbalanced state of mind through the disorienting colors and cutting, and through the close-ups which leave us uncertain of where we are or of what may lurk off-camera, just out of sight. Subtler is the way in which a particular shot will recur, to link disparate parts of the play. The dance in which Oberon and Titania cast a spell of new harmony is a case in point. In extreme close-up the man's face and the woman's move into the frame from either side until they stop, eye to eye, inches apart. Their backlit images darken the screen, which shows them at such close range that only their features, not their entire heads, are visible. Like their dance, this image is itself an emblem of the great forces come into harmony in the play. It gathers strength from ties with an earlier image: Lysander and Hermia gazing into each others' eyes as they pledge their troth and plan to flee. And it gains yet greater richness when we discover it again, utterly changed, in the ludicrous pose of Pyramus and Thisby kissing through the wall's hole.

The film abounds with so many good things, from conceptual setting to graceful subtleties of visual composition, that I am puzzled by the poor reviews. These point to a special difficulty the film encounters with a general audience, a difficulty minimized for us as teachers and critics of Shakespeare's plays by our interest in the verse and in the interpretation of the play. Hall's documentary camera techniques call into play realistic cinematic conventions which may distort a true response to the film as a film. Because we associate close-ups and handheld cameras with film documentary, especially

with television news reporting, the film is in constant danger of seeming to be merely a film of actors acting. If this convention prevails, as it did for about one-third of the British reviewers, the film fails. The modern clothes and setting then seem a cute attempt to be up-to-date, "rather as if," Hall "had assembled a house party of brilliant people and said: 'Let's make a movie!'" [Felix Barker, in the *Liverpool Echo*, 1 February 1969]. The interplay between posing and ironic reality collapses. The special effects, devoid of magic, only irritate. To argue that Shakespeare films are a film genre unto themselves, while true, substitutes a lesser truth for a greater. For the play itself, as its stage history attests, is of a strange, mixed genre, constantly calling attention to its actors as actors, playing with our suspended disbelief at every turn, and tempting us to dismiss it, with Pepys, as merely "insipid." Perhaps more than Hall guessed when he said it "may not be a film at all, [*The Sunday Times,* 26 January, 1969] the film is a true rendering of Shakespeare's *Midsummer Night's Dream.* Like the play itself, it challenges its audience to set their notions of conventional film aside, to believe with Hippolyta that this most rare vision does indeed grow to something of great constancy. (pp. 531-34)

Michael Mullin, "Peter Hall's 'Midsummer Night's Dream' on Film," in Educational Theatre Journal, *Vol. 4, No. 27, December, 1975, pp. 529-34.*

PRODUCTION:

Peter Brook • Royal Shakespeare Company • 1970

BACKGROUND:

Together with Harley Granville-Barker's 1914 staging, Peter Brook's production in 1970 with the RSC is one of the most significant revivals of *A Midsummer Night's Dream* in this century. Set in a white box surrounded by catwalks and hung with trapezes, this *Dream* severed nearly all ties with tradition; even Mendelssohn's musical accompaniment was reduced to a brief passage blaring out of a loudspeaker. Circus tricks and acrobatics further emphasized the artificiality of the production, which sought to create an atmosphere of theatricality rather than illusion. In addition, influenced by Jan Kott's essay on *A Midsummer Night's Dream* in his *Shakespeare, Our Contemporary,* Brook stressed the play's darker theme of passionate sexuality.

COMMENTARY:

Clive Barnes   (review date 28 August 1970)

[*Barnes maintains that the RSC's staging of* A Midsummer Night's Dream *was "a magnificent production, the most important work yet of the world's most imaginative and inventive director."*]

Once in a while, once in a very rare while, a theatrical production arrives that is going to be talked about as long as there is a theater, a production that, for good or ill, is going to exert a major influence on the contemporary stage. Such a production is Peter Brook's staging of Shakespeare's "A

Midsummer Night's Dream," which the Royal Shakespeare Company introduced here tonight.

It is a magnificent production, the most important work yet of the world's most imaginative and inventive director. If Peter Brook had done nothing else but this "Dream" he would have deserved a place in theater history.

Brook has approached the play with a radiant innocence. He has treated the script as if it had just been written and sent to him through the mail. He has staged it with no reference to the past, no reverence for tradition.

He has stripped the play down, asked exactly what it is about. He has forgotten gossamer fairies, sequined eyelids, gauzy veils and whole forests of Beerbohm-trees.

He sees the play for what it is—an allegory of sensual love, and a magic playground of lost innocence and hidden fears. Love in Shakespeare comes as suddenly as death, and when Shakespeare's people love they are all but consumed with sexual passion.

Brook's first concern is to enchant us—to reveal this magic playground. He has conceived the production as a box of theatrical miracles. It takes place in a pure-white setting. The stage is walled in on three sides, and the floor is also white. Ladders lead up the walls and on the top are scaffolds and rostrums from which actors can look down on the playing area like spectators at a bullfight.

The fairy characters—Oberon, Titania and Puck—are made into acrobats and jugglers. They swing in on trapezes, they amaze us with juggling tricks, Tarzan-like swings across the stage, all the sad deftness of clowns.

Shakespeare's quartet of mingled lovers, now mod kids humming love songs to loosely strummed guitars, are lost in the Venetian woods. The trees are vast metal coils thrown down from the walls on fishing rods, and moving in on unwary lovers like spirraling metallic tendrils. And in this wood of animal desire the noises are not the friendly warblings of fairyland, but the grunts and groans of some primeval jungle.

Sex and sexuality are vital in the play. Oberon and Titania, even when quarreling, kiss with hasty, hungry passion—no shining moon for them—and the lovers seem to be journeying through some inner landscape of their own desires toward maturity.

The sexual relationship—with the wittiest use of phallic symbolism the stage can ever have seen—is stressed between Titania and her Bottom. Yet the carnality of the piece is seen with affectionate tolerance rather than the bitterness the playwright shows in "Troilus and Cressida," and this tolerance, even playfulness, suffuses the production.

Brook is a magician and he gives us new eyes. Here, for reasons admirably supported by the text, he has Theseus and Hippolyta (that previously rather dull royal couple whose wedding provides the framework for the play) played by the same actors as play Oberon and Titania. At once the play takes on a new and personal dimension. The fairies take on a new humanity, and these human princelings, once so uninteresting, are now endowed with a different mystery, and the gentle, almost sad note on which the play ends has a feeling of human comprehension and godlike compassion to it. It is most moving.

Two other characters take on dual assignments. Philostrate, that court master of ceremonies for Theseus, is also, naturally enough, Puck, and, rather more puzzlingly, Egeus, the angry father of Hermia, whose opposition to her marriage sets off the action, is also Peter Quince, one of the mechanicals. Presumably the purpose is to bring the play within the play more closely into the main structure, for just as Egeus initiates the real action, so Quince initiates the inner play. But it savors of a literary rather than dramatic device.

Puck is the key figure in this version. Looking like a more than usually perky Picasso clown, he bounces through the action with happy amiability, the model of toleration. John Kane plays him delightfully, performing his tricks with a true circus expertise and acting with unaffected delight.

The Theseus/Oberon and Hippolyta/Titania of Alan Howard and Sara Kestelman are special pleasures, and the mechanicals with the terrible tragedy of "Pyramus and Thisbe" are the best I have ever seen, with David Waller's virile Bottom particularly splendid.

But the star of this dream is Peter Brook himself, with his ideas, his theories and above all his practices. Of course he is helped—first by the samite-white pleasure palace devised by his Los Angeles-based designer, Sally Jacobs, and the richly evocative music and sound score provided by Richard Peaslee. But Mr. Brook is the genius architect of our most substantial pleasure.

He makes it all so fresh and so much fun. After a riotously funny and bawdy courtship of Titania by Bottom, the two leave the stage to, of all wonderful things, Mendelssohn's Wedding March, and all hell breaks loose, with confetti, paper streamers and Oberon himself flying in urbane mockery across the stage.

And Brook uses everything to hand—he is defiantly eclectic. It is as though he is challenging the world, by saying that there is no such thing as Shakespearean style. If it suits his purpose he will use a little kathakali, a pop song, sparklers borrowed from a toyshop, dramatic candles borrowed from Grotowski. It is all splendid grist to his splendid mill. Shakespeare can be fun, Shakespeare can be immediate, Shakespeare can most richly live.

Clive Barnes, *"Historic Staging of 'Dream',"* in The New York Times, *August 28, 1970, p. 15.*

Irving Wardle (review date 28 August 1970)

[*In the excerpt below, Wardle judges Brook's revival of* A Midsummer Night's Dream *a masterpiece. He praises all aspects of the production, but particularly admires the gymnasium-like stage setting, which, he claims, removed "the sense of being earthbound": it was "natural here for characters to fly."*]

After a good, if not vintage season, Stratford rounds off its year with a masterpiece. By which I mean that Peter Brook's version of *A Midsummer Night's Dream* marks the apex towards which the R.S.C. has been moving for the past two years: and that it brings Brook himself to a new point of rest. You could not have predicted what he would do with the play; but after seeing the production you feel you ought to have known, as it is a simple and inevitable crystallization of what has gone before.

Like the R.S.C.'s previous shows it is set in a bare lofty room. The difference is that Brook's designer (Sally Jacobs) has converted it into a gymnasium with ropes and trapezes suspended from the flies and a railed gallery running round the top. This serves several purposes.

It provides an environment for the *Dream* which removes the sense of being earthbound: it is natural here for characters to fly. Also it offers a range of entirely manmade images (even the trees are coils of wires let down on fishing rods) that set off the natural images of the text. Again it provides the greatest extension so far of the company's efforts to develop bodies as well as voices.

In this sense, the production relates back to Meyerhold and biomechanics: the ideal of a troupe of crack gymnasts skilled in clowning and all the tricks of the circus. In this way Brook's company give the play a continuously animated physical line, occupying the whole cubic space of the stage as they shin up and down vertical ladders and stamp about on enormous stilts. Some of the effects are breath-taking: like the nuptials for Titania and Bottom (David Waller) where the stage is deluged in confetti and a purple-gowned Oberon swings across on a trapeze to the roar of Mendelssohn's Wedding March.

A smaller example is Puck's magic flower, here shown as a spinning juggler's plate which he and Oberon nonchalantly toss from wand to wand.

However, Brook is at least as much concerned with the voice as he is with the body. And what he offers is another answer to the question of false stage rhetoric. It consists of a running musical accompaniment (by Richard Peaslee) mainly scored exotically for percussion—autoharps, tubular bells, bongos. These punctuate the action to provide atmosphere and a sense of occasion. He also uses a guitar. The effect these have on the text is to make it natural for characters, at moments of high emotion, to pass over into song: sometimes lyrical, like the lovers, sometimes barbaric like John Kane's war dance "Up and Down" as Puck.

The interpretation to which these styles give substance is one of social harmony expressed by means of emphasizing the parallels between the three groups of characters. We are accustomed to seeing them as inhabitants of different worlds. Brook shows them as members of the same world. Aegus's loss of his daughter is matched by Oberon's loss of his Indian boy. "This same progeny of evils comes from our debate" [II. i. 115-16], says Titania; and as Sara Kestelman delivers it, reclining on the huge scarlet ostrich feather that serves as her bower, the line is meant to embrace the whole action.

Thus Theseus is doubled with Oberon, both played with sovereign magnanimity by Alan Howard. Hippolyta doubles with Titania and Philostrate with Puck.

Brook has done two things here. He has made some reversals simply to produce a thrill of the unexpected: as in the beefy male fairies and a Snug (Barry Stanton) whose lion really does alarm the ladies. And he has altered other traditional emphases to express the main theme. You see this first in the Bottom-Titania wedding, an occasion for real sexual revels and not a joke against an outclassed clodpole.

But the point comes out most strongly in the mechanicals' play. The joke this time is not against them. The audience are not invited to join with the nobility in sneering at these crude performers. The play is a meeting between friends. At Pyramus's line "I come without delay" [V. i. 203] all the lovers

join in the song. And the event closes on a note of calm social harmony. "Meet *we all* by break of day" [V. i. 422], Oberon says to the assembled stage. And the cast leave by way of the aisles shaking hands with the house. A marvellous evening.

Irving Wardle, "To the Heights on a Trapeze," in
The Times, *London, August 28, 1970, p. 9.*

Peter Brook and Ronald Hayman (interview date 29 August 1970)

[*In the excerpt below, Brook discusses his conception of* A Midsummer Night's Dream. *He places special emphasis on the merging of romance and realism in the Pyramus and Thisbe sequence in Act V, claiming that one must "revise one's views of the entire play in relation to why it is that the play couldn't exist, couldn't have its meaning without this last act."*]

At an early rehearsal of *A Midsummer Night's Dream* at Stratford-on-Avon one of the actors asked Peter Brook "How can you define what it is we're looking for?" His answer was that the work they were doing would take them in a thousand different directions but it was all towards a definition which couldn't be formulated in advance. If it could, the work wouldn't be worth attempting.

Brook has never been one to pursue straight lines. "I believe that the only way one finds anything is through the radar system of finding one point, two points, three points, and somewhere in between those is what you're looking for. For this reason I've really spent all my working life in looking for opposites. For instance very early on, if I worked in Shakespeare, I'd then want to do a commercial comedy, if I'd worked in television, I'd want to go to opera. This is a dialectical principle of finding a reality through opposites."

His choice of *A Midsummer Night's Dream* as his first Shakespearian production since his *King Lear* with Paul Scofield in 1962 can be seen in these terms. "It seemed that having worked on the *Marat-Sade, US, Oedipus* and the series of King Lears that's spread over seven years, including two for the film, it was absolutely essential to go to another part of the world where there was a different sort of life and joy."

But how does a director like Brook approach a play like the *Dream?* The first thing is always a series of exercises, some physical, some vocal, some improvisational, aimed to make the actors work more freely together as a group. "This is something that always has to be renewed. The fact that the group worked well last week doesn't mean that it will this week."

The second thing is to arrive at what he calls "a collective understanding" of the play, which can't be achieved simply by making an explanatory speech, "because eventually the quality of the result depends on a shared understanding, not on one man's view. For an actor to go on the stage with the conviction that really carries to an audience, he has to know what he's talking about, to believe, to be inwardly committed. An actor who is representing something which he knows to be true because he's shared in the discovery has no embarrassment about presenting it. On the contrary, he wants it to be known."

Working on *US,* Brook started off by asking his actors what they all believed about the war in Vietnam. "In the case of the *Marat-Sade,* we could use the true, lived material of each of the actors, who nearly always had had an encounter with

Alan Howard as Oberon, Sara Kestelman as Titania, David Waller as Bottom, and John Kane as Puck. Act IV, scene i.

madness. Three quarters of the families of the world have madness in them. 'Anybody seen a madman?' Everybody said 'Yes. I know one. I am one'. But get a group together and say 'What do fairies mean to you?' No good answers will come out of that. 'Anybody seen a fairy?' 'No'. 'Are you a fairy?' Blushes. One voice saying 'Well, maybe. Yes'. But until you get past that stage, you can't start working on the *Dream*. First-hand experience is needed and the only first-hand experience you can get is trying to explore the text, using specific acting methods. Where someone in a library uses intellectual and analytical methods to try to discover what a play is about, actors try to discover through the voice, through the body, through experiment in action.

"In those exercises on *The Tempest* which were seen in public at the Round House, there was a Japanese actor who, by approaching Ariel through his breathing and through his body, made Ariel something very understandable. A certain force became tangible in something which to the Japanese was easy to understand because in the basis of the Noh theatre, from which he came, there was a certain type of sound, a certain type of cry, a certain type of breath. The idea of that force was truly represented. It could be discussed because it had suddenly happened. There it was amongst us. It was no longer force, an abstract movement, it was *force,* a reality, something which could even influence other people."

Brook believes it is wrong to direct the *Dream* as if the fairies, the aristocrats and the mechanicals belonged to three different worlds. "The more one examines the play, the more one sees how these worlds interweave." He has the same actor playing Oberon and Theseus, the same actress Titania and Hippolyta, the same actor Puck and Philostrate.

He is also, as always, very conscious of how deliberately Shakespeare uses prose sequences. In the *Dream* the mechanicals' scenes are written in prose. "The prose world in Shakespeare always suggests that one has to look outwards; the verse world is a world in which you look inwards into the text in the sense that it's a concentration of the meaning. One can't start with a sense that one has to embroider. But the prose portions demand turning into a flesh and blood existence for which realistic elements have to be found. If you think in terms of social realism about a group of artisans attempting—because they believe in it passionately—to put on a romantic play, that play of Pyramus and Thisbe at once takes off in a different direction. This isn't an interpretation but a direction dictated by a realism which, while ill-applied to a poetic world, is directly called for by a prose world."

Brook also realizes how important it is to solve the problem of why Shakespeare, who by the time he wrote the *Dream* did nothing by accident, put the play of Pyramus and Thisbe in the key position. Instead of ending the play, as he could have done, with the reconciliation of the lovers, which comes at the end of Act Four, he built the whole of Act Five around the play-within-the-play. "One has then to revise one's views of the entire play in relation to why it is that the play couldn't exist, couldn't have its meaning, without this last act."

"Is there a short answer to that question?"

"I think so", Peter Brook said, "but I can only express it in performance."

Peter Brook and Ronald Hayman, "Life and Joy,"
in The Times, *London, August 29, 1970, p. 7.*

Helen Dawson　(review date 30 August 1970)

[*In the following review, Dawson asserts that in this production, "the play and its poetry leap into almost Oriental clarity, and the audience, uncluttered by romantic 'scenic' tradition, goes through an additional experience: propelled by the play, the imagination begins to race."*]

Whenever Peter Brook decides to direct a classic, you can be sure that he has some interpretive idea which will cut through the play like a laser. His historic new production of *A Midsummer Night's Dream* at Stratford is no exception; it is radical, full of thought, and, theatrically, a triumph.

Magic, now, is discredited; 'bewitching' no more than a casual adjective, even in the theatre where once it was taken for granted. As Brook says in his book, *The Empty Space:* 'We must open our empty hands and show that really there is nothing up our sleeves. Only then can we begin.' Once we are out of childhood, the closest we come to magic is through our dreams; in this extra-terrestrial world we meet that part of ourselves which we bury under social convention.

The key to this production comes when Theseus rebukes Hermia for refusing to marry Demetrius. 'Take time to pause,' he tells her [I. i. 83], and in the pause before the new moon, the play (the dream, the magic) takes place, peopled by the subconscious personalities of Theseus and Hippolyta before their wedding; of Hermia, Lysander, Demetrius and Helena before they finalise their love.

'Everything seems double' [IV. i. 90], says Hermia when she wakes at the end. In the dream Theseus becomes Oberon and Hippolyta Titania. Sara Kestelman's Titania is a woman of taut sensuality who falls for Bottom out of a lust which she could never own to in court, but which Theseus (Alan Howard, pale and authoritative) has recognised in her and, as Oberon, can encourage out of his own unspoken desire to see her purity sullied and his jealousy vindicated. Hermia's stern nobleman father, Egeus, becomes the gentle Quince, and Philostrate, Theseus's tame Master of Revels, turns into Oberon's wild-boy, Puck.

For the two pairs of lovers there is no direct transformation; their dream fantasies are more direct. For instance, when Hermia declines to sleep with Lysander, 'So be distant, and good night, sweet friend' [II. ii. 60] (and one of the fairies pulls him back from her), it is no accident that she dreams of the serpent, and in her dream wakes to find Lysander gone and her fears and Helena's hopes realised. Their roles reversed, Helena has a superfluity of love and Hermia has none.

For his setting Brook has seized on the theory that 'The Dream,' unlike most of Shakespeare's plays, had no original source, but was culled from the jumble of entertainment available to Elizabethans in fairs and halls. Sally Jacobs's sets and costumes evoke a Big Top, with a balustrade round the top for musicians and chases. It is not only a valid device, but one which bursts with invention. With none of the usual scampering behind bushes, the play and its poetry leap into almost Oriental clarity, and the audience, uncluttered by romantic 'scenic' tradition, goes through an additional experience: propelled by the play, the imagination begins to race.

To an accompaniment of drums and metallic rumblings, tinsel darts and bright clashes of costume colour, the production abounds in circus tricks and excitements. Puck and Oberon swing over and in on the trapeze; the 'love in idleness' potion is juggled on spinning plates; Bottom as the ass has a black clown's nose; Titania's couch is a huge, scarlet ostrich feather; and Hermia, when she's rejected, hangs from the trapeze, fighting like a wounded monkey.

But, not unexpectedly, it's not all fun. As in a dream—and a circus—there are moments of stark terror, at times reminiscent of Brook's 'Marat/Sade,' when the tent turns into the high walls of an institution, when characters scuttle in fear through Puck's grotesque stilt legs. The fairies are streaked through with cruelty; an uneasily ambiguous bunch who seem to be warning 'Don't meddle in illusion.'

There are also moments of genuine, fresh beauty, when the relationships, especially between the young lovers, take on a new, altogether realistic, dimension. And I've never seen the Mechanicals handled with more wit or lively affection. Solid, cloth-capped workmen, they are not merely 'jokers' but personalities linked to both court and forest.

The cast, as so often under the Brook baton, seem to pull themselves technically several notches higher, while at the same time giving slightly anonymous, team performances. However, David Waller's Bottom is outstanding, a rich comic creation, beautifully in control; Frances de la Tour's Helena is a lank, loose-limbed original; John Kane's Puck fairly bubbles and Barry Stanton is a lovely, fat Snug.

Finally, another Brook hallmark: at the end, when Puck blesses the house, and Theseus and Hippolyta strip off their wedding finery to face the audience, there is a moment of solemnity, a sinking in of 'great constancy,' before an abrupt change of key as the cast pelt up the aisles, shaking hands with the audience. A further reminder that there are good directors and very good directors, but there is only one Peter Brook.

> Helen Dawson, "Doubling Up for a Triumph," in The Observer, August 30, 1970, p. 19.

Benedict Nightingale   (review date 4 September 1970)

[Nightingale offers a dissenting view of Brook's Midsummer Night's Dream. He considers it "humourless and pretentious" and "surely Brook's most dispiriting production."]

If a director is called Peter, he is sure to be British; if he's British he's sure to be called Peter. So concluded a writer in the New York Times recently—and no doubt Brook, the most theatrically adventurous of the clan, was still somewhere near the front of her mind. He has given us the Scofield Lear, the Marat-Sade and, less happily, US; but all that was in the early and middle Sixties, and we have heard little from him since, at any rate on stage. My own last contact with him was through the medium of a television set, an odd, uncanny vision, which bothers me still. There he sat, hunched, furrowed, brooding, and, with every appearance of terrible intellectual struggle, enunciated more convoluted platitudes than one would have believed possible in so short a time. Was it really the Big British Peter? If so, what would his next production be like? As humourless and pretentious as this? Well, the answer is at Stratford, a Midsummer Night's Dream to strain the faith of admirers. The mountain has laboured and brought forth, among other things, Mickey Mouse.

This, presumably, is what his Bottom is meant to evoke. Why else should he have a tiny black bulb for a nose, small black ears instead of the conventional ass-head, and huge black clogs for feet? The actual purpose of the innovation isn't so

clear; but then nor is much else in the production. It takes place in a slightly smaller version of the plain white box we've seen so often at Stratford: ladders lead up the sides to a gallery at the top. Those players who aren't onstage stand up there, gazing down at those who are, and intermittently grate, scrape and bang at the rails, making rough music. Music of a slightly smoother kind is provided by two small percussion sections, also aloft. The trees of the forest are represented by enormous springs dangling from what look like aluminium fishing rods, Puck's magic flower by a steel plate twirling on a steel wand; players noisily wave big blunt saws and hurl shrieking silver and blue torpedoes at each other. It is a bizarre, metallic business: Shakespeare as he might be conceived by a science fiction addict, or, indeed, performed by enthusiastic Vegans; the Dream 2001 AD.

Perhaps this is the point. The romantic imagination nowadays isn't so exclusively filled with visions of spotted snakes, musk-roses, luscious woodbine and the other exotica invoked by the spirits in the play. We have seen Oldenburg as well as Rousseau, read Ballard as well as Keats. There's no reason why the nightmares of a technological age should not include processed minerals as well as animals and vegetables. But this little perception cannot justify the production as a whole, and there are other oddities still to be explained. Why Mickey Mouse? Why should the young bloods be dressed in what look like Marks and Spencer blouses, and the fairies in baggy silver pyjamas, like Japanese wrestlers? What are we to make of a Puck in billowing yellow silks and a blue skullcap, who swings on a trapeze above the bickering lovers at a time he's supposed to be offstage, and still manages to mistake their identity afterwards? 'I'll put a girdle about the earth / In forty minutes' [II. i. 175-76], cries this fantastical Chinese rabbi from his perch, grinning foolishly; and we do not believe him for a moment. Only a humourless man could have staged this. There are also times when one feels that only a cynical one could be in control. The archetypal Hollywood mogul, thinking a scene dull, will call for gratuitous tit; and some of Brook's innovations seem analogous. Does the verse limp, the acting labour? Very well: put the speaker on a swing or stilts, make him scramble up ladders or wrestle with his betrothed on the ground, let him deliver his lines as if they are a pop-song, or, if they're meant to be sung already, sob them like a raga. All this happens in Brook's perverse Dream, and more.

The invention, though profuse, seems quite arbitrary. It is a hectic, abrupt journey from the Hayward Gallery to Disneyland, from Billy Smart's Circus to International Wrestling on ITV, from August Bank Holiday, Isle of Wight, to the grind and clank of the industrial Midlands. Brook would doubtless declare that all this is perfectly intentional, and argue that most invention is as arbitrary as most other. No one knows what fairies look like. Is it really necessary for them to be fey queers on tiptoe, with wings and wands? Why not solid bodies, capable of sending Bottom spinning into the audience? And why one period's costumes rather than another's? It's a reasonable reply; but insufficient. External invention must surely be commensurate with the internal demands of the text: there's a point after which it simply draws attention to itself, regardless of relevance. But then, again, Brook might well admit that this point has been left far, far behind by his production. Indeed, if one may attribute any overall purpose to him, it is to turn the play into a gigantic skylark, in which any vivid excrescence is justified and (fashionably enough) the audience is involved as much as possible. Characters wink and joke at us, not bothering to disguise the fact they're actors, and, at the final curtain, bound out and wring our applauding hands.

Some seemed delighted to find the bard thus supercharged; but, whatever the gain to them, he is surely the loser. What chance of subtlety from an Oberon precariously balancing in mid-air? Characterisation suffers; so does plot. It is even harder than usual to follow the emotional fortunes of such gabbling, writhing lovers. More to the point, there's no indication that Brook has given much thought to the reason Shakespeare wrote this play rather than another: he won't hound or sleuth out a meaning. Perhaps we're meant to read something into the unusual solemnity of a *Pyramus and Thisbe* during which the assembled courtiers contemplate their own mortality; but that scarcely takes us very far. The oddity of it is that Brook's controversial friend and influence, Professor Kott, is never more persuasive than when he condemns the sentimentality with which the *Dream* has been swaddled since Mendelssohn and before: in no other Shakespeare play (he suggests [in *Shakespeare Our Contemporary*]) is 'eroticism expressed so brutally'. The effect of Brook's interpretation is to sentimentalise it once again, and in a new, more insidious way. His manic decoration has deprived it of suffering, fear, horror and, apart from one moment, when Bottom's phallus is crudely mimed by the fairies, even of lust.

Shouldn't it, then, at least be funny? Alas, the mechanicals are a drab crew, apart from David Waller's eager, gentle Bottom. His controlled pathos somehow survives a production that manages to swamp and swallow most others: so (just) do Ben Kingsley's Demetrius, Mary Rutherford's Hermia, Sara Kestelman's Titania and Alan Howard's Theseus. Mr Howard also plays Oberon, and there's more doubling of the kind, for no clear reason except economy. And I laughed once only, and that at no appropriate moment. Little point lingering over what is surely Brook's most dispiriting production. . . .

Benedict Nightingale, "Dream 2001 AD," in the New Statesman, *Vol. 80, No. 2059, September 4, 1970, p. 281.*

Kenneth Hurren　　(review date 5 September 1970)

[*Hurren gives a sharply negative review of Brook's production, regarding it "a bleak comment on the wayward standards of contemporary Shakespearian criticism that this impertinent travesty" was "received with tolerance and even fervour."*]

The stage of the Royal Shakespeare Theatre at Stratford-upon-Avon—a theatre still visited by a great many simple souls from home and abroad in the innocent belief that it is here they will find a touch of reverence for the Bard—would seem to me the last place in the world to be placed at the disposal of a director like Peter Brook as a sort of private playpen wherein to indulge his bizarre whims and anarchic fancies. That, however, is the way things are.

Last week Mr Brook had at a piece that is described, with some effrontery, as William Shakespeare's *A Midsummer Night's Dream* on the cover of a programme book that offers a number of depressing quotations having to do mostly with the limitless freedom of dream fantasies and the advantages of bare stages in isolating a work of art (as a picture is isolated on the wall of a gallery) and in according a proper emphasis to the spoken word—all intended, I fear, to brainwash the congregation into accepting Mr Brook's little show as a valid revolt against tradition. It is, of course, nothing of the kind, but simply a tiresomely self-indulgent display of directorial gimmickry at the expense of a work that, in its traditional form, has been known to enchant an auditor or two in its time. Old Sam Pepys, to be sure, thought it 'the most insipid ridiculous play that ever I saw in my life,' but it can never have been quite so ridiculous as Mr Brook makes it.

It is performed as a circus entertainment within the harshly white walls of a gymnasium, but the stage is not altogether bare: there are a few pillows for reclining upon, a giant scarlet feather fan (that is to serve in due course as Titania's bower), and great spiral coils of wire suspended on fishing rods from the catwalk around the top of the walls, and I'd raise a sceptical eyebrow at anyone who felt this paraphernalia to be less distracting from the spoken word than more conventional items of scenery. You may, on the other hand, be grateful for any distraction from the words as they happen to be spoken here: 'I know a bank,' remarks Oberon as prosaically as if he were referring to Lloyds or Barclays, swinging the while on a trapeze and spinning a plate on a stick.

Trapezes figure prominently throughout as perches for the immortals, among whom Puck is a kosher clown in skull-cap and baggy pants, sometimes appearing on stilts, and the attendant fairies are drably got up as prisoners of war. On the whole, they are less of a nuisance up there than they are on the ground, where they are apt to disport themselves in smutty horseplay with Bottom and Titania (Mr Brook lets slip no opportunity to vulgarise the action with sexual innuendo at every level) or to strip the hapless Snug to his G-string. The lovers, when they are not singing their couplets to pop guitar music, are a quartet of tumblers who include a Demetrius played as a swarthy version of Harpo Marx, and a Helena whose long hair is so frequently hanging over her face that it is hard to say when she is coming and when she is going.

The dream, in the main, is that of Duke Theseus, who sees himself as Oberon (Alan Howard takes both parts in attitudes that alternate between boredom and derision) and Hippolyta as a Titania who seems phallus-fixated to the point of nymphomania, an idea that ignites so little enthusiasm in Sara Kestelman that she plays the roles with the expressionlessness of the embalmed. As to the music, while Mendelssohn may not be to Sir Denis Brogan 'absolutely first-class,' I think he could give cards and spades to Richard Peaslee who makes a dominant supplementary contribution, raucously scored for bongos, bedsprings and plastic tubing.

It is a bleak comment on the wayward standards of contemporary Shakespearian criticism that this impertinent travesty has been received with tolerance and even fervour. I should have suspected its most fascinated audience to be a convention of psychiatrists; for myself I find Mr Brook's hang-ups of rather less interest than Shakespeare's play. (pp. 248-49)

Kenneth Hurren, "Disenchantment," in the Spectator, *Vol. 225, No. 7419, September 5, 1970, pp. 248-49.*

J. C. Trewin　　(review date 12 September 1970)

[*In the excerpt below, Trewin stresses Brook's fidelity to Shakespeare, despite the iconclasm of his production of* A Midsummer Night's Dream. *"I have seldom heard the verse uttered with so much clarity and music," he asserts.*]

Some nights are markers in the history of the stage: those, for example, when Olivier played Richard III, the Royal Court found *Look Back In Anger,* and Peter Brook directed *King Lear* at Stratford. Now here is another Brook creation, *A Midsummer Night's Dream,* also at Stratford, that should live in record as Granville-Barker's so different *Dream* has lived since 1914.

If somebody had told me, even ten years ago, that I should have applauded a revival of this play set in a stern white box with unvaried lighting, a Wood of coiled wire suspended from fishing-rods, and Puck, on one trapeze, joining Oberon, on another, in the plate-spinning routine of a circus, I might have assumed that it was all a stray nightmare. In fact, it was the most exciting *Dream* within memory.

We have met the fantasy in so many forms; over-decorated and under-decorated, as a swooningly Victorian album or as a Jacobean masque. The Wood has been a complicated forest, an austere, moon-silvered thicket, or a garden in Regent's Park. Nobody has ever transfigured it in the Brook manner; moreover—this is the point—he has done so without damage to his poet. Though it is a director's creation, it is that of a director working with a dramatist: I have seldom heard the verse uttered with so much clarity and music.

Brook gets us to listen because he treats the *Dream* as something none of us has heard or seen before. His bare, clinically white stage, with an upper gallery on three sides, is the blank sheet upon which he writes the play, illustrating it with the most unexpected vigour and invention. Always he gets the verse to reach us as if it were new, spoken by characters who are never the stereotypes of a hundred revivals.

Visually, thanks to Sally Jacobs, it is a world of unsullied primary colours, startling against the unadorned background and beneath the strong lighting that never changes though the verse can transform it: when Oberon says "as black as Acheron" [III. ii. 357], the stage becomes so to our imaginations. We are made to imagine: sight and hearing are sharpened. Brook employs some of the disciplines of the circus: trapeze-work, the spinning of the silver dish that holds "the little western flower" [II. i. 166], even a moment's uncanny stilt-walking for Puck. While we watch, admiring technical dexterity, not knowing what may follow, we are listening also to Shakespeare unfussed.

On three or four occasions Brook has a passage sung mock-operatically. It does no harm; indeed it can be heightening. I must have heard *A Midsummer Night's Dream* nearly a hundred times, but I cannot recall so fresh an impact, so new a spirit of wonder. It does not harm our valued memories, it is simply the great tripartite fantasy re-thought by a genius of the contemporary theatre: his own dream, compact of subtleties. I shall not cease to think of his union of the worlds, the doubling—rather the merging—of Theseus and Hippolyta with Oberon and Titania, sub-conscious selves released in dream and night; the spectacle of Titania upon her scarlet ostrich-feather bed above the frenzies of the Wood; the affectionately-observed Mechanicals whom we appear to be meeting for the first time; the ubiquitous lemon-breeched Puck, clown, djinn, and master of the ceremonies, and naturally doubling with Philostrate; such a surprise as the whirl of confetti and the thunder of the Wedding March—enter Mendelssohn—while Bottom is borne off at the end of the first half; the sight of an infuriated Hermia clinging to her trapeze; and that enchanted calm at the last before the company

breaks suddenly from its stage, shaking hands left and right—"Give me your hands" [V. i. 437]—as it comes up through an astonished auditorium.

I have not assembled these impressions in any special order because the main thing is the knowledge that, however Brook illustrates Shakespeare, it is Shakespeare that matters. Brook has simply polished the mirror. I am grateful to the entire company, in particular to Alan Howard, Sara Kestelman, Frances de la Tour, and John Kane; but this will go straight into the records as Brook's *Dream*—with a word for the musical contrivances of Richard Peaslee.

J. C. Trewin, "Peter Brook's Creative Dream," in The Illustrated London News, *Vol. 257, No. 6841, September 12, 1970, p. 33.*

Peter Brook and Peter Ansorge   (interview date October 1970)

[*In this discussion of his production of* A Midsummer Night's Dream, *Brook comments on some of the play's darker elements and their influence on his conception of the play, observing that "Oberon's cool intention is to degrade Titania as a woman."*]

The quartet of sleeping lovers lolled perilously upon swings suspended from the flies: Bottom lay motionless below seeming dead to the world. On another side of the stage, Oberon was waiting to catch a spinning plate on a pole tossed down by Puck from a high balcony. He missed, shrugged ('Take 342!') and tried again. In the front stalls of the Stratford auditorium Peter Brook was watching the fraught rehearsal of *A Midsummer Night's Dream* calmly and without any visible signs of anxiety or doubt.

Brook surveys his actors like a subdued Moses bearing a hidden decalogue in his hands. He is directing the *Dream* unaided by the obvious pretty, pretty fairy enchantments. Props and movements have been shaped from a circus ring rather than a haunted wood. He doesn't worry when things go wrong—the actors must make their own magic. Mistakes are part of the performance, risks to be taken in the mastery of stage illusion.

During the second week of rehearsals, when the text had yet to be opened, the actors had improvised a happening around the theme of the *Dream*. 'It had extraordinary force and interest,' states Brook. 'But like all happenings it can never be repeated—it was there once and gone.'

The Tempest Roundhouse experiment notwithstanding, far from neglecting the text of a play, Brook's involvement in a work which interests him is total. For this Shakespeare comedy, his actors must never be allowed to forget that they are playing; in the context of continual stage happenings, a world 'swift as a shadow, short as any dream' [I. i. 144].

'After a long series of dark, violent, black plays I had a very strong wish to go as deeply as possible into a work of pure celebration. *A Midsummer Night's Dream* is, amongst other things, a celebration of the arts of the theatre. On one level the actors have to display a physical virtuosity—an expression of joy. Hence our production at Stratford involves acrobatics, circus skills, trapeze acts. Equally, certain parts of the play cannot be played without using a Stanislavskian sense of natural character development. There's the play we all know—and also a hidden play, a hidden *Dream*. That's the one the actors set out to discover for themselves.

'The *Dream* is a play about magic, spirits, fairies. Today we don't believe in any one of those things and yet, perhaps, we do. The fairy imagery which the Victorian and even post-Victorian tradition has given us in relation to the *Dream* has to be rejected—it has died on us. But one can't take an anti-magical, a down-to-earth view of the *Dream*. When I directed *Titus Andronicus* at this theatre sixteen years ago I was convinced that the play wasn't just a series of gory events but was a *hidden* play—the drama behind *Titus* was a ritualistic expression of a primitive cycle of bloodshed which, if touched, would reveal a source of immense, atomic power. In the same way, the interest in working on the *Dream* is to take a play which is apparently composed of very artificial, unreal elements and to discover that it is a true, a real play. But the language of the *Dream* must be expressed through a very different stage imagery from the one that served its purpose in the past.

'We have dropped all pretence of making magic by bluff, through stage tricks. The first step must be moving from darkness to daylight. We have to start in the open—in fact we begin in a white set and white light (the only darkness in the entire production occurs during the public encounters between Theseus and Hippolyta). We present all the elements with which we are going to work in the open. This is related to one of the key lines in the play when the question arises about whether the man who is going to play the lion should be a real lion or only pretend to be real. Out of this academic and very Brechtian discussion comes the formulation that the actor should say to the audience, 'I am a man as other men are' [III. i. 43-4]. That is the necessary beginning for a play about the spirit world—the actors must present themselves as men who are like all other men. It's from the hidden inner-life of the performer that the magic, the unfolding possibilities of the play, must emerge. The core of the *Dream* is the Pyramus and Thisbe play which doesn't come at the end of a highly organised work just for comic relief. The actor's art is truly celebrated in this episode—it becomes a mysterious interplay of invisible elements, the joy, the magic of the *Dream*. The play can become an exploration, through a complex series of themes, of what only the theatre can do as an art form.'

Brook has several of his actors doubling, even trebling their roles in the play. Most notably Alan Howard and Sara Kestelman play both Theseus-Hippolyta and the fairy king and queen Oberon-Titania. Was this for thematic or economic reasons?

'There were two motives. Firstly I wanted to do the play with a small group. There is a quite different quality of involvement with such a group than with a large cast where the actors come on, do a little bit and then disappear for the rest of the evening. When I directed the RSC experimental group in a version of Genet's *The Screens* we used a small group in which one actor played two, even three, roles. In this way you can take an actor much further—if he reappears in a different part during a performance. Close to this was the fact that in the *Dream* there are no set characters—the more you study the comedy it becomes a comment on what makes a dream; each scene is like a dream of a dream, the interrelation between theme and character is more mysterious than at first sight. Theseus and Hippolyta are trying to discover what constitutes the true union of a couple, what can bring about the

conjunction whereby their marriage can become true and complete. Then a play unfolds like a dream before their wedding in which an almost identical couple appear—Oberon and Titania. Yet this other couple are in an opposition so great that, as Titania announces in language of great strength, it brings about a complete schism in the natural order. She claims that her dispute with Oberon is the cause of the whole world going awry. Thus on the one hand we have a man and woman in total dispute and, on the other, a man and woman coming together through a concord found out of a discord. The couples are so closely related that we felt that Oberon and Titania could easily be sitting inside the minds of Theseus and Hippolyta. Whether from this you say that they *are* actually the same characters becomes unimportant.'

I then asked Brook if he shared Jan Kott's view of the *Dream*—that far from being a 'celebration' the play contained a darker, more sinister exploration of love than is normally suggested. 'Most definitely. Kott wrote very interestingly [in his *Shakespeare Our Contemporary*] about the play—though he fell into the trap of turning one aspect of the play into the whole. The *Dream* is not a piece for the kids—it's a very powerful sexual play.

'There is something more amazing than in the whole of Strindberg at the centre of the *Dream*. It's the idea, which has been so easily passed over for centuries, of a man taking the wife whom he loves totally and having her fucked by the crudest sex machine he can find. We had a long discussion about this at one point in rehearsals—we listed all the alternative animal-mates with which Titania might have been presented by Oberon. One realises that every other animal could have left Titania with a certain sexual nostalgia—it's a sort of romantic dream for a woman to be screwed by a lion or even a bear. The ass, famous in legends for the size of its prick, is the only animal that couldn't carry the least sense of romantic attachment. Oberon's deliberate cool intention is to degrade Titania as a woman. Titania tries to invest her love under all the forms of spiritual romance at her disposal—Oberon destroys her illusions totally. From Strindberg to D H Lawrence, one doesn't find a stronger situation than that. It's not only an opposition between this ethereal woman and a gross sensuality that's coupled between Titania and Bottom—but the much darker and curious fact that it's the woman's husband who brings this about—and in the name of love! Yet there's no cynicism in Oberon's action—he isn't a sadist. The play is about something very mysterious, and only to be understood by the complexity of human love.' (pp. 18-19)

Peter Brook, "Director in Interview," in an interview with Peter Ansorge, in Plays and Players, *Vol. 18, No. 1, October, 1970, pp. 18-19.*

Peter Thomson   (review date 1971)

[*In the excerpt below, Thomson assesses the early critical reaction to Brook's production as well as offering his own judgment. "More than anything I have ever seen," he concludes, "this production declared its confidence and delight in the art of performance. In doing so, it went, for me, beyond the meaning of the play to a joyous celebration of the fact that it was written."*]

Peter Brook's production of *A Midsummer Night's Dream* is the sensation of the 1970 season. Those who did not respond to it will feel compelled to argue against it. Those for whom it was a uniquely joyful experience will regret the cribbed

David Waller as Bottom, Sara Kestelman as Titania, and fairies. Act III, scene i.

confinement of the cavillers, who lost the light for a handful of prejudices. I am decidedly of the second party, and can only with hesitation undertake to analyse an experience that came to me whole. I think I understand now what Brook means when he describes himself [in his *The Empty Space*] as a man 'searching within a decaying and evolving theatre'. It is not enough that the Royal Shakespeare Company should serve Shakespeare. It must be prepared, from its position of privilege, to serve the British theatre, which finds itself, in 1970, threatened materially by, for example, a new minimum wage for actors, and spiritually by a loss of faith in the holiness of its art. One member of the *Dream's* cast told me that working with Peter Brook was 'fantastic. It changes your life.' England has a bad record in its treatment of wayward theatrical genius. Some of the attacks on Peter Brook ring like repeating history, but no one to whom I talked at Stratford was ready with outright condemnation of *A Midsummer Night's Dream*. One Shakespearian scholar confessed that he shut his eyes during the performance, loving the way it was spoken, hating the way it was presented. And yes, it was superbly spoken, despite the fact that Brook gave no textual notes throughout the rehearsal period. I choose to believe that the actors spoke well because the director had renewed in them a generous anxiety to communicate with the audience. It was no accident that the programme notes featured Meyerhold's insistence that, 'There is a fourth *creator* in addition to the author, the director and the actor—namely, the spectator . . . from the friction between the actor's creativity

and the spectator's imagination, a clear flame is kindled.' At the end of the performance Puck's 'Give me your hands, if we be friends' [V. i. 437], was taken as the cue for the actors to leave the stage and walk through the auditorium shaking hands with the audience. It was the culmination of a feast of friendship. I was moved.

The design by Sally Jacobs set the play among white walls rising to about eighteen feet and topped by a practical gallery from which actors not on stage were constantly surveying those who were, and contributing where necessary to the mechanics of the staging. Two upstage doors, much narrower than their Elizabethan counterparts but similarly placed, provided the only access at stage level, but there were ladders at the downstage end of both the side walls, and trapezes slung from the flies could lower and raise Oberon, Puck, Titania and the four fairies. The costumes were vivid, of no single period, aiming at beauty and the actors' comfort. Puck was in a glossy yellow clown-suit and blue skull-cap. Demetrius and Lysander wore smocks of the currently popular smudged pastel design over pressed white flannels, Helena and Hermia long, side-slit dresses with the same smudged pastel decoration. Oberon wore deep purple, Titania bright green, the Mechanicals the working clothes of British labourers in the age of austerity. The Fairies, unobtrusive amid the colour, wore practical suits of grey silk. Against white walls, costume stands out. So do properties. The trees were coiled wire mobiles, hung out from the gallery, which produced metallic music as they twisted and settled. Hermia, waking alone at the end of [Act II, Scene ii], was threatened and snared by them in a nightmare realisation of 'the fierce vexation of a dream' [IV. i. 69]. At the amazing end of [Act III, Scene i] (immediately followed by the interval), the stage was a bedlam of flying plates and flashing tinsel darts, the wild confetti for the 'marriage' of Titania and Bottom. The play's magic was replaced by circus tricks. Brook has described the reasoning:

> today we have no symbols that can conjure up fairyland and magic for a modern audience. On the other hand there are a number of actions that a performer can execute that are quite breathtaking. So we went to the art of the circus and the acrobat because they both make purely theatrical statements. We've worked through a language of acrobatics to find a new approach to a magic that we know cannot be reached by 19th century conventions
> [*The Daily Telegraph*, 14 September 1970].

I am not convinced of the necessity for the substitution, but its effectiveness in the theatre can be assessed only in the theatre; and even there not argued, only perceived or denied. At [II. i. 246], Puck swings down on a trapeze, spinning a plate on a rod. Oberon, on a lower trapeze, looks up to ask,

Hast thou the flower there? Welcome, wanderer . . .

[II. i. 247]

and Puck leans over to tip the still spinning plate on to Oberon's rod—'Ay, there it is' [II. i. 248]. The plate does not *become* the flower. Instead, the act of passing it becomes the *magic* of the flower. In order to harry Lysander and Demetrius in [Act III, Scene ii], Puck climbs on six foot stilts and darts around the stage in a new-established convention of invisibility that makes stage poetry out of a scene normally surrendered to a dead convention. I feel no inclination to defend any of Brook's decisions. I doubt whether the play could have been so well spoken if it had been seriously falsified. It should, however, be recorded that there was doubling of Theseus and Oberon, Hippolita and Titania (the change at [IV. i. 102] was simply managed, though with remarkable poignancy, by having Oberon and Titania walk up to the stage doors, don cloaks and turn to walk downstage as Theseus and Hippolita), Philostrate and Puck, Theseus' courtiers and the fairies, so that the lovers carried with them into their dream all the familiar faces of the Athenian court. And it should also be admitted that a man more musically accomplished than I would annotate the variety of Richard Peaslee's score where I can only applaud it. More than anything I have ever seen, this production declared its confidence and delight in the art of performance. In doing so, it went, for me, beyond the meaning of the play to a joyous celebration of the fact that it was written. And it did all its work in full view of the audience. I am reminded of another of Peter Brook's stated beliefs: 'This is how I understand a necessary theatre; one in which there is only a practical difference between actor and audience, not a fundamental one.' (pp. 125-26)

Peter Thomson, "A Necessary Theatre: The Royal Shakespeare Season 1970 Reviewed," in Shakespeare Survey: An Annual Survey of Shakespearian Study and Production, *Vol. 24, 1971, pp. 117-26.*

John Russell Brown   (essay date 1971)

[*In the following excerpt, Brown disputes the supposedly liberating effect of Brook's staging of* A Midsummer Night's Dream, *arguing that the director made Shakespeare subservient to his own theatrical theories and interpretation of the play.*]

Shakespeare is unique and those who present his plays in the theatre should try to take this into account: usual ways of working may be quite inappropriate.

Matthew Arnold's description of Shakespeare's special qualities has become proverbial:

Others abide our question. Thou art free.
We ask and ask: Thou smilest and art still,
Out-topping knowledge.

In our own words, most of us would agree that we cannot nail down his purposes or be sure that we understand. Returning to a play after a few years, we realise that we have seen only what we had looked for, and that as we have changed so, it seems, has he. But we are also aware of a direct, involving engagement and, like Keats, we will not sit down to read *King Lear* again without some prologue, at least a moment of adjustment:

once again the fierce dispute,
Betwixt Hell torment and impassion'd Clay
Must I burn through . . .

Shakespeare seems to draw us into his creation, into fresh discovery and active imagination: we 'burn through' a recreation of the play in our own minds.

Standing further back from individual plays, we, like Dryden, wonder at the range and power of his mind: 'He was the man who of all Modern, and perhaps Ancient Poets, had the largest and most comprehensive soul.' Coleridge was later to call him 'myriad-minded', in that phrase catching the bafflement that mixes with our admiration. The apparent ease with which he wrote is at once the most attractive and most astonishing of his qualities. Dryden called it 'luck': 'All the Images

of Nature were still present to him, and he drew them not laboriously, but luckily. . . . 'But while Ben Jonson praised the naturalness of his writing—

Nature herself was proud of his designs,
And joy'd to wear the dressing of his lines,

he also knew that the 'joy' depended on craftsmanship, each line being 'well turned and true filed' as in a blacksmith's forge.

Besides these old encomiums, scholars and critics today have added to our appreciation, showing verbal complexity, theatrical variety, social awareness, psychological perception, intellectual grasp and scepticism. No theatre producer could read all that has been written, let alone judge each opinion and find means to reflect what he has thought in theatrical productions. The readiest response is to stage Shakespeare according to current theatrical methods and the perception of the moment, and trust Shakespeare to survive. So we should go to the theatre to see new facets of his plays, knowing that in five years' time we shall see still more.

I have long supposed that this was the only sensible course for playgoers or for producers. But to spend one's time wholly in the pursuit of 'something new' is to run the risk of being 'too superstitious', as the apostle Paul told the men on the Hill of Mars. If the Shakespeare devotee is able to build up a composite impression of the plays from the many partial renderings he has seen, must every play-goer go through the same progression? Must each view be limited by another man's momentary perception? Journalistic criticism of Shakespeare productions reflects the interest which is centred today on the task of deciphering the 'director's intentions' in a production. A director describing his work will explain what is 'the whole fascination of the centre part of the play to me', and how that has influenced his staging.

The history of Shakespeare in the theatre shows how each age has, indeed, seen the plays only through the various filters of individual interpretive artists. But in the present century there is a new situation, for now the filter is more likely to be provided by a director than by an actor: we talk of Peter Brook's *Dream,* Peter Hall's *Dream,* or Zeffirelli's *Romeo.* The nature of the intervening filter is changing, for while an actor has to bring himself along with his interpretation and work out his recreation of Shakespeare's character in daily contact with Shakespeare's words and with his own complete personality, the director never has to live with what he has created. Good directors do respond widely to the text, will 'live' through the rehearsals using all their experience of life and all their intuitive responses as well as their intellectual grasp of the play and their verbalisation of the fascination that the text has for them; but this is not the same kind of engagement as an actor's, working on a single play with other actors over the course of months or, perhaps, of whole years. Moreover the director has much greater power over the play than any one actor. He can, with his designer, reduce individualised characters to an almost uniform appearance through which the actors would have to work crudely to make any individual impression: see, for example, the all-red costumes for a recent Stratford production of *Much Ado* (1968) in which prince and soldier were scarcely distinguishable, or the current *Hamlet* (1970) where the whole court is dressed in regulation white, trimmed with fur, and boots. The director can set the play in a period that forces the actors to assume a range of mannerisms which limits their rhythms, tones and responses, and this assumption of a period may well take their attention away from more basic aspects of their task: see, for example, the current version of *The Merchant of Venice* (1970) at the National Theatre in London, which is set in Victorian streets and drawing rooms.

Today Shakespeare does not 'abide' the question of audiences. Directors are working all the time to make their own *answers* abundantly clear, by underlining with all the contrivance of set, costume, lighting, sound and the drilling of actors (and invention of improvisations); by placing of visual emphasis; by grouping and movement; by verbal emphasis and by elaborate programmes and public-relations operations. Shakespeare is not free; he is not still. We do not 'ask', for all the time we are being 'told and told'. Nothing much happens 'luckily', and if it does, it is assimilated into the defined and high-powered presentation of a particular 'interpretation'. What is forged in the smithy of the rehearsal-room is nothing 'natural', but a clear, surprising, challenging, unavoidable interpretation of Shakespeare: 'something new'. (pp. 127-28)

The choice of a unifying idea for a production, and its expression in settings, costumes, interpolations, by-play, verbal emphasis, manner of performance, limits the presentation of what Shakespeare has written. It concentrates on one single meaning for almost every ambiguous line. It enlarges one incident and diminishes, or cuts completely, some other incident that is capable of contrary emphasis. The productions are not myriad-minded; Shakespeare is not free. If questioned about this procedure, I suspect that most directors would answer that to gain power, a production must be simple, must not dissipate its effectiveness, must lead in one way not several and must build up climaxes. They would also explain that Shakespeare is often difficult to understand and that their additions serve to clarify his obscurities.

To these usual attitudes, Peter Brook offers some contrasts. In company with Nunn, Barton, Hands and Miller, this director assumes an individual way of working. He refuses to 'take a categorical position' in approaching a production: 'I often drive people mad by not making up my mind, but I don't believe it's really a fault. In a work context, the eventual clarity I hope for comes not from any dogmatism, but an encouraged chaos from which the clarity grows' [*The Observer*, 10 August 1970].

The first step towards a production is a series of exercises for the actors, physical, vocal and improvisational, which aim at making the 'actors work more freely together as a group'. The next is to seek a 'collective understanding' of the play, by using specific acting methods to explore the text through voice and body, through experiment in action. Instead of thinking about the meaning of words, the actors are encouraged to see how they can speak them, represent, support or contrast them. They criticise each other's work and wait for something to come right. Peter Brook tells the story of experimental rehearsals for *The Tempest*, when:

> A Japanese actor who, by approaching Ariel through his breathing and through his body, made Ariel something very understandable. A certain force became tangible in something which to the Japanese was easy to understand because in the basis of the Noh theatre, from which he came, there was a certain type of sound, a certain type of cry, a certain type of breath. The idea of that force was truly represented. It could be discussed because it

> had suddenly happened. There it was amongst us. It was no longer force, an abstract movement, it was *force*, a reality, something which could influence other people [*The Times*, 29 August 1970].

By asking the actors to respond to the text and to various tasks of the director's invention, different ways of presenting characters and incidents are evolved in random patterns. From these the most 'forceful' are chosen, and so, 'in place of a lack of an intention, an intention appears' [*Plays and Players*, October 1970].

Is this 'new' way of directing the means to 'free' Shakespeare, to avoid fixing a production according to a director's 'interpretation' or 'view', Peter Brook's *A Midsummer Night's Dream* in the 1970 Stratford season has been hailed as a revelation by many playgoers: does it provide hope for a specially appropriate production method for Shakespeare?

In the acting some results are obvious. Peter Thomson reports in [the 1971] issue of *Shakespeare Survey* that the actors found their work 'fantastic', but it is noticeable that this is because they are working 'with Brook', not with Shakespeare. At least half of their task must have been getting accustomed to the trapezes, coiling wires and stilts, and to the wayward percussive music and sounds that all derive from Brook's decision to work as in a circus, whenever possible. This idiom seems to have been chosen to encourage a 'display of physical virtuosity—an expression of joy'. However, in these skills the actors remained amateurs, and nothing was attempted like the silence that falls in a circus as danger is confronted. The revealing all-white stage seemed suitable for a ballet or gymnastics, but only a sporadic attempt was made to move with dancer-like precision or authority. The technical hurdles have been introduced to thrust the actors into unknown territory so that they court discovery, rather than to display the effortless skill of artistic achievement. Variety of style seems to have been pursued for much the same reason. Movement varies from solemn simplicity (and often cliché) to novel ingenuity. On occasion the speaking is noticeably slow, especially when the words are about death or virginity, or about the actor and his art, dream and reality. At times movement and noise obliterate speech, or make so strong a counter claim for the audience's interest that words can scarcely be followed. At other times, the drama seems to be going on inside the minds of motionless and inexpressive performers, and the pace is so slow that either the audience loses interest or is forced to find it for itself in general curiosity.

The production met with such good-will that many of the audience seemed wholly satisfied. When Peter Thomson writes: 'I feel no inclination to defend any of Brook's decisions. I doubt whether the play could have been so well spoken if it had been seriously falsified', he sounds as though he is accepting a piece of novel showmanship entirely in its own terms. He goes on to say: 'More than anything I have ever seen, this production declared its confidence and delight in the art of performance. In doing so, it went, for me, *beyond the meaning of the play* to a joyous celebration of the fact that it was written . . . ' This is not criticism, it is capitulation. But it does suggest that Shakespeare's play might have become open to the audience, with no directorial interference of note, beyond the surface interest of the performance itself.

But if we wish to ask how the production served the play, we must go beyond recording pleasure or distaste. Nor is this difficult, for certainly a single interpretation had been found during the actors' explorations under the director's guidance, and this has been unambiguously presented. Time and again, the audience is forced to take the play in one comparatively simple way. Helena and Theseus hold fixed kneeling positions for soliloquies and so contradict the energy and light rhythmic variety of the writing. The Mechanicals parade on to the stage accompanied with blaring noise that makes them far more broadly comic and assertive than the words alone imply, and quite alter the textual contrast (and similarity) between their speeches and Helena's preceding soliloquy. Certain words are chosen for repetition, usually by a listener, and so are underlined as they are not in the text. Laughter is provided on stage with no direct cue in Shakespeare's words, and while the audience remains silent. Helena's quarrel with Demetrius is made funny by the boy falling on to the floor, the girl crawling on to his back, and he trying to crawl from underneath. Bottom is carried off to Titania's bower accompanied by large phallic gestures and cries of triumph, when the concluding words in that incident suggest delicacy and silence:

> Come, wait upon him; lead him to my bower.
> The moon, methinks, looks with a wat'ry eye;
> And when she weeps, weeps every little flower,
> Lamenting some enforced chastity.
> Tie up my love's tongue, bring him silently.
>
> [III. i. 197-201]

Hippolyta and Titania, Theseus and Oberon, are openly doubled as if the actors' task was to make what likeness exists between the pairs as obvious and inescapable as possible, and to minimise the very considerable differences. Verbally certain phrases are given overwhelming importance by pauses and exaggerated enunciation, which only directorial decision could permit. One such item picked out for emphasis is 'cold . . . fruitless . . . moon' [I. i. 73], so that the incidental phrase becomes a posed invocation, at least an evocation, for which the pace of the action (and of the metre) must be suspended. The actors seeking 'force', 'clarity', 'reality', or 'something which could influence people', are not presenting a free Shakespeare. Above all, they are trying to impress what they, themselves, have found, and Peter Brook has chosen.

Speaking after the rehearsals were complete, Peter Brook was obviously committed to one particular interpretation. While he quotes the text in his own support, it is noticeable how easily he contradicts it, or misrepresents it. Now he is far more concerned with what the experiments have thrown up, not only from the text but also from his own and his actors' experience, predilections and theatrical improvisation. So in an interview, he has said that: 'Theseus and Hippolyta are trying to discover what constitutes the true union of a couple . . . ', but what he should have said is that this issue came to interest the actors who had the task of presenting the two characters. I can find nothing in the text that suggests this concern, and it is quite as likely to derive from the fantasies of the experimenting and questioning actors as from the subtextual possibilities of the play. Speaking of Oberon, Brook put the dramatic point in extreme terms of 'total' love, whatever that means (it is not a Shakespearian phrase): 'a man taking the wife whom he loves totally and having her fucked by the crudest sex machine he can find . . . Oberon's deliberate cool intention is to degrade Titania as a woman'. The director has here left the text far behind. First, Oberon is a 'creature of another sort', a fairy not a man. Second, he does not choose a 'sex machine' of any sort, but expects Tita-

nia to have more general 'hateful fantasies' [II. i. 258] and is prepared for her to 'love *and languish*' for any 'vile thing' [II. ii. 27, 34]. When Oberon has enchanted Titania, he still does not know what she will 'dote on' [III. ii. 3], and hearing of Bottom's transformation says, specifically, that 'This falls out better than I could devise' [III. ii. 35]. Finally, the object of devotion is not an ass, but a man with an ass's head who never says a word suggesting an intention to fuck her, crudely or otherwise. Bottom's first thought is of how to escape, his second of answering Titania's attendants with requisite courtesy. When Titania is seen 'coying' his cheeks and kissing his ears, he is irritated by an itch, feels hungry, and then announces simply—or perhaps ambiguously—that he is tired. The director, with his actors to help him, has discovered something that is not in the play-text at all, but in the reactions, predispositions, theatrical consciousness and fantasies of their own, and he enforces this upon the audience's attention with elaborate business, noise, vocal reactions and climactic placing at the end of the first half of the performance.

Most critics have proclaimed a new way of staging Shakespeare after seeing Brook's production, but what seems newest in his work is the theatrical playing with the text in order to invent business and discover an interpretation that suits his own interests and the actors with whom he is working. This is said to release the potential of the text, but in fact the 'chaos' with which rehearsals began led to a limited, eccentric, single-minded (and rather simple-minded) interpretation. Once more the director has fixed the production so that certain points are made without ambiguity and without any danger that the audience could overlook them. Will anyone find a way of presenting Shakespeare freely? Could an audience be allowed to find 'meaning' for themselves, be struck with whatever force or reality that their own imaginations can observe? Could there be a direct audience contact with the stage and with Shakespeare's creation, or do the necessities of theatrical art, the need for preparation and obvious excitement, preclude this open-ended experience? Could theatrical craftsmanship be allied to a production which seemed as unstrained, as 'easy' and 'natural', as Shakespeare's writing? And as ambiguous, reflective, invitingly difficult, and alive?

To seek for such a way is, I believe, of utmost importance. It would not rediscover the 'essential' Shakespeare or explain anything in the plays for good and all. In no way would it lead to a museum production, seeking an elusive 'Elizabethan' accuracy of speech or behaviour. But it would bring Shakespearian qualities to the theatre, and allow audiences to respond in ways that are generally recognised as appropriate to Shakespeare's genius. The audience might become seekers—askers of questions, as Arnold would say—whereas, at present, they are invited to accept and share other people's answers. (pp. 131-34)

John Russell Brown, "Free Shakespeare," in Shakespeare Survey: An Annual Survey of Shakespearian Study and Production, *Vol. 24, 1971, pp. 127-35.*

J. L. Styan   (essay date 1977)

[*In the following excerpt from his assessment of Brook's revival, Styan declares that the production's self-conscious theatricality caused the audience to feel "an inescapable demand for its collaboration in a common endeavor."*]

All-white sets of plain curtains or flats date back to J. B.

Sally Jacob's set design (1970).

Fagan in the twenties. They encouraged a non-realistic image for Shakespeare, but the tired eyes of the spectator inhibited attention as well as illusion. The practice matured somewhat with the three-sided white box design, lit harshly from above, conceived by Christopher Morley for Trevor Nunn's Stratford season of 1969, particularly for *Pericles* and *The Winter's Tale*. Nunn's professed purpose was to focus upon the actors and their relationships in 'a kind of chamber architecture' [*Plays and Players,* September 1972] which must have made the open stages shake their heads. In *The Winter's Tale,* the set served to symbolize a white nursery world of innocence as well as to mark reality from illusion by a lighting change from yellow to blue for Leontes's first-act asides, unhappily suggesting that in his jealousy he was also subject to schizophrenic hallucinations. Peter Brook had moved in a similar direction, notably with his violently Artaudian production of Peter Weiss's *Marat/Sade* (1964), where his plain cold set was planned primarily to achieve a Brechtian effect of alienation. The ultimate setting of this kind was demonstrated by Sally Jacobs for Brook's Stratford production of *A Midsummer Night's Dream* in 1970.

After Kott's essay, 'Titania and the Ass's Head', erotic versions of *The Dream* had proliferated, the most notable example being John Hirsch's production at Stratford, Ontario in 1968. Brook, however, did not seek the key to the play in its sexual theme, but in its element of magic. In his *Orpheus*

essay of 1948 he had long before attacked the tradition of 'gauzes, ballets and Mendelssohn' associated with this play, and by coincidence a Regent's Park Open Air Theatre production in the summer of 1970 had disproved the idea that a pastoral setting provided a fitting background: 'The main casualty, of course, is magic. You cannot have magic in an environment loud with passing aircraft and where actors are obliged to trumpet their lines to reach the back row' [Irving Wardle, *The Times,* 7 June 1970]. Brook sought the magic not in the fairies, who could as well be stage hands as ballet dancers, but in the play itself, as Helen Dawson observed [in the *Observer,* 30 August 1970]:

> The key to this production comes when Theseus rebukes Hermia for refusing to marry Demetrius. 'Take time to pause', he tells her, and in the pause before the new moon, the play (the dream, the magic) takes place, peopled by the subconscious personalities of Theseus and Hippolyta before their wedding; of Hermia, Lysander, Demetrius and Helena before they finalise their love.

Brook's problem was to find the appropriate substitutes for gauzes and ballets in all the visual and aural elements of his stage, and in the total style of performance. The result? 'The traditions of a lifetime have been torpedoed into infinity! Every accepted canon of stage-mounting has been thrown to the winds. And for what! The quaint simplicity of a child's

Christmas toy-box' [Norman Marshall's *The Producer and the Play*]. But this was the response of *The Stage* to Granville-Barker's *Twelfth Night* in 1912.

Sally Jacobs's set was variously seen as a three-sided white box with white carpet, a squash court, a clinic, a scientific research station, an operating theatre, a gymnasium and a big top. Two doors were cut in the back wall, two slits in the sides, two ladders set at the downstage edges, and a gallery or catwalk round its top allowed the musicians and fairies to gaze down at the players fifteen feet below in the box. Dawson found it to be 'not only a valid device, but one which bursts with invention', and Irving Wardle thought it 'removes the sense of being earthbound: it is natural here for characters to fly' [*The Times*, 28 August 1970]. Into this space the immortals could indeed descend on trapezes or manipulate flexible metal coils on the end of rods to suggest trees. For John Russell Brown, 'this was a machine for acting in' [*Shakespeare Survey* 24, 1971], and at the same time the actors acting in it were the visible puppets of the machine.

The box was lit with a fierce white light, and when drums rolled the whole company swooped into the arena in long white capes: not unlike the actors in Williams's *The Comedy of Errors,* their entrance bluntly declared that they were performers, and that thereafter the audience would be participants in their game. Capes flung off, the actors suddenly became characters in primary colours, Theseus in purple, Hippolyta in green, Egeus in blue, Philostrate in black with a tall cap, the lovers mostly in white. Philostrate later became Puck in billowing yellow silk breeches and a little blue cap, while the fairies were less than characters in their baggy grey judo pyjamas. With a great scarlet feather hammock hanging high above them, awaiting an occupant, the purple and yellow figures swung loosely on trapezes in their white open space.

The audience was to look into this magic box, not only to see the magic, but also to be shown what was up the magician's sleeve. Brook explained [in the *Daily Telegraph*, 14 September 1970],

> Today we have no symbols that can conjure up fairyland and magic for a modern audience. On the other hand there are a number of actions that a performer can execute that are quite breathtaking. So we went to the art of the circus and the acrobat because they both make purely theatrical statements.

For a month Brook had made the actors practise their tricks in improvisation and rehearsal, and in this setting the audience willingly accepted any invention of the company. The show was indeed breathtaking. The purple flower became a twirling plate on a juggler's wand, passed spinning from Puck to Oberon, a magic image in itself (II. i). . . . 'The plate does not *become* the flower', Peter Thomson commented [in *Shakespeare Survey* 24, 1971]; 'instead the act of passing it becomes the *magic* of the flower.' Thus, for her nightmare, Hermia was shown frantic in a jungle of the coiled wire (II.ii). For his assignation with Titania, Bottom was carried to his scarlet bower of feathers in a shower of streamers and paper-plate confetti, backed by the blare of Mendelssohn's Wedding March as Oberon swung across the stage on a rope (III.i).

The lovers were more athletes and tumblers than dancers, chasing up and down the ladders and round the gallery. On Lysander's 'Withdraw and prove it too' [III. ii. 255] to Demetrius, Hermia threw herself sideways across a door to prevent his going, and as if by a miracle he saved her from falling to the floor. Thereupon he hung her on a trapeze and her 'O me! You juggler! You canker-blossom!' [III. ii. 282] was screamed to Helena as she dangled and kicked the air helplessly. At the end of this scene, Puck's teasing of Lysander and Demetrius in the wood had them chasing in confusion round the legs of giant stilts, on which Puck seemed to have a supernatural power to control their movements. In an interview with Ronald Hayman for *The Times* [29 August 1970], Brook made this point: 'Where someone in a library uses intellectual and analytical methods to try to discover what a play is about, actors try to discover through the voice, through the body, through experiment in action.'

Through all this, the players who were not on stage watched those below, on occasion shooting blue and silver darts across the space and making sounds with musical saws and plastic tubes. Richard Peaslee's two small percussion groups provided an intermittent accompaniment of music from bongo-drums, guitar, autoharp or zither, bed-springs and tubular bells. Frequently the verse lines shifted into mock-operatic arias, as for Lysander and Hermia on 'Fair love, you faint with wandering in the wood' [II. ii. 35ff.], Demetrius's 'So sorrow's heaviness doth heavier grow' [III. ii. 82ff.], Puck's 'Up and down' [III. ii. 82ff.], and Helena's 'O weary night' [III. ii. 431ff.], and 'Sixpence a day' by the mechanicals [IV. ii. 19ff.]. One would think that in all this the lines would be drowned. True, the text was often at variance with the action, but J. W. Lambert was not alone in reporting a 'subtle sculpting of phrase' [*Drama*, Autumn 1971] and J. C. Trewin decided that 'the more closely we watched the actors' unexpected virtuosity, the more we heard of the play, better spoken than most people had ever known' [*Peter Brook: a Biography*].

The fairies were no longer thought of as decorative, but as functional. They appeared as hefty circus hands when they swept up the confetti, as familiar spirits when they physically controlled the movements of the lovers and demoniacally trapped them in their steel forest, and as amoral trolls when they stripped Snug of his trousers and created an obscene phallus for Bottom. Yet throughout the proceedings and all their busy interventions they remained calm and casual as puppet-masters should.

The mechanicals were very sober workmen, no longer the butts of the play, but keen amateur actors whose play was important to them. The customary laughs were missing, and Quince's tears of joy when Bottom returned in time to play Pyramus were genuinely moving. For his ass's head, Bottom wore no smothering fur, but a button nose, ear muffs and clogs, so that while he looked like a circus clown his facial expressions remained realistic to a degree: at least in this respect, the imagination was not free to run riot. Quince's men were treated as individuals, not stereotypes, so that their rehearsals were afforded an unusual dignity. Consequently, the play scene was unfunny, and Snug's lion really did alarm the ladies. Miriam Gilbert carefully noted the effect of Pyramus's dying speech:

> Pyramus's death speech is fairly sincere. When Theseus says, 'This passion, and the death of a dear friend, would go near to make a man look sad,' he looks across at Hippolyta, as if he's testing her. And she responds, as I think he wants her to, with 'Beshrew my heart, but I pity the man' [V. i. 288-90]. Theseus smiles. After Pyramus dies, there are again flip remarks, but Theseus remembers something else as he says, 'With the help of a surgeon,

he might yet prove an ass' [V. i. 310-11], and the second half of the speech is directed out to the audience, slowly, musingly, challenging us to remember that Pyramus is Bottom who was an ass in the forest.

When in earnest Bottom spoke his line, 'No, I assure you, the wall is down that parted their fathers' [V. i. 351-52], it was as if he were speaking the solemn moral of the piece for the benefit of all the lovers on the stage. So much sobriety among so much revelry seemed a curious contradiction, but the integration was strongly assisted by a controlling device of the director's. In *The Merry Conceited Humours of Bottom the Weaver* (1646), the pre-Restoration droll derived from *A Midsummer Night's Dream,* Theseus had doubled with Oberon and Hippolyta with Titania; it is probable that this was also the practice of the Lord Chamberlain's Men in the first production (*c.* 1595), since perforce they regularly doubled the roles in a play whose characters exceeded their number. Although Benedict Nightingale declared [in *New Statesman,* 4 September 1970] that the doubling in Brook's production was done 'for no clear reason except economy', it was apparent to many that his intention was to suggest that the dream in the wood near Athens was a premarital fantasy of the Duke and his bride. The result was that the different groups within the play, the lovers, the fairies and the mechanicals, whose activities are usually set in contrast with one another, seemed more of a kind. The idea of the doubling was made neatly theatrical. Theseus and Hippolyta simply shed their white cloaks at 'dusk', and assumed them again at 'daybreak', by standing in each door to be dressed. Philostrate, Theseus's master of the revels, also became Puck, master of Oberon's magic. The device was made visible: the audience was to participate as omniscient observers.

The new unity of the court and the wood scenes in addition introduced an unaccustomed and darker mood into the comedy. The high spirits of the dream were constantly undercut by the memory of the real problems facing the mortal lovers. Thus, Oberon's desire to punish, even degrade, the Titania he loved became a sobering issue. And Helen Dawson was careful to report that the wood scenes were 'not all fun':

> As in a dream—and in a circus—there are moments of stark terror, at times reminiscent of Brook's *Marat/Sade,* when the tent turns into the high walls of an institution, when characters scuttle in fear through Puck's grotesque stilt legs. The fairies are streaked through with cruelty; an uneasily ambiguous bunch who seem to be warning, 'Don't meddle in illusion'.

Theseus's melancholy extended to the last act, when his grave tone underscored the central concept of the imagination which 'bodies forth / The form of things unknown' [V. i. 14-15]. Dawson considered that Brook's interpretive idea cut through the play like a laser: 'In this extra-terrestrial world we meet that part of ourselves which we bury under social convention', and upon Theseus's rebuke to Hermia, 'Take time to pause', all parties to the play were submitted to Shakespeare's idiom of the supernatural.

Needless to say, opinions about Brook's *Dream* were radically divided. Those who disliked it could not see past the surface of the production, Kenneth Hurren finding it 'a tiresomely self-indulgent display of directorial gimmickry' [*The Spectator,* 5 September 1970] and J. W. Lambert was troubled that the director's 'commentary' on the play 'though

often stimulating and enriching, may swamp its subject' [*The Sunday Times,* 13 September 1970]. David Selbourne, who watched rehearsals, summarized this position when he argued that the production was 'technically brilliant', but a 'director-shaped commodity' [in *Culture and Agitation*]. However, a leader in *The Times* [29 August 1970] sought to resolve the contradiction between the eccentric setting and performance, and the shrewd and thought-provoking ideas many spectators perceived. The article asked the question, 'How, beyond an identity of text, is Mr Brook's production related to William Shakespeare's play?', and answered,

> This is not the kind of production that seeks to reconstruct the performance that Shakespeare and his company are most likely to have devised. There have been such essays in theatrical scholarship. Being original, the Stratford production is not one of them. Being also appropriate, it is not at the opposite pole either, where the play is treated as if it were no more than an idea, or a structure, or a source of invention, rather in the way Joyce or Sartre has made use of Greek myth. In versions of that kind the producer does not respect the natural limits imposed by the text. He feels free to contrive situations and to characterize the *dramatis personae* as he fancies. Being appropriate, the Stratford production is not of that kind either. . . .
>
> A good Shakespeare production is true to the original in a sense other than textual accuracy or resemblance to how it might have been at the Globe. One begins to see why Plato needed his doctrine of Forms. The question is easily resolved if one is allowed to have a Form of the *Dream* laid up in heaven. Productions of the play to be good would have to resemble the Form of it, the resemblance being not one of copying but of congruence. So it would come about that for all the trapezes, juggling, helical wire trees, and general non-Elizabethanism, the Stratford production is not just good theatre but a true production of the *Dream.*

Just as the poet cannot explain his meaning in terms other than those of the words of his poem, so Brook could not express his sense of a play in terms other than those of performance. The Platonic Form lay hidden there, valid and (one would think) scholarly, awaiting discovery. How close are we here to Wilson Knight's concept of 'interpretation'?

Audiences can hope to perceive the meaning of Shakespeare's *A Midsummer Night's Dream* only by allowing it to expand the mind and senses. Performance which does not close the windows of the play is the proper stimulus for such perception, and Brook's approach was to deny all stage illusion, leaving a sufficient vacuum to be filled by the imagination of the spectator. Dawson, the most enthusiastic of the critics, found that Brook made the play and its poetry 'leap into almost Oriental clarity', and that her mind began to race. The actors never hid the *fact* of performance, and although this might seem to be merely a modish alienation-effect, in practice the audience felt an inescapable demand for its collaboration in a common endeavour. Theseus and Hippolyta spoke their opening lines to the audience as they knelt ritualistically on cushions. Egeus's complaint was spoken as a challenge to the audience. Helena's first-act soliloquy, 'How happy some', [I. i. 226ff.], was dropped in the audience's lap. In III.ii, Hermia and Demetrius momentarily froze in front of Oberon for Puck's 'This is the woman, but not this the man'[III. ii. 42]— 'a moment of stylization which reminds us once more that we are watching a play, which can be stopped, started, controlled, speeded up, slowed down, at will' [Miriam Gilbert]. Puck's 'Lord, what fools these mortals be!' [III. ii. 115] was again for the audience. When the lovers greeted the dawn, they held hands in a line facing the house, sharing their wonder: 'Why then we are awake' [IV. i. 198]. Oberon's closing verses, 'Through this house each fairy stray' [V. i. 402], embraced the whole theatre, and on Puck's 'Give me your hands, if we be friends' [V. i. 437], the whole company turned to the audience, ran up the aisles and shook hands with everyone they could. It was the audience's triumph they wished to share. (pp. 223-31)

> *J. L. Styan, "Shakespeare, Peter Brook and Non-Illusion," in his* The Shakespeare Revolution: Criticism and Performance in the Twentieth Century, *Cambridge University Press, 1977, pp. 206-31.*

Richard Proudfoot (essay date 1980)

[*Proudfoot provides a survey of Brook's* Dream, *with special reference to the director's theories of staging.*]

By [the late 1960s] Brook's association with the Royal Shakespeare Company had become more intermittent than in the early 1960s. With the founding, in Paris in the spring of 1968, of his International Centre for Theatre Research, Brook moved into a new phase of his career, as theatrical researcher, directing not just a production but a living theatre-laboratory, in which a small international group of actors, designers, musicians and writers would explore all aspects of acting technique and styles and would search for a theatrical language capable of addressing audiences anywhere in the world. These preoccupations were to take Brook first to Persepolis in 1971 then, the next year, on a trek across North-West Africa. They also explain some features of his 1970 production of the *Dream* for the Royal Shakespeare Company which, at the time, took both audiences and critics by surprise.

Discussion of this celebrated production is complicated by the proliferation of published material about it. There are the usual reviews, including those for the world-wide tour, and interviews with Brook himself, but many of the company have also recorded their views and reminiscences. In 1974 the RSC even published, in conjunction with the Dramatic Publishing Company an 'Authorized Acting Edition' of 'Peter Brook's *Production of A Midsummer Night's Dream*'—a dramatic document beside which 'Pyramus and Thisbe' and its prologues pale into theatrical insignificance. It is strange that Brook should have sanctioned a publication so plainly antithetical to his continued assertion that theatre is ephemeral and that a production of a play is *always* an answer to the play's questions appropriate to a particular time, place, company of actors and audience. However, much valuable comment on the production is included.

With the *Dream,* Brook met head-on the dilemma of the theatrical researcher who also directs for the commercial theatre: the life of the theatre resides in the spontaneous interplay of actor, text and audience, but the business of theatre depends on the performance being repeatable, a reliably marketable commodity. Brook's *Dream* endeavoured to make a peculiar kind of appeal to the imagination of its audiences, but one main source of its success, apart from its novelty, was the prestige of his own name, another the growing popularity of one of his leading players, Alan Howard.

The eight-week rehearsal period began with two weeks in which the text was hardly used at all: two weeks of questioning, of exploration of ideas and theatrical techniques. Then came a month of playing with the unusual properties used in the fairy scenes and of physical exercises to prepare the actors for the acrobatics and circus tricks which the ideas of director and designer required of them. Brook decided to double four pairs of roles, thus reducing the size of his cast and facilitating the chosen method of rehearsal. The doubles were Theseus/Oberon (Alan Howard), Hippolyta/Titania (Sara Kestelman), Puck/Philostrate (John Kane) and Egeus/Quince (Philip Locke). The four fairies demanded by the text also served as stage hands.

After the opening, Brook's ideas about the *Dream* were widely publicised. These were characteristic: the need to interweave the actions involving fairies, 'aristocrats' (the lovers apparently included) and mechanicals; the difficulty of finding stage techniques to create the play's magic for a materialistic modern audience; a determination that the play dealt covertly with dark sexual passions; and the propositions that 'the core of the *Dream* is the "Pyramus and Thisbe" play' and that 'It's a sort of celebration of the theatre arts' [*Plays and Players,* October 1970].

A good general description was given by Rosemary Say [in the *Financial Times,* 28 August 1970], who also raised some of the points around which critical debate revolved. 'Peter Brook . . . is more determined than ever to compel us to take a creative part in his production. This time we are to be bullied into getting our imaginations to work. His method, lively and inventive, just gets by—particularly when he allows Shakespeare to take some part in the proceedings from time to time. The stage is white-walled and empty. An iron gallery runs round the top where those members of the cast not immediately taking part stand to look down on the play in the manner of overseers supervising a factory floor. Two trapezes hang on black cords and a vast red plume is splashed across the back wall. The actors spill on the stage, a garish mixture dressed in King's Road-type shirt and trousers, white silk cloaks and dresses of hard primary colours. Last come the artisans, a gang of workmen carrying planks, sandwiches and mugs of tea.' For others, the set had different associations, among them 'circus big top', 'squash court', 'polar bear pit at the zoo', gymnasium, play-room—even the Elizabethan stage, with its tiring-house wall, two large upstage doors and gallery above and behind the stage.

A widely admired feature of the performances was, once more, clarity: 'Never have I heard the verse more beautifully spoken, every line comes across as if the thought behind it had just been born in the actor's mind' [*Jewish Chronicle,* 4 September 1970]. Even a tendency for verse, especially that of the lovers, to modulate into song provoked little strong dissent. Clarity was also the key to the fairies and the magic flower. No illusion was allowed, the means of the fairies' teasing of the mortals were as visible as the devices of 'Pyramus and Thisbe'. The programme quoted from [Brook's] *The Empty Space*: 'It is up to us to capture [the audience's] attention and compel its belief. To do so we must prove that there will be no trickery, nothing hidden. We must open our empty hands and show that really there is nothing up our sleeves. Only then can we begin'. A circus trick represented the magic flower: a spinning plate was passed from wand to wand by Puck and Oberon (and sometimes dropped) as they swung on the trapezes. The nearly continuous musical background was carefully orchestrated. The whole cubic space of the stage was filled, by action on the trapezes; by the hoisting up of Titania's featherbed; by Puck on high stilts misleading Lysander and Demetrius; by the metallic coil 'trees' dangled on fishing-rods from the gallery by the fairies; and by the athletic running, jumping and climbing of the lovers. The lovers were denied lyricism, almost becoming the knock-about comics of the play. Hermia in particular was constantly in motion, being caught horizontally across doorways or snatched up by trapeze, indignantly crying 'Puppet!'. A still centre was afforded by the solemnity with which the mechanicals set about rehearsing their play. In performance, its effect was to provoke in the courtly audience not laughter but a hushed involvement. Titania's encounter with Bottom, the climax before the interval, was remarkable for the physicality of her lustful assault and culminated in a triumphant and ithyphallic hymeneal procession, to the accompaniment of flying streamers and Mendelssohn's wedding march, while Oberon swung wildly above on his trapeze.

The allusion to Mendelssohn pinpointed the iconoclasm of the production. Not only was an older stage tradition left far behind but, for at least one reviewer, Shakespeare's text too. John Russell Brown [in his essay in *Shakespeare Survey* 24] spelt out, in acid tones, the exact degree and detail of infidelity into which Brook's pursuit of that 'hidden play' so 'very powerfully sexual' had led him, demolishing point by point Brook's most extreme allegation about Oberon—that Shakespeare's King of Fairies is to be seen as 'a man taking the wife whom he loves totally and having her fucked by the crudest sex machine he can find'.

For the professional skill of the actors, no praise could be too high: they performed feats far beyond normal expectation (if hardly up to circus standard). They also succeeded remarkably in embodying Brook's idea of the play as having 'no set characters' and of each scene as being 'like a dream of a dream'. Reviewers frequently spoke of 'the actors' rather than 'the characters'. One crystallised the compelling quality of the performance with the words: 'The company seem not to act in it but to belong in it' [*South Wales Evening Argus*, 31 August 1970]. Audiences left the theatre happy. So did most critics, though hindsight left some of them puzzled. The puzzles included the doubling. It undoubtedly contributed to the coherence of performance-style, but the conception of Oberon and Titania as subconscious projections of the unavowed desires of Theseus and Hippolyta found little to sustain it in the text and other doublings, notably that of Egeus and Quince, were even harder to rationalise. The mating of Titania and Bottom seems even further from the sense of this play, so much concerned with the power of imagination rather than of passion. The end of the play was another *tour de force* of production. For the final entry of Oberon and Titania, Alan Howard and Sara Kestelman had to change roles on stage, removing the cloaks which identified them as Theseus and Hippolyta. During their speeches, the other actors, 'whistling softly', also removed their coloured cloaks, to reveal white clothes beneath, and moved slowly downstage, led by Oberon, intoning his final speech on a solemn monotone. The ritual solemnity of the moment (of which the speech gives no hint) was followed by Puck's epilogue. After it, as the prompt-book has it, 'all off stage and into auditorium, shaking hands with audience'. This last action, cued by 'Give me your hands if we be friends, / And Robin shall restore amends' [V. i. 437-38], rejected the overt sense of requesting applause.

Audiences responded fairly well to the demand for reciprocity, though in doing so they were submitting to an intention imposed on them rather than expressing a spontaneous wish of their own. As the *Scotsman* reviewer drily put it, 'at times the players' easy chumminess with the audience throws up more barriers than it casts down' [29 August 1970]. The solemnity of the ending, recognised as the touch of Brook, was an unsuccessful attempt to impose a meaning at odds with the obvious festivity suggested by the lines. This production, though verbally faithful to the complete text and clear in projecting it, ended by revealing that Brook's search for his 'hidden play' was proceeding not *through* Shakespeare's words, but *beside* or *beneath* them. Brook seemed to have grown tired of the constantly shifting suggestiveness of Shakespeare's language. Rejecting a style of 'Shakespearian acting' equated (perhaps unfairly) with the mouthing of verse in a 'poetry voice', he had reached an opposite extreme, where experiment and analysis led, not to renewed expressiveness but to rigid imposition of patterns of inflection and rhythm derived from rehearsal exercises rather than the spontaneous recreation of feeling in performance. Brook's choice of the *Dream* seemed, at last, to owe more to a preoccupation with acting technique than to a vital curiosity about Shakespeare's meanings. Its rejection of a sentimentalising stage tradition was dearly bought. By robbing it of human particularity, by reducing the fairies to subconscious projections of the humans, by rarifying the mechanicals into the Pirandellian heart of a mystery, Brook in his turn risked a sentimental reduction of the play, a confinement of its range and fantasy within a setting as modishly pretty and as thoroughly distracting as a whole forest of palpable-gross Beerbohm trees. (pp. 166-70)

Richard Proudfoot, "Peter Brook and Shakespeare," in Drama and Mimesis, *Cambridge University Press, 1980, pp. 157-89.*

PRODUCTION:

John Barton • Royal Shakespeare Company • 1977

BACKGROUND:

In the first RSC production of *A Midsummer Night's Dream* since Peter Brook's iconoclastic presentation, John Barton directed a traditional staging of the play in 1977. Although conventional and featuring realistic settings, this production also contained a markedly aggressive Oberon and half-human, half-animal fairies that transformed themselves into rocks, stumps, and other elements of the scenery. Critics praised Barton for demonstrating that fresh, vivid presentations of *A Midsummer Night's Dream* need not be revolutionary.

COMMENTARY:

Robert Cushman   (review date 15 May 1977)

[*In the moderately favorable review excerpted below, Cushman stresses the traditionalism of Barton's 1977 production of* A Midsummer Night's Dream; *"I almost expected to hear Mendelssohn," he states.*]

The lesson of *A Midsummer Night's Dream* may be that you never get out of the wood. Certainly that seems to be the up-shot of John Barton's new production at Stratford. When we enter the theatre, mottled shadows, leaf-patterned, cover the back wall of the set. They fade to invisibility during the opening scene in the Athenian court, but once re-established they are a fixture. The final revels—the marriages and the performance of 'Pyramus and Thisbe'—take place in their shadow: almost it seems by their permission.

It makes perfect sense; we are explicitly told that the fairies who rule the wood also rule the world, and without their intervention the last act of the play would never happen. They make up its unseen audience; if Mr. Barton has sacrificed some of the surprise of their final celebratory appearance he has made it seem perfectly logical. He has also made it an occasion of genuine joy; the choreographer Gillian Lynne is listed as his co-director, and the lyric accomplishment of this sequence, as of much else in the evening, must surely be credited to her.

It is something at Stratford in 1977 to see greenery that actually looks green; something, too, to find fairies who might have been taken from some sumptuously eclectic collection of children's picture-books. (There are even children present to play Peaseblossom, Cobweb, Moth and Mustardseed; with so much tradition about, I almost expected to hear Mendelssohn, but there are limits. Actually, by the Renaissance-Gothic standards that are established here, Mendelssohn would appear a strident modern.)

The politics of this fairyland are complicated; Titania has a copious train, but they all seem to be double agents working for Oberon. And though there is plenty of majesty in Marjory Bland's white-goddess performance, she cannot be said to stand much of a chance. OK or not, Oberon rules; you might guess as much from the casting. In a mainly young and un-tried company the experienced Patrick Stewart stands alone. Generally thought a dour plain actor he has in fact (witness his Moor in 'Titus Andronicus') a considerable flair for the exotic. This Oberon, 'come from the farthest step of India' [II. i. 69], bronzed physically and vocally, is night to her day. When he threatens her the lights go down; when she defies him they go up again.

But though sinister, Mr. Stewart stops short of malevolence; his attitude to Puck ('I saw but *thou* could'st not' [II. i. 155]) is patronising but protective. Leonard Preston is a cheery hobgoblin but capable, in his description of the lost-soul graveyard sprites, of real dread. Mr. Barton, in fact, has thought out his fairy kingdom, even to the details of magic applied without anaesthetic. When Lysander receives the love-juice, he writhes violently; Titania, loving an ass, tries a few enthusiastic 'hee-haws' of her own and her revulsion when his true nature is revealed is not, for once, passed over.

The lovers run to type; there are not really too many ways of playing them. Marilyn Calsworthy adds to the treasurable list of funny languishing Helenas. Some of the mechanicals, too, are easily recognisable in outline, though transfigured by sheer intensity of performance; so Snug's declaration that he is 'slow of study' [II. i. 67] seems in Brian Coburn's performance as shattering a stroke of genius as anything in Shakespeare. (It is beautifully capped when Quince absently hands him the massive script intended for Pyramus.)

Richard Griffiths's Bottom, however, is a true original; not a shover, but a man quietly sure of his own talents, though

still capable of modest musing when their full extent is revealed. He is gentle and a very good choice for Pyramus; he might also make a good Thisbe. (I would not myself cast him as the Lion.) The first entrance of this fellowship transforms the play, which gets off to a chilly start. By the end, all is harmony. It is ritual to say of a Stratford production that it will probably improve; this one is pretty good already.

Robert Cushman, "In Perfect Harmony," in The Observer, *May 15, 1977, p. 30.*

Bernard Levin　(review date 15 May 1977)

[*In the excerpt below, Levin asserts that there are "two John Bartons in one body," one who is responsible for presenting the fairies as "hideous bald freaks" in this production, and the other who is "equipped with a rich visual imagination, meticulous at balancing the three levels of the play, and seized of the harmony with which it is filled."*]

Sooner or later the RSC had to undertake the daunting task of re-producing *A Midsummer Night's Dream,* despite the fact that the magic which Peter Brook wrought with it set a standard by which productions of the play will be judged for decades to come. The lot has fallen upon John Barton, and the play has opened the RSC's Stratford spring season.

There are two John Bartons in one body. There is Barton-Mephistopheles, responsible in his time for some memorable atrocities, and clearly at work here in such notions as turning the fairies into hideous bald freaks out of a fifteenth-century Temptation of St. Anthony, Oberon into a Red Indian, clad only in a loin-cloth and going berserk from time to time, and many of the speeches into handy pause-holders, some lines ("You - may - do - it - ex - tempo - o re" [I. ii. 68]) being so strewn with them that the audience could have a substantial meal in the course of a single pentameter, one course in each pause.

So much for the black angel; but there is also a white one, Barton-Faust. He is here clearly steeped in the text, equipped with a rich visual imagination, meticulous at balancing the three levels of the play, and seized of the harmony with which it is filled.

As in all the best versions, Faust wins. The lightness of Mr. Barton's touch in the quadruple quarrel, funnier than I have ever known it, and the firmness of his grip on the play-scene (where the comparison with Brook's account is at its most cruel), which never broadens too far, are typical of a production that begins in uncertainty, and is flawed throughout, but at its extensive best fully justifies the RSC's decision to wait no longer.

Patrick Stewart's Oberon, despite the handicap of his get-up, is virile and ethereal at the same time, and Leonard Preston's Puck, an impish puppy at the heels of the Fairy King, provides an excellent accompaniment. The Bottom of Richard Griffiths is absolutely right: never conscious that he is being funny, he is thus ten times more so. But the outstanding achievement is that of Marilyn Galsworthy as Helena; pretty as porcelain, she is delicately musical in the coloured verse and delightfully self-mocking and childlike in the plain.

Some of the diction is shocking: there is no excuse for "Helenar-adieu" or "Helenar-I love," and how many more times do I have to explain that the imperial votaress is not a female elector on her way to the polling station? But all in all, I am inclined to think that Heraclitus was wrong when he said that a man cannot step twice into the same river.

Bernard Levin, "Lullabies of Broadway," in The Sunday Times, *London, May 15, 1977, p. 37.*

John Elsom   (review date 19 May 1977)

[*Elsom detects an uncertainty behind this traditional presentation of* A Midsummer Night's Dream, *contending that Barton had not "used his imagination to show us anything different from our normal expectations of the* Dream.*"*]

By now, *A Midsummer Night's Dream* at Stratford-upon-Avon will probably have settled down into an enchanting production; but a fortnight ago, when it opened, it seemed a little fussy. Was it necessary to bring a gun into the woods to liven up the lovers' scenes, which, in any case, seemed over-choreographed—too many little lines given quick cross-stage movements? Why did Richard Griffiths's Bottom go down on all fours for his roaring match with Brian Coburn's Snug? Should Patrick Stewart's Oberon have delivered karate noises while waving his staff at Marjorie Bland's Titania? What was he trying to prove?

These are niggling points, fussy criticism, in fact, and let nobody be put off by them; but they could indicate an uncertainty behind this production for which the Royal Shakespeare Company have no reason to feel ashamed. Honest doubt can be a valuable state of mind; and, in this case, the RSC had every reason to feel apprehensive. This production is virtually without stars, though Stewart might count as one; and the RSC were nurturing the younger and less experienced members of their company for major roles.

Also, the last RSC *Dream* was the Peter Brook version in 1970, a hard act to follow; and these two productions could not be more dissimilar. Brook was trying to alter our ideas about magic and fairy woods, by doing without the sylvan spells altogether. He set the whole affair in a white-walled gymnasium, with trapezes for Oberon and Puck, juggling, whirling tubes and a large, hanging red feather for Titania's bower. It is hard to forget that inventiveness; and it would be easy to underrate the imagination behind the current production, which, by comparison, seems alarmingly trad.

The fairies actually look like those from slightly bizarre nursery books, with Mabel Lucie Attwell bodies and Mervyn Peake heads. Leonard Preston's Puck has a shock of red hair, uncombed like Struwwelpeter, turned-out ankles and a Max Wall bottom. The permanent set at Stratford undergoes a transformation for the glade, with trees springing up as if under an enchantment, a little mist and a leafy mould blanketing the ground, into which the spirits can sink, camouflaged by their colours.

John Napier's designs explore images which Brook, years ago, rejected as clichés. Nor are any liberties taken with the text, unless the absence of Philostrate be counted as one; nor are startling new interpretations imposed on the performances, unless the rippling muscles, black hair and athletic Indian body of Stewart's Oberon come as too much of a surprise. John Barton, who directed, has not used his imagination to show us anything different from our normal expectations of the *Dream*; but rather to brace up an orthodoxy which was in danger of becoming flabby. Sometimes, the rejection of the familiar can become a rather easy kind of inven-

tiveness, a creativity through rebellion, and Barton, on this occasion, has set his face against the novelties.

The acting discovery in the RSC's cast is undoubtedly Griffiths, whose Bottom looks like an over-ripe pear. His stomach seems to have slumped to below the knees, although it swells proudly around his thighs, before tapering sharply towards his shoulders, hunched in thoughtful introversion, and a stalk of a head, moustached for added dignity. His Bottom takes acting seriously. He is delicately absorbed in his own brilliance, fluttering his hands and bashing around his voice. His problem is lack of talent, so that, even when he does do something well, such as the last crooning lament, it comes too near for comfort to something which has turned out badly.

Other company members were impressive, too: Leonard Preston, Marjorie Bland, Stewart, of course, and Marilyn Galsworthy as a lively and petulant Helena. As the months pass, we may well look back to this production as one which brought a valuable transfusion of new blood to the RSC; and it may have another significance, too. It may have scotched the RSC habit of believing that new productions of well-known plays require special justifications for their presences within the repertoire. If this proves so, it will be particularly appropriate that Barton has taken a lead in nudging the RSC back to conventionality. He has not been slow to experiment before, even to the point of rewriting Shakespeare. (p. 661)

John Elsom, "Family Dreams," in The Listener, *Vol. 97, No. 2509, May 19, 1977, pp. 661-62.*

Sally Aire   (review date July 1977)

[*In the following review, Aire contends that this RSC production offered a relatively narrow, restricted interpretation of* A Midsummer Night's Dream; *nevertheless, it was "magical, delightful, and . . . hilariously funny" within the limits it set itself.*]

A Midsummer Night's Dream is a play about enchantment, and enchantment is the prime quality of John Barton's production at the main RSC theatre, Stratford. It is magical, delightful, and more often than is usual with this play, hilariously funny. But is this really all there is to it?

From the snatches of criticism included in the programme notes, it appears that commentators have sought to justify the dramatic function of Theseus almost more than any other character. It is true that (in this production, at least) Theseus only really registers in 'the lunatic, the lover and the poet' speech [V. i. 2-22], where the Old Man himself is actually directly addressing us. But if we cease to think of Shakespeare's treatment of the two kingdoms, mortal and fairy, as a creation of 'two separate worlds . . . skilfully blended', but see them rather as separate faces only of one integrated world, the dark and the light, instinct and reason, primitive and cultured, then therewith ceases any problem about the dramatic function of Theseus or Hippolyta. What is Theseus but the human, reasoning, mortal side of Oberon?

If this interpretation of the play's presenting the dual nature of one world rather than the 'skilful blending' of two, still leaves some gaps unstopped, it does come some way towards recognising the kind of integral whole which every Shakespeare play presents. Nor, indeed, is this idea new—Brook has doubled Theseus and Oberon, and Frank Dunlop at the Young Vic back in '67 with Cleo Laine as Titania (and superb music by John Dankworth) illuminated this play for me in a way which is becoming increasingly rare. It is *not* a matter of 'finding something new to say about the Old Man'—one has simply to fall into the cliché of talking about eternal truths . . .

This, however, is not John Barton's object in the current RSC production. The piece is played for sheer enchantment. The fairies are magical: costumed in cobwebs, wispy wigs and what looks like magnified constituents of John Innes compost, they sink into the forest floor in perfect camouflage. They are most successful in their stiller passages. I couldn't help feeling that they are somewhat over-choreographed—reacting with rather predictably 'sinister' gestures on the more obvious bits of text. Cobweb and colleagues are beautifully played by very small boys, a creepy combination of childish bodies and voices and old men's heads and faces.

Unfortunately, Titania seems quite out of key with her earthy, demonic train. She shines forth like a fairy-tale fairy queen, complete with wings and flowing hair; mercifully she has abandoned her wand, although we fear it may be lurking, topped by a glittery star, somewhere just off the stage. The darkness is lacking in this interpretation of the role. We miss the elemental cruelty of her 'And for night tapers crop their waxen thighs / And light them at the fiery glow-worm's eyes / . . . / And pluck the wings from painted butterflies . . .' [III. i. 169-70, 171]. Marjorie Bland's Titania is a beautiful, gracious rather middle-class lady, who makes a command to steal the squirrel's horde of nuts sound like a proposal of an expedition to the new High Street macrobiotic delicatessen. So her rage is too well-mannered to convince. Yet she does succeed magnificently at the moment of the play's psychic climax—as she and Bottom 'gently entwist'. Patrick Stewart's superb Oberon is darker, crueller, more overtly sexual, a more successful interpretation. Brown-skinned and loinclothed, he is the most manly Oberon I have yet seen (unlike the effete Oberon of Robert Stephens' TV performance, 'My fairy lord' [III. ii. 378], indeed!). But, having channelled so much elemental masculinity into Oberon, one takes something away from the conventional playing of Puck. He must now become less the phallic Robin Goodfellow, and more of the mischievous pixie, and Leonard Preston's version of the role emphasises the muddle and the humour, becoming as near a clown as thematic considerations allow.

If Theseus and Hippolyta appear stiff and formal and all but narratively redundant (after all, if your subtext is being played for you by another actor, there's not much else you can do), this is not true of the other mortals. I was a little taken aback, worried even, at Helena's first entrance but, once I had accepted the new idiom of the interpretation, I found the lovers a real revelation. The quarrel scene deserved and got a round of delighted applause. Never have I seen (or even imagined) it so athletic, virtuosic and hilarious.

The role of Bottom is what I think one could call 'a gift' for an actor. But so were the talents given to the stewards in the parable, and one of them buried his gift in cold clay. Not Richard Griffiths. His playing of Bottom (the bestial, rather than the genital aspect of the play's sexuality) is oafish, aggressive even, but has a streak of genuine kindness that is utterly endearing. The detail of this totally integrated and complete performance is meticulous (the hand, for example, fractionally extended to Thisbe at the end of the 'play', and which Flute ignores . . .). Indeed the whole 'mechanicals' aspect of the piece is a delight, played not so much for the scathing

sniggers they earn from Hippolyta, as for our full-bellied laugh of totally sympathetic response to the clumsy well-meaningness of the artisans. For once, this production does not patronise them. Particularly moving is their lament for the 'translated' Bottom.

It is during this lament that the music of this production is at its best. This particular number—a sort of glee turned inside out, is brilliant in its simplicity. The 'rough' music of the 'tongs and the bones' [IV. i. 29] also works well, although even here the rhythm could be less formal. At other points the music is less successful, most notably in the 'spotted snakes' passage [II. ii. 9-26], which comes over as automatic, pretentious and vapid.

Choreography, too, succeeds only in places. It is best among the fairies although there is rather too much self-conscious 'movement' (not unlike a green room exercise) during some of the spoken text. It is at its least easy during the dances of Oberon and Titania, which appear slightly old-fashioned, formal, and tailored for actors, rather than allowing them to become dancers.

Yet, details apart, John Barton's production is a totally integrated whole within the limits it sets itself. The setting (apart from hideous village-hall black flats with daylight between, which mercifully don't survive the sticky opening scene) is refreshingly minimal—the large fern-like plants conjured by fairies from the roll-up forest floor. The play licks along at tremendous speed, fluent and wholly enjoyable. (pp. 22-3)

　　　　　Sally Aire, in a review of "A Midsummer Night's Dream," in Plays and Players, *Vol. 24, No. 10, July, 1977, pp. 22-3.*

J. Fuzier　(review date October 1977)

[*Fuzier extols Barton's production of* A Midsummer Night's Dream, *claiming that it was "sheer delight throughout . . . the RSC at its best—flawless to the last detail, and Shakespeare as one likes it.'*]

John Barton's production of *A Midsummer Night's Dream*, the first new item on the bill of the 1977 season at Stratford, should be a great success judging from the enthusiasm of its early audiences. It has nothing in common with the last RSC production of the play, Peter Brook's 1970 circus show, which was performed on an empty space stage, with flying trapezes hanging from the loft, and had everything except magic and poesy, which are the web and woof of the work, and the web and woof of Barton's *Dream*.

The set used is the 'wooden O' designed by John Napier for all the productions of the 1976 season: a serviceable set, which there were good reasons—other than the financial ones—to make last at least another year. It suggests a natural glade, with dark recesses under the backstage gallery, and it needed only a few trees to conjure up the enchanted forest in which most of the action takes place. Thus, there are trees, and ferns, and mossy boulders, and a profusion of brown, red, and yellow leaves realistically sticking to the garments of all those who rested their tired limbs on the bestrewn floor. There are fairies and elves who look like fairies and elves, feathery diminutive creatures, half-human, half-animal, with an uncanny talent for transforming themselves into rocks, stumps or logs every time men are in sight—creatures of night all, shy, harmless, though vaguely frightening. Titania

(Marjorie Bland) has gorgeous ethereal robes, and reigns supreme on this fantastic world. Patrick Stewart, as Oberon, could not resist displaying once more his harmonious musculature, and went about majestically, brandishing, in the Red Indian style he seems to favour, a spear-like magic wand. He and Titania formed an impressive kingly couple, and were more than a match for Theseus and Hippolyta (Richard Durden and Carmen Du Sautoy, both excellent). As for Puck, he was no airy Ariel, but a sturdy Robin Goodfellow with a bristling head of red hair and a remarkably hairy chest to match. Leonard Preston played the part with great gusto, and boisterously blundered his well-meaning from lover to lover to the soothing anticlimax of a queer, fairy-tale ending. In the lovers' scenes, a fair balance was kept between sentimental and slapstick comedy, and Paul Whitworth (Lysander), Pippa Guard (Hermia), Peter Woodward (Demetrius), and Marilyn Galsworthy (Helena) got all the laughs that could legitimately be got without ruining the romance of the play. Griffith Jones was a worthy Egeus, and the mechanicals were perfect. Richard Griffiths (Bottom) was a splendid ass, actor and stage-director, and he and his fellows (Norman Tyrrell, Duncan Preston, Keith Taylor, Leon Tanner and Brian Coburn) entertained the Athenian court and the Stratford audiences with one of the most hilarious *Pyramus and Thisbe*'s I have ever seen.

It is to be hoped that this production, which is sheer delight throughout, may last more than one season. It is perfect teamwork—the RSC at its best—flawless to the last detail, and Shakespeare as one likes it. (pp. 73-4)

> *J. Fuzier, in a review of "A Midsummer Night's Dream," in* Cahiers Élisabéthains, *No. 12, October, 1977, pp. 73-4.*

Roger Warren (review date spring 1978)

[*In the following excerpt, Warren maintains that Barton's RSC production "beautifully reconciled" the contrasting "combination of courtly formality and rich, vivid evocation of the English countryside" in* A Midsummer Night's Dream.]

A Midsummer Night's Dream has always seemed to me a particularly Elizabethan play, in that its combination of courtly formality and rich, vivid evocation of the English countryside has a strong flavour of Elizabeth's own court and its progresses. This flavour was caught with particular success in Peter Hall's Elizabethan country house version, especially in the 1962/3 revival. It was totally absent from the celebrated Peter Brook version. J. L. Styan in *The Shakespeare Revolution* . . . claims that 'those who disliked [Brook's] could not see past the surface of the production'; but the meaning of a play is not to be arbitrarily separated from the style and language in which it is expressed. The wood, the wild flowers, the juxtaposed court and rural worlds are essential features of the play. They are not merely its 'surface'; they make it what it is, and to neglect them, treating them merely as symbols for something else ('a celebration of the arts of the theatre', for instance) is to jettison not just the surface of the play but its essence as well. (p. 141)

John Napier's set for Mr. Barton's version beautifully reconciled court and countryside: a formally designed wooden floor with a central motif suggesting a Renaissance view of man (or even, perhaps, Oberon as he was subsequently presented). This floor was later covered by a huge, many-coloured silk cloth decorated with leaves, backed by trees, and lit by

an exceptionally imaginative overhead system, a particularly useful feature of which was to isolate characters in white light at the lovers' reaction to the magic juice or Puck's confusing of the duellists or the mechanicals. The sense of a magic forest was also conveyed in mime by a group of grotesquely masked male and female fairies; these masks were perhaps too sinister for spirits who inhabit muskrose buds and sing a charm *against* sinister creatures; there was some confusion here.

Clearly Mr. Barton wanted to stress the varied ancestry of the fairies, quoting David Young in the programme: 'a curious mixture of wood spirits, . . . household gods, pagan deities'. The most striking, and much the most successful, treatment was of Oberon. 'A prince from the farthest steep of India, shadowy and exotic', says Mr. Young, and Patrick Stewart was virtually naked, muscular and dark-skinned, with long curling black hair in a headband. He began Part Two reclining on the floor playing panpipes, a pastoral god, for all the world like Nijinsky's *Après-midi d'un faune*. However surprising this may sound, the strength of the approach lay in the ease with which Mr. Stewart could switch from these exotic associations to a casually humorous 'I wonder if Titania be awaked' [III. ii. 1], or to a direct, compelling delivery of all the great speeches: 'I know a bank' [II. i. 249] and especially the central, crucial 'But we are spirits of another sort' [III. ii. 388] had maximum impact, totally persuasive. This Oberon could range from benevolence there to fury elsewhere and to exceptional sensuous tenderness at 'wake you, my sweet queen' [IV. i. 75], cradling Titania in his arms. An outstanding performance.

Against these exotic beings, the mortals were sturdily Elizabethan, court and lovers in resplendent black and white—though Helena seemed oddly scruffy, rather like Ophelia after being dragged out of the brook and left to dry. Was this self-neglect her melancholy reaction to Demetrius's desertion, or was it, perhaps, the cause of it? It wasn't hard to see why Demetrius should prefer the enchanting, musically spoken Hermia of Pippa Guard. The lovers' scenes went with boisterous gaiety, aided by a large musket with which Demetrius went in pursuit of Lysander and a lute upon which Lysander accompanied Helena's maudlin reflections about school-days with Hermia. These scenes strongly recalled Peter Hall's version, as did Richard Durden's secure bringing out of Theseus's ironic humour at 'Saint Valentine is past' [IV. i. 139] and 'No doubt they rose up early *To observe the rite of May*' [IV. i. 132-33], which Mr. Hall was the first to make plain. But whereas his Theseus was humorous throughout, a wryly pragmatic country duke, Mr. Durden was otherwise young and vigorous, a striking Elizabethan gallant.

Court and wood were well balanced, contrasted yet related. In the very first court scene, the many references to the moon were emphasized, delivered up and out front, anticipating the influence of moon and moonshine in the wood later. After the return to court, some of the trees remained in half-light, as did some of the fairies, 'bodying forth / The forms of things unknown' [V. i. 13-14] as Theseus spoke of them, and so ironically counteracting his scepticism. The white-clad court lay down to sleep in a circle around the edge of the stage as the fairies blessed them. They later joined in with the blessing, rather oddly; and even more oddly they awoke and raised themselves into sitting positions at Puck's reference to the graves letting forth their sprites.

The mechanicals were beautifully unforced, getting laughs

off the lines, not off gags. The play scene was hilarious, as almost always, but also something more: picking up Granville-Barker's query, quoted in the programme, as to 'just how bad their play was meant to be', there was a sense, almost, of near-integrity, certainly a determination on Bottom's part to get things right, whatever the obstacles. Faced with having to stab himself through a magnificent but stubbornly impenetrable breastplate, he applied himself with slow, calm logic to the problem, and took all the time in the world to get his lyre into a suitably aesthetic position before expiring grandly but slowly. Richard Griffiths conveyed Bottom's self-absorption not by boisterous rant but by solicitous advice to Quince and the others. This quiet, warm, very human performance was the chief gain of the production's declared policy of using largely untried actors; but for Titania (especially opposite *this* Oberon), more is needed. Marjorie Bland spoke with the direct clarity that characterised the production but lacked that complex sense of identification with the world around her that should make the 'progeny of evils' [II. i. 115] seem of direct concern to her. (pp. 141-43)

Roger Warren, "Comedies and Histories at Two Stratfords, 1977," in Shakespeare Survey: An Annual Survey of Shakespearian Study and Production, *Vol. 31, 1978, pp. 141-53.*

PRODUCTION:

Ron Daniels • Royal Shakespeare Company • 1981-82

BACKGROUND:

Director Ron Daniels blended lavish Victorian realism, conscious artifice, suggestions of ballet, and magic tricks in the 1981 RSC production of *A Midsummer Night's Dream.* The fairies in this controversial and disturbing version of the play were grotesque and menacing china doll puppets; the very opulence of the costumes and sets for Theseus's hall betrayed their theatricality; and the woodland scenes took place amid the disordered devices and props of countless previous stage productions. Critics were divided over this presentation of the play. Some found it vital and energetic, while others deemed it a confusing mélange of half-formed ideas. After opening in Stratford-upon-Avon, Daniels's production was taken on provincial tour and then to the Barbican Theatre in London in 1982.

COMMENTARY:

Robert Cushman   (review date 19 July 1981)

[*In the following review of Daniels's 1981 RSC staging of* A Midsummer Night's Dream, *Cushman contends that despite the artifice of the Victorian setting, this production was "actually playing very straight with us." According to the critic, Daniels recognized that "we still have a traditional view of fairyland."*]

History-books suggest that the greatest twentieth-century production of *A Midsummer Night's Dream* was not Granville-Barker's or Peter Brook's, but Tyrone Guthrie's in the Thirties, with Victorian sets and costumes, Ninette de Valois

ballets, and Mendelssohn music—everything, in fact, we have been taught to despise. But, of course, extremes meet; Mr. Brook's production, ostentatiously demystifying, only substituted one form of artifice for another, while Ron Daniels's new Stratford version, which returns to the full panoply of Victoriana, is actually playing very straight with us.

Maria Bjornson's lovely set is a nineteenth-century stage, a blown-up Pollock print; the production acknowledges that we still have a traditional view of fairyland and takes off from there. This is 'The Dream' in a special society and a special theatre, one whose devices are lovingly and knowingly employed, most consummately when painted flats descend for Puck's befogging of the lovers 'Pyramus and Thisbe' becomes a Saturday-night melodrama, backed by yet more pastiche chords from Stephen Oliver (whose setting of 'ye spotted snakes' would, in a better world, make the charts).

Not everything works; the minor fairies as glove-puppets misfire, because we actually look at the manipulators, and the mechanicals are more winsome than hilarious, their tone set by John Rogan's dear old Irish Quince. (Mr. Rogan is always playing a dear old Irish something). But the relationship of Geoffrey Hutchings's bantam Bottom and Juliet Stevenson's Titania is well sketched in.

Mike Gwilym doubles a courtly, caring Theseus with an Oberon who does the beautiful bits beautifully and whose deliciously held pause before asking Puck 'what *hast* thou done?' [III. ii. 88] is worth the price of admission, which at Stratford these days is saying something. And the lovers are as good as I remember; better as regards the men, to whom Philip Franks and Simon Templeman give their full measure of rapture, folly and self-righteousness.

Meanwhile Jane Carr, while keeping all her comic expertise, at last succeeds in finding a classical rhythm (more successfully, to my surprise, than Harriet Walter's Helena); her stage-stomping cadenza on her rival's '*height,* forsooth' (the italics are hers, and heavy) is irresistible. Finally, Joseph Marcell makes Puck's farewell both a logical end and a teasing new beginning, which is the test of any 'Dream.'

Robert Cushman, "Bubbling!" in The Observer, *July 19, 1981, p. 31.*

Robert Hewison   (review date 19 July 1981)

[*Hewison offers a mixed review of Daniels's production in the excerpt below. He finds this staging visually "ravishing" but dislikes the presence of the puppeteers who operated the fairies. These figures, whose "black working clothes and dirty faces" suggested an "industrial proletariat of millhands and match-girls," created a "distracting fourth social class in the play."*]

"A Midsummer Night's Dream," it is believed, was originally created as a marriage entertainment, and it features a royal wedding. It is entirely appropriate that Ron Daniel's new production, which opened at Stratford this week, will be playing on July 29.

In the interest of comedy—and perhaps the contemporary mood—the class distinctions between Fairy King and Queen, court life and rude mechanicals have been somewhat democratised. Oberon and Titania are doubled as Theseus, Duke of Athens, and Hippolyta, Queen of the Amazons. Mike Gwilym and Juliet Stevenson retain a certain *hauteur* in both roles, but theirs is a semi-bourgeois court at the end of the 19th century. In the opening scene the frogging both on Theseus's uniform and Hippolyta's dress suggest the designs for Kenneth Macmillan's ballet "Mayerling," but any tragic overtones are quickly dispelled by the youthful gaucheries of the crossed lovers, Hermia (Jane Carr), Demetrius (Simon Templeman), Lysander (Phillip Franks) and Helena (Harriet Walter).

The lovers are played all for comedy and none for courtliness, and Jane Carr has a particular success as the plump soubrette raging against her taller rival. Aristocratic pretensions are shed as all four lovers progressively lose their outer clothes in the snags and snares of the forest.

Because there is so much Offenbach in the lovers' scenes, the rude humour in the traditionally comic parts must be proportionately less. Bottom and his colleagues are not rude mechanicals, but bowler-hatted tradesmen, and Geoffrey Hutchings shows admirable restraint as the Weaver with a passion for amateur theatricals. This does not make Bottom's scenes any less funny and, of course, the final performance of "Pyramus and Thisbe" is hilarious, but the restraint makes for a much better balance within the play. My only regret is that Bottom does not appear to be enjoying the final Morris dancing bergamasque. Stephen Oliver's music is discreetly right throughout.

The designer, Maria Björnson, has taken a heavy hint from the theatrical sub-text, and produces a visual style that is part-Pollock Toy Theatre, part-Victorian pantomime. The most controversial element is the use of hand-operated puppets, like china dolls, to represent the fairies. This creates a distracting fourth social class in the play, the puppeteers, whose black working clothes and dirty faces suggest an industrial proletariat of millhands and matchgirls. (I realise that this may be pushing the late-nineteenth century parallel too far). The dolls are grotesque, not charming, and Ron Daniels is right to point up the element of black magic and evil in Oberon and Titania's dissension.

The overtones of ballet return in the presentation of Titania and Oberon, and the doubling of parts creates neat touches which suggest that Hippolyta and Theseus are more constrained versions of the same personalities. Joseph Marcell is a coal-imp of a Puck, but he, and indeed all of the cast, is not quite attentive enough to the verse. Visually, however, the production is ravishing. It is tautological to say that "A Midsummer Night's Dream" is magical, but the RSC's "consultant on magic," Ali Bongo, has done his work.

Robert Hewison, "Midsummer Merry-Making," in
The Sunday Times, *London, July 19, 1981, p. 41.*

Benedict Nightingale   (review date 24 July 1981)

[*In the following excerpt, Nightingale admires certain aspects of this presentation of* A Midsummer Night's Dream, *notably its treatment of "Theseus's subconscious hostilities towards Hippolyta," but regards much about the production merely "tricksy and confusing."*]

The new *Dream* has been described as the RSC's salute to the Royal Wedding; but, if so, it's an ambiguous one, with something akin to two fingers sprouting from the patriotically outstretched arm. The reason I say this is that Ron Daniels's production combines the doubling of real and fairy king and queen with the suggestion, also made in the famous Brook

version ten years ago, that Oberon's revenge on Titania reflects and resolves Theseus's subconscious hostilities towards Hippolyta, his bride-to-be. In other words, Chuck might feel better about Di if he imagined her having sex with a prole with a donkey's head.

Such, at any rate, is the inference I take from the transformation of the faces Mike Gwilym and Juliet Stevenson present each other: cold, wan, almost funereal at first, and then, after they've swapped their courtly blacks for leprechaun shimmer and flitted through the glades, surprisingly warm and friendly. I rather enjoyed this, as I did Mr. Daniels's gleeful handling of the other lovers, dominated by Jane Carr's Hermia, a raging skivvy capable of booting over and stomping on her swain; but not the rest of the production, which too often seemed tricksy and confusing. Why, when the cardboard arches of Theseus's Ruritania are swept away, are they replaced by an equally illusory fairyland, with Moth, Cobweb *et al* reduced to droll dolls manipulated by drably dressed puppeteers? 'Lovers and madmen,' runs the evening's key line, 'have such seething brains, such shaping fantasies, that apprehend more than cool reason ever comprehends' [V.i. 4-6]. The point would be more convincing if the shaping fantasies provided by Mr. Daniels were richer, wilder, and more overwhelming.

Benedict Nightingale, "Professional," in New Statesman, *Vol. 102, No. 2627, July 24, 1981, p. 22.*

Nicholas Shrimpton   (review date 31 July 1981)

[*Shrimpton presents a markedly negative assessment of this RSC production of* A Midsummer Night's Dream. *"The account of the imagination, the sense of disrupted natural harmony, the comments on love, the exploration of theatrical illusion, even the psychological points made . . . by the doubling of Theseus and Hippolyta with Oberon and Titania—all these things [were] scrambled and diminished," the critic contends.*]

After the Penny Plain of the 1960s, the Royal Shakespeare Company has gradually been turning Twopence Coloured. The Theatre of Cruelty gave way to *commedia dell'arte,* empty spaces to crowded chambers, ferocity to fantasy and fun. The change continues apace. If it is nothing else, a Stratford production of *A Midsummer Night's Dream* in the style of the Victorian "Juvenile Drama" is a milestone in this long march through the dramatic conventions.

The door of Ron Daniels's theatrical toyshop opens onto a scene straight from Pollocks. The Brook white box could hardly be further from us. Swags of canvas cloud hang stiffly in the heavens. Flats and cutout wings present a palace of Theseus in the highest Victorian taste. To the tinkling music of an off-stage piano, Hippolyta enters in a crinoline, escorted by Theseus as Colonel of the Ruritanian Imperial Guard. All is decorum and drawing room manners. The Duke reclines on a chaise-lounge to receive his troublesome deputation, and admonishes Hermia in the clipped tones of a premature Noel Coward.

Mutton-chop whiskers and frock-coats do not, of course, make this a Victorian production of *A Midsummer Night's Dream.* The Victorians themselves were acutely conscious of the ancient and Athenian setting of the play, and certainly never attempted what to them would have been modern-dress staging. When Tyrone Guthrie directed his pastiche of a Victorian *Dream,* at the Old Vic in 1937, he put his fairies in ballet skirts, his mechanicals in Greek tunics, and revived the Mendelssohn score. Daniels does none of those things. Instead he hides a conventionally rumbustuous mid-twentieth century production behind a thin Victorian veneer.

The effect is bright and jolly, and the toy-theatre manner sometimes helps to conceal the stiffness of Shakespeare's construction. But the superficiality of the conception prompts an unworthy suspicion. With a Victorian smash-hit on its hands in *Nicholas Nickleby,* is the RSC suffering from stylistic cross-infection? Does everybody, at least when handling comedy, suddenly want to inhabit the 1830s? Certainly it is hard to find any very profound intention behind the choice of dress. The fairies are plastic dolls (seemingly inspired by Peter Blake's paintings), manipulated by actors in proletarian clothes from the pages of Mayhew. If a point is being made about the class structure, however, it remains obscure. Peter Brook uncovered social implications far more effectively by the simple device of casting as the mechanicals actors who actually looked like tinkers, tailors and carpenters.

Elsewhere the Victorian reference seems straightforwardly decorative. The hunting scene looks more convincing than usual when played in pinks and toppers, and crinolines lend some additional comic business to the fight between Helena and Hermia. Little else can really be claimed for the idea. Its source, I fear, is the weakest part of *Nicholas Nickleby:* the Crummles' cod production of *Romeo and Juliet.* The mechanicals' play here is given as a similar burlesque of what we (wrongly) assume to have been standard nineteenth-century theatrical practice. Members of our premier dramatic company should have better things to do than repeatedly send up a misconception about the professional standards of their grandfathers.

Many productions of *A Midsummer Night's Dream* in the last ten years, it must be said, have been casting about for ideas, and the reasons are obvious enough. Twice in this century the play has been made the pinnacle of a short period of theatrical innovation, once by Granville-Barker in 1914, then by Peter Brook in 1970, and such peaks leave troughs beyond them. The more coherent recent attempts at reinterpretation have based themselves on abtruse scholarly ideas about Elizabethan Neo-Platonism and its view of love and marriage. After such well-intentioned obscurity, it's perhaps no bad thing to see the play as a wholesome romp in colourful costumes.

But the slightness of this reading rapidly infects even those portions of the text which need no intrusive interpretation to render them significant. The account of the imagination, the sense of disrupted natural harmony, the comments on love, the exploration of theatrical illusion, even the psychological points made (following standard modern practice) by the doubling of Theseus and Hippolyta with Oberon and Titania—all these things are scrambled and diminished. There are occasional felicitous touches, such as the moment when Theseus carelessly steps halfway across the mechanicals' footlights for "The best in this kind are but shadows" [V.i. 211]. Mere touches, however, cannot redeem the general slackness of the verse speaking (John Burgess's Egeus is an honourable exception) and the persistent uncertainty of tone.

Mike Gwilym does his best to sparkle as Theseus and to smoulder as Oberon. In both roles he remains indecisively marooned between the sinister and the benign. If that's a problem for him, it's a worse one for the minor fairies. Dizzy-

ing transitions between appearances as cannibal dolls from a horror-movie and as kindly nature spirits, with an occasional function as *corps de ballet* thrown in for good measure, leave the audience (and, I should imagine, them) thoroughly confused.

The mechanicals have a good running gag about the forgetting of Snug's name, and a sharp perception of Flute's adolescent smuttiness. But Geoffrey Hutchings is a distinctly lightweight Bottom and, as a team, they content themselves with the easiest effects. As so often when *A Midsummer Night's Dream* is played as a romp, in fact, the best opportunities fall to Hermia. The doll-like Jane Carr, plump, genial and awesomely spirited, seizes them eagerly. She ends up the queen of the toybox.

Nicholas Shrimpton, "Frisky Juveniles," in The Times Literary Supplement, No. 4087, July 31, 1981, p. 875.

Gareth Lloyd Evans (review date Winter 1981)

[*In the following excerpt, Evans offers a mixed review of Daniels's production of* A Midsummer Night's Dream. *This presentation was "all done for fun," but it was "raucous, dangerous, even menacing fun," he notes. Evans adds that "A Midsummer Night's Dream seems condemned to be a sort of laboratory specimen vulnerable to all kinds of interference" in such stagings.*]

[The R.S.C.'s production of *The Winter's Tale*] contains some notable examples of the decay in speaking and acting which seems to have infected a number of the younger members of the company. Who would have thought that one could have lived long enough to hear that line about the daffodils [IV.iv. 118] spoken as if the actress had a Mars bar halfway down her throat, or to see a Florizel move with such illgrace. Of such stuff are productions flawed.

But whether triumphant or run-of-the-mill the R.S.C. never ceases to arouse interest and incite debate. Its other midseason production—*A Midsummer Night's Dream*—coincided with three Shakespearean events, in all catering for a formidable, even terrifying, array of scholars, graduate students and R.S.C. addicts gathered together for lectures, seminars, workshops, bun-fights, ego-trips and incessant yatter about the Bard. *The Dream* coked up their boilers incredibly—wild adherents of Jan Kott were waylaid by marauding bands of Brechtites, who themselves were enfiladed by furtive platoons bearing banners with the device "Peter Brook will never walk alone". In the distance a lonely figure was surrounded by a mob of fierce Marowitzians ignoring his plea—"William Shakespeare wrote it".

Ron Daniels' production indeed encouraged both neurotic and considered speculation about its sources, and plainly only he knows where he got it from. Whatever the answer is it was a theatrical success in the very best traditions of showbusiness—efficient in execution, brisk in pace, versatile in effect, entertaining in form and spirit. Whether you consider the obvious enjoyment it generated for a large proportion of its audience was purchased at too high a price is a matter for your own aesthetic sensibilities.

The set impersonates a Victorian theatre and I suspect (though it is not absolutely clear) that we are intended to assume that we are seeing a dress rehearsal of a performance of the play. The acting, therefore, is highly theatrical and, since it is in late Victorian opulent mode, it is visually sensational, with its glittering star-clusters, its swirling fog, garish costumes, and special effects contrived by the R.S.C.'s magic consultant, Ali Bongo.

But, and this is what drove those scholars and afficionados out of their minds with yattering speculation, Mr. Daniels confounds us by doubling Theseus and Oberon and Titania and Hippolyta, by making his fairies into puppets manipulated by humans, by inducing from Jane Carr as Hermia a frantic turn rather than a performance. Even more baffling, Mike Gwilym plays both Duke and King Fairy with unrelenting ill-temper and Juliet Stevenson seems to find little to differentiate her performance of Amazon Queen and Queen Fairy.

The possibility that the academic influence of Jan Kott with its emphasis on the play as a vicious nightmare is strong is increased by the malevolence of the puppets and the curious reluctance of Theseus to accept the status which the text so clearly gives him—that of reconciler. Moreover the virtual absence of any attempt by any actor or actress to release the superb lyricism of Shakespeare's language suggests a deliberate policy of reducing the sweeter virtues of the play's spirit. It is all done for fun, but it is raucous, dangerous even menacing fun.

By far the most pleasing adherence to Shakespeare's text in spirit comes from the mechanicals. John Rogan (Peter Quince) and, again, Geoffrey Hutchings (Bottom) lead a group of amateur thespians, awkward, a bit thick, embarrassed, well-meaning and lovable—this is Shakespeare's vision and it is superbly expressed.

Would that the rest, for all its ingenuity, had attained the sense of authenticity and unforced comedy achieved by Bottom and his men. But *A Midsummer Night's Dream* seems condemned to be a sort of laboratory specimen vulnerable to all kinds of interference. (p. 12)

> Gareth Lloyd Evans, "Shakespeare in Performance," in Drama, London, No. 142, Winter, 1981, pp. 10-12.

Irving Wardle   (review date 17 June 1982)

[*In the excerpt below, Wardle observes that Daniels's production pushed the play to a "non-illusionist extreme." The "toy-theatre" settings and puppet fairies, he claims, demonstrated "the force of the oldest theatrical conventions; the magic inherent in doorways, traps, and ropes—devices that fool nobody, and yet can still fool everybody when rightly used."*]

One lasting legacy of Peter Brook's production of this play is to have stripped off its ethereal reputation. Apart from Egeus's unaccountable failure to notice that his daughter has run away from home, it is an indestructibly robust piece of plotting at every level from the court drama to the events in Titania's bower.

Ron Daniels's production, the first Stratford show to arrive at the Barbican, acknowledged this fact by pushing the play to a non-illusionist extreme.

The setting and style are mid-Victorian: not only in Maria Bjornson's toy-theatre palace interiors and cut-out woodland glades, but also in the magical mechanics, costume references, and in Stephen Oliver's music, which supports the action as in the old Lyceum melodramas sometimes carrying

the text over into song. Going beyond the Victorian limit, Mr Daniels presents the fairies as rod-puppets in the hands of manipulators.

The evident purpose is to demonstrate the force of the oldest theatrical conventions; the magic inherent in doorways, traps, and ropes—devices that fool nobody, and yet can still fool everybody when rightly used.

The opening Athenian scene, seems to promise an entirely different kind of play. It is very stuffy, overdressed and respectable, with the sound of pastiche Mendelssohn drifting in from an adjoining room.

As the production develops, this is an absolutely necessary preparation. Here are the young lovers, rolling across the carpet in crinolenes, casting their eyes up to heaven as they take eternal vows and strike heroic postures. Shortly they will be chasing each other, and (in the case of Harriet Walter's whiningly distraught Helena) losing her skirt.

Most electrifying among these transformations is that of Jane Carr's Hermia from a pallid little victim, transmitting as much martyrdom as a muffin, to the enraged harpy of the woods. "PUPPET" she screams at Helena's ill-judged accusation, and takes off like a Sidewinder, reducing the boys as well as her rival to a flattened heap on the floor.

At Stratford I thought the immortals paid a poetic penalty for the tricky stagecraft; and Mike Gwilym still strikes me as a needlessly bad-tempered Oberon. But what he and Joseph Marcell's Puck (costumed like Grimaldi) do achieve is to combine enchantment with solidly corporeal acting.

One triumph of the approach is Mr. Gwilym's raid on the bower, where he has a fist fight with the puppets before managing to work his spell on the genuinely ethereal Juliet Stevenson. And the moment of Bottom's transformation releases an amazing box of tricks, with hats flying like frisbees over the stalls, and scenic pieces dancing up and down in a cascade of changing lights.

The mechanicals, despite their sober working-class suits, remain sublimely unaffected by the surrounding changes. I have seen them funnier; but never more self-respectingly believable than in Geoffrey Hutchings's master craftsman Bottom, showing beard samples to John Rogan's Quince, and making something quite passable of Pyramus's death speech, before he finds he cannot lie down.

> Irving Wardle, "Enchantment and Solid, Bodily Acting," in The Times, London, June 17, 1982, p. 10.

Anthony Masters   (review date August 1982)

[*In the excerpt below, Masters maintains that Daniels's production created a "nonsensical gap" between the artificiality of the fairy scenery and the "meticulous realism of Theseus' drawing-room, giving the actors "nothing to relate to."*]

Perched on gilt chairs in the massively pillared salon, red plush drapes behind them, aspidistras to right and left, sit a young Victorian couple: Theseus and Hippolyta. Once again, the RSC have not only done a Shakespeare comedy but done it up—with, as usual, a delicious pastiche score from Stephen Oliver. Once again, they have entrusted this particular play to a largely inexperienced, second-eleven cast. And, as if this were not enough, there is Ron Daniels's central idea. Taking his cue from Theseus' obscure but evocative words about imagination, he finds his milieu for the play's magical and menacing 'other world' in the act of theatre itself, and dumps those scenes solidly within the pantomime conventions of the time: cloud-painted flats, tinsel tat for the fairy king and queen, wooden fairy puppets.

Such a cerebral solution, keeping magic within inverted commas rather than meeting the challenge of making an audience feel it, leaves a nonsensical gap between those scenes and the meticulous realism of Theseus' drawing-room, and gives the actors nothing to relate to. Juliet Stevenson, as Titania, has to lie on what looks like a putrefying chaise-longue festooned with cobwebs and bits of tree, and fall magically asleep beneath a heavenly host of little wooden dolls and eight all-too-corporeal actors manipulating them. My heart went out to her.

Burdened by such a weight of concept (and not helped by this huge new theatre), the comedy has difficulty taking off. The direction of the mechanicals shows a lack of relish and affection. Geoffrey Hutchings (Bottom), tentatively overacting as a Victorian weaver too roundly good-natured to cause trouble up at t'mill, and John Rogan (Quince) are honest and endearing actors both, but the scenes don't blossom as they should do and the Pyramus play turns out old, crude gags, as though aware that the average audience laughs anyhow. (Some time, a director should sit down and think out what unforeseen disasters—and triumphs—*might actually happen* in this sort of amateur dramatics.)

Only two members of the cast have a really good evening. Jane Carr and Harriet Walter (Hermia and Helena) show themselves superb natural comediennes—Miss Carr not surprisingly, but Miss Walter's comic gifts are a glorious revelation. Looking (as an Osborne character once said) like a female version of Emily Brontë, she combines inventive absurdity with pathetic glimpses into plain-Jane loneliness before beautiful men start unaccountably falling at her feet. Miss Carr, meanwhile, has a field day with the prim propriety she sustained like a fig-leaf throughout the most scandalous perversities of *What The Butler Saw*. The forest scenes are as full of farcical knockabout as ever, perhaps more, but her energy and precision make every flying tackle a delight and actually, at one point, earn her three laughs in the course of one undistinguished line.

Mr Daniels's trenchant, disturbing talent does show well in the slow, brooding first scene of heavy fathers and stifling social pressures. He finds an unconventional pattern of comic climaxes in the big forest scene. There are even moments when the production's good and bad selves seem to co-exist: Oberon viciously attacks Titania's puppets in a sequence simultaneously fatuous and sinister. (And the puppets' expressive movements are really exquisite throughout.) But there is not enough to suggest that this is a play Mr Daniels ought to have been let loose on. I felt myself longing for Richard Cottrell's Bristol (and London) Old Vic production with its black and silver forest and its black and silver fairies. (pp. 32-3)

Anthony Masters, in a review of "A Midsummer Night's Dream," in Plays & Players, *No. 347, August, 1982, pp. 32-3.*

Gary Jay Williams (review date Summer-Fall 1982)

[*Williams stresses the "rich and dark conception" of this production. "Daniels's world for the play," he states, "seemed to me one filled with apprehension, echoing with lament, and his intuitions very dark at the edges."*]

Any production of *A Midsummer Night's Dream* in these last twelve years since "Brook's *Dream*" (yes, twelve years), has risked comparison. The Royal Shakespeare Company's current, somewhat controversial production has been seen both as a nostalgic return to the Victorian world of Vestris, Phelps or Charles Kean and as a reverse image of the Peter Brook-Sally Jacobs white box of 1970. Neither was intended and neither characterization does the new production justice. Directed by Ron Daniels, the new staging comes out of a rich and dark conception, richer for the consideration than any since Brook's anxiously bright circus.

Its young lovers inhabit a high Victorian court of red velvet swag curtains and potted palms, crinolines and fitted frock coats, dove-grey spats and chin-high collars. The forest world they flee to is an old backstage world made of muslin flats and wicker prop trunks, remnants of a Victorian theater, faded and askew, dimly luminous in oil lamp footlighting on a vast stage that is enveloped by a black cyclorama. And the fairies they meet there are small doll puppets, china doll spectres, some cracked, some sans eyes, sans hair, sans arms. The Titania and Oberon they serve are king and queen of a world of melancholy stage tinsel. It is an effecting production that moves one siftingly through this play again; and it leaves one to reflect on what we have passed through since the magic flower was a silver platter spinning on a lucite rod, passed from Puck to Oberon, high on their trapezes. It is also, as Brook's was, a production which holds a dialogue with the theatrical traditions of this play as it seeks to engage our imaginations anew.

The RSC production directed by Ron Daniels was developed at Stratford-upon-Avon in 1981, moved early this year to the RSC's northern base at Newcastle-on-Tyne and may move into the RSC's new London home in the Barbican Arts Centre. (The RSC's two theaters there will replace their locations at the Aldwych and the Warehouse). It is a production susceptible to readings that locate the old, familiar play among fond Victorian trappings which arouse a vague nostalgia. But there also has been some puzzlement and downright irritation over its weird puppet fairies. Michael Billington of the *Guardian* was both puzzled and skeptical, saying, "I began to feel like Ben Jonson's Zeal-of-the-Land Busy, bursting in on a puppet show crying, 'I will no longer endure your profanations.'" Robert Cushman of the *Observer* decided that it was a production that was "actually playing very straight with us," returning to "the full panoply of Victoriana," after Brook's "ostentatiously demystifying" version. And if its puppets "misfired," much else charmed, including Maria Bjornson's set, "a blown-up Pollock [toy-theater] print," the comic young lovers, and the play of "Pyramus and Thisbe" as "a Saturday night melodrama." Michael Coveney of the *Financial Times* was the more patiently exploring of the morning-after reviewers, sensing a movement toward reconciliation underlying the production. Cushman's review is probably the more representative response, but certainly one is not dealing here (as he suggested) with a fond Victorian recreation such as Tyrone Guthrie's 1937-1938 toy theater production at the Old Vic. (Even then Guthrie had his tongue in his cheek.) Ron Daniels made the comment that he went

into rehearsals of *A Midsummer Night's Dream* feeling that
it was a play "filled with unease;" he made a passing comparison to *Timon of Athens,* which he has recently directed at The
Other Place in Stratford (of which he is the Artistic Director), and ventured that Shakespeare was both thrilled and
frightened by the possibilities of his dream play. Daniels's
world for the play seemed to me one filled with apprehensions, echoing with lament, and his intuitions very dark at the
edges.

In the Theseus's palace setting of the first scene, there is indeed the suggestion of a Pollock toy theater print, but a
strangely ominous one. A huge classical triumphal arch upstage center is framed by matching wing sets right and left,
painted in such skillful perspective as not only to deceive but
to underscore the deception in a theatrically self-conscious
virtuosity. Overhead hang great Baroque clouds in violets
and blues, and the setting is amberlighted from shell-shaped
footlights. Beneath the painted architraves, pillars, and statuary are potted palms painted on discernible netting. There is
the note of grand Charles Kean Victorian classicism here, but
the evocation is not that of the charming miniature. The
monumental artifact glooms around the actors; they seem
small and ruled by it. Costumes and demeanor are scrupulously high Victorian. Through the central archway, with its
red velvet, gold-fringed portier, the males parade the entering
ladies in their vast bustles and trains, as if at some grand ball
of 1865, and sit them picturesquely on the single, tufted black
leather divan at right. Much in the text is alive to the Victorian context, such as: Egeus's list of indictments against Lysander, who "hath bewitched the bosom of my child . . . with
verses of feigning love, . . . bracelets of thy hair, rings,
gawdes, . . . nosegays" [I. i. 27, 31, 33, 34]; there are the
lovestruck males and chaste girls who must not chase them,
and all the talk of virginity and maiden-pilgrimages, primrose
beds and sweet playfellows, dowager aunts, and roses fading
on the cheek; all the establishment rhetoric festooned with
sententiae, and all the youthful promises blossoming into
vows by Cupid's bow and Venus's doves. The young lovers
here are appealing, as usual; what is unusual here is that Theseus and Hippolyta seem vaguely uneasy caretakers of this
court world, as if perhaps it were only illusory and their
hearts were not in the keeping up of appearances.

As we move to the mechanicals gathering to cast their play,
and then on into the forest with the fairies and the lovers, the
RSC stage becomes a stage. Theseus's palace "flies" in our
view. The mechanicals help stage hands brace flats and set
props. Upstage on the raked stage, in the far shadows of the
ambering footlights, are seen an ancient Victorian lighting
machine for sunsets and sunrises (such as we will later see silhouetting Oberon and Titania), a wind machine, and a wicker
prop basket. Quince and company, in nineteenth century
working class dress, rehearse beside a standing bracket of gas
jets. They are, throughout the play, more winsome and thoroughly earnest than hilarious. Later, in the lovers' chase, a
cutout tree flat flies in up left to hang askew, and another flies
in backward down right, showing "Act I, Sc. 3" lettered on
its backside. When Puck taunts Lysander and Demetrius into
their would-be duel within this would-be wood, they flounder
beneath a billowing sky canvas that has been lowered on two
stage-wide batterns. The forest of lovers' confusion, then, is
one made of fragments of theatrical illusion in disarray; this
is the other side of Theseus's toy-theater palace. The land of
imitation has been turned inside out, and one could get lost
amidst the trappings of transformations and illusion. Mike

Gwilym doubles as Theseus/Oberon, and Juliet Stevenson as
Hippolyta/Titania. Puck is played by a black actor (Joseph
Marcell) as symmetrically proportioned as a puppet and costumed like one, and he has a small black look-alike among
the puppet fairies. One suspects that were one to ask where
illusion begins and ends here, neither Theseus nor Oberon,
Titania nor Hermia, Bottom nor Puck, would know. An uneasiness hangs in the air around the scattered theatrical remains of an age that once was very sure. The tone of Mike
Gwilym's Oberon is one key to this; the puppets are another.

The fairies first emerge from the wicker prop basket like colored streamers (some are dolls trailing diaphanous fabric and
some are streamers on sticks). They are operated by cast
members all in black, their faces veiled or smudged, unobtrusive, though not, like Japan's Bunraku operators, at pains to
perfect an illusion. Created by the production designer Maria
Bjornson, the puppets range from one to three feet high, are
variously rod-manipulated, and are not complexly articulated. Their details are not discernible beyond the first few rows,
and most spectators will have an impression of them as a
strange assortment of china dolls, each unique and all in various stages of disintegration and decay. Their operators often
move them in large sweeping, diving motions, and on the vast
stage against the black cyclorama, they seem like small, white
macabre souls, darting silently in the blackness. They scatter
in the winds at Oberon's first entrance ("Ill met by moonlight, proud Titania" [II. i. 60]), which he makes like a demon
king in a pantomime, riding up on an iron spiral staircase that
emerges through a trap amid theatrical smoke and blue
lights. They hover in the air, protectively, around Titania,
and they watch anxiously as the fairy king and queen quarrel,
shifting and darting, their puppet limbs sometimes clacking
quietly in the silence like bones.

Since Harley Granville-Barker's fairies of 1914—gilded oriental miniatures out of Leon Bakst—the fairies have been everything imaginable—though more often than not, imaginable has been the problem. This is not the first time they have
been puppet creatures. Frank McMullen directed a Yale production of 1962 using marionettes which were operated from
the grid, had pre-recorded voices, and danced a ballet for Titania. But the RSC's puppets are not scaled down, neo-
romantic Sadler's Wells toe dancers nor any kind of charming wee folk. Daniels's use of them evolved out of the rehearsal process. "Costumed adults make no sense," he commented, "so I tried puppets. Once I tried them, I found things
grew." He came to see them as "the neglected children of a
parental quarrel," that quarrel between Oberon and Titania,
the archetypal parental Male and Female, whose dissension
("These are the forgeries of jealousy . . ." [II. i. 81]) alters
the very seasons. Theirs is a quarrel that breeds "a progeny
of evils," of which, says Titania, "We are their parents and
original" [II. i. 115, 117]. And so, an ineffable sadness clings
to these "neglected children" as they hover about the fairy
king and queen and over the remnants of illusion on the dim
stage. The sense of loss they convey goes far beyond Pinochio
pathos. They seem to wait in eternity for the mending of a
world long broken. They are not so much like disintegrating
dolls as haunting relics of belief or souls no longer prayed for,
within an inch of vanishing irrecoverably in the night wind.
They attack Oberon when he comes to work the charm on
Titania, and audiences gasp when Oberon strikes one of the
brittle heads fiercely, the dust and sequins flying. At the end
of the play he seeks to make his peace with them, and the
black puppet Puck, at first unsure, takes his offered hand.

Gwilym's Oberon sets the tone of the production. Though he has grace, he has no stage-heroic countenance or rolling vowels. His small eyes sit low in his skull beneath a high forehead. His Oberon is a mystery, disquiet and reflective, an almost mournful Oberon. His costume is a suit of glittering golds and purples, with sash and baggy pants, theatrically gaudy, perhaps that of a genie from a Pollock toy theater *Aladdin,* two-pence colored. Juliet Stevenson's Titania is a solid, pretty girl, warm and maternal, a perfect fairy queen for a home-town children's theatre. Her dress is vaguely that of the romantic ballet stage, but over-tinseled and spangled with green and blue sequins. Behind the skirt, one can glimpse the hoop structure supporting the illusion.

The centerpiece of the production becomes the reconciliation dance after Oberon has awakened his queen and taken the charm from her eyes. He shows her the sleeping Bottom, whose ass's head is for once quite ugly, as if kindly to say, "you see on what thin ground we stand." Daniels has spoken of "the existential sense behind the play:"

> I am how you look at me. Look at me with love,
> and I am loveable. Look at me with hate, and that
> is how I shall appear—ugly.

And so a world of shadows is answered in the dance. It is a slow, simplified ballet in the classical manner, in which Titania twirls figures around Oberon. It is not so very beautifully danced (they are not Robert Helpmann and Moira Shearer), and we and they know it is not. It is, rather, made for us to allow it and them to be pretty, and it ends in Titania and Oberon's anxious, close embrace, as if this were indeed the one dance left to dance upon the edge of a vanishing enchantment.

Daniels plays other minor variations on his motif that we make our own truth and beauty. When Puck scatters the frightened mechanicals in the wood, their bowler hats fly out over the audience and boomerang back in a Saturday matinee magician's trick, and upstage the twinkling stage stars sink suddenly from sight. Bottom traditionally wraps himself in a blanket when he whistles alone in the dark with the ass's head on him; here, the blanket is a piece of a stage drop, with grommets along the edge. In the final court scene, as Theseus/Oberon is saying "The best in this kind are but shadows . . . ," he finds himself astride the footlights set up for "Pyramus and Thisbe," one foot in and one foot out, and he finds a familiar resonance in the rest of the line: " . . . and the worst are no worse, if imagination mend them" [V. i. 211-12]. The costuming of Bottom as Pyramus renders Pyramus like a large Sicilian puppet, vestige of another venerable theatre of belief. Other things I cannot quite integrate: the mechanicals' entrance in the forest is made in sou'westers and umbrellas, to rehearse in the "rain," the sound effects of which we hear; and in one of Puck's entrances, he is lowered slowly from the grid riding on what appears to be a bomb, or is it heavy stage weights?

As I have said, some simply seek out the familiar play here amid fond Victorian trappings, and others go away irritated about oddities and novelties. Perhaps Daniels could have clarified its shape, but then the conception is not one susceptible to hard-handed handling. It is not a production that has the impact of "Brook's *Dream*;" rather, it is one that lingers, traveling the winding side streets of the mind. Its lovers are comic and engaging, yes, especially the diminutive Hermia of Jane Carr, with her small clenched fist of an angry voice. And

its mechanicals are likeable, prosaic lads. But we are aware of something more as we watch the company create the play amid the worn theatrical artifacts which in an earlier era conjured belief. Pervading all is the sense that they know it has been given to them to find the means to create faith here among the ruins. They are well-disposed, not disdainful, toward these relics of ancient belief-making; the better perhaps to understand how belief works. (The rehearsal period included study groups on Victorian stagecraft.) They are anxious and intent, yearning for means to faith of their own. This yearning is reminiscent of Brook's *Dream,* and like that production, this one would place its stake on irrational faith (which the play itself certainly suggests). But here no anxious claim is made to the exclusive authenticity of exuberant, erotic young love; there is no promise of a new and glorious replacement of an old world of deceit, no ecstatic born-again salvation.

Here, the sense of surrounding darkness is palpable and the yearning is for some personal reconciliation of light and dark. In response, the production creates the dance of a fairy king and queen of deeper shadows, a dance in which beauty exists and truth is as sure as it ever can be by virtue of what they and we, together, make of the dance. Another image of reconciliation occurs at the end, when Oberon and the black puppet Puck shake hands, making the fairy family whole, a compact made against the void between ephemeral spirits. These moments of reconciliation are quite poignant in the theatrical moment, and they probe very near the suggestion in Shakespeare's play that poets and lovers, actors and spectators can, probably, with imagination and faith, create order and purpose in a shadow-world: but it is a precarious dance. (pp. 60-4)

> *Gary Jay Williams, "A Dance for Our Disbeliefs: The Current 'A Midsummer Night's Dream' of the RSC," in* Theater, *Vol. 13, No. 2, Summer-Fall, 1982, pp. 60-4.*

COMPARISONS AND OVERVIEWS

William Winter   (essay date 1892)

[*Winter surveys the American stage history of* A Midsummer Night's Dream *and provides a consideration of the most "suitable method in the acting" of the play. "The essential need of acting, in a portrayal of this play," he states, "is whimsicality—but it must be whimsicality exalted by poetry."*]

A Midsummer Night's Dream was popular in Shakespeare's time. Mention of it, as impliedly a play in general knowledge and acceptance, was made by Taylor, the water poet, in 1622 [in his *Sir Gregory Nonsence*].

A piece called *The Fairy Queen,* being Shakespeare's comedy, with music by Purcell, was published in London in 1692. It had been acted there, at the Haymarket—the presentation being made with fine scenery and elaborate mechanism. There is another old piece, called *The Merry-Conceited Humours of Bottom the Weaver.* This was made out of an episode in the Dream, and it is included in the collection of farces attributed to Robert Cox, a comedian of the time of Charles I., published in 1672. A comic masque, by Richard Leveridge, similarly derived, entitled *Pyramus and Thisbe,* was performed at Lincoln's Inn Fields theatre, and was published in 1716. Two other musical farces, with this same title and origin, are recorded—one by Mr. Lampe, acted at Covent Garden, and published in 1745; the other by W. C. Oulton, acted at Birmingham, and published in 1798. Garrick made an acting copy of *A Midsummer Night's Dream*—adding to the text as well as curtailing it, and introducing songs—and this was played at Drury Lane, where it failed, and was published in 1763. Colman reduced Garrick's piece to two acts, and called it *A Fairy Tale,* and in this form it was tried at Drury Lane, and published in 1764 and 1777. Colman, however, wrote: "I was little more than a godfather on the occasion, and the alterations should have been subscribed Anon." The best production of this comedy ever accomplished on the English stage was that effected by Charles Kean, at the Princess's theatre, London,—managed by him from August 1850 till August 29, 1859.

The first performance of *A Midsummer Night's Dream* given in America occurred at the old Park theatre, for the benefit of Mrs. Hilson, on November 9, 1826. Ireland, in his valuable records [*Records of the New York Stage*], has preserved a part of the cast, rescued from a mutilated copy of the playbill of that night: Theseus, Mr. Lee; Bottom, Mr. Hilson; Snout, Mr. Placide; Oberon, Peter Richings; Puck, Mrs. Hilson; Titania, Mrs. Sharpe; Hippolita, Mrs. Stickney; Hermia, Mrs. Hackett. On August 30, 1841 the comedy was again revived at that theatre, with a cast that included Mr. Fredericks as Theseus, W. H. Williams as Bottom, Mrs. Knight as Puck, Charlotte Cushman as Oberon, Mary Taylor as Titania, Susan Cushman as Helena, Mrs. Groves as Hippolita, Miss Buloid (afterward Mrs. Abbott) as Hermia, and William Wheatley as Lysander. The next revivals came on February 3 and 6, 1854, at Burton's theatre and at the Broadway theatre, rival houses, with these casts:

	At Broadway.	*At Burton's.*
Theseus	F. B. Conway	Charles Fisher.
Lysander	Lannergan	George Jordan.
Demetrius	Grosvenor	W. H. Norton.
Egeus	Matthews	Moore.
Bottom	William Davidge	W. E. Burton.
Quince	Howard	T. Johnston.
Flute	Whiting	G. Barrett.
Snug	Fisk	Russell.
Snout	Henry	G. Andrews.
Puck	Viola Crocker	Parsloe.
Oberon	Mme. Ponisi	Miss E. Raymond.
Titania	Mrs. Abbott	Mrs. Burton.
Hippolita	Mrs. Warren	Mrs. J. Cooke.
Hermia	Mrs. Nagle	Mrs. Hough.
Helena	A. Gougenheim	Mrs. Buckland.

Great stress, in both cases, was laid upon Mendelssohn's music. At each house it ran for a month. It was not revived in New York again until April 18, 1859, when Laura Keene brought it forward at her theatre, and kept it on till May 28, with C. W. Couldock as Theseus, William Rufus Blake as Bottom, Miss Macarthy as Oberon, Miss Stevens as Helena, Ada Clifton as Hermia, and herself as Puck. It was a failure. Even Blake failed as Bottom,—an acute critic of that period, Edward G. P. Wilkins, describing the performance as "not funny, not even grotesque, but vulgar and unpleasant." Charles Peters was good as Thisbe. The stage version used was made by Richard Grant White. That same theatre subsequently became the Olympic (not Mitchell's, but the second of that name), and there, on October 28, 1867, under the management of James E. Hayes and the direction of Joseph Jefferson, who had brought from London a Grecian panorama by Telbin, *A Midsummer Night's Dream* was again offered, with a cast that included G. L. Fox as Bottom, W. Davidge as Quince, Owen Marlowe as Flute, Cornelia Jefferson as Titania, and Clara Fisher as Peasblossom. Telbin's panorama displayed the country supposed to lie between Athens and the forest wherein the Fairy Queen and the lovers are enchanted and bewitched and the sapient Bottom is "translated." Fox undertook Bottom, for the first time, and he was drolly consequential and stolidly conceited in it. Landseer's famous picture of Titania and the ass-headed Bottom was copied in one of the scenes. Mr. Hayes provided a shining tableau at the close. Mendelssohn's music was played and sung, with excellent skill and effect—the chief vocalist being Clara Fisher. Owen Marlowe, as Thisbe, gave a burlesque of the manner of Rachel. The comedy, as then given, ran for one hundred nights—from October 28, 1867 till February 1, 1868. The stage version used was that of Charles Kean.

The next production of *A Midsummer Night's Dream* was effected by Augustin Daly, at the Grand Opera House, on August 19, 1873. The scenery then employed was of extraordinary beauty—delicate in colour, sensuous in feeling, sprightly in fancy. Fox again played Bottom. The attentive observer of the stage version made by Augustin Daly,—and conspicuously used by him when he revived the piece at his theatre on January 31, 1888,—would observe that much new and effective stage business was introduced. The disposition of the groups at the start was fresh, and so was the treatment of the quarrel between Oberon and Titania, with the disappearance of the Indian child. The moonlight effects, in the transition from act second to act third, and the gradual assembly of goblins and fairies in shadowy mists through which the fire-flies glimmered, at the close of act third, were novel and beautiful. Cuts and transpositions were made at the end of the fourth act, in order to close it with the voyage of the barge of Theseus, through a summer landscape, on the silver stream that rippled down to Athens. The third act was judiciously compressed, so that the spectator might not see too much of the perplexed and wrangling lovers. But little of the original text was omitted. The music for the choruses was selected from various English composers—that of Mendelssohn being prescribed only for the orchestra.

The accepted doctrine of traditional criticism—a doctrine made seemingly potent by reiteration—that *A Midsummer Night's Dream* is not for the stage, need not necessarily be considered final. Hazlitt was the first to insist on that idea [in the *Examiner,* 21 January 1816]. "Poetry and the stage," said that famous writer, "do not agree well together. The attempt to reconcile them, in this instance, fails not only of effect, but of decorum. The ideal can have no place upon the stage, which is a picture without perspective. The imagination cannot sufficiently qualify the actual impression of the senses." But this is only saying that there are difficulties. The remark applies to all the higher forms of dramatic literature; and, logically, if that doctrine were observed in practice, none of the great plays would be attempted. *A Midsummer Night's Dream,* with all its ideal spirit, is dramatic; it ought not to be lost to the stage; and to some extent, certainly, the difficulties can be surmounted. In the spirit of a dream the play was written, and in the spirit of a dream it can be acted. (pp. 169-75)

With reference to the question of suitable method in the acting of *A Midsummer Night's Dream* it may be observed that too much stress can scarcely be laid upon the fact that this comedy was conceived and written absolutely in the spirit of a dream. It ought not, therefore, to be treated as a rational manifestation of orderly design. It possesses, indeed, a coherent and symmetrical plot and a definite purpose; but, while it moves toward a final result of absolute order, it presupposes intermediary progress through a realm of motley shapes and fantastic vision. Its persons are creatures of the fancy, and all effort to make them solidly actual, to set them firmly upon the earth, and to accept them as realities of common life, is labour ill-bestowed. To body forth the form of things is, in this case, manifestly, a difficult task: and yet the true course is obvious. Actors who yield themselves to the spirit of whim, and drift along with it, using a delicate method and avoiding insistence upon prosy realism, will succeed with this piece—provided, also, that their audience can be fanciful, and can accept the performance, not as a comedy of ordinary life but as a vision seen in a dream. The play is full of intimations that this was Shakespeare's mood. Even Bottom, the consummate flower of unconscious humour, is at his height of significance in his moment of supreme illusion:

> I have had a dream,—past the wit of man to say what dream it was:—Man is but an ass if he go about to expound this dream. Methought I was—there is no man can tell what. Methought I was, and methought I had—But man is but a patched fool if he will offer to say what methought I had. The eye of man hath not heard, the ear of man hath not seen, man's hand is not able to taste, his tongue to conceive, nor his heart to report, what my dream was.

The whole philosophy of the subject, comically stated, is there. A serious statement of it is in the words of the poet Campbell:—

> Well may sleep present us fictions,
> Since our waking moments teem
> With such fanciful convictions
> As make life itself a dream.

Various actors in the past—although *A Midsummer Night's Dream* has not had great currency upon the stage, at any period, whether in England or America—have laid a marked stress upon the character of Bottom. Samuel Phelps, upon the London stage, was esteemed excellent in it. He acted the part in his production of the Dream, at Sadler's Wells, and he again acted it in 1870 at the Queen's theatre, in Long Acre—now demolished. On the American stage William E. Burton was accounted wonderfully good in it. "As Burton renders the character," says Richard Grant White, "its traits are brought out with a delicate and masterly hand; its humour is exquisite." And William L. Keese, in his careful biography of Burton, makes equally cordial reference to that achievement of the great comedian: "How striking it was in sustained individuality, and how finely exemplified was the potential vanity of Bottom! What pleased us greatly was the vein of engaging raillery which ran through the delivery of his speeches to the fairies." Burton produced the Dream at his theatre, in 1854, with such wealth of fine scenery as in those days was accounted prodigious. The most notable impersonation of Bottom that has been given since Burton's time was, probably, that of George L. Fox. Self-conceit, as the essence of the character, was thoroughly well understood and expressed by him. He wore the ass's head, but he did not know

that he was wearing it; and when, afterward, the vague sense of it came upon him for an instant, he put it by as something inconceivable and intolerable. His "Not a word of me!" [IV. ii. 34]—spoken to the other hard-handed men of Athens, after his return to them out of the enchanted "palace wood"—was his finest single point. Certainly it expressed to the utmost the colossal self-love and swelling pomposity of this miracle of bland and opaque sapience. The essential need of acting, in a portrayal of this play, is whimsicality—but it must be whimsicality exalted by poetry. (pp. 181-84)

> William Winter, "Fairy Land: 'A Midsummer Night's Dream'," in his Old Shrines and Ivy, Macmillan and Company, 1892, pp. 163-86.

Harold Child　(essay date 1924)

[*In the excerpt below, Child traces the English stage history of* A Midsummer Night's Dream.]

Meres mentions *A Midsummer-Night's Dream* in *Palladis Tamia* (1598). The title-page of the quarto of 1600 says that it had been publicly acted by the Lord Chamberlain's servants. In 1624, a Protestant writer, John Gee, mentions in his book, *New Shreds of the Old Snare*, the comedy of '*Piramus and Thisbe*, where one comes in with a Lanthorne and Acts Mooneshine.' In his *Works*, published in 1630, John Taylor, the water-poet, calls the play by its true name, and quotes the prologue to the clowns' tragedy (Address to Nobody, prefixed to *Sir Gregory Nonsence his Newes from No Place*). Evidently, the play, or some part of it, held the stage in the reigns of James I and Charles I; but the title given to it by Gee might suggest that already the popularity of the clowns had led to their being separated from the comedy, as they have been since in a hundred theatres, and in innumerable school speech-days. They were certainly so separated after the closing of the theatres in 1642. Their rehearsal and performance were turned, as Francis Kirkman records in *The Wits*, into one of the 'humours and pieces of Plays, which . . . were only allowed us, and that but by stealth too, and under pretence of Rope-dancing, or the like.' This 'droll,' called *The Merry Conceited Humors of Bottom the Weaver*, was published separately by Kirkman and Marsh in 1661, and included by Kirkman in *The Wits* in 1673. The characters are the clowns, Oberon and Titania (who are 'doubled' with 'the Duke and Dutchess') and 'Pugg.' It is pure Shakespeare.

The droll was popular; the comedy as a whole did not suit the taste of the Restoration. It was one of the Shakespeare plays chosen by Killigrew for the King's company when he and D'Avenant divided the repertory; but only one performance of it under his management is recorded: that which Pepys saw at the theatre in Verestreet on September 29, 1662: 'To the King's Theatre, where we saw "Midsummer's Night's Dream," which I had never seen before, nor shall ever again, for it is the most insipid ridiculous play that ever I saw in my life.' True, it offered him 'some good dancing and some handsome women, which was all my pleasure'; and his words imply that this was not the first time that it had been given since acting began again; but the production was probably simple and without the allure of spectacle. It was not till later in the seventeenth century that the theatre, having elaborated its scenic devices and created a taste for display, discovered that some of Shakespeare's comedies made good raw material for scenes, machines and music. In 1692 Betterton produced at the Queen's Theatre (formerly called Dorset Garden, and famous under D'Avenant for spectacle) an operatic and spectacular piece, *The Fairy Queen* (published by Tonson in 1692), founded upon Shakespeare's play. The course of the comedy was not much altered, except that Hippolyta was left out, and the clowns' play was transferred to the third act and performed in the wood. The object of this change was doubtless to leave more room in the last act for the spectacle, of which each act had one and the last act the most sumptuous, with a chorus of Chinesas, a dance of six monkeys, a Chinese garden, and what not. Shakespeare's verse was much changed to suit the contemporary taste; and music by Henry Purcell was among the attractions of what seems to have been Betterton's supreme achievement in this kind of thing. 'The Court and Town,' says Downes, the prompter, 'were wonderfully satisfy'd with it; but the Expences in setting it out being so great, the Company got little by it.' That story has been heard in the theatre since. By 1703 *The Fairy Queen* had shrunk to be a one-act interlude in a concert.

Betterton's example was soon followed and outdone. During more than a century, the comedy was frequently and ruthlessly adapted into an opera. John Rich, carrying on at Lincoln's Inn Fields the tradition of spectacle and music, produced there, on October 19, 1716, as an after-piece to Thomas Jevon's farce, *The Devil of a Wife*, a work by Richard Leveridge, entitled *The Comick Masque of Pyramus and Thisbe* (published in 1716). Leveridge did much what the droll had done before. He took the clowns and left out the lovers; and he is scarcely to be blamed, seeing that his little masque was 'composed in the high stile of Italy'; that is, as a jest at the craze for Italian opera. Three musicians, Semibreve, Crochet and Gamut, attend a rehearsal of the clowns' play and use up some of the Athenians' comments, adding many all their own. Everyone sings, including the lion. With Spiller as Bottom (replaced by Leveridge himself when Bottom assumed the singing part of Pyramus), the mock opera was played more than once as an after-piece to *Timon of Athens*, and at least once after *The Gamester*. At Drury Lane on January 9, 1723, the clowns' play, pretty much as Shakespeare wrote it, was pitchforked by Charles Johnson into *Love in a Forest*, his version of *As You Like It*, for the amusement of the banished Duke and his fellows in the forest. On January 25, 1745, Covent Garden produced, as an after-piece to *The Miser*, an enlarged version by the German musician, John Frederick Lampe, of Leveridge's mock opera, with many new songs, Beard playing Pyramus and Mrs Lampe Thisbe. For ten years this Leveridge-Lampe travesty was all that the stage knew of *A Midsummer-Night's Dream*. They were acting it as late as 1754.

Then, in February, 1755, a grand new perversion of the play was presented by Garrick at Drury Lane. It was called *The Fairies* (published 1755), and the compiler (probably Garrick himself) turned the tables on the previous adapters by leaving out the clowns and with them, of course, the ass's head, thereby obscuring the story of Oberon and Titania. The prologue attributed the play to 'Signor Shakespearelli'; and on seeing in the cast the names of Signor Curioni as Lysander and Signora Passerini as Hermia we do not need to be assured that this 'blessed exhibition,' as Tate Wilkinson called it [in his *Memoirs of his Own Life*], was but another opera. The music was chiefly by Smith. The songs were taken from many sources, including Shakespeare's other plays, Dryden, and Milton. The dialogue was cut freely, though but little rewritten. Beard, a famous singer, was the Theseus, and the fairies were all played by children. Four performances are recorded,

and the whole run was estimated at nine. But Garrick's Drury Lane had not done with *A Midsummer-Night's Dream*. During Garrick's absence abroad, a piece bearing that title was performed on its stage in November, 1763 (printed 1763). Whether Garrick himself, or his deputy, the elder Colman, were responsible for it—and each blamed it on the other—it was a dead failure, and was performed no more than once. It was an opera, of course, with the clowns this time partially restored, though most of their play was left out; and with Yates for Bottom, Baddeley for Flute, and Parsons for Starveling, that part of it at least must have been well acted and sung. Colman saved what he could of it by cutting out Theseus and Hippolyta and the lovers (though Miss Young had played Hermia and Mrs Vincent Helena) and making the opera into an after-piece, which he called *A Fairy-Tale*. This proved a useful little stop-gap. It is found on the stage of Drury Lane as late as 1768, and again at the Haymarket in the summer of 1777, when it was first printed. The clowns' play is left out altogether, and though Bottom is lured off by Puck there is no mention of his wearing the ass's head when he returns—his natural clownishness being sufficient, it must be presumed, to make Titania's passion ridiculous. The last news of the play in the eighteenth century is from Bath, where in March, 1794, Blisset plays Bottom in a *Comical Tragedy of Pyramus and Thisbe*, and a fortnight or so later Elliston plays Bottom in *A Midsummer-Night's Dream*. What relation this piece or these pieces bore to Shakespeare's work there is no telling now.

The eighteenth century had evidently been puzzled about the unity and proportions of a play composed of three pretty distinct elements: fairies, human lovers and clowns. It had picked and chosen, generally the clowns. The nineteenth century very soon shows someone at least trying to see the play as a whole, instead of snippeting it into after-pieces and burlesques. In January, 1816, John Philip Kemble, nearing the end of his reign at Covent Garden, produced (but did not act in) a version by Frederic Reynolds (printed 1816)—an operatic version still, with music by Henry Bishop, supplemented with songs by Arne and Smith. Thus did Reynolds enter on his evil, successful career of making operas out of Shakespeare. 'Not acted 50 years,' says the bill: 'not acted two hundred years, and not yet to be acted' would have been nearer the mark. John Kemble's production not only borrowed from the two Drury Lane versions: it went back to Betterton by misplacing the clowns' play so as to leave room in the last act for a display, not indeed of Chineses and monkeys, but of the victories of Theseus. The scenery and pageantry are recorded as very elaborate and splendid; and with Liston as Bottom, Emery as Quince, Miss Stephens as Hermia, Miss Foote as Helena, Miss Sally Booth as Puck and Mrs Faucit as Titania, the acting ought to have been very good. But by 1816 certain people had discovered that Shakespeare knew his job as playwright better than to deserve such alteration; and one of them, Hazlitt, was moved to a famous outburst. In *The Examiner* of January 21, 1816, he wrote: 'All that is fine in the play, was lost in the representation. The spirit was evaporated, the genius was fled; but the spectacle was fine: it was that which saved the play. Oh, ye scene-shifters, ye scene-painters, ye machinists and dressmakers, ye manufacturers of moon and stars that give no light, ye musical composers, ye men in the orchestra, fiddlers and trumpeters and players on the double drum and loud bassoon, rejoice! This is your triumph; it is not ours: and ye full-grown, well-fed, substantial, real fairies, . . . we shall remember you: we shall believe no more in the existence of your fantastic tribe. . . . All that was good in this piece (except the scenery) was Mr Liston's Bottom.' He sums up with a principle favoured in his time: 'Poetry and the stage do not agree together. . . . The *ideal* has no place upon the stage, which is a picture without perspective; every thing there is in the foreground. That which is merely an airy shape, a dream, a passing thought, immediately becomes an unmanageable reality.'

The theatre listened to Hazlitt no more than it has listened to any critic. He had been in his grave two years when, forgetting even John Kemble's attempt to give the play as a whole, Covent Garden squeezed into a musical version of *All's Well That Ends Well* a masque called *Oberon and Robin Goodfellow*; and a year later, in November, 1833, Alfred Bunn serves up at Drury Lane an after-piece in two acts, with music which Professor Odell describes [in his *Shakespeare—from Betterton to Irving*] as 'compiled from all the Midsummer Night's Dreams that had disgraced the stage from Garrick to Reynolds.' A decade after Hazlitt's death, however, some of his, or Coleridge's, or Lamb's, ideas about Shakespeare as poet and playwright had penetrated into the theatre; and, to judge from contemporary accounts, Hazlitt himself might have approved the production of *A Midsummer-Night's Dream* given by Mme Vestris and Charles Mathews as a play, not an opera, in November, 1840, during their second season at Covent Garden. J. R. Planché, who made the version for them, kept closely to Shakespeare. He used nothing that was not in Shakespeare's original: he even saw that Shakespeare's own ending to the play made a better final scene for it than any pageant of them all. Some attempt at archaeological accuracy in the dresses seems to have resulted, at any rate, in beauty; the scenery, by the Grieves, aiming also, in its degree, at fidelity to ancient Athens, was much admired; and the music, composed and selected by T. Cooke, included 'Mendelssohn's celebrated overture.'

Samuel Phelps's production at Sadler's Wells in October, 1853, would have come yet nearer than that of the pioneer Mme Vestris to convincing Hazlitt that poetry and the stage might agree together, and that a stage moon might give light. From the accounts left by Henry Morley and others, this may be concluded to be the most Shakespearian production that had ever been given; and at least it was not surpassed in the nineteenth century. Bottom was one of Phelps's best parts, and he played it again in September, 1870, at the Queen's Theatre, Long Acre. But better even than the acting of Phelps and of his capable, undistinguished company at Sadler's Wells was the dream-like, fairy-like atmosphere of the whole production. When Charles Kean staged the comedy at the Princess's Theatre in October, 1856, with a cast that included neither himself nor his wife, but gave Bottom to Harley and Puck to a child of eight named Ellen Terry, he lost the dream and the fairy feeling. He cut Shakespeare down a good deal to make room for spectacle, some of which (especially that obvious absurdity, a shadow-dance by fairies) was severely blamed by good critics. The whole was found wanting in poetry, no matter what its archaeological pretensions and its splendour. And this fault of missing the poetry may be charged against some subsequent productions. There have been a good many in the last three or four decades, all attempting, not all succeeding, to get back to Shakespeare's own idea of the unity and the proportions of his play. Mr F. R. Benson gave it in London in 1889 and 1890. Daly gave it—only moderately altered—at Daly's Theatre in 1895, with Miss Ada Rehan not at her most interesting as Helena. Tree very sumptuously gave it at Her Majesty's Theatre in 1900;

and again in 1911, when Mr Arthur Bourchier replaced him in the part of Bottom and the poetry of the enchanted wood was sought by means of live rabbits on the stage. In contrast with this were the sound, unextravagant production by Mr Oscar Asche at the Adelphi in 1895; and the pretty version of Mr Oscar Barrett at the Crystal Palace in 1896. In 1908 the Oxford University Dramatic Society essayed it; in 1916 the boys of Bradfield College gave it freshly and pleasantly in their Gray Pit, or Greek theatre.

In 1914 the twentieth century brought its ideas of the production of Shakespeare to bear on the comedy that had puzzled the eighteenth and mainly defeated the nineteenth. Those ideas include the abandonment of elaborate staging and of archaeological accuracy. By means of an 'apron-stage,' more or less corresponding to the Shakespearian platform-stage, and of simple, easily changed scenery, they attempt almost continuous performance of the complete text; and they replace archaeology with a distinct poetic or 'atmospheric' convention for each play. A capital instance of these aims was given by Mr Granville Barker's production of *A Midsummer-Night's Dream* on the temporary 'apron-stage' of the Savoy Theatre. Details in the production were hotly attacked, and nothing in it more hotly than Mr Norman Wilkinson's scenery and costumes, in which the fairies were remarkable for their Oriental style and their gilded faces—Eastern creatures, and made of moonshine. There was some freakishness about it all; but the production achieved, within its rather strange convention of style, its purpose, which was to preserve the proportions of Shakespeare's play as he left them, and to steep the whole in the strangeness of moonlight and of dream. The play was staged on similar lines at the Kingsway Theatre in November, 1923. (pp. 160-68)

> *Harold Child, "The Stage-History," in* A Midsummer-Night's Dream *by William Shakespeare, edited by Arthur Quiller-Couch and John Dover Wilson, Cambridge at the University Press, 1924, pp. 160-68.*

Ralph Richardson   (essay date 1957)

[*A distinguished British actor, Richardson performed the role of Bottom in numerous productions, including Tyrone Guthrie's 1937 production at the Old Vic Theatre. In the following excerpt, Richardson offers a selective overview of the stage history of* A Midsummer Night's Dream. *This essay first appeared as the introduction to the Folio Society edition of the* Dream *(1957).*]

The stage history of *A Midsummer Night's Dream* has been, in miniature, much the same as those of its more popular fellows in the Shakespeare canon—it has reflected the passing pageant of theatrical fancy. The text has been decimated to provide at least one opera, Oberon has been played by a succession of women, and the fairies have appeared in gold, in green, in red, as Romantic ballet dancers and as street urchins. But the play's inherent qualities have kept it consistently before the public. There are, of course, innumerable opportunities for scenic extravagance and ingenuity, opportunities of which every age has taken full advantage. Although it contains no great role, it does have a well balanced cast of characters excellently chosen for their variety, all of them amusing to watch and exciting to perform. But above all there runs through the play an atmosphere of enchantment and gaiety which unifies the diverse elements, the boisterous 'mechanicals', the comedy of mistaken identities, the touches of malevolence and the poetry, into one, timeless whole.

It is generally accepted that 'The Dream' was not originally written for the public, but as a masque for a private celebration, and, to judge from the events in the play itself, almost certainly for a wedding. It was then recast into its present form for public performance at the Globe, between 1598 and 1600. A most imaginative reconstruction of an early performance is the theme of *Moonlight at the Globe* by Ronald Watkins. As he shows, the actual scenic resources would have been slight but extremely well adapted to the quick pace of the action and to the broad daylight in which the play was given. Both these factors have been completely lacking in the playhouses which have existed since the Restoration, where scenery has tended to slow down the action and swamp the poetry.

Undoubtedly at its first, private, performance, *A Midsummer Night's Dream* would have had that lavish decoration that the Elizabethans were wont to give their masques, and the provision for this did not disappear from the text when the play was translated to the public stage. It is not surprising, then, that although the actual play did not please at the Restoration, it did provide a quarry for the anonymous librettist of *The Fairy Queen,* an opera-spectacle by Purcell. The pedestrian level of the adaptation and its complete negation of the original poetry is saved by Purcell's vividly pictorial music. Although no longer Shakespeare, *The Fairy Queen* is still enjoyable entertainment, as those who saw its revival at Covent Garden in 1946 can testify.

During the eighteenth century *A Midsummer Night's Dream* appeared irregularly, but with the middle of the nineteenth it entered a new phase in its history. An early female Oberon, Madame Vestris, an actress of considerable personality, at Covent Garden, and Samuel Phelps at Sadlers Wells, re-established 'The Dream' in public favour. From then on, for some sixty years, most of the actors and actresses of note appeared in it. Ellen Terry played Puck in 1856; Phelps, George Weir, Arthur Bourchier, Oscar Asche, Nigel Playfair, Beerbohm Tree, all played Bottom; Lysander was played by such matinée idols as Lewis Waller, Basil Gill, Forbes Robertson; and Hermia and Helena by Ada Rehan, Lilah Macarthy, Laura Cowie, Mrs Benson and Julia Nielson.

The productions in which they all appeared were models of historical accuracy and realism, for this was the order of the day. The British Museum was ransacked for designs to deck Theseus' palace, and A Wood near Athens became the butt of all those who disliked their stage forests full of real rabbits, real bracken and real waterfalls. A revolution was due. It came in 1914, a year that saw the disintegration of so much that had been accepted for so long. Harley Granville Barker, whose productions, in the words of a contemporary critic, 'had already swept the stage of some of its close clinging cobwebs of convention', turned his attention to 'The Dream'. *The Daily Telegraph* describes 'the apron stage, the decorative curtains for a background and only two set scenes . . . The Palace of Theseus is a place of massive white columns with black decorations and a background of star-spangled black yielding to reddish-purple.' The Wood seems also to have been of a striking simplicity and to have set the pattern for most of the subsequent revivals.

My own first meeting with 'The Dream' was when I studied it with my schoolmaster in the manner prescribed for the ex-

amination. Everything about the play was anatomized—the internal and external evidence, the strong and weak endings, the sources of the plot—a dry-as-bones examination with never one word to let in the idea that the work had been written first and foremost as a work of entertainment, of delight and of laughter. All that was a strict taboo, something quite unheard of, but as far as I was concerned, this attempted desecration was completely unsuccessful.

It has always seemed to me that from every point of view *A Midsummer Night's Dream* is a perfect play, and I feel that Pepys' dislike of it is one of the oddest curiosities of literature.

It is certainly perfect from the actor's point of view. Every single part in it is a joy to play, and an actor, in his desire to play all of them, might well echo the similar sentiments of Bully Bottom.

There are no difficulties with any of them, no awkwardness to overcome, no unaccounted links missing, no shady corners of obscurity—the only difficulty lies in drawing them to perfection.

But even though I have never seen a bad production of the play, I have equally never seen a perfect one. The demand for a flawless string of matched pearls is all but impossible to realize.

When I myself study a part in Shakespeare, I try to find out all I can about it, reading the text in as many forms as possible, including a photostat that I possess of the first *Folio*. But I am always conscious of the fact that Shakespeare—in the printed page or acted on the stage—must always come to us at second hand, and that the real naked body of the play will never be embraced by man in this world; the incarnation existed only once in time—in the mind of the author William.

I have had the happiness of essaying many parts in this play, and I have played Bottom in many productions. Once, to my shame, when I was nineteen, I fell asleep in the part, while waiting out of sight behind the fairy bank after the ass's head had been taken off. I also played the part in Tyrone Guthrie's production at the Old Vic in 1937. The whole production was a deliberate harking back to the Victorians, with Mendelssohn's music, Taglioni fairies, and the spirit of 'tuppence coloured' pervading everywhere. It was produced at Christmastime in that pantomime atmosphere of magic and high spirits which has made this one of the best loved of all Shakespeare's plays. (pp. 77-9)

Ralph Richardson, "A Midsummer Night's Dream," in Introductions to Shakespeare: Being the Introductions to the Individual Plays in the Folio Society Edition, 1950-76, *Michael Joseph, 1978, pp. 77-9.*

Roger Warren   (essay date 1982)

[*In the excerpt below, Warren compares two 1981 productions of* A Midsummer Night's Dream, *the first a performance of Benjamin Britten's operatic version of the play directed by Peter Hall at the Glyndebourne Music Festival; the second is Ron Daniels's RSC staging at Stratford-upon-Avon. Warren lauds the Glyndebourne production, judging it a "complex, absorbing blend of Britten's and Peter Hall's responses to Shakespeare's play, executed with exceptional professional flair and imagination." He is much less admiring of Daniels's offering, claiming it is "less a coherent interpretation than a series of haphazard effects from the Victorian theatre."*]

Both Benjamin Britten and Peter Hall made notable contributions to the interpretation of *A Midsummer Night's Dream* in the early 1960s, Britten in an operatic version so imaginative as to amount to a re-creation of the essence of the play, Peter Hall in a developing series of RSC productions which brought out the close relationship between the court and the surrounding countryside, set in an Elizabethan manor house which was easily transformed into a wood. When he came to direct Britten's opera at Glyndebourne in 1981, he developed this approach still further, modifying it to reflect the distinctive qualities of Britten's score. The total impression was of a complex, absorbing blend of Britten's and Peter Hall's responses to Shakespeare's play, executed with exceptional professional flair and imagination.

The opera begins in the wood, introducing passages from Shakespeare's first act later, and Britten makes this wood a living presence, expressed in orchestral sighs and breaths, marked 'slowly animating'. Peter Hall and John Bury, his designer, established this presence from the outset: in dim light, branches, bushes, and logs, animated by black-clad mutes, moved mysteriously and absolutely precisely to the musical phrases, on a shiny floor which reflected the light in such a way as to hint at the water-logged weather of Titania's account. Puck (Damien Nash, a boy-actor of astonishing flexibility) was a cockney urchin; the other boy-fairies combined Elizabethan doublets and helmets with pixies' ears, fairy guardsmen ('pensioners') who carried branches like halberds and who snapped to attention in perfect unison at the percussion flourish which emphasizes that they 'serve the Fairy Queen'.

At Stratford Peter Hall had captured Shakespeare's blend of the courtly and the rural by dressing Oberon and Titania in splendid Elizabethan court clothes whose fabric also suggested cobwebs and gossamer, with bushy, misty grey wigs. At Glyndebourne this was taken a stage further: Oberon's wig was streaked with black like a badger, and the combination of this with his pale face, ear-ring, and Elizabethan ruffed collar matched Britten's emphasis on the weird and non-human in the part. James Bowman has unusual vocal power for a counter-tenor, but neither he nor Ileana Cotrubas (Titania) had the clarity of diction or variety of personality to dominate quite as much as both Shakespeare and Britten require. Perhaps they blended a little too closely with the dark foliage; at any rate, when the moon came out with the arrival of the lovers, four outstanding performers projected their roles with precisely the clarity and authority that seemed lacking in the fairy rulers, and so the centre of gravity moved from the fairies to them.

This was certainly a major development from Peter Hall's first Stratford version in 1959, when John Russell Brown complained in *Shakespeare Survey 13* that the lovers' scenes were presented as a 'continual, unrelieved and not very resourceful burlesque'. Although the basically humorous approach remained, it was toned down in subsequent revivals, and their Hilliard finery replaced by a more workaday, comfortable Jacobean style, which the Glyndebourne lovers also wore, and which became progressively dirtier in the wood. But the characterizations at Glyndebourne were much subtler, eloquent and impassioned, without any loss of humour. Indeed, these were the best performances of these parts I have ever seen anywhere, greatly helped by the composer: Britten expands Hermia's 'I swear to thee' [I. i. 169] into a passionate duet which Ryland Davies and Cynthia Buchan projected

with beautiful clarity. The other pair was better still: Dale Duesing's Demetrius had so much personality that he almost (but not quite) unbalanced the quartet: 'O Helen, goddess, nymph, perfect, divine' [III. ii. 137] was a tremendous moment; it led to a superbly paced quarrel, phrases whipping back and forth at breakneck speed with no loss of rhythmic precision. Britten transforms Helena's saccharine recollections of schooldays with Hermia into something more heartfelt; Felicity Lott managed a delicious transition from the velvet glove here to the claw within when she calls Hermia a 'vixen' and—fatal word—'puppet': the rhythms at this point exactly suggest Hermia's increasing rage, and she was beautifully supported by the constantly changing reactions of the other three, from amusement to nervousness to genuine alarm. This was a major climax, a blend of humour and human feeling which is absolutely characteristic of Shakespearian comedy.

While Peter Hall fully brought out the way in which Britten unerringly captures this blend here and in the Titania/Bottom encounter, he was able to draw on his earlier productions to bring off Britten's less inspired treatment of the play scene. Theseus is introduced here for the first time, and the doggerel of *Pyramus and Thisbe* is interpreted in terms of the threadbare cliché of much nineteenth-century Italian opera. Sir Peter gave the scene a real context by introducing the Elizabethan country-house atmosphere of his Stratford versions, warm red brick, casement windows, a log fire, and a trestle stage for the mechanicals. The mechanicals themselves played strictly in character without labouring Britten's jokes, with very funny results: they took their acting very seriously, especially Patrick Power's Flute, flinging himself into Thisbe's florid lament with a full-throated eloquence which irresistibly recalled celebrated Spanish tenors taking themselves equally seriously in just such threadbare repertoire as Britten is parodying. The return of the fairies was magical in every sense: as they gathered outside the windows, there was a powerful sense of a country house surrounded by a wood whose living presence had been so strongly established earlier. In his epilogue Puck swept the hall and reset the furniture as vigorously as, an act earlier, he had shaken the very last drops of magic juice into Lysander's eyes, exactly matching Britten's celesta phrase. Such down-to-earth detail is very characteristic of Peter Hall's approach to *A Midsummer Night's Dream*: 'Fairy tales must be concrete if they are to be human and not whimsical' [*The Sunday Times,* 26 January 1969].

At Stratford, meanwhile, were spirits of another sort. Ron Daniels set his RSC *Dream* in 'a society which was straightlaced yet could surrender to misrule at night' [*The Times,* 3 July 1981]: in a red-carpeted throne-room, Theseus and Hippolyta gingerly approached what the programme synopsis called 'a marriage of convenience between two strangers' wearing the stiff, formal military frogging of opposing sides, Hippolyta like the other women imprisoned in a vast crinoline. But this throne-room was so obviously penny-plain, tuppence-coloured that the over-all impression was less of a real society, straightlaced or otherwise, than of a Victorian stage set; but any idea that we might be watching a Victorian production of the play itself vanished when their 'misrule at night' took place, not even in a Victorian idea of a wood, but on the empty stage of a Victorian theatre, as was made clear by the downstage flat which had its frame side facing the audience.

Puck flew down on a counter-weight, and Peaseblossom and the rest were puppets manipulated by actors so that they could at the same time be small and yet be whirled rapidly around the stage; they were also extremely sinister (one with a smashed face), very like those hideous Victorian dolls beloved of the makers of horror films: the newts and blind-worms would have had heart-failure at the sight of this bunch. Oberon had to fight his way past a mass attack of screeching dolls to get at Titania's bower. There was no consistency about this fairy world: if their small size would have enabled them to creep into acorn cups, their nastiness instantly contradicted their opening phrase about cowslips and 'fairy favours' [II. i. 12]; even their threat to those newts and blind-worms was thwarted by the Victorian lullaby their manipulators were given to sing; and Oberon and Titania, in Arabian Nights glamour, were scarcely sinister at all.

The internal contradiction characterized the whole production. There seemed no reason why lovers fleeing from even a straightlaced society should wander on to the stage of a deserted theatre, nor why the mechanicals should rehearse there under umbrellas, in sou'westers and oilskins (which would obviously have made sense in a rainy wood). It seemed less a coherent interpretation than a series of haphazard effects from the Victorian theatre: tree borders flew in as Demetrius arrived in the 'wood'; Titania's bower was a prop tree-trunk built upon a chaise-longue; border lights flashed as the ass's head (scrawny and ugly, like the puppets, with buck teeth) appeared; cloud cloths were dropped to the floor behind and over the top of which Puck misled the duellists; the play scene was a mixture of pantomime (Pyramus in harlequin tights and Thisbe as the 'Dame'), music-hall (a piano commentary), and morris-dance (with Bottom, of course, wearing the horse's head).

The strengths and weaknesses of the performances seemed almost unrelated to the approach. The mechanicals were under-powered but had one nice moment of sheer consternation at the suggestion that they should learn their parts 'by tomorrow night' [I. ii. 100-01]. Helena's appearance as an adult Alice-in-Wonderland lent new edge to her nostalgia about schooldays with Hermia, but conflicted with Harriet Walter's Elizabethan directness elsewhere. The lovers' big quarrel scene was played for gales of laughter as in other productions, with Jane Carr's screeching housemaid of a Hermia, terrorizing not merely Helena but the men too, well over the top. They were laid to sleep not in pairs but in a general heap, enabling Mike Gwilym to wring even more wry humour than usual from Theseus's 'No doubt they rose up early to observe / The rite of May' and from his ironic greeting 'Good-morrow, friends. Saint Valentine is past' [IV. i. 132-33, 139] Simon Templeman made so much of Demetrius's lyrical speech about his rediscovered love for Helena that he moved Juliet Stevenson's Hippolyta to influence Theseus to overbear Egeus's will, although according to the production's theory they are 'two strangers'; and however 'straightlaced' his society, even at the start this courteous, considerate Theseus seated Hermia beside him to try to persuade rather than bully her out of opposition to her father, as the text of course suggests.

Mike Gwilym and Juliet Stevenson also played Oberon and Titania. The production seemed to offer no real connection between the two couples, and this doubling led, as it always does, to contrivance: their dance of amity had to be greatly prolonged, using stand-ins towards the end of it, to enable

them to change into elaborate Victorian riding outfits for their reappearance as Theseus and Hippolyta; and the dance itself, though well executed, uncomfortably suggested less a modern use of the Victorian theatre to convey nocturnal liberation than an old-fashioned balletic production; so did the follow-spots and the officious musical backing for Oberon's 'I know a bank' and 'we are spirits of another sort' [II. i. 249; III. ii. 388], which isolated them from their context in a quite unnecessarily artificial way. Mr Gwilym overcame these and the other liabilities by the sheer authority of his speaking and his personality; and he gave Miss Stevenson the sympathetic support in her finely delivered speech about the progeny of evils which Mr Daniels's context denied her. Indeed, I felt that these two very strong performances would have been even better in an interpretation, like Peter Hall's, derived from the language and events of the play. But it was certainly good to hear them both making the most of Theseus's and Hippolyta's hunt speeches, and to watch Mr Gwilym's relaxed, varied, good-humoured control of the play scene, unobtrusively handing out drinks to his guests at a soirée in the throne-room: it was the final irony that the production's stage-within-a-stage wasn't used when the text actually asks for one. (pp. 144-47)

Roger Warren, "Interpretations of Shakespearian Comedy, 1981," in Shakespeare Survey: An Annual Survey of Shakespearian Study and Production, Vol. 35, 1982, pp. 141-52.

STAGING ISSUES

Percy Fitzgerald   (essay date 1908)

[In the excerpt below, Fitzgerald offers suggestions regarding several aspects of staging A Midsummer Night's Dream, including the presentation of the fairies, the music, and the dancing.]

How are we to deal with fairies? This form of the supernatural has really suffered, if it has not been destroyed, by the conventions of the modern theatre. The notion of fairies in the Midsummer Night's Dream has furnished an excuse for a sort of grand pantomimic exhibition—crowds of little girls flitting about among the trees, each, it may be, carrying an electric lamp. They wind in and out, in serpentine fashion, uttering little chirps or screams. Sometimes a dance is arranged. It is, in fact, a sort of ballet show.

Now, our bard's idea of the supernaturals was that fairies should form an element of his play, and each should have a distinct individuality; they were to be characters. When he exhibits a ghost, he does not present a crowd; when he shows us witches, he makes each speak; when he introduces servants, he does not need a whole retinue, but gives each servant an individuality, much as Molière did later.

Oberon and Titania are important personages, people of great power, who control the course of the play, particularly in the case of the four lovers—Bottom, etc. They make long speeches, have their quarrels, and, in fact, dominate the whole piece. It is impossible to have respect for their power when we see them heading bands of little children, capering about, carrying lights, etc., and also, for no reason, so much smaller than themselves. There is no rule that a fairy should necessarily be a child. At the same time, it may be conceded that there is something pretty and poetical in such exhibitions. No, the notion of a fairy must be conveyed by the acting—by a sort of quaint uncanniness or queerness and oddity, with a certain airiness of bearing.

And this brings us to the difficult question of the class of performer that would be suitable to present them. Children or Lilliputian figures is an arbitrary assumption. Childhood has no necessary connexion with fairyland. Oberon and Titania are important acting parts, and no 'green girls' could do justice to them. Oberon should be played by a trained, intelligent youth, and Titania by a young woman. Then, for their retinue: no children again, for if the King and Queen be of mature age and stature, there is no reason why their followers should be of tender years—nay, it seems rather absurd. But again the real solution lies in the acting. It should be the *acting* of a fairy, according to our imagination and our lights. There should be a sort of airiness and irresponsibility, as though earthly matters were beneath them. This, of course, cannot be taught, but comes of instinct. With, say, a dozen graceful girls, with wings, if you like, each *acting* her part—constantly in movement, uncertain, peeping, hiding, disappearing—a telling effect would be produced.

Yet with all this we might be inclined to make an exception here, and be tolerant in this special case; for the spectacle of these flitting children is exceedingly pretty and poetical, and to Mendelssohn's lovely illustration much must be allowed. We must not be too rigidly reforming. (pp. 52-3)

. . . . .

The question of Shakespeare's music is a large and interesting one. It seems to be admitted that Mendelssohn, in his *Midsummer Night's Dream,* is the only writer who found the right tone, measure, and quantity. You but hear a few bars of his enchanting strains to feel that it is true Shakespeare. Even the last three or four—the high treble 'thirds'—bring the whole drama before you. But who can touch *that* lyre? Accompanying his spoken text with music has been tried, and will not do. Mr. Bouchier in his *Macbeth* revival has, however, supplied a good deal of this element. The composer, a good musician, furnished a troubled, stormy overture, presaging the contending passions of the play. The notion of an overture is too conventional, and even vulgar—it is a sort of flourish of trumpets anticipation; whereas the play should begin in its own calm way, without any such noisy heralding. We cannot conceive of an overture to *Hamlet.* Mendelssohn's is so exquisite, that it has become an exception, and the play is in the nature of a fairy masque.

In this *Macbeth* revival there was something almost comic in the Scotch turn given to some of the music, so much so that we expected to see the pipers entering skirling. As it was, there seemed to be Scottish airs worked in, and almost suggesting reminiscences of Rob Roy.

There is nothing so destructive of illusion and dramatic effect as the stage music as it is commonly rendered. It is supposed to colour or intensify the situation. We know that the moment has come by the conductor getting into his seat, and beginning to *beat* time for the moving strains, his waving arms being conspicuous in the middle of the stage. Here is at once a link with the prosy outer world; it brings us down to earth again. It would be different were the executants wholly concealed, the music floating upwards from some unseen region.

How absurd in the *Midsummer Night's Dream,* when the fairies are fluttering about in their dances, crossing and re-crossing in the shadows, to see the fiddlers hard at work over their shaded lamps, and the conductor in evening dress, as prosaic as possible, whose moment has *now* come, gesticulating away at Mendelssohn's music. Usually the play is interrupted, and the song is virtually performed for the audience. The singer stands forward and pretends to play his lute, while the orchestra accompanies. (pp. 57-8)

There is a notable song in the *Midsummer Night's Dream*—'I know a Bank'—which is a truly awful example of this purview. This lilt has been extraordinarily popular, and has set many an old head nodding. It is firmly established, is believed in as something almost Shakespearean itself. We know the formula and cue for orchestra—symphony, etc. Two presentable fairies come forward smiling, and go through the whole in thirds, warbling away melodiously with trills and flourishings, so as to enrapture all the hearers. It finishes triumphantly and to applause, and is, of course, encored. No one knows what it is all about, or why such warbling should be introduced. Yet in the text it is quite intelligible. Oberon wishes to enchant Demetrius, and sends to Puck for a certain magic flower. Puck returns with it, on which Oberon—

> I pray thee, give it me.
> I know a bank where the wild thyme blows,
>
> [II. i. 248-49]

and where Titania sleeps. With the juice of the flower he will anoint her eyes, and he further directs Puck to take the juice and anoint Demetrius' eyes. All this detail is lost or overlooked by the introduction of the modern harmonized song.

Thus Oberon's speech has been turned into a song, which was never intended by the author; and therefore the invariable rule should be that only what Shakespeare intended to be a song should be set to music, and that music should always take the shape of a spontaneous utterance, without interruption of symphony or elaborate accompaniment.

Again, in the same play, how the moderns have distorted the beautiful fairy machinery! Thus Puck asks a fairy, 'Whither wander you?' She answers him in a bit of careless poetry—

> Over hill, over dale,
> Through bush, through briar,
>
> [II. i. 1-3]

giving him also information about the King. The composer, however, must seize on this as a splendid opportunity, for a showy solo, one very difficult and effective. Puck has to stand aside, look on and listen, while she—a female vocalist, introduced for a purpose, say Miss Parkina—is at the footlights for at least ten minutes, with roulades, *fortes,* etc., to say nothing of ensuring a certain encore. The vulgarity of this is inconceivable, and is wholly undramatic. (pp. 60-1)

In many of the Shakespearean dramas we have a dance introduced, and here comes the opportunity for the spectacular stage manager, who can only deal with it after his favourite methods; in fact, he knows no others. The leader, who has been sitting low down among his fellows, suddenly jumps into his high seat, taps his desk, raises his arm. The King and his lords seat themselves, and from the wings, right and left, run on or skip on a large number of girls, who group themselves down near the footlights and start off with their muscular antics. They keep their faces to the audience all the time, and really dance *for* it, and not for the seated royalties; and the movement goes on for several minutes. But how should it really be? First, such dancing as is furnished in a palace for the entertainment of the royal owner would ordinarily be supplied by a few performers—say, three or four, or half a dozen at most. They would perform their measures at the side, in obtrusive, graceful way, old-fashioned, and without jumps or boundings. The eye should rest on them as on a piece of tapestry or a scene by Watteau. The dance should be blended with a play, and not be an introduced episode.

In short, it might be said that in every instance where our author has directed music to be introduced as an aid to the dramatic interest, it has been seized on as an opening for actually destroying the beauty of the situation. The action is violently interrupted, the fiddlers become obstreperous, and the singer with a good voice, 'specially engaged' intrudes himself. But Shakespearean is, or should be, an inspiration to the musician. Mendelssohn alone has been thus inspired. It is not too much to say that his *Midsummer Night's Dream* music, when played in a concert-room, brings up all the images of the beautiful fairy play. We are conscious of the presence of the elves, and the exquisite pathetic passage at the close of the overture ever suggests the general dreaminess. Sullivan in parts of his *Tempest*—notably the 'Yellow Sands' motive—has something of the same tenderness and fitness. (pp. 61-2)

> *Percy Fitzgerald, "Shakespearean Ghosts, Apparitions, Witches, Etc.," and "Music-Dancing," in his* Shakespearean Representation: Its Laws and Limits, *Elliot Stock, 1908, pp. 34-56, 57-62.*

Cecil Sharp (essay date 1914)

[*Sharp composed the music for Harley Granville-Barker's renowned 1914 production of* A Midsummer Night's Dream. *In the following excerpt, he considers various problems involved with composing music for this play, assesses several alternative solutions, and explains why he decided to employ folk-songs in his score. The timeless quality of these pieces, he argues, is ideally suited to the* Dream. *"By using folk-music in the Shakespearean play," he states, "we shall then be mating like with like—the drama which is for all time with the music which is for all time."*]

The artistic significance of the music, songs, dances, &c., in the Elizabethan poetic drama is usually under-estimated, and it is often and far too hastily assumed that costumes, scenery, and music had but a small share in its production. Mr. G. H. Cowling, in his 'Music on the Shakespearian Stage,' has, however, shown that the drama of Shakespeare's time, so far from being purely a literary production, made a sensuous appeal, not only to the ear with poetry and music, but also to the eye with dress, properties, and painted scenes; and that "whilst the imagery of verse cast a glamour over the imaginative effect of the drama on the intellect and the emotion, there were music and colour for the senses."

If we accept this opinion, and regard the musical scenes and interludes in Shakespeare's plays as no mere decorative additions of minor import, but rather an integral part of the drama, designed to heighten its effect and carry on the action, their adequate treatment becomes a matter demanding serious consideration. Unfortunately, the question is hedged with difficulties, and the right handling of the songs and music in the acting of Shakespeare presents to the musician a problem of a troublesome nature.

Where the original music used in Shakespeare's day has sur-

vived, the simplest and, perhaps, the safest course—though not necessarily the ideal one—is to retain it. But how are we to treat songs like those in 'A Midsummer Night's Dream,' for which not a single note of contemporary music has been preserved? Three ways lie before us: (1) we may adapt Elizabethan music that was originally set to other words; (2) compose music in the Elizabethan idiom; or (3) commission a composer of our own day to write original music.

To the adoption of the first method there is one grave objection. The text and the music of the Elizabethan song are so closely interwoven—the one is so exact a counterpart of the other—that the substitution of other words for the original ones, even when this can be done without the alteration of a single note of the music, will only produce a piece of palpable patchwork, artistically worthless.

The second alternative may be summarily dismissed. The Shakespeare play is the last place into which any one would wish to introduce anything of the nature of a "fake."

There is far more to be said for the third method, though even to this many will take objection. It will be urged that modern music is out of place—an anachronism—in an Elizabethan play. With this, however, I do not agree. Indeed, I am prepared to go further, and question whether, artistically, it is advisable even to retain those Elizabethan settings of Shakespeare's songs which have happily survived. A great many of these are admittedly very beautiful and characteristic. The retention, however, binds us to the Elizabethan attitude towards Shakespeare, and, by stamping the dramas as mere Elizabethan products, lessens the force of the appeal which they would otherwise make to modern ears. To us Elizabethan music must always sound strange, unfamiliar, archaic, and, to some extent, "precious."

The archæologist will not, of course, accept this view of the matter. The question, however, lies outside his province; it concerns the artist, not the antiquary. To the artist the fact that the plays were written in the days of Elizabeth is a matter comparatively of small import—little more than a mere accident. Shakespeare himself was infinitely more than an Elizabethan. The message he delivered to his contemporaries has, as time has proved, reached far beyond them. Shakespeare the man was an Elizabethan; Shakespeare the artist and dramatist belongs to all time.

This is not to assert that there are no features in the plays which betray their Elizabethan origin. On the contrary, there are a great many. But these are not mainly the essential elements—those qualities which make the dramas a living force at the present day. We shall, of course, have to discriminate between the essential and the accidental. Some of the "accidents" may not admit of rejection or variation without incurring artistic loss, such as, for instance, the special form of stage used in Shakespeare's day; while others, *e.g.*, the roofless auditorium, it would be mere pedantry to retain. Each case must be judged on its own merits, and upon artistic, not archæological considerations.

It is so with regard to the music. The musician, if he feels that Elizabethan music sounds strange and archaic, may reject it and substitute music of his own. He is entitled to claim full liberty to settle the matter in his own way, realizing, of course, that his own experiment will sooner or later be itself superseded.

This, indeed, is the fate that has now overtaken Mendelssohn's incidental music to 'A Midsummer Night's Dream,' though it won the admiration of his contemporaries, whose ideals it faithfully reflected.

We of the present generation are no longer under the influence of the wave of German Romanticism which swept over this country sixty or seventy years ago, and to us, therefore, his music comes as an echo of a past age—the expression of an ideal which is not ours. And this must always be so, for the evolution of the art of music has been continuous: each generation of composers has been occupied with the solution of particular technical and æsthetic problems. Consequently the music of every epoch is distinguished by certain musical figures or idioms which, to the musical historian, bear evidence of the date at which it was composed.

While, then, we admit the right of the modern musician to set the songs in Shakespeare's plays in his own way, we must not forget that this, at best, is a temporary solution of the problem. Finality can only be attained by making use of music which possesses the same characteristic of permanence and freshness as the drama itself—music which is impervious to the passage of time, and will satisfy equally the artistic ideals of every age.

Now, folk-music is the only music which fulfils these requirements. It is undated; it belongs to no period; it is a growth, not a composition—the product of evolution, not the work of an individual. It is timeless in that it flows beneath the surface ripples set up by the passing fluctuations of taste peculiar to this or that epoch. Tolstoy maintained that no art was worthy of the name but that which was either created by the peasant, or which could be understood and appreciated by him. Without endorsing this proposition, it may at least be claimed that the music of the peasant is, in one sense, the only permanent music, because it appeals insistently and with equal force to every age.

By using folk-music in the Shakespeare play, we shall then be mating like with like—the drama which is for all time with the music which is for all time. An attempt to show that this is practicable—or, at any rate, might become so in more capable hands—is being made in the present production. Almost every tune used in the course of the music is either a folk-air or derived from one. It would, of course, have been easy, by decorating the tunes with modern harmonies, to destroy their folk-character and convert them into music indistinguishable from that of our own day, and thus defeat our ends. This pitfall, however, can be avoided—as is being done in the present case—by the simple expedient of using diatonic harmonies only and eschewing modulation.

That this is an experiment, and a bold, perhaps an audacious, one, is freely admitted. Those who wonder why it has not been made before should remember that it is only within the last few years—*i.e.,* since our folk-music has been collected—that it has become possible.

We know, of course, that this is a question which is not going to be decided on theoretical or logical grounds. If the method advocated is to carry conviction, it must be because the folk-tune is artistically better suited for the purpose in question than any other kind of music. Now the employment of folk-music ensures, or at least renders feasible, a simple and direct treatment of the text which will preserve the rhythm and beauty of the language, instead of obscuring its meaning. Throughout its evolution the music of the folk-song has always been subservient to the words, the embellishment and

interpretation of which has been its sole purpose. The only repetition of the text that the folk-singer ordinarily allows himself is the "doubling" of the last few words of the stanza.

Is not this precisely the musical treatment that we should wish to accord to Shakespeare's songs? If they are to have their full effect, they must be rendered concisely and tersely, without verbal repetition, and in such a manner that every syllable of the text may be distinctly heard; and with the utmost brevity too if the musical scene or interlude is to fall into its proper relation with the drama—*i.e.,* to aid and carry on the action of the play, not to arrest it.

Mendelssohn, of course, had another aim than this. He proceeded as though he were composing a secular cantata to be performed in a concert-hall. To him the words were mere pegs upon which to hang his music, and consequently he never scrupled to mutilate the text and obscure its meaning. The two methods may be best exhibited by comparing the folk-song setting of 'You Spotted Snakes' [II. ii. 9ff.] with Mendelssohn's treatment of the same words. In the first case the only repetition is of the last two lines of the choral refrain, and the words are set in such a way that there is no reason why every syllable of the text should not be heard as clearly as if it were spoken. In Mendelssohn's hands the words become an inextricable tangle. The phrase "So, Good-night," or "So, so, Good-night," is reiterated no fewer than twenty-two times in each stanza; while at the end of the four-lined verse allotted to the First Fairy the words "Hence away!" are arbitrarily interpolated—words which do not belong to the song at all, but are directed to be *spoken* by the Second Fairy at the conclusion of the lyric. However beautiful the music may be in itself, such a treatment of the text is quite indefensible. Moreover, the lengthening of the scene which this method involves not only delays the action of the drama, but also gives the scene an importance and prominence which it was clearly never intended to usurp.

In the arrangement of the dances a similar principle has been followed. The movements have all been adapted or developed from those of the English folk-dance. The figures and steps, for instance, of the dance in the first act have been taken mainly from the Country Dance, and those of the two dances in the fifth act from the Sword Dance.

No attempt has been made to produce a realistic effect. The absence of the requisite accommodation for a large orchestra, and the lack also of any available body of expert dancers in this country, would alone have rendered this impossible, even if it had been considered appropriate. The dances are, therefore, frankly conventional, and set throughout to folk-tunes of regular eight-bar rhythm.

Although the folk-dance bears the same relationship to the ballet as folk-music to art-music, there is this important difference to be noted. For while supreme within its own sphere, folk-music consists of unharmonized melody only, always used in the service of some other art—poetry, dance, or drama—and covers, therefore, but an infinitesimally small part of the ground exploited by the art-musician. The folk-dance, on the other hand, is far less restricted in its range. Indeed, it is questionable whether the art of dancing will ever be carried very far beyond the point to which the peasant dancer has taken it. At any rate, it cannot be said that any of the attempts to extend it have so far been successful. These have usually resulted in the invention of movements that are acrobatic, and, as such, appeal to the sense of wonder rather than that of beauty, or meaningless, or pretty in a tiresome, superficial sort of way. That the futility of such developments is now becoming generally recognized is shown, on the one hand, by the waning popularity in this country of the panto-mimic ballet of the Italian School, and, on the other, by the enthusiasm recently aroused by the Russian Ballet, the steps and figures of which are very intimately related to those of the folk-dance. All, indeed, that the Russians have done is to adapt the figures and movements of their native dances to freer and more irregular rhythms, to blend them in fresh combinations, to adapt them to a larger number of performers, and, above all, to develope a technique which, in the nature of things, the folk-dancer was never able to achieve.

If an English Ballet is ever to be established comparable with that of the Russians, it will assuredly have to be based in like manner upon our own folk-dances. Perhaps the tentative and modest effort that has been made to develop our native dances for the purposes of this production may incite others to make further and more adequate attempts in the same direction. (pp. 210-11)

> *Cecil Sharp, in a review of "A Midsummer Night's Dream," in* The Athenaeum, *No. 4502, February 7, 1914, pp. 210-11.*

Harley Granville-Barker   (essay date 1914)

[*The following excerpt is drawn from Barker's preface to his acting edition of* A Midsummer Night's Dream, *which was first published in 1914, the same year as his controversial production. Barker presents a wide-ranging discussion of various aspects of staging the* Dream.]

'September 29th, 1662, . . . and then to the King's Theatre, where we saw *Midsummer Night's Dream,* which I had never seen before, nor shall ever again, for it is the most insipid, ridiculous play that ever I saw in my life. I saw I confess some good dancing and some handsome women, which was all my pleasure.' How many of us nowadays would dare confide that even to a cipher diary? But Pepys, as usual, is in the fashion. Shakespeare was out-moded, and the theatre manager was already bolstering up his mere poetry with sensuality and display. We have, of course, reformed all that. Still, if I must choose between this cheerful Philistine and the pious, awe-struck commentator, who tells me that 'The germs of a whole philosophy of life are latent in the wayward love scenes of *A Midsummer Night's Dream*' [Georg Brandes, *William Shakespeare: A Critical Study*], I turn rather to Pepys. He has done less to keep Shakespeare from his own. If you go to a theatre to scoff you may remain to enjoy yourself; if you go to pray (once in a while) you likelier leave to patronise.

Why waste time in proving that *A Midsummer Night's Dream* is a bad play, or proving otherwise, since to its deepest damnation one must add: Written by a man of a genius for the theatre, playwright in spite of himself? Does not vitality defeat doctrine? The opening of the play may be bad. The opening speech surely is even very bad dramatic verse. There is nothing much in the character of Theseus; there's nothing at all in Hippolyta. The substance of the opening scene is out of keeping both with its own method and with the scope of the play. But before the end of it, earlier than usual even in his later days, Shakespeare has begun to get into his stride. If he couldn't yet develop character he could write poetry and—

. . .O happy fair!

Your eyes are lode-stars; and your tongue's sweet air
More tuneable than lark to shepherd's ear,
When wheat is green, when hawthorn buds appear.
[I. i. 182-85]

At the sound of that we cease to demand from Helena—for the moment at least—any more material qualities. How he could and seemingly couldn't help but flower into verse! It was still a question, I suppose, whether he remained a poet or became a dramatist. He was in every sense nearer to 'Venus and Adonis' than *Macbeth.* If he hadn't been a man of the people, if he hadn't had his living to earn, if he hadn't had more fun in him than the writing of lyric poetry will satisfy! If it was he made the English theatre, did not the theatre make him what he is—what he might be to us?

Next come the clowns. It is necessary, I am ashamed to say, to remark that Clown does not, first of all, mean a person who tries to be funny. A clown is a countryman. Now, your Cockney audience finds a countryman comic, and your Cockney writer to this day often makes him outrageously so. Shakespeare presumably knew something about countrymen, and he made the simple discovery and put it into practice for the first time in this play that, set down lovingly, your clown is better fun by far than mocked at; if indeed apart from an actor's grimaces he had then been funny at all. Later on Shakespeare did this, as he did most other things, better, but he never did it so simply. If Shallow and Silence [in *2 Henry IV*] are finer, they are different; moreover, though countrymen they are not clowns. If Dogberry [in *Much Ado about Nothing*] is as good, he hasn't, for me, quite the charm. There are little sketches in the last plays; that delightful person, for instance, at the end of *Antony and Cleopatra* with his, 'I wish you joy of the worm' [V. ii. 279]. But from the moment Bottom, gloweringly mistrustful of poor Snug, asks, 'Let me play the lion, too' [I. ii. 70], from that moment they have my heart, all five, for ever. It is a little puzzling to discover just how bad their play is meant to be. Did Quince write it? If he is guilty of 'Now am I dead' [V. i. 301], then, is not the prologue a plagiarism? But a good deal of more respectable playwriting than this was plagiarism, as who knew better than Shakespeare? I suspect he was of two minds himself on the point, if of any at all.

Then come the fairies. Can even genius succeed in putting fairies on the stage? The pious commentators say not. This play and the sublimer parts of *King Lear* are freely quoted as impossible in the theatre. But, then, by some trick of reasoning they blame the theatre for it. I cannot follow that. If a play written for the stage cannot be put on the stage the playwright, it seems to me, has failed, be he who he may. Has Shakespeare failed or need the producer only pray for a little genius, too? The fairies are the producer's test. Let me confess that, though mainly love of the play, yet partly, too, a hope of passing that test has inspired the present production. Foolhardy one feels facing it. But if a method of staging can compass the difficulties of *A Midsummer Night's Dream,* surely its cause is won.

Lacking genius one considers first how not to do a thing. Not to try and *realise* these small folk who war with rere-mice for their leathern wings, that goes without saying. In this play I can visualise neither a beginning nor an end to realism of either scenery or action. Nor yet to use children. To my mind neither children nor animals fit with the theatre. Perfect in their natural beauty, they put our artifice to shame. In this case one is tempted, one yields a little, over Cobweb and Co. It's possible, even probable, that children served Shakespeare. But I expect that the little eyasses of that time were as smartly trained in speaking verse as is a crack cathedral choir now in the singing of anthems. That there might be a special beauty, an impersonal clarity, in a boy's Oberon or Titania I can well believe. To take a nearly parallel case, who would not choose to hear treble rather than soprano through Bach's *Matthew Passion?* This is an interesting point, and it opens up the whole question of the loss and gain to pure poetry on the stage by the coming of women players. But where are our children with the training in fine speech and movement? Stop beneath the windows of an elementary school and listen. Or worse, listen to the chatter of a smart society gathering; in the school playground at least there is lung power. It will take some generations of awakening to the value of song and dance, tune and rhythm, to re-establish a standard of beauty in the English language.

The theatre might help if it were allowed. Though, first of all, heaven knows, it needs to help itself. One may say that the tradition of verse-speaking on the English stage is almost dead. So much the better. Our latest inheritance of it, at the least, was unsound, dating not from Shakespearean times, the great age of verse, but from the 'heroic' days of Rowe and Otway; later from the translators of 'the immortal Kotzebue' and the portentous Sheridan Knowles. Comic verse found its grave (at times a charmingly bedizened grave) in the rhymed burlesques of Planché and Byron. But Shakespeare was a classic and must be spoken 'classically,' and what you couldn't speak classically you had better cut. Look at the Shakespeare prompt books of even the last few years and see how mercilessly rhymed couplets were got rid of, blots upon the dignity of the play. From this sort of thing William Poel has been our saviour, and we owe him thanks. In the teeth of ridicule he insisted that for an actor to make himself like unto a human megaphone was to miss, for one thing, the whole merit of Elizabethan verse with its consonantal swiftness, its gradations sudden or slow into vowelled liquidity, its comic rushes and stops, with, above all, the peculiar beauty of its rhymes. We have had, of course, individual actors or speakers of taste and genius (one instances Forbes-Robertson), and there might be now and then a company inspired by such scholarly ideals as Benson could give, but Poel preached a gospel.

What else was Shakespeare's chief delight in this play but the screeds of word-music to be spoken by Oberon, Titania, and Puck? At every possible and impossible moment he is at it. For Puck's description of himself there may be need, but what excuse can we make for Titania's thirty-five lines about the dreadful weather except their sheer beauty? But what better excuse? Oberon is constantly guilty. So recklessly happy in writing such verse does Shakespeare grow that even the quarrel of the four lovers is stayed by a charming speech of Helena's thirty-seven lines long. It is true that at the end of it Hermia, her author allowing her to recollect the quarrel, says she is amazed at these passionate words, but that the passage beginning 'We, Hermia, like two artificial gods' [III. ii. 203] is meant by Shakespeare to be spoken otherwise than with a meticulous regard to its every beauty is hard to believe. And its every beauty will scarcely shine through throbbing passion. No, his heart was in these passages of verse, and so the heart of the play is in them. And the secret of the play—the refutation of all doctrinaire criticism of it—lies in the fact

that though they may offend against every letter of dramatic law they fulfil the inmost spirit of it, inasmuch as they are dramatic in themselves. They are instinct with that excitement, that spontaneity, that sense of emotional overflow which is drama. They are as carefully constructed for effective speaking as a messenger's speech in a Greek drama. One passage in particular, Puck's 'My mistress with a monster is in love,' [III. ii. 6] is both in idea and form, in its tension, climax, and rounding off, a true messenger's speech. Shakespeare, I say, was from the first a playwright in spite of himself. Even when he seems to sacrifice drama to poem he—instinctively or not—manages to make the poem itself more dramatic than the drama he sacrifices. And once he has found himself as a playwright very small mercy has he on verse for its own sake. He seems to write it as the fancy takes him, badly or well, broken or whole. Is there a single rule he will not break, lest his drama should for a moment suffer? Is there a supreme passage in the later plays but is supreme more in its dramatic emotion than its sheer poetry? Take for an extreme instance the line in *King Lear,* 'Never, never, never, never, never' [V. iii. 309]. Can you defend it as poetry, any more than you can defend 'Oh, Sophonisba, Sophonisba, oh!' [in James Thompson's *Tragedy of Sophonisba*]? As a moment of drama what could be more poignantly beautiful? Whence comes the tradition that a blank verse play is, merely by virtue of its verse, the top notch of dramatic achievement? Shakespeare's best work, seen alive in the theatre, gives, I maintain, no colour to it. Verse was his first love, his natural medium—the finest medium for the theatre in general of his day, I'll admit. But how far he was, in principle and practice, from those worthy disciples who have for these centuries and do indeed still attempt to drag us wearily up their strictly decasyllabic pathway to Parnassus, only a placing of their work and his side by side in the living theatre will show. It has all come, I suppose, from learned people elevating him to the study from the stage. Despite the theatre; it revenges itself. I digress.

The fairies cannot sound too beautiful. How should they look? One does one's best. But I realise that when there is perhaps no really right thing to do one is always tempted to do too much. One yields to the natural fun, of course, of making a thing look pretty in itself. They must be not too startling. But one wishes people weren't so easily startled. I won't have them dowdy. They mustn't warp your imagination—stepping too boldly between Shakespeare's spirit and yours. It is a difficult problem; we (Norman Wilkinson and I—he to do and I to carp) have done our best. One point is worth making. Oberon and Titania are romantic creations: sprung from Huron of Bordeaux, etc., say the commentators; come from the farthest steppe of India, says Shakespeare. But Puck is English folklore.

How should the fairies dance? Here I give up my part of apologist to Cecil Sharp. I only know they should have no truck with a strange technique brought from Italy in the eighteenth century. If there is an English way of dancing—and Sharp says there is—should not that be their way?

And what tunes should they sing to? English tunes. And on this point Sharp has much to say—more sometimes than I can quite follow him in. I have no doubt there is a lyric missing at the end of the play, and to set a tune to the rhythm of Oberon's spoken words seems absurd. If this most appropriate one we borrow from *Two Noble Kinsmen* is not Shakespeare's (Swinburne thought it was), I'm sorry. I'm sorry, anyway, if it's vandalism, but something has to be done.

Finally, I divide the play into three parts. I don't defend the division; it only happens to be a convenient one. I can't defend any division, and some day I really must ask a modern audience to sit through two hours and a half of Shakespeare without a break; the play would gain greatly. This is less absurd, that is all, than the Jonsonian five act division of the Folio, for which, of course, there is no authority. (pp. 33-9)

> *Harley Granville-Barker, "Preface to 'A Midsummer Night's Dream',"* in his *Prefaces to Shakespeare, Vol. VI, P. T. Batsford Ltd., 1974, pp. 33-9.*

Margaret Webster   (essay date 1942)

[*Webster advocates stressing romanticism rather than realism or experimentation in productions of* A Midsummer Night's Dream. *She argues that "if we can persuade our audience to accept enchantment, we shall not need identifiable oaks, nor raucous green stylizations."*]

A MIDSUMMER NIGHT'S DREAM is as moon drenched as ROMEO AND JULIET is shot with stars. The moon is not in a malignant phase, but her radiance sheds a disturbing magic this midsummer night, holding all the play in an opalescent enchantment, where everything seems "translated." Only with Theseus' hunting horns at dawn and the music of his hounds does the thin, silver mist dissolve, and a world emerge in which lovers are mortal men, trees are trees merely, and Bottom can scratch his ear without the inexplicable feeling that it has grown long and hairy. Not until THE TEMPEST will Shakespeare write a play with elements as delicately ethereal as these.

Our scenic problem is thereby the more complicated. We can so easily crush the flowerlike fragility of Titania by requiring her to sleep upon a bumpy bank, a little grayed with honest theatre dust, amid a laborious forest, with real rabbits, as in Sir Herbert Tree's production, to keep her company and "add a touch of verisimilitude to an otherwise bald and unconvincing narrative." We need, once more, a mood, an atmosphere, in which anything may happen, a setting which suggests but does not specify. Enchanted woods have been with us from the earliest fairy stories we learned as children; if we can persuade our audience to accept enchantment, we shall not need identifiable oaks, nor raucous green stylizations.

There is nothing difficult for the actors in this play. We are apt to discount the lovers, with a secret fear that they are a bore, and to let the clowns loose with free, galumphing feet. The lovers need not be wearisome. As usual, when Shakespeare is writing lovers in sets, the women are better than the men. Both Helena and Hermia are vivid enough and tartly contrasted. If Helena will play a rather silly girl in love as a rather silly girl in love, and not moan for our sympathy all the time, she will be fully rewarded by our surprised delight when the worm turns, and upbraids her dearest friend with all the armory of feminine cattiness assured of male support. There is some very elegant fooling in the quarrel scene between the quartet.

Nor need Demetrius and Lysander lugubriously accept the usual fate of stooges, if they will play for the enchantment of the wood and make us realize the depths of bemused and driveling sentimentality to which its magic has reduced two ordinarily upstanding and normal young men. In the play's

first and last scenes they are both drawn lightly but quite firmly; what they establish in these scenes will govern the degree of comedy to be extracted from their moonlit aberrations. Even so percipient a critic as Mr. Van Doren has condemned them as "dolls"; but any actor with imagination knows better, and the play will lose if he cannot establish their humanity.

For the lovers, more clearly even than Theseus and Hippolyta, form the link between the honest, tangible, homespun craftsman's world, peopled by the so-called clowns, and the airy dimension which Oberon and Titania inhabit. Puck knows both worlds and partakes of them. But to him the mortal world represents every reasonable idea standing idiotically on its head; whereas, to the lovers and clowns, Titania's domain dissolves all reliable and stable values in fluidity and bewilderment. Bottom, of course, is the most deeply entangled, and in him the most solid of the earthy elements is emmeshed by the most delicate fabric of the fairy world.

For Titania's attendants, Shakespeare adopts the conventional ideas of his time concerning fairies, and it is hard to see what different idiom we can use on our stage. We shall probably have to use children as he did, and see to it that no brash precocity or excess of song and dance jars against the musical burden of the play which Oberon and Titania so delicately carry.

The clowns are straightforward stuff. They are apt to emerge a trifle encrusted with tradition, which has gathered as thick as barnacles around them. One piece of business has come down from Shakespeare's own time, from a contemporary reference to the fact that Thisbe, in killing herself, falls on the scabbard instead of the sword. Since that time every possible change has been rung on the comic possibilities of the Pyramus-Thisbe interlude; these variations have persisted in actors' minds, and have been preserved and added to from generation to generation.

Many of them remain genuinely, if not very subtly, funny. The director must select judiciously, and above all, keep the fooling spontaneous and not allow it to stretch out interminably in order to meet the contribution of every actor in the play. "Simpleness and duty" are accredited to the amateur actors [V. i. 82], and the fun can be heightened if they do remember that they are supposedly playing to the Duke and his companions, and do not too freely caricature the traditions of village-hall theatricals. The scene offers limitless possibilities. We may treat it with temperance and do nobody any harm.

In other scenes than this the Clowns are dogged with tradition. Starveling is supposedly deaf. When he is told that he is to play Thisbe's mother, he has for generations interpolated: "Thisbe's brother?" *"Mother!"* replies the united troupe. Flute has immemorially protested that he has "a beard—" "Huh?" from his companions, "—coming!" But the Clowns are genuine, human, and indestructible. We fall for them today as they did in Elizabethan London. This is a lighthearted, irresponsible piece of mischief and magic; let us lend our best ears to its melodies and warm our hearts at its humanity. The moonlit Shakespearean heavens will not often be so beautifully cloudless, nor his lyric gift of song so purely melodious. (pp. 155-58)

> *Margaret Webster, "The Early Plays," in her* Shakespeare Without Tears, *Whittlesey House, 1942, pp. 135-58.*

Herbert Farjeon   (essay date 1949)

[*Farjeon offers an impressionistic discussion of issues related to staging* A Midsummer Night's Dream, *with particular reference to the portrayal of the fairies. "A charming diminutive effect is achieved when children are dressed as grown-ups," he contends, though he acknowledges that it "might not be an entirely satisfactory solution" to the problem of representing these magical creatures.*]

Shakespeare wrote two great pastoral plays: *As You Like It,* the scene of which is laid in the Forest of Arden, and *A Midsummer Night's Dream,* with its Wood near Athens. Of these two plays *A Midsummer Night's Dream* is the more magical and mysterious; and if you would inquire the reason, you might find it in the answer that, while the Forest of Arden is the Wood near Athens, and while both are English to the last acorn, night is more magical and mysterious than day. The Forest of Arden is for the sun-worshippers. Here it is perpetual high noon. We shall never know what sleeping accommodation the Banished Duke provided for his contented followers. We shall never know how Rosalind behaved by twilight—whether she maintained her triumphant buoyancy, or whether, when the horn of night had sounded in the glade, she subdued her wit to a gentler quality.

We shall never know how Oberon and Puck would have rung the changes on the love of Silvius for Phebe, of Phebe for Ganymede, of Orlando for Rosalind, and of Rosalind for no woman. But just as the Forest of Arden is governed by the sun, so is the Wood near Athens governed by the moon. This wood is wet with night. The tiniest sounds prick as piercingly through the darkness as the stars prick through the vault of heaven. And as you thread your way between the trees, stumbling over a root or a shoot or a lover, to where Titania in a cup of light decks her gentle ass with coronets of flowers, the smell of a century of dead leaves rises with a strength and sweetness unknown to-day.

If a psycho-analyst were to ask me to "associate", as I believe it is called, beginning from the starting-point of *A Midsummer Night's Dream,* my first response would be "Wet woods at night"; and after that perhaps I should blab out, "Three-legged stools", for Puck, you may remember, plays pranks with three-legged stools, and the immortal fairy-stuff in this play is made firm and fibrous because it is not merely of the air or even of the earth, but of the cottage.

When he created, or perhaps one should say when he reincarnated, Puck, Shakespeare was not so much fairy-conscious as kitchen-conscious. What a loss we should have sustained if, in the last scene of all, Puck had come to bless the house with a wand instead of a besom! We must remember that it was the housewives who invented the fairies, and that the true fairyland is therefore to be found, not in the hazy nowhere to which timid fancies gravitate, but between four solid walls of brick and mortar. The Wood near Athens is the home of the newts and the bats and the screech-owls and the spotted snakes. It is not the home of the fairies. It is their playground. When their revels are at an end, they vanish, but not into thin air. They vanish into the linen-press of Mistress Quince, into the oven of Mistress Flute, into the milk-pan of Mistress Starveling. And it is because Shakespeare understood their origin and because he had grown up with them under a thatched roof that he made them so much more alive than Theseus and Hippolyta. Hippolyta may have been an Amazon and Theseus a mighty hunter before the gods, but it is

in Oberon that we see the man of action and in Titania the mate who must be won with more than wooing.

Perhaps there is no comedy by Shakespeare containing more beautiful music than *A Midsummer Night's Dream.* It is for the nose and for the ear rather than for the eye, and if you wander through the woods on a summer night, you can scarcely fail to smell it and to hear it, though you may fail to see it. But it would be a mistake to infer from this statement any sympathy with the objection to stage representations of *A Midsummer Night's Dream* which is based on the mathematical calculation that fairies five, or even four, feet high, could never drown in the honey-bag of a humble-bee. A playgoer who cannot imagine that four feet are half an inch can never have looked at the stage through the wrong end of his opera-glasses and should give up the theatre altogether. This particular objection may disappear when the play is broadcast, but even so he may be troubled to account for the fact that Pease-Blossom has a mouth like a Loud Speaker. The playwright uses his imagination to the best of his ability, but all his efforts will be vain if the audience does not bring its own imagination to his support. After all, it entails little effort. For as Theseus says, at the close of his famous speech on the lunatic, the lover and the poet:

> How easy is a bush suppos'd a bear!
>
> [V. i. 22]

What *is* to be done about those fairies? What did the Elizabethans do about them? What sort of a spectacle did they present in Shakespeare's time? Nobody can say for certain. But is there not an illuminating suggestion in that most illuminating pamphlet by Mr. Ernest Law on *Shakespeare's "Tempest" as Originally Produced at Court?* Mr. Law, considering the problem of Ariel, suggests a costume similar to that described by Ben Jonson for Jophiel in his *Masque of the Fortunate Isles.* Here is Ben Jonson's direction:

> *Enter, running, Jophiel, an airy spirit . . . attired in light silks of several colours, with wings of the same, a bright yellow hair, a chaplet of flowers, blue silk stockings, and pumps, and gloves, with a silver fan in his hand.*

Pumps, gloves, and a silver fan! Not an ideal flying costume according to the lights of Drury Lane. Yet Jophiel was a flying fairy. It is with these words that he opens the Masque:

> Like a lightning from the sky,
>   Or an arrow shot by Love,
> Or a bird of his let fly;
>   Be't a sparrow, or a dove:
> With that winged haste, come I,
>   Loosed from the sphere of Jove,
>   To wish good night
>   To your delight.

In some such way might we not formalize the retinues of Titania and of Oberon into diminutive courtiers and ladies-in-waiting, with capes and ruffs and wings and chaplets? It might not be an entirely satisfactory solution, but a charming diminutive effect is achieved when children are dressed as grown-ups. And it would be better, I swear than presenting these fairies like choristers out of *Iolanthe,* or tricking them out in the customary gauzy flummery, which makes them look like secondary schoolchildren who have temporarily abandoned their spectacles to give a Christmas breaking-up entertainment. If you believe in the gods and the heroes and the little people, they are as solid as goats. It is only the doubters who dress their fairies in gauze. (pp. 48-50)

Herbert Farjeon, "'A Midsummer Night's Dream': Random Notes," in his The Shakespearean Scene: Dramatic Criticisms, *Hutchinson & Co. Ltd., 1949, pp. 39-49.*

Lincoln Kirstein   (essay date 1960)

[*In the following excerpt, Kirstein analyzes several facets of producing* A Midsummer Night's Dream, *including the music, dancing, and settings, and discusses how these were treated in Jack Landau's production for the 1958 American Shakespeare Festival at Stratford, Connecticut.*]

This essay was prompted by a production at the American Shakespeare Festival in Stratford, Connecticut, in 1958. The production was directed by Jack Landau, with settings by David Hays, costumes by Thea Neu, music by Marc Blitzstein, and with dances arranged by George Balanchine. The essential aim was to follow Shakespeare's original intention as closely as possible.

A Midsummer Night's Dream was probably devised originally as part of the entertainment at a noble marriage. The marriage itself would have taken place in broad daylight, "after the toune be rysen with honours and reverence," and the play would have been performed that night at the wedding feast. Noble weddings were splendid enough to cause the early Puritans to rail at their vain shows. Several such weddings have been suggested as the occasion of the play, the most probable being that of Elizabeth Carey and Thomas Berkeley in 1596. Many masques and entertainments for weddings survive, and splendid weddings are sometimes called for in plays of the period.

That any play can be visualized in a variety of styles goes without saying. If *A Midsummer Night's Dream* was first offered as part of a wedding celebration, it was surely enacted later on the London stage, with appropriate alterations. The play as we have it can be thought of as having an ending for production in a private house, with Puck sweeping the Hall before bed-time, and another ending for the playhouse: a final dance. In the 1958 Connecticut production there was a synthesis of the two endings. The aim was not antiquarian accuracy, but an imaginative re-creation of an entertainment composed by a great poet for a splendid occasion.

Productions of this play in the last century suffered from too much spectacle, but our younger and more analytical directors turn increasingly to the text itself. There is more wizardry in the spoken verse, if said with conviction, care and charm, than any painted canvas or miraculous dress-making can manufacture. And so, for this production, we cleaved to the word as written, and tried to echo the author's intention.

The play takes place in the palace of the Duke of Athens, in a workmen's room or shop, and in a near-by forest. The original performing-area was probably the Great Hall of a manor house. Such a house was large enough to accommodate Queen Elizabeth when she was the guest of one of her great nobles on one of her summer "progresses." With its barns and dependencies, the house might have had to care for three hundred bag-and-baggage carts, a huge staff of domestics (besides the regular house-servants), and the court guests, horses, grooms and retainers.

This manor house is no fortress. We are no longer in the medieval world of heavy masonry-bearing walls, slit windows, and surrounding moats. Society is reflected in the play. Egeus is the conventional squire, the father of a country family. Theseus is more justice of the peace than great captain: magistrate, not tyrant. His soldiers are gentlemen armed for the hunt rather than a fight. His realm is not a castle but a country house. Charlecote, the home of Sir Thomas Lucy, connected by tradition with Shakespeare's youthful poaching imbroglio, would be an excellent model.

The structure of a Great Hall in a country house in which a Queen could have been welcomed, or a duchess married, determines the style and often the movement of the play. The scene is not changed by complete changes of setting, but by means of simple visual props or descriptions in the verse. The actors perform, not within a square proscenium, curtained and foot-lit, but at the far end of a huge oak-beamed room, whose heavy slate roof is supported by massy timbers, and through whose high, lead-paned lights we can see the surrounding trees. The movement passes up and down, in front of and behind a splendid ornamented staircase which has two symmetrical flights of steps, each leading by at least one turn to the gallery above which gives off to the upper bedrooms. One can imagine, outside, formal knot-gardens of box or yew, with topiary birds and sculptured hedges. Beyond is the deer park which merges imperceptibly into Oberon's oak wood.

In Stratford, Connecticut, the theatre is built, inside and out, of a silvery brown, tobacco-colored South American teak. No curtain separates the spacious apron of the raked stage from the auditorium. When the audience has assembled, lights dim in the hall and rise on the stage, to mark the start of a play. For this particular play, we first see the far end of an Elizabethan Great Hall. Broad twin steps turn up toward a balcony, fronted by a pierced foliate grill. High above hangs a large verdure tapestry, a greeny blue forest of thin-trunked trees, recalling the background of the great series of Unicorn tapestries in the Cloisters Museum. Their style is medieval rather than renaissance, like the rest of the play, as if these hanging had been part of inherited house furnishings, in the owners' family for generations.

The action of this production started in dumbshow, with the company of mechanicals, each in character, as houseservants preparing the Hall for the marriage festivities. Hence it was clear from the first that they were members of a Warwickshire estate's staff, not Athenian workmen. They raised to the rafters great cut-out initials, a double-monogram, T and H, in late Tudor script, for Duke Theseus and his Hippolyta. Having made the Hall ready, the mechanicals withdrew, taking much care to behave silently and properly. The master of ceremonies of the ducal household then prepared the way, and Theseus, a lordly but faintly comic figure made his entrance and began his speech which opens the play.

The verdure tapestry suspended above the gallery was a device of focal importance. In the transformation of the timbered Hall into the Forest, outdoors, the figured stuff of the tapestry magically divides. It then spreads to thrice its size, and surrounds the entire acting area with shimmering leafage. At the end of the play it shrinks, to become woven tapestry again. There is a final glint of starlight through its texture, to reflect fading embers from an unseen fireplace, which Puck sweeps tidy just at cockcrow.

The treasure of sung, danced and partly-instrumental music

descending to us from Shakespeare's time is incalculably rich. One may find in it a dazzling, indeed confusing wealth of material with which to adorn the plays.

European travelers in Elizabeth's time often remarked that the English were a nation of musicians. Paul Hentzer, a German visitor in 1598 wrote:

> The English excel in dancing and music, for they are active and lively. . . . They are fond of great noises that fill the air, such as the firing of cannon, drums and the ringing of bells. . . . Actors represent almost every day comedies and tragedies to very numerous audiences; these are concluded by a variety of dances accompanied by excellent music and the excessive applause of all those that are present. . . .

The source of musical life, no longer the church, was rather the court, and later the town. The rising merchant class took over the taste of the court for musically-based shows.

Shakespeare's plays abound in references to music, and the lilt of clear song or plucked strings, is interwoven in the whole texture of *Dream.* As for specific music to accompany the various parts of the play, there are as many possibilities as there are directors.

For our production, the music was specially composed by Marc Blitzstein, an experienced theatre-musician. He was inspired by antique precedent, but made music for his own time. Since the company enjoyed the services of Russell Oberlin whose voice is one of the most beautiful counter-tenors now singing, much floating, liquid melody with words, and even in simple vocalization in extended cantilena, was given to his pure, soaring notes. The instrumental accompaniments were discreet, except for the ruder and more percussive dance portions and the underscoring for the play of Pyramus and Thisbe.

In Shakespeare's time social dancing on the aristocratic level approached theatrical spectacle in its calculated ostentation. Folk-dancing of country or townspeople continued a medieval tradition, including the Morris and other seasonal festival dances derived from Italy, France and Spain. All of these dances were embroidered with flashier steps and figures for theatrical use.

It was customary to end the plays with a dance, as in *A Midsummer Night's Dream* and *Much Ado About Nothing.* A Swiss traveler in 1599 saw *Julius Caesar* (probably Shakespeare's, at the Globe), and reported: "At the end, as is their custom, they danced, two in men's and two in women's clothes, wonderfully well together." A month later he saw another play, and again, "they performed the English and Irish dances." The Irish dance was possibly a jig, a comic danced ballad, accompanied by pipe and tabor.

In *Dream,* dances of various kinds are called for on different occasions. If the play has any connection with a public festival, it would be May Day, which the atmosphere and action sometimes suggest. On May Day there were elaborate dances and celebrations. In the City of London midnight fires were lit to celebrate the passage of the sun through the zodiac's highest arc, and boys leapt over the fires, for good luck, and to cleanse their souls. The play, however, is not specifically connected with the festival of a particular date. Rather, it is set in a countryside where all the folk celebrations were familiar, and it was common knowledge, for instance, that fairies

dance in rounds or fairy-circles. There were at least two kinds of fairy-rings, a green circle surrounded by a bare brown circumference made by bad fairies, and a brilliant green in the midst of a lush meadow caused either by good fairies or by a fungus.

Titania and Oberon often refer to the fairy-lore of the time. Titania calls, "Come, now a roundel, and a fairy song" [II. ii. 1]. A roundel (or roundelay) was a round-dance to the accompaniment of the dancers' singing. In Act II, Scene 1, the First Fairy (who is traditionally both the first dancer and a singing soloist) explains:

> And I serve the Fairy Queen,
> To dew her orbs upon the green.
>
> [II. i. 8-9]

That means that the fairies must refresh the bruised grass of the fairy-rings, which have been crushed in the tramp of the fairy-measures.

Titania's hint enables us to imagine the floorplan of the fairies' dances as somewhat complicated:

> The nine-men's-morris is filled up with mud,
> And the quaint mazes in the wanton green,
> For lack of tread, are undistinguishable.
>
> [II. i. 98-100]

The Nine Men's Morris is a game of Midland shepherds, something like a game of checkers cut in deep turf. "The quaint mazes" may refer to traces of a child's game, or, more probably, to tracks left by rural sports and dances on the village green. In any case in a contemporary production of the play, it would be wise to combine a bit of art with a bit of folk-dance, just as Shakespeare mixed in his verses to be sung the old folk-song and the new art-song. The publications of the English Folk Dance Society, while they generally apply to social rather than theatrical forms, provide a mass of basic material.

Towards the end of the play Duke Theseus asks:

> Come now; what masks, what dances shall we have,
> To wear away this long age of three hours,
> Between our after-supper and bed-time?
>
> [V. i. 32-4]

The after-supper was dessert, with sweetmeats. Philostrate offers a rich list of entertainments, all derived from Italian models: the kind of pompous shows which European princes from Parma to Paris published, in splendid editions, to impress their peers, wherever policy demanded. Philostrate suggests a battle of centaurs, to be sung (accompanied, we can imagine, by the harp, by a choreographed scene) by an Athenian eunuch, to the harp. Inappropriate for a marriage, the Duke will none of that. Well then, "The riot of the tipsy Bacchanals, / Tearing the Thracian singer in their rage" [V. i. 48-9], that is, the story of Orpheus. But Theseus chooses the "tedious brief scene" [V. i. 56] of Pyramus and Thisbe, and after that maladroit amusement is over, Bottom asks:

> Will it please you to see the epilogue, or to hear a
> Bergomask dance, between two of our company

Theseus disdains the epilogue, and the First Folio says *A Dance of Clowns.* Bottom was correct when he said "*hear* a Bergomask dance" [V. i. 353], for the Bergamasco was a sung dance. It derived, however remotely, from a dance of the Italian peasants of Bergamo. The Italian buffoons used to imitate the rustic Bergamaschi, and their Commedia dell'Arte was popular all over Europe. There is, however, no real reason to introduce the characters of the Commedia into this play, though their familiar figures have been used as decorative features in many recent productions. John Playford, whose *English Dancing Master* (1650) is a source-book of folk-music, described the country dance as calling for "kissing, shaking hands, clapping, stamping, snapping the fingers, peeping, wiping the eyes." The handkerchief, to hold and to wave, was an important accessory.

Actors are not necessarily trained dancers, and in the Bergamask dance they can be as rude and hearty as possible. Mistakes are only the funnier if the simple pattern be performed with rustic energy. In the Connecticut production, George Balanchine made a fairly elaborate transition from the comic play to the finale. The Bergamasco started with Nick Bottom and Robin Starveling, then Peter Quince, Tom Snout and Snug the joiner joined in. It was a five-handed country dance that could have been called by any square-dance caller; but then, imperceptibly, the gentry were invited to join the mechanicals. Hermia and Helena, followed by Hippolyta (who in her wedding-dress looked like a portrait by Zuccaro of Elizabeth herself) were swung into the pattern. But the weight of their skirts, as well as the grandeur of their status, slowed the dance down and brought heels back to the floor. The clowns respectfully made their bows and modestly withdrew, while their places were taken by the noble guests Lysander and Demetrius, and finally the Duke himself. The music changed from rough and quick to slow and stately; the dance became a version of Pavan, an Italian figure supposedly inspired by the spreading peacock (*pavo*), in which the robes and skirts of the nobility could be displayed to the greatest advantage. Balanchine's steps were very simple, but the style of the actors' execution of them, the light and atmosphere of the long day ending, the formal exchange of the mixed partners, who after all the adventures had regained their loving opposites, the twin stairs to be gained for beds above, provided a touching and beautiful climax to the poetry of the occasion.

Our ballet has not had a good effect on recent productions of Shakespeare, for the dexterity of trained dancers seems to accentuate the limited range of actors, and make it seem awkwardness. If actors can be taught the traditional court-bow and curtsey, and perform them with formal elegance and simplicity, that is enough. To learn to bow and curtsey is harder than one might imagine. Americans have not the habit of saluting, or even recognizing status: we have no Court of St. James as model for ballroom behavior. In America the most beautiful public reverences are seen in the opera-house and concert-hall, in recognition of the audience's acclamation. There are infinite varieties of meaning—gratitude, modest mastery, consideration, exact judgment of partner or public—which may be expressed and made legible in the simple inclination of the neck and head, the bend of the knee, the management of the skirts. But this requires study and practice. In this play the most important element in performing the dances is not virtuosity but neatness. The stage represents, essentially, a ballroom, and the dances are more analytically social than brilliantly theatrical.

In our theatre, this play could suitably end with a masque of fairies, in which Oberon and Titania recapitulate their quarrel over the Indian boy, leaving Puck to sweep the place clean of evil and ill luck. There is danger that such a dance might

develop into a divertissement, delaying the final lines which are, after all, the key to the play. But there is ample precedent for elaboration. In Connecticut, the wealth of stairs and traps on the stage encouraged a magical ending molded into the movement of the actors. Morning was not far off; the fire from the great imaginary chimney had burned to dozing embers. Stars glittered like hundreds of sequins through the translucent green verdure of the tapestries. Only a few graceful steps, turns and exchanges were needed to make all creatures vanish, and leave Puck his epilogue. With a puff of smoke he blew out his cheeks and the whole hall vanished. The applause he had begged for overwhelmed him.

Who were the fairies; what did they look like? Well before 1400 the Wife of Bath, on her way to Canterbury [in Chaucer's *Canterbury Tales*] said that they were even then hard to come by:

> Tholde dayes of the Kyng Arthour,
> Of which the Britons speken greet honour,
> Al was this land fulfild of faierye.
> The elf queene with hir joly compaignye
> Daunced ful ofte in manye a grene mede;
> This was the olde opinion, as I rede.
> I speke of manye hundred yeres ago;
> But now kan no man se none elves mo.

The point is often made, just before and after Shakespeare's time, in ballad and broadside, that fairy-folk are little, visible by mortals mainly between midnight and dawn. Reginald Scott in his *The Discouerie of Witchcraft* (1571) compounds confusion. All the types he mentions have appeared, at one time or another, in the court masques derived from the Italian models:

> . . . In our childhood our mothers maides have so terrified us with . . . bull beggars, spirits, witches, urchens, elves, hags, fairies, satyrs, pans, faunes, sylens, kit with the cansticke, tritons, centaurs, dwarfes, giants, imps, calcars, conjurors, nymphes, changelings, Incubus, Robin goodfellow, the spoorne, the mare, the man in the oke, the hellwaine, the fierdrake, the puckle, Tom thombe, hob goblin, Tom tumbler, boneless and such other bugs, that we are afraid of our own shadowes. . . .

How Pan, Silenus, fauns, tritons and centaurs, creatures with an ancestry from Ovid, got mixed up with purely English, Scotch and Irish countryside figures is a grateful topic for the learned. But it seems to have been conceded that although early fairies were taller than humans, Elizabethan fairies were small, not evil, while elves were mischievous but not lethal.

The Mad Pranks and Merry Jests of Robin Goodfellow (printed in 1628, but thought to have been circulated as early as 1588, and perhaps consulted by Shakespeare) is filled with suggestions for modern designers:

> . . .There were with King Obreon a many fayries, all attyred in greene silke: all these with King Obreon, did welcome Robin Goodfellow into their company. Obreon took Robin by the hand and led him in a dance: their musicians were little Tom Thumb; for hee had an excellent bag-pipe made of a wren's quill, and the skin of a Greenland louse; this pipe was so shrill, and so sweete, that a Scottish pipe compared to it, it would no more come neere it, than a Jewes-trump doth it to an Irish harpe. . . .

It seems that fairies were, by and large, green more than any other color, probably grasshopper- or grass-green; by extension, iridescent, with insectile antennae and froggy dapplings. In *The Merry Wives of Windsor* (Act IV, Scene 4) the fairies are described as black, white, gray and green. *The Fairy Tradition of Britain,* by Lewis Spence, may be consulted for microscopic particulars. He instances variants from the canonical green:

> As for more or less modern fairies, the residual figures of an ancient tradition, perhaps the best models are Arthur Rackham's beautiful water-colors in his gift edition of the play. It is unfortunately out of print, but available in libraries. He more than any other artist illustrated the spirit of the Song of Robin Goodfellow:
>
> . . .Round about, little ones, quick and nimble,
> In and out wheele about, run, hop or amble.
> Joyne your hands lovingly: well done, musition!
> Mirth keepeth man in health like a phisition . . .
> Make a ring on the grasse with your quick measures,
> Tom shall play, and Ile sing for all your pleasures. . . .
>
> (pp. 16-26)

Lincoln Kirstein, "On Producing 'A Midsummer Night's Dream'," in A Midsummer Night's Dream *by William Shakespeare, edited by Charles Jasper Sisson, Dell Publishing Co., Inc., 1960, pp. 16-27.*

John Simon (essay date 1971)

[*The excerpt below is drawn from Simon's review of Peter Brook's production of* A Midsummer Night's Dream *during its New York run. He offers a point-by-point challenge to both Brook's conception of the play and his theories of staging.*]

Do masterpieces need to be reinterpreted for every revival? Are there, perhaps, no more masterpieces left at all—as Artaud proclaimed and some eminent critics and men of the theater were only too eager to corroborate lately? What is needed, according to Robert Brustein, the most intelligent and temperate of the antimasterpiecers, is "willing[ness] to approach classical works with complete freedom, even if this means adapting them into a modern idiom" [*The Third Theatre*]. Oddly enough, Brustein seems to see no significant difference between directorial reinterpretations—as when, say, *King Lear* is so edited, staged, and acted as to make it resemble a work by Beckett (Peter Brook's production); and authorial versions, as when Dryden or Giraudoux writes a wholly new *Antony and Cleopatra* or *Electra*.

In his new-found role as producer and director, Brustein seems to contradict, or at least relax, his former critical standards. Thus, to bolster his argument in favor of irreverence to masterpieces, he is perfectly willing to adduce numerous examples for which he himself has no use: why, for instance, bother to mention such experiments as Dryden's with *Troilus and Cressida*, which, as Brustein states, was "a hash" of the original? And I cannot fathom what the difference is between the Stratford, Connecticut, *Much Ado,* set "in Spanish Texas around the time of the Alamo" and reprehended by Brustein; and Lowell's version of *Prometheus Bound,* as staged by Jonathan Miller, with the Greek setting or Caucasian crags abandoned for "a vague seventeenth-century background— probably Spain during the Inquisition" and defended by

Brustein—indeed produced by him for the Yale Repertory Company.

The objection to leaving masterpieces more or less as they are is that they were produced by "companies . . . more often dedicated to perpetuating the past than illuminating it, and, as a result, ended up looking more like museums than living organisms." Brustein is writing here about the Old Vic and Comédie Française, and though his intent is to decry old-fashioned productions of classics, the subject of the sentence is "companies"; in truth, it is they who end up looking like museums (and presumably blameworthy), not the practice of letting a masterpiece remain itself. This, of course, raises the question of what is wrong with a museum as long as it preserves and displays its treasures accessibly and tastefully? Do we have to repaint a Cézanne or rebake a Minoan terra-cotta to bring it up to date?

The main issue, however, is precisely how to maintain the quality of a living organism in a play. The failure to do this in so-called conventional productions does not stem from setting and staging the play logically and consistently, from not manhandling the author's text and intentions (to the extent that they are knowable), and from not being palpably and provocatively different from every other mounting of the play that ever was. The failure—and it is common enough—lies in offering a routine, bloodless production along well-trodden lines, in which the play's sights and sounds and ideas are not experienced afresh. Certainly a good production is one that suggests that we are enjoying the play with new eyes, new ears, new minds; but this does not mean that it should be revamped beyond recognition, beyond respecting at least the basic intentions and givens contained in it. To be sure, it is much easier to dazzle by doing things differently with a vengeance—say, converting outdoors into indoors, Venice into Vienna, women into men, romance into satire, etc.—but true artistry is to make things both the same *and* different.

Take, for example, *A Midsummer Night's Dream,* these comments being a preamble to a discussion of its new production by Peter Brook for the Royal Shakespeare Company, now imported by David Merrick. *Dream* can be laid in Athens, in Shakespeare's England or in an imaginary world of the poetic fancy. Or any two of these, or all three places may be combined, and suggestions of time present can of course be legitimately introduced. All of these valid options allow for an individual vision on the part of the director and designer, yet would not clash with what is in the text or with the best tradition of *Dream* productions. Within this set of plausibilities one can work wonders of resourcefulness and empathetic sensitivity.

Indeed, Peter Brook has not taken significant liberties with the time of the play. Although Puck looks like a character from the commedia dell'arte, and the lovers wear mod tie-dyed togs, the period of the production is pleasantly indeterminate. But something jars even here: the costumes (by Sally Jacobs, who also designed the scenery) tend to have an inexpensive, humdrum look about them: not quite Grotowskian poverty, but a kind of flimsy, school-production economy. Where the licence—or licentiousness—comes in is with the locale, the spatial concept of the production, which is topsy-turvy, cute and perverse without shame or surcease. To revert to Brustein: " 'No more masterpieces' means treating the theatre as informally as a circus tent, a music hall, a prize ring—a place in which the spectator participates rather than worships, and offers the stage something more than the condescension of applause."

I find that remark genuinely puzzling. Why is applause a form of condescension? It is a convention as good as any other—say, shaking hands or tipping one's hat—and has a perfectly acceptable symbolic value. It is, moreover, boisterous and informal in character. Furthermore, at the circus and the music hall, two of Brustein's suggested locations, applause is very much the order of the day. At prize fights it is not, but I doubt whether Brustein would be happy if one of his stage productions were constantly interrupted with shouts of "Sock him!" or "Kill him!" and the various jeers and howls the punched flesh is heir to. And what about audience participation? In none of the mediums Brustein describes does the spectator participate in any tangible way; indeed, Brustein has treated with just contempt most audience-participation theater. Clearly what is meant is some sort of emotional involvement, and this is available from any good play in a decent production, however unexperimental it may be. The key word in Brustein's statement, I dare say, is "worships": he is rightly incensed by the sheeplike audiences that flock to the various temples of culture, absorb their monthly quota of self-improvement (or self-promotion), dutifully clap their hands where they are supposed to, and remain basically uninvolved throughout.

But the trouble with a theater that wants to jolt the masses out of their torpor is that it tends to see the problem in simple black-and-white terms. Over here the snobbish, bourgeois audience in their black-and-white evening regalia, pompously or jadedly applauding their fiftieth *Romeo and Juliet* in which an effete Romeo and an elocutionary Juliet vow their love under and on the identical balcony with the selfsame pear-shaped B.B.C. diction all over again. But over there the *Romeo and Juliet* that takes place in the bohemian section of some modern city, with a drug-pusher Romeo wooing the daughter of the illegal liquor-traffic king, the words emerging tough and nervous from the top and bottom of a fire escape, and the audience all involved young people in unregimented clothing and at the edges of their seats with excitement. Not so. One can get radical productions that are absolutely awful, whereas an essentially traditional mounting may be brilliant, its conventionally attired audience genuinely aroused. Innovation can take place subtly, in details, in peripheral matters, slight shifts of emphasis or interesting new technical devices, or a lovely new musical score. Such innovation is less spectacular and more difficult to achieve, yet it will make the tenth go at a great play perfectly rewarding for an intelligent audience. How often, after all, do most of us get to see even so popular a classic as *A Midsummer Night's Dream?* Surely not more often than we hear in concert a major piece of music, yet we do not expect that to be rewritten. What I am saying is that we must not allow our justified indignation with boring productions or complacent spectators goad us into senseless retaliatory measures that cannot reclaim a blasé or boorish audience, but may obscure and destroy the meaning and beauty of a play.

Oddly enough, Brook's *Dream* has strong suggestions of the circus and music hall, and even some of the physical violence of the prize fight. The stage is a dazzling white box set with two swinging doors in the back wall, narrow black ladders bisecting the side walls (these ladders can be pushed aside and thus make a passage), and where the side walls come closest to the proscenium, a further pair of ladders and poles. A nar-

row gallery runs around the top edges of the set. There the actors not in a given scene tend to congregate and watch their colleagues act; from there too they create such special effects as lowering huge wire coils suspended from fishing rods to become the trees of the enchanted forest. Also up there are a brace of musicians who produce mostly percussive or electronic obstreperousness; onstage, there is a chap who follows the actors around playing a flamenco guitar; the fairies will perform a raga while slowly rising and descending on swings—at other times, they may launch into a rock concert.

The air above the stage is troubled. Titania, on her bed made of one enormous scarlet feather, is sometimes afloat in it; Oberon and Puck swing through it on trapezes or ropes, sometimes passing a whirling disk to each other from wand to wand, a disk that represents the flower with the magic juice; Hermia is hoisted up into it by ropes and pulleys (all visible to the audience) when Lysander suspends her from a crossbar; the fairies, as noted, go up and down in it, making music. But the aerial traffic is not only in bodies: there are silver and blue tinfoil planes shot through this space by the actors on the catwalk; when Titania's body is being belabored by the donkeyfied Bottom, and a p.a. system blares out a deliberately scratchy rendition of Mendelssohn's Wedding March, all kinds of streamers and paper plates are hurled at the stage, a litter that Puck is seen sweeping up with a rake as the curtain descends.

Let us dwell for a moment on Titania and Bottom. The ass's head here consists of a pair of hound's or faun's ears, a bulbous Mickey Mouse nose, and heavy wooden clogs suggestive of hooves. A fairy then sticks an arm ending in a fist through Bottom's thighs, so that he seems to have a huge erect phallus topped with a monstrous glans; thus accoutered (the arm waves up and down), he falls on Titania. Now this is clearly, like much else in the production, influenced by Jan Kott, whose essay on *Dream* [in *Shakespeare Our Contemporary*] makes it out to be Shakespeare's most bestially erotic play. According to Kott, Shakespeare picked the donkey because it "was credited with the strongest sexual potency and among all quadrupeds was supposed to have the longest and hardest phallus." Kott then goes on to visualize Titania as one of those very fair, flat-chested, tall Scandinavian girls he used to see in the Latin Quarter "clinging tightly to Negroes with faces grey or so black that they were almost undistinguishable [sic] from the night." The "grey" was thrown in, I suppose, because it is the color of asses; otherwise, the statement makes perfect sense as the utterance of a sniggering puritanical clod. Titania, according to Kott, then rapes the ass Bottom, "the lover she wanted and dreamed of " without daring to admit it; their lovemaking is meant "to rouse rapture and disgust, terror and abhorrence." We can now add to the other characteristics of Kott his proneness to absurd sexual fantasies. How does our critic gloss Oberon's line about the next thing Titania will see: "She shall pursue it with the soul of love"? [II. i. 182]. "As a punishment Titania will sleep with a beast." I would not have thought that "the soul of love" was instant intercourse; even less plausible is it to assume that Oberon expressly destines Titania for the largest-membered beast there is in the Renaissance bestiaries, since his list of possibilities includes the monkey, the lynx, and the cat, with which she could scarcely have had sex at all. The encounter with the ass-headed Bottom—and surely Shakespeare was largely motivated by the pun arse (ass), bottom—was pure accident. Moreover, as the scene is written, there is not the slightest need to suppose that the transmogrified tinker and the Fairy Queen ever consummated their love.

And now here is Peter Brook, in an interview, discussing "the most extraordinary demonic notion of having the Queen fornicate with a physically repellent object—the Ass. And why does Oberon do it? Not out of sadism, anger or revenge—but out of genuine love. It is as though in a modern sense a husband secured the largest truck driver for his wife to sleep with to smash her illusions about sex and to alleviate the difficulties in their marriage." Well, that's a mighty queer concept of genuine love and the ways to alleviate marital difficulties—to say nothing of it as an interpretation of the play. Oberon, I repeat, does not know what chance will turn up before the waking Queen, and it would be a sorry truck driver indeed whose organ would be the size of a cat's. And of course what one may do under the spell of the magic juice has nothing to do with one's secret yearnings, which is made explicit when Titania, disenthralled of the drug, looks at the sleeping Bottom and says, "O, how mine eyes do loathe his visage now" [IV. i. 79]. No comment on the phallus, which only the fevered Freudianizing of Kott and Brook dragged in in the first place.

But that other Pole, Jerzy Grotowski, is equally and no less dismally relevant to this production. The glaringly white set, which gives one a bad case of snow blindness, is the kind of environment Grotowski dreams up for his productions. It also reminds one of Peter Brook's remark in his book, *The Empty Space:* "A true image of necessary theatre-going . . . is a psychodrama session in an asylum." And so an asylum ward becomes the sole setting for all of *A Midsummer Night's Dream* (why not? it worked for *Marat/Sade,* didn't it?), an asylum that is also a circus, and a nice place for an orgy: the floor is conveniently strewn with cushions. From Grotowski, too, Brook may have derived the idea of doubling his actors. Theseus becomes Oberon; Hippolyta, Titania; Philostrate, Puck; Aegeus, Quince. The first three doublings can be defended as stressing the parallel between the fairy and human worlds. But is this underscoring desirable? Surely the play wants to point to certain differences as well as similarities; to make the aerial and Athenian rulers identical obscures the interplay of likeness and unlikeness, and reduces much of the playing to mere tours de force. There is no reason whatever, though, for Aegeus' becoming Quince, especially since the actor in question is questionable enough even in a single part.

This brings us to the performers. The Athenian lovers are all remarkably unprepossessing. Lysander, like Aegeus, is portrayed as a lisping fag; Demetrius looks like a faintly brutish mod cab driver. Hermia is a mousy nonentity; Helena a gawky, plain, desperately sex-starved tomboy. Like most of the other actors, they speak with commonplace accents, often with poor diction, and their lovemaking is of the crudest sort: wrestling bouts, pratfalls, leaps on top of one another, strangleholds, even an occasional travesty of a *Pietà.* Often the actors cannot be heard at all. Words are blithely mispronounced: Theseus, rather unbiblically, gives us an eye for an aye; Helena pronounces erring as airing—which admittedly is as arrant as it is errant. Titania's attendant fairies include one lumpish fattie, Theseus-Oberon is pallid and unregal, Titania vaguely dumpy. Puck is a chunky fellow who comes on rather tougher and more domineering than usual, but who swings well from ropes, walks nimbly on stilts, and juggles passably: when the spinning plate drops on occasion, it is impossible to tell if this is an accident or a deliberate comic ef-

fect. The artisans, on the other hand, are made much less undignified than usual, but whether in order not to offend a working-class audience or to help contribute to the general upending of the play is open to question.

By confining the entire action to a white box, by making various characters interchangeable, by using drab actors and flat speech, etc., Brook systematically depoeticizes the play. Much acclaim has been given his avoidance of cardboard forests, fake moonlight, winged fairies, and so forth—as if we could now finally see what the play is all about and hear the words properly against an uncluttered background. But this is sheer nonsense: an imaginative set designer, a stylish costumer, a good lighting man can create images that are suggestive rather than factitious, not ineptly naturalistic but stylized and bewitching. And only in a suitable setting can Shakespeare's lines exude their full meaning and poetry. A bare stage might just do it, too, but a *mise en scène* that contradicts the words or overillustrates them—as when Hermia is called a puppet while being hoisted aloft by a bar on which Lysander suspended her—draws attention to the director's cleverness or capriciousness, to a superimposed absurdism or demented literalness, but not to what Shakespeare wrote. Alas, a Brook for a Shakespeare is not a fair exchange.

So the comedy is reduced to farce in the first half of the play—but farce with nasty overtones. In the second half, the comedy is turned into something rather somber and depressing, again only to demonstrate that the author is putty in the director's hands and that the director really knows what a modern audience needs. So the mechanicals' play becomes less ludicrous, almost pathetic; the comments on it by the wedding couples are made to come out sour, even mean, instead of merely ironically bantering; the final arrival of Oberon, Titania, and their train is imbued with a kind of melancholy, and accompanied by the ominous soughing of the wind: it is as if the fairies were abandoning the mortals forever to their mortality. So Brook turns this airy pageant (with some serious overtones, to be sure) into a dark comedy, which it was never meant to be. Even the songs, which might be presumed to defy Brook with their lyricism, are brutalized by Richard Peaslee's musical settings: drum beats, weird echo-chamber effects, rattles and crashes, rock, unmelodiousness.

The enchantment stamped out, the performances divested of magic, love turned into lust, the *Dream* changed into nightmare—what remains when everything is overthrown, dismantled, shattered? There remains the supreme magician, Peter Brook, who fancies himself the Prospero of the occasion but is really its Sycorax. And what exactly is Brook's fascination with the male arse all about? In *Marat/Sade* he gave us Marat's bare behind; here it is Snug who is twice stripped to tiniest briefs made from a Union Jack. Why does Helena duck when her suitors are about to kiss her each from his side, with the result that they end up bussing each other? Why does the waking, bewitched Demetrius reach passionately for Puck's genitals—especially since none of the mortals except Bottom is at any other time able to see the fairies? Why do the fairies wave about colored plastic tubes of a vaguely phallic sort? But never mind the epicene aspects of this production, which may, after all, be quite harmless. It is the eclecticism, the contrariness, the helter-skelter of it that makes it self-defeating. Peter Brook once surprised a young film maker by telling him that he should shoot his film both in black-and-white and in color and then intercut the two.

Why? Because it would create an interesting effect. A mania for injudicious experimentation is what characterizes the director's work in the theater too. In the case of a minor play like *Marat/Sade* or *Titus Adronicus* this can work well enough; with *King Lear* and even *A Midsummer Night's Dream* it undercuts and diminishes the playwright's achievement.

But, say the champions of reckless innovations, this brings new audiences into the theater. What kind of audience, however, would come just to see Brook's cleverness? And how could they see the forest for the coiled-wire trees? And would this lead them to the appreciation of respectable theater (by which I do not mean long-faced and anemic), or would they remain fixated at this anal level? These are questions that cannot easily be answered; still less can they be easily dismissed. I believe that a passable revival such as the current one of *A Doll's House,* ably and conservatively staged by Patrick Garland serves the theater better than all these Brookish fireworks. (The attendants at the Theseus-Hippolyta nuptials actually bring in tapers surrounded by Christmas sparklers.) It may be that there won't be large theater audiences without this kind of bait; and it may be that the days of the theater as a popular art are numbered, or even over. Would that be so bad? If the theater became an élite art, like architecture or contemporary poetry or classical music, giving it few company but fit, I for one would not grieve. Render unto television, popular movies, rock concerts what is theirs and *who* is theirs, and let the rest of us get down to the serious business— or art—of theater. (pp. 314-22)

> *John Simon, "Spring, 1971," in his* Uneasy Stages: A Chronicle of the New York Theater, 1963-1973, *Random House, 1975, pp. 313-38.*

FURTHER READING

REVIEWS AND RETROSPECTIVE ACCOUNTS

Addenbrooke, David. *The Royal Shakespeare Company: The Peter Hall Years.* London: William Kimber, 1974, 334 p.

> Overview of Hall's career, including his several productions of *A Midsummer Night's Dream* in the 1950s and 1960s. This work also features two interviews with the noted director.

Agate, James. " 'A Midsummer Night's Dream': Mendelssohn's Music." In his *Brief Chronicles: A Survey of the Plays of Shakespeare and the Elizabethans in Actual Performance,* pp. 43-6. 1943. Reprint. New York: Benjamin Blom, Inc., 1971.

> Review of Harcourt-Williams's 1929 Old Vic revival of *A Midsummer Night's Dream,* with special reference to music in the staging of the play. This production featured John Gielgud in the role of Oberon.

———. "No Fairies for Titania" and "The 'Dream' Again." In his *The Contemporary Theatre: 1944 and 1945,* pp. 151-53, 154-56. London: George G. Harrap and Company Ltd., 1946.

> Two reviews of Nevill Coghill's 1945 Haymarket production of *A Midsummer Night's Dream* with John Gielgud as Oberon.

Allen, Shirley S. "Samuel Phelps, Last of A Dynasty." *The Theatre Annual* VIII (1950): 55-70.

> Survey of the illustrious nineteenth-century theater manager's career, including his outstanding 1853 production of *A Midsummer Night's Dream.*

Alvarez, A. "Interpreting Dreams." *New Statesman* LVII, No. 1474 (13 June 1959): 824, 826.

> Admires Peter Hall's "imaginative control" in his 1959 Stratford-upon-Avon presentation of the *Dream.* Alvarez claims that this production regained for the play "some of the vigour and seriousness it must originally have had," and yet, he notes, it was "touched by none of the heavy pedantry that goes with scholarly correctness."

Ansorge, Peter. Review of *A Midsummer Night's Dream. Plays and Players* 18, No. 11 (August 1971): 47.

> Considers the 1970-71 RSC production of the *Dream* "the most accessible of Peter Brook's theatrical experiments."

Atkinson, Alex. Review of *A Midsummer Night's Dream. Punch* CCXXXVI, No. 6201 (17 June 1959): 813-14.

> Judges Peter Hall's first presentation of the *Dream* at the Shakespeare Memorial Theatre "enchanting." "No wood," Atkinson maintains, "was ever more delightfully haunted."

Atkinson, Brooks. Review of *A Midsummer Night's Dream. The New York Times* (22 September 1954): 33.

> Considers Michael Benthall's Old Vic production a "heavy, slow-footed 'Dream'." This review is of a performance of the comedy at the Metropolitan Opera House in New York.

Barbour, Charles M. "Up Against a Symbolic Painted Cloth: *A Midsummer Night's Dream* at the Savoy, 1914." *Educational Theatre Journal* 4, No. 27 (December 1975): 521-28.

> Close analysis of the printed version of Harley Granville-Barker's groundbreaking production of the *Dream.*

Barnes, Clive. "A Magical 'Midsummer Night's Dream'." *The New York Times* (21 January 1971): 27.

> Praises Brook's production of the *Dream* as "a celebration of life and fancy, of man and his imagination, his fate, and the brevity of his brief candle in the light of the world."

Benson, Frank. "My First London Venture." In his *My Memories,* pp. 285-304. 1930. Reprint. New York: Benjamin Blom, 1971.

> Recollection of the difficulties Benson encountered in his first London engagement, which included a production of *A Midsummer Night's Dream.*

Brahms, Caryl. "To the Woods." *Plays and Players* 6, No. 10 (July 1959): 13.

> Offers a balanced assessment of Peter Hall's 1959 RSC staging of *A Midsummer Night's Dream.*

Brown, Ivor. "Eastward Ho!" *The Observer* (28 March 1954): 11.

> Contains a review of George Devine's Shakespeare Memorial Theatre staging of *A Midsummer Night's Dream.* Brown praises the portrayals of the mechanicals, but generally censures the production as "murky and unmagical."

Byrne, M. St. Clare. "The Shakespeare Season at The Old Vic, 1957-58 and Stratford-upon-Avon, 1958." *Shakespeare Quarterly* IX, No. 4 (Autumn 1958): 507-30.

> Describes Michael Benthall's 1957 presentation of *A Midsummer Night's Dream* at the Old Vic as "a very delightful production."

Clurman, Harold. Review of *A Midsummer Night's Dream. The Nation* (New York) 220, No. 21 (31 May 1975): 668-70.

> Admires the "genial robustiousness" of the Yale Repertory Theater's 1975 production of Henry Purcell's operatic version of the *Dream.*

Croyden, Margaret. "The Achievement of Peter Brook." In her *Lunatics, Lovers and Poets: The Contemporary Experimental Theatre,* pp. 231-85. New York: McGraw-Hill Book Company, 1974.

Comprehensive analysis of Brook's renowned 1970 RSC production of *A Midsummer Night's Dream* and other works.

Cushman, Robert. "Fairy-tale Time." *Observer Review* (28 November 1982): 33.
Favorable evaluation of Bill Bryden's National Theatre revival of *A Midsummer Night's Dream.* The critic declares that he preferred this staging to Peter Brook's landmark production.

Darlington, W. A. "Old Vic on Stage at Scottish Fete." *The New York Times* (1 September 1954): 31.
Negative review of a performance of Michael Benthall's *Dream* in Edinburgh. Darlington argues that this production's blend of music, ballet, and spectacle overwhelmed the play's humorous elements.

David, Richard. "Stratford 1954." *Shakespeare Quarterly* V, No. 4 (Autumn 1954): 385-94.
Mixed review of George Devine's production at Stratford-upon-Avon. "It was slick, it was efficient, it was streamlined, it kept the audience purring throughout," David states, "but to achieve this slickness poetry and magic had to go by the board."

——. "Plays Pleasant and Plays Unpleasant." *Shakespeare Survey* 8 (1955): 132-38.
Generally negative evaluation of George Devine's 1954 Shakespeare Memorial Theatre presentation of *A Midsummer Night's Dream,* a production which featured half-human, half-animal fairies. David admires the "intellectual treats" this staging offered, but concludes that they were "not enough."

Dehn, Paul. "The Filming of Shakespeare." In *Talking of Shakespeare,* edited by John Garret, pp. 49-72. London: Hodder & Stoughton, 1954.
Includes a brief consideration of Max Reinhardt's film adaptation of *A Midsummer Night's Dream,* stressing its relation to the director's stage versions of the play.

Dukere, Bernard F. Review of *A Midsummer Night's Dream. Educational Theatre Journal* XXIII, No. 1 (March 1971): 93-4.
Examines Peter Brook's revolutionary 1970 production with the RSC. Dukere maintains that this staging was "enormously entertaining and triumphantly successful."

Eaton, Walter Prichard. "Do You Believe in Gold Fairies?" In his *Plays and Players: Leaves from a Critic's Scrapbook,* pp. 234-40. Cincinnati: Stewart & Kidd Company, 1916.
Reviews Granville-Barker's staging of *A Midsummer Night's Dream* at Wallack's Theater in New York. "You leave the theater a bit bewildered" after this performance, Eaton observes, "but admitting that, after all, you never knew before that 'A Midsummer Night's Dream' could be such an interesting play."

Evans, Gareth Lloyd. "Shakespeare in Stratford and London, 1981." *Shakespeare Quarterly* 33, No. 2 (Summer 1982): 184-88.
Includes a review of Ron Daniels's RSC revival of *A Midsummer Night's Dream.* "This production," Evans states, "was, arguably, a mixed-up amalgam of Brook's theatricality, Kott's misguided intellectuality, the RSC's own contemporary obsession with Dickens . . . and a few personal quiddities of the director."

Feingold, Michael. "Yale's 'Dream' Grew from a Unified Vision." *The New York Times* (8 June 1975): 5.
Defends the "organic quality" of the Yale Repertory Theater's presentation of *A Midsummer Night's Dream* set to Henry Purcell's music. This production was "a fully realized interpretation of the play," Feingold contends.

Findlater, Richard. Review of *A Midsummer Night's Dream. Plays and Players* 353 (February 1983): 24-5.
Deems Bill Bryden's 1983 National Theatre production at the Cottesloe "one of the more successful post-Brook productions of this elusive play in my experience."

Gascoigne, Bamber. "A Dream of Fair Women." *Spectator* 208, No. 6983 (27 April 1962): 539.
Laudatory assessment of Peter Hall's second revival of *A Midsummer Night's Dream.* "The 'magic of the theatre' is a cliche," Gascoigne observes, "but it remains the most apt description of the dancing lightness of certain very rare productions. Peter Hall's is one of these."

Gelb, Arthur. "Extravagant Dream." *The New York Times* (29 September 1954): II, 1, 3.
Conversation with Michael Benthall during the New York run of his 1954 Old Vic production of *A Midsummer Night's Dream.*

Griffiths, Trevor. "A Neglected Pioneer Production: Madame Vestris' *A Midsummer Night's Dream* at Covent Garden, 1840." *Shakespeare Quarterly* 30, No. 3 (Summer 1979): 386-96.
Reconstruction of this important nineteenth-century staging of the play.

——. "Tradition and Innovation in Harley Granville-Barker's *A Midsummer Night's Dream.*" *Theatre Notebook* XXX, No. 2 (1976): 78-87.
Detailed analysis of Barker's 1914 production in terms of his departures from established staging techniques.

Gussow, Mel. "Stage: Haunting Shakespeare's 'Dream'." *The New York Times* (15 May 1975): 48.
Review of the Yale Repertory Theater's presentation of Henry Purcell's operatic version of *A Midsummer Night's Dream.* Gussow finds it a "haunting, lustrous 'Dream'."

Helpmann, Robert. "Formula for Midsummer Magic." *Theatre Arts* XXXVIII, No. 9 (September 1954): 76-7, 95.
Description of Michael Benthall's 1954 Old Vic presentation of *A Midsummer Night's Dream* by the actor who played Oberon and choreographed the production.

Hewes, Henry. "A Dream for Mortals." *Saturday Review* (New York) LIV, No. 6 (6 February 1971): 48, 62, 66.
Evaluation of Peter Brook's RSC staging of *A Midsummer Night's Dream* during its New York run. Brook's presentation, Hewes contends, was "a milestone in the history of Shakespearean production."

Hunt, Hugh. "Granville-Barker's Shakespearean Productions." *Theatre Research* X, No. 1 (1969): 44-9.
Covers Barker's revolutionary 1914 revival of *A Midsummer Night's Dream* at the Savoy Theatre. This production, Hunt stresses, "was a complete departure from the prettiness of a Victorian fairyland."

Hurren, Kenneth. "Minority View." *Spectator* 226, No. 7460 (19 June 1971): 854-55.
Unfavorable review of a performance of Peter Brook's *Dream* at London's Aldwych Theatre.

Joseph, Bertram L. Review of *A Midsummer Night's Dream. Drama Survey* 2, No. 2 (October 1962): 206-11.
Assesses Peter Hall's second staging of the play at Stratford-upon-Avon. Joseph finds numerous shortcomings in this production but admits that "visually the set was delightful."

Kauffmann, Stanley. Review of *A Midsummer Night's Dream. The New Republic* 164, No. 8, Issue 2930 (20 February 1971): 24, 35.
Contends that there was much about Peter Brook's RSC staging of the *Dream* that was seemingly arbitrary and conceptually undeveloped.

Keown, Eric. Review of *A Midsummer Night's Dream. Punch* CCXXVI, No. 5923 (24 March 1954): 419-20.
Evaluates George Devine's *Midsummer Night's Dream* at the Shakespeare Memorial Theatre in Stratford-upon-Avon. "The magic of the *Dream*" was missing in this production, Keown

contends, because the poetry was "only hauled along, like a ton of coals."

Kerr, Walter. "Seductive 'Dream'." *The New York Times* (25 May 1975): 5.
Ironic review of the Yale Repertory Theater's 1975 production of *A Midsummer Night's Dream*. Kerr claims that eighteenth-century composer Henry Purcell's music was "irrelevant" to this staging "but charming to listen to."

————. "The Play is Scanted in the Scurry." *The New York Times* (31 January 1971): 5.
Maintains that the acrobatics of Peter Brook's presentation of *A Midsummer Night's Dream* obscured the play's deeper meanings.

Kingston, Jeremy. Review of *A Midsummer Night's Dream*. *Punch* 259 (9-15 September 1970): 376-77.
Mixed review of Peter Brook's innovative staging of the play. Kingston expresses several reservations, but concludes that this production was "a marvel full of marvels."

Kroll, Jack. "Placing the Living Shakespeare Before Us." *The New York Times* (7 February 1971): 1, 9.
Laudatory review of Peter Brook's revival of *A Midsummer Night's Dream*. Kroll asserts that this production was "a triumph of courage, good faith and artistic sensitivity."

Kuner, Mildred C. "The New York Shakespeare Festival, 1967." *Shakespeare Quarterly* XVIII, No. 4 (Autumn 1967): 411-15.
Includes an unfavorable appraisal of John Hancock's dark interpretation of *A Midsummer Night's Dream* in a 1967 New York production.

Lambert, J. W. Review of *A Midsummer Night's Dream*. *Drama*, No. 102 (Autumn 1971): 15-30.
Judges Peter Brook's RSC production "enormously enjoyable, wonderfully funny, splendidly spoken to reveal a hundred insights and nuances lying fallow in the text, mind-expanding."

Mahon, Derek. "Two Excellent Shakespeare Productions." *The Listener* 85, No. 2203 (17 June 1971): 798-99.
Review of Peter Brook's staging of *A Midsummer Night's Dream* during its London run at the Aldwych. "The play," Mahon states, "is about magic, the production magical."

Manvell, Roger. "Theatre into Film." In his *Shakespeare and the Film*, pp. 114-32. New York: Praeger Publishers, 1971.
Contains an assessment of Peter Hall's 1968 screen adaptation of *A Midsummer Night's Dream* and an interview with Hall.

Marowitz, Charles. "Brook: From 'Marat/Sade' to 'Midsummer Night's Dream'." *The New York Times* (13 September 1970): 7.
Discussion of Brook's *Dream* with particular emphasis on the production's relation to the director's career.

Review of a *Midsummer Night's Dream*. *The Nation* (New York) 100, No. 2591 (25 February 1915): 231.
Assesses a performance of Granville-Barker's production during its run at Wallack's Theater in New York. The critic admires this staging, stating that it was "the result of careful study and earnest conviction."

Review of *A Midsummer Night's Dream*. *New-York Daily Tribune* (19 April 1859): 5.
Evaluation of Laura Keene's production at her theater in 1859. "As an exhibition of scenery, costume, mechanical effects, and general display," the reviewer argues, this staging was unparalleled.

Review of *A Midsummer Night's Dream*. *The New York Times* (22 April 1859): 4.
Judges Laura Keene's 1859 production of the play at Keene's Theater "skillfully cast and gracefully rendered."

"Director Breaks 'Dream' Tradition." *The New York Times* (3 June 1959): 30.
Admires the "engaging freshness" of Peter Hall's 1959 revival of *A Midsummer Night's Dream*. The reviewer particularly praises Charles Laughton's performance as Bottom, stating that the actor made this role "not a tour de force of knockabout farce but an endearing character study."

Nightingale, Benedict. "Tripping Gaily." *New Statesman* 81, No. 2100 (18 June 1971): 858-59.
Sharply negative assessment of Brook's revival of *A Midsummer Night's Dream*. Nightingale deems this production a "berserk circus."

"South American Casino." *The Observer* (7 June 1959): 22.
Review of Peter Hall's first RSC presentation of *A Midsummer Night's Dream*. The critic censures this production as a "send up" of Shakespeare's play.

O'Connor, John J. Review of *A Midsummer Night's Dream*. *The New York Times* (19 April 1982): C 20.
Lauds Elijah Moshinsky's BBC television production of *A Midsummer Night's Dream*. "Magically," O'Connor claims, "Mr. Moshinsky's conception weaves its spell from beginning to end."

Pierce, G. M. Review of *A Midsummer Night's Dream*. *Cahiers Élisabéthans*, No. 21 (April 1982): 61-2.
Balanced consideration of the BBC television production of *A Midsummer Night's Dream* directed by Elijah Moshinsky. Pierce draws particular attention to the high quality of the performances.

Richie, Donald. Review of *A Midsummer Night's Dream*. *The Drama Review* 15, No. 2 (Spring 1971): 330-34.
Thorough assessment of Peter Brook's RSC production of Shakespeare's comedy. In this presentation, Richie asserts, the director "made us believe, for one moment at any rate, in the great and apparently undying dream of love and human understanding."

Roberts, Peter. Review of *A Midsummer Night's Dream*. *Plays and Players* 5, No. 5 (February 1958): 15.
Admires the "very happy balance between the knockabout of the mechanics and the light fantasy of the fairies" in Michael Benthall's 1957 staging of the *Dream*.

————. Review of *A Midsummer Night's Dream*. *Plays and Players* 18, No. 1 (October 1970): 42-3, 57.
Consideration of Peter Brook's enormously successful production with the RSC. Roberts particularly stresses the exuberance and energy of this revival.

————. Review of *A Midsummer Night's Dream*. *Plays and Players* 357 (June 1983): 34-5.
Favorable evaluation of Bill Bryden's 1983 National Theatre presentation of the *Dream*. The critic especially admires Robert Stephens's Oberon. "His way of re-issuing mint-fresh the famous passages of poetry . . . made stale by over quotation" was "quite a revelation," Roberts claims.

Rudin, Seymour. "Theatre Chronicle: Winter-Spring 1971." *The Massachusetts Review* XII, No. 4 (Autumn 1971): 821-33.
Includes a laudatory assessment of Brook's presentation of *A Midsummer Night's Dream* during its New York run.

Rutherford, Malcolm. Review of *A Midsummer Night's Dream*. *Plays and Players* 10, No. 12 (September 1963): 47.
Moderately favorable review of Peter Hall's second RSC staging of the play. This production, Rutherford asserts, was "more of a continuous romp than a perfect whole," but "pleasing nonetheless."

Seddon, George. "Hall's 'Dream'." *The Observer* (16 June 1963): 29.
Mixed review of a London performance of Peter Hall's second

production of *A Midsummer Night's Dream*. This revival, Seddon asserts, was "the only *Dream* I have not found unbearably tedious."

Shrimpton, Nicholas. "Hot Ice and Wondrous Strange Snow." *The Times Literary Supplement*, No. 4108 (21 December 1981): 1492.
Disparaging review of the BBC television presentation of *A Midsummer Night's Dream* directed by Elijah Moshinsky. Shrimpton judges this an incoherent interpretation that merged "reckless" romantic fantasy with "austere historicism."

Simon, John. "Bardicide." *New York* 4, No. 6. (8 February 1971): 48.
Unfavorable appraisal of Peter Brook's revival of the *Dream*. Simon especially censures this production's "twistings and distortions" of Shakespeare's play.

Sprague, Arthur Colby. "Shakespeare on the New York Stage 1954-1955." *Shakespeare Quarterly* VI, No. 4 (Autumn 1955): 423-27.
Presents a mixed review of a New York performance of Michael Benthall's 1954 Old Vic production of *A Midsummer Night's Dream*.

Sullivan, Dan. "Opium Dream." *The New York Times* (30 June 1967): 23.
Negative evaluation of an "avant-garde" production of *A Midsummer Night's Dream* directed by John Hancock. "Where Shakespeare gives us light-hearted merriment," Sullivan contends, Hancock gave us "heavy-hearted (sometimes heavy-handed) irony, and something close to despair."

Taylor, John Russell. "Shakespeare in Film, Radio, and Television." In *Shakespeare: A Celebration, 1564-1964,* edited by T. J. B. Spencer, pp. 97-113. Baltimore: Penguin Books, 1964.
Includes a brief consideration of Max Reinhardt's screen adaptation of *A Midsummer Night's Dream*. Taylor notes that this was "not, clearly, a 'serious' approach to Shakespeare at all, and yet, strange to relate, a remarkably successful film."

Review of *A Midsummer Night's Dream*. *The Times*, London (16 May 1923): 12.
Assesses W. Bridges-Adams's 1923 offering at Stratford-upon-Avon. Though this production cannot rank with the Shakespeare Memorial Theatre's best work, the critic states, its "outstanding virtue" was that it was "played for entertainment and not for reverence."

Review of *A Midsummer Night's Dream*. *The Times*, London (26 January 1945): 6.
Deems Nevill Coghill's 1945 Haymarket revival of the play "a charming performance."

Review of *A Midsummer Night's Dream*. *The Times*, London (24 March 1954): 5.
Divided judgment of George Devine's Stratford Festival presentation of the *Dream*. Although the production impressed him with "the good taste of the stage spectacle," and "the richness of the drollery," the reviewer maintains, it did "not enchant."

Trewin, J. C. "Country and Town: 1886-1890." In his *Benson and the Bensonians*, pp. 50-66. London: Barrie and Rockliff, 1960.
Recounts the circumstances and the critical reception of F. R. Benson's 1889 production of *A Midsummer Night's Dream* at the Globe Theatre in London.

——. "A Most Rare Vision: 1970." In his *Peter Brook: A Biography*, pp. 173-92. London: Macdonald & Co., 1971.
Comprehensive overview of the director's landmark production of *A Midsummer Night's Dream*.

——. "Brook's Dream Abroad." *Contemporary Review* 221, No. 1282 (November 1972): 244-48.
Analyzes Peter Brook's production of *A Midsummer Night's Dream* in relation to the stage history of the play.

Wardle, Irving. Review of *A Midsummer Night's Dream. The Times*, London (11 June 1971): 8.
Evaluates a London performance of Brook's RSC staging of Shakespeare's comedy, with particular attention to the changes and developments in the production since its first presentation at Stratford the previous year.

——. Review of *A Midsummer Night's Dream. The Times*, London (26 November 1982): 11.
Offers a favorable assessment of Bill Bryden's production of the play at the Cottesloe Theatre.

Warren, Roger. "Shakespeare in England, 1982-83." *Shakespeare Quarterly* 34, No. 3 (Autumn 1983): 334-50.
Includes a review of Bill Bryden's National Theatre staging of *A Midsummer Night's Dream* at the Cottesloe. Warren admires the "rough-and-ready effectiveness" of the playing and the "homely context" of this production.

Watts, Richard, Jr. "Films of a Moonstruck World." *The Yale Review* XXV, No. 2 (December 1935): 311-20.
Analysis of Max Reinhardt's film adaptation of *A Midsummer Night's Dream*. The critic argues that the failure of this work demonstrates the difficulties inherent in transferring Shakespeare to the screen.

Williams, Gary Jay. "*A Midsummer Night's Dream:* The English and American Popular Traditions and Harley Granville-Barker's 'World Arbitrarily Made'." *Theatre Studies* 23 (1976/1977): 40-52.
Comprehensive study of Barker's landmark production, focusing on its innovations and violations of stage traditions.

Williams, Harcourt. "My Watch." In his *Old Vic Saga*, pp. 79-96. London: Winchester Publications Limited, 1949.
Includes a brief recollection of the author's 1929 Old Vic production of *A Midsummer Night's Dream* with John Gielgud as Oberon.

Worsley, T. C. "Stratford." *New Statesman* XLVII, No. 1203 (27 March 1954): 400, 402.
Brief consideration of George Devine's Shakespeare Memorial Theatre presentation of *A Midsummer Night's Dream*. This production was "enjoyable in many of its parts," Worsley asserts, "but decidedly not memorable as a whole."

COMPARISONS AND OVERVIEWS

Foulkes, R. A. Introduction to *A Midsummer Night's Dream* in The New Cambridge Shakespeare, edited by R. A. Foulkes, pp. 1-41. Cambridge: Cambridge University Press, 1984.
Contains a section on the stage history of the play.

Jorgens, Jack J. "Max Reinhardt and William Dieterle's *A Midsummer Night's Dream*" and "Peter Hall's *A Midsummer Night's Dream*." In his *Shakespeare on Film*, pp. 36-50, 51-65. Bloomington: Indiana University Press, 1977.
Provides detailed analyses of these two screen adaptations of Shakespeare's comedy.

Merchant, W. Moelwyn. " 'A Midsummer Night's Dream': A Visual Recreation." In *Early Shakespeare*, Stratford-upon-Avon Studies 3, edited by John Russell Brown and Bernard Harris, pp. 165-85. London: Edward Arnold (Publishers) Ltd., 1961.
Constructs a history of the stage images and settings employed in productions of *A Midsummer Night's Dream*.

Sprague, Arthur Colby. "A Midsummer Night's Dream." In his *Shakespeare and the Actors: The Stage Business in His Plays (1660-1905)*, pp. 50-5. Cambridge, Mass.: Harvard University Press, 1944.
Scene-by-scene description of the stage directions and treat-

ments of characters in productions of the *Dream* throughout its stage history.

Stedman, Jane W. "Victorian Imitations of and Variations on *A Midsummer Night's Dream* and *The Tempest*." In *Shakespeare and the Victorian Stage,* ed. Richard Foulkes, pp. 180-95. Cambridge: Cambridge University Press, 1986.

Discusses the numerous nineteenth-century adaptations and derivatives of the *Dream.*

STAGING ISSUES

Granville-Barker, Harley. "Shakespeare's Progress." In his *On Dramatic Method,* pp. 68-116. New York: Hill and Wang, Inc., 1956.

Includes a section on *A Midsummer Night's Dream,* in which Barker discusses his interpretation of the comedy. "The whole play," he asserts, "is conceived as music, and in this is its integrity."

————. "Preface to *A Midsummer Night's Dream*." In his *Prefaces to Shakespeare,* Volume VI, pp. 94-134. London: B. T. Batsford Ltd., 1974.

Influential and far-ranging analysis of the staging of the *Dream* by the eminent director.

Kott, Jan. "Titania and the Ass's Head." In his *Shakespeare, Our Contemporary,* translated by Boleslaw Taborski, pp. 213-36. New York: W. W. Norton & Company, 1964.

Controversial examination of the elements of violence, sexuality, and cruelty in *A Midsummer Night's Dream.* Kott's views

had an immediate and significant impact on the staging of this comedy.

Lewis, Allan. "*A Midsummer Night's Dream*—Fairy Fantasy or Erotic Nightmare?" *Educational Theatre Journal* XXI, No. 3 (October 1969): 251-58.

Assesses the influence of Jan Kott's views on contemporary productions of Shakespeare's comedy and compares such stagings to traditional romantic presentations.

MacCarthy, Desmond. "The Production of Poetic Drama." *New Statesman* II, No. 45 (14 February 1914): 597-98.

Argues that the scenery and costumes for stagings of *A Midsummer Night's Dream* should be suggestive rather than prescriptive and should support, not overwhelm, the poetry of Shakespeare's play.

Selbourne, David. *The Making of* A Midsummer Night's Dream. London: Methuen, 1982, 327 p.

Production journal, featuring week-by-week reports on the preparation and rehearsal of Peter Brook's innovative RSC staging of the *Dream.*

Watkins, Ronald. *Moonlight at the Globe: An Essay in Shakespearean Production.* London: Michael Joseph Ltd., 1946, 136 p.

Detailed analysis of all facets of producing *A Midsummer Night's Dream,* including settings, music, and costumes.

———— and Jeremy Lemmon. In *Shakespeare's Playhouse: A Midsummer Night's Dream.* Tottowa, New Jersey: Rowman and Littlefield, 1974, 150 p.

Passage-by-passage reconstruction of a performance of the *Dream* in Shakespeare's lifetime.

THE TAMING OF THE SHREW

Two factors obscure the early stage history of *The Taming of the Shrew*. There is no record of the play until it appeared in QUARTO form in 1631, and there is little evidence to suggest its composition date. Most scholars agree, however, that it was probably written in the early to mid-1590s. A remarkably similar play, *The Taming of a Shrew*, was anonymously written within a few years of Shakespeare's comedy. Some scholars assert that this was a source for the Shakespearean work, but others believe that *A Shrew* is merely a "bad quarto" version of *The Shrew*. While the two plays are structurally and thematically similar, Christopher Sly, the drunken tinker who appears in both comedies, persists throughout *A Shrew*, whereas he disappears from *The Shrew* after Act I, scene i. The problem of Sly's disappearance has prompted scholars to speculate about whether Shakespeare purposely excised the Sly material from the latter part of his play or whether it was deleted by a later stage manager or editor. Irrespective of scholarly hypotheses, the Christopher Sly dilemma has challenged the creativity of numerous directors, who have variously interpreted his role in Shakespeare's play over the past four centuries.

The title page of the 1631 Quarto claims that *The Taming of the Shrew* was performed by the KING'S MEN at the GLOBE and BLACKFRIARS theatres. Since the King's Men did not regularly perform at Blackfriars until 1610, the play had apparently been in the company's repertoire for several years. Presumably, then, *The Taming of the Shrew* was staged more than once during Shakespeare's lifetime. Records indicate that it was still being produced as late as 1633, when it was acted at the court of Charles I.

From about this time, however, until the mid-nineteenth century, Shakespeare's comedy generally appeared only in heavily adapted forms. Sometime between 1604 and 1617, John Fletcher wrote a sequel entitled *The Woman's Prize; or, The Tamer Tamed*. Fletcher modified Shakespeare's story, presenting Petruchio as a widower who takes a new wife named Maria. Through the course of the play, Maria effectively turns Petruchio's taming techniques against him until in the end he surrenders in much the same way Kate does in the original version. If Fletcher's play works at all, H. J. Oliver argued, it is "only by sacrificing completely the character of Petruchio—as Shakespeare did not sacrifice the character of Kate—and so fails as an 'answer,' even a jocular one" (see Further Reading). Another popular adaptation, *Sauny the Scot: Or, The Taming of the Shrew: A Comedy*, was first presented during the Restoration period by John Lacey. Lacey greatly altered Shakespeare's text, casting Petruchio's servant Grumio in the lead role. The name "Sauny" is apparently a derivation of "Sanders" or "Saunders," the servant's name in *A Shrew*. Lacey's adaptation held the stage for decades, appearing as late as 1732 at Goodman's Fields Theatre.

Other early eighteenth-century adaptations focused solely on Christopher Sly and the Induction. Charles Johnson's farce *The Cobler of Preston* was staged at DRURY LANE on 3 February 1716, featuring Sly as the hero. Christopher Bullock of LINCOLN'S INN FIELDS—Drury Lane's rival company—

received word of Johnson's project and, in an effort to undermine his competitor, rushed his own version of *The Cobler of Preston* to the stage on 24 January. Bullock's scheme succeeded, for his version won over audiences and was frequently performed until 1759. Another variation of *The Taming of the Shrew* was James Wordale's *A Cure for a Scold* (1735), a two-act farce adapted from Lacey's *Sauny the Scot*. These versions were all supplanted in 1754, when David Garrick, the renowned eighteenth-century actor-manager, presented *Catherine and Petruchio*—the most famous and enduring adaptation of *The Taming of the Shrew*. Garrick's version omitted much of the original play, most notably the Induction. He divided the comedy into three acts, simplifying the Bianca/Lucentio subplot to focus on the courtship of Katherina and Petruchio. Since the adaptation was a considerable abridgment, Garrick often presented it with his altered version of *The Winter's Tale*, providing an original prologue to join the two plays. Immensely popular, *Catherine and Petruchio* was presented before English and American audiences for more than a century. Many prominent Shakespearean actors took the part of Petruchio, including John Philip Kemble, William Charles Macready, and Henry Irving. Such eminent actresses as Sarah Siddons, Helena Faucit, and Ellen Terry portrayed Katherina.

A movement away from the preference for Garrick's adaptation began in 1844, when Shakespeare's *Taming of the Shrew* was completely restored and presented by Benjamin Webster at the HAYMARKET THEATRE. This ambitious venture was initially proposed by J. R. Planché, who felt that two actors in Webster's company, Louisa Nisbet and Robert Strickland, were ideally suited to play Katherina and Christopher Sly. Intrigued by Planché's idea, Webster commissioned his associate to restore the original text of the play. Well known for his antiquarian interests, Planché recommended staging the production in an Elizabethan manner to underscore the company's dedication to Shakespeare's text. Planché felt that the comedy was a perfect subject for Elizabethan staging, for the restoration of the Induction encouraged the presentation of the play proper with little or no elaborate scenery. This proposition was a bold one, for extravagant scenery was the rule rather than the exception in Victorian theaters. Opening in March 1844, the production was welcomed by contemporary critics. Even those who did not entirely agree with its austere staging, recognized its ingenuity. Commentators applauded the performances of Nisbett and Strickland, justifying Planché's initial casting decision, but Webster's performance as Petruchio was less favorably reviewed. The production enjoyed a successful run throughout 1844 and was revived in 1847. Many years later Planché proudly reflected upon the role he had played in the ingenious staging: "My restoration of this 'gem' is one of the events in my theatrical career on which I look back with the greatest pride and gratification."

Other attempts to restore the original text to the stage followed Planché and Webster's, even though leading artists of the period continued to present Garrick's adaptation. In 1856, Samuel Phelps produced Shakespeare's *Shrew* at

Sadler's Wells, playing Christopher Sly in a performance which drew high praise from critics. Henry Morley claimed that Phelps's representation accurately expressed "Shakespeare's sketch of a man purely sensual and animal, brutish in appetite, and with a mind unleavened by fancy." Commentators also acclaimed the performances of the rest of the company. As one critic concluded, "the competent spectator will retire from the performance with a higher appreciation of the comedy . . . [than] the manner in which it is normally acted." No attempt to restore the original text of *The Taming of the Shrew* was made in America, however, until three decades after Phelps's production. The eminent stage-manager Augustin Daly was the first to do so in 1887, but he added embellishments of his own. Daly included all of the original elements of Shakespeare's play—the Induction, the Bianca/Lucentio subplot, and the Katherina and Petruchio story—but he rearranged scenes, omitted lines, and borrowed material from Garrick's *Catherine and Petruchio* to make the play conform to his own dramatic preconceptions. The production opened in New York on 18 January 1887 and featured the accomplished Shakespearean actress Ada Rehan as Katherina. The revival was an immediate success among theater-goers and critics alike, and it ran for more than 120 performances. One critic maintained that this production "will be remembered as the most successful venture of Mr. Daly in the Shakespearean field." After the production's successful New York run, Daly took it to the Gaiety Theatre in London, where it debuted on 29 May 1888 and again met with critical acclaim. Ada Rehan received special recognition for her brilliant portrayal of Kate. One critic professed that to "translate into the measured language of criticism the impression of fire, the strength, the versatility of Miss Ada Rehan's impersonation of Katherine is not possible." Rehan continued to play Katherina in Daly's numerous revivals of the play, and her portrayal of the shrew is considered by many critics the best ever given.

In 1913 John Martin Harvey produced *The Taming of the Shrew* with the help of the celebrated actor-manager, William Poel. Martin Harvey wanted to present an Elizabethan revival of the play and felt that Poel, the founder of the Elizabethan Stage Society, would be an invaluable consultant to the project. Martin Harvey later claimed that Poel showed scant interest in designing the setting, however, and was more interested in "the necessary 'cuts' to be made in the play . . . than the decoration of it." The production debuted on 10 May 1913 at the Prince of Wales Theatre, featuring Martin Harvey as Petruchio. Critical reaction to the presentation was markedly favorable. Commentators recognized the attempts to exhibit the play in an Elizabethan manner and to emphasize acting rather than scenery. One critic who commented admiringly on the production suggested that theater-goers were becoming more "fully alive to the advantages of the method, and would demand more of its excercise."

The next significant presentation of *The Taming of the Shrew,* however, demonstrated no adherence to this method. In the early 1930s Alfred Lunt and Lynn Fontanne, the husband and wife acting team, interpreted the play as a knockabout farce and used outrageous stage business to entertain their audience. Fearing that their irreverent treatment of the play would meet with a harsh reaction from New York critics, the Lunts took their show on tour throughout America. Having won critical acclaim with virtually every engagement, the Lunts decided to bring their production to the Guild Theatre in New York on 30 September 1935. The stage business for the Lunts' slapstick production was overwhelming, with a clown band, tumbling dwarfs, acrobats and jugglers, and numerous eccentric props. Theater critics responded enthusiastically to the production, taking great pleasure in the Lunts' ability to add rollicking humor to nearly every line of the play. Joseph Wood Krutch, for example, described it as "distinctly exhilarating," Brooks Atkinson praised it as "most exceeding funny," and Edith J. R. Isaacs maintained that it provided great entertainment for New York audiences who had "forgotten the circus and probably never knew good vaudeville." The Lunts' popular production ran for 128 performances at the Guild Theatre before resuming its tour of major American cities.

A more subdued approach to the play was offered by George Devine in 1953 at the Shakespeare Memorial Theatre. Devine was one of the first modern directors to provide a play-within-a-play framework for the comedy by restoring Shakespeare's Induction and incorporating the epilogue from *A Shrew*. This interpolation afforded Devine the opportunity to implement Christopher Sly into the action of the entire play. Moreover, the sustained presence of Sly allowed Devine to probe the theme of dream versus reality and to underscore the plays various levels of theatrical illusion. Critics applauded Devine's textual innovations and praised his representation of the other characters as creatures of Sly's imagination. Devine revived the production in 1954 and continued to win acclaim from reviewers who preferred his subdued approach to more flamboyant ones.

Six years after this revival, John Barton adapted elements of Devine's production into his own, which debuted on 21 June 1960 at Stratford-upon-Avon. Like Devine, Barton presented the play as a romantic comedy and incorporated the epilogue from *The Taming of a Shrew,* but he heightened the emphasis on theatrical illusion even more than Devine had done. Taking advantage of a recently-installed revolving stage, Barton arranged one side of it as the exterior of a country inn and the other side as its interior. When the action shifted from outside to inside, the players moved through the backdrop and took their positions on the other side of the stage as it revolved before the audience. During the revolution, a green-room was revealed between the two sets, with players rehearsing lines, playing cards over ale, and changing costumes. Peter O'Toole and Peggy Ashcroft received general acclaim for their portrayals of Petruchio and Katherina. T. C. Worsley asserted that O'Toole could "seize a scene and spin it round his little finger with a minimum of visible effort." Critics noted, however, that one drawback to O'Toole's performance was his inability to control the volume of his voice. "He yelps when he means to roar," Worsley recalled. Ashcroft pleasantly surprised commentators, who initially assumed she was cast against type for the role of the shrew. According to Kenneth Tynan, she "[confounded] all prophesy by demonstrating herself ideal for the part." Maurice Daniels restaged Barton's *Taming of the Shrew* one year after its successful run at the Shakespeare Memorial Theatre. Daniels's addition of more slapstick comedy generally met with disdain from critics. Richard Findlater disparaged the production for its "alarming addiction to crude knockabout," and Tom Milne maintained that the slapstick comedy generated "acres of mild tedium." For the most part, however, commentators praised the cohesive performances of the players in the revival, offering special praise for Vanessa Redgrave and Derek Godfrey in the roles of Katherina and Petruchio.

The modern trend to emphasize the play-within-a-play structure of *The Shrew* continued with Michael Langham's 1962 staging at Stratford, Ontario, and Trevor's Nunn's Royal Shakespeare Company production in 1967. Langham treated Christopher Sly as an integral component of the entire play. The actors performing in the play concentrated on the tinker as their main observer, going to great pains to make sure he fully understood the dramatic action. This focus on Sly gave the production a cohesive, well-balanced perspective that reflected, as Henry Hewes expressed it, Langham's "gradually acquired supremacy" in the art of open theater direction. Perhaps the most unusual innovation in this production was its concluding action. After the final scene, the characters portraying Katherina and Petruchio stood exhausted, regaining their composure while the other players packed up the props. As the troupe began to leave the country inn, Petruchio walked past Kate, threw his arm around the actress who had played Bianca, and walked off stage with her. This underscored the notion that what had just transpired was only a play and contributed to the motif of theatrical illusion. Trevor Nunn used the play-within-a-play framework to achieve a cohesive balance between the various elements of his production. Nunn also introduced a great deal of slapstick comedy into the presentation, hoping to integrate the pathos of romantic comedy and the silliness of knockabout farce. J. C. Trewin recognized this dichotomy, noting that although the production was ostensibly "an uproarious brawl," it was "in retrospect far subtler than we may think at the time." John Higgins also praised the mixture, maintaining that "the comedy is all the better for having an occasional undercurrent of true emotion." Opening at Stratford-upon-Avon on 5 April 1967, Nunn's production enjoyed a highly successful run before moving to the Aldwych Theatre later in the year.

Another noteworthy event in the history of *The Shrew* occurred in 1967: the release of Franco Zeffirelli's film adaptation of the comedy, with Richard Burton as Petruchio and Elizabeth Taylor as Katherina. To allow for an extended development of the scenes between Petruchio and Kate, Zeffirelli deleted the Induction and heavily cut the Bianca/Lucentio subplot. Nearly every critic found fault with his excision of the text, and most of them attacked other aspects of the film as well. David Robinson panned it as "muddled and self-indulgent," maintaining that Zeffirelli's interpretation was more "dark and cruel" than Shakespeare ever intended the comedy to be. Penelope Houston commented on the film's breakneck speed, noting that it came across as "less of a fine Renaissance restlessness than of a fussy, spasmodic garrulity." Gerald Kaufman, too, deprecated the manic pace, stating that so much action occurs so quickly that "the spectator's dearest wish is that, if only for a moment, everyone will stand still and shut up." As for the featured performers, Stephen Farber maintained that Burton was permitted "to ham gruesomely and to rely on a favorite manic laugh all too regularly," while Taylor's voice was "gratingly shrill and monotonous." There was, however, a measure of favorable commentary regarding Zeffirelli's effective presentation of a dream-like Paduan landscape that skillfully expressed the play's inherent artificiality.

In the following decade, the most significant production of *The Taming of the Shrew* was Michael Bogdanov's unorthodox staging for the Royal Shakespeare Company in 1978. Bogdanov defied previous interpretations, presenting the comedy as a "male chauvinist fantasy," steeped in biting irony. The tone was established at the beginning of the play, just as theater-goers were taking their seats. A disturbance broke out between an usher and an unkempt drunk, who broke away from her grip, jumped onto the stage, and proceeded to tear down the elegant Italianate set, exposing a backdrop of scaffoldings and catwalks. The audience was aghast until the drunkard's language revealed that this was in fact part of the Induction and he was Christopher Sly. After the Induction, Bogdanov treated the interior play as Sly's misogynistic fantasy, enhancing this conception by doubling the roles of Sly and Petruchio. In Bogdanov's interpretation, Petruchio's sole objective was to conquer Katherina and win her dowry. The last scene showed the result of his savage taming, with Kate, tendering her speech of submission with complete sincerity while the men sat around a gaming table, smoking cigars and drinking whiskey. Kate's masochistic submission to Petruchio's cruelty suggested that his apparent victory was double-edged, for now he had to live with his servile creation. This bitterly ironic touch allowed Bogdanov to make a strong statement against male chauvinism. Critics appreciated the technical values of the production, but reacted strongly to Bogdanov's chilling interpretation. As "compulsive as the production is," Tamie Watters wrote, "it is not Shakespeare[;] Bogdanov blots out the glimpse of harmony that surfaces in every Shakespearean play. The broken Katherina of the final scene is enough to set the Bard's teeth on edge" (see Further Reading).

A much more traditional interpretation of *The Taming of the Shrew* was offered by Jonathan Miller in his 1980 BBC television production. Constrained by the limited time-frame allowed for the program, Miller deleted the Induction. He staged the rest of the play as a straightforward representation of the Elizabethan precept that a wife must recognize the authority of her husband. Prior to the show's premiere, skeptics questioned Miller's casting of John Cleese, a comic actor with no previous Shakespearean training, in the role of Petruchio. In the estimation of most commentators, however, Cleese gave a memorable performance. In keeping with Miller's emphasis on obedience and authority, Cleese's Petruchio was both puritanical and compassionate in his treatment of Kate. Stanley Wells praised Cleese for his "deeply thoughtful performance, convincing us of the seriousness of Petruchio's intentions." David Sterritt found the depiction "at once precise, carefully modulated, and ever-so-slightly insane." The production itself received generally favorable reviews, with Andrew Sinclair, for example, claiming that it was "as fresh and appealing as Shakespeare could possibly be," and Michael Ratcliffe praising its "very nice balance between domesticity, intelligence, and tenderness."

The Taming of the Shrew continues to be one of Shakespeare's most frequently performed comedies. Among the more noteworthy recent stagings were Toby Robertson's 1986 presentation, featuring Timothy Dalton and Vanessa Redgrave, and a 1987 revival by Jonathan Miller. Robertson offered an uncomplicated interpretation of the play at the Haymarket's Theatre Royal, introducing a great deal of slapstick comedy to accentuate its farcical nature. As Katherina and Petruchio, Redgrave and Dalton virtually guaranteed a large box office draw, and many critics praised their performance as the embattled couple. The rest of the production, however, was not as well received. Sheridan Morley considered it a "semi-showbiz knockabout" belonging more to the genre of Cole Porter's *Kiss Me Kate* than true Shakespearean comedy. Stella Flint described it as a production "with no subtle motivation, no psychological insight, no emotional depth or demand." Jonathan Miller's 1987 revival with the Royal Shakespeare Company, on the other hand, fared better among critics. In essence, the production reprised Miller's highly successful television adaptation, but this time the director offered a more insightful treatment of the Elizabethan ethic of wifely obedience by making his interpretation as historically accurate as possible. To downplay any potentially misogynistic implications, Miller used period costumes and Renaissance music to underscore the fact that this represented an Elizabethan perspective. Miller's historical treatment of the play demonstrated that *The Taming of the Shrew* still remains open to a variety of readings. Indeed, its capacity to survive and flourish in so many forms may explain why the play has continued to challenge directors, entertain audiences, and confound critics for nearly four centuries.

REVIEWS AND RETROSPECTIVE ACCOUNTS OF SELECTED PRODUCTIONS

PRODUCTION:

David Garrick's *Catherine and Petruchio* • 1754-1870

BACKGROUND:

This adaptation of *The Taming of the Shrew* was first produced in 1754 by the eminent eighteenth-century actor-manager David Garrick. Garrick deleted many scenes in the original play to emphasize the courtship of Petruchio and Katherina. The adaptation was thus a greatly abbreviated version of *The Shrew* and Garrick often presented it as part of a double bill with his altered version of *The Winter's Tale. Catherine and Petruchio* was so successful that it became the accepted stage version of Shakespeare's play for more than a century. Among the prominent Shakespearean actors who played Petruchio in this adaptation were John Philip Kemble, William Charles Macready, and Henry Irving. Notable Catherines included Sarah Siddons, Helena Faucit, and Ellen Terry.

COMMENTARY:

Thomas Davies   (essay date 1808)

[*Davies was a bookseller and actor, as well as the author of the* Life of David Garrick *(1780) and* Dramatic Miscellanies: *consisting of Critical Observations on several Plays of Shakespeare (1784). In the excerpt below, Davies justifies Garrick's adaptation of* The Taming of the Shrew, *claiming that "the loppings of this luxuriant tree of the old poet were not only judicious, but necessary to preserve the pristine trunk."*]

Among the plays of Shakespeare which Mr. Garrick revived, were *The Winter's Tale,* and *The Taming of the Shrew;* each of these comedies being reduced by him into three acts, and called *Florizel and Perdita,* and *Catherine and Petruchio:* they both pleased the audience greatly; he often introduced them to the public by a humorous prologue of his own writing, in which he criticised the various palates of the public for theat-

rical representation, and compared the wine of Shakespeare to a bottle of brisk Champaign. *The Taming of the Shrew* was not altogether written in Shakespeare's best manner, though it contained many scenes well worth preserving. The fable was certainly of the farcical kind, and some of the characters rather exaggerated. The loppings from this luxuriant tree of the old poet were not only judicious, but necessary to preserve the pristine trunk. Woodward's Petruchio was, perhaps, more wild, extravagant, and fantastical than the author designed it should be; and he carried his acting of it to an almost ridiculous excess.

Mrs. Clive, though a perfect mistress of Catherine's humour, seemed to be overborne by the extravagant and triumphant grotesque of Woodward; she appeared to be overawed as much by his manner of acting, as Catherine is represented to be in the fable. In one of his mad fits, when he and his bride are at supper, Woodward stuck a fork, it is said, in Mrs. Clive's finger; and in pushing her off the stage he was so much in earnest that he threw her down: as it is well known that they did not greatly respect one another, it was believed that something more than chance contributed to these excesses. (pp. 311-12)

> Thomas Davies, "Chapter XXIV," in his Memoirs of the Life of David Garrick, Vol. 1, *revised edition, 1808. Reprint by Benjamin Blom, Inc., 1969, pp. 311-15.*

The Times, London   (review date 30 December 1867)

[*In this unsigned review of Garrick's* Catherine and Petruchio, *the critic praises Ellen Terry's performance as Kate, but admonishes Henry Irving for his inability to achieve the "gentlemanlike rollick" evident in the character of Petruchio.*]

[The] delightful little comedy *Katherine and Petruchio,* which was carved years ago out of Shakespeare's *Taming of the Shrew,* is new to the boards on which it is now performed, and is, indeed, put on the stage with all the care that would be bestowed on a veritable novelty. In this the part of Katherine is played by Miss Ellen Terry—not, as has been incorrectly rumoured, by her elder sister, who, unfortunately for the public, has retired from the stage. She takes a view of the character which departs from the usual routine, and which, perhaps, better than any other, accounts for that tamed condition of the shrew in the last act, which, if the lady is made too confirmed a virago, will appear sudden to all who share the opinion of the profound student of human nature, Captain Macheath, when he declares his predilection for women of spirit, adding that they make excellent mistresses, but "plaguey bad wives.' The ebullitions of passion in the early scenes belong, according to Miss E. Terry's interpretation, rather to the spoilt child than to the confirmed vixen, and as speedily as possible she makes the audience perceive that she really feels an interest in the suitor she is enjoined to marry, and that her resistance to the match is the result of waywardness, not of dislike. The speech she utters after her conversion to the now less docile sister may be taken as a model of quiet elocution, so sensibly, so feelingly, and with so unequivocal an appearance of moral conviction is it delivered. We cannot say she is supported with the utmost efficiency by her Petruchio. Mr. H. Irving, who made his London *début* at the St. James's Theatre about a twelvemonth since, is a very valuable actor, and the manager of the New Queen's has shown great judgment in securing his services. His representation of the gamester in Mr. Boucicault's *Hunted Down*—an excellent piece, never appreciated according to its deserts—and the drunkenness of despair proper to Harry Darnton in the latter portion of the *Road to Ruin,* were in their way perfect; but Petruchio is just one of those parts which apparently he cannot hit. Those who are old enough to recollect the late Mr. Charles Kemble's Petruchio will easily bring to mind the gentlemanlike rollick with which he carried off the extravagancies of the shrew-tamer, showing that at bottom he was a man of high breeding, though for the nonce he found it expedient to behave like a ruffian. No impression of this kind is left by Mr. H. Irving. His early scenes are feeble, and when he has brought home his bride he suggests the notion rather of a brigand chief who has secured a female captive than of an honest gentleman engaged in a task of moral reform. Moreover, before he takes his position as a speaker of blank verse certain defects of articulation require emendation.

A review of "The Taming of the Shrew," in The Times, *London, December 30, 1867, p. 9.*

The Times, London   (review date 10 October 1870)

[*The anonymous critic offers a generally unfavorable review of* Catherine and Petruchio, *except for the "creditable" debut of Miss Alleyne as Kate. He also believes that Miss Alleyne ought to have revived Shakespeare's original play rather than Garrick's adaptation.*]

Entirely redecorated by Mr. E. W. Bradwell, under the direction of Mr. Walter Emden, opened by Miss Alleyne, the Globe Theatre on Saturday night presented a very pretty appearance. Everything was new and bright, and the act drop, representing Shakespeare's old Globe Theatre on the Bankside, Southwark, conveyed an impression that something of the higher order would be attempted in the beautiful house. This was confirmed by an address, written by Mr. Walter Lacy, and spoken by him after the conclusion of an introductory farce.

The main piece of the evening was the abridged version of Shakespeare's *Taming of the Shrew,* commonly played under the title of *Katherine and Petruchio.* The fair vixen was represented by Miss Alleyne, who modestly professes herself a novice. Her voice and appearance are greatly in her favour, she speaks with discrimination, and her manner generally recalls that of Miss Neilson. Of the character of Katherine she takes somewhat too amiable a view, keeping the "shrew" in the background, and more plainly revealing the loving nature which ultimately leads to the reconciliation of the tamer with the tamed. But altogether it was a most creditable *début.*

In our opinion, had Miss Alleyne, who confesses inexperience, been better advised, she would have revived, not the farce, which was always played as an after piece at the patent theatres, but Shakespeare's entire comedy, with the character, Christopher Sly, after the fashion in which, some years ago, it was admirably reproduced at the Haymarket Theatre by Mr. Benjamin Webster. She would thus at once have marked out her theatre for what is technically called a "speciality," and, at the same time, would have concealed the weakness of her company. Comparatively few persons have seen the comedy, but everybody is familiar with the farce, which is associated in all memories with the names of our greatest comic actors. Mr. Fairclough, who plays Petruchio, doubtless does his best, and he is a good declaimer, but of the buoyant, joyous gallant represented by Charles Kemble or James

Wallack he has no more notion than Mr. Cathcart has of Grumio. Sad errors, too, are there in the general conduct of the piece, showing that oblivion of tradition does not necessarily cause improvement. The leg of mutton which provokes the rage of Petruchio was really burnt to a cinder, the cap which he rejects was really ugly. Now, the whole gist of the play consists in the assumption of motiveless rage by a man who wishes to put to shame the unreasonable ill-temper of his bride. The wrath of Petruchio on beholding such a joint as is served up at the Globe Theatre would have been simply natural in a fiery gentleman of the 16th century who had not attained that masterly control over passion which is the boast of the nineteenth. Had the old comedy been revived with all its strange appointments, in a sound archæological spirit, the defective details would have been lost in the novelty of the spectacle.

A review of "The Taming of the Shrew," in The Times, *London, October 10, 1870, p. 6.*

Athenaeum   (review date 15 October 1870)

[*In this unsigned review of Miss Alleyne's 1870 production, the critic attacks Garrick's* Catherine and Petruchio *for taking great liberties with Shakespeare's text, noting that many key lines in the adaptation represent misinterpretations of the original play.*]

Of the three pieces with which on Saturday the Globe Theatre re-opened under the management of Miss Alleyne, one only, the least considerable, is a novelty. *Board and Residence,* by Mr. Conway Edwards, is a farce presenting in a slightly altered form materials, which in one shape or other are continually exhibited. It owes its title to the fact, that the adventures depicted take place in a boarding-house, and that the lovers with whose entanglements it deals, present themselves in the guise of would-be lodgers. Its merit, like its story, is exceedingly slight. Katherine and Petruchio, as Garrick's version of *The Taming of the Shrew* is entitled, came next. This piece, which has for a hundred years been the subject of constant praise, is, as acted, a thoroughly contemptible production. Shakspeare's meaning is violated with a hardihood and irreverence not to be found in any of the adaptations of Dryden, Cibber, or Tate. The very spirit of the play is altered, the hero is turned into a buffoon, and his associates become clowns of pantomime. Future generations may be interested to know that in 1870, when scholarship had exhausted itself in dissertations upon Shakspeare, and when facsimiles of his original text had come within the reach of all, a work purporting to be his *Taming of the Shrew* was presented at a west-end theatre, in which such liberties were taken as no other author of reputation has ever had to endure. When in the course of attempting the cure of his wife, Petruchio bears her to his house, and refuses, in her own pretended interest, to permit her to eat one of the meats cooked for her, or wear a portion of the finery provided, the process of reformation is that of showing how utterly violent and unreasonable he can be. As acted, however, Petruchio ceases to be unreasonable. The meat provided is indeed black as a coal,—so black, as to smurch the face and dress of the cook, at whom Petruchio throws it. A not wholly unreasonable man at whose table such a dish was presented might be pardoned a strong display of indignation. Much the same may be said of the gear brought by the tailor. The dress of which Katherine says—

I never saw a better fashioned gown,
More quaint, more pleasing, nor more commendable,

is a worn, faded, and ridiculous garment no woman of taste or reason would consent to wear. The carelessness and blindness which permit managements to continue these farcical devices for extracting a laugh cannot be too strongly condemned. In an address spoken after the performance by Mr. Walter Lacy, the management took credit to itself for producing Shakspeare's plays in a building named after his old house on the Bankside. The resemblance of the new play to the old is scarcely greater than that of the modern theatre to the famous edifice after which it is named. Mr. Fairclough enacted *Petruchio* with much extravagance. As *Katherine,* Miss Alleyne made her first appearance in an important part. Nervousness, sufficiently pardonable under the circumstances, marred a performance which was not destitute of merit. The expressions changed too quickly, until the facial play resembled grimace. Passions succeeded each other upon Miss Alleyne's face with such rapidity that the effect became absolutely bewildering. The costumes worn by the actress were over-elaborate. There was promise, however, in the representation, much of the dialogue being effectively spoken, and some of the gestures being well chosen. Mr. Cathcart's *Grumio* was amusing.

> *A review of "The Taming of the Shrew," in* The Athenaeum, *No. 2242, October 15, 1870, p. 507.*

The Illustrated London News   (review date 15 October 1870)

[*The anonymous critic comments on the 1870 presentation of* Catherine and Petruchio, *arguing that Shakespeare's play, not Garrick's adaptation, should have been chosen for performance.*]

The reopening of the Globe with a Shakspearean revival, thus making the third London theatre where the legitimate drama for a time may be regularly witnessed, naturally demands particular attention. The purpose of managements in reproducing the most excellent old pieces should be the making of a fair experiment whether they retain or not their popularity. To try this properly, the Shakspearean revival should be placed on the boards not only with new scenery, but with the best and most practised actors. Such plays, unless well acted, are desecrated; and should be intrusted only to veteran performers, who are skilled to show them in the best light. In this manner only can old plays be expected to compete with new, commended as these are by special companies, who at our modern theatres represent them in the finest manner. But, alas! this theory finds little favour in actual practice. Too obviously the theatre is taken, not for the due interpretation of Shakspearean art, but for the introduction of some new performer who seeks to establish a reputation by appearing in the principal *rôle*; the rest of the characters being for the most part misrepresented by the members of a "scratch" company. Of these, two or three are perhaps respectable actors, forced into an ungenial position by stress of weather, and the remainder lamentably incompetent to the business. Of course we except from this charge the experiment now making at the Queen's, where the revival of "The Midsummer Night's Dream" has the advantage of being performed by recognised artists fully capable of sustaining their respective *rôles*. We wish that we could extend this compliment to the essay now making at the Globe, which, with Mr. Walter Lacy as stage-

manager, was started on Saturday, under the direction of Miss Alleyne. The piece selected was the Garrick-Kemble arrangement of Shakspeare's robust comedy of "The Taming of the Shrew." The original in its entirety ought to have been represented, and not this adulterated abridgment. When produced at the Haymarket, under Mr. Webster's management, a few years since, it proved eminently successful, and that good example might have been now followed with advantage. Miss Alleyne undertook herself the part of Katharine, and was thus introduced to the audience in the metrical address previously spoken by Mr. Lacy:—

> A young and scarce-tried actress to your view,
> Will first assault you as the untamed shrew.

Here confession is made that it is not the popularity of Shakspeare which is upon trial, but the talents of a fair novice, bold enough to take a playhouse for herself. It is important that this should be understood, in case the run of the revived comedy should not be satisfactory. Miss Alleyne dressed the part superbly, as might have been expected, and showed no small degree of merit in her assumption. A certain degree of crudeness and unfinish was inevitable, for actresses cannot be made at a pinch; a term of sedulous practice and serious study is needful before a strong Shakspearean character can be even decently performed. Allowing for the nervousness of a first night, we can fairly accredit Miss Alleyne with the possession of much vigour and spirit, which occasionally made themselves felt and seen, even in a startling manner. A further acquaintance with the part will lead to more discrimination and more "smoothness," which Shakspeare himself teaches players, through Hamlet, as expedient "even in the storm and whirlwind of passion" [*Hamlet,* III. ii. 6-7]. Mr. Fairclough, as Petruchio, was cautious to a fault, and treated the text with a reverential care for which he merits commendation. He was certainly not a great Petruchio, but he was a good one, and established a claim to be well-considered by the audience. Mr. Cathcart as Grumio was still more satisfactory, and the rest of the dramatis personæ were respectably filled. The scenery and costumes are new and costly—though the latter are not always appropriate.

> *A review of "The Taming of the Shrew," in* The Illustrated London News, *Vol. LVII, No. 1618, October 15, 1870, p. 411.*

PRODUCTION:

Benjamin Webster and J. R. Planché • Haymarket Theatre • 1844

BACKGROUND:

Webster was the first director to present the original version of *The Taming of the Shrew* after nearly two centuries of neglect. He also played Petruchio in this production. J. R. Planché is credited with the initial conception of restoring the play; he felt that Louisa Nisbett and Robert Strickland—two actors in Webster's company—were ideally suited to perform the roles of Katherina and Christopher Sly. Planché also recommended an Elizabethan staging of the play—a bold proposal in an age when extravagant productions were the norm. Theater critics acclaimed the presentation's ingenuity, although many were not entirely receptive to Webster's austere staging. Encouraged by the production's success, Webster presented it again in 1847.

COMMENTARY:

Punch, or The London Charivari   (review date 1843-44)

[*In this unsigned review, the critic satirically praises Mr. Stuart's performance as the lord, a role which demands nothing more than various movements and gestures once the Induction is over.*]

During the whole performance of the *Taming of the Shrew*, in five acts at the Haymarket Theatre, Mr. STUART sits in one corner of the stage, as the Lord before whom the play is acted. Nothing can be finer than the acting of Mr. STUART from first to last, in the very arduous character assigned to him. There is something truly Shaksperian in his treatment of the wand which he holds in his hand, and which he twiddles about, from time to time, between his fingers, with a nice appreciation of the highly dramatic situation in to which he is thrown by the towering genius of the Swan of Avon. In the fourth act, Mr. STUART rests his right arm on an adjacent chair: but the point we admired most was, the truly Elizabethan jerk he gave to his left leg in the middle of the banquet scene.

We understand that a deputation from the Shakspeare Society intend waiting on Mr. STUART, to thank him for the zeal with which he has adhered to the original text, by not opening his mouth. But it will be suggested to him, that a wink at Katharina, in the third act, might be introduced with effect, as showing that the Lord before whom the play is acted might be trying to gain the attention of the very pretty woman who is representing the principal female character.

A vote of thanks is nightly proposed in the Green-room to Mr. STUART, for his able, impartial, and unimpassioned conduct in the chair: and we have heard it intimated that he will be offered an engagement at Covent Garden Theatre, as Chairman at all the League meetings.

A review of *"The Taming of the Shrew,"* in Punch, or The London Charivari, *Vol. 5-6, 1843-44, p. 143.*

The Times, London   (review date 18 March 1844)

[*The anonymous critic commends Webster and Planché for reviving the original version of* The Taming of the Shrew, *deeming it "one of the most remarkable incidents of the modern theatre." The reviewer especially admires the spare, Elizabethan staging. He also compares the relative merits of Shakespeare's play and the anonymous* Taming of a Shrew.]

There is perhaps no play in the whole series of the British drama about which there is so much discussion as the *Taming of the Shrew;* and there is so much reason in what is advanced in favour of conflicting opinions, that it is next to impossible for the occasional student of such matters to come to a satisfactory determination as to the points at issue.

All, we believe, now agree that the play is founded on the anonymous comedy of the *Taming of A Shrew* (with the indefinite article), which is contained in the collection familiar to all who take an interest in early English literature by the name of the "Six old plays." The edition used in the collection

was printed in 1607, but an earlier edition was printed in 1594, and is now in the possession of the Duke of Devonshire. The "induction" in which Christopher Sly figures as the chief personage, the notion of having the comedy itself played in his presence, and all the incidents belonging to *Katharine and Petruchio* are based upon the anonymous play. Indeed, in the older work the fortunes of Sly are more consistently followed out. In Shakspeare's version, after he is made to wish the play were over, he seems to be forgotten altogether; but the earlier dramatist has him regularly taken out of the Lord's house shortly before the conclusion of the play; and when it is terminated we find him borne back to the spot whence he was taken, considering the finery he has witnessed to be no more than a dream. The underplot of Bianca in Shakspeare's play is likewise derived from the anonymous one, but it is considerably modified, whereas the "business" of the other portions is actually transferred from one play to the other. The anonymous play has been assigned to Greene and to Marlowe. Mr. Knight, in his *Pictorial Shakspeare,* gives strong arguments in favour of Greene, particularly calling attention to the style of Greene's acknowledged plays, which certainly bear a great resemblance to the language of *Taming of* A *Shrew.* The two pair of lovers vie with each other in crowding together mythological allusions, in a manner most pedantic, and most wearisome to the reader, and all who have read Greene will recollect that this is one of his most striking peculiarities. There is also a passage in Greene's "Groatsworth of Wit" which is corroborative of the opinion that he wrote the play in question.

We advise those of our readers who are interested in such matters to read together the comedy which is in the "Six old plays" and Shakspeare's *Taming of the Shrew,* as perhaps they could not have a finer exhibition of the power of drawing real character—of vivifying dull, lifeless stage puppets with the true breath of life. In his own play Shakspeare has not added one material incident to the portion which relates to the "shrew," and yet by his boldness of colouring, he has made the incidents which he had at hand assume tangible substance, and has created a character (Petruchio) original, complete, and perfectly distinguished from all other characters whatever. The dialogue of the older drama is frequently feeble and meager in the highest degree, as if written for the mere purpose of connecting such practical jokes as beating the servants, &c.; and Ferrando (so is the "tamer" called) is as close an approach to a no-character as possible. Let the reader compare this Ferrando with the bold, reckless, good-humoured, and withal, selfish Petruchio, let him compare the dull clown Sander, in the older play, with the quaint and humorous Grumio into which Shakspeare expanded him, and he will say, "Verily, the hand of a master has been here."

The same praise cannot be extended to the underplot that is awarded to the part relating to Petruchio, and to the fresh and natural "induction," which Mr. Knight properly calls "one of the most precious gems in Shakspeare's casket." The part relating to Bianca and her suitors, though an unquestionable improvement on the bombastical pedantry of the lovers in the older play, is still weak and abstract, and notwithstanding there are some opinions to the contrary, we believe it is pretty generally agreed that this part does not proceed from Shakspeare. Mr. Collier, in that most useful book, the *History of Dramatic Poetry,* throws out a hint that it may be the production of William Haughton, author of a comedy called *Englishmen for my Money.*

The great point in dispute among commentators is the period at which the play which is now called Shakspeare's was written. In favour of this adaptation being one of his earliest productions, is the argument brought forward by Mr. Knight, that he would hardly have condescended to undertake the work of re-modelling in the zenith of his fame, and another argument, founded on the occasional introduction of that sort of doggrel Alexandrine measure in which *Gammer Gurton* is written, and which in rhythm is nearly identical with the old Teutonic metre, as shown in the *Nibelungen lied.* This measure is known to have been most liberally used in those plays which are acknowledged to be Shakspeare's earliest productions. On the other hand, we have in favour of the opinion that it was written after 1600, the facts that it is not mentioned in Mere's enumeration of plays in 1598, and that "Baptista" is properly used for a man's name in this play, whereas in *Hamlet,* which is assumed to be written in 1601 at the earliest, it is improperly applied to a woman. Singularly enough in the old anonymous play a similar error is committed, and "Valeria" is the name given to the man servant, who appears as Tranio in Shakspeare. As for the argument that Petruchio, when he says—

This is the way to kill a wife with kindness.

[IV. i. 208]

actually alludes to Heywood's *Woman Killed with Kindness,* which was produced after 1600, we agree with Mr. Knight in doubting, whether we have a right to assume that any such allusion was intended. Indeed, Mr. Collier, who is in favour of the later date, but who confesses that his opinion on the subject has often varied, seems himself to have given up this argument, for though he uses it in his "history," which was published in 1831, he does not refer to it in his edition of Shakspeare, which appeared within the last two or three years, but chiefly relies on the silence of Mere and the word Baptista. These, we believe, are the heads of the controversy, and those who would go further into it will find ample material in the works to which we have referred.

The short play of *Katharine and Petruchio,* to which the public has been for years accustomed, was published in the year 1756 by David Garrick, who omitted all the parts not relating to the characters who give the name to his abridgment. Of all the alterations that have been made of our old plays, this one appears to us the most excusable. The part selected was perfect in itself, and *Katharine and Petruchio* has always been a most amusing little piece.

Nevertheless the greatest credit is due to Mr. Webster for reviving the play in the shape in which we find it in Shakspeare's works, and for producing it in a style so unique that this revival is really one of the most remarkable incidents of the modern theatre. It was a suggestion of Tieck's that the plays of Shakspeare should be acted on the sort of stage which existed in the time of Elizabeth and James I., and although the revival at the Haymarket does not exactly follow this suggestion, still it is in the same spirit, and allows an audience to judge of the effect of a play unaided by scenery. The "induction," in which Christopher Sly is discovered drunk by the sporting lord, is played in the ordinary manner, before a scene representing an inn; but when he is removed into the hall, there is no further change, but the play of the *Taming of the Shrew* is acted in that hall, two screens and a pair of curtains being the whole dramatic apparatus. By the mere substitution of one curtain for another, change of scene was indicated, and all the entrances and exits are through the cen-

tre of the curtain, or round the screens, the place represented being denoted by a printed placard fastened to the curtain. This arrangement, far from being flat and ineffective, tended to give closeness to the action, and by constantly allowing a great deal of stage room, afforded a sort of freedom to all the parties engaged. The audience did not in the least seem to feel the absence of scenery, and though the play lasted three hours and a half, the attention of the house never failed, and a play could scarcely go off with more spirit.

The comedy was, on the whole, efficiently acted. Mrs. Nisbett, as "Kate the curst," had an opportunity of displaying all that petulant vivacity for which she is unrivalled, while, at the same time, as the "tamed" Katharine, she acted with a degree of feminine delicacy and gracefulness which formed a most pleasing contrast. The impressive and really eloquent manner in which she delivered the concluding speech on the duty of wives to their husbands, drew down repeated shouts of applause. Webster, as Petruchio, showed that a less hurried study of the arduous part would have made him a very able representative, many portions he performed with very striking effect, while others seemed marred by the nervousness arising from a sense that the text was not wholly at his command. The drunken tinker, Sly, was played with great unction by Strickland, who, attired in his newly acquired finery, rolled about the stage in a state of the most vague astonishment. Bianca, Lucentio, Hortensio, and Grumio, were played by Miss Bennett, Hall, Howe, and Buckstone, and it should be remarked that the underplot of the play, which has hitherto been omitted, went off with excellent effect. The players who appear in the "Induction," were so made up as to give a sort of resemblance to Shakspeare, Ben Jonson, and Richard Tarleton. The costumes were very handsome and appropriate, and the whole does great credit to Mr. Planché, under whose superintendence the play was produced. A drop-scene has been painted for the occasion, representing a view of London, with the Globe Theatre as one of the principal objects.

The house was well filled, and the piece was announced for repetition every evening amid the most enthusiastic applause.

A review of "The Taming of the Shrew," in The Times, *London, March 18, 1844, p. 5.*

The Athenaeum   (review date 23 March 1844)

[*In this unsigned review, the critic questions the "pedantic affectation of accuracy" in Webster's revival of* The Shrew. *Addressing the issue of stage scenery, the critic argues that even though Shakespeare wrote his plays for performance on a bare stage, Webster's adherence to such a stricture was not "essential to the representation of the Comedy in its integrity."*]

Extremes meet, says the proverb; and of this familiar truth we have a notable instance in the theatrical world. At a time when the ingenuity and skill of the scene-painter, stage-machinist, and property-man have been taxed to the utmost to make the mimic scene faithfully represent the localities of a drama, whether the scene be laid in a real or an ideal world—above the clouds or under the waves—on shipboard or an enchanted isle;—when every approximation to supposed exactness in this particular is hailed as a new triumph of scenic art, and recorded as a step in advance towards the complete restoration of Shakspeare to the stage—at this very time the manager of the Haymarket, who professes to have the same object in view, finds it necessary to the perfect revival of the text of the 'Taming the Shrew,' to represent the comedy without any scenery whatever, just as it might have been performed in Shakspeare's time, in a private house, or on the stage before scenes were in use! The "Induction," however, is represented with all the modern accessories of scenery: Christopher Sly is ejected from a scenic alehouse, and installed in the "lord's" chamber, with a substantial bed and pictured splendour. This being the place whereon the comedy is supposed to be acted, a couple of screens and a curtain, divided in the middle, form a veil to hide the actors off the stage, and labels affixed to the curtain denote the changes of scene; Sly being present as a spectator during the whole time. It is needless to protest against such pedantic affectation of accuracy as this, or to point out the absurdity of sacrificing five acts of Comedy to a farcical "induction" of two scenes; since it is obvious that the opportunity afforded by the peculiar construction of the play, was seized upon by the manager for the sake of giving a feature of novelty to the representation: no one can suppose for a moment that this was essential to the representation of the Comedy in its integrity; for after the first scene, Sly and his host are heard no more of, and their subsequent appearance being unwarranted by the text, they carried on in dumb show the device that Shakspeare dropped altogether, after it had served his purpose. In strict consistency, therefore, the comedy and its induction ought to have been acted both alike; either without or with scenery. The personal resemblance to Shakspeare and Ben Jonson, aimed at in the dressing of the players, and the drop scene of London copied from Hollar's print exhibiting the old theatres on Bankside, are attempts to carry the audience back to the early period of the stage, which, in proportion as they are successful, give rise to a comparison between the past and present generation of players, unfavourable to the latter; for though there is no standard of comparison, the incidental allusions (in Hamlet especially,) to the acting in those days, indicate a higher kind of sentiment, and more impassioned declamation, than characterize contemporary actors. Mr. Webster's previous assumption of Shakspeare's semblance made his subsequent misconception and undignified personation of *Petruchio* more glaring; and Mrs. Nisbett's personal attractions procured immunity for a degree of vulgarity, that would hardly have been tolerated in the smooth-faced striplings who played the women's parts in Shakspeare's time. The impression conveyed by their performance is that of a scolding vixen suddenly converted into an eloquent advocate and example of obedience in a wife, by a salutary dread of the tyranny of a brutal husband: those who see nothing more than this in the 'Taming the Shrew,' will be satisfied with this performance; and delight, as the audience did, in the buffooneries in which Mr. Buckstone, as *Grumio,* revelled with his usual gusto. Mr. Strickland's *Sly* is humorously droll. (pp. 275-76)

A review of "The Taming of the Shrew," in The Athenaeum, *No. 856, May 23, 1844, pp. 275-76.*

The Examiner (review date 23 March 1844)

[*The anonymous critic describes Webster's and Planché's production as "an odd experiment," maintaining that "as a curiosity, the piece is worth seeing." The emphasis on Elizabethan staging, the critic argues, added no significant dimension to this mediocre production.*]

An odd experiment was tried at this house on Saturday. Not only was the *Taming of the Shrew* brought out as written by Shakspeare, but it was made a means of exhibiting the ancient

Robert Strickland as Christopher Sly.

English method of representing plays, without scenery. When *Christopher Sly* is taken from the front of the inn, where he is first discovered, and placed in the *Lord's* house, there is no further change. The players, to represent the comedy of the *Taming of the Shrew,* fit up the apartment by placing two screens at the back: hanging curtains between them, as well as on each side of the stage. The different localities are then indicated by placards. Thus, the first scene is marked by a scroll inscribed 'Padua, a public place;' the second, 'the same, front of Hortensio's house,' and so on. It was a needless pedantry, but pedantry is sometimes curious.

As a curiosity, the piece is worth seeing. The industry and taste of Mr Planché, whose talent in matters of this kind is well known, have been employed in its production. But if any enthusiast argues from it that plays without the aid of scenery are to prove attractive, he is wofully mistaken. Precisely the opposite inference ought to be drawn. Supposing an attraction to exist here, it is pretty certain that the restored play does not supply it, for the underplot of *Bianca* is weak in the last degree; and certainly, though Mrs Nisbett and Strickland are reasonably good representatives of *Katharine* and *Sly,* the performance of Mr Webster in the rather important character of *Petruchio* is enough to show that it will not be discovered in the acting. No; this very absence of scenery, in an age when scenes are every-day things, becomes in its turn a scenic effect. More persons came to see how a stage was fitted up in the sixteenth century, than for any other purpose whatever. Let a series of plays on the same principle be acted, and observe the result.

Some of the dresses—Mr Planché's foible—were preposterous enough. *Petruchio's* wedding-dress, for example. And before Mr Webster assumed it, he had gravely presented himself to the audience, as one of the poor players, evidently *made up* for no less a person than the author of the play. This was a very equivocal compliment to the Great Immortal!

A review of "The Taming of the Shrew," in The Examiner, *No. 1886, March 23, 1844, p. 181.*

The Illustrated London News   (review date 23 March 1844)

[*The anonymous critic maintains that although Webster's and Planché's production lacked the "gew-gaw accessories" normally associated with the stage, excellent acting, particularly by Miss Nisbett, contributed to its overall success.*]

The revival of this curiosity of dramatic construction in its original form was a hazardous experiment in these days, when the scenic display of the painter, the gorgeous costumes of the taylor—the clever tricks of the machinist, and a story told in Pantomime, intermixed with graceful dancing, together with an inconveniently crowded stage, are the *"artes et insidias"* by which a manager can hope for public patronage. It proved successful, nevertheless, and shews that the mere gew-gaw accessories of the stage are not necessary when there is the *"mens divinior poetæ"* present. None but the genius of Shakspeare could entertain an audience through so many scenes undiversified by anything but the Proteus wit of the immortal Swan of Avon. The said wit, however, is often coarse and puerile, with miserable plays upon words, but ever and anon comes a passage of transcendant intellect and knowledge of humanity. The Induction (which no doubt gave birth to the plot of "The Devil to Pay," in which Mrs. Jordan and Mrs. Davison were so great in the part of *Nell*) was represented for [the] first time in our days, and most admirably, too, particularly the part of *Christopher Sly*, which was personated *"ad unguem"* by Strickland, for as

> The thirsty earth soaks up the rain,
> And drinks, and gapes for drink again,
>   [Abraham Cowley, *Drinking*]

so did the tinker of his embodiment, "a thirsty soul" too,

> Accept the challenge and embrace the bowl.

As to the "getting up" of the piece nothing could have been better. Scenery there was not, but its absence was not missed in the general effect produced by some excellent acting. Mrs. Nisbett was by far the best *Katherina* (as the bills call her) that we have ever seen. A word or two here relative to the change in the spelling of the names of the *dramatis personæ*. *Petrucio* is certainly more consonant with the general pronunciation than *Petruchio*, in which the *ch* would be hard; but why retain *Katherina*, which in two instances is anti-Italian?

Webster played in some of the boisterous scenes of the comedy with great spirit, but, to use a vulgar saying, he cowed rather than humbled the saucy *Kate*: there was more the rude tyrant than the haughty gentleman about him. Mrs. Nisbett gave a new phase to the character of *Kate;* she did not sud-

denly sink into the abject slave of her husband's whim, but now and then broke out into short ebullitions of the hasty temper she was wont to indulge in. Her softening down to gentleness was "fine by degrees" and her irascibility "beautifully less." In short, as we have before said, her Kate was the best we have ever seen, for through the veil of the termagant the lady was still visible.

Miss Julia Bennett as *Bianca,* "walked in beauty," for she had little else to do. The rest of the *dramatis personæ* remain in the *statu quo* of their respectability. By the way, it cannot be a great treat for Strickland and his fair attendants (one standing all the while) to remain on the stage, or one side of the proscenium, or before the public. It is true the interval between the supposed acts is very short, but it is a pity that *Sly* could not have been allowed to indulge in a running commentary upon what he "doubly sees," which would be a great relief to the monotony of the scene. The *tout ensemble* is excellent in the extreme, and proves that the lessee, or proprietor, which ever he may be, is a man of most judicious management and speculation. The scene which precedes the drama is not in the happiest manner of Marshall—it is too *clay*-y—and the Shaksperian overture is a sorry medley of tunes that have been huddled together most clumsily. It is said in the bills to be the composition (?) of Sir H. R. Bishop; if so, we are sorry for it.

The whole revival, however, is got up in good spirit, and evinces much taste and veneration on the part of the liberal manager for the true and legitimate drama.

A review of "The Taming of the Shrew," in The Illustrated London News, *Vol. IV, No. 99, March 23, 1844, p. 189.*

The Times, London   (review date 27 October 1847)

[*In this unsigned review, the critic praises Webster's restored version of* The Taming of the Shrew *as "a creditable achievement" over the still-popular adaptation,* Catherine and Petruchio. *The reviewer calls attention to the Elizabethan staging, the performances of Webster and Louisa Nisbett, and the success of Mr. Keeley in the part of Grumio.*]

The revival of the entire play of *Taming of the Shrew,* instead of the abridgment called *Katharine and Petruchio,* was a very creditable achievement on the part of Mr. Webster; for not only was there the merit of restoring an original work in the place of a fragment but, the play being acted in the "Lord's" house, the effect was given of the ancient method of dramatic representation in England, when the art of scene-painting was unknown, and the only decoration was a placard inscribed with the name of the place.

The *Taming of the Shrew,* put upon the stage in this style, was acted last night, a period of a few years having elapsed since the first revival. Mrs. Nisbett is the best Katharine on the stage. Perhaps, last night she was a degree less spirited than on some former occasions, but she thoroughly understands the rising, impatient temper of the "shrew," and the portion in which she is reduced to gentleness is rendered with perfect quietude and great delicacy. Mr. Webster throws a hearty violence into the obstreperous scenes of Petruchio, and the crack of the whip is the certain signal for peals of laughter. Grumio was probably never so well played as by Mr. Keeley. This genuine actor, who can be droll without buffoonery, manages to infuse a rich humour into the most trivial phrases of the character, and decks it out with such a variety of significant but inobtrusive gestures, that, seemingly without effort, he always makes it one of the most prominent on the stage. The Haymarket is a new theatre for Mr. Keeley, but he has made a thorough "hit" in it, and at the fall of the curtain was called after Mrs. Nisbett and Mr. Webster.

The parts of the drama which do not relate to Petruchio and his bride, necessarily suffer from that deficiency of light comedians which is felt on the existing stage. As far as our London experience goes, no blame can be attached to any individual *entrepreneur* for the want in this respect. There is not a manager of greater spirit or liberality in promoting the drama than Mr. Webster, and the weaknesses in what may be called the general "utilities" of a company represent a weakness in the present theatrical age. To young Mr. Vandenhoff we would suggest, in the few Latin words which Lucent cites, an adoption of the English instead of the Italian mode of pronunciation, or at any rate let him not adopt a compound of the two. Mr. Brindal, too, who acts Tranio, should be informed that the penultimate of "Redime" is short. A greater attention to metre generally would do much towards an improvement in our actors, and prevent many trippings in sense as well as sound. With Christopher Sly, the drunken tinker of the Induction, Mr. Lambert took great pains, and showed some talent in the various expressions with which he listened to the play. Mr. Rogers, as the Lord, looked stately enough, but his air was rather that of a suppressor than of an encourager of the drama.

But, allowing for the deficiencies of the time, the *Taming of the Shrew,* as represented at the Haymarket, is a very interesting performance, and should be witnessed by all who would get a notion of the old method of dramatic exhibition. It was heartily relished last night by a very crowded audience.

> *A review of "The Taming of the Shrew," in* The Times, *London, October 27, 1847, p. 5.*

Henry Crabb Robinson   (journal date 6 November 1847)

[*Robinson is remembered as an insightful and outspoken commentator on the literary world of nineteenth-century London. The recollections chronicled in his* Diary, Reminiscences, and Correspondence, *published two years after his death in 1867, provide an astute assessment of literary trends and society during his lifetime. In the following excerpt, Robinson briefly praises Webster's 1847 production of* The Taming of the Shrew *as a "novelty in the getting up," expressing particular interest in the unusual scenery.*]

I had more than usual pleasure in seeing *The Taming of the Shrew* according to Shakespeare's text. A novelty in the getting up. An imitation of the ancient stage in its simplicity—a curtain and an inscription instead of a scene. A drop scene was introduced representing from Hollar London in Shakespeare's age—a very pleasing view—it looked very large—St. Paul's and the bridge and the Southwark church and the Globe Theatre, all very interesting. Webster a coarse Petruchio and Mrs Nisbett an adequate Catherine.

> *Henry Crabb Robinson, in a journal entry dated November 6, 1847, in his* The London Theatre, 1811-1866: Selections from the Diary of Henry Crabbe Robinson, *edited by Eluned Brown, The Society for Theatre Research, 1966, p. 183.*

James Robinson Planché   (essay date 1872)

[*Planché was a nineteenth-century English dramatist and musician. His plays—*The Island of Jewels *(1849) is considered his best—were better known for their extravagant effects than for their literary quality. He also wrote numerous libretti for opera, including Weber's* Oberon, *and English versions of* The Magic Flute *and* William Tell. *The following excerpt is taken from his autobiography, first published in 1872. Planché recalls his conception of staging* The Shrew *in its original form and his notion of having Sly remain on the stage throughout the entire play. He declares the revival a great success, particularly praising the performances of Louisa Nisbett as Katherina and Robert Strickland as Christopher Sly.*]

The season 1846-47 was signalised by the return to the stage of that charming woman and actress, Mrs. Nisbett, then Lady Boothby, and for the second time a widow but slenderly provided for. During her brief sojourn in Derbyshire she had endeared herself to all classes, particularly the poor, in the neighbourhood of Ashbourne, by whom her memory was cherished long after her leaving it, as I can avouch from personal experience when visiting in that locality in 1851.

Her engagement suggested the idea to me of reviving "The Taming of the Shrew," not in the miserable, mutilated form in which it is acted under the title of "Katharine and Petruchio," but in its integrity, with the Induction, in which I felt satisfied that excellent actor Strickland would, as *Christopher Sly,* produce a great effect.

It also occurred to me to try the experiment of producing the piece with only two scenes—1. The outside of the little alehouse on a heath, from which the drunken Tinker is ejected by the hostess, and where he is found asleep in front of the door by the nobleman and his huntsmen; and, 2. The nobleman's bedchamber, in which the strolling players should act the comedy, as they would have done in Shakspeare's own time under similar circumstances—viz., without scenery, and merely affixing written placards to the wall of the apartment to inform the audience that the action is passing "in a public place in Padua,"—"a room in *Baptista's* house,"—"a public road," &c.

Mr. Webster, to whom of course I proposed this arrangement, sanctioned it without hesitation. I prepared the comedy for representation, gave the necessary instructions for painting the two scenes, and made the designs for the dresses.

One difficulty was to be surmounted. How was the play to be finished? Schlegel says that the part "in which the Tinker, in his new state, again drinks himself out of his senses, and is transformed in his sleep into his former condition, from some accident or other, is lost." Mr. Charles Knight observes upon this: "We doubt whether it was ever produced, and whether Shakspere did not exhibit his usual judgment in letting the curtain drop upon honest *Christopher,* when his wish was accomplished, at the close of the comedy, which he had expressed very early in its progress—

> 'Tis a very excellent piece of work, madam lady—would
> 't were done!
>
> [I. i. 253-54]

Had Shakspeare brought him again on the scene in all the richness of his first exhibition, perhaps the patience of the audience would never have allowed them to sit through the lessons of "the taming school." We have had farces enough *founded* upon the legend of *Christopher Sly,* but no one has ever ventured to *continue* him. I was the last person who would have been guilty of such presumption, but after studying the play carefully, I hit upon the following expedient:—

Sly was seated in a great chair in the first entrance, O.P., to witness the performance of the comedy. At the end of each act no drop scene came down, but music was played while the servants brought the bewildered Tinker wine and refreshments, which he partook of freely.

During the fifth act *Sly* appeared to fall gradually into a heavy drunken stupor; and when the last line of the play was spoken, the actors made their usual bow, and the nobleman, advancing and making a sign to his domestics, they lifted him out of his chair, and as they bore him to the door, the curtain descended upon the picture. Not a word was uttered, and the termination, which Schlegel supposes to have been lost, was *indicated* by the simple movement of the *dramatis personœ*, without any attempt to *continue* the subject.

The revival was eminently successful, incontestably proving that a good play, well acted, will carry the audience along with it, unassisted by scenery; and in this case also, remember, it was a comedy in *five* acts, without the curtain once falling during its performance.

No such *Katharine* as Mrs. Nisbett had been seen since Mrs. Charles Kemble had acted it in the pride of her youth and beauty. Strickland justified all my expectations. As powerful and unctuous as Munden, without the exaggeration of which that glorious old comedian was occasionally guilty. Buckstone was perfectly at home in *Grumio;* and Webster, although the part was not in his line, acted *Petruchio* like an artist, as he acts everything.

Of the Induction, which had been for so many years neglected, that intelligent critic, Charles Knight, says:—

> We scarcely know how to speak without appearing hyperbolical in our praise. It is to us one of the most precious gems in Shakspere's casket. If we apply ourselves to compare it carefully with the earlier Induction upon which Shakspere formed it, and with the best of the dramatic poetry of his contemporaries, we shall in some degree obtain a conception not only of the qualities in which he equalled and excelled the highest things of other men, and in which he could be measured with them, but of those wonderful endowments in which he differed from all other men, and to which no standard of comparison can be applied.

My restoration of this "gem" is one of the events in my theatrical career on which I look back with the greatest pride and gratification. (pp. 295-98)

James Robinson Planché, "Chapter XXVIII," in his Recollections and Reflections: A Professional Autobiography, *revised edition, 1901. Reprint by Da Capo Press, 1978, pp. 292-300.*

Jan McDonald (essay date 1971)

[*McDonald examines in detail J. R. Planché's restored version of* The Taming of the Shrew *and its contemporary critical reception. He places the production in the context of nineteenth-century theories of Elizabethan staging and notes that Planché's innovations won few converts among Victorian producers of Shakespeare's plays.*]

It is to J. R. Planché that we must give credit for the idea of reviving *The Taming of the Shrew,* under Benjamin Webster's management, at the Haymarket Theatre in March 1844. He attributes his choice of this play to the return to the stage of Mrs Nisbett, then Lady Boothby, whom he thought would make an ideal Katharine, and he was encouraged in his desire to present the original text, including the Induction, by the presence in the Haymarket company of Strickland, whom he thought particularly suited to the part of Christopher Sly.

It is not surprising that the renowned antiquarian Planché was anxious to present the original text and eschew what he calls 'the miserable, mutilated form' of Garrick's *Catharine and Petruchio,* but it is perhaps more difficult to understand why, thirty-seven years before William Poel's famous First Quarto *Hamlet,* the idea of presenting a play in what current opinion held to be an Elizabethan style should have occurred to him.

Perhaps the 'play within the play' structure of the *Shrew* is the main factor. This does present problems to any producer, and the solution of presenting it as originally done may come quickly to him. Possibly, too, Planché was influenced by the work of Tieck in Germany. Tieck, first as *dramaturg* of the Court Theatre in Dresden, and later at the Prussian Court, had presented Shakespeare's plays in a setting that imitated freely the Elizabethan stage as he conceived it. The ideas expressed in *Der junge Tischlermeister* (1836) anticipated the Munich *Bühnenreform* of 1889, and, by the time of his death in 1853, Tieck had presented *The Merchant of Venice* (1821), *Twelfth Night* (1836), *A Midsummer Night's Dream* (1843) and *Macbeth* (1851) according to his principles. Planché would almost certainly have heard of his work, as Tieck was in fairly frequent correspondence with John Payne Collier, Crabb Robinson and Charles Kemble—the last had visited him in 1834—and it is well known that his ideas were current in England. *The Times* review of the Haymarket *Shrew* does indeed refer to them.

The contemporary English views on Elizabethan staging are expressed by John Payne Collier [in his *English Dramatic Poetry*] and Edmund Malone [in his edition, with James Boswell, of *The Plays and Poems of William Shakespeare*]. Collier, like Malone, disallows the use of any painted and movable scenery on the stage—Malone defines scenery as 'a painting in perspective on a cloth fastened to a wooden frame or roller'—although both recognize the use of movable properties. Collier writes, 'Hangings on the stage made little pretension to be anything but coverings for the walls'. Malone believes that for tragedy the curtains were black, and when they became worn they would be painted with pictures. Until the Restoration, these curtains ran upon a rod and opened in the centre. They were usually composed of arras and worsted. The back curtains in the Haymarket *Shrew* were made of tapestry, and did have a centre opening.

Two other nineteenth-century ideas on Elizabethan staging, particularly relevant to this production, should be mentioned here: first, the idea that the place of action was written on a placard or board. Collier cites as authorities the Induction to *Cynthia's Revels* by Ben Jonson, and Sir Philip Sidney's *Apologie for Poetrie:* 'What child is there, that coming to a play and seeing Thebes written in great letters upon an old door, doth believe it is Thebes', and Collier adds a quotation from *A Fairy Pastoral, or the Forest Elves,* ' . . . you may omit the sayd properties, which be outward, and supplye their places with their nuncupations only in text letters'. In the Haymarket production, change of place was indicated by change of placards, attached to the tapestry curtain, the actors changing the notices as they left the stage in preparation for the next scene.

Secondly, Malone describes thus the method of presenting 'a play within a play'.

> The court or audience before whom the interlude was performed, sat in the balcony or upper stage, *for the nonce,* the performers entered between the curtain and the general audience, and on its being drawn, began their piece addressing themselves to the balcony, and regardless of the spectators in the theatre, to whom their backs must have been turned during the whole performance!

Collier disagrees with this, citing the stage direction in *The Spanish Tragedy,* 'He knocks up the curtain', as an indication that the performers were discovered in, or acted in the alcove. Wisely Planché did not attempt to copy Malone's idea. His 'stage audience' sat downstage right and downstage left, giving them a side view of the players, and the action took place facing the real audience.

There is no mention of a balcony or upper level in the Haymarket production. Perhaps it was felt that the play did not demand it.

Neither Malone nor Collier stresses the importance of the apron in the Elizabethan stage structure, and in 1843 Webster had greatly reduced the size of the Haymarket apron, 'a useless portion of the stage', as he described it, in order to accommodate more orchestra stalls. One could take it that what we regard as the great advantage of the Elizabethan stage, namely the intimacy between actor and audience, was not present in 1844, but *The Times* review does comment on the 'closeness of the action'. Perhaps the presence of the stage audience well downstage brought the actors more to the front.

The text used was probably the Folio text. Poel's antiquarian interests took him to the bad quarto of *Hamlet* for *his* revolutionary production, but Planché did not go back to the 1594 *Taming of a Shrew* for his script. Planché was of the opinion that the 'epilogue' was not lost, as Schlegel thought, but had never been written. In Planché's opinion no writer, not even Shakespeare, could finish the legendary Sly. At the last line of the Katharine and Petruchio story, the actors bowed, and the nobleman's servant lifted Sly out of his chair, and carried him offstage. Thus, wrote Planché, 'the termination which Schlegel claims to have been lost was indicated'. Action supplied the lack of words. The *Morning Post* review of the first performance complains that at the end of the *fourth* act the stage audience went off stage and left the players to amuse themselves by finishing without any audience. At the end of the play the lord entered and paid the players. They exited, and Sly was borne across the stage asleep. No other reviewer mentions this, and, indeed, *Punch* describes a jerk of the leg given by Stuart, playing the Lord, during the banquet scene, which would indicate the presence of the stage audience during the last act. It is possible that the fourth act exit was changed, either during the first run in March, 1844, or for the 1847 production. Planché in his *Recollections,* does confuse the two.

The play opened on a typical Victorian painted scene 'representing an inn' which Planché describes as 'a little alehouse on a heath, from which the drunken tinker is ejected by the hostess, and where he is found asleep in front of the door by the lord and his huntsmen'. Then occurs the only scene

change to the Lord's bedroom, where the Katharine and Petruchio story is enacted by the strolling players, made up 'so as to give a sort of resemblance to Shakespeare, Ben Jonson, and Richard Tarleton', in an attempt to give added Elizabethan flavour. (pp. 157-60)

The lord and his servant are downstage left, Sly and his party downstage right. They remain there throughout, their only contribution to the action being that Sly and the others were plied with drinks during the 'very short' intervals. The critic of *The Illustrated London News* complains that Sly could very profitably have contributed comments during the course of the action, as of course he did in the old *Taming of a Shrew* (1594), but clearly this was not done.

The set for 'the play within the play' presents some problems. *The Times* review states that 'two screens and a pair of curtains' were 'the whole dramatic apparatus'. The actors could make exits and entrances round the screens as well as through the centre gap in the curtain. It is difficult to ascertain . . . whether the screens referred to by *The Times* were the outer ones—modified Serlian wings very accurately decorated with Tudor ornamentation as one would expect under Planché's supervision—or the inner pilasters, which are only vaguely outlined.

The second problem is whether the side curtains between the pilasters and the wings were in fact practicable. Frank Marshall, in Volumes 3 and 4 of his edition of Shakespeare (1922), quotes Howe, who had played the part of Hortensio in this production, as saying these side curtains were maroon-coloured and were 'looped-up'—which would imply they were for decoration only—but a quotation from *The Times* review would lead one to believe that they were used. 'By mere substitution of one curtain for another, change of scene was indicated.' Without the prompt-book it is impossible to tell, but a scathing letter to *Oxberry's Weekly Budget* signed 'K', describes the set as 'two blankets suspended from a rod', and would add weight to the view that the second set of curtains was merely decorative. (pp. 160-61)

[Attached] to the back curtain [was] the placard indicating the place of action. The *Morning Post* criticizes the stage-management on the first performance, complaining that the place of action and the placards did not change simultaneously.

The last interesting feature of the setting was the drop-scene which preceded the drama, painted by Charles Marshall from Hollar's print of the Bankside, included to add to the Elizabethan flavour, but in a typically Victorian way. It was generally praised, except by the critic of *The Illustrated London News,* who considered it too 'clay-y', and the critic of the *Morning Post* who, although liking the scene, thought the painting of the water 'unfinished'.

The Elizabethan costumes in general were praised, and, considering Planché's interests, were no doubt reasonably accurate. They were thought 'very handsome and appropriate' by *The Times,* although a sarcastic critic in *Bentley's Miscellany* suggests that, since written notices were used to indicate scenes, costumes could have been shown in the same way, the actors wearing placards attached to the appropriate parts of their persons, reading 'a slashed doublet of fine green velvet' or 'a handsome pair of scarlet hose'. A more serious comment on the dressing of the Induction characters as real Elizabethans, comes from the *Athenaeum* critic. He felt that this led the audience to expect a type of acting very different from that which existed on the stage in his day, and writes, 'Webster's previous assumption of Shakespeare's semblance made his subsequent misconception and undignified personation of Petruchio more glaring'. Since so little was known of Elizabethan acting styles, and since the critic bases his ideas entirely on Hamlet's speech to the players, perhaps this is not a serious criticism, but clearly the disguises in the Induction were not uniformly approved.

The Shakespearean overture by Sir Henry Bishop is interesting. It is probably the same as that used in the gala performance given at Covent Garden in December 1847, in order to raise funds to restore Shakespeare's house. It consists of themes, previously written or chosen by him for earlier Shakespeare revivals, *Twelfth Night*, *The Tempest*, *A Midsummer Night's Dream*, *The Comedy of Errors* and *As You Like It*, the only new theme being one for *Macbeth*, together with pieces by Ford and Arne. Bishop's biographer, Northcott, does not include the 1844 Shakespearean Overture in his list of works, although the 1847 version is mentioned. The critic of *The Illustrated London News* did not approve—'The Shakespearean overture is a sorry medley of tunes that have been huddled together most clumsily. It is said in the bills to be the composition (?) of Sir H. R. Bishop; if so we are sorry for it'. The interval music, to cover the plying of Sly with liquor, was under the direction of the Haymarket's regular conductor, Thomas German Reed, and was an arrangement of madrigals by Festa and Wilbye, and traditional English airs. Since the intervals were relatively short, the amount of music was minimal.

The cast (from a playbill for 27 March 1844) was as follows:—

Baptista – Mr. Gough	Tranio – Mr. Bindal
Vincentio – Mr. Tilbery	Biondello – Mr. H. Widdicomb
Lucentio – Mr. Holl	Pedant – Mr. Sauter
Hortensio – Mr. Howe	Katharina – Mrs. Nisbett
Gremio – Mr. James Bland	Bianca – Miss Julia Bennett
Petrucio – Mr. Webster	Widow – Mrs. Stanley
Grumio – Mr. Buckstone	Sly – Mr. Strickland
	Lord – Mr. Stuart

With a few qualifications as to Webster's own performance, the acting was universally praised. This leads us to consider two points: firstly, while it is true that Webster had assembled around him at the Haymarket a very distinguished company, it is possible that, for the first time, the nineteenth-century critics were able to see acting untrammelled by complicating setting and costumes. As far as I can ascertain, there was no new style of playing approximating to Poel's 'tunes', that went with the new setting, but, and this leads me to the second point, the actors would have much less time between acts and scenes than they would have in a conventional production. They were not cumbered by complicated settings and innumerable properties, and this perhaps led to the speed and vivacity of playing that the critics comment on; and, since they were relying on themselves and each other more than on the props of spectacle, the style of setting could have led to the development of the accomplished 'ensemble' playing mentioned by the critic of *The Illustrated London News*.

Mrs Nisbett's performance excited ecstatic reviews, even from those who did not approve of the whole production. The *Morning Post* critic, who regarded the evening as a bore, attributes the volume of applause at the end to her delivery of her last speech, expounding the duties of a wife. This speech was described by the *Theatrical Journal* critic as 'an elaborate fin-

ish to an exquisite performance'. The quality she added to the part was that 'she did not suddenly sink into the abject slave of her husband's whim, but now and then broke out into the short ebullitions of hasty temper she was wont to indulge in' (*Theatrical Journal*), and that she always maintained her dignity so that 'through the veil of the termagant, the lady was still visible' (*Illustrated London News*). *The Dramatic Mirror*, referring to the 1847 revival, praises both her 'buoyancy and spirit' and 'her delicacy' and proclaims her 'the best Katharine on the stage', a view echoed by the critic in *Oxberry's Weekly Budget*—'a most beautiful piece of acting'. The only murmur of dissent came from the critic of the *Athenaeum*, who made the point that, since Webster was so intent on being Elizabethan, the part of Katharine should have been played by a boy, and adds: '. . . Mrs. Nisbett's personal attractions procured immunity for a degree of vulgarity that would hardly have been tolerated by smooth-faced striplings who played women's parts in Shakespeare's time'.

Webster as Petruchio was not so highly praised. It was generally felt that he was uneasy in the part which was of 'too high a cast for him' (*Theatrical Journal*). Therefore he rushed the lines (*Times*). *The Illustrated London News* felt that there was more of the rude tyrant than the gentleman about him. Westland Marston, while acknowledging that Webster had 'few faults', wrote that his Petruchio 'seemed really violent and angry, and showed little enjoyment of the part he was masquerading'. The *Morning Post* agrees about the coarseness, and complains about 'sing-song' delivery.

Nisbett shared the acting honours, not with Webster, but with Strickland as Sly, who was praised for his by-play, although, says the *Morning Post* critic, according to the original text he ought to have been in bed, not walking about in a dressing-gown and slippers. There is little indication as to what the by-play may have been. We only know it was 'humourously droll'. 'He was drunk all over, yet not dead drunk, or mad drunk, or half drunk; but in a twilight state, between part drunkenness and future sobriety' (*Dramatic Mirror*).

The other notable performance was Buckstone's Grumio. He played the part with his 'usual gusto' (*Athenaeum*) and was 'a relief to dreariness' for the *Morning Post* critic, who tells us that the piece of business when Grumio draws his sword and follows Petruchio from the stage, presumably after the abortive wedding banquet in Act III Sc. ii, earned three rounds of applause. He is criticized however by the same critic for 'a nasal twang' which was not felt to fit with the characterization.

The only other actor reviewed at length was Stuart who played the Lord, and he was the subject of an ironic review in *Punch*.

> Nothing can be finer than the acting of Mr. Stuart from first to last in the very arduous character assigned to him. There is something truly Shakespearian in his treatment of the wand which he holds in his hand, and which he twiddles about, from time to time between his fingers, with a nice appreciation of the highly dramatic situation into which he is thrown by the towering genius of the Swan of Avon. In the fourth act, Mr. Stuart rests his right arm on an adjacent chair but the point we admired most, was the truly Elizabethan jerk he gave to his left leg in the middle of the banquet scene. . . .

The Times says the whole performance took three and a half hours. This seems extraordinarily long, especially as only one scene change is required and the act intervals were so short. Did they merely seem short to a Victorian audience? The Shakespearean overture would last about 12-15 minutes. One of the 1847 playbills announces the *Shrew* performance for 7 p.m., and second prices at 9, but, of course, the second-price audience could have seen the end of the *Shrew* for their money. Clearly the speed of delivery of Webster's company kept them a long way from observing the 'two-hours' traffic' of the stage.

One must now consider the general press and public opinions of the experiment. The newspapers were divided. Those *for* the Elizabethan setting included *Bentley's Miscellany, The Dramatic Mirror, John Bull, The Illustrated London News, Oxberry's Weekly Budget, The Theatrical Journal* and *The Times.*

Bentley's Miscellany praised the economy and simplicity of the production: 'Here at one blow by the substitution of a contrivance beautiful in its simplicity, the whole army of scene-painters, carpenters, and shifters are ingeniously swamped'. *The Illustrated London News* concurred, writing that the success of the *Shrew* showed that 'mere gew-gaw accessories of the stage are not necessary when there is the "Mens divinior poetae" present'. *The Times* explained that the setting gave 'closeness to the action, and, by constantly allowing a great deal of stage room, afforded a sort of freedom to all parties engaged'. An advantage of the setting noticed by *The Dramatic Mirror* reviewer was that the simple staging 'permitted the undivided attention of the audience to the business of the drama'. *John Bull* took the opportunity to point out that this production showed that if there was a decline in the drama, it was not due to a decline in public taste, for Webster's intelligent experiment had been 'attended with complete success'. To sum up those 'in favour': what they liked was the simplicity and economy of the setting, which they felt helped not only the actors, in giving them freedom of movement, but also the members of the audience, who were forced to use their imaginations, and could and did listen to the words of the play with more attention than was necessary or possible in a spectacular production.

Those 'against' range from the ironic reviewer of Stuart's performance in *Punch* to the furious 'K' whose letter was printed in *Oxberry's Weekly Budget. Punch* continues his irony in a later issue. On learning that the spectacular *Der Freischütz* is scheduled for the Haymarket, the writer suggests that the incantation scene be got up after the manner of *The Taming of the Shrew.* Moon, clouds, smoke, lightning, blue fire, lizards, toads, boas and bears, are to be represented by placards hung at appropriate points.

Bentley's Miscellany, although favourably disposed in the main, ends on a warning note. If Webster's experiment was carried to its logical conclusion 'the imagination of the public (could be) at last educated to so high a point that they may be able to read a play at home, and fancy themselves at the theatre'.

More serious complaints were launched by the critics of the *Morning Post* and the *Athenaeum.* The *Morning Post* critic found the production a bore, first because of the restoration of the original text:

> [The managers] overlook the fact that the original text was not altered until it had been tried and found wanting in dramatic interest. We must plead

guilty to the impeachment of preferring the pleasant abridgement of it in *Catherine and Petruchio* to the long, wearisome and yet unfinished comedy of five acts, with its preliminary induction without a conclusion.

The applause of the audience at the end is attributed to the snob appeal of the play. Told it was the *real* thing, the audience had to like it, but there was little applause or laughter during the performance. The charge of being boring was also implicitly levelled against the production by Charles Kemble when, in a letter to *Punch,* he wrote 'Prince Albert will, in a short time, wholly renounce the idols of the Opera and as a most convincing proof of his belief in Shakespeare, sit out the *Petruchio* of Mr. Webster'.

The *Athenaeum* accuses the management of gimmickry and 'pedantic affectation of accuracy', but does perhaps make a valid point in objecting to the inconsistency of style in presenting the Induction with typical Victorian scenes, and 'the play within the play' in an imitation of the Elizabethan manner. It is in this point that the spirit of the Haymarket revival differs most from Poel's. Within a Victorian conception of a Tudor hall, the play was performed in what roughly approximated to an Elizabethan stage. The tone of the whole production was not Shakespearean or Elizabethan as Poel understood the words.

The most virulent attack, and that which most clearly shows the rage for spectacle that had such a strong hold on the nineteenth-century theatre, comes from the letter in *Oxberry's Weekly Budget.* The writer, 'K', agrees that the restoration of the text might well be justified, but the restoration of the 'primitive beauty' of the stage condition was 'a miserable failure'. Shakespeare, he claims, would have loved nineteenth-century methods of staging, and, like the critic of the *Athenaeum,* he levels the charge of 'pedantic affectation' against the production.

In general, however, the reception seems to have been favourable, and Webster revived the production for fourteen performances in October/November 1847. Howe claims this was not so much of a success, but *The Times* critic found it a very interesting performance, and 'the effect was given of the ancient method of dramatic representation in England, when the art of scene painting was unknown'. *The Illustrated London News* records that the house was well filled.

There were few major changes in cast. Webster and Nisbett continued as Petruchio and Katharine, but Vandenhoff took over from Holl as Lucentio, and Keeley from Buckstone as Grumio. Lambert played Sly. Webster, if we are to believe the critic of the *Dramatic Mirror,* had improved, and was less guilty of the 'coarseness' that was complained of in his earlier interpretation. He showed 'an hilarious freedom and boldness in his bearing that conveyed to us a perfect idea of a choleric man without the blustering vulgarity of the bully, or the rudeness of an illtempered brute'. Crabb Robinson, who did not see the first production, still complains of 'coarseness'. From *The Illustrated London News* review, we learn that Webster continued 'with much effect on the audience' the traditional cracking of the whip in the character of Petruchio.

Keeley was praised for his 'rich and quiet drollery' and *The Times,* although not the *Dramatic Mirror,* preferred him to Buckstone. The performances of the minor characters were inferior to those of the original production. *The Times* felt greater attention should have been paid to metre, and criticized Vandenhoff's trick of pronouncing the Latin in the passages with Bianca, according to Italian, not English pronunciation. Vandenhoff replied almost in the terms of a Stanislavskian actor, citing Lucentio's birthplace Pisa, and upbringing in Florence, as authorities for his choice of pronunciation. Rightly, however, *The Times* reviewer points out that, on this level, the whole play should be in Italian, and the fact that Bianca repeated the Latin phrases in an English way led to a jarring inconsistency.

Lambert as Sly was not so highly praised as Strickland, but he did 'take great pains and showed some talent in the various expressions with which he listened to the play' (*Times*). What was missed was Strickland's 'unctuous drunkenness'. Rogers, as the Lord, in place of Stuart, apparently looked more like a suppressor than an encourager of drama.

Clearly Webster did not regard the revival as a failure, as he chose scenes from Acts I and IV to be his contribution to the Shakespeare Night at Covent Garden on 7 December 1847, 'in aid of the fund for the purchase and preservation of Shakespeare's House'. Other excerpts presented included scenes from *Henry IV*, parts I and II, *Henry VIII, Two Gentlemen of Verona, Romeo and Juliet, The Merry Wives of Windsor, The Tempest, The Winter's Tale,* and the programme involved almost all the leading actors in London. The setting of the extracts from the *Shrew* is described in the programme as 'A Gothic Hall'. It is possible that this was merely stock scenery from Covent Garden, but the specific nature of the other set descriptions, 'Juliet's bedroom', 'The island before the cell of Prospero', 'A street in Verona' would lead one to believe that the set of the *Shrew* was the set of the second scene of the Induction, i.e., the Lord's bedroom, and that it was performed in more or less the same way at Covent Garden, as it had been in the Haymarket.

Another money-making venture, the publication of a book called *Selections from Shakespeare's Plays as represented at the Royal Italian Opera, Covent Garden* (1847), leads to some confusion about the extracts actually performed. In the first place, the text quoted is not from Shakespeare's play, but from Garrick's alteration, revised by J. P. Kemble. It is impossible to believe that Webster's company, having restored the original text in 1844, and revived it only a month before this performance, would have gone back to *Katharine and Petruchio* for the gala. One must suppose that the compiler of the book was confused, and used the wrong text—no doubt an indication of the currency of the Garrick version at this time. Secondly, the extracts printed are very short—fifty-one lines in the first extract and only twelve in the second—hardly enough to give any idea of the play. And lastly, although the full cast, except for the Induction characters, is listed in the programme, in the printed text only three appear—Katharine, Petruchio and Grumio. In the printed extract Grumio has only three lines, yet *The Illustrated London News* records that Keeley was specially called for after the performance. The *Selections,* then, was probably thrown together, very hurriedly, and gives very little clue to what was actually performed.

Webster's contribution to the evening is not noticed particularly, most press attention being given to the prologue by Charles Knight, spoken by Samuel Phelps, and the inadequate acoustics of Covent Garden for Shakespeare.

The results of the production are disappointing. Webster did not try any other play on an Elizabethan stage, although public reaction had on the whole been favourable. *Katharine and Petruchio* was still performed, and although Phelps revived the original text at Sadler's Wells in 1856, he did not use Elizabethan staging. The only follow-up was in Edinburgh in February 1849, when the Garrick text plus the Induction was performed 'in the Baron's Hall, fitted up for a temporary theatre as in days of yore'.

A totally contrasting production of the full text was used by Augustin Daly to open his new theatre in 1893, but the settings were lavish. 'Mr. Daly, wisely considering that the omission of proper scenery was by no means essential, has mounted the play with liberality and good taste'.

The theatre had to wait for Poel before it gave widespread recognition to Planché's idea. Poel was apparently not influenced by the Haymarket productions, as he calls his *Hamlet* 'the first revival of the draped stage in this country or elsewhere'. But we must beware of attributing too much foresight to Planché. As Stanley Wells points out, Planché was as much the forerunner of the Kean—Irving—Tree tradition, as of Poel's Elizabethan stage. He no doubt felt that *The Taming of the Shrew* was particularly suited to this treatment, and perhaps the accusation of some critics that he was only pursuing 'novelty' for its own sake could be justified. He was still presenting an Elizabethan stage within a Victorian setting. Let us not, however, ask too much of Planché and Webster. They were attempting to reconstruct an Elizabethan stage, without the benefit of a sixteenth-century education, or of the discoveries of the next hundred years, but with the possible disadvantage of their knowledge of all the conventions and trappings of a Victorian theatrical experience. Neither William Poel, nor Walter Hodges, nor any other restorer has had the advantage of this type of education, and their ideas are as much the product of their own time and experience as Planché's were of his. We must, therefore, give him credit for the idea, and for recognizing the interesting possibilities that arose from his experiment. He wrote in *Recollections and Reflections*: 'My restoration of this "gem" is one of the events in my theatrical career on which I look back with the greatest pride and gratification'. (pp. 161-69)

Jan McDonald, " 'The Taming of the Shrew' at the Haymarket Theatre, 1844 and 1847," in Essays on Nineteenth Century British Theatre, *edited by Kenneth Richards and Peter Thomson, Methuen & Co. Ltd., 1971, pp. 157-70.*

PRODUCTION:

Samuel Phelps • Sadler's Wells Theatre • 1856

BACKGROUND:

Phelps was a renowned nineteenth-century actor-manager. His production followed the trend set by Benjamin Webster and J. R. Planché a decade earlier, presenting the original *Taming of the Shrew* rather than Garrick's abbreviated adaptation. The production offered a cameo appearance by Phelps, who drew high praise from contemporary critics for his brilliant portrayal of Christopher Sly.

COMMENTARY:

The Times, London   (review date 17 November 1856)

[*The anonymous critic compares Phelps's* Shrew *to Webster's earlier revival, noting that Phelps did not adopt Webster's scant use of scenery. Additionally, the critic highly commends Phelps's performance as Christopher Sly.*]

In the year 1844 Mr. Webster, the manager of the Haymarket, revived the *Taming of the Shrew,* in the place of the shortened piece which, under the title of *Katharine and Petruchio,* had long supplanted it on the London stage, and considerable interest was excited on the occasion. Not only had the piece in the form which is ascribed to Shakspeare remained unacted since (perhaps) the Restoration of Charles II, but the performance of the play (as distinguished from the "Induction") in the "Lord's" Palace allowed the representation of a drama without scenic decoration, at a time when the graver portion of the public were beginning to suspect—not without reason—that the decorative artist threatened to obscure the poet. The "Induction" had, indeed, its appropriate scenery, like any ordinary work, but as soon as the tinker had taken his place in the hall, and the tale of the Shrew-tamer commenced, the plan of the mimic action was simply indicated by placards. From the success of this experiment some of those enthusiasts who are always dreaming of theatrical revolutions, and fancying they will result in a supreme reign of dramatic poetry, inferred that a good time was at hand, when scenery would vanish altogether, and a white board, inscribed "Rome" or "Padua," would be sufficient for an imagination already rendered active by the beauty of dialogue. We need scarcely say that the expected change never came. *The Taming of the Shrew,* being a play within a play, was too exceptional in its form to be a precedent for dramatic production in general, and, even if this had not been the case, it might easily have been seen that the sort of interest occasioned by the absence of scenery depended entirely on the novelty of the arrangement. Half the play-goers in London might be anxious to see how a play would look without decorations, but, curiosity once satisfied, the ordinary method would be preferred. So far was the practice of making stage adornment an especial consideration, checked by the revival of 1844, that it has steadily progressed since that period, and has now reached a culminating point which we conceive is hardly to be passed.

Mr. Phelps, who revived the *Taming of the Shrew* on Saturday, does not go so far as Mr. Webster in the restoration of the old method of stage contrivance. Christopher Sly and his party sit in the front of the stage and look upon a performance adorned after the usual fashion. Before the play is far advanced the tinker is carried off insensible, and from this point the distinction from the ordinary mode of representation vanishes altogether.

The great feature in the revival is the Christopher Sly of Mr. Phelps, who, although much less abundant in words than the other comic characters with which the same gentleman has occasionally delighted his public, is coloured and elaborated with all the care that denotes a strong predilection on the part of the artist. Mr. Phelps proposes to himself the exhibition of a thoroughly low and grovelling nature, still further debased by the least poetical form of drunkenness, and not a detail does he miss that can contribute to the realization of a stupid sensuality. So low is the intellectual condition of the debauchee that when his animal side is not touched his face literally wears no expression at all. What with innate dulness, and what with "small ale," he is not bright enough to be

greatly startled at finding himself transformed into a lord; a palace and a dead wall will strongly resemble each other when dimly seen through the medium of a dense fog. When his attendants strive to impress him with a belief in his own grandeur his surprise is of the slowest kind, being chiefly indicated by the instinctive manner in which he wheels round his face towards each successive speaker, clearly oblivious of all that has been said by the rest.

When Christopher Sly is borne from the stage the audience are left free to bestow their undivided attention on the play, properly so called, and certainly more amusement was never created within the walls of a theatre than by the process of shrew-taming as exhibited on Saturday by Mr. Marston and Miss Atkinson in the characters of Katharine and Petruchio. They both played with admirable spirit, and every crack of the whip by the gentleman, and every frown or stamp on the part of the lady stirred up the stormiest satisfaction. Whether much is gained by the restoration of the whole story of Bianca may be fairly doubted, inasmuch as this underplot is carried on by a great number of feebly drawn personages, and is far more complex than entertaining. However, it is set down in *Shakspeare,* and that is a good and sufficient reason at Sadler's-wells.

A review of "The Taming of the Shrew," in The Times, *London, November 17, 1856, p. 7.*

The Athenaeum   (review date 22 November 1856)

[*In this unsigned review, the critic recognizes the theatrical significance of Phelps's restored version of* The Shrew, *asserting that "the competent spectator will retire from the performance with a higher appreciation of the comedy" than can be derived from "the manner in which it is ordinarily acted."*]

An important revival was placed on the stage on Saturday at [Sadler's Wells],—the twenty-ninth, as it is stated on the bills, of the Shakspearian dramas introduced by the present management to the audiences of Islington. 'The Taming of the Shrew,' with the Induction, was performed *in extenso,*—Mr. Phelps himself undertaking the portrait of *Christopher Sly.* An Asiatic air surrounds this little introductory romance, which is, as we know, of Oriental origin, as witness the adventures of Abou Hassan, and of Alo-eddin; but the immediate authority of Shakspeare and his predecessor was the historian Henterus, who tells the story of the Duke of Burgundy, Philip the Good. A similar incident has been fixed on Charles the Fifth, and told of the Emperor by Richard Barckley, in his 'Discourse on the Felicitie of Man.' Shakspeare has not, however, made so much of the Induction as had the preceding playwright from whom he borrowed the design, and has dismissed Sly long before the termination of the play; whereas in 'The Taming of *a* Shrew' he concludes the action, thus making a complete framework for it, and realizing the notion of a play within a play. But our greater bard has touched up the text, both of this Induction and the drama that follows, and set the stamp of his genius on the rude work of an elder hand. We have already pointed out Mr. Phelps's peculiar excellence in certain eccentric characters, and think that he has done well to add *Sly the Tinker* to *Bottom the Weaver* [in *A Midsummer Night's Dream*] and *Mr. Justice Shallow* [in *Henry IV, Parts I and II* and *The Merry Wives of Windsor*]. The elaborate, minute touches bestowed by the artist on these small parts bring out the wonderful genius of the dramatist by whom they were created or improved. They subject them, as it were, to the action of a microscope, and reveal what were else invisible. The process, of course, would be tedious were it adopted on a large scale, but applied as it is to "these brief instances," it is instructive and suggestive. Mr. Phelps, at any rate, never appears so great an actor as when he is doing these little things. Here he is at once effective, original, and beyond critical censure. The whole play went off admirably; the more comic characters attaining full relief by the retention of the whole of the scenes and situations, so admirably distributed for the purposes of alternate repose and action. As now acted, we can estimate this production as a work of Elizabethan art; and the competent spectator will retire from the performance with a higher appreciation of the comedy, as such, than he can gain from a mere perusal, or the manner in which it is ordinarily acted.

A review of "The Taming of the Shrew," in The Athenaeum, *No. 1517, November 22, 1856, p. 1439.*

The Illustrated London News   (review date 22 November 1856)

[*The anonymous critic comments on Phelps's performance of Christopher Sly as a man "wholly moved by his instincts" and on the advantages of presenting* The Taming of the Shrew *in its entirety.*]

On Saturday "The Taming of the Shrew" was revived, with "the Induction," usually omitted in representation. Mr. Phelps boasts on his playbill of this being the 29th Shakspearean revival produced under his management of this theatre. Out of thirty-seven plays this is, indeed, a fair proportion, and we believe a feat not previously achieved by any management. With respect to the present the merit consists in reviving the whole of the play, including the Induction; for, in an abridged form, under the title of "Katherine and Petruchio," the comedy has been frequently acted both in town and country. It has been treated with little reverence indeed; being regarded as a farce in its general action and rough outline. One of the plays which Shakspeare altered rather than created, the rude material exposes itself through his embellishments. It was preceded by a drama, entitled "The Taming of *a* Shrew," and George Gascoigne's comedy of the "Supposes," from which the underplot is derived, the incidents being similar in both, but the motives different. Even the Induction is to be found in the prior play, the *Hostess* being substituted by Shakspeare for a *Tapster,* but both beginning with the ejection of *Christopher Sly* from the alehouse. The *Tinker,* however, in the old play, is continued throughout it; whereas Shakspeare drops him with the first act; and thus the notion of a play within a play is more fully carried out in the rough draught than in the amended copy. Probably at this time Shakspeare had conceived, and partly written, his "Midsummer Night's Dream," and was not willing to anticipate *Bottom,* the weaver, by *Sly,* the tinker. In the old play, the situation of his awaking, and concluding that the whole was a dream, is carefully elaborated. Such portions of the induction, however, as Shakspeare did take he much improved, adding to them both colour and character. We dwell the more on this point because, in the cast of the present revival, Mr. Phelps has selected the part of *Christopher Sly* for his own. It is now thoroughly understood that Mr. Phelps has a special aptitude for the impersonation of low-comedy character parts, and it was therefore justly expected by his admirers that a banquet of humour was in store for them by his adoption of the person of the emparadised tinker. It may stand

safely by the side of *Bottom,* the weaver, and is to all intents as richly elaborated. *Sly,* under the influence of drink, is little better than a machine, and wholly moved by his instincts. His head turns mechanically from one to another when spoken to, like a clairvoyant under the influence of mesmerism. Gradually his impulses are awakened, and he then shows somewhat of his native humour; the various traits of which were so excellently delineated that the house was convulsed with laughter. We may add that the most uproarious merriment also rewarded the efforts of Mr. Marston and Miss Atkinson, as *Petruchio* and *Katherine.* The effect was incomparably greater than any ever produced by the performance of the same play in its usual abridged form. Why is this? It is true that some of the passages usually omitted are dull, tedious, and "lead to nothing;" but they serve the purpose of relief and contrast; and it is owing to the dramatist's exquisite distribution of light and shade that the comic scenes come out with so much more potency in their natural order than in that imposed upon them in the compressed version. Another instance, this, to demonstrate how much less wise in general is the player than the poet, and to inculcate reverence towards works which bear on them the divine impress of genius. The revival in full of "The Taming of the Shrew" is likely to teach this lesson, and if it does no more it will have answered no mean purpose and done no little good.

A review of "The Taming of the Shrew," in The Illustrated London News, *Vol. XXIX, No. 831, November 22, 1856, p. 521.*

Henry Morley   (review date 6 December 1856)

[*Morley was a nineteenth-century English scholar, editor, and dramatic critic whose writings often focused on the various relations between literature and the stage. As a member of the School for Dramatic Art, his chief goal was to raise the standard of the acting and drama of his day. Morley also contributed essays and reviews to the* Examiner *from 1850 to 1864. Many of his dramatic criticisms were collected and published in 1891 as* The Journal of a London Playgoer from 1851 to 1866. *In an originally unsigned review, reprinted below, Morley presents a detailed description of Phelps's performance as Christopher Sly, maintaining that the actor excellently filled out "Shakespeare's sketch of a man purely sensual and animal."*]

The *Induction* to the *Taming of the Shrew* enables Mr Phelps to represent, in *Christopher Sly,* Shakespeare's sketch of a man purely sensual and animal, brutish in appetite, and with a mind unleavened by fancy. Such a presentment would not suit the uses of the poet, it could excite only disgust, if it were not throughout as humorous as faithful. Mr Phelps knows this, and, perhaps, the most interesting point to be noted in his *Christopher Sly* is that the uncompromising truth of his portraiture of the man buried and lost in his animal nature, is throughout, by subtle touches, easy to appreciate but hard to follow, made subservient to the laws of art, and the sketch, too, is clearly the more accurate for being humorous;—throughout we laugh and understand.

Hamlet and *Christopher Sly* are at the two ends of Shakespeare's list of characters, and, with a singular skill, Mr Phelps, who is the best *Hamlet* now upon the stage, banishes from his face every spark of intelligence while representing *Sly.* Partly he effects this by keeping the eyes out of court as witnesses of intelligence. The lids are drooped in the heavy slumberousness of a stupid nature; there is no such thing as a glance of intelligence allowed to escape from under them; the eyes are hidden almost entirely when they are not widely exposed in a stupid stare. The acting of this little sketch is, indeed, throughout most careful and elaborate. There is, as we have said, no flinching from the perfect and emphatical expression of the broader lights and shadows of the character. *Christopher* is, at first, sensually drunk, and when, after his awakening in the lord's house, the page is introduced to him as his lady wife, another chord of sensuality is touched, the brute hugs and becomes amorous. Of the imagination that, even when there are offered to the sensual body new delights of the appetite, is yet unable to soar beyond the reach already attained, Mr Phelps, in the details of his acting, gives a variety of well-conceived suggestions. Thus, to the invitation—"Will't please your mightiness to wash your hands?" [Ind. ii. 76]—*Christopher,* when he has grasped the fact that a basin is being held before him in which he must wash, enters upon such a wash as sooty hands of tinkers only can require, and, having made an end of washing and bespattering, lifts up instinctively the corner of his velvet robe to dry his hands upon.

The stupidity of *Sly* causes his disappearance from the stage in the most natural way after the play itself has warmed into full action. He has, of course, no fancy for it, is unable to follow it, stares at it and falls asleep over it. The sport of imagination acts upon him as a sleeping draught, and at the end of the first act, he is so fast asleep that it becomes matter of course to carry him away. The *Induction* thus insensibly fades into the play, and all trace of it is lost by the time that a lively interest in the comedy itself has been excited.

> *A review of "The Taming of the Shrew," in* The Examiner, *No. 2549, December 6, 1856, p. 773.*

PRODUCTION:

Augustin Daly • Daly's Theatre • 1887

BACKGROUND:

Daly's production of *The Taming of the Shrew,* which opened at Daly's Theatre in New York on 18 January 1887, was immensely popular with audiences and theater critics, running for more than 120 performances in its first season. The following year, Daly took his production to London's Gaiety Theatre, where it met with similar acclaim. The production featured Ada Rehan, the accomplished Shakespearean actress, as Katherina. Many critics regard her portrayal of Kate the most outstanding in the play's stage history. Appearing with Miss Rehan were John Drew as Petruchio, William Gilbert as Sly, James Lewis as Grumio, Otis Skinner as Lucentio, Joseph Holland as Hortensio, and Frederick Bond as Tranio. In succeeding years, Daly restaged the popular production numerous times, especially when his theater faced financial decline and he needed a guaranteed success.

COMMENTARY:

The New York Times   (review date 19 January 1887)

[*The anonymous critic offers a favorable review of Daly's*
Shrew, asserting that it "will be remembered as the most successful venture of Mr. Daly in the Shakespearean field."]

The Shrew was tamed successfully at Daly's last evening. And a noted theatrical success it was, to be added to the long list of similar successes that have marked the career of the enterprising and oft-time daring manager Augustin Daly, to whom theatregoers of New York owe so much in the way of pleasure. A novelty in theatricals was promised, and a novelty was given, and the great crowd that filled the theatre had but words of praise for that novelty, for a prettier shrew than Ada Rehan never was tamed, and every man in the audience envied John Drew, the tamer.

It was a social event, as Daly's first nights always are; a sort of family gathering of friends in social and business life, as first nights at Daly's have come to be. They welcomed Miss Rehan and Mr. Drew, Mrs. Gilbert and Mr. Lewis, Miss Dreher and Mr. Skinner and Mr. Bond much in the kindly spirit accorded to people of "our set" who tread the boards for charity's sake before an audience of social friends. They summoned Mr. Daly twice to the footlights. As the play progressed the social welcome as of friend to friend gave way to that oft-time heartier, more cordial, and sincere welcome of art admirers to the actors whose art warms up the cockles of even the somewhat chilled heart of society. More cordial or more sincere and hearty plaudits actors never get than those given last night during the progress of Shakespeare's revivified comedy, "The Taming of the Shrew."

It was an audience that assembled to give welcome to the first presentation in this country of the comedy that was flattering alike to actors and manager. For there were present in addition to the regular first nighters an audience critical, but not coldly critical. That could not well have been, for the mass of the audience would not permit that, and swayed the coldly critical ones with them to enthusiastic auditors. Club men, to whom enthusiasm is "bad form," dropped in with the rest to the enjoyment of the hour, and the arrogant termagant Ada Rehan, her conversion to a dutiful wife, the rich costumes, fine stage pictures, and elaborate stage setting, will form the topic of conversation for some time longer than the ordinary nine days' wonder.

"The Taming of the Shrew," as it was done last night, will be remembered as the most successful venture of Mr. Daly in the Shakespearean field. This energetic manager has produced several of the supreme poet's works, always with lavish expenditure, and after much thoughtful preparation. His early revivals of "Twelfth Night," and "As You Like It" are still remembered, but these, as well as the sumptuous dress he gave to "Love's Labor's Lost," and the spirit and splendor of "The Merry Wives," at the first Fifth-Avenue Theatre, would not stand the test of comparison with his latest achievement for many reasons. "The Taming of the Shrew" was completely successful last evening because it was well acted, with vim and humor, apt perception of character, and delicacy of touch; because it was richly mounted, with scenes that aided the players to preserve the illusion of time and place, while of sufficient beauty to elicit admiration on their own account, and dresses such as Italian gallants and clowns and pedants wore in the sixteenth century; because in the adaptation of the poet's text and the needful arrangement of the episodes scholarly discretion was joined with managerial tact, and while the omissions were warranted by good taste, the additions to the original dialogue were few in number and equally tasteful, and the new "business" was all in keeping with the tone of the play. It was a performance of poetic comedy, so beautiful, so graceful, and so merry that the eye was dazzled, the ear captivated, and the senses charmed. It was true to the poet's conception, and highly creditable to the understanding, the enterprise, and the sagacity of the manager. The work done was all new. There were no available precedents to consult as to the mounting of the play, the costuming, or the business of the stage. The traditions preserved in the bungling afterpiece called "Katherine and Petruchio," with few exceptions, were disregarded, and the production was distinctly different from either of the two revivals of the comedy famous in the history of the London stage. Following Shakespeare's own idea, the characters of the Induction dropped out of sight after the first act, and the interludes taken from the old play attributed to Greene were not brought into use. The attention of the spectator, at first held by the mystified tinker and his cajolers, was gradually diverted to the gayety, the sentiment, and the intrigue of the mimic play, and not again recalled from the romantic atmosphere of the poet's Padua to the English castle or the alehouse on Wincot heath. So Shakespeare wrote the play, and so, we are bound to believe, he intended it to be performed. The production must be judged entirely on the basis of Shakespeare's own play, without reference to any existing "prompt books," or any previous representation of the work. The alterations in the text were not important, and most of the elisions had been made in order to keep the performance within the allotted three hours. Katherine's first scene was omitted, and the incidents that result in the submission of the shrew to her husband's will were compressed into one lively scene in the house of Petruchio. The coarse allusions and positive vulgarity that did not offend the audiences of the Globe Theatre in Elizabethan days were wisely eliminated. The whole of the lively intrigue to secure the hand of sweet Bianca, involving courtly Lucentio and gallant Hortensio, old Gremio, the comic servants, the true Vincenzio and the false one, was retained, and the closing passages introduced the test of the three wives and the triumph of transformed Katherine over herself and her husband.

The acting was surprisingly good in all parts for a company so closely confined, during most of the year, to modern comedy. The Katherine of Miss Rehan, however, was of greater merit than any other individual performance. In appearance she was a superb figure, and the gradations of temper in her earlier scenes with Petruchio, her simulation of fright in the stormy episode that begins the honeymoon, and the delicate art with which the submission of the woman to the man was depicted demonstrated the constantly increasing skill of this fine actress and her keen insight. Katherine, at the beginning the personification of shrewishness, was in the denouement a sweet and sympathetic personage. The portrayal was admirably finished and consistent with the poet's creation, though it may be doubted if, for that very reason, it was wholly true to nature. Mr. Drew was picturesque, forcible, and easy beyond expectation as Petruchio. Mr. Lewis and Mrs. Gilbert made a quaintly comical pair as Grumio and Curtis. Miss Dreher was a vision of loveliness as Bianca, Mr. Skinner and Mr. Joseph Holland embodied very successfully the two young gallants and Mr. Frederick Bond bore the part of that apt and amusing rascal, Tranio, with excellent effect. All of these players received special tributes of praise from the audience; but sound and valuable work was done also by Mr. Fisher, Mr. Leclercq, Mr. Wood, Mr. Moore, Mr. Wilks, and Miss Gordon, and in the Induction, which was all capitally done and continuously entertaining, Mr. George Clarke as

the whimsical Lord had authority and dignity, and Mr. William Gilbert was very droll as befuddled but self-satisfied Christopher Sly. The incidental music, arranged by Mr. Widmer, including Bishop's setting of "Should he upbraid," sung by Miss St. Quinten, was all charming.

"Mr. Daly's Great Triumph," in The New York Times, *January 19, 1887, p. 1.*

Amélie Rives   (review date June 1887)

[*Rives contends that although Daly's revival has run through more than one hundred consecutive performances, it nevertheless remains an entertaining production.*]

One of the chief pleasures of the winter has been the revival at Daly's Theatre of the *Taming of the Shrew;* and no less a pleasure has been its success, because that promises to secure to us similar pleasures hereafter. The success of the revival has been signal. The performances proceeded every successive evening to the one-hundredth repetition, and the play held the stage to the end of the season. Every performance has been witnessed by a crowded house, and every seat has been engaged long in advance. The secret of such success is worth ascertaining, for this one event has disposed of a familiar impression, that Shakespeare's dramas can no longer compete with the modern plays except in the very unusual event of the appearance of a remarkable genius.

The revival of the *Taming of the Shrew* has demonstrated that Shakespeare has not lost his hold of the modern theatre, if the different conditions of the theatre in his time and ours are duly perceived and regarded. The first consideration is completeness of setting in scene and costume; the second is fitting adaptation of the play to the character and talent of the company; the third is a general superiority in the company, which secures a uniform excellence in the representation; and the fourth is that precision and perfection in the detail of action which gives the impression of entire ease and spontaneity. All these conditions were attained at Daly's in this revival. When the play was first acted by her Majesty's servants at "the Blacke Friers and the Globe," in 1596—if that was the year, upon which point the editors differ—it is easy to fancy the bareness of the setting and the dependence upon the boisterous fun of the story. But the play as seen at Daly's would have been a delight to Shakespeare himself, like the beautiful modern editions of his dramas.

It is, by the general agreement of the commentators, a composite work. Grant White says that at least three hands are evident in it, and Mr. Winter, in his introduction to the play as revived this winter, says that Shakespeare never claimed it as one of his works, and it was first published in the folio of 1623 after his death. It was an older play, perhaps by Robert Greene, rewritten. But the original story is like Emerson's road that dwindles from a highway to a squirrel-track, and finally runs up a tree. It is supposed to be drawn from a translation from Ariosto. The Induction is supposed also to be traced to an actual incident at the marriage of Duke Philip the Good of Burgundy, in 1440; and again it is referred to a ballad of unknown old date; and finally Knight thinks it is of Eastern origin, being found in the *Arabian Nights;* and so doubtless it vanishes in a sun-myth.

The Induction and the taming are full of that boisterous liveliness which belongs to Boccaccio and the old Italian stories, but which alone would not hold a modern audience for a hundred nights. The success depends, as we said, upon a thorough appreciation of the play and complete adaptation to its representation of adequate talent, and then the admirable setting and perfect movement of the whole. All this we had at Daly's. There is little wit in the drama. It is largely horse-play in the taming scenes. The motive is the subjugation of an imperious temper by a well-feigned superior obstinacy carried out inflexibly, but in entire good-humor. To this result the company at Daly's co-operated with a remarkable evenness of intelligence and skill. It is especially a spirited, breezy, open-air play, and it was rendered with the utmost spirit. The performance had a freshness which was truly extraordinary when the "damnable iteration" of a hundred and more consecutive nights is considered.

The modern taste which this revival gratified demands fidelity to the scene—the reproduction of the air and temper and spectacle belonging to the story quite as much as the adequate representation of the characters and the repetition of the words. The perception of this taste and demand, and their gratification, explain the great success of Henry Irving. As the modern opera of Wagner and his compeers subordinates the virtuoso and the trained individual vocal skill to the general effect of a drama told in music and action for its own sake, and not for the distinction of the performers, so the modern presentation of the drama must give the very aspect and pressure of the time. We must walk in Padua and be entertained in Petruchio's country house, and all that we see and hear—all the bright circumstance—must lap us in Italian airs, and in a world of faery beyond our own.

This was the exquisite charm of Irving's production of the *Merchant of Venice*. We were transported to the Adriatic shore. There were the palaces, the bridges, the canals. The air was full of song and the murmur of revelry. Here passed the hurrying maskers with echoing gibe and laughter. There under the arching bridge glided the lighted gondola, the floating bower of love. It was all mystery and melody and romantic form; the throbbing hum of music for dancing; the dark dominos of revellers; the sudden gleam of a stiletto; the folded embrace of lovers; the moonlit gardens of Belmont:

> In such a night
> Did Jessica steal from the wealthy Jew,
> And with an unthrift love did run from Venice.
> [*The Merchant of Venice*, V.i.14-16]

All this was in the beautiful suggestion of Irving's setting of the *Merchant of Venice*. It was imaginative, poetic, and lingered in the memory like sweet music or a lovely picture.

The *Taming of the Shrew* is not poetic; but it is Italian, and it belongs to the Boccaccian world. To recall that world, therefore, to show us its figures and fill us with its spirit, so that we enjoy without submitting enjoyment to criticism, is what Daly's revival does, and so it achieves its triumph. It has produced universal and innocent pleasure; and its happy ending, with the picture of Paul Veronese turned into life and gayety and music, is one of the mimetic scenes that will not be forgotten. (pp. 152-53)

> *Amélie Rives, in a review of "The Taming of the Shrew," in* Harper's New Monthly Magazine, *Vol. LXXV, No. CCCCXLV, June, 1887, pp. 151-55.*

The Times, London   (review date 30 May 1888)

[*The anonymous critic highly praises Daly's revival of* The Taming of the Shrew *at the Gaiety Theatre, describing it as a production "mounted with perfect taste and with at least as much archeological correctness as an intelligent public requires."*]

The Daly Company have not been content to apply their refined and elegant methods of comedy to the modern repertory alone. Last night they gave us Shakespeare in the form of a "restored" version of *The Taming of the Shrew*, and it may be said at once that, with the exception of Phelps's revival of five-and-twenty years ago, no such rendering of this play has been seen on the English stage. Shakespearian plays are seldom or never acted in their entirety for a variety of reasons, the best of which is their great length; but few have suffered so much from the pruning knife as *The Taming of the Shrew*, which was cut down by Garrick to the proportions of a three-act farce, and in that form has held the boards ever since. Phelps went back in a great measure to the original text, but his example has never been followed by any English actor or manager, and until it occurred to Mr. Daly last year to attempt a resuscitation of the piece in the shape in which it left Shakespeare's hands it seemed as if this comedy were fated to rank as the most despised and rejected of the poet's productions. The commentators, it is true, have not taught us to look upon *The Taming of the Shrew* with a very reverent eye. Tieck stands alone in considering it as exclusively Shakespeare's handiwork—it being generally supposed that the play called *The Taming of a Shrew*, published in 1594, was done by an anonymous writer, and that this was afterwards taken in hand and improved by Shakespeare. Be that as it may, *The Taming of the Shrew* dates from Shakespeare's earliest period. There is reason to suppose, moreover, that as it now stands it is incomplete, seeing that Christopher Sly, after figuring in the Introduction and the first act as the personage before whom the play within the play is performed, is lost sight of altogether. Schlegel opines that the closing scene of the play, in which we ought to see the tinker rousing himself from a drunken sleep, has been lost. In the edition of 1594 there exists such a scene, but whether Shakespeare in the exercise of his discretion cut it out, or whether he added something of his own that subsequently escaped the attention of the printers, is a moot question. As the result of these various considerations *The Taming of the Shrew* has received but scant justice from its professional interpreters. So at least it would now appear, in view of this splendid revival of the comedy, which, sumptuously mounted, and acted with admirable spirit and point, keeps the house throughout its five acts in a state of continuous merriment.

The Introduction is a quaint scene, and the only one in the entire range of Shakespearean drama where the costume of the poet's own day, and of Warwickshire to boot, can be displayed. It occupies but ten minutes or so in representation, and by a dexterous use of curtains leads us in without any pause in the action from Sly's bedchamber to the "Square in Padua," where the story of Katherine and Petruchio opens. The drunken tinker, who amid his fictitious grandeur persists in calling for a "pot o' the smallest ale" [Ind.ii.1.ff.], is a person of a merry humour, and it is with some regret that we see him at the close of the first act drop out of the action. But as the modern stage is managed it would probably have a distracting effect upon the house were Sly and his consort to sit throughout the play at what is known as the "prompt side," the spot whence in this production they view the earlier scenes. Shakespeare contemplated no such mingling of real and fictitious characters under the eye of the spectator, for in his time, as Mr. Daly reminds us, when a play was produced within a play the sham audience was accommodated in a gallery at the back of the stage overlooking the actors' platform. As such an arrangement is, however, incompatible with modern conditions as to scenery, there seems to be no reasonable means of retaining Sly nowadays as a spectator of the comedy supposed to be given for his entertainment. Nor, indeed, is he long missed. The action of the play proper speedily absorbs the attention of the house, and if any stickler for form is disposed to wonder at the tinker's absence, he is free to conclude that that worthy has fallen asleep and been put to bed—a supposition sanctioned by Sly's tumbling off his chair in the first act, and by his sage remark with reference to the play, "'Tis a goodly work, I would 'twere done" [I. i. 253-54]. So much for the difficulty of carrying the Introduction to a logical conclusion. It is still open to the spectator to hold with Garrick that, in the circumstances, it is not worth while to introduce such a prelude at all.

Besides the Introduction, Mr. Daly restores the underplot of the play concerning the loves of Hortensio and Bianca. The scenes so introduced are not particularly interesting in themselves, but they serve to throw into relief the relations of the stiff-necked heroine and her subjugator. In the purely farcical version of *The Taming of the Shrew* the importance of such relief appears to have been under-estimated. It is difficult otherwise to account for the greatly increased interest which Mr. Daly and his company have been able to arouse in this play. Those who have known it only in the current acting form will be agreeably surprised at the wealth of dramatic material thus brought to light, and at the unsuspected force of Miss Rehan and Mr. Drew's embodiment of the leading characters. Admirable indeed is the performance of these accomplished comedians. Miss Rehan is a shrew of imposing and dignified mind, yet not without the suggestion of a flaw in her woman's armour by virtue of a certain winsomeness of manner and a pride not far removed from coquetry. Mr. Drew, on the other hand, asserts his masculinity in every note and every gesture, over-awing, not his victim but his prize by sheer force of lung and muscle. Both play in the farcical key, rightly esteeming that to tone down their extravagant scenes in the modern manner would be to whittle them away to nothing. Mr. Drew wields his long whip with the dexterity of a cowboy. There is, in short, nothing of the namby-pamby in the performance; a policy of half measures, even in the throwing about of the leg of mutton upon which Katherine hopes to dine, would be disastrous, and much of Miss Rehan's and Mr. Drew's success is due to their appreciation of that truth. Miss Russell, Mr. Lewis, Mr. Fisher, Mr. Leclercq, and Mrs. Gilbert all find places in the cast, which, indeed, taxes the strength of Mr. Daly's company. The play is mounted with perfect taste and with at least as much archæological correctness as an intelligent public requires. In the banqueting scene, upon which the curtain falls, a glee party sing "Should she Upbraid" to Bishop's well-known music. Archæologists may be horrified at this defiance of their theories, but the effect is pretty and, we will add, appropriate in the extreme.

A review of "The Taming of the Shrew," in The Times, *London, May 30, 1888, p. 9.*

Ada Rehan as Katherina.

The Athenaeum   (review date 2 June 1888)

[*In this unsigned review, the critic regards Daly's revival as a "triumphant . . . vindication of Shakspeare as an acting dramatist." The critic asserts, moreover, that* The Taming of the Shrew *is decidedly more entertaining than its "detestable abridgement,"* Catherine and Petruchio.]

The success of 'The Taming of the Shrew' as presented by the Augustin Daly Company is a triumphant, and it is to be hoped final, vindication of Shakspeare as an acting dramatist. The managerial dictum that "Shakspeare spelt ruin and Byron bankruptcy" was refuted by the enduring success obtained at different theatres with 'Hamlet,' 'Romeo and Juliet,' 'Much Ado about Nothing,' 'A Comedy of Errors,' 'Measure for Measure,' 'Twelfth Night,' and 'As You Like It.' All that Mr. Chatterton was justified in asserting was that Shakspeare as acted under the Chatterton management at Drury Lane "spelt ruin." A vindication more ample was in reserve. The Dramatic Students were the first to show that a comedy which had long been proclaimed unactable could be witnessed with delight, and two of the largest West-End houses have seen plays resting under the same imputation mounted for a run. At the Lyceum Miss Anderson has tested 'The Winter's Tale' with most satisfactory results, and now at the neighbouring house, the Gaiety, 'The Taming of the Shrew' has been received with applause.

So far as is known the present is the third revival of the play as Shakspeare wrote it. Until the middle of last century, when Garrick produced his detestable abridgment 'Catharine and

Petruchio,' no record of its performance in any form is accessible. In Garrick's farce a series of admirable artists, from Mrs. Pritchard and Kitty Clive to Miss Ellen Terry and Mrs. Bernard Beere, have played the heroine. Kemble, when for the second time he revived this piece, christened it 'The Taming of the Shrew,' and in this Mrs. Charles Kemble acted, Mrs. Siddons having appeared in the previous revival. Ben Webster first tried the public with 'The Taming of the Shrew' upon the return of Mrs. Nesbitt, then Lady Boothby, to the stage. Mrs. Nesbitt was the Katherine; Webster, Petruchio; Keeley, and subsequently Buckstone, Grumio; Howe, Hortensio; and Strickland, Christopher Sly. Phelps in December, 1856, added 'The Taming of the Shrew' to his long list of Shakespearean revivals, and himself played Christopher Sly. It is noteworthy, however, that 'Catharine and Petruchio' was soon afterwards substituted for the original version.

Belief in Shakspeare has been hard to inculcate. Genest, who is merciless upon Dryden, Tate, Davenant, Cibber, and other adapters of Shakspeare, says that Garrick "has done little more than omit the weak part of 'The Taming of the Shrew,' and has thereby made the best afterpiece on the stage"; and the editors of the 'Biographia Dramatica' go into ecstasies over it. In fact, nothing Garrick has done conveys a poorer idea of his abilities than his treatment of the play and the traditions as to its acting he has transmitted.

Upon its revival at the Gaiety 'The Taming of the Shrew' proved not only an exhilarating entertainment, but, as was to be expected, a poetical treat. It does not, of course, claim to be a comic masterpiece, such as is 'As You Like It' or 'Twelfth Night.' It ranks, in fact, with 'A Comedy of Errors' as farce. But the poetry is there if adapters and managers will only retain it. There were moments in Tuesday's representation when the mind was filled with sympathy, and the laugh of mirth was arrested by that strange spasm of emotion which poetic beauty is apt to provoke. To account, however, for what Garrick would have regarded as a miracle, there was no special merit of representation. In four characters only, and two of these subordinate, could the performance be said to be good; in one only was it inspired. Miss Ada Rehan has entered into the very soul of Katherine, and furnishes a representation of the character not to be surpassed in loveliness and in originality. She shows Kate as a woman of the passionate red Italian loveliness to which the Venetian school of painting has accustomed us, and has dressed her in brocades so rich in colour and warmth that Titian himself might have designed them. Her appearance as she entered fuming upon the stage in the second act, or again when she sat, the centre of a wedding banquet, in her father's hall in Padua, is one of the things that will haunt the memory. Meanwhile, her movements had something of the rage of a captured animal, and her outcries were such as an actress less inspired by her subject and less sure of her resources dared not have employed. It is difficult, however, to believe that some of Miss Rehan's predecessors—Kitty Clive, whose temper must have fitted her for the part, Mrs. Siddons, or others—may not have equalled her in the character. Mr. John Drew meanwhile, though picturesque, easy, and natural as Petruchio, is not an ideal exponent. He plays well up to Miss Rehan, and is successful in showing the admiration with which he is filled for the prize he is winning. Mr. Lewis is, of course, an intellectual Grumio, and Mrs. Gilbert is an acquisition in the small part of Curtis. Mr. Otis Skinner, moreover, spoke pleasantly and correctly as Lucentio. Mr. William Gilbert was, however, hopelessly at sea in Christopher Sly, and the exponents gener-

ally of the remaining characters call for no mention. All that pretty and poetical scenery and admirable dresses could do for the piece had mean time been done, the musical accessories were delightful, and taste was everywhere apparent. The removal at the end of Act I. of Sly and his surroundings, arranged by Mr. William Winter, is quite defensible. Shakspeare after the play is once launched ceases to concern himself with the bemused tinker. Why should others not follow the example?

While full credit, then, is due to Mr. Daly's management, there is nothing to detract from Shakspeare's claim to the chief responsibility for the success. Whether the play will prove lastingly attractive remains to be seen. If not, all that can be said will be that the lovers of the Shakspearean drama are sceptical and hard to reach, or few. At any rate, 'The Taming of the Shrew' is an immeasurably finer work than the often-praised 'Catharine and Petruchio.' The scenes in Petruchio's house were shorn of much of the extravagance ordinarily exhibited in England, but were yet too full of buffoonery.

A review of "The Taming of the Shrew," in The Athenaeum, *No. 3162, June 2, 1888, p. 706.*

The Saturday Review   (review date 2 June 1888)

[*The anonymous critic offers a favorable review of Daly's* Shrew, *asserting that "[to] translate into the measured language of criticism the impression of fire, the strength, the versatility of Miss Ada Rehan's impersonation of Katharine is not possible."*]

The performance of Mr. Augustin Daly's version of the *The Taming of the Shrew* at the Gaiety on Tuesday fully justified the remarkable favour bestowed upon it by the New York public when produced last year. Hitherto Londoners have, for the most part, enjoyed small opportunities of estimating the powers of the Daly Company of Comedians, individually and as an artistic society, in the class of drama most congenial to them. In the lighter Shakspearian comedy and in the comedy of the Restoration they have achieved the highest distinction. The *The Taming of the Shrew* is not perhaps one of those plays which Charles Lamb had in mind when he insisted on the divorce of the ideal from the stage, and circumscribed the art of the actor who aspired to Shakspearian parts with a quaintly determined *ne plus ultra*. Nevertheless, there is a large element of poetic illusion in the *The Taming of the Shrew,* sufficient, indeed, to test the artistic capacity of the Daly Company in this direction, and it must be admitted that it is hard to conceive the reader of Shakspeare, however exalted his standard of excellence, who would not recognize in Tuesday's performance an interpretation that transcended his ideal. It was altogether a complete vindication of the player's art. Here and there arose points, of course, that were of questionable value or gain; but they do not in the least affect the merit of the representation as a whole. Mr. Daly's acting version is in many respects a Shakspearian restoration, though there is nothing of the restorer, as he is commonly known, in the skill and good taste that distinguish it. Nor will any student of Elizabethan literature fail in commendation of Mr. Daly's inclusion of the Induction scenes and his introduction of a musical interlude in the admirably designed banquet scene of the last act. The chorus of boys, led by Miss St. Quentin, who sang Bishop's "Should he upbraid" from a balcony overlooking the festive hall, was perfectly in accord with tradition; and the character of Bishop's music—which was charmingly sung, by the way—is sufficiently akin to that of the Elizabethan madrigalists to propitiate sticklers for propriety. No defence of the Induction is needed. It belongs to the play, and ought never to have been allowed to lapse from its presentment. The old playgoer, who is nothing if not retrospective, might reasonably find the Christopher Sly of Mr. William Gilbert a little too alert, a little deficient in the characteristic humour of the toper who never drank sack. Only a simple, slow-witted creature, as Sly undoubtedly is, would be quite so readily fooled, so swiftly convinced of his "amendment." Mr. Gilbert plays the part of the awakened tinker with a febrile activity, and shows almost a preternatural intelligence until he accepts the situation. In this he departs from stage tradition. On the other hand, nothing could be more humorous than his bearing towards the courtiers and the page who masquerades as his wife; while his acting as an uninterested spectator of the play is excellent. He does not forget that the play's the thing, to which the Induction is but the curious vestibule; and he is careful not to exaggerate into distractive elements his grunts and snores, his odd walking starts and objurgatory glances, his occasional slidings to the floor and awkward stumblings to his seat. Considering the injunctions of their host to the players, it is natural that the actors should not altogether ignore him. The situation is completed by the whimsical and entirely judicious by-play of Mr. James Lewis as Grumio.

To translate into the measured language of criticism the impression of the fire, the strength, the versatility of Miss Ada Rehan's impersonation of Katharine is not possible, if the chill of a most unjust reserve is to be avoided. Analysis of an impression so rich and complex inevitably leads to bafflement. In storm and in calm, in the later scenes of submission, and during the process of being schooled by the stings of Petruchio's fantastic humour, Miss Rehan's Katharine was a marvellous demonstration of art. The very excellence of her fellow-comedians—markedly of Mr. John Drew's Petruchio and Mr. Charles Fisher's Baptista—seemed rather to enhance the unique force and charm of her acting in the second and third acts, and supplied a striking proof that the actor who dreads this form of competition, or succumbs to it, has nothing of the artist in him. Thus the supreme moments of Miss Rehan's acting—if such may be cited from a performance so exquisitely in keeping, so vitally consistent—were precisely those where Miss Phœbe Russell, as the sweet and gracious Bianca, Mr. Charles Fisher, and Mr. John Drew were also ascendent. Of course these are chiefly what are called "situations," as in the lively scene where Katharine flouts Bianca and Baptista interposes, and where, subsequently, Katharine's gibing at Petruchio culminates in defiance. But the whole wooing of Petruchio, and the grotesque scenes between the two in Act IV., on the return to Petruchio's house, were equally convincing and delightful. Miss Rehan very happily suggested throughout that temperament, not mere "temper," was the source of Katharine's shrewishness. Under all her splendid pride of bearing and freakish outbursts of passion the innate womanliness of her nature was apparent. Petruchio worked no miracle, save in the eyes of the faint-hearted suitors and the general vulgar. Mr. John Drew's Petruchio completely responded to Hazlitt's conception of the part. It was played in the spirit of masterful self-confidence, with untiring vivacity, and a flow of animal spirits that ceased not until the final triumph, when Katharine is commanded to appear before Lucentio's guests. The slight touches that showed Petruchio to be a sly detective of the

progress of his experiment were given with delicate art, as also was his sense of the humour of it. The Baptista of Mr. Charles Fisher was excellent in all respects. The humour of the serving-man Grumio found a representative of original method in Mr. James Lewis, whose dry enunciation of a point and diverting by-play were alike admirable. The Gremio of Mr. Charles Leclercq was in some respects a pleasant variant from the conventional race of stage greybeards. The amusing speech in Act III., descriptive of the wedding, was a notable example of picturesque utterance. For the rest, Mr. Otis Skinner was an agreeable Lucentio; Mr. Frederick Bond, as Tranio, was spirited; Mr. Joseph Holland, as Hortensio, was a good representative of the fervid lover, and Mrs. Gilbert—it is needless to say—was all that is desirable in the small part of the housekeeper Curtis. The play is elaborately mounted, the final scene especially being a beautiful example of effective painting and arrangement, and Mr. Henry Widmer's orchestra, with an excellent selection of music, merits commendation. (pp. 655-56)

> A review of "The Taming of the Shrew," in The Saturday Review, London, Vol. 65, No. 1701, June 2, 1888, pp. 655-56.

Punch   (review date 30 June 1888)

[In an unsigned review, the critic awards "unqualified praise" to Ada Rehan and enthusiastic notice to John Drew.]

One visit to the Daly Co., now performing The Taming of the Shrew at the Gaiety, will make it evident to the student of the English Drama that Theatrical America must have been discovered by the KEMBLES, with Mrs. SIDDONS, followed by MACREADY, PHELPS, COMPTON, and BUCKSTONE, whose good old traditions have not yet been discarded as is evidenced by the occasionally deep tones and courtly gestures of the leading members of this company, and in the peculiar mannerisms of the low comedians. What first struck me, after the remarkable performance of Miss ADA REHAN as Katherine, was Mr. JOHN DREW's clever embodiment of Petrucio; and passing over the cut-and-dried comic business of Mr. JAMES LEWIS as Grumio, Mr. F. BOND as Tranio, and Mr. CHARLES LECLERCQ as Gremio, I was delighted with Mrs. GILBERT as Curtis, whom the Americans have changed into an old woman after SHAKSPEARE had made a man of him. Miss PHOEBE RUSSELL looks quite Burn-Jonesian as Bianca. About the others, with the exception of Mr. WILLIAM GILBERT, the exponent of Christopher Sly, there seemed to me to be an amateurishness which was quite inexplicable. But the two, on whom the success of this Elizabethan Farcical Extravaganza depends, are worthy of the greatest praise, of which to Miss REHAN must be allotted the lion's share.

About the spelling of Petruchio's name there is admittedly some slight difference of opinion, but about the pronunciation of it as spelt in the Daly Company's bill, "Petrucio," there is a good deal of difference among the Daly Company themselves, seeing that the same person is called at one time "Petruzzio," at another "Petrooshio," and again "Petrutchio," according to the taste and fancy of the individual. If the correct spelling be Petruchio, the correct pronunciation would be "Petrukio." The absence of uniformity in such a matter is a note of indecision in stage management, and throughout the piece there is constant evidence of their still being bound hand and foot by the old theatrical red-tape of the Kemble-Macready tradition, of which the English stage has well rid itself by a series of Emancipation Acts, passed by the leaders of generations of oppressed players "nobly struggling to be free."

Mr. DREW, as the mad-cap, strong-willed, gay and gallant *Petruchio,* has to thank nature for nothing, and art for everything. He doesn't look the part at all, but plays it within a few inches of as well as it is ever likely to be played. To impersonate a man acting a part, and to avoid appearing theatrical and self-conscious, is exceedingly difficult, though just within the resources of dramatic art.

For Miss REHAN as *Katherine* I have unqualified praise. She looks the shrew, she acts the shrew, she exhibits such demoniac possession as can only relieve itself by inarticulate cries of anger, and by violence of action sudden and uncontrollable. When being starved into submission, Miss REHAN so enlists our sympathies, even in the most outrageously farcical situations, that the men in the house begin to think what a cowardly brute is *Petruchio,* and what a shame it is to use this splendid creature so cruelly, when she might have been conquered by kindness. But *Petruchio* is right; if *Katherine* had once got outside a good square meal, he and his cowboy whip, his Buffalo Bill swagger and his burlesque bluster would have had as much effect on SHAKSPEARE'S *Katherine* as it has on the audience who are in the secret. And then to note how Miss REHAN wins the audience who remain spell-bound by her wise and gentle delivery of that excellent lecture on the duties of wives towards their husbands, with which the play practically finishes,—the sentiments of which lecture I noticed were greeted with rapturous applause by the elder male portion of the audience, while better halves appeared to be suddenly particularly engaged in getting at their opera-cloaks and wrappers. I wonder how Mrs. WILLIAM SHAKSPEARE liked this finishing speech; that is, if dear ANNE was alive at the time, and ever went to the Theatre to see her husband's pieces. The sort of pantomime "hurry" music played at the entrance of *Katharine* is a mistake, though quite in keeping with the old-fashioned notion of the character which Miss REHAN utterly dispels.

When the Daly Company has left us, the truth concerning this performance of *The Taming of the Shrew,* will be summed up in two lines,

> REHAN the Shrew
> And *Petruchio* 'Drew'.

I advise anyone who doesn't believe in the possibility of this piece being acted nowadays, to go and see Miss REHAN as *Katherine,* and I fancy they will remain of the same opinion still, as, without her, where would this muddle-plotted whimsical farce be? But *with* her it is something to be seen. . . .

> *" 'Daly' News," in* Punch, *Vol. XCIV, No. 2451, June 30, 1888, p. 301.*

John Drew   (essay date 1922)

[*A member of the renowned late-nineteenth-century Drew acting family, Drew was considered one of the outstanding actors of his day. He often performed opposite Ada Rehan in Augustin Daly's acting company, appearing in such classics as* As You Like It *and* The School for Scandal, *but he is best remembered for his Petruchio in* The Taming of the Shrew. *In the following excerpt, Drew recalls his performance as Petruchio in Augustin Daly's memorable 1887 production of* The Taming of the Shrew, *noting the novelty and popular success of this presentation.*]

"Get onto Jacob Earwig," said James Lewis, who was standing back of me. He looked over my shoulder toward the prompt-entrance.

He was playing *Grumio,* one of my servants in *The Taming of the Shrew,* but in all the excitement and tenseness of that night, January 18th, 1877—the most important first night in the history of Daly's Theatre—he was sufficiently calm to call attention to a man in evening dress sitting in the first entrance and holding out a magnificent, beaten-silver ear trumpet.

Later, when I got a chance to look that way I saw that it was Horace Howard Furness, the Shakespearian scholar. He was very deaf. Certainly, for no less a person than Furness would Daly have departed from his rigidly enforced custom of allowing no one behind the scenes. I did not dare look at Lewis during the rest of the performance for fear that I, in my first-night nervousness, might laugh and blow up.

As with most actors, Lewis remembered the parts he himself had played, and in an old farce called *Boots at the Swan* there was a deaf old man, the low-comedy character, and his name was *Jacob Earwig.*

The production of *The Taming of the Shrew* was much heralded in advance. All during rehearsals we were led to believe that this was to be a great and history-making production. The strange fact is that it was. Nothing that Daly had hoped for the production before the first night turned out to be too extravagant. It was at once taken up and acclaimed by the press. For years afterwards this performance of *The Taming of the Shrew* was talked of as an historical event, and certainly it was the highest point of achievement in Daly's career of many successes. It was perhaps a surprise to the public, but no more so than it was to us, that a company which had made its success in light comedies from the German should reach its highest point in a Shakespearian comedy. We had not been very happy or successful in *The Merry Wives of Windsor.*

By 1887 the four principal actors of the Daly Theatre were so firmly intrenched in the public's favor and so much identified with the succession of plays that Daly would not run the risk of leaving one of this group out of the cast. Accordingly, into the trivial and unimportant rôle of *Curtis,* a retainer of *Petruchio,* he put the ever popular Mrs. Gilbert. *Curtis* is really a man's rôle, but there was precedent for Daly's putting Mrs. Gilbert into the part, as a Mrs. LeBrun had played *Curtis* when Clara Morris played *Katherine* and Louis James *Petruchio* at the Academy of Music some years before. In the whole line of light comedies Mrs. Gilbert and Lewis had played opposite each other, and *Curtis* enabled her to play a low-comedy scene with *Grumio,* which was played by Lewis on this occasion.

At the end of the performance Horace Howard Furness, being already on the stage, was the first to reach us. He congratulated Ada Rehan, the *Katherine,* and me, the *Petruchio.* I do not see how he could have heard any of the play even from his vantage point in the first entrance, for he was so deaf that it was necessary to shout into his ear trumpet.

Katherine was that night, and always remained, the greatest part in Ada Rehan's long list of performances. *Petruchio* was to me the most grateful rôle that I have played. It has everything that the player of high comedy can desire: telling speeches and effective situations; in fact, everything that makes for and makes up a great part. Since *Petruchio* is a great Shakespearian character, it may be imagined how gratifying it was to be told by everyone whose opinion and judgment I regarded that I had come out of the effort successfully.

The Taming of the Shrew was really a novelty in 1887. A short version of the play known as *Katherine and Petruchio* had been played by a number of tragedians when they wanted a rest. This garbled version, which consisted mainly of the horse-play scenes in which *Petruchio* brandishes his whip and the leg of mutton about the stage, had been played by Edwin Booth. It was this version that Clara Morris and Louis James had played; in fact, for stage use the play had come to be known as *Katherine and Petruchio*. The Daly production went back to the play as written and *The Induction* was restored. Presumably, the characters in *The Induction* were then played for the first time in America.

Christopher Sly, a drunken tinker, is observed by a lord and his servants as they are coming from a hunt. *Sly* has been thrown out of an alehouse. It occurs to the lord to dress this fellow up and when he comes round to serve him with all ceremonies and make him believe that he is a great lord. The real lord has his page, a part very well played by the youthful Willie Collier, dress up as a woman and pretend to be the wife of *Sly*. When everything is ready the real lord, dressed as a servant, comes to him and says:

> Your honor's players, hearing your amendment,
> Are come to play a pleasant comedy:
> For so your doctors hold it very meet,
> Seeing too much sadness hath congeal'd your blood,
> And melancholy is the nurse of frenzy;
> Therefore, they thought it good you hear a play
> And frame your mind to mirth and merriment,
> Which bars a thousand harms and lengthens life.
>
> [Ind. ii. 129-36]

Sly answers: "Marry, I will; let them play it" [Ind. ii. 137].

By this time they have made *Sly* believe that he is really a lord. He and the page, dressed as his lady, sit at the side of the stage down left, and then the play begins. They are removed after the first act and they do not appear again, but the whole action of the play is supposed to be before this tinker and his lady.

After the one-hundredth performance of *The Taming of The Shrew* there was a supper on the stage of the theatre. Of this the *New York Herald* recorded:

> Mr. Augustin Daly's supper, given to his company and a few invited guests on the stage of his theatre yesterday morning, was a remarkable event in several ways. It commemorated the one-hundredth night of a Shakespearian revival of more than usual splendor and it brought together many remarkable men.
>
> The company sat down at one-half past twelve and rose at five in the morning. A great circular table occupied the entire stage. Its center was a mass of tulips and roses. Around its outer edge sat forty participants. Think of a supper at which General Sherman acted as toastmaster, at which Horace Porter made an unusually clever speech, Mark Twain told a story, Bronson Howard and Wilson Barrett spoke, at which Miss Ada Rehan made a neat and charming response when her name was called, at which the ever young Lester Wallack

commended in the heartiest way the brother manager whose guest he was, at which Willie Winter read a poem of home manufacture. Imagine all this and add to it countless witty stories that were told around the board, think of the wine glasses that clicked, think of the champagne that bubbled, think of the pretty women, think of the weird surroundings (the dark cave-like auditorium and the brilliantly lighted stage).

(pp. 88-93)

John Drew, in his My Years on the Stage, *E. P. Dutton & Company, 1922, 242 p.*

Marvin Felheim   (essay date 1956)

[*Felheim provides an evaluation of Daly's successful staging of* The Taming of the Shrew, *focusing on the producer's cuts and revisions of the original text.*]

On January 18, 1887, the unflagging Daly staged [a] major Shakespearean production, *The Taming of the Shrew*. This revival was unquestionably his most successful venture into the field of Shakespearean drama and, from all accounts, must be reckoned one of the truly great presentations of the play. Inasmuch as Daly restored the two scenes of the Induction, and made the main play four acts in length, the production deserves to be described as the first American attempt to present the play in any reasonable resemblance to its original pattern. As such it superseded the popular short farce, *Katherine and Petruchio,* which had held the stage in America since 1768, when it was first given at the John Street Theatre by Lewis Hallam's company.

The success of Daly's revival was instantaneous. Ada Rehan created a furor as the shrew. The initial run of the piece lasted until April 30, for a consecutive showing of 121 performances, a remarkable record for a Shakespearean revival. Subsequently, of course, the comedy remained constantly in the repertoire of the Daly company. Its first important replaying occurred a year later, at the Lyceum Theatre, London, during the third European tour of the troupe. And on August 3, 1888, a performance was given at Stratford-on-Avon for the benefit of the Library Fund of the Shakespeare Memorial. According to Judge Daly, this was the first performance of the play ever given there. Its success prompted the installation of a gift from Daly, a statue of Ada Rehan as Katherine.

After the English triumph, Daly produced the play in Paris at the Vaudeville Théâtre. There, Constant Coquelin, the great comedian, saw the performance and consequently determined to play Petruchio. The French version, by Paul Delair, called *La Mégère Apprivoisée,* was given by Coquelin in Paris and later (1892) in New York.

Ada Rehan continued to star in the play, and Daly continued to produce it through the years. Theatrical records list an imposing total of revivals. Indeed, Daly frequently came to use the play as a means of reviving his fortunes after a failure and to hold the stage until a new piece could be prepared. The popularity of this production—and of Miss Rehan—never waned. Her interpretation of Katherine has been accepted by critics as one of the finest ever given.

Despite pretensions about the completeness of his text, Daly nevertheless perpetrated many minor and several major excisions, amounting in a few speeches to actual mutilation. True enough, both scenes of the Induction were restored (to allow William Gilbert histrionic success as Christopher Sly) with almost literal fidelity, but the rearrangements of the rest of the comedy rendered this textual scrupulosity ironical. In fact, the Induction seems to have been retained mainly so that Daly could advertise his devotion to "pure" Shakespeare; further, it provided a novelty for audiences; and finally, the second scene allowed for the mounting of a most lavish bedroom set, an example of the opulence which contributed to Daly's sense of fitness in Shakespearean production.

The changes which Daly made were largely confined to the play itself. First of all, he reduced Shakespeare's five acts to four by telescoping Acts III and IV into one act of three scenes. The jumble in the latter is most confusing. For scene I, he used all of Shakespeare's Act III (both scenes); as scene 2, he combined scenes ii and iv of Act IV, in both of which the subplot of Tranio, Hortensio, Lucentio, and Bianca is featured so that there is no appreciable distortion; but for scene 3, he had, consequently, to telescope scenes i, iii, and v of Act IV. The result is a single scene dealing with the "taming," which may be satisfactory in terms of setting (Petruchio's house in the country), but speeds up the process so rapidly that the illusion of reality is lost and the characters of both Katherine and Petruchio become so exaggerated that the change, particularly in Katherine, seems arbitrary and contrived rather than properly motivated.

A second kind of revision consisted of rearrangement and reassignment of lines to allow Ada Rehan to star. Her entrance was postponed till the second act. She was thus allowed, wrote Towse, to start her performance "at the highest pitch of quivering indignation at her command." She "thereby secured a most picturesque and effective entrance." But the effort of maintaining this concept "left her without any reserve force for climaxes. Consequently, her performance was lacking in light and shade, and grew weaker instead of stronger toward the end." Once on stage, however, she remained the star. To give her a curtain speech in Act II, Daly interpolated twelve lines from Garrick's version. In Act III, her appearance was again delayed until after Bianca's wedding ceremony. Both she and Petruchio were eliminated from Act IV, scene I (Shakespeare's V, i). Finally, the lines of the last scene were reordered to give Katherine the final speech of the play. On a somewhat lesser scale, Daly made certain revisions for John Drew as Petruchio. He was allotted Tranio's lines of Act I, scene ii, 274-279, to give him the curtain speech of Act I, and with Katherine, he shared the distinction of being eliminated from Daly's Act IV, scene I, the scene in which the involvements of the Bianca subplot are settled.

In connection with this reordering of lines, Daly's greatest blunders were committed in his altering of the famous Katherine-Petruchio duet of Act II. The changes here involve a third type of revision, the elimination of words, phrases, and lines for the sake of refinement. As a result, the lines about wasps, arms, and coxcombs went the way of "lechery" and "belly" and this delightful scene frequently shrinks into vapidity. In place of the lines excised, Daly substituted a few meaningless speeches simply to allow Katherine to speak as much as the taunting Petruchio. After his line, "And, will you, nil you, I will marry you" [II. i. 271], she echoed, insipidly, "Whether I will or no?" Again, after Petruchio's "With gentle conference, soft and affable" [II. i. 251], she interposed, "This is beyond all patience;—don't provoke me." Lastly, after Petruchio's challenge, "For I am he that's born

to tame you" [II. i. 276], she can only answer, "Indeed! We'll see, my saucy groom." In place of her answer, "Yes, keep you warm," to his question, "Am I not wise?" [II. i. 265-6] Daly had her say, "Yes; in your own conceit, keep yourself cool with that or else you'll freeze"; to this Petruchio replied (Daly's version), "Marry, warm me in thy arms, sweet Kate," instead of Shakespeare's "Marry, so I mean, sweet Katherine, in thy bed" [II. i. 267]. To bring out Ada Rehan's best talent—a certain archness—Daly inserted for her, following Petruchio's "That she shall still be curst in company" [II. i. 305], the lines, "A plague upon such impudence! O, for revenge! I'll marry him—but I will tame him!" And thus for the moment, the whole play was metamorphosed into the taming *by* the shrew.

Other examples of the third kind of revision are numerous. "By Saint Jeronomy!" [Ind. i. 9] was omitted. The word, "God," was changed to "Love" or to "Heaven." The word, "whoreson," and the phrase, "lewd and filthy," were deleted. And "bedfellow" appeared as "wedded wife."

There were, of course, dissenting voices amidst the almost universal acclaim tendered *The Taming of the Shrew*. "Interesting and attractive" as he found the Daly version, Percy Fitzgerald thought the Adelphi Theatre production with Oscar Asche and Miss Brayton, directed by Otho Stuart, better. Although Jerome K. Jerome considered Miss Rehan's Katherine "magnificent," he always regarded Drew in Shakespeare as "A Yankee at the Court of King Arthur." A. B. Walkley admired Miss Rehan and Drew but labeled the other performances "feeble . . . crude . . . soporific." These adverse criticisms, it will be noted, are mainly English. American critics, except Towse, found nothing to condemn.

The success of the revival led Daly to provide a sumptuous banquet on the occasion of the hundredth performance. A round table, seating forty-nine, was set up backstage with "an immense circular bed of roses as its centre." Among the distinguished guests were Bronson Howard, Mark Twain, General Sherman (who acted as toastmaster), the Honorable R. O'Gorman (Mayor of New York), Laurence Hutton, Lester Wallack, William Winter, Horace H. Furness, and selected members of the Daly company (the Big Four). After a most elaborate meal, most of the guests made short speeches. Daly's was the most interesting, for he spoke of his intentions in reviving Shakespeare.

> I fully believe that where the sole purpose in producing a Shakespearean play is to make money by spectacular profusion, disaster is likely to result. . . . Ever since I began management, now some 18 years, I have devoted a period in every season to the production of a Shakespeare play or an old comedy. None of these productions was ever offered by me to the public with the expectation that it was destined to popular favor by reason of the outlay made upon it.
>
> I freely confess that I did not anticipate the enormous popular success of this revival. My motive has been to give, in return for the very large share of popular support which I have always received, an opportunity to my own generation of seeing the works of our greatest masters in their best shape; and if this purpose has resulted in my accomplishing what might be deemed a great managerial success, then I am willing to be credited rather with a worthy motive than with unparalleled foresight and sagacity.

To vindicate Shakespeare, I set my judgment against that of Garrick, and you have the result. Shakespeare was right.

(pp. 238-42)

Marvin Felheim, "Shakespeare, New Style," in his The Theater of Augustin Daly: An Account of the Late Nineteenth Century American Stage, *Cambridge, Mass.: Harvard University Press, 1956, pp. 219-84.*

————————

PRODUCTION:

John Martin Harvey • The Prince of Wales Theatre • 1913

BACKGROUND:

Martin Harvey produced this version of *The Taming of the Shrew* in collaboration with William Poel, the celebrated actor-manager and founder of the Elizabethan Stage Society. Martin Harvey, whose previous productions were more commercially oriented, sought Poel's help in creating a sixteenth-century staging of the play. Martin Harvey claimed that Poel, however, was more interested in the question of textual cuts, and that he devised most of the scenery himself. Nevertheless, both contemporary critics and scholars who have assessed the production retrospectively have drawn attention to Martin Harvey's indebtedness to Poel. The production debuted on 10 May 1913 with Martin Harvey in the role of Petruchio, Charles Glenney as Sly, and Nina DeSilva—Martin Harvey's wife—as Kate.

COMMENTARY:

The Times, London (review date 12 May 1913)

[*The anonymous critic praises Martin Harvey's Elizabethan staging of* The Shrew, *maintaining that he and William Poel had now won over a rising number of theater-goers who became more "fully alive to the advantages of the method," and who would henceforth "demand more of its exercise."*]

We hope that some careful chronicler is at work making notes of one of the most interesting things in the theatrical history of our time—the return to common use of Elizabethan method of staging Shakespeare. For it seems pretty certain now that this is no piece of archaeological affectation, but a movement that will spread, because it answers to a public demand. Very likely Mr. William Poel created that demand; and he worked, as pioneers are used to working, for years without recognition. Then the public got to know and on Saturday evening at the Prince of Wales it looked (just as it looked recently at the Savoy) as if the public were now fully alive to the advantages of the method, and would demand more of its exercise. The "new way" advertised by Mr. Martin Harvey is only the old way of Mr. William Poel, his conjutor in the production—the Elizabethan way of continuous action, with merely the patent drawing of "traverses" and moving of properties to mark the changes of place and the advance of time. The conventions of this method of production are at least harder to swallow than the conventions of the "re-

alistic" method: and since it makes no pretence that anything but a play is toward, we are auditors not merely unhindered but positively helped by obvious indications that a play it is.

To have had a place in one of the first few rows of stalls on Saturday was to have tasted a surely Elizabethan dramatic flavour. It was to be as close to the stage as the groundlings were to the platform: it was also (as it happened) to share with the players the full beams of what in Elizabeth's time was the blessed sun, and on Saturday the unblessed limelight. And just in front, now companioned by his excellently acted boy-wife, and now by the gamesome lord, was Christopher Sly himself, an auditor too, and continually seeing cause to be an actor, only restrained by his companion from climbing on to the stage; as simple as Sir Roger de Coverley in his capacity for illusion, and as free as a child in his expression of his likes and dislikes. We found not only the Induction (which was given in full) but the presence of Christopher Sly in the audience a great help. We had seen the troupe of players arrive in their gaudy clothes of red and yellow. We knew they were only players. It left us free to enjoy this "pleasant conceited historic" as a piece of hearty fun, without bothering about its ethics or calculating its probability or its likeness to life.

The whole play, Induction and all, was over in two hours and a half, and that with one or two of the characters lacking the speed and spirit that Mr. Martin Harvey set as the model. We happened to be a little too close to the stage to see the full effect of the scenes, but it was plain that they were well designed, and Mr. George Kruger's costumes were rightly brave and fantastic. That is to say, the pleasure of the eye had been properly considered; and the rapid speaking of the verse—notably in the cases of Mr. Harvey as Petruchio and Mr. Gordon McLeod as Tranio—was a lively pleasure to the ear. And if the company as a whole was not remarkable, it was at least able to keep the thing going, which is the great requisite with such a play. Mr. Martin Harvey himself made a Petruchio almost first-rate. He preserved the charm of the man; bluster as he would, he never became a brute. And Miss de Silva took her taming in a properly humorous spirit, with a kind of half-smile at the wild wilfulness of the delightful Termagant who had rushed her into marriage. Among the rest Mr. Charles Glenney, Mr. Franklin Dyall, and Mr. Michael Sherbrooke were prominent in their contributions to this very gay and unpretentious production.

A review of "The Taming of the Shrew," in The Times, *London, May 12, 1913, p. 8.*

John Palmer (review date 17 May 1913)

[*Palmer applauds Martin Harvey's production, remarking that it provided audiences with an unqualified Shakespearean dramatic perspective by emphasizing vigorous acting rather than decorative scenery. The robust comedy was incarnated in Charles Glenney's spirited portrayal of Sly, the critic notes.*]

Do I suffer from some strange affliction, or is the theatre really becoming a happy place? During the last few weeks I have enjoyed myself everywhere—at Drury Lane, at the New Royalty, at the Haymarket, at the Prince of Wales. A word of self-congratulation is due, of course, to a circumspect selection of plays. Knowing it is a critic's duty, not, as some would have it, to be merry and bitter at the expense of conscionable wretches who do their best, but to seek out and hold fast that which is admirable and praiseworthy, I consistently avoid places that incite in me feelings of anger, tedium, despitefulness, or an urgent necessity to unpack the heart in words. I choose the theatres of my visitation with well-weighed scruples of the ceaseless eremite. Nevertheless, as my readers are well aware, plays and players have not invariably, till now, found in my eyes perpetual favour. What, then, can be happening? Is it the theatre which changes, or is it I? Am I at this moment—soul-curdling reflexion—prematurely at the threshold of that comfortable middle-age of the critic when all seems precisely as it should be in the best fed of possible worlds? Or is the English theatre surpassing itself in a succession of good deeds that beggar the catalogue? When Donna Anna arrived in Hell she told Don Juan that she could not possibly be there because she felt no pain; whereat Don Juan assured her she was undoubtedly in Hell; that, since she felt no pain, there could possibly be no mistake that Hell was her just and natural environment; and that in heaven she would be like an English audience at a classical concert. Your devil is at home in Hell, and thinks he is in heaven. I think I am in heaven at Drury Lane, at the New Royalty, at the Haymarket, at the Prince of Wales. Where am I in sober and absolute fact?

At the Prince of Wales Theatre, watching Petruchio's taming of Katherina in the equally appreciative company of Christopher Sly, I was beyond doubt in heaven, so far as my impressions are to be trusted. Not only was this entertainment delightful in itself, but it suggested conclusions to gladden the heart of all who are interested in the restoration, after nearly three hundred years, of Shakespeare to the English stage. Playgoers are coming to realise that Mr. Poel's judicious restoration of the conventions of Shakespeare's theatre, so far as they can be fitted into our modern houses, is not mere Elizabethan antiquarianism, or a craze for novelty. How this restoration is a necessary prelude to a re-establishment of Shakespeare as a dramatic poet I have too often urged to risk a further repetition. The heartening thing about this production of Mr. Martin Harvey at the Prince of Wales is its demonstration that the English public is at last awake. Mr. William Poel begins at last to be a public man—now that he has retired. His methods are accepted without exclamation. Mr. Martin Harvey presents "The Taming of the Shrew" with Shakespearean incursions into the auditorium; with curtains, screens, and the minimum of baggage; with a clear recognition that Shakespeare's drama was poetical-rhetorical. Playgoers frankly enjoy themselves; and the critical small dogs wag their tails where twelve months ago they yelped at Mr. Barker's company for exceeding the speed-limit. Ça ira. It only remains now for Sir Herbert Tree to refuse any longer to handicap himself and his players in a desperate attempt to be Shakespearean in conditions as far as possible removed from those with which Shakespeare was familiar. Then we shall be entirely happy; and begin to suspect that Shakespeare for the study was, after all, nothing but the despairing cry of a generation that had never really known Shakespeare for the theatre.

I am not sure that this revival of "The Taming of the Shrew" is not, all round, the most authentic piece of Shakespeare yet offered in the West of London. The decoration and the costumes are, for their business, better than those of the Savoy revivals. The end of Shakespearean decoration of the scene or of the player is that it should be inconspicuous; that it should not interfere, or in any way compete, with the text. The only reason for dressing Shakespeare's people at all is that costume, in a Shakespearean play, would be more con-

spicuous by its absence than the most flamboyant theatrical haberdasher could make it by its presence. The decoration of Mr. Harvey's "The Taming of the Shrew" is ideal. It neither offends by an overwhelming insistence that it is original and beautiful; nor comes short of filling the eye. It asks for no independent recognition. It does not posture as a competitive fine-art.

> Costly thy habit as thy purse can buy,
> But not expressed in fancy
>
> [*Hamlet,* I. iii. 70-1]

seems to be the idea of Mr. Poel and Mr. George Kruger and Mr. Dodson; and a better one were very hard to find. As to the scenes, no better backgrounds for this merry-conceited history are readily imaginable—I, at any rate, am unable to imagine them—than those against which Mr. Harvey and his men are thrown into such bold relief at the Prince of Wales. The decorations as a whole asserted, so far as they transgressed decorum in asserting anything, that the play and the players were the thing. This is the summit of good stagecraft where Shakespeare is concerned.

The play, certainly, we had as never before this side of the seventeenth century—Shakespeare's own play delivered with the rushing impetuosity and vigour that he asked, and undoubtedly got, of Burbage and his men. How utterly in the robustious momentum of its delivery did we lose all the small misgivings of these flaccid times as to Petruchio's gentility! Does one rebuke the whirlwind that it knocks off one's hat, and does not stay to apologise? Mr. Martin Harvey got right into the heart of his admirable enterprise. His conduct was a perpetual invitation to Katherina that she should with him enjoy the excellent jest of matrimony; and, when she at last was persuaded to see the immense fun of being married to Petruchio, we realised she would not for the world have missed it. Miss N. de Silva was especially admirable at the turning-point. This Petruchio was a good fellow. Happily he was married to a good fellow, able to appreciate the humour of his wooing.

Mr. Martin Harvey's players all had spirit for the occasion; but Mr. Charles Glenney's Christopher Sly had more. Much of the success of Mr. Martin Harvey's revival was due to this presence of Christopher Sly. The true Shakespearean grin,

> Broad as ten thousand beeves at pasture,
>
> [*The Spirit of Shakespeare,*i]

was incarnate in Mr. Glenney's extraordinary realisation of Christopher. Mr. Glenney must actually be seen to be believed. I despair of conveying to anyone who has not seen him the vivid sense he gave of all in Shakespeare's comedy (intruding into moods the most fantastic and enskyed) that smells of fresh earth, that shows the meanest of men as the dear fools of God, and cleans as with a rushing wind Nature's necessary and sufficient evil of the day. There are things in Shakespeare's "The Taming of the Shrew" that can only be enjoyed through the eyes of such as Mr. Glenney's Christopher. He is our interpreter; he sets the pace of our merriment. Simple and dirty fellow, he is the measure of our capacity to inherit the really good things of the earth. (pp. 609-10)

John Palmer, in a review of "The Taming of the Shrew," in The Saturday Review, *London, Vol. 115, No. 3003, May 17, 1913, pp. 609-10.*

John Martin Harvey (essay date 1933)

[*Martin Harvey was an eminent turn-of-the-century English actor-manager. He began his career as a member of Henry Irving's Lyceum acting company and eventually became its manager in 1899. In his inaugural production as manager of the Lyceum, Martin Harvey portrayed Sydney Carton in* The Only Way, *an adaptation of Dickens's* A Tale of Two Cities. *Throughout his long career, he offered memorable interpretations of such characters as Hamlet, Richard III, and Oedipus Rex, but audiences always associated him with the melodramatic role of Sydney Carton. Here, Martin Harvey discusses the circumstances surrounding his 1913 revival of* The Shrew. *He describes his innovative treatment of Sly, who, following the Induction, watched the performance from the front of the house as if it were being staged solely for his amusement, as well as the characterization of Kate and Petruchio. Nina De Silva's Katherina conceded her husband's dominance with grace and humor, while Martin Harvey's Petruchio tamed his wife with kindness rather than brutality.*]

No work ever gave us greater pleasure in its preparing and acting than this delightful comedy of Shakespeare [*The Taming of the Shrew*]. I had only seen Augustin Daly's production many years ago, and it had left very little impression on me, though, of course, my wife and I used to play Garrick's bowdlerized version during our Lyceum Vacation Tours, so I was able to approach its interpretation with a mind clear of any traditions, admirations and unconscious cerebrations. This may not have been an advantage, but at least it gave me freedom of invention. My conception for the staging of this play was described in an address at the Exhibition of Scenic Designs, which I had the honour of opening at the Municipal Art Galleries in Manchester. I said:

> The main points of difference between this production and those that have been staged since Shakespeare's time are two. First, the action of the play is continuous, with the exception of one break in the middle to give breathing-time to the actors as well as to the audience: for perhaps two and a half hours would be too long to expect an audience to remain seated. Second: the drunken tinker, 'Christopher Sly', remains present, not only through the early part of the play (as in the generally accepted version) but throughout the entire performance. The play is acted indeed, as Shakespeare clearly indicated, for his amusement.

You remember the story, of course. A sporting "Lord" comes upon a drunken tinker ('Christopher Sly') asleep under a hedge and, with the help of his servants, makes him believe that he is in reality "a mighty lord" himself who "has slept and dreamed these fifteen years" [cf. Ind. ii. 79]. Then, for his amusement, an entertainment is arranged by a troupe of strolling players who by chance have just arrived at the "Lord's" country house. This entertainment is the play, *The Taming of the Shrew,* as we know it.

It is, as I have said, performed for the amusement of the drunken tinker; but, for reasons which I perhaps can indicate, 'Sly', in the generally accepted version of the play, disappears from the scene shortly after the play begins, i.e., after what is known as "The Induction." Now, before this well-known play of Shakespeare's there was an earlier one on the same subject called *The Taming of A Shrew,* in which some commentators discover the hand of Shakespeare in certain passages. In this earlier play, 'Sly' remains on the stage throughout the entire performance, and at the end is carried out by the 'Lord's' servants and deposited near the alehouse where he had been originally discovered.

For what my opinion is worth, I think that the reason why Shakespeare, in the second version of the play, cut 'Sly' out after the Induction is that the low comedian, to whom the part of 'Sly' would be given, took too many liberties with his part—in fact, that he 'gagged' shamefully—and diverted the attention of the audience from the play proper. This he could easily do, for on the Elizabethan stage he probably occupied the gallery which ran across the back—the stage-direction in the printed play reads "enter Sly aloft." From this position he could dominate the play and attract more than a legitimate amount of attention to himself to the hurt of the play proper, and it would be almost impossible to prevent him from doing so. He was almost certainly an owner of shares in the Theatre, and could not be dismissed, as he would be if—well, if he were a member of *my* company! Shakespeare would, therefore, have the annoyance of seeing attention diverted from his play, which was proceeding on the stage, by the "gags" and interpolations of the comedian playing 'Sly'; so in his new version of the play 'Sly' is cut out altogether after the Induction. But this course leads to certain dilemmas, because, after all, the play is performed for the special amusement of 'Sly'. So I have taken the liberty of restoring him to his old prominence; but, instead of having him seated in a gallery at the back of the stage, I have put him in the front of the theatre—where the musical director usually sits—practically as one of the audience. Here he sits, therefore, with his *back* to the audience, you see; and his comments upon the 'taming' process seem to afford as much delight to the audience to-day as they did in the days of Elizabeth.

Before designing the setting for the play I had sought the co-operation of Mr. William Poel, founder of the Elizabethan Stage Society, whose Shakespearean productions upon a platform stage and without scenery, are famous. I had watched my own children give scenes from Shakespeare in the drawing-room, and had seen how little scenery was missed. I wanted Poel to advise me as to how far he had found his own audiences would accept a Shakespearean play without scenery. He was kind enough to come down several times to Birmingham for this purpose, but his interest in the matter seemed confined to the necessary 'cuts' to be made in the play rather than the decoration of it. The result was that I carried on my own growing conception of the *décor.*

My final arrangement was that the entire action of the play was carried through in one scene. This scene was a stylized representation of a gorgeous summerhouse in the architecture of the early fifteenth century. The back of this scene was open to the illimitable gardens of the Lord's mansion and in this summerhouse the players presented their comedy to the bemused 'Sly', who sat, as I have said, in the orchestra from which the musicians had been banished. Any change of scene was suggested by the actors themselves, who moved into this Hall either such screens as could be found in the house of their Princely host crudely to represent a street, or else some trellis-work covered with leaves cut from the neighbouring garden to represent a leafy lane; or again, some of the Lord's own hangings were let down from the ceiling of the hall for interior scenes. Furniture was deliberately placed in position in front of the audience by the members of the troupe, and 'Sly,' in the unforgettable person of Charles Glenny, made humorous comment on the entertainment provided for him. Some of these comments are not to be found in Shakespeare!

but Glenny's 'gags' were so absolutely irresistible that I believe Shakespeare himself would have roared with delight at them. This keeping of 'Sly' in front of the house with his back to the audience not only prevented him from attracting too much attention, but gave the actors unsuspected opportunities for legitimate comedy which they could introduce with propriety when the play was at last performed for its original purpose, viz.: for the amusement of 'Sly.'

The costumes designed by George Kruger Gray and inspired by the designs of Benozzo Gozzoli for the frescoes in the Riccardi Palace, in Florence, were the most striking I have ever seen on any stage, and their brilliant colouring emphasized the joyous festivity of the whole entertainment. After a few performances in Hull, Glasgow and Edinburgh, we took the play to my old home, the Prince of Wales's Theatre, in London, where it was received by the Press with a unanimous chorus of approval. Sir Sidney Lee wrote:—"I am sure you catch the spirit of the work to a degree quite impossible in the older elaborate style. It was an artistic feast all through." Edmund Gosse said—"It was a most brilliant and successful performance, far exceeding in merit any others—and I have seen several—which have been attempted in recent years." Professor Oliver Elton:—"I shall read it now (*The Shrew*) with a mind relieved—sure that William Shakespeare meant it to be taken lightly and brilliantly in your way, and not in the brutal traditional way. If he (William Shakespeare) did not mean the lady to see the jest, so much the worse for him!" Professor Elton's comment refers to the reading my wife and I gave of our respective parts. She played Katherine as a 'Shrew,' yes, but her surrender was the whimsical surrender of one who should say: "Let the man have his way, it saves a lot of trouble and seems to keep him happy," while being in love with him all the while. As for my own conception of Petruchio, I see in him one of the greatest gentlemen Shakespeare ever drew. He had the almost unique distinction of being a man who did not mind a "scene." How the "brutal traditional way" of which Professor Elton wrote, could ever have been accepted in spite of the obvious care that the author takes in explaining the motive and method of Petruchio's 'taming' is a mystery. *Who first introduced that maddening whipcracking?* As if any woman of breeding and spirit could be "tamed" like a circus beast! This method of reducing a woman to obedience by such means is to degrade a high-spirited comedy to the receptiveness of the audience of a penny gaff. Shakespeare gives no shadow of excuse for it; on the contrary, Petruchio declares that "all is done in *reverent care of her* ('Katherine') and that his taming process is "the way to kill a wife with *kindness*" [IV. i. 204, 208].

The opinions of the Press—so unusually unanimous—were boiled down by my Secretary at this time. I was so proud of this general approval that I venture to quote it in its entirety.

> A win all along the line for what was described on the programme as the New Way of producing Shakespeare, but is really the only true way. *The New Way is the Only Way.* The chief reason for this is that the New Way is the old original way for which Shakespeare designed his plays. There was nothing merely eccentric, nothing odd for the sake of oddity. Mr. Martin-Harvey has devised a scheme of things rich in colour and of ample variety. Above all the *spirit of jollity* ran through the performance; there was red blood in the veins of the old farce. To have a place in the stalls on Saturday was to have tasted a surely Elizabethan flavour. We found the presence of Christopher Sly in the audience a great

help. Mr. Harvey has exalted the bibulous tinker into a most important and conspicuous personage. Having finished his own special contribution to the stage picture, Sly descends to the level of the stalls, and from the seat that ordinarily might be the conductor's chair, sits first with his page 'wife' and later with the nobleman who has gulled him out of his senses, and drinks, and reflects the humour of the play. Mr. Charles Glenny's Sly was a *notable performance*, rolling and bibulous and rustic, a very model of a Shakespearean clown.

The comedy is thus given with only one break, which comes naturally enough at the point where Petruchio carried Katherine off after their mad marriage. Even more original, however, was the way in which the comedy was acted. What we saw was manifestly a performance by actors for the benefit of the bemused Sly, to be paid for out of the purse of the young Lord. We had seen the troupe of players arrive in their gaudy clothes of red and yellow. More than once the players looked to the tinker for their applause, and after one of the scenes he mounted on the stage and insisted on an introduction to Katherina. We knew they were only players. It left us free to enjoy this 'pleasant conceited historie' as *a piece of hearty fun,* without bothering about its ethics or calculating its probability or its likeness to life. To this end Mr. Martin-Harvey's Petruchio is absolutely the best we have ever had. Among other things he can move about this open stage and do just what he wants with a grace and command and free spirit that no other actor can quite show. The old incessant artillery, like cracking the cart-horse whip, is not the conqueror of 'Kate the Curst' at the Prince of Wales'. It is an intellectual conquest. Mr. Martin-Harvey's Petruchio hypnotises Katherina into reasonableness. His Petruchio was a delight from beginning to end, a gentleman and man of humour throughout. Miss N. de Silva gave us such a charming Katherine that we fell in love with her from the very first. It had great moments. She took her taming with a kind of half-smile at the wild wilfulness of the delightful Termagant who had rushed her into marriage. She suggested very pleasantly the lady's sense of humour and her enjoyment of Petruchio's whims. The lines:

Pardon old father, my mistaking eyes
That have been so bedazzled by the sun—
　　　　　　　　　　　　　　　[IV. v. 45-46]

could not have been more brilliantly given, delivered as it was with a mute appeal to Petruchio as to whether it was sun or moon. The play ended with a gay chain dance of all the performers across the stage and back again—in which Christopher Sly joined—and after a generous offering of applause everybody went away delighted. Mr. George J. Dodson, the painter of the decorations and Mr. George Kruger Gray, the designer of the costumes, must be praised for their tasteful work. This is the summit of good stagecraft where Shakespeare is concerned. Anyone who failed to enjoy Saturday's presentation of the 'pleasant conceited historie' must have been a jaundiced critic. We shall be surprised if all London is not presently flocking to the Prince of Wales' to show its appreciation of 'The New Way.'

(pp. 410-16)

While the audiences were equally enthusiastic, the old cloud descended upon us. Shouts of joyous laughter, an unexceptionable Press, the emphatic praise of the scholarly, and—an average nightly return of £41! I said: "We'll run it for four weeks no matter what it plays to; for this is a good thing." The average nightly receipts *before* we produced it in London were, Glasgow £148, Edinburgh £152, even poor little Hull £100! *Res ipsa Loquitur!* (pp. 416-17)

> John Martin-Harvey, "The Taming of the Shrew,"
> in his The Autobiography of Sir John Martin-
> Harvey, Sampson Low, Marston & Co., Ltd., 1933,
> pp. 410-17.

Cary M. Mazer (essay date 1981)

[*Mazer examines Martin Harvey's production of* The Taming of the Shrew, *deeming it heavily influenced by William Poel. Martin Harvey, Mazer asserts, achieved a successful production by combining elements of both Poel's Elizabethan style and Max Reinhardt's technique known as the New Stagecraft.*]

Of all Poel's followers and debtors, the only one to evolve a vital form of production was Martin Harvey, though he applied Elizabethan principles directly to only two productions and evolved a separate style for each. These two productions represent, in several ways, the best and worst of Edwardian experiments in Elizabethanism. The first, *The Taming of the Shrew* (1913) exercised a greater conventional freedom, integrating features of the New Stagecraft into an Elizabethanist frame; the second, *Henry V* (1916), represented a return to archaeologism through the transformation of the Elizabethan stage into a pictorial showcase.

The Elizabethanism of *The Taming of the Shrew* was inspired, as it was for Webster and Planché, by the performance frame offset by the Induction. As with the production seventy years before, the later production was actually an exercise in archaeology, here enhanced with features of the New Stagecraft learned from Reinhardt.

Harvey claimed [in his *Autobiography*] that the inspiration for the production was independent of contemporary trends in Elizabethanism: "I had watched my own children give scenes from Shakespeare in the drawing-room, and had seen how little scenery was missed;" and he furthermore claimed that Poel's assistance, solicited for the production, was limited "to the necessary 'cuts' to be made in the play rather than the decoration of it." However, Poel's contribution appears to have been greater than this, to judge by the preparation/rehearsal copy housed in the London Museum: the margins contain a running dialogue of suggestion, response and counter-suggestion between the collaborators, the principle aim of which was the development and elaboration of the performance format of the players, and a means of including the theatre audience into the frame of Christopher Sly and the arbitrary 1490 setting of the Induction.

The production was Elizabethanist insofar as it was set in a permanent neutral locale according to the scenic resources of a group of itinerant players, dressed in motley, and carrying with them properties, screens and curtains in a wagon. The neutral locale was a hall in a summer house of the Lord, opening up, past a terrace, onto a garden. This was depicted by a series of arches framing the stage, a balustraded rostrum upstage with two conventionalized trees, and a view of a landscape on the backcloth with a wide road receding into the distance. The players entered along the rostrum and played their

scenes upon it and upon the stage proper, with Sly watching the play throughout from a bench placed at the forwardmost edge of the apron, built into the orchestra pit several steps down so that sight-lines were not obscured for the theatre audience. The screens were moved by hand by extras and stagehands dressed either as members of the travelling company or as servants in the Lord's house. Through these means Harvey was able to present a fluid and continuous production, and to steer clear of the disturbing social implications of the play by emphasizing the romping, athletic *commedia* aspects of the performance.

But in many ways Harvey's *Shrew* had more in common with the New Stagecraft than with Elizabethanism. Harvey had acted for Max Reinhardt in *Oedipus* at Covent Garden in 1912, and was touring with the production when he first rehearsed and produced *The Shrew*. He therefore had, as part of his touring equipment, a portable apron stage, proscenium masking, and equipment for front-of-house lighting. The servant/stagehands are recognizable Reinhardt devices. But more significant is the way Harvey chose to integrate the style of the staging of the Induction with that of the play proper. Rather than having a naturalistic setting into which the players would bring a purely theatrical display, Harvey used decorative front curtains reminiscent of most Edwardian experiments in Elizabethan staging. The act drop parted at the beginning of the induction to reveal an imitation tapestry depicting an Italianate landscape: the device of using a tapestry which is at once decorative and pictorial is reminiscent of Tree's use of them for outdoor scenes in his 1905 *Hamlet*. For the scene in the Lord's chamber, the tapestries parted, revealing another set of decorative curtains, of white Roman satin with large decorative medallions; these medallions were indicated in reference to the Lord's "wanton pictures." The full set was revealed only just before the entrance of the players.

In staging the play itself, Harvey also blurred the line between the modern performance and the semi-improvisational piece performed within it. [In his *The Theatre of Max Reinhardt*] Huntly Carter described one scenic effect: "In the second half of the play a large canopied seat with a table in front occupied the center of the stage whenever a scene was supposed to be taking place in Petruchio's house. These properties were so arranged that they could be hoisted into the flies while a screen scene was being played." The suggestion here is that the technical machinery of the stage was used in ways which would be impossible in a Lord's country house. Harvey's own retrospective description illustrates how he tried to excuse this under the guise of the enframed Elizabethan performance:

> Any change of scene was suggested by the actors
> themselves, who moved into this Hall either such
> screens as could be found in the house of their
> Princely host crudely to represent a street, or else
> some trellis-work covered with leaves cut from the
> neighbouring garden to represent a leafy lane; or
> again, some of the Lord's own hangings were let
> down from the ceiling of the hall for interior scenes.

So Harvey explained even the Lord's curious fly system according to the archaism of the performance. He also revealed the characteristic Edwardian obsession with pictorial appropriateness (trellises and leaves for gardens, curtains for interiors, etc.). The promptbook further reveals Harvey's traditional use of Edwardian alternation: although changes were effected by visible stagehands, he did use downstage "street" scenes, formed by a configuration of curtains and potted hedges, to mask the placement of heavier pieces of furniture, such as a fifteen-foot long table for the last scene. (pp. 77-9)

[One] example of an attempt to bridge the gap between the modern audience and the implied Elizabethan audience of a revivalist production can be found in Harvey's *Shrew.* Christopher Sly, placed on a bench at the front edge of the sunken apron stage, served as an intermediary between the modern audience and the Renaissance travelling players enacting the play. The promptbook in the London Museum contains the following note for the interval:

> Suggestion: all guests follow *Pet. & Kath.* off the terrace leaving the stage empty—save for *Lord.* Sly climbs from his seat [in] the orchestra (Kath. and Pet.) to be brought before him in pantomime of course. They are brought back & Sly congratulates them & offers them drink. Kath. refuses of course—Pet. can laughingly accept. They all retire together. Stage is left empty. Music or partsinging during interval.

While it is unclear whether this business was indeed used, we can nevertheless see in this clever curtain call a reminder to the audience that they could directly share in the response of a drunken tinker to a skeletal performance employing non-representational decor, as well as an encouragement to the audience to patronize the bars in the foyers. (p. 81)

> Cary M. Mazer, *"Shakespeare and the Elizabethan Revival,"* in his Shakespeare Refashioned: Elizabethan Plays on Edwardian Stages, *UMI Research Press, 1981, pp. 49-84.*

Jan McDonald   (essay date 1982)

[*McDonald examines the collaboration of Martin Harvey and William Poel to produce* The Taming of the Shrew *in 1913. Through letters exchanged between the co-directors, as well as prompt-book markings and Martin Harvey's autobiography, the critic traces their respective contributions. He concludes that although it appears the production was ultimately "more Harvey than Poel," this cannot be reliably determined.*]

The production of *The Taming of the Shrew* in the spring of 1913 was the occasion of the "alliance" of William Poel and Martin Harvey, and the attempt at reconstruction which follows is based on a set of unpublished letters from Poel to Harvey, dating from August 1912 to May 1913, the promptbook, and sketches of the set, which I was fortunate enough to acquire some years ago.

At first sight, the collaboration seems unlikely. Martin Harvey, the matinée idol, was a product and supporter of the actor-manager system that Poel abhorred for its commercialism, but the correspondence reveals that both men were interested in a change of direction at this stage in their careers.

Martin Harvey wrote in his autobiography, "I sought the co-operation of William Poel, founder of the Elizabethan Stage Society, whose Shakespeare productions upon a platform stage and without scenery are famous. I had watched my own children give scenes from Shakespeare in the drawing-room, and had seen how little scenery was missed. I wanted Poel to advise me as to how he had found his own audience would accept a Shakespeare play without scenery".

There may have been another reason for Harvey's interest. He appeared in 1912 in the title role of Reinhardt's celebrated production of *Oedipus,* with Lillah McCarthy, Granville Barker's wife, as Jocasta. Barker was then preparing the first of three brilliant but outrageous Shakespearean productions, *The Winter's Tale,* performed at the Savoy in November 1912. It is not presuming too much to imagine that during the rehearsal period of *Oedipus,* the two men discussed new approaches to the staging of Shakespeare. We know that Barker must have been in evidence, for his detailed notes to his wife on her playing of Jocasta imply his presence at rehearsals. It is likely that the ambitious Harvey wanted to mount the "new Shakespeare" bandwagon.

He first approached Poel in August 1912 with the idea of a joint production of *Richard III.* Poel, at this time, was disillusioned and tired. A letter to Harvey, dated 6 November 1912, reveals that he intended to give up directing plays on his own, and meant to act in future as a kind of *mise-en-scène* consultant. He refers to his forthcoming production of *Troilus and Cressida* for the Elizabethan Stage Society as his last. "The winding up of thirty years' work is of course a busy moment in one's life . . . I am also so very anxious now to be satisfied with working for others and not for myself." He was currently collaborating with Bridges-Adams on a production of Sybil Amherst's *The Book of Job,* presented 28 November 1912. He was also rather short of funds, and the correspondence with Harvey is peppered with requests for fees and expenses.

In addition it is only fair to say that Poel respected Harvey as an actor. In 1908 he had tried to sell him the production of *Everyman* for £250. "I think you would act the role admirably and your artistic temperament and great popularity with your public would make the play a great success with your management." In fact, Harvey did play Everyman in 1923, but in Von Hoffmannstahl's version of the piece.

Harvey, as the statement from his autobiography implies, was principally interested in getting Poel's advice on décor. It was perhaps typical of Poel that in the event he was prepared to give advice on anything but. In answer to Harvey's request, Poel replied, "Perhaps I ought to point out to you that, in my opinion, the success of a play on Elizabethan lines does not depend as much on the setting, as upon the complete alteration of methods of elocution and stage-management— that is action—methods which might not be popular either with your actors or audiences".

Considering that even the dedicated Granville Barker had found being shut up by Poel for three weeks to "learn the tunes" of *Richard II* somewhat tedious, one is not surprised that Poel had some reservations about inflicting his methods on a regular commercial company. What is interesting about this letter is that it shows that Poel is becoming less antiquarian in methods of staging. It is on the delivery of the verse and on the blocking that he places most emphasis.

338

He does show, however, that in his new role as consultant, he is prepared to satisfy consumer demand. He asks for details of the size of the apron, whether there have to be any scene changes, and whether Martin Harvey wanted any of the cast to enter through the auditorium, a practice that he himself had used with great success in *Everyman*. "You will easily realize that I must have some definite form of platform in my mind's eye before I can be arranging the movement." He also in the same letter asks for a cheque. His fee was two guineas a day, for six hours' work.

At this point the whole project almost came to grief, because Martin Harvey abandoned the idea of *Richard III,* and proposed instead *The Taming of the Shrew*. Perhaps he felt, as Benjamin Webster had done before him, that this play with its Induction, its setting in the Lord's house and its visiting troupe of actors performing there, lent itself more readily to the Elizabethan method. Poel was disappointed. He put forward a counter-proposal of *Much Ado,* and then suggested *Macbeth*. The *Shrew* Poel felt had been well enough done in the regular commercial theatre in the recent past. There had just been a successful production by Oscar Asche and Lily Brayton. He also thought that Harvey should choose tragedy rather than comedy for his first venture, especially after his great success in Reinhardt's *Oedipus*. He concedes the point, however, with a typically acid comment. "But I suppose the Shrew has the most money in it. English audiences seem to delight in seeing the same thing over and over again. I suppose it might be all right with striking costume effects and quaint music."

Another problem emerged when it became clear that Harvey intended to cut the sub-plot altogether, surprising perhaps, since the actor-manager talks elsewhere of "Garrick's shamelessly dismembered version of Shakespeare's *The Taming of the Shrew*". But actor-managers throughout the nineteenth century had the habit of expressing horror at Restoration and eighteenth-century Shakespearean texts, before proceeding to exercise their own butchery on the plays. Poel pointed out that it would only run one and a half hours minus the "underplots", "in which case you will want another strong piece in the bill, and this would be well, because it might justify shortening the play. Otherwise omitting the underplots will run you foul of the critics, because one of the great objects of the Elizabethan Method is to afford more time for getting in more of the text". Since there was a permanent architectural background and continuous action, time was not wasted on elaborate and lengthy scene changes. It is interesting to note, however, that Poel's own production of *Troilus and Cressida,* on which he was working at the same time as "advising" Harvey on *The Shrew,* was cut considerably, and according to some critics, injudiciously. Poel believed that in *Troilus and Cressida* the dialogue held up the action, and so went to work with his blue pencil.

The idea of a double-bill became increasingly attractive to Poel, when it occurred to him that *Jacob and Esau,* a sixteenth-century interlude, which he had produced the previous February would be the ideal companion piece. Martin Harvey would have none of it, however, and *The Shrew* was presented on its own.

Harvey later complained that he had asked Poel to discuss décor but all *he* had done was talk about cuts. The correspondence scarcely deals with these, but they may have been discussed at one of the production meetings (for which Poel

charged two guineas plus expenses). The promptbook, however, provides evidence of the final acting version.

Some 668 lines are cut out of a play of just over 2,500. The play was given in two acts, the interval being taken between the end of the wedding scene (Act III Sc. 2), and the arrival of the couple at Petruchio's house. Most of the cuts are accounted for by the fairly extensive excisions in the Pedant/Vincentio sub-plot, although the bones of it remain. Lucentio's description of his father in Act I Sc. I, and the whole of Act IV Sc. 4 (i.e. when the Pedant impersonating Vicentio meets Baptista) is omitted. Much of the "low comedy", for example the scene between Curtis and Grumio in Act IV Sc. I, goes. This may well have been at Poel's suggestion, for he admitted to Harvey that it was primarily the horseplay that made him dislike the play.

The overall effect of the cutting is to focus the attention on the Petruchio/Katharine story, and, perhaps more significantly, to build up the character of Petruchio, and to stress those aspects of it that Harvey wanted to develop. All references to Petruchio's initial intention to marry Katharine for her money are cut, such as Petruchio's line, "Wealth is the burden of my wooing dance" [I. ii. 68], and the one made famous by *Kiss me Kate,* "I come to wive it wealthily in Padua" [I. ii. 75]. So is Grumio's comment,

> Give him gold enough and marry him to a puppet . . .
> Why, nothing comes amiss, so money comes withal.
>
> [I. ii. 78-9; 80-1]

It might be felt that this removed all Petruchio's motivation for tackling the rich shrew, but according to J. T. Grein [in *The Sunday Times* of 21 May 1916], Harvey played the part as "a jovial smiling Italian gentleman who seemed to get immense fun out of an experiment". In addition, while Petruchio is allowed to dress up in a bizarre fashion for the wedding, Tranio's line, "Yet often times he goes but mean apparelled" [III. ii. 73] is omitted, the implication being that Petruchio, when he is not shrew-taming, is immaculate. . . . Harvey said, "As for my conception of Petruchio, I see him as the greatest gentleman Shakespeare ever drew". He disliked the stage tradition of horse-whipping his wife into submission. His was, according to *Lloyd's News* "an intellectual conquest. Martin Harvey's Petruchio hypnotizes Katherina into reasonableness." However, as Grein put it, "Indeed, so amiable, smiling, smooth-tongued and polite was he in the first act that he seemed inconsistent with the Petruchio that Shakespeare drew"—an instance perhaps of the actor-manager wanting to be loved?

Other cuts show that he certainly wanted to be applauded, for on several occasions a scene is stopped immediately after Petruchio's exit, e.g. at the end of Act III Sc. I (i.e. Harvey's Act I), the scene ends with Petruchio's lines,

> Fear not, sweet wench, they shall not touch thee, Kate!
> I'll buckler thee against a million
>
> [III. ii. 238-39]

Petruchio lifts Katharine on his shoulder and exits, omitting the exchange between Baptista, Bianca and the others, and the play ends similarly with the exit of Katharine and Petruchio, cutting the Hortensio/Lucentio exchange.

Minor cuts are made for the usual reasons of prudery, for example, all references to beds, maidenheads and the like are excised, and of obscurity, for example the classical references to Ovid and Aristotle in Lucentio's speech in Act I, but the really unforgivable and, perhaps, inexplicable cut is the massacring of Kate's last speech, which is cut from 44 lines to 17. Could the actor-manager not bear his leading lady, even if she were his wife, to have such a protracted last word? According to Grein, Nina de Silva played "her final surrender more in the nature of making the best of a bad job than of submission to a superior will. Indeed one felt there was some reluctance in her yielding, and that her rebuke to the Widow and Bianca proceeded rather from pose than from conviction". This interpretation is borne out by Harvey himself, who writes that hers was "the whimsical surrender of one who should say 'let the man have his way, it saves a lot of time and it keeps him happy', while being in love with him all the while". Katharine's playing the last scene with a smile is certainly a viable reading but why omit

> My mind has been as big as one of yours
> My heart as great, my reason haply more.
>
> [V. ii. 170-71]

which would help this interpretation? The disembowelling of this speech, whoever was guilty of it, shows little feeling for either the verse, the message or the comedy of the play.

Originally the co-directors' plan was that Poel would prepare a promptbook with movements and cuts indicated. But later he writes to Harvey telling the latter how to make one, ". . . buy two I/-copies of the full text (Cassell's National Library for preference) then cut out the pages and cut out all Act and scene headings, and paste the leaves into a scrapbook so that they make one continuous movement".

Poel received the promptbook, and a sketch of the set on 21 October. This, and Martin Harvey's subsequent comment that he had carried out "my own growing conception of the décor" makes it clear that the final version was the latter's work. However, Poel was pleased with the result. "I like it very much," he wrote. "It is simple yet dignified." He then proceeded to work out the "movements" as he put it, a task he enjoyed, but he withdrew from preparing a detailed scheme of moves on 6 November, "because, as the staging is not strictly Elizabethan the movements and the changes of curtain must be a matter more or less of experiment and modifications. And it would help matters not to be too definite"— an indication perhaps that Poel was finding producing a play by proxy rather hard, and that he would prefer to work things out on the set with actors. He suggested a meeting, which was no doubt more sensible in terms of the theatrical end product, but in the absence of a transcript of the discussion, provides no evidence for the theatre historian.

The set basically consisted of five sets of curtains:

(1) Tapestry curtains at the first groove position, used as a backing for the inn in the Induction, where Sly is found by the Lord.

(2) What are referred to as "nude women curtains", set immediately in front of the tapestry ones, used as a backing for the Lord's bedroom. The idea for these came from the Lord's lines,

> Carry him gently to my fairest chamber
> and hang it around with all my wanton pictures. . . .
>
> [Ind. i. 46-7]

(3) Black and red curtains at the second groove position, used for Bianca's wooing scene.

(4) Silver and grey curtains at the third grooves, used for all the other scenes in Baptista's house.

(5) Pink curtains at the fourth grooves, used for Petruchio's house.

Curtain backings were used for interiors. The exteriors were done with screens, and door- and windowpieces when required.

The full set, with movable trellises covered with laurel leaves, was used for the first scene of the play proper, a public place in Padua, for the procession from the church, and for the final banquet. The laurel pieces differently set, so as to make "a leafy lane" provided the backing for the journey of Katharine and Petruchio back to Padua.

The very back of the scene showed an unchanging vista of the Lord's garden. The idea was that the whole of the play proper took place in the Lord's summer house. The moving of the screens and laurel pieces and of the furniture and props was done by the "actors", and the curtains were let down as if they were the Lord's hangings. Sly and the Lord sat in the orchestra "in the musical director's place", and Sly made frequent comments on the action from there, which as Harvey said "were not Shakespeare, but were irresistible".

As Poel had pointed out, the setting was hardly Elizabethan. Scene changes were minimal, allowing almost continuous action. There was an embryonic apron, built over part of the orchestra pit, with steps going down to accommodate Sly and the Lord, but when an upper level was needed in the scene in which Vicentio questions the Pedant, who is at a window, a bookflat, steps, a windowpiece and a doorpiece were found ready waiting behind the drapes. The setting is a modification of normal nineteenth-century décor, rather than an imitation of Elizabethan staging. Despite the fact that the production was billed as being done in "The New Way", it is fairly clear that Martin Harvey was using drapes in a much less imaginative fashion than Barker had done some months earlier in *The Winter's Tale* and *Twelfth Night*.

Poel told Martin Harvey on 13 November, "I have now visualized the play—the whole of it and hope it will come out as actable for your company and to your liking". Another discussion was arranged for 26 November, but Poel was becoming increasingly involved in *Troilus and Cressida,* "hard and anxious work". At the same time he was playing Keegan in a revival of Shaw's *John Bull's Other Island,* so it is unlikely that he would have had a great deal of time for discussion.

The promptbook does not give very detailed moves, and such groupings as are indicated more often than not show the old-fashioned scheme with principals in the centre and the others gathered round them in a semi-circle. One move that Poel did discuss at some length, however, was the possibility of Katharine and Petruchio entering through the audience on their return from Petruchio's house. He is enthusiastic about this idea, but as he says, if they are to enter this way in Act II, then they must leave through the audience at the end of Act I. "This with the horse might be difficult, unless the horse could be brought down stage as far as the apron so that the curtain could come down leaving the four of you outside for a moment and then rise again for you to take the call. For myself I like the idea of Katharine never leaving your horse after her return from the church. It suggests that you did not trust her with her friends."

Neither the horse nor the entry through the auditorium found its way into the finished production. At the end of Act I Petruchio put Katharine on his shoulder, and carried her off by the R.U.E. to the cheers of a group of 12 children and a fanfare from the musicians. All principals on SR crossed to SL and looked after the couple. The Stage Direction then reads *PICTURE,* a nice nineteenth-century tableau in the midst of all this ersatz Elizabethanism. After the Act call Petruchio came forward and shook hands with Sly. For the return journey through the aforementioned leafy lane, Katharine and Petruchio entered through R.I.E. In fact, if the convention is that the play is taking place in the Lord's summer house, it would break it rather to go rushing off through the auditorium, with or without a horse.

The costumes, designed by George Kruger Gray, were we are told [by Harvey] "inspired by the designs of Benozzo Gozzoli for the frescoes in the Ricardi Palace in Florence", another echo of nineteenth-century antiquarianism. The costumes are certainly Italianate in design, rather than Elizabethan, and one may assume, therefore, that Poel did not have a hand in their design, since he still believed that Shakespeare should be played in Elizabethan dress. *Troilus and Cressida* was all stomachers and ruffs.

Poel came in again in March to advise on music. His regular musician, Dolmetsch, was in Paris, and so he suggested that Martin Harvey engage a young lady, called Rosabel Watson, who could "produce the music of the period with violins and cellos, so that only the real expert could tell the difference. The performers would all be ladies, but they could dress up as young men".

The production opened in Hull and came to the Prince of Wales' in London on 10 May. Poel saw it on 15 May. He wrote to Martin Harvey, "You have brought out in an admirable way the joyousness and brightness of the comedy, and removed the horseplay which has always been offensive to me. I limit my criticism, therefore, in great part to the movement"—a clear indication that his advice had not been taken nor his suggestions followed. He goes on, "I like the action to tell a story so that if the words were removed the audience would still know what it was all about. But, you are no doubt right in saying that it is a matter of indifference to the audience".

In general, the production was well reviewed, with comments like "The new way is the only way". *The Saturday Review* called it "the summit of good stagecraft", "the liveliest revival of the play seen in our day". One critic commented that Katharine and Petruchio were so far removed from reality that even the suffragettes could not object to her surrender to him.

Harvey was apparently satisfied. From a commercial point of view the production did well in the provinces drawing over £100 in nightly returns, but despite critical acclaim it was not a financial success in London with average nightly box office takings amounting to only £41. It has been suggested that the popular success of Laurence Irving's *Typhoon,* currently at the Haymarket, drew away the crowds.

Martin Harvey reproduced the play as part of his scheme to mount a Shakespeare season in 1916 to promote the idea of a National Theatre, and so he clearly thought it worth repeating. He also invited Granville Barker to remount his three famous productions, but these did not materialize.

Perhaps it is impossible to reconstruct what each director contributed to a joint production, but it seems clear that what ultimately emerged was more Harvey than Poel. Or was it? An editorial note in *The Mask* raises doubts.

> Who will deny that there was sack and canary in the "Taming of the Shrew" as produced by . . . , but here we come to a broken sentence. Who *was* it produced by? Was it produced by Mr. Harvey *and* Mr. Poel, or was it produced by Mr. Poel alone? Never have we seen anything like that from Mr. Poel's hand before and very little of that character from Mr. Harvey's. It seemed to us to be all Barker.

Further enquiries were made, and in the following April appeared the tantalizing comment [in *The Mask*], "We now know, for one of the gentlemen has told us. But this is amongst the secrets we shall enjoy keeping." (pp. 64-72)

> *Jan McDonald, "An Unholy Alliance: William Poel, Martin Harvey and 'The Taming of the Shrew',"* in Theatre Notebook, *Vol. XXXVI, No. 2, 1982, pp. 64-72.*

PRODUCTION:

Alfred Lunt and Lynn Fontanne • The Guild Theatre • 1935

BACKGROUND:

Lunt and Fontanne, the celebrated husband and wife acting team, presented a highly farcical interpretation of *The Taming of the Shrew.* Fearing that their irreverent treatment of the play would meet with disdain from New York theater critics, the Lunts first took their production on tour throughout America. After receiving widespread critical acclaim, however, the pair decided to stage their production at the Guild Theatre in New York, where it opened on 30 September 1935. Much to the Lunts' surprise, New York critics also responded enthusiastically to their boisterous rendition of the play. The production ran for 128 performances before resuming its tour of major American cities. In addition to Lunt and Fontanne in the starring roles, the cast included Richard Whorf as Sly and Sydney Greenstreet as Baptista. The Lunts revived the production for one week in 1940 to benefit the Finnish Relief Fund.

COMMENTARY:

Brooks Atkinson   (review date 1 October 1935)

[*Atkinson was the dramatic critic for* The New York Times *from 1926 to 1960. Upon his retirement from that post, the Mansfield Theatre in New York was renamed the Brooks Atkinson in honor of his contribution to the theater. His publications include* Skyline Promenades *(1925),* Henry Thoreau: The Cosmic Yankee *(1927), and* East of the Hudson *(1931), as well as many collections of his dramatic criticism. In the following excerpt, Atkinson describes the carnival-like mood of the Lunts' production, remarking that the two actors "have more gusto for every sort of stage hocus-pocus than any other performers on the American bulletin boards."*]

Good friends, the tumult in Fifty-second Street last evening was Shakespeare. Alfred Lunt and Lynn Fontanne were pouncing on "The Taming of the Shrew" and playing it in the Guild Theatre like a game of ninepins. Most exceeding low, my friends, and most exceeding funny, for "The Shrew" is cabotinage and the Lunts have stuffed it with all the horseplay their barn loft holds. Beginning with the befuddled Christopher Sly induction, they have improvised a performance as the vagabond mummers of an ideal age might play it in a nobleman's courtyard. "Oh, this learning, what a thing it is" [I. ii. 159], one of the characters says. Oh, this tumbling and revelry, how uproarious it is when pace is keen and the humor is midriff merriment. There is not a single grain of pedants' dust in this tan-bark version of "The Taming of the Shrew." Fifty-second Street is always a midway when the Lunts are appearing there.

Even in Shakespeare's time "The Taming of the Shrew" was a low tale for an afternoon of elementary fooling. Shakespeare and some unknown playmaker merely adapted it from a standard farce that had almost the same title and much the same mischief. The Lunts have drawn on both for this carnival junket—adding a band with drums, a troupe of tumblers, a cluster of midgets, a pair of comic horses and some fine songs set to good beer-garden music by Frank Tours.

If you complain that you cannot hear the lines nor decipher the Bianca plot, you are well within your rights. There is no time for clarity or exposition when the comedians are riding the whirlwind. Since he was an actor, Shakespeare will not object to a brace of good actors using his cluttered script for a public holiday. After all, lines are a nuisance. Pantomime is a sounder comedy medium. What you are offered by way of compensation is Richard Whorf's seedy Christopher Sly, who is as drunk as a waterfront stew, and a rag-tag and bobtail of prancing performers in a costume antic.

For Kate's father there is Sydney Greenstreet—corpulent, frightened, bewildered, hopeful. For Grumio, Horace Sinclair, who is a red-faced clown. For Biondello, George Meader, who can fill a song with joy. For Bianca, Dorothy Mathews; for Tranio, Bretaigne Windust; for Lucentio, Alan Hewitt, and for Curtis, Alice Belmore Cliffe, who looks jolly, and is.

For Petruchio and Katherine, well, here are the actors who have more gusto for every sort of stage hocus-pocus than any other performers on the American bulletin boards. Miss Fontanne is playing with a painful knee injury that doubtless handicaps her in the running broad jump and hundred-yard dash. But it does not curb the choler of ugly Kate. When she bellows from a room upstairs, the actors huddle in the corner and tremble. When she stamps on Petruchio's foot, he is stamped for all time. She is a pathetic creature when hungry, and a broken mare when Petruchio's training has exhausted her, and she is a lady of poise and breeding when in the last scene she teaches married women their duty.

As Petruchio, Mr. Lunt plays with incomparable bounce and humor, beaming with mischief, grimacing at the audience and vigorously driving the performance before him. The production is hung with gay settings by Carolyn Hancock and dressed in carnival trappings by Claggett Wilson. Mr. Gribble has directed the whole affair with the versatility and dispatch of a musical comedy ringmaster.

All Shakespeare needs at any time is actors. He has them here. Obviously, the Lunts have enjoyed devising this production. Audiences are always in luck when good actors are enjoying themselves.

Brooks Atkinson, "Alfred Lunt, Lynn Fontanne, Theatre Guild, 'The Taming of the Shrew,' All and Sundry," in The New York Times, *October 1, 1935, p. 27.*

The Literary Digest   (review date 12 October 1935)

[*The anonymous critic comments on the Lunt/Fontanne* Shrew, *praising their reinstatement of the element of "swift, boiling farce" that has often been omitted from the play.*]

There is no fun in the breadth and length of Manhattan to match the thumping picnic which the Theater Guild, assisted by notions and roars from Alfred Lunt and Lynn Fontanne, has made of "The Taming of the Shrew."

Ancient fiddle-faddle, always supercargo in previous revered productions, has been cut away with whacking slices. Pure comic prancing has been displaced by swift, boiling farce, and the result is a whirlwind of action combining outrageous humors, scuffling horse-play and rich gusto.

It is Shakespeare as thousands have wanted to see him and as scholars and pompous actors in concert have for years prevented him from being seen.

This is a production which utilizes the rare *Christopher Sly* induction, popping that debauched and majestically drunk tinker into a royal box from which, munching oranges and howling imprecations at the players, *Sly* becomes an authentic, ribald force in the play's scheme.

It was *Sly* who was in that "Pleasant, Conceited Historie, called 'The Taming of a Shrew' " which Shakespeare must have read assiduously if, indeed, he did not write it. Here, in this monstrously bumptious version, the pedants of Shakespeare have but little chance. Their only chance is to say whether Will cribbed from the earlier play (1570) or was its mysterious author. Having explained that, they may retire: the Elizabethan romp of the Guild's "Shrew" is no place for their beards or their sad, profound eyes as heavy as the eyes of a bloodhound.

The first performance in New York was a breathless one for the audience, and two reasons lay behind that ill-suppressed suspense: one, the blasting speed of the production gave them small chance to breathe and, two, Miss Fontanne came to that exhausting, careening performance with her left knee in all but steel casings. Strenuous, lusty rehearsals had dislocated a cartilage.

Her pain was great, her reliance on that knee a free gamble. At any minute it might have buckled under her. She played her *Katherine* the night before, at dress rehearsal, from a front row seat in the Guild Theater, sitting there roaring *Katherine's* defiance of *Petruchio* and all mankind with her accustomed vigor. Opening night, determined to play it through, she lashed her knee into docility, grimaced away the stabs of pain and turned in a *Katherine* who was a shouting, clawing, clubbing virago.

The spectacle of the duet-performance of Miss Fontanne and Mr. Lunt aroused critics to rare expressions of approval.

Lynn Fontanne and Alfred Lunt as Katherina and Petruchio

Robert Garland, in the New York *World-Telegram,* describes the extravaganza and adds:

> Her *Katherine* is every inch a shrew, shrill and bois-
> terous in a venerable tradition. To lift a phrase from
> Noël Coward, here is a woman who should be
> struck as regularly as if she were a gong. Frankly,
> you don't take stock in her last-minute meekness.
> Neither does her *Petruchio.*

That *Petruchio* is one of the best things Mr. Lunt has done,
a lady-killer with a twinkle in his voice, determination in his
eye. You gather that he rather likes his Kate the way she is,
that his faith in her reformation is tempered by a touch of the
humor which is merely common sense.

The settings are graciously and gracefully in the romping
mood of the production, a production which runs to Elizabethan tunes sung in the manner of a Times Square croon, to
fantastic midgets, flaming costumes, to horses made up of
two men and some old skins.

This pranking with the play and its *décor* upsets no one, dis-
tresses no one. Rather, it is counted blessed relief from old
and more formalized productions.

"This dolling-up has not been done with any particular reverence for a classic," writes Burns Mantle in the New York
Daily News. "Why should it be? Shakespeare had little reverence for the sources of supply from which he took it. No, it
has been done with purposeful intent of making a comedy
into a slapstick farce that will remain sufficiently intelligent
to please many people and offend few."

Only one doubtful note issued from Manhattan's critics. It
was sounded by Richard Lockridge in the New York *Sun:*

> They have so earnestly shaken the professors out of
> Shakespeare that they have very nearly shaken the
> play out, too. Dwarfs and bright costumes, songs
> and dances and the like are all very well, but in this
> case they obscure the story a little. The play has
> been cut deeply to minimize the intricacies of the
> plot and there has been an evident effort to touch
> only the high spots. . . . Add to this the inescap-
> able fact that neither of the Lunts speak their lines

too clearly and you have something which is neither quite circus nor altogether play.

Gilbert W. Gabriel, in the New York *American,* is graveled by no such sighs for disturbed Shakespeare.

"Here's 'some' Shakespeare," he rushes to announce, "obviously, openly done for Lunt and Fontanne's sakes, which means for very expert fun's sake, for loud and rapid laughter's sake, for high holiday, for lovely mischief, for the sport. . . . The gaiety of it grew steadily with the evening. The Guilders loved it tempestuously. The players danced their thanks for the audience's thanks . . . and Will Shakespeare must have chuckled and said the immortal equivalent of 'Gee whiz' from across the Styx."

"Taming the Shrew with Whips and Midgets," in Literary Digest, *New York, Vol. 120, October 12, 1935, p. 20.*

Joseph Wood Krutch   (review date 16 October 1935)

[*Krutch was an American dramatic critic who wrote theater reviews for the* Nation *from 1924 to 1959. His critical essays are remembered as scholarly and penetrating, indicating that he was not a mere reporter of the playhouses, but an insightful commentator on drama as literature. Here, Krutch contends that Lunt's fine acting and the production's lively pace contribute to "a distinctly exhilarating" presentation of* The Taming of the Shrew.]

At the Guild Theater Mr. Alfred Lunt is taming Miss Lynn Fontanne in expert and exhilarating fashion. The play is gentle Shakespeare's most ungentle farce, and when the irresistible Katherine meets the immovable Petruccio, hell breaks loose in Padua. By comparison the late unpleasantness between Guelphs and Ghibellines was a mere difference of opinion and it is doubtful if the last invasion of the Lombards was quite so disrupting.

It is my misfortune never to have seen Otis Skinner and Ada Rehan engage in this particular fracas. I did, however, once observe the gallant Sothern tenderly correcting the saintly Marlowe (whose acidity was never more than Ph.6.8); and those who, like me, got their first idea of the play's possibilities from such decorous exhibitions have some lively shocks in store for them. Miss Fontanne is a Katherine who hides a few links of sausage in the bosom of her wedding gown, and Mr. Lunt is a Petruccio who can, and does, give his bride a kick in the pants. To be sure, he also carries the traditional horsewhip, but such gentle persuaders are little necessary to a man who can squeeze the wind out of his wife with one arm or sit on her stomach when the occasion seems to call for something of the sort.

The Guild is not, of course, the first producing organization to see in "The Taming of the Shrew" its knock-about possibilities. A few years ago Mary Ellis and Basil Sidney gave a rousing performance in the same play, but their production as a whole was a bit skimpy and it has remained for the Guild not only to throw to the winds all academic solemnity but also to go the limit so far as the decoration and other incidentals are concerned. When Mr. Lunt and Miss Fontanne are not busy with the principal business of the evening, the stage is kept in lively tumult with incidental activities of every sort. There are acrobats, jugglers, two splendid prop horses of the highest mettle, and, for serving men, more dwarfs than the

entire House of Morgan could hold on its assembled laps. The result, as I previously indicated, is distinctly exhilarating.

Probably the acting honors of the evening go to Mr. Lunt, who, to be sure, has the fattest part. Still, it is no easy task which is set him. For two hours and a half he must mistreat a handsome lady abominably without losing the sympathy of the audience, and he manages the business by somehow giving the impression that he is high-spirited and desperate rather than merely brutal and that, if it does not exactly hurt him more than it does his victim, it is at least all for her own good. Miss Fontanne makes the most of her slighter opportunities and plays the grand transformation scene in which, at her husband's request, the sun becomes the moon and then the sun again with a fine sense of comedy. There is something grim about her acquiescence which suggests that though Kate is no longer cursed there will be moments in the future when her *eppur si muove* will not be sotto voce. As the befuddled spectator, Christopher Sly, Richard Whorf deserves more than a word of praise for his antics. His comment from the box, " 'Tis a very excellent piece of work: would 'twere done" [I. i. 253-54], is one which, at other times, dramatic critics have often made for themselves, but the second half of it has seldom been less appropriate than on this occasion.

Joseph Wood Krutch, "A Real Shrew Really Tamed," in The Nation, *New York, Vol. CXLI, No. 3667, October 16, 1935, p. 448.*

Stark Young   (review date 16 October 1935)

[*Young was an American dramatist, director, author and critic. He served on the editorial staffs of both* The New Republic *and* The New York Times, *earning a reputation as one of the best critics of acting in America. Among his successful publications were a novel entitled* So Red the Rose *(1934) and a translation of Chekhov's* The Seagull *(1939). In the excerpt below, Young commends the Lunt/Fontanne production of* The Taming of the Shrew *as a creative presentation in keeping with the Shakespearean tradition of joyous comedy.*]

There is one thing that various reviewers and spectators are sure to say about "The Taming of the Shrew" at the Guild Theatre. They will say, meaning to praise it, that this presentation of Shakespeare's play is not bothered by any reverence or tradition, in sum that the Lunts are taking the bard easy. Nothing could be worse tosh. There are two kinds of irreverence to Shakespeare: one is to think him dull and all outdated; one is to believe, or profess, that regardless of centuries and despite human weakness, in dramatist and audience, every word in him is immortal. With the Lunts it is the very opposite of irreverence. They believe in the delight inherent in the piece they undertake for us, in the deep power of joyous humor; and they know that nothing is less Shakespeare than a good deal of the Shakespearean tradition. The famous Daly-Rehan form of "The Taming of the Shrew," for example, was only a patch-up of the Garrick version, whole scenes added, and divers bits, no doubt.

When they were devising the present production, the Lunts saw, of course, its limitations, partly due to epochs so separate as the English Renaissance and America today, partly due to the differences in humor, the woman question, the stage possibilities, et cetera; and partly to Shakespeare himself's having thrown the piece off for what it was worth, as apt to the occasion and hilarity. He struck the note of his show when he opened it with hunting gentlemen and their dogs, Silver, Clowder, Echo, Belman, along with Christopher Sly, et cetera, et cetera. In a manner of speaking, everything is left to lump it in "The Taming of the Shrew"; and this the Lunts knew also. They were quite right to invest that play within the play with a contrasting palatial elegance and rich riot. Such was the Renaissance and nobody could know that better than Shakespeare. Such was England, bawdy, magnificent, dirt and brocades, as the Venetian ambassador wrote back to the Council.

The Katherine and Petruchio are brilliant performances, in roles where the difficulties spread out beyond our time almost. You can see that Miss Fontanne and Mr. Lunt recognize perfectly the play's earlier simplification of the problem of men and women's combat. The sly overtones that these two modern players give to the whole version of this sex struggle, Shakespeare, if he came into the stalls at the Guild, would himself appropriate, for he was ever ambitious of the centuries and greedy for all time. He would admire the fresh application of his matter. Anybody who thinks that Miss Fontanne means, as she recites it, Katherine's last speech to settle the question for good is much mistaken. She merely lets it serve to outline the battle launched, but at the same time, neatly indicates that modes in warfare may change without war's ending. A player's comment must be seen in his playing—if we are to have art—and for an actress nowadays to seem to take Katherine's last speech in perfect seriousness would mean only nonsense or some forced quaintness in the scene. Miss Fontanne is further defended by the bounce and eloquence of the lines themselves, not to speak of what Katherine is doing to the other two ladies. We remain by no means convinced that the speaker is depressed or very much broken.

I have never seen Mr. Lunt or Miss Fontanne better in stage movement, or in bold, assured stage make-up that renders them almost masks. In the theatre, the style of acting never leads but follows the play and the idea behind its production. Thus the first problem in this production of "The Taming of the Shrew" is to get all the present company's performance into one key. The baroque intention of the whole production needs to pass into and throughout all the playing, the players need time to strive for that. The key has been excellently devised. It appears in Mr. Claggett Wilson's costumes, which are beautifully Italian Renaissance and are dramatic to the piece; and in the scheme for and designs of the settings. It appears in the opening and closing pageantry employed. Many of the scenic pieces have great charm and stage variety. Whether some of these could be richer in tone and in scale and still not interfere with the acting is a question that might be considered. The Baptista of Mr. Sydney Greenstreet was admirable; it achieved a new drawing that brought the character into interesting lights.

The second chief need for this production is an audience. Mr. Lunt and Miss Fontanne have devised something that boldly reminds us of the fact that a good portion of the theatre art is the audience. Riding in, for example, on those fantastic artificial horses, one of them handsome, one grotesque, or tripping through passages of rowdy poetry, and all that whirling confidence and gusto so plainly meant to be shared with the audience—what could that not become with spectators awake to circus and bravura in the theatre?

Stark Young, "Wayward Glamor," in The New Republic, Vol. LXXXIV, No. 1089, October 16, 1935, p. 274.

Grenville Vernon   (review date 18 October 1935)

[Vernon maintains that the principal actors' often unintelligible speech was the only detriment to an otherwise enjoyable performance.]

"The Taming of the Shrew" is essentially a farce, and a farce the Theatre Guild and the Lunts have made it, and with a vengeance! They have decorated it with dwarfs and tumblers and horses made of men; they have beribboned it and bedecked it, and, the purists would add, perhaps bedevilled it; they have made of it a hilarious extravaganza. Yet as there is nothing artistically sacred in this particular Shakespearean play, indeed it is probably only partly Shakespeare's, they ought not to be condemned for their liberties, if those liberties add gaiety to the proceedings, and if they do not take away from the play itself. Now gaiety the Guild production certainly does have, and real gaiety is a rare thing in a theatre largely given over to vulgarity or neurasthenia, as the New York theatre is today, and so another score must be chalked up to the credit of the Guild. But what happens to the plot of the play is another matter, and there are moments when it disappears amid the confusion of movement and the shouting of the performers, and the characterization of Katherine and Petruchio becomes hazy indeed.

After all, we do like to hear the words of a speech, and there were some of Miss Fontanne's and Mr. Lunt's in which half of what they said escaped me. Mr. Lunt was in particular an offender, and this is a pity, for Mr. Lunt is one of the outstanding actors on the stage, and possesses a brilliancy both of personality and artistic method which makes him unique. There are those who hold that his technique is artificial, and it certainly is not the technique to be employed in the strictly realistic drama, but it has a dash, a *brio,* and an imagination which make his performances, and those of his partner, Miss Fontanne, shine out brilliantly amid the mass of capable but uninspired acting of the contemporary American theatre. It is therefore doubly a pity that his enunciation and pronunciation should be progressively getting worse and more incoherent. Admirable as was his impersonation of Petruchio, his speech was at times almost that of a foreigner.

Miss Fontanne never looked more lovely than as Katherine, nor acted with greater verve, but she too seemed to have caught some of her partner's vocal deficiencies. However, she proved herself a mistress of Elizabethan farce, though she did little with the one truly Shakespearean speech of the play, the one which begins, "A woman moved is like a fountain troubled" [V. ii. 142]. She seemed to miss the charm and womanly surrender of the lines. The Christopher Sly, given in its entirety in the Guild production, was most amusingly impersonated by Richard Whorf, and admirable performances were given by Alan Hewitt as Lucentio, Bretaigne Windust as Tranio, Sydney Greenstreet as Baptista, Barry Thompson as Hortensio, George Meader as Biondello, and David Glassford as Vincentio. Under the direction of Harry Wagstaff Gribble the crowds moved with gusto and color, and Claggett Wilson's costumes were a feast for the eye.

Grenville Vernon, in a review of "The Taming of the Shrew," in The Commonweal, Vol. XXII, No. 25, October 18, 1935, p. 612.

Brooks Atkinson   (review date 20 October 1935)

[Atkinson contends that much of the success of the Lunts' pro-

duction was the result of its exploitation of the play's farcical elements.]

If it were not for the gusty "Taming of the Shrew," which is now filling the Guild Theatre with guffaws, votaries of Shakespeare might be down with despair. Shakespeare is heavy company when he is indifferently performed. For a good many years Broadway has been keeping him safe on the book shelf—high up and in a gloomy corner. But there was a sudden Shakespeare recrudescence last Spring—stimulated, perhaps, by the fervor of the Cornell "Romeo and Juliet." The Lunts began trouping with the rousing burlesque act which has now settled in Fifty-second Street; Philip Merivale held out the promise of "Macbeth" and "Othello"; the Reinhardt film version of "A Midsummer Night's Dream" began to sharpen expectation, and nearly everybody hoped to play Hamlet. Leslie Howard's prince of melancholy is a midwinter prospect. But Mr. Merivale's revivals have already been dismantled, and the Reinhardt film has turned out to be only a photographer's orgy. Once more it is plain that the best of actors cannot guarantee a Shakespeare "intelligible," as Dryden put it, "to a refined age."

It is no reflection upon the broad farce which the Lunts have improvised to say that "The Taming of the Shrew" is the easiest play of the lot to produce. Although it offers many staging problems it has none of the sweetness of imagination, subtlety of characterization, intellectual significance or grandeur of verse that try the ingenuity of actors who come to grips with the tragedies. "The Taming of the Shrew" seems to have been originally only a stop-gap farce knocked together at about the time Shakespeare was writing "The Merry Wives of Windsor" and just before he went seriously to work upon "Much Ado About Nothing," "As You Like It," and "Twelfth Night." It was frankly adapted from a familiar play of unknown authorship entitled "The Taming of a Shrew" and George Gascoigne's "Supposes." No one knows how much of the farce Shakespeare wrote and how much was scribbled by another hand; but proceeding on the unctuous theory that the best of it is Shakespeare, the pundits have granted him the Petruchio and Katherina plot and cursed his collaborator with the intricate and heavy-footed Bianca embroglio. If "The Taming of the Shrew" has any value in the golden treasury of Shakespeare it is only as proof of the boisterousness of his sense of humor. At this sunny period of his career, when he was an accomplished poet and a talented, spirited writer of plays, he had an appetite for common buffoonery.

The Theatre Guild revival is animated by the same impulse. The actors gambol across the Bianca plot as swiftly as possible, hoping that it will not sober the evening more than necessary; they waste no beauty on lines which, as a matter of fact, are not jewels of dramatic poetry. But, believing in farce and theatre entertainment, they have dusted off all the lumberroom gags that might suit any uproarious occasion and abandoned themselves to horseplay. The midgets impress me as being superfluous: midgets are seldom good actors. But the tumblers and the trick horses are capital material for low skullduggery, and the brisk entrance of the players to the rattle of drums is a trenchant theatre flourish, signifying a good time.

As for Christopher Sly, he has always been a nuisance in "Shrews" that did not dispense with him entirely. But Richard Whorf's befuddled, coarse, snoring, belching, thickwitted neighborhood drunk is a masterpiece of vulgarity, and the direction has made him a more integral part of the perfor-

mance than he is of the play. What Cornell's "Romeo and Juliet" was to romantic tragedy the Lunts' "Taming of the Shrew" is to farce. "And for your reading and writing, let that appear when there is no need of such vanity" [*Much Ado about Nothing*, III. iii. 20-2], Dogberry counseled his watch. There has been plenty of scholarship in the making of the Lunt revival, but it has used books for inspiration rather than instruction. Shakespeare would admire a theatre that could do so much more for his play than he did. Being a busy man, working for the most part under pressure, he did not have time for a circus as versatile as this one. If the "Shrew" is modern it is because the Lunts have made it so.

> Brooks Atkinson, "Bard of Passion and Beauty," in The New York Times, *October 20, 1935, p. 1.*

Edith J. R. Isaacs   (review date November 1935)

[*Isaacs was an American dramatic critic who served as editor of* Theatre Arts *from 1919 to 1945. Her critical essays provided discerning analyses of the stage, and for twenty-five years she exercised significant influence on the American theater as a whole. Isaacs maintains in this excerpt that while the Lunt/Fontanne production of* The Taming of the Shrew *enjoyed marked popular success on its American tour, New York audiences may not be wholly receptive to its boisterous comedy.*]

More than delighted whispers have been coming in for months from the towns in which, last spring, Alfred Lunt and Lynn Fontanne played their gay and rowdy version of *The Taming of the Shrew.* Packed houses, it is reported, greeted them wherever they went, but packed houses might well greet any play that presented the Lunts in good comedy roles. Writing comedy is a difficult enough task in a democratic nation that offers little material for the ordinary basis of social comedy; playing comedy, and playing it with high style, is obviously even more difficult, and the Lunts have earned every whit of the popular favor with which they are received for their accomplishment. So good audiences were only one measure of their success in this Shakespearean venture. Much more important was the report that the audience and the players everywhere had such a good time; the fun and brilliance, the jest and color that moved at top speed across the stage seemed to have infected every auditorium, and what pleasure the players gave to the house came back to them again with more than an echo.

Such things do not happen in New York, not, at least, with the sophisticated subscription audiences at the Theatre Guild. Here, too, this Katherine and Petruchio have earned praise and applause, as well they may. But it is hard to imagine a less cooperative audience. And how long the performers can go on giving their performance in the boisterous, Elizabethan inn-yard vein that is the key-note to their production, before a crowd that has forgotten the circus and probably never knew good vaudeville, remains to be seen. The playing does not need much analysis. If you know the give-and-take method with which Alfred Lunt and Lynn Fontanne play their double-edged comedy, you know how it goes. The production and costumes by Claggett Wilson are a dazzling exaggeration. The settings by Carolyn Hancock are bright and right Italian. Richard Whorf overdoes, deliberately, the already overdone drunk of Christopher Sly. Sydney Greenstreet plays Baptista's oversize, bargaining fatherliness to exactly the right measure. George Meader adds a lovely voice to the good acting of Biondello, and you can both hear and understand most of the other members of the company. William Shakespeare's *The Taming of the Shrew* is as good theatre with Alfred Lunt and Lynn Fontanne as ever it was. (pp. 821-22)

Edith J. R. Isaacs, in a review of "The Taming of the Shrew," in Theatre Arts Monthly, *Vol. XIX, No. 11, November, 1935, pp. 821-22.*

John D. Beaufort   (review date 6 February 1940)

[*Beaufort reviews the Lunts' 1940 revival of* The Taming of the Shrew, *commenting favorably on their portrayals of Petruchio and Katherina, as well as Richard Whorf's Christopher Sly.*]

For Finland, if not for Shakespearean purists, Alfred Lunt and Lynn Fontanne rolled their caravan up to the stage door of the Alvin Theater last night to begin a week of performances in "The Taming of the Shrew." Out ambled a large company of strolling minstrels, mimes, mummers, three acrobats, four midgets, a stuffed cow, a brace or two of stuffed geese, some horses, and a barrel of paraphernalia to astonish even the prankish bard of this spirited piece.

With Herbert Hoover in one box to make a speech of thanks, and Christopher Sly in another to heckle the tardy, the Lunt-Fontanne or "Hellzapoppin" folio went off with a bang to the evident delight of all who were there in tribute to Finland.

It is a boisterous romp. One might well believe Mr. Lunt's assertion, in a curtain speech, that after 33,000 miles of travel, the company is weary but willing. More willing than weary, judging by the wholehearted manner with which each player threw himself into the violent exercises of these comic horrors.

Harry Wagstaff Gribble has given full heed to Mr. Lunt and Miss Fontanne in contriving the broad buffoonery which marks the play's progress—from the preamble involving drunken Christopher Sly to the final flight tableau of Katharine and Petruchio in love's chariot. It is a braw sight.

As Sly, Richard Whorf embellishes the customary Shakespearean text and the conceits of an earlier play with grunts, groans, and other laryngeal explosions. He does everything but fall out of his box and, if the responding laughter gets any more vociferous, I shouldn't be surprised to hear that he has done that, one night.

Mr. and Mrs. Lunt—a fig for all this professional formality!—give just the sort of performance that all their numerous admirers want them to give. The teamwork of "the Lunts" has become a sentimental trademark in theaterdom—they have acted together almost constantly since their marriage in

Lynn Fontanne and Alfred Lunt as Katherina and Petruchio.

1922—and it is no wonder that almost everyone, from romantic Westchester matrons to Broadway denizens, gets a sort of double-barrelled impact from their familiar tricks. It is a familiarity that does not, somehow, breed contempt, and here, of all plays, is one which they may exploit to the full.

Here is Mr. Lunt to inject the occasional and expected hint of guttural into a laugh or a line. Here is Miss Fontanne to make a passage of dialogue her own by a hard, scraping, yet vibrant manner of delivery. Here is a series of exits and entrances and exits which probably only the Lunts could devise and certainly only they could play. And yet this does not even hint at the quality of their joint performance, which, like a passage of program music, does not seem subtle until one attempts to reduce it to print. As Harry and Irene, Elizabeth and Essex, Jupiter and Alcmena, or as Katharine and Petruchio, at least half the fun comes in watching them enact Mr. and Mrs. Alfred Lunt.

It is not strange under the circumstances that the coterie of players who, in some cases, have been in several Lunt-Fontanne successes should behave as a sort of acting family whose little idiosyncrasies have become familiar. For instance, Sydney Greenstreet, an accomplished veteran, can invariably win a laugh by merely drawing in his breath with the sound of a pneumatic dredger. Francis Compton (Gremio) has also become a known and welcome member of the troupe. The work of the entire company is satisfactory, but Philip Bourneuf, Alan Hewitt, Norman Stuart, S. Thomas Gomez, Charles Bowden, William La Massena, and both Harry Be Gar and Don Morrell (the prankish horses) seem to merit individual mention.

John D. Beaufort, "The Lunts and Shakespeare," in The Christian Science Monitor, *February 6, 1940, p. 11.*

Brooks Atkinson   (review date 6 February 1940)

[*Atkinson describes the 1940 Lunt/Fontanne revival of* The Shrew *as "a little milder" than their critically acclaimed 1935 performance, yet as full of vitality.*]

Finland's loss is our gain this week. In support of the Finnish Relief Fund, Alfred Lunt and Lynn Fontanne have brought back their incomparable version of "The Taming of the Shrew," which they acted at the Alvin last evening. More than four years have gone by since this bit of Shakespearean horseplay first convulsed Fifty-second Street in the Guild Theatre just across the way, and almost two years have passed since the Lunts last appeared in New York. Even without "The Shrew" it would cheer up the town to see the Lunts enjoying themselves on a stage again, and with "The Shrew" reunion becomes carnival. For their staging of the familiar farce by Shakespeare is one of the theatre's master works. One week is much too short to have another look at it. Every theatregoer ought to add this production to his memory-book of creative theatre.

Technically, it is a revival. And it would actually be a revival if the Lunts were not calling the tune. One of the most remarkable things about them is the enthusiasm they preserve about their work in the theatre. They are never finished with anything they are doing. And their "Shrew" antic is a case in point. It is not only exuberant in every detail, but a little milder than it was on the memorable evening of Sept. 30, 1935, when it first opened in Gotham and added uproarious-

ness to an ancient farce. Look closely and you may find an idea from "Amphitryon 38" in it now. And how about that dead fish that crossed the stage for a laugh in "The Sea Gull"? Hasn't Mr. Lunt put it into a bird cage now? At any rate, Miss Fontanne and he have raised the curtain with as much eagerness as though they had never staged "The Shrew" before.

For this theatregoer's personal enjoyment they have painted the lily a trifle too gaudily. Like a three-ring circus, which is perhaps the model, it is too full of material, and it begins to lack spontaneity. All the details are worked a little too hard; and the deliberation of the plan begins to show through. But if this is a fault it is on the right side. For the masquing, the vaudeville, the band, the buffoonery, the carnival singing, the acrobatics, the costumes, the candid scenery and Richard Whorf's clowning as Christopher Sly makes a "Taming of the Shrew" that accepts the original Elizabethan plan of trumpery farce and adds to it all the gagging of fond old theatre. It is inspired barnstorming by a troupe of singularly accomplished comedians.

Broad as the general style of fooling may be, there are subtleties enough in the acting. Not everything is bounce and physical mummery. For Mr. Lunt and Miss Fontanne, and also Sydney Greenstreet, who is their most valiant prime minister, can give a line a comic edge by intonation, gleam or expert timing. They are the best actors for classical-farcical and historical-comical occasions. And as usual you will find them surrounded with a company that is worthy of them, and that probably reflects honesty of leadership. Fay Baker, Philip Bourneuf, Byron McGrath, Francis Compton, Alan Hewitt, Norman Stuart, Edith King and the others play like free artists caught up in the merriment of a good time on the stage.

Many thanks to every one concerned for the good-will, skill and high spirits. Among the things Finland has accomplished is a glimpse of two of our most cherished actors in one of their happiest improvisations. For only one week, folks!

Brooks Atkinson, "Lunt's and Fontanne's 'Taming of the Shrew' Comes Back for the Finnish Relief Fund," in The New York Times, *February 6, 1940, p. 17.*

PRODUCTION:

George Devine • Shakespeare Memorial Theatre • 1953 and 1954

BACKGROUND:

Devine initiated a new era in the stage history of *The Taming of the Shrew* by presenting the entire shrew taming sequence as a play within the context of the Christopher Sly story. To accentuate this play-within-a-play structure, Devine framed the play proper by beginning with the Induction from *The Taming of the Shrew* and concluding with the epilogue from *The Taming of a Shrew*—a device subsequently adopted by several other producers of this comedy. This approach allowed Devine to underscore various levels of theatrical illusion and to redefine themes considered unpalatable by modern audiences. Critics esteemed Devine for launching the play in this new direction and for endowing it with an unusually subdued tone. Devine presented it again at Stratford in 1954, when it was described by some critics as the season's best offering. Cast members in the key roles of the 1953 production included Marius Goring as Petruchio, Yvonne Mitchell as Katherina, Michael Warre as Christopher Sly, and Donald Pleasence as Grumio. In the 1954 restaging, Kevin Michell appeared as Petruchio, Barbara Jefford played Kate, and James Grout portrayed Sly.

COMMENTARY:

The Times, London　　(review date 10 June 1953)

[*In this unsigned review, the critic applauds Devine for focusing more on comedy than farce and thus presenting the play with "complete simplicity." The reviewer remarks that Yvonne Mitchell's Kate is shrewish "not by nature but by affection," while Marius Goring's Petruchio is perceptive and good-humored.*]

This piece [*The Taming of the Shrew*] has been so variously interpreted in recent years that producers now may well feel that the tax on their ingenuity has become unbearably onerous. Mr. George Devine uses a rich Renaissance setting but orders the fun with complete simplicity. The pleasant result is to reveal that there is more of comedy and less of farce than is commonly supposed in the young Shakespeare's treatment of the old wife-taming plot that came his way in the ordinary course of play-making.

It is true that Mr. Devine has had to suit his production to a shrew who is not very formidable and to a tamer who is not very fierce; but he has succeeded in making a virtue of the players' lightness. Miss Yvonne Mitchell cleverly presents Katherina as a girl who has not the imagination to see how her overbearing ways strike others. She is a shrew not by nature but by affection, and the proud-minded girl deserves what she gets—a rude awakening by a peremptory wooer. Mr. Marius Goring, with a pleasing show of high spirits, suggests a Petruchio who perceives the good nature of the girl he has undertaken to woo for her money and is resolved to bring it to life by his own methods, which are admittedly eccentric but carried out without a particle of ill-humour.

Katherina's lesson is rough, but it teaches her the truth about herself, and in the light of this interpretation her sermon at the end is indeed the keynote of the whole episode. We see her, then, not as a wife cowed by a brutal husband but as a woman who has been brought by rough and devious ways to a genuine happiness. Thus the comedic values of the piece, primitive though they may be, are preserved, as they seldom are when farce is given the upper hand, and Petruchio is left clinking his glass in appreciative glee at his own triumphant masterfulness.

Mr. Devine has taken great pains with the minor parts, and he and we are rewarded by some admirable little performances. Miss Mary Watson is a lively and characterful Bianca; Mr. Tony Britton is the smoothly humorous wooer in masquerade; Mr. Donald Pleasence is excellent as Petruchio's servant; and from the lips of Mr. Donald Eccles we get the full flavour of Gremio's enraptured description of the wedding kiss coming off with a clamorous smack that the whole church echoed. In short the light acting and the rich

scenery combined to make a delightful evening's entertainment.

A review of "The Taming of the Shrew," in The Times, *London, June 10, 1953, p. 10.*

Antonia White　　(review date 12 June 1953)

[*White characterizes Devine's* Shrew *as a production which "turns a boring play into a spectacle . . . never less than delightful to the eye and, at moments, magical." The scenes which feature Yvonne Mitchell and Marius Goring are remarkable for vitality and dramatic tension, she notes.*]

Few people can be enthusiastic over the *Shrew* as a play. However, like *Much Ado,* it has two famous acting parts and it gives scope to a producer. George Devine uses this scope to the full and by doing so turns a boring play into a spectacle which is never less than delightful to the eye and, at moments, magical. He makes brilliant use of the idiom developed in the days when he, Glen Byam Shaw and Michel St. Denis were responsible for the Old Vic and which goes back to the Compagnie des Quinze and the London Theatre Studio. Not only is this *Commedia dell' Arte* treatment ideally suited to this romping play within a play but Devine manages to give what is little more than a rather brutal farce a lyrical overtone. Vivienne Kernot's settings and costumes are quite exceptionally beautiful. There is a richness and solidity about the décor which is a relief after the flimsiness of so many modern stage sets which made the actors appear so much more substantial than the walls against which they lean. The lighting is admirable; so mellow that at times, with the subdued colour harmonies of the dresses, one seems to be looking at a living Giorgione. At the end, when the bright figures fade like a dream and Sly wakes from his fuddled dream, there is a moment of pure magic.

As a play, the *Shrew* only comes to life when Katharina and Petruchio are on the scene. The amount of life generated by this pair is electrifying and refreshing. Marius Goring's Petruchio is a comic triumph. He is bold and sparkling, lively without being fidgety and full of humorous charm. Yvonne Mitchell looks like a lovely wild Italian gipsy and plays with such fire that one almost believes her to be a real girl of uncontrollable passions. I say "almost" because a real girl would surely have shown more nervous exhaustion after Petruchio's quite authentic torturing, and this Kate hardly changed her key after two sleepless nights. But, in the last act, battered and gay, she was delicious and, in the final speech where the tamed falcon coos like a dove, extraordinarily moving. The tension engendered by this pair, the way they suggest profound attraction underlying surface quarrelling makes one think how admirable they might be as Beatrice and Benedick.

Nearly all the other parts were well played except, to my mind, the sham Lucentio, whose constant facial contortions were not only irritating to watch but seemed to bear no relation to what he was saying or hearing. This was all the more evident because Tony Britton, the real Lucentio, acted so admirably with his face that one was aware of all his feelings and reactions even when he was neither speaking nor being spoken to. Two special commendations should go to Michael Warre's Christopher Sly, which he and the producer had built up into a considerable part by excellent mime, and to Mary Watson's demure minx of a Bianca. (pp. 755-56)

Antonia White, in a review of "The Taming of the Shrew," in The Spectator, *Vol. 190, No. 755, June 12, 1953, pp. 755-56.*

Clifford Leech   (review date October 1953)

[*Leech, an Elizabethan drama scholar and editor, produced numerous studies on the plays of Shakespeare and his contemporaries, including* Shakespeare's Tragedies and Other Studies in Seventeenth Century Drama *(1950),* Shakespeare: The Chronicles *(1962), and* "Twelfth Night" and Shakespearian Comedy *(1965). Here, Leech asserts that Devine's production of* The Taming of the Shrew *was a great success with the audience, who were delighted by the atmosphere of "an Elizabethan jest-book."*]

The readiness of the world to come to Stratford, conferring prosperity without precedent on its Memorial Theatre, has this year made it possible for two Stratford companies to function simultaneously: one, under the direction of Mr. Anthony Quayle, is touring in Australia and New Zealand; the other, under Mr. Glen Byam Shaw, has further strengthened Stratford's hold on its own public. The extension of activity has been accompanied by an increased self-confidence in the presentation of this season's plays. One no longer feels, as one did till quite recently, the straining of every nerve to dazzle and bemuse a gaping audience. Rather, one has the impression that the producer of each play has staged it in accord with his own, not a vaguely fancied public's, taste. (p. 461)

Stratford has come a long way from the Portuguese *Romeo and Juliet,* the Byzantine *Winter's Tale,* the Victorian *Hamlet,* the skilfully trimmed *Measure for Measure* of quite recent years. This does not mean that a producer's legitimate exercise of fancy, within the framework of the play's given world, has been altogether inhibited. In Mr. George Devine's handling of *The Taming of the Shrew,* the *A Shrew* ending was employed and, when Sly had spoken his last words, the strolling players came across the stage, leaving the lord's house and, wearied with their craft, making their way to bed. Sly gazed at them, puzzled and half-guessing, as the curtain came down. The effect was not labored, and it gave to the rough *A Shrew* text a hint of the formal and the human that had its own delight. (p. 462)

The Shrew, set—after the Induction—in the great hall of a lord's house, attempted no romanticizing of Katherina: she was simply a shrew successfully tamed, and the jest was found good: before her final entry Petruchio silently prayed, and the audience was delighted to find that his methods were crowned with success. It was delighted too by the antics of Sly, who was often caught up in the action as he wandered in his interest and excitement from one part of the hall to another. The atmosphere was that of an Elizabethan jest-book, and the playing had a becoming lack of subtlety. Miss Yvonne Mitchell and Mr. Marius Goring took their opportunities with vigour, though perhaps Mr. Goring, when he spoke from the balcony the concluding soliloquy of IV.i, was a shade portentous. That the producer and the actors had difficulty in interesting us in the Bianca-story was hardly their responsibility. (p. 463)

Clifford Leech, "Stratford 1953," in Shakespeare Quarterly, *Vol. IV, No. 4, October, 1953, pp. 461-66.*

T. C. Kemp   (essay date 1954)

[*Kemp was an English dramatic critic, lecturer, and author who wrote for the* Birmingham Post *from 1935 to 1955. A great admirer of Sir Barry Jackson, Kemp explored the eminent director's career in his* Birmingham Repertory Theatre: the Playhouse and the Man *(1944). He also collaborated with J. C. Trewin on a history of the Shakespeare Memorial Theatre entitled* The Stratford Festival *(1953). Here, Kemp offers a favorable review of Devine's production, noting that the director interwove the play's comic and romantic elements with great effectiveness.*]

George Devine's production of *The Taming of the Shrew* took a new way with the old farce. We were kept always informed that we were watching a play within a play, on this occasion in the handsome hall of an Elizabethan mansion, designed by Vivienne Kernot. The towers of Padua were to be glimpsed through the windows, but we were aware that the English alehouse was on the heath just around the corner. Marius Goring took a civilized way with Petruchio. Here was no heavyweight champion battling for a wench, but a fellow of some sensitiveness and perception. He had his own humorous values and his own sense of the dramatic. He gave the impression that Petruchio was watching this taming business with the anxious eye of an artist. When Katharina was unusually rampageous, he had a moment of hovering anxiety lest he should not be able to bring her to heel again. When he had so achieved, he let out his triumph on a fine flow of rolling speech. This was a whimsical trainer teaching his pupil how to behave for her own good. By the time that he and Katharina were on their way back to Padua and that perverse argument about the sun and the moon was being thrashed out, we realized that this couple had fallen deeply in love, and Petruchio's "Kiss me, Kate!" was not so much a command as an invitation. Yvonne Mitchell's Katharina consorted consistently with this particular Petruchio. She was attracted by her would-be trainer, and watched him with sulky feminine interest. When she realized that she was beginning to fall in love with this unpredictable but masterful gallant from Verona, she gave him a smile which promised that the armistice, once signed, would be permanent. By reducing the whipcracking to a minimum and keeping the circus tricks at a reasonable distance from the customary bear-baiting, the producer touched the training quite firmly with romance. This new feeling for the old farce was most agreeable. (pp. 126-27)

T. C. Kemp, "Acting Shakespeare: Modern Tendencies in Playing and Production," in Shakespeare Survey: An Annual Survey of Shakespearian Study and Production, *Vol. 7, 1954, pp. 121-27.*

The Times, London   (review date 2 June 1954)

[*The anonymous critic offers a favorable review of Devine's production, praising Keith Michell's and Barbara Jefford's performances as Petruchio and Katharina.*]

This [*The Taming of the Shrew*] is a production carried over from last year to become the most satisfying thing so far of the present season. It has not been easy this year to pinpoint redeeming features in the work of the young company. Their speaking of verse is plainly inadequate to the needs of the Stratford stage, and necessarily this inadequacy has had the effect of more or less blotting out much acting that in itself was pointful, intelligent, and spirited. Now in a piece that makes but slight poetic demands these hitherto dimly described merits emerge clearly. We get a performance that

Yvonne Mitchell and Marius Goring as Katherina and Petruchio.

deals with the vigorous verse vigorously and is wholly delightful in its buoyant animation.

It was always a good production, and it is rather better served
this time than last. The play needs all the help that a producer
can give it if the wife-taming plot is to be put across to a modern audience as a piece of rough but not unhealthy horseplay. Mr. George Devine makes the judicious use of the anonymous quarto of *The Taming of a Shrew* to cover the central
crudity in as many separate wrappings of illusion as it will
bear. We are never allowed to forget that we are watching a
performance by poor strolling players in the hall of a rich Renaissance house and that they have been commissioned to
play down to the simple credulity of a drunken tinker in such
a way as to amuse the sportive lord from whose idle mind the
jest has sprung.

Mr. Devine manages this double illusion with admirable inventiveness. He is much helped by Mr. William Devlin's silent eloquence as the lord fascinated by the successful working out of his whimsical scheme and also by the restraint with
which Mr. James Grout, as Christopher Sly, dodges about
the fringes of the mimic play. The final wrapping of illusion
is perhaps one too many. It seeks to pass off the whole affair
as something the tinker has dreamed and then introduces figures so like those of the strolling players that the confusion
of the tinker's mind as it wrestles with Pirandellian complexities spreads to our own. Beyond question, however, the

spatchcocking of the two plays gives the play an agreeable
sense of depth.

Mr. Keith Michell, whose Tybalt [in *Romeo and Juliet*] earlier in the season caught the attention with its cat-like intensity, plays Petruchio with a gusto which recalls the late Douglas Fairbanks and with a manner of his own vaguely suggesting that romance is in him consenting to mock itself. Romance insists that Petruchio shall fall in love with Katharina
at first sight and, having thus paid homage to itself, gets fairly
down to business and spares the loved shrew nothing till she
kneels for peace. It is a rapid, bustling, and inspiriting performance. Mr. Michell is well partnered by Miss Barbara Jefford, who wears Spanish dark hair and deepens out of all recognition the affected voice which quite spoiled her Desdemona [in *Othello*]. She is not afraid to be violent in her tantrums,
but is not yet quite happy in her moments of solemn bewilderment. Miss Muriel Pavlow plays Bianca with a complete realization that the artificiality of the young lady's wooing calls
for all possible romantic charm. This she supplies, and is fortunate in her Lucentio who is lightly and gracefully handled
by Mr. Basil Hoskins. Mr. Leo McKern finds room to make
a most pleasing grotesque of Petruchio's servant, and Miss
Rosalind Atkinson is a good hearty ale-wife.

A review of "The Taming of the Shrew," in The
Times, *London, June 2, 1954, p. 2.*

Ivor Brown (review date 6 June 1954)

[*Brown was a British author, dramatic critic, and editor. As a
critic, he regularly contributed to such periodicals as the*
Guardian, Saturday Review, Observer, Sketch, *and* Punch.
His works include Shakespeare in his Time (1960), *Shakespeare and His World* (1964), *and* Shakespeare and the Actors (1970). *In the excerpt below, Brown describes Devine's interpretation of* The Shrew *as "a fantastic dream." Such a perspective, he remarks, allows the director to present a more fanciful characterization of Katherina and Petruchio and to mitigate the play's brutality.*]

George Devine's production of *The Taming of the Shrew*
(Stratford-upon-Avon) effects a double rescue. It saves the
company from any feeling of inferiority that may have been
inflicted on it earlier this year, and it saves the author from
the crudity of the comedy, which is now as little liked as any
in the canon. By ending with Sly awake again and with the
players departing to find another patron or a tavern public,
he gives the piece true pattern. He also creates the impression
of a fantastic dream. Thus the humours of cruelty are mitigat-
ed. Petruchio and Katherina are now figures of fancy, half in
love from the start, he a laughing cavalier, and not only a fortune-hunting bully-boy, and she a flashing beauty whom anybody would love to coax into kindness. Perhaps Shakespeare
did not intend such softening of his tigress-taming act. But
modern taste prefers the story turned to fancy-free. It is also
a great pleasure to have pictorial Shakespeare once again. Vivienne Kernot's set and costumes are not only charming to
look at, but a great aid to the players, which recent essays in
austerity have hardly been. The whole company are seen at
their best. Barbara Jefford is an admirable Katharina, with
a blaze of eloquence as well as of temper; she speaks her closing lines to perfection. Keith Michell is a lightweight
Petruchio, with a disarming smile in a commanding part,
more inclined to crack a jest than a whip. Sometimes the pace
is excessive, and Leo McKern's characteristically amusing
Grumio might give us more chance to hear his lines. I was

never much taken by Bianca until I saw Muriel Pavlow in the part. Those who shrink in apprehension from this play need have no fear. They will be reconciled.

Ivor Brown, "House Full," in The Observer, *June 6, 1954, p. 6.*

Richard David (review date Autumn 1954)

[*David salutes Devine's* Taming of the Shrew *as one of the best productions of the 1954 Stratford season, according particular praise to Barbara Jefford's spirited performance as Katherina.*]

A. E. Housman's test of true poetry was that it brought tears to his eyes and made his hair stand on end. There is, alas, no such simple touchstone of the excellence of a theatrical performance. Even when the effect made is purely a poetical one, it comes to the hearer through a diffracting medium, upon the sounding-board of the personality of the actor, who can magnify the value of a perfectly ordinary piece of writing or mar a passage of genius. In general, however, theatrical effects are seldom simple, even when the extra dimension contributed by the actor has been discounted. There are the visual impressions made by the spectacle, whether purely pictorial or reinforced by the emotional context of the play. There is the satisfaction to be drawn from a dramatic "stroke," be it recognition, reversal, unexpected (or expected) denouement, or mere coup de théâtre, as well as from its shaping and timing by the actors. There is the pleasure given by any manoeuvre well executed or by an adroit piece of teamwork, which may be a matter of acrobatics or Shakespeare's "set of wit well played"; and there is the excited apprehension of the purpose and spirit and artistic shape of the play manifesting itself in bodily form and taking to itself substance and extension as the performance proceeds. In each production, in each performance, different elements may predominate, though it is a poor one to which they do not all contribute some share, reinforcing and counter-pointing each other. Rarely, very rarely, all are present together in full strength, and then the spirit of delight seizes on the spectator and for one evening he is rapt in an ecstasy whose particular elements he cannot analyze or even remember, though the mere thought of the whole, years after, may still produce a Housmanian raising of the hackles.

The Stratford season of 1954 provided no such ecstasies. (p. 385)

The two comedies, one fantastical the other farcical, were both directed by George Devine, who controlled them with a deft skill that kept them gaily spinning from start to finish. Of *A Midsummer Night's Dream* little more need be said. It was slick, it was efficient, it was stream-lined, it kept the audience purring throughout, and never can the four plots that compose the play have seemed neater or more neatly interwoven; but to achieve this slickness poetry and magic had to go by the board. Motley's set was an "arrangement" of chromium plating and neon lights, with a "practicable" burrow for Puck. The lovers were reduced to accomplished puppets. The fairies, bird-feathered and shrill, achieved a superhumanity beyond the range of the conventional butterfly wings, but at the expense of the homeliness that must surely be an ingredient of Shakespeare's faery. The moon that presided over this *Dream* was the moon of science fiction not of Warwickshire. It is true of course that under such a crisp, hard influence some parts of the play can still survive and even flourish. The

clowning of the rude mechanicals could hardly have been bettered, and there was a taking droll of a Puck; but even these might have made a richer and more memorable effect against a more luminous background.

A method unsuited to *A Midsummer Night's Dream* succeeded to admiration with *The Taming of The Shrew*. That the Induction might not be left hanging in the air, as in the normal version of the play, Devine had legitimately imported, from what is now thought to be a "bad quarto" of the play, some further interpositions of Sly and a final scene in which, once more asleep, he is carried back to the tavern steps and wakes to believe the whole adventure a dream. Sly's share in the action was very adroitly managed, largely by means of a most ingenious set designed by Vivienne Kernot. This was in effect the fireplace, staircase, and one panelled wall of an Elizabethan hall, but standing isolated in a wide open space, with a whole clockmaker's shop of pinnacles, balconies, and bell-towers grafted onto it. By focussing on particular parts of the structure, effects of great realism could be produced (for example in the scenes directly concerned with the fooling of Sly). Widen the view, and there plain to see was a pantomime set; widen it again and it took in Padua, Italy, the whole world. The plan recalled Herbert's verse:

> A man who looks on glass,
> On it may stay his eye;
> Or, if he pleases, through it pass,
> And then the heaven espy.

The skill of the director resided in the management of these sudden changes of focus, and in the sleight of hand whereby Sly and his fellows were flitted from one corner of the stage to another, so that their presence was always felt yet was never obtrusive, never cramped the freedom of the inner action. It was a happy touch that made the players at one point allow the gratified Sly a trotting-on part in the play within the play, as one of the horses in Petruchio's cavalcade.

The cast ably supported the director. The teamwork was admirable, the comedians were brisk and to the point, the intriguers set out their plots crisply and clearly. William Devlin added a great deal of plausibility and humanity to the whole by his playing of the Lord who sets on foot and controls the entire action, phrasing his part of the Induction with a natural fluency and grace that provided a model of verse-speaking, while for the rest his benevolent presence in the background, churchwarden pipe in hand, held both the Sly plot and the play within the play together. As Katharina, Barbara Jefford gave a magnificent performance. She shirked nothing of the fieriness—her "Ha!" was terrifying—but from the start she was sympathetic as well; and she managed the startling transition from untameable to tamed with a delicacy and pathos that made it seem almost possible. Though her Petruchio remained more of a stage figure, without Katharina's glow of inner life, Keith Michell nevertheless brought an ample liveliness and windswept vigor to the part, and there was never for a moment any feeling that he was playing second fiddle to Miss Jefford.

The story of the Shrew gains enormously, at least for modern audiences, from its framing in the Sly sub-plot. The double artifice makes palatable not only the creaky humor of Pantaloon and Harlequin and the burlesque of the clowns, but also those scenes, such as Katharina's binding and beating of her sister, or Petruchio's hurling the meat at the servants, which are too roughly Elizabethan for our tastes. And at any moment (such is the flexibility of drama) the play can soar out of its framework, which drops away and is forgotten in the instant. Such a moment was the first meeting of Katharina and Petruchio, Petruchio in swashbuckling pursuit of any wife, so long as she has money, Katharina in a rage against all mankind. They meet—and practically nothing happens. Petruchio falters for a moment in his speech, and continues in a tone even lighter and more outrageous than before. Katharina is suddenly still, like a pointer that checks at game. And there for you, presented with the utmost precision and certainty, the utmost economy of means, is love at first sight.

At the end of the play came another and even more striking instance of this sudden expansion and enrichening of quality. The old gag of the husbands who cannot control their wives is played out, and Katharina proceeds to prescribe to the offending wives the duties they have neglected. It is not in itself a particularly fine speech, though it has kinship to the great "aria" with which Berowne reproves the shamefaced lovers in *Love's Labour's Lost* and requires virtuoso performance. This it received from Miss Jefford; for the first and only time in the season she pulled out all the stops—by which I do not mean any elaborate, or mannered, or sonorous performance, but one employing all the rich variety of tones, perfectly matched to the meaning, that this actress commands. When one had smoothed the prickling hairs back into place, and wiped away the tears, one could only bewail that the season had offered her no other opportunities of this kind. (pp. 392-94)

> Richard David, "Stratford 1954," in Shakespeare Quarterly, *Vol. V, No. 4, Autumn, 1954, pp. 385-94.*

PRODUCTION:

John Barton and Maurice Daniels • Shakespeare Memorial Theatre • 1960 and 1961-62

BACKGROUND:

In his 1960 production of *The Taming of the Shrew*, featuring Peter O'Toole as Petruchio and Peggy Ashcroft as Katherina, Barton employed the play-within-a-play structure developed in the previous decade by George Devine. Barton also took advantage of a recently-installed revolving stage to heighten the production's emphasis on theatrical illusion. Barton designed one side of this stage as the exterior and the other side as the interior of a country inn. As the stage revolved between interior and exterior scenes, it revealed a green-room where players were shown in various stages of preparation. O'Toole received generally favorable reviews from theater critics. Ashcroft confounded critics, who believed her cast against type as Kate, by portraying a memorable shrew. Also in this production, Jack MacGowran appeared as Christopher Sly. Maurice Daniels redirected the presentation in 1961-62, featuring Derek Godfrey and Vanessa Redgrave in the leading roles and Roy Dotrice as Sly.

COMMENTARY:

T. C. Worsley   (review date 22 June 1960)

[*Worsley reports the audience's enthusiastic response to Barton's production and notes that O'Toole and Ashcroft complemented each other well in this "high-spirited, quick-mettled farce."*]

The Taming of the Shrew is always popular with audiences, which is perhaps to say that the emancipation of woman is less complete than we sometimes like to think. Certainly, you might have judged so by the merry applause with which last night's performance was greeted at Stratford. But one thing is certain: that to prove some such point is not the aim. The aim of this well-tried old farce is simply to make us laugh, and judged by that standard, the new Stratford *Shrew* is an undoubted success.

We have seen many ingenious versions of the play at Stratford—we even saw a cowboy one once. But Mr. John Barton returns us to the old fashion. We are under thatched roofs, outside the old inn, and Christopher Sly is drunk across the doorstep. Soon the old trick is played on him: He is dressed as a lord, with his lady beside him, and the players are giving for his special pleasure *The Taming of the Shrew.*

It is the merit of this production—and I, personally, find it a rare merit in this particular play—that very little is tedious. We are perfectly safe of course, with our Katharine and Petruchio. Dame Peggy Ashcroft is not an obvious choice for the Shrew. But a great actress can find some merit in almost any part. Dame Peggy finds enjoyment in this one. She enjoys every moment of her tantrums, of her humiliation, and of her surrender. And what she enjoys we inevitably enjoy, too.

Her style is perhaps something a shade higher than the plain farce going on all around her. But she knows how to match another performance exactly, so that she plays in with Mr. Peter O'Toole perfectly. This young actor is now high on the way up, and he fully justifies the hopes that are held out for him. He has swagger, attack, vivacity. He can seize a scene and spin it round his little finger with a minimum of visible effort. His only possible weakness lies in his voice. He yelps when he means to roar. But training will remedy this. Altogether, these two, she with her perfection of assured technique, he with his fresh and sprightly talent make a fine centre to the play.

For the rest, farce is the order of the day, and a very lively, high-spirited, quick-mettled farce it is. It ranges, from another of Patrick Wymark's slow-talking, moon-faced loons, to Paul Hardwick's excellently judged comic timing as Baptista. It takes in Dinsdale Landen's commedia dell'arte clowning, and Ian Holm's whey-faced mouthing as the ancient Gremio. It includes innumerable pieces of comic invention in the production, and never for one moment lets the audience slip.

The new Stratford revolve was much in evidence, and I found the use made of it not entirely happy. It huddled the action forward into an uncomfortably confined space and made the Stratford stage seem for once too small. The actors could only do their best not to trip over each other and their props. That they overcame this obstacle so well is a tribute to the growing discipline of this immature but talented company.

> T. C. Worsley, in a review of "The Taming of the Shrew," *in* The Financial Times, *June 22, 1960, p. 19.*

can do most things on the stage, but broad and robust farce has not hitherto seemed to be much in her line.

She played the part, however, at the pace and with the simple directness that farce demands and made a considerable personal success. Also, over and above the rough-and-tumble stuff, she contrived to give the shrew a depth of character that is unusual.

She managed to suggest a woman of high spirit who had found it so easy to dominate those about her all her life that she had become a termagant, much as a drug taker becomes an addict. At the bottom of her heart she wanted nothing better than to be mastered in her turn, and her final surrender to Petruchio had about it, therefore, a sense of profound relief—a knowledge that with this man, and with this man alone, she could find the peace of mind that was otherwise beyond her reach.

> W. A. Darlington, " 'Taming of the Shrew' Staged in Britain," in The New York Times, *June 22, 1960, p. 29.*

Peggy Ashcroft and Peter O'Toole as Katherina and Petruchio.

W. A. Darlington   (review date 22 June 1960)

[*An English dramatist and critic, Darlington served as theater critic for the* Daily Telegraph *for several years. He was also the author of such theoretical works as* Through the Fourth Wall (1922) *and* Literature in the Theatre (1925). *Here, Darlington contends that amid rumors of some actors challenging Barton's unusual directoral techniques, the production successfully ran with "speed and certainty." Peggy Ashcroft, the critic remarks, lent an unusual degree of complexity to the role of Kate.*]

When the London drama critics arrived at the Shakespeare Memorial Theatre here tonight to see the opening performance of "The Taming of the Shrew," they found the air full of rumors.

The director of the play, John Barton, is not a professional theatre man but a don from Cambridge University. The story was that his methods of production had been so unusual that some of the leading players had objected to them, with the result that Peter Hall had had to take over the final rehearsals.

Whether these rumors had truth in them or not, Mr. Barton's name appeared in the program as sole director; and the play went over with a speed and certainty that showed that any difficulties there may have been had been successfully smoothed over.

The main interest lay in the appearance of Peggy Ashcroft as Katharine the shrew. She is an accomplished actress who

Kenneth Tynan   (review date 26 June 1960)

[*Tynan was a prolific dramatic critic and author whose reviews appeared over three decades in* The Spectator, The Observer, *and* The New Yorker. *Laurence Olivier appointed Tynan the first literary manager of the British National Theatre in 1963, with which he remained affiliated until 1973. In the following excerpt, Tynan offers high praise for Barton's production, expressing particular appreciation of Ashcroft's performance as Kate, who "confounds prophesy by demonstrating herself ideal for the part."*]

At Stratford-upon-Avon we have a vigorous and thoughtful production of *The Taming of the Shrew*—a more inhuman play, I have always felt, than even "Titus Andronicus," since it argues (as nobody in "Titus" does) that cruelty is good for the victim. Yet one must concede "The Shrew" a certain ghastly candour; having shown us that the basis of marriage is economic rather than romantic, it does not shrink from the corollary—that a wife is essentially a piece of property, and must expect to be treated as such. In Petruchio's words:—

> She is my goods, my chattels: she is my house,
> My household-stuff, my field, my barn,
> My horse, my ox, my ass, my anything.

[III.ii.230-32]

Tenderness and affection are her rewards for good behaviour; she cannot demand them as rights. At heart, the play deals not with the taming of a shrew but with the training of a premature feminist to take her place in Elizabethan bourgeois society.

John Barton's direction is full of wideawake scholarship. Preserving the unities, he restricts the action to the courtyard and snuggery of an inn; it is here that the mummers gather to amuse Christopher Sly. As soon as the Induction is over, Shakespeare abandons his gullible tinker; Mr. Barton keeps him on stage throughout, and justifies his presence by borrowing lines from the non-Shakespearean "Taming of a Shrew," in which Sly staggers off at the end to practise on his wife what Petruchio has preached.

The device works splendidly, "framing" the play as its author never did. Inside the frame there is some lovely, jocular acting by a predominantly youthful company that seems, as

Benson might cricketingly have said, to have no tail. Peter O'Toole plays Petruchio in a vein of snaky, complacent stealth, interspersed by eruptions of infectious music-hall extravagance. Like many of his colleagues, he knows how to alternate flights of rhetoric with sudden comedic descents to the tone of everyday chat.

Peggy Ashcroft, in prospect an impossible Kate, confounds prophecy by demonstrating herself ideal for the part; it was her predecessors who were impossible. This is no striding virago, no Lady Macbeth *manquée;* instead, we have a sulky, loutish girl who has developed into a school bully and a family scold in order to spite Bianca, the pretty younger sister who has displaced her as father's favourite daughter. Her fury is the product of neglect; Petruchio's violence, however extreme, is at least attentive. He cares, though he cares cruelly, and to this she responds, cautiously blossoming until she becomes what he wants her to be. The process is surprisingly touching, and Dame Peggy plays the last scene, in which the rival husbands lay bets on their wives' obedience, with an eager, sensible radiance that almost prompts one to regret the triumph of the suffragette movement.

Kenneth Tynan, "The Economics of Murder," in The Observer, *June 26, 1960, p. 24.*

Eric Keown   (review date 29 June 1960)

[*Keown commends Ashcroft's distinctive portrayal of Katherina in Barton's production of* The Shrew, *reporting that she created "a shrew to strike terror into the hearts of men."*]

In his production of *The Taming of the Shrew* at Stratford John Barton includes passages from the rival play, published in 1594, *The Taming of a Shrew,* to round out the story of Christopher Sly, who now remains to the end. This gives weight to the idea that the play is for his entertainment, and allows him to go off fired by ambition to reform Mrs. Sly. It is doubtful if the experiment is justified, but at any rate in Jack MacGowran Mr. Barton has a Sly worth entertaining, a richly gawping tinker.

This is otherwise a fairly straightforward production, memorable only because Peggy Ashcroft, coming to the play late in her career, makes a shrew to strike terror into the hearts of men. She is not the kind of shrew who, out of perversity, enjoys being trampled on, but a high-powered termagant who pulls no punches. When she arrives *chez* Petruchio she looks as if she had gone a full fifteen rounds with Floyd Patterson, and when her dinner is whipped away it is more than one can bear. The part is alien to her temperament, but she makes it hers by sheer comic skill; and the lectures to the less disciplined ladies at the end she carries off splendidly.

Peter O'Toole, who is this year's most interesting recruit to Shakespeare, is an unashamedly romantic Petruchio, a little mannered perhaps but equipped with the fire and determination needed to bring Dame Peggy's Katharina to heel. Elizabeth Sellars decorates the thin little part of Bianca charmingly. Paul Hardwick gets amusement from the paternal embarrassment of Baptista, who would have plenty to talk about with Lear. I thought Patrick Wymark much funnier as Grumio than Dinsdale Landen was as Biondello. Mr. Landen's was a straight music-hall act; but others were enchanted by it. The pace was good, and Alix Stone's rustic set, an inn one side and an interior the other, seemed to me an intelligent use of the revolving stage.

Eric Keown, *in a review of "The Taming of the Shrew," in* Punch, *Vol. CCXXXIII, No. 6249, June 29, 1960, p. 923.*

J. C. Trewin   (review date 2 July 1960)

[*Trewin is a British dramatic critic, editor, and author whose reviews have appeared in* The Observer, The Illustrated London News, The Sketch, The Birmingham Post, The Listener, *and* The Times Literary Supplement. *In addition, he has written numerous theatrical biographies and dramatic studies, including* The English Theatre (*1948*), Stratford-upon-Avon (*1950*), Mr. Macready: A Nineteenth-Century Tragedian (*1955*), Shakespeare on the English Stage: 1900-1964 (*1964*), Shakespeare's Plays Today (*with Arthur Colby Sprague, 1970*), *and* Peter Brook: A Biography (*1971*). *In the following excerpt, Trewin maintains that although Peggy Ashcroft was plausible in the second half of* The Taming of the Shrew, *it is impossible to conceive of her as a termagant. In Trewin's opinion, the production as a whole lacked the ingredients for success.*]

If I had had to set down quickly a dozen of our leading actresses who might be cast for Katharina, Dame Peggy Ashcroft's name would not have appeared. There is, I agree, no reason why an actress—and especially such an artist as Dame Peggy—should not be cast sometimes against type: indeed, this can often bring the best results. But there are times to pause, and certainly I would have paused before coupling

John Barton's 1960 RSC production. Act V, scene ii.

"Shrew" and "Ashcroft": names quite extraordinarily foreign to each other.

Dame Peggy, as we know well, can freeze the stage as Hedda. To see her as a termagant takes a strong imagination. Still, it is her part in the Stratford-upon-Avon revival of "The Taming of the Shrew," and we arrived at the Shakespeare Memorial Theatre rather in the mind of the man from Sheffield in the famous comedy. "Show me!" he said. We waited for Dame Peggy to show to us Katharina Minola, renowned in Padua for her scolding tongue, a woman "intolerable curst, and shrewd and froward, so beyond all measure" [I.ii.89-90].

She duly appeared, wearing flame-colour, with an auburn wig. Courageously she bit into the part, grappled with Petruchio, wielded a three-legged stool, used a hop-and-a-jump to indicate anger, tried hard to assure us that she was a virago. It was a bold attempt, acting against the grain. But one thing Dame Peggy could not disguise. Although she sought to use Katharina's blistering tones, her voice remained obstinately (and delightfully) Ashcroft: if you closed your eyes the termagant disappeared, and so, quite often, did Shakespeare's play.

The second half was different. Kate the tamed became plausible, the more so because Dame Peggy did not allow the woman to sag into a mere slavish docility. The Kate we saw on the way back from Padua, stroking along the Petruchio she had come to understand, was genuine and recognisable (her querying pause at "so bedazzled with the—sun?" [IV.v.46] had the night's loudest laugh). And we could recognise the Kate who spoke that long and dire speech at the last: for me the straggler among all Shakespearean show-pieces. Here was Dame Peggy in her high authority as an actress. Because we have this aspect of Katharina for much of the second half of the play—something we are inclined to forget—the casting is less capricious than it had seemed.

Still, I cannot believe in Dame Peggy as a termagant. If any member of the first-night audience dropped into the Picture Gallery next day and studied the famous Ada Rehan portrait, blazing from the wall, he would have known at once what was wrong. Now, when we have considered Dame Peggy and observed that Peter O'Toole could summon Petruchio's swagger with appropriate ease (and without a whip)—though he really need not have brought those film-recalling bagpipes—there is little to add. The farce has so often been done so well at Stratford that the latest revival appeared to be over-anxious. We had fragments from the source-play that established the strollers at work before the transiently ennobled tinker—Jack MacGowran as a Sly majestically fuddled—and John Barton, Stratford's assistant director, had clearly tried to aerate the romping. It seemed, for all that, to be oddly dispirited: the Stratford company this year is short of comedians, and at the première nothing much emerged from the manœuvring. Dinsdale Landen was an acrobatic Biondello, but he sacrificed clarity to vigour.

I do remember Ian Richardson's voice as the Nobleman—he continues to be Stratford's one real find this season—Mr. MacGowran's Sly with his air of a fuddled woodpecker, and the way in which Paul Hardwick, the Baptista, would bring out a speech simply by under-stressing it. For the rest, I felt that the evening was doughy: the cake had not risen.

J. C. Trewin, "Out of Order," in The Illustrated London News, *Vol. 237, No. 6309, July 2, 1960, p. 34.*

A. Alvarez   (review date 2 July 1960)

[*Alvarez briefly reviews Barton's production, arguing that it "has all the advantages of pictorial brilliance, an increasingly polished company, and . . . unpedantic scholarship."*]

The Stratford season gets better and better. John Barton's production of *The Taming of the Shrew* has all the advantages of pictorial brilliance, an increasingly polished company, and a little unexpected and unpedantic scholarship. He has used extracts from an earlier, non-Shakespearean version of the play to round off the Christopher Sly episode, which is another of those bits Shakespeare never blotted. The result is not only a superb reconstruction of an Elizabethan production, with every inch of Alix Stone's setting put to use; it also places the play. For *The Shrew* is, by Shakespeare's own standards, a piece of hackwork. By emphasising the play within a play and joke within a joke, Barton sets both the inerter verse and more tedious brutality at a distance. The dead wood becomes an intriguing curiosity and what is lively seems even livelier.

He also has the advantage of Peggy Ashcroft's Shrew. Usually, I find Dame Peggy plagued by a terrible genteelness; whatever the circumstances, she seems to remain both young and nice at heart. But as Katharina her vice has no chance. Instead, it re-emerges as an unexpected tenderness under all the raging, spitting and wonderfully timed awkwardness. The vitality was there—she hopped like a rabbit at the start—but it deepened at every turn into feeling. As Petruchio, Peter O'Toole spat and shouted perhaps a little too fiercely at times, making his physical panache seem dangerously like coarseness. But for the most part, he matched Dame Peggy depth for depth. One can't ask more. Jack MacGowran gave a beautifully attentive performance as Sly and Dinsdale Landen slid and leaped with a vengeance. (pp. 14-15)

A. Alvarez, "Waste Land Revisited," in New Statesman, *Vol. LX, No. 1529, July 2, 1960, pp. 14-15.*

Alan Brien   (review date 15 July 1960)

[*Brien offers a generally favorable review of Barton's production. Among the show's few weaknesses, he declares, was Peter O'Toole's voice, which "had the curiously hollow, sawn-off deadness of an old record played through a tin horn."*]

The Taming of the Shrew . . . engagingly and effectively mixes scholarship with slapstick. [In this production,] the audience has been considered before the text and rightly so. There is a lot of sliding down stairs on bottoms, staggering on the edge of balconies, and show-off leaps over recumbent colleagues. None of this is anywhere indicated in the play (which also advantageously incorporates scenes from an earlier non-Shakespearian version), but equally none of it contradicts the sense or the mood of what is after all pretty much of a competent pot-boiler. The director, John Barton, has brilliantly utilised the revolving stage and the rabbit-hutch set to give us glimpses of the strolling players conning lines and changing costumes in their behind-scenes tiring-room.

To judge from some reviews, no critic has ever even heard of a masochistic wife with a cock-of-the-walk husband—as if every marriage today were based on the principles of Ibsenite idealism. *The Taming of the Shrew* is not so old-fashioned and brutally outmoded as it is often pictured. Mr. Barton was right to persuade Peggy Ashcroft to play Kate as an unhappy man-hater who yearned to be slapped down into yielding domesticity without any winks or nudges to a modern audience. She began a little too hoppity-jumpity, like a stiff marionette, but soon settled in a smooth, irresistible flowing performance, glittering with intelligent insights. Peter O'Toole looked and reared like the right stallion to tame such a sulky nightmare of a bedfellow, but his voice had the curiously hollow, sawn-off deadness of an old record played through a tin horn. It was almost as if his much-publicised nose bob had removed the resonant sounding board which vibrated through *The Long and the Short and the Tall.* Apart from giving Sly a twelve-year-old child as a wife, John Barton has moved with extraordinary sureness and confidence through the often tedious tomfoolery of the play and the supporting roles are all played with this company's usual vigour and gusto.

Alan Brien, "Obstacle Courses," in The Spectator, *Vol. 205, No. 6890, July 15, 1960, p. 101.*

Lisa Gordon Smith   (review date August 1960)

[*Smith contends that while Barton's production was commendable, his use of the revolving stage created a distraction that at times resembled "Piccadilly Circus in the rush hour."*]

It is a well known theatrical fact that ninety-nine producers out of every hundred, when faced with something "new" in the way of stage equipment, will be unable to resist the temptation to exploit it instead of using it.

John Barton is one of the ninety-nine, even though in many ways a commendable one, in respect of his reaction to the newly installed revolve at Stratford. After the first few whirls I began to recall childhood memories of accepting challenges to see how many rides I could take on the merry-go-round without turning green.

As for the actors, it really did take all the running they could do to stay in the same place, for some of them had the additional hazard of having to rush up and down stairs as well as round and round in order to finish up where they began—before our very eyes. It was all very gay and amusing and afforded some pleasant glimpses of the actors in the play-within-the-play swigging ale between scenes; but did at times bear some resemblance to Piccadilly Circus in the rush hour.

Katharina is not one of Peggy Ashcroft's best roles. Her temper in the early scenes does not entirely convince, but even less so does her conversion, which has very much the flavour of being a put-up job. If one did not know the play, it would lead one to expect some kind of *volte face* which would finally turn the tables on Petruchio.

Peter O'Toole is a splendidly swashbuckling shrew-tamer with an expansively grand manner which it is a pleasure to watch, and there is splendid playing from Jack MacGowran as Christopher Sly.

Dinsdale Landen is memorably funny in the broad comedy role of Biondello and James Bree equally memorable in the more subtle and intriguing part of the plotting Tranio, adding to the pleasures of the evening with beautifully expressive timing and gesture.

Elizabeth Sellars made Bianca so smug a miss that one's sympathies were entirely with her sister in the hair-pulling scenes and I was sorry that the potentially comic scenes between her rival lovers were played down to the minimum. (p. 23)

Lisa Gordon Smith, in a review of "The Taming of the Shrew," in Plays and Players, *Vol. 7, No. 11, August, 1960, pp. 23, 31.*

Robert Speaight   (review date Autumn 1960)

[*Speaight was a British actor, author, and lecturer. He began his career on the stage playing leading Shakespearean roles at the Old Vic. Speaight wrote several dramatic studies, including* William Poel and the Elizabethan Revival (*1954*), Nature in Shakespearean Tragedy (*1956*), The Christian Theatre (*1960*), Shakespeare on the Stage: An Illustrated History of Shakespearian Performance (*1973*), *and* Shakespeare: The Man and His Achievements (*1977*). *In addition, he was the British dramatic critic for* Shakespeare Quarterly *during the 1960s and early '70s. Here, Speaight comments favorably on Barton's production of* The Shrew, *praising its honest adherence to Shakespeare's text.*]

The Taming of the Shrew is a play that I have always cordially disliked; but I should have remembered that there was a time when I even turned up my nose at *Much Ado,* until Mr. Douglas Seale's production revealed it to me at Stratford two years ago. It is in this sense that Mr. Barker's production of *The Shrew* was a revelation. It had, for me, the character of finality. An older and almost forgotten England relived before one's eyes. Social and moral values, long since discarded; humours that hardly survived outside the Music Hall; a tradition of genial and unsentimental caricature—all this was in the air as one left the theatre. When at last I retired to bed, I could not sleep for thinking of it; and I am thinking of it still.

I say "English" advisedly, because attempts are constantly being made to turn the play into an Italianate Harlequinade. "Commedia dell' Arte" are three words that spring easily to the lips of clever young producers who wince at boot and saddle. Now the first merit of Mr. Barker's production is not its inventiveness, which is unfailing, but its honesty, which is absolute. If you cannot look a play of Shakespeare's in the eye, you had much better not look at it at all. This is the Shrew that Shakespeare drew, tracing its pedigree right down from Chaucer and Langland, and from the carvings that a curious eye may discover on the choir-stalls of an English, or a French, cathedral. For the assumptions which lie behind *The Taming of the Shrew* were still common to all Europe; we find them in Villon and Rabelais, as well as in Ben Jonson, just as we catch their later echoes in Molière rather than in Congreve.

Nothing is more universal than an inn—unless it be a church; and the inn which Miss Alix Stone had designed for Mr. Barker suggested all the difference between an inn and a community center—and that is all the difference in the world. Having decided to use his revolve, Mr. Barker did not overdo the trick. Two faces to one set, not too frequently changing, were enough. But of course the best of inns is nothing without actors at the bar. Here Dame Peggy Ashcroft and Mr. Peter O'Toole—Stratford's latest discovery—had seen straight to the heart of the question. If the *Shrew* is to succeed, it is essential that we should like Petruchio and Katherine, and that they should be seen to like each other. It is not easy to dislike Dame Peggy, even when she is cudgelling her sister, and she made it clear to us, in a flash of fine acting, that she had fallen in love with Petruchio at first sight. There is tenderness and humor underneath these tantrums and this tyranny, a certain Shakespearian delicacy, which the exigencies of farce had not been able to dispel and which these two performances marvellously disclosed. I have seen nothing in the theatre more spontaneous and yet more accurately judged than the scenes which Dame Peggy and Mr. O'Toole play together. Time and again the rhythm hit one in the pit of the stomach—which is where all good acting should hit one, unless it is to hit one in the pupil of the eye.

Round these two a number of excellent performances clustered; but there remained the problem of Sly. Some producers dislike Sly so much that they cut him out altogether; this has actually been done at Stratford. Others have him acted for considerably more than he is worth. But Mr. Barton and Mr. MacGowran tactfully fade him in and out. He is very much there at the beginning, and rather touchingly so at the end. The play is over; the actors have changed and are off to their next one-night stand; and Mr. MacGowran wanders in their wake, ruminating about his wife in Sligo. This was magnificent, though it was not Shakespeare; the perfect end to an irreproachable evening. (pp. 446-47)

> *Robert Speaight, "The 1960 Season at Stratford-upon-Avon," in* Shakespeare Quarterly, *Vol. XI, No. 4, Autumn, 1960, pp. 445-53.*

Gareth Lloyd Evans   (review date 1961)

[*Evans notes that although the players in Barton's production of* The Taming of the Shrew *gave solid performances, the presentation itself had "the certain rashness of inexperience."*]

John Barton's production of *The Taming of the Shrew* had . . . very much the quality of farcical entr'acte. The symmetry which he gains by grafting on Shakespeare's text parts of the anonymous *Taming of A Shrew,* enabling him to keep Christopher Sly in the action throughout, is marred somewhat by a restlessness and illogicality of action created by the use of the revolve. The Tinker is constantly looking for the play. Moreover, in a play rather slavishly Italian in atmosphere and reference, the desiccated Dürer set strikes oddly at first. But Barton clings to the notion that farce must thumb the nose at expectation, and in general the production's self-conscious bubbling deviousness is acceptable. Hortensio is stiff-upper-lip English, Biondello an acrobat-grotesque, Petruchio flashingly Italian, Grumio, Northern Music Hall, and Bianca pussyfooting from a French finishing school. The architecture of the play's surrounds is clever undergraduate review—the Marlowe Society with its hair down. But the production jumps beyond the cul-de-sac of farce in the acting of Peggy Ashcroft and Peter O'Toole. One wondered if her limpid brilliance had enough coquettish rage, and if her patient maturity would suit with O'Toole's crackling youth. The result is unusual and wonderfully successful. Together they create a balance of forces. Both are tamers and both are tamed. Petruchio's fire and fury has moments of gentleness, Kate's stamping anger has moments of surprised awe. The keynote is wild respect growing into immense love, and, in the end, there is an insistent sense of two witty collaborators in a game the result of which is unbreakable devotion. These performances, together with that of Ian Holm—a fuddy-duddy Gremio, and Paul Hardwick—a virile Lord Baptista—are perhaps wiser than the production which, for all its comedy, has the certain rashness of inexperience. (pp. 164-66)

> *Gareth Lloyd Evans, "Shakespeare Memorial The-*

atre, 1960," in International Theatre Annual, *No. 5, 1961, pp. 154-69.*

Richard Findlater   (review date 14 September 1961)

[*Findlater criticizes Daniels's production for its artificial imposition of Sly between the audience and the play and its "alarming addiction to crude knockabout." One redeeming virtue of the presentation, Findlater asserts, was the team of Vanessa Redgrave and Derek Godfrey.*]

Not content with Shakespeare, this Stratford version—first launched by the Avon last year and now redirected by Maurice Daniels—includes extracts from an anonymous "shrew" play of 1594, in order to bolster the importance of Christopher Sly.

Throughout the story of Kate and Petruchio, the drunken tinker and others are there on the stage, intrusively and insulatingly, as an audience in front of an audience. In theory, this alienation effect gives the director a good excuse for exaggerated theatricalism, by insisting on the rather perfunctory Shakespearian fact that the play within a play is performed by visiting barnstormers. It also is intended, no doubt, to make up for the unfunniness of the text by squeezing comic business out of Sly's interruptions. And it provides a neater frame into which the shrew's tale can be fitted with the help of some pretty and ingenious stage pictures.

Yet, on balance, I disapprove. It is not that *The Taming of the Shrew,* heaven knows, is beyond improvement; but rather that by interposing Sly between the actors and the public the

Peggy Ashcroft as Katherina.

whole play is distanced in the wrong way, and a kind of arty, gimmicky, desperately self-conscious staginess is fostered.

This production, indeed, in one respect, shows the worst side of the recent Stratford record: that alarming addiction to crude knockabout which, every now and then, convulses the Royal Shakespeare Theatre company in both Stratford and London. Here there is a prodigious amount of falling down, jumping about, wheezing, tittering, bottom-kicking, face-slapping, served up—for the most part—with a carefully plotted precision which lacks the oil of true farce-playing, and which is painfully, yawningly, *joyless*. The text is gabbled at a terrific lick, and I found Grumio, for one, almost completely inaudible.

Still, this *Taming of the Shrew* also shows Stratford at its best. Visually, it is a delight, with Alix Stone's costumes, beautifully harmonising autumnal red, brown, buff and orange, lit by John Wyckham.

That often treacherous revolve comes into its own, for once most apt and valuable, swinging round Miss Stone's excellent two-faced set and the players with it in a swirling theatrical rhythm, where machinery somehow helps to catch a kind of playfulness which eludes some of the actors.

What's more, the play is buttressed by some of the Royal Shakespeare Theatre Company's sturdiest talents. In spite of the laboured comic drill of the production, such artistes as Patrick Wymark (Baptista), Clive Swift (Grumio) and Peter Jeffrey (Lucentio) give their puppets a distinctive life. And, in all, the movement of the play—if not its speaking—gains notably from the fact that its cast are accustomed to working together as a team.

Most important of all, however, is the couple at the heart of the play—the shrew and her tamer. Everything else fades into insignificance if these loving enemies are played with the right kind of blaze and humour and compassion. That is how they were played at Stratford in 1960 by Dame Peggy Ashcroft and Peter O'Toole, and that is how they were played last night at the Aldwych—in a very different way—by Vanessa Redgrave and Derek Godfrey.

As Petruchio, Mr. Godfrey can deploy to the full—with subtle and irresistible effect—that brand of self-amused irony which, in other roles, has sometimes seemed awry. He is enjoying the joke, and we enjoy it with him—because (unlike some of his hapless colleagues) he is not required to *force* us into enjoying it; because its fundamental brutality is camouflaged, by the conspiracy of sympathy between this Petruchio and his Kate; because he is a real person, not just an exercise in swaggering panache.

This means, of course, that Petruchio's character has been partly sentimentalised in the production—as in the final scene where, commanding Kate to come before him as an example to the other men's wives, he is shown as gripped by fear that she will disobey at the last. Such pangs of self-doubt are scarcely warranted by the Petruchian text.

In Miss Redgrave's Kate, moreover, there is too much sweetness from the start. She is, rather too obviously, *playing* at being a bad-tempered girl and enjoying her reputation as a virago. Petruchio's conquest is immediate, at the first glance, and so his final victory is all the smaller for being postponed so long after her initial surrender. Miss Redgrave is a little stilted in both speech and movement. But this stiffness, I am

sure, will disappear as the play wears into the repertoire; and for the rest, who cares?

Vanessa Redgrave has the rare theatrical benison of being able to touch the heart with a kind of happy grace, a lyrical tenderness, a kindling sincerity that is among the main pleasures of my playgoing in recent years. Kate does not, as I had hoped, noticeably extend her range. But in this role she shows again what a skillful and sensitive artist she is. There was some doubt about how the aggressive theatricalism of this production could accommodate her kind of realism. Could such sincerity survive such style? Miss Redgrave has solved this problem in her own way, which is the way of any good artist. She gives Kate all the life she can bring to her, and that is a great deal. Enough, in fact, to make it worth sitting through all those terribly unfunny jokes two or three times, just to see her.

Richard Findlater, in a review of "The Taming of the Shrew," in The Financial Times, *September 14, 1961, p. 16.*

Tom Milne   (review date 21 September 1961)

[*Milne asserts that with the exception of the well-acted Katherina and Petruchio scenes, Daniels's production was lackluster and contained "acres of mild tedium."*]

One of the more unwarranted assumptions about that mythical beast, the National Theatre, is that we are likely to find anything to put in it, apart from disconnected flashes of acting talent.

Britain, of course, has always been the true home of the cult of the Great Actor. At the turn of the century, when such men as Stanislavsky, Antoine, Appit, Craig, Copeau and Reinhardt were laying the basis for the conception of the modern theatre as a fusion of play, acting and design under the creative control of one single man (the director), Britain was mainly in absentia. Gordon Craig found so little use made of his ideas that he left the country, just as Granville Barker later gave up working in the theatre. The British theatre has come round a little, especially in modern plays, but still remains divided in its loyalties. Given a classical play, where stars can be let loose, it tends to let the play go hang in order to let the audience thrill to Great Acting. (It took an Italian, Zeffirelli, to show what could be done with *Romeo and Juliet* by treating it as a play, rather than as an excuse for the acting of the leading parts.)

This week, two of the heirs presumptive (or, at least, pretenders) to the National Theatre throne are on show with the sort of thing which one may not unreasonably expect to find on the bills of our future pride and glory: The Royal Shakespeare Company with *The Taming of the Shrew* (at the Aldwych), and the Old Vic with *Dr Faustus*. Neither play is self-sufficient, in that each has a number of viable scenes, linked by acres of mild tedium which cry out for the shaping hand of a director willing and able to impose order on the play as a whole. Both plays are left to fend for themselves, and understandably founder.

The Taming of the Shrew ('Re-directed by Maurice Daniels from the 1960 Stratford-upon-Avon production') starts with the inestimable advantage of having Vanessa Redgrave's luminous Katharina on which to build. The part does not offer much opportunity for building a three-dimensional character, but she seizes every chance. In her first scene with her father, for example, she clearly indicates that her shrewish temper is simply a defence against the crushing boredom of her pedestrian family. We have at once the sketch of a passionate creature as yet unawakened, and her look of rapturous delight when she is carried off by Petruchio shows he really is the knight in shining armour that she needs.

This Kate is well-matched by Derek Godfrey's witty and urbane Petruchio, who has exactly the right romantic power to awaken such a girl. The feeling sparked off between the couple is deep and true, and as the horseplay in their scenes is kept to a minimum, we can concentrate, through the light banter, on the growth of their love up to Kate's final declaration of obedience. The delicious touch of irony which Vanessa Redgrave adds to this speech amplifies the suggestion that she submits to Petruchio, not because woman must submit to man as her natural master, but because she loves him.

Outside the Katharina-Petruchio scenes, however, the production falters. With a more-or-less realistic love affair, the *commedia dell'arte* leaping and frothing of the minor characters is merely embarrassing, as though they came from another world entirely. It is high time that certain comic short-cuts used in the classics were listed and formally banned: these would include ancient lovers so staggery that they cannot keep upright, servants who prance and wildly wave their limbs, eyebrows raised in constant surprise, bottom kicking, and falling over. Even the best of the supporters, Patrick Wymark as Baptista and Ian Holm as Gremio (an ancient lover), have a strained note. Is it really so difficult to produce this play either with Kate and Petruchio as *commedia* characters, or the minor characters as human beings? (p. 1564)

> Tom Milne, "The Taming of the Director," in Time
> & Tide, Vol. 42, No. 38, September 21, 1961, pp.
> 1564, 1566.

V. S. Pritchett   (review date 22 September 1961)

[*Pritchett is a highly esteemed English novelist, short story writer, and critic. In the excerpt below, he argues that although Daniels's production was overburdened with unnecessary stage business, the players' solid performances saved the presentation.*]

There is far too much old Aldwych knock-about and a plethora of 'business' in Maurice Daniels' new version of last year's Stratford production of *The Taming of the Shrew*, now at the new Aldwych. But it has spirit. And the cast must certainly be congratulated on one achievement: if anything is thrown at them as they rush about the stage they catch it brilliantly—and quite a lot is thrown. Something had to be done with a hack play that does not hang together, has no clear intention and goes on 40 minutes too long; and the producer correctly saw that he had to give every action a wit of its own. The character of Katharina is so vaguely sketched that it gives a lot of freedom to the actress. Vanessa Redgrave takes it that Katharina is a beastly, obstreperous schoolgirl who is astonished by love at the first sight of Petruchio and fights, tooth and nail, yet with a palpable pleasure in the certainty of surrender, against the humiliation to her pride. This reduces the drama of her situation, but increases its piquancy; and, at the end, we have the pleasant impression that now the snarling prefect has been exorcised, the proud woman will carry on with an enemy worthy of her mettle and her tenderness, and with subtler weapons. Vanessa Redgrave has a

Vanessa Redgrave as Katherina and Derek Godfrey as Petruchio.

naive, bounding, headlong loveliness marred only when her occasional grins of contentment during the horseplay get a shade broad; but in the final kneeling scene she was dignified and moving—the timing was very fine and she visibly grew into a woman. Derek Godfrey's Petruchio had an easy vitality which must have helped enormously.

The whole cast was neatly characterised, and Roy Dotrice as Christopher Sly, Shakespeare's notion of a mass-viewer out of his depth, was very sharp. The play may be a mess but this, I suspect, is because Shakespeare was given two or three old scripts and was told to run them together, give them a bit of class but keep them commercial. The real shrew in the play is not Katharina but the widow whom the wretched Baptista has to marry. Untamable, I would say.

> V. S. Pritchett, "Old Aldwych," in New Statesman,
> Vol. LXII, No. 1593, September 22, 1961, p. 400.

Bamber Gascoigne   (review date 22 September 1961)

[*Gascoigne argues that Daniels overemphasized the concept of a play-within-the-play approach to* The Shrew. *In his effort to present the action at a level appealing to Sly's simple sense of humor, Gascoigne maintains, Daniels added unnecessary slapstick comedy to the production, thus making it unbearable for a discriminating audience.*]

The date of *The Taming of the Shrew* is unknown, but it is probably later than 1594, the year in which another author's play called *The Taming of a Shrew* was printed. This play, which Shakespeare perhaps rewrote and enlarged a year or two later, made much more use of Christopher Sly, the tinker whom a nobleman finds in a drunken stupor and dresses up as a rich lord, and for whom the company of strolling players perform the comedy of the shrew. In Shakespeare's version Sly interrupts the comedy only once, after the first scene. He is already nodding off, and his one critical comment when he is nudged awake is: "Tis a very excellent piece of work; would 'twere done" [I.i.253-54]. He presumably sleeps from then on; we hear no more of him, whereas in the 1594 play he had interrupted throughout the evening and had gone home at the end, dressed once again in his rags, determined to set about taming his own shrewish wife.

The Aldwych production, redirected by Maurice Daniels from last year's Stratford production with Peggy Ashcroft, takes all these interruptions by Christopher Sly and fits them into Shakespeare's text. The grafting gives several excellent moments—as when Sly, using his new lordly power to rectify an old tinker's grudge, prevents the arrest of two characters with a cry of 'I say we'll have no sending to prison'—but the good moments are outweighed by two severe disadvantages. The first is that it is difficult to provide a large enough stage audience to watch the play with Sly. For most of this production Sly and his 'lady'—a male servant hastily decked out in dress and wig—sit by themselves at the side of the stage. In their lonely vigil they seem more like bird-watchers than playgoers.

The second disadvantage is much more serious. The play-within-a-play convention has tempted Mr. Daniels to direct the comedy of the shrew in a style that will appeal to the oafish Sly. This means the most mechanical type of knockabout farce. When doors are opened, the people coming in and the people going out bump heads neatly in the middle. A clown, faced with a long speech about Petruchio's arrival, gabbles it incomprehensibly, but his capers while doing so are nothing short of regimental; and when he has breathlessly reached the end he reclines on the ground, one, two, three, takes a carrot from his pocket and starts eating it. Actors are reduced by such antics to comic robots who, miraculously, can form almost articulate words. Never mind the sense; the wonder is that they can speak at all.

The Taming of the Shrew, indeed, takes its place as a brave new advance in the Stratford company's assault on the spoken word. After seeing Peter Hall's recent productions one can only conclude that his regime actually shares Christopher Sly's taste in theatre, his preference for 'a Christmas gambold or a tumbling trick' [Ind.ii.138]. For, after all, the idea of playing to please Christopher Sly can't even claim any antiquarian authenticity, any element of 'this is how it must have been in Shakespeare's time.' Sly's solitary interruption at the end of the first scene makes it quite plain that he found Shakespeare's comedy a most infernal bore.

The only relief from all the grunting and grinning comes in the encounters between Petruchio and Kate. Derek Godfrey is astoundingly versatile. He can blow rich notes from a most improbable-looking horn or piercing whistles through his fingers; he can accompany himself pleasingly on a lute; he can strut about like a turkey-cock; and besides all this he can act. Petruchio's confident arrogance may give an actor an almost sure-fire role, but there is plenty in this production to put a less good one off his aim.

The part of Kate is more problematical. She tends to seem either exaggerated before her taming or tepid after it. Vanessa

Redgrave's Kate, a most magnificent beast with a great pile of red hair, errs if anything in the first direction—I would have welcomed a hint that there was something besides natural viciousness in her cruelty to her sister—but she comes completely into her own in the later scenes. This is a creature who has been well worth the taming, and she complies with Petruchio's idiocies about the sun and moon not abjectly but with a smile: she has for the first time found a relationship with a human being and she is prepared to humour the man's foibles. So her final speech about the role of wives becomes a private exultation between Petruchio and herself, instead of just a sickening homily on obedience. Before closing this short but rich list of credits, Roy Dotrice's racy performance as Christopher Sly must be mentioned. And Alix Stone's set has a certain Hansel and Gretel charm.

Bamber Gascoigne, "Tinker's Fuss," in The Spectator, Vol. 207, No. 6952, September 22, 1961, p. 387.

Caryl Brahms   (review date November 1961)

[Brahms maintains that Daniels's revival of Barton's Taming of the Shrew lacked the theatrical magic of the original production. The critic also expresses a strong preference for O'Toole's Petruchio over Godfrey's.]

In the matter of professional playgoing, like George Bernard Shaw, I have never flinched from martyrdom. And again like G.B.S., by far the heaviest demand ever made upon me by the public weal is that of devoting my nights to the theatre and my days to writing about it—particularly of late, when I have been limping through thrusting foyersful in the rehabilitation stage, post-operation. If, as Shaw puts it, I had known how exceedingly trying this experience would be, I am not sure that I would not have seen the public weal further!

No amelioration was to be found in the Stratford-cum-Aldwych gallery either, where Mr. Peter Hall flung Miss Vanessa Redgrave into the breach caused by the departure of Madame Leslie Caron. It was unfair to our next Dame Sybil, eager as she is from the triumph that her Stratford Rosalind [in As You Like It] has been, to sling her on in a part which Dame Peggy has made her own with a Petruchio less resilient—to say the very least—than Mr. Peter O'Toole in the part, in a production "redirected" from that of 1960.

"Where is the life I used to live" sang Petruchio in Mr. Derek Godfrey's careful baritone, to which I thought I heard Shakespeare's voice replying from the Shades "Where is the magic we used to make?"

Mr. Maurice Daniels's reproduction goes tumbling after the John Barton-Peter Hall lightning tempo which brought stroke after stroke of brilliant staging in its desperate wake never quite catching up with it, while his cast goes tumbling and mumbling after him, and Miss Alix Stone's admirable and capacious set keeps right on turning round. Indeed, not the least of many sadnesses was the way that Mr. Ian Holm (Gremio) in particular—because one expects so much of him—mugged and wumped and fell about—true his audience fell about too, in another sense; equally it is a clown's job to make his audience laugh. And with Mr. Holm in the lead there followed a train of ancients and their retainers all mugging, all wumping, all snatching at something—anything to be funny with—coercing instead of coaxing our laughter from us; daring us not to laugh, and to be fair, reaping our laughter time and time again.

The difference, perhaps—or one of the differences—between the good actor and the great actor is that your great actor can so take over a part that it is impossible ever to see some other player in the part without thinking of him. Mr. O'Toole is a great—I do not use the word lightly—Petruchio. Writing of his performance in another place I find that I said:

> What in particular has the Stratford *Taming of The Shrew* to send the heart home singing? It has a great actor, out of the oven but not yet out of the mould—it has Peter O'Toole's Petruchio.

It was a mould that must have been hard put to it to contain the heady yeast of Mr. O'Toole's rebellious personality.

> But that from the restraint Mr. O'Toole has forced himself to endure, there will emerge a master is no longer in question. A master? A Macbeth. A Lear . . . from a splay-tongued, loose-limbed lumbering and rebellious jig-saw of a man we suddenly found Mr. O'Toole all in one piece and a considerable technician.

In other words an untidy-seeming genius had reached out into history to make a part his own.

Does Mr. Derek Godfrey reach out into history? No. For one thing he is too smooth; too careful. But we must not fall into the trap of blaming Actor A because he is not Actor B, so let us examine what Mr. Godfrey does in fact bring to his Petruchio. Mr. Godfrey is something of a surprise packet in that he is always so much better than I had expected him to be—the other side of the coin, therefore, to Miss Redgrave of whom one's hopes are so high that from time to time it is inevitable that they should come a cropper with her. Mr. Godfrey on the other hand contrives to be wittier, warmer, more technically complete, more robust and with greater variety than I had foreseen. All these qualities he brings to his Petruchio without for a moment blotting out the role's true owner.

Dame Peggy Ashcroft, like Dame Edith Evans, does not defy age so much as appear to detach herself from that catastrophe. With Vanessa Redgrave it is not so. We are at all times conscious of her youthfulness in a way that we are not conscious with your routine ingenue. Youth is Miss Redgrave's most golden stock-in-trade. It is for this golden youthfulness that we must love her—and for her serious intent and courage. Courageous it was for an actress so young to have a bash at the Shrew, and a bash is exactly what she gave us. No doubt that she is a brave one. But there is more than swing and swagger in Katharina—there is an eyebrow—the raised eyebrow of irony—the eyebrow that recognises that there is a twist about the taming of the Shrew—that the hand extended on the ground to do Petruchio ease at one moment is capable of swinging up and catching him one across the ear, the next. This our mild honeygirl, Miss Redgrave, misses completely. And it is only one of many things that are lacking from her Shrew—shrewishness among them. A tomboy, yes. A Kate of Kate Hall, no. And this is not her fault but rather her willingness to try her luck too far, too soon (or Mr. Hall's audacity for her) which is to blame.

In the matter of playgoing, as we agreed at the beginning, I have never flinched. But I went back to the *Shrew* in search at least of some of the magic I have met with in this patchwork piece. Leaving the Aldwych the other night I overheard a scrap of conversation. "Well," said a young woman, pushing me off the pavement in her rush to get away, "It's better than school was, anyway!" A thought that both Mr. Hall and the present writer may well examine. (p. 15)

> *Caryl Brahms, in a review of "The Taming of the Shrew," in* Plays and Players, *Vol. 9, No. 2, November, 1961, pp. 14-15.*

The Times, London   (review date 24 April 1962)

[*The anonymous critic comments on the success of Daniels's production, noting that* The Shrew *is an excellent vehicle for developing an acting company's cohesiveness. The critic especially praises the commanding performances of Godfrey and Redgrave.*]

By including this play in the programme for yet another season Mr. Peter Hall is showing it a favour that its content is not interesting enough to justify. The choice becomes explicable when one perceives how well *The Taming of the Shrew* suits a director's purposes, if his aim is to establish a company having a style of its own.

The play does so for the reason that it is, when regarded as a whole, a play about acting. The story of Baptista's two daughters and their suitors is in itself a performance given, as we do not need reminding, by a company of strolling players whom a Lord, for reasons of his own, that is for the mystification of his drunken guest Christopher Sly, employs for the evening. They have to sell the story to the Lord and his guests before selling it to us, who form the secondary audience.

They can only do this if they work together as a troupe, creat-

Ian Holm as Gremio, Ian Richardson as Tranio, and Paul Hardwick as Baptista.

ing their opportunities as time goes on and pressing their advantages home. The primary audience, the Lord and guests, must also be drawn into the game and have a part to play in making us participate in and enjoy it. All this, one can see, must be excellent training for a theatrical company.

Mr. Hall had reason to feel tonight that his own people had profited by it, for there was no doubt about their success with the secondary audience. Miss Alix Stone, the designer, and Mr. John Wyckham, who has planned the lighting, see to it that the arrival of the players pushing their cart and carrying their baskets, with Mr. Paul Hardwick in a fur cap representing their doyen, is a moment of sudden excitement not without a strange pathos.

Right at the end when the Lord, the musicians and one or two favoured spectators—Sly has gone by then—look down on the supper at Lucentio's house, the scene with its chiaroscuro looks like a Mannerist picture, and once again there is an emotional excitement, a hovering of pity, somewhere in the atmosphere.

Sly (Mr. Clifford Rose) and the Tapster (Mr. Hugh Sullivan) are unaware of this as they walk off at the very end. For them it is now a question of putting together the story of the night's play if they can. But we, the secondary audience, have more to take away than that. We have the sensation of having shared in something very lively, human and with certain moments of truth.

If the sub-plot, turning on the wooing of Bianca, has no moments of truth, it is here, nevertheless, a legitimate part of the composition. The comic picture is a more subtle one for the antics and, if your ear is quick enough to follow it, the patter of Mr. Barry MacGregor (Biondello), and Mr. Ian Richardson (Tranio), and Mr. Clive Swift (Grumio), and the ripe good humour of Mr. Hardwick's Baptista. Without this background the principals, Mr. Derek Godfrey and Miss Vanessa Redgrave, could hardly present two such characters of solid interest as they, in fact, do.

Mr. Godfrey's Petruchio is first and last the leading man of the little company, their most picturesque and flaunting figure. To the tips of his fingers he is theatre.

Miss Redgrave's Kate is something more than that. There is a melancholy, almost a despair, about her at the beginning when no one has the force to oppose her in her scenes of shrewishness, and at the end there is a breaking down into a sort of rapturous first childhood hitherto denied to her. Her performance is now an entirely satisfactory comic short story of a young woman's life.

As for the stage itself, it is disconcerting to find Sly and the Lord now at one point on the touchline, now at another, now up aloft, now down below. But no area of the stage escapes the supervision of the director and the planner of the lighting, and no part of it that is used to bring out some legitimate aspect of the situation in the play.

> *"A Kate Comic and Entire,"* in The Times, *London, April 24, 1962, p. 14.*

John Russell Brown   (essay date 1966)

[*Brown is a British scholar, director, editor of several Shakespearean plays, and associate director of the British National Theatre. His works include* Shakespeare and his Comedies *(1957),* Shakespeare's Play's in Performance *(1966),* Shakespeare's Dramatic Style *(1970),* Free Shakespeare *(1974),* Shakespeare in Performance: An Introduction through Six Major Plays *(1976), and* Shakespeare and His Theatre *(1982). Here, Brown argues that the success of Daniels's 1962 revival of* The Taming of the Shrew *was due to the experienced, introspective performances of Godfrey, Paul Hardwick as Baptista, and Ian Holm as Gremio, as well as the performers' familiarity with the text.*]

The Royal Shakespeare Company's productions at Stratford-upon-Avon in 1962 provide useful examples of contemporary Shakespearian acting, for their achievements were of diverse kinds. A revival of the 1960 production of *The Taming of the Shrew* showed some talents of the company to best advantage. Elaborate comic business obscured the dramatic line of the play as a whole but provided many farcical incidents that could be performed vigorously and ostentatiously. Doors were slammed, heads slapped, plates tossed, postures held, lines underlined or thrown away with controlled gusto. This was a competitive style of production in which everyone was allowed to be assertive and single-minded. (p. 180)

Undoubtedly the actors can feel gratified by the 1962 season, for they were often effective, playing strongly for the audience's immediate attention. But if we ask how well they served Shakespeare's plays, their success will appear far smaller. Perhaps the most common and noticeable failure was the inability to give an impression of intelligence. Shakespeare often requires an actor to speak as if he were thinking quickly, cunningly or subtly; sometimes he must say one thing and seem to think about another, sometimes he must seem to enjoy alacrity of mind, or to turn desperately to it because his passions have been inexplicably aroused. On such occasions the pursuit of immediate effectiveness betrays the actors to clumsiness. (p. 181)

The actor who thus pursues effectiveness alone may be said to be afraid of subtlety. How else can we account for the protracted moment at the end of the first scene between Petruchio and Katharine in the Stratford *Taming of the Shrew?* This was played so broadly for sentiment, the lovers gazing in each other's eyes while Petruchio strokes his lady's calves, that the whole 'game' of the play was given away: these two would *have* to love-ever-after. It gave a strong moment of feeling at the beginning of the play and engrossed the audience's interest, but Katharine's final victory was shorn of all its surprise and much of its pleasure; the general strategy of Shakespeare's progressive revelation of the bases of character was defeated at the outset. (p. 182)

A further achievement of the 1962 season at Stratford was not gained by its general pursuit of effectiveness. This was the playing of Derek Godfrey, Paul Hardwick and Ian Holm in *The Taming of the Shrew,* as Petruchio, Baptista and Gremio. Occasionally they all acted too broadly and were too indulgent in accepting details of comic business, but this was the second or third season in which these players had appeared in these roles, and their acting had been refined by practice and complicated by further knowledge. Many points were now rejudged by instinct or vigilant self-criticism, and seemed to gain new meaning and deeper effect. Derek Godfrey's

> O, how I long to have some chat with her!
>
>   [II.i.162]

could now suggest both assurance and something like self-mockery. Both Ian Holm and Paul Hardwick could turn a jest so that it aroused pity as well as laughter, and by making their two old men draw close together in adversity they suggested unconscious subtextual reactions and enhanced the whole play by a comic demonstration of a coupling of practical interests to offset the various couplings of love. This was not superimposed on the text, but a revelation of a part of Shakespeare's play which would be missed in less subtle performances and probably in the most painstaking reading of the words alone. As the plot unfolds, these two characters do, in fact, speak in new agreement and the action does require that they should stand or sit by each other's side. At the latest possible moment in the comedy, Baptista gives money to Katharine; so Gremio had offered money at his instigation to purchase Bianca, but now the money is a gift without conditions. These actors had had practice to make perfect their characterisations, and they were often drawn by the text to discover the various 'faces' of their roles: a single line gave a double impression; subtextual concerns were suggested through certain qualities of the text; gesture effected what words could not. So they were able to present characters responding at various levels of consciousness and to contribute to the general wit and enjoyment of the play.

These few, matured performances were made possible by years of familiarity with a text and with the practical problems of each role in performance. And they point the way to the most necessary condition for improving our Shakespeare productions: his plays require skilled, subtle, strong and imaginative performances, and so actors must work consecutively, patiently and ambitiously. (pp. 190-91)

> *John Russell Brown, "Acting Shakespeare Today,"*
> *in his* Shakespeare's Plays in Performance, *Edward*
> *Arnold (Publishers) Ltd., 1966, pp. 180-92.*

PRODUCTION:

Michael Langham • Stratford Festival, Canada • 1962

BACKGROUND:

Langham's production of *The Taming of the Shrew* emphasized the play-within-a-play structure by including the epilogue from *The Taming of a Shrew*. To further heighten the sense of theatrical illusion, Langham improvised a concluding vignette in which, after the players had finished performing for Christopher Sly, the actor who had played Petruchio walked past Kate, threw his arm around the actress who had portrayed Bianca, and left the stage with her. Innovations such as this one elicited high praise from theater critics. John Colicos appeared as Petruchio, Kate Reid played Katherina, and Hugh Webster portrayed Sly.

COMMENTARY:

Walter Kerr   (review date 21 June 1962)

[*Kerr is a Pulitzer Prize-winning American dramatic critic, essayist, and playwright. Throughout his career, he has written theater reviews for such publications as* Commonwealth, *the*

New York Herald Tribune, *and the* New York Times. *In the following excerpt, Kerr applauds the creativity of Langham's production of* The Shrew, *particularly his idea of ending the play on a curiously wistful note. Unhappily, the critic remarks, the director's inventiveness did not extend to his treatment of the relationship between Kate and Petruchio.*]

Far and away the most fetching conceit in director Michael Langham's conceit-studded production of "The Taming of the Shrew" is the curious sigh on which it closes. Mr. Langham has suddenly remembered that it is always sad when the players go.

The "Shrew," of course, is full of players who are really playing in triplicate: they are performing in jest for Christopher Sly, in earnest for the noble Lord who is paying them, and then, most generously, for all the rest of us. In due time, and after they have bolted in and out of church, hurtled tables hither and yon, and slapped at one another until the air is a rattle of thunder-claps, the whole compounded performance comes to its hearty, muscular, grinning conclusion.

In that moment—with just a faint suspension of breath to show that something is passing—a world closes down like the last light of day. Petruchio, so triumphant over Kate only a moment ago, is now leaning against a pillar as though his energies could never be restored, his shoulders limp with an actor's weariness. Kate, the virago who has not for a moment stood still, stands alone, looking at no one as the stage properties are hustled past her, waiting for her composure to return. The supporting company, instantly characterless and briskly indifferent, cares only about packing the cart for the journey into the night.

And when Petruchio has breathed out his tensions and become a mere player again, he moves past Kate without so much as a nod to her. Starting down the road that will end somewhere in another performance, he throws his arm about Bianca, who is obviously his real love. A play is a play, and even when it is well done, 'tis done.

One of Mr. Langham's special gifts as a director—already handsomely demonstrated in earlier productions here—is his instinct for what is true about artifice. He is constantly pointing his finger at any artifice the playwright may have deliberately employed, and then, if possible, doubling and quintupling it as though the universe were a round-dance. If a tumbler's cart comes rolling precipitously down a steep ramp, it must spin wildly to a stop, spilling its luggage indiscriminately about the stage in order to accent the instability of a player's life. If choirboys belong at the Petruchio-Kate wedding, what is wrong with having them lose their heads exactly as everyone is doing, leaping upon one another's shoulders and skipping rope in their bright red cassocks? The stage, like life, is an elaborate game, and there is fun to be found in the simultaneous precision and abandon of its conscious elaboration.

The fun of this "Shrew," then, is located in the clockwork reconciliation of Petruchio and his outraged servant: they embrace twice and then crash their heads together as though the sequence were a universal law. It is in Sly's various and dogged attempts to slip into one of the parties the principal characters are always giving, and in the invisible manner in which he finally joins an unreal world. It is in pedants who nearly drown in their mighty Venetian ruffs, and in the blazing fire of bright orange feathers that is summoned up from some fireplace logs.

Sometimes the fancifulness overbusies itself, one comes to wish that a clown could mention a horse without automatically slipping into a canter. And in all of the inventive insistence that we see reality as an eternal act of pretending (which Shakespeare himself has surely built into this apparently simple farce), there is some failure to give full attention to the core of the contest. The relationship between Kate and Petruchio is almost entirely arbitrary, and that hurts.

Kate, for instance, isn't exactly a girl you would care to tame. In Kate Reid's rushed and headlong attack on the role, she is malicious enough to approach her sister with a hangman's noose in her hands, nearly as though she meant business; and the fast rasp of her voice through two-thirds of the play permits Petruchio to hear very little that is private behind it. Miss Reid recovers ground precisely as she submits to some of her lover's more preposterous pronouncements, and the nicest thing she does all evening is to start with surprise and delight when her lordly employer kisses her at the close of the performance; but the sense of a woman beneath the virago comes late.

John Colicos' Petruchio is steadily better stuff. Flinging out his words as though he had just shaken them in a dice box, arrogantly tossing the curliest hair since Little Lord Fauntleroy last got into a fight, piously requesting that Kate say grace and leading her with demented delicacy through a few graceful dance steps ("Be merry, Kate"), he is a buccaneer whose very grin seems to bite. The match will be a better one, though, when these two discover something personal between them.

Among the zanies who scatter like leaves before their director's formalized whirlwind, Hugh Webster, Eric Christmas, Bernard Behrens and Lewis Gordon are especially blithe and brisk. And Tanya Moisewitsch's dazzling costumes—beginning with the 18th century and spiraling backward through time as the play turns in on itself—crown Mr. Langham's purpose majestically. They clothe a world of lively puppets with mannerly grace.

> *Walter Kerr, in a review of "The Taming of the Shrew," in the* New York Herald Tribune, *June 21, 1962, p. 12.*

Henry Hewes (review date 7 July 1962)

[*Hewes is an American dramatic critic who wrote for the* Saturday Review *from 1951 to 1977. In the excerpt below, Hewes comments favorably on Langham's production, noting how his "gradually acquired supremacy" in the art of using the open stage contributed to his presentation of* The Taming of the Shrew's *play-within-a-play structure.*]

The tenth Stratford Shakespearean Festival of Canada offers a sampler of three approaches to Shakespeare production, of which the most successful is the one Michael Langham has applied to "The Taming of the Shrew." Here, Mr. Langham again demonstrates his gradually acquired supremacy in the art of using this unique open stage. And just as evident is Tanya Moiseiwitsch's unwavering artistry in bringing color and style onto the neutral wooden U—which this season has been remodeled slightly toward W.

The presentation begins with the delightful spectacle of tattered Christopher Sly as he is suddenly showered with all the voluptuous elegance Shakespeare and Miss Moiseiwitsch can supply. But as gorgeous as this is, Mr. Langham understands

that no pleasure can ever equal the glory achieved in the imagination of the person experiencing the spectacle, and that the secret of the open stage is to get imaginary sights, happenings, and forces to occur in the mind of an audience within a split second of the moment they come into the heads of the performers.

Thus the most effective of all the trappings the practical-joking Lord offers Sly is nothing we actually see, but an imaginary wanton painting of "Io, as a maid, and how she was beguiled and surprised—as lively painted as the deed was done" [Ind.ii.54-6]. While describing the painting, Sly, portrayed nicely as a cautious vulgarian by Hugh Webster, tilts his head so as better to inspect the lascivious detail of the horizontal figures. He is immediately interrupted by the Lord, who calls his attention to a painting of a lovely though solitary Daphne, but, after giving the Daphne a quick glance, he surreptitiously returns to his head-tilted perusal of the livelier former picture.

In giving us the play's main plot, Mr. Langham has balanced the whipped cream of the costumes with an economically realistic presentation of the story. John Colicos's Petruchio is less a dashing romantic than he is the hard head of a household that requires money to maintain it. His taming of Kate is pursued strictly out of economic necessity, which gives Mr. Colicos a point of occupation that keeps him from some of the gratuitous posing that so often attends a performance of Petruchio. And Kate Reid plays her namesake as more shrewd than shrewish. Petruchio doesn't tame her by his virility and the penetration of a love-starved girl's emotional fortress. He simply forces her to see that she will be better off living under his system. Similarly the clowns led by Peter Donat's Hortensio, Bernard Behrens's Tranio, and Eric Christmas's Grumio have a realistic concern with material assets.

However, this approach does not dull the fun. Indeed, it would be hard to imagine a madder and more effective wedding scene than the one Mr. Langham has staged. Petruchio enters in a cart that roars down an incline to a perilous stop center stage, captures his elusive bride by the arm, rushes her along a red carpet up the steps into the church, and after the brief offstage ceremony, tumbles the entire procession of choir boys and wedding guests with a whirlwind exit.

> *Henry Hewes, "Canadian Capers," in* Saturday Review, *Vol. XLV, No. 26, July 7, 1962, p. 17.*

Robert Russell (review date July-August 1962)

[*Russell contends that although Langham's production of* The Taming of the Shrew *was skillful, Kate Reid and John Colicos failed to project a convincing interpretation of seduction and affection.*]

Michael Langham, who has based his reputation on his magical touch with the poetic comedies, has chosen to approach this production [of *The Taming of the Shrew*] in a basically traditional way (in contrast with Tyrone Guthrie's drastic and arbitrary transposition of the same play to the American wild west, during the Festival's second season). This is in fact a play-within-a-play, and Michael Langham has shown great skill in his handling of the framework scenes, wherein a jaded lord drags a drunken tinker home for the pleasure of fooling him into believing that he too is an aristocrat. The lord then invites a strolling group of *commedia dell'arte* players home to entertain the besotted tinker with their version of *The Taming of the Shrew*. Throughout the performance of this play-within-a-play, we are watching not only the *commedia* fable, but the earthy and amusing reactions of the drunken tinker, brilliantly played with gusty realism by Hugh Webster. Since the main play is really enacted by a group of strolling players, this gives the Stratford company an opportunity to play with a flamboyant, exaggerated style, with much lifting of eyebrows and striking of poses, and parading in wildly romantic costumes. Having excused his theatrical inclinations with this device, Michael Langham proceeds to run riot with the production, until it becomes a tasteful but extravagant romp. At times it appears he will go overboard and lose us in the exuberance of his vision, but he somehow always manages to remain just inside the limits of our acceptance, and the play moves swiftly and perfectly through to its series of unwinding finales.

Kate Reid . . . played the female lead, and . . . surprisingly, something failed to function. In spite of many brilliant moments in her work, she failed to win our sympathy. The same was true of John Colicos: in spite of his amazing enthusiasm and zest for the task at hand, we never felt his affection roused for his new-tamed bride. In fact, poor Kate's situation is quite touching. She's a fine spirited beast, and her shrewishness should be turned by love to something finer. It is very important that we see her emotions engaged, then tortured, and finally won. For herein the playwright states his case for love, honour and obedience in most effective terms. Brilliant as the production is, it fails to examine the psychological processes of seduction and affection, upon which Shakespeare constructed the whole framework of his play. The actors may possibly be able to correct this in later performances; as it is, in spite of the splendour of the costumes, the unity and near-perfection of the comic vision, and the traditional elegance of the speech, I was left with the feeling that the play was heartless and meaningless, and that though the evening was by no means wasted, this was certainly not a definitive production of *The Shrew*. (p. 313)

> Robert Russell, *"On Interpreting Shakespeare—Four Dimensions of Reality,"* in Canadian Art, *Vol. XIX, No. 4, July-August, 1962, pp. 311-13.*

Jack Winter (review date September 1962)

[*Winter commends Langham for his masterful incorporation of* The Shrew *and* A Shrew *into one cohesive play that makes good use of Christopher Sly's presence from beginning to end.*]

Since it rewrote *King John* in 1960, Stratford has excelled in first-rate productions of the second-rate. (How Canadian can you get!). This year it compiles a *Taming of the Shrew* which makes Shakespeare's version look like Fletcher's sequel.

The programme notes do not mention a dramaturge, so presumably director Michael Langham is responsible for the doctored script. Shakespeare's *Taming of the Shrew* (Folio, 1623) is gap-ridden, needlessly involved, and ultimately truncated. By an integrated use of the anonymous *Taming of A Shrew* (1594 or earlier), Langham has overcome many of these problems. His most brilliant innovation is in carrying the induction past [I.i.254] and through to the end. Langham thus provides himself with a comic play which distracts from and almost excuses the difficulties remaining in the text. Clumsy exposition is accounted for by causing it to be addressed to the sottish Sly. Confusing intrigues and counter-

intrigues are made clear by various asides to the Sly entourage. And the audience is liberated to an unselfconscious enjoyment of the play's slapsticks when it thinks that the frivolity is aimed at Sly.

The Christopher Sly sub-plot provides a tone as well as a framework. In the beautifully paced induction we are at first linked to Sly by our sympathy for his plight. We are then replaced by him. He becomes audience to the play and we become audience to him and to the play. Gradually, our inhibitions are discarded, and we respond to the play within the play as to something twice removed from life. Theatricality reigns.

Visually, this *Taming of the Shrew* is Langham's most inventive production. Disguises are kept clear through multiple costume changes by dressing each character in his own colour. Stage business is plentiful, but rarely upstages the dialogue. For example, Katherine's and Petruchio's smutty stychomythia is cleverly matched to the business of a stubbed toe. The patterns on stage are consistently delightful. At one point there are four distinct groups of auditors to the main action: Lucentio and Tranio who watch Bianca, the "acting company's" bored musicians and prompter, a rapt Christopher Sly, and the Stratford audience itself.

The characterizations—appropriately—are of *commedia dell' arte* dimensions. Particularly notable are William Needle's Gremio, a *dottore* with *pantalone* overtones, and Eric Christmas's Grumio, a *zanne* of the first water. John Colicos (Petruchio) provides a *harlequin/capitano* who is weak of voice, but energetic enough for two. Kate Reid's Katherine is almost a masterpiece. She allows her characterization wit and intelligent self-awareness. Except in her final monologue which she delivers moralistically she also manages to suggest that this Shrew is tamed only for the moment and only for the purpose of securing herself a mate.

Certain summer-stock tendencies persist. The players wait for their laughs, and this bad habit tends to drain rather than entertain the audience. The pace and costuming are also somewhat unremitting. Miss Moiseiwitsch's costumes are beautiful but unmodulated, and the absence of darker shades sometimes makes the stage appear blinding and overcrowded.

In the second part at the height of the complication Christopher Sly intrudes into the middle of the play and is politely ejected before the action resumes. The hilariousness of this un-Shakespearean gesture is a symptom of the play's total success. No directorial excesses can obscure the energy and healthiness which pervade this production. (p. 125)

> Jack Winter, *"Stratford, 1962,"* in The Canadian Forum, *Vol. XLII, No. 500, September, 1962, p. 125.*

Wes Balk (review date Fall 1962)

[*Balk offers high praise for Langham's production of* The Taming of the Shrew, *noting that Sly was the presentation's "most appealing character."*]

"But damn it all! The two festivals are almost the same age. Why should theirs be so much better than ours?" The speaker is obviously no Canadian, but an immature and rather inarticulate American who, in spite of the fact that he knows about Art transcending national boundaries, cannot ignore the chauvinistic envy he feels while reveling in the Stratford Festival in Canada. And it does his mood no good to read that artistic director Michael Langham is already worrying about the possible death of the Shakespearean boom (at the very height of its popularity) and the necessity for expansion (which has in fact already begun very happily with *Cyrano de Bergerac*). Our querulous American realizes with a pang that the Canadian Festival is setting standards which we can only wave at and wish for in another Stratford, 1,000 miles away in Connecticut. (p. 195)

One brief comparison between the festivals will not solve anything, but it may indicate some of the causes of the contrast. Take the respective stages, for example. Both were altered this year, and one can only commend the American Festival for removing the universally derogated potato-chip bowl; but its replacement is hardly an improvement: a nineteenth-century bastard compromise, by proscenium out of forestage, with curtains, cyclorama, set pieces and scene changes. The redesigner, Eldon Elder, is only the latest candidate to tackle the Connecticut dilemma, which arises from the attempt to please all the people all the time. This lack of philosophic and artistic continuity can only be harmful; the necessary Shakespearean scene-flow has been hobbled, and one is reminded more of Broadway on each successive visit.

The Canadian stage, on the other hand, has not only kept its philosophic concept intact, but has strengthened and clarified it, probably because Tanya Moiseiwitsch, the original designer, also did the altering. The Ontario changes are simple: the forestage is unchanged, whereas the back area is broadened and opened up; the balcony has been raised eight inches, and the playing area beneath it has been further enlarged by removal of four superfluous pillars; the seldom-used side balconies, a tentative gesture in the direction of Elizabethan reconstruction, have been removed and the side entrances beneath them have been broadened and heightened. While the Connecticut stage retreats, the Ontario stage advances in both the symbolic and literal senses of the word; in Connecticut the forestage has become a modified apron, whereas in Ontario it is more naked and commanding than ever.

Alterations are made to be used, and Mr. Langham took immediate advantage of his, especially those large side doors. Three times in his production of *The Taming of the Shrew* a gaily decorated cart careered through the stage-right door, down a ramp and diagonally across the forestage, each time with Petruchio as its main charioteer. To complement these farcical pulsations, the same cart was lugged uphill three times, the final painful climb taking full advantage of the cart-journey complex. At the end of the play-within-a-play, the cart carried the worn-out actors up the ramp and on to their next performance—a poignant fable of the theatre in miniature; old age and rebirth in one. The stage was left in a dull drab mood, and the poignancy of the departure might have won the day but for Christopher Sly.

Shakespeare opens the *Shrew* with an Induction which establishes Sly as the butt of a huge practical joke. But after a brief episode at the end of the first scene of the play-within-the-play he is forgotten. Why? Scholars have gone to some lengths to show, on one hand, that there *is* a textual gap, and, on the other, that the gap is part of Shakespeare's meaning. Mr. Langham cut through this mass of speculation in the best Elizabethan tradition; he decided that the Sly incident should frame the play, and called upon appropriate scenes from the anonymous play *The Taming of A Shrew* to do so. It was well

worth it. Christopher Sly turned out to be the most appealing character in the show; so appealing, in fact, that the spectators found it difficult to pass from his level of reality to that of the play-within-a-play. But none of the players was to be denied his place in the sun-light of suspended disbelief, and, with this one exception, the levels of reality (there are at least four) meshed perfectly. The poignancy of the players' departure was created by one such Pirandellian meshing, but the play regained its clown cap in the final scene depicting Sly's return to *his* real world. The irrepressible little vulgarian awoke on the tavern steps and reflected that he would go home to his wife since he had learned how to tame a shrew. Thanks to the playing of Hugh Webster, the bittersweet tonal relationships were left in their proper perspective.

The characters of Petruchio and Kate were also brilliantly portrayed. He was an intelligent, witty and sensitive gentleman who was forced through economic necessity to treat Kate as he did; and there was none of the brutal sadism so often seen in the part. She was not just a shrew, but another strongwilled and intelligent being, a suitable mate for a man who had found neither partner nor match in the world. The final proof of his victory—when Kate wins a wager for him by appearing at his command—received a spontaneous burst of applause, not because a woman had been bullied into submission, but because two unique individuals had found and understood each other. The whole performance demonstrated once again that farce succeeds far better when taste and humanity are used to complement slapstick and hilarity. (pp. 195-96)

> *Wes Balk, in a review of "The Taming of the Shrew," in* Drama Survey, *Vol. 2, No. 2, Fall, 1962, pp. 195-200.*

Peter D. Smith   (review date Autumn 1962)

[*Smith maintains that Langham's successful production of* The Taming of the Shrew *was indicative of the director's careful, yet unobtrusive style.*]

If box-office receipts are the measuring-stick of success, the 1962 season at Stratford, Ontario, was the best yet. This is, after all, what one might have expected. The choice of plays was in itself enough to insure some degree of success: *Macbeth,* the play that had been asked for more often than any other since the Festival began; *The Tempest,* very much in fashion, and just the thing to show this stage to its best advantage; *The Taming of the Shrew,* a romp that cannot fail to please when presented by a good company. (p. 521)

The Taming of the Shrew is the first play to be repeated at Stratford. When it was produced by Tyrone Guthrie in 1954 (the second season), it was given the full Guthrie treatment and ended up as a riot of a farce set in the Wild West in its wildest days. The 1962 production was just as typical of *its* director's style, coming with the hallmark of care and unobtrusive thought stamped upon it.

Glitter and life filled the stage throughout, but we were always conscious that we were watching theatrical glitter, for the "play within the play" was always apparent, and with it a justifiable flamboyance. Not only did Mr. Langham preserve the Induction but, taking lines from *The Taming of a Shrew,* he gave Sly a life of his own at all times during the play and rounded the whole thing off by having Sly resolve to try for himself the methods he has just seen in practice. At every point the actors in the central play showed that they were act-ing for Sly; all the asides were addressed to him, small ges-tures reassured him as he followed anxiously the fortunes of the lovers, and when, at the end of Act III the crowd left the stage to enjoy Baptista's feast, Sly, to the consternation of the Lord, dashed off with the rest of them. The effect of course is two-fold: on the one hand this episode in the fairy-tale of the battle of the sexes is removed one stage further from reali-ty and its extravagance is accordingly made more acceptable; and, on the other, the audience, paradoxically, is given a keener sense of participation as they happily become involved in Sly's own enthusiasm.

There is a remarkable unity to be found in a Langham pro-duction. One senses that all those taking part have grasped the point and that all are moving in the same direction: there is something of the inevitability of all great art. Just as Miss Tanya Moiseiwitsch's costumes always blend into an inte-grated pattern where nothing stands out that is not meant to, so too the actors work as a harmonious team evidently enjoy-ing themselves, with each taking his moments of prominence skillfully and fitting them into the general plan.

There were some memorable performances in this produc-tion: a major one in that of John Colicos, who was a Petruchio with greater resources than many and greater vari-ety both in speech and movement. With this performance Mr. Colicos more than fulfilled the promise of 1961: he seems cer-tain to go on to even more notable successes. In lesser roles, William Needles as Gremio, Eric Christmas as Grumio, and Bernard Behrens as Tranio all demonstrated why they are so successful season after season in such parts. They seem to find that they are as keenly challenged and become as much involved in the business of theatrical creation when they bring all their talents to bear on the lines that Shakespeare wrote for his old playboys and young menservants as they would be if they were playing Brutus, Shylock or Iago. Hugh Webster as Sly made an auspicious first appearance. At all times his whole being was engaged: his initial bewilderment was moving and his eventual conviction of his rise in the world just as touching: above all his open-hearted, simple-minded attachment to the players acting for his delight was a captivating part of a rich performance.

The ladies did not fare so well. The one part of the production that jarred was to have Bianca appear as a vain and empty-headed nonentity, a creature that no Gremio, however senile, no Hortensio, however absurd, no Lucentio, however inexpe-rienced, would have gone to much trouble to win. As Katha-rine the Shrew, Kate Reid, though bringing to the part her considerable talent and experience, nevertheless failed to match the style of Mr. Colicos. She unfortunately seems un-able to rid herself of the tendency to come too soon to a cli-max, to become incomprehensible as she speaks more and more loudly, and to lapse into an irritating selection of irrele-vant gestures and postures. (pp. 521-22)

> *Peter D. Smith, "'Toil and Trouble': A Review of the 1962 Season of the Stratford, Ontario, Festival," in* Shakespeare Quarterly, *Vol. XIII, No. 4, Au-tumn, 1962, pp. 521-27.*

Arnold Edinborough   (review date 1963)

[*Edinborough credits Langham with a "sensitive and compre-hensive" interpretation of Shakespeare's* Taming of the Shrew.]

Canada's Shakespeare Festival at Stratford, Ontario, cele-brated its tenth season last summer. In more sophisticated countries, where the tradition of theatre runs deeper, there would be little to crow about in a mere ten-season record. But when the first Stratford season opened in a big-top circus tent, there can have been only a few visionaries who thought that such a venture in Canada would last as long as ten years. (p. 152)

In a sense the tenth festival was a miniature of what the festi-val now stands for and what it has accomplished. The three Shakespearian plays were *Macbeth, The Taming of the Shrew,* and *The Tempest*—one play aimed at students (*Mac-beth* is a 'set' text), one at the tourists and one for the general public who might like to build up their repertoire of plays seen. The first of these was directed by an English director, Peter Coe, and was a failure; the second was directed by an expatriate Englishman, Michael Langham, and it was a great success; the third was directed by a native Canadian and it was competent only.

Coe, with that English passion for doing something new to stimulate the jaded appetites of Londoners, completely in-verted the values of *Macbeth* and produced it as if Shake-speare did not believe in witches and thought Macbeth had no nobility. (p. 153)

[This] is not the first time that an English director has tried to blind the locals with his own brilliance and to dim the brightness of Shakespeare. Guthrie did it, notably in his 1954 production of *The Shrew,* and that may be why *The Shrew* was chosen for reworking (it is the only play to be given two productions as yet). The second *Shrew* was directed by Langham who, in the eight years that he has been artistic di-rector of the festival, has emerged as one of the most sensitive, most resourceful Shakespearian directors now working in the theatre—and one of the most scholarly.

Not for Langham the obvious symbol, the cheap effect and the heartless cutting of lines to avoid a dramatic difficulty. He, indeed, added lines, for his *Shrew* was done as a play within a play and the irony of Sly (thrown out by one shrew and ready to be welcomed roughly in by another) was brought out by filching a final scene from the old *Taming of A Shrew*—a final scene which made the irony poignant: only on the stage do men wive it wealthily and/or happily.

On this tightrope between dream and reality, between dra-matic illusion and audience absorption, Langham balanced his conception beautifully. Petruchio (subtly played by John Colicos) was false to his nature but true to his ideals. Hortensio and Lucentio, disguised, were false to their station and to their ideals. Bianca rightly, therefore, played her father fair and her lovers false. The pace being kept up, the illusion being deftly portrayed and sustained, the whole play was such a whirl of disguise, deceit and dishonesty that Sly's bewilder-ment at the end and his slinking away made us wonder which was foul and which was fair, much more than *Macbeth* did.

To achieve such reaction from what is often thought of as a fustian play is proof that a director of Langham's calibre can do more for Shakespeare than a library full of emenders, crit-ics and scholars. It also proves that a stage like Stratford's, and the atmosphere of carnival and genial criticism which a summer festival properly mounted can produce, does won-ders for actors, audience and author alike. What had been first shown in Langham's excellent 1961 production of *Love's Labour's Lost* was here triumphantly reaffirmed—that a director who moves away from his text (like Coe) does so at his peril and at the peril of his actors, whereas a director who moves, through a sensitive and comprehensive reading of the text, towards his author, can make old cloth shine like new satin. (pp. 153-54)

Arnold Edinborough, "Canada's Achievement," in Shakespeare Survey: An Annual Survey of Shakespearian Study and Production, *Vol. 16, 1963, pp. 152-54.*

PRODUCTION:

Franco Zeffirelli's Film Adaptation • 1967

BACKGROUND:

Zeffirelli's film adaptation of *The Taming of the Shrew,* which featured Richard Burton and Elizabeth Taylor in the lead roles, was released in 1967. In an attempt to provide greater focus on the taming scenes, Zeffirelli deleted the Induction and cut vast portions of the Bianca/Lucentio sub-plot. Several reviewers harshly decried Zeffirelli's excisions as too severe and attacked his interpretation of the play's major themes. Many commentators also admonished Burton for misinterpreting Petruchio and faulted Taylor for her lack of classical acting experience. Nevertheless, most critics reacted favorably to Zeffirelli's scenic effects, maintaining that the director successfully subverted the realistic quality characteristic of film and replaced it with a sense of artificiality generally reserved for the stage.

COMMENTARY:

Walter Lucas   (interview date 25 July 1966)

[*Lucas records Burton's and Zeffirelli's optimism regarding the forthcoming release of the film version of* The Taming of the Shrew.]

For Richard Burton, Elizabeth Taylor, and Franco Zeffirelli, filming the recently completed "Taming of the Shrew" was an act of faith. The Burtons received no salary for playing Shakespeare's Petruchio and Katharina. They will share in whatever profits there may be.

But Mr. Burton is confident that the production will be "the first Shakespearean film ever to become an immediate commercial success." The Welsh star has always believed "The Shrew" to be one of the Shakespearean plays that lend themselves to the screen. (Five or six other cinema versions have been made.)

"It is robust and vital," he says. "Its language is relatively simple. The story is both tender and sweet, horrendous and earthy—all ingredients that have made a success of other adaptations from the classics."

For Mr. Zeffirelli "The Shrew" is the latest work of a director who has more or less dedicated his career to the works of the Bard.

"I have always felt," he said in a recent interview, "that I

could break the myth that Shakespeare on stage or screen was only an exercise for the intellectual. I want his plays to be enjoyed by ordinary men equally; the worker and countryman who would even pay his good money to go and see some play like this one on the screen. This has been my objective in directing the 'Taming of the Shrew.'

"Working in complete harmony with a great Shakespearean actor like Richard Burton and an actress of the caliber of Elizabeth Taylor, and a highly experienced cast from London, I have been able to invest the characters with human feelings and failings and social relationships such as you and I and millions of others have—not just make them vehicles for sonorous verse," declared the Italian director.

When the idea of making a movie of "The Shrew" first occurred to Mr. Zeffirelli, he faced the prevailing and frequently proved argument that "there's no money in filming Shakespeare."

"Certainly the records seem to bear this out," he agreed. "I doubt if any Shakespearean movie, except Laurence Olivier's 'Henry V' has been a box-office success."

A "guardian angel," he said, led him to the Burtons. When he was searching for money without much success, someone suggested he approach the famous couple, and they responded immediately. With the Burtons backing him, "there was no difficulty in getting Columbia to pick up the rest of the tab."

Incidentally, this is Richard Burton's first attempt at Shakespeare on the screen. It is Elizabeth Taylor's first venture into Shakespeare in any medium.

Walter Lucas, "The Burtons in 'The Taming of the Shrew'," in The Christian Science Monitor, *July 25, 1966, p. 6.*

John Russell Taylor   (review date 28 February 1967)

[*Taylor asserts that Zeffirelli's adaptation does not overcome the problem all directors face when creating a film version of a Shakespearean drama, namely, how to preserve most of the original text even though the average audience is unable to understand the language.*]

Since Franco Zeffirelli wants to forget his only previous feature film, a "rosy realist" comedy, we may fairly take this Shakespearian extravaganza as his official debut as a film director. Filming Shakespeare, of course, is to plunge in at the deep end: the traps are innumerable, and no director yet has managed to avoid them all. Moreover, the comedies are if anything the worst. You have to preserve a reasonable proportion of the original words if you are not to be accused of betraying Shakespeare, but at the same time you have to face the fact that many of the words are not even comprehensible, let alone funny, to a non-specialist audience, and to do something about it.

Mr. Zeffirelli with his fellow adapters, Paul Dehn and Suso Cecchi d'Amico, clearly recognizes the difficulty, but wavers alarmingly about what its solution should be. For the first half the words (such as are not cut) are buried in bustle and business, so that the majority of the audience, on whom the endless puns on the word "Kate" are lost anyway, will at least have something to look at. This spreads out the plot excessively, and does not really distract us from the gap at the centre. The second half is at least less ornate; instead the script is cut to the bone, and everything is concentrated on the two stars, Elizabeth Taylor and Richard Burton, in the hope no doubt that they will carry the film on sheer star appeal.

Here, with everything working for them, they do not do too badly, though Mr. Burton is a little stodgy for Petruchio and Miss Taylor a little shrill for Katharina. Earlier, though, they tend to vanish completely into the sumptuous decor. Mr. Zeffirelli's method is rather that of an orchestral wizard trying to write a concerto for two frail solo instruments. In his National Theatre production of that other tiresome play *Much Ado about Nothing,* at least the instruments (Maggie Smith and Robert Stephens) were incisive enough to cut through the heavy, crowded orchestration; here they are swamped until the composer realizes that he must orchestrate lightly if they are to hold their required place in the ensemble.

Still, there are compensations. The film, thanks to the lush colour photography of Oswald Morris and some really splendid sets and costumes, does look marvellous. The Lucentio-Bianca part of the plot, though slashed to the point of incoherence (no hint, for instance, of why the whole elaborate deception is necessary in the first place) is decorated by two fresh and attractive young players, Natasha Pyne and Michael York. And Michael Hordern as Baptista repeats his feat of *A Funny Thing Happened on the Way to the Forum* by nipping in and snapping up most of the film's real laughs so quickly that no one else seems any the wiser.

John Russell Taylor, "Zeffirelli's Sumptuous 'Shrew'," in The Times, *London, February 28, 1967, p. 8.*

David Robinson   (review date 3 March 1967)

[*Robinson maintains that Zeffirelli's "muddled and self-indulgent" interpretation of* The Shrew *results in a darker comedy than Shakespeare intended. Taylor is surprisingly effective as a pathological virago, the critic declares, and Burton gives a solid performance as a nasty, brutish Petruchio.*]

The Taming of the Shrew has given Shakespeare's successors more difficulty than most of his plays, by being based on assumptions of the inequality of the sexes that were probably already reactionary in Elizabethan times. Significantly, the great revival of the play's stage popularity was in mid-Victorian times, when lip-service to the idea of masculine domination was for the moment fashionable. This popularity was prolonged into the present century, generally speaking, either by developing a lyrical-romantic vein (Petruchio as a gay, fantastic suitor word-bandying with an unwilling bride) or, perhaps with more literary justification, treating it as a red-nose farce in the popular low-comedy theme of the nagging woman.

Franco Zeffirelli has doubled and redoubled the difficulties in this film version, by making Katharina a case in morbid psychology. And to give added conviction to this reading, Elizabeth Taylor (whose casting I had feared, quite without justification in the event, might prove the film's undoing) plays this sick-minded Katharina extraordinarily well. Given the interpretation, this is as good a Katharina as you could hope for.

She is first glimpsed as a single large, beautiful, malevolent eye glowering through momentarily opened shutters; then as a virago, yelling from an upper window and hurling down joint-stools at her father below; then brutally beating up her younger sister. Stark-mad or wondrous froward? There is no doubt which. When Petruchio first braves her, she is pacing her bare chamber, wild-eyed and stray-haired, quite as deranged as *Suddenly Last Summer.*

In this condition all the upbraiding and teasing, all the talk of suitors and forced marriages looks (as Miss Taylor plays her responses) like a brutal series of taunts and aggravations. And to them is added, worst of all, Petruchio. Even to Shakespeare there must have been something unlovable about Petruchio. His courting is altogether callous: "Wealth is burthen of my wooing dance . . . Be she as foul as was Florentius' love, As old as Sybil, and as curst and shrewd as Socrates Xantippe, or a worse . . . I come to wive it wealthily in Padua" [I. ii. 68-75]. His humour is all malice: "A mad-brain rudesby, full of spleen . . . Hiding his bitter jests in blunt behaviour" [III. ii. 10-13].

The Zeffirelli/Richard Burton Petruchio is nastier still. He is dirty, coarse and drunken; and his house is Slut's Hall. Here Kate is not tamed so much as broken. Even Hazlitt, who thought the whole thing a joyous witty lark, acknowledged that "The situation of poor Katharina, worn out by his incessant persecution, becomes at last almost as pathetic as it is ludicrous." With Taylor often very touching as a sick-mad girl, and Burton as a sadistic boor, the situation ceases altogether to be comic and is instead a Hammer horror in the *Gaslight* mould.

Miss Taylor's weakest scenes are her first, in which the natural roughness of her voice is not the right violence for the wild-cat, and her last, where she is hampered by banal direction. Between these points she perceives the continuity in Katharina's development (or rather, in this instance, collapse). Around this unexpected strong centre, the film dangles like an unpegged bell-tent about its pole. Burton's Petruchio is solid enough, according to its lights, but the rest of the players have a sheepish undirected look. Even fine comedians like Michael Hordern, Cyril Cusack and Victor Spinetti are encouraged to flog about within the narrowest limits of their range. And the juveniles (Michael York and Natasha Pyne) are in the frailest stage tradition of Shakespearean juveniles.

Zeffirelli's approach to the problem (for modern English ears, to say nothing of Italian ones) of understanding Shakespeare's language has seemed to be, here as in *Much Ado About Nothing,* to distract the audience from the words as much as possible. Sometimes you feel (wrongly I am sure) a positive contempt for the text in the lengths Zeffirelli will go to to stage diversions to take your mind off it.

There is something to be said for the method if the diversions are really pretty or funny. But the knockabout only rarely comes off here. The chase between Petruchio and Katharina in a prop-laden granary has its moments (mainly due to Taylor again) but the attempts to liven up the Gremio and Tranio bits don't make them much funnier than Elizabethan clowns usually are. (One might have thought, incidentally, that the play gave Zeffirelli clown trouble enough, without dragging in additional bits and pieces from other plays, like the clown song from *Twelfth Night.*)

The effort after prettiness is more positive. Oswald Morris' and Luciano Trasatti's colour photography is handsome. The first shots of Lucentio and Tranio riding out of one of those zig-zag back-drops from the Quattrocento masters and wearing, with pleasant inconsequence, clothes that seem to come from The Triumph of Maximilian, is enchanting. And the design throughout betrays a similar care. But it is largely negated by Zeffirelli's quite surprising ineptitude in composing groupings on the screen. Again and again the extravagant hurly-burlies of activity into which he launches extras and principals alike (distractions, again, from the rigours of following the often indistinct dialogue) are as ugly as they are irrelevantly busy. A lesson in contrasts is afforded by Eisenstein's triumph of *mise-en-scène, Ivan the Terrible,* which by almost malicious chance BBC-2 showed the night before the Royal Film Performance of the Zeffirelli film. Here groupings are handled with conscious and elaborate artifice, but every movement of every figure within the frame is calculated to produce new, exciting, composed pictures.

As *mise-en-scène The Taming of the Shrew* is muddled and self-indulgent; as Shakespeare it is evasive; as comedy it is dark and cruel. One had hoped for much more from Zeffirelli. But then, one had not hoped for half as much from Miss Taylor; and since it is upon her tremendous following at the box-office that the film's ultimate success will depend, everyone connected with the film is likely to be quite happy.

David Robinson, *"A Suitable Case for Treatment,"*
in The Financial Times, *March 3, 1967, p. 26.*

John Coleman   (review date 3 March 1967)

[*Coleman presents a generally unfavorable review of Zeffirelli's film adaptation of* The Shrew, *concluding that it "is a weird masterpiece of camouflage."*]

Franco Zeffirelli's *The Taming of the Shrew* is very good-looking and noisy, rather as if it were ashamed of its background. The publicity accompanying it seems to have similar reservations, nervously acknowledging the debt of a trio of script-writers—Mr Zeffirelli, Paul Dehn and Suso Cecchi D'Amico—to one Shakespeare 'without whom they would have been lost for words'. The trouble is that no one seems to have made his mind up about just how closely the film was going to hew to the Elizabethan text. The result is compromise, interpolation, the odd downright wilful misreading: but, above all, a drowning turbulence of action. When the film does settle down for a minute or two to giving the words—Shakespeare's words—full value, as when Burton's Petruchio tenderly relishes the lines:

> With silken coats and caps, and golden rings,
> With ruffs and cuffs, and farthingales,
>   and things
>
>   [IV. iii. 55-6]

(though these are, in fact, misplaced), the effect is almost unwarrantably stunning. Other irritations would include the apparently endorsed leer Alfred Lynch's Tranio is allowed to assume midway through the comment, 'That wench is stark mad, or wonderful froward' [I. i. 69]. Now *froward,* meaning 'peevish' or 'perverse', occurs more often in *The Shrew* than in any other Shakespearian play, a key-word if ever there was one. Here Mr Lynch says 'forward' instead: hence the sidelong smirk. But why? And why again should the beautiful closing clown's song from *Twelfth Night*—'For the rain it raineth every day' [V. i. 389ff.]—be purloined to adorn this revel?

I don't feel these criticisms to be hair-splitting because in other places Zeffirelli shows himself aware that the text is still

playable as it stands. His film is nearly brave and, with most of the cast he assembled, could have been tremendous: performers like Cyril Cusack (Grumio), Victor Spinetti (Hortensio, a role cut to ribbons), Michael Hordern as the shrew's father, and the young sub-plot lovers, Michael York and Natasha Pyne, could have given far more, given in turn their chance. But all is subordinated to the big, boisterous and box-office flyting of Mr Burton and Elizabeth Taylor's Kate. This has its moments. Mr Burton has a fine apprehensive laugh, a sort of self-winding heh-heh, which works wonders early on: alas, it soon lapses into a lazy mannerism. Miss Taylor makes her plump, lovely presence compensate for some poor speaking. They chase, tumble and brawl with an élan that occasionally recalls Fairbanks and Pickford in the Hollywood version of 1928. They fall through a floor on to sheep-shearings, straggle on horseback through drenching rain, steadily break up bedsteads and dressers and warming-pans. The emphasis on destruction and humiliation becomes obsessive.

But then this is a difficult, unpleasant, ambiguous play to convert into a vehicle for two of the few remaining cinema stars. It needs genuine actorish playing to make the brutal taming of Kate endurable, let alone meaningful. As it is, it may be that Zeffirelli took a wrong decision early on. His *Shrew* looks splendid, Renaissance, with fumy yellows and ochres and reds and great, tumultuous groupings. At a guess, it would look remarkable stopped at any frame. (It was photographed by Oswald Morris and decorated by John de Cuir and too many others to mention, though they all deserve it.) Maybe a less steamy and atmospheric production would have better assorted with both the play and its glamorous principals. Greater stylisation, a soft-pedal on realism, might have turned out something as arresting as another recent Zeffirelli go at Shakespeare, that Sicilian *Much Ado* for the theatre with Maggie Smith and Robert Stephens superlatively going through their paces. I can't shake off the feeling that this film is a weird masterpiece of camouflage.

John Coleman, *"Sound and Fury,"* in New Statesman, *Vol. 73, No. 1877, March 3, 1967, p. 303.*

Gerald Kaufman   (review date 9 March 1967)

[*Kaufman asserts that Zeffirelli's film version of* The Shrew *is nothing more than "a good-natured bore." The constant swirl of activity becomes tiresome and overwhelms the dramatic action, the critic contends.*]

If art were judged by its pretensions alone, then the outstanding films of the month would be Joseph Losey's *Accident* and Franco Zeffirelli's *The Taming of the Shrew.*

The Taming of the Shrew is, at any rate, far from pretentious. Zeffirelli has set out, quite simply, to produce a pleasing film version of the Shakespeare comedy. If he has failed it is not because he and his co-script-writers (Suso Cecchi Damico and the inevitable Paul Dehn) have massacred the original dialogue—though this they have undoubtedly done. Orson Welles took an even more merciless axe to the text of *Othello* and emerged with what, in the view of some critics, was in cinematic terms an unmistakable work of art. *The Taming of the Shrew* turns out to be a good-natured bore not because so many liberties have been taken but because the interpolations are unsuccessful.

The aim of making the film sumptuous visually is hampered

by the shoddiness of the sets and fuzziness of the Technicolor. The intention to beguile the eye with swirling movement breaks down because so much is perpetually going on that the eventual effect is simply fussy. Dogs run about incessantly; characters hurl artefacts either to the floor or at each other; the entire cast at frequent intervals breaks into hearty communal applause or rowdy communal laughter. People fall about; or swing, Tarzan-like, on ropes; or run pointlessly after one another across roofs. After a couple of reels of this, the spectator's dearest wish is that, if only for a moment, everyone would stand still and shut up.

Swept helplessly along by this tide of indefatigable activity, the film's roster of delightful performers puts up a commendable struggle against the total submersion which afflicts both plot and sub-plot. Victor Spinetti—made, for some reason, to look like Despina in one of her *Così fan tutte* impersonations—plays Hortensio with the preoccupied air of an anxious hen. Michael Hordern (the shrew's distracted father) delivers his dialogue as a series of meaning-fraught gasps groping wildly for contact with the surrounding iambic pentameters. As Petruchio and Katharina, Richard Burton and Elizabeth Taylor contribute their now celebrated double-act: the one strutting, the other snarling, and both at their magnetic best in a farcical wedding scene of whose existence Shakespeare was never remotely aware.

Gerald Kaufman, "No Messages," in The Listener, *Vol. LXXVII, No. 1980, March 9, 1967, p. 330.*

Penelope Houston   (review date 10 March 1967)

[*Houston contends that the constant action in Zeffirelli's film adaptation gives the viewer the impression not of "a fine Renaissance restlessness," but "a fussy, spasmodic garrulity."*]

Anyone who has ever managed to catch up with the Fairbanks-Pickford *Taming of the Shrew* will remember one justly famous credit title: the acknowledgment to a Mr Sam Taylor for 'additional dialogue.' For years, these brave, ill-chosen words were liable to be quoted as the definitive instance of Hollywood gaucherie, philistinism and disrespect to great authors. And one might suspect that they've been remembered by someone concerned with the Zeffirelli, or Taylor-Burton, *Shrew*. Paul Dehn, Suso Cecchi d'Amico and Zeffirelli himself—whose screenplay credit could be for dialogue reduction—skittishly recognised their debt to 'William Shakespeare without whom they would have been at a loss for words.'

This credit, really, sets the tone of the film: an indefatigable, hammering playfulness which more or less assumes that no one will be paying much attention to those words they are never at a loss for. (An honourable exception: Michael Hordern, poaching harassed laughs as Baptista with the same tip-and-run technique he used a few weeks ago as a Roman dotard.) But almost every production of this play, I find, has the effect of sending one back to the text, convinced that there must be some wisp of poetry, some extra shred of wit, which by an oversight in the production has got lost along the way. Of course there never is; and this version, which pares the Bianca-Lucentio sub-plot almost into incomprehensibility, at least has the merit of cutting some of Shakespeare's more dispensable dialogue.

Actors, one supposes, like the play because it gives them a chance to throw the furniture at each other while still keeping

classical company. Directors must like it because so much needs doing to so little text. Zeffirelli's film predictably encrusts it with decoration: the amount of scuffling, scrapping, flouncing, mopping and mowing that goes on in the background suggests that Padua is in a more or less permanent state of nervous agitation.

All in all, though, the impression is less of a fine Renaissance restlessness than of a fussy, spasmodic garrulity which actually undercuts some of its own effects. Given the richness of costume, and a muted, almost autumnal colour scheme of greens and russets and reds, the film should be marvellously pleasurable to watch. Some of it undeniably is; but one is reminded again that stage pictures are not screen pictures—that one of the harder things to do in a film is to hold a crowd scene in balance, so that there seems to be some point to all the bustling. Zeffirelli actually manages it best in a quieter scene: the long wait before Petruchio's tatterdemalion arrival at the wedding, with the crowd massed like a sulky football queue in the city square.

A pantomime wedding, with the bride making a headlong dash at the altar, the priest pulling shameless faces, and Petruchio taking a swig at the consecrated wine, is very latterday Italianate: Shakespeare, Sicilian style. It's preceded by a silly, pretty sequence in which Petruchio chases Kate around storerooms and apple lofts and over rooftops, and followed by one in which the luckless Shrew gets tipped off her donkey into a pond and left to make her own damp way home. All of which Elizabeth Taylor stands up to, at any rate, with a trouper's spirit. It would be an understatement to say that Miss Taylor is hardly a Shakespearian actress, but then this is hardly a Shakespearian *Shrew*. Richard Burton's Petruchio is rather on the Long John Silver side, piratically boorish, commanding his ruffianly crew of servants as though they were all at sea with the hatches battened down.

No question, either, that for this Petruchio Kate's dowry remains emphatically the first of her attractions. I can't remember a production which lays more stress on the financial side of the marriage bargain, even to the extent—perhaps an inflationary measure—of upping the stakes for the final wager. For all its extravagances, this is by no means a romantic *Shrew*. Perhaps, after all, there is still one more permutation left on the play: the definitive, anti-romantic, marxist version. (pp. 286-87)

Penelope Houston, "Shrewdly Cut," in The Spectator, *Vol. 218, No. 7237, March 10, 1967, pp. 286-87.*

Carey Harrison   (review date Spring 1967)

[*Harrison provides a mixed review of Zeffirelli's film adaptation, praising the superbly constructed Renaissance Paduan setting, but charging that the acting is not in keeping with the traditional mood of the production.*]

Watching the edges of a Zeffirelli production is always a delight. His tableaux are exquisitely composed, his use of movement imaginative, and for once the extras are energetic and enthralled. You can even imagine that these people inhabit the sets, with their children and their dogs. But this is not the imaginative condition of watching an Elizabethan play. True, this is a film, not a play, and must be judged on its own terms, but no one with an understanding of the relation of the parts to the whole in a successful work could effectively hope to make a good film using the playwright's words in so significantly altered a setting.

It must be said that were it not for Shakespeare's lines (without which the scriptwriters would be 'at a loss', the credits tell us) this *Taming of the Shrew* could be a most engaging trifle. Far from being at a loss, the film's most successful moments in fact come between the lines, when Zeffirelli explores a storybook Padua, full of charming pageantry. But when all this is consigned to the background, it takes Zeffirelli's good taste with it, and in the foreground we are treated to the other aspect of his productions, weary farce, tasteless caricature, and a hysteria of grimaces. The central relationship fails because Elizabeth Taylor's Kate is too shallow to make a worthwhile conquest for even the most penurious Petruchio (though the production stresses apologetically that he is only doing it for the money). It is a shrill performance, offering Burton no challenge. By way of balance, Burton undermines the wit of the piece, playing Petruchio as a drunken peasant who owns land but sups with his slaves, rather than a swain fallen on bad times. The poetry and the flamboyance are not wholly missing, merely a little damp. Of the supporting cast, the young lovers are dull, and the comics more hysterical than funny. Only Michael Hordern as Baptista sustains the grotesquerie with success. But even these successes, verse from Burton, farce dotage from Hordern, are no kin of the material mise-en-scène, the detail of the sets, the extras with faces out of Renaissance portraiture.

And yet, if the film had offered a Shrew with character, it would have been an entertaining story, disorganised and often vulgar, but very pretty to watch . . . This is hardly a re-creation of the 16th century, Padua warts and all, but it is imaginative, and permits one to dream about the Renaissance with renewed excitement. Zeffirelli's next film project is *Romeo and Juliet* as a *cinéma-vérité* documentary (his words) on Renaissance Verona. Which takes us back to the very first point: one can't help feeling that only a man without a concept of the way parts of an art work relate to the whole could cherish this ambition; or a man who neither understands nor profoundly likes Shakespeare for what he is. (pp. 97-8)

> *Carey Harrison, in a review of "The Taming of the Shrew," in* Sight and Sound, *Vol. 36, No. 2, Spring, 1967, pp. 97-8.*

The Shakespeare Newsletter (review date September 1967)

[*The anonymous critic takes delight in Zeffirelli's film adaptation of* the Taming of the Shrew, *noting that it is infused with a truly Shakespearean "joy of living."*]

From a director who once directed an Italian *Hamlet* who said, "To be or not to be, what the hell!" we may expect anything and everything. Accordingly, *The Taming of the Shrew* directed by Franco Zefferelli is a completely uninhibited production, tempestuously acted by the co-producers Elizabeth Taylor and Richard Burton whose cinematic and private lives have given them ample experience.

Although Zefferelli, Paul Dean, and Suso Checchi D'Amico are credited with preparing the script, the opening footage of the film gives some credit to Shakespeare "without whom we would have been at a loss for words." To these script writers goes the credit, one supposes, for introducing Feste's *Twelfth*

Night song "The rain it raineth every day" [*Twelfth Night*, V. i. 389ff.], an additional scene where Petruchio wakens Kate for the return to Padua saying it is seven in the morning while she screams that it can be no later than two, and much more.

To the director goes the credit for a more than spectacular wooing scene with a wild chase through a sausage packed smoke-house, a large barn, and over precarious rooftops, one of which collapses, dropping them into a mountain of shorn wool. Through this they tussle amain until Kate drops wearily, and won. It was obvious from her actions earlier, however, that she was not too displeased with her new suitor.

I would not have missed the performance for anything. If Shakespeare was aborted it was done in a Shakespearean manner. The joy of living is manifest throughout. True there is more slapstick farce than Shakespeare would have introduced—it does detract from the romantic element in the play—but as Moira Walsh said in *America* magazine "a sizable segment of the mass movie-going public, who would not ordinarily be found dead at a performance of Shakespeare" will be content to sit through this performance.

Since an adequate setting could not be found in Padua, the film was shot in Rome at the De Laurentin studios. The photography and color are excellent. The full glory of the high and low side of Renaissance life is revealed. The soft-focused cameras retained all the glorious color while rounding off (with a fog filter) the sharp edges of the buildings and landscapes. Some of the scenes seemed to have been painted by the Italian masters. . . .

Not all the critics were happy about the production. The *New York Times* critic said "Don't bother to brush up on your Shakespeare" if you are going to see this film. He found it overacted; "it all grows a bit tedious." Brendan Gill, in *New Yorker* said that there are no villains in this play but Franco Zefferelli. He gave us too many "stone arches and tiled roofs and dusty alleys . . . heaped-up fruit stands and braying asses and overexuberant aristocrats and caponized priests and cretinous peasants." The actors "hurl themselves . . . against the Zefferelli juggernaut, but in vain."

The *Time* magazine critic found Elizabeth Taylor to be the ideal Bawd of Avon and Richard Burton "a kind of King Leer." He found the film "a salty salvo in the war between the sexes" and concluded that "When a classic is treated as deathless, it dies; by being brash and breezy, Zefferelli has breathed new life into an old text."

The bearded Mr. Burton was generally praised for his fine reading of the blank verse while Miss Taylor was usually censured. The *Vogue* magazine critic wondered "to hear so thin a voice emanating from so rich a source."

> *"The Burton-Taylor 'Taming of the Shrew'," in* The Shakespeare Newsletter, *Vol. XVII, September, 1967, p. 33.*

Stephen Farber (review date Fall 1967)

[*Farber charges that Zeffirelli's imagination "is simply not filmic, and the harder he works" at adapting* The Shrew *for the screen, "the worse for the comedy."*]

The Taming of the Shrew, or The Son of Virginia Woolf, can be best understood as cashing in on last year's success; people will apparently never tire of peeping on a fantasy version of the Burtons' homelife. As disguised voyeurism the film may have its rewards, but as entertainment it has very few. Shakespeare's text has been drastically cut, which wouldn't have been bothersome (the play is hardly one of his masterpieces) if director Franco Zeffirelli had found less oafish ways of "opening up" the play. It seems that for most of this long movie roofs are falling in, tables of food overturning, ladies wallowing in mud. The wit and tension in the dialogues between Petruchio and Katharina are lost because Zeffirelli has them running an obstacle course while they bicker—this to make the material cinematic, in case someone misses the point. The film has been filtered through a sort of burnt sienna light that gives it the muted golden haze of many Renaissance paintings, and is indeed lovely to look at, but as a series of stills, not moving pictures. Zeffirelli's imagination is simply not filmic, and the harder he works, the worse for the comedy. Nor has he been of much service to the actors. Burton and Taylor both have their moments, but he has been permitted to ham gruesomely and to rely on a favorite manic laugh all too regularly; and although her face is expressive as well as lovely, her voice is as gratingly shrill and monotonous as in her pre-*Woolf* acting. A couple of the supporting performances register more comfortably—Natasha Pyne's sly but abbreviated Bianca, Michael Hordern's craggy, vulgar father of the bride. Most everyone seems anxious to break into song, and they sometimes do, most spectacularly when Petruchio brazens out a line from *Kiss Me Kate*. Somebody in the front office must have known he was stuck with an overweight mutation.

> Stephen Farber, in a review of "The Taming of the Shrew," in Film Quarterly, *Vol. XXI, No. 1, Fall, 1967, p. 61.*

Jack J. Jorgens   (essay date 1977)

[*Jorgens presents a comprehensive analysis of Zeffirelli's film version of* The Taming of the Shrew, *exploring such aspects as the lively farce, the complexity of the taming process, and the significance of the saturnalian festival. The critic argues that Zeffirelli treats* The Shrew *as a "festive comedy," with Kate and Petruchio as dissenters against a restrictive society.*]

The Taming of the Shrew has more than one layer of reality. The main story of the marrying of Baptista's daughters is framed by another story—the duping of Christopher Sly—which distances the main tale, shares themes with it, and casts a certain ambivalence over it. . . . [*The*] *Shrew* is part romance, focusing upon love and based upon the stock New Comedy situation: the old block the coupling of the young, the blocks are removed, marriages are celebrated, and harmony is restored. In other respects, however, *Shrew* differs from the later comedies. It has fewer characters of complexity and warmth. It is not as genteel and aristocratic in tone—less lyrical and fantastic, less witty, less philosophical, less sentimental about love. The deluding of the drunken tinker by aristocratic pranksters into thinking he is a lord awakened from a bad dream is less genial than Bottom's dream. There is something cruel about it, and though the ending has either been omitted by Shakespeare or is lost, we sense that Sly must inevitably be disillusioned.

This comedy is not set in some never-never land—Illyria, Arden, a wood near Athens—but in Warwick, Padua, and the country near Verona. It has a tough, bourgeois, urban

strain and a note of crass materialism which counterpoints with, and to some extent undermines, the romance. Despite his talk of winning his daughters' affections, Baptista is a merchant driving a hard bargain. He goes along with Petruchio and the false Lucentio because he thinks they have gold and social position, not because they have won Bianca's and Kate's love. Petruchio comes to "wive it *wealthily* in Padua," and though his motives may change during the course of the play, commerce never entirely disappears. Uncharacteristic of romantic comedies, which take us to the threshold of marriage but not—like *Othello* or *Winter's Tale*—inside, the marriage of the hero and heroine comes in the middle of the play and, as in *Merry Wives of Windsor*, their remaining struggles remove some of the idyllic gloss from that institution.

The most realistic element of the play, however—the one that offends modern sensibilities the most—is the taming of Kate. George Bernard Shaw, posing as an irate woman who had just seen the 1888 producing starring Ada Rehan, labelled *Shrew*

> one vile insult to womanhood and manhood from first to last. . . . Of course, it was not Shakespear. Instead of Shakespear's coarse, thick-skinned money hunter who sets to work to tame his wife exactly as brutal people tame animals or children— that is by breaking their spirit by domineering cruelty—we have Garrick's fop who tries to "shut up" his wife by behaving worse than she. . . . In spite of [Petruchio's] . . . winks and smirks when Katherine is not looking, he cannot make the spectacle of a man cracking a heavy whip at a starving woman other than disgusting and unmanly.

To a feminist, *Shrew* is either a piece of male chauvinist wishful thinking, asserting that woman's will can be broken and in the end both she and the man will be the happier for it, or it is a confirmation that the rebel in comedy—and, by implication, in society—must ultimately toe the mark. Neither of these is very funny (or perhaps we should say both are *painfully* funny).

Kate has been interpreted in many ways. Perhaps she is a real shrew, full of self-hatred, contempt for kindness and love, and uncontrollable rage, who is shouted down by a male shrew, trained by a lion tamer, or subjected to primal scream therapy by "Dr. Petruchio." Perhaps she is a neglected daughter who envies the favorite Bianca and seeks both the love and the figure of authority in a husband that she missed in her father. Perhaps she is not a shrew at all, but merely shrewd, playing the same game Bianca plays but angling in a different way and for a better prize. Whichever Katherine predominates, viewed with cold, Monday-morning eye, *Shrew* is not entirely humorous, especially if Kate's final speech is taken at face value.

But *Shrew* contains farce as well as romance and realism. It is a play not for a sober Monday morning but for a drunken Saturday night, a vacation from morality, psychology, and seriousness, in which we can sit back and laugh at a caricature of the battle of the sexes, free of the need to be understanding and fair or even to pass judgment. From this perspective, it is enough that there be plenty of knockabout physical humor, that the struggle be lively and entertaining and the action varied (as in any monster movie). It doesn't really matter who wins (would the play really change if, as in *Merry Wives,* the women tamed the men?), for the enjoyment is in the intrigue, curses, and pratfalls, in seeing con artists conned and the everyday world turned into a madhouse.

Franco Zeffirelli, in his boisterous film of *Shrew,* which pits Richard Burton against Elizabeth Taylor, plays up the romance and sentiment, tones down the realism, and revels in the farce. Petruchio and Kate are in love from the moment they set eyes on each other. Their struggle, really a mutual taming, is "the old game"—they test each other, school each other (the other schoolmasters are fakes). When they come to an agreement, it is much more like real-life marriage than the pallid Lucentio-Bianca soap bubble which is pricked in the end. Crass, drunken, self-serving, and materialistic at the beginning, Petruchio, without being rendered impotent, becomes civilized, witty, and dignified by the end. Twice Kate chooses Petruchio over the collection of fops and old men in Padua: by maintaining silence behind the stained glass window when Petruchio announces their wedding on Sunday, and by following him in the rain when he leaves her at Padua's gates and rides toward his crumbling, moth-eaten mansion.

Petruchio's "taming" of Kate in this film has several dimensions. He is the plebeian, taking down a peg a spoiled, egotistical, well-fed, rich girl, teaching her about humility, patience, and recognizing a will other than her own. He is the bohemian teaching her to disdain wealth and luxury, to avoid the bourgeois obsession with appearances and a confusion of values by subjecting her to wetness, cold, fatigue, hunger, pain, and the ridicule of her inferiors. Petruchio, who tests the silver of Baptista's goblets before broaching the subject of marriage and cries "my twenty thousand crowns!" as Kate jumps out the window to escape him, changes too. Like most good teachers, he learns as he teaches.

> To me she's married, not unto my clothes.
> ....
> Well, come my Kate; we will unto your father's
> Even in these honest mean habiliments.
> Our purses shall be proud, our garments poor,
> For 'tis the mind that makes the body rich;
> And as the sun breaks through the darkest clouds
> So honor peereth in the meanest habit.
>
> [III. ii. 117; IV. iii. 169-74]

Petruchio is also a playful actor who, unlike the uncreative maskers and unconscious hypocrites of Padua, enjoys taking on roles, is self-aware, and has a sense of irony.

In the beginning, Kate is encased in the role of "shrew," cast in it by frightened, ineffectual men and crafty (though on the surface, submissive) Bianca and kept in it by her refusal to capitulate. She is trapped in a negative image of everything in Padua that she hates, and in that sense she is an imitation of it. Petruchio, her knight in tarnished armor, opposes the frozen, the negative, the uncreative. As D. A. Traversi said [in his *Approach to Shakespeare*], "Petruchio is in effect revealing the *real* Kate to herself. . . ." In cursing him, fighting him, fleeing him, Kate is infinitely more alive and inventive than in dealing with lesser men. Perhaps she learns humility, but she also learns not to be tied to the literal when she must say it is seven o'clock when it is two, or when she must call the sun the moon. In one of the funniest scenes in the film, Kate learns that her husband's "commands" are an invitation to humorous invention. With delicious, devilish innocence, she greets grey-bearded Vincentio as a budding virgin whose parents are blessed in "her." Greeted with his bewildered look as he peers around the head of his horse, she

realizes her "mistake" and delivers a mock apology for having her eyes dazzled "by the . . . sun?" (she looks to Petruchio; he nods yes) [IV. v. 46]. By raining blows on his servants (the first time we see Petruchio he chases Grumio around the fire, boots him, and rams him into Hortensio's door), making impossible demands, and causing the faults he scolds (he trips the servant who brings the water), by decimating the fashionable clothes prepared for Kate to wear to Bianca's wedding and placing the blame on the poor craftsmen, Petruchio shows Kate her own image. He forces her to see that she must be more forgiving. "Patience," she says, "I pray you, 'twas a fault unwilling" [IV. i. 156]. "I pray you, husband, be not so disquiet. The meat was well if you were so contented" [IV. i. 168-69].

> PETRUCHIO: First kiss me Kate, and we will.
> KATE: What, in the middle of the street?
> PETRUCHIO: What, art thou ashamed of me?
> KATE: No sir, God forbid, but ashamed to kiss.
> PETRUCHIO: Why then let's home again. Come sirrah,
>   let's away.
> KATE: Nay, I will give thee a kiss. Now pray thee, love,
>   stay.
>
> [V. ii. 143-48]

(In the film, Kate holds her own, for she gives him a most unsatisfying peck on the nose.) What he demands, in place of both conformity and rebellion, is tolerance, strong bonds between people, kindness, forgiveness.

For Zeffirelli, Kate's "submission" at the end is a kind of *rite de passage,* a demonstration that she understands what Petruchio has been trying to teach her. After a taste of domestic warfare with Petruchio, a close look at the meanness and vulgarity of the widow and Bianca, and a glance at the children playing with the dogs before the lavish banquet table, Kate seizes the opportunity of the wager to make a pact with Petruchio. With delightful irony, she, who has terrified men by smashing furniture, bellowing, and raining blows on them, bodily hauls the widow and Bianca before their husbands and describes the *frailty* of women. Using her new-found sense of role playing, she uncovers the real shrews and feeds the males present such an eloquent and unconditional surrender to male domination that they are all taken in. But the speech isn't really to them; it is to Petruchio. Beneath her irony, she enunciates the paradox at the heart of love in all of Shakespeare's romantic comedies: give all and you will get all. Kate's fluid shifts in tone, playful hyperbole, love of doing the unexpected, and obvious awareness of her double audience constitute her farewell to the narrowness and rigidities of Kate the shrew. Her offer of "love, fair looks, and true obedience" [V. ii. 153] to Petruchio's *honest* will," an important qualification, confirms her new-found humility and expresses gratitude for his freeing her from a sterile role. This time there is no hesitation when he asks for a kiss. And if the audience has missed the point and thinks Kate's spirit broken, to the delight of the crowd in the film while Petruchio triumphs over the losers of the wager, Kate sneaks out of the room and makes him begin the chase anew.

Zeffirelli has little use for the realism in the play. For instance, Shakespeare's refusal to be "poetical" and lyrical in the play has been overruled, for the film is loaded with pleasant but syrupy melodies in the best Hollywood tradition. (This is one of the few Shakespeare films where the audience comes out humming the music.) Broad comic acting emphasizes the typical nature of the characters: stooped, pathetically outclassed Baptista, Hortensio the effeminate fop, the pantaloon Gremio, Lucentio the handsome young suitor, Grumio and Tranio the tricky servants, the pedant laden with books and peering through spectacles, the Puck-like Biondello, who peers like a faun through the greenery while Lucentio and Bianca make love in the garden. Whatever ironic perspective Shakespeare provided by making the main action a crude entertainment for a drunken, deluded tinker trying in vain to get his "wife" into bed is gone, for like many theatrical directors, Zeffirelli has omitted the frame story altogether.

There are touches of vivid realistic detail in the film: the children taunting the "wife-stealer" in the stocks and the "drunkard" in the cage near Padua's city gates, tough-looking men and whores, Gremio's bad breath, Hortensio's getting hairs from his false beard in his mouth, Petruchio's ugly, gap-toothed servants, giant dogs eating meat scraps by the banquet table at Bianca's wedding, the ticks Petruchio picks from his dog and shows to squeamish Hortensio, the filth that covers everything at Petruchio's seedy, gothic house, and the downpour that drenches Petruchio and Kate. But these are used for comic effect, and work to heighten the colorful, rich portrait of renaissance Italy. From the opening moments when Lucentio and Tranio, riding in a gentle summer rain, spy Padua haloed with a rainbow beyond a pastoral vision with shepherds, sheep, and greenery, the film is a beautiful idyll bathed in golden and rose-colored light. The central stylistic device, derived from the language of a play uncharacteristically lacking in verbal ornament, is the epic catalogue, the heaping on of detail. Reading verbal floods in Shakespeare—like Gremio's description of his city and country houses, the verbal portraits of Petruchio's outrageous wedding costume and the desecrated marriage ceremony, Grumio's list of tasks the servants were to have performed, and Petruchio's enumeration of rich garments Kate will wear to Bianca's wedding—Zeffirelli created visual equivalents in shots full of sensuous surfaces, color, and motion. Vicariously we devour fancy dishes and drink fine wine, eat symbolic apples, roll in the grass, lie in huge soft beds, sing bawdy love songs, swing on a trapeze and then drop into a bin of raw wool, splash with choirboys in the fountain outside the church, and ride through the rain.

Apart from sentimental romance, Zeffirelli's major emphasis is upon farce. The film delights in harmless violence and festive destruction. Kate smashes shutters and stained-glass windows, splinters music stands and lutes, rips out the bell rope which Petruchio tugs upon so daintily, and tears loose a railing to hurl at him. Petruchio drunkenly knocks over wine glasses and pulls down curtains at Hortensio's house, smashes through railings and brick walls, and falls through the roof in Baptista's barn. He pummels and spits upon his servants, bisects a hat with a family sword causing the haberdasher to faint, tears dresses, hurls food, overturns the dinner table, and makes a shambles of the wedding bed.

This *Shrew* revels in farce's extravagant expenditures of energy and comically accelerated actions: wooing and winning in half an hour, running down the aisle at the wedding, rushing down a muddy mountain on a donkey, spinning half-plucked chickens on a spit. It delights in absurdly complicated situations, as when an avalanche of babbling suitors and schoolteachers falls upon bewildered Baptista, or distracted Vincentio confronts fraudulent versions of himself and his son. It has farce's shallow characterizations and lack of reflective passages. Above all, its primary structural device, the chase,

which is repeated in endless variations, is straight out of the Keystone Cops. Tranio chases Lucentio, the singers chase Bianca, Gremio and Hortensio follow Tranio who follows Lucentio who follows Bianca home, and both Lucentio and Petruchio pursue their servants. In the longest chase of the film, Petruchio pursues Kate until he catches up with her at the altar. But the pattern of pursuit does not stop there. Kate rides after Petruchio and Grumio in the rain, the servants chase the chickens with meat cleavers, and so on to the end of the film where Petruchio's chase of Kate is renewed (this time, we suspect, she will not run too hard).

In filming *Shrew*, Zeffirelli obviously provided a pleasant vehicle for Richard Burton and Elizabeth Taylor. But he also redefined, perhaps even revealed, its central action. For most critics and directors, the essence of the play is the "taming" of Kate, or at least the mutual taming of Kate and Petruchio; and certainly the director's radical compression of the Bianca plot makes them even more prominant. But, important as it is, the "taming" is not the heart of the film. Rather, it is the good-natured but thorough assault of Kate and Petruchio on Padua and Paduan values. Zeffirelli turns loose two rebels against hypocrites, greedy pantaloons, time-servers, blind idealists, tricky maidens, and crafty widows. They declare war on respectability, duty, religion, sighing literary romance, and narrowing materialism.

In a fine discussion of *Shakespeare's Festive Comedy*, C. L. Barber argues that *A Midsummer Night's Dream, The Merchant of Venice, Love's Labour's Lost, As You Like It, Twelfth Night* and *Henry IV, Part 1* are rooted in saturnalian festivals and other outbursts of "folly"—May Games, the Lord of Misrule, Morris Dances, Masks, Disguisings—which survived in Elizabethan England from the middle ages. In complaining of the European cousins of these revels in 1445, the Dean of the Faculty of Theology at Paris seems almost to be writing a commentary on Zeffirelli's *Shrew*:

> Who, I ask you, with any Christian feelings, will not condemn when priests and clerks are seen wearing masks and monstrous visages at the hours of Office: dancing in the Choir, dressed as women, panders, or minstrels, singing lewd songs? They eat black-pudding at the horn of the altar next the celebrant, play at dice there, censing with foul smoke from the soles of old shoes, and running and leaping about the whole church in unblushing, shameless iniquity; and then, finally, they are seen driving about the town and its theatres in carts and deplorable carriages to make an infamous spectacle for the laughter of bystanders and participants, with indecent gestures of the body and language most unchaste and scurrilous.

Ultimately, if anthropologists are correct, both these festivals and comedy go back through Rome and Greece to ancient seasonal rites of the death of the old year and birth of the new. "The holiday occasion and the comedy are parallel manifestations of the same pattern of culture, of a way that men can cope with their life." By removing Shakespeare's frame story of Christopher Sly and replacing it with a frame of his own—the saturnalian revels of the students of Padua—Zeffirelli emphasizes that *Shrew* is also a "festive comedy" saturated with the exhilaration of holiday, that Petruchio and Kate are allied with the saturnalian forces which stand the everyday on its head and turn reason inside out. As Zeffirelli sees it, the comedy is not primarily about a taming, but about a release of Dionysian energies. As in Alf Sjoberg's *Miss Julie* and Fellini's

Amarcord, the opening saturnalian ritual defines what follows.

When the film opens, Lucentio and Tranio arrive in Padua on the first day of the new academic year. It is first celebrated solemnly as they witness a beautiful cathedral service in which a boys' choir sings and a Bishop leads the students in prayer. But suddenly a cannon is fired and pandemonium reigns as Zeffirelli provides us with a marvelous condensation of saturnalian motifs. Death, the archenemy of comedy, is mocked as a decorum-shattering funeral winds its way through the streets. A mitred Bishop wearing a mask of a pig strides with great dignity at the head of the procession of mourners carrying a staff crowned with a grinning skull sporting a rakishly slanted turban. In place of the beautiful choir music, we hear raucous songs and obscene chants. The "corpse" (the Old Year) is a skinny, lecherous old man in a white nightcap and nightgown who will not stay dead and has to be forcibly restrained from attacking women (some of them students in drag) along the way. He is treated most indecorously—pummeled with a broom, shaken, tossed high in the air and caught on his bier. The figurative royalty of the procession are the King and Queen, represented by giant masks, but the real queen—the Madonna—is a giant whore who displays her mammoth breasts and strides brassily down the street on foot-high chopines. Chivalry, embodying the height of medieval civilization and encompassing religion, feudal loyalty, and romance, is reduced to a ludicrous knight on a hobby horse, wielding a padded, three-pronged lance. Nearly everyone in the procession wears a mask, many with animalistic features, symbolizing the casting off of civilized identities for more elemental ones. What seems to be an unexpectedly romantic, gentle song sung by several revellers to Bianca, as a figure in a beaked mask lowers a hook to lift her veil, turns out to be bawdy: ". . . give me leave / To do for thee all that Adam did for Eve / I'll do it well, gentle maid, I'll do it well."

This rowdy procession with its chaos of shouts, songs, and shrieks of laughter, completely disrupts the daily routine in Padua, routs seriousness and pretensions to dignity, overturns the hierarchies of power, and dissolves boredom and drudgery. It challenges the populace, tests their sexual prowess, creative energy, thirst, appetites, and late-night endurance. It renews communal feeling by replacing social and economic competition with an orgy of hospitality. Part of the idyll is that modern urban paranoia is banished and creative anarchy reigns, cementing the society together and making life—fraught as it is with failure, sickness, and death—more tolerable.

This new frame was a perceptive stroke, and it is interesting to see how many of its themes carry over into the other parts of both play and film—the theme of masking, for instance, of confused or transformed identities. Everyone in the play wears a mask of some sort: Lucentio and Hortensio the masks of "schoolmasters," Kate is "the shrew," Petruchio "the patient wooer," Tranio is "Lucentio," and Bianca "the meek and dutiful daughter." Vincentio has the dreamlike experience of meeting his own double. The overturning of hierarchies also recurs: daughters and sons rule the fathers, servants become masters. In both the opening procession and the rest of the film the central activity is male pursuit of the female. Kate refers specifically to the Madonna-whore when she shrieks at her father "would you make a whore of me among these mates?" [cf. I. i. 58] Above all, it becomes clear that in assaulting conventional society, Petruchio and Kate are Lord and Lady of Misrule, two bulls crashing through the Paduan china shop. Their courtship burlesques courtly love. Petruchio, who has absorbed Christopher Sly's coarseness and love for the bottle, is no genteel poetical wooer, and Kate, who hurls stools and kegs at suitors and breaks lutes over their heads, lacks the disposition of a Maiden Fair. Their destruction, like that in the Marx brothers' *Night at the Opera,* is an expression of contempt both for culture and for things (recall Petruchio's schoolings), an assault on the old order. The life of decorative luxury, condensed by Zeffirelli into the wine glasses, rich curtains, stuffed bed, and bath water strewn with rose petals at Hortensio's house, is put in its place by Petruchio's bumblings and smashings, socks with holes, and delicate swishing aside of the rose petals to dampen his fingers so as to daub his eyes and ears.

The wedding of Kate and Petruchio is, like the funeral procession, a travesty and a sacrilege. Petruchio arrives two-and-a-half hours late, drunk, dressed in garish clothes (traditional for the Lord of Misrule) including a huge striped pillow adorned with pheasant feathers, carrying dead game birds, and blowing kisses to ladies in the crowd. Enraged, Kate invites him with a smile, then shoves him down the steps, puts down her veil, and races down the aisle, with Petruchio, the children, and guests scrambling in behind her. And all the while, an incongruously beautiful, slow "Gloria" is sounded by organ and chorus in the background, recalling the opening religious ceremony. Once at the altar, Petruchio falls asleep, has a coughing fit, gulps down the holy wine with an oath, shoves the mousy, protesting priest to the floor, fumbles for the ring and laughing stupidly displays it to the crowd. He caps his performance by stopping Kate's mouth with a kiss at the "will" of *I will not!* The traditional wedding dinner is deflated in midjollity as Petruchio carries Kate out into the rain and leaves the guests to celebrate without them. It is replaced by the inelegant, parodic repast of half-plucked chickens and pudding poured over someone's hat, served by filthy, leering cutthroats amid the wreckage at Petruchio's house; and even this is delayed by Petruchio's comically prolonged grace and then destroyed as he rages that the meal is not fit for the starving bride. The wedding night becomes a blow on the head with a warming pan, a bed ripped apart, and—for the groom—a night on a hard bench.

Also following Shakespeare's lead, Zeffirelli turns the wooing of Kate into a mock epic, continuing the travesty of chivalric valor in the opening procession. When Petruchio, Hortensio, Gremio, and the rest back away in fear upon hearing Bianca scream, our hero boldly declares:

> Think you a little din can daunt mine ears?
> Have I not in my time heard lions roar?
> Have I not heard the sea, puffed up with winds,
> Rage like an angry boar chafed with sweat?
> Have I not heard great ordnance in the field
> And heaven's artillery thunder in the skies?
> Have I not in a pitched battle heard
> Loud 'larums, neighing steeds, and trumpets' clang?
> And do you tell me of a woman's tongue?
>
> [I. ii. 199-207]

Then a spirited Sousa-like march is played by a totally anachronistic full marching band on the sound track as Petruchio strides down the street, followed by lesser mortals, to ring the bell at Baptista's house. In another display of comic heroism, Petruchio, while casting the commercial values of Padua in the teeth of the guests ("she is my goods, my chattels" [III.

ii. 230]) "rescues" Kate from the bridal dinner (like Erroll Flynn) to the accompaniment of shouts, thunder, and lightning flashing against Grumio's pathetically short sword (Petruchio has lost his).

In "comedies of the green world," as Northrop Frye calls them, it is usual at the end for "a new society to crystallize around the hero" [*Anatomy of Criticism*]. The Lord and Lady of Misrule do not reject order altogether. They simply seek a period of release from imprisoning things and rigid identities in order to humanize society and make discoveries about themselves. Like the lovers and Dukes who flee to the forest in *A Midsummer Night's Dream* and in *As You Like It*, or Bassanio who voyages to Belmont to hazard for Portia, Petruchio and Kate journey from the city to their decrepit country house, where they are reborn. But once Kate has invaded the male enclave and restored it to order, and the seeds of harmony between herself and Petruchio are sewn, like the other voyagers, they make a return. The concluding banquet celebrates a new harmony between parents and children, the old order and the new.

Still, in the film the reconciliation and transformation at the end are not complete. At the dinner Bianca's mask drops, now that she is a wife, and, as was foreshadowed in her earlier outbursts of temper, she becomes a "shrew." The joke is on the newly married men, for not only have they lost the bet, they have yet to fight the battles that Kate and Petruchio have fought, and, quite frankly, they don't look up to it. As in Shakespeare, the hero and heroine do not remain at the center of the supposedly renewed society but assert their superiority by leaving it. Petruchio is ultimately bored with Padua ("eat and drink, eat and drink" [cf. V. ii. 12]) and finds chasing the playful, inviting Kate much more interesting. For once the rebels in a comedy are not absorbed by society, but maintain their independence to the last.

Zeffirelli has not made a perfect film of *The Taming of the Shrew*. Though the cuts in the Bianca plot, which has not aged well, are justified and well executed, and the new opening is both functional and entertaining, one misses Christopher Sly and the doubleness he lends to the play proper. One could do with less mindless baritone laughter from Richard Burton and more acting, and one would like to see as much care lavished on the lines as on the decor and the farce. Nevertheless, it is a better and more thoughtful film than the surprisingly vitriolic attacks on it by many critics would lead one to believe. Given the broad style of the play, with its obvious humor and shallow characterization, it is unreasonable to demand the same subtlety and sophistication we demand of films of *Hamlet*. And, certainly given the sober temper of our times, there is nothing wrong with Zeffirelli's attempt to revive in Shakespeare's comedy a film version of the Saturnalian Revel. (pp. 66-78)

> *Jack J. Jorgens, "Franco Zeffirelli's 'Taming of the Shrew',"* in his Shakespeare on Film *Indiana University Press, 1977, pp. 66-78.*

Michael Pursell   (essay date 1980)

[*Pursell evaluates Zeffirelli's film version of* the Taming of the Shrew, *remarking that in this adaptation the director maintains the kind of tonal and thematic balance usually limited to a stage production. Zeffirelli's use of visual techniques achieves an artificiality similar to that of a stage backdrop, the critic notes. The film is successful precisely because Zeffirelli*

avoids the temptation offered by the medium to develop the play's more realistic dimensions.]

Zeffirelli's two films *The Taming of the Shrew* and *Romeo and Juliet* seem to me among the most aesthetically successful film adaptations of Shakespeare to date. Such a statement naturally invites controversy in that purists of either side would say that an aesthetically successful adaptation is a contradiction in terms; that in the last analysis the verbal nature of a Shakespeare text cannot be reconciled with the visual nature of film. Zeffirelli's films go some way towards refuting that view.

Before looking in detail at *The Taming of the Shrew,* it is perhaps worth making two points. One is that Zeffirelli's films are essentially visual and cinematic in their conception. They do not exist simply to record and transmit a performance of a play; rather, they *are* in every aspect of their visual realization an interpretive performance—the medium of film itself impinges on the transmission of the text and its meanings. One needs only to compare Zeffirelli with Olivier to see this. In the latter's films the visual realization furnishes merely a more or (frequently) less realistic background to the enunciation of the Text—it supplies decor instead of being an integral interpretive element. Zeffirelli does not treat film as a transparent medium in this way, and this raises the second point: Cinematic adaptation is necessarily a blend of the verbal and the visual, the ultimate aim being, presumably, the integration of the visual realization with the text so that each supports and enriches the other. The attendant danger of audiovisual pleonasm this produces will at times necessitate editing of the text. This seems to be a small price to pay in cases where a director is manifestly sensitive to the tone and spirit of a play, and where his fidelity to these emerges in his visual approach. Such fidelity is obvious in Zeffirelli, where he converts those textual devices so vital to the tone of each play into visual equivalents. The result in each case is a film true to the spirit of the text that is at the same time fluent, lively and quite lacking in that ponderous verbal or visual redundancy that is all too frequent in filmed Shakespeare.

Filming the *Shrew* immediately presents a number of problems, all connected with that device unique in Shakespeare— the Induction. Far from being simply an animated prologue or comic hors d'oeuvres, this device has quite clear tonal and thematic functions. On a thematic level, its characters and action prefigure those of the play proper, from the comic inversion of Sly being kicked out by the termagant hostess to the Lord's elaborately staged jest that articulates a major unifying idea in the play—that of "supposes." From this point of view Zeffirelli could conceivably have ignored the Induction altogether, insofar as the play's popular appeal does not rest on any thematic concerns announced in it, but rather on the comic battle of the sexes in the play proper. To leave out the Induction might truncate the play's more subtle thematic concerns, but enough would remain to satisfy most audiences. It is, I think, to Zeffirelli's great credit that he does not adopt this easy solution.

In fact, he cannot ignore the Induction because it functions on a tonal as well as a thematic level. As its title suggests, the Induction is a device for drawing us into the world of the play, providing a bridge, via the earthy Warwickshire humor of Sly, between us and that world. At the same time, by establishing a play within a play, the Induction keeps us at one remove from fictional Padua, so that the total effect is to enable us to experience the play as "real" while being aware of the play as a play. It is obvious, of course, that all theatre exhibits a basic duality such as this—the stage is at once a stage and an imaginative elsewhere; we accept in the theatre an illusion that is visibly neither real nor realistic. This duality is so commonplace that it forms an unremarked, tacit assumption on the part of players and audience alike; an assumption without which theatre simply would not function. Shakespeare wants us to remark it though, hence the stress on the Induction as a framing device that gives an additional, unusual degree of reflexive awareness to the fiction. In this respect, the Induction serves to adjust very precisely the basic duality of the theatre experience—an adjustment that creates a tonal balance that is vital if the play is not to be misunderstood. Once the play within the play begins we are, thanks to the Induction, sufficiently involved to treat the characters seriously as people, yet sufficiently detached to see their clash as comic, despite the violent verbal and physical action. The mood is comic without being flippant; serious without being solemn. As the major figure in the Induction, the Lord twice refers directly to his moderating function, and I think it is clear that without some tonal guidance it would be easy to adopt extreme responses in the play's initial stages—it could appear as harmless and superficial farce, or a callous and cynical tale of the triumph of mutual self-interest over genuine feeling.

All this is achieved with such ease in the theatre that it might hardly seem to be an issue at all. Yet the transfer of so quintessentially theatrical a work to film poses problems that Zeffirelli cannot overlook if he is to remain faithful to the spirit and tone of the text. Tone for Zeffirelli must have been very much an issue, since any alteration threatens a serious imbalance. The core of the problem is that, unlike theatre, the tacit assumption between spectator, players and director in film is that there is *no* duality—that film proffers an unassailable, autonomous and wholly unreflexive diegesis.

Given this, the necessary tonal balance can be established only by some visual equivalent of the Induction. This device must be visual because Zeffirelli can neither use Shakespeare's Induction nor wholly ignore it. He can't use it because logically he would then have to present the play proper *as a play,* which makes nonsense of filming it in the first place. In any case, in the theatre we are inducted into the play to a considerable extent; to film the Induction would put quite the wrong emphasis on subsequent scenes—they would lack the qualified but necessary illusionist element. Filmed theatre remains exactly that, as Olivier's films amply demonstrate. He can't ignore the Induction because he would then be using a straightforward photographic realism as in *Romeo and Juliet.* Such a "realist" approach would have a two-fold effect. Firstly, placing the characters and action firmly in some sort of alternative real world would emphasize the reality of, say, Katharina's anguish or Petruchio's avarice, at the expense of the comic balance. Similarly, Baptista would become much like Capulet in *Romeo and Juliet*—a repugnant figure using his daughter as a counter in a social/financial transaction. Secondly, the reality of the setting and consequently heightened seriousness of our reaction would by contrast reveal the ludicrous impossibility of conventions like multiple disguise and love at first sight. In terms of its action, the play simply cannot be taken as a credible representation of real events. Disguises that *work* are only possible in non-realistic fiction. Yet how can this be captured in a medium that demands consistent realism in its locations if we are not to dismiss it as "theatrical" in the Olivier sense? Zeffirelli must somehow moderate the realism that makes the seriousness of Kate's

predicament too vivid and the play's conventions ridiculous, without falling into the trap of having his characters stuck in a theatre or wandering through cardboard studio sets. Visually the film must lie, as the play does in the theatre, somewhere between real and unreal, belief and disbelief, involvement and detachment. Words cannot help here—they can't make an image credible if it is not, nor can they make it seem false if it's visually convincing.

Zeffirelli adopts a number of related visual techniques to solve his problem. The first of these is to eschew location shooting and contrast to many a studio location, Zeffirelli's Padua is convincingly solid and three-dimensional—in other words it appears to be consistently realistic. Another is that it seems to ramble over an area that apparently defies studio presentation. Then, too, its realism of detail is carried through to an almost fanatical degree—worn cobbles, dirt-encrusted murals and many other small details attest to the precision with which Zeffirelli has sought to create a credible, lived-in environment. The success of this can be judged by glancing at any of the "exterior" shots.

At the same time this is only a partial solution. It avoids clumsy theatricality, and it does help prevent Padua from seeming too divorced from reality. Nevertheless, while Zeffirelli needs to remove the action from the real world, he doesn't therefore want to confine it to the studio, and fanatical realism of detail notwithstanding, that would be the result were he to involve no other technique. Another danger is that this combination of studio location and realism of detail could be taken as an attempt to mislead or deceive the viewer—asking him to take what he sees as real. Even a hint of this kind of trick can seriously damage a film's credibility. The studio locations are patently not real, and it would be useless for director or audience to try to pretend that they are.

Initially, Zeffirelli manoeuvres us into accepting the studio location—and the whole realistic/artificial mixture so familiar in theatre and so difficult on film—through a carefully contrived visual contrast that to some extent substitutes for the Induction.

In the film's opening shot the Panavision screen is filled by an enormous painted background of the Italian countryside. The foreground is occupied by a passing shepherd and his flock. A road winds away into the distance where two figures approach on horseback. It is raining. As the figures draw close we cut to shot two, which offers a mid-shot of them with some dialogue that establishes them as Lucentio and Tranio. Again, it is clearly raining. Lucentio declares his intention to study in Padua, whereupon we cut to shot three—another painted landscape, this time showing Padua nestling in "fruitful Lombardy" complete with rainbow over the town. Lucentio's speech takes us across the next cut to shot four, where we find ourselves deep in the town, tracking along one of those highly realistic streets.

These three shots constitute the establishing scene and are worth some attention, for what they help to establish is the kind of world in which these characters move; a world at once credibly realistic and colorfully unreal. These twin strands of apparent realism and obvious artificiality are clear in each shot. The painted background of shot one, for example, is persuasively naturalistic at first glance, and the imperceptible blending of painted background space and real foreground space reinforces this feeling. Yet a second glance reveals that it is, in fact, a painting. Again, the fact that Zeffirelli fills the Panavision screen with it momentarily disconcerts us by sheer size—it must surely be real—but finally this strategy positively invites us to detect the falsity of the thing. By allowing the painted scene to dominate the opening shot, Zeffirelli ensures that we are at once intrigued by its apparent realism yet aware of its artificiality. He thus announces the kind of world the film will present, while persuading us to accept—if only temporarily—the mixture of realistic and artificial; an acceptance stimulated by the honesty of the shot, its intriguing realism and imperceptible line of demarcation between foreground and background. Other elements of the shot naturally contribute to this. The presence of the shepherd emphasizes real as opposed to painted space, yet Lucentio and Tranio quite literally appear to ride out of the latter and into the former. The shepherd and his sheep are real enough, yet immediately bring associations of the pastoral; a highly artificial, non-realistic type of fiction.

Shots two and three amplify these twin strands. The rain of shot two is a nicely realistic touch—somehow we don't expect it—yet the same shot clearly reveals it to be that convenient studio rain that falls in front of the camera but not on the actors. In shot three the rainbow is a perfectly naturalistic touch, but with inevitable associations of non-realistic, idyllic fiction.

Zeffirelli could hardly make it plainer that we are being invited to participate in a realistic kind of illusion; an environment predominantly false but intriguingly realistic. This emphatic opening statement is not quite the tonal balance the play needs, though, and it is here that Zeffirelli makes use of contrast. In contrast with the establishing scene the realism of shot four is so overwhelming that we accept it—we treat it as real—almost without hesitation. In the cut, the emphasis has shifted significantly, from the predominantly artificial and false to the predominantly realistic. Since the establishing scene has prepared us for some degree of overt falsity in the image, we accept the studio location where we would normally reject it. In fact the only obviously false element is the light, and Zeffirelli has coped with that problem too. In this way, Zeffirelli creates initial conviction in a studio location, persuading us to treat as real a location we know and see is not. This is closely analogous to the balance created by the Induction in the theatre.

Maintaining that balance is something else. To do this, Zeffirelli makes the most of the contrast. The Padua of the fourth and all subsequent shots is alive with fascinating and purposeful peripheral activity; an artisan finishing a statue, housewives with washing, men gossiping and so on. This activity rapidly escalates as the students gather at the University to inaugurate the new academic year, until it takes over the image. After the ceremony, the screen becomes almost literally a riot of energy, activity and color. It is impossible not to become caught up in this and surrender to the intensity of it, so that by this time we are definitely treating the illusion as real. Yet it is at this point that Zeffirelli brings up the titles, as if once again to remind us that it is only an illusion after all. If I seem to exaggerate the care he takes, I can only refer the reader to the contrast between the establishing scene and the post-wedding donkey ride. In the latter, there is no trace of a painted landscape; everything is solid and real, unlike Petruchio's castle. Here again it is raining, but not "studio" rain—rather a downpour that drenches everyone over an area seemingly beyond the scope of studio presentation. Such

consistent handling of detail pervades the film, and it is a prime source of its tonal coherence.

Shakespeare's Induction is, conceivably, separable from the play it precedes. Zeffirelli's establishing scene is not. Despite the contrast it facilitates, it must not be too distinct from the more realistic Padua; they must both be acceptable images of the world of the film. Zeffirelli achieves this link and at the same time solves the problem of the short-lived effect of the contrast through one of the film's most striking visual characteristics—its use of color.

The whole film appears to have been shot through an ochre or sepia tinted filter. The effect is a mild alteration of color values better described as a bias rather than a tint, since no colors are lost or even seriously distorted. The resulting tones and hues are deliberately evocative of Renaissance painting, and by making both establishing and subsequent scenes resemble each other in this way, the color bias makes them both clearly images of the same fictional world: They resemble each other more than either resembles the real world.

The color bias also helps sustain throughout the film the required tonal balance. It impinges on the highly realistic studio sets so that they are literally seen in a new light: Not the studio light that is always an inadequate and detectable substitute for daylight, and which falsifies everything it touches; rather a light that in conjunction with the studio realism recreates the effect of Renaissance painting in offering a world in touch equally with realism of detail and imaginative visual creation. Being an optical effect, the color bias affects all the elements of the image equally, adding a degree of intentioned unreality to an otherwise highly realistic scene. Paradoxically, this enables us to believe in the studio locations, at least enough to create the tonal balance. It is clear, I think, that the studio location must itself be consistently realistic if there is to be any level of credibility at all: Our belief in the painted landscape, for example, lasts less than the running time of the first shot. That we accept the obviously artificial light and color is partly a result of the contrast, of course, as well as the delicacy of the effect and the fact that it clearly cannot be taken as some inept attempt to simulate reality. It is only through light and color that Zeffirelli can achieve his tonal adjustment; he has made maximum use of those elements of the image most amenable to expressive distortion. As a result of the color bias the whole image gravitates towards the required real/unreal limbo so common in theatre and so unusual in film.

If our response to fictional Padua is elusively balanced between belief and disbelief then the most striking aspect of the color bias is that it creates this balance by itself, irrespective of the particular content of the image. The sensuousness of the color, present in all color films but exaggerated here, contains an implicit contradiction. As Alex remarks in *A Clockwork Orange,* "it's funny how the colors of the like real world only seem really real when you viddy them on the screen." At the same time, this heightening effect makes the illusion all the more apparent. In the *Shrew* the color immediately and effectively secures our belief in that it makes the image vivid—that is, engaging to the senses. One obvious reason for this is that an ochre bias emphasizes "warm" colors (yellows, oranges, browns) that attract us, without excluding others (greens, blues or even blacks and whites). One great advantage of this bias is that it can assimilate most colors without any violent or unharmonious effect, while at the same time promoting an increased awareness of materials and surfaces—the effect of the color bias on, say, the velvets and brocades of the costumes makes them noticeably more tactile than normal. This doubly inviting effect of warm colors in association with a tactile sense of surfaces is something Zeffirelli plays up for all it is worth: Flaking walls; pitted stone; heavy tapestries; dirt-encrusted murals and so on figure in the background of almost every scene. Indeed, it is this sense of the tactile so closely bound up with the color that both compels and anchors our belief in the world of the film. Yet at the same time, and despite the strength of this sensuous involvement, it is quite obvious that the colors do not have their natural value, and the optical interference that produces this change is quite clear. The effect is to distance us, making us aware of the illusion. The color bias therefore tugs gently in opposite directions throughout the film. To the extent that the color bias induces us to believe in the image and to disbelieve it, it functions as a permanent equivalent of the Induction that draws us into and keeps us at one remove from Padua.

In film such a device cannot be merely introductory. In the theatre, the Induction sets the tone, and the collective will and imagination of the audience sustain it. In film, no amount of audience participation or effort can affect the inherent credibility or otherwise of a photographic image. The viewer is unable to maintain a balance that the image does nothing to support. Once established, such a balance must be maintained through the camera; it must stem directly from some permanent visual technique.

The final element of this technique is the film's use of the Panavision format. The effect of this is to foster the realism of Padua by including peripheral activity in the image without undue emphasis, and by providing a highly tactile visual fringe, as it were, around the central action. Together these create a feeling that Padua is an autonomous fictional world, and the extension of the Panavision image beyond the immediate limits of visual attention tends to draw us into this fictional world. This is why Panavision is commonly thought of as more "realistic" than standard 1.33:1 format. Yet at the same time the Panavision format is not so wide that the controlling and organising function of the frame is lost, as it is in Cinerama. We are thus simultaneously encouraged to see the image as fictional world, without losing sight of the image as image—again, a balance wholly appropriate to the tonal and thematic requirements of the text.

Zeffirelli has then been faithful to the tone of his original while at the same time making a genuinely cinematic adaptation of it. Yet the success of the *Shrew* is thematic too, for in transposing verbal into visual devices Zeffirelli has brought attention to the play's themes much as the Induction does.

The play's two contrapuntal plots are connected with each other and with the Induction through the idea of "supposes"—a word having the meaning of "substitutes" or "counterfeits". The play begins with supposes of a most basic sort. We suppose the Lord and his attendants to be who they say they are, rather than actors. Sly too takes them at their word, and becomes the victim of an all-embracing suppose that leads him to believe he is an aristocrat. He and we watch a play that supposes itself to be in Padua, and which we eventually suppose to be real. The same theme recurs on the level of plot; Baptista is a victim of Lucentio's supposes (disguises), yet Lucentio is himself the victim of a much subtler suppose—that Bianca is a timid and obedient wife. Katherina goes through the process of becoming what Petruchio "sup-

poses" her to be in his early speeches to her. The whole process reaches it absurdly comic conclusion when Kate, in response to Petruchio, "supposes" old Vincentio to be a "young budding virgin."

The film retains all the plot manoeuvres and dialogue that are specifically related to this theme. In lieu of the Induction's clear opening articulation of theme, we have Zeffirelli's establishing scene, studio realism, color bias and screen format. All these arguably help to articulate the "supposes" idea. The Panavision format encourages and limits our belief in Padua as an autonomous fictional world—a basic suppose on a par with our belief in the play in the theatre. The color bias reinforces this, so that just as Sly is caught up in his suppose, so are we in ours:

> Or do I dream? Or have I dreamed till now?
> I do not sleep: I see, I hear . . .
> I smell sweet savours and I feel soft things.
>
> [I. i. 69-71]

Like Sly, we cannot resist the proffered illusion. "Would not the beggar soon forget himself?" says the Lord, and he and we do just that. "He cannot choose" [I. i. 41-2], comes the reply; nor can we. Yet our response to the film is closely analogous to that of a theatre audience's even in the qualifications that limit belief and involvement. Peripheral awareness of the Panavision frame parallels the audience's awareness of itself and the stage in the theatre. In the establishing scene the painted landscape introduces visually the idea of "supposes" simply by fooling us momentarily. We think the painted scene is real but it turns out not to be. By contrast, Padua seems realistic and believable even though it isn't, in fact, either of those things.

With the natural exception of the establishing scene, Zeffirelli's visual techniques are permanent. This means in effect that the idea of "supposes" is kept constantly before us; that the film's every image is in a sense a metaphor for the unreliability of surface appearance. Seen from this point of view, Zeffirelli's visual approach is deeply implicated with the play's themes of Supposes and Metamorphosis; themes which would otherwise emerge only through a truncated text operating entirely on the level of plot and dialogue. Zeffirelli has succeeded in substituting for some of the play's verbal effects visual equivalents of no less strength or subtlety, so that the film is not just recorded theatre or transmitted performance decoratively enhanced, but a *film,* that is, a visual experience where image and text each enhance and elucidate the other.

The *Shrew* is not a freak. One could, space permitting, advance similar arguments concerning the visual realization of tone and theme in *Romeo and Juliet.* Whatever the relative success or failure of such devices, Zeffirelli's two films are important at least insofar as they raise directly the theoretical problems of to what extent film and Shakespearean text can be reconciled. (pp. 210-18)

Michael Pursell, "Zeffirelli's Shakespeare: The Visual Realization of Tone and Theme," in Literature/Film Quarterly, *Vol. 8, No. 4, 1980, pp. 210-18.*

PRODUCTION:

Trevor Nunn • Royal Shakespeare Company • 1967

BACKGROUND:

Nunn followed the recent trend in producing *The Taming of The Shrew* and presented it with close attention to the play-within-a-play structure. He also attempted to blend slapstick comedy with a serious treatment of the play's thematic issues. Although dramatic critics were divided on the question of whether he successfully integrated these divergent elements, nearly everyone praised the performances of Janet Suzman and Michael Williams as Katherina and Petruchio.

COMMENTARY:

The Times, London   (interview date 1 April 1967)

[*In an unsigned interview with Trevor Nunn shortly before the opening of his production of* The Shrew, *the critic relates some of the director's perceptions regarding the play's themes and characters. The interviewer reports that Nunn was especially interested in the comedy's depiction of the conflict between appearance and reality.*]

Despite the changes in policy and Shakespearian production styles that have taken place at Stratford-on-Avon during the last 20 years, one thing has remained impressively constant: the readiness of successive theatrical regimes to give talented young directors their head. In the days of Sir Barry Jackson, a 21-year-old Peter Brook produced a haunting, Watteauesque *Love's Labour's Lost.* Peter Hall was 25 when, during the era of Glen Byam Shaw, he began his Stratford career with a production of the same play. And now that Mr. Hall is himself in charge, he is showing a similar faith in the gifted young: at 26, Trevor Nunn is an associate director of the Royal Shakespeare Company, has three major productions to his credit and is now directing *The Taming of the Shrew,* which opens the new Stratford season on Wednesday.

When it comes to *The Taming of the Shrew,* Mr. Nunn talks with that attention to textual detail that is the hallmark of the post-Leavis generation of ex-Cambridge producers. His first crucial decision was to do it with a company of only 13. "You could have 43 people on stage if you wanted—piles of sluts, whores and the usual Shakespearian addenda. But it's perfectly logical to do it with 13. It starts with the decision anyone directing *The Shrew* has to make—whether or not to do it as a play-within-a-play. Do you ignore the Induction and go for hot sun, white walls, Padua, Renaissance Italy? Or do you say that it's an entertainment within a given framework? If you decide the latter (which I suppose is the reverse of the Zeffirelli treatment) you begin in front of a tavern on a heath in Warwickshire, with snow on the ground and a group of actors turning up to put on a performance."

To most spectators, the play itself usually emerges as a highly effective, boisterous Elizabethan farce but Mr. Nunn thinks it is a rather richer play than that suggests. For one thing, it touches on the conflict between appearance and reality that is one of the classic Shakespearian themes. "There is a massive amount of disguise in the play. One part of it—the Bianca subplot—is also based on Ariosto's *The Supposes* and this word 'suppose' is used constantly throughout the play. One

can also take this theme a stage farther and ask how much one can trust what the characters say about themselves. For instance, Petruchio's first few speeches make it clear that he's a young man who's just left home and has 'come abroad to see the world' [I. ii. 58]. But then we find him saying just after that—'Have I not in my time heard lions roar? Have I not heard the sea puff'd up with winds?' and so on [I. ii. 200ff.]. He obviously hasn't heard or seen any of these things—in fact, he's a sort of Elizabethan Billy Liar.

"Unfortunately, *The Shrew* has always been a bit of an embarrassment to scholars and critics. They're always busy looking for 'the hand of Shakespeare' in it. But there seem to me two indications that it's the work of a great playwright. First, it shows Shakespeare's extraordinary awareness of the mood of his audience. It was originally played, as far as we know, in a building called the Theatre in Shoreditch which was used a lot for bear-baiting as well. So there'd probably be blood and straw all over the place where the audience went in. What could be better judged to follow that sort of entertainment than *The Taming of the Shrew,* which has just the right amount of physical violence? Secondly, there is this overall perception of the appearance and reality theme."

Petruchio and Kate themselves, Mr. Nunn sees as essentially young and evenly matched. ("There isn't a *per se* physical triumph. In the wooing scene, for instance they're pitting their wits against each other as well as their strengths".) To play them he has Michael Williams (who took over the role of the counter-revolutionary hero in *Tango*) and Janet Suzman (lately Rosalind [in *As You Like It*], Portia [in *The Merchant of Venice*], and Ophelia [in *Hamlet*] at Stratford). And that splendid comic actor, Roy Kinnear, makes his Shakespearian stage debut as Baptista. Mr. Nunn tells me that to ensure authenticity his cast have been busy learning to juggle, tumble and sing and acquire all the professional attributes of an Elizabethan company on tour. And then, full of apologies, he rushes off to further rehearsals, rather like a chef who has an important dish on the boil and doesn't want to leave it out of sight for too long.

"Young Man Looks at 'The Shrew'," in The Times, *London, April 1, 1967, p. 7.*

B. A. Young   (review date 6 April 1967)

[*Young maintains that Nunn's production was marred by too much slapstick comedy. As a result, the players were unable to introduce any subtlety into their performances.*]

What's to be done with Christopher Sly?

Shakespeare took him over with the rest of the play when he made his version of an earlier, anonymous, piece called *The Taming of A Shrew* but he very soon got tired of him. At the end of Act I he is asked how he likes the entertainment provided for him, which is the actual play about Katharine and Petruchio. "'Tis a very excellent piece of work," he replies. "Would 'twere done" [I. i. 253-54]. Thereafter he disappears.

Everyone knows better than Shakespeare nowadays, and Trevor Nunn in this production has made Sly a key figure. He doesn't actually give him much more to do, though he keeps him actively interested in the play-within-a-play throughout the evening, and even borrows some words for him from *The Taming of A Shrew.* But it is a basic factor in this production that what we are seeing is a performance given by a company

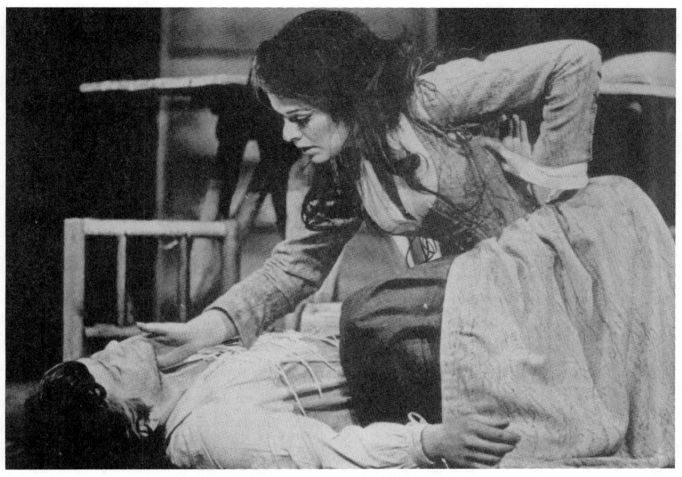

Michael Williams as Petruchio and Janet Suzman as Katherina.

of strolling players in a country inn to gratify the whim of an eccentric Lord to play a trick on a drunken tinker.

This means that we are to be deprived of any kind of polish in acting or production. The action takes place on the straw-strewn floor of the inn, with benches running along either side for Sly and the Lord and his minions to watch from. There is no scenery, the players extemporising what they need out of benches, tables and so on. The inn is luckily equipped with plenty of entrances; it also has a marvellous folding roof that turns inside out when required to transport us from exterior to interior and vice versa.

This admirable set is the work of Christopher Morley, and it gave me more pleasure than anything else in the evening excerpt perhaps Guy Woolfenden's music. This is played by a quartet of minstrels on a variety of medieval wind instruments including a krummhorn; the minstrels sit with the rest of the Lord's retinue and strike up a gay tune at the drop of a hat.

I got less pleasure out of the playing of the company. Mr. Nunn has, rightly according to his vision of the play, insisted on a slapstick, rough-and-tumble style the whole evening. Never have so many bottoms been slapped, so many feet been tripped over, so many running gags run into the ground. Bianca's trio of suitors and their hangers on chase Baptista

about the stage like a rugger scrum. Grumio and the tailor finish their encounter by putting basins on their heads and fighting a mock duel on the table.

This kind of thing is all very well in moderation, but moderation is along way off here. There's a bit of business for almost every line. It is even applied in places where business can have no other effect than to deprive the lines of their due impact. When Petruchio teases Kate by telling her that what she has just (to oblige him) called the moon is actually the sun. Kate laughs hysterically for two minutes, lies down full length on the ground, and agrees "It is the blessed sun!" [IV. v. 18].

One result is that the play is prolonged to well over three hours' duration. Another, more serious, is that no one has a chance to put any kind of subtlety into the acting. Michael Williams is Petruchio; his Cockney accent may be forgiven if he is supposed to be no more than a member of a troupe of strolling players, but could he not have made the character more than a shouting young cad? Does he ever fall in love with Kate, and if so when? Is he in fact concerned with anything more than concluding this performance, which has already sent Sly to sleep, and collecting his money from the Lord?

Janet Suzman does much better with Kate. She gives a fine, spirited performance that stands out among the rest as being something more than merely comic. Roy Kinnear's performance as Baptista stands out too, of course; he is in his element in this kind of thing and gives a lesson to the rest of the company in controlled farce-playing. And just once he spoke a "straight" line so movingly that it suggested that he has more than this to give.

> B. A. Young, in a review of "The Taming of the Shrew," in The Financial Times, *April 6, 1967, p. 26.*

Irving Wardle (review date 6 April 1967)

[*Wardle describes Nunn's* Shrew *as "a marvellously enjoyable show" and commends the director for calling attention to the motifs of disguise and fantasy.*]

Following the example of other Shakespearian directors who first made their name with the early plays, Trevor Nunn confirms the promise of last year's *The Revenger's Tragedy* with a brilliant production of *The Taming of the Shrew,* which sets the play in the full context of Shakespeare's development.

Among other things, the production does justice to the wife-breaking comedy. It also includes the Induction and draws on the anonymous earlier *Shrew* play to keep Christopher Sly continuously on the stage, interrupting the actors to demand changes in the script (whereupon they go into a huddle round the prompt book while a juggler entertains the company), and finally awakening in the cold inn yard and vowing to apply the shrew-taming lesson to his own wife.

Thus presented, the play emerges as an intricate variation on the Shakespearean theme of false appearances, and the interchangeability of dream and reality. The Stratford Theatre, the Warwickshire Inn, the streets of Padua and the disguises of the actors (one finds Katharina and Petruchio doubling as a pair of officers) become a series of dissolving perspectives, none more "real" than any other. Sly himself looks forward to Bottom [in *A Midsummer Night's Dream*] and Caliban [in *The Tempest*], and elsewhere the production echoes Hamlet's advice to the players and the duels of Beatrice and Benedict [in *Much Ado about Nothing*]. It is a blueprint for the poetry to come.

The acting troupe is firmly characterized as a collection of all-rounders, as skilled in tumbling, dancing and scene-setting as in delivering the lines. Before the play they present a mimed prologue in masks, and at climaxes they are prone to form up into rings and chorus lines to the accompaniment of a scratch wind ensemble. Everything gives the appearance of being joyously improvized. Petruchio's equestrian arrival is made on a barrel, discharging a pistol into the air; and he makes his first entry as a blind beggar carrying a hat round the circle of spectators. Mr. Nunn knows how to use his constricted acting area to advantage, as in the early Paduan scenes, where the importunate suitors crowd round the perspiring Baptista (Roy Kinnear) like a rugger scrum.

Although the atmosphere is rough and the company at the inn gleefully rub their hands before the woman-quelling begins, the actual scenes between Petruchio and Katharina are as humanized as I have ever seen them. The shock-haired Michael Williams, a Latin cowboy in baroque stetson and vast yellow codpiece, and Janet Suzman, a boyish shrew with humour always playing at the corners of her mouth, both come over as very young and much more in the process of self-

discovery than in exhibiting any ingrained brutality. Their quiet first encounter is plainly one of love at first sight; and when the war begins it is in the spirit of a game.

If anything Mr. Nunn has piled on an excess of comic detail; one could do with fewer funny voices and less boisterous crowd response. But it is a marvellously enjoyable show, and Christopher Morley's set—which unfolds from a wintry exterior to the timbered inn room—is the best piece of machinery to have appeared on this stage since *The Wars of the Roses.*

> Irving Wardle, "Shrew Set in Its Full Poetic Context," in The Times, London, *April 6, 1967, p. 12.*

Jeremy Kingston (review date 12 April 1967)

[*Kingston praises Nunn's response to the challenges posed by* The Taming of the Shrew, *singling out his presentation of the Induction and the Katherina and Petruchio wooing scenes.*]

Two problems face any director of *The Taming of the Shrew* (Stratford-upon-Avon). If the Christopher Sly induction is included—setting the play proper within a play—what is to be done with Sly after Shakespeare forgets about him? Second, how to treat the Katharine-Petruchio episodes? Why is Kate shrewish? does he really tame her? at what point does true love enter in? Trevor Nunn successfully solves both these problems. By adding scenes from the anonymous, contemporary *Taming of A Shrew* (which might even be a corrupt version of Shakespeare's *Shrew*) he closes the evening with Sly waking up outside the alehouse having "dreamed" how to control his own shrewish wife. Tottering homeward he is passed by the cloaked players laden with burdens and babes in arms—homeless wanderers—hurrying out of his life into the shadows. With this framework sustained around the main story and a country audience watching from either side of the rush-strewn stage, the players can give performances in a riper, broader style than would otherwise be permissible.

If the audience sitting out in front were the only audience Roy Kinnear's fraught Baptista would seem too much of a performance. As it is, this piece of casting is a stroke of genius. Usually presented as an uninteresting aged parent, we are given instead the company's fat man and actor-manager, anxiously gasping his interpretation of such a part while worrying about his troupe. The expressions on Mr. Kinnear's gleaming pink-jelly face again and again convert a commonplace line into something ludicrous. In the second half Mr. Nunn's comic invention flags but until the wedding his production is the funniest I can remember. John Kane makes a splendid clown of Biondello, reaching the height of absurdity with his impersonation of Petruchio's terrible, shoulder-shotten, glandered horse.

Gone are the days when a Petruchio strode about the stage like Douglas Fairbanks cracking a horsewhip and spreadeagling Kate across his knees for a hiding. But this production avoids the opposite, equally irritating, interpretation which implies that her reformation is insincere. Janet Suzman plays her as an intelligent woman turned shrewish, one supposes, from scorn for the feeble Paduan gallants; finding in Petruchio at last a man whose readiness to reject accepted behaviour is on a par with her own. In his first major role for the company Michael Williams is a chubby, puckish Petruchio and bubbling over with good humour and a sense of the ludicrous. From the beginning it is made clear that each recognises in the other a worthy partner, and Miss Suzman and Mr. Williams skilfully blend the knock-about comedy with tenderness in their first encounter. At the end of Kate's final speech on the duties of wives Petruchio's "Why, there's a wench!" [V. ii. 180] is not the conqueror's cry of triumph but a lover's quiet wonder at what his therapy has wrought. (pp. 539-40)

> *Jeremy Kingston, in a review of "The Taming of the Shrew," in* Punch, *Vol. 252, No. 6605, April 12, 1967, pp. 539-40.*

J. C. Trewin   (review date 15 April 1967)

[*Trewin contends that while Nunn's presentation was "an uproarious brawl," it was nevertheless also characterized by unexpected subtlety.*]

The comedy is over, and from the alehouse on the heath a shadowy procession of strolling players moves off into the dark—watched muzzily by Christopher Sly, the tinker restored now to his former state. Fleetingly, at the Royal Shakespeare Theatre, I thought of Henley's "Into the night go one and all," doubtless an unexpected line to drift through the memory at the end of *The Taming of the Shrew*.

But, then, Trevor Nunn's revival, which opens the Stratford-upon-Avon season, always keeps the imagination alive. I have never been more conscious of the strolling players as a unity, a troupe prepared to do practically anything, to tumble or dance or sing, even to juggle. (There is a play as well.) The night's engagement is an odd one, to run through a comedy for the benefit of a drunken tinker; but the patron, a jesting Lord, will pay handsomely, and there is plenty of room for manoeuvring in the alehouse. It is Mr Nunn's excellent device to keep the play there instead of shifting Sly to the nobleman's mansion. What we get is a revelling hullabaloo (any Italian atmosphere is entirely incidental) within the rough-timbered alehouse on a winter night.

I daresay Mr Nunn, in his quest for comic decorations, has worked too anxiously. Really there is little reason why we should be reminded, visually, of cowboy films, the Keystone Cops, the Seven Dwarfs, and so forth and so on. Still (as Stratford knows) the *Shrew* has always been regarded as fair game for a director; and here the strange thing is that, at the last, we do forget the irrelevances and think only of the sudden fading of a dream. Moreover, among all the furious slapabout, the tale of Petruchio and Katharina is established from the first as genuine—from the moment when, in a phrase from another play, the headstrong girl and the smiling fortune-hunter "change eyes": the rest will follow. It is pleasant, I think, that Kate, suddenly, should realise the comic side of it at the line, "Then God be bless'd, it is the blessed sun" [IV. v. 18], on that wild journey back to Padua with Petruchio.

Janet Suzman, overwhelmed by laughter, acts this scene as confidently as she swirls through the early rages or speaks the ultimate homily. She is an entirely persuasive Kate, partnered by the ever-smiling Petruchio of Michael Williams, fortune-hunter who, in quest of a dowry, finds treasure more lasting. Round this splendid pair the company is in a tumult that I can summarise in that deathless poetic phrase of Adam Lindsay Gordon, "Flash! bang!" One performance, in particular, emerges from the turmoil: Roy Kinnear as Katharina's father. On the stage Mr Kinnear is a man born for woe. Now, battered and squeezed through the night, trembling like an

indignant blancmange and always on the edge of unexpected tears, he provides a new sort of Baptista. We may find in future that it has [altered conventional] ideas of the usual grave and substantial citizen of Padua.

Certainly I believe we shall discover that Mr Nunn's production stays with us. Superficially an uproarious brawl, it is in retrospect far subtler than we may think at the time; and subtlety in this particular context is a surprising word.

> *J. C. Trewin, "Strolling Players," in* The Illustrated London News, *Vol. 250, No. 6663, April 15, 1967, p. 35.*

Peter Roberts   (review date June 1967)

[*Roberts criticizes Nunn's production of* The Taming of the Shrew *for its overreliance on slapstick comedy. Slapstick, Roberts asserts, "needs to be brilliant if it is not to produce a groan instead of a grin."*]

The encouragement of youthful talent would seem to be a determining keynote of the two new productions that initiate this year's season at Stratford-on-Avon. I am not talking, of course, of the interpretation that Trevor Nunn's production puts on *The Taming of the Shrew* nor, indeed, of John Barton's direction of *Coriolanus*. I mean the enlightened self-interest that prompts the Royal Shakespeare Company to promote leads from within its own ensemble rather than draft in big guns from outside to set this year's festivities booming. Thus while London was offered Elizabeth Taylor and Richard Burton in Zeffirelli's Old Master print of *The Shrew,* Stratford came up with Janet Suzman and Michael Williams as Katharina and Petruchio. And a week later it was the RSC's own Ian Richardson who was chosen in *Coriolanus* to challenge recollections of what Laurence Olivier and Anthony Quayle contrived with this uncongenial son of Rome.

Too high expectations, based on what he achieved last year at Stratford-on-Avon with *The Revenger's Tragedy,* may partly account for the disappointment I felt with Trevor Nunn's work on *The Taming of the Shrew*. I salute, of course, the sensible decision to lift a few lines from that other play, *The Taming of A Shrew,* which enables the production to conclude as well as begin with Christopher Sly. Whether it is Shakespeare himself or, more likely, a careless publisher who is to blame for the fading out of the character, the arrangement has always been untidy and unsatisfactory. The retention of Sly, of course, marks the point at which Nunn's stage production proceeds in the opposite direction to the line taken by Zeffirelli's film, which omits him entirely. The price you pay for Sly's presence throughout the evening, naturally, is that the main action must be conducted as a play-within-a-play with the stage audience reacting purposefully on the sidelines and encircling the players with their space-taking crowd work. Sly also means that you have to settle for Elizabethan Warwickshire rather than plump, as Zeffirelli did, for the splendour and squalour of Renaissance Italy. Of course the play-within-a-play framework fits into the currently fashionable exercise in beating Pirandello at his own game on the shifting nature of reality—but it would take a pretentious director and a pretentious spectator to put that sort of gloss on the farcical rough and tumble of *The Shrew*.

I recommend the visitor to Stratford this summer to take note of an undoubtedly intentional inconsistency in the style of this production. The opening and closing sections of the play,

Charles Thomas as Tranio, Roy Kinnear as Baptista, and John Kane as Biondello.

where Christopher Sly is rescued from the freezing Warwick-shire snow and then cast out into it again, are staged with painstaking verisimilitude. It's enough to set one reflecting on the social inequalities of Merrie England, and as the company of actors troop off disconsolately behind their wagon one is reminded of Mother Courage and the harshness of *her* life on the open road. But once Christopher Morley's ingenious set dissolves to the interior of the Tudor Lord's mansion and the players get under way the production veers into an exuberant freewheeling style that admits anachronistic visual jokes like Petruchio turning up to his wedding in a cowboy outfit, an apparent fugitive from the Beverly Hillbillies. The roughness of the slapstick, we may take it, is explained by the fact that it is performed by Elizabethan mummers who were thus sing-ing for their supper and didn't bother to do so with overmuch finesse. My complaint is that slapstick, like a pun, needs to be brilliant if it is not to produce a groan instead of a grin. And running gags must be self-sustaining. Mr Nunn's device of getting his players reluctantly to freeze to respectful atten-tion at each mention of Petruchio's late father, like a depart-ing spectator caught by the National Anthem, gets less funny at each reprise. Or so at least I found it.

As far as the play's central romance is concerned, I have al-ways cherished a production in which the director would have the courage to cast Katharina in a way that would justi-fy her envy of her younger sister and her shrewishness gener-ally. A gorgon wooed exclusively for her dowry, who could pull that off? It would take a Madge Brindley or a Peggy Mount. Instead the rôle is invariably entrusted to the compa-

ny's Juliet, ineffectually disguised with a lock of matted hair and a frown. Janet Suzman abandons the impersonation sooner than most for no sooner has she clapped eyes on Petruchio than, before you can say *coup de foudre* [thunder-clap], it is love at first sight, just like the star-crossed lovers at the Capulets' ball. The ensuing courtship is an elaborate joke in which each indulges the other in pretending to be beastly. And Michael Williams' Petruchio really isn't beastly at all—shortish and smiling he's really a charming little fell-er. On the fringe there's a wildly overpitched Bianca from June Watts and Roy Kinnear going through his familiar slap-stick routine as Baptista. (pp. 17-19)

> *Peter Roberts, "Home-Grown," in* Plays and Play-ers, *Vol. 14, No. 9, June, 1967, pp. 16-19, 58.*

John Higgins   (review date 4 August 1967)

[*Higgins applauds Nunn's "vaudeville" interpretation of* The Shrew, *remarking that the director maintained "an occasional undercurrent of true emotion" throughout the performance.*]

The versatility of the current young Aldwych company is re-markable. The two Shakespeare productions in the London repertory could scarcely be more contrasted—David Jones's approach to *As you like it* is soft and decorous, almost rever-entially responsive to the play's beauties; Trevor Nunn takes every kind of liberty with *The taming of the shrew*, tossing it this way and that—yet much the same cast moves from the one to the other apparently without a sigh or a strained muscle.

Shrew came into London last night, with Christopher Sly still well to the forefront as at Stratford, cackling away at the play before him like one of those daft old ladies occasionally met in the stalls who catch up with the jokes minutes after everyone else.

At times the performance looks not so much like a *Shrew* as a *Big bad mouse,* with many of the lines, particularly in the first half, sent up rotten. "We will go walk a little," cries Roy Kinnear, a sweating Baptista crushed against a table by half a dozen substantial bodies. Yet in the madness that Trevor Nunn puts into the production there is a method: he reveals the play as gag-ridden as Baptista is hag-ridden by his daughters.

The moving spirit of the production is vaudeville, in the pratfalls, the dousings with cold liquid, the actors lining up arm in arm across the stage. Yet the comedy is all the better for having an occasional undercurrent of true emotion. When Kate first claps eyes on Petruchio she knows that he is *Der Richtige* [the right man], and so the end of the play, which can be so weak, has its effect. In a much wilder way Trevor Nunn has blended farce and feeling with some skill as has Michael Blakemore in *Joe Egg.*

The cast is the same as that described by B. A. Young at Stratford. Janet Suzman, one of the most improved actresses of the year, is a splendidly aggressive and clever Kate, a high-kicking, vigorous filly simply awaiting the right jockey. There is none of the old stand-offishness and she manages to suggest that much of Kate's violence stems from genuine passion. This is a performance to set beside her admirable Celia [in *As You Like It*].

The style of the production leaves Petruchio less limelight than usual, and I'm not sure that Michael Williams's back row forward stockiness is ideal for the part. (Perhaps Howard Keel's superbly husky shrew-tamer in *Kiss me Kate* ruined the market.) But within its perky, randy limits the interpretation will do well. There is no weakness in the cast, and Charles Thomas (Tranio) and John Kane (Biondello) are outstanding. Roy Kinnear goes his own imperturbable comic way with his own imperturbable assurance, and not least of Trevor Nunn's triumphs is to slot this idiosyncratic Paduan gentleman into distinctly alien surroundings.

I've yet to come across a *Shrew* without dull patches, but the Aldwych production, despite its three hours playing time, cuts them down to a very minimum.

> *John Higgins, in a review of "The Taming of the Shrew," in* The Financial Times, *August 4, 1967, p. 20.*

John Peter   (review date 4 August 1967)

[*Peter briefly reviews Nunn's* Shrew, *commending the strong ensemble playing and asserting that the production "makes for a highly sophisticated entertainment."*]

This is the second play to be transferred from Stratford-on-Avon this season and it fully justifies the praise it received when it opened there.

Trevor Nunn's production keeps the plot firmly in its overall context as a play within the play. The characters arrive as a bedraggled crew of players and they never lose the sense of being members of a *commedia dell'arte* type troupe. Their business is to impersonate stock types of stylized comedy; and, accordingly, the acting acquires the added dimension of actors playing actors playing their parts.

Handled as it is here by Mr. Nunn, such an approach makes for a highly sophisticated entertainment: it combines the abandonment of knock-about farce with the artificial detachment created by two sets of spectators. When the two kinds of comedy explode together the production has some superb moments of madness: notably when Sly, infuriated at police intervention in the play, stops the show to put things right. (By the way, the angle at which he and his companions sit on stage makes some of the action invisible to those on the right hand side of the stalls.)

Broadly stylized as the production is, it makes its impact mostly by splendidly organized company acting, with a few individual performances which take wing on their own. Janet Suzman as Katharina makes heavy weather of being a comic puppet with a distressed pout; but when her arch humour is allowed full play she has some vibrant and splendid moments.

> *John Peter, "Fusion of Comedies," in* The Times, *London, August 4, 1967, p. 6.*

Frank Marcus   (review date December 1967)

[*Marcus observes that by emphasizing* The Taming of the Shrew *as a play performed before Christopher Sly, Nunn accomplished two objectives. First, there was no need for an Italianate setting, which often runs counter to the text's Northern quality, and second, by accentuating Petruchio's position as an actor, his misogyny is ameliorated.*]

With the Royal Shakespeare Co's *The Taming Of The Shrew* we are on . . . familiar territory. . . . Not that Trevor Nunn's production is free of innovation. He not only includes the Christopher Sly scenes (confined originally to the opening), but uses him again at the end, with material borrowed from a similarly titled play by an unknown contemporary of Shakespeare's.

He starts with Sly, having been evicted drunk from a Warwickshire inn, passing out in the snow. Enter a Lord and his retinue, who decide to while away the evening by picking up the drunk peasant, pretending that he's a nobleman whose every wish is their command. Arrival of a troupe of shabby, freezing players, wheeling their prop cart. They're invited to perform before the bemused befuddled Sly. *The Taming Of The Shrew* begins.

This achieves two results. No attempt is made at an Italianate setting, which spares us the incongruity—so jarring in [Zeffirelli's] film version—between a sun-drenched Latin locale and the unmistakably Northern quality of the text, and it neutralizes the repulsive actions of Petruchio: he's only acting in a play.

He further softens the latter aspect of the play by establishing a conspiratorial bond between Petruchio and Katharina, so that the final humiliations are played tongue-in-cheek. Unknown to the others, they're playing a game. They have everybody on; they're a kind of Elizabethan Bonnie and Clyde. I'm not at all sure that this works. At the risk of being accused of having been nobbled by the National Theatre, I must point out that a troupe like the one depicted would not have contained women, and that a boy-Kate would have fought Petruchio with more, not less, physical brutality. And an Elizabethan audience, reared on bear baiting and cock fighting, would have relished the scenes of the shrew's humiliation. In this version, Katharina was conquered at her first encounter with Petruchio; she was broken in too soon. Their courtship lacked tension.

Within this framework, the performances are vivid, if conventional. Janet Suzman is a lean, intelligent Katharina: the sort of intense girl one sees squatting on the floor in Hampstead, sipping coffee from a pottery mug. Michael Williams has the right brash and arrogant masculinity as Petruchio. That dexterous balloon, Roy Kinnear, turns the mild distraught Baptista into a Paduan Oliver Hardy: a really creative comedy characterization. John Kane mimes brilliantly as the servant Biondello; his description of Petruchio's approach to the wedding was a memorable piece of virtuoso acting. Elsewhere, we have the usual anthology of comic mannerisms: the Aldwych stutter, twitch, squint, belch, and an abundance of ancient jaws, working away like pistons.

A good, lively production, a bit too restless and raucous for my taste. (pp. 81-2)

> *Frank Marcus, "New Approaches," in* London Magazine, *n.s. Vol. 7, No. 9, December, 1967, pp. 78-84.*

PRODUCTION:

Michael Bogdanov • Royal Shakespeare Company • 1978

BACKGROUND:

Bogadnov offered an unorthodox approach to *The Taming of the Shrew* in his 1978 production. Rather than treating the play as a farce or a romantic comedy, he interpreted it as a bitter satire on male chauvinism. Bogdanov employed various techniques to cultivate this interpretation: doubling the characters of Christopher Sly and Petruchio, emphasizing the themes of money and greed, and likening Petruchio's wooing of Katherina to a hunt. The production was highly controversial. Critics were disarmed by Bogdanov's ironic interpretation, but they also acknowledged that it offered audiences an increased appreciation of Shakespeare's comedy. Bogdanov's *Shrew,* which featured Jonathan Pryce as Sly and Petruchio and Paola Dionisotti as Kate, opened in Stratford-upon-Avon and moved to the Aldwych Theatre the following year.

COMMENTARY:

B. A. Young   (review date 5 May 1978)

[*Young maintains that Bogdanov's highly farcical treatment of* The Shrew *allowed him to move the dramatic action effortlessly through the play's various levels of unbelievability.*]

When I can believe in it, I find *The Shrew* a very unattractive play. Of Michael Bogdanov's modern dress production for the RSC. I believed only the first two minutes, for he has inherited the opening used by his predecessor at the Young Vic. As we settle in our seats, the theatre staff are arguing with a drunk who wanders about the stalls, drinking beer from a bottle and speaking some very un-Shakespearean dialogue. Not until he has found his way to the stage and started a riot that utterly destroys the disappointingly unfashioned decor do we realise that this is Christopher Sly, the tinker for whose benefit the subsequent romance is to be performed.

When the new scene is set, an unrepresentative affair by Christopher Dyer consisting mostly of open iron staircases, Sly mixes with the other characters, still a little unShakespearean. He has already disposed of his "wife." He also disposes of himself in the first scene, slinking away after Kate and so depriving us of my favourite line, "'Tis a very excellent piece of work, would 'twere done" [I. i. 253-54].

The play continues on a highly farcical level, but now keeping faithfully to the text between the slapstick adornments. I was able to believe in it only as far as I can believe in Feydeau, but because the company proves itself so adept at the farcical style. I never felt that embarrassment which farce engenders when it is impossible. Paola Dionisotti plays Kate, apt casting with her Jack Hulbert profile. She makes her first entry with an incoherent yell. The barbed wire stretched over Baptista's gates might have been put there as much to keep her in as to keep her sister's suitors out.

Her own suitor enters on a motorbike, Grumio on the pillion. They are a fine couple, Jonathan Pryce as confident as a politician and as casual as a punk rocker. David Suchet confirming the fine impression he made as Caliban on Tuesday with a Grumio that might have come from Moliere. Mr. Pryce makes his Kate smile too early in his wooing when he picks up an ornament from Baptista's desk and uses it as a microphone; but she does not smile much thereafter, for she is absolutely tame after her short sharp honeymoon, and when she delivers her great anti-Women's Lib speech after her sister's wedding it is clear she is lost for ever.

Her sister Bianca is Zöe Wanamaker, easily approachable by the right man, who is Antony Higgins' Lucentio, but unpromising material for Kate's new crusade. Tranio (Ian Charleson) turns himself expeditiously from a servant suggesting a Scottish lawyer into a young man of flamboyant pride such as his master might have been glad to be.

Mr. Bogdanov is up to all sorts of tricks. He marches a military band around the stage. He finds an opportunity for Tranio and Lucentio to be discovered in a cafe with their trousers off. He gives Baptista (nicely played by Paul Brooke, who knows how to be funny when he is doing nothing) an electronic calculator with which to reckon the relative values of Bianca's suitors. It catches fire when Tranio adds his contribution. The guests at Kate's delayed wedding shiver beneath umbrellas until Petruchio arrives disguised once more as Christopher Sly with a pantomime horse upstage instead of his Honda.

The story, or rather the stories, of *The Shrew* are so fantastic that there is ample justification for playing it this way, as long as it is done as expertly as it is done here. Mr. Bogdanov has, however, not found a way out of the Christopher Sly problem. Shakespeare simply put him to sleep and forgot about him. In Shakespeare's immediate source, Sly has dreamed the whole thing. Sly doesn't say so in this production which ends as Shakespeare ended it, with the men congratulating themselves; but this is as good an explanation as any—if you must have an explanation of such a joyous evening.

B. A. Young, in a review of "The Taming of the Shrew," in The Financial Times, *May 5, 1978, p. 19.*

Irving Wardle　(review date 5 May 1978)

[*Wardle praises Bogdanov for his inventive interpretation of* The Taming of the Shrew *as a brutal play offering "no nonsense about love at first sight between Petruchio and Katherine." Jonathan Pryce, doubling as Christopher Sly and Petruchio, gave an insightful performance, Wardle asserts.*]

To spectators of the old school, the opening of Michael Bogdanov's production will be a sight for sore eyes. There is, regrettably, no curtain, but there is everything else: plywood pilasters, wobbly loggias, a perspective street scene framing a beefy classical statue.

There is also a bit of trouble going on between an usherette and a drunk who clambers up on stage and demolishes Chris Dyer's set to a smoking ruin, dumping spectators back in the usual open spaces of this company's house style.

The drunk, needless to say, is Christopher Sly, who passes out and awakens in a luxurious bathtub, being scrubbed by a gang of deferential heavies who gradually ease him out of the freewheeling additional dialogue into Shakespeare's formalities and thence to the play within the play.

The main justification for all this is that it gives Jonathan Pryce the chance to play both Sly and Petruchio. As he disappears into the second role, never to reappear in the first, the pattern does not make much sense, but who cares, given the superlative quality of Mr Pryce's performance and the experience—too rare at Stratford—of a brilliantly irreverent young director who keeps the stage in cartwheels for three hours?

If one must find a serious defence for this glorious entertainment, it is that it acknowledges the *Taming of the Shrew* to be an ugly play. Mr Bogdanov stands no nonsense about love at first sight between Petruchio and Katharina.

Just as Sly is picked up by red-coated huntsmen, so Petruchio hunts down his own prey. No tender feelings are involved. Production scores by presenting the central plot with full savagery, and surrounding it with a fantastic wealth of farcical business.

We see the starving Katharina sprinting round the catwalks of her Gothic prison in pursuit of a Grumio (David Suchet) who has got hold of a sandwich. Paul Brooke's Baptista tots up the rival suitors' offers on a calculating machine that goes up in smoke when Tranio (Ian Charlson) puts in his bid. The final demonstration of wife-taming takes place in a Monday Club atmosphere full of cigar smoke and rumbling "hear hears".

All this offsets the brutality of the main story, which takes some offsetting with Mr Pryce in control, arriving on a motorbike and laying the crash helmeted Grumio flat with a vicious knee jerk. Direct physical violence comes almost as a relief in the work of this alarming actor; what really rivets the tension is the fear of what he may do next.

You know he is confined inside the role, which he delivers with fine, snarling precision, but you never can tell where those reptilian movements and spasms of murderous energy are going to stop. "He that knows better how to tame a shrew now let him speak. Eh?" [IV. i. 210-11], he says, raking us with a derisive gaze, and then turning on his heel, stuffing a bottle into his pocket.

His Katharina is Paola Dionisotti, his match in spleen and forbidding looks, but not entirely entering into the role of victim. It is unclear at which moment she begins to crack, and there is an element of personal irony in the final submission foreign to a game of unconditional surrender.

Irving Wardle, in a review of "The Taming of the Shrew," in The Times, London, *May 5, 1978, p. 13.*

John Elsom　(review date 11 May 1978)

[*Elsom comments favorably on Bogdanov's production of* The Taming of the Shrew, *describing it as a "male chauvinist fantasy."*]

The Taming of the Shrew at Stratford starts with a joke previously tried out at the Young Vic recently, in that Christopher Sly is a lout in the audience, waving a bottle of Newcastle Brown, and generally making a nuisance of himself. The RSC, however, extend the idea in various ways. Sly breaks up the minor Italian opera set with its red drapes; and when he falls asleep, he dreams of becoming Petruchio, the part he eventually plays, with the usherette who tried to control him becoming Katharina. *The Shrew* is thus presented as a male chauvinist fantasy.

That scheme works so well that I would have liked Michael Bogdanov, who directed, to have dispensed with the rest of Shakespeare's Induction, where the lords come in from hunting to dress Sly in rich clothes and provide him with a wife. Bogdanov piled symbolism on symbolism by making the hunt itself represent what men do to women, with the baying hounds and the braying horn closing the production as well as opening it.

This heavy sexist gloss detracted from a production which was otherwise cheerful and imaginative. Jonathan Pryce (Sly and Petruchio) brought a tense alertness, with quick flashes of mime, a grating determination and a happy flamboyance to his job of shrew-taming; while Ian Charleson was a quick-witted Tranio. Paola Dionisotti's Katharina looked formidable; and the final scene where she describes a wife's role becomes a reversion from sadism to masochism which alarms even Petruchio. Jonathan Pryce removed his foot quickly when she offered to put her hand under it. The surrounding cast was excellent, with Paul Brooke's Baptista and David Suchet's Grumio outstanding; and after the early havoc, Chris Dyer's set is a delight, with simple levels, spaces and stairs, providing the possibility of an easy flow to the whole play. (p. 612)

John Elsom, "Family Ties," in The Listener, *Vol. 99, No. 2559, May 11, 1978, pp. 611-12.*

Benedict Nightingale　(review date 12 May 1978)

[*Nightingale admires Bogdanov's innovative emphasis on the play's male chauvinist elements. He particularly calls attention to the portrayal of Paduan society as mercenary and hypocritical, and to Pryce's steely—at times, unnerving—recreation of Petruchio.*]

At an Edinburgh Festival some years ago I sat behind a lady who intermittently stumbled to her feet and, in a ringingly genteel Morningside voice, asked the actors why they didn't 'bloody stuff it'; and at Stratford last Thursday it looked as if there might be a similar embarrassment. Who was the un-shaven lout in the third row, shouting and singing and strug-gling with an usherette? Wasn't it Jonathan Pryce, the actor billed to play Petruchio? Yes, it was, and presenting so plausi-ble a display of alcoholic rage that I was momentarily con-vinced he had been given the boot and was taking an ugly re-venge on the RSC hierarchy. Then he yelled, 'I'm not having any bloody woman tell me what to do', scrambled on to the stage, proceeded to demolish the pillars and podia of the dolly Padua built upon it, collapsed in a stupor—and all was sud-denly clear. This was an induction to Shakespeare's own 'in-duction' to the *Shrew,* and Pryce was Christopher Sly, the tin-ker who is duped by passing huntsmen into believing himself to be a wealthy nob just recovered from the delusion of sup-posing himself a drunken yob.

The director, Michael Bogdanov, is pretty cavalier with cuts, colloquialisms and costumes. One moment Pryce is wailing 'hey, lads, get off, will yer?' at the flunkeys who are bathing him; and the next he is in a leather jacket and on a high-octane motorbike, roaring into what appears to be a modern Italian piazza. But, again, the point is clear. We are about to witness a male supremacist's fantasy, the longed-for revenge of the Sly clan upon its uppity women. Katherine, as the cap-sule enemy is called, is not only to be starved and browbeaten into abject surrender. She is to reward her persecutor with a fat fortune provided by her father. This is the way Bogdanov copes with the problems that the *Shrew* notoriously poses for contemporary consciences. His Shakespeare, so far from identifying himself with Petruchio's ploys, is sitting some-where apart with you, me and the other right-thinking peo-ple, boggling at the cruelty and crudity of it all.

An intolerable liberty? Well, John Arden once wrote that there were so many corrections to the view of Agincourt as a lovely war within the structure of *Henry V* that 'one is forced to wonder if the author had not written a secret play inside the official one'. Something similar may perhaps be claimed of the sexual chauvinism the *Shrew* appears to propa-gate. Certainly, Bogdanov is only following Shakespeare's lead when he emphasises that it's money rather than love that absorbs many of the characters, not least Petruchio himself, who readily admits that he's come to 'wive it wealthily in Padua' [I. ii. 75] and is remarkably quick to quiz Baptista about the size of Katherine's dowry. And the old man isn't the least offended, since he is no less mercenary than his pro-spective son-in-law, and promptly proves it by auctioning off his younger daughter, Bianca. As Bogdanov graphically but not unjustly elaborates this particular scene, he sits hunched over a vast gilt desk, the epitome of the mafioso-turned-magnate, totting up the value of one suitor's argosies on an automatic calculator and skimming through the latest digest of farm prices when another boasts of his milch-kine and oxen. And the very last image the production offers is of the servant Grumio clambering across a table to retrieve the wager that Katherine's compliance has won his master, while Petruchio himself swaggers offstage with his wife hanging off one hand and a 20,000-crown cheque from her father in the other.

This isn't a society likely to produce Romeos and Juliets, or even Beatrices and Benedicks. Paola Dionisotti's Kate is a hard-faced bitch with a strident voice, a mean temper and, hidden somewhere beneath, the masochism to relish Petruchio's more imaginative outrages; and Bianca, usually the play's romantic nub, is played by Zoe Wanamaker as a spoiled minx, capable of crackling derisively at a lovelorn ad-mirer. If the younger sister is superficially more agreeable, it's because she has been more successful in the running contest for the status of father's pet. Her venomous, flouncing exit after Baptista shifts his approval, followed by Katherine's slightly dazed one, suggests that the two of them have ended by swapping roles and that from now on Bianca will be the shrew. Padua, it seems, is that sort of place, a competitive, grasping, cynical, hypocritical and really rather horrible city. A city in which well-fed men slouch indolently over their port, baying 'hear, hear' when one of their number extracts a particularly ignominious confession of inferiority from his woman. A city where the sound of the hunting-horn echoes symbolically over the walls. A city in which a man as unscru-pulous and deadly as Jonathan Pryce's Petruchio is all too sure to thrive.

This is a terrific performance, packed with anger and aggro, and by no means lacking in finesse. Notice the triumphant lit-tle wriggle of the tamer's shoulders when his animal first sub-mits, or the secret clenching and stretching of his fist when he tests her obedience in Baptista's circus-ring. The lapses, such as they are, are verbal not physical, and principally a tendency to scramble the last words of a sentence, so that 'a little din can daunt mine ears' [I. ii. 199] becomes an odd 'lit-tle din can daunt miners' and 'mildness praised in every town' [II. i. 191] a still more puzzling 'mildness praised in Everton'. A season with the RSC should help Pryce. And a season with Pryce might help the RSC. As I watched him at work, a rab-bit to his snake, I began to wonder if we hadn't all become a little too satisfied with the company's acknowledged vir-tues, its coldness and sophistication, its feeling for irony and itch for complexity, its knack for giving five or six simulta-neous meanings to one flattish line. Hasn't it become exces-sively chary of the glands and the gut, the stomach and smok-ing bowels? Who knows, we may remember this very arrest-ing *Shrew,* with its unnerving Petruchio, as a significant twist in the RSC's continuing progress. (pp. 648-49)

Benedict Nightingale, "Wiving It," in New States-man, *Vol. 95, No. 2460, May 12, 1978, pp. 648-49.*

Lorna Sage   (review date 19 May 1978)

[*Sage admires Bogdanov's daring interpretation of the struggle between Petruchio and Kate as a hunt and a mercenary trans-action. Ending the play in a "depressed deadlock," however, left the audience more "grumpy than thoughtful."*]

Audiences of *The Taming of the Shrew* at Stratford are in for a diverting first ten minutes. The stage, to start with, is an ele-gant, pastel-painted box, complete with a green view into an Italian garden. "That's funny", muttered a lady behind me darkly, "I've *never* seen a proscenium arch here before . . . it *is* modern *dress,* isn't it?" She need not have worried: just when everyone has had time to develop a thorough dislike for the smug little set, there is the unmistakable noise of someone making a scene, and Jonathan Pryce, lacking a ticket and clutching a bottle, is pursued to the front of the auditorium by an outraged usherette. He leaps on to the stage (everyone has now got the idea), "destroys" the scenery, "fuses" the

Michael Bogdanov's RSC production. Act V, scene ii.

lights and generally tears the picture-frame apart, in a euphoric ritual of liberation.

It is beautifully done (the rest of the cast rushing round in undress, helping the stage manager etc), and works very well, even if it is hard to believe that Stratford would ever employ such a shrewish usherette. As a way of dealing with one of Shakespeare's more elaborate and mysterious early pieces of "induction"—drunken Christopher Sly conned into believing he is a lord, and forced to watch the play—it seemed altogether ingenious and intelligent. And it imparts the right degree of sketchiness to the "real" set: a bleakish assemblage of ladders and levels inhabited by comicstrip Italians. Jonathan Pryce goes off to get into character for Petruchio, and the business of the play proper grinds into motion.

As the programme notes announce, director Michael Bogdanov is mainly interested in two themes: the image of man the huntsman, and the female reflection of that, women as chattels. He has made over Shakespeare's Padua (always rather too insistently Italian, with characters catechizing each other on place names as if to prove he had got the geography right) into a version of Italy as a Third World country, with petty domestic dictators in morning coats wheeler-dealing in dowries. You are made very conscious, for instance, of the men as a solid, plural power bloc, while the

women are lone, foxy individuals, competing with each other as well as battling fathers and husbands. Woman is singular: Paola Dionisotti as Katharina decidedly so. She looks tremendous; lantern-jawed, her frizzy brush of hennaed hair cut in a sort of wedge, so that although the play doesn't offer her much scope for establishing just what a shrew is, you know very well thirty seconds after her first entrance, skinny and quivering in an ecstasy of humiliation over her father's efforts to marry her off—"is it your will / To make a stale of me among these mates?" [I. i. 57-8].

For all that, it takes the production a fair time to get back to the level of the opening partly because of the sheer amount of machinery involved in the subplots surrounding all-too-marriageable Bianca (very well done by Zoe Wanamaker, as a sly, simpering bitch). With the central wooing scene, however, it gathers pace again, and you get an appropriately paradoxical sense of liberation as Katharina and Petruchio demolish the mystification surrounding marriage—not (in this production) because erotic sparks fly, but because of the naked necessity of the bargain they strike, he gambling for the money ("I come to wive it wealthily in Padua" [I. ii. 75]) and the sport, she because his steamroller tactics let her off the hook her hysterical spinsterhood has hung her up on for all to see. The wedding that ends the first half is thus played as glorious (anti-) climax: everyone standing around with umbrellas waiting for a groom who finally arrives to make a brutally frank speech about chattels, and manages to insult his bride in about six different positions. Jonathan Pryce does Petruchio here Groucho Marx style, helped out by Ian Charleson who, as his sidekick Tranio, does a more than passable impression of Harpo. Very funny, except that the lady in question is not a pneumatic, tough, sentimental Margaret Dumont.

This means that the second half is altogether less fun. The play's images of hunting and the analogies between the techniques for taming a hawk and taming a woman (cold, hunger, lack of sleep) are placed squarely in the foreground. Petruchio not only tames Kate, but exhausts himself, and Jonathan Pryce allows a weary edge of self-disgust to creep into the jokes. The final scene, where the three new husbands lay bets on their wives, is given a boozy, depressed postprandial, post-hunt feel; Kate's famous speech ("But now I see our lances are but straws" [V. ii. 173]) is delivered in a spiritless, unreal voice and received without appreciation by the men, and with smouldering resentment by the women. The main feeling is shame—and that the systematic deformation of Kate's character (the deformity of submission on top of spite) is being revenged in the weariness and boredom of the men. When Petruchio says "we'll to bed" it sounds as though they have been married for years. It is an interesting and courageous (not to say feminist) way to interpret the play, but though it works in theory, I am not so sure in practice. It is very difficult to accept an emotional curve that starts with exhilaration and ends in depressed deadlock, and I had the feeling that the audience emerged into a damp afternoon more simply grumpy than thoughtful (as was intended). Still, a good production, that suffers, characteristically, from trying to make too much sense.

Lorna Sage, "The Shrew's Revenge," in The Times Literary Supplement, No. 3972, May 19, 1978, p. 555.

Cahiers Élisabéthains   (review date October 1978)

[*The anonymous critic asserts that while Bogdanov's production of* The Taming of the Shrew *had some delightfully irreverent and innovative moments, the presentation lacked unity of tone and execution.*]

From the moment when Sly, with the dress and manners of a modern lower-class Englishman, began shouting drunkenly from the stalls toward the balcony about some grievance connected with his ticket while an usher nervously tried to placate him, we knew that this would be an iconoclastic production. Sly proceeded to a random demolition of the elaborate Italianate set (complete with statue upstage centre), fell asleep amid the wreckage, and the Lord entered from hunting. After this symbolic destruction of traditional Shakespeare, anything went in a wild romp sometimes more reminiscent of *Hellzapoppin'* than of *The Taming of the Shrew.*

Petruchio (Jonathan Pryce, who also plays Sly) entered in Act I on a motorcycle; in Act III his vehicle was a horse out of vaudeville, a way of showing how much Michael Bogdanov cares for the tight coherence of Shakespeare's play. An eight-piece brass band played and marched onstage part of the time. Kate smashed a wooden chair over a baronial table so massive it took six stagehands to move it on and off. Baptista (well played by Paul Brooke as an overfed Italian businessman in dark glasses and a double-breasted suit) totted up

the offers of Gremio and Tranio/Lucentio for Bianca's hand on an adding machine. It was a wild night at the theatre.

Even a purist like me occasionally enjoys irreverent treatment of icons, and there were moments when the self-conscious anachronism (multiple karate chops in approved Mafia fashion for Grumio in the *knock me here soundly* scene [I. ii. ff.]), and the insertions (*What raiment will your honour wear today?"* [Ind. ii. 4] Sly [sullenly]: *My name's not Raymond, it's Christopher*), and the breakneck speed of the slapstick action (Sly took a fast but elaborate bath stage centre, and Lucentio and Tranio were caught in compromising dishabille by a sidewalk-café waiter as they made their costume change in the street) were amusing enough. But the production could not sustain itself after intermission, and there were dreadfully slow moments in Act V. One reason is that Bogdanov, Paola Dionisotti in a red wig, and the rest of the cast took Kate's story and psyche more than half seriously while the rest of the play was fair game; a real disjunction in tone between Kate and the rest grew progressively as the evening wore on. What can you say about a production that plays Kate's speech out of Paul's Ephesians about obedient wives with solemn seriousness, even to the extent of having Petruchio move uncomfortably and respectfully away when she tries to kiss his foot, after shenanigans that make the Burton/Taylor film look tame? In an ensemble like that Miss Dionisotti could hardly be expected to produce a distinguished reading of the role, and quite clearly she did not.

As Sly/Petruchio Mr Pryce had a problem that challenges any actor who tries to double the roles. How can the coarse and mindless Sly survive into the aristocratic and shrewd Petruchio without making the finesse of Petruchio's taming ludicrously incongruous? All Sly and Petruchio really have in common are energy and self-confidence. And if Sly does not survive into the main plot, what is the point of doubling the roles? Pryce, a brilliant Sly, was a much less successful Petruchio, because the bearing and some of the voice carried over and I found his Petruchio more dishevelled than clever. The most telling moment was his arrival for the wedding drunk in exactly Sly's manner. (It was of interest to observe that when Pryce read excerpts from Shakespeare in Holy Trinity at the Sunday, April 23 Birthday Service the physical bearing was still toned-down Sly though the voice had altered entirely.)

Among the best Bianca (Zoë Wanamaker) was a fleshy, empty-faced bleached blonde in a tacky hyper-pleated silk skirt. Lucentio (Anthony Higgins) was suitably callow without the usual overplayed moonings; he succeeded as Licio too. David Lyon's Hortensio was too suave for the fumbling Cambio he became. Ian Charleson tried misguidedly to distinguish his Tranio from his Lucentio by doing the former in what I suppose was intended as an Irish accent. The delight of the evening was David Suchet, who played Grumio in the manner of an unintelligent and totally loyal bodyguard out of an American gangster film.

I could have easily dispensed with the gratuitous obscenity written into the text (why is it that directors so often think Shakespeare's bawdy inferior to their own?). Sly tried fiercely to get his head under his 'wife's' skirts while Bartholomew the Page squirmed in misery. Petruchio called the tailor *a three-inch thing* and the latter huffily retorted that his horn was a foot long. Other intrusions into the text may not have been intentional (Kate's *You wilt,* Petruchio's *thus have I po-*

litically begun my reign [IV. i. 188], and the two pronunciations of the name *Biondello*).

Samuel Schoenbaum praised the R. S. C. in *The Times Literary Supplement* not long ago for retreating from the directorial self-indulgence of recent years into restraint and textual orthodoxy. The 1978 *Taming of the Shrew* did not participate in the "new restraint"; we are put on notice in an amusing litotes in the programme notes: "Certain parts of the text have been cut or rewritten." It is tempting to find a symbolic significance in the interference at one performance by two members of the audience who mounted the stage from the stalls to try to save the set during Sly's wanton demolition. They had to be forcibly restrained from their intended rescue of the Royal Shakespeare Company. (pp. 102-04)

A review of "The Taming of the Shrew," in Cahiers Élisabéthains, *No. 14, October, 1978, pp. 102-04.*

S. Schoenbaum   (review date 27 October 1978)

[*Schoenbaum argues that the combination of Petruchio's brutality and the "soft-core sentiment" of his apparent change of heart at the conclusion was unconvincing. Far from being a fresh interpretation of* The Shrew, *Bogdanov's production suggested the director's essential antipathy toward the play.*]

Michael Bogdanov's *Taming of the Shrew* opens with a coup de théâtre by now so well publicized that it cannot come as a real surprise to many spectators; rather, we look forward to it with much the same expectation of vicarious delight stirred, in times past, by the mayhem in a Laurel and Hardy film. Before the house lights dim we become aware of an uproar in the aisle. A roughly dressed man, grasping a bottle, quarrels loudly in a prole accent with the usherette, then proceeds to clamber on to the stage and wreck the set—one of those tacky, pastel-flavoured, Italian Renaissance confections, complete with proscenium arch, we used to associate with touring-company Shakespeare. Much tumult accompanies the demolition: stagehands running up and down, bits and pieces of carpentry collapsing.

It is one hell of a device for getting your public's attention. Jonathan Pryce, playing the pugnacious drunk, is as energetic in this *Shrew* as he was listless in *Measure for Measure*. He is the archetypal yob, dues-paying member of the brotherhood of football hooligans who mug old ladies and tear up the upholstery in railway carriages after the match; except that they congregate in mobs, while Pryce is a one-man mob. What Bogdanov is up to has the character of a manifesto. By violently dismantling the set, he is rejecting a whole genteel heritage of Shakespeare production. We are a long way from *Kiss Me Kate*.

Pryce goes on to become the drunken Sly, and then Petruchio. Unbearded but needing a shave, he plays the suitor as a heartless mercenary in the sex wars, with more than verbal brutality. He beats Grumio unplayfully; in his country house, after the wedding, he spits out his drink and hurls his overdone mutton to the rafters. Nothing will keep this male chauvinist pig from wiving it wealthily in Padua and then breaking his wife's spirit. As the chosen sow, Kate (Paola Dionisotti), thin-lipped, with granite jaw and permed geometric hairdo, puts up a stiff fight, but the virago is no match for the macho.

The production is, it goes without saying, in modern dress,

and may be recommended to anybody who prefers his Shakespeare on motorcycles, with brass bands. I liked the band. Lucentio's man Tranio is a Scot, a fact of which I was previously unaware. The others have a big time being sporadically stage Italians. For the scene in which Bianca's suitors offer their financial credentials, Baptista sits behind a huge desk, attended by a Mafia bodyguard in tinted specs, and enters the dowry inventory on his adding machine until Tranio shorts it. Why make this harmlessly bemused father into a Godfather? Enough, I suppose, that he is Italian and a businessman. Anyway, it is only a passing gimmick to be used and then discarded in favour of other gimmicks. Petruchio's pursuit of his quarry is presented as a hunt, complete with the off-stage baying of hounds. Among other fatuities, the souvenir programme offers old-spelling extracts from an early hunting treatise with the long *s* ignorantly represented as *f*.

At the end an ornate chandelier overhangs a green baize gaming-table for the wager scene. Kate's long speech of wifely submission resonates with discomfiting irony. As she clasps her husband's thigh, he nervously runs his fingers through his hair, then abruptly exits, leaving Grumio to scramble on to the table to gather up his master's winnings. The huntsman, having slain the deer and won his trophy, is filled with wordless shame.

It is a symptom of the prevailing philistinism of this production that Petruchio should be throughout mispronounced with a k, the Elizabethan spelling being intended as the phonetic equivalent for Petruccio. I suspect that Bogdanov despised the play for its sexist values, and felt he could come to terms with it only by exploiting to the hilt his company's unequalled resources and his own abundant invention. He mangles the script with as much abandon as he mangles his initial set, although he has the conscience to forewarn the unwary, in his programme, that "Certain parts of the text have been cut or rewritten". But what troubled me most was the combination of brutality with soft-core sentiment. Petruchio's change of heart lacks any preparation. It is rather like the last-minute conversion at the end of an eighteenth-century sentimental comedy; this *Shrew* is less razzle-dazzle with-it than Bogdanov would have us believe. I found the evening pretty depressing—the more so because just about everybody else seemed to be enjoying it enormously. (p. 1262)

S. Schoenbaum, "Alternative Shakespeare," in The Times Literary Supplement, *No. 3995, October 27, 1978, pp. 1262-63.*

J. W. Lambert   (review date Autumn 1978)

[*Lambert contends that Bogdanov succeeded in creating an innovative production of* The Taming of the Shrew, *including an ending which represents "a most chilling indictment of the materialism which has coarsened all concerned."*]

[Michael Bogdanov's version of *The Taming of the Shrew*], it is only fair to say, has met with a mixed reception, and indeed caused grave offence to some Stratford stalwarts (strange how one can't now call anyone stalwart without implied mockery): 'I can't think', cried one indignant voice, 'why they let that young man loose in the main theatre'. Initially, and appropriately for one who has taken over from Frank Dunlop as Director of the Young Vic, he seems to be approaching the piece simply as a gigantic if sharp-edged romp. We enter the theatre to find awaiting us a very pretty and stately set depicting some high renaissance scene. As the audience settles into its seats a drunken figure is to be seen weaving about in the stalls gangway. On the night I was there, at least, many of the audience were far from sure whether or not he was part of the show. An American of portly confidence behind me was in fact quite sure, and kept assuring his brood of womenfolk that, don't be silly, of course he was not a part of the show, they would soon have to throw him out. When he was proved wrong I'm afraid his loss of face audibly impaired his pleasure for the rest of the evening. Those of us familiar with the haggard glare which Jonathan Pryce assumes so easily were of course less perturbed (I don't know, though, whether this sort of lark really makes sense for the higher reaches of the auditorium) as this grubby figure, swigging from a bottle while abusing the 'usherette', eventually rushed up on to the stage and pulled all the scenery down in an orgy of violence which I fear must have satisfied the destructive impulses of a good many of us, while no doubt symbolising the revolt of the have-nots against the haves.

The wrecked stage revealed a construction of what looked like steel girders by Chris Dyer, unexpectedly satisfying as the rampage continued over and around it. The whole Induction was played for knock-about farce, much of which continued as we moved into the play: I shall not soon forget the spectacle of Anthony Higgins's Lucentio and Ian Charleson's Tranio changing clothes in a café under the appalled gaze of a waiter.

But for all the horseplay Bogdanov's direction sees to it that his actors give full value to the absolute firework display of verbal set-pieces with which the piece is studded, and which I never remember to have savoured so strongly before—Allan Hendrick's account of Petruchio's horse, Paul Webster in Gremio's description of the wedding, David Suchet's appalling story of the journey to Petruchio's country house, and of course those of the two principals themselves. The first signs of there being something more to come than fun and games is felt when even in the first half Jonathan Pryce invests the fortune-hunting Petruchio with a deep unreasonable anger, and if I have a reservation it is that he maintains the crescendo of rage too unrelievedly, inducing fatigue in the listener. Paola Dionisotti manages to get more variety into Katherina, notably opposing her refusal to be a piece of her father's property by hinting at an underlying willingness to admit the possibility of affection (and the indulgence of feminine foibles in her delight over the new hat and dress, so rudely snatched from her); until, that is, she evidently decides that there is no use in a straightforward proposal of mutual esteem. In this more or less modern-dress production (which offers a splendid plump slick tycoon of a Baptista from Paul Brooke, as well as a roaring motor-cycle—also recalling Frank Dunlop, in his 'Pop' *Dream*) the final scene achieves a force and point to me altogether new. Here, round the gambling table, complete with cigars and decanters, gather the *nouveaux riches* (all the same in renaissance Italy or London today); before them Katherina delivers her 'submission' in tones which, though without obvious irony, yet signal all too clearly to Petruchio that he has lost. As Jonathan Pryce sits grinding out his cigar, flicking at the ash with restless fingers, the assorted Beautiful People freeze into an understandably uneasy circle. The final fading image is a most chilling indictment of the materialism which has coarsened all concerned. (pp. 13-14)

J. W. Lambert, "Shakespeare for Pleasure," in Drama, London, No. 130, Autumn, 1978, pp. 11-17.

Peter Jenkins   (review date 5 May 1979)

[*Jenkins remarks on the effectiveness of interpreting Petruchio and Katherina's relationship as "a satire on male chauvinism." Bogdanov's production was richly imaginative, the critic declares, and expertly paced.*]

It was tempting to look for topical hints when last year's Stratford production of the *Shrew* arrived in London only a week before polling day, especially as Michael Bogdanov has turned the play round quite brilliantly so that the woman in the end gets the better of the men. Indeed he has turned the whole piece into a satire on male chauvinism and thereby made acceptable, as well as immensely enjoyable, a play which if left to Shakespeare would today seem a monstrous affront.

Hazlitt advised all husbands to study the character of Petruchio but Bogdanov turns him into a psychopath. The soliloquy in Act II, Scene i in which he declares how sweetly he will woo the notorious Kate is spoken while he twists a white silk scarf in what could be murderous hands. There is plenty of evidence in the original of Petruchio's being mad—on his first appearance he assaults his servant Grumio, who later in the play cries out 'Help master, help. My master is mad' [I. ii. 18]. Bogdanov's innovation, however, is to turn the entire play into the male domination fantasy of a drunken Irish tinker.

The evening begins with a superb coup de theatre as a drunk, wandered in from the embankment, eludes an usherette and climbs onto the stage where he proceeds to destroy the scenery for what looked as if it was going to be an ultra-traditional production. This is the Christopher Sly who, eventually collapsed into alcoholic stupor, is discovered by the noble huntsmen. A practical joke is played upon him to convince him that far from being a drunken tinker he is a lord and, in the original, he settles down, glass filled and wench at hand, to enjoy *The Taming of the Shrew* as done by some wandering players who conveniently arrive.

The play has been done before as Sly's dream but here Sly himself becomes Petruchio, the would-be lord over woman, and this works wonders for the sexist theme of the play.

Bogdanov's second coup comes in the final scene where Kate makes the submission which through the ages has been regarded as one of the great touching affirmations of womanhood. This is where she says, inter alia,

> Thy husband is thy lord, thy life, thy
>   keeper,
> Thy head, thy sovereign; one that cares
>   for thee,
> And for thy maintenance; commits his
>   body
> To painful labour both by sea and land,
> To watch the night in storms, the day
>   in cold,
> Whilst thou liest warm at home, secure and safe . . .
>   [V. ii. 146-51]

This speech, the great climax of the play, is turned in Bogdanov's production into a biting satire of all that has gone before, a tongue-in-cheek manifesto for the pussy-cat club. It is done with the men sitting around a green baize poker table. At the end of it Petruchio, the winner of the wager on obedience of woman, is the loser after all and as Kate stoops to kiss his foot he, ashamedly, withdraws it. The women leave the men to their cards and the play ends with the reminder of the hunting horns which first had prompted Sly's machismo dream.

Bogdanov's production is inventive at every opportunity, almost too much so in its modern Italian dress, its Glaswegian and Cockney accents, the town band playing echoes from *Kiss me Kate* and Petruchio torturing the starving Kate with the *Minceur* cookery book in hand. However the sub-plot of the *Shrew* needs all the help it can get and this production is kept moving with pastiche and allusion and plenty of good jokes. We could do perhaps without the motorbike which has become a cliche of modern Italianate Shakespeare.

As for the acting, Jonathan Pryce on occasions, I thought, went too far—for example when introducing an imitation of Max Wall—but let us in no doubt that he is a dashing and versatile actor. Paola Dionisotti for some reason made Kate into a plain Shrew but she carried off the submission speech quite brilliantly. Bogdanov's orgiastic ingenuity allows opportunities to almost every character in the play but outstanding were Paul Brooke doing Baptista as a shady stockbroker, Ian Charleson turning Tranio into a Glaswegian punter and that wonderful character actor David Suchet doing Grumio as an East End wide boy. Altogether, it was a surprising and exciting evening in the theatre.

Peter Jenkins, "Macho Dreams," in The Spectator, *Vol. 242, No. 7869, May 5, 1979, p. 34.*

G. M. Pearce   (review date October 1979)

[*Pearce maintains that significant continuity was lost in Bogdanov's production due to various changes in scene and mood. He notes with approval, however, the ways in which props and costumes underscored the theme of hunter and victim.*]

Having been prepared by posters showing men with a motorcycle for a modern dress production, it was rather surprising to find an aggressively conventional set on view on entering the theatre. The stage was flanked by two balconies and through an arch at the back of the stage was seen a typical Renaissance landscape, in front of which was a large statue depicting an abduction. There were a few delicately posed baskets to one side of the stage and formal arrangements of flowers placed high on pretentious pillars at the front. Lulled into a false sense of security by this, the irruption of a belligerent drunk on to the stage was a rude shock. Despite half-hearted attempts on the part of the cast to stop him, he had rapidly demolished the flimsy set, and suddenly one realized that it was all part of the act and that this was Sly. The bare bones of the set were revealed as a series of iron girders and staircases, lit at first by the uncompromising glare of the searchlight which has been a feature of several of Michael Bogdanov's productions. The arrival of a group of huntsmen, bearing a bloody dead fox was heralded by a brass-band and a howling noise as of a pack of wolves. The rest of the Induction carried on at this exhilarating pace with the hilarious bathing of Sly in a pink shell-shaped bath and his meeting with his reluctant so-called wife, played by David Suchet in drag. The scene of the players was omitted and Sly proceeded to observe Lucentio and Tranio plotting together to exchange roles, whilst drinking martini; then he faded away unobtrusively, only to re-emerge (on motorbike) as Petruchio, come to woo. Jonathan Pryce with his lean cadaverous face, five o'clock shadow and unkempt hair, fitted well into both roles. His lithe and agile body was as expressive as his face and he played with tremendous energy and the necessary authority

to subdue his wayward bride. Only in the last scene where Kate appears too submissive for his liking did he show himself non-plussed.

When Kate first appears, the hunting imagery of the opening scene is re-echoed in a cage of iron bars, topped with barbed wire which encloses both her and Bianca, their emprisonment being stressed by guards patrolling outside. Zoë Wanamaker turned Bianca into a sly minx who deserved such treatment just as much as her sister, and, dressed in a sexy scarlet décolleté in the final scene, looked set to make a much less worthy wife than the now submissive Kate. Juliet Stevenson (who also doubles surprisingly as Curtis) black clad as befits a widow, was a petulant and unenthusiastic wife to Hortensio, showing further the extent of Kate's transformation. Paola Dionisotti modulated her voice and looked more attractive at the end, but was more convincing in the shrewish and petulant aspects of the character, including the transition stage where she invited the audience to share her enforced acquiescence in her husband's unreasonable behaviour. She and Petruchio struck sparks off one another from their first encounter, where Petruchio's semi-prepared speech was delivered while fighting vigorously with Kate throughout, a fight full of sexual innuendo. As a shrew she wore her red hair in a fly-away frizzy style and the birds with their wings spread on her black dress emphasized again the theme of hunter and victim. Then the whirlwind courtship ended with the re-entry of the disbelieving Baptista, played with excellent comic timing by Paul Brooke, who urged Petruchio on with prize fighting gestures. Baptista's totally materialistic outlook, selling his daughters to the highest bidder is allowed to seem funny, as he tots up the marriage settlements on an adding machine. However, there is a more sinister and ruthless side to him as he offers a bribe to the police officer who has been lurking outside his gates to take the true Vincentio to gaol.

In the sub-plot as well there was strong comic acting from Ian Charleson as Tranio, who made beautiful play with accents in the scene disguised as his master, slipping from broad Scots to an educated accent and back again (when he spoke in the more educated tone, he succeeded in making total nonsense of some lines). In the interchange of roles, the use of modern costumes worked well, as Lucentio's suit was green velvet (not too far from the text), which fitted with the twenties' flavour of the rest, and with the addition of a red-spotted kerchief, gave Tranio a gangster-like appearance. The costume joke when Petruchio refuses the dress brought in for Kate lost much of its point, as the dress in question had little in the way of fussy extremes of fashion. Anthony Higgins as Lucentio was the typical presentable young Shakespearian hero, but Hortensio (David Lyon), doubling as Licio in a blond wig, made full use of his comic opportunities.

In the baggy pants of Grumio and the irrelevant pantomime horse, as well as the cheerful, though sometimes deliberately untuneful playing of the brass band who came on whenever possible, there was a strong flavour of the circus about this production. A tremendous pace was kept up till the final scene, with even greater outbursts of energy being required in the wedding scene and the abortive meal when Kate first arrives at Petruchio's house. Some scenes were reminiscent of review, particularly Bianca's wedding, which took place off stage, but just beforehand the couple bounced on the stage to allow a few trendy wedding snaps to be taken. These abrupt changes of scene and mood made it difficult to preserve the continuity of the plot and gave a somewhat uneven quality to the production. The scene of Petruchio's wager was staged with everyone sitting round a green baize table. Kate's long speech on the duties of a wife slowed down the action to end the evening on a more sober note, with a strong indication that the natural order of things had been reversed. (pp. 89-91)

G. M. Pearce, in a review of "The Taming of the Shrew," in Cahiers Élisabéthains, *No. 16, October, 1979, pp. 89-91.*

Roger Warren (review date 1979)

[*Warren maintains that while Bogdanov's production was unusual and inventive, many of its attempts to show the similarities between disparate theatrical elements were not clearly defined for the audience.*]

The opening of Michael Bogdanov's *Taming of the Shrew* exploited the current fashion for blurring the distinctions between theatrical 'realism' and 'artifice', presumably to emphasise enduring 'relevance'. After being unexpectedly faced with old-fashioned painted scenery, the audience was suddenly startled by a deceptively genuine squabble between an usherette and a drunk member of the audience without a ticket. 'No bloody woman is going to tell me what to do!' he cried, thus making the play's relevance plain. Leaping on to the stage, he tore apart all the illusory scenery, revealing a respectably contemporary series of rusty metal frames, staircases, and cat-walks. He collapsed; the lights dimmed to a spot on him, and rose to reveal the Lord and his huntsmen in sinister outline, smoothly complacent in modern red hunting outfits. 'O monstrous beast, how like a swine he lies' [Ind. i. 34] became the smugly superior comment of material well-being upon the down-at-heel. This contrast was subsequently picked up in the play itself: the Lord became Baptista, a wealthy tycoon surrounded by servants in impeccably cut morning suits, and Petruchio adopted his earlier drunk persona in the wedding scene, to achieve maximum contrast with the society outfits of the others, and to underline his emphatic 'To *me* she's married, not unto my clothes' [III. ii. 117].

The problem with most such ingenious adaptations is that they are hard to sustain; they may confuse as much as they illuminate. Apart from merely suggesting that the male/female struggle for domination is still a live issue, there was no natural transition from Sly to Petruchio: Sly just slipped off, and reappeared, riding a motor-bike, as Petruchio. The connection between hunting and Petruchio's taming methods was stressed by the doubling and by horn calls at the end (a 'death'?); but the connection wasn't really very illuminating, since in the Induction it is the Lord/Baptista who is the hunter, not Sly/Petruchio. The contrast between smoothness and scruffiness became muddled when the servants at Petruchio's country house, led by a Curtis presented (but not re-named) as a briskly efficient air hostess, were dressed in the same smart morning suits as Baptista's servants, were indeed the same servants. I could not see the point of this discrepancy between master and men, aggravated by retaining the lines about their pumps, hats, and daggers, though virtually all of Sly's lines, for instance, had been freely changed to modern colloquialisms. Again, when the establishment at the wedding responded with relieved, superior laughter to Baptista's anti-climactic dismissal, 'let them go, a couple of quiet ones' [III. ii. 240], were we meant

to feel that the unaffected violence of Kate and Petruchio was inevitably preferable, or merely a contrast?

At any rate, the production made no attempt to soften the brutality of Petruchio's methods: the first scene with Kate was a violent physical struggle, not a wit-combat. And the creation of a world dominated by a combination of male chauvinism and material greed certainly paid off in the final scene, where the dinner-jacketed speculators sat round a circular green-baize-covered gambling table, with after-dinner brandy and cigars, to indulge in a little speculation on their latest assets—wives. This self-satisfied group, with their 'hear-hears', nods, and applause, were the perfect audience for Kate's assertion of male domination; and this setting made it much easier than usual for Kate to deliver a speech which has of recent years seemed to become impossibly difficult to bring off.

That context was just as well, for otherwise Paola Dionisotti's Kate did not achieve much more than a deep-throated rage or indignation. There was certainly no hint of possible relationship, much less affection, between her and Petruchio (who, perhaps accidentally but in any case significantly, omitted 'and love' from the line 'Marry, peace it bodes, and love, and quiet life' [V. ii. 108]). Nor was there much laughter: what Petruchio calls Grumio's 'conceits' were in fact forcefully delivered complaints, David Suchet making his presence felt with every line; and Jonathan Pryce had all the necessary distinction of presence and voice for so dominating a Petruchio while avoiding rant or monotony.

Indeed, the entire production was unusual in avoiding both tedium and, even more surprisingly, slapstick business. The sub-plot, especially, gained from the absence of the second: it was unfussily laid out and clearly delivered. What jokes there were were related to character, as when Paul Brooke's Baptista, briskly calculating the rival dowry offers on an adding machine, had to pause to look up the value of Gremio's farm stock, country market prices of course being outside an urban financial speculator's orbit. (pp. 201-02)

Roger Warren, "A Year of Comedies: Stratford 1978," in Shakespeare Survey: An Annual Survey of Shakespearian Study and Production, *Vol. 32, 1979, pp. 201-09.*

James S. Bost (review date March 1980)

[*Bost salutes Bogdanov's inventive production of* The Shrew, *characterizing it as a "reflection of the awesome talent and creativity of the RSC."*]

They've been tearing down the scenery at the Aldwych throughout the summer of 1979. Statuary has been toppled, baskets of flowers have been hurled into the wings, flats have fallen on and through actors, painted drops have crumpled to the floor, and Juliet-styled balconies have plunged crazily to their demise. Add to this the sound of sirens, the whirling red lights of police wagons, and actors running amuck, and you have the most glorious opening to hit the West End since *Oh, Calcutta!*

This mayhem has been ignited by a "drunken sot" who breaks into the stalls just before curtain time, sloughs off the restraining arms of ushers, and clambers onto the stage shouting unintelligible obscenities. The sot is, in reality, *Shrew*'s Petruchio, a priceless Jonathan Pryce, hatchet man for the riotous opening. The initial stage destruction was carefully choreographed by director Michael Bogdanov for the express purpose of shocking the audience into the realization that a traditional approach to Shakespeare is to be merrily exploded into the twentieth century.

The trappings and business are irreverently modern: Petruchio and his man Grumio make their initial entrance on a motorcycle; Tranio gives the bard's verse a howling Scottish flavor; Baptista uses an adding machine to compute the wealth of Gremio and Lucentio, and the machine suddenly explodes like a trick cigar when it proves unable to compute the listing of Lucentio's real estate; Pryce gives a "Mamma Mia spaghetti and meatballs" panache to his Petruchio, at times using a pelvic thrust to become a very funny Italian stud; and, Kate's wedding has a Royal Ascot air, complete with gray flannels and top hats, and couples posed under swank umbrellas as if waiting for taxis at Covent Garden.

The play is filled with imaginative sight gags, like Grumio "maiming" himself as he unsuccessfully attempts to break over his knee a yardstick that has just moments before been broken with great ease and flourish by Petruchio. There is the picture of Baptista, Tranio, and a Pedant wearing New Year's Eve paper hats and holding dry martinis, looking like double-breasted rejects from a children's birthday party as they celebrate Baptista's acceptance of Lucentio as fit to marry the fair Bianca. And there is the picture of Petruchio tearing a piece of meat asunder in "madness" over its being underdone. Sometimes, the gags have absolutely no relevance to the action; they are commedia *lazzi* [buffooneries], inserted because this is a Hellzappoppin' type of production and because the central character is Jonathan Pryce, an actor who has an uncanny sense of timing and loose limbs that respond on the instant. For example, Petruchio gives the impression at one time that he has lost a finger because a cymbal came crashing down on his hand; after "retrieving his missing finger" Pryce stops the action for several seconds by playing the "hand coming out of the sleeve" trick.

The Slyest trick of all is Director Bogdanov's inspired opening, where any resemblance to the traditional Sly beginning is purely coincidental. Although a number of Sly's original lines are retained along with his drunken posture, a bath sequence is inserted that allows Pryce to create rakish lazzi revolving around his attempt to prevent liveried butlers from ogling his bare back-side. The Sly beginning almost backfires because Pryce, appearing in what amounts to the character of Sly, confuses the audience momentarily when he next appears as Petruchio. This doubling is perplexing because there is little discernible difference in the look or behavior of Petruchio/Sly. Furthermore, after the drunken opening the Sly side of Pryce never returns; he is assimilated into the character of Petruchio.

The purist may understandably object to such cavalier fusion of characters as well as to the whole Bogdanov approach to *The Taming of the Shrew,* but it works. The gags not only hold up, but at times help to illuminate the meaning. In all, it is grand fun, boldly and imaginatively executed and another reflection of the awesome talent and creativity of the RSC. (pp. 122-23)

> *James S. Bost, in a review of "The Taming of the Shrew," in* Theatre Journal, *Vol. 32, No. 1, March, 1980, pp. 122-23.*

PRODUCTION:

Jonathan Miller's BBC Television Adaptation • 1980

BACKGROUND:

In his BBC production of *The Taming of the Shrew,* Miller presented an archeological treatment of the play. Drawing upon research into traditional Elizabethan values, Miller attempted to recreate a setting in which a wife clearly has a duty to respect and obey her husband. Comedian John Cleese confounded critics with his competent and introspective portrayal of Petruchio as a subtle, somewhat puritanical suitor to Katherina, played by Sarah Badel. Moreover, Cleese's taming of Kate through a psychologically sensitive process diffused potential accusations that Miller had presented a misogynistic interpretation of the text. Commentators reviewed the presentation warmly, praising Miller's honest treatment of the play.

COMMENTARY:

Chris Dunkley   (review date 24 October 1980)

[*Dunkley argues that it is difficult to produce* The Shrew *in this age without somehow seeming to despise women. Miller's BBC production succeeded in part, he contends, because it treated the story "more like a single peculiar case history and less of a general attack on women." The principal reason for its success, Dunkley declares, was Cleese's inspired portrayal of Petruchio.*]

Jonathan Miller's first contribution to the BBC's complete Shakespeare canon was not so much *The Taming of the Shrew* as *The Total Transformation of the Hysterical Harridan.* It did not, quite, go over the top into pantomime, but Miller—who has taken over as producer of the entire series and also directed this play himself—pushed it breathtakingly close to the brink.

In Act 1 Sarah Badel's Kate, bosom a-heave and eyeballs swivelling, raved and roared, punched Gremio, hurled an apple at Hortensio, and floored a passing dwarf. It began to look as though the wench really was "stark mad."

You can see Miller's problem: though Katharina has been portrayed for 400 years simply as an archetypal shrew who is finally brought to heel by good old masculine domination it becomes necessary when mounting the play for a world-wide television audience in the age of feminism to dig around for alternative implications if the work isn't to seem dreadfully "chauvinistic," as they say down at the Poly.

It remains that, of course, whatever you do but, remarkably, Miller succeeded: the story did seem less deeply misogynistic than usual, more like a single peculiar case history and less of a general attack on women. The main reason, oddly, was Miller's inspired casting of John Cleese as Petruchio. Cleese being so powerfully and popularly identified with television comedies such as *Fawlty Towers,* the choice was a huge gamble but it paid off.

He played the part not as a thigh slapping bully but more like an eccentrically pragmatic social worker using the wayward client's own doubtful habits to calm her down. Once in a while the manic gleam of Basil Fawlty did shine through; and Cleese delivered lines while yawning, eating, sighing and scratching his chin—all presumably part of his proclaimed intention of avoiding the excesses of conventional "Shakespearian" delivery. He is right for plays like *Taming of the Shrew,* anyway, though he may have taken it a little far.

Yet as a whole his performance was a triumph, as was the entire production. Though even Miller cannot solve the problem of studio floors looking dreadfully flat for exteriors, the Dutch school interiors (by Colin Lowrey) were beautiful, and the abstract backgrounds, which Miller favours, highly successful. So too was his casting of so many other faces from TV sitcom in the smaller roles: Frank Thornton as Gremio, John Barron as Vincentio and most memorably, however briefly, John Bird as the Pedant.

> *Chris Dunkley, in a review of "Taming of the Shrew," in* The Financial Times, *October 24, 1980, p. 19.*

Michael Ratcliffe (review date 24 October 1980)

> [*Ratcliffe contends that Miller's BBC production "struck a very nice balance between domesticity, intelligence, and tenderness." He further notes that a large share of credit for this evenhandedness belongs to Cleese.*]

In her superb *Shakespeare in Perspective* on Tuesday—a model of the brief visual essay in which the pictures were as good as the script—Penelope Mortimer took a robust and unfashionable view of this play. Shakespeare had been fed up with the paraphernalia of courtly love at the time; Petruchio was "a high-powered hustler with no time to waste"; he was bored with "suitable" women and wanted a mate who would last. Mrs Mortimer thought the union could be lively, that he would die a violent, and slightly preposterous, death perhaps on the hunting field, and that Katharine, when asked at the end of her life what he had been like, would say "Impossible", but then "smile, at the curious collusion that was her marriage".

Away with the chains and the sexism and the guilt, then, and in with the marriage of true minds—"for tis the mind" (Petruchio says it) "that makes the body rich" [IV. iii. 172]. If this is revisionism, it is both persuasive and liberating, and, except that she also argued for an English, not an Italian, setting and for the retention of Christopher Sly and the play-within-the-play, it offered an apt prologue to the production with which Jonathan Miller has begun his reign from the Bardic chair. For this *Shrew* struck a very nice balance between domesticity, intelligence and tenderness.

Much of the credit for this must go to John Cleese, a deliberately spectacular piece of casting as Petruchio which paid off because he placed himself entirely at the service of the production and the play, thus greatly extending his own talents in the process. Save for occasional flashes of rage when his eyes seemed to spin in their sockets—as with Hortensio's silly widow at the end—or when he screamed for his slippers and stamped on his wife's little red hat in shocking pink hose, Basil Fawlty was sternly excluded from the performance, although the possibility that he might at any point erupt into it gave the show a fine, dangerous edge. This was an unusually rational Petruchio—witty and eccentric, but also quite reasonable, relishing both the hyperbolical absurdities and the

quiet monosyllables of the prose: "For you must know, I woo not like a babe" [II. i. 137].

Sarah Badel played Katharine as a nervous hysteric anxious for attention who dissolved into beauty under Petruchio's assaults, desperately running her head into one trap after another until finally joining the joke herself. When she insisted on wearing the trampled little red hat after all you knew she had got his measure and that he had met his match.

A decent cast—notably a spirited Bianca (Susan Penhaligon) and a deliciously funny Hortensio (Jonathan Cecil)—supported these two, and Miller gave a cut text both shape and pace. The play ended on a family hymn of, it seemed, thanksgiving, in which the studio lighting (John Treays), costumes (Alun Hughes) and designs (Colin Lowrey) gave the show as warm and attractive a look as they had done throughout.

> *Michael Ratcliffe, in a review of "The Taming of the Shrew," in* The Times, *London, October 24, 1980, p. 8.*

Andrew Sinclair (review date 30 October 1980)

> [*Sinclair comments briefly on Miller's BBC production of* The Taming of the Shrew, *noting that the performance was "as fresh and appealing as Shakespeare could possibly be."*]

Dr Jonathan Miller has done it again, turning penury into opportunity in his production of *The Taming of the Shrew* (BBC2). Skimpy budgets gave the first 12 of the Shakespeare plays, produced by Cedric Messina, a lean and hungry look. But in his first essay since he took over the project, Dr Miller kept his single camera steady and his wits about him, leading his actors a merry caper or leaving them in confidential two-shots right against the lens.

We were at a peephole in Padua, watching the marriage dance round the two shrewish sisters. Vermeer-like sets, Italianate costumes that looked worn rather than wardrobe-clean, a descant or two and a sense of romp and enjoyment, all these made *The Taming of the Shrew* as fresh and appealing as Shakespeare could possibly be.

The casting was inspired. John Cleese had the authority and boorishness of a good Petruchio, yet added his own brand of comic malice. He played as if to the Bard born. And Sarah Badel's Katharina certainly convinced me that she was ultimate terror tactic against the conspiracy of men. Particularly credible was her screaming tussle with her sister Bianca, played by Susan Penhaligon with a pretty forcefulness.

'There's small choice in rotten apples' [I. i. 134], one of the suitors said of the sisters; but I found great pleasure in pippins of performances from a cast that included Frank Thornton as Gremio, John Barron as Vincentio, and John Bird as the ineffable Pedant. Dr Miller has soared away at the beginning of his long responsibility. The odds are with him in the future; for the gods have given him all the gifts we need.

> *Andrew Sinclair, "Cries for Help," in* The Listener, *Vol. 104, No. 2685, October 30, 1980, p. 590.*

Stanley Wells (review date 31 October 1980)

> [*Wells argues that Miller presented a simplified version of* the Taming of the Shrew, *bypassing the play's "imaginative com-*

plexity" in favor of "a generally prosaic, literalistic mode of presentation." Individual performances were uneven, the critic remarks, but Cleese's seemingly effortless evocation of a credible Petruchio was superb.]

Jonathan Miller—acting, we must hope, in defiance of his literary consultant John Wilders—offered a simplified version of *The Taming of the Shrew* in this BBC production. To omit the Christopher Sly episodes is to suppress one of Shakespeare's most volatile lesser characters, to jettison most of the play's best poetry, and to strip it of an entire dramatic dimension. In a series announcing itself as "The Complete Dramatic Works of William Shakespeare", this leaves a serious gap.

The consequent reduction of the play's imaginative complexity was reflected in a generally prosaic, literalistic mode of presentation. We opened on a stagey Italianate market place, peripheral touches of local colour being provided by a dwarf, a juggler, an apple-eater and basket-weavers. Baptista's house had lovely interiors reminiscent of Vermeer, sunlit, uncluttered rooms opening into one another through elegant arches with some ingenious mirror effects. The peaceful setting provided an ironic contrast to Kate's fits of temperament. Later, staginess returned, particularly in the closing feast, at which nothing was eaten and precious little drunk.

If a merit of this was to throw emphasis on the actors, Miller could not be said to have evoked a consistent acting style. Some of his performers elected for a stylized, consciously comic mode. Jonathan Cecil endowed Hortensio with a sweetly naïve simple-mindedness, an eager, dim-witted charm. One of the production's few genuinely funny sequences was provided by the increasing self-absorption with which he expounded his plot to win Bianca, initially addressing himself to Petruccio but gradually losing all consciousness of his hearer, who looked on with that fascinated, if slightly abstracted, contemplation of folly of which John Cleese is a master.

As Tranio, Anthony Pedley deployed the full armoury of the farce actor, with exaggerated facial expressions and grotesque speech characteristics—dropped and misplaced aspirates, impure vowels, glottal stops, affectations of gentility. If all around him had been playing in the same mode, we might have admired; as they were not, we remained unconvinced. Actors in lesser roles descended to the kind of half-hearted improvization which may be useful in rehearsal but should be expunged in performance; "*cum privilegio ad imprimendum solum,* i'n it, eh?" [cf. IV. iv. 93] said Biondello; and the Pedant added "Was that all right?" to one of his inventions.

By contrast, other performers underplayed their comedy. But the production's main strength lay, fortunately, in the leading actors. John Cleese's splendid physical presence helps him to create strong effects with little apparent effort. We saw the taming process, properly enough, through his eyes. Apart from a few necessary moments of flamboyance and a tendency to cluck amiably from time to time, it was a deeply thoughtful performance, convincing us of the seriousness of Petruccio's intentions. He clearly but unobtrusively established his strong physical attraction to Kate, and their relationship became a wholly credible process of mutual adjustment. Cleese's comic talent came into its own in the scenes following the wedding, in which he works on Kate's body, intellect, and imagination through a series of trials.

Sarah Badel, a comely, bosomy Kate, strong in physique and

voice, matched him well. As their relationship developed and matured, we sensed, in her enjoyment of complicity, an inner understanding between the pair which robbed Kate's advice to the other wives of offensiveness and contributed to the deep satisfaction with which Petruccio spoke "Why, there's a wench . . . " [V. ii. 179].

This was not an inventively funny production, nor a deeply imaginative one. Jonathan Miller had little success in finding the play's natural rhythms and adapting them to the small screen. He ended in anticlimax with Baptista's entire household, directed by Gremio, joining in an added part-song. Domestic cosiness took over from the sense of wonder at a transformation miraculously achieved with which Shakespeare leaves us. Still, we had seen the transformation take place; and in this at least the production justified itself.

Stanley Wells, "A Prosaic Transformation," in The Times Literary Supplement, *No. 4048, October 31, 1980, p. 1229.*

David Sterritt   (review date 23 January 1981)

[*Sterritt offers a favorable review of Miller's* Shrew, *praising in particular Cleese's "precise, carefully modulated, and ever-so-slightly insane" performance as Petruchio.*]

"The Taming of the Shrew" is not exactly a monument to women's liberation. But it's a lot of fun, and—making allowances for what some call a benighted attitude—it's also substantial in a way that Shakespeare's more frivolous farces are not. Whatever their shortcomings, the main characters are real people, and real fireworks burst forth when they get together.

All these qualities stand out in the new production that airs as the third-season opener of the "The Shakespeare Plays" series from BBC. Directed by the multitalented Jonathan Miller, it's a sturdy rendition, marked by strong performances and a rousing pace. Though the humor rarely reaches laugh-out-loud levels, the lines are crisply and clearly delivered, with occasional flights of real sublimity when the poetry warrants. The settings, as well as the costumes, are colorful and credible.

The revelation of the show is John Cleese as Petruchio. As an occasional watcher of the "Monty Python" comedy troupe, whence Cleese is best known, I've always thought of him as an able buffoon—a mainstay of the frantic Python style, but not an actor of Shakespearean range. He proves otherwise here, with a performance that is at once precise, carefully modulated, and ever-so-slightly insane. Though this Petruchio clearly knows just what he's doing, he's full of surprises for us, as well as for the Katharina whose "taming" is the main thread of the play. In Cleese's hands, he's one part dapper, two parts cunning, and three parts wacky. It's a winning parlay.

In his first contribution to the Shakespeare TV series, director Miller keeps the action flowing smoothly and swiftly. More than most TV directors, he understands how to use a flexible performance area for maximum dramatic effect.

This production is no succession of flat close-ups: The background is sometimes as important as the foreground, and Miller knows how to grab our eyes by deftly catapulting us from one to the other. Because of the limitations of the TV medium, a certain amount of visual detail is lost when the focus of attention suddenly swoops into the distance. But there is a terrific gain in energy and variety.

Cleese is capably supported by Sarah Badel as a fiery yet somehow subtle Kate, who makes her presence keenly felt even when Petruchio has all the lines. Susan Penhaligon is a lovely Bianca, and a feisty roster of supporting players rounds out the cast.

"The Taming of the Shrew" remains one of Shakespeare's liveliest and most vigorous comedies. While TV is far from ideal at conveying dramatic works—lacking the immediacy of the stage and the pictorialism of cinema—its possibilities are richly exploited in this cheerfully untamed Miller production.

> David Sterritt, "Shakespeare's 'Shrew': Lots of Fun—Even if Some Say It's Sexist," in The Christian Science Monitor, *January 23, 1981, p. 19.*

Jonathan Miller and Tim Hallinan   (interview date Summer 1981)

[*In an interview with Jonathan Miller, Hallinan questions the director about various aspects of directing Shakespearean dramas for television. Miller also discusses his approach to directing* The Taming of the Shrew, *outlining his attempt to provide a creative and insightful interpretation of the play's themes and characters.*]

Hallinan. When you're producing Shakespeare for television as opposed to the stage, what does it do to your general approach?

Miller. Well, I think that television offers you the chance of removing large-scale hectoring rhetoric. It means the people haven't got to boom or to sing or to go in for that rather grandiloquent verse-speaking which often puts people off. You can be much more naturalistic. People can speak quietly in their own voice without simply descending into an ordinary modern vernacular. You can't have them doing that because it's very destructive to Shakespeare's verse if you speak as if it was ordinary modern speech.

Hallinan. It seems to me that television is inherently a more naturalistic medium. You're used to seeing the news on television.

Miller. That's right. I think that as soon as you put Shakespeare on that box where, as you say, people are accustomed to seeing naturalistic events represented, you are more or less obliged to present the thing as naturally as you can. There are, of course, limits upon that because of the sort of language that is being spoken. First of all, it comes from the past, and secondly, it doesn't come from the naturalistic past. It comes from the artistic past, and it's got a style and an idiom of its own which can't be violated. You have to allow these people to speak verse. But you have to get them speaking the verse in such a way that the audience is not aware of the fact that they're in the presence of an art form. They're only in the presence of naked communication. You have to give them the sense that when they hear those sentiments and feelings and ideas expressed in Shakespeare's language it's the only possible way in which those particular characters could have spoken; and that that's the best way to convey the ideas that they are actually trying to express.

Hallinan. What about the visual style?

Miller. Well, you have an awkward situation always, with the television, when you're taking an art form which was not intended for that medium. One has to understand that Shakespeare wrote for an unfurnished, unscenic stage without naturalistic representation of any sort. People didn't even wear colorful costumes. They simply wore modern costume, the costume of the sixteenth century, with perhaps some item which represented the past. Even in doing the Roman plays, it seems very unlikely that people wore archaeologically correct Roman costumes. Therefore I think it's very unwise to try and represent on the television screen something which Shakespeare did not have in his mind's eye when he wrote those lines. You have to find some counterpart of the unfurnished stage that Shakespeare wrote for without, in fact, necessarily reproducing a version of the Globe theatre. Because there's no way in which you can do that. You can't put one stage inside another, but you have to find some visual counterpart of that. (pp. 134-35)

Hallinan. Your production of *The Taming of the Shrew* has been described as understated, even somber. How did you approach that play?

Miller. I think that *The Taming of the Shrew* has been bedeviled in the past by a lot of horseplay, a lot of rough-house and also a tremendously flamboyant, twinkle-eyed cavalier image of Petruchio, the gay, dashing cavalier that, "By God, come kiss me, Kate," tames the young lass and brings her to heel. As with almost all of Shakespeare's comedies, it really is a more serious play than people have taken it for. The image of the dashing, moustachio-twirling cavalier is really a nineteenth-century version which has been imposed on the sixteenth-century English version portraying the character of the Puritan squire. The most important line in the play, I think, is where Petruchio says "To me, she's married, not unto my clothes" [III. ii. 117]. That is the great line which expressed Calvinism. The idea that you are, in fact, naked before the eye of God, and that that is the way you come before the eye of your partner. And that is the way you present yourself. The outward form, the decoration of your life, doesn't matter.

As for Kate, I've always wanted to get away from this game, this twinkling, bridling, high-spirited young colt image of her. These things give the audience the impression that there's going to be a great deal more humor than, in fact, there is in the play. What we want to do is to creep up quietly with comedy.

There are two plots. They're absolutely complementary, and each is just as important as the other. There are no subplots in Shakespeare; all the "subplots" are, in fact, the other side of a very carefully cantilevered structure. Shakespeare's plays are written like the domes of Renaissance cathedrals in which if you disregard one side and think of it as minor, you upset the structure. The relationship of Bianca to her suitors is there in order to give you a sense of the relationship between Petruchio and Kate. Who is the shrew, in fact, is the question that Shakespeare would have us ask ourselves. It isn't cut and dried that Kate's the shrew; she's the shrew that's mentioned, but it turns out by the time you get to the end of the play that the one who, in fact, is least obedient—the one who is shrillest and most obedient—is actually Bianca.

Hallinan. The plot of Bianca and her suitors is, it seems to me, a little bit more difficult to handle.

Miller. Well, yes, I mean it's a conventional piece of sixteenth-century artificial comedy. It's not realistic. And the great mastery of Shakespeare is his ability to show what seemed to be perfectly realistic human temperaments at work, inside the framework of a brightly-colored, simplified jack-in-the-box, old-fashioned plot. You have to come head-on into that plot and be as straightforward and as intense as you possibly can. Make each character go hell-for-leather for his or her own intention; play it with deadly intensity and seriousness, and farce will emerge from that. The conflict among all these people, each working against the others, will automatically produce comedy.

I like to work with the comedy in such a way that accessory and unexpected things are brought in on the floor, not merely in rehearsal, but right down here in the studio. There were lots and lots of things which I didn't know were going to happen until I started to see the extras, and then I began to paint with the extras. Isaac, for example, the little busybody who happened to be hanging around the edge. I saw him there. There was an inquisitive, twinkling look to him, and I said, "Why don't we have him always hanging around the edges of the plot to try and overhear it?" And then there was a policeman at the end, and I decided to use him. There was something wonderfully inviting about his tin helmet and his fat face, and I thought, "It'd be nice to sort of strike him over the head." Well, when that happened, that led on to other things and they led on to other things.

Hallinan. What would you say are the major themes of this play?

Miller. Well, I think there are several themes. One is the enduring theme of marriage and the duty of a wife to a husband and, indeed, a husband to a wife. And, of course, also, of a father to his children and of children to their father and of children to one another. Shakespeare is the great playwright of the family. He had a very clear understanding of the political theology of the family and of the relationship of the family to the state. Shakespeare was very interested in the notion of authority—authority within the family and authority within the state—and I believe that he underwrote the idea that the state, whether it was the small state of the family or the larger state of the country, required and needed the unquestioned authority of some sort of sovereign to whom everyone could defer. This was particularly important to someone like Shakespeare who had lived through, or had just emerged from, the period of the greatest turbulence in English political life. He and his contemporaries realized the absolute, vital importance of a peace imposed by someone who held within his hands the preemptive power and could inflict punishments and maintain control.

Well, in *The Taming of the Shrew* we have something very similar in that Shakespeare is extolling the virtues of the obedient wife—not the subordinate, cowed and simply docile, crushed wife—in accordance with the sixteenth-century belief that for the orderly running of society, some sort of sacrifice of personal freedom is necessary. Now, that's not something which we acknowledge or accept, but the fact that we don't acknowledge or accept it doesn't mean that we have to portray it in terms we find satisfactory. If we wish to make all plays from the past conform to our ideals and what we think the state or the family ought to be like, then we're simply rewriting all plays and turning them into modern ones. That, I think, is a species of historical suburbanism. It's we who live in the suburbs of history. The main part of human life has already occurred, and we live on a very thin rim just

on the outside of the great metropolis of history. If we insist on making the past in our own image, we show that we have a very provincial and Philistine view of human history.

What we also have here is the situation of a daughter who behaves in a shrewish, spiteful, malignant, discontented, and unpleasant way. But Shakespeare sees her as behaving like this precisely because she has lost the love of her father. Shakespeare is interested in fathers who don't distribute their love fairly. In this particular case, Baptista unfairly adores the younger daughter, and I think what happens with Kate is that she says that "you've always loved her best." In this situation of feeling unloved, she behaves unloved. This is a very common psychological consequence of the withdrawal of love from a parent. The child says, "All right, if I am unloved, I'll behave as unlovably as you think I am." When Petruchio arrives, he shrewdly sees the true person underneath the shrewishness and realizes that the best way to tame her is to demonstrate to her by behaving badly himself just what bad behavior looks like to others. He holds a mirror up to her. It's a technique child therapists sometimes use today, and this is where Shakespeare is so shrewd. Far from the taming of a shrew, then, this play is, in fact, about the teaching of a shrew, or the treatment of a shrew by allowing her to see her own image through someone who, quite clearly, adores her from the beginning.

Hallinan. Tell us about the Psalm that you're running over the end credits.

Miller. We've taken one of the Psalms which talks about the orderliness and grace and beauty of the family. It's one of the Psalms that would have been sung in the household after a meal in a Puritan household, and it somehow reconciles all the conflicts of the previous two hours. All these characters have been working at odds with one another, working against one another, trying to get their own ends. Now they are suddenly brought together in what the sixteenth century regarded as *communitas,* which is the bringing together, the unifying and harmonizing of all individual desires so that they actually work together rather than against one another. This is expressed beautifully when they all jointly sing a part song, which in itself is an expression of bringing different voices together in one harmonious performance.

It is in the medium of comedy that Shakespeare achieves his highest and most serious purposes. In *Twelfth Night,* in *As You Like It,* in *The Taming of the Shrew,* in *All's Well That Ends Well* and *Measure for Measure,* in plays which are labeled comedies, Shakespeare brings together the higher and more exalted themes of reconciliation, harmony, and peace on earth—as far as is possible, the idea of heaven.

At the end of the play, Petruchio invites Katherine to tell these foolish froward wives what their duty is to their husbands. He's not asking, as is so often thought, a broken woman to tell her colleagues or her sisters to button their lips and be obedient. He is asking a woman who has been through a complicated experience of self-discovery what is involved in submitting your will to others in the name of some larger satisfaction, such as the beauty and harmony of a family. (pp. 138-41)

Jonathan Miller and Tim Hallinan, in an interview in Shakespeare Quarterly, *Vol. 32, No. 2, Summer, 1981, pp. 134-45.*

John Cleese as Petruchio.

Kenneth S. Rothwell   (review date Autumn 1981)

[*Rothwell commends Miller for reversing the audience's normal expectations of* The Shrew *and for exploiting the television medium so effectively. The most prominent reversal, Rothwell maintains, was to cast Cleese as a sober and puritanical Petruchio.*]

In *The Taming of the Shrew,* which ushered in the third season [of "The Shakespeare Plays" on BBC] on 26 January 1981, Director Jonathan Miller filled the screen with witty surprises. Our amazement, however, stemmed not from Artaud-like effects like having Petruchio flying through the air on a rope over Kate, but rather in the simple audacity with which Miller reversed our normal expectations. The sly joke began with the casting of John Cleese of Monty Python fame as a sober, puritanical Petruchio. By "supposing" that an actor so zany as Cleese could play a Petruchio so sober as this one, Miller at once echoed a major theme of the play, even though he jettisoned the Sly Induction scene. This Petruchio completely overturns the image projected in past flamboyant portrayals by Douglas Fairbanks and Richard Burton.

Sarah Badel's Katherina is full of surprises, too, though the innovation is primarily that there is no innovation. This healthy, aggressive woman, who can throw as stormy a temper tantrum as anyone in Padua, ultimately supports traditional values as set forth in the Anglican wedding vows, which in turn reflect St. Paul's opinions on the authority of the husband. The part-song the banquet guests sing at the close of Act V (Psalm 128, "O blest is he that fears the Lord") signals Miller's view that in Shakespeare's lifetime neither

man nor woman was liberated, but each was bound (presumably in love) to the other.

Long after the tube cools off, one recollects with pleasure visually arresting bits of business: Cleese's soliloquy at IV.i, when he shatters the monotony of the talking head with an inventive catalog of yawning, scratching, rubbing of temples and nose, etc.; the sweeping servant at the opening of II.i who establishes the social framework for the Minola household at the same time that she adds a needed third dimension to the Vermeer-like *mise en scène;* the incredible whimpering of Leslie Sarony as Gregory, whose blatant scene-stealing in this energy-charged atmosphere simply adds to the general fun.

Some of this activity can as well be said to be good theatre as good television. For example, Grumio's response to Petruchio's "Villain, I say, knock me at this gate / And rap me well" [I. ii. 11-12], by exposing the literal sense of the construction, offers an instant lesson in Elizabethan grammar for people whose only knowledge of the ethical dative stems from occasional encounters with a passing redneck. Petruchio's stress on the imperative mood with Grumio foreshadows the domestic imperialism with which he later subdues Kate. Other brilliant theatrical touches include Antonio Pedley's Tranio affecting an upper-class accent while disguised as Lucentio; and Grumio's explication of the meaning of "Lend thine ear" [III. ii. 60] to Curtis, which, it develops, is intended as much to attract the audience's as Curtis' attention. Shakespeare knew how to teach actors the tricks of their trade.

In other respects, this *Shrew* is not only good theatre but adroit television. The problem of ensemble acting has been solved by getting the actors, not the camera, to move. Choreographed blocking allows as many as six actors to whirl their way through a frame, each one getting his share of proper attention. A good example occurs immediately after Kate's wedding. Against a backdrop of doorways and loggias, Baptista, Tranio, Bianca, Lucentio, Gremio, and Biondello chatter about the forthcoming feast. Almost subliminally a bouquet removed from a public fountain is handed from Baptista to Tranio to Bianca to Lucentio to Gremio to Biondello and then back to Baptista. Acting as a bond holding the scene together, it is only one of many cunning touches that make this performance so rewarding to watch. Elsewhere this same setting of doorways and loggias plausibly represents an Italian street with a juggler in the background on the church steps and transients passing by. Rather than offering a barrier to Shakespeare's language—through intelligent editing and camera work, which knows when to hold and when to move on—this realism supports rather than detracts from the spoken word. (pp. 397-98)

Kenneth S. Rothwell, "The Shakespeare Plays: 'Hamlet' and the Five Plays of Season Three," in Shakespeare Quarterly, *Vol. 32, No. 3, Autumn, 1981, pp. 395-401.*

Jonathan Miller   (essay date 1986)

[*Miller regards Shakespeare's plays as products of their own time which should not be altered or updated for the benefit of modern audiences. He argues that "one of the advantages of directing a play like* The Taming of the Shrew *is that it invites us to see that the past is a foreign country with different customs and values from our own." Miller then describes his BBC production of* The Shrew, *featuring Cleese as a perceptive man who patiently teaches his wife the necessity of obedience.*]

As a director I have modernized both Shakespeare and opera, but I think that there are dangers when people talk about 'contemporary' Shakespeare, or the 'timelessness' of the classics. While the idea of the afterlife challenges arguments about 'the authenticity' of a production, and releases a play or an opera for interpretation, it does not mean that we can justify the survival of any work *only* by making it address what is happening today. The notion of making Shakespeare relevant is often taken as a licence for quite absurd and literal transpositions into contemporary time, and assumes that no one is capable of adjusting his or her imagination to any political period other than the present. This is a form of historical provincialism, aptly described by T. S. Eliot as an overvaluing of our own times—a belief that the past is on probation, and has to prove itself by its capacity to accommodate current interests.

We cannot act or see Shakespeare today as the Elizabethans and the author did but we can take into account that our perception is a modern one without rewriting the plays to make them contemporary. Unable to re-create, or revisit the past as Elizabethans, we can establish a relationship to that past if we allow for differences, but this does not mean that we have to make the play's concerns identical with our own. By accepting how different the world referred to at the time of writing is from our own, similarities, in views and emotional experience, become much more striking. The plays are products of their time, and I hope that even when I have directed Shakespeare in modern or nineteenth-century dress, I have not lost sight entirely of the play's antiquity in my interpretation.

The best example of this overvaluing of our own time is shown in the American approach to Shakespeare; here I am thinking of directors like Joseph Papp. The American vice is seen mostly clearly in plays like *The Taming of the Shrew* which suddenly become a test case for feminism. Petruchio is portrayed as a typical male chauvinist pig, and Katharina as a bullied victim who then has to deliver her last speech, which seems to be so abjectly submissive, in a way that implies to the audience both that she is not defeated and that her submission to Petruchio is very ironic. This is sad because it demonstrates the belief that a work from the past can be performed in its afterlife only if it is made to conform to the values of the present.

In contrast, I think that one of the advantages of directing a play like *The Taming of the Shrew* is that it invites us to look at it on its own terms, and to see that the past is a foreign country with different customs and values from our own. The play at least offers us the opportunity to try to understand what is now the radically unvisitable past. Unlike Papp's approach to the play, my own enthusiastically recognizes Tudor social ideas of the function of the woman in the household without agreeing with them. When I tried to modernize the play, it was not in the sense of setting it in the present but of looking much more carefully, through contemporary eyes, at what it was expressing in the past. Conventional English productions of *The Taming of the Shrew* have had their own type of modernity, which now appears to be rather mandarin, and portrays the entire play as a mischievous and inoffensive wrong in which Petruchio becomes a moustachio-twirling cavalier.

My interpretation was very influenced by a book by Michael Waltzer. In *The Revolution of the Saints* he wrote about ideas prevalent among the Marian exiles, the Puritans who re-turned to England after exile under Mary Tudor. He stresses that for the Puritan—and by the time Shakespeare was writing, there was a substantial Puritan squirarchy—the Calvinistic view was of the world as a fallen place in which we had all inherited the sin of Adam congenitally. On this potentially unruly and unmanageable earth, sovereign authority was needed in order for there to be some kind of control. For the Puritans, there were two magistrates deputed by God to supervise order in an otherwise fallen world: in the family it was the husband and father, and in the state it was the king. The woman was required to obey, not simply because it flattered the vanity of man but because some authority had to be invested in one unquestionable person, whether or not he was necessarily qualified for this responsibility. In other plays, Shakespeare obviously makes us question whether certain officers *are* fit to occupy office. Lear is one example, a rash, foolish old man who occupies the position of the sovereign and is evidently unqualified to exercise the authority that he seems to abdicate wilfully. But in *The Taming of the Shrew*, we have an instance of Shakespeare writing about the need for order, and here is a play in which we have tuition exercised by a man and not, as is so often the case in Shakespeare, by a woman. What we see is not the bullying and subordination of an otherwise high-spirited girl, but a course of tuition as a result of which Kate learns the necessity of obedience. If you represent Petruchio as a serious man, you can take and develop the implications of lines such as '*To me she's married, not unto my clothes*' [III. ii. 117] and "*tis the mind that makes the body rich*' [IV. iii. 172] and see how consistent these are with a Puritan view. The alternative is to present Petruchio as a flamboyant bully.

When I directed *The Taming of the Shrew* for television, John Cleese took the part. I was interested in the irritability he showed in the character of Basil Fawlty but there are also strange sympathetic depths in the man that I thought could be usefully applied to the character of Petruchio. The attention that Petruchio pays to the tuition of Katharina can be portrayed much more sympathetically than it is in most productions. Unlike so many of the other suitors, he is not put off by her tantrums and there is a sense in which he is seen as a more caring character. He identifies Kate as someone worth spending time with, and sees that much of her difficulty is due to her self-image—she thinks of herself as unloved and unlovable, rejected by her father and not so favourably regarded as her sister. By suddenly becoming the subject of such detailed and apparently bullying tuition, Kate realizes that somebody has bothered to look beyond her unruly appearance and see her for the first time. It is as though she has become spiritually and morally visible in a way that she was not when simply perceived as a scold. Petruchio has recognized in her shrewish behaviour symptoms of unhappiness and, by behaving badly himself, he gives Kate back an image of herself.

Their first encounter, when Kate tries to attack Petruchio, is usually presented as a tremendous rough and tumble on stage. During the course of rehearsing the scene when Kate slaps Petruchio, something very interesting emerged. Instead of Petruchio suddenly throwing himself violently on her, John Cleese leant considerably towards her and simply went 'Hm, mm!' as if this was an interesting move on her part which had to be considered. He then said very quietly, '*I swear I'll cuff you if you strike again*' [II. i. 220]. This is a disconcerting move for which the character of Kate is unprepared, and it forces her to visualize her behaviour in a way that she would not have time to do if Petruchio had responded immediately with some comparable loud and violent move. The very fact that Kate might be ruffled by such a gesture is interesting. She looks at him then, perhaps for the first time, and sees that he is not quite like the other suitors as he is neither frightened, nor is he simply provoked into a display of rumbustious bad temper. By unpredictable behaviour in that moment he gives her back a self-image that she can evaluate. Kate begins to realize that someone who is prepared to devote so much time to her must be prompted by affection rather than by a selfish determination to have his own authority observed. But even with this slightly more subtle performance of Petruchio, his absolute commitment to the idea that there must be rule in a household can be seen throughout the play underlying the humour and sympathy.

We no longer share this view of domesticity, which is framed by theological dogma, but as a director, approaching these plays from the past, I must recognize and accommodate the production to those theological assumptions. The alternative is to frog-march Shakespeare into the twentieth century and make the plays address *our* problems, and literally identify with our values. The language then seems wrong and artificial. If, however, you allow such differences in attitudes to be visible in the production, the play comes alive and Kate's final speech is rather moving as it is an agreement to abide by the rules within a framework in which it is possible to enjoy a close affection. In contrast to Kate's rather graceful submission, the disagreeable behaviour of her sister Bianca becomes repugnant and you can then see that the real shrew is Bianca and not Katharina at all. (pp. 119-22)

> *Jonathan Miller, in a chapter in his* Subsequent Performances, *Faber & Faber, 1986, pp. 119-53.*

Graham Holderness   (essay date 1989)

[*Holderness comments on two aspects of Miller's BBC production of* The Taming of the Shrew: *the director's advocation of a naturalistic acting style and his view of the play as a serious comedy rather than a farce. Following these precepts, Miller demonstrated to his audience the relevance of Shakespeare's treatment of family relationships. In addition, he and Cleese devised a portrayal of Petruchio as a thoughtful, compassionate man who tamed Kate through the psychologically therapeutic method of mimicry.*]

The BBC/Time-Life Shakespeare series, which between 1979 and 1986 broadcast the entire canon of thirty-seven Shakespeare plays, was in its ambitious scope, scale and massive investment of cultural capital the most significant intervention to date into the reproduction of Shakespeare in performance. The series could not have been mounted at all without other more material investment: the BBC entered into partnership with the American company Time-Life TV, which in turn raised financial backing for the series from three big private corporations in the USA—the Exxon Corporation, Metropolitan Life Assurance and the Morgan Guaranty Trust Company of New York. This alliance between the British national communications medium and American private enterprise sufficiently indicates the economic and political origins of the project. It would naturally be foolish to write the series off as a predictable symptom of its capitalistic origins: but it is important to trace and measure the constraints and determinants built into the series itself as a consequence of its cultural and institutional basis.

The scale of investment and the nature of commercial underwriting (as distinct from commercial *sponsorship*) imposed one very obvious requirement on this enterprise: it should be economically viable—that is, give a direct financial return, as well as a cultural pay-off, on commercial investment. This condition necessarily entailed the preservation of the plays in consumer-durable (video-cassette) form rather than reduction to one-off transmission, and an international marketing operation. Conscious of this dependence on the market rather than on patronage and subsidy, the planners insisted that productions should aim for 'high quality' and 'durability'. What 'high quality' originally implied in such a context is predictable: 'great' directors, 'classical' actors, 'straightforward' productions—'these productions will offer a wonderful opportunity', said the first Executive Producer Cedric Messina, 'to study the plays performed by some of the greatest classical actors of our time.' The notion of 'high quality' entailed in practice a conservative respect for 'traditional' values in Shakespearean production. Jonathan Miller, who is known for his theatrical work as an innovative and experimental director, described some of the 'problems' he inherited in taking over the series, among them 'the original contract with the American co-producers—it had to be so-called traditional . . .' Cedric Messina had accepted this constraint with enthusiasm, in the belief that only 'traditional' productions would 'stand the test of time': 'We've not done anything too sensational in the shooting of it—there's no arty-crafty shooting at all. Some of them are, for want of a better word, straightforward productions.' Despite his expressed reservations Jonathan Miller accepted the Executive Producership of the series after the second season (i.e. 1980-81): and directed productions of *Othello, Antony and Cleopatra, Troilus and Cressida, Timon of Athens* and *The Taming of the Shrew.* (pp. 95-6)

Zeffirelli's film version [of *The Taming of the Shrew*] dropped the 'Induction' in favour of an elaborate deployment of filmic devices providing an alternative establishing context. The BBC/Time-Life production also dispensed completely with Christopher Sly, though it opens with a gestural scenario of realistic establishing details: a stage-set city street with bits of Renaissance local colour such as dwarfs and jugglers. The absence of the 'Induction' from the BBC version provoked in this case more reaction from critics and reviewers, particularly since the entire series is understood to represent a partially-enforced commitment to certain 'classic' virtues, such as the retention of 'complete' or at least 'full' texts. The cut provoked Stanley Wells to some asperity:

> Jonathan Miller—acting, we must hope, in defiance of his literary consultant John Wilders—offered a simplified version of *The Taming of the Shrew* in this BBC production. To omit the Christopher Sly episodes is to suppress one of Shakespeare's most volatile lesser characters, to jettison most of the play's best poetry, and to strip it of an entire dramatic dimension. In a series announcing itself as 'The Complete Dramatic Works of William Shakespeare' this leaves a serious gap [in the *Times Literary Supplement*].

In the BBC text of the play issued to accompany the series, the literary consultant actually discusses the absent 'Induction', observing only that it was 'omitted from this production as being unsuitable for the medium of television'. The director held this view:

> I find the Christopher Sly 'Induction' terribly hard

to do in any other format but the stage: it is a stage device, and it's frightfully hard to see it on television. It's a device that brings the audience into close identification with some person who is like them. It would be on television a little extra programme tagged on before the programme proper begins. On the stage it's possible to make it work much better: it's a folk style which sits rather uncomfortably in this very twentieth-century medium of domestic viewing.

There seems to have been within the corporative consensus little disagreement with this line. Henry Fenwick, who assembled production notes on each play in the series, evidently approved: 'The only cut Miller took was to remove the "Induction"—that odd and unresolved framework of the beggar Sly being duped and entertained by a wealthy lord. Its removal is by no means new, and not only did it tidy the play considerably, it also helped the seriousness of the approach'. Further endorsement of Miller's preference can be found in some interesting comments from the man directly responsible for the text, script editor David Snodin:

> In the television production of *The Taming of the Shrew* Jonathan Miller and I decided after considerable discussion to omit the whole of that curious, lengthy and disappointingly unresolved opening known as the 'Induction'. We made this decision for the following reasons: firstly, because we felt that it may confuse the viewer coming to the play for the first time, very possibly to the detriment of his enjoyment of the play as a whole; secondly, because it is an essentially theatrical device which, while it has been known to work well in a theatre before a live audience, would not come across successfully in the very different medium of television; and lastly, because it is a device which presents the play's characters as 'actors', and we felt that this would hinder the attempt, in this production, to present them as real people in a real, and ultimately quite serious situation.

The range of motives underlying this contentious decision include some attenuated legacy (if Henry Fenwick's concept of 'tidiness' has any intellectual content at all) of neo-classical theory; a conviction that television and theatrical conventions are radically dissimilar and should be kept firmly separated; a paternalistic concern for the intelligibility threshold of the uneducated viewer; a curious notion that realism of presentation is a precondition of 'seriousness' in thematic approach; and an unwillingness to expose by any alienating or metadramatic devices the theatrical mechanisms of the play's construction.

Some of these shaping influences indicate contradictory pressures inherited from the institutional context of the series itself: from the constraints imposed by the American sponsors and coproducers, and from the economic and cultural imperatives of aiming at a world-wide market. It is quite clear that in this particular case the demand for accessibility and the censorship of innovation and experiment, both imposed by the American backers, led to an infringement of that other institutional stipulation, that the series should offer authentic and authoritative versions of the plays. The director's own position *vis-á-vis* those inherited conditions was also a somewhat contradictory one: known for his theatrical work as a particularly innovative, risk-taking cultural entrepreneur, he agreed to preside as Executive Producer over a series more remarkable for its relentlessly monumental classicising than

for its creativity in the production of Shakespeare. His observations quoted above about the *Shrew* also appear contradictory: anxious to dissuade the viewer from identifying with Christopher Sly, he nonetheless apparently wanted to secure a seamless realism of presentation for a serious drama of domestic issues.

Whatever his capacities as a stage director, Miller believes in the absolute determinacy of the television medium, which he sees as imposing its own constraints on dramatic production. Television is incurably naturalistic and translates everything it touches into naturalism: 'as soon as you put Shakespeare on that box where . . . people are accustomed to seeing naturalistic events represented, you are more or less obliged to present the thing as naturally as you can' [Miller, in Tim Hallinan, "Jonathan Miller on the Shakespeare Plays"]. Miller is therefore adverse to any attempt to theatricalise television: T.V. productions should display no manneristic theatrical styles, no expressionistic acting and no mixing of conventions. (pp. 96-9)

[Miller's *Shrew*] is set according to principles of naturalistic design, with one set simulating a populous Padua street, and others representing various domestic interiors. The basic principles of costume design were of course prescribed by the contract with the American co-producers—'traditional'; that is, contemporary with Shakespeare's own time or with the historical period in which the play's action is set. In the case of the *Shrew,* this amounts more or less to the same thing; so the costumes are historically-accurate early-to mid-seventeenth-century bourgeois dress, incorporating some deliberate allusions to Renaissance visual sources.

In so far as set and costume design employed naturalistic conventions, the photographic techniques used complemented that stylistic medium. Long shots were used to represent the open street scenes, medium shots for small groupings of characters, and close-ups for moments of detailed psychological description. The typical shot, used recurrently throughout the production, is the close-up of one or more characters, using a telephoto lens, so that other characters, or gestural details of social activity, can be glimpsed out of focus behind or between the talking heads. The camera-position expresses precisely the relationship between the individual and society characteristic of bourgeois—liberal ideology: with the person fully-focused, concrete and massive; and the social environment gesturally present as 'background', but distanced and blurred. One particularly effective use of this technique involved the grouping of several characters—typically, a number of scheming, calculating men—around the camera, confiding and negotiating, with the outside world suspiciously excluded. Miller reinforced this effect by introducing a diminutive extra who would curiously penetrate the tightly-bunched circle of men to eavesdrop and pry.

Almost consistently, the production employs the fourth-wall convention of a naturalistic stage-set, with the characters wholly absorbed in and confined to their reconstructed historical reality. Very occasionally this illusion is disrupted, by a character addressing the camera direct and thus fracturing the transparent fourth wall of the camera's perspective. The only characters permitted to do this are those on the fringes of the main action—characters such as Tranio and Hortensio—who can thus be considered as 'low-life' or comic characters, able to move off the elevated plane of theatrical realism and occupy the downstage area of more direct communication with the audience. Furthermore they are only allowed the opportunity of direct address when the text leaves them alone on stage with the responsibility of uttering an 'aside', that could be delivered to no conceivable object but the audience-camera (e.g. Tranio at [II. i. 404-11]). Where on the other hand Petruchio is left alone on stage and given lines in soliloquy—such as his manifestos of strategy at [II. i. 170]: 'Say that she rail; why then I'll tell her plain . . . ' and [IV. i. 188]: 'Thus have I politically begun my reign . . . ', John Cleese delivered the speeches not as asides or direct addresses to the audience, but as meditative self-communings, introverted self-interrogations absorbedly unaware of listeners or spectators. The result is to transform speeches which must in the Elizabethan theatres have been offered direct to the audience for debate and consideration, into naturalistic representations of a psychological process of self-examination and moral inquiry. (pp. 100-01)

Although Jonathan Miller always appears to have a strong and clearly-formulated intellectual conception of a production, his theoretical approach to acting is not what we normally associate with 'director's theatre'.

> I usually have a *general* idea, then let it shape up as I find the people. The people have a very strong material influence on what the play is going to be. Whatever ideas you have about them are very often altered by the actual substance that is going to embody them, and there is no way you can impose an idea on an actor who is going to play it. Obviously one has to give them a general idea to which they must consent in order to work, but the moment to moment details of a production are very much determined by what they bring to it. And if you've got really good and talented actors they always bring an unprecedented thing . . .

> It's always said by literary critics that you ought to be able to know what a character is from the sum of all that is actually said in a play by that given character; but if that were the case, then every time the play is performed the character would be the same. What is so peculiar about a play is that every time it's performed by a different actor, under the guidance of a different director, you're actually meeting someone quite new. As director, in order to find what is meant by a particular sentence, you and the actor have to improvise what that particular person means by the sentence they're using. And you can't do that until you've somehow invented a biography for them; in the end you have to invent a person not entirely made up of all the things they say in the play.

Clearly this is no simple theory of naturalism in acting: underlying these comments are quite sophisticated notions about language and communication, and a recognition that in performance 'character' is not something keyed into the words of a text and released by the actor's delivery, but rather a new entity over-determined by a complex process of exchange between text, director and actor, within the structural determinants of a concrete cultural situation. The actor is not a directorially-dominated *über-marionette,* but an independent seeker involved in a collaborative process of improvising character: '[Miller's] directing method . . . is to create an atmosphere where the actor is freed to release his own imagination instead of being obliged to play out a pre-conceived puppet role' [Sean Day-Lewis in the *Daily Telegraph*]. Nonetheless, as the phrase about 'inventing a biography' suggests, what the actor's imagination is required to produce is a por-

trayal of character within a broadly naturalistic approach to representation. Even where the other elements of the dramatic narrative are patently non-naturalistic, the individual character's imaginary 'biography' can still be constructed.

It was from the outset fundamental to Miller's conception of the play that it is not a farce but a serious comedy. This entails, in his view, an understanding of the play as a direct address to serious moral problems of actual living, which could only be properly enacted through a medium of psychological realism. The farcical tradition in the play's performance was an inheritance to be escaped from, since it distorted the play's earnest contemplation of serious domestic issues:

> I think that *The Taming of the Shrew* has been bedeviled in the past by a lot of horseplay, a lot of rough-house and also a tremendously flamboyant, twinkle-eyed cavalier image of Petruchio, the gay, dashing cavalier that, 'By God, come kiss me, Kate', tames the young lass and brings her to heel. As with almost all of Shakespeare's comedies, it really is a more serious play than people have taken it for . . . as for Kate, I've always wanted to get away from this game, this twinkling, bridling, high-spirited young colt image of her. These things give the audience the impression that there's going to be a great deal more humour than, in fact, there is in the play [Miller in Hallinan].

In Miller's view the play is a direct address to serious issues of sexual and family relationships, interpreted historically and approached moralistically:

> It's a play about many important themes in family life—fathers who distribute their love unfairly between their children and then are surprised to find that the deprived child is behaving cantankerously; the failure of men to recognise who the truly valuable woman is and who see in cantankerousness nothing but viciousness; the failure of unsophisticated lovers to see that the young and the bland is more likely to be the shrew than Kate herself [Miller, in Ann Pasternak Slater, "An Interview with Jonathan Miller"].

These domestic themes are certainly conceived historically, but the 'importance' attached to them by the director appears to owe something to an apparent transhistorical continuity of human experience: the 'themes' defined here are clearly not confined to a sixteenth-century social milieu. It is a natural progression from such an emphasis on immanent domestic experience to the view that psychological observations and interpretations of contemporary modern behaviour can be applied retrospectively to a dramatisation of Renaissance values. The problem of 'shrewishness' raised by the play can then be understood in the light of current psychological theory: Petruchio becomes, in the words of one reviewer, 'an eccentrically pragmatic social worker using the wayward client's own doubtful habits to calm her down' [Chris Dunkley in the *Financial Times*]. In an interview with Ann Pasternak Slater Miller was reminded that in rehearsal he had compared Petruchio's treatment of Kate with techniques of therapy for problem children used at the Tavistock clinic: 'There are ways in which a skilful therapist will gently mock a child out of a tantrum by giving an amusing imitation of the tantrum immediately after it's happened. The child then has a mirror held up to it and is capable of seeing what it looks like to others' [Miller in Slater]. At that point in the production where Petruchio refuses to allow Kate to keep the cap made for her [IV. iii. ff.] John Cleese performs exactly such an act of supposedly therapeutic, though potentially severely hurtful, mimicry.

The implications of such a psychological approach for actors leads us directly back to naturalism. If the character of Katherina is seen as a kind of case-study interpreted in the light of modern psychiatry, then the task of the actor is to present as accurately and convincingly as possible a simulation of the particular psychological deviance or disturbance imputed to Shakespeare's play. This is precisely what Sarah Badel, who plays Katherina, offers in the production: she appears constantly at the mercy of violent throes of infantile emotion, often completely possessed by passions of jealousy and resentment, and even in moments of greater stability appears close to the edge of neurotic excitation and hysteria. In the closing scene, completely cured by Petruchio's treatment, she displays an achieved serenity, a complete self-possession of confidence and poise. The 'imaginary biography' constructed for Katherina by Sarah Badel falls closely into line with the director's conception of the character:

> She's a woman of such passion, or that's how I saw it, a woman of such enormous capacity for love, that the only way she could be happy is to find a man of equal capacity. Therefore she's mad for lack of love . . . he feigns madness; she in my view is teetering on the edge of it. Petruchio is the only man who shows her what she's like.

The correct way to act this personality, it is inferred, is by means of an uninhibited self-abandonment to the inner truth of the role: 'There's no point in thinking about it or defending yourself with intelligent approaches—you simply have to come on with a total declaration and not care what anybody thinks at all, because she doesn't'. John Cleese is also quoted as complying with this general line of interpretation: he describes having consulted a psychiatrist who confirmed that the technique of mimicry and impersonation is in fact a perfect therapeutic treatment for 'shrews'.

It is of course entirely possible that these illustrations of agreement between director and actors testify to a genuinely successful programme of collaboration: but it seems far more likely, given Miller's own intellectual and academic powers, that this unity of opinion was secured by an involuntary and painless process of directorial domination. And what Miller's presuppositions required happened to be what the actors were all too willing to provide: convincing naturalistic depictions of credible human behaviour. The achievement of realism was in turn abundantly rewarded by reviewers, always looking to be 'moved' and 'convinced' by accurate representations of 'life'. Stanley Wells: 'John Cleese's . . . was a deeply thoughtful performance, convincing us of the seriousness of Petruchio's intentions. . . . their relationship became a wholly credible process of mutual adjustment' [Wells]. Or Chris Dunkley: 'Miller succeeded: the story did seem less deeply misogynistic than usual, more like a single peculiar case history and less of a general attack on women' [Dunkley].

What then happens to Miller's naturalistic propensities when they are applied to the self-evidently ostentatious artifice of the Bianca-plot? What scope is there for realism of characterisation in the context of a highly formalised Italianate comic structure? The contradiction posed here was certainly grasped very firmly in the director's mind:

> The plot of Bianca and her suitors is . . . a conventional piece of sixteenth-century artificial comedy. It's not realistic. And the great mastery of Shakespeare is his ability to show what seemed to be perfectly realistic human temperaments at work, inside the framework of a brightly-coloured, simplified jack-in-the-box, old-fashioned plot. You have to come head-on into that plot and be as straightforward and intense as you possibly can. Make each character go hell-for-leather for his or her own intention; play it with deadly seriousness, and farce will emerge from that [Miller in Hallinan].

Such a method will of course produce different results in different cases, and some of the results are unlikely to be naturalistic: as in the instances for example of purely comic characters whose 'imaginary biographies' could never be anything other than single-dimensional caricatures. But even in this context a certain measure of realism was encouraged. Susan Penhaligon, who plays Bianca, shows how under Miller's tutelage it was possible to construct a biography even for the part of Bianca:

> With Jonathan everybody is important. I know every director will *say* that but when it comes down to rehearsing, because of time or whatever, a lot of directors don't put it into practice. Jonathan does. He creates an atmosphere where you can go up to him at any time and talk for half an hour about your character—even if you've got two lines he'll build up a whole background for you so you know what you're saying.

In this particular case that 'background' proves to be a 'how many children had Lady Macbeth' biography of Bianca: 'she is as strong as Kate but had probably dealt with the family situation better than Kate: she'd learned to get her own way by smiling . . . Bianca was spoiled', and so forth. This example illustrates what seems to have been an instinctive consensus between director and actors in this production: an easy reconciliation of a particular directorial conception with the naturalistic presumptions and propensities of actors themselves. The interpretative result was recognised as identical with Miller's explicit intentions; Bianca was greeted by critics as a spoiled child who masks her spite and self-interest with a facade of sweetness. The corollary of Miller's sympathetic revaluation of the role of Katherina is that another woman should be obliged to bear the title of 'shrew'.

It is hardly surprising that other figures of the sub-plot proved rather less adaptable to the dominant naturalistic style. Miller's casting appears to have been an explicit acknowledgement of this, since he fitted a team of very well-known comic actors—familiar especially from numerous and frequent television appearances—with the roles of Gremio, Tranio, Hortensio, and the Pedant. These characters were all recognised by reviewers as playing appropriately within the discourses of comedy and farce: 'some of the performers', Stanley Wells noted, 'elected for a stylised, consciously comic mode' [Wells]. Other critics drew the inevitable parallels with the familiar television forms of humorous sketch and situation-comedy: 'There was something of Capt. Peacock in *Are You Being Served?* about Frank Thornton's vain Gremio, a touch of Reginald Perrin's boss C. J. about John Barron's commanding Vincentio, and the fruits of many familiar comedy sketches in John Bird's fuss-pot Pedant' [Day-Lewis]. It was clearly the director's intention, in casting so many inhabitants of television comedy, to mix the serious and comic modes within the production. In doing so he permitted the

Bianca-plot to approach perilously close to exactly the kind of self-reflexiveness the production team was so determined to avoid:

> Actors in lesser roles descended to the kind of half-hearted improvisation which may be useful in rehearsal but should be expunged in performance: *'cum privilegio ad imprimendum solum,* i'n it, eh?' said Biondello; and the Pedant added 'was that all right?' to one of his comic inventions [Wells]. . . .

[The] production earned the condemnation of the same critic for permitting dramatic modes to be mixed at all. Those aspects of Miller's directing that approach more nearly to the spirit of Elizabethan stage practice again meet the reproof of an attenuated and irrelevant neo-classical criticism.

The most inspired, and in my view the most successful reconciliation of these serious and farcical tendencies, was the casting of John Cleese as Petruchio. Cleese was of course the best-known comic performer in the cast, a veteran of such brilliantly innovative television comedy programmes as *Monty Python's Flying Circus* and *Fawlty Towers:* Miller's motive for casting Cleese in a production dedicated to rediscovering seriousness in the *Shrew* seems to have been a gamble that paid off. Stanley Wells, as we have seen, found the portrayal 'deeply thoughtful . . . convincing us of the seriousness of Petruchio's intentions' [Wells], while Sean Day-Lewis found the 'fortuitous reference back to the distracted existence of Basil Fawlty and his shrewish wife'—('be she as old as Sybil . . .')—to be 'no disadvantage'. One reviewer suggested that the collision of serious and comic modes in Cleese's performance may not have been fortuitous at all:

> Its success was due not to a decision to treat Petruchio comically, but to Miller's perception that the Basil Fawlty persona which is John Cleese's distinctive role has a terrible kind of manic seriousness. This Cleese brought with him, with the result that a steely, authentically puritanical—almost Cromwellian—character emerged [John Naughton in the *Observer*].

Notwithstanding these various attempts to reconcile the serious and the comic within a unified style, the distinction of the performance seems to me to reside in the distancing and doubleness of Cleese's delivery. His performance stands out from those characterisations which hew closely to naturalism, as a sustained and inspired deployment of Brechtian alienation-effect. Cleese is never entirely naturalised within his role, as other comic characters contrive to be: his delivery of the lines always preserves a certain ironic distance, as if he found difficulty not only in taking them seriously himself, but in the idea that anyone possibly could take them seriously at all. The result is a beautifully-composed detachment, which allows to the part of Petruchio a unique doubleness and self-reflexive ironical consciousness. Towering above his strange mixed company of Stanislavskian soul-searchers and music-hall comedians in creative innovation as well as in height, Cleese is easily the most admirable component of the production. (pp. 104-11)

> *Graham Holderness, in his* Shakespeare in Performance: The Taming of the Shrew, *Manchester University Press, 1989, 133 p.*

PRODUCTION:

Toby Robertson • Theatre Royal, Haymarket • 1986

BACKGROUND:

In his 1986 production, Robertson offered a straightforward interpretation of *The Taming of the Shrew,* embellishing its farcical nature with significant amounts of slapstick comedy, but generally imposing no directorial viewpoint on the text. In the estimation of most theater critics, this otherwise inferior production was barely rescued by the professional caliber of Vanessa Redgrave's Katherina and Timothy Dalton's Petruchio.

COMMENTARY:

Stella Flint   (review date June 1986)

[*Flint admonishes Robertson for a shallow interpretation of* The Shrew, *with "no subtle motivation, no psychological insight, no emotional depth or demand."*]

The engagement to play at Theatr Clwyd in North Wales, of Vanessa Redgrave and Timothy Dalton had been rumoured for months. Finally they were announced in *The Taming of the Shrew* and *Antony and Cleopatra* with a transfer to the London Haymarket envisaged. The prospect was exciting.

The Shrew opened with stillness, sounds of revelry, muted, distant. Simon Higlett has conjured a rich sixteenth century interior. Around a horse-shoe setting, the golden brown of brocaded curtains allows glimpses, across wide alcoves of mullioned windows, above porticoed doors of deep wood panelling or sweeps impressively to the floor. The mellow glow gradually lightens and the best is done already.

Every door is viable, but the upper drapes remain, save one, closed. Only the consideration of showing different locations is exploited. Speculations on the delights of a chase, the surprise of improbable happenings come to nothing. The play, according to director Toby Robertson, is 'a jolly romp' and, we soon gather no more: an excuse for gimmickry and knockabout, with no subtle motivation, no psychological insight, no emotional depth or demand.

The limitations of this interpretation are manifold. The pace must be rapid and quick fire. Speeches tumble out; the verse metres stressed to the point of obliterating sense. Frequently one questions whether lines are understood by those in smaller parts. Only in rare moments of tranquility does the poetry, tantalisingly, breathe.

The crucial relationship between Katherine and Petruchio is developed only superficially: one is left unsatisfied and uncertain. Miss Redgrave, having made public her view that Kate is simply an obnoxious woman, wild and ungoverned, no feminist, produces a first scene of flailing arms and indeterminate North country accent. Discomforted by her encounter with Petruchio she continues in a state of passive bemusement. Her parries are out of puzzlement rather than a powerful personality challenged for the first time by an equal intelligence. The sexual aspect is scarcely explored: one brief sequence of caresses, the final submissive kiss, with little between to suggest the smouldering fire that is being brought to a blaze. Yet the cues of growing warmth are acknowledged, B-movie style, by soft music and flickering firelight and, at one point a brazier at which the men must needs warm their rears.

Timothy Dalton, dashing pell-mell through his wooing has neither breath nor energy for pursuit or a snatched dalliance in spontaneous physical contact. Constantly referring to his 'Kat' he plots, plans, and executes his scheme as with the veriest bird of prey. He watches all night, allowing no sleep, starving his victim. There is neither comedy nor cruelty in his actions. Returning to Kate's father's house, the two can stand apart to witness Bianca's betrothal, and we feel no rapport, no union between them. Neither has truly suffered in their mutual ordeal.

The consciousness that these are entertainers, in a frivolous calling, is strong. The page, in woman's finery to play Sly's wife, parades in Kate's new gown, as authentic as the set, and suggests the sleezier side of modern drag. The anachronism is echoed later by a pretty Victorian parasol and more especially, by sudden snatches of song and dance, painfully so by a passage in rapping style, accompanied by clicking fingers, the whole cast mimicking a galloping coach.

The process of rehearsal and production seems to have been cumulative. Instead of refining ideas in accordance with a defined intention evolved by cast and director, *The Shrew* has become encumbered with bright notions. Together these result in a misbegotten jumble, a damp squib of a 'jolly romp'. If strict measures are applied, the West End may see a very different show. Alternatively one might surmise that, with much North American experience, Toby Robertson has, with Christopher Selbie and their assistant Jeremy Raison devised the whole thing with tourists in mind. (p. 23)

> *Stella Flint, in a review of "The Taming of the Shrew," in* Plays & Players, *No. 393, June, 1986, pp. 22-3.*

Irving Wardle   (review date 12 June 1986)

[*Wardle compliments Robertson for his courage in presenting* The Shrew *as a play about a husband's "right of supremacy," even though it may be an unpopular theme for modern audiences.*]

It has become a habit among recent directors of this comedy to suggest that it is really making a point about money, or brainwashing, or the Puritan ethic—anything rather than its manifest subject of the "right supremacy" of husbands.

It takes some originality, not to say courage, to present the piece at its face value, as Toby Robertson does in the second of his Theatr Clwyd productions. In such performances you are always left with the impression of a foolproof play that happens to be saying something totally unacceptable. The present version leaves that contradiction unresolved; but, thanks to the partnership of Vanessa Redgrave and Timothy Dalton, it at least eliminates any sense of sadistic cruelty and convincingly transforms the taming exercises into lovers' games, relating more to the world of *As You Like It* than *The Duchess of Malfi*.

The opening duel, played as a flight-and-pursuit game with Petruchio seizing every punch or kick and changing it into a caress, establishes the rules of the game. Redgrave's Kate, hands stuffed into the pockets of an Elizabethan trouser-suit, achieves comic supremacy through her mastery of the arts of defeat, showing a wonderful variety of enraged response to

each disarming setback—stamping and grinding her teeth through Petruchio's tender speeches as he holds her captive by her braces or hauls her back from the brazier when she totters freezing into the matrimonial home.

Even in the central taming scenes, it is comic detail, such as the sight of her eyes ravenously scouring the table while in the act of prayer, or of Petruchio showing off the "lewd and filthy" cap as an animated codpiece, that hold the stage; not the sense of hunger and exhaustion. As Redgrave plays it, Kate's conversion comes in a moment when she is alone and suddenly sees the light, undergoing a radiant transformation rather than having her will broken. It may sound implausible but, given the strength of affection that she and Mr Dalton put into the final scenes, it is irresistible at the time.

Played on an adapted version of Sean Higlett's *Antony and Cleopatra* stage, the production makes full use of the Christopher Sly material, keeping him in view almost throughout and thus emphasizing the sportive nature of the show by presenting it on a plank and two step-ladders in the Lord's house.

The sense of a partly improvised occasion is also strengthened by Sylvester McCoy's Tranio, a superb piece of clowning, especially when he goes into foppish disguise, manipulating the false Vincentio like a ventriloquist's doll and asking "have you ever been to Pisa?" [IV. ii. 93] while listing over as if in a high wind. On Tuesday night a moustache came off, and McCoy had a ball with that.

The surrounding company are not strong on individual personalities, but their timing and style are immaculate.

> *Irving Wardle, "Cruelty Convincingly Transformed," in* The Times, *London, June 12, 1986, p. 19.*

Christopher Edwards   (review date 21 June 1986)

[*Edwards maintains that Redgrave and Dalton were "well worth watching" as Katherina and Petruchio, but the production left some of the play's principal questions unaddressed.*]

This is a production that takes you back in time to the way Shakespeare was performed some 25 years ago; with a proscenium arch, conventional props and *sans* governing 'concept'. Indeed, it is the very opposite of 'director's theatre'. You come to see stars playing leading roles and it must be said that both Vanessa Redgrave and Timothy Dalton are well worth watching. The play, however, is left to speak for itself and what have been called 'all the awkward sexual and political questions' are left unaddressed. The shrew, Kate, has her peevish spirit broken by her husband and, at the end, delivers the famous submission speech in recognition of the prevailing social hierarchy: 'Thy husband is thy lord, thy life, thy keeper, / Thy head, thy sovereign. . . . / Such duty as the subject owes the prince, / Even such a woman oweth to her husband . . .' [V. ii. 146-56]. Just as she moves to abase herself at Petruchio's feet he catches up her hands and kisses her. Here, under Toby Robertson's direction this key moment expresses a sense of realised domestic freedom.

Kate's family stand amazed at the character's transformation and so too have several critics. No irony? No lever for the modern feminist point of view? Vanessa Redgrave, of all actresses, playing this part in this way? (We still await some satiric reinterpretation of Grumio's line from the play about 'an old trot with ne'er a tooth in her head' [I. ii. 79-80]). The production could in fact be defended as feminist. Here, you might say, we see Kate as utterly accepting of the dominant civil order and to witness her so completely in that world is a more radical statement, precisely because there is no ironical counterpoint. But that would be too nice an interpretation and in any case there seems to be no serious complaint about the evening's comparative innocence. True, we might miss some of the excitement often provided by the RSC but the warmth of the laughter in the Haymarket suggests that orthodox commercial Shakespeare has a ready public. And what a relief to be out of the Barbican's totalitarian concrete bunker.

Vanessa Redgrave's Kate is broadly played and very funny. Her early, untamed Kate is a coltish, gawky schoolgirl of pouts, grimaces and stamping feet. In her outfit of velvet culottes and bobbing blonde curls it is as if the spirit of St Trinians had got inside Little Lord Fauntleroy. But the play really belongs to Timothy Dalton's excellent Petruchio. There is not a trace of the demented sadist we have encountered in recent years. Instead here is Hazlitt's idea of the part. Dalton acts the assumed character of the mad-cap railer with complete presence of mind, with conscious theatricality and without a particle of ill humour. It is an engaging and sympathetic performance and if the pleasure of the production becomes rather more muted in the second half this is largely the fault of the play. (pp. 32-3)

> *Christopher Edwards, "Moments from History," in* The Spectator, *Vol. 256, No. 8241, June 21, 1986, pp. 32-3.*

Sheridan Morley   (review date 25 June 1986)

[*Morley contends that Robertson's "semi-showbiz knock-about" production seemed more like a rendition of* Kiss Me Kate *than Shakespeare's play.*]

After an *Antony and Cleopatra* that was far more her than him, Vanessa Redgrave and her *Haymarket* company seem keen to right the balance in the *Taming of the Shrew* which now joins their repertoire at the Theatre Royal. Here Timothy Dalton, a somewhat wimpish Antony, is allowed to come into his own as the full matinée-idol Petruchio, and the only surprise of the production, apart from Redgrave's oddly muted Katherina, is that having gone farcically this far towards *Kiss Me Kate* the directors, Toby Robertson and Christopher Selbie, didn't let their ever-eager cast loose on the full Broadway musical rather than this semi-showbiz knock-about.

Certainly they've had some very good ideas about the play, one of which is the reinstatement of the full Christopher Sly subplot usually cut from more classical renderings. What this does is to establish the notion of a band of strolling players coming to a country house and performing, largely for the benefit of a drunken tinker, an impromptu extramarital comedy about a man going to wive it wealthily in Padua. Shakespeare is thus once again conjured by the Redgrave players from an old costume basket, and a permanent set which proved useless to *Antony* comes into its own for a romping farce unusually devoid of any chauvinist overtones.

The problem for any director coming now to *The Shrew* is how to handle Kate's last-minute decision to lay herself under Petruchio's heel: here it is done in a remarkably unsex-

ist way, with Miss Redgrave able, as only she can, to suggest that she has suddenly fallen in love and that nothing else really matters as much as that. When, therefore, she goes down on one knee to him, and he rapidly joins her on that level, the battle of the sexes becomes suddenly irrelevant and everyone is off the social hook.

> *Sheridan Morley, "Road Running," in* Punch, *Vol. 290, No. 7592, June 25, 1986, p. 44.*

Jean-Marie Maguin   (review date October 1986)

[*Maguin responds favorably to Robertson's production, deeming it "an interesting rendering of the play with sentiment always richly stirring beneath the farce." Dalton's Petruchio was a "physically convincing" although "mentally reluctant" shrew tamer, Maguin maintains, and Redgrave's Kate was "well gauged throughout."*]

Ever wished to see your Shakespeare straight (meaning in period dress and without motorbikes or motorcars purring across the stage, in other words without the type of added reagent the R. S. C. has got us used to)? The production of *The Taming of the Shrew* at the Theatre Royal, Haymarket is your opportunity. The same company, headed by Vanessa Redgrave and Timothy Dalton, alternates the play with *Antony and Cleopatra.*

The set designed by Simon Higglet consists in a crescent of recognizably classical urban architecture, affording five separate doors, and framing the relatively small playing area of the theatre's stage. It serves both *Antony and Cleopatra* and *The Taming of the Shrew*. Panelled doors, classical windows, flying-buttresses vainly reaching out in space accentuate the feeling of depth. Patterned hangings of neutral colour draped from the top between the openings, and a massive iron chandelier make the set usefully convertible to indoor scenes. Throughout the production boards shown to the house and the audience on stage by one of the company of players indicate locations.

There is virtually no use of an upper-stage level except when the Pedant addresses the genuine Vincentio from a window ledge above the main central door (this is the position allocated to Cleopatra when she seeks refuge in her monument).

As is often the case, the directors have incorporated some elements from *The Taming of a Shrew* in Shakespeare's text as we have it. These are essentially the epilogue and Sly's drunken insistence that the characters in the framed play shall not go to prison following Vincentio's grave charges, whereupon Pat Nedler—in charge of the lighting—wittily turns on the lights in the auditorium, dazzling Sly with the confirmation that indeed the presence of an audience would appear to indicate that it is only a play. He staggers back, blinded, into his chair, stage right, only to lapse into the final narcosis during which he will be returned to his estate as tinker. It is a pity that the programme—otherwise helpful in its inclusion of photographs of the production—does not mention the borrowings from the anonymous play. What the programme does, on the other hand, is stress the main interpretative feature of the induction in this production: the Lord is "possibly Mr. W. H.", and "the author", surreptitiously added to the number of "your honour's players" with the Ms of the play prominent in hand, is glossed as being "probably Mr. W. S.".

The production elegantly bears out the invention to the last. Much to his amazement and delight, The Lord, Mr. W. H., is urged by his good friend Mr. W. S., to take successive parts in the production ranging from that of Curtis—which the recruited amateur falls to rehearsing silently but enthusiastically as the curtain drops for the interval prior to the homecoming of Petruchio and Kate—to that the tailor and that of the officer called by Vincentio: an officer's bonnet is clapped on his head at the last minute much to Mr. W. H.'s amazement and delight—he does look all of his famous thousand pounds! Much of the zest of the production is to be found in this imaginative handling of the frame play.

There is good acting all round. Timothy Dalton is a physically convincing, though it seems mentally reluctant, tamer. His sensitivity creates poignant moments with Kate when the rhythm is almost embarrassingly slowed down as for the reconciliatory kiss in the street for instance. With Mr. Dalton it is more obvious than with many predecessors in the part that the contrariness and general gutting of the place are but parts of a regrettable but necessary plan, a completely orthodox reading of the play and yet one which many interpretations, chief of which Richard Burton's in the film, had blurred in making much of a joyfully but genuinely choleric Petruchio.

Vanessa Redgrave's performance as Kate is well gauged throughout, from the original romp—a serious test of physical fitness as Petruchio blocks the lashing foot as though in a vice and proceeds to dragging Kate hopping on one foot to and fro across the stage. Miss Redgrave too has treasures of doubt and delicacy which we are soon allowed to glimpse and which finally climax in that controversial speech on the subjection of wives to their husbands. This is delivered without a trace of irony, with wholehearted conviction. When the actress makes for putting her hand under his boot, Timothy Dalton anxiously reaches out to prevent the humiliating gesture. The audience did not seem to have any trouble with this straightforward if unfashionable rendering of the end.

On the whole, the combined effect of Mr. Dalton's and Miss Redgrave's interpretations supports the notion that Petruchio feels genuine love for Kate very early in the play, and that the best cure he can find for her diseased humour only shows the measure of his affection and concern.

Sylvester McCoy's active Tranio comes as a useful reminder of the importance and richness of the part in the play. He endlessly struts about and preens himself in his master's clothes, lets out peals of mechanical laughter, trips up Gremio with gleeful viciousness, and insists on punctuating his arrogant rhetoric by thrusts of his codpiece in an amusing caricature of a fop. His using the drunk Pedant as a live puppet whose arms and hands point and head nods as and when he impells them is a piece of regular and effective farce. He resumes his servant status with good humour, and the remaining traces of his former tics provide minimal but titillating evidence that he has not left his wit behind.

The whole company deserve praise for their performances. Special mention must be made of Robert O'Mahoney as Gremio, of Bunny May as Grumio, of Christopher Bowen as Lord and accessory parts.

Some singing and dancing occasionally introduced (including a pleasant catch on the "taming school" theme) indicate that this *Taming of the Shrew* while straighter than most does not set out to be strait-laced. It is an interesting rendering of the play with sentiment always richly stirring beneath the farce. (pp. 91-3)

Jean-Marie Maguin, in a review of "The Taming of the Shrew," in Cahiers Élisabéthains, *No. 30, October, 1986, pp. 91-3.*

COMPARISONS AND OVERVIEWS

Charles E. L. Wingate   (essay date 1895)

[*Wingate provides an extensive account of actresses who have played Katherina through the end of the nineteenth century, concluding with Ada Rehan, who, in Wingate's opinion, was "[the] true Shakesperian Katherina."*]

One night when Edwin Booth, in "Catherine and Petruchio," was playing the all-conquering husband to the shrew of Jean Hosmer, he threw the audience into a paroxysm of laughter, and the actress into embarrassed perplexity, by turning the lady's fair face into a zebra countenance, with alternate black and white stripes. This he did by having secretly laid heavy lamp-black over his mustache before he fervently kissed his unsuspecting theatrical wife in the scene upon the stage.

Apparently it was a stock joke in former days; for I find that John Wilkes Booth played the same trick on Josephine Orton, and that other actors did not hesitate thus to increase the applause.

But "Catherine and Petruchio" is not "The Taming of the Shrew," although the Garrick farce may boast the dubious glory of having usurped the place of the Shakespearian comedy. Twice only in the records of the English stage, and once only in American annals, do we find the original work presented in its entirety.

Nearly a century and a half ago, Garrick set aside the clumsy Lacy adaptation called "Sawney the Scot; or, The Taming of a Shrew," in which Margaret, as our heroine was then called, was subdued only by attempts on the part of her husband to bury her alive; and Garrick also cast away both Bullock's and Johnson's farces bearing the same name, "The Cobbler of Preston." In their stead he gave an abridgment of Shakespeare's work, making it simply a three-act farcical afterpiece. Several scenes, including the Induction and the love episodes of Hortensio and Bianca, were omitted entirely, and other scenes were transposed.

On the 18th of March, 1754, Davy brought out his version at Drury Lane, with awkward Mrs. Pritchard as Catherine, and graceful Woodward as an extravagant, fantastical Petruchio, while the famous harlequin Yates acted Grumio. Poor Yorick! One day, when Yates was in his ninety-seventh year, he fell into such a furious passion because his housekeeper failed to have his favorite dish of eels for breakfast, that he dropped dead in his room.

Then came saucy-tongued Kitty Clive, undoubtedly delighting in the fiery snappishness of her character. She showed the spectators a very realistic bit of acting one night, when the vengeful Woodward, seeking to pay off an old-time grudge on spiteful Kitty, thrust his fork into Catherine's finger, as they sat quarreling in the supper scene, and then, in pushing her off the stage according to the directions, exceeded those directions by throwing her down in earnest on the floor. Up rose the hot-tempered actress, now thoroughly enraged, and with talons and tongue gave the reckless Petruchio a genuine taste of what a shrew could do when treated brutally.

Ever since Garrick's day, actors who have aimed at displaying versatility have presented the light afterpiece as a contrast to the tragic drama with which they opened the bill. That actresses, too, have not scorned to show their skill at varied impersonations was illustrated in 1757, when eloquent Mrs. Fitzhenry (or, as she was sometimes known, Mrs. Gregory) first passed through the agonies of a Lady Macbeth, and then, in the same evening, fumed and fretted as Catherine in the afterpiece.

Seventeen years later the droll Mrs. Hippesley-Green, of whom we have heard as Hermione, was a Catherine to lively Lewis's Petruchio; and then came Mrs. Crawford (formerly Mrs. Spranger Barry), trying in vain to lift her worthless ex-lawyer husband, the last in her threefold list, into prominence as a Petruchio.

Stately Mrs. Siddons acted in the farce with spirit, but, as might be expected, without seeming at home in the character. Boaden thought the little piece well enough played "if you could get over the conviction that such a physiognomy as that of the actress never could belong to a termagant. Of a petulant, spoiled girl the transformation might be expected. The incidents are farcical, and the whip and the crockery made noise enough for the joke's sake, but there never could be an atom of farce in Mrs. Siddons."

John Kemble was the Petruchio not only to his great sister, but also to his lesser sister-in-law, the black-eyed enchantress, Mrs. Charles Kemble (*née* Decamp).

We know of the "big Mr. Kemble" (Stephen), who could play Falstaff without stuffing, but his wife, another heroine of the farce, was of a different build from her husband. She was pretty, even if not lovely, had a musical, silvery voice, and was possessed of talent. In Katharina, said a writer in *Blackwood's Magazine* sixty years ago, "We have more than once been delighted to see her play the devil; to her it was not every man, we can assure you, that was able to be a Petruchio." This latter statement may well be believed when one recollects that on a certain night, while uttering the sweetly maternal words of Lady Randolph, "My beautiful, my brave," as she bent over young Norval, she deliberately, out of pure spite, proceeded to nip a piece out of her fellow-actor's shoulder with her own sharp, white teeth.

In 1828 "The Taming of the Shrew" had some of its stolen text restored; but as there were added songs and musical accompaniments enough to make the production operatic, the four performances it received were undoubtedly all that the mixed-up version deserved. To the Petruchio of Wallack there appeared as Catherine, in this May performance, the young lady whose songs had but recently won applause at the Italian Opera House, Miss Fanny Ayrton.

A half-century ago Benjamin Webster, managing the Haymarket Theatre in London, thought to catch the public eye with the first production, since Shakespeare's day, of the entire original play. He even went farther than a mere reproduction of text. The method of the old Blackfriars' Theatre was adopted by making one scene do duty for every act, and that scene showing simply a wall hung with tapestry. At the intervals in the play a servant would enter to fasten upon the screens the placards, labelled in turn, "A Bedchamber in the London House," "A Room in Baptista's House," and

"Padua; a Public Place." Charming Mrs. Nisbett has the honor of going upon record as the first Kate the Curst of whom the world can ever know; while the Petruchio in this 1844 production was Webster; the Grumio was waggish John Baldwin Buckstone.

Characters full of animal spirits were always Mrs. Nisbett's favorites, as sprightliness in action and exhilaration in humor came to her naturally. In her time she was almost as great a favorite as Mme. Vestris, and to the mind of the late Westland Marston, the noted playwright, was on the whole a finer actress, possessing keener perception of character and consistency, and displaying more naturalness than the Olympic player. "Her forehead," said Marston, "though rather low, was wide; her eyes brilliant and expressive; the oval of her face was relieved and thrown out by a waving wreath of dark hair. Her neck was long and stately, her form lithe and elastic, and her stature tall. She had even more animation than Vestris, but not the insinuating languor with which the latter sometimes contrasted it. Mrs. Nisbett had a laugh which swept away and charmed one by its freshness and fulness, by its music, and by its union of refinement with abandon."

The story is told that, in the Haymarket production, the part of Christopher Sly, the cozened tinker of the Induction, was offered to Strickland, a great favorite in those days with the pit, and that he accepted it on condition of having his hot drinks, during the performance, real brandy-and-water. But so often did he have his glass filled that the horrified manager found the bill for brandy for a single evening amounting to eleven shillings sixpence, and worse than that, found Strickland in such a speechless state of drunkenness when "The Shrew" was over that he could not possibly appear in the afterpiece for which he was cast. In fact, Sly's brandy-and-water killed poor Strickland; for he rolled home one night after the play, then rolled out of bed with his head downward, and was found the next morning dead, the result of apoplexy.

In Webster's production the tinker was on the stage through the entire five acts, watching the mimic play. The custom in Shakespeare's day, when a play was acted within a play, as in this case, was to erect at the rear of the stage a gallery whence the supposed spectators could watch the mimic actors on the stage below them, thus not impeding the view of the real audience.

Samuel Phelps, at Sadler's Wells, on the 15th of November, 1856, contrasted his production of the entire comedy with Webster's revival by giving "The Shrew" a liberal equipment of scenery and costumes. The manager himself had several times played Petruchio in the Garrick farce; but for this great performance,—making the twenty-ninth Shakespeare play revived by the conscientious student, at the renovated East end theatre,—he relinquished the leading *rôle* to Marston, and himself played Christopher Sly. Yes, the actor who had impersonated Hamlet and Brutus and kindred parts, for the sake of his art essayed now the *rôle* of the drunken boor. As Prof. Henry Morley points out, he did it admirably, by giving to the face of the tinker an utter lack of intelligence, and by imbuing him simply with an animal nature.

To the manly, humorous Petruchio of Marston appeared a shrew depicted by Miss Atkinson with great force, though perhaps somewhat in excess. Her gradual submission and final speech were gracefully and admirably rendered. This lady was the last of the leaders in the famous Sadler's Wells casts. Three years before the production of "The Taming of the Shrew," Phelps had opened his season without a heavy tragedy lady, being unable to find a player to suit him. As he wanted to produce several tragedies in which such an actress was indispensable, the manager was in a quandary until he heard from his prompter of a certain Dublin actress who, though young, had a fine figure for the stage, and was full of talent. On the strength of this report Phelps engaged Miss Atkinson, and set down the Queen in "Hamlet" for her opening *rôle.*

"She was very like her predecessor, Miss Glyn," writes Mr. Frederic Robinson, formerly her associate at Sadler's Wells, but now an actor of America, answering the inquiries of the writer regarding this actress of whom the printed records say so little, "but she had a smaller nose and a more massive chin. She was entirely without education, but was very apt and made great progress." In one respect she must have resembled our famous friend Mrs. Pritchard, whom Dr. Johnson so vigorously scolded, inasmuch as she often had to seek out Mr. Robinson, before playing a part, in order to correct her orthoepical defects. But, as he says, she very seldom had to be told anything more than once. After a year or two under Phelps's tutelage she became very successful in the heavy Shakespearian characters, playing nearly all of them at Sadler's Wells for the first time in her career. "She was the best Emilia in 'Othello' that I ever saw," says Mr. Robinson, "and made quite a hit in the part, in 1859, at the Friedrich Wilhelmstadt Theatre, in Berlin;" to which may be added that the Berlin papers also highly praised Mr. Robinson's Iago. Miss Atkinson remained with Phelps until he gave up Sadler's Wells.

A word to record the appearances of Helen Faucit and of Ellen Tree in the Garrick farce, and a mention to the fact that Ellen Terry marked her first appearance with Henry Irving by playing Katharina to his Petruchio—then we leave the English stage.

Here in America, the beginning—and, so far, the end—of the history of "The Taming of the Shrew" dates with Mr. Augustin Daly's revival of the comedy, first seen at Daly's Theatre, New York, on the 18th of January, 1887. Marie Seebach, to be sure, appeared in a German four-act version, without the Induction, given in America in 1870, under the title of "Die Widerspenstige;" but all else is the history of the farce "Catherine and Petruchio."

The first Katharina of America was Miss Cheer. It was rather curious that this lady, destined to become the leading actress of her day, should have chosen a farce in which to make her *début* in the Colonies, but such was the case. On the opening night, Nov. 21, 1766, of the first permanent playhouse in America, the ugly brick Southwark Theatre of Philadelphia, our rival of Mrs. Douglass played Kate, in the afterpiece, to the Petruchio of Hallam; the chief play of the evening being "Douglas," with Mrs. Douglass as Lady Randolph. (pp. 265-75)

Among other impersonators of the two characters in the farce have been: Mrs. Mason and Cooper in 1814; Mrs. Duff as Katharina in 1822; Mrs. Darley and Macready in 1827; Fanny Kemble and Charles Kemble, at the Park Theatre entertainment in New York in honor of John Howard Payne, the author of "Home, Sweet Home," on the occasion of his return to his native land, Nov. 29, 1832; Mrs. Charles Kean as Katharina in 1836; Mrs. Sharpe and W. B. Wood in 1839; Miss Vandenhoff and her father in 1839; Mrs. Mowatt as Ka-

tharina in 1845; Mrs. James Wallack, Jr., and Hamblin, Mrs. Hoey and Couldock (both of whom are now living), in 1850; Laura Addison and Hamblin at Niblo's Garden, New York, in an entertainment that included, among other attractions, the appearance of Adelina Patti, then eight years of age, on Dec. 3, 1851; Ada Clifton and Edwin Booth in 1862.

Then came Fanny Davenport to the Petruchio of Edwin Booth, Clara Morris to the Petruchio of Louis James, Agnes Booth to the Petruchio of Mr. Wheelock, and—but it is useless to record the list further. These were all participants in the productions of the farce. The true Shakespearian Katharina has appeared but once; she was Ada Rehan, the fiery Shrew of the Daly production. Miss Rehan's haughty bearing, sharp action, and quick, nervous gesture; her compressed lips and piercing glances,—all befitted the *rôle,* while her interpretation of the character was as graceful as it was vigorous. The change of spirit, during the taming and after, was manifested in such natural manner as to make one easily imagine the submission actually carried out, without too great a contradiction of characteristics.

Mr. Daly approached the work in rightful spirit. The length of the piece, including the Induction, necessitated some cutting; but this was done carefully and without impairing, to any grievous extent, the sequence of incidents retained. The original text called for revision in parts where touches of coarseness that might have been tolerated in a past age are now to be condemned; but the Induction, as was intimated, was given practically complete. The chief portion of the play, the true "Taming of the Shrew," as supposedly acted before the pseudo-noblemen, was presented by Mr. Daly's company with all the secondary as well as primary plots detailed. The artifices of the rival lovers for Bianca's hand, the rather unfilial act of Lucentio in assenting to the scheme of the old pedant usurping the place of the absent father, and the final test of submission of the three wives, were presented, in addition to the scenes that embrace the truly Shakespearian manœuvres of Petruchio, Katharina and the serving-man Grumio. The chief situations of the latter trio, the scenes wherein the taming of Katharina is made complete, were put into one scene in the Daly arrangement.

So unique was this performance that a mention of all the principals in the cast will not be amiss. There was John Drew, rightfully conceiving the character of Petruchio, in that he preserved at all times behind the assumed roughness the signs of admiration for the woman and of genuine pleasure in the pointed joke that he was so successfully playing. There, too, were James Lewis, comical and quaint as Grumio, and Mrs. G. H. Gilbert, cleverly acting Curtis. Charles Fisher read the lines of Baptista in such a way as to bring out with fidelity the true meaning at all times; while Otis Skinner as Lucentio, Joseph Holland as Hortensio, Charles Le Clerq as Gremio, were well in keeping with their characters. Frederick Bond presented a merry-hearted, bright Tranio; Miss Virginia Dreher gave, by her personality, an attractive picture of Bianca, the sweet sister of the Shrew. In the Induction William Gilbert's delineation of perplexity in the bed-chamber, and his subsequent vain-glorious assumption of lordship, made Christopher Sly productive of humorous enjoyment to the audience, although the impersonation too often bordered on the edge of caricature.

Mr. Daly has several times repeated "The Taming of the Shrew" in New York and in other cities of this country, and has also presented the play in London; but no new Katharina has yet appeared to contest the honors with Miss Rehan. (pp. 278-81)

Charles E. L. Wingate, "Katharina (The Taming of the Shrew)," in his Shakespeare's Heroines on the Stage, Thomas Y. Crowell & Company, 1895, pp. 265-81.

William Winter   (essay date 1915)

[*Winter was a conservative American dramatic critic who eschewed innovation, theatrical realism, and non-Anglo-American actors. He served as dramatic critic for* The New York Tribune *from 1865-1909 and wrote several theatrical biographies. In the following excerpt, Winter chronicles some late nineteenth- and early twentieth-century productions of* The Taming of the Shrew, *often comparing them to Augustin Daly's "brilliant representation" featuring Ada Rehan as Katherina. Included in his account are the performances of Constant Coquelin, Elsie Leslie, E. H. Southern, Julia Marlowe, and Margaret Anglin.*]

Daly's version of "The Taming of the Shrew," with Miss Rehan as *Katharine,* was presented far and wide, not only in the United States and Canada, but in England, France, and Germany, and everywhere it was opulently successful. When Miss Rehan first acted *Katharine,* the favorite comedian John Drew was associated with her, as *Petruchio,* and he was the first actor, in America, to play the part in what is, substantially, the original comedy,—if comedy it can be called which partakes so considerably of the nature of farce. After Drew left Daly's company, 1892, and became a star, George Clarke played *Petruchio,* to Miss Rehan's *Katharine,* and later, after Daly's death, 1899, the part was acted, in association with her, first by Charles Richman, and then by Otis Skinner. Drew invested the swaggering wooer with a charm of manly grace, and contrived to make the Taming process sufficiently boisterous, without any infusion of the brutality which could easily be justified, from Shakespeare's text, by the actor who should choose to employ it, but which would cause a disagreeable effect. Clarke was the best *Petruchio* seen on our Stage since the time of Edwin Booth,—making him a rough, resolute, rollicking, devil-may-care young man, shrewd and sensible in mind, abrupt in manner and speech, and tempering his fiery behavior with a certain quizzical, even kindly humor. His first entrance was superbly made. He seemed an incarnation of vigorous health, a person in the full enjoyment of life, careless of everything, and free and happy. His performance was all of one piece and it never flagged: it possessed the brightness and fluency of the acting which is governed by a clear design and vitalized by right feeling well controlled. Richman and Skinner, who were acquainted with Clarke's personation, followed the general course which he had indicated. Richman "looked" the part exceedingly well, and his fine person, animated countenance, and boy-like amiability of temperament made him agreeable in it, though he did not impersonate the character. Skinner's *Petruchio* was a pictorial, dashing blade, who revelled in the tumult of the Taming Scenes.

The brilliant representation of "The Taming of the Shrew" that was given in Paris, in the summer of 1888, at the Gaiety Theatre, by Augustin Daly's company of comedians, headed by Miss Rehan, aroused extraordinary public interest, and it was attended by at least one important consequence. The eminent French comedian Constant Coquelin (1841-1909), having seen Daly's production, became desirous of acting

Petruchio, and, under his auspices, with himself in that character, an adapted French version of Shakespeare's play presently made its appearance on the Paris Stage. That version, made by Paul Delair, is entitled "La Mégère Apprivoisée." It is based on Daly's arrangement of the original, in as far as the scenes implicating *Katharine* and *Petruchio* are concerned, but it largely curtails the incidents of the wooing of *Bianca,* and it excludes the Induction. It is comprised in four acts. On January 24, 1892, Coquelin appeared in that play, at Abbey's Theatre (now, 1914, the Knickerbocker), New York, acting *Petruchio,* in association with the accomplished actress Jane Hading, as *Katharine,* and gave a spirited, artistically finished performance, again showing himself to be a capital low comedian and a master of the technical resources of his vocation. Jane Hading gave a weak imitation of Miss Rehan, devoid of charm, and,—which was singular, considering how clever she had elsewhere shown herself to be,—devoid of art: probably the part did not interest her. One piece of Coquelin's stage business indicated the notion he had formed of *Petruchio's* character. In the course of the Taming *Katharine,* overcome with weariness, fell asleep, and thereupon *Petruchio,* with much parade of affectionate solicitude, covered her person with his cloak, to keep her from the cold,—coincidently, as is the absurd custom of the French Stage, signifying to the audience, by elaborate pantomime, the chivalric beauty of his uxorious conduct. Yet this loving husband (in Shakespeare's play) has declared his disposition and purpose by remarking:

> If she chance to nod, I'll rail and brawl,
> And with the clamor keep her still awake.
>
> [IV. i. 206-07]

And that he is true to his word is ruefully certified by *Katharine* herself, who plaintively declares:

> I, who never knew how to entreat, . . .
> Am starv'd for meat, *giddy for lack of sleep,*
> *With oaths kept waking,* and with brawling fed.
>
> [IV. iii. 7-10]

The production of "The Taming of the Shrew" that was effected by Elsie Leslie, first at the Colonial Theatre, Peekskill, May 11, 1903, and (afternoon) May 12, at the Manhattan Theatre, New York, is remembered as the first, and, indeed, the only one, thus far, ever made, combining Garrick's version of Shakespeare's play with the Induction as it stands in the original. Miss Leslie acted *Katharine,* and Jefferson Winter acted *Petruchio.* At the time of that venture Daly's superb revival was fresh in public recollection, and the presentment made by those young players was, by some judges,—forgetful that "comparisons are odorous,"—viewed as presumptuous, and censured as exemplifying the enormity of taking "liberties" with Shakespeare. That censure seemed odd, in view of the world-wide acceptance which has been accorded to Garrick's alteration of "The Shrew," and likewise to the Farmer-White-Dowden Doctrine that Shakespeare was really not the author of the play, but only a contributor to it, of the Induction and the *Katharine* and *Petruchio* scenes. If that be authentic (which I do not believe) it would follow that Miss Leslie and her associates spoke the purest "Shakespearean text" of "The Taming of the Shrew" that has ever been spoken, because they acted only the Induction and the scenes in which *Katharine* and *Petruchio* appear. The freaks of criticism, however, are more amusing than important. Miss Leslie and her players were, I believe, the first to appear conspicuously in *Katharine* and *Petruchio,* in New York, subsequent to the time when Daly's sumptuous production had made "The Shrew" almost the exclusive property of that manager and Miss Rehan. With Daly's production they could not hope, and did not attempt, to compete. The scenery with which they invested the play was "sharked up" in haste, and the setting was insignificant. Some of the stage furniture, though, was part of that which had been used by Daly,—hired from an auction company. The dresses were appropriate, in every instance, some of them being rich and handsome. Elaborate and agreeable incidental music was specially composed for the production, by that excellent musician Frederick W. Ecke. The acting, throughout, was exceptionally good.

Miss Leslie had formed a clear and correct ideal of *Katharine,* and she expressed it in bold yet graceful demeanor, simple, natural action, and a fluent delivery. Her *Shrew* was a spoiled young beauty, high-spirited, self-willed, impulsive, of a fiery temper, discontented with her circumstances and with herself, impatient of restraint, yet not unwomanly,—not lacking in latent amiability. She maintained a vigorous spirit throughout the scenes of conflict, made every point neatly and precisely, and evinced a peculiar gentleness of temperament at the close. In her delivery of such speeches as "I pray you, husband, be not so disquiet" [IV. i. 168], and "The more my wrong, the more his spite appears" [IV. iii. 2], there was a certain plaintive, wistful note, almost pathetically indicative of *Katharine's* rueful sense of unavoidable, and not wholly unwelcome, impending subjugation. The sweetly submissive closing speeches were spoken with finely simulated feeling. The pervasive characteristic of the performance was fantastic girlishness of condition, now bitter, now sweet. The impersonation of *Petruchio* by Jefferson Winter was marked by sustained vigor, rough humor, continuous action, and fluent, expressive vocalism. If the performance had been given by an actor of established repute,—such, for example, as Walter Montgomery or Lawrence Barrett, in old times,—it would have been universally and cordially approved. By the public the merit of the performance was immediately recognized, and it did not entirely lack critical commendation; but relationship of the actor to a veteran dramatic critic was remarked, and the opportunity then occurrent to evince hostility toward the father by disparagement of the son was not altogether neglected. Among Miss Leslie's associates excellent performances were given by the veteran, Edwin Varrey (one of the best of actors and of men) as *Baptista,* Robert Payton Gibbs as *Grumio,* Richard Webster as *Sly,* Thomas Hadaway as *Biondello,* Spottswoode Aiken as the *Tailor,* and Annie Alliston as *Curtis.*

A revival of "The Taming of the Shrew" was accomplished by E. H. Sothern and Julia Marlowe, September 18, 1905, at Cleveland, Ohio, and on October 16, following, they presented their production at the Knickerbocker Theatre, New York. The scenery was good and the dresses were handsome. The Induction was omitted, and the play was condensed to four acts, which had been so unskilfully cut and arranged as, practically, to make the story incoherent, and also to render the performance almost unintelligible, except to persons familiar with the original. The acting, at its best, was extravagant and turbulent, and, in general, it was commonplace. There is, undoubtedly, warrant in the text for performing "The Shrew" in a farcical spirit, but there is no warrant for degrading it into an exhibition of clamor and empty buffoonery. Miss Marlowe, as *Katharine,* was, at times, beautiful to see, but, because of her frequent use of shrill vocalism, seldom agreeable to hear. Her delivery of the text was, of course, in-

telligent, and, likewise,—which was not true as to that of her associates in the representation,—it could be understood. No intimation was given by her, at any point, of latent, womanlike sweetness in *Katharine's* nature, and her performance was rendered the more unsympathetic by pervasive self-consciousness and by her obvious disposition to amuse herself rather than to interpret the character and amuse her audience. Sothern, as *Petruchio,* was indistinct in articulation, harsh, sharp, brittle, and explosive in vocalism and, seemingly, intent on an expeditious exemplification of fume and bluster. The associate players, aiming at rapidity, only succeeded in augmenting a distressing effect of confusion and chatter. Mr. Sothern and Miss Marlowe have gained their worthy professional reputation and prosperity by many thoughtful, careful, often admirable productions and performances: it is a pity that actors so important and influential should ever forget that whatever is worth doing at all is worth doing well. They have practically dropped "The Taming of the Shrew" from their repertory.

The eminent Italian actor Ermete Novelli,—who made his first appearance in New York, March 18, 1907, at the Lyric Theatre, as *Papa Lebonnard,*—presented an Italian version of "The Taming of the Shrew," April 13, that year, and performed as *Petruchio.* Signora O. Giannini played *Katharine.* Novelli, in several comedy characters which he impersonated on our Stage, proved himself an excellent comedian. His *Petruchio* was spirited and jovial, and to that extent, if no other, was commendable. He introduced some of the same inappropriate stage business which had been done by Coquelin,—the cloaking of *Katharine,* in her sleep, etc. But Shakespeare in Italian fares even worse, if that be possible, than he does in French. Novelli's achievement as *Petruchio* was merely casual. He closed his first New York season with that performance, April 13; acted in three short plays, April 15, at the Waldorf Hotel, and on April 17 sailed for Italy.

The most recent production of "The Taming of the Shrew" which requires notice in this chronicle is that made by Margaret Anglin, who appeared in it as *Katharine.* The first performance occurred, October 10, 1908, at Melbourne, Australia; on September 22, 1913, Miss Anglin first acted the part in America, at the Columbia Theatre, San Francisco; and, on March 19, 1914, she presented it, at the Hudson Theatre, for the first time in New York. Miss Anglin's revival of "The Shrew" is chiefly notable as being *the first* presentation of it in America strictly according to the original. The text was somewhat cut, but no words were used other than those in the Folio. At first Miss Anglin presented the Induction; later, before bringing her version to New York, she excluded it. The play, as presented here, was comprised in four acts, divided into ten scenes, showing eight places. The scenery was commonplace and uninteresting, but it served its purpose. The dresses were appropriate, and in some instances rich and handsome. The frequent changes of scene and the prolix display of the Taming incidents caused an effect of extreme tediousness. The cast included Eric Blind as *Petruchio,* Miss Ruth Holt Boucicault as *Bianca,* Pedro de Cordoba as *Lucentio,* Sidney Greenstreet as *Biondello,* and Max Montesole as *Grumio.* The performance, as a whole, was execrable,—slow, heavy, colorless, and inane.

Miss Anglin's assumption of *Katharine* was the worst embodiment of hers that I have seen. The *Shrew,* however curst and froward, is "young and beautiful" [cf. I. ii. 86]: Miss Anglin presented her as ponderous, mature, and frumpish, without distinction, charm, vivacity, or even a suggestion of latent sweetness of womanhood. Her utterance was shrill and painful. During the First Act she emitted, at frequent intervals, a parrot-like screech, as indicative of her rage at *Petruchio's* behavior. Throughout the play she was pettish, fretful, and unpleasant; never either forceful, sympathetic, or interesting. If that is the *Shrew* that Shakespeare drew, then the sooner she is permitted to "die in oblivion" and the public, as far as she is concerned, to "return unexperienced to the grave" [IV. i. 83-4], the better it will be. In the scene at *Petruchio's* country house Miss Anglin's *Katharine* wore a nondescript dress, put on, presumably, because of injury to her raiment when "her horse fell, and she under her horse" [IV. i. 73-4]. Much of her stage business was trivial,—such, for example, as climbing on a chair and turning back the hands of a clock, before she would assent to *Petruchio's* assertion that at two o'clock 'tis seven. On the journey back to *Baptista's* House this *Katharine* became overcome by fatigue and fell asleep, whereupon *Petruchio* threw away his whip, and,—though there had not been the slightest intimation of even good-will between them,—developed a touching solicitude for his shrewish wife, raised her in his arms, wrapped his cloak around her, and supported her from the scene, she, meanwhile, clinging to him, with an air of affectionate dependence. Miss Anglin, finally, delivered the speech "Fie, fie, unknit that threatening, unkind brow," etc., [V. ii. 136.ff] as if it were mere mockery,—implying that it is hypocritical, a jest, secretly understood between *Petruchio* and his wife.

Mr. Blind is large and muscular in person and loud and strident in voice; crude in method, though apparently experienced, as an actor; and perfectly self-satisfied. "How was Mellish?" whispered Henry Irving,—stretched upon a sick bed,—when Mellish had, as an understudy, taken his place, as *Napoleon.* "Mellish," answered Harry Loveday, "Mellish—why—Mellish—why—he *was firm as a rock!*" "Ah, yes," said Irving; " 'firm as a rock,'—and just about as interesting, I fancy!" Mellish is one of the best actors on our Stage to-day, but there are many who are fairly described as about as interesting as a rock, and Mr. Blind is one of them. He spoke the lines of *Petruchio,* made the motions, did the usual business, and "got through." There are scores of such commonplace actors on our Stage any one of whom would give a performance just as good and just as unimportant. Mr. Montesole as *Grumio* and Mr. Greenstreet as *Biondello* deserve special record, for the reason that they were so completely and wickedly bad. Many of the low-comedy parts in Shakespeare are mere bits,—quaint, whimsical, eccentric, interesting for a few moments, and useful as cogs in his dramatic machinery. It has, unhappily, come to be thought essential that every actor who appears in any one of these minor parts should make a pother about it, assert himself, and in every possible way intrude upon public attention. That was the method (in as far as there was any method) exhibited in these two performances. *Biondello* is a comic bit, and he has one exceptionally difficult speech to deliver. Mr. Greenstreet presented him as a gross caricature of humanity, a clumsy, greasy, loathsome lout, and his treatment of that speech,— "Petruchio is coming, in an old hat and a new jerkin," etc., [cf. III. ii. 43-4]—with its wheezy, inarticulate, meaningless utterance and clown-like grimace, would have disgraced the callowest amateur that ever afflicted his friends in back-parlor entertainments at a country house. Mr. Montesole, as *Grumio,* was even worse,—a scarecrow, with hair and complexion never seen on any human being, except in this sort of "Shakespearean revival," with two heavy semicircles of

brown paint drawn around his chin and lower face, and blotches of blue paint as big as half-dollars around his eyes; idiotically grotesque, inhuman in method and speech, and altogether a prodigy of abominable ineptitude and indurated self-conceit. That woful exhibition was sapiently pronounced to be "Shakespearean": perhaps, in the worst possible sense, it was. Shakespeare seems to have seen some such fellows, and he has left a description of them: fellows that, "neither having the accent of Christians, nor the gait of Christian, pagan, nor man," address themselves to the "barren spectators," "capable of nothing but inexplicable dumb shows and noise"! [*Hamlet;* III. ii. 31-2; 41; 11-12]. (pp. 527-40)

William Winter, " 'The Taming of the Shrew'," in his Shakespeare on the Stage, second series, *Moffat, Yard and Company,* 1915, pp. 481-540.

Tori Haring-Smith   (essay date 1985)

[*In the first section of the excerpt below, Haring-Smith presents a detailed examination of David Garrick's 1754 afterpiece adaptation of* The Taming of the Shrew, *concluding that it offers only "pat answers" to the questions raised in Shakespeare's play. She also delineates the adaptation's stage history in England and America from its first performance to the end of the eighteenth century. In the second section, Haring-Smith analyzes the revival of the play-within-a-play staging of* The Taming of the Shrew—*an approach initiated by George Devine in 1953 and further developed by John Barton in 1960. She also examines how this reading was successfully implemented by such directors as Michael Langham and Trevor Nunn in later productions.*]

[In 1754] David Garrick first staged his three-act farce *Catharine and Petruchio,* undoubtedly the most important of the many revisions of *The Taming of the Shrew.* Except for the three-night run of an operatic *Shrew,* this adaptation was the sole version of Shakespeare's *Shrew* on the English and American stages from 1754 to 1844. The play, designed as a short afterpiece, was the sixth most popular Shakespearean play on the stage from 1754 to 1800. Charles Beecher Hogan [in his *Shakespeare in the Theatre, 1701-1800*] records 234 performances of the farce during that time. By contrast, during the fifty years before *Catharine and Petruchio* was staged, there were only 124 performances of all four earlier adaptations of *The Taming of the Shrew* combined. *Catharine and Petruchio* continued to be staged until the early twentieth century, when afterpieces were no longer stylish and Augustin Daly had proven how successful the full *Shrew* could be.

Garrick solves the problem of disunity among the three plots of Shakespeare's play by presenting only one—the taming of Katharine, whom he renames Catharine. Although he eliminates the Induction and subplot (Bianca is married to Hortensio when the play begins), Garrick follows the outline of Shakespeare's main plot closely, cutting it to fit the time requirements of an afterpiece. The result is a farce that emphasizes four scenes: the wooing, the wedding, the dinner, and the Tailor's visit to which is attached a version of Katharine's final speech.

Garrick trims away most of the pure comedy, concentrated in the subplot, and retains most of the slapstick. The low humor helped make acceptable the accelerated taming process of *Catharine and Petruchio,* and it was not objectionable to critics who repeatedly pointed out that the afterpiece was only distantly Shakespeare's and not taken from one of his best works at that. The combination of farce and heavy-handed cutting leaves no room for significant character development, so Garrick redefines the characters of Petruchio and Catharine to make their motives simple and explicit. In so doing, he gives both of them more acceptable personalities: they are still the shrew and the merry adventurer, but in the end, they are also a loving couple who share control of their marriage.

Garrick's Catharine is stronger than Shakespeare's and more clearly motivated before her wedding, but honestly submissive in the end—a determined but refined Catharine who is beaten at her own game. The demonstration of her early shrewishness is confined to breaking the lute over the Music Master's head, an action that takes place offstage. She first appears onstage in the wooing scene, which is cut to avoid the bawdiest puns. Because this abridgement omits Catharine's early protestations and her sauciest jokes, this Catharine seems to agree to the match more readily. Perhaps to combat this impression, Garrick supplies her with a clear motive for marrying Petruchio—the desire to tame him. Before she gives him her hand, she echoes Lacy's Margaret [in *Sauny the Scot*], saying in an aside: "A Plague upon his Impudence. I'm vex'd—I'll marry my Revenge, but I will tame him." Garrick's Catharine is clearly on the offensive, making the taming process a two-way battle. She closes Act I, declaring:

> Why yes. Sister Bianca now shall see
> The poor abandon'd Cath'rine, as she calls me,
> Can hold her Head as high, and be as proud,
> And make her Husband stoop unto her Lure,
> As she, or e'er a Wife in Padua.
> As double as my Portion be my Scorn
> Look to your Seat, Petruchio, or I throw you.
> Cath'rine shall tame this Haggard;—or if she fails,
> Shall tye her Tongue up, and pare down her Nails.

But even this strong Catharine is finally subdued in Petruchio's taming school. Just as Garrick makes Catharine's strength explicit in the first act, so he underscores her final humility. When Baptista asks her, "Ar't not alter'd Kate?" she replies, "Indeed I am. I am transform'd to Stone," and then "So good a Master cannot chuse but mend me." It is possible that Catharine is calling Petruchio a good master only because he has prompted her to do so—she may believe this no more than she believes that the sun is the moon. This reading, however, does not seem to be Garrick's intent, since he emphasizes her servility when he adds these lines for Bianca:

> Was ever Woman's Spirit broke so soon!
> What is the Matter, Kate? hold up thy Head,
> Nor lose our Sex's best Prerogative,
> To wish and have our Will.

Catharine's final speech on wifely duty is abbreviated and frequently interrupted. Her revelation no longer receives our undivided attention, and she loses the spotlight in the last scene.

We hear very little from Catharine after the first act, and Petruchio becomes the central character, stealing two out of three curtains. Garrick's Petruchio follows the same taming recipe as Shakespeare's Petruchio, but his character is less ambiguous. Garrick assures us that his tamer is not habitually violent; one of Petruchio's servants remarks: "He kills her in her own Humour. I did not think so good and kind a Master cou'd have put on so resolute a Bearing." To maintain the picture of Petruchio as a gentleman, Garrick cut the opening scene in which Petruchio beats Grumio. *Catharine and*

Petruchio begins instead with Petruchio's advertisement of his qualifications to Baptista. Knowing that Petruchio is usually a gentleman reassures us that Catharine will merely be teased, and then only briefly. In the end, Garrick gives us a glimpse of the real Petruchio, a man who is willing to "doff the lordly Husband; an honest Mask, which I throw off with Pleasure" and to assure his bride:

> Far hence all Rudeness, Willfulness and Noise.
> And be our future Lives one gentle Stream
> Of mutual Love, Compliance, and Regard.

Even his mercenary motives are gone, for when Baptista offers him a second dowry for a second daughter, he refuses, saying, "My Fortune is sufficient. Here's my Wealth: Kiss me, my Kate."

The play closes not in a draw but a compromise. Petruchio, a true gentleman, has transformed Catharine from a shrew into a loving wife, and their marriage promises to be happy and ordered. Catharine delivers the beginning of her lecture on wifely duty, and Petruchio finishes it, reciting the play's moral as he takes his wife by the hand and brings her forward.

> How shameful 'tis when Women are so simple
> To offer War where they should kneel for Peace:
> Or seek for Rule, Supremacy, and Sway,
> Where bound to love, to honour and obey.

Petruchio rules his household, but he is no longer a tyrant: Catharine is tamed, but she is not humiliated. Whereas Lacy satisfied the Restoration appetite for ribaldry, Garrick brought his audience a moral farce. Because this marriage conformed to contemporary standards and because Catharine was reclaimed from her temper, she was not pitiable.

Catharine and Petruchio was undoubtedly one of the most popular adaptations of the works of Shakespeare—only Nahum Tate's *King Lear* and Colley Cibber's *Richard III* have longer stage histories. Garrick's contemporaries often viewed him with the same reverence they applied to Shakespeare himself. Some critics, like Arthur Murphy [in his *The Life of David Garrick*], made extravagant claims for the Garrick version:

> The original play is, perhaps, the worst of all our great poet's productions. It is supposed to be presented before some great lord in his palace, and, by consequence, loses all power of imposing on the minds of an audience. It cannot for a moment pass for reality. It is a wild, confused, and almost inexplicable fable, crowded with superfluous scenes and unnecessary characters; forming all together a chaos of heterogeneous matter, a wilderness without a path to guide you through the labyrinth. Garrick, however, saw his way. He was like a man travelling over a rugged country, who, amidst the rocks and desert wastes that surround him, perceives great order and beauty in several parts. From the whole he had the judgment to select the most coherent scenes, and, without intermixing anything of his own, to let Shakespeare be the entire author of a very excellent comedy.

Others of his contemporaries, however, condemned *Catharine and Petruchio* as firmly as modern critics do. Then, as now, the afterpiece was considered "a mangled three-act affair." Dr. Johnson [in *Works of Samuel Johnson*, ed. Arthur Sherbo] must have been dismayed by the single-plot play since he felt that the two plots of Shakespeare's *Shrew* were "so well united, that they can hardly be called two without injury to the art with which they are interwoven." In 1850, G. G. Gervinus remarked [in his *Shakespeare Commentaries*] that Garrick had unfortunately "expunged the more refined part, the plot for wooing of Bianca, and . . . debased the coarse remainder into a clumsy caricature." John Drew [in his *My Years on the Stage*], who played Petruchio in Daly's famous restoration of *The Taming of the Shrew*, dismissed Garrick's version as mainly "the horseplay scenes in which Petruchio brandishes his whip and the leg of mutton about the stage."

In transforming Shakespeare's play into a moral farce, Garrick removed all ambiguities from Shakespeare's text. His characters' simple, explicit motives eliminate the tension in Shakespeare's play. Garrick's gentlemanly tamer is no real threat to his bride, and his shrew is clearly tamed but not beaten. *Catharine and Petruchio* may have satisfied playgoers of the eighteenth and nineteenth centuries, but it is a thin version of Shakespeare's play, lacking the original imagery, rich themes, full-bodied characters, and complexity. Shakespeare's play raises questions; Garrick's only offers pat answers.

Because the play was so popular in its time, many of the great actors and actresses of the eighteenth and early nineteenth centuries played in it. The first performance was staged at Drury Lane on 18 March 1754, as an afterpiece to *Jane Shore*. The night was a benefit for Mrs. Hannah Pritchard, who took the female lead, playing opposite Henry Woodward. Her clear, strong voice, fine sense of timing, and ability to identify completely with her character were her great assets. Thomas Davies declared [in his *Memoirs of the Life of David Garrick*], "Her delivery of dialogue, whether of humour, wit, or mere sprightliness, was never, I believe, surpassed, or, perhaps, equalled." Thomas Gilliland was also impressed by her "easy, unaffected manner of speaking" and remarked on her dignity of character. This dignity combined with her skill in spirited comedy and repartee made her an excellent Catharine. Even her large figure, a liability in many roles, suited the shrew. Henry Woodward, who played Petruchio intermittently until 1775, was also well suited for his part. Seemingly a confirmed misanthrope, he terrified many members of the acting company with his quick temper. His specialty was vivacious, outlandish characters. Thomas Davies described his acting vividly:

> He was an actor, who, for various abilities to delight an audience in comic characters had scarcely an equal. His person was so regularly formed, and his look so serious and composed, that an indifferent observer would have supposed that his talents were adapted to characters of the serious cast; to the real fine gentleman, to the man of graceful deportment and elegant demeanour, rather than to the affecter of gaiety, the brisk fop, and pert coxcomb. But the moment he spoke on the stage a certain ludicrous air laid hold of his features, and every muscle of his face ranged itself on the side of levity. The very tones of his voice inspired comic ideas; and though he often wished to act tragedy, he never could speak a line with propriety that was serious.

This combination of temper and good humor fit Garrick's conception of Petruchio perfectly.

Despite this winning combination, the play must not have been an overwhelming success since Garrick did not offer it

again that year and kept it on the shelf until 1756. The revival on 21 January 1756, however, was a hit. Woodward reappeared in the role of Petruchio, Kitty Clive played Catharine, and Richard Yates remained in the role of Grumio, a role soon to be assigned to Ned Shuter. This production fascinated the audience since it was no greenroom secret that Mrs. Clive and Henry Woodward did not get along well. Perhaps, therefore, the battles between Catharine and Petruchio were more real than most.

> In one of his mad fits, when he and his bride are at supper, Woodward stuck a fork, it is said, in Mrs. Clive's finger; and in pushing her off the stage he was so much in earnest that he threw her down: as it is well known that they did not greatly respect one another, it was believed that something more than chance contributed to these excesses.

A number of critics agreed that Woodward's acting on that occasion was more boisterous than usual. Davies remarked, "Woodward's Petruchio was, perhaps, more wild, extravagant, and fantastical than the author designed it should be; and he carried his acting of it to an almost ridiculous excess." Mrs. Clive was no one to take such treatment calmly, and Tate Wilkinson reported that "her talons, tongue, and passion were very expressive to the eyes of all beholders." She was famous for her farcical scolds and viragoes, and would have been a very effective Catharine—even if she had not been facing an enemy in the role of Petruchio. Davies left this description of her performance:

> Mrs. Clive, though a perfect mistress of Catherine's humour, seemed to be overborne by the extravagant and triumphant grotesque of Woodward; she appeared to be over-awed as much by his manner of acting, as Catherine is represented to be in the fable.

Mrs. Clive was, by all accounts, neither beautiful nor particularly bright, but she had a natural talent for low humor. The fact that her Catharine was more boisterous than Mrs. Pritchard's may account for the great success of the play in 1756.

After the fame of the performance of 21 January spread, this farcical afterpiece became a standard part of the repertory of most actors and actresses. Editions of *Catharine and Petruchio* published in the late eighteenth century indicate that even in these farcical performances, actors and actresses exaggerated the changes Garrick had initiated in order to make the play's characters even more attractive. In these editions, Petruchio is presented as more reasonable and less mercenary. Grumio does not comment in Act I on his master's love of money, nor does Baptista describe Catharine's wedding as the result of a mad venture "in a desperate mart." These later editions close Act II with Petruchio and Catharine exiting to the bridal chamber, and eliminate Petruchio's after-dinner soliloquy about taming Catharine like a wild falcon. While this change softens Petruchio's character, it also omits the servant's line, "I did not think so good and kind a Master cou'd have put on so resolute a Bearing." Perhaps this assurance that Petruchio is actually sane and gentlemanly became redundant because Petruchio's character had been improved in so many ways. Not even Catharine is allowed to criticize his behavior: her complaints that he treats her worse than a beggar are cut, as is her retort,

> My tongue will tell the anger of my heart,
> Or else my heart, concealing it, will break,
> And rather than it shall, I will be free,

Even to the uttermost, as I please, in words.

These acting editions also excise Baptista's threat to disinherit Catharine if she refuses to marry Petruchio, making her seem less victimized and more willing to be wed. Even Bianca is less recalcitrant and does not resist Petruchio's suggestion that Catharine explain her wifely duties to her. With these changes, the final scene is more of a public reconciliation than a trial for Catharine. Her speech on wifely duty is reduced from forty-four lines to about ten, and Petruchio does most of the talking, making his dominance unmistakable.

In the late eighteenth century, Garrick's afterpiece crossed the Atlantic and gained popularity in America. From 1750 to 1774, it was the third most frequently staged Shakespearean play, surpassed only by *Romeo and Juliet* and *Richard III.* Because many of these performances shared the bill with circus and tumbling acts, we can assume that they, too, were highly farcical. This blatant but sure-fire distancing technique was probably the wisest choice for actors who have been called [by Charles Shattuck in his *Shakespeare on the American Stage: From the Hallams to Edwin Booth*] "competent but unremarkable." The early American actors were, of course, Englishmen who had come to the new world to escape religious, political, and personal problems. Most of them were of the Old School and practiced extremely formal verse delivery and stilted, stiff movements. All American companies needed actors desperately and often recruited people with no other qualifications than physical attractiveness. In addition to these handicaps, American actors faced a relatively untutored audience. To succeed, they had to rely on the surest method for making a play go—in this case, broadly farcical acting.

Catharine and Petruchio was first staged in America by David Douglass and the American Company at the Southwark Theatre in Philadelphia on 21 November 1766. The Catharine for this performance was Margaret Cheer, an Englishwoman who had joined the company in 1763. She had not been trained as an actress, her only qualifications being beauty and natural talent, but later accounts of the early American stage describe her as an excellent actress. Although few records of early American performances survive, one Philadelphia critic left this picture of Margaret Cheer's histrionic capabilities:

> There is no necessity of destroying the least articulate Beauty of Language, thro' Fury, Eagerness, or Passion; Miss Cheer never loses the sweetest accent, or faulters in the Clearness of Expression, from any or all those Causes, though I believe she is equally delicate, and capable of feeling the Force of Passion.

The Petruchio in this first staging was Lewis Hallam, Jr., a better known actor but not an especially good one. Joseph Norton Ireland [in his *Records of the New York Stage from 1750 to 1860*] describes Hallam as

> slightly above the middle height, erect and thin, but strong, vigorous and graceful—being an accomplished fencer and dancer. A slight cast in one eye, resulting from an injury in his youth, . . . materially heightened the expression and effect of his features in humorous parts.

He practiced the Old School methods and his vocal delivery was "excessively declamatory, in moments of high passion lapsing into gabble and rant." Other members of the first American cast for *Catharine and Petruchio* were:

Hortensio: David Douglass	Music Master: Mr. Allyn
Grumio: Owen Morris	Peter: Stephen Woolls
Baptista: Mr. Tomlinson	Bianca: Mrs. Thomas Wall
Biondello: Thomas Wall	Curtis: Catherine Maria Harman

Douglass was a mediocre actor, but Owen Morris was one of the finest low comedians in America at that time. Despite inadequacies in the acting of some individuals, the show was a success.

New Yorkers first saw *Catharine and Petruchio* when Douglass and his company staged it at the John St. Theatre on 8 January 1768. This production also starred Margaret Cheer and Lewis Hallam, Jr., supported by the same cast as in 1766 with the exception of the Tailor, now played by tall, handsome John Henry, and Bianca, assumed by young, petite Maria Storer. This performance presented *Catharine and Petruchio* as an afterpiece to *Romeo and Juliet,* a common combination on the early American stage. Again the play succeeded, and it became the most frequently performed comedy at the John St. Theatre in the 1767-1768 season. The American Company continued to stage the play every year until the Revolution closed many of the theatres. The only other company to perform Garrick's afterpiece before the war was the New American Company, which first offered *Catharine and Petruchio* in Annapolis on 3 June 1769, with a cast headed by Mrs. Walker and William Verling.

The war closed all theatres except those staffed by the British military. One troupe, led by Sir Henry Clinton, performed *Catharine and Petruchio* at the Theatre Royal in New York during the 1779-1780 season. Seven days before the performance, they were still advertising for a promptbook, so the performance undoubtedly consisted of little more than characters shouting at one another while exchanging blows and throwing dishes.

On 4 October 1785, only two weeks after the John St. Theatre opened for its first post-war season, *Catharine and Petruchio* was back on the professional stage again, this time with Mr. Hallam's Petruchio taming the Catharine of Mrs. Allen. When John Hodgkinson became co-manager of the American Company in 1792, he took over the role of Petruchio, a part that he had earlier played in Bath. This versatile actor-manager, described by William Dunlap [in his *A History of the American Theatre*] as "too fleshy to appear tall," had suffered an eye injury which left one eye smaller than the other, adding archness to his expression in comic roles. Because he shared many traits with the shrew-tamer—vanity, greed, aggressiveness, and boastfulness—he was naturally suited for the role. His mobile face and versatile voice also helped make his Petruchio a great improvement over the stilted tamer of Lewis Hallam, Jr.

The last performance of *Catharine and Petruchio* at the John St. Theatre is memorable primarily because of its unusual audience. The frigate *John Adams,* carrying captured pirates, had anchored in New York harbor. These prisoners were granted leave to go to the theatre on the night of 5 March 1805 in order to witness a double bill of *Blue Beard* and *Catharine and Petruchio.* Whether they understood a word of either play is doubtful, and perhaps it is better that they did not. At least they saw one of America's better actresses, Elizabeth Johnson, described by George Odell [in his *Annals of the New York Stage*] as "a highly finished representative of ladies of fashion, and of what we know as high comedy heroines. Probably no better actress in this line has ever appeared in America."

The kind of farcical treatment that Garrick's afterpiece received in America and England at this time was typical of its treatment throughout the nineteenth century. During the next one hundred years, actors would gradually add gags to the play, perverting its logic and obscuring its characters until audiences would hiss it from the stage. (pp. 15-22)

. . . . .

Directors of broadly farcical *Shrews* present the world of the play as joyful, exuberant, and full—sometimes too full—of life. The settings and costumes are bright and rich, and the characters feel no pain. By reducing *The Shrew* to a clown act, these directors avoid confronting the play and its themes. They laugh off its message and make no attempt to unify its three plots—the duping of Sly, the wooing of Bianca, and the taming of Kate. They are concerned primarily with the story of Katharine and Petruchio, and the other two plots become important only as they affect the taming procedure.

But during the 1950s and 1960s, directors at the Shakespeare Memorial Theatre reexamined *The Shrew* and reevaluated its characters and themes, focusing on the play-within-a-play structure and the prevalence of playacting in *The Shrew*. From this perspective, Sly gained new importance. In the three-ring *Shrews,* the tinker had become just another clown. His story was forgotten at the end of the Induction, which only served to get Sly onstage, and the Epilogue was rarely performed. But directors like John Barton added the Epilogue and other sections of *The Taming of a Shrew* to the First Folio text in order to give Sly more purpose and to define more clearly the play-within-a-play structure. They ensured that the audience would not forget that Katharine and Petruchio were simply roles adopted by two members of a troupe of strolling players. The actors changed costumes in full view of the audience, called on their prompter when they forgot lines, and even joined the stage audience when they were not playing their roles. At the end of the play, as Sly awoke beside the alehouse, the players could be seen in the distance, travelling on to their next one-night stand.

By including the Epilogue, these directors stressed the theme of deception in *The Shrew*. The play began with the lord's plan to dupe Sly and ended with Sly's realization that he was not a nobleman. As Sly is deceived, so (according to this interpretation) Katharine and Petruchio deceive themselves. Katharine believes that she is a fierce shrew, but she is really a love-starved woman; Petruchio believes that he is a mercenary bully, but he is really an affectionate suitor. In the subplot, Lucentio poses as Cambio, Tranio as Lucentio, Hortensio as the Music Master, the Pedant as Vincentio, and Bianca as a sweet young thing. These deceptions are all part of the larger illusions of the actors as characters and the play as reality. During the performance, Sly keeps this distinction prominent by his inability to understand it. He interferes with the players to keep Lucentio from being jailed, and the lord must remind him, "My lord, 'tis but a play. They're but in jest." Illusion is layered on top of illusion in a series of Pirandellian Chinese boxes—an RSC actor plays the role of an Elizabethan actor who in turn plays Lucentio who poses as Cambio.

In their productions, directors like Trevor Nunn extended this reading of the play to make *The Shrew* not only a play-

within-a-play, but also a play about plays—a statement about the theatre and the power of theatrical illusion. They focused on the contrast between the gay and wealthy world of Padua and the dreary world in which Sly and the players live. Sly is no more than a miserable, drunken tinker, and the strolling players, who have slept in ditches and walked for miles carrying heavy bundles, are ragged and exhausted. But through the power of the play, actors and spectators are transported to a world of silly slapstick, generous dowries, and happy endings. For the duration of the main play, the grubby reality fades; Sly becomes a lord, and the players become wealthy and carefree. When the last lines have been spoken, however, the magic of the theatre fades, Sly totters off to his wife, who will surely beat him, and the players exchange their finery for rags. The farce is encased in pathos, making the experience of the play pleasurably bittersweet.

George Devine was the first major director to use the expanded Epilogue, which completed the stories of Sly and the strolling players. His production opened on 9 June 1953 at the Memorial Theatre in Stratford-upon-Avon with Yvonne Mitchell as Katharine, Marius Goring as Petruchio, Michael Warre as Sly, and Donald Pleasence as Grumio. The show was revived on 1 June 1954, with a new cast led by Keith Michell and Barbara Jefford.

After a conventional Induction, Sly was carried into the lord's hall where he sat on a large bed at stage right or stood on a balcony to watch the players. He was fascinated by the performance and often joined the action—helping Tranio and Lucentio exchange cloaks, playing the rear end of one of the horses, and intervening to protect Grumio from Petruchio's temper. Sly offered the actors a drink now and then, and he and Grumio became good friends. But at times he mistook the play for reality. When Petruchio shouted, "Where's my Kate?" [cf. III. ii. 110] the tinker looked under his bed to see if she was hiding there. Between scenes, Sly wandered onto the playing area, and when he leaned against a pedestal just as a stagehand was removing it, he fell flat. Devine stressed Sly's confusion in the Epilogue; just as the tinker had convinced himself that he had only dreamt about shrew-taming, he turned to see the familiar players, now in their ordinary clothes, walking off into the dawn. Antonia White, the critic for the *Spectator,* called this "a moment of pure magic."

Vivienne Kernot's scenery for this production reflected its concern with illusions. The play was set in the hall of an Elizabethan mansion with elegantly ornate furniture and richly inlaid wooden walls, some of which periodically became transparent to reveal the stylized towers of Padua in the distance. The lighting was soft, giving the stage an air of unreality, and changes in the lighting could make the hall substantial or insubstantial.

> By focussing [the light] on particular parts of the structure, effects of great realism could be produced. . . . Widen the view, and there plain to see was a pantomime set; widen it again and it took in Padua, Italy, the whole world [Richard David, in "Stratford 1954"].

As in many modern *Shrews,* Devine's Katharine and Petruchio fell in love early in the play and disguised that love while they tested one another and battled for position. This reading not only satisfied modern audiences, but also reinforced the theme of deception. Katharine appeared to be a confirmed shrew: she punched Bianca and Petruchio, tied her sister's hands and whipped the girl with a rope, punched wildly at Grumio when he refused to give her food, and swung a poker at Petruchio, who fortunately ducked in time to avoid decapitation. Petruchio seemed to be a hardened sadist: he beat Grumio's head against a door, kicked Grumio to the ground, used the servant as a footstool, and later sat on him. When he offered Kate some meat on the second day of their marriage, he extended the dish to her and raised the cover, only to slam it down on her finger as she reached for the food. But neither character was really vicious, and even as they fought they were falling in love. Richard David described their first meeting:

> They meet—and practically nothing happens. Petruchio falters for a moment in his speech, and continues in a tone even lighter and more outrageous than before. Katharine is suddenly still, like a pointer that checks at game. And there for you, presented with the utmost precision and certainty, the utmost economy of means, is love at first sight.

Neither was willing to drop this mask of belligerence until Kate agreed to call the sun whatever Petruchio liked, and then rushed over to embrace her husband.

To highlight the romantic comedy in this taming and to invite playgoers to consider the play more seriously, Devine tempered—but did not eliminate—the farce. Most of the slapstick was generated by the servants and Sly: Tranio kicked Biondello, who in turn booted the Pedant; Grumio fell backwards out of a window; and Sly and the Hostess took turns walloping each other with a warming pan.

The production was very successful and was hailed as the best production of 1954 at the Memorial Theatre. Most critics, bored with mad-cap *Shrew*s, were delighted by this new, less frantic approach. A typical headline read: "The 'Shrew' at Stratford: Thoughtful Rather Than Flamboyant" [*The Daily Telegraph*]. John H. Bird of the *Evesham Journal* wrote, "Gone is the over-rumbustious romp, the excessive invention and the incongruous costumes. Brisk, bustling at times, the 1954 production has a fine polish and a certain loveliness." *The Times* critic praised the 1953 production for revealing "that there is more of comedy and less of farce than is commonly supposed in the young Shakespeare's treatment of the old wife-taming plot." Yet Devine's production included enough slapstick to satisfy those few reviewers who demanded a roughhouse *Shrew*. In sharp contrast to the reception of other modern *Shrew*s, only one critic complained that the horseplay was excessive.

The critics applauded Devine's full treatment of the framing story that raised the issue of illusion in *The Shrew* but did not belabor it, giving the play what *The Times* called "an agreeable sense of depth." For the first time, critics noted that *The Shrew* had dramatic shape and therefore could have a more subtle theme than the statement of wifely duty embodied in Katharine's final speech. Devine's production prepared the way for more serious interpretations of *The Taming of the Shrew,* even though the core of his play was still the taming of Katharine.

John Barton, who next staged *The Shrew* in Stratford-upon-Avon, heightened the emphasis on the power of theatrical illusion. His production opened on 21 June 1960, with Peter O'Toole as Petruchio, Peggy Ashcroft as Katharine, and Jack MacGowran as Sly. Barton accentuated the contrast between the world of the play and reality by setting the main play not in a spacious and elegant Jacobean hall, but in the confined

area of a rustic thatched inn, described by one reviewer as "tatty." Alix Stone, the set designer, used the revolving stage to alternate scenes between the exterior and interior of the inn. Both the courtyard and the inner room were surrounded by windows and balconies from which patrons and kitchen wenches could watch the strolling players perform. A staircase connected one side with the other, so that as the stage revolved, actors scrambled up the stairs, over the wall, and into the other half of the set. In front of the inn, Stone built a heavy gray picture frame proscenium which further confined the playing area. One critic reported, "The result, from the front, is now a picture frame stage with a quasi-Elizabethan stage set within it and within this, again, one finds the play." By increasing the number of frameworks for the play, Barton emphasized the levels of illusion in it. By tricks of lighting, this set in muted colors was transformed during the players' performance into "a place of bustling, bubbling comic licence." Because the dingy inn was so different from wealthy Padua, the transformation wrought by theatrical illusion was very impressive.

Barton expanded the Induction by adding lines from *The Taming of a Shrew* and highlighting the actors' roles as players. The company entered pushing their cart and carrying bundles. They discussed their repertory with the lord and then made arrangements for the props they would need. They brought with them a prompter, who spent most of his time crouching under the open wooden staircase, feverishly thumbing through his promptbook. Occasionally, he appeared as a minor character—usually a messenger—and delivered his lines in an amateurish singsong fashion. As the stage revolved, the audience could see between the exterior and the interior a greenroom where the prompter rehearsed the actors, and the players changed clothes, played cards, and guzzled ale. The audience was given numerous glimpses like this of the actors out of character. At one point, Katharine waved to the audience from the greenroom as the stage spun around. Although these players were poor and ragged, they were light-hearted both on and off the stage. They filled *The Shrew* with music and sang as they travelled on at the end.

The plot of the Induction was unchanged except that the lord kept Sly at the inn rather than transporting him back to his mansion. The tinker watched the performance from a variety of locations: he sat on the stairs, on the ground and on benches, and, as the scene shifted from outside to inside, he and the lord, who posed as a servant named Sim, scrambled over the stairs to follow the action. Sly commented on the play as if it were reality, and he intervened to stop Vincentio from being incarcerated. As he ran onto the playing area shouting, "We'll have no sending to prison; that's flat," the actors stood amazed, lost their cues, and had to wait for the prompter to get them started again. During the closing scene, Sly fell asleep on a bench in the courtyard, and, after the last lines of the play, was rudely awakened by the hostess. Robert Speaight [in "The 1960 Season at Stratford-upon-Avon"] paints this picture of the closing scene:

> The play is over; the actors have changed and are off to their next one-night stand; and Mr. Mac-Gowran [Sly] wanders in their wake, ruminating about his wife in Sligo. This was magnificent, though it was not Shakespeare; the perfect end to an irreproachable evening.

Like Devine, Barton presented the taming story as a romantic comedy in which both Katharine and Petruchio pretended to be more belligerent than they really were. In the early parts of the play, Peggy Ashcroft, who did not usually play rough-and-tumble roles, was convincingly shrewish. She poked at Bianca with a stick, pulled her sister's hair, broke her father's cane over her knee, bit Petruchio, and threw stools and shoes at him. This kind of violence provoked Eric Keown to remark [in a review in *Punch*], "She is not the kind of shrew who, out of perversity, enjoys being trampled on, but a high-powered termagant who pulls no punches." But it was soon apparent that she was attracted to Petruchio. At the end of the wooing scene, she offered her cheek to Petruchio to kiss, and when he ignored her, she slapped him. One reviewer [in *The New Statesman*] felt that she exhibited "an unexpected tenderness under all the raging, spitting and wonderfully timed awkwardness. The vitality was there—she hopped like a rabbit at the start—but it deepened at every turn into feeling." Several critics believed that she wanted to be tamed, and by the end of the Tailor scene, remarked Harold Hobson [in *The Sunday Times*], this Kate was "so patient, so unresisting, so pale, so wearied, with the unshed tears dwelling in her eyes, that the brutal, vulgar farce is transfigured with beauty and pathos." She lifted her role above farce and, according to one astonished reviewer, was "even subtle." Peter O'Toole's Petruchio was also a poseur. When pretending to be a rough shrew-tamer, he seemed to Milton Shulman [in the *Evening Standard*] "the most aggressive, virile, dominating Petruchio in years. Any woman who stood in his way would be blown apart by a puff or a sneeze." When he arrived for the wedding playing bagpipes, he looked to Gareth Lloyd Evans [in the *Stratford-upon-Avon Herald*] like "a mixture of Chief Running Water and a berserk Macbeth." But this rough exterior hid the real Petruchio, who never used a whip on his bride, always showed good humor, and fidgeted nervously as he waited for Kate to answer his summons in the last scene.

Barton's *Shrew* had a fair amount of slapstick in addition to its romantic comedy. When Grumio fired his blunderbuss, everyone on the stage fell flat. Petruchio leaped over Grumio as he began his "Have I not heard . . . " speech [I. ii. 200.ff], and when Katharine pulled a stool out from under her suitor, he remained seated—on nothing. Most of the slapstick, however, was assigned to Biondello, an acrobatic clown with a cockney accent who slid down banisters, turned somersaults, and raced offstage imitating a car screeching around a corner.

Barton's *Shrew* was very popular, largely because of the fine performances of Peggy Ashcroft and Peter O'Toole. The critics applauded Barton for taming the farce usually associated with *The Shrew*. The critic for *The Times* wrote, "For racy and boisterous farce we are given in lavishly comic detail a gently amusing antiquarian spectacle, and the curious thing is that this spectacle has the effect of taming farce by introducing into it overtones of comedy." Norman Marshall [in his *The Producer and the Play*] rated this *Shrew* one of the best Shakespearean productions between 1955 and 1960 because it transformed "a cruel and loutish farce into a light-hearted, charming comedy." But there was no consensus about Barton's heavy emphasis on the play-within-a-play structure. Several reviewers thought it was labored, and faulted Barton, a Cambridge don, for being too scholarly. Other critics praised this new interpretation for making "what is lively [seem] even livelier," and Robert Speaight admired the production "not for its inventiveness, which is unfailing, but its honesty, which is absolute."

This popular production was revived twice, appearing next at the Aldwych on 13 September 1961, and then returning to Stratford where it was selected to open on Shakespeare's birthday in 1962. Peter Hall, director of the RSC in the early 1960s, included *The Shrew* in the company's repertory for a couple of years because, as a play about acting, he thought that it was a good training-ground for a company of actors trying to develop a distinctive style. Both revivals starred Vanessa Redgrave and Derek Godfrey and were directed by Maurice Daniels, who reproduced Barton's *Shrew* with few changes. He used Alix Stone's set, emphasized the play-within-a-play, and presented Katharine and Petruchio as lovers. But Daniels increased the slapstick in his revivals, transforming the servants and the characters in the subplot into *commedia* caricatures who overacted, gabbled incoherently, turned cartwheels, and chased one another around the stage. Tranio and Biondello had numerous battles; Hortensio fell over Gremio as the two men tried to hide from Kate; Grumio executed a backwards somersault off the dinner table; and Baptista got his nose caught in a battered lute. Pat Williams of the *Sunday Telegraph* described the servants as "little gibbering gnomes who belong in 'Beyond the Fringe'; puppies barking and tumbling at their master's heels." As might be expected, the critics firmly rejected this kind of horseplay as distracting, illogical, and "painfully, yawningly *joyless.*"

To unify the production's tone, Daniels made the tamer and his shrew more energetic. Derek Godfrey's Petruchio throttled the Tailor with a tape measure and cracked his whip as he dragged his bride away from the wedding. During the Tailor scene, Petruchio ripped Katharine's new dress off her bit by bit, and Grumio raced over to cover her with the Tailor's oversized bill. The key to Godfrey's performance was speed.

> Derek Godfrey's deft Petruchio makes an exit after the first duologue with Kate in which the door seems to open and shut in mid-line, with nothing left of him but the applause. He later whirls her off, over his shoulder, at a speed which leaves her hair travelling horizontally behind. And when he throws her seven-course dinner off the table a smart slip-field of a serving-man catches the lot, ending with a pitcher over his head, and I'd say the whole scene takes five seconds [*Financial Times*].

Vanessa Redgrave's shrew was no less lively. According to J. C. Trewin [in "The Old Vic and Stratford-upon-Avon, 1961-1962"], "On her first entrance, Miss Redgrave, in a swirl of tangerine, got some of us to think of Ada Rehan's shrew as it flames from a portrait in the Royal Shakespeare Picture Gallery." During the wooing scene, she threw stools at Petruchio and spit in his face.

Daniels compensated for his added roughhousing by making it obvious that Katharine and Petruchio fell in love at first sight and battled simply to test one another. Despite the farce, the main plot remained a romantic comedy. The wooing scene closed as Petruchio massaged Katharine's calves while the two lovers gazed into each other's eyes. John Russell Brown wrote [in *Shakespeare's Plays in Performance*] that this business "gave a strong moment of feeling at the beginning of the play and engrossed the audience's interest," but also defeated Shakespeare's "progressive revelation of the bases of character."

As in the Barton *Shrew,* the fine acting of the principal players, who both conveyed the complexity of their characters, was the highlight of the show. Godfrey's Petruchio was "no brutish bore, but a philosopher" who was "honest and un-malicious, yet unswervingly determined." Although Redgrave as Kate was occasionally vixenish, she was generally more sympathetic than shrewish—a performance for which she received the *Evening Standard* Award for Best Actress in 1961. Tom Milne of *Time and Tide* wrote that this Kate

> clearly indicates that her shrewish temper is simply a defence against the crushing boredom of her pedestrian family. We have at once the sketch of a passionate creature as yet unawakened, and her look of rapturous delight when she is carried off by Petruchio shows he really is the knight in shining armour that she needs.

Petruchio's taming methods forced her to grow out of her childish temper and into a loving woman. Her final speech was "a private exultation between Petruchio and herself, instead of just a sickening homily on obedience."

By 1962 the set, the character interpretations, and the actors' performances of the principal roles were familiar, and the reviewers were able to consider the subtler aspects of the show. Critics were more aware of the play-within-a-play structure and the actors' double roles as Elizabethan strolling players and as characters within a play. *The Times* remarked, "Mr. Godfrey's Petruchio is first and last the leading man of the little company, their most picturesque and flaunting figure. To the tips of his fingers he is theatre." The critics pointed out that the "strange pathos" of the framing story contrasted with "the swirling movement of the play within a play." J. C. Trewin, who had disliked Barton's production in 1960, praised Daniels's Epilogue highly [in the *Birmingham Post*] and concluded that "a *Taming of the Shrew* that can move one as well as exhilarate is something to be heard and observed."

Barton's influence was not restricted to the Royal Shakespeare Company. In 1962, Michael Langham emphasized the play-within-a-play structure of his *Shrew* staged at Stratford, Ontario, with a cast led by John Colicos and Kate Reid. William Needles, who had played Petruchio in Guthrie's 1954 production, took the role of Grumio. The actors delivered their lines to Sly and gestured to help him understand the play. Hugh Webster's tinker, who remained onstage throughout the performance, was both charming and boozy. During the Induction, the servants directed Sly's attention to the "wanton pictures" on the walls. Even though in Langham's set both the walls and the pictures were invisible. Sly tilted his head to inspect the obscene picture of Io closely. When the lord moved on to describe the next and less provocative picture of Daphne, Sly glanced at it, then surreptitiously returned his gaze to Io. One critic said of Webster's Sly:

> At all times his whole being was engaged: his initial bewilderment was moving and his eventual conviction of his rise in the world just as touching: above all his open-hearted, simple-minded attachment to the players acting for his delight was a captivating part of a rich performance [Peter D. Smith, in " 'Toil and Trouble': A Review of the 1962 Season of the Stratford, Ontario, Festival"].

Sly's performance helped focus the audience's attention on the players themselves rather than on their roles. Walter Kerr left this vivid description [in *New York Herald Tribune*] of the "curious sigh" on which Langham ended his *Shrew*:

> In that moment—with just a faint suspension of

breath to show that something is passing—a world closes down like the last light of day. Petruchio, so triumphant over Kate just a moment ago, is now leaning against a pillar as though his energies could never be restored, his shoulders limp with an actor's weariness. Kate, the virago who has not for a moment stood still, stands alone, looking at no one as the stage properties are hustled past her, waiting for her composure to return. The supporting company, instantly characterless and briskly indifferent, cares only about packing the cart for the journey into the night.

And when Petruchio has breathed out his tensions and become a mere player again, he moves past Kate without so much as a nod to her. Starting down the road that will end somewhere in another performance, he throws his arm about Bianca, who is obviously his real love. A play is a play, and even when it is well done, 'tis done.

As Peter Smith recognized, Langham's completion of the framing story lent the production a satisfying unity.

By making the main play broadly farcical, Langham accentuated the contrast between the exhaustion of the actors as they slowly departed and their energy when they were in character. Katharine and Petruchio participated in the slapstick—Petruchio, a money-conscious mad-cap, arrived for the wedding in a cart which rolled wildly downhill, and Kate, a true shrew, threatened Bianca with a hangman's noose. The Pedant wore a huge ruff and orange feathers, Petruchio and Grumio bumped heads repeatedly, and Biondello cantered around the stage as he described the appearance of Petruchio and his horse. The critics did not object to Langham's inclusion of so much horseplay because the pathos of the framing story helped offset the farce.

When Trevor Nunn, one of the young, energetic, and intelligent directors drawn to the RSC in the 1960s, produced *The Shrew* in 1967, he followed the tradition of stressing the play-within-a-play structure. What Barton and Daniels had implied about the power of theatrical illusion, Nunn made explicit. His *Shrew* opened at the Memorial Theatre on 5 April 1967, with Michael Williams and Janet Suzman in the principal roles. After the Stratford run, the show was taken to the Aldwych in the fall of 1967 and then on tour in 1968.

Nunn envisioned the Renaissance performance of Shakespeare's *Shrew* taking place at the Theatre in Shoreditch after a bearbaiting session. The actors' ability to transform an area strewn with bloody straw into aristocratic Padua illustrated for him the magic of the theatre. In his rehearsal notes, reproduced in the program of the play, Nunn explained his concern with the contrast of theatrical illusion and reality in *The Shrew*:

> One of Shakespeare's sources for *The Shrew* was Ariosto's *I Suppositi*, translated by Gascoigne as *The Supposes*, a play about "posing," of assuming identities other than one's own. Shakespeare's genius lies in the elaboration of Ariosto's theme of appearance and reality, of masks behind masks. . . . Infinite regression is not as complex an idea as it sounds. The labels on bottles of Camp coffee, for instance. An army officer is being served by his Indian batman with coffee from a tray. On the tray is a bottle of Camp coffee on which an army officer is being served by his Indian batman with coffee from a tray. On the tray is a bottle of Camp coffee on which etc to infinity—or, rather, we can suppose

it to recur infinitely. Where does such a sequence begin and where does it end? The idea of Chinese boxes is similar. Where then is the reality of *The Shrew?* Is it in the Royal Shakespeare Theatre, or in the Warwickshire that is presented within it, or in the play that is presented within that, or in the deceptions those actors acting actors, acting parts, then openly perpetrate on each other, or is it in the more subtle deceptions of self-knowledge within these characters? When is anybody acting or posing, what do we accept, and what reject, where is the basis of truth in this ever diminishing or ever expanding fantasy? It's a theme that Shakespeare never leaves, throughout Hamlet's madness, Lear's judgement that "robes and furred garments hide all" [*King Lear,* IV. vi. 164], to Prospero's valediction, "Our revels now are ended" [*The Tempest,* IV. i. 148]. It is only embryonic in *The Shrew,* but it is excitingly and undeniably there.

Christopher Morley's set for Nunn's *Shrew* reflected the contrast between reality and theatrical illusion. When the Induction began, the audience saw the exterior of an uncompromisingly real inn set in a snowy landscape. Sly was ejected from the inn and fell asleep in the snow, where he was discovered by the lord. When the nobleman proposed his practical joke, the stage revolved and the roof of the inn lifted up to reveal the interior of the building with wooden-slatted walls, rush-strewn floor, rough wooden stools, beef drying in the rafters, and a stone chimney with a blazing fire. The small boxlike room was warm and light, a haven from the snowy evening. In this confined area, the players performed *The Shrew,* transforming the rustic inn into bright Padua. After their performance, the illusion of the play faded as the players and spectators went back out into the cold night and the set revolved to hide the warm interior of the inn. As Sly tottered homeward, he was passed by "the cloaked players laden with burdens and babes in arms—homeless wanderers—hurrying out of his life into the shadows."

The players, described by Hilary Spurling [in the *Spectator*] as "a higgledy-piggledy travelling company," had arrived blue with the cold but, once hired, scurried around the small room searching for props like a dishcloth and leg of lamb. Their bright costumes looked well-worn, and they acted most of the play without scenery—for the garden, a board with a single sprig of greenery stood in the middle of the room. With only thirteen actors in the troupe, individual actors often played several parts. Katharine and Petruchio, for example, donned helmets and doubled as the officers called to arrest Vincentio. Their prompter remained in full view of the audience, and when the actors lost their lines, they turned to him while Biondello entertained the stage audience with his juggling. J. C. Trewin was impressed by this detailed portrayal of an Elizabethan travelling troupe: "I have never been more conscious of the strolling players as a unity, a troupe prepared to do practically anything, to tumble or dance or sing, even to juggle" [*Illustrated London News*].

Sly, the lord, the hostess, and other patrons of the inn watched the performance from benches on either side of the room. Sly cackled away "like one of those daft old ladies occasionally met in the stalls who catch up with the jokes minutes after everyone else" [*Financial Times*]. As in Barton's production, he confused the illusion of the play with reality. He joined Petruchio in beating Grumio, asked repeatedly when "the fool" would appear, and intervened to stop Vincentio's arrest. This last interruption confused the players,

who huddled around their prompter as he refashioned the plot to suit Sly's demands.

A mime, one of the most artificial of theatrical forms, preceded the main play, which was filled with farce and so made no pretense at realism. Players tripped, fell off stools, overturned tables, and kicked one another in a variety of places. Every fall was punctuated with a toot or a drumbeat from offstage. Petruchio arrived for his wedding wearing a cowboy hat and oversized codpiece with an obscene green feather sticking out of it, and he rolled Katharine away from the ceremony in a barrel. The wooing scene looked like a Three Stooges routine. Petruchio kicked Katharine, and she, in retaliation, kicked him. He fell down, pretending to faint, and as she went for some wine to revive him, he popped up again. Seeing this, she turned and slapped him hard enough to knock him down again. When Petruchio climbed up on a table, Katharine kicked it over and then sat down on a bench which Petruchio kicked over, pinning her underneath. When the bench was fully loaded with Petruchio, Baptista, Gremio, and Tranio, she arose, sending the men rolling across the stage. The character of Baptista, so often lost in the crowd of minor characters became, in the hands of Roy Kinnear, a central figure in the farce.

> We are given . . . the company's fat man and actor-manager, anxiously gasping his interpretation of such a part while worrying about his troupe. The expressions on Mr. Kinnear's gleaming pink-jelly face again and again convert a commonplace line into something ludicrous [*Punch*].

Janet Suzman's Katharine and Michael Williams's Petruchio merely pretended to be a shrew and a bully, reinforcing the contrast between reality and illusion. When Katharine entered for the wooing scene, she did not see Petruchio and, thinking no one was in the room, momentarily relaxed her grotesque grimace. When Petruchio suddenly appeared, they stood gazing at each other and the audience realized that this was love at first sight. Petruchio, described as "gay, boyish, endearing, and sincere," was exhausted after the wooing scene and dropped his pretense of invincibility as Grumio hauled him away. Jeremy Kingston [in *Punch*] characterized Petruchio's final line, "Why there's a wench. Come and kiss me Kate" [V. ii. 180], as "not the conquerer's cry of triumph but a lover's quiet wonder at what his therapy has wrought."

Nunn's production was very well received; one critic hailed it as "one of the finest productions staged at Stratford for a very long time." Most reviewers especially admired the way in which Nunn balanced farce and pathos. J. C. Trewin observed, "Superficially an uproarious brawl, it is in retrospect far subtler than we may think at the time; and subtlety in this particular context is a surprising word." As Cecil Smith pointed out [in "Royal Troupe Stages 'Shrew' at Ahmanson"], the Epilogue was especially touching because of the strong contrast between the wild and energetic farce in the main play and the quiet departure of the weary players. Most critics agreed that the farce was appropriate entertainment for the stage audience at the inn and for the real audience in the theatre. Colin Frame wrote [in the *Evening News*], "It is all shameless playing to the gallery, and with the gallery I stand and cheer." A small number of critics, however, declared that the farce was excessive and "drearily unfunny." Irving Wardle complained [in *The Times*], "One could do with fewer funny voices and less boisterous crowd response," but he conceded, "It is a marvellously enjoyable show."

Several critics commented on Nunn's use of the play-within-a-play structure, and most agreed with R. B. Marriott [in *Stage and Television Today*] that it was "a triumph of imaginative interpretation" which gave the production a pleasing coherence. J. C. Trewin praised Nunn for weaving together all the various elements of his *Shrew* to produce the impression of "the sudden fading of a dream." (pp. 149-62)

The trend in stage interpretation of *The Shrew* initiated by Barton and Devine has more promise than the practice of smothering Shakespeare's text with slapstick as if it were Garrick's *Catharine and Petruchio*. The new emphasis on the play-within-a-play structure solves many of the basic problems of staging *The Shrew*. It can distance the play by allowing the audience to see the actor behind each character; the characters become merely imaginary constructs. This technique is as artificial as *commedia*, but instead of removing all the humanity from the figures onstage, directors like Langham replace our sympathy for the characters with an interest in the actors. Because Sly and his retinue are the primary audience for these productions, we can dismiss any facet of the play which displeases us—a character, plot incident, or its message—simply by arguing that it was designed to entertain the stage audience, not us. The players in a *Shrew* like Nunn's can overact grotesquely and clown shamelessly without being censured because they are merely an unpolished Elizabethan travelling company. But this interpretation should not be used as an excuse for unlimited clowning that will drown Shakespeare's characters and themes.

Productions like those examined in this chapter unify the three plots to give the play thematic coherence and place it within the larger context of other Shakespearean and Renaissance works with the same concern for the opposition between illusion and reality. *The Shrew* is most interesting when this general theme is presented in specific terms and becomes a statement about theatrical illusion or about the tensions within Renaissance society. Seen from this perspective, the play gives us a glimpse of the young Shakespeare reflecting upon the powers of this newfound medium. Without pretending that *The Shrew* is a masterpiece and without reducing its value as simple entertainment, directors like Barton, Nunn, and Langham have prepared the way for more sophisticated and subtle productions of Shakespeare's *Taming of the Shrew*. (pp. 166-67)

Tori Haring-Smith, in her From Farce to Metadrama: A Stage History of "The Taming of the Shrew," 1594-1983, *Greenwood Press, 1985, 280 p.*

Tice L. Miller   (essay date 1986)

[*Miller presents a critical survey of numerous post-war productions of* The Taming of the Shrew, *describing the various ways in which many of the play's most problematic elements have been interpreted.*]

The Taming of the Shrew remains one of Shakespeare's most popular comedies in spite of opposition from feminists offended by the story of a woman tamed by a man. This is due, in part, to the practice of many postwar directors to play down the brutality of the Kate-Petruchio relationship and suggest other meanings in Kate's final speech ("Fie, fie! Unknit that unkind brow . . . " [V. ii. 136ff.]). A number of productions (Stratford, Ontario, in 1981, for one) turned Petruchio into a kind of social worker interested in modifying Kate's shrewish behavior. Related to this was Jonathan Mil-

ler's Chichester version of 1972 in which Anthony Hopkins played a puritanical Petruchio "motivated by a sincere, semi-religious disapproval of " (Ronald Hayman [in *The First Thrust: The Chichester Festival Theatre*]) the pampered Kate of Joan Plowright. The humor in such interpretations is not always easy to discover.

Other productions have worked on the premise that Kate and Petruchio fall in love at first sight, then decide to play the more conventional roles for everyone else. The danger here is of too early a climax to the action. Nevertheless, Keith Michell and Barbara Jefford managed the notion brilliantly in George Devine's 1954 restaging of his 1953 Stratford-upon-Avon production. In Gerhard Klingenberg's Zurich staging of 1978, after the lovers fell for each other on the instant, they continued their relationship as an "amorous game" (Balz Engler [in "Shakespeare in Switzerland"]). The Petruchio and Katharina in the 1978 Virginia Shakespeare Festival production also were first-sight lovers, and the concept helped greatly to give their characters the depth necessary to balance the production's broadly comic periphery.

Still other directors have suggested that Kate gains the upper hand but realizes that she must seem submissive; she then delivers her final speech with an ironic touch, such as a wink to the audience, sharing her secret that all is not as it seems. Among the variations on softening the ending was that at the Boston Shakespeare Company in 1977 in which S. Proctor Gray made Katharina's speech work by "directing the first lines with a harsh irony toward the widow, and the final lines with a loving tenderness toward Petruchio. [Petruchio's] amazed response . . . was sufficient to redeem [him] in the eyes of the fiercest feminist" (Virginia M. Carr [in "Boston Shakespeare Company"]). On the other hand, Christoph Bruck and Wolf Bunge's Berliner Ensemble version in 1980 let the speech begin seriously, with Kate relishing the annoyance of her listeners, then had her turn ironically aloof to her own remarks: "Finally, when Petruchio bowed to kiss her outstretched hand, she drew it back and led him away: she knew how to play the social game to her advantage" (Eva and Günter Walch [in "Shakespeare in the German Democratic Republic"]). Director Roger Hendricks Simon at the Folger in 1980 had Katharina actually seduce Petruchio during the speech: "It worked to defuse the potentially sexist bomb and left the audience with a genuine sense of *con*-summation" (Jeanne Addison Roberts [in "Shakespeare in the Nation's Capital"]). In Wilford Leach's 1978 New York Shakespeare Festival mounting, Meryl Streep appears to have been properly submissive for her final speech; however, when she and her Petruchio, Raul Julia, began to exit at opposite sides of the stage during the curtain calls, she signalled that hers was the way to go and he, with a shrug, dutifully followed. Some Kates are so ironic at the end that there is no question that their "submissiveness" is moot. The George Sand-like Kate in Michael Maggio's 1979 Illinois Shakespeare Festival production, for example, swung a revolver in her hand during her tongue-in-cheek delivery of the lecture.

A popular means of not dealing directly with the main story has been to mock it by turning the production into a knock-about farce. A persistent complaint by critics of such productions is that the minor characters are generally made into dolts and simpletons, while the shrew and her tamer struggle unsuccessfully to retain their integrity as witty and knowing lovers; the "deeper" currents of the play, then, are commonly imperilled by the zaniness of the conception. Nevertheless, the approach, when supported by truly funny business, is usually appreciated by audiences. Not least among such productions was Judd Parkin's in 1978 at Ashland, Oregon, which seemed to find a reason for laughs in every line. Instead of beginning with the Induction, Parkin inserted a boisterous Punch and Judy show, a song tied to the theme of the play, and a fiery encounter between the protagonists. "From the opening street scene to the closing, no holds were barred" (Allan C. Dessen [in "Oregon Shakespearean Festival"]). Daniel Sullivan's Seattle Rep production of 1980 was intended as farce and nothing but farce: as Charles Frey noted [in "Shakespeare in Seattle"], "things went from bed to wurst as the actors hustled through the first half riding sawhorses, knocking at falling gates, throwing Bianca's food, and drawing from their scabbards sausages instead of swords." Of like approach was Richard McElvain's 1981 Boston Shakespeare Company mounting, "a rollicking crowd-pleaser in which men dressed in rich velvet costumes featuring brilliantly-colored codpieces whacked one another (and the women) with much good humor" (Elizabeth H. Hageman [in "Shakespeare in Boston and Cambridge"]). In West Berlin, radical director Peter Zadek made the *Shrew* into a bizarre farce filled with outlandish nonsequiturs, "including an outsize rabbit, a cat leading dogs on a leash, and an Arab with a prayer carpet trying to keep Petruchio's horse from eating the palm leaves" (Wilhelm Hortmann [in "Opposites"]). There were also Zadek's "customary transvestism and the split-second change of costume, sex, and roles by several actors" (Hortmann).

Directors have turned also to the *commedia dell'arte,* the circus, and vaudeville for a unifying concept which turns the play into a farcical romp. In addition to the 1954 Tyrone Guthrie version, Gerald Freedman's 1960 New York Shakespeare Festival's *Shrew* drew from the Marx Brothers and other comedians reminiscent of the commedia; William Ball's 1976 American Conservatory Theatre version imitated the real thing and became a definite *Shrew* in the United States—mainly because it was filmed and then broadcast on public television. At Stratford, Ontario, the same year Jean Gascon directed a successful version that incorporated dancer-like commedia figures who served as prop shifters, and an onstage audience. Gascon's fantastications included "golden bolts of lightning that could be carried by hand when a storm was needed, a paper rainbow that appeared on cue, a two-piece articulated horse, a fireplace where daintily-painted flames were activated by the turning of a crank" (Berners W. Jackson, 1973 [in "Shakespeare at Stratford, Ontario, 1973"]).

Directors also have enlarged the Christopher Sly role by adding material from *The Taming of a Shrew,* long considered by some a source play but more recently thought to be a bad quarto version of Shakespeare's play. In these examples, Sly is used as a framing device for the main action and frequently gets involved in the action of the play. Before describing some productions which have used this device, an aside made by Eleanor Prosser [in "Shakespeare in San Diego"], reviewing the 1962 San Diego *Shrew,* with its added dialogue from *A Shrew,* might be considered: "Am I alone in preferring Shakespeare's version? Sly's interruptions really are not very funny and the epilogue is a pedestrian anticlimax. Why not let Sly go to sleep, wake him with a rousing dance at the end, and stop?" Judging by the remarks of other critics, however, the Sly interpolations usually provide a frame that is not only amusing but thematically appropriate. However, Prosser's

comment would not have been considered misguided to viewers of George Devine's 1953 and 1954 mountings at Stratford-upon-Avon, where the snoozing Sly, having been carried back from the lord's Elizabethan mansion to the tavern steps, woke to gaze with a puzzled expression at the strolling players departing wearily for bed as the curtain fell. "The effect was not labored, and it gave to the rough *A Shrew* text a hint of the formal and the human that had its own delight" (Clifford Leech [in "Stratford, 1953"]). At Stratford, Connecticut, in 1956, Mike Kellin's Sly remained awake watching all the action from a bed in an upper gallery "except when, shortly before the second intermission, he broke into the action to run across the stage calling for a cup of small ale" (Richard Hosley [in "The Second Season at Stratford, Connecticut"]). For the 1980 Folger production Sly sat with pride in the audience in the seat of the Folger Library's Director. At Stratford, Ontario, in 1981 he was situated in the balcony over the stage, occasionally meddling, as do so many Slys, in the action. In Toby Robertson's Huntington Theatre Company revival of 1983, set in a Tudor manor house, Sly was ensconced before the hearth to watch the Players. When Petruchio tossed the burned meat to a servant, it was so hot that it was thrown from one person to another until it ended up in Sly's hands (and mouth). Several productions, such as Nagle Jackson's at San Diego in 1971, have used the Sly frame to point up the role-playing aspect of the characters in the main plot. The players keep reminding the audience that they are actors, and continually involve Sly in the fun. At the close of Jackson's version the *A Shrew* ending was applied so that, "as Sly turned for home to tame his own shrewish wife, he saw the troupe of players leaving town. A Jack Benny take, and the point was well made: 'Do I dream? Or have I dream'd till now?' " (Lynn K. Horobetz [in "Shakespeare at the Old Globe, 1971"]). The Klingenberg revival not only used the *A Shrew* materials, but the director/translator wrote seven brief passages himself to sustain it. At the end, when Sly woke up in the gutter and noticed a ring on his finger, he realized that his experiences possibly had happened in reality. The theme of illusion versus reality (a popular topic for program notes when the director seeks to elaborate on the play's meaning) was emphasized by contrasting the brutal treatment of Sly by the Lord's retainers as compared with the dreamlike beauty of the play-within-the-play. . . . John Barton's 1960 Stratford-upon-Avon production, followed in 1962 by Michael Langham's rendition at Stratford, Ontario, were among those that furthered the use of the frame.

Some recent productions have doubled Sly with Petruchio; this was done in Lee Stetson's 1979 Venice Beach presentation and in Edward J. Feidner's 1979 Champlain Festival showing, for example. In the latter Kate was also the Hostess: "The backlash came . . . when Petruchio failed to disconnect himself from Sly. In the resulting identity crisis, . . . Petruchio turned into a boorish oaf" (Kenneth S. Rothwell [in "Champlain Shakespeare Festival"]. Gillette A. Elvgren, Jr.'s well-liked *Shrew* at Pittsburgh in 1980 featured a Sly who joined the main plot as the Pedant, as did the Folger's production the same year.

Directors have been drawn to the *Shrew* because it can withstand extensive adaptation and modification, enabling them to put their personal signatures upon their productions. They have set the play in such unlikely places as Cleveland's Little Italy, the American Southwest, Nigeria, New South Wales, and the American West. Updating the setting and adding topical allusions allows them to bring a fresh touch to the play and to appeal to local audiences not knowledgeable about the traditions of Shakespeare performance. Tyrone Guthrie's Wild West setting at Stratford, Ontario, in 1954 was in this tradition; it offered a broadly farcical treatment that included sight gags and pranks from vaudeville. There have been several rootin', tootin' Western *Shrews* since; one was James Dunn's San Francisco production of 1979, previously seen at the Edinburgh Festival. Dunn parodied familiar Hollywood cowboy songs, character-types, and situations, but sometimes these were intrusive rather than pertinent. Among others in this mode were two in 1980: Theatre 40's in Beverly Hills and Nagle Jackson's for the Shakespeare Festival of Dallas. Both had Petruchio hog-tie Kate in their first encounter. Revolutionary Europe in the 1830s was the background chosen for Michael Maggio's 1979 offering, with its cigar-smoking Kate dressed in a mannish coat, vest, and slacks, and a Petruchio depicted as "a cock-of-the-walk Napoleon": "Putting Kate in the era of George Sand made a viable bridge between Shakespeare's violent shrew and contemporary feminist indignation without subduing her to either" (Richard P. Wheeler [in "Illinois Shakespeare Festival"]). Padua in 1934 was the locale for Mark Lamos' 1979 California Shakespeare Festival production so that the idea of a modern woman residing in a machismo-oriented Fascist world could be explored. The Cafe Capulet was a central element of the clothesline-adorned town square. Anne McNaughton's 1981 San Jose Repertory presentation moved the time frame even closer by selecting Italy in 1947 and playing Petruchio as a macho Italian-American G.I. Barnet Kellman's North Carolina Shakespeare Festival staging of 1977 set the *Shrew* in modern Italy and peopled the stage with all the characters with which the audience might be familiar from Italian movies. Italian accents were used (as in several other such modern dress adaptations) and topical allusions inserted: for example, "A silken doublet! a velvet hose! a scarlet cloak!" was revised to "double-knit pants and Gucci shoes!" Pamela Hawthorne set her upbeat and preppy 1984 Missouri Repertory Theatre *Shrew* in a modern Italian town with Pepsi bottles, Cinzano signs, and racing bikes.

A few directors also have gone against the grain and attempted to graphically depict the violence and brutality of the play. Their intentions are suggested by the tendentious treatment accorded Kate's final speech in Charles Marowitz's ideologically radical adaptation, originally seen in 1973 at his Open Space in London. A 1978 Danish production of this *Shrew* displayed the adaptor's determination to turn the play into a feminist tract about a woman "reduced to the status of chattel and sexual object" (Ingeborg Nixon [in "Shakespeare in Denmark"]). Kate's speech was placed at the beginning as a prologue which was delivered "with sweet and confident irony, the cupped-hand gesture of the closing lines continuing into the wave of a clenched fist that signaled liberty and equality rather than war." When she spoke the same speech at the end of the play proper, it was "with the dullness of an automaton, under the remote control of Petruchio, who was enthroned above and behind her" (Nixon). Marowitz himself directed the piece in Norway in 1979. In Andrew Kennedy's opinion, Shakespeare's comedy had been transformed "into a decadent Jacobean tragedy, . . . with post-Artaud scenes of psycho-physical horror" concerned with the relations between a pair of sadists [in "Shakespeare in Bergen"]). Katariina Lahti's Swedish production of 1980 was a harsh indictment of sexual role-playing. Petruchio was an obnoxious male chauvinist who conquered Kate in an outright battle of the sexes. Kate totally capitulated, without irony, at the end,

and when Petruchio realized "what a docile, suppressed, and vapid creature his wife had become" (Gunnar Sorelius [in "Shakespeare in Sweden"]), he looked at a dove he held in his hand—symbolizing the submissive woman—and then broke its neck. Michael Bogdanov's 1978 RSC rendition focused on the plight of women in a male-dominated society. Kate lost not her shrewishness but her sense of personal dignity. And Keith Digby's 1980 [in "Illinois Shakespeare Festival"]). production in Edmonton, Alberta, depicted Petruchio as the cause of Kate's physical and mental collapse; brainwashed, she delivered her final speech as a sermon. These were controversial productions, not especially popular with either audiences or critics.

American directors have tended to treat the play as a farce, not a comedy; an exception was R. O. Ceballos' 1978 version at the Shakespeare Festival of Cincinnati; the usual physical brutality was clearly absent, and the taming of the shrew was a victory of words and wit. Kate's lesson changed her into "a woman who could transcend her own preconception about her importance. . . . Her final speech . . . was addressed very pointedly to both men and women: everyone must play a pre-established social role" (W. L. Godshalk [in "The Shakespeare Festival of Cincinnati"]). Only Petruchio, watching "the role he had essentially created," remained aloof as she spoke: "For Kate and Petruchio the future was left open-ended, their relationship fraught with possibilities" (Godshalk). Such comedic approaches are more common in England. Yvonne Mitchell in Devine's 1953 *Shrew* was not romanticized: "She was simply a shrew successfully tamed, and the jest was found good: before her final entry Petruchio silently prayed, and the audience was delighted to find that his methods were crowned with success" (Leech). Marius Goring's Petruchio "was a whimsical trainer teaching his pupil how to behave for her own good" (T. C. Kemp [in "Acting Shakespeare: Modern Tendencies in Playing and Production"]). Barry Kyle's 1982 RSC rendition took a traditional approach which did not attempt to justify Petruchio's cruel actions but did show a Kate in need of discipline and self-knowledge which comes from her encounter with Petruchio. Critics were divided in their reception because many felt that Kyle had not come to terms with the cruelty in the play. This is a challenge which any contemporary director faces. In the 1980s, how does one deal with the play's cruelty without turning the production into a rant on sexism and thereby ruining its popularity with audiences? (pp. 661-66)

Tice L. Miller, "The Taming of the Shrew," in Shakespeare Around the Globe: A Guide to Notable Postwar Revivals, *edited by Samuel L. Leiter, Greenwood Press, 1986, pp. 661-84.*

STAGING ISSUES

Ernest P. Kuhl (essay date 1921)

[*Kuhl argues that the Induction to* The Taming of the Shrew *is nothing more than a device used by Shakespeare to furnish "a farcical atmosphere for a farcical story." Once Sly had served the function of helping set the tone of the play, the dramatist had no further interest in the character.*]

A solution satisfactory to all scholars for the early disappearance of Sly is yet forthcoming. The play as it stands naturally leaves something to be desired, for it obviously is not well rounded out. To account for this flaw many suggestions have been made, some of them being less plausible than others. Ulrici thought that the dramatist intended the closing of the old farce, *A Shrew,* to be reproduced in his own, a statement that rightly has been questioned.

It does not seem probable that Professor Schelling's recent observation [in his *A Book of Homage to Shakespeare*] is the key to the solution, namely, that the dramatist wearied, dropping the adventures "when the play within the play was at an end." There was no need of any great creative work; in fact *A Shrew* contains all the necessary remarks of Sly, speeches that the later playwright might have used had he wished. For indeed he borrowed freely from the Induction of the old work, helping himself to this good bit and that as was his practice in general. Moreover it is difficult to imagine Shakspere's tiring of one of his comic creations. It would be more plausible to assume that the poet was guilty of carelessness, a charge to which he was to lay himself open (to all appearances) even in his mature dramas. But this reason seems unsatisfactory also, since the tinker plays not a small part in the Induction, and (as we shall later see) his exit seems carefully planned.

Elze [in his preface to Schlegel and Tieck's *Shakespeare*] and others have remarked that the end was lost. The difficulty with this view is that Sly should appear somewhere between his dropping out of sight (close of I, i.) and the epilogue. This he actually does in the older play. It is hardly conceivable that he should merely "sit and mark" silently for nearly five acts. If he is too drowsy to make comments, he is also too sleepy to stay awake. He was too garrulous a creature to remain unheard. Neither could he have slept through four or more acts, and then make remarks. There would be nothing *apropos* for him to say: he had witnessed none of the taming scenes; in fact he had not even seen Petruchio. He could hardly point a moral when he had not had a glimpse of the tamer! Probably the best theory is that stated by Professor Neilson [in his introduction to *The Taming of the Shrew* (Cambridge edition)]: "in the necessity of clearing the gallery, from which Sly is viewing the stage for the appearance of the Pedant from a window in v. i." This theory, however, conflicts with evidence (shortly to be presented in full) that Shakspere in the beginning deliberately planned Sly's exodus.

Is not the solution of the problem to be found in the belief that the drunken tinker was dismissed for artistic (and psychological) reasons? To imagine *The Shrew* with Sly's occasional remarks, let us see what the author of *A Shrew* has actually done. Greater exhibition of improbability and lack of realism could not well be found. No sooner is the rogue completely intoxicated than he is asked to witness a play; his observations are to be based on life in the academic city of Athens. But being in a stupor he is naturally in no fit condition to witness a theatrical performance. To complicate matters his physical condition grows worse, since he calls repeatedly for more "small ale." Yet through the greater part of the spectacle he remains mentally alert and imperturbable. Not until near the close of the fourth act does drowsiness overcome him, and he falls asleep, being carried out at the close of that act. Though he misses entirely the final, and important, act in which the audience sees the shrew completely conquered, he appears in the epilogue to point the moral.

For Shakspere to have pursued a like method would have been a transgression of all laws of realism. Let us see what changes were made in the composition of *The Shrew*. The Induction opens with Sly completely intoxicated just after he has been put out of an ale house by an irate hostess. Being unconscious he is presently picked up by a lord returning from a hunt. As soon as the lord's house is reached the tinker is bathed and put in a warm bed, and then made to believe that he is a lord just awakening from a long sickness. Meanwhile a consuming thirst overcomes him, and he begins to call for "small ale." Under these circumstances Sly is obviously not fit to play his part for long, though (as has been shown) not realized by the author of the old drama. But Shakspere was too familiar with the power of the "invisible spirit" for that: Falstaff's famous apostrophe to sack as well as the drinking scenes in *Othello, Antony and Cleopatra,* and elsewhere, is proof on that point. We are not surprised to learn, therefore, that when the comedy for his benefit is about to begin he lapses into a state of lethargy, for he now reverts to prose after several speeches of blank verse; and that at the close of the first scene he is not only bored but has actually been nodding. Shakspere consequently was remaining firm on the rock of human nature; there was nothing else to do, provided he was to remain true to his art.

Another, in some ways more important, reason for the tinker's disappearance is the following. His presence and comments would dissipate the spectator's interest in a remarkably clever and entertaining plot. The title of the farce is significant: not (as in the old play) the taming of *a* shrew, but of *the* shrew. In making the change Shakspere presumably had a purpose (cf. '*The* Winter's Tale'). Is it too much to suggest that the dramatist wished to compose a farce that should be a masterpiece? This is what he was to do in the other types of drama; and it may not be wholly without significance that *The Shrew* was probably his last farce.

As for scattering the interests of the audience, Shakspere throughout his plays was a master in centering attention. Everywhere in his best comedies and tragedies there is one characteristic—a unity and welding of the whole piece. This singleness of effect is, according to Creizenach [in his *The English Drama in the Age of Shakespeare*], the outstanding feature in Shakspere. His contemporaries seek "separate effective situations," and not an "organic whole." A notable instance occurs in *Antony and Cleopatra.* The flattening out of subordinate characters and events (the latter sometimes completely obliterated) is at times amazing. MacCallum in his masterly treatment of the play [in *The Roman Plays,* 2 ed.], observes how the facts of history are warped to suit the dramatist's purpose: that nothing must interfere with the overpowering infatuation of the Roman for the "serpent of old Nile." And again the same writer notes that everything is done "to concentrate the attention on the purely personal relations of the lovers." In *Macbeth,* to mention but one other instance, this unity of impression is got with consummate skill. Bradley [in his *Shakespearean Tragedy*], in speaking of the ironing out process of minor personages, sees no reason "why the names of the persons should not be interchanged in all the ways mathematically possible."

Now *The Shrew* exhibits this quality to a high degree. Scholars beginning with Dr. Johnson have praised the superb handling of the various threads of the play. In fact the parts are not distinct, but one and indivisible. The closing scene of the farce is in this respect unsurpassed even in Shakspere. Every detail, particularly noticeable in the last dozen lines, is carefully managed. The final speech, led up to by two or three preceding speeches, is perfect in its focussing of interests. The compactness of these few lines, the rapid dénouement, the breathless interest all testify to Shakspere's plan of welding the various parts of the farce into a perfect whole. If the poet then reveals such care in this matter could he possibly have wished to defeat his very purpose by introducing Sly? He wanted totality of effect, a characteristic, as we have seen, of his mature works. The only way to have it was to sacrifice everything in favor of the tamer and the shrew; for it does not seem probable in view of these facts that Shakspere would permit a puppet to engage the attention of the spectators. *The Shrew* with him would have a defect; without him it is a finished piece of work.

Furthermore, there is evidence of a definite nature indicating that the dramatist while composing the Induction deliberately planned Sly's dismissal. We have seen that the rogue was physically and mentally beyond his depth: his closing remarks (end of I. i.) reveal his drowsiness and boredom:

> *First Serv.* My lord, you nod; you do not mind the play.
> *Sly.* Yes, by Saint Anne, do I. A good matter, surely;
>   comes there any more of it?
> *Page.* My lord, 'tis but begun.
> *Sly.* 'Tis a very excellent piece of work, madam lady:
>   would 'twere done!
>
> [I. i. 249-54]

From these lines it would seem clear that the poet had no further intention of keeping the tinker.

Additional testimony of a peculiarly interesting character supports such a view. The reference in the Induction of the old play to the moral *A Shrew* would furnish all husbands has been entirely omitted by Shakspere. This omission can hardly be accidental. Moreover scholars have observed that the old play rounds out completely; but has the nature of the conclusion been carefully noted? Making all due allowances for a drunken and illiterate rogue's inability to keep awake, we yet have the inartistic ending of *A Shrew,* namely, its lesson.

> *Sly.*   Who's this? Tapster? Oh, lord, sirrah, I have had
>   The bravest dream to-night, that ever thou
>   Heardest in all thy life!
> *Tapster.*   Ay, marry, but you had best get you home,
>   For your wife will course you for dreaming
>   here to-night.
> *Sly.*   Will she? I know now how to tame a shrew!
>   I dreamt upon it all this night till now,
>   And thou hast waked me out of the best dream
>   That ever I had in my life.
>   But I'll to my wife presently
>   And tame her too, and if she anger me.

That Shakspere on artistic grounds could have retained such an ending is, in the light of his other plays, highly improbable. To be sure the author of the old play has done well enough with the moral as such. But that is not the problem before us. Shakspere, in omitting the allusion to it in his Induction, did not intend that *The Shrew* should point a lesson, Hazlitt notwithstanding. Let us grant for the moment that Sly's benediction would not have dissipated the interests of the audience; it yet would have been an inartistic ending, wholly unlike anything in Shakspere. Therefore, once granted that the moral could not be superimposed, what excuse was there for

keeping Sly on the stage? He had never, it will be remembered, seen a play,—another touch in *A Shrew* which was dropped by Shakspere. Unlike Polonius, therefore, he could not criticise its art. Nor could it be in the manner of a climax to have him dismiss the spectators, with the request that he be left alone with his wife. And it certainly would be an anti-climax to have the play end with another of his requests for ale! What, therefore, *could* he say or do?

Of course, the question Why did the poet write the Induction at all? still remains. There is, when all is said and done, the imperfection. Apparently he saw the difficulty early, if indeed not from the beginning. For, if the observation above is correct, he planned the dismissal of the rogue in the Induction. At any rate, the humorous references to the Midlands—seemingly reminiscences of his youth—indicate that the poet enjoyed the writing of this prologue. The added concreteness and richness of detail, in which the framework of the source is clothed with flesh and blood, is likewise of the poet's best. One noticeable improvement stands out, in the substitution of the hostess for the tapster of *A Shrew;* and the dialogue that follows between the drunken tinker and the hostess foreshadows what is soon to come in the scenes at the Boar's Head Tavern. Of irksomeness and weariness, therefore, no hint appears in this preface.

Assuming that the dramatist may have seen from the first the inevitable imperfection, we may imagine that he argued in one of two ways. He could have reasoned that the flaw was not venial; no one can urge that the slip is worse than some others that might be mentioned: for instance the untimely disappearance of old Adam [in *As You Like It*], as well as the Fool in *Lear.* Indeed these two apparent blunders seem the result of carelessness or indifference, for (unlike Sly to all appearances) no provision for their going had been made. Obviously in the very nature of the form the bit of inartistic fault in *The Shrew* is more conspicuous. However, it is unlikely that Sly, anymore than Adam or the Fool, was missed by the audience, and Shakspere did not write for critics of another age. The spectators, once engrossed in the doings of the tamer and the shrew, forgot all about the tinker. Or, in the second place, the poet may have argued that he would like to try his hand at an innovation. Quiller-Couch has shown, in a stimulating book [*Shakespeare's Workmanship*], that the dramatist throughout his career never wearied of experiments. Inasmuch as an Induction does not appear in any other play, Shakspere may have wished to see the effect of one on the audience. It lay before him in his source; why not use it? Why not, especially, when *A Shrew* as we know, was popular. The choice of a theme familiar to his audience upon which to build a comedy or tragedy was, moreover, his usual practice.

At all events, the lively and graceful lines in the Induction testify to his pleasure in composing it; the spectators presumably were entertained by it, forgetting all about Sly in their enjoyment of the inimitable farce to follow. Hence, for all practical purposes the rogue had served his usefulness, in that he had given a novel setting to a good play. In short, the Induction had furnished a farcical atmosphere for a farcical story. The way to the dramatist was then left open to write a farce that has proved to be his masterpiece, in which he was to obtain a totality of effect that the tinker's presence would make impossible; a farce, the technique of which equals the master's best achievements in comedy and tragedy. (pp. 321-29)

Ernest P. Kuhl, "Shakspere's Purpose in Dropping

Sly," in Modern Language Notes, *Vol. XXXVI, No. 6, June, 1921, pp. 321-29.*

C. J. Sisson   (essay date 1955)

[*Sisson examines problems the Induction raises for stage directors, maintaining that the absence of an epilogue may be the result of improper text deletions before the play was printed in the First Folio of 1623. He also explores modern reactions to Petruchio's taming of Kate.*]

The Taming of the Shrew is generally looked upon to-day as a play for groundlings, for the actor and for the box office, not for the critic (whether daily, weekly, or bookly) nor for the intelligentsia. Yet for Hazlitt, no mean critic, it was the only real "problem play" in Shakespeare. Dr. Johnson found it admirable in construction, and very diverting and sprightly. But the play has now, and for long, been under a critical cloud, scholar and critic vying in emulative rivalry of distaste, which has spread widely even into our schools, and is indeed becoming orthodox and established. One perfunctory notice of the 1954 *Shrew* at Stratford was chiefly taken up with a statement of the critic's dislike of the play as a brutal, revolting farce, not to be approved however performed, a simple excommunication of a work of dramatic art by a master. Strong protests have been made even against its use for reading in schools, as conducive to juvenile delinquency or at least to bad manners. Broadcast currency was recently given to a nauseous interpretation of the play as Shakespeare's revenge upon his wife, the mother of his three children, for her shrewishness (of which there is, of course, no evidence whatever).

André Maurois, in a recent article in a French newspaper, declared it to be a capital fault in dramatic criticism to be governed by the fashions of the day and to neglect historical and general criteria. In this instance the prevalent moral and aesthetic distaste for certain plays of Shakespeare (for *The Shrew* is not alone in being under a cloud) derives largely from the fashions of yesterday. The weight of Victorian refinement and sentimentalism lies heavy upon us still. Such once popular guides to opinion as Morton Luce's *Handbook to Shakespeare* (1906) have exercised an influence traceable most unexpectedly, and ineffaceably, even in a world striving at all costs to be modern in its critical outlook, and Hollywood's idolatry of woman has joined hands with gallant memories in England of the Lady of Shalott.

The odd thing is that this seems to be a purely masculine reaction to the play. Actresses battle for the joy of playing Katherine, who is in fact the most spirited woman's part in Shakespeare, along with another Katherine, Kate Percy [in *1 Henry IV*], and Beatrice in *Much Ado,* all young women with a marked leavening of shrewishness in their being. They are indeed young women of authentic Elizabethan vintage. The delight of the feminine part of the audiences which revels in the play is not all unthinking merriment. They emerge moved, thoughtful too, and questioning with themselves, especially the young married women, who somehow envy Katherine after all. It is astonishing to me that the plain facts of the play are obscured by blind prejudice. When the play opens Katherine is unhappy, at odds with herself and the world, discontented, *dépaysée* [out of her element]. When it ends, she is radiant and secure, mistress of herself, and is at peace with the universe. To consider the play as a mere farce, to play it as a farce, is plain *lèse majesté,* and reduces a true

comedy to the level suggested by the title *Kiss Me Kate,* which in French becomes *Embrasse-moi chérie,* a Palais Royal title if ever there was one. But producers have gone against the tide of critical fashion, and Petruchio's whip, a feature of Restoration and later productions, no longer comes near Katherine.

For the producer, the chief problem is the Induction, the setting of the main play in the framework of a performance by a travelling company before a Lord in his country house, as part of the Lord's elaborate jest upon a drunken tinker, Christopher Sly. It is also taken generally as his only opportunity for originality, for the play in other respects plays itself and can hardly go wrong if the "book" is followed. The Induction, indeed, looms large in most productions and usurps upon the main play as an accompaniment and running commentary throughout. This arrangement, of course, presents obvious difficulties. Sly and his bed, the Lord and his servants, occupy part of the stage, which is thus denied to the play itself. (It is clear that the Elizabethan setting avoided this difficulty by using the upper stage or balcony stage for the Induction, as the Folio stage-directions prove.) Shakespeare's "book" provides nothing for them to *say,* and the yawning void is filled up with "business" which has to be invented to give them something at least to *do.* The result is, for the vast majority of audiences, a series of tiresome distractions from the absorbing and complex action of a tightly constructed play, and the intrusion of charade upon drama, a continuous obstacle to that suspension of disbelief which is dramatic illusion. There is obvious inconsistency in playing the Page's impersonation of a lady at the level of Belles in Battledress, for the servants of an Elizabethan Lord were often not untrained in playing, the Lord himself expressly trusts their capacity for acting their parts, and boys played women's parts on the professional stage. There is room enough for some finer distinction between the amateur actors (the Lord's men) and the professionals performing the main play. (Some distinction, as Mr. Glen Byam Shaw pointed out to me, is necessary to any thoughtful production.) Shakespeare's actors would have been capable of this, and his audience of appreciating it, as would indeed modern actors and audiences. These problems arise only in the continuance of the Induction throughout the play and into an Epilogue.

It is well known that the authoritative text of the play, the text of the First Folio of 1623, gives no support to this continuance of the Induction throughout the action, or to the conclusion of the play in a final return to the Induction ending with the departure of the travelling company and the awakening of Sly. In the Folio, the Induction is a prologue-framework. After a brief comment at the end of the first scene of the play the characters of the Induction disappear for good from "aloft", where the curtains are drawn, and there is no Epilogue. The material for the continued Induction and for the Epilogue all comes from the text of the 1594 quarto play *The Taming of a Shrew,* long thought to be the source used by Shakespeare but now generally agreed to be a corrupt, pirated, improvised text of his play. There can be little doubt that the Induction as given in the quarto points, however imperfectly, to the original form taken by Shakespeare's play. Why then have the later Induction passages disappeared in the Folio text, which is so manifestly the true text, resting upon a prompt-copy? Explanations offered, such as a mere accident of the printing-house, or truncation to economise in cast for travelling, are very unconvincing. The Folio text gives evidence of revision during the history of the play before

1623, during the thirty years of its career since its writing in 1592-3. It may well be that the later parts of the Induction were cut for those very reasons which have here been urged against the continuation of the Induction in a modern production, as Benson cut the whole in his Stratford production. We may not unreasonably recall Hamlet's protest against the abuse of clownery interfering with the necessary business of a play. The cut was probably made upon a later revival of the play, if we accept the evidence of the quarto as reflecting the original acting version. The comment at the end of the first scene of the play would then be an accidental survival, due to imperfect deletion in the "book" of the play. There are examples of such survivals elsewhere in the Folio. If so, the Folio text represents the final, approved, acting text of the play, restricting the Induction to the function of a Prologue but I see no reason for doubting that it was done by Shakespeare in consultation with his fellow actors.

If it is argued that the play as a whole is rounded off, the circle completed, by the Induction-Epilogue, it can be argued with at least equal force that its omission brings the play to an end upon a magnificent curtain, hard upon the climax of its action, and avoids an anti-climax, mainly in dumbshow, following upon the most awkward of intervals between the play and the Epilogue. Another attraction of the Epilogue is the opportunity it gives of dignifying the play with an esoteric interpretation as a commentary upon life and art, upon "the baseless fabric of a vision" caught and made permanent only by art. But I do not believe that this was in the early Shakespeare's mind. *The Shrew,* indeed, is recalcitrant to critical voyages of discovery, in the modern style, of new-found lands of Shakespeare. With Sly as a star part, again not without Chaplinesque touches of pathos and mystery, it becomes impossible in a modern production to dismiss him from the play after the Prologue. He must be amply provided for, and share the curtain. On Shakespeare's stage, I suspect, the part of Sly was doubled with that of Grumio in the revised version of the play. But this would perhaps offend against modern stage decorum.

We may well consider the function and operation elsewhere of a continuous Induction and Commentary upon a play enclosed within it. Fletcher's *The Knight of the Burning Pestle* makes it clear that in such a structure for comedy the principal interest naturally resides in the Presenters, to use the Elizabethan term, and that the intention of the play as a whole is essentially satirical, in this instance social satire allied with satire upon popular literary taste. To such an end the device is entirely suited. It is indeed an admirable vehicle for the explicit purpose. But the formula cannot be applied to *The Taming of the Shrew.* Whatever canons of dramatic art are brought into operation here as general and historical criteria, to use Maurois' phrase, they are those of romantic comedy. The play must moreover be judged in the light of some reasonable familiarity with the outlook and the principles of Elizabethan English society, with the life and the people of Shakespeare's day, with the world reflected in the play. Does anyone, even the most incurable survivor of Victorian romanticism, deny that *The Taming of the Shrew* has a happy ending, for Katherine as for Petruchio? The audience, at any creditable performance of the play, is left in no doubt after the curtain. It is as vain to plead that Katherine ought to be resentful as it is to urge that Isabella in *Measure for Measure* should not have been so fussy about committing a deadly sin. Marriage was a serious affair to the Elizabethans, as also to most Second Elizabethans. The marriage service which sanc-

tifies it is still concerned with the future, with promises and undertakings. It is a sacred contract. "Marriage," said G. K. Chesterton, "is a duel to the death." And Shakespeare, in *The Taming of the Shrew,* shows how with two swordsmen worthy of each other's steel both, paradoxically, can win. I wish I could be as secure of the enduring happiness of Bassanio and Portia [in *The Merchant* of Venice], of Ferdinand and Miranda [in *The Tempest*], as I can of Katherine and Petruchio. To be able to think thus of the matter is evidence enough that the play is neither satire nor farce, but true comedy. (pp. 25-7)

C. J. Sisson, in a review of "The Taming of the Shrew," in Drama, *London, No. 38, Autumn, 1955, pp. 25-7.*

Karl P. Wentersdorf   (essay date 1978)

[*Wentersdorf examines the framing device in* The Taming of the Shrew, *arguing that another Christopher Sly scene originally ended the play, but was somehow lost or excised before the play was included in the First Folio. In a portion of his essay not reprinted here, Wentersdorf presents a table that shows the distribution of virtually all the characters throughout the play and indicates, as well, which characters enter at the beginning of a scene and which ones remain on stage to the end.*]

The weight of modern critical opinion leans rather heavily toward the view that Shakespeare's interest in Christopher Sly did not end with the opening scenes of *The Taming of the Shrew.* Those two scenes, now known as the Induction though they are not distinguished thus in the First Folio, introduce the drunken tinker Sly and show him being duped by a Lord into believing that he himself is a nobleman and married to a beautiful lady (the Lord's page in disguise); and they leave him, anxious though he is to go to bed, as he settles down to watch from "aboue" the presentation of a "pleasant Comedie," acted by travelling players who have arrived to entertain the real Lord:

> *Beg.* Marrie I will let them play, it is not a Comontie, a
>   Christmas gambold, or a tumbling tricke?
> *Lady.* No my good Lord, it is more pleasing stuffe.
> *Beg.* What, household stuffe.
> *Lady.* It is a kinde of history.
> *Beg.* Well, we'l see't:
> Come Madam wife sit by my side,
> And let the world slip, we shall nere be yonger.
>   [Ind. ii. 137-43]

With this, the second scene of the Induction comes to an end. Trumpets sound a flourish, two players (Lucio and Tranio) enter, and the play within the play begins.

There has naturally been some difference of opinion as to why the Folio text, the only surviving version of Shakespeare's original play, does not end with scenes showing Sly being removed from his point of vantage "aboue" and taken back, in a drunken sleep, to the place in front of the alehouse where he was first discovered. The "bad" anonymous Quarto entitled *The taming of a Shrew,* with its similar plot lines and parallel though differently named characters, does have such scenes. The alternatives are clear: either Shakespeare did not complete the framework story, having tired of the Sly business or perhaps never having intended to develop it beyond the end of the episodes surviving in the First Folio, in which case it was left for the mediocre writer responsible for the patchwork text of *A Shrew* to invent the conclusion to the framework that is found in the Quarto; or one must assume that Shakespeare did write some final scenes for Sly. Critics favoring the latter assumption, which seems to me much the more reasonable of the two, have offered two possible though not mutually exclusive explanations for the disappearance of the scenes before the manuscript used as text-copy arrived at the printing-house: either the last leaf of the manuscript, containing the conclusion of the Sly framework, had somehow been lost, or the play had undergone at some time in its history a revision dictated by the necessity for staging the comedy with a smaller cast. According to Alexander, when Shakespeare first wrote *The Taming of the Shrew,* "some time before the closing of the theaters in 1592," he then had "at his disposal a company of considerable size that would allow the tinker and his aristocratic attendants to sit and watch the Shrew piece," and it was this version of the play that was reflected in the corrupt Quarto version; at some time after 1592, however, "the Sly business was cut down as too demanding in personnel." (pp. 201-02)

From [a casting] analysis, it is evident that in the original Shakespearian version, in which the Sly framework was hypothetically complete, the number of actors with speaking parts required to stage V.i-ii was sixteen (not counting a minimum of five supernumeraries for servants, attendants, and an officer): there are eleven roles for adult actors (Sly and Lord "aboue"; Baptista, Vincentio, Lucentio, Petruchio, Gremio, Hortensio, Tranio, Grumio, and the Pedant) and five boys' roles (the Page "aboue"; Biondello, Katherina, Bianca, and the Widow). Without excision, doubling is impossible for the sixteen major roles. Since two of the eleven adult characters in V.i-ii are found only in the later part of the play—the Pedant first appears in IV.ii, Vincentio in IV.v—economy in casting could be effected by cutting the Sly episodes from IV and V, in which case the actors of Sly and the Lord could double as the Pedant and Vincentio, and the boy-actor who played the Page disguised as Sly's Lady could double as the Widow.

The world of the Elizabethan theater is known to have gone through a period of considerable financial difficulty and professional disruption during the plague years of 1592-1594. There is a considerable body of evidence pointing to the abridgement of plays to permit staging by smaller companies. For this reason, the abridgement theory as an explanation for the loss of the final part of the Sly framework carries conviction.

There is some internal evidence in *The Taming of the Shrew* which, though it does not necessitate acceptance of the abridgement theory, certainly supports it strongly. The surviving framework elements include, in addition to the two scenes of the Induction, a brief inter-scene episode at the end of the third scene (I.i in modern editions):

> *Exeunt. The Presenters aboue speakes.*
> I. *Man.* My Lord you nod, you do not minde the play.
> *Beg.* Yes by Saint Anne do I, a good matter surely: Comes there any more of it?
> *Lady.* My Lord, 'tis but begun.
> *Beg.* 'Tis a verie excellent peece of worke, Madame Ladie: would 'twere done. *They sit and marke.*
>
> [I. i. 249-54]

It has been argued, strange as it may seem, that this passage indicates the point at which Sly and his attendants leave the play. Alexander, who characterized such an interpretation as "singularly inaccurate," rightly insisted that the stage-direction "They sit and marke" is an unmistakable indication

of the author's intention that the Presenters, seated in the gallery "aboue" and watching the action taking place on the platform stage, were to remain and observe the whole process of taming that was just about to begin. That Sly should drink too freely of the Lord's sack and ultimately fall into a stupor has no effect on the watching of the comedy by the other Presenters, though it turns out to be a convenient preliminary to the final episode in which Sly is transported back to the spot where he was originally found.

This inter-scene episode calls to mind the kind of brief scene which Shakespeare elsewhere uses as a special structural device to mark the passage of dramatic time. Such technical scenes often introduce nonce characters; they seldom advance the action in any way and could be removed without affecting the story line in any markedly disruptive fashion; yet in the Elizabethan theater, with its customary continuous action, the excision of such scenes would have created time problems. Consider the episode of the Scrivener in *Richard III:* in III.v, the Dukes of Gloucester and Buckingham plot to induce the citizens of London to appeal to Gloucester to ascend the throne, and the scene ends with Gloucester's cynical comments on his preparations for this goal; at the beginning of III.vii, Buckingham reports to Gloucester on the citizens' initially unfavorable reaction to the scheme; and covering the passage of time between these two important episodes is a fourteen-line scene (III.vi) in which the Scrivener soliloquizes on Hastings' indictment. Similarly in *2 Henry IV,* V.iii, when Falstaff—in Gloucestershire—hears that Prince Hal has become king, he rushes off to London; at the beginning of V.v, in Westminster (after four lines spoken by the Grooms), Falstaff enters to await the new king's approach; and the time occupied by Falstaff's long ride back to the capital is covered by the brief episode (V.iv) in which the Beadles arrest Hostess Quickly and Doll Tearsheet. And in *Julius Caesar,* III.ii, after Antony has stirred up the crowd against the conspirators, he is informed that Octavius has arrived in Rome and he goes off to meet him; at the beginning of IV.i, Antony and Octavius enter with Lepidus to discuss the measures to be taken against the conspirators and their supporters; and the time lapse between these two historically significant incidents is bridged by the brief scene (III.iii) in which Cinna the Poet is attacked by the Roman mob. All of these short scenes are structurally necessary, even though from the standpoint of a smooth and logical development of the story line they could be described as expendable.

This Shakespearian technique in the structuring of scene sequences has been noted and discussed by various scholars. It was observed that in plays written before 1608 (when the King's company acquired the Blackfriars Theater, Shakespeare habitually avoided exits immediately followed by reentrances of the same characters, and this practice came to be known as the "Law of Reentry." The nature of the so-called law was summarized by Irwin Smith [in "Their Exits and Reentrances," *Shakespeare Quarterly,* 18 (1967)]:

> Shakespeare avoided having a character enter the stage at the beginning of an act or scene after having been on stage at the end of the preceding act or scene. He did so because intermissions were unknown in the public playhouses for which he wrote all his earlier plays, and because, with act following hard upon act and scene upon scene, the player who departed at the end of an act or scene and then reentered at the beginning of the next, would be reentering immediately. An immediate reentrance

could only seem futile and bewildering. Presumably the player departed in the first instance in order to accomplish some dramatic purpose, perhaps to make an imaginary behind-the-scenes journey. . . . Any such journey must inevitably occupy some dramatic time, however much that time might be foreshortened in performance; but if the player returned immediately, his reentry necessarily denied that any time had elapsed, and thus denied that he had accomplished the purpose for which he departed.

If there was no necessary piece of action to be developed while the journey or other off-stage business was being undertaken, Shakespeare neatly solved the problem by inserting a short "time-lapse" scene.

It is conceivable that one or other of the later Sly episodes was a scene of this nature, having been created partially for its comic effect but primarily to suggest the passage of time. In this case, its excision might have left some detectable irregularity in the Folio text.

For indications as to where Sly episodes may have occurred in the original play, we have to rely on the corrupt text of *A Shrew*. The "bad" Quarto lacks a counterpart to the first inter-scene Sly episode cited above, but it has an episode at the point corresponding to I.ii < > II.i in modern editions of the Folio text:

> Then *Slie* speaks.
> *Slie. Sim*, when wil the foole come againe?
> *Lord.* Heele come againe my Lord anon.
> *Slie.* Gis some more drinke here, souns wheres The Tapster, here *Sim* eate some of these things.
> *Lord.* So I do my Lord.
> *Slie.* Heere *Sim* I drinke to thee.
> *Lord.* My Lord, heere comes the plaiers againe.
> *Slie.* O braue, heers two fine gentlewomen.

The disappearance from the authorial text of an episode parallel to this has not left any trace in the Folio: II.i begins with a clear change in location and characters. Curiously enough, there is an irregularity at this point in the Quarto. The last line of the Sly episode, "O braue, heers two fine gentlewomen," is spoken as the Players enter, but the characters who appear are 'Tranio' and 'Kate.' In the Folio version, II.i opens with the entrance of Katherina and Bianca, the two principal gentlewomen making their first appearance in the play; and it seems to me that the Sly episode in the Quarto must here embody the reporter-writer's memory of the action in the Shakespearian version.

The Quarto contains three further Sly episodes before the conclusion now known as the Epilogue. One is a very brief comment on a courtship scene between 'Lucentio' and 'Bianca' (a scene that is the counterpart to IV.iv in the Folio):

> *Slie. Sim*, must they be married now?
> *Lord.* I my Lord.
>   Enter *Ferando* ['Petruchio'] *and Kate and*
>   *Sander* ['Grumio']
> *Slie.* Looke *Sim* the foole is come againe now.

The next episode occurs in the course of the Quarto counterpart to Shakespeare's V.i, when 'Tranio' and the 'Pedant' are impersonating 'Lucentio' and 'Vincentio': in the Quarto text, 'Vincentio' orders that the impersonators be arrested, and it is at this point that Sly interrupts from "aboue":

> Then *Slie* speaks.

> *Slie. I* say weele haue no sending to prison.
> *Lord.* My Lord this is but the play, theyre but in iest.
> *Slie.* I tel thee *Sim* weele haue no sending,
> *To* prison thats flat: why *Sim* am not I *Don Christo Vari?*
> *Therefore I* say they shall not goe to prison.
> *Lord.* No more they shal not my Lord,
> They are runne away.
> *Slie.* Are they run away *Sim?* thats wel,
> Then gis some more drinke, and let them play againe.
> *Lord.* Here my Lord.
>   *Slie* drinkes and then fals a sleepe.

Since this episode occurs in mid-scene, it does not serve a purely structural purpose. It does, however, bring the attention of the real audience to Sly's continuing presence, to his simulated concern at what is going on in the comedy, to his increasing state of inebriation, and to his lapse into drunken slumber, this time for good.

The next inter-scene episode is by far the most interesting. It occurs in the Quarto at the point corresponding to V.i < > ii in *The Shrew,* that is, immediately before the finale of the play within the play. The preceding scene takes place out-of-doors and includes the already mentioned business of the attempted arrest of the impersonators; 'Lucentio' begs his father's forgiveness, 'Vincentio' grants it, and the scene ends with 'Baptista,' 'Vincentio,' 'Lucentio,' 'Hortensio,' and the others leaving to attend the wedding feast. The inter-scene episode follows:

> *Slie* sleepes.
> *Lord.* Whose within there? come hither sirs my Lords
> A sleepe againe: go take him easily vp,
> *A*and put him in his own apparell againe,
> *A*nd lay him in the place where we did find him,
> Iust vnderneath the alehouse side below,
> But see you wake him not in any case.
>   *Boy.* It shalbe don my Lord, come helpe to beare him
>   hence.
>   *Exit*

This serves the immediate dramatic purpose of alerting the real audience to the impending reversion of Sly to his former poverty-stricken existence. Immediately after the withdrawal of the Lord from "aboue," with his attendants carrying off the sleeping tinker, 'Lucentio,' 'Hortensio,' and 'Tranio' enter to continue the post-banquet merry-making of the finale.

The absence of a Sly episode at V.i < > ii in the Folio version very definitely creates a problem. Scene V.i takes place, as in the Quarto, out-of-doors, and the location is twice emphasized in the course of the dialogue. Petruchio, on his way with Katherina to attend the celebration of Bianca's wedding, brings Vincentio to the house where his son is lodging:

> *Petr.* Sir heres the doore, this is *Lucentios* house,
> My Fathers beares more toward the Market-place,
> Thither must I, and here I leaue you sir.
>   [V. i. 8-10]

Before he exits, there follows the exposure of the fraudulent Vincentio, during the course of which Baptista, Bianca, and Gremio appear. At the end of the scene, as they all go off, Petruchio holds Katherina back for a moment and there is a brief exchange, again underscoring the location:

> *Kate.* Husband let's follow, to see the end of this adoe.
> *Petr.* First kisse me *Kate,* and we will.
> *Kate.* What in the midst of the streete?
>   [V. i. 142-44]

Thus as they exit, attended by their servant Grumio, the audience is reminded that they have not quite completed their trip to Baptista's.

At the beginning of the immediately following scene, which takes place inside Lucentio's house, all of these characters re-enter for the celebration *subsequent* to the nuptial feast at Baptista's house. The Folio stage-direction reads as follows:

> *Enter Baptista, Vincentio, Gremio, the Pedant, Lucentio, and*
>> *Bianca. Tranio, Biondello Grumio, and Widdow:*
>>> *The Seruingmen with Tranio bringing*
>>>> *in a Banquet.*
>>>>> [s.d. V. ii. 1]

It is odd, to say the least, that the names of Petruchio and Katherina are missing from this entrance, even while the direction brings on their servant Grumio! The omission, however, is only one of several that have to be corrected in modern editions of the play. Carelessness with both entrances and exits is one of the notable characteristics of the Folio text. That Petruchio and Katherina were intended by Shakespeare to appear with the others at the very beginning of the scene is evident from the fact that they are addressed personally in the first speech of the scene, and that Petruchio is the first to comment on that speech:

> *Luc.* At last, though long, our iarring notes agree,
> And time it is when raging warre is come,
> To smile at scapes and perils ouerblowne:
> My faire *Bianca* bid my father welcome,
> While I with selfesame kindnesse welcome thine:
> Brother *Petruchio*, sister *Katerina*,
> And thou *Hortentio* with thy louing *Widdow:*
> Feast with the best, and welcome to my house,
> My Banket is to close our stomakes vp
> After our great good cheere: praie you sit downe,
> For now we sit to chat as well as eate.
>> *Petr.* Nothing but sit and sit, and eate and eate.
>>> [V. ii. 1-12]

There is not the slightest indication, here or elsewhere, that Petruchio and Katherina were originally intended to come on stage some time after the rest.

This anomaly has not passed unnoticed. In his recent article on the "Law of Reentry," Irwin Smith points out that although there are approximately 750 scenes in the Shakespearian canon, there are not more than sixteen reentrances that conceivably represent departures from the dramatist's habitual practice. One of these is the situation at V.i < > ii in *The Taming of the Shrew*. In nearly all of the sixteen cases, Smith argues, the departure is more apparent than real. He suspects that in several of the sixteen instances, the supposedly reentering character had not really exited in the first place (so that there was really no question of reentry). Regarding the few remaining doubtful cases, he feels that "since Shakespeare clearly made it his concern to avoid immediate reentrances, we should probably find that he has done so in the doubtful instances also, if we knew all the facts relating to their presentation on the Elizabethan stage."

In his discussion of the problem at V.i < > ii in *The Shrew*, Smith concludes that this is one of the instances in which the breach of the "Law of Reentry" is more apparent than real:

> Petruchio and Katherina are on a street before Lu-

centio's house at the end of V.i, and are inside the house at the beginning of V.ii. They are not listed among the persons who enter at the beginning of the latter scene, but their entrance cannot be long delayed, since they are addressed at line 6 and Petruchio speaks at line 12. I suggest that they are absent from the stage only momentarily, if at all. At the beginning of V.ii the stage curtains open to reveal the rear stage as the interior of the house, with serving-men bringing on a banquet, and Petruchio and Katherina merely pass from the platform, as the street in front of Lucentio's house, to the rear stage as its interior. Their reentrance, if in fact they do not remain continuously in view of the audience, thus does little violence to the rule.

In brief, the problem, according to Smith, is really nonexistent because the supposedly reentering characters (Petruchio, Katherina, and Grumio) either leave the stage "momentarily" or not at all.

It is true that at the end of V.i, Petruchio and Katherina are on the street in front of Lucentio's house, and that at the beginning of V.ii they are inside the same house, attending a celebration honoring the new bridal pairs. What Smith seems to have overlooked, however, is that when Petruchio enters with Katherina in V.i, he is en route to the house of his father-in-law Baptista, which "beares more toward the Market-place" [V. i. 9]. He explains to Vincentio, "Thither must I" [V. i. 10]; and, of course, not only he and Katherina but all the others must make their way to Baptista's for the nuptial celebration. It can never have been true, therefore, that Petruchio and Katherina "merely pass from the platform, as the street in front of Lucentio's house, to the rear stage as its interior." Dramatic propriety makes it impossible for them to remain, as Smith implies might have been the stage practice, "continuously in view of the audience." On the contrary, there can be no doubt that Shakespeare intended Petruchio and Katherina to leave by one of the side doors, in the already indicated direction of the market-place, on their way to Baptista's. Furthermore, some time elapses between V.i and V.ii, during which—and it is Lucentio's opening speech which reveals the fact—the "great good cheere" [V. ii. 10] of the wedding banquet has been enjoyed at Baptista's house. It is only when this feast is over that the bridal couples and their guests, as listed (though incompletely) in the opening stage-direction of V.ii, can repair to Lucentio's lodging for the final celebration and the wagering.

In the text as it stands, there is an unmistakable violation of the Shakespearian "Law of Reentry." The anomaly strongly suggests that there has been some dislocation of the text at this point in the manuscript handed to the printer of the Folio. The simplest way to account for the irregularity is to posit the original existence of an intervening episode, however brief, that would cover—adequately for dramatic purposes—the supposed passage of several hours of real time. With a Sly episode at this point comparable to that in the Quarto, there would be no breach of the "Law of Reentry." Such a scene, however, implies the existence of a final episode or Epilogue returning the still sleeping tinker to the place where he was first found, in front of the alehouse. I therefore believe that the irregularity at V.i < > ii is a second piece of evidence supporting the theory that the framework was complete in Shakespeare's original version of *The Taming of the Shrew*.

How does the theory of abridgement fit in with current views as to the provenience of the copy-text for the First Folio's *Taming of the Shrew*? The theory was set forth long before there was any serious discussion regarding the nature of the copy-text. In 1928, Wilson argued [in "The Copy for *The Taming of the Shrew*, 1623," in the New Cambridge text] that the Folio text was printed from a carelessly made transcript of the author's holograph, a transcript that bore evidence of use in the playhouse. Chambers likewise felt [in his *William Shakespeare*, I] that the manuscript had doubtless "been used as stage-copy." The prevailing view today is that the copy-text was in all likelihood Shakespeare's holograph. The fullness and indefiniteness of some of the stage-directions suggest the hand of the author; the irregularity with regard to character-names and speech-prefixes and the omission of entrances and exits are typical of the carelessness that Shakespeare evidently permitted himself in preparing the dramatic manuscripts he handed to his fellows. If the signs that are sometimes adduced as evidence of a bookkeeper's handling of the autograph manuscript have been correctly interpreted, then the intervention was erratic and tentative, and much tidying up was needed in the preparation of the fair copy, which would have to be licensed by the Master of the Queen's Revels before it could be used to stage the play. Irregularities of the kind surviving in the Folio text could hardly have been tolerated in the official prompt-book.

Given the likelihood that circumstances calling for an abridgement did arise in the years 1592-93, where and how could it have been carried out? Would the owners of the drama have abridged their licensed prompt-book? It would certainly have been an easy process, since it was a common Elizabethan practice to indicate the excision of passages or scenes in manuscripts by enclosing them in brackets or by drawing a line down the margin, parallel to the segment to be cut; where such methods were used, the cut passages could be restored at any time without difficulty. But if this kind of abridgement *was* made in the original playbook, it cannot have directly affected the transmission of the text, since the playbook does not appear to have been used as the copy-text in 1621.

The abridgement is therefore most likely to have been carried out on the authorial manuscript with all of its imperfections. Now if those imperfections, as perpetuated in the Folio text, are such as to negate any supposition that Shakespeare's holograph could have been used as prompt-copy by the full company during the original staging, would the mere excision of certain scenes have made it any the more usable by the smaller company for which the abridgement *ex hypothesi* was made? Must it not be assumed that these players would have needed a fair copy, too? One reason, of course, for the preparation of the original fair copy (in addition to the desirability of having a readily legible and internally consistent prompt-book) was the necessity for providing the Queen's censor with a clean manuscript that he would agree to read for the purpose of licensing. Now if a licence had already been obtained for the complete text, no further permission would have been needed for a mere abridgement. Furthermore, if the company making the abridgement were in financial difficulties, it is surely conceivable that the actors would have revised the author's original draft, by excising the later Sly scenes, and would then have used the shortened draft as a makeshift prompt-book. In the circumstances, it would be hazardous to suggest that a fair copy of the shortened version would have been called for; the authorial manuscript, with certain episodes cut out, might well have been considered ad-

equate for staging purposes, particularly since the play itself was already a well-established part of the company's repertory.

All of this is speculative and does not explain why the omitted scenes were not restored for the printing of the play in the First Folio. Even if the cancelled scenes had literally been cut out of the revised authorial draft or made illegible, why were they not restored from the full text in the company's official prompt-book? In their address to the readers of the First Folio, Shakespeare's fellows advertised the plays as being no longer "maimed" but now "cur'd, and perfect of their limbes," yet they seem to have forgotten or ignored the need for restoring the ending to the framework of *The Taming of the Shrew*. One realizes that it would be anachronistic to expect from Heminges and Condell anything like modern editorial attitudes regarding the faithful reproduction of the author's original intentions, even down to the smallest details, yet there remains a feeling of uneasiness at the thought that these "editors," true men of the theater, should not have bothered to reinstate at least the concluding scenes of the conceptually brilliant—and in the theater undoubtedly highly successful—framework of *The Shrew*. One possible explanation is that they believed the revision to have been carried out with Shakespeare's approval and therefore that the shortened text constituted an authentic if artistically less satisfactory version. Another possibility is that the licensed playbook containing the original ending was missing from the players' library of prompt-books when the printer called upon them to supply copy-text for *The Shrew;* the playbook of *The Winter's Tale* seems also to have been missing at the time when the printing of the First Folio was getting under way. (pp. 204-15)

Karl P. Wentersdorf, "The Original Ending of 'The Taming of the Shrew': A Reconsideration," in Studies in English Literature, 1500-1900, *Vol. XVIII, No. 2, Spring, 1978, pp. 201-15.*

Michael W. Shurgot   (essay date 1981)

[*Shurgot explores the various dimensions that can be added to the experience of* The Taming of the Shrew *when it is represented on the stage. He demonstrates this theory by describing how a performance of the Katherina and Petruchio courtship reveals a greater complexity of character than can be derived from a mere reading of the text.*]

J. Dover Wilson once remarked of *The Taming of the Shrew* [in his introduction to the Cambridge edition] that "although it reads rather ill in the library, it goes rather well on the stage." Wilson's remark separates the two distinctly different ways of experiencing a Shakespearean play. The first is "literary": an encounter with the text as a piece of literature to be studied, where such factors as our preconceptions of the play or knowledge of its sources, our previous readings of the play, and our knowledge of its "place" in Shakespeare's "development" all contribute to how we "see" or want to see a particular work. The second is "theatrical": an encounter with the play as Shakespeare originally intended it to be experienced—on the stage—where the sensory data of the production, including the director's use of lighting, blocking, props, music, his direction of the actors, and the actors' own interpretations of their roles may forge in our mind a new appreciation and understanding of a play we thought we knew quite well.

While reading (and carefully re-reading) Shakespeare's plays are certainly valuable and necessary for the teacher/scholar, nonetheless the "theatrical dimension" of Shakespeare criticism during the past two decades has shown clearly the error of judging how a play "reads" in the library independently of how it "goes" on the stage; or, what is worse, of assuming that the only valid criterion for judging one of Shakespeare's plays, either alone or compared with another, is a "scholarly" reading of the "literary" text. Dramaturgical considerations of Shakespeare's plays demand a more sensuously alert encounter with his words, and ask us to remember that in the theatre his text creates and energizes all that we see and hear. Dramaturgical considerations attempt to explain how he engages his audience's full participation in his plays, and how the contrasts and emphases of his "visual effects" complement a play's dramatic poetry to create "total theatre."

Theatrical criticism challenges one to perceive the dramaturgy implicit in Shakespeare's text, and meeting that challenge in the text of *The Shrew* provides a possible solution to Dover Wilson's dilemma. He is absolutely right about the play's theatrical appeal, yet he fails to see that the reasons for its stage success lie within the very text that he finds such a poor companion in the library. Although reading *The Shrew* may never be as intellectually stimulating as reading, say, *The Merchant of Venice* or *Hamlet* or *The Winter's Tale,* nonetheless when we examine the text of *The Shrew* as a theatre script we find ample evidence of why the play—*as a play*—goes well. In order to appreciate the dramatic energy of *The Shrew,* we must begin with Shakespeare's dramatic presentation of Petruchio and Katherina, for throughout the play the dynamics of their roles demonstrate forcefully how characters who may appear simplistic or "one-dimensional" on the page become complex and multi-dimensional on the stage and thus contribute enormously to a play's stagecraft.

Summarizing Shakespeare's achievement in comic characterization, M. C. Bradbrook writes [in her *The Growth and Structure of Elizabethan Comedy*] that while he adhered to the principle that comedy displays character, he "profoundly modified it by deepening and strengthening each separate character, developing the relationships between different characters, until the characters *became* the plot." Bradbrook adds that Shakespeare evolved a form of "interior metamorphosis" among his comic figures that permitted them "to develop," rather than being "transformed by some exterior violence" as often happens in earlier (e.g., Lylian) Elizabethan comedy. In the taming plot of *The Shrew,* Shakespeare invests his principal characters with a psychological and physical *vitality* noticeably lacking in the Bianca plot, and this vitality is the key to appreciating how Shakespeare exploits for maximum theatrical effect the idea contained in his folk tale sources. Shakespeare's portrayal of Petruchio and Katherina from a theatrical perspective, the perspective of their physical relations, reveals how he creates from their intriguing conflict what Styan calls "total theatre," and how he theatrically involves his audience emotionally in the vital presence of the major characters and so in the play that they play out before us.

Following the "enormous explosion of energy" in the Induction, in which Shakespeare foreshadows in Sly's "transmutation" the change of personality that will occur in Katherina, the principal figures of the play are introduced and their types clearly presented. Katherina reveals her choleric nature in sharp, biting retorts to several other characters: to Hortensio's "No mates for you, / Unless you were of gentler, milder mould [I. i. 59-60], Kate immediately responds with the threatening, angry, explosive, and seemingly irrational aggression that marks her speech and action throughout most of the play:

> I' faith, sir, you shall never need to fear.
> Iwis it is not half way to her heart;
> But if it were, doubt not her care should be
> To comb your noodle with a three legg'd stool,
> And paint your face, and use you like a fool.
>
> [I. i. 61-5]

In a scene replete with polite conversation, Petrarchan raptures, and covert scheming, Kate's threatened violence stands apart and announces a socially disruptive, egocentric personality. Clearly she is one of the "raging fires" that are about to consume the stage—a "devil," a "fiend of hell"; in Tranio's phrase, "stark mad or wonderful froward" [I. i. 88, 69]. Kate's exit lines, following her father's polite, but feeble attempt to order her about ("Katherina, you may stay" [I. i. 100]), indicate her fierce independence that obviously plagues Baptista (and his traditional wedding formulae) but that paradoxically attracts Petruchio in II. i.: she retorts, "Why, and I trust I may go too, may I not? / What, shall I be appointed hours, as though (belike) / I knew not what to take and what to leave? Ha!" [I. i. 102-04]. The content of her early speech establishes tension between her and the predominant social environment, even as her tone and staccato rhythm immediately identify her as a major theatrical "force." Clearly, Kate *is* shrewish.

Yet Tranio's explanation to Lucentio that Baptista has kept Katherina "closely mew'd . . . up" because she "will not be annoy'd with suitors" [I. i. 183-84] is only partially correct. Kate's interest in and jealousy of Bianca's admirers are clearly evident in II. i., when the bound Bianca enters, naively assuming that Kate covets only material attractions, her garments and jewels. Kate, however, envies Bianca for her suitors, not just her fine attire: "Of all thy suitors here I charge [thee] tell / Whom thou lov'st best; see thou dissemble not" [II. i. 8-9]. Kate's envy indicates a natural longing for physical affection; hearing and seeing her cruel treatment of Bianca, we witness Kate's extremely "curst," volatile character. But while Kate may desire the active attention that Bianca receives, she resolutely determines that any such wooing will be conducted in her own manner. She will not alter her personality to attract the likes of Hortensio or Gremio, yet in her jealous rage she strikes Bianca attempting to force her to identify the favored wooer. When her father enters, Kate laments that she must "dance barefoot" on her sister's wedding day, that she is doomed to "lead apes in hell," and then departs, complaining, "I will go sit and weep, / Till I can find occasion of revenge" [II. i. 35-36]. H. B. Charlton [in his *Shakespearian Comedy*] thinks Katherina's pathetic claim is "widely out of character," but he fails to observe either the vigorous sincerity of Kate's desires for masculine company or the physical display of the complexity of her emotions at this point. She may indeed seek means of revenge, as any shrew would. But she may very likely "go sit and weep" also, frustrated by Bianca's "silence," and by her own solitude and failure to attract suitors.

Petruchio's entrance is even more rowdy than Kate's. His impatience with Grumio's word-game leads him to wring his servant's ear, employing the violence that Kate merely threatened in her first entrance. As Kate's aggression and impatience dominate her behavior in the previous scene, so Petruchio's description to Hortensio of his travels and his singular attitude regarding women and wooing emphasize his own unruly, indomitable character:

> Signior Hortensio, 'twixt such friends as we
> Few Words suffice; and therefore, if thou know
> One rich enough to be Petruchio's wife
> (As wealth is burthen of my wooing dance),
> Be she as foul as was Florentius' love,
> As old as Sibyl, and as curst and shrowd
> As Socrates' Xantippe, or a worse,
> She moves me not, or not removes at least
> Affection's edge in me. [Whe'er] she is as rough
> As are the swelling Adriatic seas,
> I come to wive it wealthily in Padua;
> If wealthily, then happily in Padua.
>
> [I. ii. 65-76]

Grumio's "Nay, look you, sir, he tells you flatly what / his mind is. . . . Why, nothing comes / amiss, so money comes withal" [I. ii. 77-8, 81-2] informs Hortensio and the audience that Petruchio means exactly what he says. Petruchio's concern with the material rewards of his wooing is central to the play; he is initially interested in Kate because her father is wealthy, and he is utterly unconcerned about her being, as Hortensio warns him, "intolerable curst / And shrowd and froward, so beyond all measure" [I. ii. 89-90]. Instead, he assumes that any woman of any temperament—be she a toothless "old trot" or have as many diseases as "two and fifty horses" [I. ii. 81]—will suit him provided her dowry suffices, an attitude towards marriage consistent with his obstinate, tenacious, and immensely self-confident nature. Petruchio will "board [Kate], though she chide as loud / As thunder when the clouds in autumn crack" [I. ii. 95-6]; having heard lions roar, the sea rage, and "great ordnance in the field," [I. ii. 203], "a woman's tongue" is to him less frightening than "a chestnut in a farmer's fire"—"Tush, tush, fear boys with bugs" [I. ii. 207, 209-10].

Intermingled among the various "supposes" and disguises of the developing Bianca plot through II. i., Petruchio's brash, boasting tone clearly establishes him, like Kate, as a significant theatrical force. Shakespeare's dramatization of Kate's and Petruchio's predominant characteristics in carefully juxtaposed scenes creates considerable anticipation within a theatre audience about the pair's eventual meeting. Kate's and Petruchio's language and tone exhibit considerable energy, but their interests are diametrically opposed; Petruchio's "business asketh haste" [II. i. 114], while marriage is "not half way to [Katherina's] heart" [I. i. 62]. Indeed Petruchio's impatience and bullishness prior to his meeting with Kate suggest that his stated willingness to marry her only because of her dowry is just what Grumio says it is: a "humor" that he says Hortensio should allow Petruchio to follow while it "lasts." The sense of spontaneity in this arrangement, and the sheer improbability of its succeeding, are reinforced by Grumio's description of the rhetorical (and possibly physical) violence Petruchio will use on Kate; by Petruchio's hyperbolic and seemingly irrational enthusiasm for Kate after Hortensio enters from her music lesson "with his head broke"— "Now by the world, it is a lusty wench! / I love her ten times more than e'er I did. / O, how I long to have some chat with her!" [II. i. 160-62]; and especially by Petruchio's short dialogue with Baptista. To Baptista's sensible caution that "specialities" can be arranged between them only "when the special thing is well obtain'd, / That is, her love; for that is all

in all" [II. i. 128-29], Petruchio responds, "Why, that is nothing; for I tell you, father, / I am as peremptory as she proudminded" [II. i. 130-31]. Petruchio assumes that both the process of winning Kate's affections and those affections themselves are "nothing"; he has decided even before meeting her that the actual "taming" of Kate will pose no challenge to his own rough, burly nature. Yet a theatre audience, having *heard* Kate's scolding tongue and having *seen* two examples of her violent temper in action by this point in the play, senses the folly of ignoring the wishes or usurping the will of a woman as independent as she. Petruchio is certainly something of a braggart soldier, a "madman in his senses" [William Hazlitt, in his *Characters of Shakespeare's Plays*]; but the combination of his cavalier attitude towards wooing Kate and her capacity for violence creates an anxiety, suspense, and uncertainty about this couple's initial meeting that we may not sense when reading the play but that creates in the theatre the interplay between stage and audience that keeps spectators alert and receptive.

The core of *The Shrew* is the clash between the two irascible individuals whom Shakespeare outlines in the early scenes of the play. Petruchio uses two tactics: first, in their initial encounter, a parodic portrayal of the courtly Petrarchan lover; and second, especially at the wedding and later at his estate, a frenetic, strident imitation of Kate's shrewishness that provides ample comic entertainment on the stage and simultaneously teaches her the social consequences of her habitual behavior. Petruchio's deliberately exaggerated mimicry of Kate supports his contention that he woos "not like a babe" [I.i.137]; and his well-calculated, ironic tactics indicate some depth in his character, for he has the presence of mind to perceive exactly how Kate must be tamed. In his soliloquy in II. i., Petruchio explains his "spirited" wooing:

> Say that she rail, why then I'll tell her plain
> She sings as sweetly as a nightingale;
> Say that she frown, I'll say she looks as clear
> As morning roses newly wash'd with dew;
> Say she be mute, and will not speak a word,
> Then I'll commend her volubility,
> And say she uttereth piercing eloquence;
>
> [II. i. 170-76]

By deliberately contradicting Kate's moods and actions Petruchio intends to exasperate her and so to anger her: and the more angry she becomes, the more reason he will have to be angry; and the more angry he is, the more his behavior will resemble hers; and the more his behavior resembles hers, the more blatant it will be to Kate why she must change if she is to acquire what she desires, including Petruchio himself. Furthermore, while Petruchio's calculated "wooing" scheme may seem priggish on the page, in the theatre it is the perfect prologue to the ensuing debacle; a theatre audience, from what it already knows of Kate's personality, senses that an explosion between her and Petruchio is imminent. Merely anticipating Kate's reaction to Petruchio's planned baiting of her increases the audience's uncertainty and anxiety about them and thus stimulates its anticipation of and fascination with their actual encounter. In Petruchio's soliloquy Shakespeare captures his audience in one of the two most highly charged, tense, and theatrically effective moments in the play; for here the dual energy fields in his text are about to converge and collide.

The collision is violent, explosive, bawdy, and dramaturgically rich. Shakespeare juxtaposes stichomythia and longer verse paragraphs to create a rhythmic variety within Kate's and Petruchio's dialogue that directs the theatre audience's response to what it sees and hears. The violence and bawdy of their dialogue are confined primarily to the stichomythia of [II. i. 197-241 and 262-66]; within these lines they exchange increasingly clever sexual puns, and several explicit and implicit stage directions in the text indicate Kate's striking Petruchio, his threat to retaliate, and her attempt to elude him. But the farcical electricity during these few moments is balanced by a series of verse paragraphs, all spoken by Petruchio, that establish his verbal dominance in the scene and emphasize the importance of what he says in them for the remainder of the play. Shakespeare places these verse paragraphs very carefully: two frame the stichomythia; the first of these two and another frame the entire scene between Petruchio and Kate; and in general the paragraphs are juxtaposed against Kate's short, one- or two-line responses so that the audience hears her far less than it hears Petruchio; thus Kate's attempts to respond to his verbal mastery of their encounter, however threatening her words, appear unconvincing. The rhythm of this scene, in other words, tells the audience that Katherina has met her match; and this rhythm dominates their relationship until the final moment of the play.

Throughout his verse paragraphs, Petruchio ironically praises Kate in a courtly manner, noting her "mildness," her "virtues," and asserting that he finds her "passing gentle," and "courteous." In an attempt to convince her that she may become something more than a shrew detested by every man she has met, he creates an image of something else she may become: a woman praised for her physical beauty, admired for her chastity, and loved for her energetic yet thoroughly compatible, pleasant disposition. However, when Petruchio flatly declares "will you, nill you . . . upon Sunday is the wedding-day" [II. i. 271, 298], Kate angrily responds that she would rather see him "hang'd on Sunday first" [II. i. 299] than marry him. Her preference for the gallows is simply another version of her violent reaction to Hortensio's assumption that she might wish to learn the lute. Petruchio's bold declaration that Kate is to marry him, regardless of her wishes, elicits from her precisely his—and the audience's—expected response; Katherina will not allow herself to appear pliant to another's will, and having been challenged by Petruchio's caricature of her own nature, she responds the only way she knows: by being as characteristically "curst" as possible.

Like Sly the tinker, Petruchio has little patience with formality for its own sake; fascinated by Kate's challenging, volatile character, attracted to her beauty, and satisfied with her dowry, he decides for both of them that marriage is imminent:

> For by this light whereby I see thy beauty,
> Thy beauty that doth make me like thee well,
> Thou must be married to no man but me;
> ....
>   Never make denial;
> I must and will have Katherine to my wife.
>
>   [II. i. 273-75, 279-80]

Curiosity about Kate's beauty is something new in Petruchio, the first indication of his developing affection for her. He expresses his romantic interest in Kate, whom he initially wished to marry only because of her father's money, as he simultaneously frustrates her selfish, uncompromising will.

Throughout the play, his manifest sexual interest in her is evident in his overtly farcical and often severe abuse, yet Petruchio's tactics are intended to convince Kate of his love for her by making her see herself as others have. Only when she realizes that her barriers to romantic love are self-created will she begin to appreciate Petruchio's actions.

In describing to Baptista, Gremio, and Tranio his first clash with Katherina, Petruchio resorts to a fictional idealization, yet this fiction embodies the romantic situation she desires:

>   O, the kindest Kate,
> She hung about my neck, and kiss on kiss
> She vied so fast, protesting oath on oath,
> That in a twink she won me to her love.
> O, you are novices!
>
>   [II. i. 307-11]

Petruchio is exactly what Kate says he is: a "half lunatic, / A madcap ruffian and a swearing Jack, / That thinks with oaths to face the matter out" [II. i. 287-89]. Yet by combining an imitation of Kate's usual behavior with a suggestion of Petrarchan language and mannerisms, he elicits from her an emotional reaction that, judged by her weeping at his failure to arrive at the church promptly, is quite sincere. Petruchio and Katherina have " 'greed so well together" [II. i. 297] on the volatility and independence of their personalities, and the proper ordering of their wills is the business of the remainder of the play. For only when they have agreed on the traditional relationship between husband and wife can Petruchio's fiction become reality.

For a theatre audience, the most engaging feature of the first two acts of the play is this ironic discrepancy between what it has *seen* between Petruchio and Kate and what it hears him *say* about what it has seen. The comic debacle in II. i. is violent and centrifugal, implying that these two people could not survive together for very long in one room, let alone cohabitate for a lifetime; whereas Petruchio's fiction, which "in plain terms" [II. i. 269] summarily describes a sacramental union, is peaceful and centripetal. Petruchio's fictional account of his madcap encounter with Katherina jolts an audience into an awareness of the comical irony it has just seen/heard, and this irony creates the uncertainty about the Petruchio-Katherina relationship that sustains an audience's interest in the only way through which Petruchio's fiction can become real: playing out the drama itself. It is as if those qualities in Katherina which Petruchio ironically conjures up in II. i., her being "pleasant, gamesome, passing courteous, / But slow in speech, yet sweet as spring-time flowers"; her inability to "frown," to "look askaunce"; her lack of pleasure in being "cross in talk"; and the "gentle conference, soft, and affable" with which she "entertain'st [her] wooers" [245-46, 47, 49, 51, 50] were themselves fictions that must become real if the marriage that Petruchio confidently predicts can ever succeed. Regardless of how well we know the text of *The Shrew*, when watching the play in the theatre we are unavoidably fascinated by the comical irony that Shakespeare has created by Act II and simultaneously intrigued by the visual and verbal clash between Petruchio and Kate that we realize is inevitable in the remainder of the play.

Petruchio's behavior at their wedding is consistent with his antics at his country house. Throughout Acts III and IV his own deliberate, hyperbolic shrewishness vividly mirrors Kate's. The farcical violence of these two acts, which one cannot wholly appreciate when reading the play, creates "total theatre" for an audience as it sees numerous visual images of Petruchio's self-confessed "game" as he plays with Kate; while that game itself, and Kate's reaction to it through IV. iii., increase an audience's anxiety about just how these two people can possibly achieve marital peace.

When the astonished Gremio asks "Was ever match clapp'd up so suddenly?" [II. i. 325] he speaks for the entire theatre audience whose sense of the irony of this marriage is heightened by Shakespeare's placing it in the middle of the play only two short scenes after Petruchio's and Katherina's last appearances on stage. This sense of irony is intensified by Biondello's frantic report that Petruchio, who had asserted "We will have rings and things, and fine array" [II. i. 323] at the wedding, comes to the ceremony "a monster, / a very monster in apparel" [III. ii. 69-70]. Petruchio's motley visually signals his disdain for ceremony and tradition and announces him as both symbol and cause of the chaos that follows. Kate's reaction to this self-centered folly is predictable; she responds indignantly to his order to leave immediately after the ceremony, reversing suddenly her crying after he failed to appear promptly:

> For me, I'll not be gone till I please myself.
> 'Tis like you'll prove a jolly surly groom,
> That take it on you at the first so roundly.
>
> [III. ii. 212-14]

Kate "will be angry," for she sees that "a woman may be made a fool, / If she had not a spirit to resist" [III. ii. 216, 220-21]. Her "spirit" is exactly what motivates Petruchio's desire to tame her; but at this point her spirit only succeeds in eliciting from him an even stronger assertion of *his* determination to dominate her:

> Obey the bride, you that attend on her.
> Go to the feast, revel and domineer,
> Carouse full measure to her maidenhead,
> Be mad and merry, or go hang yourselves;
> But for my bonny Kate, she must with me.
> Nay, look not big, nor stamp, nor stare, nor fret,
> I will be master of what is my own.
>
> [III. ii. 223-29]

Petruchio is rude, irreverent, possessive, egocentric, and very clever. The stage directions implicit in line 228 (above) indicate that he has again, as in II. i., thoroughly aroused Kate's anger, which he then uses to justify his outrageous, yet sportive chauvinism. Kate shall be what he says she is: his goods, his chattels, his household stuff, his barn, his ox, his "any thing" [III. ii. 230-32]. As in II. i. Petruchio again verbally dominates this small, hectic scene. The accelerating rhythm of his verbal abuse parallels the rising friction between himself on the one hand and Kate and the wedding guests on the other. As the scene climaxes, so do Petruchio's histrionics: claiming that they are "beset with thieves," [III. ii. 236] he orders Grumio to draw forth his weapon as they "rescue" Katherina from the astonished guests. Obviously reveling in his characteristically self-created role of "protector," Petruchio comically and quite self-consciously magnifies the actual situation. Petruchio's brandishing his sword may seem silly and unwarranted "in the library," but it exemplifies Styan's point that the eye and ear are inseparable in Shakespeare's stagecraft. Petruchio's sword-play at this critical moment vividly heralds the hyperbolic "taming" he employs later and is also an entirely appropriate phallic symbol that indicates visually his wish to tame Kate in order to establish a mutually satisfying sexual relationship with her.

Petruchio's antics after the wedding crown a dynamic scene that increases an audience's ironic insight into the play and also its anxiety about the play's main characters. Petruchio gladly acts out Kate's view of him—a "half lunatic, / A madcap ruffian and a swearing Jack" [II. i. 287-88]—because doing so is part of his plan. Having been told in II. i. that he intended to woo Kate with some "spirit," the audience knows what Petruchio is up to; but she does not. Thus the audience's emotions are pulled two ways: exhilaration at the sheer bravado and energy of Petruchio's performance; and sympathy, albeit comically muted, for the victim of his improvised lunacy—his wife! Furthermore, despite its privileged knowledge of Petruchio's motives the ironic discrepancy between how an audience expects newlyweds to interact and what it sees/hears on the stage heightens the sense of the improbable and bizarre in the couple's relationship. That both Petruchio and Katherina are, in Bianca's words, "madly mated," [III. ii. 244] is far more evident in the theatre than in the library, as is Petruchio's determination to teach Kate the social consequences of her shrewish behavior. In the final moments of Act III we note the beginning of a change in Kate's personality as she realizes for the first time the effects on others of a will as strong and uncompromising as her own.

The trek to Petruchio's country estate is, by Grumio's account, terrifying. Clearly Petruchio is being deliberately cruel to Katherina: "By this reck'ning he is more shrew than she" [IV. i. 85], remarks Curtis. Yet it is all part of his game that, as Hazlitt says, Petruchio plays "without a particle of ill-humor"; for the terrible journey plainly amplifies his frantic behavior at the wedding and anticipates the last stages of his psychologically severe but ultimately successful mimicry of Kate's obstinacy. In these ironic tactics we witness further evidence of Petruchio's personal interest in Katherina; if he did not strongly desire her as a compatible sexual partner, he would not go to such extremes to forge the secure bond evident in Act V.

His plan involves denying Kate those basic necessities of life—food, clothes, and rest—for which, having been "Brought up as best becomes a gentle-woman" [I. ii. 87], she has never had to "entreat." His throwing about of the meal that, as Kate admonishes him, "was well, if you were so contented" [IV. i. 169], is a counterpart to Kate's breaking Hortensio's instrument over his head; Petruchio wishes Kate to see how unnecessary and ridiculous such activity is. Further, events that seem to a *reader* to be an unwarranted extension of the couple's feud have just the opposite effect in the theatre. Petruchio's actions at this late point in the play increasingly frustrate an audience's expectations of normal marital activity: the lack of a proper, solemn wedding ceremony; the couple's hasty, frenzied exit from the communal feast; their horrid journey; the lack of any clear signal from Petruchio that he intends soon to consummate this marriage; and the sustained, noisy antagonism between them at his estate theatrically emphasize the constantly increasing tension between the reality of this relationship and Petruchio's ironic, idealized, yet still unrealized version of it in II. i.

When Petruchio damns the tailor's gown, the result is predictable: Kate objects: "I never saw a better-fashioned gown, / More quaint, more pleasing, nor more commendable. / Belike you mean to make a puppet of me" [IV. iii. 101-03]. Having again angered her, he again mimics her. He is knowingly and monstrously wrong about the clothing; the cap and gown were no doubt made "According to the fashion and the time"

[IV. iii. 95], and indeed Kate recognizes the quality of the tailor's "ruffling treasure" [IV. iii. 60]. It is now Petruchio who is "deceived," but quite deliberately; he pursues his game with the bewildered tailor for its own mad sake.

That Petruchio's actions throughout Act IV are intentionally exaggerated and carefully calculated for their effect on Kate is evident from the soliloquy that he addresses to the audience, thus involving us personally in his "plot" and soliciting our approval. Employing imagery from hawking, he explains both his desire for Kate's obedience to his will and his genuine love for her. The "faults" that he finds about the meal and the "making of the bed" are "undeserved" [IV. i. 199-200]. Further, he actually *is* doing all "in reverend care of her," [IV. i. 204] killing her with an ironical kindness that only a woman of Katherina's temperament could appreciate. Thus Petruchio's attitude towards Kate has changed noticeably: the man who decided spontaneously to woo her "while the humor last[ed]" [I. ii. 107-08] has matured into a loving husband who truly cares for Kate and wishes to establish a compatible relationship with her; indeed, Petruchio's integrity is such that his taming has her interests in mind as well as his own. But Kate must discern herself what Petruchio has told the audience, and the change in her personality is evident only after she has carefully scrutinized the mirror Petruchio fashions for her and has fully appreciated his "game" or "sport" for what it really is.

Kate's understanding of Petruchio's sport is evident on their journey back to Padua. During their whimsical mock-debate about the sun and moon, she accepts Petruchio's astrological decrees because she perceives in his fantastic insistence that he can control the heavens an image of lunacy, of a madcap game pursued simply to reiterate a point. The substance of his remarks does not matter. Lest Petruchio rashly decree that they return to his house, Kate agrees with his nonsense:

> Forward, I pray, since we have come so far,
> And be it moon, or sun, or what you please;
> And if you please to call it a rush-candle,
> Henceforth I vow it shall be so for me.
>
> [IV. v. 12-15]

Her playful, witty tone shows that she recognizes the obvious practicality of playing a game whose rules she has painfully learned. As the sun and moon seemingly depend for their existence on Petruchio's whim, so apparently do the age and sex of the confused old man, Vincentio. The brief exchange among Vincentio, Petruchio, and Kate anticipates the farcical, disguised identity of the false Vincentio who encounters his adversary in V. i., and simultaneously signifies the final stage in Kate's appreciation of her husband's sport. In addressing Vincentio as "Young budding virgin, fair, and fresh, and sweet" [IV. v. 37], Kate has at last, as Ralph Berry remarks [in *Shakespeare's Comedies*], "adopted Petruchio's mode. . . ."

The final scene of the play must be viewed in relation to the "controversy" of V. i. The complicated "supposes" and false identities of the Bianca-plot produce human relationships that, under testing, yield neither a sense of individual self-knowledge nor of mutual understanding. Conversely, Katherina's long speech exemplifies love and understanding between herself and Petruchio. Once she has understood his perspective, she is perfectly willing to assume her place within the traditional design of marriage. The solidity of their union is achieved through their different, yet equally necessary changes evident on the stage: through the educational trial with Petruchio, Katherina realizes the evils of shrewishness; whereas Petruchio learns that a woman may be loved for her beauty and merits, not just her dowry. Petruchio's and Katherina's "interior metamorphoses" are thus the heart of this play precisely because they develop out of the clash between the energetic, fascinating personalities that Shakespeare makes so vocally and visually compelling.

The final moments of *The Shrew* are its most intense, most theatrically potent. As Petruchio orders Kate to lecture Bianca and the widow on their wifely duties, the rhythm of their relationship suddenly changes; Kate now vocally dominates the scene with the longest speech of the play. The sheer length of Kate's sermon commands the audience's attention, and as she concludes, her offer to place her hand beneath Petruchio's boot creates a moment, a situation that can be fully exploited and appreciated only in the theatre. The longer Kate remains in a submissive posture, the longer her hand lies beneath Petruchio's boot, and the longer he waits to respond, the greater the dramatic tension. In this final instance of the uncertainty and anxiety about these characters that Shakespeare maintains from II. i. onward, his stagecraft is most evident. Because of what the audience has just heard from Kate, because of its memory of their feud, and because of Petruchio's harsh tone to Kate when she returns with the other women—"Katherine, that cap of yours becomes you not; / Off with that bable, throw it under-foot" [V. ii. 121-22]—an audience again expects an authoritative response from Petruchio. But this expectation is suddenly shattered by Petruchio's wonderfully playful, "Why, there's a wench! Come on, and kiss me, Kate" [V. ii. 180]. Shakespeare finally releases his audience from the ironic tension of the taming plot in an appropriately abrupt, unceremonious manner. The hyperbole of Kate's speech suggests that she is as gamesome here as Petruchio has been all along, but an audience cannot be sure of her attitude (or his) until they kiss and joyously head for the nearest bedroom. [J. L.] Styan [in his *Shakespeare's Stagecraft*] asserts that Shakespeare created stage contrasts assuming that an audience would deduce meaning from them; and what a theatre audience will deduce from the vivid contrast between Kate's long speech and her sudden dash off the stage with Petruchio is that these two people are about to begin the normal but hitherto frustrated rhythm of marital love with a marvelous gusto. Petruchio's fiction—"O, the kindest Kate, / She hung about my neck, and kiss on kiss / She vied so fast, protesting oath on oath, / That in a twink she won me to her love" [II. i. 307-10] is about to become reality in a sexual embrace.

In order to appreciate Petruchio and Katherina as dramatic characters, we must see them in the theatre, for only there can we recognize how the theatrical energy of their encounter evolves from and is sustained by the fullness of their presence. In place of the unreflective, unfeeling figures generally present in farce and in the traditional shrew-taming story, Shakespeare substitutes "two intelligent people [who arrive] at a modus vivendi" [Berry]; similarly, in place of the often physically brutal taming of a wife in numerous contemporary versions, he substitutes a theatrical process in which his characters arrive at an active self-knowledge that permits the fulfillment of mutual desires. And in these substitutions lies an early sign of Shakespeare's comic mastery, for Petruchio and Katherina are indeed the plot of this play. (pp. 327-40)

Michael W. Shurgot, "From Fiction to Reality:

Character and Stagecraft in 'The Taming of the Shrew'," in Theatre Journal, Vol. 33, No. 3, October, 1981, pp. 327-40.

Ellen Dowling   (essay date 1983)

[Dowling addresses the question of Christopher Sly's function in The Taming of the Shrew, noting the several ways in which productions have handled the Induction. "The play can be," Dowling concludes, "a hit without Christopher Sly. But something is always lost."]

Critics of Shakespeare's The Taming of the Shrew have long been fascinated with Christopher Sly—"by birth a pedlar, by education a cardmaker, by transmutation a bear-herd" [Ind. i. 19-20], and, by his creator's artistry, a minor comic masterpiece. Many have discoursed at great length on Sly's reason for being, establishing thematic links between the Sly story and the Shrew story, and pointing out parallels between the tinker who becomes a lord and the shrew who becomes a lady. For these scholars, the question is what to make of Sly and his retinue. Directors and producers of the play, on the other hand, have long pondered the question of what to do with the "Presenters," and in the theatre, where scholarly debate must lead eventually to practical decision-making, the first choice any director of Shrew must make is whether or not to cut the Induction. For most directors, it is not a simple decision.

The early stage history of The Taming of the Shrew offers scanty information to a director seeking precedents for cutting or keeping the Induction. Christopher Sly and company appear in both the 1596 quarto edition of The Taming of a Shrew and the 1623 folio edition of The Taming of the Shrew—more or less: more in A Shrew, where the drunken tinker is given several opportunities to interrupt the action of the play he is watching, and where, at the end, he awakens to find himself once more in a field outside an alehouse, discusses with the Tapster ("Hostess" in The Shrew) the strange dream he has had, and leaves the stage determined to try out Ferrando's (Petruchio's) taming methods on his own wife back home; and less in The Shrew where Sly is heard from no more after [I. i. 254]. So we can assume that audiences then were entertained by Sly in one form or another, as they most likely were again in 1633 when "The Taminge of the Shrew" was "revived" at St. James's for the King and Queen. But thirty-four years later Sly had disappeared from the stage. In 1667, Samuel Pepys saw a production Sauny the Scot; or, The Taming of the Shrew, an adaptation of A Shrew by John Lacy, a member of the King's Company. Lacy cut the Induction and re-arranged the plot to make "Sauny" (from "Sander," Grumio's counterpart in A Shrew) the main character. Sly was briefly resurrected in 1716, when two rival playwrights, Charles Johnson and Christopher Bullock, wrote their versions of the Sly story, both entitled The Cobler of Preston, but he was buried once again in the mid-eighteenth century when David Garrick produced his enormously popular Catherine and Petruchio. It was not until 1844, nearly 100 years later, when Benjamin Webster decided to produce the Folio version of The Taming of the Shrew, Induction and all, that Sly was restored to his original place in the theatre and his permanent place in Shakespearean criticism.

Since that time, most professional directors and producers (75% of them, in over sixty-five productions staged in the

U.S. and Europe from 1844 to 1978) have chosen not to cut the tinker and his play-acting confederates. Significantly, when directors or producers have chosen to cut Sly, they usually feel obligated to explain their decision. In an interview published in The New York Times after the opening of their highly controversial, rough-and-tumble version of a Sly-less Shrew in 1905, Julia Marlowe and E. H. Sothern defended their decision to cut Sly by resting their case on the textual authority of "Fleay, Furnivall, and Furness," claiming that "it is the only indubitably spurious portion of the Text" and "has nothing to do with the play proper." Others have cut the Induction "for purposes of expediency" (as Brooks Atkinson assumed in his review of Richard Boleslavsky's 1925 production at the Klaw Theatre, New York City), or in deference to their audiences: R. O. Ceballos, director of the 1978 Shakespeare Festival of Cincinnati, claimed in a program note that "Since it's become standard to drop the Sly scenes, most of the audience—not familiar with the text—would have questioned whether they were watching Shakespeare." On the contrary, more likely most of them—at least the experienced playgoers—would have wondered, "What happened to Christopher Sly?"

The most important questions that need to be raised at this point are: 1) Why do so many directors choose to keep Sly (when cutting him would seem to be the easier choice—fewer actors to cast, fewer lines to work on, less scenery, less complicated staging); and 2) what theatrical effect does his presence have on the style of the play as a whole?

One practical reason why so many directors choose to keep the Induction is that it allows them to simplify the physical setting of the play. Once the basic set—the Lord's house—has been contructed, the subsequent scene changes can be facilitated by the Players themselves, who may carry their own props and furniture on to the stage, set up a drop cloth or curtain from which to make their entrances, and hang placards indicating "A Street in Padua," and so on. A simplified set design like this is not only economical but it also eliminates the kind of scenic clutter to which most nineteenth century theatres were (and some twentieth century theatres are) addicted. J. R. Planché, the designer who first suggested to Benjamin Webster that he replace Garrick's Catherine and Petruchio with Shakespeare's original play, believed that this simplicity of style was the concept's chief attraction. Not all nineteenth century critics were ready for this innovation in stage design—the Athenaeum reviewer dismissed the whole idea as "pedantic affectation of accuracy"—but most agreed with The London Times reviewer who praised the production, calling it "one of the most remarkable instances of modern theatre," and stressing that the staging "tended to give closeness to the action, and by constantly allowing a great deal of stage room, afforded a sort of freedom to all parties engaged."

Yet the play can also be performed without the Induction—as it was by the American Conservatory Theatre company in 1973—and still retain the ambiance of a commedia dell'arte romp put on by a band of wandering players atop wagon-stages, so one must not conclude that the presence of Sly and company is a prerequisite for simplified staging. What is necessary, most directors who keep the Induction believe, is the theatrical distancing effect which Sly's presence has on the audience. In the theatre, as Larry S. Champion has pointed out [in his The Evolution of Shakespeare's Comedies], the Induction "serves constantly to draw the filter of fiction before us lest we be tempted to forget that Kate is a purely artificial figure of farce and, like many an armchair critic, to become indignant that Shakespeare could consider such cruel mistreatment of womankind as comic. . . . " With this idea in mind, Max Reinhardt chose to retain the Induction in his 1909 production at the Deutsches Theater, Berlin, believing that this alone "would excuse Petruchio's intolerable behavior." And Tyrone Guthrie, in both his 1939 production for the Old Vic and his 1954 production at Stratford, Ontario, chose to do likewise, claiming that the play, "without the framework, loses its best reason for being."

Reviewers have generally concurred favorably with the director's choice to play it all to Sly. *The London Times* reviewer who saw Martin Harvey's 1913 production at the Prince of Wales Theatre felt that Sly's presence enabled the audience to relax: "It left us free to enjoy this 'pleasant conceited historie' as a piece of hearty fun, without bothering about its ethics or calculating its probability of its likeness to life." As modern sensibilities about women's rights were raising the consciousnesses of most would-be admirers of Petruchio, a reviewer of Harcourt Williams' 1931 production at Sadler's Wells could claim, with some relief, that "the taming of poor Kate, which commonly grates harshly upon our polite ears, suddenly acquires the curious grace which belongs even to the roughest horse-play in a novel of Boccaccio." Richard David, reviewing George Devine's 1954 production at Stratford-upon-Avon likewise felt that the double artifice made "palatable" the "creaky humor" of the play proper, and enabled modern audiences to endure those scenes "which are too roughly Elizabethan for our tastes."

With Sly there to "soften the blow," the bounds of farce can be pushed to their furthest limits. If, as a reviewer of Ben Iden Payne's 1940 production at Stratford-upon-Avon claimed, the Induction enables the director to keep the comedy "on the plane of a drunken tinker's hallucination," then, as the reviewer of John Burrell's 1947 production at the Lyceum Theatre concluded, "hardly anything in it can be too theatrical," and, as in Trevor Nunn's 1967 production for the Royal Shakespeare Company, "the players can give performances in a riper, broader style than would otherwise be permissible." Sly's presence thus has a two-fold effect on both the play and the audience, as Peter D. Smith, reviewer of Michael Langham's 1962 Stratford, Ontario production has noted: "On the one hand this episode in the fairy-tale of the battle of the sexes is removed one stage further from reality and its extravagance is accordingly made more acceptable; and, on the other, the audience, paradoxically, is given a keener sense of participation as these happily become involved in Sly's own enthusiasm."

Once a director has decided to keep the Induction, he or she must then make several more important decisions, the first being to decide what is to happen to Sly and the others after I.i. According to the Folio, after Sly's last "enthusiastic" interjection (" 'Tis a very excellent piece of work, Madam lady. Would 'twere done" [I. i. 253-54]) the stage direction reads, "They sit and mark." Does this mean that they unobtrusively watch the rest of the play until the audience forgets all about them, or is Sly expected to extemporize throughout, playing off the actors playing to him?

Some directors have chosen to simplify the problem by removing Sly all together after I.i., a solution first advanced by Samuel Phelps in his 1856 production at Sadler's Wells. Phelps himself played the drunken tinker and received acco-

lades from reviewers who thought his performance, though of so brief a duration, outshone that of all the other actors, including Mr. Marston and Miss Atkinson, who played Petruchio and Kate. The reviewer from *The Examiner* found Sly's disappearance after I.i. thematically logical and dramatically effective, given the lushness of Phelps's performance and his emphasis on the tinker's overwhelming dim-wittedness, and asserted that "The stupidity of Sly causes his disappearance from the stage in the most natural way after the play itself has warmed into full action. He has of course no fancy for it, is unable to follow it, stares at it, and falls asleep over it. The sport of imagination acts upon him as a sleeping-draught, and at the end of the first act he is so fast asleep that it becomes matter of course to carry him away." Augustin Daly repeated this procedure in his highly successful 1887 production in New York and 1888 production in London. William Gilbert's Sly was, understandably, so overshadowed by Ada Rehan's Kate and John Drew's Petruchio that the *Athenaeum* reviewer felt justified in claiming that the sleeping Sly's removal at the end of I.i, was "quite defensible. Shakespeare after the play is once launched ceases to concern himself with the bemused tinker. Why should not others follow his example?" On the other hand, Andrew Leigh, playing Sly in Henry Cass's 1935 Old Vic production, gave such a masterful comic performance that *The London Times* reviewer was moved to praise the Induction as "a gleam of farce that shines on human vanity and exhibits in penetrating light the cruelty of farce itself " and to lament that "too soon poor Christopher gives sign of falling asleep and the taming itself takes the stage from him." In spite of these notable exceptions, the decision to close the curtains on a sleeping Sly is rarely made in the theatre, a fact that may attest to Sir Arthur Quiller-Couch's feeling that something about this choice just doesn't seem right: "After all," he has said [in his Introduction to the New Cambridge Edition of *The Taming of the Shrew*], "it is not the way of authors to invite public attention so subtly to the dullness or insipidity of their own compositions."

A more practical disadvantage of this choice is that it wastes acting talent. As J. Dover Wilson has pointed out, "To keep three players up on the gallery throughout the play, speaking only occasionally and never able to help out the main action by doubling, would have seemed a crime to any practical stage manager of the period, unless he were very rich in actors." To circumvent this "crime," some directors have experimented with a wide range of doubling possibilities, including the interesting procedure of doubling Sly and Petruchio. Oscar Asche tried this first in 1904, rather unsuccessfully, in Robert Atkins' opinion, since this caused "an act-long wait between the Induction and the play itself, which made nonsense of the close attachment of the one to the other." Fritz Leiber played both Sly and Petruchio in a Chicago Civic Shakespeare Society production in 1930, and, more recently, Jonathan Pryce doubled a boorish, scenery-wrecking Sly with a leather-coated, motorcycle riding Petruchio in Michael Bogdanov's 1978 production for the Royal Shakespeare Company. (Reviewers of this production seem to agree with Mel Gussow of *The New York Times* that this concept had little thematic or structural relevance to the play, but that it encapsulated wonderfully the "outrageous anything-goes attitude of the director.") The logistics of changing Sly into Petruchio and back again to Sly are, as can be imagined, rather complicated, since Petruchio is supposed to step on stage immediately after Sly's last interpolation at the end of I.i., and has only two lines of dialogue between Lucentio and Hortensio at the end of the play during which, if the director so desires, to change back into Sly.

A more popular—and less problem-ridden-choice is to double the Presenters with characters who appear later in the play proper: the actor who plays the Lord, for example, could easily be doubled as Vincentio, his servants could become Petruchio's servants, Sly's "wife" could appear again as the Tailor or the Widow or Biondello—there are many possibilities. Sly could be pressed into service as the Pedant, as he was in Claude Gurney's 1937 New Theatre production and in the Young Vic's 1974 production, or the actor playing Sly could double as Petruchio's horse, as he did in Margaret Webster's 1951 production at the New York City Center, and in George Devine's 1953 and 1954 productions at Stratford-upon-Avon. For a small company with a limited supply of actors, keeping the Induction, then fading it out at the end of I.i. and recycling the actors in other parts may well be the most economically feasible decision.

The majority of professional directors, however (most of whom have not had to worry about a limited supply of actors), have chosen to keep the Presenters on stage throughout the play so as to never let the audience forget that they are watching a play-within-a-play, and to emphasize that "distancing" and "softening" effect described earlier in this essay. Quite a few directors have taken their cue from Quiller-Couch, who theorized that Shakespeare deliberately omitted any further lines for Sly, intending that the actor who played him feel free to extemporize and comment (verbally or nonverbally) on the action taking place before him.

Left to his own devices to comment on and participate in the play, the actor playing Sly (with, of course, the coaching of the director) has many choices. He can react non-verbally throughout the play, as D. Hay Petrie did so successfully in Andrew Leigh's 1917 production at the Lyric Theatre, prompting *The London Times* reviewer to exclaim: "His is an extraordinarily good piece of acting, notable for the industry with which, condemned to silence, he presses the members of his body into the service of eloquence. His lips, his eyebrows, his fingers are admirably expressive; his lusty motions of applause and his silent confidences are a weightier commentary than words." Or he can verbalize his reactions, as M. Donnio did in Gremier's 1924 French production in New York City, bursting out irreverently in English slang whenever he felt so moved. He can wander around the stage to get a better view, as in George Devine's 1953 and 1954 Stratford-upon-Avon productions, and occasionally participate directly in the slapstick: he can assist in whacking Grumio (Guthrie's 1939 Old Vic production), steal a whiskey bottle from one of the players with a butterfly net, Harpo Marx fashion (Norman Lloyd's 1955 Stratford, Connecticut production), or he can rush on stage—much to the consternation of the Lord—to join the wedding feast at Baptista's house (Michael Langham's 1962 Stratford, Ontario production). The possibilities for Sly's active participation are many, and interestingly enough, his antics always appear to add to rather than detract from the audience's focus on the play proper; I found not one review where an extemporizing Sly was accused of upstaging the Shrew story. On the contrary, many reviewers considered Sly the hit of the show and devoted more space to praising him than any of the other principals. Sly's particular appeal, most reviewers agree, is his childlike sense of wonder and enchantment, which adds immeasurably to the audience's own enjoyment of the play. A typical example is The

London Times reviewer's assessment of Bernard Miles's performance as Sly in John Burrell's 1947 production at the New Theatre: "The whole action is warmed through with the good-natured fellow's childlike, if flamingly bibulous, appreciation of its simple excitements and all the brutality is warmed out of it. With the tinker and his mock wife aloft on a great bed, surrounded by the sportive nobleman and his amused friends, the play enacted on the floor below them becomes an Elizabethan romp. The tinker's delight in his entertainment, never relaxed and never overdone by Mr. Bernard Miles, communicates itself irresistibly. . . . "

So theatrically appealing has Sly's presence been to some directors that they have chosen to pad out his part by including sections from *The Taming of a Shrew.* Harcourt Williams appears to have been the first (in 1931) to add the Epilogue from *A Shrew,* and since that time, although most scholars have defended Shakespeare's choice (if, indeed, it was his choice) to omit an epilogue (they consider it too anti-climactic), the directors who have chosen to follow Williams' example—notably Tyrone Guthrie (1939), John Burrell (1947), Margaret Webster (1951), George Devine (1954), Craig Noel (1962), Michael Langham (1962), and Trevor Nunn (1967)—have met with marked success. *The London Times* reviewer of Ben Iden-Payne's 1936 production at Stratford-upon-Avon, for example, felt that "the dove-tailing of the two pieces is . . . harmless and even necessary. It sets the comedy more firmly in what seems to be its proper place, and it sends us away with echoes of something better than Kate's claptrap about the duties which a wife owes to her husband, lord, and master." George Devine was also praised for his "judicious use" of the epilogue from *A Shrew,* which enabled him "to cover the central crudity in as many separate wrappings of illusion as it will bear." The Epilogue not only contributes to the "rounding off" of the play, but also, as Arnold Edinborough, reviewing Langham's 1962 production, noted, to the highlighting of the central irony of the play, that "only on the stage do men wive it wealthily and/or happily."

It must be stressed that the decision to keep Sly on stage throughout the play does not necessarily force the director into a no-holds-barred, anything goes, boisterously farcical production. Although W. Bridges-Adams refused to have anything to do with Sly during his tenure as director of the Stratford-upon-Avon Shakespeare Festival from 1920 to 1933, asserting that Kate and Petruchio would certainly dislike "having twenty preoccupied and irrelevant types around them on the stage—to say nothing of a bed—at that perfectly thrumming moment when they are alone together for the first time," most directors who choose to keep Sly find, as Richard David noted about George Devine's 1954 production, that "at any moment (such is the flexibility of drama) the play can soar out of its framework, which drops away and is forgotten in the instant." In spite of (or with the assistance of) Sly on the stage, Kate and Petruchio can fall in love at first sight, or on the way home from their "honeymoon," or at the end of the play, or never. Kate can give her last speech ironically (with a knowing wink to the audience or to Sly), or conspiratorily (with a knowing wink to Petruchio), or absolutely sincerely (and then Sly winks at *us*—after all, it's *his* dream). The play proper can be performed as all-out farce or romantic comedy or a happy combination of both. And any production can be panned for going too far in any direction, with or without the assistance of Sly.

What matters most, then, is the additional level of illusion which Sly's presence adds to our appreciation of the play on the stage. In the study, we may quickly forget all about Sly after I.i, but in the theatre, if the director has retained him, we will be made constantly aware of what J. Denis Huston has called Shakespeare's "hall of mirrors" effect:

> Shakespeare begins a play, which is then apparently re-begun as a more conventional play, in which a Lord decides to stage a play, but he is interrupted by a group of players, who themselves come to offer service in the form of a play to this Lord, who talks with them about yet another play, which they have acted in the past but which they are not going to present this evening, when a player-Lord will observe their performance of a play staged after the 'real' Lord and his servants have played out their play with the player-Lord, who will [possibly] sleep through the play which Shakespeare, himself playing through this mind-boggling series of false starts, will utimately present to his audience [in " 'To Make a Puppet': Play and Play-Making in *The Taming of the Shrew*"].

The play can be—has frequently been—a hit without Christopher Sly. But something is always lost. (pp. 87-93)

> *Ellen Dowling, "Christopher Sly on the Stage," in* Theatre History Studies, *Vol. III, 1983, pp. 87-98.*

FURTHER READING

REVIEWS AND RETROSPECTIVE ACCOUNTS

Beckerman, Bernard. "The 1965 Season at Stratford, Connecticut." *Shakespeare Quarterly* XVI, No. 4 (Autumn 1965): 329-33.
    Criticizes the "irrelevant" theatrical inventions in Joseph Anthony's production of *The Taming of the Shrew.*

Berry, Ralph. "Stratford Festival Canada." *Shakespeare Quarterly* XXXIII, No. 2 (Summer 1982): 199-202.
    Offers a mixed review of Peter Dews's production, which lacked "intensity" but "improved as it went along."

Brower, Brock. "Shakespeare's 'Shrew' With No Apologies." *The New York Times* (6 August 1978): D1, 5.
    Interviews Meryl Streep and Raul Julia about their preparation for playing Katherina and Petruchio in Wilford Leach's New York Shakespeare Festival presentation of *The Taming of the Shrew.*

Coleman, Emily. "Gags & Good Intentions Can't Tame a Shrew." *Life* 59, No. 4 (23 July 1965): 13.
    Maintains that Joseph Anthony's production at Stratford, Connecticut was "hardly satisfying from anybody's point of view."

Curtis, Anthony. Review of *The Taming of the Shrew. Drama,* No. 133 (Summer 1979): 52-53.
    Asserts that the doubling of Sly and Petruchio in Michael Bogdanov's RSC production of *The Taming of the Shrew* gave the play more coherence. The depiction of the inner play as Sly's dream, Curtis argues, created "an unfailing inventiveness" that made the production work well.

Cushman, Robert. "The Rumpscuttle." *Observer Review* (1 May 1983): 30.

Comments on Barry Kyle's adept handling of *The Taming of the Shrew*'s several plots in the RSC production of the play.

Duncan-Jones, Katherine. "Psychologically Speaking." *The Times Literary Supplement,* No. 4407 (18-24 September 1987): 1019.
    Praises Miller's RSC production as "a festive, highly entertaining *Taming of the Shrew* with plenty to please the eye and ear."

Edwards, Christopher. Review of *The Taming of the Shrew. Plays and Players,* No. 358 (July 1983): 30-31.
    Disparages Kyle's RSC *Taming of the Shrew,* describing it as "a dire production; an embarrassing camp farrago; tabloid Shakespeare."

Elsom, John. "Shrews." *The Listener* 90, No. 2334 (20 December 1973): 864-65.
    Criticizes Clifford Williams's "flippant" treatment of *The Taming of the Shrew* in the 1973 RSC production.

Garebian, Keith. "The 1981 Stratford Festival." *Journal of Canadian Studies* 16, Nos. 3 & 4 (Fall-Winter 1981): 199-204.
    Favorably reviews Dews's lively direction, remarking that the performance was dynamic and exuberant.

Griffin, Alice. "The Season at Stratford." *Theatre Arts* XXXVIII, No. 9 (September 1954): 24-25, 92.
    Offers a favorable review of Tyrone Guthrie's "nonconventional" Stratford, Ontario production and comments on his interpretation of the inner play as Christopher Sly's dream.

Hewes, Henry. "Triple 'en Tente.' " *The Saturday Review* XXXVII, No. 31 (31 July 1954): 33-4.
    Provides a mixed review of Tyrone Guthrie's Stratford, Ontario production. While the inner play was effectively represented as a dream sequence, Hewes asserts, there was too much slapstick comedy.

Hughes, David. "How the Fat Knight Got a Fresh Face." *The Sunday Times,* No. 8157 (26 October 1980): 41.
    Interviews Jonathan Miller, who declares that his goal as leader of the BBC Shakespeare project is "to keep the plays intimate, to quieten them for home viewing."

Jackson, Berners W. "Shakespeare at Stratford, Ontario, 1973." *Shakespeare Quarterly* XXIV, No. 4 (Autumn 1973): 405-10.
    Maintains that Jean Gascon's unsympathetic treatment of *The Taming of the Shrew* imparted a prevailing sense of artificiality to his production.

James, John. "Breaking the Rules." *The Times Educational Supplement,* No. 3651 (20 June 1986): 30.
    Asserts that Timothy Dalton's performance as Petruchio was the only virtue of Toby Robertson's misdirected presentation of *The Taming of the Shrew* at the Theatre Royal.

Lambert, J. W. "Plays in Performance." *Drama,* No. 86 (Autumn 1967): 16-28.
    Praises the performances of Janet Suzman and Michael Williams as Katherina and Petruchio in Trevor Nunn's RSC production.

Leech, Michael. "Canada." *Plays and Players* 20, No. 7 (April 1973): 58-59.
    Contends that Jean Gascon's awkward direction and the players' uneven performances led to an overall lack of focus in the Stratford, Ontario production.

Marshall, Margaret. Review of *The Taming of the Shrew. The Nation* 172, No. 18 (5 May 1951): 429-30.
    Argues that Clare Luce's fierce facial expression throughout Margaret Webster's New York City Center production allowed her to display only one dimension of Kate's shrewishness.

Morley, Sheridan. "The Nation's Health." *Punch* (17 May 1978): 830.

Praises Michael Bogdanov's "inventive" production for the RSC. "Kate emerges as the final winner on points," Morley remarks.

―――. "Another Roaring Girl." *Punch* (11 May 1983): 59-60.
Asserts that Barry Kyle's RSC production was unconvincing because the interpretation of Petruchio vacillated between that of a chauvinist and "a more subtle and liberal lover."

Review of *The Taming of the Shrew. The New Statesman and Nation* XVII, No. 423 (1 April 1939): 494.
Maintains that Tyrone Guthrie's "harlequinade" production at the Old Vic Theatre was brilliantly done. The reviewer complains, however, that some key actors were inaudible.

Nightingale, Benedict. "The Furies in Yorkshire." *New Statesman* (5 October 1973): 491.
Criticizes the excessive stage business and the actors' generally inadequate performances in Clifford Williams's RSC production.

Novick, Julius. "Stratford II." *The Nation* 201, No. 3 (2 August 1965): 65-7.
Asserts that Joseph Anthony's production at Stratford, Connecticut was "easier to like than to admire."

O'Connor, Garry. Review of *The Taming of the Shrew. Plays and Players* 21, No. 2 (November 1973): 46-47.
Contends that although the comedy of Clifford Williams's RSC production was "a barnstorming riot," the actors gave unconvincing performances.

―――. Review of *The Taming of the Shrew. Plays and Players,* No. 409 (October 1987); 20-1.
Maintains that Miller's 1987 RSC production of *The Taming of the Shrew* displayed both "wit and intelligence."

Peter, John. "Reviving a Domestic Drama." *Sunday Times Review* (15 June 1986): 49.
Briefly comments on Toby Robertson's *Taming of the Shrew* at the Theatre Royal, featuring Timothy Dalton as Petruchio and Vanessa Redgrave as Katherina.

―――. "Taming the Text With Intelligence." *Sunday Times* (13 September 1987): 57.
Asserts that Jonathan Miller's insightful interpretation reflected the level of theatrical intelligence a Shakespearean play deserves.

Pettigrew, John. "Stratford's Festival Theatre, 1973." *Journal of Canadian Studies* IX, No. 1 (February 1974): 3-9.
Argues that while Jean Gascon's production was "an energetic romp," his interpretation was "more mask than revelation of the strengths of Shakespeare's play."

Ratcliffe, Michael. "A Cross to Bear." *The Observer Review* (13 September 1987): 25.
Brief notice of Jonathan Miller's "unusually truthful, moving and funny" RSC presentation of *The Taming of the Shrew.*

Shaw, Fiona. "An Actor's Diary." *Drama* (London), No. 166 (1987): 53-54.
Describes the evolution of her interpretation of Katherina in Jonathan Miller's 1987 production. Shaw observes that "Kate deals with domestic political reality like an over-zealous student after a crash course in Elizabethan neo-platonism."

Simon, John. "Brush Off Your Shakespeare." *New York* 11, No. 35 (28 August 1978): 111-12.
Disparages Wilford Leach's New York Shakespeare Festival production for reducing the play's more complex issues to nothing more than "meaningless hokum."

Spurling, Hilary. "Rapier of the Week." *The Spectator* (14 April 1967): 428-30.

Briefly reviews Trevor Nunn's RSC production, noting that the director's interpretation focused on the "artificiality" of the play.

Review of *The Taming of the Shrew. The Times,* No. 47,135 (6 August 1935): 8.
Contends that Iden Payne's "well-intentioned" production at the Shakespeare Memorial Theatre "somehow missed fire" because of the poor performances by the supporting actors.

Review of *The Taming of the Shrew. The Times,* No. 48,266 (29 March 1939): 14.
Maintains that although there were instances of excessive "romping" in Guthrie's Old Vic production, the overall effect was one of "freshness and gaiety."

Review of *The Taming of the Shrew. The Times,* No. 50,910 (5 November 1947): 7.
Praises John Burrell for including the Induction in his production of *The Taming of the Shrew* at the New Theatre.

Review of *The Taming of the Shrew. The Times,* No. 53,103 (1 December 1954): 7.
Argues that Denis Carey's Old Vic production nearly achieved an ideal comedic balance by depicting Kate as both a shrew and an obedient wife. The reviewer adds, however, that the presentation was burdened by excessive stage business.

Trewin, J. C. "Shakespeare in Britain." *Shakespeare Quarterly* XXX, No. 2 (Spring 1979): 151-58.
Disagrees with Bogdanov's interpretation of the taming scenes as a "hunt" in this "second-team" RSC production of *The Taming of the Shrew.*

Warner, Marina. Review of *The Taming of the Shrew. The Sunday Times,* No. 8169 (18 January 1981): 38-39.
Holds that Jonathan Pryce's performance as Sly destroying mock-scenery at the beginning of Michael Bogdanov's 1978 RSC production was so realistic that "members of the audience were often moved to restrain him."

Warren, Roger. "Shakespeare in England." *Shakespeare Quarterly* XXXIV, No. 3 (Autumn 1983): 334-40.
Asserts that Barry Kyle's treatment of the Sly scenes in his RSC production illustrates how the director "was clearly at pains to distinguish between the different layers of the play."

Watters, Tamie. " 'Love's Labours Lost' But Its Box Office Gains." *The Christian Science Monitor* (25 June 1979): 11.
Contends that although Bogdanov's production was "compulsive," it was not Shakespearean. Petruchio's taming of Kate in the final scene, Watters argues, would have "set the Bard's teeth on edge."

Wood, Roger, and Clarke, Mary. "The Taming of the Shrew." In their *Shakespeare at the Old Vic,* pp. 141-44. London: Adam and Charles Black, 1956.
Praises Paul Rogers's performance as Petruchio in Denis Carey's otherwise unsatisfactory Old Vic production.

Young, B. A. Review of *The Taming of the Shrew. The Financial Times* (30 April 1979): 15.
Assesses Michael Bogdanov's RSC presentation of *The Taming of the Shrew,* emphasizing the thematic significance of the Induction for the rest of the play.

COMPARISONS AND OVERVIEWS

Allen, Shirley S. "Phelps and Shakespeare: Manager." In her *Samuel Phelps and Sadler's Wells Theatre,* pp. 200-51. Middletown, Conn.: Wesleyan University Press, 1971.

Briefly discusses Phelps's 1856 production of *The Taming of the Shrew*, noting that contemporary critics found it "a dull play."

Bradbrook, Muriel C. "The Function of a Complex Variable: Shakespeare at Stratford." *Shakespeare Translation* 8 (1981): 75-8.
Examines recent trends in producing Shakespeare's plays. Bradbrook offers remarks on Michael Bogdanov's 1978 "deconstruction" of *The Taming of the Shrew,* as well as Jonathan Miller's 1980 production, interpreted as "an act of the imagination."

Findlater, Richard. "Sir Laurence Olivier." In his *The Player Kings,* pp. 204-37. New York: Stein and Day Publishers, 1971.
Records that Laurence Olivier was first noticed by the press when at the age of fourteen he portrayed Katherina in a choir-school production of *The Taming of the Shrew.*

Freedley, George. *The Lunts.* Liverpool and London: Charles Birchall and Sons, 1957, 134 p.
Surveys the Lunts' contributions to the stage and screen, providing contemporary dramatic criticism of the Lunt/Fontanne *Taming of the Shrew.*

Gow, Gordon. "Shakespeare Lib: Gordon Gow Talks to Three Shakespearean Feminists." *Plays and Players* 20, No. 9 (June 1973): 18-21.
Interviews Susan Fleetwood, Janet Suzman, and Diana Rigg, who discuss their interpretations of Katherina and other Shakespearean female characters.

Grebanier, Bernard. "Henry Irving and Ellen Terry." In his *Then Came Each Actor: Shakespearean Actors, Great and Otherwise, Including Players and Princes, Rogues, Vagabonds, and Actors Motley, from Will Kemp to Olivier and Gielgud and After,* pp. 277-316. New York: David McKay Company, 1975.
Briefly describes the performances of Henry Irving and Ellen Terry in a late nineteenth-century production of *Catherine and Petruchio.*

Greenfield, Thelma N. "The Frame Plays." In her *The Induction in Elizabethan Drama,* pp. 97-120. Eugene, Ore.: University of Oregon Books, 1969.
Compares and contrasts different aspects of the Inductions to *The Taming of a Shrew* and *The Taming of the Shrew.*

Manvell, Roger. "The Arrival of Sound: the First Phase of Adaptation" and "The Italians and Shakespeare: Castellani and Zeffirelli." In his *Shakespeare and the Film,* revised edition, pp. 23-36, 97-100. Cranbury, N. J.: A. S. Barnes and Company, 1979.
Discusses two film adaptations of *The Taming of the Shrew:* the 1929 version starring Mary Pickford and Douglas Fairbanks, Sr., and the 1967 version with Elizabeth Taylor and Richard Burton.

Morris, Brian. Introduction to *The Taming of the Shrew* by William Shakespeare, edited by Brian Morris, pp. 1-150. London and New York: Methuen & Co., 1981.
Gives great attention to the numerous early adaptations based on one aspect or another of Shakespeare's original play.

Oliver, H. J. Introduction to *The Taming of the Shrew* by William Shakespeare, edited by H. J. Oliver, pp. 1-75. Oxford: Oxford University Press, 1982.
Provides a comprehensive stage history of *The Taming of the Shrew.* Oliver often incorporates revealing contemporary critical remarks on how the play was received at various periods in the last four centuries.

Price, Cecil. "Plays." In his *Theatre in the Age of Garrick,* pp. 142-174. Totowa, N. J.: Rowman and Littlefield, 1973.
Addresses Garrick's "well-made farce" *Catherine and Petruchio,* which held the stage until 1886.

Spencer, Hazelton. "The Taming of the Shrew." In his *The Art and*

Life of William Shakespeare, pp. 136-41. New York: Harcourt, Brace and Company, 1940.
A detailed discussion of the play's stage history.

Sprague, Arthur Colby. "Shakespearian Playgoing." In his *Shakespearian Players and Performances,* pp. 150-76. 1953. Reprint. Westport, Conn.: Greenwood Press, Publishers, 1969.
Examines various productions of Shakespeare's plays during the late 1940s and early 1950s. Sprague cites Nugent Monck's 1951 *Taming of the Shrew* as an example of that director's "enviable sureness of touch."

———, and Trewin, J. C. "Additions to the Text." In their *Shakespeare's Plays Today,* pp. 51-65. London: Sidgwick & Jackson, 1970.
Comments on different ways that directors have elected to end *The Taming of the Shrew* and round off the story of Christopher Sly.

Tanitch, Robert. *Ashcroft.* London: Hutchinson, 1987, 160 p.
A photographic study of Peggy Ashcroft's contributions to the stage. Tanitch briefly discusses Ashcroft's role as Katherina in John Barton's 1960 production at the Shakespeare Memorial Theatre.

Wells, Stanley. "Television Shakespeare." *Shakespeare Quarterly* XXXIII, No. 3 (Autumn 1982): 261-77.
Explores the effectiveness of producing Shakespearean plays for television. In cutting the Induction, Wells asserts, Jonathan Miller's BBC production reduced *The Taming of the Shrew* "by an entire dimension."

STAGING ISSUES

Alexander, Peter. "The Original Ending of *The Taming of The Shrew.*" *Shakespeare Quarterly* XX, No. 2 (Spring 1969): 111-16.
Argues that the epilogue to Shakespeare's *Taming of the Shrew* was omitted at some point in the 1590s because Pembroke's Men did not have the funds to support a large cast. The emendation persisted until the play's first printing, Alexander hypothesizes, when the Sly business in I.i was reproduced but the finale was not.

Greenfield, Thelma Nelson. "The Transformation of Christopher Sly." *Philological Quarterly* XXXIII, No. 1 (January 1954): 34-42.
Maintains that the Induction has an organic relationship to the rest of the play. Greenfield also compares the Induction with framing devices in *The Taming of a Shrew* and other Elizabethan dramas (see *SC* 9).

Jayne, Sears. "The Dreaming of the Shrew." *Shakespeare Quarterly* XVII, No. 1 (Winter 1966): 41-56.
Argues that the best way to incorporate the Induction into *The Taming of the Shrew* is to treat the entire inner play as Sly's dream. Jayne's theory holds that after Sly falls asleep at the end of I.i, he becomes Petruchio in a dream sequence. As a dashing heroic figure, Sly fulfills all of his desires, only to wake up at the end of the play as himself once again (see *SC* 9).

Margarida, Alice. "Two 'Shrews': Productions by Lunt/Fontanne (1935) and H. K. Ayliff (1927)." *The Drama Review* 25, No. 2 (Summer 1981): 87-100.
Offers an extensive analysis of the Lunt/Fontanne and H. K. Ayliff productions of *The Taming of the Shrew,* focusing on stage business and scenery in those presentations.

Sprague, Arthur Colby. "The Comedies." In his *Shakespeare and the Actors: The Stage Business in His Plays (1660-1905),* pp. 3-75. Cambridge, Mass.: Harvard University Press, 1944.
Examines the stage business of various productions of *The Taming of the Shrew* from the perspective of prompt-book entries and eyewitness accounts.

Webster, Margaret. "The Early Plays." In her *Shakespeare Without Tears,* pp. 135-58. New York and London: Whittlesey House, 1942.
    Proposes ways of interpreting the characters of Sly, Katherina, and Petruchio to make a production of *The Taming of the Shrew* more effective (see *SC* 9).

THE TWO GENTLEMEN OF VERONA

As one of William Shakespeare's fledgling works, *The Two Gentlemen of Verona* has never enjoyed the same high praise as his later plays. Considered an apprentice-like attempt at romantic comedy, *The Two Gentlemen* is burdened with problematic plot development, uneven verse, and a notoriously awkward ending. For all of its shortcomings, it does reveal flashes of Shakespeare's genius. Nevertheless, the evident lack of artistry in this play has led many scholars to speculate about the circumstances of its composition. The most widely held opinion is that *The Two Gentlemen* is one of Shakespeare's earliest plays, written when he was still a young playwright and had not yet perfected his poetic style. Another theory suggests that the play was composed in fragments throughout Shakespeare's early career, with the highly problematic fifth act hastily prepared to fill a sudden gap in his theater company's repertory schedule. Although the play may have been written as early as 1593-94, the first recorded reference to it is in Francis Meres's *Palladis Tamia* (1598). Unfortunately, Meres offered no information regarding an actual performance of the play, leading most scholars to conclude that it was either never performed or so unpopular that it did not merit recognition. Although it appears *The Two Gentlemen* was not successful in the dramatist's lifetime, Shakespeare found use for many of its elements in more than one later comedy. The relationship between Julia and Lucetta becomes more firmly developed in the characters of Portia and Nerissa in *The Merchant of Venice;* the Julia-Proteus-Silvia love triangle reappears in a more polished form in *Twelfth Night* with Viola, Orsino, and Olivia; and Launce foreshadows such famous clowns as Touchstone in *As You Like It* and Feste in *Twelfth Night.*

Just as no evidence exists to suggest that *The Two Gentlemen* was performed in Shakespeare's lifetime, there is no record of a production in the century and a half after his death. Indeed, the first recorded performance did not occur until 1762, when David Garrick, the celebrated eighteenth-century actor-manager, directed an altered version of the play. It was adapted by Benjamin Victor, a theatrical historian, who amended almost all of the play's ambiguous and contradictory elements, and added his own verse where he deemed it necessary to refine the text. In an advertisement for the production, Victor stated that while *The Two Gentlemen* is "adorned with several poetic flowers such as the hand of Shakespeare alone could raise," nevertheless the comedy "abounds with weeds." Victor intended to remove "the rankest of those weeds," and he took the liberty of adding two scenes of his own creation to the fifth act. Garrick's production of *The Two Gentlemen* opened on 22 December 1762 at Drury Lane. The most noteworthy member of the cast was Richard Yates, the famous English comedian, who played Launce. Even with two such prominent individuals associated with the production, it was presented only six times, the last performance taking place on 2 February 1763. Clifford Leech maintained that the play's poor showing can be related to the quality of Victor's adaptation. He noted that "Victor's additions are largely in prose, occasionally in halting verse. He has done a neat job on the play, showing where he found it faulty. . . .

If he had written better, his version might have held the stage longer" (see Further Reading).

The original version of *The Two Gentlemen* was produced on 17 April 1784 at Covent Garden, but only one performance was given. John Philip Kemble attempted revivals of the play in 1790 and in 1808, both of which were dismal failures. It was not until 1821 that a production of *The Two Gentlemen* enjoyed even moderate success. This achievement came with Frederick Reynolds's operatic version of the play at Covent Garden. Music for the production was composed by Henry Rowley Bishop, and J. H. Grieve designed an extravagant pageant which was staged in the middle of the play. Reportedly, the pageant was a magnificent spectacle and ran nearly half an hour. It included such marvels as the changing of the four seasons, Cleopatra's galley, and a mountain which exploded to reveal a temple of Apollo. This lavish pageant, rather than the play itself, attracted theater-goers. As one reviewer noted, "[the] first three acts were dull . . . but in the fourth, the Carnival was displayed in more than its customary glories." Henry Crabb Robinson, whose diaries offer comprehensive documentation of London theaters in the early nineteenth century, was not amused by *The Two Gentlemen of Verona* itself: "Only the pageant saves the piece. That is splendid. The Seasons, Elements, and Cleopatra's car are the most gorgeous productions I ever saw." Primarily because of the pageant's popularity, Reynolds's version of *The Two Gentlemen* enjoyed a successful run of twenty-nine performances. Over the next seventy years, several other eminent Shakespeareans attempted to produce the original version of *The Two Gentlemen*. In 1841 William Charles Macready directed a revival at Drury Lane, but it met with failure. Similarly unsuccessful were Charles Kean's productions at the Parke Theatre, New York in 1846 and at the Haymarket Theatre, London in 1848. A few years later, Samuel Phelps staged the play at Sadler's Wells, as did Osmund Tearle at Stratford-upon-Avon in 1890. These productions, too, suffered apathetic receptions.

In 1895 Augustin Daly, the American dramatist and manager, felt certain he could successfully revive this unpopular play by altering the text as Victor had done more than a century before. The production opened on 21 February 1895 at Daly's Theatre in New York, and featured Ada Rehan, the accomplished Shakespearean actress, as Julia. Even with Rehan's help, however, the *The Two Gentlemen* sustained a run of only twenty-six performances through 19 March 1895. Daly tried to stage it again some months later in his theater in London, but it barely lasted the week of July 2-7. Bernard Shaw, the celebrated dramatist and critic, was present on the opening night of Daly's London revival and wrote a condemnatory review of the production. Shaw found fault not merely with Daly's production of *The Two Gentlemen,* but with his whole theory of dramatic composition. He reprimanded the producer for making the play more "a vaudeville" than a romantic comedy; in his opinion, this conception aptly reflected "Mr. Daly's theory of how Shakespeare should have written plays." At about the same time, another renowned Shakespearean actor-manager, William Poel, also attempted to revive *The Two Gentlemen*. His first production, presented at the Merchant Taylors' Hall on 30 November 1896, included chase scenes up and down the theater aisles, with the outlaws' forest attack taking place in the vestibule. The play suffered from actors' poor performances, however, and was presented only once more the following year. Several years later, Poel returned to the play at the request of Beerbohm Tree, the eminent turn-of-the-century actor-manager. Tree was in charge of the Shakespeare Festival at His Majesty's Theatre in London when he asked Poel to stage *The Two Gentlemen* in 1910. For this production, Poel instituted two mechanical innovations that enhanced the play's effectiveness: an apron over the orchestra pit so that the audience could hear the actors' lines clearly and front lighting on the balconies facing the stage. These innovations accented the introspective and vigorous performances of Poel's young acting company, making his production a great success. Poel's accomplishment was not soon forgotten, for in a letter written to him on 18 April 1916, Prince Antoine Bibesco offered high praise for the 1910 production of *The Two Gentlemen*. Bibesco asserted that "[having] been present at a Shakespearean performance given by you a few years ago at His Majesty's I realise that you are really the only man that has given an adequate idea of the way Shakespeare should be played."

Other revivals of *The Two Gentlemen* continued to appear throughout the first half of the twentieth century without, however, gaining much critical recognition. It was not until 1952 that a twentieth-century production of *The Two Gentlemen* won substantial acclaim. Critics maintained that Denis Carey's production at the Bristol Old Vic captured the theme of youthful vitality which Shakespeare's play is obviously intended to celebrate. Led by John Neville, the young actors in Carey's presentation gave vigorous performances, creating a rare cohesiveness that contributed to the play's success. Carey's revival became so popular that the Bristol Old Vic and its young company were elevated to a position of national eminence. Another critically acclaimed production of *The Two Gentlemen* was presented in 1957 by Michael Langham at London's Old Vic. Langham gave the play an early nineteenth-century Italian setting, rather than its traditional Elizabethan one. He toned down Shakespeare's depiction of the conflict between love and friendship—a dichotomy modern audiences frequently find unpalatable—by interpreting the play as a romantic fantasy. In the Elizabethan context of the play, love submits to principles of friendship; in Langham's treatment of the theme, love is an all-consuming entity capable of undermining the bonds of friendship. Another aspect of offering the play from a romantic perspective gave greater depth to the characters of Proteus and Valentine, casting them as Byronic and Shelleyan figures. While most critics applauded Langham's innovations, the play was not a popular success, running for only thirty-one performances. Langham attempted to revive the production in the following year, assembling a new cast and taking it on a tour of Canada and the United States. Sponsored by the Stratford, Ontario Festival, Langham's company performed at the Phoenix Theatre in New York on 18 March 1958. Critical response to the well-attended production varied widely, judging it anywhere from a "dullish affair" of a "nothing play," to a "sheer delight."

In 1960 Peter Hall offered the first production of *The Two Gentlemen* to appear at Stratford-upon-Avon in several decades. It opened the season as part of Hall's master plan to present the steady maturation of Shakespeare's poetic genius through a chronological progression of six comedies. Commentators found merit in Hall's concept, yet his initial production was not successful. Several critics maintained that one of its most significant problems was a recently-installed revolving stage at the theater, which Hall apparently felt obliged to use frequently. According to many critics, the stage revolved so swiftly that the actors were unable to follow stage directions comfortably, and thus some of their movements appeared awkward and unnatural. Additionally, the actors' concentration on the moving stage was so intent that their line delivery suffered greatly. As a result of these distractions, commentators maintained, the play's inherent vigor—a crucial element for its success—was lost. From the viewpoint of several critics, another detriment to the play was Renzo Mongiardino's scenery. In many scenes, the background was so overpowering that it overshadowed the events unfolding on stage. This problem, coupled with the complications of the revolving stage, contributed to what was generally considered a disastrous failure. Throughout the production's run at Stratford, critics had much to say about the play's painfully visible shortcomings. Alan Brien remarked that the production was "a bore—and a bore made more infuriating by the unsuccessful attempts to smarten and enliven it," and A. Alvarez noted "[the] stage twirled so constantly and fast that it seemed at times more like *Carousel* than Shakespeare." At least one critic, Richard Findlater, defended Hall's production from such harsh remarks, although he did not completely endorse it. Findlater argued that while other critics held Hall responsible for "tarting [*The Two Gentlemen*] up and taking the mickey out of it in that disrespectful way . . . I am not so sure that, for this particular play in the circumstances of 1960 Stratford, the complaint is apt. For if you play this comedy straight, you are likely to knock it right back into the grave." The grave, however, is where *The Two Gentlemen* stayed for the next decade.

Robin Phillips was the next director to attempt a major production of *The Two Gentlemen of Verona*. In this inventive production, which opened at Stratford-upon-Avon in 1970, Phillips afforded *The Two Gentlemen* a modern, albeit highly fantastic, setting. The actors appeared onstage dressed in bathing suits and sun glasses, while the action took place at such diverse locations as a beach in Verona and a university campus in Milan. With this exotic milieu Phillips accentuated the play's absurd comedic elements, offering a more satirical exploration of the love and friendship contest than most productions had previously considered. Another departure was a backdrop screen through which silhouettes conformed to the action onstage, giving a pronounced focus to key scenes in the production. A deviation in characterization added a new dimension to the two gentlemens' contest not implicit in Shakespeare's text. Proteus was portrayed as physically inferior to Valentine, leading him to betray his best friend and pursue Silvia in order to prove his masculinity. These inventions all contributed to the production's popularity at Stratford, where it was performed before large audiences throughout the 1970 season. Reception of Phillips's production was generally favorable, and critics described it as a highly entertaining, although not introspective, depiction of Shakespeare's early comedy. J. C. Trewin, for example, wrote that once Phillips had "chosen an unattractive form of modern dress, he could have made hay of the night. Still, he does remember his dramatist. While nobody would be hyperbolical about the production, it is far better than one might have feared, occasional silliness apart." Robert Speaight was more admiring, stating that "Mr. Phillips deserved our applause for rescuing [*The Two Gentlemen*] from neglect and for proving its power to entertain." Phillips revived his successful production of *The Two Gentlemen* five years later during the 1975 season of the Stratford, Ontario Festival. With the help of his co-director David Toguri, Phillips added even more outrageous comedy to the new production. Perhaps the most significant addition was the satirical portrayal of Silvia not as the innocent victim of Proteus's schemes, but as a rich and wilful heiress who manipulated her suitors' affections for her own amusement. Another invention included the depiction of Antonio and the Duke of Milan as cigar-smoking Mafia godfathers. Much like his 1970 production, Phillips's revival of *The Two Gentlemen* was highly praised by dramatic critics and theater-goers alike.

In an effort to attract audiences to lesser plays in the Shakespeare canon, John Barton offered an experimental double bill production of *The Two Gentlemen of Verona* and *Titus Andronicus* at Stratford-upon-Avon in 1981. In order to present both plays in a single performance, significant cuts were made from the text of each. Barton removed 850 lines from *Titus Andronicus* and 515 from *The Two Gentlemen,* trimming the entire production to just under four hours. To lure audiences normally disinclined to see Shakespeare's less popular dramas, the two plays were shown for the price of one. Most reviewers agreed that Barton's excessive revisions of Shakespeare's text did more harm than good. The scenery and costumes were the principal innovations of this production. To emphasize the double bill concept, Barton combined the sets of both plays into one informal conglomeration of crates, ropes, props, and costumes—much as an itinerant troupe of Elizabethan players four centuries ago would have assembled. The effect was heightened when the players not acting in a particular scene quietly observed the action from the background, yet in full view of the audience. Despite these novelties, Barton's double bill received consistently unfavorable reviews from theater critics. Gareth Lloyd Evans remarked that "[double] bills have a respectable heritage, being part of the nineteenth-century theatre table d'hote menu, but John Barton's coupling of *Titus Andronicus* and *The Two Gentlemen of Verona* was a terrible dish to serve." Similarly, Sheridan Morley contended that "this whole John Barton endeavor is gimmicky and aimless in the extreme. The plays have nothing in common beyond their construction in the early 1590s, and neither is improved by the *Reader's Digest* canter through the highlights of the text." While Roger Warren did not criticize Barton as harshly as many of his contemporaries, he nevertheless pointed out that the production was unable to transcend the flaws of the original play. According to Warren, "the final impression is that we are on familiar but still experimental ground, the humour and humanity still separate strands rather than integrated with the confidence of, for instance, *A Midsummer Night's Dream.*"

In recent years, two productions of *The Two Gentlemen of Verona* have been presented to wider audiences in less traditional contexts. In 1971 Joseph Papp produced a musical adaptation of the *The Two Gentlemen* sponsored by the New York Shakespeare Festival in Central Park. The production's outrageous comedy not only attracted large audiences to the open air theater, but also won remarkably favorable reviews from dramatic critics. Buttressed by its success in Central Park, the hit musical comedy enjoyed a popular run on Broadway in the following year. Commentators had mixed feelings, however, about the integrity of John Guare and Mel Shapiro's altered text. Brendan Gill observed that "they have

been so wisely thorough in their ruthlessness; the Bard has been thrown out with the bath water, and only his tender and amiable spirit remains" (see Further Reading). More recently, *The Two Gentlemen* was performed under the auspices of BBC Television Shakespeare in England. Directed by Don Taylor, the performance was aired on 27 December 1983. The production drew mixed reviews from critics, who found fault with Taylor's satirical interpretation of the Elizabethan love theme, but praised the strong performances of the production's young cast. Another noteworthy aspect of Taylor's production was the scenery. The Renaissance buildings, courtyards, and staircases set against an unreal blue sky reminded Sandy Craig of that period's paintings in that "they give the illusion of having no depth, of being all surface" (see Further Reading). Taylor emphasized the theme of artifice throughout his production, stressing a significant aspect of *The Two Gentlemen of Verona*. In Craig's words, it is a play "about surfaces, not depths . . . It is a play about the play of ideas, not about the psychology of love."

REVIEWS AND RETROSPECTIVE ACCOUNTS OF SELECTED PRODUCTIONS

PRODUCTION:

David Garrick • Drury Lane • 1762

BACKGROUND:

This production is the first recorded performance of *The Two Gentlemen of Verona*. Benjamin Victor, the noted theatrical historian, substantially revised Shakespeare's original play, refining the various textual inconsistencies by cutting lines and rearranging scenes. Victor also created a comedic sequence at the end of the play which involves Speed playing a joke on Launce, adding greater dimension to the barrage of events in the last act. Under the direction of Garrick, one of the most prominent eighteenth-century actor-managers, *The Two Gentlemen of Verona* opened on 22 December 1762 and ran through six largely unsuccessful performances. The principal actors in this production included Mr. Holland as Proteus, Mr. Obrien as Valentine, Mr. Yates as Launce, Miss Bride as Silvia, and Mrs. Yates as Julia.

COMMENTARY:

Benjamin Victor   (essay date 1762)

[*Victor briefly comments on his adaptation of* The Two Gentlemen of Verona *in a 1762 advertisement for the play, explaining that his revisions are only meant to preserve the "several poetical flowers" in a comedy that "abounds with weeds."*]

It is the general opinion that this comedy abounds with weeds, and there is no one, I think, will deny, who peruses it with attention, that it is adorned with several poetical flowers such as the hand of a Shakespeare alone could raise. The rankest of those weeds I have endeavoured to remove; but was not a little solicitous lest I should go too far and, while I fancy'd myself grubbing up a weed, should heedlessly cut the threads of a flower.

The other part of my design, which was to give a greater uniformity to the scenery and a connection and consistency to the fable (which in many places is visibly wanted), will be deemed of more importance if it should be found to be executed with success.

As to the two additional scenes of Launce and Speed in the last act, I shall leave them to the candid judges of dramatic composition whether they contribute any thing to the representation, or afford any amusement to the reader.

> *Benjamin Victor, in an excerpt from* Shakespeare, The Critical Heritage: 1753-1765, Vol. 4, *edited by Brian Vickers, Routledge & Kegan Paul, 1976, p. 525.*

The Monthly Review   (review date January 1763)

> [*In an unsigned review, the critic praises Victor's adaptation of* The Two Gentlemen of Verona *as an improvement over Shakespeare's original play.*]

Although this Comedy is generally reckoned as one of Shakespeare's worst Performances, and even by many thought so meanly of, as to be deemed the Work of some inferior hand, in which Shakespeare bore but a very small Part; yet hath it been so much more favourably regarded by the present Editor [Benjamin Victor], as to be thought worth all the pains he hath taken to improve it. He observes, in his previous advertisement, that "it is the general opinion, that this comedy abounds with weeds;" but he thinks no one who peruses it with Attention, will deny, "that it is adorned with several poetical Flowers, such as the hand of a Shakespeare alone could raise."—The rankest of the weeds he has endeavoured to remove, and we think with a careful and skilful hand.—Another part of his design was "to give a greater uniformity to the scenery, and a connection and consistency to the fable, which in many places is visibly wanted:" wherein we apprehend our Editor hath not been unsuccessful. He has also inserted two additional scenes in the last act, of a humorous cast, and which, in our Opinion, are not inferior to any other parts, of the same kind, in the original.

> *A review of "The Two Gentlemen of Verona, a Comedy," in* The Monthly Review, London, *Vol. XXVIII, January, 1763, p. 75.*

George C. D. Odell   (essay date 1920)

> [*Odell examines Benjamin Victor's 1762 adaptation of* The Two Gentlemen of Verona, *describing the numerous textual changes and additions he made to the original text.*]

[Benjamin] Victor, the chronicler of the stage and its doings, adapted [*The Two Gentlemen of Verona*], and had it produced at Drury Lane on December 22, 1762. His Advertisement to the printed copy is more fearsome in sound than is warranted by a study of his adaptation. The preamble, as usual, states the author's aim to be the removal of "the rankest of those weeds" in which "this comedy abounds." The other part of his design was to give greater uniformity to the scenery. "As to the two additional scenes of Launce and

Speed in the last act," he leaves them to "the candid judges of dramatic composition."

There is a very great deal of shifting of Shakespeare's order in the first two acts, all to gain the desired unity. For instance, Proteus enters in the second scene, reading Julia's letter, though the scene of Julia's tearing his letter, etc., does not come till later. There is new matter for Speed. In the parts immediately following, in Julia's chamber, three scenes of Shakespeare are violently run together—her letter scene with Lucetta, her parting with Proteus (Shakespeare's Act II, Scene 2) and her subsequent resolve to follow him to Milan (Shakespeare's Act II, Scene 7). This, of course, permits all the events at Milan to be played consecutively, without further return to Verona. No doubt unity of place must be purchased at any sacrifice of meaning or sense in the situation. In Act II, now at Milan, there is an extra trial for Silvia, in which, to protect herself from the love of Thurio, she throws herself on the love and protection of Valentine. The famous "bit" of Launce with the dog and Speed is transferred to Milan; but here it has no sense, since he has been a long time from Verona. Acts III and IV are practically Shakespeare intact, except that there is an added scene for Eglamour and Silvia at the Abbey. The fifth act involves the matter of the flight to the forest, the episodes of the brigands, etc. This is enlivened by the two new scenes for Launce spoken of in Victor's advertisement. In the first Launce enters the forest, followed by Crab, and indulges in a long soliloquy expressing his fright. "We are lost and undone! What will become of us? What could my master mean by sending me into this frightful forest," etc. Enter three Outlaws, who present their guns at Launce, and drag him out. The second of these new scenes begins after the Duke has given his consent to Valentine's marrying Silvia. Speed rushes in, claps on a disguise, and tells them all to prepare for sport. Brigands drag in Launce and his dog; they threaten to kill him. They offer to let him and the seemingly unmoved dog draw lots to see which shall die. Launce says he cannot live without his dog. All laugh, he recognises them, and happiness crowns the event. (pp. 374-75)

> *George C. D. Odell, "The Plays: 'The Two Gentlemen of Verona,' 1762," in his* Shakespeare from Betterton to Irving, Vol. I, *1920. Reprint by Constable and Company, Ltd., 1921, pp. 374-75.*

PRODUCTION:

Frederick Reynolds • Covent Garden • 1821

BACKGROUND:

On 29 November 1821 Reynolds's musical production of *The Two Gentlemen of Verona,* which included a magnificent pageant in the middle of the play, opened at Covent Garden. The text of the play was significantly cut in order to accommodate the pageant, which ran nearly a half hour and included such spectacles as the changing of the four seasons, Cleopatra's galley, and a mountain which exploded to reveal a temple of Apollo. This extravagant stage show was immensely popular, but it completely overshadowed the play itself. Largely due to the pageant, the production enjoyed a successful run of twenty-nine performances.

J. H. Grieve designed the scenery and Henry Rowley Bishop provided the music for the production. The principal actors included Mr. Abbott as Proteus, Mr. Jones as Valentine, Mr. Liston as Launce, Miss Hallande as Silvia, and Miss Tree as Julia.

COMMENTARY:

European Magazine   (review date 29 November 1821)

[*In the following excerpt, the anonymous critic offers high praise of the extravagant pageant in Reynolds's production of* The Two Gentlemen of Verona, *although he maintains that the rest of the play was monotonous.*]

'The Two Gentlemen of Verona,' was this evening revived with an abundance of music, splendid scenery, and surpassing machinery. Whether this perversion of Shakespeare into melo-drame have 'nothing of offence in it,' may be a question; but if the offence could be palliated, it must be in the case of the present play, one the feeblest and most incomplete of all the hasty works of it's great author; so much so indeed, as to have been doubted by many competent judges, if it were really his. The love of Valentine, and the inconstancy of Proteus; the lofty resolution of Sylvia, and the gentle constancy of Julia, were to-night embellished with illuminated palaces and triumphant galleys; catches and glees in forests, and a blazing mountain! The first three acts were dull, with the occasional exhilaration of songs by Miss Tree and Miss Hallande; but in the fourth, the Carnival was displayed in more than its customary glories. The opening of the scene displayed the Ducal Palace and great square of Milan illuminated, golden gondolas on the river, and all the usual appendages of a foreign gala, masquers, dancing girls, and mountebanks. The pageant then commenced, with a display of the Seasons. Spring came enthroned on a pile of unblown flowers, which the nymph touched with her wand, and the buds were turned into blooms. Then came Summer in the midst of corn, which grew into golden heads at her touch. Autumn followed, with a similar conversion of leaves and stems into melting grapes and blushing apples, and Winter closed the pomp by a view of Lapland with a shower of snow; while dancing nymphs, reapers, and shivering Laplanders, filled up the intervals. Next came the elements, Earth moved on in majesty, seated in a car drawn by lions over clouds; and Air was a portrait of Juno, attended by her peacocks.—Fire had Vulcan in his forge, illuminated by showers of his own sparks; and Water was green robed, with a pair of pigmies sounding Conch shells, and seated upon Dolphins. The stage was then suddenly invaded by water, and on it's bosom rolled Cleopatra's galley, covered with silks and gilding. The Queen lay classically sofa'd upon the deck, and the Nymphs and Cupids flew and fanned about her with picturesque fidelity. This was followed by a splendid scene of the Palace of Pleasure, all gaiety and glory, which was also succeeded by a view in the Duke's gardens, with a lake, a castle, a bridge, and an artificial mountain reaching to the clouds, the explosion of which discovered a gorgeous Temple of Apollo, rich in all that is bright and brilliant; and dazzling the spectators until the drop scene covered the catastrophe. The applause which had before been most lavish, rose to enthusiasm at this spectacle, which it is but justice to say, was most magnificent. Its only fault being its too great length, which has been since remedied.

There was also rather too much music in the Play; and of this

the two glees harmonized from If o'er the cruel Tyrant Love, and Pray Goody, were the most popular. Sylvia's songs were, however, also clever compositions, and Julia's duet with Master Longhurst, displayed both to much advantage.

Jones, who bore the character which, we believe, was once played by John Kemble, threw much spirit into the true lover, and bold outlaw, Valentine. Abbott played Proteus very ably, and Farren's Sir Thurio was the 'high fantastical,' both in his acting and his dress. Liston was a good Launce, and his dog Crab was a fine quiet animal of the Newfoundland breed, which bore much pulling about the stage with much equanimity. Miss Tree performed and sang most sweetly as Julia, but was tasked by too many songs, and Miss Hallande both sang and acted extremely well as Sylvia. We have spoken of the general preparation of the play, which was most costly and striking; and though something more than either song or scenery is essential to continued popularity, 'The Two Gentlemen of Verona,' we think, discovers all the longevity, that the managers could reasonably anticipate, for its lavish expense well deserves public remuneration. The whole play is very materially transposed and altered from the original, and many of the scenes display Mr. Reynolds's blank verse in company with Shakespeare's.

A review of "Two Gentlemen of Verona," in The European Magazine and London Review, *Vol. LXXX, December, 1821, p. 570.*

Henry Crabb Robinson   (diary date 3 December 1821)

[*Robinson is remembered as an insightful and outspoken commentator on the literary world of nineteenth-century London. The recollections chronicled in his* Diary, Reminiscences, and Correspondence, *published two years after his death in 1867, provide an astute assessment of literary trends and society during his lifetime. In the excerpt below from his diary, dated 3 December 1821, Robinson mentions seeing Reynolds's production of* The Two Gentlemen of Verona. *While the play itself was not entertaining, he holds, the pageant was the best he ever saw.*]

Lounged at the Surry institution and then went to Covent Garden. Hardly amused by the *Two Gentlemen of Verona*—Liston's Launce and Miss Tree's Julia alone pleasing—The Two Gentlemen worthless in themselves were represented by Jones and Abbott. Only the pageant saves the piece. That is splendid. The Seasons, Elements, and Cleopatra's car are the most gorgeous productions I ever saw—Talk of a Coronation—psha!

Henry Crabb Robinson, in a diary entry on December 3, 1821, in his The London Theatre: 1811-1866, *edited by Eluned Brown, The Society for Theatre Research, 1966, p. 98.*

European Magazine   (review date 6 December 1821)

[*In the excerpt below from an article first published in* European Magazine *on 6 December 1821, the anonymous writer describes an accident which befell Mr. Abbott as he played Proteus during a performance of Reynolds's* Two Gentlemen of Verona.]

'The Two Gentlemen of Verona' had this evening rather a tragical denouement, from an accidental wound given to Mr. Abbott as Sir Proteus while fencing in the banditti scene at the close of the fifth act. From the piercing shriek of Mr. A.

the injury was at first apprehended to be really dangerous, but was speedily ascertained not to have touched the eye, although the cheek was laid open by Mr. Comer's sword. The audience would not suffer the play to proceed farther, and Mr. Abbott was instantly conveyed home from the theatre in a carriage.

A review of "The Two Gentlemen of Verona," in Eyewitnesses of Shakespeare: First Hand Accounts of Performances 1590-1890, edited by Gāmini Salgādo, Barnes & Noble, 1975, p. 80.

European Magazine   (review date 17 December 1821)

[The following excerpt is taken from a review that first appeared in European Magazine on 17 December 1821. The anonymous critic reports that Mr. Abbott, who played Proteus in Reynolds's Two Gentlemen of Verona, returned to the stage, fully recovered from an accidental stab wound received during a performance two weeks before.]

We are equally happy in being enabled to announce the recovery and re-appearance of Mr. Abbott; and the continued success of 'The Two Gentlemen of Verona.' The injury sustained by Mr. A. having been much less than was at first apprehended, we are gratified in congratulating both himself and the public upon his resumption of his professional exertions this evening. The temporary indisposition of Miss Hallande since our last notice, introduced a Miss Boyle from Dublin for a few evenings as Sylvia; and also as Zelinda in 'The Slave'; in both which characters she was very favourably received; though she is certainly far more au fait as an actress, than a singer. Her compass and power of voice, both appearing to us quite inadequate to sustain the vocal heroines of Covent Garden. The gorgeous spectacle attached to Shakespeare's comedy, continues to attract crowded audiences, and elicit unbounded approbation. So much so, indeed, that when gazing upon Cleopatra's galley, we forget that the Cydnus can have no business at Milan; and that Venetian Carnivals are not even yet naturalised amongst the Milanese. The last scene also by Pugh, of an opening in a forest by moonlight, forms a display of quiet tranquil beauty, that we have never seen exceeded. (pp. 80-1)

A review of "The Two Gentlemen of Verona," in Eyewitnesses of Shakespeare: First Hand Accounts of Performances 1590-1890, edited by Gāmini Salgādo, Barnes & Noble, 1975, pp. 80-1.

The Theatrical Observer   (review date 17 January 1822)

[In the following review, the anonymous critic offers a brief account of various performers in Reynolds's production of The Two Gentlemen of Verona at Covent Garden.]

THE TWO GENTLEMEN OF VERONA, and the PANTOMIME, drew a very numerous Audience to this Theatre last Night. The Pit was full,—the Galleries nearly so,—the Dress Boxes respectably attended,—and the other Circles rather indifferently so,

Mr. JONES was very deficient in the words of his character. Mr. BLANCHARD performed the part of Speed with his usual success: and we noticed with much pleasure in the last scene but one of the fourth act, an attention to the lighter shades, which denoted the Master—On being surrounded by the Robbers, Speed labours under the greatest fear, and, with

much vehemency entreats Sir Valentine to accept their offer of electing him as their Captain; on his doing which, the timid servant instantly became the courageous comrade, and Mr. B giving the full effect to this, after a few minutes of examination, changed the cock of his hat to that assumed by the Banditti, and in other respects evinced a desire to imitate their manners and habits. These are but trifles, yet these trifles pourtray the mind of the Actor; and as we are often severe when we perceive "trifling" encroachments upon the propriety of the stage, we are alike ready to notice every treat of talent and study. We must congratulate Mr. Mongrel on his improvement in the character of Crab; his knowledge of the stage, and confidence, during his performance, have very much increased since his debut, and he seemed to have imbibed a very favorable idea of the passing events, as on the wag of his tail being referred to for an answer to a question, with much precosity of talent, he gave the unexpected reply to the great amusement of Messrs. Liston and Blanchard.

A review of "The Two Gentlemen of Verona," in The Theatrical Observer, No. 64, January 17, 1822, p. 254.

Sybil Rosenfeld   (essay date 1967)

[The excerpt below is taken from an essay on Shakespearean scene designs by J. H. Grieve. Rosenfeld briefly examines the spectacular pageant Grieve devised for Frederick Reynolds's 1821 production of The Two Gentlemen of Verona.]

In 1821, J. H. Grieve . . . had three Shakespeare productions to his credit, the two others being 2 Henry IV and The Two Gentlemen of Verona. This latter was in a musical version by Reynolds and Bishop who had already collaborated with Grieve in their Comedy of Errors in 1819. Scenically it was distinguished by a set of four new scenes of carnival in the square of Milan. The pretext for this is in the Duke's words:

Come let us go: we will include all jars
With trumpets, mirth, and rare solemnity,

[V. iv. 160-1]

duly adapted to 'Now, on to Milan; where will end all jars'. The four scenes were: (1) the four seasons and four elements in procession with Cleopatra's barge sailing down the Cydnus; (2) palace of the hours, morning, noon, evening and night by Wright; (3) an artificial mountain in the gardens of the Duke of Milan which exploded and discovered (4) the Temple of Apollo. This pageantry lasted half an hour, though subsequently curtailed, and necessarily involved much cutting of the text. Opinions on the scenery differed. The Theatrical Observer considered it 'exceedingly splendid and beautiful' but the critic in Drama was carping: he surmised that the scenery had been painted for some Venetian play and merely used for The Two Gentlemen. He found alarming errors at a time when topical accuracy was the vogue: 'There is a view of St Mark's palace, which is admirable in every respect but the church, which is a very indifferent representation' since its west front had been carelessly supplied with seven doors instead of the actual five. The error, he continues, could have been avoided if the scene painter had viewed Barker's panorama in the Strand. Worse was to follow: 'The scene announced in the bills as the grand square of Milan' was guilty of including what was obviously the Venetian Doge's Palace with an opening leading to St Mark's. As for Cleopatra's galley, it 'filled the whole frame of the stage' and the writer concluded in a vein of admiration: 'this play has borne the arts of stage machinery and scenic decoration to the highest pitch'. The *Morning Post,* after defending the musical version on the ground that it restored an unattractive play to popularity, added that the production was 'distinguished by one of the most gorgeous pageants that can be conceived . . . a representation of the Carnival with all its gaieties and amusements'. The audience is said to have risen to the spectacle and shaken the house with applause. Indeed it was so popular that it was later detached from the play and presented with the coronation spectacle from *The Exile.* (pp. 107-08)

> Sybil Rosenfeld, *"The Grieves Shakespearian Scene Designs,"* in Shakespeare Survey: An Annual Survey of Shakespearian Study and Production, *Vol. 20, 1967, pp. 107-12.*

PRODUCTION:

Augustin Daly • Daly's Theatre • 1895

BACKGROUND:

Daly was an eminent nineteenth-century American dramatist and actor. His production of *The Two Gentlemen of Verona* was first performed in New York on 21 February 1895. For his presentation, Daly cut and rearranged much of the original text to make the plot run more evenly. The play was not well received by New York theater-goers, however, playing only twenty-six times through 19 March 1895. Daly tried to revive it at Daly's Theatre in London some months later, but it ran for only one week. After attending a performance in London, Bernard Shaw severely criticized Daly for using his unusual dramatic theories to make an already flawed play even more bewildering. In this unsuccessful production, the two gentlemen were played by Mr. Worthing and Mr. Craig. Mr. Lewis appeared as Launce, Maxine Elliot as Silvia, and Ada Rehan as Julia.

COMMENTARY:

Bernard Shaw   (review date 6 July 1895)

[*Shaw, an Irish dramatist and critic, was the major English playwright of his generation. In his Shakespearean criticism, he consistently attacked what he considered Shakespeare's inflated reputation as a dramatist. Shaw did not hesitate to judge the characters in the plays by the standards of his own values and prejudices, and much of his commentary is presented—as a recent editor, Edwin Wilson, remarked—"with an impudence that had not been seen before, nor is likely to be seen again." Shaw's hostility toward Shakespeare's work was due in large measure to his belief that it was interfering with the acceptance of Henrik Ibsen and the new social theater he so strongly advocated. Shaw served as theater critic for the* Saturday Review *from 1895-98. In the excerpt below, Shaw harshly criticizes Daly's production of* The Two Gentlemen of Verona, *finding fault with all aspects of his interpretation of the play. He regards the production as nothing more than "a vaudeville," attacking in particular Daly's textual alterations, his scenic effects, and the music.*]

The piece founded by Augustin Daly on Shakespeare's "Two Gentlemen of Verona," to which I looked forward last week,

is not exactly a comic opera, though there is plenty of music in it, and not exactly a serpentine dance, though it proceeds under a play of changing coloured lights. It is something more old-fashioned than either: to wit, a vaudeville. And let me hasten to admit that it makes a very pleasant entertainment for those who know no better. Even I, who know a great deal better, as I shall presently demonstrate rather severely, enjoyed myself tolerably. I cannot feel harshly towards a gentleman who works so hard as Mr. Daly does to make Shakespeare presentable: one feels that he loves the bard, and lets him have his way as far as he thinks it good for him. His rearrangement of the scenes of the first two acts is just like him. Shakespeare shows lucidly how Proteus lives with his father (Antonio) in Verona, and loves a lady of that city named Julia. Mr. Daly, by taking the scene in Julia's house between Julia and her maid, and the scene in Antonio's house between Antonio and Proteus, and making them into one scene, convinces the unlettered audience that Proteus and Julia live in the same house with their father Antonio. Further, Shakespeare shows us how Valentine, the other gentleman of Verona, travels from Verona to Milan, the journey being driven into our heads by a comic scene in Verona, in which Valentine's servant is overwhelmed with grief at leaving his parents, and with indignation at the insensibility of his dog to his sorrow, followed presently by another comic scene in Milan in which the same servant is welcomed to the strange city by a fellow-servant. Mr. Daly, however, is ready for Shakespeare on this point too. He just represents the two scenes as occurring in the same place; and immediately the puzzle as to who is who is complicated by a puzzle as to where is where. Thus is the immortal William adapted to the requirements of a nineteenth-century audience.

In preparing the text of his version Mr. Daly has proceeded on the usual principles, altering, transposing, omitting, improving, correcting, and transferring speeches from one character to another. Many of Shakespeare's lines are mere poetry, not to the point, not getting the play along, evidently stuck in because the poet liked to spread himself in verse. On all such unbusinesslike superfluities Mr. Daly is down with his blue pencil. For instance, he relieves us of such stuff as the following, which merely conveys that Valentine loves Silvia, a fact already sufficiently established by the previous dialogue:

> My thoughts do harbour with my Silvia nightly;
> And slaves they are to me, that send them flying:
> Oh, could their master come and go as lightly,
> Himself would lodge where senseless they are lying.
> My herald thoughts in thy pure bosom rest them,
> While I, their king, that thither them importune,
> Do curse the grace that with such grace hath blessed them,
> Because myself do want my servant's fortune.
> I curse myself, for they are sent by me,
> That they should harbour where their lord would be.
> [III. i. 140-49]

Slaves indeed are these lines and their like to Mr. Daly, who "sends them flying" without remorse. But when he comes to passages that a stage manager can understand, his reverence for the bard knows no bounds. The following awkward lines, unnecessary as they are under modern stage conditions, are at any rate not poetic, and are in the nature of police news. Therefore they are piously retained.

> What halloing, and what stir, is this to-day?
> These are my mates, that make their wills their law,
> Have some unhappy passenger in chase.

They love me well; yet I have much to do,
To keep them from uncivil outrages.
Withdraw thee, Valentine: who's this comes here?

                                                    [V. iv. 13-18]

The perfunctory metrical character of such lines only makes them more ridiculous than they would be in prose. I would cut them out without remorse to make room for all the lines that have nothing to justify their existence except their poetry, their humour, their touches of character—in short, the lines for whose sake the play survives, just as it was for their sake it originally came into existence. Mr. Daly, who prefers the lines which only exist for the sake of the play, will doubtless think me as great a fool as Shakespeare; but I submit to him, without disputing his judgment, that he is, after all, only a man with a theory of dramatic composition, going with a blue pencil over the work of a great dramatist, and striking out everything that does not fit his theory. Now, as it happens, nobody cares about Mr. Daly's theory; whilst everybody who pays to see what is, after all, advertised as a performance of Shakespeare's play entitled "The Two Gentlemen of Verona," and not as a demonstration of Mr. Daly's theory, does care more or less about the art of Shakespeare. Why not give them what they ask for, instead of going to great trouble and expense to give them something else?

In those matters in which Mr. Daly has given the rein to his own taste and fancy: that is to say, in scenery, costumes, and music, he is for the most part disabled by a want of real knowledge of the arts concerned. I say for the most part, because his pretty fifteenth-century dresses, though probably inspired rather by Sir Frederic Leighton than by Benozzo Gozzoli, may pass. But the scenery is insufferable. First, for "a street in Verona" we get a Bath bun coloured operatic front cloth with about as much light in it as there is in a studio in Fitzjohn's Avenue in the middle of October. I respectfully invite Mr. Daly to spend his next holiday looking at a real street in Verona, asking his conscience meanwhile whether a manager with eyes in his head and the electric light at his disposal could not advance a step on the Telbin (senior) style. Telbin was an admirable scene painter; but he was limited by the mechanical conditions of gas illumination; and he learnt his technique before the great advance made during the Impressionist movement in the painting of open-air effects, especially of brilliant sunlight. Of that advance Mr. Daly has apparently no conception. The days of Macready and Clarkson Stanfield still exist for him; he would probably prefer a watercolour drawing of a foreign street by Samuel Prout to one by Mr. T. M. Rooke; and I dare say every relic of the original tallow candlelight that still clings to the art of scene-painting is as dear to him as it is to most old playgoers, including, unhappily, many of the critics.

As to the elaborate set in which Julia makes her first entrance, a glance at it shows how far Mr. Daly prefers the Marble Arch to the loggia of Orcagna. All over the scene we have Renaissance work, in its genteelest stages of decay, held up as the perfection of romantic elegance and beauty. The school that produced the classicism of the First Empire, designed the terraces of Regent's Park and the façades of Fitzroy Square, and conceived the Boboli Gardens and Versailles as places for human beings to be happy in, ramps all over the scenery, and offers as much of its pet colonnades and statues as can be crammed into a single scene, by way of a compendium of everything that is lovely in the city of San Zeno and the tombs of the Scaligers. As to the natural objects depicted, I ask whether any man living has ever seen a pale green cy-

press in Verona or anywhere else out of a toy Noah's Ark. A man who, having once seen cypresses and felt their presence in a north Italian landscape, paints them lettuce colour, must be suffering either from madness, malice, or a theory of how nature should have coloured trees, cognate with Mr. Daly's theory of how Shakespeare should have written plays.

Of the music let me speak compassionately. After all, it is only very lately that Mr. Arnold Dolmetsch, by playing fifteenth-century music on fifteenth-century instruments, has shewn us that the age of beauty was true to itself in music as in pictures and armour and costumes. But what should Mr. Daly know of this, educated as he no doubt was to believe that the court of Denmark should always enter in the first act of "Hamlet" to the march from "Judas Maccabæus?" Schubert's setting of "Who is Silvia?" [IV. ii. 39ff.] he knew, but had rashly used up in "Twelfth Night" as "Who's Olivia." He has therefore had to fall back on another modern setting, almost supernaturally devoid of any particular merit. Besides this, all through the drama the most horribly common music repeatedly breaks out on the slightest pretext or on no pretext at all. One dance, set to a crude old English popular tune, sundry eighteenth and nineteenth century musical banalities, and a titivated plantation melody in the first act which produces an indescribably atrocious effect by coming in behind the scenes as a sort of coda to Julia's curtain speech, all turn the play, as I have said, into a vaudeville. Needless to add, the accompaniments are not played on lutes and viols, but by the orchestra and a guitar or two. In the forest scene the outlaws begin the act by a chorus. After their encounter with Valentine they go off the stage singing the refrain exactly in the style of "La Fille de Madame Angot." The wanton absurdity of introducing this comic opera convention is presently eclipsed by a thunderstorm, immediately after which Valentine enters and delivers his speech sitting down on a bank of moss, as an outlaw in tights naturally would after a terrific shower. Such is the effect of many years of theatrical management on the human brain.

Perhaps the oddest remark I have to make about the performance is that, with all its glaring defects and blunders, it is rather a handsome and elaborate one as such things go. It is many years now since Mr. Ruskin first took the Academicians of his day aback by the obvious remark that Carpaccio and Giovanni Bellini were better painters than Domenichino and Salvator Rosa. Nobody dreams now of assuming that Pope was a greater poet than Chaucer, that "Mozart's Twelfth Mass" is superior to the masterpieces of Orlandus Lassus and Palestrina, or that our "ecclesiastical Gothic" architecture is more enlightened than Norman axe work. But the theatre is still wallowing in such follies; and until Mr. Comyns Carr and Sir Edward Burne-Jones, Baronet, put "King Arthur" on the stage more or less in the manner natural to men who know these things, Mr. Daly might have pleaded the unbroken conservatism of the playhouse against me. But after the Lyceum scenery and architecture I decline to accept a relapse without protest. There is no reason why cheap photographs of Italian architecture (six-pence apiece in infinite variety at the bookstall in the South Kensington Museum) should not rescue us from Regent's Park Renaissance colonnades on the stage just as the electric light can rescue us from Telbin's dun-coloured sunlight. The opera is the last place in the world where any wise man would look for adequate stage illusion; but the fact is that Mr. Daly, with all his coloured lights, has not produced a single Italian scene comparable in illusion to that provided by Sir Augustus Harris at Covent Garden for "Cavalleria Rusticana."

Of the acting I have not much to say. Miss Rehan provided a strong argument in favour of rational dress by looking much better in her page's costume than in that of her own sex; and in the serenade scene, and that of the wooing of Silvia for Proteus, she stirred some feeling into the part, and reminded us of what she was in "Twelfth Night," where the same situations are fully worked out. For the rest, she moved and spoke with imposing rhythmic grace. That is as much notice as so cheap a part as Julia is worth from an artist who, being absolute mistress of the situation at Daly's theatre, might and should have played Imogen [in *Cymbeline*] for us instead. The two gentlemen were impersonated by Mr. Worthing and Mr. Craig. Mr. Worthing charged himself with feeling without any particular reference to his lines; and Mr. Craig struck a balance by attending to the meaning of his speeches without taking them at all to heart. Mr. Clarke, as the Duke, was emphatic, and worked up every long speech to a climax in the useful old style; but his tone is harsh, his touch on his consonants coarse, and his accent ugly, all fatal disqualifications for the delivery of Shakespearean verse. The scenes between Launce and his dog brought out the latent silliness and childishness of the audience as Shakespeare's clowning scenes always do: I laugh at them like a yokel myself. Mr. Lewis hardly made the most of them. His style has been formed in modern comedies, where the locutions are so familiar that their meaning is in no danger of being lost by the rapidity of his quaint utterance; but Launce's phraseology is another matter: a few of the funniest lines missed fire because the audience did not catch them. And with all possible allowance for Mr. Daly's blue pencil, I cannot help suspecting that Mr. Lewis's memory was responsible for one or two of his omissions. Still, Mr. Lewis has always his comic force, whether he makes the most or the least of it; so that he cannot fail in such a part as Launce. Miss Maxine Elliot's Silvia was the most considerable performance after Miss Rehan's Julia. The whole company will gain by the substitution on Tuesday next of a much better play, "A Midsummer Night's Dream," as a basis for Mr. Daly's operations. No doubt he is at this moment, like Mrs. Todgers, "a dodgin' among the tender bits with a fork, and an eatin' of 'em"; but there is sure to be enough of the original left here and there to repay a visit. (pp. 10-12)

Bernard Shaw, "Poor Shakespeare," in The Saturday Review, *London, Vol. 80, No. 2071, July 6, 1895, pp. 10-12.*

Marvin Felheim   (essay date 1956)

[*Felheim comments on Daly's 1895 production of* The Two Gentlemen of Verona, *noting that even Daly's significant text revisions and insertions could not rescue this unpopular play from failure.*]

Although *Twelfth Night* had been a sprightly revival, Daly's subsequent production, *The Two Gentlemen of Verona,* was a dismal failure. Viola and Rosalind provided material worthy of stars but to mold Julia into the central figure of *The Two Gentlemen of Verona* Daly not only had an insufficiently drawn personality to work with, but he was also inextricably involved in a minor play which could not stand up under his rough handling. Such worth as there is in the play he distorted so ridiculously that Shaw labeled the revival "a

vaudeville . . . founded by Augustin Daly on Shakespeare." To this Shaw added a general condemnation of that "school" of managers which considered Shakespeare "a wretchedly unskillful dramatic author."

The distortions in this play not only resulted in rearranged scenes and lines but also frequently succeeded in making the plot and the characterizations even less distinct than Shakespeare had left them. For example, in Daly's Act II, scene I (Shakespeare's I, iii and II, ii), by the curious omission of the first 44 lines of I, iii, the surrendering of Proteus' lines to Julia, and the strange ordering of the two scenes, Julia enters to bid Proteus goodbye immediately after his father finishes telling him he is to go to Milan. How she could have found out the news other than by sheer intuition is a mystery. However illogical her entrance at that point may be, the rearrangement gives her the first scene curtain speech of Daly's Act II.

As a matter of fact, Miss Rehan speaks the curtain lines in all four acts as well as in the above-mentioned scene. Daly's Act I ends with Julia's soliloquy from Shakespeare's Act I, scene ii. To close Act II, she speaks lines 34-38, transposed to follow lines 80-90. By ending Act III with Shakespeare's IV, ii, Daly manages a third act curtain speech for Julia. Finally, at the conclusion of the play she not only recites Valentine's lines from Act V, scene iv, but also speaks an epilogue transferred from *The Famous History of the Life of King Henry the Eighth.* (pp. 255-56)

When Kittredge asserted that the final scene of the play "sacrifices everything to crude sensationalism," he was referring to Shakespeare's treatment. To increase the "sensationalism," Daly added a storm, merely for purposes of scenic effect since there is no indication in the text of any change of climate. In a bitter mood as a result of the many excesses of this revival, Archer ventured the ironical suggestion that Mr. Daly be appointed "Honorary President of the Elizabethan Stage Society" since his revivals were "object lessons in support of the Society's tenets"—that Shakespeare should be recited word for word on a bare platform.

Public disapproval was more effective than Archer's irony. In New York, *The Two Gentlemen of Verona* was presented only twenty-six times, from February 21 through March 19, 1895. In London, it lasted the week of July 2-7, 1895. It was never revived again by Daly. (p. 257)

Marvin Felheim, "Shakespeare, New Style," in his The Theater of Augustin Daly: An Account of the Late Nineteenth Century American Stage, *Cambridge, Mass.: Harvard University Press, 1956, pp. 219-84.*

PRODUCTION:

William Poel • Merchant Taylors' Hall • 1896

BACKGROUND:

Poel was a celebrated English actor and producer, as well as a leader of the late nineteenth-century Elizabethan Revival. His first attempt at producing *The Two Gentlemen of Verona* occurred at Merchant Taylors' Hall on 30 November 1896. Although he used several innovative theatrical effects, such as chase scenes up and down the aisle, the production was unsuccessful, largely because the cast was unable to master the elocutionary techniques required of them. Poel offered the production again at the Great Hall of the Charterhouse on 18 January 1897, but it too met with failure. At the invitation of Beerbohm Tree, the influential turn-of-the-century actor-manager, Poel directed a second revival of *The Two Gentlemen of Verona* for the Shakespeare Festival at His Majesty's Theatre in London on 20 April 1910. For this memorable and well-received production, Poel had an apron constructed over the orchestra pit, thus bringing the actors forward and allowing their voices to be better heard by the audience.

COMMENTARY:

A. B. Walkley　(review date 21 April 1910)

[*Walkley praises the successful Elizabethan staging of* The Two Gentlemen of Verona *as "a feather in the cap" of the production's director, William Poel.*]

A "Shakespeare Festival," consisting, like the present, of a series of "turns" by different companies presenting Shakespeare in a variety of styles, would certainly not be complete without a performance from the Elizabethan Stage Society. Their style, as everybody knows, is the archaic. They reproduce the "platform stage," the dresses, the "rhetorical" acting, and, generally, such conditions as can be reproduced, of Shakespeare's own period. Of course, what they cannot reproduce is the Elizabethan audience with the Elizabethan frame of mind, so that what was originally natural is now quaint: and that will seem to most people reason sufficient to dispose of the society's avowed "principle that Shakespeare's plays should be accorded the build of stage for which they were designed." Nevertheless, it is good to see the principle now and then carried out, for it certainly helps us to a better knowledge of Shakespeare: and *The Two Gentlemen of Verona* did, in fact, furnish last night an entertainment of absorbing interest, while the puerile complications and improbabilities of the intrigue, which a "realistic" modern setting would only have made more glaring, became of little account. The "literary" quality of the play, the verve of its dialogue, the lyric beauty of many of its passages, came out with unusual freshness and in clear-cut relief. And, better still, one got far more satisfactorily than one could get in a modern setting the "atmosphere" of the play, the atmosphere of warm, romantic amorism. You were made to feel more than ever how *The Two Gentlemen of Verona* is a brilliant fantasia on what Pascal called "les passions de l'amour" [the passions of love]— love as a constant devotion in Valentine and as in Julia, as mingled coquetry and tenderness in Silvia, as spiritual idealism in Sir Eglamour, and as Donjaunism in Proteus. Who cares where Shakespeare found his plot or how little trouble he took to make it probable? What one cares about is the beauty, the youthfulness, the passionate mood of the whole thing—the mood, beyond all cavil, of a man, like St. Augustine in his youth, "in love, with love." And no Elizabethan costumes can make that mood seem archaic. On the contrary, one is constantly being reminded of modern analogues—now of some "Italianate" trifle of Musset's, then of the *marivaudage* [frivolous bantering talk] of Marivaux, and again of the romantic fervor of Cyrano de Bergerac serenading his *précieuse.* Even the lightness with which Proteus's fickleness is

condoned strikes a "modern" note—for, after all, the Donjuanism of Proteus is a Donjuanism *pour rire* [in jest], say rather the conscienceless, almost childlike irresponsibility of Pierrot.

Blended with associations of modern romance such as these, one had the amusement of the antiquarian interest—the quaintly hideous farthingales and ruffs of the ladies, the authentic dresses of the men copied from frescoes in the hall of the Carpenters' Company, and the delightful music by Robert Johnson (1600) for "Who is Silvia?" [IV. ii. 39ff.]. Nor was the characteristically Shakespearean element of the epicene lacking. Both Valentine and Panthio were played, and capitally played, by ladies. All concerned spoke their lines with admirable distinctness and, where the verse demanded it, a nice observance of the Elizabethan pronunciation. The fooling of the two clowns was "right" Shakespearean. Indeed, the whole affair was thoroughly enjoyable and a feather in the cap of the indomitable enthusiast, the founder and director of the society, Mr. William Poel.

A. B. Walkley, in a review of "The Two Gentlemen of Verona," in The Times, London, April 21, 1910, p. 12.

Robert Speaight　(essay date 1954)

[*Speaight was a British actor, author, and lecturer. He began his career on the stage playing leading Shakespearean roles at the Old Vic. Speaight wrote several dramatic studies, including* William Poel and the Elizabethan Revival (*1954*), Nature in Shakespearian Tragedy (*1956*), The Christian Theatre (*1960*), Shakespeare on the Stage: An Illustrated History of Shakespearian Performance (*1973*), *and* Shakespeare: The Man and His Achievements (*1977*). *In addition, he was the British dramatic critic for* Shakespeare Quarterly *during the 1960s and early '70s. Here, Speaight examines Poel's two productions of* The Two Gentlemen of Verona, *noting that the second, at His Majesty's Theatre in 1910, was a large success.*]

[For his 1896 production of] *The Two Gentlemen of Verona,* Poel borrowed the Merchant Taylors' Hall. There was no built-up stage, but the audience was raised on tiers. The design for the costume of the two gentlemen was taken from some frescoes painted about the middle of the sixteenth century on the walls of the Carpenters' Hall. The outlaws were dressed as Halberdiers, after a design used in the Fishmongers' Pageant of 1609, and they made their entrance through the audience to the accompaniment of flag and drum. Schubert's setting for "Who is Sylvia?" [IV. ii. 39ff.] seemed an evident anachronism and a new melody was composed by Arnold Dolmetsch.

Poel had invited Lugné-Poë, the celebrated director of the Théâtre de l'Œuvre in Paris, to come over for the performance, and Lugné-Poë afterwards described his impressions in *La Nouvelle Revue* (1 March 1897). We learn from him that the minstrels' gallery of the Hall served, naturally enough, for Sylvia's balcony, and that when Valentine went into exile he passed through the middle of the audience, acting his part all the time. Hardly had he left by the door through which the audience had come in, than the noise of the outlaws' attack was heard in the vestibule. Sylvia escaped in the same way, running after her lover, and accompanied by a servant. And then came the Duke in chase of his daughter, turning round when he had almost reached the exit to give a last instruction to the servants who were still on the stage. A moment later he, too, was attacked in the vestibule. At the end everyone returned through the audience to the rolling of a drum, and it was on the stage proper that Valentine persuaded the outlaws to submit to the Duke who had been their prisoner. "Everything combined," wrote Lugné-Poë, "to make us relive naïvely and sincerely the glorious flowering of English dramatic art."

The production, however, was not a success. The speaking was monotonous and inaudible, and once again, in reading the criticisms, one has the impression of half-trained actors struggling to acquire a technique of elocution which they could not master and did not understand. In the process all spontaneity was lost. The play was given on the 30 November 1896, and repeated in the Great Hall of the Charterhouse on 18 January 1897.

Poel's second production of this play was one of his most important contributions to the Elizabethan Revival. In 1910 Beerbohm Tree, who had an impresario's nose for novelty, invited him to present *The Two Gentlemen of Verona* during the Shakespeare Festival at His Majesty's. This was to ask the wolf to step into the sheep-fold, for Tree's way with Shakespeare was the popular illustration of everything Poel condemned. But he was in no mood for compromise when he led his half-trained troupe of semi-amateurs within those sumptuous and slightly vulgar precincts. The young Bridges-Adams, only recently down from Oxford, was his Assistant Stage Manager, under Nugent Monck, and he has described to me his first meeting with the great reformer.

He found Poel wrapped in a grey muffler, nibbling at a biscuit and sipping a glass of milk. In front of him a lady, shimmering with sequins and no longer in her first youth, was in an attitude of visible distress. Poel's voice was raised in querulous criticism: "I am disappointed," he said, "very disappointed indeed. Of all Shakespeare's heroes Valentine is one of the most romantic, one of the most virile. I have chosen you out of all London for this part, but so far you have shown me no virility whatsoever."

Yet the production had beauties which lingered in the memory; among them, Nugent Monck's inn-keeper nodding to sleep over his lantern. For the first time an 'apron' was built out over the orchestra pit of His Majesty's and front lighting installed in the balconies. Beerbohm Tree may have smiled at the austerity of Poel's Elizabethan way, but the apron and the front lighting were retained for his own *Henry VIII* two years later. And they have now become a commonplace of Shakespearian production. It was the thin edge of the Elizabethan wedge and no one has since dislodged it.

The production was described by A. B. Walkley as "an entertainment of absorbing interest. The literary quality of the play, the verve of its dialogue, the lyric beauty of many of its passages came out with unusual freshness and clear-cut relief." He thought that the Elizabethan convention, for all its stiff archaic quaintness, gave one far more of the play's atmosphere—its "romantic amorism"—than could ever have been conveyed by a modern setting. And it brought to mind a number of more recent analogies—some "trifle of de Musset," some "*marivaudage* of Marivaux," or the "fervour of Cyrano de Bergerac serenading his *précieuse*" (*The Times;* 21 April 1910). This production was to be remembered. Six years later, in a letter to Poel, Prince Antoine Bibesco paid him the following tribute:

Having been present at a Shakespearian perfor-

mance given by you a few years ago at His Majesty's I realise that you are really the only man that has given an adequate idea of the way Shakespeare should be played (18 April 1916).

(pp. 119-22)

Robert Speaight, "The First Experiments," in his William Poel and the Elizabethan Revival, *William Heinemann Ltd., 1954, pp. 90-131.*

PRODUCTION:

B. Iden Payne • Shakespeare Memorial Theatre • 1938

BACKGROUND:

Payne's production of *The Two Gentlemen of Verona* met with moderate success upon opening at Stratford in 1938. The play featured Francis James as Proteus, Gyles Isham as Valentine, Jay Laurier as Launce, Peggy Livesey as Silvia, and Valerie Tudor as Julia.

COMMENTARY:

The Times, London   (review date 20 April 1938)

[*In the excerpt below, the anonymous critic contends that despite Shakespeare's imperfect characterizations in* The Two Gentlemen of Verona, *the actors in Payne's production gave admirable performances.*]

If producers of Shakespeare are never guilty of wishing that they were dealing with lesser works, they mostly respond with notable eagerness to the challenge of one of Shakespeare's lesser plays. This early comedy, absent from the Stratford repertoire since 1925, and from the London professional stage for even longer, stirs Mr. Iden Payne to his smoothest and liveliest. The design of the piece is obvious, and in the end crude, the behaviour of the characters improbable to the point of silliness. Yet it was made to appear tonight as a pretty tale of love and friendship told by a young poet with a still uncertain touch, but with magical moments, as when Silvia is commended in song and Valentine and Julia speak of love, and with sudden delightful rushes of the humour that was later to flow so deep and broad. This pretty tale is set dancing lightly against a deep-toned Italian background, which some may think unimaginative in its detailed naturalism, and others hold to be justified by the rich colours which it sheds upon the action. The important thing, however, is that the tale dances unfalteringly from beginning to end, helped on its way by skilful grouping and a freshness of invention that never confuses the means with the end.

So far as individual performances go it is Mr. Jay Laurier's evening. This comedian finds in Launce a character almost perfectly suited to his humour, and whenever he is on the stage we are in contact with something that is more than a mere foreshadowing of greater things to come. Launce may be the first of a line of clowns leading ultimately to Touchstone [in *As You Like It*], but we have no great wish to see Mr. Laurier play this remote descendant. We are satisfied to have him in the first degree of Shakespearian clowning, tearfully reproaching his cruel-hearted cur for having no more pity in him than a dog, and drenching with simple humour the brittle wit of Speed. Yet Mr. Andrew Leigh carries off Speed, a dry fool if ever there was one, by sheer sprightliness, a notable achievement.

All the chief romantic characters are continually vexed by the ghosts of their descendants, but the actors cannot help that. Miss Valerie Tudor's Julia might grow into a Viola [in *Twelfth Night*], the Proteus of Mr. Francis James into an Iachimo [in *Cymbeline*]. This is to praise the actors of those parts, and similar praise might be given to Miss Peggy Livesey and to Miss Pauline Letts, who contribute to the prettiness and gaiety of the evening.

> *A review of, "The Two Gentlemen of Verona," in* The Times, *London, April 20, 1938, p. 8.*

Ivor Brown   (review date May 1938)

[*Brown was a British author, dramatic critic, and editor. As a critic, he regularly contributed to such periodicals as the* Guardian, Saturday Review, *the* Observer, Sketch, *and* Punch. *His works include* Shakespeare in His Time (1960), Shakespeare and His World (1964), *and* Shakespeare and the Actors (1970). *Here, Brown maintains that although* The Two Gentlemen of Verona *is probably one of Shakespeare's most flawed plays, viewing a production such as Payne's offers one the chance to see how this "poor play is well-nigh translated into a species of excellence."*]

A NOTE ON BAD PLAYS.

Some, no doubt, will be shocked to hear that both the plays to which my title alludes are by Shakespeare and will be ready to hurl charges of blasphemy and heresy. But I do not think that the suggestion would have ruffled Shakespeare himself; he evidently did not believe that his plays were "for all time," since he did nothing to preserve their texts. As a man of the theatre, he knew that the surprise in "The Merchant of Venice" could hardly be very surprising after a year or so, much less after three hundred and thirty years. He also knew, I fancy, that "The Two Gentlemen of Verona" was the crude work of a prentice hand and, indeed, he admitted as much by putting into later plays, and then vastly improving, several of the notions attempted in this one.

Shakespeare may have had a fair conceit of his own poetical powers (the Sonnets certainly suggest as much), but it would have staggered him to know that every line and facet of his theatre-work would be scrutinised three centuries later as though it were some species of Holy Writ. Had he known that, he would doubtless have left his plays and papers in good order and would have tidied up and carefully revised much which was written under pressure, hastily. Yet Shakespeare has had the luck. Think of the efforts made by actors and decorators to mask his failures, to make his bad jokes seem passable, his puns endurable. Every year, for example, at Stratford-on-Avon a just and, on the whole, well appreciated feature of the Festival is the revival of one of the pieces rarely acted, such as "Troilus and Cressida," or "All's Well That Ends Well."

This year the choice has fallen on "The Two Gentlemen of Verona," an early play with a fatuous plot about a faithless friend who stole his companion's sweetheart, practised the most abominable deceits, and was at once and as easily forgiven as if his offence had been some mild discourtesy or trivial breach of manners. The play abounds in Shakespeare's

favourite tricks, dressing a girl as a boy, and pretending that she is unrecognisable to her lover because she has exchanged skirt for breeches. Its verse only occasionally deviates into poetry and the quibbling of the clown Speed is an exasperating kind of facetiousness. And yet one can, at Stratford, watch it all with great pleasure. For we know how to titivate Shakespeare until a poor play is well-nigh translated into a species of excellence. The Veronese scene looks so pleasant that we forgive the story for the sake of the scene, and the part of the second clown, Launce, is so richly played by Mr. Jay Laurier and built up with sound music-hall "business," brilliantly executed, that the sparseness of humour in the text does not eventually matter. Launce, so treated, becomes a great comic character. (pp. 828, 830)

> *Ivor Brown, "The World of the Theatre," in* The Illustrated London News, *Vol. 192, May 7, 1938, pp. 828, 830.*

St. John Ervine   (review date 26 August 1938)

[*Ervine asserts that Payne's production of* The Two Gentlemen of Verona—*the "dullest" play he has ever seen—"did nothing to reduce its dullness." In Ervine's opinion, the production was "as flat as last year's unbottled stout."*]

If Shakespeare had died immediately after the first performance of "The Two Gentlemen of Verona," no one would have had the faintest idea of the potentialities he had had within him, and he would now figure only in footnotes to histories of English drama. The play, according to Sir Edward Chambers's chronology, is the seventh in the order of composition, being preceded by the three parts of "King Henry VI.," "Richard III.," "The Comedy of Errors," "Titus Andronicus," and "The Taming of the Shrew." It is the worst of the seven, and its production must have dismayed its author's admirers who can scarcely have failed to feel that he had shot his bolt. A few months later, however, he produced "Romeo and Juliet." Very little is known about the composition of "The Two Gentlemen of Verona." We do not, for instance, know on what date it was performed for the first time, and its place in the order of composition is largely based on conjecture. But it is certainly an early work as we might deduce from the "notes" for other plays it contains. Here are hints for "Romeo and Juliet," "The Merchant of Venice"— the scene in which Portia discusses her suitors and the reference to rings, for example—"As You Like It," and "Othello." Proteus is surely a "note" for Iago, and Julia is the first of the Shakespearean heroines to disguise herself so thoroughly by putting on a man's attire that no one, not even her lover, recognises her or even perceives a resemblance. . . . "The Two Gentlemen of Verona" is one of the dullest plays I have ever seen, and its production and performance at Stratford did nothing to reduce its dullness. The play marks, in my mind, almost the end of Shakespeare's apprenticeship and period of experiment. The young author, aware of his rustic accent and inclined to feel abashed in the presence of smart gentlemen from the universities, endeavoured to make a dramatist of himself by imitating what he thought were his betters. He followed their example in his work, repeating their tricks and using their artificial situations as if he were convinced that no other way of writing was open to him or to anybody else. He was to continue in that delusion for another play, "Love's Labour's Lost," before he could bring himself to shake off the bondage of the tradition which had imposed upon him and write out of his own nature and knowledge; but when he did free himself, how magnificently he was delivered. "Love's Labour's Lost" was followed by "Romeo and Juliet." There were hints in the first of these two plays of the emergence of the author of the second. The play is artificial in its arrangement, but it has natural characters in it, and it contains some lovely lines. Recall the speech, spoken by Biron in the fourth act, scene III, in which he details the additions made to every power by love:

> For valour, is not Love a Hercules.
> Still climbing trees in the Hesperides?
> Subtle as Sphinx: as sweet and musical
> As bright Apollo's lute, strung with his hair.
> [*Love's Labor's Lost,* IV. iii. 337-40]

It was a poet, not an imitation university wit, who wrote that last line.

"The Two Gentlemen of Verona" is a lazy man's play, dashed off in haste and without much effort to keep its characters in some semblance to human beings. Iago, in "Othello," is a hard man to understand, but who can make head or tail of Proteus, his "note," in this piece? This unstable sentimentalist, shifting his affections from lady to lady without rhyme or reason, and stooping to the meanest betrayals of his friend, Valentine, defies understanding or affection. How Julia, who is a spirited girl in petticoats, but becomes a ninny in tights, brings herself to marry this fellow after the humiliations he puts upon her, is a problem impossible to solve. We can only conclude that she wrapped her brains in her petticoats and left them in Verona while she went adventuring after Proteus in Milan. The ease with which Valentine pardons Proteus and commends him to Julia's pity is beyond belief. My heart went out to Silvia, when, from her balcony, she rated the faithless fellow:

> my will is even this:
> That presently you hie you home to bed.
> Thou subtle, perjured, false, disloyal man!
> Think'st thou I am so shallow, conceitless,
> To be seduced by thy flattery,
> Thou hast deceived so many with thy vows?
> [IV. ii. 93-8]

The last act is a clutter of manufactured reconciliations and pardons, none of which has any foundation in human nature; and it is evident that Shakespeare, tired of the tedious stuff when he began to give it shape, was so bored with the whole business by the end that he threw it on to the stage without attempting to give it any veracity. Mr. Giles Isham made a manly looking Valentine, but his part has less authority than is given to the part of Proteus, in which, however, Mr. Francis James was unimpressive. Mr. James has a good voice, but he is excessively mannered, and he lacks emotional authority. Miss Valerie Tudor was excellent as Julia in petticoats, but ineffective as Julia in tights, and Miss Peggy Livesey was an admirable Silvia. The part of the clown, Launce, was performed by Mr. Jay Laurier, who has hitherto graced the music-hall stage. He seemed reluctant to leave it, and brought all its buffooneries with him to Stratford. I could scarcely believe my eyes when I saw him indulging in the commonest kind of low comedy in his first scene, especially when he tried to lay the dust with his tears. Mr. Laurier brought out a sodden handkerchief, as large as a face towel, and wrung it, so that a tumblerful of water fell into his hat! He even placed his shoes, instead of his hat, on his head! . . . A number of elderly ladies were delighted with his humour, and if their delight is all of Mr. Iden Payne's intent, then the buffoonery is justi-

fied, but he surely cannot have forgotten Shakespeare's bitter complaint of comedians who *will* say and do more than is set down for them. The best part of this production was the charming scenery designed by Mr. J. Gower Parks. The rest was as flat as last year's unbottled stout.

St. John Ervine, "The Stratford Memorial Theatre—II," in The Observer, *August 26, 1938, p. 11.*

PRODUCTION:

Michael Langham • Old Vic • 1957

BACKGROUND:

Langham's production of *The Two Gentlemen of Verona* opened on 22 January 1957. His unconventional, early nineteenth-century setting supported his examination of the force of love and its far-reaching implications from a non-Elizabethan perspective. Langham muted Shakespeare's problematic theme of friendship, which modern audiences find difficult to accept, focusing instead on love as an all-consuming entity which can and does undermine a close bond like friendship. This romantic treatment of the play also gave greater depth to the characters of Proteus and Valentine, casting them as Byronic and Shelleyan figures. While Langham's innovative treatment of the original text won him critical acclaim, the play was not a popular success, running for only thirty-one performances. He tried to revive the production a year later, taking it on a tour of the U. S. and Canada, under the sponsorship of the Canadian Shakespeare Festival. The performance given at New York's Phoenix Theatre on 18 March 1958, however, enjoyed even less success than the London production. The principal actors for the Old Vic production included Keith Michell as Proteus, Richard Gale as Valentine, Robert Helpmann as Launce, Ingrid Hafner as Silvia, and Barbara Jefford as Julia. The Stratford Festival Company production included Lloyd Bochner as Proteus, Eric House as Valetine, Bruno Gerussi as Launce, Diana Maddox as Silvia, and Ann Morrish as Julia.

COMMENTARY:

The Times, London   (review date 23 January 1957)

[*In an unsigned review, the critic contends that Langham's conversion of* The Two Gentlemen of Verona *from a traditional Elizabethan comedy to a Gothic romance imaginatively concealed some of the play's original inconsistencies.*]

The Bristol Old Vic revealed some years ago how much unsuspected charm the stage could still draw from this piece of experimental Shakespeare; and evidently the parent company has learnt the trick. It is not quite the same trick, but it works no less well.

Mr. Denis Carey set the comedy dancing lightly and gaily to its fifth act tumble into burlesque. Mr. Michael Langham trusts less to balletic inspiration than to carefully considered and well invented stage effects, and the comedy marches spiritedly to its inevitable collapse in the preposterous reconciliation scene.

Renaissance Italy becomes the Italy of early nineteenth-century romance. The men wear curly brimmed tall hats and the women dresses that, however elaborate, derive from the riding habit, and Miss Tanya Moiseiwitsch has constructed a set of flower-entwined pillars which, with a simple change of backcloth, can become Verona, Milan, or the Mantuan forest.

For once, the bold pitching of a play out of its accepted period seems to help rather than to tease the imagination. *The Two Gentlemen of Verona* is full of difficulties for a modern audience. Love is represented as a passion so powerful and inexplicable that even its shadow—the false appetite excited by another's possession of a chaste maid's affections—can overwhelm all other considerations and impel friend to betray friend. The rival claims of comrade and mistress may have been a live topic of debate among youthful Elizabethan courtiers, and it may have pleased them to hear it discussed in high romantic terms. To us the matter seems singularly unsuited to the requirements of high romance. Proteus, false alike to Julia and Valentine, is so far from our conception of a romantic hero that he seems wholly undeserving of a happy ending to the troubles he has made for himself; and the reconciliation with Julia and Valentine is so absurdly arranged that we are bound to greet it with hoots of derisive laughter. But the change of period sets us at a remove from the Elizabethan conception of romance and somehow makes it easier for us to enjoy, as though we were in but not of it.

Mr. Keith Michell plays Proteus on exactly the right note of romantic youth so fiercely driven by passion that he is utterly unaware that he is turning into a knave. Mr. Richard Gale gives him a serviceable opposite number in a brightly ingenuous Valentine. And Miss Barbara Jefford is shiningly sincere as the Julia who pathetically but bravely pursues her wayward lover for the woman's simple reason that she loves him.

Mr. Robert Helpmann is a good Launce, and if he is inclined to force the touch of fun needlessly it must be remembered that the actor is playing all the time against a dog, and "Duff" happens to be the sort of dog who establishes himself with the audience and misses no chance of ramming his advantages home. Mr. Dudley Jones gives a brisk account of the word-playing Speed, and Mr. Derek Godfrey's quizzical Duke of Milan is always neatly in the picture.

A review of "The Two Gentlemen of Verona," in The
Times, *London, January 23, 1957, p. 30.*

J. C. Trewin   (review date 2 February 1957)

[*Trewin is a British dramatic critic, editor, and author whose reviews have appeared in the* Observer, *the* Illustrated London News, *the* Sketch, *the* Birmingham Post, *the* Listener, *and the* Times Literary Supplement. *In addition, he has written numerous theatrical biographies and dramatic studies, including* The English Theatre (*1948*), Stratford-upon-Avon (*1950*), Mr. Macready: A Nineteenth-Century Tragedian (*1955*), Shakespeare on the English Stage: 1900-1964 (*1964*), Shakespeare's Plays Today (*with Arthur Colby Sprague, 1970*), *and* Peter Brook: a Biography (*1971*). *Here, Trewin maintains that although Langham's direction of* The Two Gentlemen of Verona *made the flawed play entertaining, the production suffered from poor acting.*]

This week I have to celebrate together the bicentenary of John Philip Kemble's birth—he was born at Prescot, in Lan-

cashire, on February 1, 1757—and the addition of "The Two Gentlemen of Verona" to the Old Vic's Five-Year-Plan.

These hardly seem to go with each other. John Philip Kemble was, so to speak, the noblest Roman of his day. Trained originally for the Catholic priesthood, he went on the stage—he was the son of an actor and an actress—and worked unremittingly for its good. True, he was often marblecold; his speech could be laboured and formal and his pronunciation curious (he would say "varchue" for "virtue," "airth" for "earth," "hidjus" for "hideous"). Yet he was a classical actor of nobility: a man in our short record of First Players: Burbage, Betterton, Garrick, Kemble, Edmund Kean, Macready, Irving (and take your choice from our own time).

What has "Black Jack," as they called him, Kemble of Drury Lane and Covent Garden, Sarah Siddons' brother, to do with "The Two Gentlemen of Verona," Shakespeare's slightest comedy? It has always amused me to read that Kemble revived it—as much as to remember that a greater actor, Macready, also played Valentine (in 1841, and to his own displeasure), a nice piece of personal miscasting. Kemble, whose version was acted at Drury Lane in 1790 and Covent Garden in 1808, arranged a "Two Gentlemen" with various transpositions, that worked fairly well, though it was never meant for purists. He added some extraneous and stilted matter of his own—not that the average playgoer was likely to remember anything in this piece as he would a Kemble interpolation in "Twelfth Night."

I am ravished by the names that he chose to give to Shakespeare's innominate outlaws. He calls them Ubaldo, Luigi, Carlos, Stephano, Giacomo, Rodolfo, Valerio, and the programme must at least have looked well-dressed. Kemble had long retired when Frederick Reynolds provided for Covent Garden, in November 1821, "The Two Gentlemen" as an operetta rich in songs, duettos, and glees. The cast included personages called Philippo and the Genius of Pleasure. The songs included settings of sonnet-fragments, "That time of year thou may'st in me behold" and "When in disgrace with fortune and men's eyes." Rodolfo, Carlos, Ubaldo, and Stephano—Kemble's names remaining—sang "Now the hungry lion roars" from "A Midsummer Night's Dream" [V. i. 371]; and passages from "Love's Labour's Lost," "The Taming of the Shrew," and "As You Like It" were among others dragged into song in what must have been a perplexing mosaic.

In fact, until lately, "The Two Gentlemen" has rarely been fortunate. Was it not of this (in a Daly revival) that Shaw wrote in 1895: "A man who, having once seen cypresses and felt their presence in a North Italian landscape, paints them lettuce-colour, must be suffering either from madness, malice, or a theory of how nature should have coloured trees, cognate with Mr. Daly's theory of how Shakespeare should have written plays."?

In recent years the comedy of echoes—for that is what it is—has had some better luck. Denis Carey, with the cast of the Bristol Old Vic, produced it beautifully a few years ago: its first performance in Waterloo Road since Robert Atkins's day (1923). I need not repeat now—and it would take columns—the long run of resemblances, early drafts and suggestions, that must delight a listening Shakespearian: Julia and Lucetta, for example, are setting the scene for Portia and Nerissa, and there is much else that Shakespeare would work up later. Thus, already, "Romeo and Juliet" must have been

John Morris as Sir Eglamour, Derek Francis as Thurio, Robin Close and Thomas Johnston as servants, Dudley Jones as Speed, Keith Michell as Proteus, Richard Gale as Valentine, and Ingrid Hafner as Silvia. Act II, scene iv.

sparking in his mind. A good deal of the verse has the freshest charm of youth. The line, "O, how this spring of love resembleth The uncertain glory of an April day!" [I. iii. 84-5] speaks accurately for the piece.

I am sorry to say that, except when Barbara Jefford's Julia is with us—again we mark her delivery and beautiful carriage of the head—the verse is not well-treated at the Vic. A lot of it is just rattled off; Keith Michell and Richard Gale, as the two gentlemen, Proteus and Valentine, are especially to be blamed. But, for once—and it is rare that one can suggest it— Shakespearians should not let this worry them greatly. They should visit the Old Vic if only to observe the liveliness and wit with which Michael Langham (director) and Tanya Moiseiwitsch (designer) have put the comedy forward to the early nineteenth century: to a date a little later than Kemble's death. It is a period of romantic attitudes and curly-brimmed toppers, one of a general pleasant lushness. Keith Michell's Proteus, looking like Byron, sets the period note immediately, though afterwards we may think rather in terms of the romantic-minded Pickwickians; Snodgrass and Winkle would have found themselves in very good company; Tupman, too, no doubt [all in Dickens's *Pickwick Papers*].

The play is gently mocked (though I cannot agree with the

burlesquing of "the fair Sir Eglamour"), the patterns are elegantly pictorial, the "business" has a nice easy resource. Now and again, too, the dog Crab appears—with Robert Helpmann in tow—and takes the play in charge. Fond though I am of dogs of every breed, I feel usually that a dramatist who uses one is cheating, playing on the sympathies of his audience. But Crab is an exception, and certainly this Crab is: he is a solemn golden labrador called Duff—owned by Keith Michell—and, throughout, he surveys the play with a mild grandeur of his own. (p. 198)

J. C. Trewin, "Tragical—Comical—Historical," in The Illustrated London News, Vol. 2305, February 2, 1957, pp. 198-99.

Philip Hope-Wallace   (review date 2 February 1957)

[*Hope-Wallace argues that although Langham's production of* The Two Gentlemen of Verona *became more unrealistic as the show progressed, the Byronic, Italian setting augmented his interpretation by giving the play a "dream-like detachment."*]

'Producer's Shakespeare' can be a penance but if it turns an 'impossible' play into a success, who really minds? The answer is: a lot of self-appointed guardians on the Bard Board.

If they would prevent such things as Tyrone Guthrie's recent Edwardian *Troilus and Cressida* or this delightful Byronic *Two Gentlemen* devised by Michael Langham then I cannot side with the solemn-sides.

Apart of course from the scenes for Launce (the original Idle Jack) and his dog Crab which are among the delights of the evening, the play becomes steadily more unbelievable as it goes on. Putting the whole thing into early nineteenth century costume, with the two gentlemen appearing more or less as Byron and Shelley might have looked in Naples, the producer gives the plot a dream-like detachment which makes it much easier to take.

Thinking now in terms of the extravagance of the Gothic revival and the Romantic Movement we accept behaviour which seems wantonly foolish to the cousins of Romeo and Juliet. For the preposterous renunciations of the last scene, Mr Langham has quite legitimately—so I think—superadded a threat of suicide and Werther-like pistol play, all of which illumines the text without spoiling it. The speaking was not up to much; the 'April day' came out like a champagne cork. But the young company had been given much ingenious 'business' and much latent talent was disclosed. Keith Michell was excellent. It was delightful to see Barbara Jefford and Rosemary Webster doing the mistress and maid letter scene so funnily. Robert Helpmann dressed like Kate Greenaway's Jackanapes tries not to be played off the stage by a most amiable, blinking Labrador, sleek and loved, rather than the disreputable cur Crab should be. I'm not sure the master wasn't a little incast too, but the scenes had the house in stitches which is what matters.

> *Philip Hope-Wallace, in a review of "The Two Gentlemen of Verona," in* Time & Tide, *Vol. 38, No. 5, February 2, 1957, p. 127.*

Caryl Brahms   (review date March 1957)

[*Brahms argues that Langham's production lost its Shakespearean perspective by departing from the traditional Elizabethan setting. What resulted, Brahms continues, was not a faithful examination of Shakespeare, the dramatist, but a "Regency masquerade."*]

It is a scene of some enchantment, this Verona, which Miss Tanya Moiseiwitsch has designed for our delight, with the soft blue blur of distances and the soft green smudge of trees; with fluted urn-crowned columns linked with climbing ivy and with rich romantic drapes hanging from indefensible places, so that I was reminded of the ballet to which I was sentenced some years ago in which The Spirit of the Drapes (I quote the cast list) came down from—would it be some interplanetary space-pelmet—to bind up the leaping villain hand and foot, thus rendering him harmless—and not a beat too soon for the present writer.

It is, then, a series of delectable Regency prints into which we are invited, in the Waterloo Road, and when, by a simple re-arrangement of these drapes we find that we have been whisked from an exterior to an interior, swiftly, soundlessly and without evident recourse to back-stage staff, we are immediately reconciled to the drape convention.

And, of course, if blue-green vistas of Verona, Milan and A Wood Near Mantua were all, how grateful the playgoer would be to Miss Moiseiwitsch—of all the top-ranking stage-designers in this country the one who builds and peoples her

worlds in the searching light of her own integrity. She has given the uncertain glory of this Shakespearean play a pleasant place in which to breathe, to grow, to glow, to sparkle and so to commend itself to the more frivolous among the audience.

But those drapes were to prove the symptoms of something far more sinister than honest arras.

For soon it was made clear to us that Mr. Michael Langham, the producer, had no faith in his author at all. In his frantic search of some plus to make sense of a nonsense he hit upon the early nineteenth century. Mr. Langham's Two Gentlemen, skipping a couple of centuries, traded-in the ruffs and doublets of the Elizabethan stage for the stove-pipe pants and coloured swallow-tails of the Regency buck, and his Two Ladies sailed the stage in curls and crinolines.

And what has this caper done to the play besides taking our minds off it each time a character came on in a change of costume? It has turned an Elizabethan piece of a secondary, but nonetheless certain, inspiration into a Regency masquerade—a kind of verbal *Carnaval* without Messrs. Schumann, Beidmeier and Fokine, and very nearly without Master Shakespeare.

The producer has, by tricking out his plot with this and that and the vapours and by much general prepostering, pointed up its weaknesses and directed its passions and its poetry to a conclusion as foregone as the artificial flowers in a milliner's posy.

Granted that this trick with time was one way of skating over the thin ice of one's author's intentions, how insecure can a producer get?

There remains, fortunately, a great deal of lovely, lively fun and poetry in this comedy of plotwise errors; and I am compelled to admit that the poetry seemed to me to be better realised than I had remembered it in Mr. Denis Carey's Bristol production that came to London a few years ago, though perhaps there was less unforced fun and high spirits than bubbled in the earlier production, which also served to present the music of Mr. Julian Slade to London.

But to the Two Gentlemen under review—or rather to one of them—the more instantly arresting of the two.

Mr. Keith Michell's Proteus is vigorously and incisively played. But Mr. Michell is altogether too purposeful and single-minded an actor to play a poor man's Romeo. In the fulness of time we may find him an admirable Petruchio [in *The Taming of the Shrew*] with plenty of bombast, for he is a red corpuscled actor rather than a step-son of the aristocracy of Denmark.

Miss Barbara Jefford anchored her Julia nicely midway between hope and despair. There was a deal of quiet accomplishment in her playing and a calm feminine competence that made me feel I was watching Miss Eileen Herlie through two widths of nainsook on a Saturday afternoon.

I wish I could have liked Miss Ingrid Hafner's Silvia better, for I daresay her decisive diction deserves a warmer appreciation than I can find for it. Certainly she was hampered by a monstrous wig that lent her the impression of a gallant frigate towing a battleship. However, I can at least record that in her swooning scene Miss Hafner is the mistress of the finest stage-fall that I remember seeing in the English theatre.

I have left till last the two most endearing performances of the evening—the first by Duff, the dog, who plays Crab the dog; and second by his master (Mr. Robert Helpmann's Launce) who so faithfully dogged the dog's footsteps.

Firstly, let me commend this play to your diary—it has a magic of its own, even though you may question the methods of the magician. (p. 15)

Caryl Brahms, "Stove Pipe and Crinoline," in Plays and Players, *Vol. 4, No. 6, March, 1957, pp. 14-5.*

Muriel St. Claire Byrne   (review date Autumn 1957)

[*Byrne credits Langham's production of* The Two Gentlemen of Verona *as an entertaining revival of one of Shakespeare's least performed plays. She also offers a detailed discussion of the Regency costume, noting how it helped restore the play's inherent tone of gaiety.*]

Michael Langham's production of *The Two Gentlemen of Verona* (31 performances) takes to itself the credit of having provided the most diverting entertainment of the season. Should one ask more of this play, or are we entitled to believe that the youthful author's intention was to poke some good-humored fun, prettily spiced with light irony, at certain fashionable attitudes then current in life and literature, in order

Robert Helpmann as Launce and Duff as Crab.

to divert? The play's record for this century suggests that the theatre has regarded it as unsuitable for general enjoyment. Until the Bristol Old Vic company brought their successful 1952 production to London the score was: Old Vic-Stratford, 1916; Old Vic, 1923; Stratford, 1925 and 1938—not an encouraging total. It is not its artificiality which has in the past kept it out of the Old Vic repertory: *Love's Labour's Lost* can boast performances there in 1906, '18, '23, '28, '36, '49 and '54, not to mention the famous Westminster Theatre production of 1932. The trouble with *The Two Gentlemen* is that one of them isn't. The average playgoer writes off Proteus as one complete cad and the end of the play as simply silly. He agrees with Launce that his master is a kind of knave, and his instinctive reaction . . . is to think Valentine a fool and say, What about Sylvia's feelings, and Julia's? and to push the whole thing aside with irritation: it cannot be taken seriously and it is not funny. If the actors decide to guy the conclusion and get the audience to laugh with them they will get their curtain applause, but it will not save the play, as such.

The Bristol company got away with a straight presentation because they were beautifully produced, were carried to town on the tide of success, and delighted the select audience, largely theatrical and academic, that flocks to the Old Vic for these special limited runs, by the sheer youthful zest and freshness of their playing. "Do the boys carry it away? Ay, that they do!" I have spoken of this year's Old Vic company as young, but these things are comparative. It is old or middle-aged in relation to those charming young people from Bristol, to whom, we could allow, such attitudes and affectations were natural. To try to do anything of the same kind with the 1956-7 company, in my opinion, would have been to court disaster. Given these more sophisticated players, however, it was possible to underline the fact that Shakespeare was cocking a humorous eye at certain contemporary affectations and applying to them the same kind of delicately ironic treatment that delights us when we meet it in Jane Austen. To point these things for the average playgoer who does not read his Elizabethans is not so easy: he is unmoved by the debate between the rival claims of friendship and love. But he does read his Jane Austen and he has generally met his Lydia Languish [in Richard Brinsley Sheridan's *The Rivals*] and her sentimental elopement with its amiable ladder of ropes and conscious moon. Let Tanya Moiseiwitsch's decor and costumes transport us to the age of Byronic heroes and *Northanger Abbey,* and we know at once where we are. The sentiments and the clothes go perfectly together. There is an essential frivolity about Regency costume which persuades us to abandon our disapproval of Proteus and our concern for the ladies' feelings as irrelevant. If the producer can make us agree to accept it as artificial comedy, set in an age where we take romantic absurdity for granted, he can restore to the play a gaiety with which I believe its author tried to endow it and which was captured by the Bristol company with accent on youth.

The charming set, complete with practicable, ivy-mantled tower with window, amiably adapts itself in a moment to Verona, Milan and the Forest Glade, reminding us, with its subtle harmonies of green, blue and brown of a Paul Sandby gouache, properly heightened for theatrical purposes. The young gentlemen are clean-shaven, the one darkly Byronic, the other blondly Shelleyan: the Duke and Thurio are handsomely bewhiskered, the latter looking like half a dozen portraits of royal dukes rolled into one portly figure. The ladies seem to have walked out of the pages of *Ackermann's Reposi-*

tory and *La Belle Assemblée;* and Sylvia at the ball is Fanny Kemble Twopence Coloured as Juliet. Incidentally, Julia as page to Proteus was becomingly garbed in a period livery, that is, genuine male costume, instead of one of the late 18th century epicene travesties that ousted from the stage the proper costumes of disguised Shakespeare heroines. The gentlemen are all extremely elegant in their uniforms or their frilled shirts, tall hats, dress pantaloons, strapped trousers and voluminous swirling cloaks. Proteus at the ball which opens Act III is a most striking figure, all in very dark red. There is much appropriate theatrical invention to divert. Thurio is groomed and barbered and tight-laced for his proxy-wooing: Valentine's departure into exile is heralded by his luggage—this is a laugh: it is the hat-box that does it—: the Milan scenes are taken into the open air and enlivened by a display of afternoon archery, with a *vie de Bohème* artist thrown in to paint Sylvia's portrait, and by a ducal ball, complete with period waltz and sound of revelry by night, which makes a lively background to Proteus' betrayal of his friend and to the Duke's "discovery" of Valentine's elopement plans.

In such an atmosphere the play becomes a consistent whole. The preposterous ending is prepared for from the start and comes as a perfect climax, with its sensibility and its swooning and a threat of suicide with a pistol by the repentant Proteus to give a plausible period cue for Valentine's offer to surrender Sylvia. Derek Godfrey as the Duke, Derek Francis as Thurio, Keith Michell as Proteus and Richard Gale as Valentine were most stylishly and consistently within the picture; and the final comment, most effectively delivered by Mr. Michell, went right home with the audience: "O heaven! Were man but constant, he were perfect" [V. iv. 110-11]. Mr. Godfrey, quizzical and monocled, made his central scene, first with Proteus, then with Valentine, the stylistic high-light of the play. His syncopated timing, to deal with the farewells of departing guests which punctuated the scene, heightened the tension very skilfully; and the gravely sympathetic-ironic manner in which he interrogated Valentine was suggestively reminiscent of Gilbert's Mikado. If line after line in these speeches does not bear out the producer's evident belief that this is not a heavy father but the dramatist's humorous comment upon the conventional figure, then the young Shakespeare is more naive than either Mr. Langham or I take him to be. Barbara Jefford was a charming Julia, loving, sincere and natural, and at her most vivid in her scenes in boy's disguise. She and Lucetta (Rosemary Webster) made a lively affair of the letter scene, which delighted the audience. Launce and Speed were less helped by the convention than their betters. Duff, a darling plum-duff of a dog, looked as if he had stepped straight out of the pages of Turbervile. John Morris gave a charming little sketch of a gossamer but gallant and gentle Sir Eglamour (in pale grey, and steel-rimmed spectacles), who must have been in constant demand as a chaperone for young ladies escaping to forests to join exiled lovers. The company was in good fettle and very much on its toes, though there were regrettable passages when Proteus and Valentine just gabbled, nor were they the only offenders. But it was first and foremost a producer's and designer's triumph with a much neglected play. Mr. Langham has a great sense of style, a delicate touch and a sense of the theatre. We incline to be captious about stylized productions of Shakespeare. Success in this kind is a rarity, and is to be esteemed as such. (pp. 469-71)

Muriel St. Claire Byrne, "The Shakespeare Season

at the Old Vic, 1956-57 and Stratford-Upon-Avon, 1957," in Shakespeare Quarterly, *Vol. VIII, No. 4, Autumn, 1957, pp. 461-92.*

Mary Clarke   (review date 1957)

[*Clarke offers a favorable review of Langham's 1957 production of* The Two Gentlemen of Verona, *noting the effectiveness of the nineteenth-century Gothic romance setting.*]

The Two Gentlemen of Verona is one of Shakespeare's very early comedies. It has been neglected for many years, dismissed because of its inconsistencies and often declared to be the work of several authors. Yet much of it is Shakespeare's unquestionably; the lyric *Who is Silvia?* [IV. ii. 39ff.] is hardly surpassed in all his plays and the quality of constancy, which he later portrayed so strongly in Viola [in *Twelfth Night*] and Imogen [in *Cymbeline*], is already present in Julia. The comedy scenes, nearly all in prose, are assuredly from the same pen that was to create Bottom [in *A Midsummer Night's Dream*] and Dogberry [in *Much Ado About Nothing*] and Falstaff. If the play was in fact written by Shakespeare in 1593 he would have been scarcely thirty years old at the time and most of the inconsistencies can be attributed to the youthful carelessness of a young man who preferred to pour out his heart in words rather than to go back and check up his references.

Dr. Johnson's rebuke on this point has the amused tolerance of a headmaster dealing with a gifted but careless schoolboy: '. . . the author conveys his heroes by sea from one inland town to another in the same country; he places the emperor at Milan, and sends his young men to attend him, but never mentions him more; he makes Proteus, after an interview with Silvia, say he has only seen her picture; and, if we may credit the old copies, he has, by mistaking places, left his scenery inextricable. The reason of all this confusion seems to be that he took his story from a novel, which he sometimes followed, and sometimes forsook, sometimes remembered, and sometimes forgot.'

The play, then, is almost certain to fail if taken too seriously. Bristol and Regent's Park, however, have shown in recent years that it can still hold the stage happily if well directed and lightly played. *The Two Gentlemen* is, in fact, creeping back into favour and its progress towards popularity must have been helped by Michael Langham's production at the Old Vic.

Langham worked from the premiss that although the young men and women all profess to be most horribly in love and can think and talk of nothing else, there is no reason why the audience should not smile at their extravagance. Helped by his designer, Tanya Moiseiwitsch, he moved the play forward to the Italy of the early nineteenth century, thus giving his characters kinship with those of the Gothic novels (many of which, such as [Horace Walpole's] *The Castle of Otranto* and [Ann Radcliffe's] *The Mysteries of Udolpho,* are also set in Italy) and also with those of *Nightmare Abbey*—Thomas Peacock's brilliant burlesque of the Shelley-Byron circle. The result of this treatment was that the audience reacted with laughter rather than disapproval to the passionate change of heart in Proteus and the finish became an excuse for greater merriment rather than a heavily contrived happy ending.

The setting was an Italianate garden with a semi-circular stairway at the left of the stage, some broken pillars, flower-entwined, and at the right a tower covered in ivy with a Gothic window high up and out of reach. The base of the tower was supported on a circle of pointed arches. Changes in back-cloth moved the scene from Verona to Milan or the forest on the frontiers of Mantua.

The costumes of the period, becoming alike to men and women, helped the players to catch the right mood of self-conscious romanticism. Proteus, his hair dressed in dark curls on his forehead, wore a wine-dark suit with flying tails and a Byronic collar; in his first scenes he clutched a book of poems—an agonized lover before he opened his mouth. The more cheerful Valentine was dressed in blue. Julia's first gown, in russet-coloured silk, trimmed with coppery swathes of tulle and with pale green sleeves, was something a Jane Austen heroine might have sighed after. Silvia and the courtiers in Milan were a little in advance of their country cousins from Verona, in the matter of fashions. Silvia's first costume was a brilliant flame-coloured riding habit; while she later changed into a simple but elegant white Empire gown. The Duke was imposing in black and white, Thurio apoplectic in crimson.

The play opened in the garden of Proteus' house. Sailors carrying bundles of luggage hurried across the stage and down the steps at front, while Proteus and Valentine walked slowly and sadly behind them. Valentine, full of cheer and confidence, was very different from his friend who seemed to walk in a daze of love, regretting his friend's departure yet scarcely hearing his words of farewell. He woke up, however, to indulge in the quick battle of words with Speed and then, hand on heart, went mournfully back into his house.

The same garden served for Julia and Lucetta, only their entrance was from the right instead of the left. Lucetta was dressed pertly and prettily in primary colours and was a self-possessed young woman, more than a match for her mistress. When Julia inquired, with great show of indifference, *What think'st thou of the gentle Proteus?* [I. ii. 14], she responded with a merry peal of laughter before crying, *Lord, Lord! to see what folly reigns in us!* [I. ii. 15]. When Julia finally left alone to collect the scraps of her torn letter, she sank down on her knees in a flutter of taffeta to croon over every word. She was still in this position when Lucetta returned and was hard put to it to carry off the situation with a desperately prosaic, *Well, let us go.* [I. ii. 129].

The following scene showed Antonio, a country gentleman returned from the shoot, talking easily with his very old and very sober servant, Panthino, as the latter pulled off his boots and substituted slippers. In the background, Proteus leaned against an ivy-clad pillar; a book in his hand and the other hand to his brow. When called by his father, he fell straight into the trap of saying politely he would like to join Valentine and then found himself sternly ordered to do so. Alone, he sighed over his fate:

> "O, how this spring of love resembleth
> The uncertain glory of an April day,
> Which now shows all the beauty of the sun,
> And by and by a cloud takes all away!"
>
> [I. iii. 84-7]

There might, in his mind, have been some connection between the metaphor of the cloud and the person of Panthino who returned at that moment to hasten him.

The first scene in Milan was enlivened by having the ladies and gentlemen of the court indulge in archery practice at the back of the stage while Valentine and Speed had their little conversation at the front. Silvia's entry was dazzling; her brilliant gown, red-gold hair and trim little figure would have made her the centre of interest had she not been the daughter of a Duke. The farewell of Proteus and Julia, a hastily snatched moment of unhappiness, was constantly interrupted by distant calls for *'Julia!'* or else *'Proteus!'*. Eventually, Panthino, who had gone down the front steps ahead of his master, returned to say irritably *Sir Proteus, you are stay'd for* [II. ii. 19]. The next arrivals on the scene were Launce and his dog. Launce came straggling along with a bundle in one hand and the dog's lead in the other, wailing into a large handkerchief. The dog sat cheerfully by while the scene of leavetaking in the Launce family was demonstrated to him, and occasionally eyed his master with an expression of pity or contempt or else yawned widely to the audience. When Launce and Crab had been hustled away by Panthino, the scene returned to Milan. There Silvia sat for her portrait and amused herself by teasing the wealthy Thurio, an elderly Regency rake. The Duke here first showed his disapproval of Valentine; he amiably delivered the news that Proteus was on his way to Milan and was greeted with such a tumult of eager explanations from Valentine that he withdrew a little and put up his monocle to observe this impetuous, too-talkative young man. Valentine's excitement was not dampened, however, and he ran gladly to greet Proteus and to present him to Silvia. Proteus lifting her hand to his lips was struck dumb by her beauty; at that moment was Julia forgotten. After the departure of Silvia, though, he managed to converse reasonably with his friend and throughout this episode there was much by-play with the unfinished portrait of Silvia which had been left by the artist on his easel.

At the conclusion of his soliloquy, *Even as one heat another heat expels* [II. iv. 192], Proteus remained in a corner of the stage in a pensive, lovesick attitude, throughout the brief scene between Speed and Launce. His thought thus seemed to continue straight into his next soliloquy:

> "To leave my Julia, shall I be forsworn?" (a vigorous nod)
> "To love fair Silvia, shall I be forsworn?" (another nod)
>
> [II. vi. 1-2]

The scene then returned to Verona for Julia's decision to follow Proteus despite Lucetta's more worldly warnings. After her exit, crying

> "Come, answer not, but to it presently;
> I am impatient of my tarriance."
>
> [II. vii. 89-90]

came the only intermission.

The second half of the play began with dancing in the gardens of the Duke's palace. Everyone took part and old Sir Eglamour became quite dizzy with the merriment and the whirling figures of the dance. There were plenty of drinks being carried round by servants and after gulping down enough to give him courage, Proteus revealed Valentine's secret to the Duke. The Duke's method of dealing with Valentine was cat-like; the claws hidden by a velvet paw of seeming trust, he consulted the boy about a proposed elopement of his own. Poor Valentine, growing ever more uneasy and transferring, with exaggerated casualness, from one arm to the other the cloak which hid his rope ladder, survived the torture well until the Duke's cheerful demand, *I pray thee, let me feel thy cloak upon me* [III. i. 136]. Then he dropped everything and stood aghast like a schoolboy while the Duke read his letter to Silvia.

The banishment of Valentine, Proteus' hypocritical sympathy, the comments of Launce and his discussion with Speed as to the merits of his prospective wife were played straight through in the same scene. There followed the even more hypocritical behaviour of Proteus when he pretends to sympathize with the Duke's plans for marrying his daughter to Thurio.

There was a change of backcloth for the next scene, and by dim lighting the stage was transformed into a darkly romantic forest. The outlaws emerged from the shadows at the front of the stage, and Valentine and Speed made their entry across the narrow fringe of stage which divides the audience from the apron. One of the outlaws remained on this forestage throughout the scene, silhouetted against the general picture.

Returning to Milan, Julia in her boy's clothing was found alone and miserable by the Host who took her into the Duke's garden to look for Proteus. This scene was played before the entry of Proteus so that Julia, hidden by a pillar, heard his serenade and all his treachery. Silvia, leaning from her Gothic window, accepted the flowers and garlands brought to her but sternly rejected Proteus' pleas of love.

After this late-night interlude, the lighting changed to morning sunshine as the frail and gentle Sir Eglamour came chirpily down the steps carrying a posy of flowers for Silvia. Her request to be taken to join Valentine caused him a moment of disappointment but with selfless devotion he agreed to assist and accompany her.

Afterwards came Launce to grumble at Crab for cur-like behaviour and then Proteus, accompanied now by Julia (disguised as Sebastian a page), to grumble at Launce. Silvia was already on her way to meet Sir Eglamour when Julia met her, but she stopped to send for her picture and to talk for a moment before running happily away. Julia, left alone, had a panic-stricken moment when Silvia's pretty maid began to show an interest in 'Sebastian'.

Sir Eglamour and Silvia duly met by one of the Gothic arches at the front of the stage, now representing Friar Patrick's cell. Friar Patrick himself and also Friar Lawrence were represented as onlookers and even as they pronounced blessing they realized what was afoot. The interview between Thurio and Proteus, with Julia as onlooker and commentator, took place while Thurio was being dressed, shaved, prinked and preened and curled by an army of valets. As he lay back in his chair, lather on his cheeks and curling irons in his hair, the Duke arrived in a fury and amid the general consternation the curling irons were forgotten until a strong smell of smoke gave warning that Thurio's top curls were afire.

The mass exit down the front steps of the stage, each character crying wildly *I'll follow!* for some different reason, brought gales of laughter from the audience and laughter continued almost uninterrupted until the end of the play. Silvia's wail when captured by the outlaws, *O Valentine, this I endure for thee!* [V. iii. 15], was pure Mrs. Radcliffe. Proteus with a pistol, Valentine crying *Ruffian!*, Silvia swooning, Julia fainting—all this played at speed with mock heroics was capital fun and when Proteus proclaimed with a deadpan expression and sententious tone:

> "O heaven, were man

> But constant, he were perfect!"
>
> [V. iv. 110-11]

he got the biggest laugh of the evening.

The Duke and Thurio were carried on by the outlaws and dumped unceremoniously in the middle of the stage. Very much aware of the outlaws' weapons, Thurio could not disclaim Silvia quickly enough. The Duke, drawing himself up to his full height, opened his mouth to remonstrate but then noticed the pistol pointed at his heart and changed his speech into one of reconciliation. The last laugh of the play came as the evil-looking brigands surrounded the Duke, and Valentine proclaimed solemnly:

> "They are reformed, civil, full of good,
> And fit for great employment, worthy lord."
>
> [V. iv. 156-57]

Michael Langham certainly obtained full co-operation from his players in this experimental change-of-century production. Keith Michell in voice, bearing and expression was exactly right as a Proteus who was half Byron, half Scythrop [in Peacock's *Nightmare Abbey*]. Barbara Jefford saw the absurdities as well as the sincerity of Julia and Richard Gale made a cheerful, extrovert Valentine. Ingrid Hafner, a twenty-year-old actress from the Old Vic School at Bristol, had her first important part as Silvia. She spoke clearly and prettily with a nice understanding of what she was saying (a quality not to be taken for granted among actors) but did not attempt any very deep characterization. Derek Godfrey was a Duke who would have consorted happily with Wellington, and Derek Francis with a few bluff hahs and haws made much of the tiny part of Thurio. As the two clowns, Dudley Jones accomplished easily the word-play of Speed and Robert Helpmann, as Launce, made a brave stand against the scene-stealing tactics of his dog who must, said *Punch,* 'have won the Golden Bone at R.A.D.A.' John Humphry was unbelievably solemn and very funny as Panthino while David Dodimead played both Antonio and the leader of the Outlaws, giving welcome strength to two small but important parts. In all, the production was an admirable example of true repertory acting where all parts contribute to the play itself and no star performer imposes his personality too strongly.

The Two Gentlemen, first produced on January 22nd, 1957, had an excellent press and enjoyed the usual extra publicity that is always lavished on the dog who plays Crab (in this case, Keith Michell's golden labrador Duff). Unfortunately, however, the play did not attract very large audiences and was withdrawn on March 23rd after thirty-one performances.

Mary Clarke, "The Two Gentlemen of Verona," in her Shakespeare at the Old Vic. *The Macmillan Company, 1957.*

Robert Coleman   (review date 19 March 1958)

[*In the following excerpt, Coleman praises Langham's "discerning direction" in his 1958 revival of* The Two Gentlemen of Verona.]

The Stratford (Ontario) Festival Company has won an enviable reputation with its revivals of the classics. Notably with the works of Shakespeare. Since some of us haven't the time or the money for a pilgrimage to Canada, T. Edward Ham-

Richard Gale as Valentine, Barbara Jefford as Julia, Keith Michell as Proteus, and Ingrid Haffner as Silvia. Act V, scene iv.

bleton and Norris Houghton have brought the eminent organization to us.

The Festival Company opened its visit to our Phoenix Theatre Tuesday evening with "Two Gentlemen of Verona." Though it is one of the Bard's earlier and lesser pieces, it should prove interesting to all with a fondness for the First Gentleman of Stratford-on-Avon. It is a prophecy of finer comedies to come.

Here, we have Master Will experimenting, searching for a style. Here, we have the sassy, philosophical servants, the girl posing as a boy, the intrigue, within intrigue, that were to mark such later and weightier works as "Twelfth Night" and "As You Like It." Here, we have a few of the neatly phrased quotations with which they would be more richly equipped.

In a review of "Two Gentlemen of Verona" by G. B. Shaw, the heading was "Poor Shakespeare." But G. B. might have observed that it's a better comedy than most other dramatists are capable of fashioning. Played to the hilt, as it is in this instance, it is beguiling fun. It has its rewards.

We are particularly grateful to the Stratford company for doing it, as it is seldom presented professionally in this century. When offered over here by the Keans some hundred years or more ago, it shocked the aisle-sitters a bit. For that was

a rather puritanical era, averse to the ways of the Renaissance.

As you may recall, "Two Gentlemen of Verona" has to do with Valentine and Protheus, who go to the Court of Milan in search of preferment. There, they both fall in love with the Duke's daughter, Silvia. Protheus, already affianced to Julia back home, betrays his friend to further his own interests.

But eventually Valentine gets Silvia, and Protheus his faithful Julia. And the two friends are reconciled. Now that's what riled the critics in the 1800's: the placing of friendship over love and romance. There was nothing cynical about the drama guides of that period.

Eric House, Lloyd Bochner, Douglas Rain, Diana Maddox, Ann Morrish, Bruno Gerussi and Douglas Campbell act the leads with just the right tongue-in-cheek air, under Michael Langham's discerning direction. Eric Christmas, George McCowan, Powys Thomas, Eric Berry, Amelia Hall, Roberta Maxwell and Helen Burns also have the right approach to their roles.

Tanya Moiseiwitsch has designed a production that is at once simple and gala. Light blue drapes and brownish set pieces, against a black backdrop, suggest many locales with fluidity.

The costumes, quite attractive, seek for timelessness, to avoid dating.

Shakespeare's introduction of "well-bred outlaws" and "low-class brigands" must have put ideas into the heads of W. S. Gilbert and Edmond Rostand for their "Pirates of Penzance" and "The Romancers." We can only wonder why Master Will never pursued this satiric bent in subsequent plays.

Robert Coleman, "Bard's Comedy Well Done," in
Daily Mirror, *March 19, 1958.*

Walter Kerr   (review date 19 March 1958)

[Kerr contends that although Langham's 1958 production of
The Two Gentlemen of Verona *was "not terribly exciting," it generally triumphed over the plot complications in Shakespeare's text.]*

Shakespeare was something of a novice when he wrote "Two Gentlemen of Verona," and it's nice to know that he made good, later.

The funny thing about the play, now that the Stratford Festival Company of Canada has given us one of our rarer opportunities to see it, is that in it Shakespeare seems such a stock-company version of himself.

Here are all the convenient plot complications in which "women change their shapes and men their minds," quite neatly dovetailed. Here are the low comics—with and without their sad-eyed dogs—explaining that their walking sticks understand them (lean on a walking-stick and it will understand you, if you really want to pursue this joke).

Here are disarming heroines, belligerent fathers, treacherous lovers, and rope ladders that can be hung from balconies—and they all seem to exist in a rather finished, rather routine, shape.

Good work, and hack work. Where, you wonder from time to time, are the unformed and perhaps disorderly flashes of real genius?

Well, of course there are some. When a coquettish Julia, intelligently played by Ann Morish, asserts her maidenly modesty by refusing to look at a love letter, becomes decidedly petulant the moment the letter is out of her reach, manages to get it back and then—out of maidenly modesty—tears it into shreds, the ugly truth about feminine psychology has been handsomely hinted at. Portia [in *The Merchant of Venice*], and better yet Beatrice [in *Much Ado About Nothing*], may still come to be written.

When the world of polite, and politely devious, lovemaking is fancifully crossed with a forest band of murderous brigands ("Were you banished for so small a fault?" [IV. i. 31] they ask a fellow who has just killed a man), that odd and special universe in which cutthroats and cads can consort with beguiling innocents and never injure them is somewhere in the offing.

Bruno Gerussi finds some small pleasure in Launce's tear-drenched account of his farewell to his family (only the dog wouldn't cry), and it's fun for every one when Diana Maddox—a Silvia wrapped in a scarlet cloak—is whisked into the air and carted treacherously away crying "Oh, Valentine, I endure this for thee!" [V. iii. 15]. (You may find yourself tempted, now and then in the evening, to murmur "Oh, Shakespeare. I endure this for thee," but not too urgently).

What have the Canadian actors, operating at something less than full strength, managed to do for so minor, and mild-mannered, a work? They have spoken it very clearly, which is no mean consideration. They have successfully imagined—in Douglas Campbell's cigar-chewing parent, in Eric Christmas' shy little suitor, in Douglas Rain's light-footed and whinnying Speed—certain fresh attitudes and engaging inflections for extremely familiar types. Director Michael Langham's conceit of tossing the whole romantic daydream into a powdered-wig eighteenth century gives him an opportunity for some minuet posturing that is prettily lighted, and Tanya Moiseiwitsch's background of ivied arches is as stunning as it is simple.

I think the one thing that might have lifted a gentle scholarly exercise into vivid practical theater is missing: the impact of personality over and above the craftsmanlike trial-flight that Shakespeare wrote. The production simply adds competence to competence, which is quite enough for the conscientious student but not terribly exciting for anybody else.

Walter Kerr, " 'Two Gentlemen of Verona' Is Revived at the Phoenix," in New York Herald Tribune, *March 19, 1958, p. 22.*

John McClain   (review date 19 March 1958)

[McClain argues that Langham's attempt to revive The Two Gentlemen of Verona *failed because it is a "nothing" play. "[If] the Bard's imprint were not upon it," he remarks, "there is serious doubt that anybody would do it, ever."]*

Viewing the proceedings from this pew it seemed passing strange that the Canadian Shakespeare Festival company should have chosen to open their short repertory at the Phoenix Theatre last night with "Two Gentlemen of Verona." This is a "nothing" play whose single virtue is that it features the services of an amiable dog; if The Bard's imprint were not upon it there is serious doubt that anybody would do it, ever.

So why should our neighbors from the North stick their necks out? Perhaps because they felt it was an important challenge, and one which by unusual direction and mounting might create more interest than the conventional selections. This is laudable, but I'm afraid it didn't work.

The malleable sets designed by Tanya Moiseiwitsch are most attractive, and it seemed to me that Michael Langham had scraped the bottom of the barrel to extract the last morsel of humor from the situations.

But the play itself is fairly charm resistant, and there are not, frankly, enough players in this contingent with the stature to bring brilliance out of banality.

Protheus is one of the most vacillating, disloyal and (to me) dreary young men in the history of the spoken word; his alleged pal, Valentine, is an ethereal dope; even the two girls, Julia and Silvia, could be readily replaced. How they finally pair off becomes a matter of minor moment.

In their various assignments I thought the two girls, Ann Morrish and Diana Maddox, were quite capable, but I didn't think that either Eric House, as Valentine, or Lloyd Bochner, as Proteus, had the flair and flamboyance that might have given the evening a lift. On the other hand I thought Douglas

Campbell did; his Duke of Milan is an authoritative and classical parody.

The Canadian company, in this version, have chosen to move the events up to the beginning of the Nineteenth Century, and the costumes are thus more imaginative. There is a quite delightful dance sequence and, of course, the song "Who Is Sylvia" [IV. ii. 39ff.] sung by William Cole.

There is little point in pursuing "Two Gentlemen of Verona" further; it is Shakespeare at his cute and captious worst, and this isn't the aggregation that will alter the impression.

> John McClain, "Shakespeare Troupe Offers Poor Opener," in New York Journal-American, *March 19, 1958.*

Lewis Funke   (review date 19 March 1958)

[*Funke asserts that while Langham's 1958* Two Gentlemen of Verona *was "an exceedingly lovely production," some of the play's comedic elements were lost through the emphasis on the courtly tradition.*]

Although Shakespeare lovers know that their idol wrote "Two Gentlemen of Verona," it may be observed without too much argument that comparatively few of them have ever seen it performed on the stage professionally. It is one of the earlier comedies, a prelude to the more finished products that were to come.

Last summer the New York Shakespeare Festival troupe presented an uninhibited and boisterous version in Central Park and last night the Stratford Festival Company of Canada gave it a regal and stately production at the Phoenix.

Since some scholars believe that the play was presented before the court and, indeed, it is written in courtly style, this approach that director Michael Langham has endorsed has tradition on its side. The result is an exceedingly lovely production. Everyone is quite elegant and regal in handsome costumes designed by Tanya Moiseiwitsch and the simple setting, also by Miss Moiseiwitsch, is bewitchingly effective.

There is fluency in the action, the single set being utilized for scenes in Verona, Milan and the forest near Mantua. Everyone speaks the lines clearly and devotedly, and there is a nice over-all pictorial quality. But to at least one observer the courtliness becomes just a bit too courtly. There is just a little too much polish in everything for the sake of a play that could do with a little more of the comic thrust.

"Two Gentlemen of Verona," you may recall, is a comedy based on love, mistaken identity and plain low-down knavery. Protheus, leaving behind a devoted Julia, proceeds to Milan and there falls in love with Silvia, beloved by his dearest friend, Valentine. Protheus, a cad, indeed, disclosed to Silvia's father his friend's plan to elope with Silvia, thinking that then he will have a chance to press his suit. It all gets pretty much entangled, but in the end everything is put to right, the knots untangled. Amid all this there are flashes of the master's wit and some of the text is lovely to hear. But it is a secondary work that a livelier point of view could help.

The players are first-rate. Eric House is a suitably ardent Valentine who at first scoffs at love but eventually himself became tangled in its clutches. Lloyd Bochner as the two-timing Protheus is an effective suitor, with the right touch of skulduggery in his character. Ann Morrish's Julia is beguil-

ing and touchingly earnest, while Diana Maddox' Silvia is cool, gay and most attractive.

There are also nicely etched contributions by Eric Christmas as an old and doddering, never-say-die wooer (Sir Eglamour), and Douglas Campbell, whose Duke of Milan is robust and decisive. The roles of the clowns are played by Bruno Gerussi (Launce) and Douglas Rain (Speed). Mr. Gerussi's Launce is humorously simple-minded, sniveling and bewildered, and he manages the business with his dog rather well. Mr. Rain is cocky enough and sprightly, too.

That this Canadian company has come by its plaudits honestly cannot be gainsaid. It has style, intelligence and an affection for the work in hand. And it knows how to speak the verse with clarity and a touch of music. Credit it, too, with courage in undertaking for this New York debut a play such as this. "Two Gentlemen" may be courtly all right, but a little letting down of the hair could, perhaps, prove most beneficial.

> Lewis Funke, in a review of "The Two Gentlemen of Verona," in The New York Times, *March 19, 1958, p. 35.*

PRODUCTION:

Stuart Vaughan • New York Shakespeare Festival • 1957

BACKGROUND:

This production of *The Two Gentlemen of Verona* opened on 22 July 1957 in New York's Central Park. Rather than exploring the complex, yet ill-formed themes in the play, Vaughan elected to fully exploit the play's comedic elements. As a result, virtually every line of comedy was underscored, giving the play a vitality which attracted and entertained large audiences. The principal players included Sheppard Kerman as Proteus, Robert Blackburn as Valentine, Jerry Stiller as Launce, Peggy Bennion as Silvia, and Ann Meara as Julia.

COMMENTARY:

Lewis Funke   (review date 23 July 1957)

[*Funke praises Vaughan's production of* The Two Gentlemen of Verona *for its "slapstick and mock melodrama." Although Vaughan's brand of comedy became tedious at times, Funke continues, it nevertheless saved the play from becoming "limp fare."*]

New York's biggest theatre bargain—the free Summer Shakespeare Festival—returned to Central Park last night with a broad and raucous rendition of "The Two Gentlemen of Verona." And, if there also is a touch of "The Black Crook" in the current incarnation, it is completely intentional and felicitous.

This is not one of the more frequently played in the comedies in the Shakespeare collection. Without the slapstick and the mock melodrama it could prove limp fare, indeed. Director Stuart Vaughan, who recently staged the troupe's immensely successful "Romeo and Juliet," once again has used intelligence in bringing to life this antic on the foibles of love and romance.

There is barely a line of comedy that isn't underscored. Nor is an opportunity for a sight laugh overlooked. Some of this emphasis gets a little tedious, to be sure, and occasionally even a touch of silliness creeps in. But the general effect is satisfactory as the more than 1,500 spectators indicated by their laughter and hearty response.

This is free Shakespeare but it isn't shoddy Shakespeare. There are energy and enthusiasm in the production. And there is youth, which helps. Valentine, Proteus, Silvia and Julia are young lovers, in fact, full of vanity, boastfulness, whims and high spirits.

Robert Blackburn as the ardent, double-crossed Valentine, plays with a free and easy style; Paul Stevens as the deceitful Proteus brings a proper stroke of the rogue to the role; Anne Meara as the betrayed Julia gives the part a tomboyish quality that succeeds in winning laughter, and Peggy Bennion is a lovely Silvia, the one for whom the song and verse "Who is Silvia?" [IV. ii. 39ff.] were written.

To Jack Cannon and Jerry Stiller have gone the clownish characters and, allowing for some over-eager moments in which they believe themselves on a vaudeville stage, they do well enough. Mr. Stiller's Launce is especially good, as he should be, in the soliloquy over his dog Crab and again in his recounting of Crab's misbehavior among his betters. Mr. Cannon's Speed is highly energized, a bit too much so at times. Effectively humorous contributions are made also by Robert Geiringer, Albert Quinton and Joseph Shaw.

John Robertson's lighting helps considerably and Bernie Joy's costumes are gay and colorful. The Summer Shakespeare Festival troupe, which had hoped to tour the city's parks with all its productions—it did with "Romeo and Juliet"—has decided to settle down in the area of Central Park's Belvedere Tower to conserve both its finances and its strength. Until Aug. 9, with the exception of Mondays, it will be giving "The Two Gentlemen of Verona." If it no longer can visit the boroughs it would not be unwise for the boroughs to visit it.

> Lewis Funke, "Antics in Park," in The New York Times, *July 23, 1957, p. 21.*

Harold Clurman   (review date 31 August 1957)

[*In the excerpt below, Clurman commends Vaughan's production for capturing the virility inherent in the text of Shakespeare's* Two Gentlemen of Verona.]

Having complained sufficiently, I have been looking for something to be cheerful about. I found it—in Central Park.

Very near the geographical heart of Manhattan there is a Summer Shakespeare Theatre where in the open air an organization calling itself the Shakespeare Workshop has been giving a series of productions of the Bard's plays more satisfactory than any I have seen hereabouts for a long time.

The first production I saw was a thoroughly captivating one of the delightfully inconsequential *Two Gentlemen of Verona.* This is Shakespeare in his most youthfully bubbling vein—refreshingly lighthearted, full of animal spirits, bursting with the promise of genius.

The director, Stuart Vaughan, has understood the basic tenet of Shakespearian production: everything must be activated. Speech must form part of a fabric of sustained movement and visualization in a spirit either of overflowing festiveness or passion. The keynote is virility. Here obscenity is preferable to a vapid prettiness. Abandon is closer to Shakespeare than gentility.

The entire cast is to be congratulated. The clowns were really funny. The lovers, handsome and winning, were mercifully without either of the two besetting sins in such performances—cuteness and stuffiness—and their lady loves were robust, reminding us that the original actors of these parts were young men. Here was a consummate ensemble—down to the best cast dog I have ever seen on the stage. (p. 98)

> Harold Clurman, in a review of "The Two Gentlemen of Verona," in The Nation, New York, Vol. 185, No. 5, August 31, 1957, pp. 98-9.

Euphemia Van Rensselaer Wyatt   (review date October 1957)

[*Wyatt argues that Shakespeare's immature play is strengthened in Vaughan's production by both the director's imagination and the actors' dedication "to transmute a young poet's ebullience into lively farce."*]

From the sadness of *Romeo and Juliet,* the New York Summer Shakespeare Festival turned to one of the earliest comedies [*The Two Gentlemen of Verona*]—a light-hearted trifle Shakespeare adapted from the sixteenth-century Portuguese novel, *Diana,* which contained the mistaken identity—the girl masquerading as a page to plead her own cause with her lover—as well as forest outlaws, all of which Shakespeare found good enough material to use again. There is even the first version of Portia's famous catalogue of her suitors but this time it is the lady who invites the maid's comments. Shakespeare evidently enjoyed the scene with the robbers because in *As You Like It* he ennobled them for the Forest of Arden. Perhaps he had played Robin Hood as a boy in the woods of Warwickshire!

No company seems better able to transmute a young poet's ebullience into lively farce. To strengthen the characterizations, the director, Stuart Vaughan, unleashed his imagination to show the cheery little Duke of Milan as an amateur horticulturist whose choicest treasures together with pruning shears and watering-pot were wheeled about behind him by some varlets. Sir Thurio, Sylvia's elderly suitor, was always practicing his fencing on a dummy labeled "Valentine" while Sir Eglamour, Knight, made his one scene climactic with a broadsword too large for comfort. The lockets with their ladies' portraits worn by Valentine and Proteus were almost pie size and the trees of the forest were suggested by young dancers in green in arboreal poses. Carnival scenes with bears and acrobats marked the passage of time.

Jerry Stiller was more than at home as Launce, the yokel servant of Proteus, who appeared with his dog, Crab, said to be the sourest dog that ever lived. It seems a bit unkind for Shakespeare thus to describe the only canine appearing in his casts but the dogs in the audience—of whom my poodle was one—took it all in good part. Launce and Crab made many friends. Speed, Valentine's valet was a wily domestic with a beard. To vary the scenes with the ladies, Sylvia was seen reviewing the results of a shopping expedition, while Julia plotted her escapade as a page from behind a screen where she was having her bath.

Anne Meara was a very lively and charming young Veronese lady with a voice that carried well as a page. Robert Blackburn and Paul Stevens were excellent as the honorable Valentine and the dishonorable Proteus whose faithlessness to Julia results in his singing "Who is Sylvia, what is she—?" [IV. ii. 39ff.] so we must forgive him as did Valentine. Robert Geiringer was delightful as the busy gardener, the Duke of Milan.

The stage had been repainted blue as more suitable to comedy and some pretty changes in the archway indicated palace or garden. The costumes were fantastic and attractive; the pace swift and jocund. (pp. 67-8)

> *Euphemia Van Rensselaer Wyatt, in a review of "Two Gentlemen of Verona," in* The Catholic World, *Vol. 186, No. 1111, October, 1957, pp. 67-8.*

PRODUCTION:

Peter Hall • Shakespeare Memorial Theatre • 1960

BACKGROUND:

Hall's production of *The Two Gentlemen of Verona* opened at Stratford on 5 April 1960. His intention was to present it as the earliest in a progression of six Shakespearean comedies. Thus, it was to be displayed with all its limitations so that people who saw the entire sequence of plays could witness Shakespeare's steady maturation. While the concept was not without merit, Hall's *Two Gentlemen of Verona* was unsuccessful for reasons other than Shakespeare's immature artistry. According to many critics, one of the biggest problems with the production was the recently-installed revolving stage at the theater, which Hall felt obliged to use more than was necessary. The audience became distracted by the actors' inability to concentrate on the delivery of their lines and maintain their proper place on the moving stage at the same time. Renzo Mongiardino's overpowering scenery provided further distraction and was difficult to move efficiently between scenes. As a result of these various complications, much of the play's vigor was lost. Those who played the major roles in the production included Derek Godfrey as Proteus, Denholme Elliot as Valentine, Patrick Wymark as Launce, Susan Maryott as Silvia, and Frances Cuka as Julia.

COMMENTARY:

***The Times,* London   (review date 6 April 1960)**

[*In this anonymously published review, Hall's production of* The Two Gentlemen of Verona *is deemed "restless and fussily visual." The critic asserts, moreover, that the players' uneven performances reflect the difficult play which "demands polished acting in proportion to its limitations."*]

The most likely explanation of Mr. Peter Hall's restless and fussily visual production of *The Two Gentlemen of Verona,* which opened this year's Memorial Theatre season, would

rest on the play's neglect. Although well known as a medley of themes more satisfactorily handled in the later comedies and hence well chosen to begin the sequence planned, it usually stays on the shelf; and in any case it demands polished acting in proportion to its limitations. Presumably it has been decided that a young company cannot be expected to play it straight.

On the other hand the play's neglect is something of a mystery, for any impatience roused by the formal interplay of its quartet of lovers is short-circuited by the clowns who provide a satirical commentary. The formula, enriched by humour, also becomes airborne by poetry good enough to make the reputation of any less eminent author, so that we may resent a production which seems to lack faith in the dramatic impact of verse admired by Middleton Murry and Professor Wilson Knight. When the lines are broken up to the point of saying: "Hope . . . is a lover's staff " [II. i. 248] and of giving verbal emphasis to the sands on which leviathans dance, we may feel that Sir Laurence Olivier's felicities ought not to become general practice.

Mr. Derek Godfrey, a handsomely Italianate Proteus, misuses his excellent voice a great deal in this way, and is given no chance to develop the sombre theme hinted at by this character. It is a pity, because the contrast he makes with Mr. Denholme Elliott's Valentine, one subtly experienced and the other innocent, solves at a glance any problems raised by their vulnerable friendship. Mr. Elliott, indeed, is almost too benevolent, not far from Aguecheek in simplicity [in *Twelfth Night*]. In fact his kindly personality makes the robbers' choice of him as their leader more than usually incredible. He comes off best in the scene with the Duke where a rope ladder is discovered under his cloak.

Neither of the two ladies can be accepted outside a burlesque rendering of the courtly setting. Whether to-day's taste approves it or not, the element of social distance and of a sticky protocol is inseparable from much of the drama and the emotion. The frequent scampering exits, reduce any atmosphere of chivalry to a minimum, like the notion of Sir Eglamour as a doddering greybeard and of the Duke as tetchy rather than formidable. Miss Susan Maryott is attractively pretty and feminine in a pantomime context and Miss Frances Cuka, ill at ease in her male disguise, imposes her own kind of emotional integrity and impish humour in the earlier scenes. She shows remarkable confidence in direct address to the audience and often discovers lyrical freshness.

Not surprisingly in a production which even sets the robbers brawling among themselves before Valentine enters, the clowns are at home. Mr. Jack MacGowran brings Speed to life and Mr. Patrick Wymark, assisted by a Birmingham accent, takes his time over Launce, with a justified confidence in the part. Once he draws an authentic laugh of the George Robey type by delaying a harmless word and the small dog which partners him has pathos and a neat economy of movement.

> *"Fussy Production Opens Stratford Season," in* The Times, *London, April 6, 1960, p. 15.*

Alan Brien   (review date 8 April 1960)

[*Brien harshly criticizes Hall's production of* The Two Gentlemen of Verona *and its distracting staging techniques. He condemns the production as "a bore—and a bore made more infu-*

riating by the unsuccessful attempts to smarten and enliven it.'']

The Stratford Shakespeare season opened an inch or two with *Two Gentlemen of Verona*—as dull and mechanical a bread-and-butter entertainment as was ever churned out by a twenty-six-year-old for the box office of 1589. But if it has to be performed, there is only one way to perform it—and that is the way it is written. Peter Hall seems to have assumed that no one listens to Shakespeare's words any more and that he can safely tart it up, whizz it round, ham it about like television spectacular ballet.

Mr. Hall seems to have taken literally Shakespeare's remark about 'the two hours' traffic of our stage' [*Romeo and Juliet*, Prol. 12]. Round and round on the revolve go Mantuan arches, bulbous trees, gold-inlaid fireplaces, sepulchral towers, blind beggars, carolling servingmen and an occasional actor like rush hour in Piccadilly Circus. For some reason, Mr. Hall is afraid that the audience will object to the incredibility of a girl disguised as a boy—so all the men are dressed in skirts and most in peek-a-boo bangs. (The fact that this makes nonsense of all Shakespeare's jokes about girls in a cod-piece, and turns the sly fantasy of lords in farthingales into silly fact, does not appear to have occurred to him.) He is also worried that Proteus may be accepted as an admirable figure so he directs Derek Godfrey to signal each scrap of skullduggery with elaborate eye-rolls, deafening sniffs, sinister gargles, and pantomime grimaces. To eke out the text, Mr. Hall has written in some memorable dialogue of his own such as 'Ah ha' and 'Hmm hmm' and 'Tch tch' and 'Ho ho ho ho' to punctuate the duller colloquies. Where a point might seem obscure to the modern non-listener, he has not hesitated to syncopate the lines to give them an entirely different meaning. The clowns of Patrick Wymark and Jack MacGowran inject a little ripe humour into the sad charade, but even here one of Shakespeare's most obscene and dateless squibs slides by without raising even one dirty guffaw. Frances Cuka, as Julia, is cast entirely against physique and technique so that her squeaky feminine endings, her intoxicated giggles, her girlish embarrassments seem only a parody of her brilliant performance in *A Taste of Honey*. This production of *Two Gentlemen of Verona* is a bore—and a bore made more infuriating by the unsuccessful attempts to smarten and enliven it. (p. 507)

Alan Brien, "A Taste of Hamburger," in The Spectator, *Vol. 204, No. 6876, April 8, 1960, pp. 506-07.*

A. Alvarez   (review date 9 April 1960)

[*Alvarez argues that while Hall apparently has a firm understanding of Shakespeare's plays, his production of* The Two Gentlemen of Verona *was marred by some unnecessary staging techniques. Most distracting was Hall's use of a revolving stage, but in addition, Renzo Mongiardino's scenery was overwhelming.*]

The new dispensation at Stratford is in. The theatre now has a revolving stage, an apron jutting into the stalls and a new resident director. The opening production of *The Two Gentlemen of Verona* seemed designed chiefly to show off these assets. The stage twirled so constantly and fast that it seemed at times more like *Carousel* than Shakespeare; the leading characters each took their turn on the apron stage, trying to break down the fourth wall and buttonhole the audience; and Peter Hall tried nearly every trick in the book to relieve the

monotony of very early Shakespeare. But it's heavy going: the plot and development are conventional and the verse monotonous. Yet I'm not at all sure that the play's longueurs are as inevitable as he makes them seem.

Granted Mr Hall has great advantages as a Shakespearean director. He seems to know what the plays mean now, as though, alone among the producers, he'd read critics later than Granville Barker. He has respect for the language as poetry and does his best to force a high standard of verse-speaking on his cast. But he has a vice: he is a sucker for a pretty scene; and in Renzo Mongiardino he has a designer all too able to pander to him. The stage was so littered with ivied ruins and bits of decaying gilded interiors that it looked like an opulent, tinted Piranesi. Pretty enough in itself, I admit, yet it contrived to make an immature play seem altogether decadent. Mr Hall's direction dragged accordingly. There were so many pauses while the stage ground round to show off the scenery, picturesque extras hobbled in and out providing atmosphere and the characters paused to imply meanings that weren't there, that the play's one saving grace was lost. I mean its vigour. Despite this production, *The Two Gentlemen* is not sober, serious and dark-varnished; on the contrary, it has freshness, bounce and precious little else.

The vigour survives only with the comics. Patrick Wymark, aided by a talented, deadpan dog, was a brilliant Launce, exuding a massive, stricken humour which was perfectly offset by Jack MacGowran's more vulnerable, pattering style as Speed. The rest of the cast was mixed. Denholm Elliott and Susan Maryott, as Valentine and Sylvia, matched each other, sensitivity for sensitivity. Both have voice, delicacy, gentleness but no reserves of power. Miss Maryott, however, who gamely fought robbers and a slipping wig at the same time, has that haunting and haunted look that might make her a fine Juliet. Derek Godfrey's Proteus and Frances Cuka's Julia were another matter entirely. Mr Godfrey apparently can't yet distinguish between a renaissance gallant and a plain wide-boy. His idea of wit is to pull a sour face and strenuously massacre the metre. Miss Cuka did the same, but self-deprecatingly. Eric Porter was a strong, stylish and witty Duke of Milan. Raymond Leppard provided excellent music.

Obviously, the company has yet to settle down. Obviously, too, Mr Hall will find plays that really interest him as the cycle of comedies moves on. On this occasion, he seems to have decided that the play, as a play, was worthless except as a way of showing off his newly installed equipment. So he sacrificed everything to a fey, twilit atmosphere. It may not be much of a sacrifice but it did for *The Two Gentlemen*.

A. Alvarez, "Dark-varnished Comedy," in New Statesman, *Vol. LIX, No. 1517, April 9, 1960, p. 518.*

Alan Pryce-Jones   (review date 10 April 1960)

[*Pryce-Jones considers Hall's* Two Gentlemen of Verona *a failure, not only because of the distracting set and costumes, but also because of the actors' poor performances.*]

[The Stratford-on-Avon] *Two Gentlemen of Verona* seems all set and clothes, with Shakespeare a long way behind. Peter Hall is unlucky in beginning his cycle of Shakespearean comedy with this irritating play; but there was no reason to turn it into a producer's nightmare—with the revolve whizzing round so urgently that the cast had to cling to scraps of olde

Verona as they flew by. The clothes evoked Clouèt and Ten-niel in equal proportions; and there was one moment when poor Valentine—bravely carried through after a muted fashion by Denholm Elliott—was forced to grovel about in skirts and a shoulder-length blonde wig, looking for all the world like Alice after she had eaten the wrong mushroom. Denholm Elliott is far too good an actor to be exposed to such mortifications, and he was not much helped either by the Proteus of Derek Godfrey, who wore no wig at all and had worked out his part in a quite other convention, or by the Silvia and Julia of Susan Maryott and Frances Cuka, each in her own way departing still further from the central unity of style which alone could make this play bearable.

Luckily the comics were well up to scratch, and Launce's dog, who always steals the evening anyhow, was admirably bland, to offset the contrasted humours of his master, Patrick Wymark, and Jack MacGowran's Speed. The best performance of the evening was Eric Porter's as the Duke. Peter Hall is a brilliant young director, and he is unlikely in the later comedies to be exposed to such perils as those imposed on him by a young and perfunctory Shakespeare, but this is a shaky start to the season.

> Alan Pryce-Jones, "Into the Wilderness," in The Observer, *April 10, 1960, p. 23.*

Eric Keown   (review date 13 April 1960)

[*Keown maintains that although Hall had intended to present* The Two Gentlemen of Verona *as an example of an immature*

Patrick Wymark as Launce and Jack MacGowran as Speed.

Shakespearean comedy, that approach does not excuse the production's weaknesses.]

Peter Hall's idea of showing us Shakespeare's development through a sequence of six of his comedies is such a good notion that it seems ungrateful to quibble with his first offering. *The Two Gentlemen of Verona* is a very unequal play, but from recent productions we have a pretty close idea of how much can be made of it; and that is much more than is achieved by the new company at Stratford. Mr. Hall has presumably had his pick, and we expected acting of distinction; it is disappointing to find a lack of authority running right through the cast, and a general level of performance below that of many repertories in my experience. The first night of a new season is not, however, the time to make sweeping judgments and next week, in *The Merchant,* we may easily see a great improvement.

Mr. Hall's alterations to the Stratford stage are so clearly right that one wonders, as always in the face of imaginative reform, why they weren't made long ago; a short apron now projects into the auditorium, with solid benefits to hearing and intimacy. He is probably right, too, to have installed a big revolving stage, though this production of his bears out my feeling that no producer, however restrained, can resist the temptation to play unnecessary tricks with such deceiving mechanisms. *The Two Gentlemen* is a very straightforward comedy needing no great changes of scene, and the only result of putting it on a turn-table is to make the cast form embarrassed little processions to get to the other side.

Renzo Mongiardino's sets are quite attractive, though Silvia must have lived very vertically in her bijou lodge cottage. The dresses of Lila de Lobili are much less helpful. Julia, having described the boy's clothing she will wear, comes out in a gym tunic as if about to play lacrosse. The Duke of Milan appears in the kind of joke-overcoat Flanagan is fond of, much too big for him and heavily trimmed with pantomime fur; it has the interesting effect of making Eric Porter, one of the best in the cast, actually move like Flanagan. And, most serious of all, Denholm Elliott as Valentine is engulfed in a wig that flanks his face with foolish tresses that make him a member of the Aguecheek family [*Twelfth Night*].

I thought Derek Godfrey a reasonable Proteus, though not sufficiently a cad, and I thought Patrick Wymark and Jack MacGowran, the Launce and the Speed, both had the skill in timing required by Shakespeare's clowns if they are to be tolerable. About the rest of the cast it is fairer to suspend criticism. As for Crab, the dog who played him seemed to have less interest in the drama than any animal I can remember on or off the stage.

> Eric Keown, in a review of "The Two Gentlemen of Verona," in Punch, *Vol. CCXXXVIII, No. 6238, April 13, 1960, p. 533.*

J. C. Trewin   (review date 23 April 1960)

[*Trewin asserts that Hall's production of* The Two Gentlemen of Verona *suffered primarily from the actors' poor articulation, with the exception of Derek Godfrey, whose "splendid" voice served the role of Proteus well. Also, Patrick Wymark gave an admirable performance as Launce.*]

I gather, though I have read very little that my colleagues have written about this revival [of "The Two Gentlemen of Verona"], that Shakespeare needs a stern reprimand. To-day it is the smart thing to bang away at him whenever possible, and, of course, "The Two Gentlemen of Verona" was never intended for the kind of reviewer, so sadly popular now, who reminds me of Prince Hal's view of Percy: "He that kills me some six or seven dozen . . . at a breakfast, washes his hands, and says to his wife, 'Fie upon this quiet life! I want work' " [*1 Henry IV*, II. iv. 102-05].

"The Two Gentlemen" is not a major play. It is just a mild romantic comedy, filled with the tricks that Shakespeare would enjoy using later when he knew better how to handle them. Situations and lines speak to us of excitements to be: it is, indeed, a piece that—shall we say?—can offer the intimations of immortality. In its own right, it is just a frisk round Verona (observe the name) and Milan, that must please a true Shakespearean with an ear for the early music, and baffle and exasperate the uncompromising hearties.

Peter Hall has now chosen it for the first of his sequence of comedies in the present Festival at Stratford-upon-Avon. As he did with Olivia in his revival of "Twelfth Night" a few seasons back, he has laughed without malice at the rapturous excesses of young love. One does not blame him for that; and some of the scenes—Valentine before the Duke, with the ladder of cords, and the disguised Julia with Silvia's immense portrait—are neatly and amusingly heightened. What does trouble me is the failure to keep the sound of the comedy. I am not talking now of audibility, but of the play's gentle Shakespearean music which is almost entirely lost.

I dare say Peter Hall is tired of being told this. It is "damnable iteration" (to return to "Henry the Fourth"). But, alas, it is true; and it will be a great pity if so much decorative craft, so much ingenuity, so much real skill, have to be lavished upon a production that (in its most important part, the speaking of the verse) is jarringly out of tune. Agreed, it has one splendid speaker. Derek Godfrey is Proteus. All who knew him at the Old Vic will realise that he has the tone and the manner. Denholm Elliott, the Valentine (in a remarkable wig), has a pleasantly mischievous sense of humour, though he cannot cope yet with such a set-piece as the "banished" speech ("To die is to be banish'd from myself" [III. i. 171ff.]) in which Valentine looks forward to Romeo. And the two girls, Frances Cuka, the Julia (who disguises herself as a gauche page), and Susan Maryott, the Silvia (who lives, very properly, in a tower), lack the voice to match their performances. The acting is spirited; the poetry is minimised. This will probably deceive anyone who has not read "The Two Gentlemen" into believing that the verse is poor stuff. But, though it is very young and sometimes faint, the play as a whole is a spring song that should not be maltreated.

Its Stratford company has a few able speakers. We shall know later what Eric Porter (waddling about as a bandy, peering Duke) and Ian Richardson (as Thurio who, like Cloten [in *Cymbeline*] in later years, orders a serenade), will make of parts in which they are permitted to use their sense of Shakespearian poetry. Patrick Wymark, with a Birmingham voice—you might hear him, I suppose, at Villa Park any winter Saturday—has the comedian's gift, Launce: this is the servitor with the broad speech and the dog Crab (here a nice white terrier, scene-stealing as usual). It is amusing to listen to Jack MacGowran as he tries to fit his foaming Irish accent to the lines of Speed, the secondary comedian: one part at least that nobody can defend with much enthusiasm.

The settings by Renzo Mongiardino on the new stage (which revolves too often and too self-consciously) have a romantic grace matched by Lila de Nobili's costumes. Always the stage looks good, and the little narrative flickers along with the appropriate visual charm. If only there were vocal charm to match it! However, we can imagine that Mr. Hall and his colleague John Barton will see to this as the Stratford Festival develops. Meanwhile, we can be glad that Mr. Hall has not treated "The Two Gentlemen" as Augustin Daly did in London during the summer of 1895, an occasion which drew one of Shaw's happiest notices in "The Saturday Review." Thus:

> In preparing the text of his version, Mr. Daly has proceeded on the usual principles, altering, transposing, omitting, improving, correcting, and transferring speeches from one character to another. Many of Shakespeare's lines are mere poetry, not to the point, not getting the play along, evidently stuck in because the poet liked to spread himself in verse. On all such unbusinesslike superfluities, Mr. Daly is down with his blue pencil . . .

And again:

> The scenery is insufferable. . . . For a "street in Verona" we get a Bath-bun-coloured operatic front cloth, with about as much light in it as there is in a studio in Fitzjohn's Avenue in the middle of October. I respectfully invite Mr. Daly to spend his time looking at a real street in Verona. . . .

and so on. But Daly was lucky in one thing. He had Ada Rehan for Julia. As a great personage of the English theatre said to me, a little wistfully, during the first-night interval, "It would have been something to have seen Rehan."

J. C. Trewin, "A Stratford Straddle," in The Illustrated London News, *April 23, 1960, p. 704.*

Caryl Brahms   (review date May 1960)

[*Brahms criticizes Hall's casting of the main characters in his production of* The Two Gentlemen of Verona, *deeming it "wilful to the point of lunacy."*]

So Mr. Peter Hall's reign at Stratford-upon-Avon begins. A' made a good start with a flourish of music in the foyer to play us into the theatre where one of the loveliest scenes ever to be set on on a stage rejoiced our eyes (Mr. Renzo Mongiardino). But of course there is more to *The Two Gentlemen of Verona* than the sparkle of leaves and the play of sunlight over long-basking walls.

There is, or could be—or, to be honest, should be—a sparkle of poetry and a shimmering of characters and scenes due to take form in the plays to come, which we glimpse in this salad play of Shakespeare's; a line here and a situation there that speaks to the attentive heart like the voice of an old friend.

Did we complain that Mr. Hall's last season's *Midsummer Night's Dream,* a masque set in the hall of a nobleman's manor, was insufficiently leafy? He has more than repaid us with the beauty of green glade in this. And when the glade revolves it is to open out to us new vistas of blue sky or candle-kindled hearth—the soft and glimmering beauty of poetry made visible.

Of course we do not look to Shakespeare's spring-time play for strong dramatic substance. We are not naive, us. The Old Vics, Bristol and Waterloo Road, in lively productions by Mr. Michael Langham and Mr. Michael Benthall, have put us wise to this. We look on this green play, then, as on a tree from which *Love's Labour's Lost* will in due season put on leaf and flower. It grows in a pleasant forest filled with the rou-cou of wood notes wild. But stay—what lark was that to heaven ascending? . . . A strange, arresting, dumpy little sparrow, rather, with a Salford accent and gift of tears. And who are these two gentlemen of Stratford striving to make-do with calculated middle-aged whimsy for their lack of youthful impetuosity? My admiration for the courage of Mr. Hall, is unabated. Has he not the courage to let funny lines be funny of themselves without assembling a clutter of outside business to try to make them funny? Has he not the courage to bring his play right down into the auditorium upon an apron stage? Just as he has the courage—foolhardiness some might say—to set his revolving stage spinning and send his cast sprinting from the no-longer stationary scene. He plays, in short, an old play up; but there is no glimpse of magic, no line or sudden word of poetry that this producer misses. The plays that Mr. Hall directs can breathe—and so can we. But I must not hide it that in my opinion his casting can be wilful to the point of lunacy.

First let us take that interesting young actress, that taste of honey of a girl, Miss Frances Cuka. In her we see an actress—a real actress—in the making. She can cause one's heart to miss a beat by the timing of a line, the pointing of a word. She is coarse, and warm and well aware of poetry. She could become a very fine comedienne. And no one fortunate enough to have seen her as the girl in *A Taste of Honey* will doubt that as an artist she is sincere. Her acting has that final, unfaltering ring of truth in it, but she is not of the aristocracy of players. No Edith Evans is in the making here. But rather is she rooted in that republic of lively, often unlovely, players who look to Miss Joan Littlewood for their inspiration. A player of the people for the people, then, but not a player queen. Miss Cuka being as sensible as a dish of Lancashire hot-pot would probably prefer it to be this way. She could never, I suspect, content herself with being a virtuoso of the spoken line, letting her intelligence and not her heart guide her as is the way so often with the kind of player who speaks lines "beautifully". Nevertheless she'd better get weaving with Miss Iris Warren, the distinguished specialist in speech, if she is not to break clean through illusion this season at the splendid house of Shakespeare.

And now for Mr. Derek Godfrey. It is one of the greatest difficulties of my calling that I must forever be faulting people I would most like—and let us face it, am in a position to—praise. Mr. Godfrey played the character of Shakespeare in the musical adapted from the novel I wrote with S. J. Simon, *No Bed For Bacon,* at the Bristol Old Vic last summer. I wish I could have repaid his hard work, irony and intelligence by thinking him suited to the part of a youthful, vacillating suitor, prancing in the sun—the kind of part Mr. John Neville does so well; the kind of part in which Mr. Alec Clunes used to excel in the thirties. But Mr. Godfrey was always one to linger in the shade. And no amount of fussing with a line-breaking it up to make it youthful or that appalling thing "cute"—and no amount of (understandably in the circumstances) sprinting from the scene thereafter, can put a spring in his spirit like the spring the producer requires in his gait.

Mr. Denholm Elliott smiles too much. Yet in the right part, what a rueful orphan he would make—a perfect prince consort in a puppet play rebelling against the pull of the strings. These two Veronian gentlemen cannot be as old and mirth-less as the cruel miscasting of them makes them seem to be to us.

And then Miss Susan Maryott, who we know is terribly intelligent, bends backwards to prove that as Sylvia she has settled for just being terrible.

I watched the changes of Mr. Mongiardino's delectable scenes with a rapture from which I absented myself from time to time to see these same players in the mind's eye in a play by Chekhov. Miss Maryott would simply, and rather beautifully, never get to Moscow (but how sensitively and prettily she would sigh at this foreknowledge). Miss Cuka, meanwhile, would bustle about with a lover, and a baby, and a husband and those great mooning girls, her three sisters-in-law. Mr. Denholm Elliott goes off to his rendez-vous with death, making this, his one effectual gesture in my dream play, beautifully, inevitable. And Mr. Godfrey, no longer torturing himself by twisting all the humour from a line and all the poetry from a pause, but floating into being funny, wistful, ironic and brave, as once he did as the Clown in Benthall's *Twelfth Night,* and as Chekhov's gormless husband would give him the perfect chance to do.

And now to happier players. I write of course of Messrs. Eric Porter (Duke of Milan), Jack MacGowran (Speed), Patrick Wymark and Dog (Launce and Dog). Here are players perfectly cast and satisfactorily extended. I liked the style, attack and pace of Mr. Porter, who is a connoisseur's actor; ask any actor about him. I liked, too, the Irish charm and softly imbecillic qualities of Mr. MacGowran's fool; how his Irish brogue does caress the words of Shakespeare, making his Speed a darlin' clown. I will not fault Mr. Wymark's Launce for the unblinking Birmingham in which he plays him, although he is a bigamist wedded to both his dog and his gallery, since it is all Sheep Street to a China Orange that Shakespeare's clowns addressed themselves just as brazenly to the groundlings in their day. And these three actors if they do not together make an ecstasy of casting at least we do not find them difficult to accept.

Mr. Michael Northen has surpassed himself in the matter of sunny summer: morning and afternoon and velvet night. There was a moment, however, when I heard the patter of tiny feet and saw the hurrying shadow of a stage hand passing behind the gauze, when try though I might to tell myself it was Miss Ada Rehan, dropping in from the shades to see that all was well with Verona (in spite of the dismal effort made by two singers of Verona to render Mr. Raymond Leppard's by no means complicated two-part harmonies to the song *Where is Sylvia* [IV. ii. 39ff.]) I could not convince myself.

I did not greatly care for Miss Lila de Nobili's costumes, lovely though they were in colour and texture. They were too faithful perhaps to the paintings of the period and would have benefited by some tactful transcription from the static drama of costumes on a canvas to the livelier drama of costumes for a stage.

> Caryl Brahms, "Two Rather Old Young Gentlemen," in Plays and Players, Vol. 7, No. 8, May, 1960, p. 11.

Richard Findlater   (review date June 1960)

[*Findlater defends Hall's* Two Gentlemen of Verona *from recent critical attacks, pointing out that several non-directorial factors contributed to the production's poor quality. In fact, he points out, this play cannot be effectively presented to a modern audience without the "stage pictures, machinery and 'business'" Hall has devised here.]*

For actors at the *Ur*-Stratford, April is often the cruellest month. Opening 'cold' as they do, without the buttering practice of a preliminary tour, they may look at their worst on the first night of the season. Within a few weeks the costumes begin to feel and look like clothes (if the designer knows his job or has been saved by the theatre's wardrobe staff); the wig-joins seem less visible to the naked or the inner eye as actors get used to at least two heads in a week; and voices straddle the auditorium with greater ease, if not always with greater audibility. As the season strains into May the individuals who have drunk together after rehearsals learn to work together on the stage and become a company. But on the first night, of course, it's different; and the opening performance of the 1960 season bristled with a particular, over-publicized difference. Not only were some of the leading players new to Shakespeare, having made their reputations in modern-dress drama, but the theatre itself was opening a new chapter under the direction of Peter Hall. Suffering from the news-value of his youth and his wife, Mr Hall had been widely interviewed by the national press, and the broadcasting of his admirable ambitions for a new deal—notably, in developing a continuity and coherence of style—had roused premature expectations of his inaugural production. That is one reason why, I suspect, *The Two Gentlemen of Verona* and its cast were judged somewhat more severely on first-night form than they would have been in an average Stratford year—as the April pattern of things to come.

If you consider *The Two Gents* as a particular production, not as a test-case of Mr Hall's intentions, then there is one glaringly obvious weakness—the play. Mixing low comedy and high romance, this conventional Italianate flummery is infused with the unmistakable flavour of early Shakespeare. Here is a touch (in Launce's love of his scene-stealing dog) of what Hazlitt approvingly calls Shakespeare's 'inimitable quaintness of humour' (thank God most of it *is* inimitable); here are teasing premonitions of themes, phrases and situations which flower later in greater plays; here are sudden jets of lyric beauty, as in the unstaled 'Who is Silvia?' [IV. ii. 39ff.], and little streams of light, sweet music. *The Two Gents* is, as Wilson Knight says, 'rich in typical imagery', a seedbed for the student bardolater. But as a play for a modern audience it is doomed, almost inevitably, to be a bore: a painfully bungled bit of Elizabethan hackwork, hastily knocked out—so it seems—by an apprentice author to stop a hole in the repertoire. Most of its comedy is mummified banter, and its plot is perfunctory and silly. This is dead theatre, which nobody would bother to exhume were it not for the sacred brand-name on the shroud. Few producers, indeed, disturb it in its grave: this is only the sixth time that the play has been staged in Stratford's 101 seasons. By choosing it as an opener Mr Hall seemed deliberately to court disaster, or at least to dull the edge of critical appetite. Yet having decided on a set policy for his first season—'to trace, through a sequence of six plays, the range, development and paradox of Shakespearean Comedy'—he was clearly right to begin at the beginning. Buttressed as he is by the Stratford box-office, which is still blankly immune to the ebb-and-flow of critical opinion, Mr Hall can afford to ignore the commercial manager's need to start with a bang. Yet need he have started—as the critics saw it—with such a whimper?

Gallantly defending the author against the director, most critics complained that Mr Hall was being unfair to this museum-piece. They thought, they said, that he knew better, tarting it up and taking the mickey out of it in that disrespectful way. After all, *The Two Gents* wasn't *that* bad, and Mr Hall's way of smartening it up made it seem worse. In the Stratford tradition of Shakespearean spectacular—which is what, they intimated, Mr Hall was supposed to be against—he put the scenery and the 'business' first, instead of letting the Master's words do their work. *The Two Gents* should be played straight, or not at all. Now, that is a venerable ploy which all critics use with justifiable frequency about most productions of The Works; but I am not at all sure that, for this particular play in the circumstances of 1960 Stratford, the complaint is apt. For if you play this comedy straight, you are likely to knock it right back into the grave. Unless, of course, you can camouflage its absurdities and catch its essential lyricism by matching its artifice of writing with a consistent artifice of behaviour and speech, imposing the gloss of a unified acting style. Such a style is rarely achieved under English theatrical conditions, and certainly Mr Hall cannot whistle up the ghost of it at the beginning of a Stratford season with a mixed bag of players. Should he, then, stick austerely to the text, the whole text and nothing but the text? I think not. Putting the ear before the eye is a sound theatrical principle in Shakespearean production for which I vote nine times out of ten, but *The Two Gentlemen of Verona* is the exception. A lot of it just isn't worth hearing. With a text like this, for a modern audience, you must compromise. You must depend upon stage pictures, machinery and 'business', if you are to project the play—such as it is—to a 1960 public, unless you have a 1960 ensemble. Mr Hall hasn't, but in his projection, I think, he generally succeeds.

Among other mistakes, he goes wrong in his apparent attempt to rationalize a prime convention of this romantic pastoral world—the convention of transvestism. Throughout Elizabethan and Jacobean comedy on the modern stage girls dress up as men in flagrantly transparent disguise, bustily Principal Boying it in their breeches parts, and everybody on the stage and in the audience pretends that they don't mind. But although they'll take almost *anything* from Shakespeare, I suspect that many modern playgoers—far from accepting this as a necessary bit of cultural make-believe—find it distractingly hard to swallow such casual change of sex. Mr Hall has, it seems, tried to minimize the visual absurdity of the convention by levelling the differences of dress, but has made it patently and embarrassingly ludicrous by his casting and by effectually caricaturing the girl's disguise. It may, perhaps, help an audience's suspension of disbelief to make Valentine and Proteus stride about in skirts, while Valentine peers out from beneath a dreadful, flaxen, girlish wig. But why does Mr Hall allow Proteus to appear wigless in his own contemporary-styled poll? And how could he ever permit his Julia to step on to any stage in her ugly parody of imposture? This wildly incredible 'boy' is, quite plainly, a frowsy, psychopathic schoolgirl in urgent need of a haircut and a fix from matron.

Mr Hall has also been widely criticized—with some justice—for the mechanical fussiness of his production. As if determined to show off the new revolve, just installed in the Stratford stage, he keeps it whirling round and round, whisking picturesque extras and edifices with it as it goes, an ostentatious symbol of theatricalism. Clearly this is a useful bit of stage machinery, but like all machinery in the theatre it is dangerously intrusive. In *The Two Gentlemen of Verona* no harm is done by an extra twirl or so; in *The Merchant of Venice* the director practises total abstinence; but the revolve is a temptation to future Avonside directors, a bait which the young supremo himself must learn to resist.

Yet in spite of such flaws in direction, in spite of weaknesses in casting and difficulties in restyling in spite of the play itself, Mr Hall's *Two Gentlemen of Verona* avoids disaster. For one thing, it *looks* beautiful, thanks to Renzo Mongiardino's evocative backcloths and architectural props, romantically lit by Michael Northen. There is a bit too much birdsong and not enough man-music; too many eye-catching beggars, shepherds and servants busy themselves in the background or hold graceful poses till the revolve threatens to fling them off again; and the mood is less April than October, a false autumnal mellowness for a springtime play. Over-pictorial Shakespeare may be an obstacle to the higher standards of verse-speaking which Mr Hall confidently hopes in time to establish, but in the meantime this tasteful prettification helps him to secure a certain visual and atmospheric unity which gives the play a coherence threatened by dissonance in acting style.

What's more, some of the characters—in spite of that dissonance—come freshly alive in the hands of Mr Hall's cast: Ian Richardson's Thurio and Mavis Edwards's Lucetta stand out among the smaller fry, while Eric Porter's Duke, Jack MacGowran's Speed and Patrick Wymark's Launce are all wonderful revivalists whose performances have been generally and rightly praised to the Stratford skies. And already one prize asset of the new Stratford régime has been proved: the 'apron stage' which now projects some fifteen feet forward into the audience. This architectural *rapprochement* intensifies the potential immediacy of relationship between the actor and his public. Everyone in the theatre now has a much better chance of hearing what he is saying, even when he is not sure what it means.

Nothing has changed at Stratford overnight; but if we don't keep on taking Mr Hall's temperature, and give him time to get on with the job without continual post-mortems, I see no reason—apart from the sloth of audiences and the vanity of actors—why the Shakespeare Memorial Theatre shouldn't open a new era in production about 1963. (pp. 550-54)

Richard Findlater, "Out and About," in The Twentieth Century, *Vol. 167, No. 1000, June, 1960, pp. 550-54.*

Robert Speaight   (review date Summer 1960)

[*Speaight briefly comments on Hall's production of* The Two Gentlemen of Verona, *disapproving of Lila de Nobili's costumes and praising the performances of Patrick Wymark and Jack MacGowran as Launce and Speed.*]

The Two Gentlemen of Verona was an excellent choice to begin [the 1960 Stratford season] with, because it already states a number of the themes which we find elaborated in the later comedies. Mr. Hall had seen the play in its sequence—a play where the sunshine is already throwing its long shadows—a play far removed from the "light and jocund Italianate comedy" which was all that Quiller-Couch could see in *The Two Gentlemen*. To emphasize this Mr. Hall called on Miss Lila de Nobili to provide the same sort of coloring that she had provided for *Twelfth Night*. I do not think she was so successful with the earlier play as she had been with the

later one. Her costumes were much less attractive. When Julia sets forth on what she imagines will be a happy quest, she would hardly have done so in deep mourning. Furthermore Mr. Hall decided to use his revolve. The method is convenient, and can produce, as it does here, its ingenious variations. But the isolated fragments of scenery, continually showing us a new face, have the effect of breaking up the play instead of pulling it together. We saw later [in the season] how a more restrained use of the revolve could help *The Taming of the Shrew*.

Nor did the production deploy the company at anything like its full strength. In some respects it was seriously undercast, and it was left to Mr. Patrick Wymark as Launce and Mr. Jack MacGowran as Speed to hint at pleasures in store. Admirably contrasted in personality and girth, each knows how to twist an audience round his little finger. Mr. Wymark had the bigger opportunity and how gloriously—how gluttonously—he took it! I am not in the counsels of Stratford, but I shall be disappointed if we do not see, before long, one of the finest Falstaffs of our time. One was grateful, too, for the good speaking throughout; and behind the whole production one could discern the clear outline of allegory. Sir Eglamour is not one of the greater Shakespearian roles, but his costume and make-up recalled us from the world of Machiavelli to the world of Malory—which is where this play really belongs. The perfunctory ending failed to shock because one was allowed to see what Shakespeare was getting at, even if he was getting at it crudely; to hear through these entanglements "the inly voice of love" [cf. II. vii. 18]; and to watch, in its earliest functioning, the operation of Shakespearian justice. (p. 446)

Robert Speaight, "The 1960 Season at Stratford-upon-Avon," in Shakespeare Quarterly, *Vol. XI, No. 3, Summer, 1960, pp. 445-53.*

John Russell Brown   (review date 1961)

[*Brown is a British scholar, director, editor of several Shakespearean plays, and associate director of the British National Theatre. His works include* Shakespeare and His Comedies *(1957),* Shakespeare's Plays in Performance *(1966),* Shakespeare's Dramatic Style *(1970),* Free Shakespeare *(1974),* Shakespeare in Performance: An Introduction through Six Major Plays *(1976), and* Shakespeare and His Theatre *(1982). In an excerpt from his analysis of recent productions by Peter Hall, John Neville, and Michael Langham, Brown explores Hall's directing techniques and how they added several creative dimensions to* The Two Gentlemen of Verona.]

The task of a theatre director is so complicated that it is tempting to treat the matter as one of personal taste, as did Bernard Shaw writing to Mrs Patrick Campbell, to give 'no other but a woman's reason', but think it so because we think it so. And normal difficulties are increased when Shakespeare's plays are discussed, for everyone has different recollections of earlier productions and probably their own views on how to translate the plays into modern terms and adapt them for modern theatres. Yet while it is hard to formulate general rules, we may describe individual methods and compare them. The summer of 1960, for instance, showed the work of three directors of Shakespeare, each with clearly divergent training and abilities, and so by lining up their achievements it is possible to assess a wide range of currently accepted techniques.

Peter Hall had the fullest showing at the Memorial Theatre, Stratford-upon-Avon, with a *Two Gentlemen of Verona*, a *Troilus and Cressida* (in which he had the assistance of John Barton) and a revival of a *Twelfth Night* from two years earlier. This director came to Shakespeare after staging twentieth-century plays, and the experience is mirrored in his work. It is most obvious in his attitude to speaking Shakespeare's verse and prose: he is determined to avoid stuffiness, or solemn staginess, and seeks instead liveliness, humour and point—in a word, vitality. He has had an apron built over the orchestra pit and uses it for direct and forceful contact with the audience. The clear gains of this policy are in certain comic passages where the actors have sufficient skill to sustain the size of their delivery without crudeness. Patrick Wymark as Launce animated his repetitive speeches by a variety of timing and emphasis, and based all on a sympathetic understanding of the large-minded, stubborn character who is yet at the mercy of circumstance. He made the audience wait for words, when he could do so without slowing up his performance, and so invited them to enter his view of the world of the play: correcting Speed for counting 'slow of speech' [cf. III. i. 332] among his maid's vices, he then looked in blank wonder at the audience so that the following line, 'To be slow in words is a woman's only virtue' [III. i. 334], was the necessary statement they had been waiting for, an exaggeration which satisfied where it might have fallen dead with its stale wit. Such acting is well served by Peter Hall's quest for vitality. (p. 129)

Equally clear is Peter Hall's pursuit of visual elaboration. . . . *The Two Gentlemen* had a large revolving stage, on which were set small but detailed trees and buildings—a tower, gatehouse, chimney-piece and so forth—much of it in careful, picturesque ruin. The colours here were dark blues and greens and . . . dull golds and browns, and in the background there was a painted cloth of high, bosky hills and a stormy sky. It is difficult to guess the motives for choosing to imitate Irving or Tree in this manner, for the simulated jet of water in a fountain and the stuffed doves on the gatehouse were artless enough, to modern eyes, to destroy any simple 'belief' in the 'picture'. Moreover, the whole cumbersome effort seemed at variance with the pursuit of vitality in diction. (p. 130)

A further [director's mark] is a constant pursuit of business. . . . This aspect of Peter Hall's direction can be distracting, especially when business is allowed to obliterate the connexions, contrasts and emphases suggested by the text of a play. For example, in *The Two Gentlemen*, the song, 'Who is Silvia?' [IV. ii. 39ff.], gives a moment of rest and impersonal harmony as the course of love goes out of tune and harsh, but in Hall's production it did not sound with unprecedented ease, for immediately before the outlaws had been presented as a boyish troop, harmonizing a song from *As You Like It*.

But any director's achievements must be judged by his handling of complete plays. *The Two Gentlemen* was the least well received, failing to sustain interest. Pictorial lavishness was much to blame, for invented business as the stage revolved—a beggar, a gatehouse-keeper, a singer, dances, hide-and-seek, and the duke taking his shoes off before a fire—slowed down the narrative by awaking an idle curiosity. The transitions of the play are clear and quick—ironically so at times, as when Julia's leave-taking, silent because of her 'true love', is followed immediately by Launce's complaint that his

dog at parting 'sheds not a tear nor speaks a word' [II. iii. 31]. This production consistently dissipated such effects. Moreover, the director's insistence on vitality in speaking made the 'straight' scenes far too slow. Their language is clear and bright, with rapid turns of thought, needing a light and graceful delivery; but here it sounded laboured, as when Proteus, with clenched fist, emphasized, 'I cannot leave to love, and YET I DO' [II. vi. 17]. Juxtaposed with Speed's garrulity, Valentine's 'I would it were no worse' and 'I have dined' [II. i. 163 and 171] do not need to be made large, with embarrassed movement and kissing of his letter; such underlining loses the speedy economy of the musical and sentimental contrast. Silvia's

> Well, I guess the sequel;
> And yet I will not name it; and yet I care not;
> And yet take this again; and yet I thank you,
> Meaning henceforth to trouble you no more.
>
> [II. i. 116-19]

needs a nimble grace, not ejaculatory point; there is too much of this kind of writing for that treatment. Besides slowing down the play, the search for vitality and business cheapened it: between the speeches in the letter-scene Julia chased Lucetta until she cried 'Owh!', and as she entrusted her reputation to her maid's keeping she tickled her nose and laughed; there was a special pause after Proteus had promised to serve Silvia so that the lady could giggle with pleasure. Peter Hall is to be praised for seeing point and humour in much of the dialogue, but not for stressing it so broadly. Occasionally soft lyrical utterance was encouraged, but this, which can modulate from a delivery as stylish and mannered as the writing, here sounded odd and studied. Pictorially and vocally the production was too heavy and unsophisticated: the lovers seemed like pampered children, overgrown and playing in rich and glowing clothes. Vitality and sumptuous stage-pictures did not serve the grace, clarity, wit, sentiment, excitement and fluency of the early romantic Shakespeare—the poet whom his contemporaries called 'gentle' and 'honey-tongued'. Only Launce and Speed could grow to proper stature, and their humanity seemed unrelated to anything else in the play.

In missing its style and tempo, the director also missed the romantic climax of the play. The last scene was dominated by laughter—at Silvia's 'Oooh!' as Proteus unblindfolded her (an interpolated incident), at the trotting Julia's comic faint, at Proteus' high-pitched 'were man But constant, he were perfect' [V. iv. 110-11], at the outlaws' routine pranks, and at the fuddled duke and his roguish laugh as he saw through Julia's disguise. The threatened rape of Silvia was a broad joke: Valentine's embarrassing, impossible, generous, 'All that was mine in Silvia I give thee' [V. iv. 83], was spoken so that it was hardly noticed; Proteus' repentance was a sentiment to laugh at. Much work went into sustaining a romping conclusion, but the conflict of love and friendship, and the manifestation of generosity, faithfulness and truth went unheeded. In this slow-moving production no other course was possible; the director had been too busy with other matters to attend to the development of these issues, and the style of delivery was incapable of presenting them in the dialogue Shakespeare has provided, for pauses and emphasis had already been used too lavishly; the economy and the mainspring of the comedy had been forfeit. (pp. 131-32)

John Russell Brown, "Three Directors: A Review of Recent Productions," in Shakespeare Survey: An

Annual Survey of Shakespearian Study and Production, *Vol. 14, 1961, pp. 219-37.*

PRODUCTION:

Robin Phillips • Royal Shakespeare Theatre • 1970

BACKGROUND:

The success of this production of *The Two Gentlemen of Verona,* which opened on 23 July 1970, was attributed to Phillips's creative genius. Phillips orchestrated a modern dress revival which explored the themes of love and friendship from a satirical perspective. Electing to present the play in a highly fantastical fashion, Phillips set much of it on Italian beaches, dressing the actors in bathing suits and sun glasses, and backing the set with screens producing silhouettes that conformed to the action onstage. Phillips also added a dimension to the contest between Proteus and Valentine not implicit in Shakespeare's text. Proteus was portrayed as athletically inferior to both Valentine and Thurio, thus leading him to betray them and pursue Silvia in order to prove his masculinity. With all of these creative innovations, Phillips's *Two Gentlemen of Verona* enjoyed a popular run at Stratford throughout the summer and was revived at the Aldwych in London on 22 December 1970. The production featured Ian Richardson as Proteus, Peter Egan as Valentine, Patrick Stewart as Launce, Estelle Kohler as Silvia, and Helen Mirren as Julia.

COMMENTARY:

B. A. Young   (review date 24 July 1970)

[*Young maintains that Phillips masterfully dealt with the unrealistic elements of* The Two Gentlemen of Verona *by fantasticating the characters, costumes, and scenery.*]

La dolce vita is the keynote of Robin Phillips's production of [*The Two Gentlemen of Verona*]. It's pointed out often enough how badly Proteus behaves, switching girls in midstream, running after Silvia, his best friend Valentine's mistress, stopping Valentine in his attempted flight with her. But really Valentine isn't much better. We can't doubt that he sympathizes with Proteus's antics except when they trespass on his own territory. In the last act, he comes on Proteus in the very act of ravishing Silvia in the forest. "If hearty sorrow," says the embarrassed Proteus, "be as sufficient ransom for offence, I tender it here" [V. iv. 74-6]. And immediately Valentine tells him, "Once again I do receive thee honest" [V. iv. 78].

Honest! None of them are honest in the whole bunch, from the Duke of Milan down to Launce's dog Crab (which incidentally receives a star performance from a gentle mongrel called Blackie). They are a collection of worthless aristocratic layabouts without even the depth of passion that renders Romeo's behavior tolerable. Robin Phillips has made them a pack of wealthy mods in off-King's Road gear. The gunglasses ("sun-expelling masks," Julia calls them [IV. iv. 153])

that they wear most of the time gives them a sinister aspect in keeping with their behavior.

It's hopeless to look for a hero among them. As Proteus and Valentine between them have to occupy the slot, the problem is solved by keeping them—and indeed everybody—a step or two outside reality. They are no more to be believed in as actual people than the characters of the *Commedia dell'arte.*

This works very well, especially since the characters have been fantasticated with judicious restraint. (I could do with fewer of those unspellable howls of rage, delight, and what not that so many of them give way to.) Sebastian Shaw's wonderfully funny Scoutmaster Sir Eglamour is as solemn in realisation as it is comic in conception. Clement McCallin has made the Duke laughable by giving a straight performance, and a very good one, of a figure who simply doesn't belong in those surroundings. Moreover, the surroundings themselves are comic for the same reason; courts being out of fashion in the 20th century, Mr. Phillips has sent his young people to a Milanese university where their behavior fits in very suitably.

Ian Richardson's performance as Proteus brings back happy memories of his Antipholus in Clifford Williams's *Comedy of Errors.* Once more he shows us how much he can suggest by the subtle inflection of a line, how much mockery or menace or amusement he can load into a pause of a second or two. Peter Egan as Valentine has to stand for the principles of rectitude and so has less chance to flaunt his double meanings, but he keeps up stoutly with his friend.

Estelle Kohler plays Silvia, lithe and graceful; and Julia is Helen Mirren, a blonde-wigged tigress who, in these unisexual days, need to little more than put on a trendy cap to turn herself into a boy.

Launce is one of Shakespeare's less comic comics, but he has these sweet scenes with his dog, and Patrick Stewart makes him likeable and at the same time faintly menacing; you can imagine him employed on any dirty errand for his unattractive masters, and coming back to slobber over his Crab.

Most of the action takes place by a small swimming pool, containing real water; it is the same in Daphne Dare's set, whether it is in Verona or in Milan. Behind it a steep rake leads to three big panels of scrim which can in fact be swivelled to act as entrances but which are mainly used to take projections of characters "behind the scenes." Miss Dare has been cunning in blending the rather sterile "house style" with her own poetic imagination.

B. A. Young, in a review of "The Two Gentlemen of Verona," in The Financial Times, *July 24, 1970, p. 3.*

Gareth Lloyd Evans   (review date 24 July 1970)

[*Evans contends that Phillips's production was highly successful because it treated* The Two Gentlemen of Verona *"in a spirit of affection . . . rather than disdain."*]

Doubtless few people will worry about the set for the Royal Shakespeare Theatre's "Two Gentlemen of Verona"— Shakespeare's least known and, perhaps, least loved play. It takes place, apparently, on the patio of a half-built hotel on the Italian Riviera around an inadequate swimming pool with real water. The lovers are apparently affluent undergraduates on holiday, the Duke of Milan looks like a rich roué, Proteus's father is a ruined millionaire whose eyes and belly have fallen vilely away, and Sir Eglamour is an ageing Boy Scout on the verge one suspects of a sex change. All this, and Martin Best's splendid Mediterranean music entitles it, perhaps, for the alternative title of "Carry on Rutting."

And yet, for all the many visual and thematic inconsistencies induced by such a treatment, it seemed to me to have been done in a spirit of affection for rather than disdain of this immature play. Every inhabitant of this Shakespearean Hilton is excellently played but one noticed, in particular, Clement McCallin, Terence Taplin, Sebastian Shaw, and, especially, Phillip Manikum, getting and grabbing wonderfully his first big chance as Speed.

The play is about the power of love, and lovers responses to that power. However you present it visually and however much you broaden its comedy, if you are an honest director you will in the end, recognise the serious purpose of Shakespeare's comedy. This early play like the final one—"The Tempest"—shows how love reconciles. This production, largely because of the purposeful playing of Peter Egan, Ian Richardson, Sheila Burrell, and Estelle Kohler does, eventually recognise what the play is about. Egan's manly sincerity, Richardson's consummate embracing of the lines, Kohler's vulnerable beauty and Burrell's wry poise break through in the end.

Their work was made harder by Helen Mirren who, at the moment, shoves and pushes too much. She seems to overact at every point and must learn to allow the audience to come to her occasionally rather than rush at them. This production was, in the end, a victory of professionalism over playfulness and, though it was left desperately late, of Shakespeare over the twentieth century.

Gareth Lloyd Evans, in a review of "The Two Gentlemen of Verona," in The Guardian, *July 24, 1970, p. 8.*

Irving Wardle   (review date 24 July 1970)

[*Wardle presents a mixed review of Phillips's* Two Gentlemen of Verona, *arguing that while the production had appeal, its examination of Elizabethan themes of love and friendship was obscured by extravagant humor.*]

Stratford audiences are quieter than most as they usually get their heads down for a quick survey of what past critics have thought about the play. I wonder how far Stratford's directors also read these programme notes.

For instance, the general view you glean from the notes to this production is that *The Two Gentlemen* deals with a specifically Elizabethan contest between love and friendship, and that it appears more confused and implausible to us than it would have done to Shakespeare's public. What, then, is the point of putting the characters into Italian beachware and rounding things off with a Beatles' hit? To show that young love stays much the same from age to age, or to plaster new invention over a botched original?

Both purposes seem to underly Robin Phillips's production which, to do it justice, certainly offers no neat modern reduction of Shakespeare's comic extravaganza. It seeks rather to create an equally extravagant modern counterpart, in which boxing gloves and cocktail trolleys co-exist with symbolized

forests and court protocol: a swinging pastoral bounded by the twin poles of earth-bound affection and erotic enchantment.

The result, however, makes less sense of the comedy than did last year's modest Theatregoround revival which spanned the time gap with the aid of a set presenting an Elizabethan stage in the form of a modern building toy.

Mr. Phillips enjoys more elaborate resources. Daphne Dare's ramped set is dominated by a group of revolving screens which alternatively glow like huge golden doors and carry magnified silhouettes from behind. We also get a cantilevered balcony jutting vacantly across the stage until Silvia takes possession of it after half-time. And when Antonio mooches on like a Mafia boss dropping his cigar ash into the outstretched hand of an obsequious crony, Miss Dare even arranges for him to take a dip in the water-filled trap.

It is touches like these that make up most of the show's appeal: and they have to be paid for. Once sunk, that pool sits there for the rest of the evening unused until Sir Eglamour (Sebastian Shaw in the guise of a superannuated Rover Scout) lays a home-made bridge across it to lead Silvia into the woods.

What is missing is the kind of linch-pin which Derek Smith's Duke supplied in the Theatregoround version: an ironic master of ceremonies playing along with the absurdities for the sake of the fun. Clement McCallin, the new Duke, is also an ironist especially in the ladder scene with Valentine whom he reduced to a state of wobbling one-legged misery by plying him with coffee and a cigar. But he is a dry joker who is making fun more of a few characters than of the action.

Lacking a firm centre, the show subsides into an unfocused series of separate moments and performances, some of them very good, like Ian Richardson's coldly impassioned Proteus, and the temperamentally well contrasted clowns: some not so good, like Helen Mirren's Julia, who overplays the early scenes of maidenly caprice beyond the limits of sympathy, and subsequently settles into a butcher-boy jauntiness.

Irving Wardle, "Bard and Beatles," in The Times, *London, July 24, 1970, p. 13.*

Robert Cushman   (review date 1 August 1970)

[*Cushman maintains that with the exception of Ian Richardson as Proteus, the actors in Phillips's production of* The Two Gentlemen of Verona *are incapable of fully expressing their characters' complexities.*]

The Two Gentleman of Verona (to say nothing of the dog) was the play chosen to inaugurate Peter Hall's regime at Stratford in 1960. It was by general consent a disaster, and the Royal Shakespeare Company must have had the play on their conscience ever since. Having in the course of the 'sixties successfully annexed most of the other Shakespearian comedies they square up again to the earliest and most imperfect of them. The result is delight, but delight qualified. *The Two Gentlemen* is that interpreter's nightmare, an immature play on the subject of immaturity, abounding in charm but infected by an artlessness which a generous critic might take as a ruthlessly accurate depiction of very young love. Others will blame Shakespeare.

Robin Phillips has swallowed the mixture nearly whole,

transporting the action to present-day popland, all dark glasses, Riviera sun-tans, and beachwear. Verona is one great lido, and Mr Phillips's two gentlemen disport themselves accordingly. Valentine's world is still bounded by athletics; Proteus has progressed as far as poetry-reading, and a hopeless schoolboy crush on Julia which stops considerably short of consummation: her request for a kiss at parting is met with a reproving 'Here is my *hand* for my true constancy' [II. ii. 8].

When they get to Milan (a very cool university in a state of permanent vacation) horizons broaden. Valentine's passion for Silvia now rivals his friend's for Julia though, as the heartier of the two, he has more active plans involving midnight elopements and rope-ladders. Emulation is a powerful spur and Proteus, his affections easily and instantaneously transferred, soon outgrows Platonism; by the end of this production his designs on Silvia amount to graphically-staged attempted rape. Valentine, however, arrives in the nick ('Ruffian, let go that rude uncivil touch' [V. iv. 60]) and reduces Proteus to repentant prostration.

Both of them may be assumed to have grown up a little since we first met them, though, as is usual in the genre, their ladies have outstripped them. Julia, who, as portrayed by Helen Mirren, had thought it a great giggle to follow her lover to Milan in male attire (an impressionable girl, she had perhaps been reading too many Elizabethan comedies) is much sobered by overhearing his courtship of Silvia, and matures before our eyes; Silvia, less fortunate or less demonstrative, presumably undergoes a similar annealing process offstage. She is certainly no longer the violently flirtatious (and the hell with the Courtly Love code) young lady we first met. Each ends happy in the appropriate partner's arms; indeed, another couple of minutes and we'd be watching *Oh! Calcutta!* But all this romance is thrown into sharp relief by Proteus's servant Launce; as an unusually discerning programme note remarks: 'when it comes to true devotion, there is nothing . . . to compare with Launce's selfless love for his dog, Crab.' The abiding impression left by the final tableau is that Man Gets Dog. And if that isn't news. . . .

Now there's a neat dramatic pattern. I wish I could convince myself that it all transpired at Stratford last Thursday. The outlines are there but they are blurred, partly by the unevenness of the writing, which is liable to whisk a character back to square one of his development at the clump of an iambic foot, and partly by casting which compounds the sins of the text by adding yet a third layer of immaturity. While hardly as extravagantly youthful as the text suggests, the leading quartet are, with one exception, incapable of turning their surplus sophistication to advantage.

The exception, of course, is Ian Richardson, a past master at Shakespeare's virginal young men who discovers in Proteus whorls of irony (see him convulsed at the idea of Valentine's 'corded ladder') and of poetry (he does the lyrical bits in a spotlight which would be infuriating in a richer play but serves well for this one) and having found them searches on. The effect is unsettling; this is the first time I have seen Mr Richardson in less than total control of his means. My final quarrel is with Patrick Stewart's louring Launce. That he should be a standing rebuke to his master is a sound idea, and excellent counterpoint; but to have him snarl through his great monologues is excessive. This is blatant playing against the lines, it is effective, and it is much too easy.

Elsewhere Mr Phillips has drawn from his cast some minor miracles of characterisation. I think of Antonio (Trader Faulkner) lowered solemnly and hilariously into a pool, whence he emerges to dismiss his son to Milan with a plutocratic disregard that tells us all we need to know of our hero's home life; of Lucetta (Sheila Burrell) mocking her mistress without once blowing her cool; and of Eglamour (Sebastian Shaw), a perpetual scoutmaster of impeccable chivalry and scrupulous punctuality. Daphne Dare's setting is bright and versatile, a high-diving board in Verona doubling with aplomb as Silvia's balcony in Milan. (p. 107)

Robert Cushman, "Gentlemen and Players," in The Spectator, *Vol. 225, No. 7414, August 1, 1970, pp. 107-08.*

Jeremy Kingston   (review date 5 August 1970)

[*In this brief excerpt, Kingston praises Phillips's production of* The Two Gentlemen of Verona, *deeming it "the best Stratford production this year."*]

[At] the *Royal Shakespeare Theatre*, Stratford-upon-Avon, inventive Robin Phillips worked a minor miracle upon *The Two Gentlemen of Verona*, one of the bard's trickier comedies. He sets it in the sunbaked beach and campus world of today where the boys wear tight slacks and red leather bathing trunks and the Duke is a greyhound hippy Vice-Chancellor—a very funny performance by Clement McCallin, particularly in the scene with Valentine about to elope with his daughter. The young man desperately tries to conceal the corded ladder under his gown while the Duke plies him with drink, cigar, matches and other inconvenient courtesies.

The girls can't manage the updated style required but Ian Richardson, as you might expect, uses his intense steady stare to impart suggestions of sexual distress to the aptly named character of Proteus and makes it a fascinating portrait. At every mention of the "corded ladder" he gives a delighted gurgle of incredulity that in itself is worth half the price of the ticket. Sebastian Shaw does the inadequately gallant Sir Eglamour as a mournful old Boy Scout and Patrick Stewart's dark Launce stands on the sidelines as a reminder of the real world of menace and money-grubbing. The best Stratford production this year. (pp. 212-13)

Jeremy Kingston, in a review of "The Two Gentlemen of Verona," in Punch, *Vol. 259, No. 6779, August 5, 1970, pp. 212-13.*

J. C. Trewin   (review date 8 August 1970)

[*In the following excerpt, Trewin sparingly commends Phillips's innovative revival of* The Two Gentlemen of Verona.]

There are swimming pools in Verona and Milan; cigars and coffee at the Duke's; outlawed hippies in the forest. Fashions vary between bikini and maxi; the Duke wears gown and mortarboard. Silvia is serenaded by a pop group. Sir Eglamour seems to be a Rover Scout.

The play, you may have guessed, is *The Two Gentlemen of Verona.* Visually, as directed by Robin Phillips at Stratford-upon-Avon, it is unlike any revival one has known. The voice, fortunately, is Shakespeare's. While Ian Richardson's Proteus is uttering the lines with melodious deliberation, we recognize the lyric comedy of youth at the spring, the invention in which Shakespeare says much that he will develop later. It is a gentle piece; for all its immaturity, it will hold any theatre if spoken well enough. It need not be fussed with a director's tricks.

Mr Phillips has few of these. Having chosen an unattractive form of modern dress, he could have made hay of the night. Still, he does remember his dramatist. While nobody would be hyperbolical about the production, it is far better than one might have feared, occasional silliness apart. It moves like Julia's "current that with gentle murmur glides" [II. vii. 25]; now and then the quiet voice finds such a splendour as "huge leviathans forsake unsounded deeps to dance on sands" [III. ii. 79-80]. Call it, in general, a night of calm make believe, rightly expressed by such players as Mr Richardson, Helen Mirren, and Peter Egan.

> J. C. Trewin, "A Night of Make Believe," in The Illustrated London News, Vol. 257, No. 6836, August 8, 1970, p. 28.

Peter Roberts   (review date September 1970)

[Roberts praises Phillips's production of The Two Gentlemen of Verona for its creative examination of the subtleties and ambiguities in the play's text.]

Since his first solo production for the RSC (Tiny Alice, Aldwych, January) Robin Phillips has unloaded upon us, most notably, the embarrassment of Abelard and Heloise at Wyndham's with designs by Daphne Dare. It was an agreeable surprise, therefore, to find the July opening at Stratford of The Two Gentlemen of Verona with Phillips and Dare again in tandem more a trailer for the RSC's August openings than a postscript to the breathless sexploitation of a nude Diana Rigg and Keith Michell in Ronald Millar's West End weepie.

Shakespeare, of course, must take the credit. With Helen Mirren as the Julia in Two Gentlemen disguising herself as a boy named Sebastian, who could forget that in August Judi Dench as Viola would be doing virtually the same thing in John Barton's revival of Twelfth Night at the Aldwych? And, with Peter Brook sitting immediately in front of me, I watched the lovers in Robin Phillips' production unhappily cavorting in a corded forest near Milan mindful of the fact that Brook at Stratford would be putting a cast through a similar situation for his production of A Midsummer Night's Dream on the same stage a few days later.

Of the two later comedies, I see The Two Gentlemen more as a tentative dip in the androgynous waters of the mature Twelfth Night than as a preface to the chain reactions induced by the magic potions of The Dream. Or at least that is the way I think this revival would have us view some of it. A young Shakespeare is of course dealing with adolescent love that comes and goes with the uncertain glory of an April day and, were it not for the difficulty of convincingly motivating Proteus' double-crossing of (and all too swift reconciliation with) his friend, Valentine, one would say it is a play that allows a young director to have a lot of easy fun. 'Easy' partly because the parallelisms of the two pairs of lovers (with their idealised love) and the low-life juxtaposition of their contrasted servants, Speed and Launce (with their more practical assessment of a future spouse) makes for schematic playmaking; and 'easy' because the academics write off the proceed-

ings as apprentice Bard with which you may do what you will.

And, on one level, there is a lot of jokey manipulation of the text that ensures this revival radiates happily round the auditorium. Julia's maid, Lucetta, is both upgraded and updated (with appropriate textual emendations) to be a hard-bitten Lido socialite—a sort of Mediterranean divorcée who, as Sheila Burrell plays her in gin-sodden mockery of Julia's emotional and sexual naïvety, you feel would yawn her way through Oh! Calcutta!, not to mention The Dirtiest Show in Town. And, at the other end of the play, Sir Eglamour comes wrapped from Sebastian Shaw in the trappings of an elderly Boy Scout whose elaborate bespectacled precautions to enable Silvia to traverse a ditch are rendered hilarious because the girl simply hops across it. Trader Faulkner as Antonio, Proteus's father, decides to send his son after Valentine to Milan cigar-smoking and shoulder-deep in a swimming pool that gives this revival's glimpse of Verona a decadent slant of a decidedly nouveau riche sort. And, whilst we're still in the fun and games department the dog, Crab, is performed by Blackie, a cur of the kind that would win a sneer at Crufts and a very big bone everywhere else.

But the short evening is not just a larkey sugar coating. Verbal leitmotifs in the text, such as the one about love being blind, are duly underlined by devices like having the love-lorn wear sunglasses. But the blindness in the verse prods a little deeper than that and so, I think, does this revival. And Ian Richardson's bronzed Proteus provides the principal instrument for dredging in that murky area where Shakespeare gives voice to confusions that surface in the Sonnets with allusion to 'the master / mistress' of my passion.

What is the evidence that the revival is working on these lines? Well, the ambiguity in the text is reflected in the production but I believe that it is there all the same. Robin Phillips bookends his production with what The Two Gentlemen of Verona is most famous for, the serenade, Who is Silvia? what is she? [IV. ii. 39ff.] The play opens with the singing of these lines and there is a reprise at the close. But it is not only a question of Who is Silvia? what is she? but also of Who is Valentine, What is he?

At the beginning of the play when the friends, Valentine and Proteus, have embraced to mark what proves to be only a brief separation, the latter comes downstage, flexes his arm muscles and limply dismisses his lack of an imposing physique. As Ian Richardson plays him, it is clear that his shortness compared both to Valentine and Thurio, whose lithe beachboy figure he enviously paws, is a source of lack of confidence. His double-dealing of both men is therefore motivated here not so much by the requirements of a plot borrowed from literary sources but by the spiteful jealousy of a confused adolescent. Thus when this friend and lover with all his hangups is paid the ultimate compliment of being offered his best friend's mistress at the close of play, this previously unplayable scene can be said to offer some meaning in the light of current récherché theories of displaced homosexuality. In this area Terence Taplin is suitably vacuous as Thurio and Peter Egan a tall but, on first night evidence, somewhat less than word-perfect Valentine.

Happily, the ladies and the clowns are less complicated beings. Whether anxiously trying to piece together the love-letter Proteus has sent to her or anguishedly witnessing his pursuit of Silvia later on, Helen Mirren is a fresh, sincere, golden-haired Julia. And Estelle Kohler, coolly peeling off a page of *Tatler* in response to Proteus' urgent request for a pin-up of her, makes a dignified Silvia. The Verona she inhabits proves to be a sophisticated campus where her father, the Duke, (Clement McCallin) appears as a lanky university don who carries his gown and his scholarship as lightly as he does his cocktails and his coffee. McCallin's urbane reading contrasts, as it no doubt was meant to, with Patrick Stewart's dour, black-suited account of life at the other end of the social spectrum inhabited by the dog-owning Launce.

Martin Best's musical scoring is ingeniously irreverent, even managing unobtrusively to provide 'Now is the time for us to say goodbye' as a cheeky backing to Julia and Proteus's initial leavetaking. And John Bradley, whether illuminating the three peer-through screens that are the principal feature of Daphne Dare's set or whether emphasising the text's concern with shadows and realities, does a superb job. An evening, then, when Bardolators should beware of responding overmuch to surface ingenuities lest they miss undercurrents that no revival I have seen has hitherto explored. (pp. 28-9)

> *Peter Roberts, in a review of "The Two Gentlemen of Verona," in* Plays and Players, *Vol. 17, No. 12, September, 1970, pp. 28-31.*

Robert Speaight   (review date Autumn 1970)

[*Speaight maintains that by breaking the conventions which had previously governed* The Two Gentlemen of Verona, *Phillips successfully balanced the play's light-hearted and more earnest aspects.*]

The last production of *The Two Gentlemen of Verona* at Stratford, ten years ago, sounded a very squeaky overture to the reign of the Royal Shakespeare Company; and there was every excuse for seeing whether sheer, irreverent inventiveness could not do for *The Two Gentlemen* what Clifford Williams had done so successfully for *The Comedy of Errors*. There was also the risk that in bringing the play theatrically to life its deeper qualities might be obscured. If one has to apologize for a play, it is much better not to produce it at all—and *The Two Gentlemen of Verona* needs no apology. Mr. Phillips deserved our applause for rescuing it from neglect and for proving its power to entertain—although I can imagine a production equally satisfying, if hardly as amusing as this one, where the emphasis would be romantic, in the neo-Platonic vein, rather than satirical. For what interests us here is the adumbration of future themes, and Shakespeare's skilful interweaving of them—with Julia looking forward to Rosalind [in *As You Like It*], and forgiving the most unforgivable of Shakespearian juveniles, as, in a very different context, Helena forgives Bertram [in *All's Well That Ends Well*] and Isabella Angelo [in *Measure for Measure*]. Mr. Phillips' production, with its flower children, its Turkish baths, and its highly contemporary costumes, was not so fantastic that Julia's heartbreak became inaudible; and indeed, if it had been less fantasticated, her magnanimity might have seemed incredible. It is a question of balance, and at the critical moment the balance held. *The Two Gentlemen of Verona* may be never so light a comedy—but like all the best comedies it is about serious matters, reminding us that in nothing are people more serious or more silly than in love.

Mr. Phillips not only broke with whatever conventions had hitherto governed the production of the play, but he challenged the current use of the Stratford stage. On entering the auditorium, I rubbed my eyes—could that really be an unmistakable flight of steps, and beside them a positive, even a precipitous, slope? Was it possible that the action of the play would be allowed to proceed on more than one level? By the operation of what magic had Mr. Phillips secured this concession to pictorial effect? The casting was particularly happy, Mr. Richardson's playboy Proteus warning us not to take him too seriously either in his fidelity or his falsehood, and Miss Mirren maturing from flapperdom to full feminity as she discovers how "men are deceivers ever" [*Much Ado about Nothing*, II. iii. 63]—a gay, resourceful, and immensely enjoyable performance. Here is a Viola [in *Twelfth Night*] or an Imogen [in *Cymbeline*] to look forward to. Mr. Patrick Stewart as Launce not only played the part with split-second timing and superb comic address—but he presided over the play with the air of a natural philosopher. One expected him any moment to exclaim, "Oh what fools these mortals be!" [*A Midsummer Night's Dream*, III. ii. 115], and if any actor needed a lesson in the art of picking up one's cue, or in the far subtler art of stealing the stage by doing absolutely nothing, he had only to watch the performance of Crab—Launce's inseparable, canine, companion. Mr. McCallin's Duke combined authority with absent-mindedness, and his exchange of courtesies, Castellas, and finally recriminations with Mr. Egan's Valentine was a dazzling example of high speed, comedy technique. Miss Daphne Dare's décor and Mr. Best's music were both attuned to Mr. Phillips' high-spirited, yet astringent, conception of the play. Stratford is all the better, and certainly the gayer, for what Bridges-Adams used to describe as a *machine de guerre* [engine of war]. Komisarjevsky supplied this in the 'thirties, and Mr. Phillips' secret weapon detonated with equal effect. You could hear it both in the production and the applause. (pp. 446-47)

> *Robert Speaight, "Shakespeare in Britain," in* Shakespeare Quarterly, *Vol. XXI, No. 4, Autumn, 1970, pp. 439-49.*

Peter Thomson   (review date 1971)

[*Thomson explores the "unresolved combination of quick-witted inventiveness and ponderous point-making" of Phillips's* Two Gentlemen of Verona. *Particularly provocative, according to Thomson, was the imaginative depiction of Proteus as physically inferior to his rivals, Valentine and Thurio.*]

Daphne Dare's set for *The Two Gentlemen of Verona* had a ramp and steps from mid-stage leading up to three large screens, with a heavy diving-board scaffold mid-stage left and a small pool downstage right. The forest was created by the dropping of a single batten of ropes from the flies and a dappling of the light. The costumes were basically, but not consistently, modern. It was a curiosity that the sun-drenched impression created by the clothes and emphasised by the use of sun-glasses was contradicted by a chilly lighting-plot. This was a production that opened amid ominous rumours of company quarrels, last-minute changes and threats of withdrawal. In the event it was kindly received. I found it an unresolved combination of quick-witted inventiveness and ponderous point-making. It opened with a tableau of the lovers in silhouette and a recorded echo-song, 'Who is Silvia? Who is Valentine? Who is Proteus? Who is Julia?', but addressed itself, in the main, to a clarification, along plausible psychological lines, of Proteus's misconduct. The initial exchange had an athletic Valentine, stripped for the lido, doing exercises with a beach-ball to the admiring envy of a comparatively puny Proteus, the sort of man who would never dare take off his shirt in the face of such competition. With Valentine's exit, Proteus deprecatingly felt his own muscles. The vanity and disloyalty of Proteus has, then, its origin in his sense of his own inadequacy. It is exaggerated self-awareness that impedes his farewell to Julia and, presumably, limits his capacity to love. This Proteus is a man who reads books, but only because he isn't good at games. Ian Richardson finds a precise comic image of Proteus's search for physical grace when he throws his strapped bundle of 'books for the voyage' over his shoulder in a gesture of careless abandon that Valentine might have admired, but fails quite to restrain a wince when the strap brings them round in an arc to clobber him on the left buttock. In Verona Proteus is constantly tense. In Milan he relaxes, finding Valentine reduced to love. The betrayal is confident, and Ian Richardson's 'comforting' of the banished Valentine is almost complacent. But here a director's point turns the tables. Valentine interrupts Proteus's account of Silvia's imprisonment by slapping him hard on the cheek. The blow is not well motivated, but its consequence is interesting. For the rest of the play, Proteus feels the horror of his deception in his stinging cheek. At [III. ii. 89], when Thurio pinches his face in a patronising gesture of thanks, he pulls away in pain. On other occasions he soothes his cheek nervously. Only when Valentine forgivingly kisses him exactly where he had struck him is this Proteus free of his confining self. In new delight the lovers pair off and tousle on the forest floor. Valentine's 'Forbear, forbear, I say; it is my lord the duke' [V. iv. 122] is addressed, not to the outlaws, but to Julia and Proteus—'do her up quick. It's Silvia's father!'—but the gaiety of this trick is not sustained. The play ends with a tableau, set against a reprise of the opening echo-song and following Valentine's portentous delivery of the final speech. He phrases the last line in such a way as to cast doubt on the prospect it promises:

> One feast, one house, one mutual (*pause*) happiness
> (*with an interrogatory vocal rise*).
>
>   [V. iv. 173]

Robin Phillips, the director, brought to the play a sense of humour and a dangerous desire to analyse its presentation of adolescent sexual confusion. Hence the combination of inventiveness and point-making. The invention was generally superior to the analysis. Thurio was aptly portrayed as an amorous narcissist with sun-glasses and an Italian accent, Eglamour as a sad old scoutmaster, who brought an ordnance survey map to aid in Silvia's escape; and the difficult I, iii was turned into a theatrical triumph by having Antonio, a bloated, cigar-smoking capitalist, plunge into his private pool, leaving Panthino to hold his smoking cigar and monogrammed beach-wrap. Phillips saw the play in a context of leisured society, sun-bathing and beautiful bodies. Verona was a high-class resort, Milan an open-air university, with the Duke as its avuncular Vice-Chancellor. The tone-painting was ingenious and acceptable, the analysis tendentious and speciously plausible. Julia sucked chewing-gum in I, ii, her thumb in II, vii, and rolled on to her back to say,

> Now kiss, embrace, contend, do what you will.
>
>   [I. ii. 126]

Silvia revealed a modern willingness to take the initiative in embracing her men, but escaped from Proteus's attempted rape to the comforting arms of Sebastian/Julia rather than to Valentine's. (Why?) It was in the interpretation of Launce that the dangers of a production insecurely anchored to the

text were most apparent. Phillips seems to have felt the need for a sentimental counter-balance to the blissful ignorants. His Launce knew, and could endure, everything. Patrick Stewart played him (well) in ragged black, a dour northerner against Speed's jaunty cockney. From the opening tableau, when he threaded his way among the still lovers in a springless stroll, to the curtain-call, when he stood downstage of the main group, separated by his knowingness, Launce was the unmoved observer, tearless throughout and tolerant, a man who never expected much. (pp. 120-21)

> *Peter Thomson, "A Necessary Theatre: The Royal Shakespeare Season 1970 Reviewed," in Shakespeare Survey: An Annual Survey of Shakespearian Study and Production, Vol. 24, 1971, pp. 117-26.*

PRODUCTION:

Robin Phillips and David Toguri • Stratford Festival, Ontario • 1975

BACKGROUND:

For the Canadian revival of his popular 1970 *Two Gentlemen of Verona*, Phillips repeated the many absurd elements which had made the production such a success at Stratford-upon-Avon. With the help of a co-director, David Toguri, Phillips added even more outrageous comedy to this production, which opened at Stratford, Ontario on 11 June 1975. These changes came mainly in the form of character development. Most striking, perhaps, was the satirical portrayal of Silvia not as the innocent victim of Proteus's schemes, but as a rich and wilful heiress who manipulated her suitors' affections for her own amusement. Another was the depiction of Antonio and the Duke of Milan as proud, cigar-smoking Mafia godfathers. With these additions, Phillips's Canadian *Two Gentlemen of Verona* was as successful as its predecessor had been in England. The principal actors included Nicholas Pennell as Proteus, Stephen Russell as Valentine, Eric Donkin as Launce, Jackie Burroughs as Silvia, and Mia Anderson as Julia.

COMMENTARY:

Berners W. Jackson   (review date Winter 1976)

> [*Jackson favorably reviews Phillips's* Two Gentlemen of Verona, *claiming that the actors were "full of the juice of life." He also notes that the modern dress and scenery successfully liberated the play from the restrictions of an Elizabethan setting so that the "authentic voice was there, but it seemed to be speaking in our time."*]

Four of Shakespeare's plays were produced at Stratford, Ontario this past summer, but only two of them, *Measure for Measure* and *Twelfth Night,* at the original theatre. As one of his innovations, Robin Phillips, the new Artistic Director, presented the other two, *The Comedy of Errors* and *The Two Gentlemen of Verona,* at the Festival's second theatre, the Avon, in the center of town. (p. 24)

A second company has been created for the Avon, lively, acrobatic, and exuberantly aware of *esprit de corps*. In fact it is called the "Young Company" and most of its members are enjoying their salad days, but here and there is a veteran, either of Stratford or of other stages, and the word goes round that "young" refers not to years but to attitude. Fittingly enough, in their first season, this new group was called upon to present two of Shakespeare's earliest plays, both of them directed by Mr. Phillips, who is himself not halfway through his thirties.

The production of the *Two Gentlemen* was full of the juice of youth. Mr. Phillips and his co-director, David Toguri, stuck faithfully to Shakespeare's text and found a tale for our time in his account of the preoccupation of the young with love and friendship. The setting was the Italian Riviera, or some place like it, where the wealthy take their pleasure amidst suntans and sunglasses, and their sons and daughters cavort in the miscellaneous finery of today's youth. A point needs to be made: this was not "modernized Shakespeare" in the usual sense of that phrase. The play was not made over to accommodate the fashions and furnishings of today; instead these things were put to the service of the play. This faithful adherence to the text in a modern setting had the effect of liberating Shakespeare from the bondage to time imposed by period costume and an attempt at period airs and manners, without subjecting his work to the kind of adjustments and ingenious inventions that are too often perpetrated in a misdirected search for relevance. We talk of the timelessness of Shakespeare. I have never been more aware of it than I was while watching this production of a comparatively slight play from his early years. The authentic voice was there, but it seemed to be speaking in our time, rather than to our time from across four centuries. The high school audiences at the spring previews recognized Valentine and his friends as their contemporaries, and kept giving the production standing ovations.

Stephen Russell, a large, dark young actor with the sort of physique that is designed for violent physical action and the sort of face that seems to welcome it, presented a dangerously volatile, restlessly physical Valentine who worked out with boxing gloves, threw a beach ball about, and displayed all the attributes of his type: frankness, generosity, impulsiveness, and a shortage of acumen. Nicholas Pennell played the softer Proteus as a young man not devious by nature but grasping at duplicity as the only weapon that might serve him against such as Valentine in his pursuit of Silvia. He came to contrition at the end in the same way that Valentine abandoned his anger, almost with relief. Both the relationship and the contrast that had been established between the young men throughout the play were very evident here. Their recognition of a peril passed, and the gratitude of each to the other that friendship had survived made the scene of their reconciliation more believable than its events suggest it is likely to be.

The production was enlivened by a Silvia who was not the somewhat passive maiden of the play's tradition. Jackie Burroughs made her a capricious daughter of wealth and power who could oblige Proteus with a picture of herself by simply tearing it out of a glossy magazine, and who had been brought up in the belief that whatever she did would be commended. Beneath the softness of her filmy gown you suspected the wiry body that brought her on stage in a swirling, precarious cartwheel; behind the fluttery affectations of her manner you were aware of the quick, intuitive mind of the accomplished flirt. This was a Silvia designed to unsettle the rugged Valen-

tine, fascinate the impressionable Proteus into forgetting his Julia, focus the attentions of the opportunist Thurio, and shamelessly victimize that aged cavalier, Sir Eglamour. A surprising interpretation, perhaps, but it worked so effectively in this production that you found yourself thinking of Silvia as the sort of girl who appropriated for herself the captain of the high school football team, or who called the Duke, her father, "daddy" when she wanted a new sports car. Miss Burroughs brought it off very cleverly. The tone of her voice—high, self-approving, with a hint of petulance in it—made the lines work for her without altering them or appearing to fight their meaning. In her final interchange with Proteus, for instance, she managed to be provocative and challenging, and then visibly excited by his advances, rather than resolute and admonitory and, finally, frightened. You felt she was enjoying herself, and that the touch of chagrin in her silence following Valentine's intervention was as much the result of being prevented from dealing with Proteus in her own way as of finding herself, for once, not the center of attention.

In contrast to this madcap Silvia there was a warm, single-minded, humorous Julia from Mia Anderson. In boy's clothes, Miss Anderson had a vulnerable, waif-like quality that made all the more appealing her determination to save Proteus from that immemorial condition in which a young man thinks he wants what he can't have and doesn't know that he wants what he can have.

Those in the supporting roles served the production strikingly. Douglas Chamberlain was a smoothly feral Duke of Milan, an updated Renaissance tyrant in velvet suitings and dark glasses, expensive, self-assured, and ruthless, designed to give Valentine and Silvia a hard time of it before he decided they should marry. Richard Curnock as Sir Eglamour in white suit and sun helmet looked like Colonel Sanders on safari as he emerged out of the dawn, equipped to meet every eventuality from butterflies to bandits while escorting Silvia on her flight to Valentine. Julia was served by Gale Garnett as Lucetta, a leggy sophisticate who tolerated the ardors and misgivings of her mistress with a mildly sardonic humor. J. Kenneth Campbell's Thurio was a handsome beach-boy, dedicated to the body beautiful, and vapidly affable in submitting to circumstance. Bernard Hopkins played Speed as a friendly lump of a boy, and made the part of that cheeky lad funnier and more agreeable than one would have thought possible. As Launce, Eric Donkin provided an ironic comment on the attachments of the young by making the lugubrious amusing, but he just managed to hold his own against Crab, a mongrel whose scratchings were impeccably timed, and who looked on the antics of the young with the same sad, speculative eyes that we see in portraits of Elizabethan notables. (pp. 25-7)

Berners W. Jackson, "Shakespeare at Stratford, Ontario, 1975," in Shakespeare Quarterly, *Vol. 27, No. 1, Winter, 1976, pp. 24-32.*

John Pettigrew   (review date February 1976)

[*Pettigrew praises Phillips's absurd comedic enhancements of* The Two Gentlemen of Verona, *maintaining that the emphasis on entertainment allowed the audience to overlook the play's many imperfections.*]

Stratford's twenty-third season was fine in itself and a happy harbinger for the future. That such was to be so was pretty clear within a few minutes of the opening performance of the 1975 season: the preview at the Avon Theatre of the touring production of *The Two Gentlemen of Verona* early in February. (p. 51)

I'd not seen *The Two Gentlemen of Verona* before and so was glad of a chance to see the play even though it is one of those plays that seem insistently to kill themselves by reminding one of better things to come, though it is not nearly as funny as the unintentional asininity of some solemn critical pronouncements about it (witness the souvenir programme), and though it is probably the most readily expendable of all Shakespeare's plays. . . . Mr. Phillips had directed the play before, at the other Stratford, in a production that, if Rumour speak true, made the collective hair of the Royal Shakespeare Company make like quills upon the fretful porpentine (as Jeeves would say), but that was not only a major critical success, but one that kept audiences very happy. Mr. Phillips' choice was nevertheless a daring one with which to open a new directorial career, and I find it depressing that the winter tour failed to play to packed houses and cost the Company a fair amount of money, and that audiences at the Avon were also smaller than the merits of the production deserved.

Mr. Phillips followed the general lines of his earlier production, and used a twentieth-century setting vaguely suggestive of a mixture of the Italian Riviera of the '20s and '70s with a Vic Tanny health resort equipped with cocktail bars and peopled, most unusually, with extremely athletic people; thrown in for good measure were a few *Godfather* things, society magazines, beach-boys and beach-balls, transistor radios, swimming pools, cocktail shakers, and other incongruous horrors. The Dook of Milan and Proteus' father were clearly Sicilian cigar-smoking Mafia chiefs, Silvia was a flapper who made her initial entrance cartwheeling across the stage while Speed sauntered in with a bicycle, Proteus and Valentine kissed and held hands, tremulous sentimental music ("Now we must part") accompanied Shakespeare's tearful farewells, and the men wore costumes that struck me as appalling but were, friends assured me, just the latest in men's styles—I fear me that my subsequent examination of current men's fashions assures me they were right, that my Karen Bulow ties of the 1950s are not in, and that civilization is clearly hurtling to a Full Stop. The action was frequently accompanied by grotesque cacophonies of a kind that are, I believe, called rock music. This world was curiously apparently next door to a strange jungle inhabited by a notably inept and agreeable bunch of outlaws who were given to silhouetting themselves behind the translucent panels and engaging in weird modern dances and poses while Martin Best's excellent jungly thumpy music suggested the strange worlds into which poor timorous Silvia was venturing. All this may well suggest that direction made a weak play palatable by gimmickry, but such was not so, for the nonsense was not only fun in itself but carefully used to support a production that was in essentials pure and clean—Mr. Phillips and his co-director, David Toguri, did not guy the play, but served it. I don't think—thank goodness—they made the play Relevant, but it was, most of the time, entertaining, and that is quite an achievement.

There were all sorts of good things. I liked, for example, Valentine's balancing act with a rope ladder under an academic gown while standing on one foot, holding a drink in one hand and a cigar in the other, and the perfect timing of his amazed look at the heavens when the ladder finally crashed to the ground. I liked Don Hunkin's fine rendition of "Who is Sylvia" [IV. ii. 39ff.] while J. Kenneth Campbell's Thurio

mouthed the words. And I broke up completely with the entrance of Richard Curnock's Colonel Sanders, alias Sir Eglamour, announcing that the sun began to gild the western sky as he staggered under the weight of those few things any young girl needs when venturing into outlaw-infested jungle: a large parrot cage, a few mink stoles and the odd butterfly net, several suitcases, camping stools, and other assorted safari gear. As Colonel Sanders patted Silvia's behind consolingly, it became clear that this apparent epitome of benevolence was in reality an unusually dirty old man, and I shall never really feel quite the same again about Kentucky or chicken. One is happy to report, however, that when he laid Silvia in the dust, it was only with a sudden fearful movement that swung his baggage-pole around and flattened Silvia completely in one of the most effective pratfalls I ever hope to see.

The Two Gents is not the kind of play that is going to let a new Olivier show his stuff, but that this production worked as well as it did is a tribute to the quality of the direction and acting. Young Stephen Russell did well with Valentine in his first major role, even at times getting some real feeling out of unpromising material, while Nicholas Pennell, reliable as ever, succeeded in the difficult task of remaining reasonably sympathetic while carrying on in a dastardly caddish way. Bernard Hopkins also managed a difficult feat: that of generally making us forget that Speed is the most dismal failure of a comic that Shakespeare ever drew; he even, at times— *mirabile dictu!*—made him faintly amusing. Mia Anderson languished lachrymosely and guttily as Julia, and made love to Proteus' torn-up letter with just the right mixture of the touching and the absurd. J. Kenneth Campbell was a memorable Thurio with a thick Italian accent, an even thicker head, and a set of muscles which suggested that though he'd never been a ninety-seven pound weakling he had taken every Charles Atlas course ever offered and a few extra on the side, and which gave special point to his final speech, which holds "him but a fool that will endanger / His body for a girl that loves him not" [V. iv. 133-34]. Similarly bird-brained was Jackie Burroughs' pliable frail flibbertigibbet of a femme fatale of a Silvia; her monumental lack of intelligence and perception got the production over that much-discussed hurdle near the end of the play when Valentine hands her over to Proteus, who, only twenty lines earlier, was attempting to ravish her in singularly ungentlemanly fashion—in this production, Silvia, ninny to the end, never really took in what was going on outside her tiny excuse for a mind. Eric Donkin has never given a weak performance at Stratford, and he made a good Launce. But it was, of course, Crab as himself that stole the show. Mr. Phillips seems to have an eye for dogs—his Crab at the other Stratford also drew raves. This Crab was a beast of markedly indeterminate breed but vaguely resembling a beagle on stilts that had passed through the hands of a headshrinker; he had been, if Rumour speak true, the pride of the Kitchener pound with an unexcelled reputation for scruffiness and randiness when auditioned by Mr. Phillips. Crab's sense of timing was impeccable, and was especially evident at the very first public performance in February when he came galumphing on with Mr. Donkin and then, fascinated by something backstage, presented his rear end, tail a-quiver, proudly to the audience. That induced more than moderate laughter and, it eventually getting to Crab that out behind those blinding lights there were 1,050 people looking at him, he about-faced and, peering beerily out at us made a gallant attempt at an imitation of a pointer. Mr. Donkin had to wait roughly five minutes to be heard, a star was born, and W. C. Fields doubtless turned over in his grave. (pp. 53-5)

John Pettigrew, "Stratford 1975 I. The Shakespeare Productions," in Journal of Canadian Studies/Revue d'etudes canadiennes, Vol. XI, No. 1, February, 1976, pp. 51-60.

Ralph Berry   (interview date 1977)

[*In a 1977 interview with Ralph Berry (RB), Robin Phillips (RP) discusses the challenges a director faces when presenting* The Two Gentlemen of Verona. *Phillips makes it clear that "to come to the end of the play with any resolution is a mistake."*]

RB [You] were speaking earlier about *Two Gentlemen of Verona,* and the extent to which it helped your actors to know certain things about themselves. And this tied in with the fact that in your production you make it explicitly about four young people who are very immature, who are imperfectly aware of their identities. At the end of the play they are very obviously asking questions about themselves and their relationships, and are not at all resting upon any illusory security in the text as we receive it.

RP What I feel most about that play is the infuriating hint at muscle that constantly comes up, the feeling that any moment we might develop into *Twelfth Night* or *As You Like It*—but it never does. The characters are just too young, they don't have the muscles, the development, the competences, the total personality. But then one has to say, 'You can't act that' unless it is part of the given circumstances. It is an unformed person, a person who doesn't yet know himself. He hasn't developed his own muscles; it isn't just an author who hasn't supplied them for him, it's a boy who hasn't yet discovered about the world about him, about anybody else. One feels that a lot of those characters could swap lines. They could just as easily be placed in each other's mouth; they're that undisciplined. And to come to the end of the play with any resolution is a mistake. The play does not resolve, they have not found maturity by the end. Their passions change from day to day, from minute to minute. To say by the end of the play they have now found the first footing and will continue is absurd. There is no suggestion, I think, that they will develop along certain lines. What we tried to say at the end is, 'And that's as far as it goes. But tomorrow we may well be looking in the other direction. We still have not found ourselves.'

RB And all this marries up happily with the pool-side location in Verona, which takes modernity in one direction about as far as it can go. (pp. 99-100)

Ralph Berry and Robin Phillips, in an interview, in Ralph Berry's On Directing Shakespeare: Interviews with Contemporary Directors, Croom Helm, 1977, pp. 91-104.

PRODUCTION:

David Ostwald • Oregon Shakespearean Festival • 1981

BACKGROUND:

Ostwald's production of *The Two Gentlemen of Verona* opened on 21 June 1981 at Ashland, Oregon. With an extensive background in staging operas, Ostwald elected to direct an operatic version of Shakespeare's play. Thus, rather than treating the play as a comedy, Ostwald concentrated on its more romantic elements, exploring the relationship between love and friendship. At least one critic found fault with Ostwald's interpretation, arguing that the director's liberal additions to the original play "exemplified what tends to go wrong outdoors at Ashland." The production featured Barry Kraft as Proteus, Joe Vincent as Valentine, J. Wesley Huston as Launce, Joyce Harris as Silvia, and Jeanne Paulsen as Julia.

COMMENTARY:

Charles Frey   (review date Autumn 1982)

[*Frey argues that the Ashland style of production—relying on pageantry and stylization rather than probing deeper dramatic complexities—does a terrible injustice to Shakespeare's plays. He examines Ostwald's production of* The Two Gentlemen of Verona *as an example of "what tends to go wrong outdoors at Ashland."*]

Is Ashland hurting Shakespeare?

The Ashland style of production—and there is an Ashland style despite the variety of directors, actors, and sets—often invites audiences to revel in velvet and ogle broad acting, to trade sight for sound, to skim the shallow and skip over the deep. Ashland offers throwbacks to American musical comedy, Cecil B. DeMille spectaculars, and the stuffed Edwardian stage. Boasting a budget of over $3,000,000 and more than 100,000 outdoor patrons annually, the Festival can claim commercial success. But is that success claimed at Shakespeare's expense? (p. 400)

When guest director David Ostwald, whose credits are largely in opera, imposed an operatic conception on *The Two Gentlemen of Verona,* the production exemplified what tends to go wrong outdoors at Ashland. Set in the late Middle Ages before an inert castle façade, the play opened with a long dumbshow introducing all the characters as well as personified versions of Friendship, Loyalty, and Amour. This rehearsal of the plot through mime was impossible to follow even given color-coded couples (Valentine and Silvia in blue, Proteus and Julia in orange). Operatic, too, were the costumes, so bulky as to make male actors look like puffing doormen, women like sweating divas. A medieval tourney scene was interpolated into the confrontation between Valentine and Thurio (II. iv). Thin, scratchy music piped incessantly, even while Silvia was captured by the Outlaws. Too often, the narrative line and the words of the play were dispersed into extraneous visual and aural appeals.

In its excessive stylization—the bright palette of limited range, the theme music, the over-gestured acting, the "explanatory" stage-business—this *Two Gents* harked back to elegantly stylized productions of the Royal Shakespeare Company and the National Theatre in the Fifties. Unnecessary stage business was used to provide subtextual rationalization and reductive motivation for what is really a subtle and, inevitably, protean play. Launce was integrated into the plot, for instance, not only by being included in the opening dumb-show but also by having him deliver the letter from Valentine to Proteus (I.iii), so that the audience was spared the strangeness of his entrance with Crab (II.iii) and the necessary work of connecting his situation with that of Proteus. What might have been an effective piece of business, Silvia peering out of a third-level window to emphasize her remoteness and ideality, was spoiled when she became a distracting overseer of Valentine's meeting with Speed (II.i) in direct contradiction to the Folio entrance. Launce's mocking call after Valentine—"Soho, soho!" [III. i. 189]—with the subsequent pun on *hair / hare,* was traduced into a hog-call—"Soo-ee, Soo-ee." The Outlaws were comic fumblers; they pranced about in masks while one scampered up a pole to dangle ten feet above the stage. Sylvia's rescue by Proteus, nowhere enacted in the text, was nonetheless staged.

Much of the stage business served to elevate Proteus and make Valentine and the servants look silly or irrelevant. After threatening to rape Silvia but before Valentine intervened, this Proteus of his own volition drew back as if to reconsider. The director said he conceived of Proteus as a youth confused but well-intentioned, and the actor, Barry Kraft, used considerable skills to elicit audience sympathy, even admiration, for Proteus. He never seemed malicious, only driven by his ever-for-the-moment honest passions. Thus he softened the criticism of Launce, softened his own mockeries of Thurio, softened his ill-treatment of Julia and Silvia, and gained an easy pride of place at the ending where most readers and many audiences have felt distinct ill-ease over his swift reintegration into society.

When Kraft's Proteus advised Thurio to serenade Silvia, he sank to one knee and carved a lyric inset out of a speech complicated by both awe and irony:

> For Orpheus' lute was strung with poets' sinews,
> Whose golden touch could soften steel and stones,
> Make tigers tame, and huge leviathans
> Forsake unsounded deeps to dance on sands.
>
> [III. ii. 77-80]

By prettifying this speech (as Director Ostwald prettified the whole production), Kraft never let the audience wonder whether the main emphasis here should be upon Proteus' reverence for the powers of poetry or upon Thurio's inadequacy for the task of wooing Silvia. The image of the nerve-strung lute, moreover, should resist precise imagining, and the pirouetting whales combine awe for Orphic force with a mannered application to Silvia's affections. Is she steel, stone, tiger, and leviathan at once? Or is the analogy much more soft and general: if song can do this to harsher nature, think what it may do to Silvia? The lambent ambivalence here, like the powerful yet partly illogical pun "unsounded," characterizes the larger text. Dr. Johnson bestowed a grace upon *Two Gentlemen* when he opined that, of the plays of Shakespeare, "few have more lines or passages which, singly considered, are eminently beautiful." A more common critical opinion is that "no passages and almost no single lines in this play (setting aside the whole of the song to Silvia) are particularly memorable" (Bertrand Evans). What should make Proteus' lines memorable in production is not their "beauty" but the way they typify the play as a whole in a mix of amazement and mockery over the interdependence of love and poetry.

Director Ostwald opted for a simplified conception, declaring the play "not a comedy," blunting the satire of Speed and Launce, and working instead toward a romantic story of youth's search for maturity finally revealed in the magical forest. Whatever the potential merits of such a conception, they were quite lost on the acting company. One of the leads whom I interviewed said she had contempt for the production, stressed that the director was a dance specialist who didn't care about laughs, who gave no strong direction, wanted mainly pageant effects, and "kept the actors still." For better or worse, when the visiting director left Ashland shortly after the run began, the other lead actress changed the style of her part drastically to make it more individually spirited. Two of the leads I interviewed found little to like in the text, perhaps because they had never been encouraged to explore its complexity and force. In the play's second scene, for example, Julia engages in intricate bawdiness with Lucetta [I. ii. 71-95], but this Julia plainly understood little of the joking and resorted to the common Ashland ploy of suggesting by tone and movement to her fellow actress and to the audience that the words were not *meant* to be understood.

Two Gentlemen requires a style of playing that will maximize the contrast between (1) the ceremonial public and idealizing stance of Valentine and Silvia, who are never alone with each other and rarely alone by themselves, and (2) the complicit, questioning style of Proteus, Julia, and Launce, who have among them some fifteen soliloquies. Through their soliloquies, Proteus (who has seven), Julia (who has five), and Launce (who has three) invite the empathy of audiences. We are brought closer to these than to the other characters. We become allied to their energy, strangeness, and wit, in contradistinction to the more solid, stolid lovers—Valentine and Silvia. Though Shakespeare's main interest follows Proteus, Julia, and Launce—characters of self-conflict and internal debate—the central question of the play remains "Who is Silvia? what is she, / That all our swains commend her?" [IV. ii. 39-40]. Why is love (or nature or fortune or providence or the playwright's mind) made to pay superior obeisance to vulnerable ideals of order, friendship, mildness, holiness, and light as against the protean, questioning dark? The answer given in the Ashland production came in the final scene, much the most cleverly staged. When Valentine, who had been musing with new-found authority on his struggle to keep his outlaws from "uncivil outrages," stepped forward to prevent Proteus' rape of Silvia—"Ruffian! let go that rude uncivil touch" [V. iv. 60]—the action stopped, and the audience was given time to savor a complex moment. Valentine's line was over-emphasized so as to border on the ludicrous. During an extended silence, two members of Valentine's band removed Proteus' armor, and he submitted to the shameful ceremony with postures of penitence, so that Valentine's following diatribe against him allowed a deepening portrayal of remorse. Valentine, having accepted the truth of Proteus' repentance, spoke the following line with a neutral ambiguity: "All that was mine in Silvia I give thee" [V. iv. 83]. As he accompanied the line with no physical offer to Silvia, it left open the interpretation that he meant only to extend his love for Silvia to Proteus or that he gave Proteus the compliment of trusting the offer would be refused. Julia's swoon was similarly ambiguous in that one could suspect its duplicity without receiving any clear signal from the actress, though her later words to Proteus—"And Julia herself hath brought it hither" [V. iv. 99]—were filled with reproach. By playing the scene slowly and thoughtfully, the cast led the audience to conclude, perhaps, that what Silvia, silent all the while, rightfully stood for was a certain will to constancy imparted to or discovered by the rest. As calmly and steadily played by

Joyce Harris and emphasized by the somewhat muted production, this Silvia's oft-stressed "kindness" and "mildness" seemed civilizing virtues emanating from the strength of constancy. The other three, more ardent lovers were cooled finally toward emulation of Silvia's repairing presence in "one mutual happiness" [V. iv. 173]. (pp. 400-02)

> *Charles Frey, "Shakespeare in the Northwest," in* Shakespeare Quarterly, *Vol. 33, No. 3 Autumn, 1982, pp. 400-09.*

PRODUCTION:

John Barton • Royal Shakespeare Company • 1981

BACKGROUND:

Barton's *Two Gentlemen of Verona,* paired with *Titus Andronicus,* was part of an experimental double bill at Stratford-upon-Avon. The Royal Shakespeare Company premiered the production on 26 August 1981. In order to perform the two plays in the space of one evening, each play had to be trimmed to under two hours. As a result, 850 lines were cut from *Titus Andronicus* and 515 from *The Two Gentlemen of Verona.* Most critics agreed that these drastic revisions of the text did more harm than good and diminished the overall effect of Barton's double bill concept. The major actors featured in this production included Peter Land as Proteus, Peter Chelsom as Valentine, Geoffrey Hutchings as Launce, Diana Hardcastle as Silvia, and Julia Swift as Julia.

COMMENTARY:

John Higgins　(interview date 26 August 1981)

[*The following excerpt is taken from an interview with John Barton before the 26 August 1981 preview of* Titus Andronicus *and* The Two Gentlemen of Verona *at Stratford-upon-Avon. Barton declares that if the double bill experiment is a success, similar projects will be considered.*]

The idea of putting on two Shakespeare plays in an evening for the price of one at Stratford-on-Avon this autumn came, like most RSC innovations, from Trevor Nunn. The reasons are basically economic. Stratford audiences, and particularly the American tourist element, are becoming more and more conservative. They go to what they know, or think they know, rather than seizing the chance to see the less familiar. So the *Dream* is packed out night by night, but there is some hesitation over *A Winter's Tale* and putting on a *Pericles,* say, or a *Timon* in the main auditorium would now involve a considerable financial risk. The choice for Stratford's first Shakespeare double bill has fallen on *Two Gentlemen of Verona* and *Titus Andronicus,* which start previewing tonight.

After making the selection it was natural enough for Nunn to turn to his resident play doctor, John Barton, to do the cutting to bring the plays down to an evening of less than *Gotterdammerung* proportions and to take on the direction as well. Barton has excised about 500 lines from *Two Gents* and 800 from *Titus.* It is reckoned that the total running time, including interval, will be a shade under four hours, in other words

little more than a full-length *Hamlet.* Barton, who is a far more practical man than his deceptive image of the absent-minded professor would suggest, accepts the project as "a straightforward experiment to see if a double bill of rarities can be good box-office". Probably he had not reckoned on a number of people asking for half-price tickets if they see *Two Gentlemen* only.

Stratford will be watching the outcome of the experiment with quite a lot of interest, not least because the plays are already scheduled to go into the opening season at the Barbican, assuming they are an artistic success. They will be in experienced hands: Barton, by coincidence, has already directed both as one half of a double bill, linking *Two Gentlemen* with *Dr Faustus* and *Titus* with *Friar Bacon and Friar Bungay.*

"That was long ago, back in the fifties at Cambridge, and I haven't touched either work since then. Running in tandem was all the fashion then and it was considered a good way of getting on the relatively unknown. Quite correctly. Then the fashion passed and we are now having a stab at reviving it. The essence of a successful duo is violence of contrast: that's what stimulates the theatrical excitement. Probably the best double bill I ever saw was *Oedipus* and *The Critic.* If *Two Gents* and *Titus* come off together we'll certainly be looking at the rest of the repertory—and not that the choice is very large. You have to choose plays that are cuttable and it helps if they are not too long to begin with. *Comedy of Errors* and *Timon of Athens* could work and would provide the right contrast. A probability? No, let's just say a possibility".

Unless matters are changed drastically during the previews Barton will be keeping a number of threads running through the two halves of the evening. The actors will select their props and clothes from a pile in the centre of the stage; the Elizabethan hobby horses which appear in *Two Gentlemen* will be carried through to *Titus* and so will Launce's dog Crab, who so far has snatched much more publicity than the humans appearing in the plays.

When John Barton assigned the role of Crab against a considerable canine opposition to an old English sheepdog, named Heidi, there were mutterings in Stratford about "mirror images". Barton himself now affects a shaggy, rumpled appearance from his grizzled head to his Hush Puppies. It is a long way from the dapper, romantic figure, ex-Eton and King's, who first appeared on stage in the adaptations he made for the RSC—*The Hollow Crown, Les Liaisons Dangereuses*—after Peter Hall had lured him away from the academic life to Stratford. The don in him still shines through the astute eyes, half mocking and half friendly, and his readiness to put the other side of any case simply out of a delight in argument. With 21 years of work at Stratford now behind him he is the RSC's "oldest inhabitant", happy to stay exactly where he is and let the legends thrive around him.

> *John Higgins, "The Realistic Economics of Doctoring Shakespeare," in* The Times, *London, August 26, 1981, p. 9.*

Ned Chaillet　(review date 4 September 1981)

[*Chaillet maintains that Barton's double bill production of* Titus Andronicus *and* The Two Gentlemen of Verona *was not a disaster. The plays "have missed that," Chaillet claims, "just as surely as they have missed a triumph."*]

Surgery has been done, and has been seen to be done, on the postponed and rumour-ridden Shakespearean double bill at Stratford. Some of the surgery was announced well in advance, the unkind, or perhaps occasionally kind, cuts of several hundred lines from both *Titus Andronicus* and *The Two Gentlemen of Verona* so that they might fit into less than four hours of gore and romance. Further medicine for the production by John Barton and Peter Stevenson was announced when the Royal Shakespeare Company took the rare and sudden option of cancelling the original opening night. That was more in the nature of corrective surgery, to control the titters and laughter that apparently greeted the tragedy and escaped the comedy.

A certain measure of laughter was clearly scored into the more brutal excisions of *Titus Andronicus*—carefully-subdued with regard to the rape of Lavinia (Leonie Mellinger), to the chopping-off of her hands and tearing out of her tongue, but as often as not courted through the device of open theatricality. A soldiers' camp signified by actors in pantomime horses, pots of limp greenery brought in from the wings when "ruthless" woods are required, and manic glee from the Titus of Patrick Stewart as he stirs up the sons of Tamora in a pie, all draw laughter that seems wholly expected by the company.

In the Royal Shakespeare style that reached its summit in *Nicholas Nickleby,* the actors remain on stage whether or not they are part of scenes, staying there to observe, encourage others and carry trees. Their own smiles at the deaths, mutilations and performances as two vicious family revenges are enacted in Rome would undermine any gloomy reading of the story. They force it to be considered as a morbid comedy by their consciously theatrical presence.

As well as the same set of actors, the plays share the setting, slightly altered by scattered leaves and modulations in Brian Harris's expressive lighting, but roofed by a canopy of fishnet and artfully cluttered with packing chests, bows and arrows and the bodies of the pantomime horses. Against expectations, the last round of hasty operations has brought the plays into a harmony that justifies their forced marriage. Primitive as each is in part, and from the earliest years of Shakespeare's composition, they touch on the grandeur of the later plays. In Mr Stewart's Titus there is too much of the clown to suggest either Coriolanus or Lear, but there is something of a perverted Prospero who has turned his magic to revenge. And the betrayal of friendship in *Two Gentlemen of Verona* when Proteus falls out of love with his Julia and into love with Valentine's Silvia is a foreshadowing of the complete confusion of love in *A Midsummer Night's Dream.*

The two gentlemen have been somewhat more severely hacked than Titus, but the reluctance to confront the Roman play as a tragedy is finally more damaging when a character turns to an audience uproarious with laughter and delivers a homily to "sad-faced spectators". The effect of the production is partially to reclaim a relish in gory excess, and partially to bury the genuine horrors of the play.

Comedy is the note carried over into the second play, *The Two Gentlemen,* and thanks to suitably romantic performances from Peter Chelsom as Valentine and Peter Land as Proteus, and to John Franklyn's Robbins as the irascible emperor of Milan, the comedy continues to build. It seemed from the publicity as if there was a disaster in the making,

but they have missed that just as surely as they have missed a triumph. It is instead a successful celebration of artifice.

Ned Chaillet, *"Double Bill,"* in The Times, *London, September 4, 1981, p. 15.*

John Elsom   (review date 10 September 1981)

[*Elsom offers an unfavorable review of Barton's* Titus Andronicus *and* Two Gentlemen of Verona *double bill, describing it as "second-rate and silly."*]

It is very hard to find a sensible justification for the Stratford double-bill—of a shortened *Titus Andronicus* and a mutilated *Two Gentlemen of Verona.* I suspect that the reason is sheer expediency, to get two unpopular plays produced from the canon in one go, but there is no law compelling the RSC to run through all of Shakespeare's plays in a set space of time; and *Titus* has had at least two good productions (one from the RSC) in recent years, while the memory of Peter Brook's *Titus* (with Olivier) still lingers. Apart from Patrick Stewart's performance as Titus, which cries out to be included in a full-length version, John Barton's shortened production fails on nearly every count. There may be a case for cutting this play of a thousand cuts, but not for losing its epic stature. Barton had the idea of presenting both plays as ramshackle fit-ups by a troupe of strolling players. That is a stale concept in itself—William Poel tried it out, though not with *Titus*—and it is particularly out of place on the main stage at Stratford. The success of the small-scale touring and studio Shakespeares seems to have gone to the RSC's head, so that they

Peter Land as Proteus and Bernard Lloyd as Antonio.

are now making an indulgence of what once was conceived as a necessity.

The background of props, hobby-horses, plastic trees and actors waiting around prevents the story of *Titus* from taking hold of the imagination and so all the bloodthirsty passages emerge as straight melodrama, which only Stewart could control. Sheila Hancock, coming from the unfortunately apt experience of *Sweeney Todd*, tried very hard not to relish Tamora too much; but when she came across lines like 'to massacre them all' [I. i. 450] or, in *Two Gentlemen of Verona* where she played a bandit, says of Valentine that he 'will not use a woman lawlessly' [V. iii. 14], her sense of fun was so heroically held back that it seemed even funnier.

As *Titus* lost its epic quality, so *Two Gentlemen* dealt inadequately with the idea of courtly love and the conflict between love and friendship; and this early comedy only came to life when Geoffrey Hutchings's Launce was left alone with his dog Crab and for one brief, but remarkable, shift of mood when John Franklyn-Robbins (as the Emperor of Milan) interrogates Valentine, as he is about to elope with Sylvia. It was a deadly evening, not disastrous perhaps but just second-rate and silly. (p. 386)

> *John Elsom, "Good at Heart?" in* The Listener, *Vol. 106, No. 2726, September 10, 1981, pp. 385-86.*

Sheridan Morley   (review date 16 September 1981)

[*Morley contends that while Barton's production of* Titus Andronicus *suffered from significant line cuts,* The Two Gentlemen of Verona *should have been cut altogether.*]

[The] RSC has curiously elected to cobble *Titus Andronicus* and *The Two Gentlemen of Verona* into a single double-bill, which means getting each one down to under two hours at a cost of some fifteen hundred cut lines in all. Production difficulties led to a delayed first night and an evidently last-minute decision to reverse the running order, so that the blood-letting of *Titus* now precedes the pastoral waffle of *Two Gents,* but this whole John Barton endeavour is gimmicky and aimless in the extreme. The plays have nothing in common beyond their construction in the early 1590s, and neither is improved by this *Readers' Digest* canter through the highlights of the text. On the sketchy evidence here *Titus* might have been worth doing in its entirety, despite Sheila Hancock's curious decision to play the Queen of the Goths in a Greta Garbo accent and a production which has the rest of the company chasing each other around the stage as for some comic-strip precursor of *King Lear*. They would I suspect have been happier doing the whole thing as a musical, though not even that would have helped *Two Gentlemen* which has already been cut by about two hours and should have been cut by another two. An appalling little play, no more than a shoddy dog story, given an appalling little production.

> *Sheridan Morley, "Gulag Land," in* Punch, *Vol. 281, No. 7349, September 16, 1981, p. 477.*

Stanley Wells   (review date 18 September 1981)

[*Wells praises Barton's attempt to revive the double bill tradition, which, he points out, enjoyed intermittent success from antiquity to the Victorian age. He questions, however, the wisdom of presenting two of Shakespeare's least popular plays—*

Titus Andronicus and The Two Gentlemen of Verona—*in one production.*]

Most readers and playgoers, asked to name Shakespeare's worst tragedy and comedy, would be likely to choose *Titus Andronicus* and *The Two Gentlemen of Verona.* Admittedly, both plays include fine poetry; both have strong dramatic situations; both display Shakespeare's emergent genius for characterization. In recent times, both have provoked eloquent critical defence in the face of earlier denigration and neglect. Appreciation of *Titus Andronicus* has been enhanced by discussion of its relationship to Ovid, of its Senecanism; of its place in the development of English tragedy. We have been taught to view the comedy more sympathetically by seeing it within the context of the Renaissance debate about the respective claims of friendship and love, and by examinations of its structure and its verbal counterpoint.

But difficulties remain, especially for the director who has the task of showing the plays at their best to audiences which must include many non-specialists. The horrors of *Titus Andronicus,* and the apparent disjunction between violent deeds and meditative verbal expression or response, require the most delicate handling if they are not to seem crudely melodramatic, or absurd in their artifice. Characterization in *The Two Gentlemen of Verona* is so slight that actors must feel they are required to make bricks with little straw. One of the gentlemen behaves so badly, and the other is such an ass, that they seem undeserving of the sympathy demanded for them at the conclusion; and important moments are so underwritten as to defy credulity.

So it is a brave director who undertakes either play; and though the Royal Shakespeare Company acknowledges a duty to perform even Shakespeare's least popular plays from time to time, to present both of them in one evening might seem to be passing beyond valour into indiscretion. Fears that this might be so were not allayed by a late postponement of the press night, and a sudden substitution of the performer in the role of Crab.

In the event, it is to everyone's credit that the first night went as well as it did. John Barton has chosen to stress the plays' Elizabethanism, and their theatricality. The same actors play in both: those with a big part in one play have a small one in the other. There are suggestions of a group of touring players. A placard names both plays, in the opposite order to that in which they are performed; the programme, too, suggests that the comedy will precede the tragedy. In the manner of recent productions here and elsewhere, the playing area is greatly reduced; it is defined by coatracks bearing costumes and a makeup mirror, five property baskets which can be variously re-arranged, and, to stage left, a scaffolding that can serve as an upper level, for Titus's study "above", or Silvia's tower. A great net swings down to bring the heavens forward, too. Before the performance begins, actors fraternize with the audience in a mode that is in danger of becoming modish.

The title of each play is declaimed, as are opening stage directions—perhaps to make sure we know which play is which, perhaps to sustain our consciousness of theatricality. The actors are visible throughout; concluding a scene, they retreat into the background and watch the action, seriously and sympathetically. In the tragedy, the device has a controlling effect on our emotions; Lavinia, carried off unconscious to be raped on her husband's corpse, revives as the actress in the midstage shadows.

If the performers are members of a touring company, Barton must be thought to have cast himself as their manager, one who, like his Elizabethan counterparts, has no scruples about altering the text. Like them, he is short of actors; no extras are available for crowd scenes. We stand in for the Roman populace (as, the text hints, Shakespeare may have meant *his* audience to do, too); the visible presence of the "resting" members of the company pleasantly peoples the stage in scenes which might otherwise have seemed too sparsely populated—though it is arguable that in the tragedy, at least, austerity would have been more fitting. Costumes are splendid; property trees are used to good effect; hobby-horses, if a little quaint, imaginatively suggest journeys; skilful lighting contributes to the constantly pleasing stage pictures.

Barton's way with the text here is not that of his Cibberian adaptations of *Henry VI* and *King John*. He has boiled down but not fudged up. Cuts are extensive—850 lines of *Titus*, 515 of *The Two Gentlemen*—but they are mostly "internal", within speeches. Before getting too hot under the collar about them, we may do well to recall that the only production of *Titus* to have set the Avon on fire—Peter Brook's, with Laurence Olivier as Titus, in 1955—used an adapted text from which over 650 lines had been excised.

All the same, the omissions are more damaging to the tragedy than to the comedy. Amplification is an essential rhetorical device in *Titus Andronicus;* to reduce it overemphasizes the action, detracts from its steady-paced grandeur, its sombre meditativeness. In general, Barton compensates for the conscious theatricality of his setting with naturalism in the acting, rather than aiming at the formal, emblematic stylization which has worked best in earlier productions.. . . .

I found most affecting the tableaux of grief which in the reading seem most artificial. Playing Lavinia's uncle, Marcus, Ray Jewers makes a deep impression with his quiet, stunned delivery of his elegantly descriptive speeches. Moving, too, is the coming together in suffering of the mutilated father and daughter, culminating in her acceptance of his killing her by dislocating her neck. The final holocaust leaves us appalled rather than moved; like the few surviving characters, we have supped full with horrors.

After the interval, the comedy. Nick Bicât's brazen flourishes and harsh, percussive fanfares give way to lyrical measures on woodwind and plucked strings. Christopher Morley's setting, essentially unchanged, adapts well to the new mood. The production is modest, charming, and sensitive to the play's weaknesses. The gentlemen, for once, seem really young, so are more easily forgiven. Peter Land plays an initially soppy Proteus, but finds a way to convey shame and bewilderment at the unexpected shift in his emotions. Peter Chelsom's engaging Valentine, full of boyish charm and innocence, youthfully pleased with himself, has the right mixture of comedy and romance, and develops into the most interesting character. The moment of his banishment, when he kneels to John Franklyn-Robbins's entertaining, strongly characterized Emperor, introduces a new dimension of seriousness; in the final scene, the genuineness of his concern for both Silvia and Proteus carries us surprisingly well through the notoriously difficult dénouement.

If we are less involved with the objects of the gentlemen's affections, it is because Diana Hardcastle's cold Silvia seems well able to look after herself, while Julia Swift is unsympathetically hoydenish in Julia's earlier scenes, and too stridently emotional in her later ones. Geoffrey Hutchings's Launce seems infected with the sourness of which he complains in his dog, but makes a good foil to the wholly delightful Speed of Joseph Marcell, who conveys a natural warmth and ebullience which illuminatingly humanize the often dry wordplay. Not much is to be done with the outlaws, but to have one of them played, by Sheila Hancock, as a sex-starved woman who takes a fancy to Valentine, only to find that he "bears an honourable mind, / And will not use a woman lawlessly" [V. iii. 13-14], creates innocent if irrelevant diversion.

Double bills have an honourable history. The Greeks had their satyr plays, the Elizabethans their jigs, the Victorians their farcical afterpieces. This Stratford evening lacks the elements of complete contrast, the suggestion of a necessary escape from high seriousness into frivolity, characteristic of most earlier examples. Nor does juxtaposition of the two plays cast unexpected illumination upon either. But the evening works well as a celebration of the varied talents of the dramatist and his performers; and you do get two plays—or most of two plays—for the price of one.

Stanley Wells, "*Elizabethan Doublets,*" *in* The Times Literary Supplement, *No. 4094, September 18, 1981, p. 1071.*

Christopher Edwards   (review date November 1981)

[*Edwards maintains that while both plays in Barton's production are flawed,* The Two Gentlemen of Verona *is more intelligible to modern audiences than is* Titus Andronicus.]

It is unusual enough to stage a Double Bill featuring any two Shakespeare plays, let alone two such early and immature works as *Titus Andronicus* and *The Two Gentlemen of Verona*. Although it is impossible to discover why, exactly, John Barton felt it necessary to cancel the first press night, one last minute change is evident to anyone who studies their programme carefully; the order of the Bill has been reversed so that now the evening closes with a Comedy instead of a grisly and unsatisfactory Senecan Tragedy of blood.

This is undoubtedly the right order of appearance for, despite its uneven verse and disconcerting switches of location, *The Two Gentlemen* points to the playwright's future and stands confidently at the beginning of a line of Comedies leading on to *As You Like It, Much Ado About Nothing* and *Twelfth Night. Titus,* however, stands alone in the canon and, while remarkably popular with original Elizabethan audiences, it has excited nothing but scathing critical comment since; most recently it was dismissed by T S Eliot as 'one of the stupidest and most uninspired plays ever written'. (p. 49)

The play does . . . have positive claims to being a tragedy, although this depends entirely upon whether Titus is allowed to retain the qualities of a tragic hero. There are hints of Hamlet in his assumed madness and, after he has arbitrated over the rival claims to the Roman empire and killed his virtuous son·in a quarrel, the parallel with Lear is particularly striking. All this doesn't, of course, make for greatness but as Olivier and Brook conclusively proved at this same theatre in the Fifties, the play can be made into a powerful and serious spectacle.

Barton's production however turns its back on *Titus'* tragic intensity and indulges a scholarly hunch that the formalized, patterned violence can be played as burlesque. This may well

Joseph Marcell as Speed, Geoffrey Hutchings as Launce, and Heidi as Crab.

be an interesting approach to the text but, as the nervous laughter of the audience suggests, it is not always quite clear when the burlesque is intentional.

The closing tableau, for example, is ridiculous. Titus has killed Tamora's sons and invited her to dine, unwittingly of course, on her children's flesh. Titus enters, face smeared with flour, sleeves rolled up, knotted handkerchief on his bald head and bearing aloft his preparation of 'fils de Tamora en croûte'; he resembles nothing so much as a demented chef at the seaside. After she has learned the awful truth ('there they both are, baked in that pie' [V. iii. 60]), her face registers pantomime amazement before she doubles up in horror—a reaction, I suppose, that Barton may have been seeking from his audience.

The outstanding success of Barton's approach—indeed of the whole production of the play—is Hugh Quarshie's cynical, beautifully-spoken Aaron. He seduces Tamora (Sheila Hancock), instigates most of the bloody action and in his self-delighting malice comes across as a sort of prototype Iago—only black. The casual barbarity of the world Shakespeare created here is perfectly captured in the scene where Tamora's nurse brings Aaron his newly born son. With the child cradled in one arm, a fond paternal smile still playing on his lips, he leans forward, beckons the nurse nearer and slits her

throat with about as much emotion as if he were blowing his nose.

The set remains the same for both plays; ropes, drums, baskets, costumes, pantomime horses and various other props are strewn around the stage and the cast sit around and change in full view of the audience. The idea is that we are attending a performance given by a strolling band of Elizabethan players and, with the actors occasionally announcing their own stage directions, the production takes on a mannered informality. (pp. 49-51)

Barton has cut about 500 lines from the second play on the Bill and both the production and the actors enjoy a greater measure of success. The rival claims of love and friendship were also explored in the sonnets and the later plays; here, in *The Two Gentlemen,* a love-sick Proteus betrays both his lady, Julia, and his best friend Valentine, but is eventually forgiven by both sides in a precariously balanced reconciliation scene at the end. The key to the success of the ending lies with Proteus, played with a mature blend of youthful enthusiasm and tact by Peter Land. In switching from sentimental lover to double-crossing villain, Land introduces just the right tremor of unease so that, while it may be threatened, the magnanimous world of comic romance is never actually disrupted beyond recall.

There are several other notable performances; Geoffrey Hutchings and Joseph Marcell put on a fine comic double act as, respectively, Launce and Speed. The former, in particular, suggests himself as a sort of lugubrious forerunner of later, greater wise fools like Feste [in *Twelfth Night*] and Touchstone [in *As You Like It*]. A dumpy, bouncy little actress called Julia Swift plays the part of Julia, the first of the bard's heroines to pass herself off as a boy; and Sheila Hancock [appears] as an over-sexed, blunderbuss-wielding Maid Marion dressed in Lincoln green. I think she speaks for the rest of the cast when she repeatedly fires her gun into the rafters. It is not so much that there is anything really memorable to celebrate, it is just a great relief to have put an unrewarding production of *Titus Andronicus* behind them and to be back in business with a Shakespeare play they all understand. (p. 51)

> *Christopher Edwards, in a review of "The Two Gentlemen of Verona," in* Plays & Players, *No. 338, November, 1981, pp. 49-51.*

Gareth Lloyd Evans   (review date Summer 1982)

> [*Evans disparages Barton's double bill production of* Titus Andronicus *and* The Two Gentlemen of Verona, *claiming that it was "a terrible dish to serve."*]

It is pleasing to curl one's fancy around the symmetry that London and Stratford-upon-Avon are as important today as centers for theatregoing as they were in Shakespeare's time. The steady flow of eminent and not-so-eminent itinerant companies through Shakespeare's home town in the mid- and late-sixteenth century ensured that the populace, then as now, was well entertained and that any keen citizen had ample opportunity to try and join the profession. It is true that nowadays transference is reversed, with major productions having conception and birth in Stratford before moving in willowy young maturity to London. But the symmetry is there, and a sense that the country's metropolitan heart depends mightily on the arterial flow from the environs.

It is fervently to be hoped that this pattern will survive, though it must be strongly tempting for the management to relegate the awkward, old, curmudgeonly inconvenient Memorial building at Stratford now that the spanking new London Barbican center for the Royal Shakespeare Company is opened. (p. 184)

The Royal Shakespeare Company's most notable contributions at Stratford-upon-Avon this year were three in number and can be conveniently designated as disastrous, quirky, and triumphant. Double bills have a respectable heritage, being part of the nineteenth-century theatre's table d'hôte menu, but John Barton's coupling of *Titus Andronicus* and *The Two Gentlemen of Verona* was a terrible dish to serve. It was as if a decision had been made that, since these two plays are probably Shakespeare's most inefficiently written, the opinion should be made quite clear to the audience.

Titus Andronicus suffered most, the victim of production and acting that mocked it beyond reason. Even Shakespeare's sow's ears give some glimpses of being capable of transformation into silk purses, but this Senecan hangover was studiedly subjected to denigration. The players indulged in in-jokes—an unforgivable practice in any production. Titus looked and behaved like a Sassoon blimp general; great play was made with those nursery horses that erstwhile actors have worn in plays about Archbishop Becket and King Henry meeting in

a field; Tamora's accent veered inconsistently between stage-Welsh and package-deal Gothic; "difficult" (i.e. and e.g., Latin) words were knowingly mispronounced with the suggestion that "we don't know what they mean, let's have a giggle." It is tedious and unpleasing to recall all the aberrations, but they all emanated from a failure to recognize and express the play's Elizabethan reality—a serious if exaggerated exercise in moral turpitude, mindlessness, and cruelty—and a total neglect of the dramatic potency of Titus, Aaron, and Tamora. The production also failed to recognize the fitful lyricism that flits over the play's cracked landscape like polar lightning.

The Two Gentlemen of Verona is Shakespeare's least engaging play, but in its gaucheness lie traces of true gold—indications, indeed, of the wealth to be mined later. Silvia and Julia prefigure the spirit of Viola [in *Twelfth Night*] and Rosalind [in *As You Like It*]; Launce announces the breeding of Dogberry [in *Much Ado About Nothing*], Gobbo [in *The Merchant of Venice*], and others; the chopping couplets sometimes modulate into a rhythm and melody that is a harbinger of later lyrical splendor. Not so for Mr. Barton. It was romp and rasp and roar, which gave away its paucity of invention by the tired and repetitive visualness of its comedy. This relied almost entirely on pantomimic (i.e., threatening) use of an aged blunderbuss wielded by a female outlaw (purists should consult the dramatis personae at this point). That players of the quality of Patrick Stewart, Bernard Lloyd, and Julia Swift, and a director of John Barton's sensibility, should have been involved in this abomination is incredible and melancholy. (pp. 186-87)

> *Gareth Lloyd Evans, "Shakespeare in Stratford and London, 1981," in* Shakespeare Quarterly, *Vol. 33 No. 2, Summer, 1982, pp. 184-88.*

Roger Warren   (review date 1982)

> [*Warren offers qualified praise of Barton's* Two Gentlemen of Verona, *noting that its comedic elements nicely contrasted and even played upon the serious tone of* Titus Andronicus.]

Mr Barton's interpretation of *The Two Gentlemen of Verona* must be considered in relation to his treatment of *Titus Andronicus*, which preceded it in a double-bill at Stratford.

The acting area was reduced to a very confined space at the front of the stage, surrounded by racks containing costumes, weapons, and props, and by the hobby-horses used by the Goths in *Titus* and by Silvia, Eglamour and Thurio in their flight to the forest in *Two Gentlemen*. Patrick Stewart (Titus) announced the play's title and read the opening stage directions. The actors visibly assumed their characterizations before entries and switched them off again once they were out of the acting area; they watched scenes they were not in, and often provided sound effects, such as birdsong for the various forest scenes. Perhaps surprisingly, this artifice did not on the whole rob the events of conviction. Sometimes the actors' presence . . . made interesting connections between episodes, as when the watching Julia laughed in sympathetic recognition at Valentine's confusion over the love-letter Silvia had asked him to write: it was as if, like Touchstone, she was thinking that 'we that are true lovers run into strange capers' [*As You Like It*, II. iv. 54-5].

I had feared that some of the extended lyrical passages would fall victim to the extensive cutting required to fit the two plays into one evening (850 lines from *Titus*, 515 from *Two Gentlemen*) but most of them were retained and indeed played an important part in Mr Barton's interpretation: as with the artifice of the staging, what might be considered verbal artifice was in fact used to increase rather than lessen the dramatic impact. (pp. 142-43)

The sheer contrast [of *Two Gentlemen*] with *Titus* was bound to emphasize its humorous potential, but in addition the scenes involving Eglamour and the Outlaws were able to make humorous allusions to the treatment of *Titus* earlier on. The Outlaws were without question the funniest I have ever seen, appearing in Lincoln green hoods among the prop trees from the *Titus* forest accompanied by twittering birdsong. There were nine of them, and the lines were redistributed so that the actor of Aaron could call abduction and murder 'petty crimes', and so that Sheila Hancock could give an astonishing performance as their leader: it was she who had stabbed a gentleman 'in my mood' [IV. i. 49]; she immediately fell for Valentine, praising him as a *linguist!*' [IV. i. 55] in tones of rapt admiration, and later telling Silvia with evident disappointment that Valentine would 'not use a woman lawlessly' [V. iii. 14]. She was also armed with a blunderbuss which suddenly went off, provoking an explosion of squawking from a host of 'off-stage' birds. The actors themselves could hardly keep straight faces after this, entirely pardonably: it was an irresistible climax to a marvellously funny scene, perfectly appropriate to Shakespeare's burlesque of Robin Hood outlaws. The treatment of Sir Eglamour was even more appropriate. Patrick Stewart's armour and gentlemanly manner recalled his Titus; with his lance, fluttering pennant, and hobby-horse he was the perfect image of an ageing knight errant, a White Knight or Don Quixote; in the forest he took on all the Outlaws at once, and since there were so many of them the textual problem of Silvia's chivalrous escort taking to his heels ceased to exist.

If the contrast with *Titus* intensified the humour, it also emphasized that, as Anne Barton put it in the programme, *Titus* 'looks to the past', *Two Gentlemen* to 'Shakespeare's future'. There was an unmistakable sense of returning to familiar ground as Mr Barton used humour to express the characterization of the lovers. The youth and inexperience of Peter Land's gangling Proteus was set against Bernard Lloyd's sharp sketch of his 'peremptory' father, briskly dispatching his business affairs and his son's future at the same time. This Proteus didn't 'show his love' because he didn't know how to, and beneath the humour of the letter scene Julia Swift's plump, tomboyish Julia expressed her frustration at his ineptitude: 'I would I *knew* his *mind*' [I. ii. 33]. Peter Chelsom's Valentine in particular used a nice sense of humour to convey an attractively warm personality: when Proteus said he would not flatter Silvia, this Valentine cried 'O, flatter *me*' [II. iv. 148] with a giggle, one intimate friend to another.

The lovers' extended, conceited speeches, too, like the forest speeches in *Titus*, were interpreted in the interests of character. Valentine's 'braggardism' in giving Julia the honour

> To bear my lady's train, lest the base earth
> Should from her vesture chance to steal a kiss
>
> [II. iv. 159-60]

suggested someone carried away by the delights of the conventional lover's service to his lady yet still aware of its extravagances. Julia's elaborate comparision of her love to an unhindered stream which gives 'a gentle kiss to every sedge

/ He overtaketh in his pilgrimage' [II. vii. 29-30] became a means of getting her way, without sacrificing the formal beauty of the lines. Proteus's speech about the power of poetry to make 'huge leviathans / Forsake unsounded deeps to dance on sands' [III. ii. 79-80] indicated how far he had developed from the callow youth of the opening scenes. He had visibly grown up before our eyes, gradually acquiring a sense of 'skill', speaking of 'some treachery us'd to Valentine' [II. vi. 32] with an uneasy smile which was a recognizable development from his awkwardly sagging lip at the start, and which was later transformed into something like a snarl in the rape scene. Here, Valentine tried to bring off 'All that was mine in Silvia I give thee' [V. iv. 83] as another piece of conventional behaviour, the kind of gesture Valentine would think was expected of him, while desperately hoping that Proteus wouldn't accept the offer. But although they strove prodigiously to make the episode work, the final impression was that we were on familiar but still experimental ground, the humour and humanity still separate strands rather than integrated with the confidence of, for instance, *A Midsummer Night's Dream*. (pp. 143-44)

Roger Warren, *"Interpretations of Shakespearian Comedy, 1981,"* in Shakespeare Survey: An Annual Survey of Shakespearian Study and Production, *Vol. 35, 1982, pp. 141-52.*

FURTHER READING

REVIEWS AND RETROSPECTIVE ACCOUNTS

Berry, Ralph. "Stratford Festival Canada." *Shakespeare Quarterly* XXXVI, No. 1   (Spring 1985): 87-93.
Recognizes Leon Rubin's attempt to establish a theme of youth in his production. Berry criticizes the costumes, however, deeming them "*G. Q.* new wave crossover."

Billington, Michael. "Open Air Revival." *The Times* (London), No. 57,576   (3 June 1969): 7.
Presents a favorable review of Richard Digby Day's 1969 revival of *The Two Gentlemen of Verona* in Regent's Park, London.

Carey, Robin. "Oregon Shakespeare Festival, 1974." *Shakespeare Quarterly* XXV, No. 4   (Autumn 1974): 419-21.
Briefly discusses new themes and stage techniques introduced in a 1974 production of *The Two Gentlemen of Verona* at Ashland, Oregon.

Craig, Sandy. "Upstaging the Bard." *The Listener* 110, No. 2838 (22 and 29 December 1983): 50.
Disparages Don Taylor's BBC production for its misinterpretation of Shakespeare's satirical attack on Elizabethan conceptions of courtly love.

Czarnecki, Mark. "Dark Dreams and Extravagant Visions." *Maclean's* 97, No. 26   (25 June 1984): 57-8.
A brief, unfavorable review of Leon Rubin's 1984 "jarring punk version" of *The Two Gentlemen of Verona* at Stratford, Ontario.

David, Richard. "Actors and Scholars: A View of Shakespeare in the Modern Theatre." *Shakespeare Survey* 12   (1959): 76-87.
Criticizes Langham's 1957 production of *The Two Gentlemen of Verona* for its satirical treatment of love itself rather than

"the excess of loverly behavior" that is Shakespeare's actual target.

Gardner, Edmund. "Stratford's New Staging." *The Shakespeare Newsletter* XI, No. 5 (November 1961): 35.

Praises Patrick Wymark's performance as Launce in Peter Hall's 1960 production of *The Two Gentlemen of Verona* at Stratford-upon-Avon.

Gill, Brendan. "The Bard, with Affection." *The New Yorker* XLVII, No. 43 (11 December 1971): 101.

Notes that while Joseph Papp's 1971 musical adaptation of *The Two Gentlemen of Verona* was entertaining, almost all of Shakespeare's own style was lost.

Griffin, Alice. "Shakespeare in New York City, 1956-1957." *Shakespeare Quarterly* VIII (1957): 515-19.

Comments on Stuart Vaughan's 1957 production in Central Park, praising Jerry Stiller's performance as Launce.

Hewes, Henry. "Going Bumpety Bump on the Rocky Road to Love." *Saturday Review* (New York) LIV, No. 34 (21 August 1971): 18.

Provides a favorable review of Joseph Papp's 1971 musical adaptation of *The Two Gentlemen of Verona,* particularly noting John Guare's praiseworthy lyrics.

———. "Public Joy and Private Terror." *Saturday Review* (New York) LV, No. 2 (8 January 1972): 38.

Welcomes Joseph Papp's 1971 musical adaptation of *The Two Gentlemen of Verona* to Broadway as "a merrily zany respite from the pressures of daily logic or neurotic romantic entanglements."

Horn, Robert D. "Shakespeare at Ashland, Oregon, 1957." *Shakespeare Quarterly* VIII (1957): 527-30.

Discusses some of the principal actors' performances in the 1957 production of *The Two Gentlemen of Verona* at the Oregon Festival.

Kroll, Jack. "Avon Rock." *Newsweek* LXXVIII, No. 24 (13 December 1971): 114.

Argues that while much of Shakespeare was lost in Joseph Papp's 1971 musical adaptation of *The Two Gentlemen of Verona,* superb actors made the show a huge success.

Leech, Clifford. Introduction to *The Two Gentlemen of Verona* by William Shakespeare, edited by Clifford Leech, pp. xiii-lxxv. London: Methuen & Co., 1969.

A general introduction to the play, with a section that outlines its stage history.

Nightingale, Benedict. "Holy Moustache." *New Statesman* 77, No. 1996 (13 June 1969): 853-54.

Offers an unfavorable review of Richard Digby Day's 1969 Regent's Park revival of his popular *The Two Gentlemen of Verona.*

———. "Quartered." *New Statesman* 80, No. 2055 (7 August 1970): 158-59.

Indifferently reviews Robin Phillips's production, describing it as "eccentric."

Smith, Peter D. "The 1966 Festivals at Ashland, Oregon and San Diego, California." *Shakespeare Quarterly* XVII, No. 4 (Autumn 1966): 407-17.

Maintains that while Allen Fletcher's operatic version of *The Two Gentlemen of Verona* in San Diego was a disappointment, Nagle Jackson's production at Ashland, Oregon in the same year "came off splendidly."

Review of *The Two Gentlemen of Verona. The Times* (London), No. 52,240 (20 February 1952): 2.

Offers high praise of Denis Carey's successful 1952 production of *The Two Gentlemen of Verona* at the Bristol Old Vic.

Trewin, J. C. "Shakespeare Summer." *The Illustrated London News* 253, No. 6730 (27 July 1968): 31.

Briefly reviews Richard Digby Day's 1968 production of *The Two Gentlemen of Verona,* and takes exception to Bernard Bresslaw's performance as Launce.

Warren, Roger. "Shakespeare in England." *Shakespeare Quarterly* XXXV, No. 3 (Autumn 1984): 334-40.

Maintains that while Taylor's production did not surmount the many problems present in *The Two Gentlemen of Verona,* the young cast gave a solid performance.

———. "Shakespeare at Stratford, Ontario: The John Hirsch Years." *Shakespeare Survey* 39 (1987): 179-90.

Contends that Rubin's updated version of *The Two Gentlemen of Verona* helped establish an adolescent love theme with which modern audiences can empathize.

Wells, Stanley. "Melancholy Misunderstandings." *Times Literary Supplement,* No. 4214 (6 January 1984): 14.

Describes the performances of the actors in Taylor's BBC production of *The Two Gentlemen of Verona.*

COMPARISONS AND OVERVIEWS

Barker, Kathleen. "Renaissance: 1943-1954." In *The Theatre Royal Bristol, 1766-1966,* pp. 213-20. London: The Society for Theatre Research, 1974.

Considers Denis Carey's 1952 production of *The Two Gentlemen of Verona* as perhaps the one that elevated the Bristol Old Vic to national renown.

Marder, Louis. "The Remarkable Paradox." In *His Exits and His Entrances: The Story of Shakespeare's Reputation,* pp. 42-83. Philadelphia and New York: J. B. Lippincott Company, 1963.

Records a 1924 performance of *The Two Gentlemen of Verona* at the London Old Vic where Mr. Hay Petrie, playing Launce, winked at a member of the audience. With this action, Marder believes, Petrie broke down the traditional barrier between actor and audience.

Vermiglia, Peter James. "The William Winter Correspondence and the Augustin Daly Shakespearean Productions of 1885-98." *Educational Theatre Journal* 30, No. 2 (May 1978): 220-28.

Examines William Winter's collaboration with Augustin Daly on Daly's 1895 production of *The Two Gentlemen of Verona.*

STAGING ISSUES

Grayeff, Leonie. "Open Theatre." *The Illustrated London News* 253, No. 6731 (3 August 1968): 25-7.

Explores the challenges an open air production poses for a director and his company. Grayeff focuses on Richard Digby Day's 1968 production of *The Two Gentlemen of Verona* in Regent's Park, London.

Sprague, Arthur Colby. "The Comedies." *Shakespeare and the Actors: The Stage Business in His Plays* (*1660-1905*), pp. 3-75. Cambridge, Massachusetts: Harvard University Press, 1944.

Examines the stage directions found in the prompt books for various productions of *The Two Gentlemen of Verona.*

Selected Studies of Shakespearean Production

Babula, William. *Shakespeare in Production, 1935-1978*. New York: Garland Publishing, 1981, 383 p.

Bradbrook, M. C. *A History of Elizabethan Drama*. Cambridge: Cambridge University Press, 1979 (2nd ed.), 6 vols.

Brown, Ivor. *Shakespeare and the Actors*. London: Bodley Head, 1970, 197 p.

Byrne, Muriel St. Clare. "Fifty Years of Shakespearian Production." *Shakespeare Survey* 2 (1949): 1-20.

Chambers, E. K. *The Elizabethan Stage*. Oxford: Clarendon Press, 1923 (rev. ed. 1951), 4 vols.

Foulkes, Richard, ed. *Shakespeare and the Victorian Stage*. Cambridge: Cambridge University Press, 1986, 311 p.

Godshalk, William, gen. ed. *The Garland Shakespeare Bibliographies*. New York: Garland Publishing, 1980—.

Granville-Barker, Harley. *Prefaces to Shakespeare*. London: Sidgwick and Jackson, 1927-47, 5 vols.

Grebanier, Bernard. *Then Came Each Actor*. New York: McKay, 1975, 626 p.

Gurr, Andrew. *The Shakespearean Stage, 1574-1642*. Cambridge: Cambridge University Press, 1970, 192 p.

Hogan, Charles Beecher. *Shakespeare in the Theatre, 1701-1800*. Oxford: Clarendon Press, 1952-57, 2 vols.

Holmes, Martin. *Shakespeare and his Players*. New York: Charles Scribner's Sons, 1972, 212 p.

Hotson, Leslie. *The Commonwealth and Restoration Stage*. Cambridge, Mass: Harvard University Press, 1928, 424 p.

Joseph, B. L. *Acting Shakespeare*. London: Routledge and Kegan Paul, 1960, 199 p.

———. *Elizabethan Acting*. London: Oxford University Press, 1951, 156 p.

King, T. J. *Shakespearean Staging, 1599-1642*. Cambridge, Mass.: Harvard University Press, 1971, 163 p.

Knight, G. Wilson. *Principles of Shakespearian Production*. London: Faber and Faber, 1936, 246 p.

Leiter, Samuel L., ed. *Shakespeare around the Globe*. New York: Greenwood Press, 1986, 972 p.

Mullin, Donald. *Victorian Actors and Actresses in Review*. Westport, Conn.: Greenwood Press, 1983, 571 p.

Mullin, Michael. *Theatre at Stratford-upon-Avon.* Westport, Conn.: Greenwood Press, 1980, 2 vols.

Nagler, A. M. *Shakespeare's Stage.* Translated by Ralph Manhein. New Haven: Yale University Press, 1958, 117 p.

Nicoll, Allardyce. *A History of English Drama.* Cambridge: Cambridge University Press, 1952-59, 6 vols.

Odell, George C. D. *Annals of the New York Stage.* New York: Columbia University Press, 1927-49, 15 vols.

————. *Shakespeare from Betterton to Irving.* New York: Charles Scribner's Sons, 1920, 2 vols.

Purdom, C. B. *Producing Shakespeare.* London: Pitman, 1950, 220 p.

Salgado, Gamini. *Eyewitnesses of Shakespeare: First Hand Accounts of Performances 1590-1890.* London: Chatto and Windus, 1975, 360 p.

Shattuck, Charles. *Shakespeare on the American Stage: From the Hallams to Edwin Booth.* Washington, D.C.: Folger Shakespeare Library, 1976, 2 vols.

Speaight, Robert. *Shakespeare on the Stage: An Illustrated History of Shakespearean Performance.* Boston: Little Brown and Co., 1973, 304 p.

————. *William Poel and the Elizabethan Revival.* London: William Heinemann, 1954, 302 p.

Sprague, Arthur Colby. *Shakespeare and the Actors: The Stage Business in His Plays, 1660-1905.* Cambridge, Mass.: Harvard University Press, 1944, 440 p.

Sprague, A. C. and Trewin, J. C. *Shakespeare' Plays Today: Some Customs and Conventions of the Stage.* Columbia: University of South Carolina Press, 1971, 147 p.

Sprague, A. C. *Shakespearian Players and Performances.* Cambridge, Mass.: Harvard University Press, 1953, 222 p.

Styan, J. L. *The Shakespeare Revolution: Criticism and Performance in the Twentieth Century.* Cambridge: Cambridge University Press, 1977, 292 p.

Trewin, J. C. *Shakespeare on the English Stage, 1900-1964.* London: Barrie and Rockliff, 1964, 328 p.

Watkins, Ronald. *On Producing Shakespeare.* London: M. Joseph, 1950, 335 p.

Winter, William. *Shakespeare on the Stage.* New York: Moffat, Yard and Co., 1911, 564 p.

Glossary

AMERICAN SHAKESPEARE THEATRE (Stratford, Connecticut): Playhouse established by Lawrence Langner in 1955 as the home of a summer drama festival. The polygonal design of the American Shakespeare Festival Theatre, as it was originally called, was derived from extant drawings of the exterior of the GLOBE THEATRE and was intended to combine an Elizabethan-style stage with modern equipment and techniques. In 1977 the American Shakespeare Theatre became part of the Connecticut Center for the Performing Arts, and its program was expanded to include performances by visiting artists and companies outside of the regular festival season. Among the more notable performances at the American Shakespeare Theatre were Morris Carnovsky's portrayals of Shylock and King Lear; Katharine Hepburn's Beatrice in *Much Ado about Nothing*; Jessica Tandy's Lady Macbeth; and James Earl Jones as the Moor and Christopher Plummer as Iago in a 1981 production of *Othello*.

BLACKFRIARS THEATRE: The Blackfriars Theatre, so named because it was located in the London precinct of Blackfriars, was originally part of a large monastery leased to Richard Farrant, Master of the Children of Windsor, in 1576 for the purpose of staging children's plays. It was acquired in 1596 by James Burbage, who tried to convert the property into a professional theater, but was thwarted in his attempt by surrounding residents. After Burbage died, the Blackfriars was taken over by his son, Richard, who circumvented the objections of his neighbors and, emulating the tactics of Farrant's children's company, staged both children's and adult plays under the guise of a private house, rather than a public theater. This arrangement lasted for five years until, in 1605, the adult company was suspended by King James I for its performance of the satire *Eastward Ho!* Shortly thereafter, the children's company was also suppressed for performing George Chapman's *Conspiracy and Tragedy of Charles Duke of Byron*. In 1608 Burbage organized a new group of directors consisting of his brother Cuthbert and several leading players of the KING'S MEN, including Shakespeare, John Heminge, Henry Condell, and William Sly. These "housekeepers," as they were called, for they shared no profits accruing to the actors, arranged to have the King's Men use Blackfriars alternately with the GLOBE THEATRE, an arrangement that lasted from the autumn of 1609 to 1642. Because it was a private house, and therefore smaller than the public theaters of London at that time, the Blackfriars set a higher price for tickets and, as such, attracted a sophisticated and aristocratic audience. Also, through its years of operation as a children's theater, the Blackfriars developed its patrons' taste for music, dance, and masque in a dramatic piece, as well as elements of suspense, reconciliation, and rebirth. Many critics attribute the nature of Shakespeare's final romances to the possibility that he wrote the plays with this new audience foremost in mind.

BOOKKEEPER: Also considered the bookholder or prompter, the bookkeeper was a member of an Elizabethan acting company who maintained custody of the PROMPT-BOOKs, or texts of the plays. Many scholars believe that the bookkeeper also acted as the prompter during performances, much as a stage manager would do today; however, other literary historians claim that another official satisfied this function. In addition to the above duties, the bookkeeper obtained a license for each play; deleted from the dramatist's manuscript anything offensive before it was submitted to the government censor; assembled copies of the players' individual parts from the company prompt-book; and drew up the "plot" of each work, that is, an abstract of the action of the play emphasizing stage directions.

COVENT GARDEN THEATRE: Covent Garden and its rival, the DRURY LANE THEATRE, were long the only two PATENT playhouses in England. The first theater in Covent Garden was built in 1732 by John Rich, who moved his company from LINCOLN'S INN FIELDS THEATRE to the new facility. The buildings housing the theater have twice been destroyed by fire, the first time in 1808, the second in 1856. The present structure was completed two years after the second conflagration. Covent Garden has a rich history of Shakespearean performances, and has been the theatrical home of many renowned actors and producers. John Philip Kemble and his brother Charles were each at different times actor-manager of Covent Garden, as was William Charles Macready, who made his stage debut there in 1816. Spranger Barry, Charles Macklin, Sarah Siddons, Edmund Kean, Fanny Kemble, and Helena Faucit were among the illustrious performers at Covent Garden in the eighteenth and nineteenth centuries. Since 1847 the theater has been almost exclusively devoted to the staging of opera.

DRURY LANE THEATRE: One of the foremost theaters in London from the seventeenth to the nineteenth century. Originally called the Theatre Royal in Bridges Street, this playhouse was opened in 1663 by Thomas Killigrew for his company, the King's Servants. Together with LINCOLN'S INN FIELDS THEATRE, it was one of two PATENT theaters established by Charles II. During the Restoration, Drury Lane witnessed the revival of several of Shakespeare's plays, including *Othello, Henry IV,* and *Julius Caesar.* After a fire devastated the original structure in 1672, a new playhouse—designed by Christopher Wren, the premier architect of the period—was built and opened as the Theatre Royal in Drury Lane in 1674. Forced to close in 1681 as the result of incompetent management, it reopened the following year with a resident company headed by the renowned actor Thomas Betterton. The assumption of control of the theater in 1690 by Christopher Rich resulted in the defection five years later of a large group of actors. Led by Betterton, these players successfully established a rival company at Lincoln's Inn Fields. Drury Lane has had many famous managers, including John Philip Kemble and William Charles Macready, but perhaps the greatest was David Garrick, whose numerous productions and adaptations of Shakespeare's works exerted an influence far outlasting his tenure from 1747-76. The aging theater was rebuilt in 1794, but destroyed by fire in 1809. The new structure, which was completed in 1812, still stands.

FOLIO: The term applied to a book usually made up of sheets of paper folded once to form two leaves, or four pages, of roughly equal size. The dimensions of a folded folio page may range in size from about 8 to 11 inches in width and 11 to 16 inches in height. The earliest collected edition of Shakespeare's plays was issued in this format and is commonly known as the First Folio. It was edited by his fellow-actors John Heminge and Henry Condell and published near the end of 1623. The First Folio contains thirty-six plays; thirteen of these had not been published before. Although this edition is considered authoritative for a number of Shakespeare's plays, recent textual scholarship tends to undermine this authority by calling for a broader consideration of all previous versions of a Shakespearean drama in conjunction with the Folio text.

GLOBE THEATRE: Constructed in 1599 on Bankside across the Thames from the City of London, the Globe was destroyed by fire in 1613, rebuilt the following year, and finally razed in 1644. Accounts of the fire indicate that it was built of timber with a thatched roof, and sixteenth-century maps of Bankside show it was either a circular or polygonal building, but no other evidence exists regarding its structure and design. From what is known of similar public theaters of the day, such as the Fortune and the SWAN, it is conjectured that the Globe contained a three-tiered gallery along its interior perimeter, that a roof extended over a portion of the three-storied stage and galleries, and that the lowest level of the stage included an apron extending out into the audience area in the yard. Further, there is speculation that the Globe probably included a tiring room or backstage space, that the first two stories may have contained INNER STAGEs, and that beneath the flat roof, which was also known as "the heavens," machinery was stored for raising and lowering theatrical apparatus. It is generally believed that the interior of the Globe was circular and that it could accommodate an audience of approximately two thousand people in its three galleries and the yard. The theater was used solely by the LORD CHAMBERLAIN'S MEN, later known as the KING'S MEN, who performed there throughout the year until 1609, when the company alternated performances at the fully-enclosed BLACKFRIARS THEATRE in months of inclement weather.

HAYMARKET THEATRE: The Little Theatre in the Hay, as it was originally known, was built in 1720 by the carpenter John Potter. The actor and playwright Samuel Foote assumed the management of the playhouse in 1747. As the Haymarket was not a PATENT theater, its existence was precarious, and Foote employed a number of stratagems to avoid its forced closure. Despite these efforts, it was several times suppressed by the authorities. Finally, in 1766, Foote was granted a Royal Patent permitting productions during the summer months. The Haymarket thus joined DRURY LANE and COVENT GARDEN as the only licensed playhouses and Theatres Royal. In 1820 the original building was destroyed and the present one was erected. The Haymarket has been the site of numerous significant Shakespearean performances throughout its long history, including the London debuts of such acclaimed actors as Samuel Phelps (1837) and Edwin Booth (1861). In the closing decades of the nineteenth century, Herbert Beerbohm Tree mounted a series of lavish Shakespearean productions at the Haymarket, and in 1944-45 John Gielgud staged a successful revival of *Hamlet* there.

INNER STAGE: An alcove or recess, representing a concealed or interior space, that some scholars believe was located at the rear of an Elizabethan stage. The area may have been closed off by a curtain, which could be drawn back to permit dramatic "discoveries." The staunchest defender of the theory of the inner stage or "study" was John Cranford Adams, who, in the first half of the twentieth century, postulated that this area was as large as eight feet deep, twenty-three feet wide, and twelve feet high. While many recent scholars acknowledge that numerous Elizabethan plays contain stage directions calling for some type of "discovery space," they maintain there is no external evidence of the existence of such a sizable enclosure. They point out that Johannes deWitt's sketch of the SWAN THEATRE, the only extant contemporary drawing of the interior of an Elizabethan playhouse, depicts no inner stage. These critics also maintain that action occurring on the inner stage would not be visible to a significant portion of the audience. Some scholars, such as Richard Hosley, have suggested that a simple curtain could have been hung across the rear wall or that a small booth or pavilion could have been easily erected and placed at an appropriate place on the stage; either of these devices would have provided a serviceable discovery space.

INNS OF COURT: Four colleges of law located in the City of London—Gray's Inn, the Middle Temple, the Inner Temple, and Lincoln's Inn. In the sixteenth and seventeenth centuries, the Inns were not only academic institutions, but were also regarded as finishing schools for gentlemen, providing their students with instruction in music, dance, and other social accomplishments. Interest in the drama ran high in these communities; in addition to producing their own plays, masques, and revels, members would occasionally employ professional acting companies, such as the LORD CHAMBERLAIN'S MEN and the KING'S MEN, for private performances at the Inns. Existing evidence indicates that at least two of Shakespeare's plays, *The Comedy of Errors* and *Twelfth Night,* were first performed at the Inns.

KING'S MEN: An acting company formerly known as the LORD CHAMBERLAIN'S MEN. On 19 May 1603, shortly after his accession to the throne, James I granted the company a royal PATENT, and its name was altered to reflect the King's direct patronage. At that date, members who shared in the profits of the company included Shakespeare, Richard Burbage, John Heminge, Henry Condell, Augustine Phillips, William Sly, and Robert Armin. Records of the Court indicate that this was the most favored acting company in the Jacobean era, averaging a dozen performances there each year during the period. In addition to public performances at the GLOBE THEATRE in the spring and autumn, the King's Men played at the private BLACKFRIARS THEATRE in winter and for evening performances. Because of the recurring plague in London from 1603 onward, theatrical companies like the King's Men spent the summer months touring and giving performances in the provinces. Beside the work of Shakespeare, the King's Men's repertoire included plays by Ben Jonson, Francis Beaumont and John Fletcher, Thomas Dekker, and Cyril Tourneur. The company continued to flourish until 1642, when by Act of Parliament all dramatic performances were suppressed.

LINCOLN'S INN FIELDS THEATRE: London PATENT theater converted from a tennis court by William Davenant for his company, the Duke of York's Servants. Opening in June 1661, Lincoln's Inn Fields was the first playhouse to have a proscenium arch and to use movable scenery. It was also one of the first to cast women rather than young boys in female roles. The Duke's Servants employed the theater until 1671, when the company moved to a new building in Dorset Garden and then to the COVENT GARDEN THEATRE. From 1672 to 1674, Thomas Killigrew's company, the King's Servants, performed at Lincoln's Inn Fields, before moving to DRURY LANE THEATRE. The structure then reverted to a tennis court until 1695, when a company led by the noted actor Thomas Betterton began a ten-year residency there. The theater was rebuilt and reopened in 1714 and continued to be the site of theatrical productions until 1732, after which time it was put to a variety of uses, including a ballroom, a warehouse, and a barracks. It was finally razed in 1848.

LORD ADMIRAL'S MEN: An acting company formed in 1576-77 under the patronage of Charles Howard, Earl of Nottingham. From its inception to 1585 the company was known as the Lord Howard's Men; from 1585 to 1603 as the Lord Admiral's Men; from 1604 to 1612 as Prince Henry's Men; and from 1613 to 1625 as the Palsgrave's Men. They were the principal rivals of the LORD CHAMBERLAIN'S MEN; occasionally, from 1594 to 1612, these two troupes were the only companies authorized to perform in London. The company's chief player was Edward Alleyn, an actor of comparable distinction with Richard Burbage of the Lord Chamberlain's Men. From 1591 the company performed at the ROSE THEATRE, moving to the Fortune Theatre in 1600. The detailed financial records of Philip Henslowe, who acted as the company's landlord and financier from 1594 until his death in 1616, indicate that an extensive list of dramatists wrote for the troupe throughout its existence, including Christopher Marlowe, Ben Jonson, George Chapman, Anthony Munday, Henry Chettle, Michael Drayton, Thomas Dekker, and William Rowley.

LORD CHAMBERLAIN'S MEN: An acting company formed in 1594 under the patronage of Henry Carey, Lord Hunsdon, who was the Queen's Chamberlain from 1585 until his death in 1596. From 1596 to 1597, the company's benefactor was Lord Hunsdon's son, George Carey, and they were known as Hunsdon's men until the younger Carey was appointed to his late father's office, when the troupe once again became officially the Lord Chamberlain's Men. The members of the company included Shakespeare; the renowned tragedian Richard Burbage; the famous 'clown' Will Kempe, who was the most popular actor of his time; and John Heminge, who served as business manager for the company. In 1594 they began performing at the Theatre and the Cross Keys Inn, moving to the SWAN THEATRE on Bankside in 1596 when the City Corporation banned the public presentation of plays within the limits of the City of London. In 1599 some members of the company financed the building of the GLOBE THEATRE, and thus the majority became "sharers," not only in the actors' portion of the profits, but in the theater owners' as well. This economic independence was an important element in the unusual stability of their association. They became the foremost London company, performing at Court on thirty-two occasions between 1594 and 1603, whereas their chief rivals, the LORD ADMIRAL'S MEN, made twenty appearances at Court during that period. No detailed records exist of the plays that were in their repertoire. Ben Jonson wrote several of his dramas for the Lord Chamberlain's Men, but the company's success is largely attributable to the fact that after joining them in 1594, Shakespeare wrote for no other company.

LYCEUM THEATRE: London playhouse, perhaps best known for the tenancy of Henry Irving, the renowned actor-manager. It was here, during the period 1878-99, that Irving, together with Ellen Terry, staged and performed in a series of lavish and highly successful Shakespearean productions. The Lyceum was built in 1765 as a concert hall and converted into a theater in 1794. Due to the monopoly on public performances held by the PATENT theaters, it was only intermittently used for dramatic productions, and then solely for private, benefit performances. In 1809, when the DRURY LANE THEATRE was destroyed by fire, its company made the Lyceum its temporary home and transferred its license there. When the company departed for its rebuilt playhouse in 1812, the Lyceum management was able to retain a license for performances in the summer months. Destroyed in a fire in 1830, the theater was rebuilt and opened four years later as the Royal Lyceum and English Opera House.

NATIONAL THEATRE (London): Established with a subsidy from the British government, the National Theatre, with its resident acting company, began operating at the OLD VIC THEATRE in 1963 under the direction of Laurence Olivier. Such a theater was the dream of actors and drama enthusiasts since the time of David Garrick, but it was not until late in the nineteenth century that concerted campaigns for its construction were mounted. Despite a continual series of disappointments and setbacks, the theater's supporters—including some of the most distinguished Shakespearean scholars and stage personnel—persisted, and on 22 October 1963, the company performed *Hamlet* as its inaugural production. The National Theatre's own playhouse, erected on London's South Bank, opened in 1976.

OLD VIC THEATRE: Built in 1818 as the Royal Coburg Theatre, this famed playhouse was renamed the Victoria after a visit by the future monarch in 1833. Although such noted nineteenth-century Shakespearean actors as Edmund Kean and William Charles Macready performed at the Old Vic—as it is commonly called—the works of Shakespeare himself were not staged there until 1914. In that year, the manager, Lilian Baylis, devised a program to produce the dramatist's works in repertory and cultivate the interest of the middle class. By 1923 the Old Vic company had produced every play in the canon and had established itself as a world-famous ensemble that attracted the finest actors and directors. Moreover, the theater was the only permanent home of Shakespearean drama in London. Heavily damaged in an air raid in 1941, the Old Vic was closed for the next nine years. With the founding of the NATIONAL THEATRE in 1963, the Old Vic company dissolved, although many of the actors formed the nucleus of the new company and the theater itself served as its temporary home until the opening of the South Bank playhouse in 1976.

PATENTS: Letters or charters signed by the monarch conferring a special privilege on an individual or group. After his accession, James I issued patent letters for all the London theatrical companies previously under the authority of other sponsors. Thus, a patent of 1603 brought Shakespeare's company, the LORD CHAMBERLAIN'S MEN, under royal patronage and altered its name to the KING'S MEN. Shortly after the Restoration in 1660, Charles II issued patents to Thomas Killigrew and William Davenant for the establishment of two theatrical companies, to be known as The King's Servants and The Duke of York's Servants, respectively. As these were the only two such licenses granted, Killigrew's Theatre Royal in Bridges Street and Davenant's LINCOLN'S INN FIELDS THEATRE together formed a long standing monopoly on theatrical performances. In 1674 Killigrew moved his company to a new playhouse he had constructed, the DRURY LANE THEATRE. The patent granted to Davenant eventually passed to John Rich, who built the first COVENT GARDEN THEATRE in 1732. A patent permitting plays to be staged at the HAYMARKET THEATRE during the summer months was issued in 1766. These licenses were abolished in 1843, and the monopoly enjoyed by these theaters was ended.

PEMBROKE'S MEN: An acting company formed around 1592 under the patronage of Henry Herbert, second Earl of Pembroke. By 1593 the troupe was in financial difficulties and was forced to sell many of its properties in order to pay its debts. The play-books of three dramas—*The Taming of a Shrew, The True Tragedy of Richard Duke of York,* and Christopher Marlowe's *Edward II*—were sold to book-sellers, who subsequently published them. Scholars contend that the first two works are either "bad QUARTOs" of Shakespeare's *The Taming of the Shrew* and *3 Henry VI* or plays he revised to create his dramas. This connection has led some commentators to postulate that Shakespeare was a member of Pembroke's company before he joined the LORD CHAMBERLAIN'S MEN. In July 1597, a performance of Thomas Nashe's controversial *Isle of Dogs* by Pembroke's Men at the SWAN THEATRE was judged seditious; civil authorities imprisoned three actors and closed all the London theaters. Although the playhouses were later allowed to reopen, the troupe was effectively broken and its members scattered. References to the company persist, however, until 1600, at which time, scholars believe, Pembroke's Men joined with the newly-formed company known as Worcester's Men.

PROMPT-BOOK: Acting version of a play, which was presented to the Master of the REVELS OFFICE, the official censor and authorizer of plays. Upon approving its contents, he would license the play for performance and endorse the text as the "allowed book" of the play. A prompt-book represents an alteration or modification of the dramatist's original manuscript. It generally contains detailed stage directions, including cues for music, off-stage noises, and the entries and exits of principal characters; indications of stage properties to be used; and other annotations to assist the prompter during an actual performance. The prompt-book version was frequently shorter than the original manuscript, for cuts would be made in terms of minor characters or dramatic incidents to suit the resources of the acting company. Printed editions of plays were sometimes based on prompt-books.

QUARTO: The term applied to a book usually made up of sheets of paper folded twice to form four leaves, or eight pages, of roughly equal size. The dimensions of a folded quarto page may range in size from about 6¾ to 10 inches in width and 8½ to 12½ inches in height. A number of Shakespeare's plays were first printed in unauthorized quarto editions. Some of the more reliable of these may have been derived from PROMPT-BOOK copies of the plays; others have become known as "bad quartos," because of irregularities, omissions, misspellings, and interpolations not found in later quarto or FOLIO versions of the same plays. The term "bad quarto" was first used by the twentieth-century bibliographical scholar A. W. Pollard and has been applied to as many as ten plays: The First Quartos of *Romeo and Juliet, Hamlet, Henry V*, and *The Merry Wives of Windsor; The First Part of the Contention betwixt the two famous Houses of Yorke and Lancaster* and *The True Tragedy of Richard Duke of Yorke*, originally thought to have been sources for Shakespeare's *2* and *3 Henry VI*, but now generally regarded as bad quartos of those plays; the so-called "Pied Bull" quarto of *King Lear;* the 1609 edition of *Pericles; The Troublesome Reign of King John*, believed to be a bad quarto of *King John;* and *The Taming of a Shrew*, which some critics contend is a bad quarto of Shakespeare's Shrew comedy. Both good and bad quartos are of value to theater historians, for the stage directions they contain, as well as their alterations of Shakespeare's original work, often provide clues to the ways in which the plays were performed in Elizabethan and Jacobean times.

REVELS OFFICE: Department of the British royal household which, under the direction of the Master of the Revels, was charged with superintending Court entertainments. Established in 1494 as a temporary office, it eventually became a permanent one, and the powers of the Master continually expanded. By Shakespeare's time, all plays for public performance had to be submitted to the Master of the Revels for censorship and licensing. In 1607 this requirement was extended to plays intended for publication as well. Among the principal responsibilities of the Revels Office was the provision of costumes and scenery for court theatrical productions, and the expenses thereby incurred were recorded in the Revels Accounts. Two of these accounts compiled during the reign of James I record performances at Court by the KING'S MEN of several Shakespearean plays, including *Othello, The Merry Wives of Windsor, Measure for Measure, The Comedy of Errors, Love's Labour's Lost, The Merchant of Venice, The Tempest, The Winter's Tale*, and *Henry V*. During the period of the civil war, the Revels Office was suspended. Although it was reinstituted after the Restoration, Charles II's direct licensing of theatrical companies by means of PATENTs greatly diminished its power.

ROSE THEATRE: Built in 1587 by Philip Henslowe, the Rose was constructed of timber on a brick foundation, with exterior walls of lath and plaster and a roof of thatch. Its location on Bankside—across the Thames from the City of London—established this area as a new site for public theaters. Its circular design included a yard, galleries, a tiring house, and "heavens." A half-dozen acting companies played there, the most important being the LORD ADMIRAL'S MEN, who performed at the Rose from 1594 to 1600, when they moved to the new Fortune Theatre constructed by Henslowe in Finsbury, north of the City of London. Among the dramatists employed by Henslowe at the Rose were Thomas Kyd, Christopher Marlowe, Shakespeare, Robert Greene, Ben Jonson, Michael Drayton, George Chapman, Thomas Dekker, and John Webster. The building was razed in 1606.

ROYAL SHAKESPEARE COMPANY: Resident company of the present-day Royal Shakespeare Theatre, which was founded in 1879 as the Shakespeare Memorial Theatre in Stratford-upon-Avon. The construction of a playhouse honoring Shakespeare in the town of his birth was the brainchild of Charles Edward Flower, a wealthy brewer. Flower's father, Edward Fordham Flower, was mayor of Stratford and had helped organize the Tercentenary Festival of 1864, a fortnight of Shakespearean drama celebrating the three-hundredth anniversary of the playwright's birth. After the Festival, which was held in a wooden pavilion, the younger Flower donated a riverside site and much of the £20,000 necessary to erect a permanent theater. The eclectic "modern Gothic" building opened on 23 April 1879 with a performance of *Much Ado about Nothing*. Although London critics generally disdained the annual festivals, in the succeeding years several managers mounted performances there on the dramatist's birthday. In 1886 Frank Benson assumed control of the theater and directed the festivals until 1919. During his tenure, Benson attracted leading players and ever-increasing audiences as his company produced all but two plays in the Shakespearean canon. The theater was granted a Royal Charter in 1925, the first year of profitability, but the building burned down the following year. The festival organizers commandeered the Stratford-upon-Avon Picture House until a replacement theater was completed in 1932. The 1940s and 1950s witnessed many theatrical successes as prominent London players and directors were increasingly invited to participate in Stratford productions. In 1960 director Peter Hall initiated a reorganization of the Memorial Theater that culminated a year later in the formation of a resident ensemble, the Royal Shakespeare Company, and the acquisition of a London theater for productions there.

STATIONERS' REGISTER: A ledger book in which were entered the titles of works to be printed and published. The Register was maintained by the Stationers' Company, an association of those who manufactured and those who sold books. In Tudor England, the Company had a virtual monopoly—aside from the university presses—on printing works written throughout the country. Having obtained a license authorizing the printing of a book, a member of the Company would pay a fee to enter the book in the Register, thereby securing the sole right to print or sell that book. Many registered texts were acquired by questionable means, and many plays were published whose titles were not entered in the records of the Company. However, the Stationers' Register is one of the most important documents for scholars investigating the literature of that period.

STRATFORD FESTIVAL (Ontario, Canada): Festival established in 1953 by the Canadian businessman Tom Patterson in collaboration with British scholar and director Tyrone Guthrie, who served as artistic director until 1955. Founded as a Shakespearean festival, its program was later expanded to include performances of the works of other playwrights, as well as concerts, operas, and films. The Festival maintains a resident company of Canadian actors which is augmented by guest performers. In the early years performances were held in a large tent, but a permanent structure, the Festival Theatre, was completed in 1957. Its stage, designed by Tanya Moiseiwitsch, has often been praised for successfully incorporating aspects of both modern and Elizabethan stages. In 1963 a second theater, the Avon, was opened, and the aptly named Third Stage was added in 1971. From the first, the Stratford Festival has been the scene of numerous memorable Shakespearean performances, and it has met with great popular and critical success.

SWAN THEATRE: Built in 1595-96 by Francis Langley, the Swan was one of Elizabethan London's principal public theaters. It is the subject of a 1596 drawing and verbal description by the Dutch visitor to London, Johannes de Witt. Although the original sketch no longer exists, a copy made by a friend of de Witt survives, providing modern scholars with the only contemporary illustration of an Elizabethan theater. It is represented as a wooden structure built on a flint and mortar base, and its interior is depicted as circular, with three tiers of galleries. Projecting into an open yard is a thrust or apron stage, on which rest columns, painted to look like marble, that support an overhanging "shadow" or "heavens." At the rear of the stage is the tiring house, where actors prepared themselves for their performances. De Witt shows two doors leading from the stage to the tiring house. The reliability of this drawing has been called into question by some scholars, who contend that Elizabethan stages typically had alcoves at the back of the stage, which were used to represent interior spaces. De Witt depicts no such recess. Other critics, however, insist that the drawing is accurate and that theories of such INNER STAGEs are based on insufficient evidence. Court documents in which both Langley's and Shakespeare's names appear have led scholars to postulate that the dramatist's theatrical company, the LORD CHAMBERLAIN'S MEN, at one time performed at Langley's Swan. After the dissolution of PEMBROKE'S MEN in 1597, the Swan was left without a resident theatrical company. It was thereafter employed for a variety of sporting events and other spectacles, as well as for the occasional staging of plays. The latest contemporary reference to the Swan is a 1632 allusion to its state of decay.

ISBN 0-8103-6136-1

90000>

REFERENCE